Prentice Hall
The PAGEANT of WORLD HISTORY
Gerald Leinwand

Cover Painting

Illustration from *the Book of Hours* of the Duke of Berry, early 1400s. This painting shows a procession of nobles from the court of the Duke of Berry in France. It appears in the Duke's personal book of hours, a type of prayerbook popular among the wealthy in medieval times. These costly and beautifully illustrated books first appeared in the late twelfth century, but the best examples were produced in the fourteenth and fifteenth centuries by artists in northern France and the Netherlands.

Frontispiece, next page

Procession of the Magi, 1459. The work is a fresco, a watercolor painted over wet plaster. It was painted by Benozzo Gozzoli on the chapel walls of the Medici family palace in Florence, Italy. The Medicis were a ruling family of Florence during the Renaissance.

The painting depicts a pageant of Florentine *magi,* or nobles and priests—some of whom are members of the Medici family. Although nonreligious in presentation, the painting was inspired by a meeting of Roman Catholic and Eastern Orthodox church officials. Gozzoli carried this theme of cultural interplay through the officials' clothes and headgear. Many of the officials are dressed in typical Florentine clothing and wear the signature red cap; others wear clothing more characteristic of the East, such as flowing robes and turbans.

Prentice Hall

The PAGEANT of WORLD HISTORY

Gerald Leinwand

PRENTICE HALL
Needham, Massachusetts • Englewood Cliffs, New Jersey

About the Author

Gerald Leinwand received his B.A., M.S., and Ph.D. degrees from New York University, and an M.A. from Columbia University. He was formerly President of Western Oregon State College in Monmouth, Oregon. He was Professor of Education and Founding Dean of the School of Education of the Bernard M. Baruch College of the City University of New York. He has served as a consultant in international education at East Tennessee State University and as Project Director for talented and gifted high-school students at Cape Cod Community College, Barnstable, Massachusetts. Dr. Leinwand has taught world history on television, and for many years, was a teacher in junior and senior high schools. He has written *The American Constitution: Tutor-Text, Teaching History and Social Studies in Secondary Schools*. He is also author of the forthcoming series *Questioning American Society*.

Prologue Co-Author: Muncel Chang, Lecturer at the California State University at Chico in the Department of Geography; Commissioner on the Commission on Social Studies in the Schools, Washington, D.C.; Geographic Consultant for the California State Department of Education; Founding Member of the California Geographic Alliance.

Credits

Executive Editor:
Jeffrey M. Ikler
Project Editor: Nancy Rogier
Editor: Peter Guthrie
Editorial Services: Mary Ashford, Susan Feibelman, Celeste Fraser, Elizabeth Grube, Susan Judge, Bruce Morgan, Barbara Brooks Simons, James Strickler
Map Editor: Celeste Fraser
"Art in History" Features:
Jeffrey L. Gibson, Department of the History of Art, Ohio State University, Columbus, Ohio

**"Geography in History"
Features:** Marian H. Shotwell, Stuart B. Shotwell
**Production/Manufacturing
Coordinator:** Martha E. Ballentine
Product Marketing Director: Martha G. Smith
Design Director: L. Christopher Valente
Design Coordinator: Betty Fiora
Design Production: Prentice Hall—Daniel Ashton, Michael C. Burggren, Hannah Fogarty, Susan Genser, Dayle

Silverman; Susan Gerould/Perspectives—Nancy Blodget, Claudia E. Simon
Cover Design: L. Christopher Valente, Martucci Studios
Book Design: Susan Gerould/Perspectives
Photo Researcher: Susan Van Etten
Text Maps: Mapping Specialists, Ltd., Sanderson Associates
Creative Illustration: Lonnie S. Knabel, Matthew S. Pippin
Technical Illustration: Publication Services

Reviewers/Consultants

Dr. Patricia Harris
Assistant Director of Curriculum Services
Gary Public Schools
Gary, Indiana

Dr. James Kracht
Education, Curriculum, and Instruction
Department of Geography
Texas A & M University
College Station, Texas

Stanley Kravetz
Past President of New York State Council of Social Studies
Chairperson, Social Studies
Syosset High School
Syosset Central School District
Syosset, New York

Maria Maracic Polite
Chairperson, Department of Social Studies/Teacher
Bakersfield High School
Bakersfield, California

Linda Wojtan
College of Education
University of Maryland
College Park, Maryland

CONTENTS

UNIT

1

Cradles of Civilization

UNIT

5

Journey into Modern Times

(1000–1750)   306

UNIT

6

An Age of Revolution

(1600–1848)   **430**

UNIT

8

The World in Crisis

(1914–1960)   572

xii

UNIT

9
The World Today

(1960–PRESENT)   **656**

BRIEF REVIEW

MAPS

GEOGRAPHY IN HISTORY

GRAPHS AND CHARTS

BIOGRAPHY

IN THEIR OWN WORDS

DAILY LIFE

LINKING PAST AND PRESENT

ART IN HISTORY

Letter from the Author

Dear Student,

I want to share a dream with you. I dreamed that a young person of 14 whom I was going to be teaching would become president of the United States during the first half of the twenty-first century. As a teacher, I was struck by this immense responsibility. What should I teach my student about the world as preparation for this awesome task? How could my world history course help this person to mature into an intelligent and humane president and leader of the free world?

Of course, the dream ended, and I awoke. But the questions the dream had raised continued to trouble me as I taught world history. I shared the dream with my students, and I asked them how they would answer the questions. Together, we developed a number of basic ideas that may be summarized as follows:

- We live on a very small but unique planet, and those who live on it share a common history.
- While there are many differences among the people of the world, we share a preference for peace rather than war.
- Progress is not inevitable, so we must work to make the world a better place in which to live.
- The earth's environment is a fragile one, and we have a shared responsibility to protect it.
- All people are entitled to basic human rights, including the right to organize, to express oneself freely, to be secure in one's home, to worship as one wishes, to protest nonviolently, and to be protected from arbitrary arrest, torture, imprisonment, or execution.

I thought I would write a new world history textbook based on these ideas. If such ideas are worthy for a student who might become a future president of the United States, then they should also be useful for all students. Even if you don't become president, a careful study of these ideas will help you take the first step on that long journey toward a better understanding of the world and of your place in the making of its history.

Sincerely,

Gerald Leinwand

Gerald Leinwand
West Hyannisport, Massachusetts

This book is dedicated to the loving memory of my wife, Selma, who was there at its creation and at every critical point in the book's many editions.

Geography: The Place Where History Happens

L ate on a November day in 1968, a man hiked into a narrow desert canyon in southern Nevada. Rounding a clump of rocks, he suddenly came upon an old wooden trunk standing in the open air. Metal bands around the trunk had rusted to a chestnut brown. Beyond the trunk lay the mouth of a small cave. Inside the cave were scattered the fragments of a life: tipped-over furniture, a frying pan and coffee pot, newspaper clippings from the year 1916, and a neatly carved walking stick.

A sense of mystery hung over the place. Who had lived here? Why had he or she camped out among the dry stones? And where had the person gone? Colin Fletcher, the hiker, spent the next 10 years wrestling with these questions. He crisscrossed the country, interviewing people and digging through old files. Not every tip paid off. Some clues led nowhere. Eventually, Fletcher learned that the mysterious cave dweller had probably been a Pennsylvania-born drifter who was known as "Chuckawalla" Bill.

The study of history is something like Fletcher's search for the man in the cave. Using bits of evidence, historians try to figure out the mysterious past. As surely as heat fills the desert, geography plays a critical role in their answers. This book contains some of the fragments that historians have picked up along life's trail. Piecing them together is what history means.

▲ **Illustrating History**
Historians might one day use this newspaper as evidence to recreate the story of the final days of World War II.

▲ **Illustrating History**   *The physical objects shown above helped Colin Fletcher to piece together the life of a drifter named "Chuckawalla" Bill.*

1 History Tells the Story of People on Earth

As you read, look for answers to these questions:

◆ What is history?
◆ Why is it important to study history?
◆ How do historians work?

Key Terms: history (defined on p. 2), primary source (p. 2), secondary source (p. 2)

The American historian and journalist Theodore White got his first introduction to newspaper work as a teenager when he sold newspapers on the streets of Boston. He would shout, *"Globe, Post, Herald,* and *Record* here! Papers?"* Each morning, White would scan the newspapers to find exciting headlines to shout, ones he thought would sell papers. Because White was a teenager during the early 1930s, many of the headlines he shouted are now key events in history—events you will study as you read this book.

Just as in the past, headlines in today's newspapers are tomorrow's history. If you understand what is happening in today's world, you will be better prepared for the future. In a similar way, learning about the past will help you to understand the headlines that are being made today.

How people learn about the past is the subject of these next few pages. You'll begin by finding out what history is and why it is important. You'll also read about the questions historians ask themselves as they study the events of the past.

History Connects the Past and the Present

History is the study of what human beings have done on earth. This definition is useful, but it is not really a complete one. The British scholar Edward Hallet Carr has described history as "an unending dialogue between the present and the past." Carr means that the past and the present are connected. We can learn about the present by studying the past. We can also learn about ourselves by studying the past.

To find out about the past, we examine its records. These may be written or unwritten. They may be the stone tools that primitive people once used. They may be bones, decayed ruins, or great stone monuments that have withstood the passage of time. Sometimes, the records are written ones, such as laws, diaries, and letters. Indeed, any written document, including your history notebook, has value as a historical record.

Because our knowledge of history is often incomplete, learning about the past can be a challenge. Some historical records have been lost or destroyed. Some were never preserved. Other records have been deliberately changed so that the truth may never be known. Although there are problems in the study of history, we must recognize that the study of history presents an unending challenge to find the facts and to interpret them. Rightly or wrongly, we interpret the past by the standards of the present, thus creating the dialogue about which Carr wrote.

History Helps Us Understand Our World

History has value for the lessons it teaches. A society that does not study the past may repeat its mistakes. History also has value for the light it sheds on the present. It helps us to understand our problems better. Studying the past gives us a picture of who we are, what we think, and how we have become what we are. History gives us a sense of belonging. We are members of the human community whose past is our past and whose future we will share. The past tells us that we are human beings whose progress has depended on the contributions of human beings who came before us. Our country, for example, is more than 200 years old, but the democratic system of government under which it operates is based on beliefs that existed in ancient Greece and Rome—thousands of years ago.

The study of world history has value of its own. By its very name, you can see that world history is concerned with every part of the globe. As you read this book, you will study world politics, world wars, and rulers who sought to dominate the world. You will learn about world cultures through art, architecture, and literature.

Your study of world history will introduce you to the history of other countries. In this way, you can compare their development with that of this country and see how our histories intertwine. A study of world history will help you understand points of view and values different from your own. Because people have not always understood each other, the history of the world has often been the story of conflict.

Historians Find Out What Happened in the Past

Historians try to answer questions as they study history. One question is, "What happened in the past?" Historians usually find out what happened in the past by studying written records. Written records of past events fall into two categories: primary sources and secondary sources. A **primary source** is a document, record, or written account made by someone who took part in or witnessed an event. This type of source is a firsthand account that comes directly from the past. The farther back one goes in history, the more difficult it is to find primary sources. Some examples of primary sources are diaries, letters, and government records.

A **secondary source** is a written account made some time after an event has taken place and by people who were not eyewitnesses. Secondary sources may be based on primary sources or on other secondary sources. This textbook is an example of a secondary source.

▲ **Illustrating History** *Written records, such as the Egyptian picture writing shown above, help historians learn more about the past.*

Both primary and secondary sources are valuable to historians. However, both kinds of sources must be judged for accuracy and for their importance to the topic being researched. Primary sources based on eyewitness accounts sometimes tell incomplete stories. For example, no one knows who fired the shots that began the American Revolution. As you know from your study of American history, the American Revolution began on April 19, 1775, at a battle in Lexington, Massachusetts. Although both the British and the Americans offered eyewitness accounts, historians do not know who fired first.

For a host of reasons, primary sources and secondary sources can also sometimes disagree. Analyzing differing sources can be a little like playing a baseball game without an umpire. In baseball, the umpire tells when a player is safe or out. The umpire makes the final decision with little or no room for disagreement. In history, there is no umpire to tell when something is accurate or inaccurate. The historian must study primary and secondary sources and draw careful conclusions based upon them.

Historians often draw different conclusions from historical facts. Although historians try not to take sides or favor a particular point of view, their own beliefs can affect how they interpret the facts. This explains why different historians, even when they are using identical sources, may reach very different conclusions.

Historians Find Out the "Whys" of History

History is more than finding out what happened in the past. Historians also try to find out the "whys" of history. They ask themselves three main questions: Why did a particular event take place? Why is the event important? Why did the event happen when it did? Explaining the "whys" of history is just as important as describing the "whats." Without the "whys," history has no meaning. Focusing on the "whys" in history helps us to answer larger questions: Why do we exist as we do? Why are we here?

Consider some of the "why" questions historians have asked about the pyramids of Egypt. These structures were built as tombs

3

for Egyptian rulers. Egyptian kings spent decades overseeing every detail of the building process and the making of the various objects that would be placed within the finished tombs. Why did the Egyptians build such elaborate burial places? Why did they spend so much of their lives preparing for their deaths? Why did they build tombs in the shape of pyramids? Why did they fill the pyramids with such objects as combs, chairs, and jewelry? Why were scenes of everyday life painted on the walls of the chambers inside the pyramids?

The search for answers to these "why" questions reveals another side to history: many of its secrets remain hidden. Some questions about our past have yet to be answered. For example, although historians know many things about the pyramids, they don't know precisely how they were built. They do know about the building methods ancient Egyptians used, however. From this knowledge, we know about three probable methods for building pyramids. One of these methods is illustrated in Chapter 2.

Just as history can sometimes be a mystery, the work of historians can sometimes resemble the work of detectives. Like a detective, a historian uncovers sources, traces the sequence of events, and seeks evidence to support his or her conclusions. Depending on what they research, historians often travel the world in their search for history. Just like Colin Fletcher, who traveled across the country to track down the origin of the trunk he discovered, historians travel as they study the past.

In addition, the work of a historian involves much more than sitting in a library poring over documents and books. Historians who study recent events, for example, identify and interview people who have taken part in those events. Historians who study ancient Egypt crawl through the dark corridors of the pyramids to reach the tombs inside. Historians visit battlefields, hunt for shipwrecks, trace explorers' routes, and document the lives of ordinary people as well as the lives of the extraordinary.

While historians are concerned mainly with what happened and why events took place, they must also focus on the "where" of history. Finding out where events happen combines history with geography. In the next section, you will learn what geography is and how it relates to history.

▼ **Illustrating History** *Historians have made important discoveries about the past through the excavation of shipwrecks.*

2 Geography Is Where History Happens

As you read, look for answers to these questions:

◆ Why is geography important to historians?
◆ How do the two main branches of geography differ?
◆ How does geography establish a setting for history?

> **Key Terms:** geography (defined on p. 5), physical geography (p. 6), human geography (p. 6), landform (p. 6)

Geography is the study of where things are on the earth, why they are there, and their relationships to people, things, or other places. As you read in Section 1, history is a study of what human beings have done on earth. Historians study past events and try to find out why they happened. Geography focuses on where those same events occurred. Geography also focuses on why an event happened and the consequences or significance of the event in relationship to the place where it happened. Moreover, geography considers the relationship that exists between that place and the people who live in the place.

History and geography cannot be separated. History tells you the time when something happened, and geography tells you about the place where it occurred. Time and place exist together.

Historians Recognize the Importance of Geography

Historians have always recognized the importance of studying and knowing geography. As you will learn in Chapter 2, an early Greek historian and traveler named Herodotus made a key observation about Egypt when he visited there in 440 B.C. He said that "All Egypt is the gift of the Nile." Herodotus meant that the history and growth of Egyptian civilization is closely tied to the Nile River.

Another early Greek historian, Thucydides, used geography to describe the spread of a disease that afflicted the army of Athens, Greece, around 430 B.C. This disease had come from Ethiopia, a land in northern Africa. Travelers carried it from Ethiopia to Egypt, where it infected Greek sailors. When the infected sailors returned to Greece, the disease spread to the army. Geography was important in tracing the spread of a disease, and the disease, in turn, had a powerful impact on history.

Many people seem to think that geography is simply the study of states and state capitals. Historians know that nothing could be

▼ **Illustrating History** *This satellite picture shows the Nile River, the setting for the history of ancient Egypt.*

further from the truth. As you begin this course, you will notice it starts with early civilizations and where they began. In Chapter 1, you will learn that civilizations began in four great river valleys, one in Egypt, one in the Middle East, one in India, and one in China. A good historian and geographer would ask, "Why there? What made those river valleys so special that humans would want to live there?" To answer these questions, geographers look for certain qualities in the physical landscape that humans find attractive and desirable.

One way that geographers investigate the earth is by studying the pattern of how things are distributed on the earth. All distributions can be plotted on a map. Patterns of these distributions may give the geographer some answers about why certain interactions take place. For example, if you were to plot the population of China on a map, you would notice that some places in the country are heavily settled, while other areas are almost vacant. The pattern that would emerge would clearly show all of the river systems of China, even though this was not the original intention of the map. The conclusion you would come to by looking at the map is that most of the people in China live along rivers.

Geography Has Two Main Branches

Geographers have divided geography into two main branches—physical geography and human geography. **Physical geography** is the study of the natural world. **Human geography** is the study of the patterns of human life and changes humans have made on the earth.

Physical geography. In describing the earth in terms of its physical geography, geographers ask the same questions as historians. What is happening where, why, and of what importance is it? For example, consider the seasons of the year. Some of the questions a geographer would ask about the seasons would include: Why do we have seasons? What happens during each of the four seasons? Where is the earth in its orbit

around the sun at different times of the year? Of what significance are seasons to humans? The answers would reveal that the growing of crops, the construction of dams and bridges, and religious and cultural festivals are all related to the movement of the earth around the sun.

Physical geography encompasses a wide range of topics—almost everything under the sun. Geographers who specialize in physical geography study the earth's climates, weather patterns, water bodies, and landforms. (A **landform** is a physical feature of the earth such as a mountain, an island, or a valley.) Geographers find out why mountains form, what causes earthquakes, and why earthquakes occur where they do. They learn why different places have different types of vegetation. They trace the development of water resources such as rivers, lakes, oceans, and seas. No matter what they study, they always ask, what is happening, where it is happening, why, and what is its significance?

Human geography. If you live in a major city, much of the physical, or natural, world around you has been covered up by the changes that humans have made. The study of human geography is the study of the patterns and changes on the earth made by the people. Human geography focuses on the patterns of human life and how humans have acted in changing the physical landscape. It also asks why people have acted as they have.

From the earliest human settlements, people have made marks on the land. The Great Wall of China, the ancient city of Machu Picchu in the Andes, and the monumental pyramids of Egypt, each speak of past human activity. Each example was created in response to different human desires or beliefs. People in China, for example, built the Great Wall to define their territory and to keep invaders out. People erect similar barriers today, such as the Berlin Wall in East Germany or the fence around a yard.

Changing the physical landscape leaves permanent marks on the earth. Some of these changes are centuries old and are still

▲ **Illustrating History** *Both historians and geographers study the marks people have made on the earth. Above is the Great Wall of China. Shown at right is a Roman aqueduct.*

going on today. In Asia, for example, a lack of good farmland in mountainous regions led to the creation of terraces, or "stairsteps" on the slopes. Other changes are more recent and have occurred over shorter periods of time. The Industrial Revolution, which took place in England and America in the late 1700s and 1800s, gave humans the ability to change the landscape drastically in a short time. New ideas about land ownership and how land should be surveyed changed the layout of the land. Labor-saving tools like the reaper allowed people to cultivate much larger fields.

Geographers who study the human world have discovered that people have changed the physical landscape for many reasons. A dam, for example, can serve several needs. It can provide a reservoir of water for drinking, cooking, and plumbing. It can be used to create hydroelectric power to run factories and homes. A dam can control floods or create lakes for recreation. Similarly, highways can be built for a number of reasons. Some highways are built to link cities, such as the highway between the cities of Dallas and Fort Worth in Texas. Some highways are built to bypass cities so that, for example,

people whose destination is somewhere other than Boston can travel around it instead of through it.

Geographers who study the human world have also learned that people need a supply of raw materials to change the physical landscape. In finding and using those raw materials, people add to the changes they make. People dig mines to obtain such raw materials as iron ore and coal. They build roads, bridges, and canals to transport these resources to manufacturing sites.

Human geography may not necessarily affect or be affected by the physical landscape. Changes in human geography may include the spread of an idea, a religion, or a culture. In today's world, where travel and communication occur easily, people may rapidly spread pieces of their cultural identity to another part of the world. One example of this phenomenon is the worldwide popularity of blue jeans. Blue jeans were first manufactured in San Francisco, California, in the late 1800s by American clothing manufacturer Levi Strauss. They soon became the work clothes of American farmers and laborers. Today, the wearing of blue jeans is unrelated to the type of work people do and has become fashionable in many parts of the world. Cultural exchanges through travel, television, magazines, and newspapers helped to spread the wearing of blue jeans.

As you read this textbook, you will encounter many examples of physical geography and human geography. At the end of each unit, for example, you will find a special essay about geography in history. Some of the essays focus on physical geography. Some focus on human geography.

Geography Establishes the Setting for History

As you read earlier, geography is the place where history happens. History tells what people have done on the earth and why. Geography tells where historical events happen and why they occur where they do. In your study of world history, you will learn that historical events happen for specific geographic reasons. Human settlements, for example, may take place for any number of reasons. People may settle at a trading crossroads. They may settle on a strategic hill guarding a pass or overlooking a valley. People may settle along a sheltered bay with a deep harbor. Or, they may settle next to a waterfall on a river where water power is available.

In addition to patterns of human settlement, trading and migration patterns also are established for specific geographic reasons. A river valley, a water hole, or a mountain pass may meet the requirements of a traveler. Routes of travel develop because they are discovered to be the most efficient links between distant places. These routes also may serve as paths for military invasions or peacetime movements.

Climatic conditions often affect historical events as much as landforms. For example, the Spanish navy was struck by a severe storm during its attempted invasion of England in 1588 and never fully recovered. Napoleon, the famous emperor of France, launched an invasion of Russia in 1812 that ended in disaster when winter snows fell on his ill-prepared troops. More recently, the history of the country of Bangladesh in South Asia has been directly affected by both its physical features and by its weather. Located in a fertile region where two rivers meet, Bangladesh can reap rich harvests of rice. At the same time, its people often suffer from heavy rains and flooding that threaten almost the entire country.

The need for natural resources, things in nature that people need, often is related to historical events, particularly the outbreak of war. Unfortunately, much of the history of humankind is a history of warfare. Most wars are related to the aggressor's need for raw materials or land. Oil, coal, iron ore, and other minerals have become increasingly precious. Land for living space and for agriculture is also precious. All these needs relate to geography, and all these needs can be traced through history.

SECTION 2 REVIEW

Knowing Key Terms, People, and Places
1. Define: **a.** geography **b.** physical geography **c.** human geography **d.** landform

Reviewing Main Ideas
2. Give two examples of how early historians recognized the importance of geography to the study of history.
3. Give one example of how people have changed the natural world.
4. How might climate and the need for raw materials and natural resources affect historical events?

Critical Thinking
Drawing Conclusions
5. How does the geography of an area affect the type of work that the people in that area do?

3 Five Themes Describe Geography's Framework

As you read, look for answers to these questions:

◆ What are the five themes of geography?
◆ How do the five themes of geography relate to history?
◆ How can the study of geography increase understanding of world history?

Key Terms: absolute location (defined on p. 9), relative location (p. 9)

As an area of study, geography, like history, has gone through centuries of development and change. Various geographers and geographical organizations have had different views of how geography should be studied. Recently, geographers across the United States have identified five themes of geography. These five themes make it easier for students to study the world around them. Both physical and human geography can be examined through the use of these five themes. As you read about each one, notice the ways in which it helps you to describe and analyze a place.

Location Tells Where Places Are Found on the Earth

While you know from Section 2 that geography is more than the study of where places are located, location is still an important geographic theme. Knowing where places are located is essential in world history because location is one of the pieces in the puzzle of history. Knowing that the first civilizations grew up in river valleys, for example, makes little sense if you don't know where the river valleys were located. The events of World War II mean little without knowing the location of such key countries as France, Germany, Great Britain, and Japan.

Location can be described in two ways, absolute and relative. **Absolute location** tells exactly where something is located on the earth. Absolute location is similar to an address; there is only one spot on the face of the earth for that specific place.

The most familiar system used to describe absolute location is the system of latitude and longitude. Imaginary lines on the earth pinpoint the exact location of a place. Lines of latitude extend east and west around the globe. Longitude lines extend north and south and meet at the North and South Poles. You will learn more about latitude and longitude in Section 4.

Relative location is the second major way of describing location. **Relative location** is the location of a place in relation to a known, familiar place. In describing relative location, words like "next to," "east of," and "around the corner from" are used to tell you about a location in reference to something that you are familiar with. Besides

▼ **Illustrating History** *The information cartographers, or mapmakers, include on maps often reveals distinct geographic patterns.*

giving your friends the absolute location of your birthday party ("1588 Elm Street," for example), you probably also include relative location ("next to Bear Creek on the other side of the covered bridge").

The significance of a geographic event often depends upon the event's relative location. A volcanic eruption in a remote, uninhabited place on earth may not cause much concern. If that volcano happens to be close to population centers, however, its relative location becomes very important.

The Theme of Place Describes Unique Characteristics

All places are different. Not only do they have different absolute and relative locations, they have different characteristics. Every place has unique human characteristics and unique physical characteristics. It is these characteristics that help geographers identify and describe a place.

▼ **Illustrating History** *The Golden Gate Bridge and the pyramid-shaped TransAmerica Building are two of San Francisco's signatures.*

When you sign your name to a letter or any other document, your signature identifies you and is unique to you. In geography, all places have signatures. Some of them are easily recognizable, such as the sign, "Hollywood," on the hillside above Hollywood, California. Other signatures are more complex but just as clear in telling you where you are. Look at the photograph of San Francisco on this page. Two signatures stand out. One is the TransAmerica Building (the pyramid-shaped skyscraper). The other signature is the Golden Gate Bridge. The Golden Gate Bridge is such an outstanding signature that you cannot mistake it for any other place in the world.

The people who occupy a place also help to define the characteristics of that place. Like the bridges they build, their backgrounds (German, English, Chinese, Thai, Kenyan, etc.) tells a great deal about the place where they live. Different backgrounds may give clues about languages, values, occupations, religions, customs, architecture, and beliefs. If the backgrounds of all the people in a certain place are mixed, the proportion of that mixture may tell something about the problems that may or may not exist in the place. All these become components of a place's signature.

Other characteristics of the population also describe a place. For example, a large population needs more water, food, and land than a small population. A large population responds differently to the use of local resources and to the use of the land. The skills of the people within a place also add to the overall picture of a place. Thus, human characteristics include not only the people of that place but also the things people have done in changing that place. The patterns of buildings, signs, and agriculture all indicate the special nature of the people who live there.

Physical characteristics are just as important in identifying a place. Like human signatures on the landscape, physical signatures may be simple and outstanding or complex and hidden. Diamond Head is a physical signature that identifies part of Honolulu, Hawaii. It is an extinct volcanic crater, the profile of which is unmistakable

▲ **Illustrating History** *This open-pit mine in Bingham, Utah, is an example of people interacting with their environment. What will future historians make of this method of obtaining mineral resources?*

anywhere in the world. Sugar Loaf mountain in Rio de Janeiro, Brazil, Devil's Tower, in Wyoming, or the Rock of Gibraltar in the Mediterranean Sea are other significant examples of geographical signatures.

Places may have physical characteristics that are not as obvious. Soil types, minerals, vegetation patterns, climate, river patterns, and landforms are mixed in a countless variety of ways to produce unique conditions for a place. Consider the mystery movies you have seen in which a detective has solved a crime by comparing the dirt on the shoes of the criminal with the soil of a particular place. In the same way, places have physical signatures that identify them.

The Theme of Interaction Focuses on People and the Environment

From the beginning of time, all humans have had to interact with their environment. The need for food and shelter led early people to search for places that had favorable environmental conditions. The cradles

of civilization, for example, developed along river valleys where water was plentiful and soil fertile. Where environmental conditions have not been ideal for human settlement, people have adapted to their surroundings. The crops they have grown were developed from the seeds that grew well in their climate and soil conditions. Along the steep river valleys of Asia, the scarcity of flat land caused people to carve the hillsides into terraces.

As technology has developed, humans have attempted to use and change their existing environment even more than in the past. The Netherlands' need for more land was solved by building dikes and reclaiming land from the sea. Natural resources that once lay beyond reach are now mined or used up at an increasingly rapid rate. Offshore oil, iron ore, bauxite, copper, and coal are available if we dig a big enough and deep enough hole. Timber is available not just log by log but by the freight-car load. How humans use these resources and how that use affects geographical systems on the planet is of great concern to modern geographers.

All interactions that humans have with their environments have a price. Decisions must be made on what we feel are acceptable risks and sacrifices. What effect will the destruction of the rain forests in tropical areas like Brazil have on the earth? What are the consequences of air pollution? If we build skyscrapers in earthquake zones, are we willing to accept the consequences?

The Theme of Movement Examines Links Between People, Goods, and Ideas

The fourth theme of geography—movement—investigates the relationships that develop between and among people and places. How one place is linked to another provides important clues to understanding the development of places. These patterns of travel and interaction are historically important.

The travels of Marco Polo to China in the thirteenth century, for example, had far-reaching effects. The introduction of new ideas, foods, clothing styles, and fabrics greatly influenced Western European merchants and traders. The introduction of new spices forever altered food preparation. Through preservation with spices, meats and vegetables could last longer at a time when refrigeration had not been invented. The voyages of fifteenth and sixteenth-century explorers were inspired in part by the stories of Marco Polo. These voyages eventually led to the search for colonies beyond Europe.

The movement of ideas had a significant influence upon the American Revolution. Today, the movement of ideas is seen in the magazine and television accounts of political activities everywhere. Everyone is affected by what is said, done, and communicated in places like South Africa, Afghanistan, Northern Ireland, Israel, and Iran. The spread of ideas brings about changes in the Philippines, Cuba, and South Korea.

Movement and technology have made it possible for humans to live in environments that suit them most in terms of leisure and convenience of life style. People no longer have to live in environments whose natural resources supply them with food, water, or shelter. Highways and railroads, canals and aqueducts, and power lines and satellites can supply what an environment lacks. Los Angeles, California, for example, uses power and water that come from hundreds of miles away. Japan survives as a leading manufacturing nation with very few natural

Illustrating History *Marco Polo* ▶ *contributed to the movement of ideas when he traveled to China in 1271. This thirteenth-century manuscript illustration shows Polo's fleet leaving for China from Venice, in Italy.*

resources. The iron ore, coal, timber, and oil it needs are imported from thousands of miles overseas.

Likewise, the locations of towns, factories, shopping centers, and stores are dependent upon geographic patterns of movement. Towns grew up at the crossroads of trade routes. Factories first appeared where the availability of water power was plentiful. Where people live and how they travel and shop are important considerations for the building of a new shopping mall.

The Theme of Regions Focuses on Areas With Similar Characteristics

Regions are made up of those areas that have certain unifying characteristics. There are countless ways of identifying a region. If you want to study a language region of the United States, you look for areas that contain a majority of people who speak Spanish, German, Italian, or French. A tropical rain forest makes up a climate region. A farming area might be classified as a region because of the type of crop grown there.

Geographers divide the earth into regions because they form convenient and manageable units of study. For example, a geographer may want to learn about salt deposits in desert soils. To do this, the geographer would first identify desert regions. The geographer would then study the soil in desert regions to find out how much salt it contains. Talking with desert farmers would tell the geographer how they deal with the problem of salt deposits. By comparing the different methods farmers use in each region, better solutions can be found.

The Five Themes of Geography Relate to History

Each of the five themes of geography can be used to describe and analyze the place a historical event happened. As you study world history, be careful to notice that these themes often overlap. Examples of one theme may also be used for another. For instance, the cable cars of San Francisco,

California, have been definite signatures of that city. As examples of human characteristics, they help define the theme of place. They are also examples of movement. In addition, they represent interaction between people and the environment. People built the cable cars to provide transportation up and down the steep hills of the city.

As you study world history, keep the five themes of geography in mind. You can begin by applying them to the civilizations you will study in the first unit of your textbook. Where were these ancient civilizations located? What physical and human characteristics made their locations unique? How did these civilizations interact with the environment? How were their developments transmitted from one place to another? What regions were they a part of? And what regions existed within them?

The study of geography can help you find the answers to all these questions about history. The study of geography can also provide you with essential tools for learning about history. You will find out what those tools are in the next section.

SECTION 3 REVIEW

Knowing Key Terms, People, and Places
1. Define: **a.** absolute location **b.** relative location

Reviewing Main Ideas
2. What are the physical and human characteristics of a place?
3. How does the way in which people interact with their environment affect that environment?
4. In geography, what does the theme of movement investigate?

Critical Thinking
Demonstrating Reasoned Judgment
5. Advancements in technology and improved methods of transportation have brought people closer together in spite of distances. What advantages can such a "smaller world" have?

4 Maps Are Essential Tools of Geography

As you read, look for answers to these questions:

◆ Why are maps important?
◆ What kinds of information do maps supply?
◆ How are latitude and longitude used?

Key Terms: parallel (defined on p. 16), meridian (p. 16), latitude (p. 16), longitude (p. 17)

The tradition of mapping began in the days before writing. Humans have always wanted to know where things were located in relation to other places in their known world. The people of ancient Egypt and the Middle East, for example, made maps. Drawn on clay tablets or sheets of pressed reeds, these maps often dealt with pieces of property. Accurately showing where property lines and boundary lines are located has always been a concern of people and nations.

Maps Show Places and Patterns on the Earth's Surface

Maps use symbols to show the real world. They provide a view of the world from above and show where places are located on the earth's surface. They show how land is organized and the patterns that this organization creates on the earth. By plotting the absolute location of certain types of information on a map, a geographer can see the patterns that emerge.

Population distribution, the location of hidden mineral wealth, types of vegetation, and the movements of people, goods, and ideas all create patterns on the earth. A map shows the absolute locations of these items as well as their relative locations. The relationships and linkages between and among people, places, and regions then become easier to analyze.

All Maps Contain Certain Inaccuracies

The only reasonably accurate representation of the earth is a globe. The four main properties of a map—area, shape, distance, and direction—are faithfully reproduced. However, a globe is too small to show much detail. It's also too awkward to carry around conveniently.

Think of all the maps that you have ever seen—road maps, maps of your home town, maps of the mall, and the maps your friends have drawn. All of them are drawn on a flat surface. In spite of how carefully cartographers, or mapmakers, do their work, all maps contain inaccuracies. This is because cartographers are attempting to show a curved surface on a flat piece of paper. Mapping the earth is a little like peeling an orange so that the peel comes off in one piece and then flattening the peel without having it break or distort. It can't be done!

A globe of the earth, like the skin of an orange, cannot be flattened without creating areas that are distorted. The actual distortion of the surface can be lessened if large sections of the globe are either removed or cut. However, this leaves large, blank spaces. You can also come close to eliminating the distortion if only a small area of the earth is being drawn.

The making of maps is usually done through the use of a projection. A piece of paper is placed on the outside of a globe. The paper may be flat, in the shape of a cylinder wrapped around the globe, or in the shape of a cone placed on top of the globe. A light placed in the center of the globe is turned on. The shadow lines of the continents and countries are projected onto the paper surrounding the globe. These are then traced onto the paper to form a map. All types of projections and combinations of projections have been used to make maps. All of them have distortions. None of them show all four map properties accurately at the same time on the same map.

A few examples of the many different types of map projections are illustrated on the opposite page. You can see how each one varies from all the others. A particular map projection is chosen because it most accurately shows what the cartographer or author thinks is most important. For example, showing direction and shape may be most important to a traveler, explorer, or navigator. Therefore, a Mercator projection, which shows distance and shape quite accurately, might be used even though areas are not accurate. Accuracy of land area requires an equal-area projection. The Gall-Peters projections shows area much more accurately than Mercator projection. Because of this, the size of Third World countries in relation to the size of other countries is more correct on a Gall-Peters projection. Like the Goode-

Homolosine projection, however, the Gall-Peters projection distorts shape. The Robinson projection comes closest to reality in its representation of both shape and area. Recently, it was selected by the National Geographic Society as the best available projection to use as a world reference map.

Latitude and Longitude Form the Main Grid System of Location

Virtually all maps that we use have some lines on them running from east to west and other lines running from north to south.

Types of Map Projections

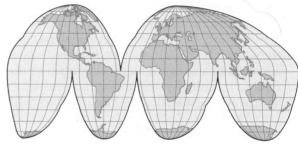

Goode Homolosine Projection

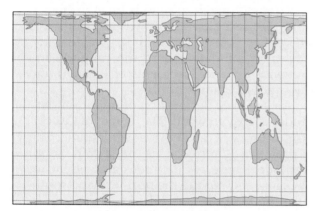

Gall-Peters Projection

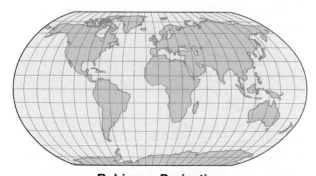

Robinson Projection

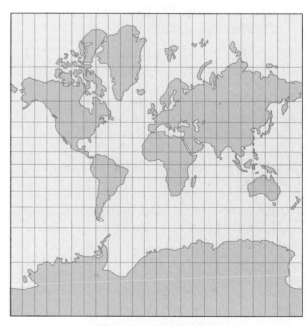

Mercator Projection

The lines that run from east to west are called **parallels.** The lines that run from north to south are called **meridians.** Together, the parallels and meridians form the grid system of location. Knowing this system is helpful in describing where something is and valuable in plotting data on a map.

The development of this grid system is taken from the natural movement of the earth. Because the earth rotates on an axis in space, two reference points are automatically established. The top of the axis on the earth is a reference point we call the North Pole. The bottom of the axis is a reference point we call the South Pole.

Parallels of latitude. Halfway between the North and South poles on the surface of the earth lies the equator, an imaginary line that is the same distance from both poles all the way around the earth. A series of parallel lines, which are actually concentric circles, are established both north and south of the equator. **Latitude** is the distance north or south as measured from the equator. All

latitude lines are measured in degrees, with the equator designated as 0°, or zero degrees. Latitude lines to the north of the equator are numbered from 1° north latitude to 90° north latitude, or the North Pole. Latitude lines to the south of the equator are numbered from 1° south latitude to 90° south latitude, or the South Pole. The closer each circle of latitude gets to the poles, the smaller it gets. This is similar to slicing an onion into onion rings.

On the surface of the earth, the actual distance between each degree of latitude is a little more than 69 miles. If a location is halfway between one degree of latitude and another, an accurate description would be impossible to give if you could only use degrees. Therefore, all degrees are divided into smaller units. One degree is divided into 60 minutes and is designated with the symbol of '. Thirty minutes would then be written 30'. Each minute is further divided into 60 seconds and is written with a ". Forty-five seconds would be written 45". Keep in mind that here the minutes and seconds are measurements of location and not measurements of time.

An accurate description of important latitudes is easy to write. The Tropic of Cancer, for example, is at 23°30' north latitude. The Tropic of Capricorn is at 23°30' south latitude. These two latitudes are significant because they define the northern and southern limits of the vertical rays of the sun. In its yearly revolution about the sun, the earth's position changes in relation to the sun. This causes the vertical rays of the sun to strike the earth at different latitudes. On June 21, the sun is directly over the Tropic of Cancer. This day is called the summer solstice and represents the beginning of summer in the northern hemisphere. On December 22, the sun is directly over the Tropic of Capricorn. The winter solstice marks the beginning of winter in the northern hemisphere.

Meridians of longitude. The other set of imaginary grid lines, called meridians, are drawn on the earth's surface and connect the North and South poles. Each meridian is the same length as all other meridians. They

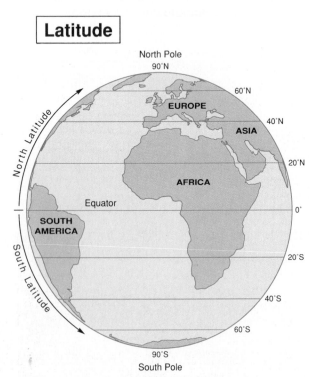

Latitude

▲ **Location** *Latitude is the distance north or south as measured from the equator.*

16

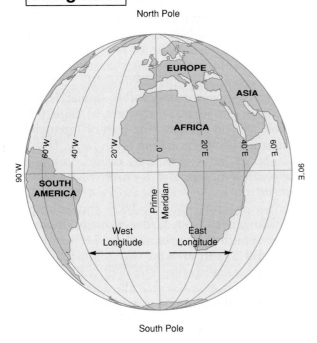

North Pole

EUROPE

ASIA

AFRICA

60°W 40°W 20°W 0° 20°E 40°E 60°E

90°W

90°E

SOUTH AMERICA

Prime Meridian

West Longitude

East Longitude

South Pole

▲ **Location** *Longitude is the distance east or west as measured from the prime meridian.*

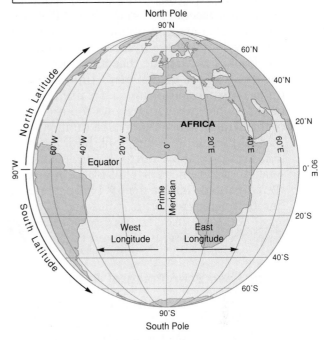

North Pole
90°N

60°N

40°N

North Latitude

20°N

AFRICA

60°W 40°W 20°W 0° 20°E 40°E 60°E

Equator

0°

90°W

90°E

South Latitude

Prime Meridian

West Longitude

East Longitude

20°S

40°S

60°S

90°S
South Pole

▲ **Location** *What continent would you be on if you were at a location 20° north latitude and 20° east longitude?*

are farthest apart as they cross the equator and come to a point at the poles. The meridian that runs through Greenwich, England, is called the prime meridian. It is designated as 0° longitude. **Longitude** is the distance east or west as measured from the prime meridian. All longitude lines drawn to the east of the prime meridian are numbered from 1° to 179° east longitude. All longitudes west of the prime meridian are numbered from 1° to 179° west longitude. East and west longitude lines meet at 180° in the Pacific Ocean.

To summarize, all latitude lines extend east-west but measure distance north or south of the equator. They are parallel to each other. Each latitude line is of a different length, and the longest is the equator.

All longitude lines extend north-south, but measure distance east or west of the prime meridian. They are not parallel to each other but vary in distance apart. They are all of the same length.

Putting this grid together now allows us to accurately plot any place on the surface of the earth. For example, you would find the city of West Berlin at 52° 30′ north latitude, 13° 20′ east longitude. The center of the harbor of the city of Rio de Janeiro, Brazil, is located at 22° 50′ south latitude, 43° 10′ west longitude. What are the proper latitude and longitude coordinates for the location of your town?

Maps Contain a Wealth of Information

Accurate location is only one type of information given to you on a map. Maps are also drawn for specific reasons and are used to show specific information or themes. Road maps, for example, are familiar to everyone. Topographic maps produced by the U.S. Geological Survey show physical features such as mountains, rivers, and plains. They also show contours, or lines that connect all points of the same elevation.

All of the information shown on a map is drawn using various lines, labels, symbols, and colors. Decoding a map is not difficult if you know something about how maps are organized and where to look. Every map in this book, for example, has a title that tells you the subject of the map. Unless everything is explained on the map itself, every map also has a key that shows the meaning of the symbols and colors used on it. Notice that all the maps in this book have a direction arrow to show north, south, east, and west. In addition, nearly all of the maps in your textbook have a scale. This scale is a line that is marked off in miles and kilometers. You can use the scale to measure distances between locations on the map.

Maps Have Been Practical Tools

People in the past have made good use of maps. All explorers, traders, travelers, military commanders, and government officials have used maps. Knowing where you are, where needed resources and materials are, and how to get there and back has been of utmost importance throughout history. A nation's existence often depends on that knowledge. Good maps made it possible for the Greeks and Romans to trade with all parts of their extensive empires. Control of those empires was also of importance.

Military operations throughout history have depended on maps. Knowing where an enemy was in relation to strategic passes, higher ground, or major resources has always been of extreme value to military commanders. Accurate mapping has become even more important today when one considers the speed and low altitude flying of modern fighter planes and cruise missiles.

Return to the reasons for maps at the beginning of this section. Throughout history, maps have served as property documents. They showed national boundary lines and the possessions claimed by various nations. Today, they are still used for that purpose. Wars are fought over the control of small pieces of territory. Treaties are signed that spell out the limits of national boundaries in great detail.

How far a nation will go to protect its property can be illustrated by a fishing rights case from Japan. International law has established fishing rights extending out 200 miles from any shoreline that belongs to a nation. About 1200 miles south of Tokyo, Japan's capital, lie the Offshore Bird Islands. These islands are only a few square feet in area and sit just above water at high tide. They are considered to be part of Japan, but the sea is slowly washing them away. If they disappear from sight, they would no longer appear on a map. The 200-mile fishing limit would no longer be measured from them, removing more than 160,000 square miles of fishing area from Japan's control. Japan is now spending approximately $225 million to build a wall around two islands smaller than your classroom. The wall will keep the islands above sea level. The Offshore Bird Islands will remain on the map and continue to permit Japan to control a great fishing resource.

Maps are as much a method of communication as writing. Information can often be transmitted more rapidly through the use of a map than in any other way. An ancient Chinese proverb says that "a picture is worth a thousand words." Maps are often worth much more than that.

SECTION 4 REVIEW

Knowing Key Terms, People, and Places
1. Define: **a.** parallel **b.** meridian **c.** latitude **d.** longitude

Reviewing Main Ideas
2. What information do maps provide?
3. Why do all maps contain inaccuracies?
4. Describe the grid system on maps.

Critical Thinking
Expressing Problems Clearly
5. Imagine that you are an ocean explorer in the days before accurate maps have been drawn. What problems would you have in planning your explorations that you would not have today?

REVIEW

Section Summaries

Section 1 History Tells the Story of People on Earth History is the story of what human beings have done on earth. Using both primary and secondary sources, historians try to discover the reasons behind the events of the past. Historians also focus on the places where past events occurred. The study of history helps us to apply the lessons of the past to present and future world decisions.

Section 2 Geography Is Where History Happens Geography is the study of where things are on the earth, why they are there, and their relationships to people, things, or other places. Location, natural resources, and the climate of an area have a major effect on how the people there live and work. The two major branches of geography are physical geography and human geography. The combined effects of physical and human geography determine much of the history of specific areas of the world.

Section 3 Five Themes Describe Geography's Framework Geographers have identified five themes of geography that help them to organize their study. These themes are: location, place, interaction, movement, and regions. Location tells exactly where something is. Place describes the unique characteristics of a location. The theme of interaction analyzes the link between people and their environment. Movement investigates how and why people, goods, and ideas move from one place to another. Regions are areas that share unifying characteristics that geographers group together for study.

Section 4 Maps Are Essential Tools of Geography Maps are important because they show places and patterns on the earth's surface. They show specific locations and the relative distances between these locations using a grid system of longitude and latitude lines. Some maps also show the physical contours and elevation of the land. Maps are invaluable as travel aids for all people, as political and economic guidelines, and as research aids for the geographer.

Key Facts

Use each vocabulary word in a sentence.

a. history
b. primary source
c. secondary source
d. geography
e. physical geography
f. human geography
g. landform
h. absolute location
i. relative location
j. parallel
k. meridian
l. latitude
m. longitude

Main Ideas

1. Why is it sometimes difficult to learn about the past?
2. Explain why a primary source might be more valuable than a secondary source.
3. How can geography influence where human settlement occurs?
4. How has technology helped humans to obtain more natural resources?
5. Why do geographers divide the earth into regions?
6. Explain how maps are made using projections.
7. What is the purpose of the scale on a map?

Critical Thinking

1. **Demonstrating Reasoned Judgment** Describe the physical geography of an area that you think would be an ideal place for human settlement.
2. **Predicting Consequences** If the natural resources of an area are continually used and not replaced, how might this affect the future of the people living there?

19

UNIT

1

Cradles of Civilization

(PREHISTORY–A.D. 500)

What is civilization? Where did it begin? As you read this unit, you will learn the conditions under which civilizations developed. You will also find out why four of the earliest civilizations grew as they did. Settlers in four great river valleys—one in Africa, one in the Middle East, and two in Asia—created lively, prosperous civilizations by building on the foundations laid by earlier people. From these beginnings rose the ancient civilizations of Egypt, the Middle East, India, and China. The map and the time line, linked by color, show where and when the cradles of civilization grew.

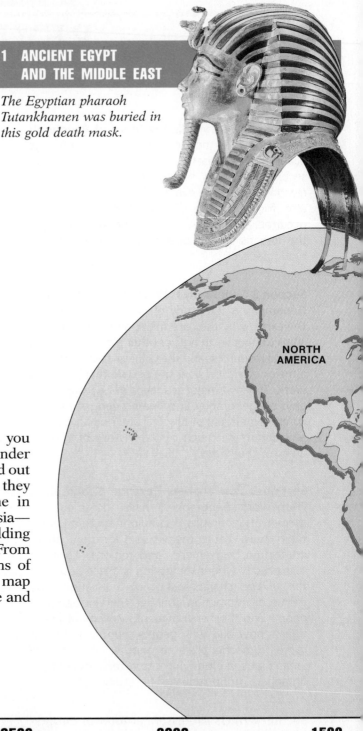

1 ANCIENT EGYPT AND THE MIDDLE EAST

The Egyptian pharaoh Tutankhamen was buried in this gold death mask.

NORTH AMERICA

PREHISTORY	2500 B.C.	2000 B.C.	1500 B.C.
■ 4000 B.C. Sumerians settle in Mesopotamia	■ 2780 B.C. Egypt's Old Kingdom, or Age of Pyramids, begins		■ 1800 B.C. Hyksos conquer
	■ 2900 B.C. Indus Valley people trade with peoples of Mesopotamia	■ 2000 B.C. Indus Valley civilization disappears	
		■ 2000 B.C. Xia family forms China's first dynasty	

20

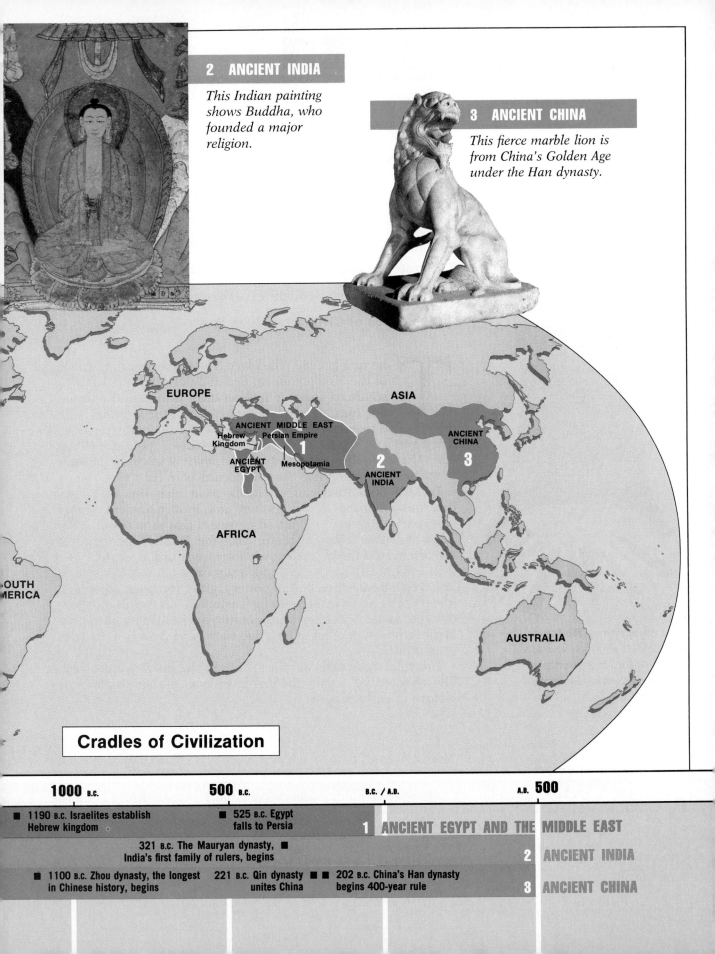

2 ANCIENT INDIA

This Indian painting shows Buddha, who founded a major religion.

3 ANCIENT CHINA

This fierce marble lion is from China's Golden Age under the Han dynasty.

EUROPE

ASIA

ANCIENT MIDDLE EAST
Hebrew
Kingdom
Persian Empire
1

ANCIENT
EGYPT
Mesopotamia

ANCIENT
CHINA
3

2
ANCIENT
INDIA

AFRICA

SOUTH
AMERICA

AUSTRALIA

Cradles of Civilization

1000 B.C.	500 B.C.	B.C. / A.D.	A.D. 500
■ 1190 B.C. Israelites establish Hebrew kingdom	■ 525 B.C. Egypt falls to Persia		1 ANCIENT EGYPT AND THE MIDDLE EAST
	321 B.C. The Mauryan dynasty, ■ India's first family of rulers, begins		2 ANCIENT INDIA
■ 1100 B.C. Zhou dynasty, the longest in Chinese history, begins	221 B.C. Qin dynasty unites China	■ ■ 202 B.C. China's Han dynasty begins 400-year rule	3 ANCIENT CHINA

Early People

(Prehistory–1000 B.C.)

1 **Scientists Help Historians Learn About Prehistory**

2 **Stone Age People Made Important Discoveries**

3 **The Bronze Age Brought Progress**

4 **The Seeds of Civilization Took Root**

▲ **Illustrating History** *The oldest shipwreck yielded bronze tools, bronze weapons, and copper ingots.*

The year is 1982. The place: 150 feet below the surface of the Mediterranean Sea at a point just off Turkey's southern coast. A Turkish diver hovers in the water. For him, the dive is part of a routine workday. The diver's job is to harvest sponges from the bottom of the sea to be dried and sold. On this day, however, the diver spots something else. There, on the ocean bottom, are small objects that he later describes as looking like "metal biscuits with ears."

Turkish and American scientists soon visit the site. They determine that the "metal biscuits" are, in fact, ancient copper bars, part of the cargo of a trading vessel that sank about 3,400 years ago. The scientists realize that the Turkish sponge diver has discovered the oldest known shipwreck in the world.

In 1984, scientists began underwater excavation of this wreck. The ship is a treasure chest of pottery, glass, weapons, tools, and jewelry. The items brought to the surface so far represent seven different ancient Mediterranean cultures. These items show that Mediterranean peoples of long ago carried on a lively trade with each other.

The shipwreck adds another piece in the puzzle of the past. This chapter will supply the first few pieces of that puzzle in its picture of early peoples.

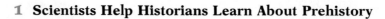

2 million B.C.	8000 B.C.	6000 B.C.	4000 B.C.	2000 B.C.
■ 2 million B.C. Old Stone Age begins	■ 8000 B.C. Middle Stone Age begins; ways of hunting improve	■ 6000 B.C. New Stone Age begins; people discover farming and live in cities	■ 3500 B.C. Written records appear	

▲ **Illustrating History** *Divers who surveyed this Bronze Age shipwreck first had to remove mud and label the many parts of the find.*

1 Scientists Help Historians Learn About Prehistory

As you read, look for answers to these questions:

◆ What is prehistory?
◆ How does science help us to learn about prehistory?
◆ What do fossils and artifacts tell us about how people lived in prehistoric times?

Key Terms: historic period (defined on p. 23), prehistory (p. 23), archaeologist (p. 24), artifact (p. 24), fossil (p. 24), anthropologist (p. 24), society (p. 24), culture (p. 24)

Discoveries about early humans, like the discovery you have just read about, give us a clearer picture of ancient history. Some-

times, these discoveries are all the more exciting because they allow us to glimpse a time long ago before the invention of writing. Written records first appeared about 3500 B.C., or 3,500 years before the birth of Jesus. Their appearance marks the beginning of a period of time that historians call the **historic period.** It includes only about the last 5,000 years. In relation to your lifetime, 5,000 years is a long time. It is brief, however, when it is compared with the span of years before written records were kept.

Historians use the term **prehistory** to describe the enormous period of time before people invented writing. Usually, historians use written records to learn about the past. Human beings, however, existed long before writing was used. To learn about prehistory, historians team up with scientists to locate and analyze the unwritten records, such as tools, monuments, bones, and pottery, left by early people.

Scientists Uncover How Prehistoric People Lived

Scientists have made many discoveries that help us to understand prehistory. Two types of scientists who investigate prehistory are archaeologists (AHR kee AHL uh jihsts) and anthropologists (AN thruh PAHL uh jihsts). An **archaeologist** uses scientific techniques to find and study the remains left by prehistoric people to learn more about their culture. These remains often include artifacts. An **artifact** (AHR tuh FAKT) is any object that was made by human beings, such as a tool, a weapon, pottery, or jewelry. Archaeologists are also interested in studying **fossils,** the hardened remains of plants and animals.

An **anthropologist** is a scientist who studies the characteristics, customs, and relationships of different societies in order to learn about their origins and development. A **society** is any group of people who live together and share a common goal. The total way of life that people in a society share is their **culture.** Anthropologists sometimes use artifacts and fragments of bone to draw conclusions about early societies and cultures.

▼ **Illustrating History** *Archaeologists must work slowly and carefully. Here, a team in Costa Rica sifts through soil.*

For archaeologists, the search for artifacts and other remains of early people is nearly always long and painstaking. The search begins when a team of archaeologists looks for places where they think early people may have lived. Once the archaeologists have found a possible location, a site is established. Small sections of land are marked off, usually with pegs and string. Then, the dig begins. Very carefully, the archaeologists begin to dig up the soil and sift through the site, one layer at a time. Any artifacts or fossils that are uncovered are carefully recorded and later analyzed.

Many times, archaeologists discover small fragments of bones and artifacts. Piecing the fragments together takes time, patience, and great skill. In 1972, for example, the archaeologist Bernard Ngeneo, who was working in Africa, spotted pieces of a skull. Day after day, he sifted through sand and gravel to locate more pieces. Each hot, dusty day yielded more small fragments of skull. It took more than a month and the help of other people to put the pieces together to form the skull of what Ngeneo and other archaeologists believed was a human who lived about 2 million years ago. The skull that Ngeneo found is a significant archaeological find because it is one of the oldest, most complete human skulls.

Imagine being one of the underwater archaeologists recovering Bronze Age treasures from the world's oldest known shipwreck you read about at the beginning of this chapter. A team from the Institute of Nautical Archaeology at Texas A&M University has spent more than four years bringing the ship's contents to the surface. First, the team made a site plan using thousands of measurements and photographs of the remains of the ship and its artifacts. An air-filled, unbreakable, clear plastic booth (which the team called the "phone booth") was lowered into the water with someone in it who could communicate with the divers as they worked. Platforms equipped with balloon devices were used to raise heavy objects from the ocean floor. This complicated archaeological project has brought to the surface bronze swords, raw ivory, amber jewelry, and gold and silver. From a historian's point of view, however, the most valuable treasure of all is the knowledge the project gives us of the distant past.

You can see that the job of an archaeologist is both exciting and demanding. An archaeologist is really like a well-trained detective looking for historical clues. Once fossils and artifacts are found, the job of determining how old they are begins.

Scientific Techniques Date Fossils and Artifacts

An important step in analyzing artifacts and fossils is dating them, or determining their ages. The layer of earth in which a fossil or artifact is found helps to determine its age. Because layers of soil and rock are laid one on top of another as time passes, the layers at the bottom of an archaeological dig are older than those at the top. Therefore, a fossil found in a rock deep underground is usually older than a fossil found in a rock nearer the surface. Analyzing the chemicals in the rock and fossils themselves also helps to determine when they were formed. For example, volcanic rocks contain a gas called argon. Scientists can analyze the amount of argon in a volcanic rock and then date the rock according to its argon content.

Using another technique that is known as carbon-14 dating, scientists can determine the age of anything that was once part of a living organism such as bones, teeth, hair, and wood. When an organism dies, the carbon-14, also called radiocarbon, contained in its cells begins to decay. By measuring the rate of decay, scientists can estimate when the organism died. The greater the decay, the older the object.

The carbon-14 method is not perfect. It cannot give reliable dating beyond 50,000 years ago. Newer, more accurate methods of dating ancient objects are being researched. Computers, for example, can greatly speed up the process of analyzing and dating fossils and artifacts.

These techniques and the work of scientists have helped to form a picture of prehistory. Of course, scientists may disagree over

▲ **Illustrating History** *This stone fragment of a horse's head, dated to between 20,000 and 10,000 B.C., offers a glimpse into prehistory.*

their findings, and new discoveries may change or add to what we know about prehistoric times. For now, we have scientists' best-educated conclusions about how early humans looked and how they lived. Knowing these facts, we can take a look into the world of prehistory.

°SECTION 1 REVIEW

Knowing Key Terms, People, and Places
1. Define: **a.** historic period **b.** prehistory **c.** archaeologist **d.** artifact **e.** fossil **f.** anthropologist **g.** society **h.** culture

Reviewing Main Ideas
2. Approximately when did written records first appear?
3. Describe the job of the archaeologist.
4. How can science help to determine the age of fossils and artifacts?

Critical Thinking

Identifying Central Issues
5. Why is it important for scientists to determine the age of artifacts?

2 Stone Age People Made Important Discoveries

As you read, look for answers to these questions:

◆ What was the Stone Age?
◆ What was daily life like for Stone Age people?
◆ What changes took place during the Old, Middle, and New Stone Ages?

> **Key Terms:** nomad (defined on p. 27), specialization of labor (p. 30)

Ice covered most of North America and much of Europe when the Stone Age began. We call this period the Stone Age because the people who lived then used tools and weapons made of stone. The Stone Age lasted from about 2 million B.C. to 3500 B.C. As the Stone Age progressed, people improved their stone-working techniques and produced more refined tools and weapons.

Historians often divide the Stone Age into three parts—the Old Stone Age, the Middle Stone Age, and the New Stone Age. Historians can only estimate when each age began and ended. Many historians believe that the Old Stone Age, or Paleolithic (PAY lee uh LITH ihk) Age, lasted 2 million years and ended around 8000 B.C. The Middle Stone Age, or Mesolithic (MEZ uh LITH ihk) Age, lasted from about 8000 B.C. to about 6000 B.C. The New Stone Age, or Neolithic (NEE uh LITH ihk) Age, lasted from about 6000 B.C. to about 3500 B.C.

Neanderthal People Learned Basic Skills

Imagine, if you can, a muscular group of people standing before a cave and looking out over a cold landscape. Some of them have stone axes in their hands and animal skins over their shoulders. What you are imagining are Neanderthal (nee AN der THAWL) men and women, one group of people who lived in the Old Stone Age. These people lived from about 100,000 to 40,000 years ago. Scientists named them after a valley in Germany where the remains were first found.

The Neanderthal people were among the first people to be classified as human beings, or *Homo Sapiens* (HOH moh SAY pee enz). The oldest known fossils of Homo Sapiens are about 375,000 years old. These skulls and skeletal remains have been found in Africa, Europe, and Asia.

How Neanderthal people looked. When one of the first nearly complete skeletons of a Neanderthal person was found in France in 1908, scientists drew some faulty conclusions about how these people looked. They said that Neanderthal people walked with their upper bodies hunched over and their arms swinging by their sides—more like apes than people. With more study, however, scientists realized that they were basing their conclusions on the skeleton of an old person whose bones were diseased and bent with arthritis.

Since then, archaeologists have found many additional Neanderthal skeletons that support the conclusion that Neanderthal people walked and looked much like modern humans. Evidence has shown that these people were muscular, about 5 feet to 5 feet 6 inches tall, and stood upright. Their brains were as big as ours, although their skulls were shaped differently. Their noses and jaws stuck forward and their teeth also were further forward than ours. Anthropologist Richard E. Leakey has written ". . . if we were able to dress a Neanderthal man and woman in modern clothes, cut their hair and put them into a modern airport, they would probably go unnoticed by the other passengers."

Neanderthal progress. Neanderthal women and men made important discoveries that later people used and developed even further. During the Old Stone Age, Neanderthal people learned to make stone tools such as axes, spears, knives, arrowheads, and chisels. From the tusks of animals, they made needles and learned to sew fur skins together to make clothing.

Neanderthal people were among the first to live successfully in colder climates. An important milestone in their development was the discovery of the use of fire. Fire kept early people warm and enabled them to cook their food and to keep enemies, especially wild animals, away at night.

Old Stone Age people were hunters and gatherers. They hunted giant prehistoric animals like the musk ox, mammoth, cave bear, reindeer, and woolly rhinoceros for meat and furs. They also gathered roots, nuts, and fruit.

To survive, the Neanderthal people had to live where there was a good food supply. If the supply of animals decreased in one place, they would move to another place and then another. People who move in search of food and have no permanent home as the Neanderthal people did are called **nomads.**

Moving, however, does not keep people from developing customs and social groups.

The Neanderthal people had both. The family, in various forms, was the basic social group. By hunting together, the family provided for its needs. It cared for its members and it defended itself against intruders. Eventually, families joined together to form larger social groups. Archaeological findings show that groups of as many as 30 people probably hunted and lived together, developing many customs.

One custom that scientists know the Neanderthal people had was the burial of their dead. Many Neanderthal skeletons have been found because, unlike earlier humans, these people buried their dead. Careful burial under a layer of earth increases the chance that a skeleton will be well preserved as a fossil.

Several interesting burial sites have been discovered that indicate that the Neanderthal people practiced burial rituals. In Asia, for example, a young child was found buried with six pairs of animal horns arranged

▼ **Illustrating History** *The Cro-Magnon people of southern France painted figures like the horse shown below on cave walls. At left are Stone Age tools.*

around his head. In Iraq, a Neanderthal man was buried with flowers arranged around his body. From an analysis of clumps of pollen fossils, archaeologists determined that the flowers were all medicinal herbs, suggesting that the man may have been considered a doctor. Although there are still many unanswered questions, Neanderthal burial rituals seem to indicate that these early people thought about the meaning of life and death.

Cro-Magnon People Advanced Rapidly

About 40,000 years ago, or around 38,000 B.C., the Neanderthal people were gradually replaced by the Cro-Magnon (kroh MAG nahn) people. These people were named after the location in southern France where their remains were first discovered.

Why or how the Cro-Magnon people replaced the Neanderthal people is not clear. Some historians think that the Cro-Magnon people may have had more advanced weapons that enabled them to destroy the Neanderthal people. Other historians think that the Neanderthal people may have been overcome by disease. It seems more likely, however, that the Neanderthal people simply changed physically over time until they could no longer be distinguished from the Cro-Magnon people.

The technology of the Cro-Magnon people advanced far more rapidly than the technology of the Neanderthal people, which helped the Cro-Magnons to accomplish the everyday tasks of living with greater ease. Cro-Magnon people made more delicate and efficient stone, bone, and wood tools than the Neanderthal people did. These later people carved fishhooks, harpoons, and fine needles from bone. They chipped away pieces of stone to make knives, scrapers, arrowheads, and spear points.

While Neanderthal people lived mostly in caves to protect themselves from wild animals, enemies, and the cold, Cro-Magnon people began to move from caves and began to build shelters for themselves. Animal skins were sometimes stretched over bones to create shelters. The dome-shaped dwellings of the Australian Aborigines (AB uh RIHJ uh neez) and Mongolians are similar to the homes that Cro-Magnon people invented. The dome-shaped home is probably the earliest and most common form of housing found throughout the world. In fact, the geodesic dome, designed by Buckminster Fuller, a twentieth-century architect, was inspired in part by the dome-shaped shelters of Cro-Magnon people.

The intellectual development of the Cro-Magnon people may be seen in the paintings they left on cave walls. A treasure trove of these paintings was found in Altamira (AHL tuh MIHR uh) in northern Spain in 1879 when a Spanish nobleman decided to explore a cave on his property. One day, he took his small daughter with him. Since the ceiling of the cave was low and he had to stoop, he looked down, but his daughter could wander about the cave freely. When she looked up at the cave's ceiling, she found it covered with colorful animal paintings that were later identified as the work of Cro-Magnon artists.

Perhaps the best known of the caves in which Cro-Magnon art may be found is in Lascaux (las KOH) in southern France. In 1940, four boys discovered the pictures in an underground cave while chasing their dog. Cro-Magnon cave art shows a great skill in observing how animals live and behave. The art also illustrates the ability of the Cro-Magnon people to express their thoughts, their dreams, their hopes and fears, and their religious beliefs.

Progress Continued During the Middle Stone Age

The Middle Stone Age (about 8000 B.C. to 6000 B.C.) was marked by gradual changes in human progress. Beginning around 8000 B.C., the glaciers of the Ice Age moved slowly north. The world's climate grew warmer, and grasslands and forests began to grow. These geographical changes set the stage for the start of the Middle Stone Age.

During the Middle Stone Age, people refined their stone work. They learned to make smaller and finer stone objects than

The First Farmers

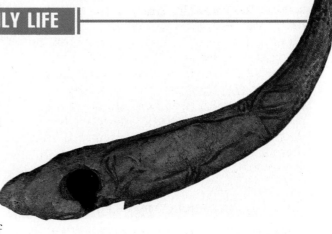

Who were the world's first farmers? No one knows for sure, but scientific evidence points to people who lived in what is now the Middle East. Archaeologists have uncovered remains of the oldest known farming communities in such Middle Eastern countries as Israel and Iraq.

One important site is Jarmo, located in northeastern Iraq. Drawn by the patches of wild barley and wheat that were growing among the hills, early hunter-gatherers settled there about 7,000 years ago.

The remains of Jarmo reveal the pattern of life in one of the world's first farming villages. Each family lived in a mud hut of several rooms. Using stone or bone tools like the one at right, the villagers grew and harvested their crops. They raised sheep and goats. When nomadic people passed through Jarmo, villagers probably traded baskets of grain for hides, wild game, and shells. From such beginnings as Jarmo, agriculture spread throughout the world.

1. What evidence suggests that farming began in the Middle East?
2. What attracted early settlers to Jarmo?

---

they had in the Old Stone Age. Their improved, sharper spearheads and arrowheads were important because they made hunting for food and defense against any enemy easier and more accurate. Small pieces of stone, probably made to insert in wood or bone handles, provided sharper cutting edges for skinning animals, preparing food, or carrying out other everyday tasks. Middle Stone Age people also made the first pottery. These clay pots and bowls allowed people to store food and water, thus making their daily lives easier.

Middle Stone Age people relied heavily on fish and shellfish for food. By making fishhooks and harpoons of bone, they increased their catches. They learned to weave nets and scrape out logs to use as canoe-like boats. Using these boats, the people were able to catch more fish and to improve their methods of travel.

Middle Stone Age people were also the first to domesticate, or tame, wild dogs. Once trained, these dogs tracked game and helped to guard and protect the people and their property.

The New Stone Age Brought Dramatic Changes

At some point during the New Stone Age, or Neolithic Age, which took place from about 6000 B.C. to about 3500 B.C., a new discovery changed human lives forever. People learned to plant seeds to grow food, thus beginning the practice of farming. Agriculture freed people from the constant search for food. Although hunting, gathering, and fishing continued, they were no longer the only ways to provide food. New Stone Age people also began to keep herds of animals, such as cattle and sheep, to use for meat.

Because of the many changes farming brought to the way people lived, historians often call the move from hunting and gathering to farming the *Neolithic revolution*.

▲ **Illustrating History**　*Shown above is Stonehenge, a ring of huge stones raised by New Stone Age people in England about 3000 B.C.*

Freed from spending their entire day hunting for food, people could devote time to other activities. They built sturdy houses and began to live in villages. They created decorative pottery, dishes, and ornaments. They learned to weave cloth from plant fibers and animal hair. During the New Stone Age, people also learned to polish stone and bone tools and weapons so that they were smooth to touch, easy to hold, and sharp to use. In addition, farmers began to use animals, such as oxen or cattle, to pull plows. As a result, farmers could plow more land and produce larger harvests.

Close to the end of the New Stone Age, another revolutionary invention took place. The first wheels and axles, made of wood, were used. Simple carts and wagons soon followed. The wheel made a dramatic improvement in the lives of early farmers and other laborers. During the New Stone Age, **specialization of labor** began. This means that people began to perform specific jobs according to their skills.

Anthropologists believe that New Stone Age people followed established customs and rules to protect themselves and their food supplies. They probably had some form of government to enforce their rules.

Religious customs and ceremonies became more detailed and elaborate than they were in the Middle Stone Age. New Stone Age people who lived in what is now southern England built Stonehenge, an enormous monument of huge slabs of rough-cut stone, about 3000 B.C. Scholars believe that some of the stones were brought to the site from a location in Wales, about 300 miles (480 kilometers) away. Although historians are not sure of the purpose of Stonehenge, it may have served as a place of worship and as an astronomical observatory. Here, people could study the position of the sun, moon, and stars, which were important to the way they lived and prayed.

SECTION 2 REVIEW

Knowing Key Terms, People, and Places
1. Define: **a.** nomad **b.** specialization of labor
2. Identify: **a.** Stone Age **b.** Neanderthal people **c.** Cro-Magnon people

Reviewing Main Ideas
3. What are the three divisions of the Stone Age? About when did each occur?
4. How did Neanderthal people obtain their food?
5. How did agriculture change human lives?

Critical Thinking
Making Comparisons
6. How did daily life during the Old Stone Age compare to daily life during the New Stone Age?

3 The Bronze Age Brought Progress

As you read, look for answers to these questions:

◆ How did the discovery of bronze change daily life?
◆ How was bronze useful in warfare and farming?
◆ What major changes took place during the Bronze Age?

Key Terms: smelting (defined on p. 32), urbanization (p. 32)

If you have ever used a rock to hammer a nail into a board, you know how hard it is to do and how much more easily the same task can be done if you use a hammer with a metal head. For the people of the New Stone Age, the discovery of metals for making tools and weapons greatly changed and improved their lives.

No one knows for sure just when or in what way New Stone Age people discovered how to make metal objects. It seems possible that about 4000 B.C., people observed that a substance bubbling from the rocks heated by their campfires could be cooled and then molded into an axe or knife with an edge that was harder and more durable than stone. Copper, as the substance came to be called, heralded the end of the New Stone Age.

Bronze Was Made From Copper and Tin

As a tool or weapon, copper is much better than stone, but it is still relatively soft. Even if it is carefully crafted, a sharp edge can be worn down easily. Probably through accident at first, copper was mixed with tin to form bronze, a harder and more durable metal than copper. The earliest bronze objects appeared about 3500 B.C. in the Middle East where evidence is found of the beginning of a metals industry.

Metalworkers gradually learned where to find copper, tin, and other metals and how to extract them from the earth and rocks. They learned how to remove the impurities that are mixed into metal ores and then how to mix the metals themselves to achieve sturdy, sharp, durable tools and weapons. As a result, the Bronze Age was born.

Although historians speak of a Bronze Age, bronze really was used by different people at different times. In fact, some people, such as those in Finland, northern Russia, Polynesia, central Africa, southern India, North America, Australia, and Japan, never used bronze at all. These people moved directly from the use of stone to the use of iron. Nevertheless, the use of bronze provides a good clue to the degree to which some ancient people advanced.

Improved Tools and Weapons Appeared During the Bronze Age

Of course, bronze tools and weapons did not replace those of stone all at once or everywhere. Then, as today, some men and women were content to use the tools they knew best. Stone tools and weapons lingered on for many generations after the introduction of bronze. Because the making of bronze was a costly process, wealthy people tended to use bronze tools and weapons more often than poor people.

At first, because bronze was scarce and expensive, it was mostly used for weapons. Soldiers armed with bronze swords, shields, and helmets could defeat enemies who did not have the strength and protection of bronze weapons and equipment.

As the use of bronze spread, it was used for more ordinary but important tools. Bronze helped farmers become more productive. With bronze digging sticks, they could plant seeds or seedlings more easily than with wooden digging sticks. With a bronze plow, farmers could make deeper and straighter furrows. With bronze tools, they could dig deeper ditches to direct the flow of water to their lands more effectively. With a bronze sickle, they could harvest their crops with a bit less backbreaking effort.

Stone Age Sport

Archaeologists have little information about when humans began to play games. In the following excerpt, the anthropologists Alyce Taylor Cheska and Kendall Blanchard explain one game they think the earliest Indian settlers of America played.

"One type of sport artifact found in the American Southeast is the chunkey stone. Chunkey is a game played among Southeastern tribes (e.g., Choctaws, Creeks) in which a player rolls the large stone along the ground, and participants compete by throwing wooden poles in the path of the stone. The object is to throw the pole as closely as possible to the point at which the chunkey stone will eventually come to rest. . . .

How [do archaeologists] determine that [chunkey stones] were used for sport or game purposes? In some cases, interpretation is based on contextual [surrounding] information. . . . For example, if a future archaeologist were to excavate a twentieth-century American site and discover a leather football, he might not recognize it as a sport device. But, if that football were to be found in association with a stadium, playing field, [etc] . . . it might seem obvious that the artifact was a sport object.

In other archaeological settings . . . the archaeologist reasons from information that he has about a living group of people to interpret the activities of a similar but extinct group of people. . . . **"**

1. Describe the game of chunkey.
2. Explain what Cheska and Blanchard mean by "contextual information."

The simple types of clay objects made during the Middle Stone Age also improved during the Bronze Age. The invention of the potter's wheel made it possible for potters to create clay pots of more uniform size and shape. The beautifully decorated clay vessels of the Bronze Age give us further evidence of the progress of the people who made them.

Simple sailing ships and understanding of how to use the wind for navigation enabled people to trade with distant communities. As this trade took place, the knowledge of how to make bronze spread.

The Bronze Age Added to Human Progress

Once bronze weapons and tools became more common, the metal-making industry began in earnest. The mining of ores, the process of removing metal from the ore, called **smelting**, and the forging of weapons all became growing industries that required societies to be reorganized.

How would people who no longer worked as farmers get fed? Would those who continued to be farmers be able to grow enough food to feed everyone? What sort of exchange could be made between metalworkers and farmers? Those who worked in the metal industry would have to earn enough to pay farmers for food they needed. Thus, trade developed whereby farmers could get the bronze plows or other farm tools needed to produce enough food for everyone.

Specialization of labor continued to grow, developing further than it had during the New Stone Age. Improved tools now allowed one person to do the work of many. Some people grew food; others made bronze tools and weapons; still others made clay pots and other vessels. Some people wove garments; some sailed ships. The development of specialized work encouraged **urbanization**, the growth of cities.

Because ores used for making metals are not found everywhere, the need to obtain ores led to increased world exploration and trade. Trade routes then had to be opened so that metal ores could be shipped to those places that wanted ores. By 2000 B.C., a

▲ **Illustrating History** *The invention of the potter's wheel during the Bronze Age allowed potters to make pots of a more uniform size and shape. At right is a bronze statue.*

network of trade routes extended across the Middle East and reached north into Europe as far as the Baltic Sea.

Materials Have Marked Human Progress

The "ages" of human progress have often been defined by the materials used during them. As you have just read, historians speak of the Stone Age and the Bronze Age. Other ages have also been defined by the metals used. In fact, our own age is known as the Age of Metals.

While people used stone tools and weapons for more than 40,000 years, men and women have used metals for no more than about 6,000 years. Although the Age of Metals is still young, societies are moving rapidly beyond the Age of Metals to the Age of New Materials.

Tomorrow's new materials will be made in the laboratory. The all-plastic automobile body is already planned for the 1990s. Airplane and automobile engines of ceramics, only remotely related to the kind of material your dishes are made of, are also already in production. These new materials may make us more fuel-efficient and hold the promise of making products that can perform a host of tasks in medicine as well as industry.

As metals grew in importance, early people took another step toward developing more advanced societies. The laboratory-made materials of the immediate future signal further advances toward a civilized society. But what does it mean to be civilized? The final section of this chapter will explore the answer to that question.

SECTION 3 REVIEW

Knowing Key Terms, People, and Places
1. Define: **a.** smelting **b.** urbanization

Focus on Geography
2. How did the geography of an area determine whether or not people could produce bronze?

Reviewing Main Ideas
3. How is bronze made?
4. What new industry began with the discovery of bronze?
5. Describe three specific ways that bronze improved agriculture.
6. How did the discovery of bronze affect the specialization of labor?

Critical Thinking
Drawing Conclusions
7. Do you think that the Age of New Materials will be the last age of discovery? Explain your answer.

4 The Seeds of Civilization Took Root

As you read, look for answers to these questions:

◆ What factors are needed to encourage the growth of civilization?
◆ How are human needs and patterns of behavior similar throughout history?

> **Key Terms:** civilization (defined on p. 34)

A **civilization** is an advanced society marked by the development and use of a written language, by advances in the arts and sciences, and by the development of laws governing human behavior. Several factors contribute to the growth of civilization. Favorable geography, the growth of cities, the establishment of a government, and the practice of religion and morality all add to the progress of civilization.

Physical Geography Helped Civilization to Grow

For civilizations to grow, they must begin in a favorable geographic environment. Climate is one geographic factor that has a profound impact on human settlement. Climate conditions that provide comfort and do not threaten life allow people to focus on improving other areas of their lives.

Just as water is essential to life, adequate amounts of water are essential to the development of civilizations. Adequate rainfall or water from rivers makes the growth of civilization possible. Rivers offer people a means of transportation and communication. They help civilizations develop by providing a way to exchange farm products, handicrafts, minerals, and information.

The natural resources of the earth are another vital geographic element. Fertile soil is necessary to a civilization because it permits farming to develop. As you can see on the map on page 35, the first civilizations began around the rich soil of four great river

valleys in Africa and Asia. The earth also yields the minerals, such as tin and copper, needed to make metals. As discussed in the previous section, the discovery and use of bronze introduced a new era of civilization.

Economic Growth Advanced Civilization

Economics refers to the ways people make a living. A people who make their living by hunting or by wandering about in search of food will not be able to make dramatic advances. The growth of civilization depends on a steady supply of food. Farming makes it possible to grow more food than is needed so that it can be stored. Once people knew food was available, they had time to domesticate their animals and build homes, schools, and religious institutions. Those who did not have to farm to survive turned to other occupations such as trade, commerce, and the making of such items as ships, weapons, farm tools, and pottery.

The Growth of Cities Encouraged Civilization

By the end of the New Stone Age, people began to live close together so that they could help one another. Cities began to grow, and civilization flourished. In fact, the word civilization is based on the Latin word *civitas,* which means city.

The food that is produced on the farm usually finds its way to the city, where the comforts that civilization makes possible are developed. In the first ancient cities, the resources were pooled to build large temples, luxurious palaces, roads, and boats seaworthy enough for long journeys. Strong walls were built around the cities so that farmers, traders, and others could carry out their activities with less worry about enemy invasions.

Government Encouraged the Growth of Civilization

Human progress depends on a stable system of government. The first governments were started because early people wanted the

34

peace and security that a government can provide. Some form of law-making body, or government, developed even among Neanderthal people. Early people looked to their governments first and foremost to protect them from enemies. For this protection, they were willing to support rulers, to pay taxes, and to fight wars. They wanted their governments to protect their property, to prevent crime, and to punish people who broke their laws. Through shared education and common experiences, people developed loyalty to their communities. In time, patriotism grew and became the cement that held a community together.

Religion Encouraged the Growth of Civilization

Early people searched for explanations of natural events they could not understand, such as eclipses of the sun or moon, thunder, lightning, earthquakes, tidal waves, and tornadoes. According to archaeologists, early people first concluded that gods and goddesses—often in the form of natural objects such as the sun, moon, earth, stars, or animals—caused these events. Later, they made gods of their kings. Through prayers to the gods, people hoped to postpone or avoid natural disasters and death.

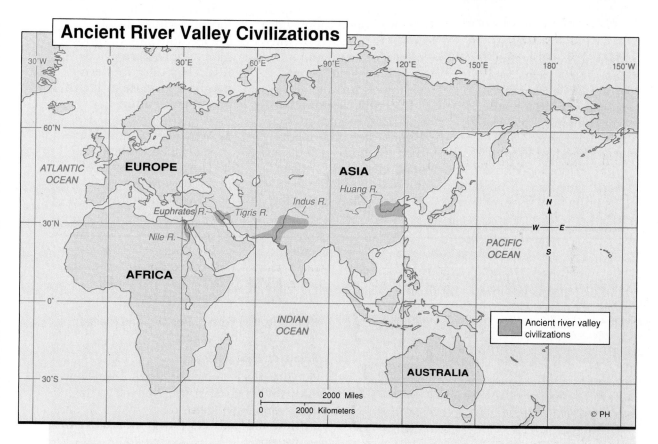

Ancient River Valley Civilizations

Focus on Geography

1. **Location**   The map shows the four river valleys in which the first civilizations began. Which civilizations were located in Asia? Which were located in Africa?
2. **Place**   Places with similar landforms and latitudes usually have similar climates. How would you expect the climates of these civilizations to compare?

Lindow Man

Near a bog, or swamp, in Manchester, England, about 2,200 years ago, a group of Celtic priests passed around a leather bag containing pieces of thin, flat bread. Each priest reached in and, without looking, chose a piece. One man in his late 20s pulled out a burnt portion—the only one in the bag. He and the others knew what this meant. In a solemn ritual, the young man was killed and flung into the bog.

According to Celtic religion, the person choosing the burnt bread was sacrificed to the Celtic gods. Those who participated in the rite hoped their gods would be pleased by the human offering and would bless the people with good fortune.

Recently, workers cutting peat, or sod, in the Manchester bog uncovered the body of the sacrificial victim. Scientists dubbed the victim "Lindow Man" after the site where he was found. Chemicals in the bog water have preserved the body in remarkable condition. An artist who studied the remains of Lindow Man made the likeness you see at left. The drawing shows what Lindow Man probably looked like.

Since the Celtic people left no written history, the few clues that Lindow Man supplies are priceless. They offer modern people a glimpse of life in an ancient culture.

1. Why was Lindow Man sacrificed to the gods?
2. How did the body of Lindow Man stay so well preserved?

As early religious practices became more complex, a special group of people was called upon to take care of the needs of the gods. These people, called priests, claimed special powers and resorted to magic to make people fear and obey them. Archaeological evidence shows that many early religions supported the practice of marriage, encouraged the stability of the family, laid down rules, or laws, for raising children and caring for the aged, and established the way the dead should be respected. In short, religions also help to build civilization.

It was in the Middle East that agriculture began, and with its beginning, early men and women took an enormous leap toward becoming civilized human beings. This geographic area of the ancient world is the focus of the next chapter.

SECTION 4 REVIEW

Knowing Key Terms, People, and Places
1. Define: a. civilization

Focus on Geography
2. What physical characteristics can hinder the growth of civilization?

Reviewing Main Ideas
3. How did agriculture help civilization to develop?
4. What does archaeological evidence show about many early religions?

Critical Thinking
Drawing Conclusions
5. Could civilization exist without government? Explain your answer.

SKILLS NOTEBOOK

Identifying Main Ideas

Authors of social studies books carefully organize their material in ways that help readers to understand it. One way authors organize their writing is by grouping all the sentences that tell about a topic into paragraphs that have a main idea. Every well-written paragraph has a main idea that can be identified.

Identifying the main idea of a paragraph can help you as you read your social studies text. Finding the main idea will help you to remember the most important points of each paragraph. Knowing main ideas is helpful when you study for quizzes or tests. Use the following steps to practice identifying the main idea of paragraphs.

1. **Find the topic of the paragraph.** Every paragraph has a topic, and the most important information about that topic is the paragraph's main idea. Therefore, the first step toward finding the main idea is to determine the topic of the paragraph. (a) Read paragraph 1 and identify its topic. (b) Identify the topic of paragraph 2.

2. **Locate the topic sentence if there is one.** In some paragraphs, a paragraph's main idea is stated in one sentence called the topic sentence. When there is a topic sentence, it is usually the first or last sentence of the paragraph. (a) What is the topic sentence in paragraph 1? (b) What is the topic sentence in paragraph 2?

3. **If there is no topic sentence, state the main idea in your own words.** Many well-written paragraphs have no topic sentence. In such paragraphs, the main idea is implied; that is, it is not directly stated. When you read a paragraph like this, you can state the implied main idea by forming your own sentence that tells the most important information about the topic. (a) Read paragraph 3 and identify its topic. (b) State the paragraph's implied main idea in your own words.

Paragraph 1

In their attempts to learn about prehistoric people, archaeologists go through a series of painstaking, time-consuming tasks. First, they try to locate places where people lived. Next, they carefully dig for remains, including artifacts and fossils such as pottery, tools, and human bones. Finally, they analyze these remains, searching for clues about the people who left them behind. Chemical analysis and computers help to date the remains.

Paragraph 2

The easiest way to pick a site that has ancient objects is by accident. This can happen when ground is excavated for a new building or highway. A riskier way to pick a site is to choose locations that could have been useful to prehistoric people. A natural shelter is one example of such a location. Recently, archaeologists have found still another way of choosing digging sites. They use aerial photographs to reveal hints of ancient building or roads, hints that are not noticeable on the ground. Thus, archaeological sites are chosen in several different ways.

Paragraph 3

Trained workers do the digging at a site. Soil must be removed carefully, a layer at a time. When an archaeologist suspects that artifacts may be discovered, he often insists that each shovelful of soil is sifted through a fine screen. This procedure is followed so no fossils or artifacts are missed or damaged. When an artifact is found, its location is marked on a site map before it is moved.

REVIEW

Section Summaries

Section 1 Scientists Help Historians Learn About Prehistory The time before written records were kept is called prehistory. Two types of scientist who study prehistory are archaeologists, who study physical remains from the prehistoric period, and anthropologists, who study the origins and development of societies. Scientific techniques such as carbon-14 dating are used to analyze artifacts and fossils uncovered during digs.

Section 2 Stone Age People Made Important Discoveries During the period that we call the Stone Age, people used weapons and tools made of stone. The Neanderthal people who lived during the Old Stone Age used crude stone tools and weapons. The Cro-Magnon people of the Middle Stone Age developed more efficient tools and weapons. The Neolithic revolution of the New Stone Age shifted people from hunting and gathering food to farming.

Section 3 The Bronze Age Brought Progress The discovery of metals around 4000 B.C. gradually led to the replacement of stone tools and weapons during the Bronze Age. People made dazzling progress in the Bronze Age. Farming methods were improved, and sailing techniques made trade with distant lands possible. The Bronze Age also saw the beginnings of urbanization, or city life.

Section 4 The Seeds of Civilization Took Root A society is civilized if it has a written language, advanced arts and sciences, and a system of government. The geographic location of a society shapes the way people live and work. Economics—how people earn their living—affects the amount of time people can devote to shelter building, education, and religion. Religion answers many questions that arise in people's lives, while government provides protection from enemies. All of these factors contribute to the growth of civilization.

Key Facts

1. Use each vocabulary word in a sentence.
   - **a.** historic period
   - **b.** prehistory
   - **c.** archaeologist
   - **d.** artifact
   - **e.** fossil
   - **f.** anthropologist
   - **g.** society
   - **h.** culture
   - **i.** nomad
   - **j.** specialization of labor
   - **k.** smelting
   - **l.** urbanization
   - **m.** civilization
2. Identify and briefly explain the importance of the following names, places, or events.
   - **a.** Stone Age
   - **b.** Old Stone Age
   - **c.** Middle Stone Age
   - **d.** New Stone Age
   - **e.** Neanderthal
   - **f.** Cro-Magnon
   - **g.** Bronze Age

Main Ideas

1. Describe two ways in which scientists have been able to study prehistory.
2. Name three important discoveries made by Neanderthal people in the Old Stone Age.
3. List four Cro-Magnon achievements during the Middle Stone Age.
4. What do scientists mean by the Neolithic revolution?
5. Name three benefits from the discovery of bronze for early people.
6. What factors influence the development of civilization?

Developing Skill in Reading History

Each chapter in your textbook has been divided into sections to organize information. For each section title below, decide what information you would expect to find in that section.
1. Scientists Help Historians Learn About Prehistory
   - **a.** the ways that scientists help historians learn about prehistory
   - **b.** the ways that scientists teach classes on prehistory for historians
   - **c.** the ways that scientists find money to pay for their experiments

2. Stone Age People Made Important Discoveries
   a. the names of early men and women who were famous for their discoveries
   b. how oxygen was discovered
   c. the types of discoveries made by Stone Age people
3. The Seeds of Civilization Took Root
   a. how New York City was founded
   b. why people were better off as nomads
   c. how early people became more civilized

Using Social Studies Skills

1. **Understanding Chronological Order** The Stone Age lasted from 2 million B.C. to about 3500 B.C. This time is divided into three periods: Old, Middle, and New. Draw a time line for the Stone Age that indicates when the following events might have occurred:
   · people are nomadic
   · pottery is used
   · seeds are planted and cultivated
   · people live in caves
   · wheel is first used
   · stone tools become smaller, more efficient
2. **Using Visual Evidence** Study the cave painting below. What conclusions can you draw about the lives of the people who did the painting?

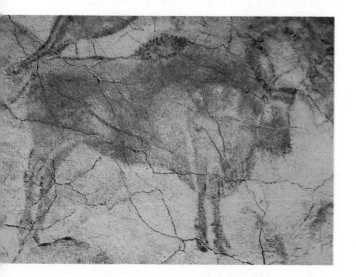

Critical Thinking

1. **Checking Consistency** Describe the first theories scientists formed about Neanderthal people. How did later additional evidence alter the way scientists thought about Neanderthal people?
2. **Distinguishing Fact from Opinion** ''People in the New Stone Age were happier than people in the Old Stone Age.'' Is this a fact or an opinion? Explain.
3. **Making Comparisons** How are Cro-Magnon cave paintings similar to urban graffiti found in cities today?

Focus on Writing

Recognizing Topic Sentences

Whether you're writing a paragraph or an essay, one of the most important writing skills is creating a topic sentence. Before you create topic sentences on your own, practice how to recognize a topic sentence.

The topic sentence states the main idea of a paragraph. An effective topic sentence strengthens the paragraph by helping the reader to understand what the paragraph is about. The rest of the sentences in the paragraph supply details or supporting information about the topic sentence. A topic sentence can appear in one of the following places in a paragraph:

· at the beginning, to give a sense of direction to the whole paragraph
· at the end, to act as a summary for the whole paragraph
· in the middle, to give a sense of direction in the paragraph following an introductory sentence or two

Look back at the section summaries on the opposite page. For each summary, tell which sentence is the topic sentence. Then, explain the purpose of the topic sentence based on its location in the paragraph.

In the Cradle
of the Middle East

(5000 B.C.–30 B.C.)

1 **The Egyptians Built a Great Civilization**

2 **Civilization Developed in Mesopotamia**

3 **Babylonia Contributed Much to Civilization**

4 **Other Civilizations Made Contributions**

Early on a November morning in 1987, a team of archaeologists huddled excitedly around a video monitor at the base of the Great Pyramid in Giza, Egypt. The picture they were about to see would be transmitted from a deep underground chamber into which they had lowered a tiny camera. Rulers in ancient Egypt built chamber-filled pyramids to use as their tombs. The archaeologists were about to find out what one particular chamber at the heart of the pyramid held.

As an image flickered onto the screen, the archaeologists could see the timbers of an ancient, wooden funeral ship. The Egyptians had buried the ship 4,600 years ago. The discovery was a major one, since only one other such boat had ever been found. Almost as exciting as the discovery itself was the manner in which it was made. For the first time, archaeologists used space-age tools to help them in their work.

These tools enabled the archaeologists to view the ship without disturbing it. The knowledge they have gained adds much to what is known about ancient Egypt. In the following chapter, you will begin your own explorations of the region.

▲ **Illustrating History**
This ancient Egyptian pendant shows a funeral boat carrying baboons and a scarab, a sacred beetle to the Egyptians.

4000 B.C.	2800 B.C.	1600 B.C.	400 B.C.

■ **4000 B.C.**
Sumerians develop the earliest form of writing

■ **2780 B.C.**
Old Kingdom, or Age of Pyramids, begins in Egypt

■ **1800 B.C.**
Hammurabi establishes a code of laws in Babylonia

■ **1280 B.C.**
Moses leads his people out of Egypt

■ **612 B.C.**
Assyrian Empire falls

▲ **Illustrating History** *These pyramids at Giza, Egypt, serve as permanent memorials for three great Egyptian kings.*

1 The Egyptians Built a Great Civilization

As you read, look for answers to these questions:

◆ How did the geography of Egypt help it to grow and flourish?
◆ What happened during each of the three major time periods of Egypt's history?
◆ What were the major contributions of Egyptian civilization?

Key Terms: hieroglyphic (defined on p. 41), cataract (p. 43), delta (p. 43), papyrus (p. 43), nome (p. 44), dynasty (p. 45), pharaoh (p. 45)

The discovery of the Egyptian funeral boat is just one of the dramatic events that have helped scholars to piece together the story of Egypt's past. One reason Egypt's history remained shrouded in mystery for so long was that no one could read the ancient Egyptian **hieroglyphics** (HI er oh GLIHF iks), or picture writings. That would change in the early 1800s. In 1799, when the French general Napoleon Bonaparte invaded Egypt, a group of his soldiers found the ancient Egyptian temples at Luxor and Karnak. At the same time, they discovered a stone tablet covered with Greek letters and Egyptian hieroglyphics. Several years later, a French scholar, Jean Champollion, used his knowledge of Greek to figure out the meaning of the hieroglyphics on the stone. His work unlocked much of the mystery of Egypt's past.

The Rosetta Stone, as the tablet was called, is one of the most important archaeological finds in the history of the world. It helped archaeologists and anthropologists to read early Egyptian writings and, thus, to gain a better understanding of Egyptian

41

GEOGRAPHIC SETTING:
Ancient Egypt and Mesopotamia

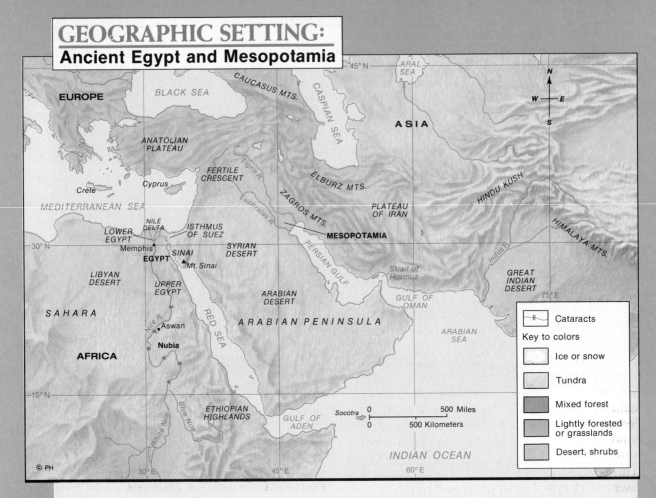

Focus on Geography

1. **Location**   Is Upper Egypt located in the northern or southern part of the Nile River?
2. **Interaction**   What physical features would have prevented the Egyptians from sailing south on the Nile River into Nubia?

society. With the discovery of the tablet, scholars learned what the ancient Egyptians thought, what they did, and how they felt. They also learned why, after prospering for many centuries, the glory of ancient Egypt faded. Although many reasons explain why ancient Egypt flourished, none is more important than Egypt's favorable geographic location.

Geography Favored Ancient Egypt

One of the key aspects of Egypt's geography was the Nile River. The Greek historian Herodotus called Egypt the "gift of the Nile." The Egyptians themselves recognized the importance of the Nile in their chant "Hail to thee, O Nile, . . . that comes to keep Egypt alive."

The Nile River, the world's longest river, begins in east Africa and flows northward for over 4,000 miles. It is navigable for most of the way except between the cities of Khartoum in the Sudan and Aswan in Egypt. Between Khartoum and Aswan, the river drops in a series of six rapids, or waterfalls, called **cataracts.** Before the river flows into the Mediterranean Sea, it deposits sand and soil it has picked up along its 4,000 mile (2,400 kilometer) journey. Over time, the deposit grows into a land triangle of sand and soil called a **delta.** The Nile Delta is the most fertile part of Egypt.

Water. Water, as you know, is one of the essentials of civilization. Because Egypt had little rainfall, it had to rely on water from the Nile. The Egypt of ancient history, then, is the valley of the Nile from the first cataract to Aswan. As you can see from the map on page 42, the delta region in the north was called Lower Egypt. The fertile lands to the south of the delta region that were within a few miles of either side of the Nile were called Upper Egypt. Because the Egyptians learned to build irrigation canals, the amount of land good for farming was 13,000 square miles (33,670 square kilometers). This area is less than the total area of Switzerland.

Rich farming soil. Each year, the Nile, swollen with rain that fell in Ethiopia, rushed northward to flood the valley and carried with it rich soil. "When the Nile inundates [floods] the land," Herodotus once wrote, "all of Egypt becomes a sea, and only the towns remain above water, looking rather like the islands of the Aegean."

When the Nile overflowed its banks, it left behind fertile, muddy soil in which the farmers could grow wheat, corn, and barley. Egypt became the breadbasket of the ancient world because it sold much of its grain to other countries. Among other major crops were flax, which was used for making linen, castor beans and sesame seeds, which were used for oils, and dates.

Usually, the Nile was a faithful friend of the Egyptians, but this was not always the case. Sometimes, the level of flooding was too low to spread the needed amount of rich soil. At other times, higher flooding than usual threatened villages and storage areas. Although the Nile would flood every year, sometimes there was too much water and sometimes too little. For example, between 2250 B.C. and 1950 B.C., too little flooding caused famines, mass deaths, and widespread confusion.

Protection from enemies. Besides providing water, geography also protected Egypt from enemies and so helped to make its long history possible. As the map on page 42 shows, deserts on either side of the river and the Sinai Desert in the northeast made invasion hard. On the north, the Mediterranean Sea offered further protection. Finally, the Red Sea left Egypt connected to Asia only by the easily defended Isthmus of Suez. Even the cataracts of the Nile offered some protection. They effectively blocked an enemy's plan to invade Egypt from the south.

Other natural resources. From Mount Sinai, near the Red Sea, the Egyptians mined gold and copper, both of which were near to the surface and extracted easily. From the mud left by the Nile, Egyptians made clay jars and pots. The Nile River and the Mediterranean Sea provided a plentiful supply of fish.

Reed plants, called **papyrus** (puh PY ruhs), were everywhere. These were used for making canoes, rafts, baskets, or sandals. The most important use of the reeds was for the making of rolls of writing material which were then used to make books.

Transportation and trade. Egypt's location—on the Mediterranean Sea and not far from Asia and Europe—is at an important crossroad of the world. While this is a marvelous location, imagine what travel would be like if you could use only your feet or ride a donkey. This was the only way the people of the ancient Middle East could journey on land from one place to another. This type of travel was hard, dangerous, and time-consuming.

The Nile River and the Mediterranean Sea, however, made travel by boat fairly easy, so the Nile valley attracted people who sought to take advantage of the valley's mild climate and fertile soil. Sailing was made easier by the wind current that blew southward from the Mediterranean Sea all summer. These winds allowed the Egyptians to travel against the Nile's current.

Upper and Lower Egypt united. Because of the Nile's benefits, most Egyptians settled along its banks. Cities grew up over time, and Egypt's population became increasingly concentrated. Because the Nile was so long, however, one system of government was not enough to unite all of Egypt's people. As a result, it was possible for one political system to develop in Lower Egypt and another in Upper Egypt.

Individual communities in these two regions formed provinces, or **nomes,** ruled by warrior nobles. Over time, two distinct kingdoms were formed. There were 20 nomes in Lower Egypt and 22 in Upper Egypt. According to legend, sometime between 3200 B.C. and 2780 B.C., King Menes of Upper Egypt united all 42 provinces of the Nile for the first time by conquering Lower Egypt.

The rulers who followed Menes wore a double crown to symbolize the unity of Upper and Lower Egypt. They built a new capital at Memphis, not far from what is now Cairo, where Upper and Lower Egypt met. The ease of travel and communication along the Nile helped the northern and southern parts of Egypt to unite. The need for the farming villages along the Nile to cooperate with one another in order to take advantage of the Nile's overflow also contributed to the unity of Egypt. The kingdom created when Upper and Lower Egypt were united lasted for centuries.

Egypt's History Is Divided into Kingdoms

Historians have divided Egyptian history into three periods. The first is called the Old Kingdom, or the Age of Pyramids (2780 B.C.–2180 B.C.). The second is called the

---

Abu Simbel

In the thirteenth century B.C., highly skilled Egyptian stonecutters and sculptors carved two immense temples into a sandstone cliff overlooking the Nile in Egypt. The stately monuments at Abu Simbel, pictured at right, remained undisturbed until the early 1960s. Then, the rising waters of an artificial lake created by the Aswan High Dam threatened to engulf them.

In a tricky salvage operation, an international team of engineers cut the monuments into 950 separate blocks and hoisted them to higher ground. There, the monuments were reassembled and reinforced. Today, visitors to Abu Simbel can again marvel at the beauty of these temples.

1. How were the monuments saved?
2. Why is it important to preserve monuments like those at Abu Simbel?

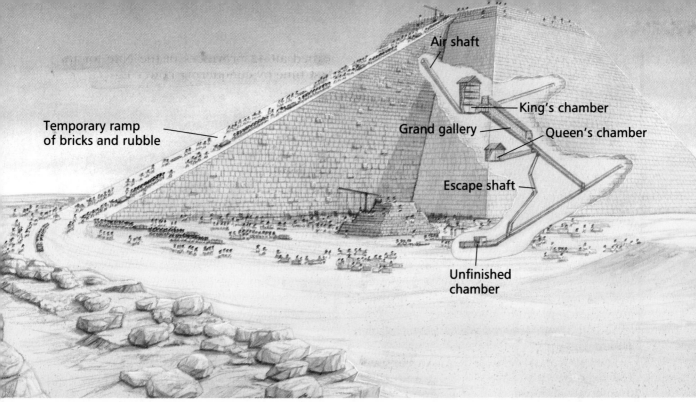

Air shaft

King's chamber

Grand gallery

Queen's chamber

Temporary ramp
of bricks and rubble

Escape shaft

Unfinished
chamber

▲ **Illustrating History** *This illustration portrays one of the probable methods for building the Egyptian pyramids.*

Middle Kingdom, or the Age of Nobles (2100 B.C.–1788 B.C.). The third period of Egyptian history is called the New Kingdom, or Age of Empire (1580 B.C.–1090 B.C.). The maps on pages 46 and 47 show each kingdom. The years between these great eras were often marked by wars, conflict, and weak rulers.

Menes and his successors made up ancient Egypt's first dynasty. **A dynasty** is a family of rulers in which the heir to the throne is a member of the preceding ruler's family. In Egypt, a child of the ruler usually succeeded to the throne.

The Old Kingdom (2780 B.C.–2180 B.C.). During the Old Kingdom, the Egyptian **pharaoh** (FEHR oh), or ruler, held all government and religious authority. Egyptians treated the pharaoh as a god. As a god, the pharaoh was believed to be immortal.

The pharaoh was responsible for the welfare of the people and even for the conditions of the land. The people believed that the pharaoh could determine such events as the flooding of the Nile and the victories of

Egypt's army. The pharaoh was also a landlord, and all nobles rented their land from him or her.

The Egyptians believed that a person's spirit lived on in the body after death. Therefore, they tried to preserve the bodies of their dead. To further protect their spirits, the pharaohs had great stone pyramids built. These pyramids were huge tombs in which the pharaohs were buried with their treasures. The walls of the pyramids were covered with pictures and hieroglyphics. The story of the pharaoh's great and good deeds was told in the picture writing. This picture writing records much of the story of ancient Egyptian times.

Although the faces of these pyramids were once smooth, builders later removed the outer slabs to create new structures. Today, separate blocks allow people to climb nearly to the top. The entrance to a pyramid is not easy to find because the pharaoh's body was not to be viewed after death. Usually, there was a small opening in the northern wall of the pyramid. To get to the vast inner chambers, a person would have to crawl along a

45

tunnel for a considerable distance on hands and knees.

The sphinx, another type of monument built by the pharaohs of the Old Kingdom, has the body of a lion and the head of a man. It is a mythical beast of ancient Egypt and represents the pharaoh as Ra, the sun god. The face on a sphinx was that of the ruler, and the body of the lion stood for the strength of the ruler as a protector. While many sphinxes were built, the most famous is at Giza.

The Old Kingdom was a productive period in Egyptian history. By the Fifth Dynasty, however, the pharaoh's authority began to decline, and the power of other authorities increased. Although heavy taxes were collected, the costly pyramids proved a drain on the treasury.

The Old Kingdom lasted to about 2180 B.C. Toward the end, the kingdom was weak, and the people suffered. The Nile's flood waters did not rise enough. Crops failed, and hunger was widespread. Nobles began to exercise greater authority over the nomes. The pharaoh was blamed for the kingdom's disasters. "Laughter had disappeared forever," wrote one Egyptian.

The Middle Kingdom (2100 B.C.–1788 B.C.). During the period of the Middle Kingdom, one powerful noble, who became known as Amenemhet I (AH men em HET), seized the title of pharaoh and moved the capital of Egypt to Thebes (theebz). He gradually restored the power of the pharaoh. In an old inscription, Amenemhet I boasts, "None was hungry in my years, none thirsted then; Men dwelt in peace through that which I wrought."

Under Amenemhet I, the kingdom prospered, and arts and literature flourished. Archaeologists have found libraries of rolled papyri packed in jars and labeled with titles. One famous story, for example, was *The Story of the Shipwrecked Sailor*, which tells about the travels and adventures of an Egyptian sailor.

Other pharaohs of the Middle Kingdom waged a successful war against Nubia, carried on trade with Kush, Mesopotamia,

Syria, and Palestine, and carried out mining operations in the Sinai. These activities helped the Middle Kingdom to stay rich and powerful.

By 1800 B.C., however, the good times gave way to centuries of renewed turmoil. Weak dynasties allowed invaders to infiltrate Egypt. None of these invaders was more powerful than the Hyksos (HIHK sohs). Between 1800 B.C. and 1600 B.C., the Hyksos ruled Egypt. These warlike people, whose name means "rulers of the uplands," had come on horseback and in horse-drawn chariots. They were armed with weapons of bronze. Thus supplied and armed, they easily defeated the weakened Egyptians. The Hyksos destroyed temples, burned cities, and

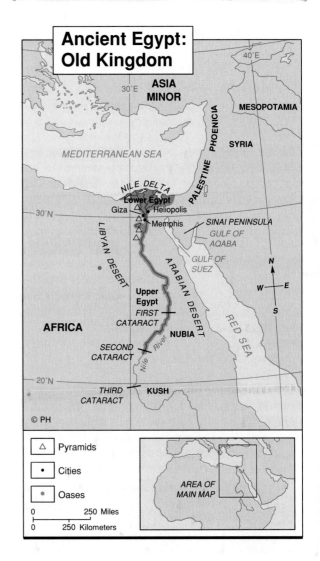

Ancient Egypt: Old Kingdom

40°E

ASIA MINOR

30°E

MESOPOTAMIA

MEDITERRANEAN SEA

PHOENICIA

SYRIA

NILE DELTA

Lower Egypt

Giza △ Heliopolis

PALESTINE

30°N

Memphis

SINAI PENINSULA

GULF OF AQABA

LIBYAN DESERT

ARABIAN DESERT

GULF OF SUEZ

N W E S

Upper Egypt

FIRST CATARACT

NUBIA

RED SEA

AFRICA

SECOND CATARACT

Nile River

20°N

THIRD CATARACT

KUSH

© PH

△ Pyramids

• Cities

• Oases

0   250 Miles

0   250 Kilometers

AREA OF MAIN MAP

destroyed art. By 1600 B.C., however, the Egyptian pharaohs had learned how to use the horse, to shoot bronze-tipped arrows from chariots, and to make shields and weapons of bronze. In time, using these improved weapons of war, they drove the Hyksos from Egypt. The end of the Hyksos prepared the way for a new period of Egyptian glory and progress.

The New Kingdom (1580 B.C.–1090 B.C.). After the Egyptian pharaohs drove out the Hyksos, they set out to make conquests of their own. The city of Thebes became important again, and a standing army, including charioteers, bowmen, and foot soldiers, was formed.

Among the outstanding pharaohs of this period was Hatshepsut (haht SHEHP soot), who ruled from 1486 B.C. until her death in 1468 B.C. (See the biography on page 48.) Because by custom the pharaoh was male, Hatshepsut would dress in men's clothes and attach a ceremonial beard to her chin. Statues of her usually show her wearing the beard.

Hatshepsut's reign was a peaceful one in which trade, not war, was carried out. She made Karnak more beautiful and expanded Egypt's trading area to the east coast of Africa. She boasted, "I have restored that which was in ruins. I have raised up that which was unfinished." During her 22-year reign, she built a great pyramid on the

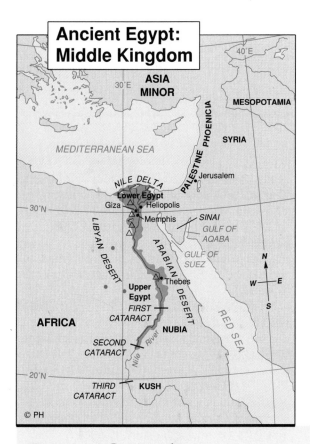

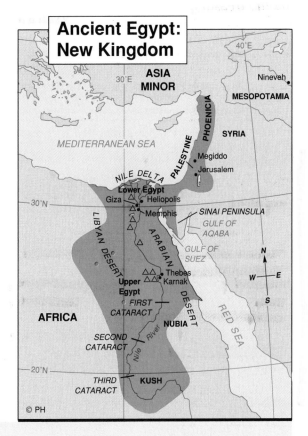

Focus on Geography

Movement These three maps show that oases became more numerous over time. How would the increase in the number of oases have affected the growth of all of Egypt?

Hatshepsut

Standing on the wharf at Thebes, the Egyptian ruler thrilled to the sight of the returning fleet of five ships, laden with ivory and gold, from the fabulous land of Punt, in east Africa. The completion of the two-year trading expedition marked another triumph in a queen's extraordinary reign.

Two other queens had occupied Egypt's throne, but neither had gone so far in holding and using power. Hatshepsut (haht SHEHP soot), pictured above left, wore the double crown of the ruler of Upper and Lower Egypt.

Hatshepsut was born sometime before 1500 B.C., the favorite daughter of Thutmose I. After her husband Thutmose II died, Hatshepsut proclaimed herself king in her own right. She brought peace and prosperity to Egypt, expanded trade, and increased building.

Her burial temple, regarded as one of the masterpieces of Egyptian architecture, still stands as a fitting memorial to the queen who has been called by one historian "the first great woman in history."

1. What was unusual about Hatshepsut's rule?
2. What were some of her accomplishments?

---

western side of the Nile in an area that came to be called The Valley of the Kings.

Her stepson, Thutmose (thoot MOH suh) III (1501 B.C.–1447 B.C.), who may have murdered his stepmother to become pharaoh, did not follow her peaceful example. Instead, in a reign of 19 years, he embarked on 17 military campaigns. For example, in 1479 B.C. at Megiddo, he conquered Palestine. He then went on to conquer Phoenicia, Syria, and finally Nubia. The latter became a valuable source for gold, copper, ivory, ebony, and slaves. Having grown well beyond its borders and having brought other countries and states under its rule, Egypt was now the leading empire of its day.

The decline of Egypt. By 1300 B.C., however, the Egyptian Empire began to falter. The first sign of trouble came in the form of annoying, small invasions on the borders of the empire. Before long these invasions proved to be serious, and the powerful Hittites (HIHT eyets) fought the Egyptian armies to a standstill. The Hittites were a part of a group of people, including Armenians, Phrygians, Lydians, and others, who moved into Asia Minor over a period of 1,000 years. In 1271 B.C., the pharaoh, Ramses II, made a peace treaty with the Hittites. Eventually, the Egyptians and Hittites became allies, but the period of Egyptian dominance appeared to be over.

By 1200 B.C., further decline set in. Ramses III was defeated by a wave of "people of the sea," a group that probably included the Philistines. The weak successors of Ramses were unable to stem the tide of invasion. After 1150 B.C., Egypt became the conquered, and by 525 B.C., Egypt fell under the power of Persia. In 331 B.C., Alexander the Great of Greece occupied Egypt. A descendant of one of Alexander's generals, Cleopatra, became the last pharaoh. In 31 B.C., after its defeat in a naval battle with Rome, Egypt became a Roman province. Egypt did not become a free nation again until A.D. 1936.

Religion Influenced the People

The Greek historian Herodotus wrote that the Egyptians were "the most religious of peoples." Religion was a major part of everyday life in ancient Egypt. In addition to the belief that the pharaohs were gods, the Egyptians believed that many other gods controlled the economy of the nation. They thought that the flooding of the Nile, the health of their animals, the size of the harvest, and success in battle all rested in the hands of the gods.

The Egyptians prayed to many gods. They considered animals such as the bull, the cat, and the crocodile to be holy. The two chief gods were Amon-Ra (AH muhn RAY) and Osiris (oh SY rihs). Amon-Ra was believed to be the sun god and the lord of the universe. As Egypt grew stronger, the worship of Amon-Ra spread to the lands that Egypt conquered. Osiris was the god of the underworld. Stories about him revolved around the idea of immortality (living forever in another world). Osiris was the god that made a peaceful afterlife possible. The Egyptian *Book of the Dead* contains the major ideas and beliefs found in the ancient Egyptian religion.

The pharaoh Amenhotep (ah muhn HOH tehp) III, who ruled from about 1407 B.C. to 1379 B.C., encouraged the worship of Amon-Ra as the one god of the Egyptians. His son, Amenhotep IV, who ruled from 1379 B.C. to 1362 B.C., went even further and tried to force Egypt to worship only one god. Amenhotep IV changed Amon-Ra's name to Aton and called Aton "the sole god, beside whom there is no other." Amenhotep IV also changed his own name to Ikhnaton. He insisted that Aton was a god of kindness, love, and mercy. He wanted all Egyptians to worship one god, and he ordered that the names and pictures of Amon-Ra and other gods be destroyed. When he tried to make further changes, it did not please those who favored the old ways. The new religion went against the traditional Egyptian way of life. When Ikhnaton died, his religious reforms died with him.

Tutankhamen returned the Egyptians to the worship of Amon-Ra. To do this, he gave

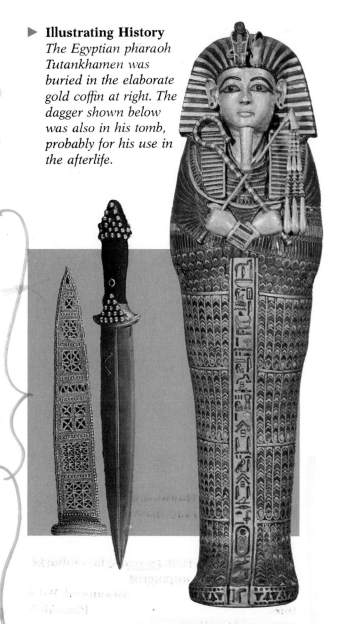

▶ **Illustrating History**
The Egyptian pharaoh Tutankhamen was buried in the elaborate gold coffin at right. The dagger shown below was also in his tomb, probably for his use in the afterlife.

great gifts to the priests of Amon-Ra. He also dedicated the magnificent temples of Karnak and Luxor to Amon-Ra. Tutankhamen also returned Egypt to its traditional religious belief of many gods.

Egyptian Society Was Organized by Class

Egyptians organized their society much like the pyramids they built. At the top was the pharaoh. Next were the members of the upper class, who included court nobles, wealthy landowners, and priests. The court

Tomb of Tutankhamen

By November 1922, Howard Carter had spent six years searching for a tomb. His financial backer, Lord Carnarvon, was ready to give up the search. In that month, however, Carter discovered the greatest archaeological find of the century—the tomb of Tutankhamen and its amazing riches. Here Carter describes his entry to the tomb.

••Slowly, desperately slowly it seemed to us as we watched, the remains of passage debris [rubble] that encumbered [blocked] the lower part of the doorway were removed, until at last we had the whole door clear before us. The decisive moment had arrived.

With trembling hands, I made a tiny breach [crack] in the upper left-hand corner. Darkness and blank space, as far as an iron testing-rod could reach, showed that whatever lay beyond was empty, and not filled like the passage we had just cleared. . . . At first I could see nothing, the hot air escaping from the chamber causing the candle flame to flicker, but presently, as my eyes grew accustomed to the light, details of the room within emerged slowly from the mist. . . . For the moment—an eternity it must have seemed to others standing by—I was struck dumb with amazement, and when Lord Carnarvon, unable to stand the suspense any longer, inquired anxiously, 'Can you see anything?' it was all I could do to get out the words, 'Yes, wonderful things.'••

1. Who was with Carter when he first entered the tomb?
2. List three words that describe the tone of the excerpt.

nobles gave the pharaohs advice and carried out their orders. Nobles who owned land spent most of their time managing their huge estates. Priests, on the other hand, spent their time performing different religious ceremonies, especially those involving the burial of the dead.

The small Egyptian middle class consisted mainly of skilled workers, government officials, merchants, doctors, teachers, artists, and scribes. Scribes wrote letters and prepared documents in the pharaoh's court, in the temples, or in the homes of wealthy nobles. Because few people knew how to read or write, scribes held an important place in Egyptian society.

The great majority of Egyptians belonged to the lower class, which was made up of two groups: peasants and slaves. Peasants worked as farmers or on farm-related activities such as irrigation systems. Burdened by poverty, hard work, and heavy taxes, they enjoyed few or no political rights. The life of the slave was even worse. Mainly prisoners of war, slaves built canals, temples, pyramids, and roads. Many slaves died young as a result of cruel treatment and overwork.

The structure of Egyptian life changed little during the period of the three kingdoms. The class system remained in place, and, in addition, the nature of the work that different classes performed generally stayed the same.

Egypt Contributed Much to Civilization

Some of the most important gifts of Egypt to later civilizations were in the fields of writing, mathematics, engineering, astronomy, and medicine.

Writing. Perhaps the greatest contribution of the early Egyptians was the writing system known as hieroglyphics. It was based on an alphabet of 24 signs. Each sign represented a basic consonant. Vowels had no signs. Egyptian papyrus was one of the world's first writing materials. Our word *paper* comes from the word *papyrus*. The scribes wrote with pens made from pointed reeds and used ink that was made from vegetable gum.

Mathematics. Egyptian numbers were clumsy to use, but they were accurate. One stroke was made for one, two strokes for two, nine strokes for nine. A different sign was used for 10 because the Egyptians had no zero.

Engineering. Egyptian engineering was based on their knowledge of mathematics. The precise construction of the pyramids shows their knowledge of mathematical principles. For example, Egyptians knew how to use the square and the right angle, and they learned how to figure the areas of triangles and other shapes. As they advanced the study of geometry, they used their knowledge in surveying and building. Egyptians knew how to use ramps—and a lot of muscle—to pull, haul, and lift huge blocks of stone into place. Some historians believe that Egyptian engineers developed the first ocean-going ships.

Astronomy. The Egyptians developed a sun calendar based on a year of 12 months. Each month had 30 days. Because this calendar was not strictly accurate, the Egyptians made an adjustment and added 5 days to the year. With this adjustment, each year had 365 days. The 5 added days usually were used for holidays.

Medicine. Egyptian medicine was quite advanced. Famous Egyptian doctors were in demand all over the world. They knew how the heart worked and how to heal and treat wounds. They knew how to take the pulse and studied the eyes of their patient for telltale signs of illness. Egyptian doctors also developed many new, different kinds of medicines.

Because the Egyptians believed the human body should be preserved for its life in the next world, they treated a dead body with oil and spices and wrapped it in linen to create a mummy. This preparation called for a high degree of medical skill.

Many Factors Caused Egypt's Decline

Egyptian civilization lasted longer than any other in history. Why, then, did it decline? One reason lies in the fact that the pharaohs did not always use their absolute power and wealth for the good of the people. Too often the pharaohs were more concerned with building pyramids and temples for their own glorification. They also spent much effort and money trying to win new lands in order to increase their territory.

Certainly, the fall of Egypt was the result of many events and factors combined. Some historians point to the lack of individual freedom as a major reason for Egypt's decline. The basic class structure of rulers and subjects did not allow for the development of a strong middle class. Meanwhile, a middle class was thriving in Greece, making strides in business, trade, and intellectual pursuits. While Egypt clung to the order of the past, other civilizations were growing around them. Thus, Egypt became open to domination by Persia, then Greece, and finally Rome.

SECTION 1 REVIEW

Knowing Key Terms, People, and Places
1. Define: **a.** hieroglyphic **b.** cataract **c.** delta **d.** papyrus **e.** nome **f.** dynasty **g.** pharaoh.
2. Identify: **a.** Rosetta Stone **b.** Old Kingdom **c.** Middle Kingdom **d.** New Kingdom

Focus on Geography
3. What geographical factors led to Egypt being called the "gift of the Nile"?

Reviewing Main Ideas
4. How did the power of the pharaohs change from the Old Kingdom to the New Kingdom?
5. Explain the importance of religion in Egyptian society.
6. Describe the "pyramid" structure of the classes of people in Egyptian society.

Critical Thinking
Drawing Conclusions
7. Why do you think that historians consider the Egyptian writing system a greater contribution than the pyramids?

The Art of Egyptian Tombs

Much of what we know of the ancient Egyptians and how they lived is told to us by the objects they left in their tombs. These tombs were meant to serve the needs of the dead person's spirit, or Ka, which would need most of the same things a person needed while alive. Therefore, a tomb would contain everything its owner had possessed—chairs, chariots, musical instruments, jewelry, wigs, games—as well as pictures and sculptures to remind the spirit of its life on earth. *Vintners and Fowlers* (which means "wine merchants and bird hunters") shows daily activities on a large estate. The estate belonged to a nobleman named Nakht, for whom the tomb was made.

We see in *Prince Rahotep and His Wife Nofret* actual portraits of the deceased. The statues represent their spirits in the presence of the Egyptian gods. The gesture of the hand over the heart indicates humility.

At right is Prince Rahotep and His Wife Nofret; *below is the tomb painting* Vintners and Fowlers.

52

2 Civilization Developed in Mesopotamia

As you read, look for answers to these questions:

◆ What is the Fertile Crescent?
◆ How did the geography of Mesopotamia challenge its people?
◆ Which nations lived in and ruled Mesopotamia?

> **Key Terms:** cuneiform (defined on p. 55), ziggurat (p. 55)

"As for me the scouts which came in my power, I have released. That I have indeed released [them] you know, still you have not sent the money for ransom. Ever since I began releasing your scouts you have consistently not provided the money for ransom. I here—and you there—should release."

These are the words of one ruler to another ruler in the ancient land of Mesopotamia (MESS uh puh TAY mee uh). Thus, hostage-taking and paying ransom are not unique to modern times. The geographic area in which these kings ruled is a land that is a part of the region known today as the Fertile Crescent.

Geography Challenged the People of Mesopotamia

A part of modern Iraq and all of Syria, Lebanon, Israel, and Jordan are the modern countries of the Fertile Crescent. The Fertile Crescent is a horseshoe, or crescent-shaped, area of good farmland. Starting in the valleys of the Tigris and Euphrates rivers, it runs along the coast of the Mediterranean

▼ **Illustrating History** *This decorated wooden panel is believed to have been carried into battle by a Sumerian prince.*

Sea as far as Egypt. As you can see on the map below, the Fertile Crescent touches Asia, Africa, and Europe. It was the crossroads of the ancient world.

The name *Mesopotamia* means "the land between the rivers." The waters of the rivers made irrigation farming possible in this dry land. The rivers were also important routes for transportation and communication and gave Mesopotamia a head start in developing flourishing civilizations.

The civilization of Mesopotamia depended upon the flooding of the Tigris and Euphrates rivers, just as Egypt's early civili-zation depended upon the flooding of the Nile. Both areas needed the fertile soil left by the rivers to grow their crops. The over-flow from the Tigris and Euphrates rivers, however, was much less predictable than that from the Nile. Therefore, it was more difficult for the people to prepare for it or to take advantage of it. Often, the flooding was so violent that the water destroyed homes and farms. Find the Tigris and Euphrates rivers on the map below.

In addition, Mesopotamia's climate was much harsher than Egypt's. Blazing summer heat gave way to harsh winter storms.

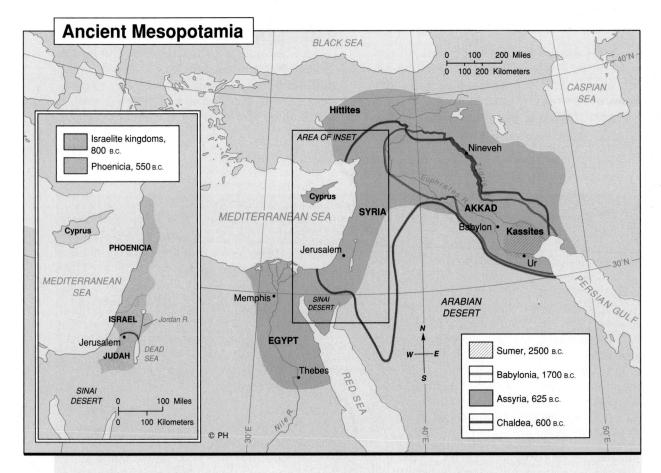

Ancient Mesopotamia

Focus on Geography

1. **Place**   Find the city of Ur. Ur was a part of what four civilizations?
2. **Movement**   What civilizations caused the Israelite kingdoms to fall?

Because of its geographic location, ancient Egypt could resist foolhardy invaders, and a united country was able to develop. In Mesopotamia, however, invasion from mountainous regions was easy. Nomads and other powerful fighters often tried to seize the wealth and splendor of the people who developed civilizations in the area. As a result, several different groups of people controlled Mesopotamia for periods of time and then disappeared. Sumerians, Assyrians (uh SIHR ee uhnz), Babylonians, and Chaldeans (kal DEE uhnz), among others, enjoyed a few centuries of power only to be conquered and finally absorbed by a more powerful people.

A Series of Rulers Controlled Mesopotamia

As early as 4000 B.C., people known as the Sumerians were living in Mesopotamia. The Sumerians lived in small, independent cities. They knew how to use the wheel and how to make tools and weapons of copper. They decorated objects with gold and silver. They also developed the earliest form of writing, called **cuneiform** (kyoo NEE uh FORM).

The early Sumerians believed that each of their cities was ruled by a separate god. They built temples as homes for these gods and added huge, pyramid-shaped towers called **ziggurats** (ZIHG uh rats) in their honor. The temple priests, nobles, and kings of each city held most of the land, which was worked by free men and women as well as slaves.

Because the Sumerians were not united by one king, their cities were often at war with one another. These wars weakened the Sumerians, whose enemies eventually attacked and conquered them.

Sargon I. In about 2500 B.C., the great Sargon I conquered the Sumerians. Sargon and his people came from the country of Akkad in northern Mesopotamia. They were not as advanced as the Sumerians, but they soon made many of the Sumerians' ways their own. Sargon united Akkad and Sumer into one strong, rich nation called the King-

▲ **Illustrating History** *Sargon, who conquered the Sumerians in approximately 2500 B.C., is pictured above in bronze. At right, a cuneiform tablet from the time of Sargon's rule shows the earliest form of writing.*

dom of Sumer. Sargon extended his kingdom west to the Mediterranean Sea, and under his rule, Sumerian civilization spread throughout the Middle East. In fact, the influence of the Sumerians was felt for many years after their civilization ended.

Hammurabi. Sometime around 1800 B.C., Hammurabi (HAH mu RAH bee) conquered the Kingdom of Sumer. Hammurabi built the mighty kingdom of Babylonia and its magnificent capital, the city of Babylon. Hammurabi's most important gift, however, is a written code of laws that tells us about the legal system of the Babylonians. Archaeologists discovered this code of laws, which was written on large pieces of black stone, in 1901.

55

Babylonia maintained its power for a few hundred years. As the map on page 54 shows, it was defeated by the Hittites, the Kassites, and the Assyrians. Babylonia would not become unified again until 600 B.C.

The fierce Hittites. The Hittites were a warlike people who first appear in history about 2000 B.C. They originally came from what is now Turkey. The Hittites, who invaded the valley of the Tigris-Euphrates about 1600 B.C., were one of the earliest people to ride horses. They made strong weapons of iron and as a result were greatly feared. Because they were the first group to refine iron ore, the Hittites are credited with starting the Iron Age in western Asia.

The Hittites invaded Syria, which was controlled by Egypt. Since Ikhnaton was busy with religious reforms at that time, he lost control of much of Egypt's northern lands. The Hittites and Egypt continued to fight over Syria. The fighting finally ended in 1280 B.C. when King Ramses II of Egypt made peace. The Hittites seem to have disappeared as a nation around 1200 B.C.

The Assyrians. The Assyrians, who lived about 300 miles (480 kilometers) north of Babylon, were also an aggressive, warlike people. They were cruel conquerors. The Assyrians would move entire groups of people to weaken their sense of national unity. They were almost unbeatable in battle, partly because they were armed with copper, bronze, and iron weapons. Riding in horsedrawn chariots, they struck terror in the hearts of their enemies.

The Assyrian Empire was the largest the world had ever seen. Between 1100 B.C. and 612 B.C., the Assyrians conquered Babylonia, Palestine, Syria, Phoenicia, Sumer, and Egypt. The great Assyrian Empire finally fell in 612 B.C. when the Assyrians were badly defeated by the Chaldeans.

The Chaldean Empire. The Chaldean Empire lasted only 74 years, from 612 B.C. to 538 B.C. It is also known as the Neo-Babylonian Empire because Babylonia became powerful once again—more than 1,000 years after the time of Hammurabi.

During part of this period, King Nebuchadnezzar (NEHB uh kuhd NEHZ uhr) ruled. He made Babylon, with its Hanging Gardens, the most splendid city of the ancient world. In 539 B.C., Babylon was conquered by the Persians, and the Chaldean Empire ended.

The Persians. Under Darius I (dah REYE uhs), who lived from 550 B.C. to 486 B.C., the Persian Empire included almost all of the civilized world. Persia extended from the Indus River to the Mediterranean Sea. Mesopotamia was just one part of this empire. Persia is credited with developing a highly effective form of government. The empire was divided into provinces, each of which was governed in the king's name.

Although Persian kings had the power to do as they wished, they usually listened to their advisers. People were generally happy under Persian rule because they were treated fairly. Conquered people were allowed to practice their own religion and keep their own language. The king also allowed each province to keep its own customs and, sometimes, its own leaders.

Until the establishment of the Roman Empire, about 500 years later, the Persian government was the strongest in the ancient world, because of its successful organization and many accomplishments. For example, the Persians improved communication and transportation with the completion of the Royal Road, which ran from Asia Minor through the empire to Susa near the Persian Gulf. Royal messengers rode horses from one relay station to the next, covering about 1,600 miles (2,500 kilometers) in 10 days. The Persians also made metal coins of equal size and weight. People could then trade more easily because they could pay with coins of a standard value.

Because peace and prosperity existed during the Persian Empire, people's attitudes were open to changes in religion. About 600 B.C., a man named Zoroaster (ZOH roh AS ter) wrote a Persian religious book. The religion he taught, known as Zoroastrianism, became the religion of Persia. As such, it strongly influenced everyday life. Zoroaster taught that the world is a battleground in which there is a constant struggle between

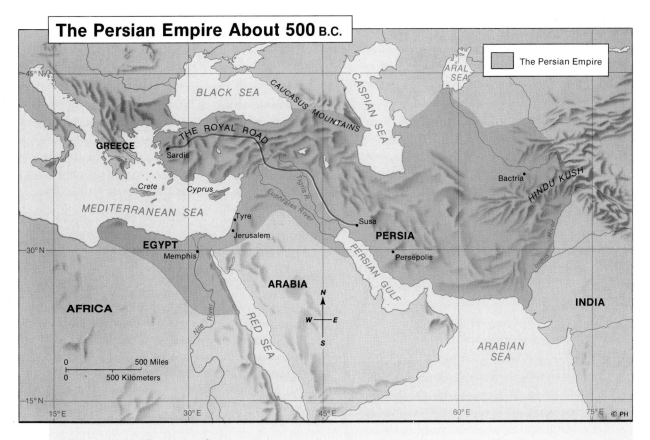

The Persian Empire About 500 B.C.

The Persian Empire

BLACK SEA
CAUCASUS MOUNTAINS
CASPIAN SEA
ARAL SEA
THE ROYAL ROAD
GREECE
Sardis
Crete   Cyprus
Bactria
HINDU KUSH
MEDITERRANEAN SEA
Tigris R.
Euphrates River
Tyre
Jerusalem
Susa
PERSIA
EGYPT
Memphis
Persepolis
Indus River
ARABIA
PERSIAN GULF
AFRICA
Nile River
RED SEA
INDIA
ARABIAN SEA

N
W — E
S

0   500 Miles
0   500 Kilometers

© PH

Focus on Geography

Movement   Find the Royal Road on the map. Caravans took two or more months to travel the length of the Royal Road. Several of the King's messengers on fresh horses could make it in about a week. How do you think the Royal Road helped the Persian Empire?

good and evil, light and darkness. Zoroaster believed that a person should always fight for the good.

As you will read in the remainder of this chapter, the early civilizations of the Fertile Crescent region made many advances in law, government, art, religion, and science. Much later, people in Greece and Rome used these ideas and expanded upon them.

The civilizations of Sumer, Babylonia, Assyria, Chaldea, and Persia each ruled over the land between the Tigris and the Euphrates rivers and made their individual contributions to world history. Many historians feel that the contributions of the Babylonians (2100 B.C.–1100 B.C.), which the next section will discuss, were the greatest.

SECTION 2 REVIEW

Knowing Key Terms, People, and Places
1. Define: **a.** cuneiform **b.** ziggurat
2. Identify: **a.** Fertile Crescent **b.** Hammurabi **c.** Sumerians **d.** Assyrians **e.** Persians

Reviewing Main Ideas
3. What lands were a part of Sumer?
4. Describe Persia under Darius I.

Critical Thinking
Predicting Consequences
5. How might the growth of Mesopotamian civilization have been different if the region had not been invaded so often?

3 Babylonia Contributed Much to Civilization

As you read, look for answers to these questions:

◆ What was life like for the people of Babylonia?
◆ How was the Babylonian code of laws organized and used?
◆ What major contributions did the Babylonians make to civilization?

Key Terms: polytheism (defined on p. 58), stylus (p. 60)

Because of its many important contributions, it is important to learn more about the Mesopotamian civilization of Babylonia. Studying about this civilization today is easier than in the past because scholars now can read the Babylonian language. For many years the language of the Babylonians was not understood. Henry Rawlinson of England, who had studied the Persian language for many years, helped to find the key to understanding the Babylonian language.

When Rawlinson served with the English army in Persia in the mid-1800s, he discovered some stories carved in the rocks of a mountain cliff called the *Behistun* (BAY hih stoon) *Rock*. The stories were written in three languages. Two of these languages were Babylonian cuneiform and Persian. Rawlinson risked his life many times to climb the mountain so he could copy every character, or letter, in the stories. The stories told how the Persian ruler Darius I, also known as Darius the Great, punished those who rose against him. Just as Greek writing on the Rosetta Stone helped scholars unlock the mysteries of hieroglyphics, so Rawlinson used his knowledge of Persian to figure out the meaning of the cuneiforms. He thus made it possible for us to know more about Babylonia and the people who lived there.

Babylonians Developed an Organized Society

Many factors influenced the structure of Babylonian society. The daily lives of the people were most affected by class lines, male/female roles, religion, and work.

Class lines. Babylonia, like Egypt, was led by a strong ruler. Class lines were clearly drawn between the rich and the poor. The scribes, who were educated, often became leading citizens. The rich owned most of the land and used slaves as workers. The free people, or the common people, were crafts workers, clerks, and farmers. The slaves were the lowest class.

Role of women. Women in Babylonia had many duties. The most important was bearing and bringing up children and looking after the family. In the course of their daily lives, women enjoyed many of the same rights as men. Women could own, buy, and sell property. They could leave what they owned to their children. Some women owned shops; others became scribes. Upper-class women had more rights than those of the lower class. As you will read later, Babylonian women had more privileges than the women of Europe had several hundred years later.

Religion's influence. Like the Egyptians, the Babylonians practiced **polytheism** (PAHL ih thee ihzm), which means they worshipped many gods. Babylonians prayed to statues representing nature gods. Among these gods were Marduk (MAHR dok), god of the earth, and Any (AY noo), god of the heavens. The Babylonians also mixed superstition with religion. They believed the use of magic would protect them from illness and evil spirits. Babylonian priests received gifts from the people who wanted to please the gods.

Work and the economy. Most people in Babylonia made their living by farming. They stored water from the rivers in open basins and then used canals and ditches to move the water to the fields. Their crops included grains, fruits, nuts, and dates.

Babylonian businesses included manufacturing and trading. Workers made cloth and clothing. They also produced bricks and metals to make houses, household utensils, and weapons. The Babylonian kings developed strict rules about trade and prices. Merchants had to pay heavy taxes to use the canals, rivers, and roads.

Instead of coins, silver was weighed out to make purchases. Borrowing and lending were common practices. Loans were made in silver, and the amount of the loan was recorded by weight.

Babylonians operated their businesses efficiently. They kept careful records of the contracts they made, of land bought and sold, and of partnerships that existed.

The Babylonians Wrote a Code of Laws

As you have read, the Babylonians set down laws that helped to govern their people. Hammurabi, who ruled around 1750 B.C., was one of the greatest kings of Babylonia. He is better known for his code of laws than for his conquests. This code was the first effort to write down all the laws Babylonians had to obey. A careful study of Hammurabi's Code tells us something about the way the Babylonians lived. It also tells us how they were governed.

The code was made up of 285 laws, which were listed under headings such as real estate, trade, and business. One feature of the code was the idea of "an eye for an eye," which means that the punishment should be equal to the crime. For example, if a poorly constructed house fell and killed the owner, the law said that the builder of the house had to die. If the owner's son was killed, then the son of the builder had to die. If a son beat his father, the son's fingers were to be cut off. What if a person were robbed, and the thief was not found? Then the city would repay the victim for the loss.

The principle of "an eye for an eye" held for those who were equal in rank but not for those who were unequal. Thus, it was possible for a noble to be treated better than a slave.

▲ **Illustrating History** *Hammurabi, shown at right, was the first to write down a code of laws all Babylonians had to obey.*

If a slave put out the eye of another slave, his or her eye was put out as punishment. But, if a noble put out the eye of a slave, then the fine was 30 shekels of silver. (A shekel is a unit of weight equal to about half an ounce.) If it were the eye of a free person, the fine was 60 shekels. Hammurabi's Code was unfair and harsh in some respects, but it was an early attempt to establish a code of laws by which everyone had to live.

Civilization Owes Much to the Babylonians

In addition to leaving the first written code of laws, the Babylonians made many other contributions to the learning of all people. They developed a system of writing based on the cuneiform writing of the Sumerians.

▲ **Illustrating History** *The Gate of Ishtar, made of glazed brick, led into Babylon.*

The Babylonians wrote on damp clay, cutting wedge-shaped marks into it with a sharp tool known as a **stylus** (STY luhs). After the surface had been written on, the damp tablets were dried and placed in glass jars in libraries, where they were grouped according to subject.

Language experts have discovered that the Babylonian language had more than 300 characters. Each character stood for a syllable. In Babylonian schools, the students studied writing, mathematics, and religion. If you think your books are heavy, just think of the clay tablets that Babylonian students carried each day.

To carry on their trade and businesses, Babylonians had to know how to count, add, and subtract. The Babylonians developed an advanced system of arithmetic based on the unit of 60. Although it is no longer used in arithmetic, the unit of 60 became the basis for telling time. The hour is divided into 60 minutes, and each minute is divided into 60 seconds. The circle of 360 degrees also comes from this counting unit.

The scientific world owes much to the Babylonians, who were interested in the stars and learned how to follow the paths of many of the planets. In most cases, Babylonian priests could predict eclipses of the moon. Our knowledge of the heavens is based in part on the observations and records of Babylonian astronomers.

As a result of their observations of space and time, the Babylonians made a 12-month calendar. Their year had 354 days. Since it takes the earth approximately 365 1/4 days to revolve around the sun, the Babylonians occasionally added a month to adjust the calendar to the earth's movement.

It is important to remember that the Babylonian and the Egyptian civilizations existed at about the same time. These countries traded with one another and sent representatives to each others' rulers. As a result, they influenced each others' culture. The Babylonians passed on their legends and stories to the Hebrews, whom you will read about in the next section. Through their contacts with the Phoenicians and the Persians, they planted the foundations of arithmetic and science, which eventually were passed on to the Greeks.

SECTION 3 REVIEW

Knowing Key Terms, People, and Places
1. Define: **a.** polytheism **b.** stylus
2. Identify: **a.** Henry Rawlinson **b.** Hammurabi's Code

Reviewing Main Ideas
3. Why were Henry Rawlinson's discovery and work so important?
4. Describe the role of women in Babylonian society.
5. Explain one way that Hammurabi's Code might be considered unfair.
6. What did the Babylonians contribute to astronomy?

Critical Thinking
Predicting Consequences
7. What do you think would happen to our civilization if there were no written codes of law?

4 Other Civilizations Made Contributions

As you read, look for answers to these questions:

◆ What contributions did the Hebrews make to civilization?
◆ How did the Phoenicians spread the gifts of the Egyptians and Babylonians?
◆ What did the Lydians contribute to civilization?

> **Key Terms:** monotheism (defined on p. 62), barter (p. 64).

As you have read in the previous sections, the Egyptians gave the world a system of writing, and the Babylonians passed on the first written legal code. Several small but important ancient Middle Eastern civilizations also made contributions that affected the history of their region and that of the entire world. The Hebrews, Phoenicians (fuh NEESH uhnz), and Lydians (LIHD ee uhnz) did not control huge empires that spread their civilizations through conquest. Instead, they provided advances in civilization through more peaceful means. The religious laws of the Hebrews continue to influence the world even today. The development of the Phoenician alphabet and the contributions of both the Phoenicians and the Lydians to trade paved the way for further exploration.

The Hebrew Kingdom Grew

Palestine, the land of the Hebrews, was not as large as either Egypt or Babylonia. Nor was it located in a great river valley. Enough rain fell, however, to permit agriculture in some parts of the country. The Hebrews plowed the land and built canals to bring more water to the drier parts of the country. Palestine was the biblical "land of milk and honey." Today, part of this land is the modern state of Israel, established by the descendants of the early Hebrews.

According to the Old Testament, the patriarch, or male leader, of the Hebrew people was Abraham, who, in about 2000 B.C., led his people away from the belief in many gods to the belief in one God, called Yahweh. Yahweh promised Abraham that his people would one day have a land of their own in Palestine if they worshipped him.

Abraham's grandson was Jacob, who was also known as Israel. It is from him that the name Israelites was applied to those who worshipped Yahweh. According to the Old Testament, Jacob had twelve sons, each of whom became a leader of one of the twelve tribes of Israel. One of Jacob's sons, Joseph, led a tribe into Egypt where they were enslaved until about 1230 B.C. Moses, another important leader, then led the Israelites out of Egypt. The Old Testament tells how the Hebrew people, or Israelites, wandered through the desert for 40 years, preparing themselves to occupy the land of Palestine

▼ **Illustrating History** *Moses holds stone tablets containing the Ten Commandments.*

that they believed Yahweh had promised them. The Old Testament tells that while the Israelites were in the desert, Yahweh gave Moses stone tablets on which were carved a code of laws called the Ten Commandments.

Moses led the Israelites to Palestine, the "promised land," but died without entering it. He was actually forbidden to enter it because he had distrusted God's word. The Israelites fought in a series of battles to establish themselves in their new land. Under the rule of their early kings—Saul, who lived about 1025 B.C., David, who reigned from 1012 B.C. to about 972 B.C., and Solomon, who lived from 973 B.C. to about 933 B.C.,—the Hebrew nation prospered.

Saul was the first king of the Israelites. He waged war against the Philistines but did not defeat them. Instead, he died in battle at Mount Gilboa. David established a capital at Jerusalem and united and strengthened the Hebrew nation. Under King Solomon, generally remembered as a wise king, the Israelites built a beautiful temple in Jerusalem and enjoyed a great respect among the people of the Middle East.

Unity collapsed, however, upon Solomon's death, and Palestine split into two kingdoms. The Kingdom of Israel was formed in the north, and the Kingdom of Judah was in the south. The Kingdom of Israel lasted for 250 years, until it was destroyed by the Assyrians in 722 B.C. In 586 B.C., the Chaldean king Nebuchadnezzar destroyed the temple in Jerusalem and enslaved the Hebrews, and the Kingdom of Judah fell.

The Persians later freed the Hebrews, and some of them returned to Palestine where they began to rebuild the temple. Although Israel was no longer an independent state, the Hebraic religious traditions lived on and had enormous influence on other religions —particularly Christianity and Islam.

The Hebrews Believed in One God and a Code of Ethics

The greatest contribution of the Hebrews to civilization was the fulfillment of the idea of **monotheism** (MAHN uh thee ihzm), which is the worship of a single God. According to the Ten Commandments, God commanded the Hebrew people not to worship other gods. Instead they were to love, fear, and pray to a single God. The commandments also instructed the Hebrew people not to steal, not to murder, not to envy another person's belongings, and to love their fathers and mothers. Like Hammurabi's Code, the Ten Commandments established a standard of conduct, one that has remained in force in many countries to this day.

The first five books of the Old Testament are called the Torah. These books cover not only ethical behavior but also tell the story of how the Hebrew people settled in Canaan and of their history as a nation in Palestine. The Talmud is an interpretation of the Torah that was begun by rabbis, or Jewish religious leaders, who were living outside of Palestine. The Old Testament and Talmud together demonstrate an effort to make people better men and women through love and prayer. The Hebrew people set aside the Sabbath as a day of religious observance, rest, and study. They also developed the idea of a messiah, or savior, who would come to establish God's kingdom on earth.

In an age when pharaohs and kings were worshipped as gods and when they could do as they wished in most civilizations, the rulers of Israel were not considered gods nor were they worshipped as gods. For example, a story in the Old Testament tells how King David's conduct displeased the prophet Nathan. Nathan went to the king and asked what should be done to a rich man who had acted unjustly toward a poor man. David said in reply, "As the Lord liveth, the man that hath done this deserveth to die." Nathan then said to King David, "Thou art the man."

If David had followed the practices of other kings of his day, he would have had Nathan imprisoned or killed for his lack of respect. Instead, David was ashamed of himself. He observed days of prayer and repentance and asked for God's forgiveness. What this story shows is that in ancient Hebrew tradition, no person, however mighty, was above the law. Over time, other societies saw the benefit of this basic principle of government. Eventually, it found its way into the United States Constitution.

The Phoenicians Spread the Gifts of Civilization

The Egyptians and the Babylonians built great civilizations, but it was the Phoenicians who spread the gifts of these civilizations. The Phoenicians were merchants and traders who carried Babylonian and Egyptian learning to other parts of the Mediterranean world. As seafarers, the Phoenicians traded throughout the Mediterranean and sailed as far as England.

The Phoenicians traded mainly crops and handicrafts. Their craftspeople made such things as metal and glass ornaments, jewelry, vases, and weapons.

As a result of their trading, the Phoenicians made contact with many people and civilizations. The Phoenicians brought many of the advancements in learning from Egypt and Babylonia to Greece. From Greece, these advancements spread to civilizations in Europe.

The Phoenicians developed an alphabet of 22 letters. Each letter stood for a single consonant sound. To these, the Greeks added vowel sounds. This alphabet was an improvement over the Egyptian hieroglyphics, and it was easier to use than the Babylonian cuneiforms. Later, the Romans made more changes to the alphabet, and it eventually became the one we use today.

▼ **Illustrating History** *These stone reliefs depict a Phoenician youth and a trading ship.*

The Growth of the Alphabet

Phoenician	𐤀 𐤁 𐤂 𐤃 𐤄 𐤅 𐤆 𐤇 𐤈 𐤉 𐤊 𐤋 𐤌 𐤍 𐤎 𐤏 𐤐 𐤑 𐤒 𐤓 𐤔 𐤕
Early Hebrew	(early Hebrew letterforms)
Early Greek	(early Greek letterforms)
Classical Greek	A B Γ Δ E Γ H I I K Λ M N O Π P Σ T Y Y Y Ξ Z
Early Latin	A B < D E F < H I I K L M N O Γ Q P ⅄ T V V V X Y Z
Classical Latin	A B C D E F G H I I K L M N O P Q R S T V V V X Y Z
Russian-Cyrillic	А Б Г Д Е Ф Г Н I К Л М Н О П Р С Т у З
German-Gothic	𝕬 𝕭 𝕮 𝕯 𝕰 𝕱 𝕲 𝕳 𝕴 𝕵 𝕶 𝕷 𝕸 𝕹 𝕺 𝕻 𝕼 𝕽 𝕾 𝕿 𝖀 𝖁 𝖂 𝖃 𝖄 𝖅
English	A B C D E F G H I J K L M N O P Q R S T U V W X Y Z

▲ **Chart Skill** *The above chart shows the evolution of the alphabet. Which language's alphabet is most closely related to the alphabet of classical Greece: English or Russian?*

The Lydians Extended Trade Routes

Lydia (LIHD ee uh), another important civilization, was located to the north of the Fertile Crescent. The Lydians are known for their system of coins that became the first true monetary system in the ancient world. The Lydians were traders, and the use of money made trading much easier. Before the Lydians developed this system, trading had been conducted by **barter**, the exchange of one product for another. With the introduction of money, bartering was no longer necessary. Croesus (KREE suhs), the king of Lydia, was thought to be the richest king in the ancient world. His kingdom fell when it was conquered by Persia in the sixth century B.C.

Archaeologists have found evidence that the people of Mesopotamia traded with the people of two other great river valley civilizations in India. The next chapter will discuss the ancient civilizations of both India and China.

SECTION 4 REVIEW

Knowing Key Terms, People, and Places
1. Define: **a.** monotheism **b.** barter
2. Identify: **a.** Abraham **b.** Phoenicians **c.** Lydians

Reviewing Main Ideas
3. How did the Ten Commandments of the Hebrews establish a lasting code of behavior for people?
4. How were Hebrew rulers different from other rulers of their times?
5. How did the Phoenicians spread civilization around the world?
6. How did the Lydians eliminate the need for bartering?

Critical Thinking
Predicting Consequences
7. How do you think that the growth of civilization would have been different without trade between peoples?

Using a Map to Observe for Detail

Maps are helpful tools that provide you with many kinds of information. They can give you details about the geography, politics, society, and economy of a place at a particular time. Knowing how to examine the information contained on maps can add greatly to your understanding of world history.

Follow the steps below to observe the details on the map on this page.

1. **Determine the kinds of information shown on the map.** Most maps contain certain elements that you can use to identify details on the map. Most maps also contain special symbols that you can learn about by reading the legend. Answer the following questions: (a) What is the title of the map? (b) What do the symbols in the legend, or map key, tell you? (c) What element on the map can you use to determine the distance between Giza and the first cataract? (d) How can you determine which direction the Nile River flows?

2. **Use the map to make detailed observations.** *Physical* maps provide information about such features as mountains, oceans, rivers, and lakes. *Political* maps show the sizes of empires or the boundaries of nations. *Economic* maps give information about such topics as trade and natural resources. A few maps give all three kinds of information. Answer the following questions: (a) Name two political features shown on the map. (b) Name two physical features shown on the map. (c) What is the approximate longitude and latitude of the city of Memphis?

3. **Study the map to draw conclusions about the historical period being studied.** You can draw conclusions by relating what you know from your reading to what you see on the

map below. Answer the following questions: (a) How can you determine the time period covered in this map? (b) What details on the map provide evidence that the Nile was the most important body of water in ancient Egypt? (c) What is the reason for including the smaller map below the main map?

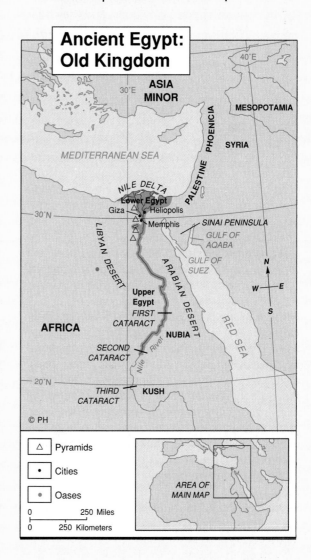

Ancient Egypt: Old Kingdom

REVIEW

Section Summaries

Section 1 The Egyptians Built a Great Civilization The Nile River was a means of transportation and a source of rich farm land for the ancient Egyptians. Egyptian history is divided into three periods: the Old Kingdom, the Middle Kingdom, and the New Kingdom. Each historical era marks the slow decline of the pharaohs' power. The Egyptians worshipped many gods, and they built great pyramids as tombs that were filled with treasures for pharaohs to enjoy in the afterlife. The Egyptians made advances in writing, mathematics, engineering, astronomy, and medicine.

Section 2 Civilization Developed in Mesopotamia Mesopotamia's civilization was greatly influenced by the geography of the Fertile Crescent. The Tigris and Euphrates rivers boosted agriculture, transportation, and communication. However, the location of Mesopotamia made foreign invasion from the surrounding mountain regions easy. Sumerians, Assyrians, Babylonians, and Chaldeans all came to power at some point in Mesopotamia's history. Each invading group, and especially the Babylonians, made its own special contributions to Mesopotamian civilization.

Section 3 Babylonia Contributed Much to Civilization Babylonian society was built along class lines. The wealthy owned land that was worked by slaves. Babylonian women, however, could enjoy many of the same rights as men. Religious practices in Babylon were polytheistic, honoring many gods. The economy depended on both farming and trade. The first written code of law in human history came from the Babylonian ruler Hammurabi. The Babylonians also made advances in writing, mathematics, and astronomy.

Section 4 Other Civilizations Made Contributions The Hebrews, Phoenicians, and Lydians made important contributions to the world. The monotheistic religion of the Hebrews formed the basis of Judaism, Christianity, and Islam. Through trade, the Phoenicians spread the gifts of many civilizations around the Mediterranean area. The Lydians were the first to base their trading economy on a system of currency.

Key Facts

1. Use each vocabulary word in a sentence.
   a. hieroglyphic
   b. cataract
   c. delta
   d. papyrus
   e. nome
   f. dynasty
   g. pharaoh
   h. cuneiform
   i. ziggurat
   j. polytheism
   k. stylus
   l. monotheism
   m. barter
2. Identify and briefly explain the importance of the following names, places, or events.
   a. Rosetta Stone
   b. Amon-Ra
   c. scribe
   d. Zoroaster
   e. Hammurabi
   f. Torah

Main Ideas

1. List three ways in which Egyptian civilization depended on the Nile River for its survival.
2. Identify two factors that contributed to the decline of the pharaohs' power and influence in Egypt.
3. Describe the historical evidence that suggests that the ancient Egyptians believed in a life after death.
4. How was the flooding of the Tigris and Euphrates both good and bad for the people of Mesopotamia?
5. Describe how the Babylonian economy worked without a system of currency.
6. What can we learn about Babylonian society from studying the content of Hammurabi's Code of Law?
7. How have the ancient Hebrews contributed to our modern concept of democracy?
8. In what ways did the Phoenicians' trading benefit their growth and that of other ancient societies?
9. What factors might have encouraged the Lydians to develop a system of currency?

Developing Skill in Reading History

Based on the information covered in this chapter, select the best ending for each sentence below.

1. Our most detailed and specific knowledge about the ancient Egyptians is the result of
   a. the discovery of the Rosetta Stone.
   b. investigating the treasures in the tombs of the pharaohs.
   c. studying Egyptian calendars and their foundation in astronomy.
2. Two things that show that Babylonian society was a mixture of tradition and progress are
   a. their superstitions and their study of astronomy.
   b. the Code of Hammurabi and the trade economy.
   c. their social structure and their polytheism.
3. The ancient Hebrews did *not* contribute to our understanding of
   a. the Bible.
   b. monotheism.
   c. trade based on a system of currency.

Using Social Studies Skills

1. **Making Inferences** Study the hieroglyphics that appear below. Then, answer the questions that follow:

a. Describe any forms that are repetitive.
b. Do the repeating forms occur in a predictable sequence?
c. Which symbol do you think needs to be deciphered first to break the code? Explain.

2. **Making Generalizations** How have coded messages been used in the modern world? Cite specific examples.

Critical Thinking

1. **Identifying Central Issues** What do the Phoenicians, Egyptians, Babylonians, and Hebrews have in common?
2. **Determining Relevance** In what ways was Mesopotamia especially vulnerable to outside invaders?
3. **Drawing Conclusions** Analyze this statement using the information presented in the chapter: ''The continual invasion of a society by conquering peoples will stifle its growth and development.''

Focus on Writing

Developing the Topic Sentence
A **topic sentence** states the main idea of a paragraph. Other sentences in the paragraph provide examples, details, or facts that support the topic sentence. Study the passage below:

> Egyptian history is divided into three time periods. The Old Kingdom was when the great pyramids were built. During the Middle Kingdom, the pharaohs declined in power. New lands were conquered by the Egyptians during the New Kingdom.

The first sentence functions as the topic sentence, and the other three sentences provide supporting details.

Read the following topic sentence: ''The Nile River was important to the development of ancient Egypt.'' Using information in the map on page 42, write three sentences to support this topic sentence in a paragraph.

Ancient India and China

(2500 B.C.–A.D. 500)

1 **Early Civilizations Rose Along River Valleys**

2 **Tradition and Religion Shaped Life in India**

3 **Rulers United India and Began a Golden Age**

4 **China's Geography Influenced Its Past**

5 **Two Dynasties Made China a Great Empire**

▲ **Illustrating History**
This fragment of stone sculpture shows a priest-king from the civilization of Mohenjo-Daro.

In the 1920s, the parched lands of western Asia yielded secrets that had been buried for thousands of years. On the west bank of the Indus River in what is now Pakistan, archaeologists excavated mounds that held important ruins. The area became known as Mohenjo-Daro (moh HEHN joh DAHR oh), or the "Place of the Dead." Mohenjo-Daro held the remains of a civilization over 4,000 years old.

An air of mystery still surrounds the site. Experts cannot decode the city's language or identify the origins of its founders. They do know, however, that these early people demonstrated great skill as urban planners.

The city's public buildings—watchtowers, a granary, an assembly hall, and a large public bath—stood on a western hill. Below the hill lay the main part of the city. Streets ran at right angles to one another. Along them, tightly packed together, stood houses made of oven-baked bricks. Each house contained an interior courtyard and a complex system of water drainage.

This architectural evidence is exciting to historians. They now believe that Mohenjo-Daro served as the center of an early Indian civilization that extended from the foothills of the Himalaya Mountains to the Indian Ocean. The chapter that follows will explore the early development of India and China.

2400 B.C.	1400 B.C.	400 B.C.	A.D. 600

■ **2000 B.C.**
Indo-Aryans move to the Indian subcontinent

■ **1500 B.C.**
Shang dynasty begins in China

500 B.C. ■
Buddhism begins in India

■ **326 B.C.**
Alexander the Great invades India

■ **202 B.C.**
Han dynasty begins in China

■ **A.D. 320**
Gupta period begins in India

▲ **Illustrating History** *The Great Bath of Mohenjo-Daro, neatly constructed of brick, has survived for more than 4,000 years.*

1 Early Civilizations Rose Along River Valleys

As you read, look for answers to these questions:

◆ What river valleys were the sites of the first civilizations in ancient India and China?
◆ What landforms separate the Indian subcontinent from the rest of Asia?
◆ What do archaeologists know about ancient India?

> **Key Terms:** subcontinent (defined on p. 69)

The discovery of Mohenjo-Daro showed that Egypt and Mesopotamia were not the only great civilizations of ancient times, although for many years they were the best known. Two other civilizations, almost as old, developed farther east on the continent of Asia. Like those in the Middle East, these ancient civilizations grew up along river valleys. Mohenjo-Daro was a part of an early civilization that developed along the Indus River valley in northwestern India. Another early civilization grew up along the Huang River in north central China. Both river valleys are shown on the map on page 70. These geographic features begin the stories of ancient India and China.

Geography Set India Apart from Asia

India, a part of South Asia, is a huge land area that is shaped like a top or an upside-down triangle. Although India is attached to the continent of Asia, it is so large it is often treated as a separate geographic region. Geographers use the term **subcontinent** to describe such large landmasses that are not themselves continents.

GEOGRAPHIC SETTING:
Asia

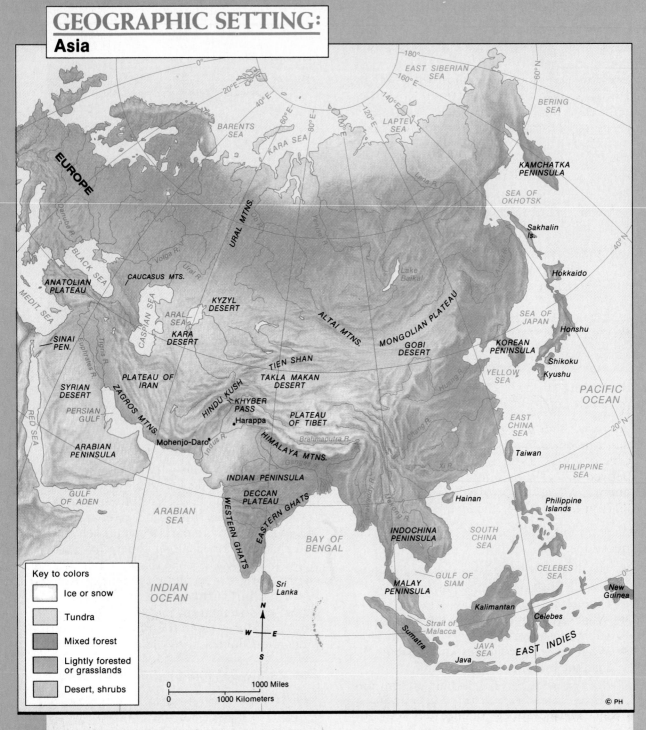

Key to colors
- Ice or snow
- Tundra
- Mixed forest
- Lightly forested or grasslands
- Desert, shrubs

0   1000 Miles
0   1000 Kilometers

© PH

Focus on Geography

Location Find Mohenjo-Daro and Harappa on the map. In what river valley were these two ancient cities located?

India's rugged geography has kept the subcontinent separate from the rest of Asia for most of its history. As you can see from the map on page 70, on its northern borders are two great mountain ranges, the towering Himalayas and the rugged Hindu Kush. The only easy land route through these commanding natural barriers is the Khyber (KY ber) Pass, which cuts into India through the Hindu Kush. Through this pass came the invading armies that attempted to conquer ancient India.

Two great rivers that flow out of the Himalayas and the Hindu Kush have played an important part in Indian history. These are the Indus and Ganges rivers. The Indus flows southwest into the Arabian Sea. Its valley was the home of India's first great civilization. The Ganges with its many branches flows eastward to empty into the Bay of Bengal. Both form wide, fertile river valleys that cut across the northern plains of the subcontinent. To the south of these plains lie deserts and rugged hills.

The center of the Indian "triangle" is the Deccan (DEHK uhn) Plateau, an area of relatively high ground between two mountain ranges called the Eastern and Western Ghats (gots). An area of level plains lies between these mountains and the sea. Frequent droughts make farming in the Deccan Plateau difficult, but the coastal plains support both agriculture and fishing.

Great Cities Appeared in the Indus Valley

The discovery of Mohenjo-Daro and the later discovery of a similar city, called Harappa (huh RAP uh), provided clues to the most mysterious of the ancient river valley civilizations. From studying these ruins, archaeologists concluded that Indian civilization was probably as old as the civilizations of Sumer and Babylonia. Archaeologists found evidence that the people of the Indus valley traded with Sumerians and Babylonians as early as 2900 B.C. Sumerian beads and pottery, for example, were found in Mohenjo-Daro. Clay seals, used by Harappan traders, were found in Sumer.

Illustrating History *The Himalaya Mountains formed a towering barrier against armies seeking to invade India.*

71

▲ **Illustrating History** *This small clay seal, found in Mohenjo-Daro, pictures a man who has been treed by a tiger.*

Almost everything else we know about the Indus valley people comes from the ruins of their cities. What do the ruins tell about the people who lived, worked, played, and died there? As early as 2500 B.C., a rich, well-organized civilization existed. The people built straight, wide city streets that ran north to south and east to west, crossing each other at right angles. The ruins also show that people lived in brick apartment houses which several families occupied. These homes had bathrooms connected to a city drainage system. At the center of each city was a fortress that had rooms for storing grain and holding religious ceremonies.

Archaeologists found evidence of trading, farming, and skilled crafts. The people used the potter's wheel and made attractively decorated pottery dishes, jugs, and jars. Children had clay toys shaped like animals and small carts. Some craftspeople made gold and silver ornaments, copper weapons, and bronze figures. The Indus valley farmers knew how to grow cotton and weave it into cloth.

Not until thousands of years later would Europeans live in such comfortable, well-planned cities. Yet, the civilization of the Indus valley disappeared about 2000 B.C. Historians are not sure why. Floods, famine, invasions, or a combination of these causes may have brought about the end of the Indus valley civilization. Historians also are not sure what happened to the people of the Indus valley. One theory is that they fled to southern India, where they became the ancestors of the people known as Dravidians. The Dravidians' language and culture today are different from the rest of India. Like the Indus valley people, they are smaller with dark skin and black hair.

The Indus valley was soon taken over by a new group of people, who were taller and had lighter skin and hair. These Indo-Aryans (IN doh AR ee enz), as they were called, played an important role in the unfolding history of India.

SECTION 1 REVIEW

Knowing Key Terms, People, and Places
1. Define: **a.** subcontinent
2. Identify: **a.** Khyber Pass **b.** Harappa **c.** Mohenjo-Daro

Focus on Geography
3. How has the physical geography of India kept it separate from the rest of Asia for most its history?
4. Why are the river valleys of India particularly suited for the growth of civilization?

Reviewing Main Ideas
5. How old do archaeologists think that Indian civilization is? Why do they believe this?
6. Describe the daily life of the people of Harappa and Mohenjo-Daro according to archaeological findings.

Critical Thinking
Expressing Problems Clearly
7. Mountain ranges can protect a country from invaders, but they can also slow the growth of civilization. Explain why this statement is true.

2 Tradition and Religion Shaped Life in India

As you read, look for answers to these questions:

◆ How was Indo-Aryan society structured?
◆ How did Hinduism and Buddhism develop?
◆ What other religions spread in India?

> **Key Terms:** rajah (defined on p. 73), caste system (p. 73), karma (p. 73), nirvana (p. 76)

The Indo-Aryans were herders who probably came from the grasslands between the Black and Caspian seas in what is now the Soviet Union. Other people from this group migrated to Persia, to the Middle East, and to parts of Europe. They spoke similar languages. Beginning about 2000 B.C., the Indo-Aryans came to the Indian subcontinent both as conquerors and immigrants. They may have destroyed the city of Harappa, causing some of its people to flee farther south. The Harappans who remained became their slaves.

The Indo-Aryans established their own government, which became the basis for the traditional Indian way of life. The Indo-Aryans first lived in tribes that were based on family groups. Each tribe was ruled by a chief and a tribal council. Later, some of these tribes joined to form small kingdoms, each of which was led by a **rajah** (RAH jah), or king. The Indo-Aryans were cattle herders, farmers, and warriors. They settled in small villages, which they then fortified against attack.

The Indo-Aryans brought new skills to India. They knew how to work metal, and they used horses for riding and pulling war chariots. Indo-Aryan warriors used bows and arrows as well as bronze weapons and armor to defeat their enemies.

The Indo-Aryan family was close-knit. Its wealth depended on the number of cows it owned. People valued the cow because it was both a beast of burden and a source of food, and so it became a sacred animal.

The Caste System Divided Indo-Aryan Society Into Classes

One important characteristic of Indo-Aryan life was the **caste** (kast) **system**. This system of social order divided Indian society into four main groups. The three highest castes were 1) *Brahmans* (BRAH muhns), or priests; 2) *Kshatriyas* (kah SHAHT ree ez), or nobles and fighters; and 3) *Vaisyas* (VYS yuhs), or ordinary people, such as merchants, farmers, and workers. A fourth caste, known as *Sudras* (SOO druhz), was made up of servants and peasants. Below these castes were the "untouchables," or outcasts. This group included the many people who did jobs believed to be unclean, such as sweeping streets. At first, there were only four castes, but over time many new castes formed.

The caste system began because the priests wanted to protect their high positions in society. When the caste system began, the rules and regulations governing relationships among castes were not nearly as strict as they later became. Differences in occupations, cultural groups, and skin color made caste divisions stricter. A member of one caste was not permitted to marry, to eat with, or to work with someone from another caste. A person could not move out of the caste into which he or she had been born. Indo-Aryans believed that a person's caste was the reward or punishment for **karma**, the good or bad deeds committed in a previous life.

Hinduism Developed in the Vedic Age

As the map on page 74 shows, the beliefs of the Indo-Aryans gradually developed into the main religion of India, called Hinduism (HIN doo IZ ehm). Indo-Aryans prayed to nature gods, including Surya, the sun, Varuna, the sky, and Signi, the fire. The leading god was Indra, who ruled thunder and storms and brought badly needed rain.

The holy songs and prayers of the Indo-Aryans are called Vedas (VAY duhz). The period in which they were composed, beginning about 1500 B.C., is called the Vedic Age. The Vedas tell the history and traditions of the Hindu faith. Priests sang them from memory, for they were not written down until hundreds of years later. One of the Vedas, the Rig-Veda, is regarded as the oldest Indian book of the Hindu religion. In the Vedas, the relationships between gods and humans are explained, as are the ways by which people can serve the gods. The Vedas also give a picture of Indo-Aryan everyday life in songs and folk tales.

The most famous of the Hindu religious books is the Upanishads (oo PAN ih SHADZ). They were handed down by word of mouth for about 300 years, from 800 B.C. to 500 B.C., before they were put into written form. The Upanishads express the idea that, over the course of many lifetimes, an individual can achieve a oneness with the world spirit, or Brahma. Each time a person dies, he or she is *reincarnated*, or born into another body, and during each lifetime, the human soul

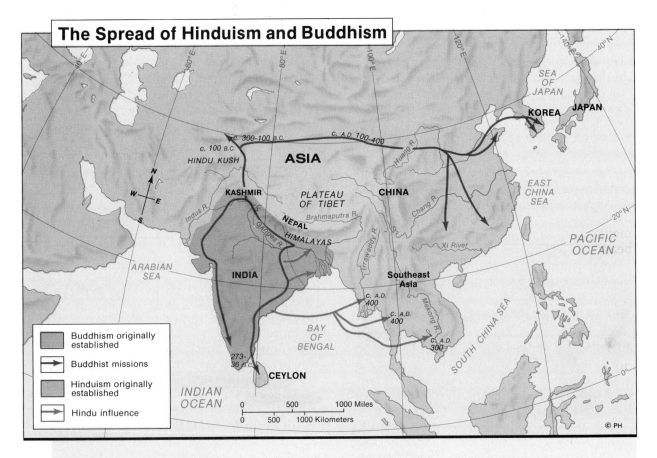

The Spread of Hinduism and Buddhism

Legend:
- Buddhism originally established
- Buddhist missions
- Hinduism originally established
- Hindu influence

Focus on Geography

1. **Regions** Hinduism eventually spread into a region dominated by another religion. Describe the region.
2. **Place** In which region would a traveller in 200 B.C. expect to see more Hindu temples—Southeast Asia, Korea, Hindu Kush, or Ceylon?

74

must try to move closer to Brahma. Hindus believe this cycle of reincarnation continues until the individual soul has reached the highest level of spiritual understanding and is reunited with the world spirit, Brahma.

The Vedas and Upanishads were written in a language called Sanskrit (SAN skrit). Along with Greek, Latin, and Hebrew, Sanskrit is one of the great classical languages of the world. Like most European languages, it also came from the language spoken by the original Indo-Aryans.

The Hindu religion has deep roots in the ancient history of India. Today, roughly 650 million people practice Hinduism, making it the most widely practiced religion in India.

Other Religious Beliefs Grew in India

The Hindu faith was not without competitors in ancient India. At about the time that Hindu priests were handing down the Upanishads, other religious teachers spread ideas of their own. One such teacher, Mahavira (mah HAH VEER ah), organized a group called Jains (jynz). They believe that all living things had souls. Therefore, the Jains maintained, they must not kill a person, a beast, or even an insect. As a result of these beliefs, devout Jains swept the street before they took even one step so they would not accidentally kill an innocent life. Some Jains also wore veils to avoid inhaling insects. The Jains, however, were a relatively small sect. A far bigger competitor to Hinduism was Buddhism.

Buddhism Began in India and Spread to Other Countries

Buddhism had its start in India about 500 B.C. Its founder was a prince named Siddhartha (sihd DAHR tah) Gautama (GOWT uh muh). According to legend, Siddhartha lived amid luxury, and his father was determined to protect him from learning about pain or sorrow. When he was almost 30, however, Siddhartha encountered illness and suffering in the form of three men: an old man, a

▲ **Illustrating History** *After seven years of living alone in the forest and thinking about life's problems, Siddhartha emerged and began to preach as Buddha. This fresco shows Buddha's first sermon.*

sick man, and a corpse. He was so moved by what he saw that he left his family, wealth, and comfortable life to live in the forest, where he could think about life's problems. After seven years, Siddhartha felt he had found the answer to why people suffer pain and sorrow and returned to the cities to spread his ideas.

To his followers, Siddhartha was known as the Buddha (BOOD ah), or Enlightened One. He wished to teach answers through talks, stories, and conversation. The Buddha saw himself as a teacher, not a god. He said

75

In their own words

Buddha's First Sermon

Five people heard Buddha's first sermon. These five were the first of millions to be influenced by his teachings. In the following excerpt, Buddha discusses the origin of suffering and the means to combat it.

❝What now is the Noble Truth of the Origin of Suffering? It is that craving which gives rise to fresh rebirth and, bound up with pleasure, . . . finds ever fresh delight. . . .

But where does this craving arise and take root? Wherever in the world there is the delightful and pleasurable, there this craving arises and takes root. . . .

Forms, sounds, smells, tastes, . . . and ideas are delightful and pleasurable: there this craving arises and takes root. . . .

What now is called the Noble Truth of the Extinction of Suffering? It is the complete fading away and extinction of this craving . . . the liberation and detachment from it.

But where may this craving vanish, where may it be extinguished? Wherever in the world there are delightful and pleasurable things, there this craving may vanish, there it may be extinguished. . . .

For, through the total fading away and extinction of craving, . . . decay and death, sorrow, lamentation, suffering, grief, and despair are extinguished. Thus comes about the extinction of . . . suffering.❞

1. According to Buddha, what is the origin of suffering, and how could an individual overcome suffering?
2. Do you think that the ideas of Buddha influence people in America today? Give examples to support your view.

that to be happy one must be unselfish. The desire for material things, he taught, was the cause of pain and evil.

The followers of Buddha taught that such things as gossiping, lying, stealing, and killing were bad. They accepted people from any caste. Buddha felt that by following the teachings of the Eightfold Path, a set of practical guidelines for living, one could reach nirvana. Nirvana is the ultimate goal of life in Hinduism and Buddhism. It is a perfect state of being and a release from the Hindu cycle of reincarnation and worldly suffering. Like other religious codes of conduct, such as the Ten Commandments, the Eightfold Path stressed right thinking, right speech, and right action.

Buddhism as a religion had great influence in India until about A.D. 200. Gradually, Hinduism absorbed many Buddhist beliefs, and over time, Buddhism merged back into Hinduism in India. Buddhist missionaries, however, took the new religion to other parts of Asia where it became the major religion in many countries.

SECTION 2 REVIEW

Knowing Key Terms, People, and Places
1. Define: **a.** rajah **b.** caste system **c.** karma **d.** nirvana
2. Identify: **a.** Indo-Aryans **b.** Brahmans **c.** Hinduism **d.** Sanskrit

Reviewing Main Ideas
3. What was life like for a member of the Sudras caste of the Indo-Aryan caste system?
4. What beliefs of the Hindu religion do the Upanishads express?
5. What did the Jains believe?
6. What did the Eightfold Path of Buddhism include?

Critical Thinking
Predicting Consequences
7. What are some of the negative consequences for the individual and for society of having a strict caste system?

3 Rulers United India and Began a Golden Age

As you read, look for answers to these questions:

◆ What were the results of Alexander the Great's conquest of India?
◆ How did Asoka help to spread Buddhism?
◆ Who were the Guptas and how did they contribute to Indian culture?

Key Terms: rajput (defined on p. 79)

During the Vedic Age, which extended from 1500 B.C. to 1000 B.C., India was made up of many small kingdoms. People followed different religious beliefs, and there was little unity among the kingdoms. These divisions made India weak.

Magadha, a strong Indo-Aryan kingdom, was the first of several kingdoms to rule northern India between 60 B.C. and A.D. 500. All Indian rulers faced serious obstacles in uniting the many Indo-Aryan kingdoms, in part because invaders regularly penetrated northern India seeking new conquests.

In 326 B.C., for example, the young Greek leader Alexander the Great invaded India. The Indians used 200 war elephants in the fierce battle that followed, and 12,000 Greek lives were lost. Still, Alexander won a great victory in northern India, which extended his empire to the Indus River. Three years later, however, Alexander died, and most of his troops left India.

Although Alexander's empire lasted only a few years, Greek rule had lasting results for India. It brought about some of the earliest contacts between European and Indian cultures. In northwestern India, where some of Alexander's followers remained after his empire dissolved, Greek culture met Buddhist culture and influenced Buddhist art, painting, and sculpture. Alexander's conquest also showed Indian leaders that without some unity, northern India would often be troubled by invasions.

The Maurya Were the First Indian Emperors

Not long after Alexander's death in 323 B.C., a young Indian noble named Chandragupta Maurya (CHUN druh GUP tuh MAWR yah) sought to unify northern India. Chandragupta conquered kingdoms from the Indus River to the Ganges River and united them into a strong nation. (See the map below.) Greeks who visited the Mauryan capital, Pataliputra (PAH tah lih POO trah), readily agreed that it was as rich and prosperous as their own cities. Chandragupta's government was a monarchy. His rule began the Mauryan dynasty, and he was the first Indian emperor to rule in India.

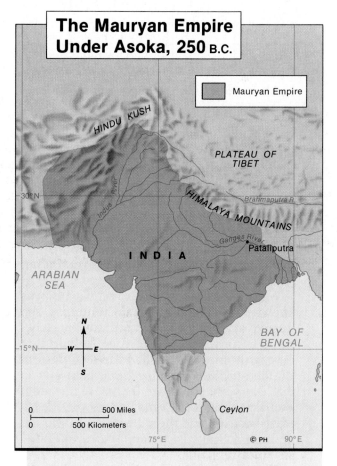

The Mauryan Empire Under Asoka, 250 B.C.

Mauryan Empire

HINDU KUSH

PLATEAU OF TIBET

Brahmaputra R.

HIMALAYA MOUNTAINS

Ganges River

Pataliputra

30°N

Indus River

INDIA

ARABIAN SEA

15°N

BAY OF BENGAL

0   500 Miles
0   500 Kilometers

Ceylon

75°E   © PH   90°E

Focus on Geography

Location What two barriers form part of the boundaries of the Mauryan Empire?

Major Events in India 2500 B.C.–A.D. 1008		
2500–1500 B.C	Harappan Age	Mohenjo-Daro and Harappa develop.
1500–1000 B.C.	Vedic Age	Indo-Aryan invaders sweep into India.
500 B.C.		Beginning of Buddhism
326–323 B.C.		Alexander the Great invades India.
323–184 B.C	Mauryan Dynasty	Chandragupta Maurya becomes first emperor.
184 B.C	Kanishka Empire	Silk Road to China opens up.
A.D. 320–500	Gupta Period	India's Golden Age
A.D. 500		Invasion by Huns
A.D. 1008		Muslim invasions

▲ **Chart Skill** *Might Alexander the Great have spread Buddhism to India?*

Chandragupta won fame as a soldier. His grandson Asoka (uh SOH kuh) won even more fame, but as a man of peace. As a great and wise ruler, Asoka deserves an honored place in world history. His kingdom was the most significant one India had seen up to that time and united nearly all of the Indian subcontinent.

When Asoka began his reign, he was known as a conqueror. Eventually, he turned against violence and war and became a convert to Buddhism. To help that new faith grow, Asoka had the teachings of Buddha written on huge stone columns so that everyone could see them. He also sent Buddhist monks to China, Japan, and Southeast Asia to spread their teachings. Although he built a Buddhist nation, Asoka tolerated all other religions.

The Mauryan kings who followed Asoka were not as wise or capable. The kingdom that Chandragupta had united by war and Asoka had united by faith fell apart. After ruling for 137 years, the Mauryan dynasty ended in 184 B.C.

Hindu Society Reached Its Height Under the Guptas

For 500 years after the breakup of the Mauryan dynasty, India knew little peace. Several groups of invaders came from the north. One of these, the Kushans (KOOSH ehnz), established the Kushan Empire in northwest India during the first century A.D. Trade along the Silk Road to China was important to the Kushans.

Another great family of rulers, the Guptas (GUP tuhz), was started by Chandra Gupta in about A.D. 320. For about 200 years, the

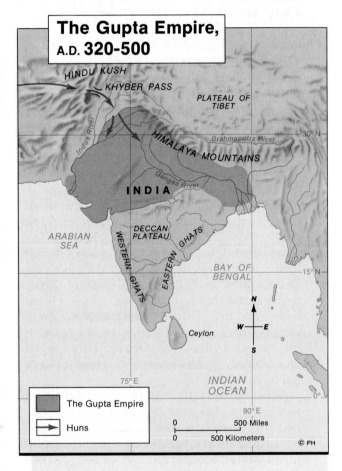

The Gupta Empire, A.D. 320-500

Focus on Geography

1. **Location** The Gupta Empire was between what physical features?
2. **Movement** Most invaders attacked India from the same direction. Describe the route and tell why it was used.

78

Asoka

Occasionally in history, a man of war becomes a man of peace. The Indian leader Asoka was such a man.

Little is known about Asoka's early life in India, but historians believe that he was trained as a soldier. Upon the death of his father in 273 B.C., Asoka became emperor of the vast Mauryan Empire of northern India. Eight years later, he led a successful invasion of southern India. The tremendous loss of life and the cruelty of battle in this invasion horrified Asoka to such a degree that he vowed never to fight again.

Not long after the war against southern India, Asoka converted to Buddhism. For the rest of his life, he worked to spread the Buddhist faith. Not only did he encourage people in his own kingdom to convert, but he also sent missionaries to convert people in foreign countries. To guide his subjects, he had the Buddhist rules of conduct carved on pillars of stone 30 to 40 feet (9.1 to 12.1 meters) high throughout the Mauryan Empire.

Asoka worked hard to improve his empire. He established a just and well-run government and ended India's harsh system of punishments. He also stopped the religious sacrifice of animals. By the time of his death in 232 B.C., India was united as never before, and Buddhism had become one of the world's most widely followed religions.

1. When and how did Asoka become emperor of India?
2. Why did he vow to give up warfare?
3. What were Asoka's major achievements?

Guptas ruled much of northern India between the Indus River and the Ganges River.

The Gupta period is called India's Golden Age. During this time, Hinduism gradually absorbed Buddhism and became once again the leading religion of India. Gupta poets and playwrights wrote beautiful works in the classical Sanskrit language. Science, mathematics, and astronomy flourished. It was a creative time for art, architecture, painting, sculpture, poetry, drama, and fables.

In the late A.D. 400s, the ferocious Huns, a tribe from central Asia, began their terrifying raids into both India and Europe. By about 600, they had brought about the fall of the Gupta Empire. Some descendants of the Huns became wealthy warrior-princes. They became part of a close-knit warrior class called **rajputs.**

For the next 600 years, Indian princes and various invaders fought for control of northern India. Invasions and warfare kept the country divided. This period of civil war lasted until the Muslim invasion in 1008.

SECTION 3 REVIEW

Knowing Key Terms, People, and Places
1. Define: **a.** rajput
2. Identify: **a.** Mauryas **b.** Asoka **c.** Guptas **d.** Huns

Focus on Geography
3. Between what two countries did the Silk Road allow trade?

Reviewing Main Ideas
4. What were two of the lasting results of Alexander the Great's conquests in India?
5. Why does Asoka deserve an honored place in world history?
6. What brought about the fall of the Gupta Empire?

Critical Thinking
Perceiving Cause and Effect
7. Why do you think that a civilization makes so many advances in art, literature, and science, for example, during periods of peace and fair rule?

4 China's Geography Influenced Its Past

As you read, look for answers to these questions:

◆ How have the size and physical geography of China affected its history?
◆ Which dynasties ruled ancient China and what occurred during each one?
◆ Who were three great Chinese philosophers and what did they teach?

Key Terms: feudal system (defined on p. 81)

Geography has always been important in China's history. Because China is large, outsiders have had difficulty conquering it. China's size has also made it difficult for rulers to unite people of different regions.

Three great river valleys divide China into northern, central, and southern regions. These are the valleys of the Huang River, the Chang River, and the Xi (shee) River. Farming in these river valleys has always been risky. Heavy rains cause flooding of farmlands, towns, and villages. Floodwaters also carry away much of the good soil. Nevertheless, most of China's people live in the river valleys. As you read in the first section, the Huang River valley was the home of the earliest civilization in China.

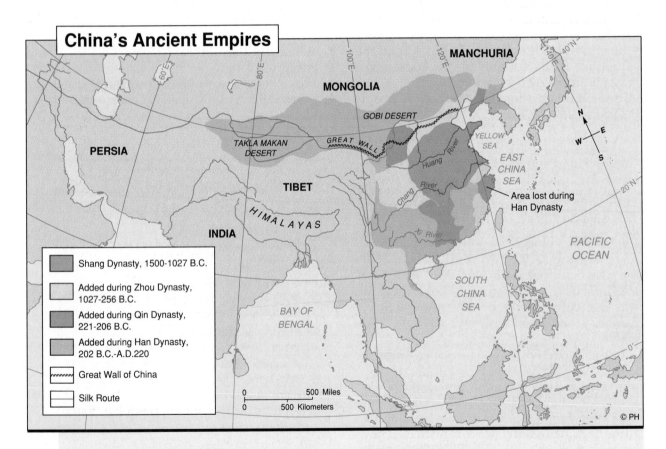

China's Ancient Empires

Shang Dynasty, 1500-1027 B.C.

Added during Zhou Dynasty, 1027-256 B.C.

Added during Qin Dynasty, 221-206 B.C.

Added during Han Dynasty, 202 B.C.-A.D.220

Great Wall of China

Silk Route

Area lost during Han Dynasty

0   500 Miles
0   500 Kilometers

© PH

Focus on Geography

Interaction   The Great Wall of China borders the Gobi Desert. Do you think the rulers who ordered it built felt the Gobi Desert was a strong barrier?

Much of the rest of China is mountainous. The north and west in particular are dry and hilly. A huge cold desert, the Gobi, is on China's northwestern border. As a result, this part of China is much less heavily populated than the crowded south and east. The Himalayas separate China from the Indian subcontinent.

Many features of China's geography have isolated the country from the rest of the world. Outsiders could enter China easily only by crossing the plains in the northeast, so invaders did not arrive until fairly late in Chinese history. For several thousand years, therefore, Chinese culture developed with little outside influence.

Several Dynasties Ruled in Ancient China

In Chinese history, events usually are recorded as taking place during the rule of a certain dynasty, rather than that of an individual ruler. China's first dynasty was the Xia [shah] dynasty (2000–1500 B.C.) Except for ancient legends, however, we know little about the Xia rulers. In about 1500 B.C., they were overthrown, and the Shang dynasty came to power.

During the Shang dynasty, Chinese artists made beautiful figures, religious objects, and weapons from bronze. Using the potter's wheel, these artists shaped clay into useful and decorative objects. The characters used in Chinese writing were also developing during this dynasty.

Although the Shang dynasty stayed in power for several hundred years, many of its rulers were vicious and amused themselves with cruel games and tortures. Shang nobles lived richly, but peasants were poor and badly treated. Both humans and animals were sacrificed in religious rites. Eventually, the Shang were driven out.

The country of the Zhou (joh) was far off in western China. From Zhou came Duke Fa, a famous fighter who made war against the dynasty of Shang and overthrew it. Taking the name Wu Wang (woo wang), this warrior-king became the first ruler of the Zhou dynasty around 1100 B.C. The dynasty lasted until roughly 256 B.C., longer than any

▲ **Illustrating History** *During the Shang dynasty, even bronze cauldrons such as this became highly decorated objects.*

other dynasty in Chinese history. As shown on the map on page 80, China under the Zhou grew to include land from the seacoast in the east and from the Chang River valley in the south.

The Zhou were strong conquerors, but they proved to be weak rulers. As in Europe more than a thousand years later, a **feudal system** developed in China. Under this system, the Zhou rulers gave small kingdoms to their friends and trusted military leaders. In return, these nobles, or landowning lords, owed military allegiance to the ruler, while he owed them protection in time of war. Under the feudal system, nobles often became more powerful than the ruler.

War, talk of war, and preparation for war ruled the lives of most nobles in feudal China. Zhou lords and their soldiers carried colorful flags as they rode off to battle. They wore suits of leather armor and carried spears and bows and arrows. They were proud of having good weapons and using them well. Even their sports centered on war and included tournaments, hunting, and practicing for battles.

As a result of the frequent wars, the strongest of the small kingdoms grew stronger. The nobles who ruled these kingdoms had the power to challenge—and defeat—the Zhou kings. In time, the Zhou rulers were kings in name only. The real power belonged to the lords who ruled the strong kingdoms on the borders of the Zhou territory.

One of the most powerful of these kingdoms was the Qin (chin) kingdom in the valley of the Wei (way) River. For more than 25 years, the Qin fought to unite the people under their rule.

Chinese Teachers Influenced People and Society

The wars during the Zhou dynasty did not lead to a decline in learning, which often happens during times of unrest. Rather, competition among the nobles and contact with other countries in Asia encouraged changes and cultural growth. Under the Zhou rulers, many new ideas thrived among the Chinese.

Three great Chinese teachers began to influence people's ways of thinking and living during the long rule of the Zhou dynasty. They were Laozi (low dzoo), Confucius (kuhn FYOO shush), and Mencius (MEHN shee ush). Each of these philosophers made many contributions to learning. Each one tried to outline a set of rules for building an ideal society.

At the same time, China was constantly torn by war. The rulers and the people began to wonder what was wrong. How could things be made better? How could people be made happier? These were some of the questions to which the philosophers, or teachers, of China sought answers during the Zhou dynasty.

Taoism. Laozi lived between 604 B.C. and 517 B.C. He taught that to find true happiness one must follow the *right way*, or Tao (dow). This belief of Laozi came to be known as Taoism.

What is the way of Tao? To explain these teachings simply, the Tao is the natural

▲ **Illustrating History** *Confucius, shown here in a statue from the Tang dynasty, taught the virtues of an ideal, orderly life.*

order of things over which people have no control. To be happy, people must allow themselves to be in harmony with the natural world. They must be humble in spirit. Trying to change the natural way would only upset the Tao and cause unhappiness.

For Laozi and his followers, laws, inventions, books, and work were not the most important accomplishments. Rather a serene life was the ideal. Laozi encouraged the Chinese to accept life as they found it. His teachings made them less anxious to change their lives.

Confucianism. By contrast, Confucius, who lived from 551 B.C. to 479 B.C., was a far more practical man than Laozi. For many years, Confucius was an adviser to the rulers of different kingdoms. When his advice was not needed or wanted, however, he would find himself looking for work. During these periods of unemployment, Confucius took time to think through his problems and those of the Chinese people. Confucius spent his life trying to find his ideal society, a society in which each person knew his or her place.

Confucius set up strict rules of behavior for certain social relationships, including the relationships between ruler and subject, parent and child, husband and wife, older and younger brothers and sisters, and even between friends. In each case, one person in the relationship was superior. Confucius taught that it was the duty of the subject to follow the ruler, the wife to follow the husband, the child to follow the parent. In this way, he believed, order would take the place of disorder in society. Each person would know his or her place and act according to established rules.

Confucius believed that rulers must set a good example for the rest of society to follow. If they set a good example, he thought, the rest of the people would be good. It was the duty of the subject to honor and obey the ruler, but it was also the duty of the ruler to set a good example. Confucius believed that people are basically good, so he felt that a perfect society is possible.

According to Confucius, a person had to show self-control in order to be good. Self-control could be achieved by following the proverb, "Do not do unto others what you would not have others do unto you." With this belief in mind, Confucius encouraged what he thought was correct behavior for all occasions. His rules soon were incorporated into the formal ceremonies that were part of Chinese life.

Honoring family ancestors was already important to the Chinese people. Confucius's ideas emphasized this idea even more. His philosophy also made people slow to change their ways. Because of Confucius, China kept its traditions longer than some other countries.

Confucius's ideas were finally written down in nine books known as the *Analects*. These classics became the guides for both family life and government organization in China. Under the Han dynasty, people who sought to enter government service had to memorize the sayings of Confucius in order to pass the required tests. Confucian ideas also spread to other countries of Asia.

Mencius. Mencius, who lived from 373 B.C. to 288 B.C., lived nearly 200 years after Confucius but followed in his footsteps in many ways. Like Confucius, he spent years looking for a ruler wise enough to use his services. Mencius, however, tried to answer the question, "What can be done if rulers are not good as Confucius expected them to be?" He decided that in such cases the people have the right to rebel. Although Mencius believed in rule by a king or queen, he insisted that a king or queen be an effective ruler. He also thought that the people were important as the real beginning of all political power. This was an unusual belief at that time.

SECTION 4 REVIEW

Knowing Key Terms, People, and Places
1. Define: **a.** feudal system
2. Identify: **a.** Gobi **b.** Shang dynasty **c.** Laozi **d.** Confucius

Focus on Geography
3. What risks are involved in living and farming in China's river valleys?
4. What geographical features of China have tended to keep it isolated from the rest of the world?

Reviewing Main Ideas
5. How did the power of the kings change during the Zhou dynasty?
6. What is the Tao philosophy?
7. What rules of behavior did Confucius think should apply to social relationships?

Critical Thinking
Making Comparisons
8. What are the similarities and differences between the philosophies of Confucius and Mencius?

5 Two Dynasties Made China a Great Empire

As you read, look for answers to these questions:

◆ Who was Shi Huangdi and how did his rule affect China?
◆ What happened to Confucianism under the Qin and Han dynasties?

Key Terms: kowtow (defined on p. 85)

By 221 B.C., the leaders of the Qin kingdom finally took control away from the weak Zhou rulers and united the small kingdoms. The Qin leader took the name Shi Huangdi (shee hwahng dee), or First Emperor.

A Strong Emperor United China Under the Qin Dynasty

Shi Huangdi was determined to unify China and rule as a strong emperor. To do so would not be easy, for the teachings of Laozi and Confucius encouraged people to accept things as they were. This outlook stood in the way of the changes Shi Huangdi had in mind. Therefore, he ordered the books of Confucius and the other philosophers burned. By destroying these books, Shi Huangdi hoped to destroy the ideas that stood in his way. Scholars who protested against his actions were either killed or banished from China forever.

Having silenced most of the educated people, Shi Huangdi then tried to silence military leaders as well. He ordered the nobles and the rulers of small kingdoms to move their households to his capital. In this way, the emperor could continually monitor their activities. Their presence at his capital also added grace and prestige to his new court. In place of tiny kingdoms, the First Emperor divided the empire into several districts. Each district was ruled by a paid official. To win the loyalty of the peasants, the emperor allowed them to own the land on which they lived and worked.

Shi Huangdi realized that he could not unite China by military strength alone. He tried other methods to bring the people closer together. He built new roads and introduced better standards of weights and measures to help increase trade. He ordered wagons to be made to a standard size and width so that they could travel easily over the new roads. In addition, Shi Huangdi made the Chinese writing system simpler, encouraged science, and built canals for irrigation and travel.

The emperor also realized that he must make his empire safe from foreign enemies. To protect lands in the north from invaders, he began the Great Wall of China. Like the building of the pyramids in Egypt, the building of the Great Wall was a huge task that required the forced labor of many people. Perhaps as many as 1 million workers had to be housed, clothed, and fed in lands far from their homes.

The Great Wall stretched inland from the Yellow Sea for about 1,500 miles (2,415 kilometers). It was about 20 feet high (6.10 meters), and 15 feet wide (4.57 meters). Guards in watchtowers kept a lookout for raiders. Built at a great cost in time and labor, the Great Wall successfully kept out China's enemies. Later emperors added to and strengthened the wall. To this day, large portions of it still stand.

Shi Huangdi did much for China. His most important contribution was transforming the country into a unified nation. Except for short periods, China has remained united to the present day. No other nation in the world can boast of a tradition of unity for more than 2,000 years.

On the other hand, the Chinese people were not happy under Shi Huangdi. They paid heavily in lives and taxes for the Great Wall. Many longed to return to the ways of Confucius. They did not forgive the emperor for burning the philosophers' books. When Shi Huangdi died in about 207 B.C., nobles and common people alike were glad that his strict rule had ended. To show his great power, however, the First Emperor was buried with thousands of life-size clay statues of soldiers and horses.

China's Secret Treasure

According to legend, a 14-year-old Chinese empress named Xilingshi went for a walk about 4,500 years ago. The empress saw a mass of cocoons dangling from the branches of a mulberry tree. She plucked a cocoon from the tree and later put it into a pot of water. To her amazement, the cocoon softened into a tangled web that could be unraveled like a ball of yarn. Xilingshi had discovered silk.

The Chinese wove the delicate threads into a fine fabric, and soon silk was all the rage among China's noble families. They kept their silk-making process secret for nearly 3,000 years, until India learned it. By the fourth century A.D. silk-making, as pictured on right, flourished throughout most of Asia.

1. Who discovered silk?
2. Why did the Chinese want to keep the silk-making process a well-guarded secret?

The Han Dynasty Followed the First Emperor

Shi Huangdi had hoped that his dynasty would last for hundreds of years, but revolts broke out soon after his death. The Qin dynasty came to an end about five years later, with the murder of his son. The leaders of the next dynasty ruled in a different way. Called the Han dynasty, it made China an even greater empire.

An unusual leader named Liu Bang (lyoo bahng) led the revolt against the Qin and became the first Han emperor. Liu was a peasant farmer who had been in the royal police. His leadership attracted other poor people of great ability. He promised them land and power when victory was theirs.

The rebels seized the throne in 202 B.C., but Liu Bang had to fight for five more years to defeat the last of the Qin nobles. Liu Bang is often called "Han Gaozu," a title that is similar to "Father of his Country." The dynasty he founded is known by the name Han after Liu's home province, or kingdom. The Han ruled for nearly 400 years, from 202 B.C. to A.D. 220.

The Han rulers realized that they had to educate loyal followers if they were to run a strong and effective government. To bring back tradition and respect for authority, they encouraged a return to the teachings of Confucius. State ceremonies were extremely formal. The act of kowtow dates from this period. **Kowtow** was a deep bow in which the head touched the floor to show respect for a superior authority.

The Han rulers also needed educated people to carry out their orders and to work in important government offices. They set up a

Chinese Dynasties 2000 BC –1220 BC		
2000–1500 BC	Hsing Dynasty	Not much is known.
1500–1100 BC	Shang Dynasty	Bronze sculpting. Period characterized by cruel and vicious leaders.
1100–256 BC	Zhou Dynasty	Feudal system develops. Period characterized by frequent wars. The ideas of Confucius, Mencius, and Laozi flourish.
221–202 BC	Qin Dynasty	Great Wall built. Confucian literature is burned.
202 BC–AD 220	Han Dynasty	Trade in silk and spices links Europe with Asia.

▲ **Illustrating History** *This flying horse dates from the Han dynasty.*

▲ **Chart Skill** *What dynasty tried to rid China of the ideas of Confucius?*

system to give examinations based on the teachings of Confucius. These exams provided a way for bright young men, even from poor families, to get jobs. Because of these tests, the teachings of Confucius became more firmly a part of Chinese thinking than they were during the Zhou dynasty.

The Han Dynasty Weakened and Fell

By about A.D. 200, events both inside and outside China weakened the Han dynasty. Barbarian tribes invaded the country's borders. A series of weak, inexperienced rulers tried but failed to drive out these invaders. In addition, government officials had grown too dependent on Confucian ideas and traditions. They could not come up with the new ideas needed to meet the challenge of the invasions. Four centuries of political confusion and fighting followed the fall of the Han dynasty.

Nevertheless, the Han dynasty accomplished a great deal. China became a huge, united empire. A rich trade in silk and spices linked it with Europe and with other countries in Asia. A single legal code was adopted for the nation. A unified writing

system was also introduced. Roads and canals were built, further uniting China by making trade, travel, and commerce easier.

SECTION 5 REVIEW

Knowing Key Terms, People, and Places
1. Define: **a.** kowtow
2. Identify: **a.** Shi Huangdi **b.** Great Wall **c.** Liu Bang

Reviewing Main Ideas
3. Why did the first emperor of the Qin dynasty destroy the books of the great Chinese philosophers?
4. What was Shi Huangdi's most important contribution to China?
5. Describe the progress made in China during the Han dynasty.

Critical Thinking
Drawing Conclusions
6. Would you conclude that the teachings of Confucius had a more positive than negative effect on ancient China? Explain your answer.

Putting Historical Events in Sequence

When you read history or any other account of events, you need to be able to figure out the sequence in which the events happened so that you can understand how they are related.

The sequence of events may be indicated in several different ways. Use the paragraphs below to practice several ways that historical events can be put in sequence.

1. **Look for a direct statement of time.** The most obvious way to determine sequence is to look for dates, such as *in 517 B.C.* (a) What two events in the paragraphs are indicated by a direct statement of time? (b) Which event occurred last?

2. **Search for phrases that are an indirect statement of time.** Indirect statements of time, such as *two centuries later,* also indicate time sequence. (a) What indirect statement of time tells when Alexander the Great invaded India? (b) What was the year of Alexander's invasion?

3. **Examine the text for words that show time relationships.** Words that show time relationships include *already, before, earlier, later, next, then, soon, finally, after,* and *following.*

(a) What word in the last sentence of the passage shows a time relationship? (b) In what year did Asoka die?

4. **Examine the passage for words that suggest cause and effect.** Words that suggest cause and effect, such as *because of, as a result, therefore, so,* can clarify the time relationship between two events because we know that causes come before effects. (a) What word in the first paragraph suggests a cause and effect relationship? (b) What is the effect in this instance?

5. **Look for verb tenses that indicate the time relationship between two events.** The following two sentences illustrate how verb tense affects time order: (1) *Indian leaders had realized the need for unity when Alexander invaded.* (2) *Indian leaders realized the need for unity when Alexander invaded.* The word *when* does not clarify the time relationship between Indian leaders' realizing the need for unity and Alexander's invasion. But, the verb tenses in each of the sentences *do* clarify that relationship. Which sentence, the first or second, states the same time relationship as the passage?

In 321 B.C., Chandragupta Maurya established the first empire over all of northern India. The way had been paved for this event by Alexander the Great, who, five years earlier, had invaded India and extended his empire into its territory. Although Alexander's rule lasted only three years until he died, his invasion made Indian leaders realize that they could be conquered by foreigners. Because of their fear of foreign domination, Indian leaders decided to unite.

Chandragupta's grandson, Asoka, strengthened the power and unity of the Mauryan empire. But, that unity had dissolved by 184 B.C., 50 years after Asoka's death.

REVIEW

Section Summaries

Section 1 Early Civilizations Rose Along River Valleys While Egypt and Mesopotamia were thriving in the ancient Middle East, a great civilization was developing in the Indus River valley in India. Rugged geography kept the Indian subcontinent isolated from the rest of the world. However, the cities of Harappa and Mohenjo-Daro were part of an advanced civilization that existed in India by 2500 B.C. The civilization disappeared around 2000 B.C.

Section 2 Tradition and Religion Shaped Life in India The Indo-Aryans conquered the Indian subcontinent around 2000 B.C. The society that they founded was organized around a rigid caste system. The Indo-Aryans' beliefs formed the foundation of India's main religion—Hinduism. Two other religions, Jainism and Buddhism, contributed their own teachings to the rich fabric of Indian religious beliefs.

Section 3 Rulers United India and Began a Golden Age India's many small kingdoms were not united during the Vedic Age, which made the country vulnerable to foreign invasions. When Alexander the Great conquered much of northern India in 326 B.C., he spread Greek culture to India. After Alexander's death, the Mauryas became India's first dynasty of rulers. Later, under the Gupta rulers, India entered a golden age when art, literature, and science flourished. The Guptas reigned until the Huns invaded India.

Section 4 China's Geography Influenced Its Past China is a huge country with three great rivers that divide it into regions and mountains that isolate it from the rest of the world. These factors allowed ancient China to develop without much foreign interference but also made the country difficult to unite. Still, several dynasties ruled ancient China. Under the Zhou dynasty, the Chinese philosophers Laozi, Confucius, and Mencius formed ideas that shaped China's culture.

Section 5 Two Dynasties Made China a Great Empire Shi Huangdi, First Emperor of the Qin dynasty, destroyed the works of Confucius and other philosophers because he wanted to bring about change in China. He centralized political and military power and began building the Great Wall of China. Liu Bang led the revolt against the unpopular Qin Dynasty. He was the first ruler of the Han dynasty, which focused on educating the people and restoring Confucian traditions. After ruling China for 400 years, the Han dynasty finally weakened and fell to barbarian invaders.

Key Facts

1. Use each vocabulary word in a sentence.
   a. subcontinent   e. nirvana
   b. rajah   f. rajput
   c. caste system   g. feudal system
   d. karma   h. kowtow
2. Identify and briefly explain the importance of the following names, places, or events.
   a. Mohenjo-Daro   f. Gupta Empire
   b. Himalayas   g. Tao
   c. Indo-Aryans   h. Confucius
   d. Vedas   i. Great Wall
   e. Buddha   j. Liu Bang

Main Ideas

1. How has the work of archaeologists added to our knowledge of early Asian civilizations?
2. What part could geography have played in the development of the Indus Valley civilization?
3. Why did Indo-Aryans feel that a caste system was a necessary part of their society?
4. How did the Mauryan emperor Asoka help to spread Buddhism, and what events in his life motivated him to do this?
5. What role did the geography of China play in its ancient history?
6. What was the function of the Confucian philosophy in the Han dynasty?

Developing Skill in Reading History

An important aspect of studying history is knowing in what order events occurred. Based on your reading of the chapter, place each group of events below in the proper chronological order.

1. _____ Ancestors of the Dravidians migrate to southern India.
   _____ The Vedic Age begins.
   _____ The Indo-Aryans invade India.
2. _____ Alexander the Great conquers northern India.
   _____ The Mauryas become the first Indian emperors.
   _____ The Kushans invade northern India.
3. _____ Shang dynasty
   _____ Qin dynasty
   _____ Zhou dynasty
   _____ Xia dynasty
   _____ Han dynasty

Using Social Studies Skills

1. **Reading Maps** China's Zhou dynasty ruled longer than any other in Chinese history. This family of rulers, from the kingdom of Zhou in western China, would eventually expand the country's borders to the seacoast in the east and the Chang River valley in the south.

   Imagine that you are a military aide to the Zhou. Based on the map on page 80, write a letter in which you describe the geographical features that must be considered before expanding to the south and the east.
2. **Interpreting Art** The inscription on the fourth-century painting on this page says that "character building is more important than appearance." What are the women in the painting doing? What does the art tell us about Chinese values?

Critical Thinking

1. **Testing Conclusions** Historians believe that people of the Indus Valley were trading with Sumerians and Babylonians by 2900 B.C. What evidence supports this conclusion?

2. **Expressing Problems Clearly** How did the ideas of Confucius both help and discourage the growth of Chinese civilization?
3. **Identifying Alternatives** How did each Chinese dynasty approach the problem of unifying this very large country?

Focus on Writing

Developing the Topic Sentence

A topic sentence states the main idea of a paragraph. **Supporting statements** contain facts or ideas related to the main idea. Within a paragraph, supporting statements give evidence for the topic sentence or clarify the main idea. Reread the opening paragraph of this chapter and identify its topic sentence and at least two supporting statements. What facts are contained in the supporting statements? What do these facts contribute to the paragraph?

Practice: Read the following topic sentence: "Geography has often played a crucial role in the development of various civilizations." Now write three supporting statements for this topic sentence using facts from the chapter.

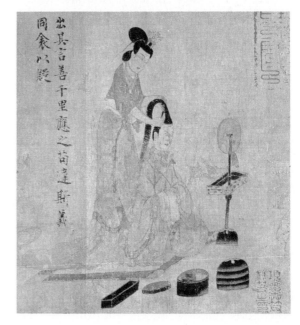

Geography in History

Cities Built on Glass, Copper, and Clay

Water and other resources made the civilizations of Mesopotamia great (see page 54). When people began to use irrigation, that once barren land bloomed with farms and cities. Elsewhere in southwest Asia, cities flourished on other resources. Although these early cities never matched the Sumerian city-states in size or importance, they shared many of the same qualities that make city life different from village life.

Basic Resources

Turkey was the ideal place for nomads to settle. In the cool, moist highlands, wheat and other grains grew naturally. Sheep and goats roamed wild. Here, basic needs could be met by farming, herding, and hunting in the same region. In time, these people began to use other available resources that turned villages into cities.

One of the largest of these early cities was Catal Huyuk (shah tahl HOO yuhk), settled in about 8300 B.C. in south central Turkey. The settlement overlooked a stream that ran through a rich plain. By 6000 B.C., its people were growing wheat, peas, and barley. From nearby mountains, they picked apples, nuts, and various berries. They also hunted.

Resources to Grow On

The mountains near Catal Huyuk helped the village to grow into a city. In ages past, volcanoes among those mountains had erupted liquid glass that hardened into dark-colored obsidian. Because the people did not have much metal, they used other materials for tools. Obsidian could be ground easily to produce a fine blade. Obsidian blades mounted on wooden shafts could be used as spears and arrows, as sickles for cutting wheat, or as knives for skinning game. Obsidian was the most widely traded resource during this time.

Catal Huyuk became the hub of the obsidian trade. Neighboring cities traded their own resources for obsidian. Some offered other minerals—white marble to make bowls, flint to make daggers and to spark flames, and sulfur for starting fires. A yellow clay called ochre could be used as paint. Some people brought jewelry made out of seashells from the Red Sea and the Mediterranean. By trading their obsidian, the people of Catal Huyuk were able to meet their needs and enjoy luxuries from far away.

Becoming a City

The prosperity that obsidian brought to Catal Huyuk made it a city of at least 6,000 people. This was a large population for that time. Some of the visitors to Catal Huyuk stayed on. Perhaps these newcomers were craftworkers, drawn to Catal Huyuk's obsidian trade.

Some of the strangers may also have come to participate in the well-developed religious life of Catal Huyuk. Religious services may have been exchanged for the resources of far-away places. This shows that in Catal Huyuk, instead of farming or making things for sale, people could make a living by performing services for others.

New Resources

Catal Huyuk was abandoned about 5700 B.C. No one knows why, but it might have declined when copper tools were introduced. As the Stone Age gave way to the Bronze Age, obsidian lost its value.

Other places in Turkey rich in copper, such as Tilki Tepe, Cayonu Tepesi, Kara Huyuk, and Arslan Tepe, began to grow. Copper was mined, made into chisels, knives, and axes, and traded with faraway places.

One Turkish city that grew after Catal Huyuk declined was Hacilar. Here, people developed a fine clay, used to make high-quality pottery, and Hacilar probably became a center for luxury goods. Manufacturing became more important than food production. This important development is one of the signs of true city life.

Focus on Geography

1. **Place** What resource helped Catal Huyuk to become a large, successful city?

2. **Location** Look at the map below. How did Turkey's resources compare to Mesopotamia's?

3. **Movement** Why were people from other towns drawn to live in Catal Huyuk?

Critical Thinking

Perceiving Cause and Effect
4. Why do you think Catal Huyuk was one of the largest of the early cities outside Mesopotamia?

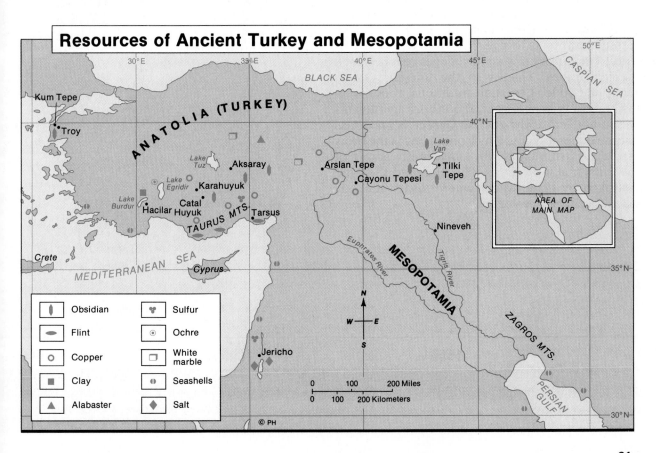

Resources of Ancient Turkey and Mesopotamia

UNIT 2

Our Classical Heritage

(2000 B.C.–A.D. 476)

Are having a say in government, being represented by fair laws, and worshipping as we choose twentieth-century privileges? As you will learn in this unit, the history of such privileges reaches back to ancient times. Thanks to the ancient Greek, Roman, and Judeo-Christian traditions, these freedoms have long been a part of our heritage. In this unit, you will learn why ancient Greece is known as the home of democracy, why Roman law is the basis of our legal system, and why Christianity is one of the world's major religions. The map and the time line, linked by color, show where and when our classical heritage developed.

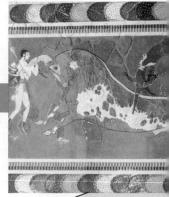

1 ANCIENT GREECE

Beautiful wall paintings like this one covered the walls of the Palace of Minos in Crete.

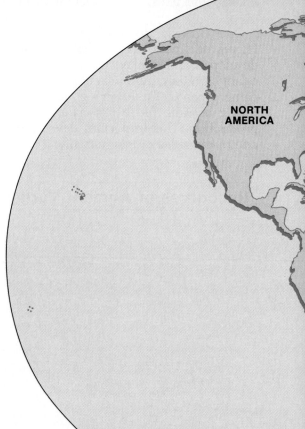

NORTH AMERICA

2000 B.C.	1500 B.C.	1000 B.C.	500 B.C.

■ 2000 B.C. Minoan civilization begins on Crete

1200 B.C. Dorian invaders conquer ■ Achaean civilization in Greece

404 B.C. Sparta defeats Athens in the Peloponnesian Wars

ANCIENT ROME AND THE ROMAN EMPIRE **2**

500 B.C. Romans drive out Etruscans ■ and establish a republic

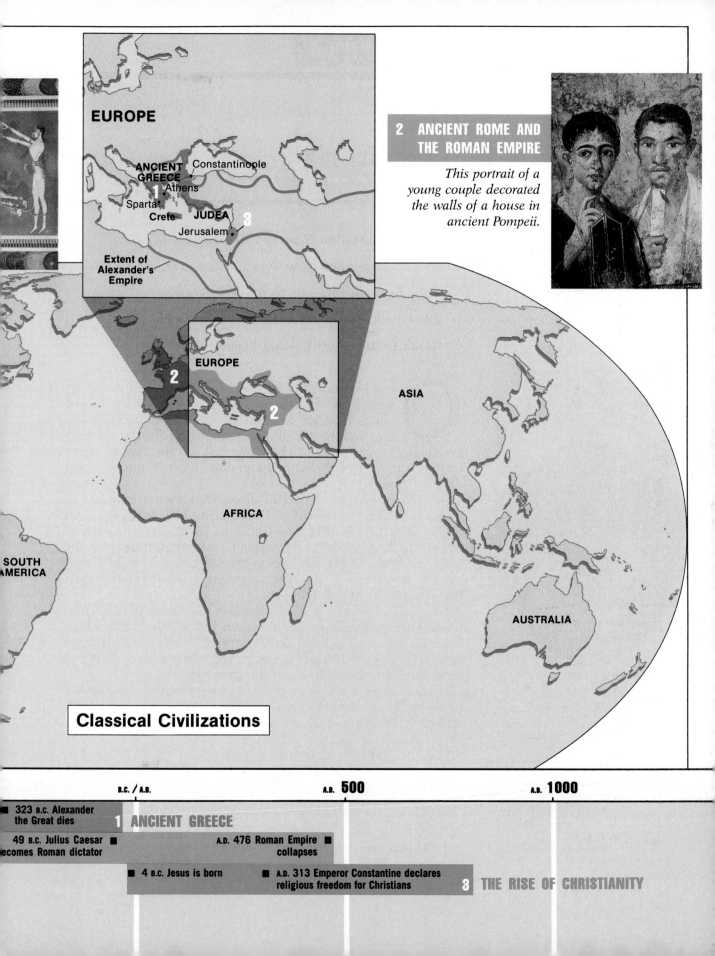

EUROPE

ANCIENT GREECE

Constantinople

Athens

Sparta

Crete

JUDEA

Jerusalem

1

3

Extent of
Alexander's
Empire

**2 ANCIENT ROME AND
THE ROMAN EMPIRE**

*This portrait of a
young couple decorated
the walls of a house in
ancient Pompeii.*

2

EUROPE

ASIA

2

AFRICA

SOUTH
AMERICA

AUSTRALIA

Classical Civilizations

B.C. / A.D.   A.D. **500**   A.D. **1000**

■ 323 B.C. Alexander
the Great dies   **1 ANCIENT GREECE**

49 B.C. Julius Caesar ■   A.D. 476 Roman Empire ■
becomes Roman dictator   collapses

■ 4 B.C. Jesus is born   ■ A.D. 313 Emperor Constantine declares
                                 religious freedom for Christians   **3 THE RISE OF CHRISTIANITY**

The Gifts of Greece

(2000 B.C.–30 B.C.)

▲ **Illustrating History**
Schliemann discovered this gold face mask in a grave near Troy.

On a hot morning in 1873, workers were turning up shovelfuls of earth at a site in northwestern Turkey when Heinrich Schliemann's (SHLEE muhn) sharp eyes caught the glint of gold. Hurriedly, the amateur archaeologist gave the workers the rest of the day off. Then leaping into the trench, Schliemann dug furiously, uncovering a dazzling treasure beneath his feet.

Schliemann believed he had discovered the ancient city of Troy. According to legend, a Greek army had destroyed Troy about 1300 B.C. As a boy in Germany, Schliemann had read about the Trojan War in a famous Greek poem known as the *Iliad*. Scholars of his day did not believe that Troy had ever existed. Schliemann, however, was convinced that there really had been a city called Troy.

Using the *Iliad* as his guide, Schliemann undertook excavations on a fertile plain in northwestern Turkey. The site had long been suspected of holding ancient ruins. During three years of steady digging, Schliemann uncovered not just one Troy but nine, buried in layers like an underground cake.

Schliemann's discovery won him recognition as the founder of the study of ancient Greece. In this chapter, you will learn about the Greeks and their way of life.

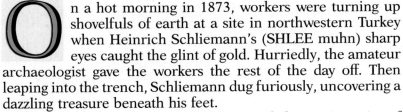

2100 B.C.	1500 B.C.	900 B.C.	300 B.C.

■ 2100 B.C.
Ionians and Achaeans invade Greece

1200 B.C. ■
Greek Dark Age begins

492 B.C. ■
Greeks defeat Persians at Marathon

338 B.C. ■
Alexander invades Greece

■ 331 B.C.
Alexander conquers the Persian Empire

▲ **Illustrating History** *The Acropolis rises above the city of Athens, Greece. These majestic buildings were used for religious purposes.*

1 A New Civilization Emerged in Greece

As you read, look for answers to these questions:

◆ How did geography shape the history of Greece?
◆ What were some of the important achievements of the Minoan and Achaean civilizations?
◆ How did the Dorians change life in Greece?

Key Terms: polis (defined on p. 97), city-state (p. 97), monarchy (p. 98)

The tales of the heroes who fought and died at Troy both reflected and shaped the lives of the people of ancient Greece. In turn, the civilization the Greeks built continues to affect the thinking and outlook of people around the world. To appreciate the remarkable accomplishments of the ancient Greeks, it is important to learn about their land and their origins.

Geography Shaped Greek History

As you can see from the map on page 96, Greece occupies the southeastern corner of Europe. There, the huge Balkan Peninsula pushes south into the Mediterranean Sea. Greece is at the southernmost end of the peninsula.

The land is rough with many mountain ranges separating deep valleys. Whereas some ancient civilizations were united by great rivers such as the Nile and the Tigris, the mountains of Greece divided people into separate communities. The mild climate let them grow crops of olives, grapes, figs, and grains. Yet, thin soils and the rough terrain limited the size of farms. Thus, the Greeks had trouble raising enough food to feed themselves. Consequently, they looked outward to the seas to find food.

GEOGRAPHIC SETTING:
Lands of the Mediterranean

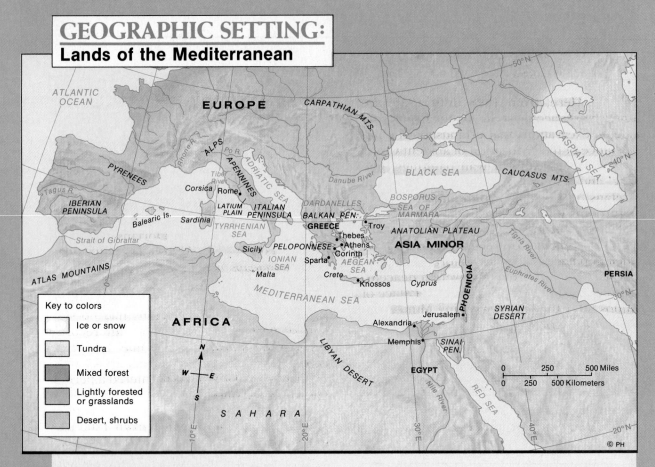

Focus on Geography

Interaction   At its height, the Greek empire spanned the entire Mediterranean region. How might the geography of the region have helped the seafaring Greeks hold their empire together?

One ancient Greek wrote, "Like frogs around a pond, we have settled down upon the shores of this sea." He might well have written "these seas." To the west of Greece lie the Adriatic and Ionian seas. To the south is the Mediterranean. To the east is the Aegean Sea.

These waters wash some 2,000 miles (3,202 kilometers) of Greek coastline. It is an uneven coastline, cut by hundreds of harbors. Offshore, many islands dot the seas. These islands provided the Greeks with step-ping stones to other lands. Greek sailors could travel for days yet never be far from the sight of land. The Greeks could also reach out to other lands for needed food supplies. In the course of trading, the ideas and learning of Egypt, Phoenicia, and other nations of the Middle East found their way to Greece. In turn, Greek ideas and customs spread from the Middle East to Asia. The island of Crete became one of the most important links in the cultural exchange between Greece and Asia.

96

People on the Island of Crete Built a Trading Empire

The island of Crete lies about 60 miles (96 kilometers) south of the mainland of Greece. Here, from 1898 until 1935, the English archaeologist Sir Arthur Evans conducted excavations that established the importance of the civilization of ancient Crete. Evans found beautiful wall paintings, pottery, and jewelry. He also found that the Cretans used copper plumbing and had bathrooms with a type of flush toilet.

At digs at Knossos (NAHS uhs) in central Crete, Evans discovered the ruins of an ancient palace. He found no forts at the site, indicating that the Cretans were a peaceful people. Evans called the ruins the Palace of Minos after the legendary King Minos who was said to have been the greatest ruler of ancient Crete. In honor of this king, Evans gave the name Minoan to the ancient civilization of Crete.

Minoan civilization flourished between 2000 B.C. and 1300 B.C. At the height of its power, Crete probably controlled a trading empire that stretched over the whole Aegean Sea. Traces of Minoan art and writing can be found at archaeological sites on the Aegean islands and in Greece. Around 1200 B.C. Minoan civilization declined rapidly due to disastrous fires and growing attacks from the outside.

European Tribes Invaded Greece

Around 2000 B.C., as Minoan civilization was expanding, invaders from the north pushed into Greece. These people probably belonged to shepherd tribes from the region of the Danube River in Europe. One tribe, the Ionians (eye OH nee ehnz), settled in central Greece and on the Aegean Islands. The Ionians founded Athens (ATH ehnz), the most famous city in ancient Greece.

A second wave of invaders, called the Achaeans (ah KEE ehnz), or Mycenaens (my seh NEE ehnz), also swept into the Greek peninsula from the north. They first settled the northern part of Greece and then gradually took over the Peloponnese (PEHL uh puh NEES), as the southern part of Greece is called. Between 1600 B.C. and 1200 B.C., the Achaeans became the greatest power in the Aegean region. They defeated the Minoans and controlled parts of Asia Minor, the peninsula in western Asia that now makes up the greater part of Turkey. Around 1300 B.C., the Achaeans attacked and destroyed the city of Troy in Asia Minor. As you will soon read, the legends surrounding this struggle later became the basis of the two greatest works of Greek literature, the *Iliad* (IHL ee uhd) and the *Odyssey* (AHD uh see).

By 1200 B.C., however, new waves of invaders poured into Greece from Europe. These invaders, known as the Dorians (DOR ee uhnz), conquered Achaean civilization. Many Achaeans fled Greece, moving to the Aegean islands of Asia Minor where they managed to preserve some elements of their culture. The invading Dorians had no system of writing. Consequently, all record-keeping disappeared. The fine arts and crafts of the Achaeans of mainland Greece also vanished. Greece then entered a period known as the Dark Age.

Little is known of the Greek Dark Age, which lasted for 450 years—from 1200 B.C. to 750 B.C. Yet, out of this time of confusion, a new culture slowly began to take shape. The Dorians became known as the Hellenes (HEL eenz), or Greeks, named after an area in northwestern Greece called Hellas. By combining their ways of life with those of the Achaeans who remained, they developed what we know as Hellenic, or Greek, civilization.

City-States Grew Powerful in the Age of Kings

The coming of the Dorians greatly changed life in Greece. The Achaeans had united the land into a strong empire. But after the Dorian invasion, Greece once again became a divided country. Separated by Greece's mountain ranges, the Dorian tribes settled into different regions and developed independently.

Political life centered on the polis. **Polis** originally meant fortress, but in time, it came to mean the city that grew up inside the fortress as well as the surrounding farms and nearby land. Another word for the Greek polis is **city-state**.

▲ **Illustrating History** *Besides these wall paintings, what other clues to Minoan life were found at the Palace of Minos?*

At first, each city-state was independent. Among the chief city-states were Athens, Thebes (theebz), Corinth (KOR inth), and Sparta (SPAHR tah). People swore allegiance to their city-state and when necessary, fought for it.

Military commanders, many of whom later became kings, ruled the early city-states. The kingship was hereditary, which means it was passed down from generation to generation in a family. This system of government in which a single person inherits the power to rule is called a **monarchy.** In addition to heading the government, the king also served as the religious leader of the polis. A detailed discussion of government in early Greece follows in Section 2.

During this time, the city-states constantly warred with each other, seeking more land. As city-states struggled for power, trade with other nations fell off sharply.

Although the city-states remained independent, some ties united the Greek people. Artisans soon began to develop new styles of pottery, and certain styles of dress became common in all the city-states. Perhaps most important, the Greeks were united by their common language. This bond of language allowed new ideas and advances to spread easily from polis to polis. The bonds of

language grew even stronger in 700 B.C. when the Greeks began to adapt the Phoenician alphabet to their language. In later centuries, the Romans adapted this alphabet from the Greeks. In still later centuries, it became the basis of our English alphabet.

SECTION 1 REVIEW

Knowing Key Terms, People, and Places
1. Define: **a.** polis **b.** city-state **c.** monarchy
2. Identify: **a.** Crete **b.** Knossos **c.** King Minos **d.** Ionians **e.** Achaeans **f.** Dorians

Focus on Geography
3. How did the geography of Greece divide the country?

Reviewing Main Ideas
4. What was government in Greece like under the Dorians?
5. How did language help unite the Greek city-states?

Critical Thinking
Perceiving Cause and Effect
6. If the island of Crete had not existed, what would have been the effect on the cultural exchange between Greece and Asia?

98

2 Greece Developed New Types of Government

As you read, look for answers to these questions:

◆ How did tyrants take control of the Greek city-states?
◆ What was life like in Sparta under the Dorians?
◆ How did democratic government develop in Greece?

> **Key Terms:** aristocracy (defined on p. 99), tyrant (p. 99), helot (p. 99), citizen (p. 100), democracy (p. 101)

By the mid-700s B.C., changes in Greek society began to affect the governments of the city-states. New forms of government emerged. Although these governments varied somewhat from polis to polis, gradually a new type of government took shape that has served as a model for many of today's governments.

Nobles and Tyrants Seized Power in the City-States

As Greece's Dark Age drew to an end in the mid-700s B.C., the power of the monarchies declined, and aristocracies took their place. As a type of government, an **aristocracy** is rule by a privileged group, usually an upper class of wealth and social position. In ancient Greece, the nobles were the ruling group. They began to gain control of large amounts of valuable farmland around the city-states. As the nobles did this, they began to exercise more and more control over the city-states and gradually seized control of the governments.

The nobles governed in their own interests. They passed new laws that stated that people who failed to pay their debts could be sold into slavery and their land could be taken away from them. Through these new laws, the nobles began to gain more land for themselves, and the slave population of Greece began to grow.

Nobles also encouraged the settlement of colonies, partly because Greece's limited farmland could not feed the growing population in the city-states. City-states sent groups of settlers to build new cities. The first colonies were started in Asia Minor and on islands in the Aegean Sea.

New colonies relieved some of the pressures on the city-states. Yet, the common people grew more and more unhappy with the rule of the nobles. By about 650 B.C., new leaders, called tyrants, rose to power with the support of the common people. Today "tyrant" means a harsh ruler. In ancient Greece, however, **tyrant** meant any ruler who seized power by force.

Often tyrants brought welcome reforms, such as reduced taxation, that improved life for the common people. Over time, however, their rule became as unjust as that of the nobles. People again pressed for changes in government.

To understand the changes in government that occurred in Greece during the period from 750 B.C. to 500 B.C., a comparison of the two leading city-states, Sparta and Athens, is helpful. These two city-states had the greatest impact on the history of Greece. They also developed very different forms of government.

Sparta Rigidly Controlled Its People

Sparta lies at the southern end of the Greek peninsula. Invading Dorians conquered the local people, and under Dorian rule, the peasants were not permitted to leave the land they worked. The Dorians made Sparta their capital. There, outnumbered five to one by the native people, the Dorians set up a harsh government under the control of military leaders.

According to legend, a lawgiver named Lycurgus (ly KUR gus) established the Spartan form of government about 600 B.C. He wanted Sparta to be strong enough to defeat all its enemies and control its **helots** (HEHL uhtz), or slaves. These were descendants of the people who had been conquered by the Dorians.

Two hereditary kings headed the Spartan government. Although some kings were able rulers, the real power lay with five elderly

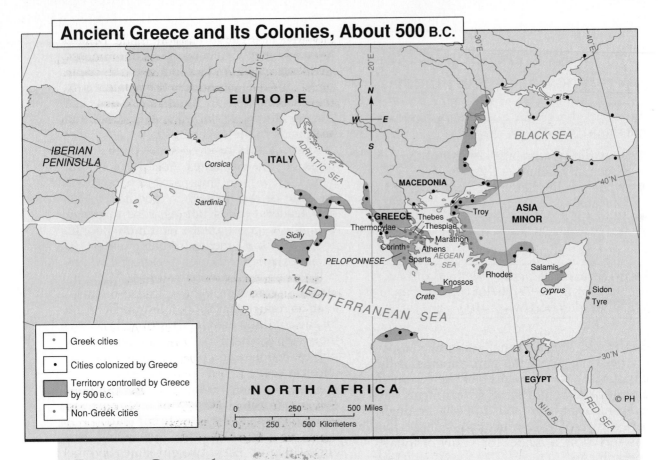

Ancient Greece and Its Colonies, About 500 B.C.

EUROPE

IBERIAN
PENINSULA

Corsica

ITALY

ADRIATIC SEA

BLACK SEA

Sardinia

MACEDONIA

ASIA
MINOR

Sicily

GREECE Thebes
Thermopylae   Thespiae
Corinth   Marathon
Athens
PELOPONNESE   Sparta   AEGEAN
SEA
Knossos
Crete

Troy

Rhodes

Salamis

Cyprus

Sidon
Tyre

MEDITERRANEAN SEA

Greek cities

Cities colonized by Greece

Territory controlled by Greece
by 500 B.C.

Non-Greek cities

NORTH AFRICA

EGYPT

© PH

Nile R.

RED SEA

0   250   500 Miles
0   250   500 Kilometers

Focus on Geography

1. **Location**   Greece colonized many cities around two of the
largest seas in the world. Name the seas.
2. **Interaction**   Would you have expected to find Greek architecture
in Tyre in 500 B.C.? Why or why not?

men called ephors (EHF orz). The ephors were responsible for the day-to-day workings of the city. Over a period of time, they became more powerful than the kings. They commanded armies, decided questions of law, and conducted business with other countries.

A **citizen** is a person who owes loyalty to a particular country and is entitled to that country's protection. Spartan citizens also played a part in government, but citizenship was limited to male landowners. Of Sparta's population of 375,000, only 10,000 were citizens. All male citizens 30 years old and older were members of the assembly, which discussed and voted on important public

issues. Thirty males over 60 years of age, called elders, made up the senate. The senate often decided which issues the assembly could handle. Besides setting an agenda for the assembly, the senate could also overrule its actions.

Sparta trained its sons and daughters to do without luxury. It expected them to live tough, active lives. Our word "spartan" comes from the way of life established in Sparta. A spartan existence is hard; it denies many of the comforts of life.

Every healthy male citizen had to serve as a soldier. The highest form of devotion a Spartan could show was to fight his city's wars and return "with his shield or on it."

Spartan boys left home at the age of 7 to begin to train as soldiers. By the age of 20, those who survived the harsh training became full soldiers. They could also marry at that age, but they still had to live in military barracks. At age 30, they became full citizens and could live in homes of their own. They continued to serve in the army until the age of 60.

Spartan girls received most of their training at home. The highest goal for a Spartan woman was to be a wife and the mother of strong, healthy children. To be unmarried or not bear children was a disgrace.

Despite the fact that women were not citizens, they held a higher position in Sparta than in the other city-states of ancient Greece. In Sparta, for example, women could inherit property and pass it on to their children. As a result, women owned nearly half the wealth of ancient Sparta. Through their part in the economy, they could exert influence and control in the city-state.

Athens Developed the First Democracy

The city-state of Athens differed greatly from Sparta. In Athens, the world's first democracy developed. The word *democracy* comes from the Greek words, *demos* and *kratia*, meaning literally, "the people rule." A **democracy**, then, is a government in which citizens rule themselves. Athenian democracy inspired those who founded America's democracy as well as many other people around the world.

Athenian democracy took shape slowly. Around 620 B.C., the Athenian ruler Draco (DRAY koh) tried to make reforms in the city-state. Draco organized laws by putting them down in a written code. Draco's code let people know exactly what the laws were and that they applied to all. The code also explained the harsh penalties for people who broke the laws. In addition, it gave a person accused of murder the right to a trial. The accused had to be proven guilty before being punished. Overall, the code helped Athens to develop a government based on written laws.

Solon (SOH luhn), an Athenian ruler in about 594 B.C., also moved the city-state closer to democracy. Solon made Draco's laws less harsh. He wrote economic and social reforms into law and ended the practice of enslaving those who failed to pay their debts. Solon also created a court for all citizens and gave all citizens the right to vote. However, citizenship was quite limited. Women and slaves could not be citizens. Only men who were born in and lived in a city-state could be citizens. Altogether, only slightly more than half of the male population of Athens were citizens. At the same time, only citizens could be members of the assembly that approved decisions made by the government.

Solon's reforms gave more freedom to the lower classes, but freed slaves, poor landowners, and laborers were not satisfied. They wanted to become citizens and gain more political power. At the same time, the wealthy classes believed that Solon had given too much of their power to the small landowners and merchants. By the time Solon left office in 572 B.C., he had lost much of his original popularity. A period of corruption then followed.

Cleisthenes (KLYS thuh NEEZ), a third democratic reformer, came to power. He

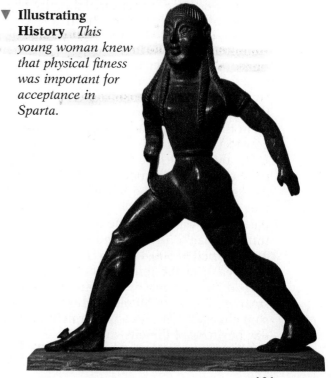

▼ **Illustrating History** *This young woman knew that physical fitness was important for acceptance in Sparta.*

101

▲ **Illustrating History** *Carved into the Parthenon, this relief suggests the role of free speech in Athenian democracy.*

gave more support to the common people. He reorganized the social and military classes and broke the power of the old noble families. Cleisthenes also permitted some immigrants and former slaves to become citizens. To protect the city-state, he introduced the practice of ostracism (AHS trah sihzm). Ostracism is banishment. Athenian citizens could vote to banish, or ostracize, from the city-state those people whom they considered dangerous.

By about 500 B.C., Athens closely resembled a modern democracy. The Athenian assembly became the lawmaking body. All free adult male citizens could now participate in the assembly. The assembly met 40 times a year to discuss and vote on issues. The Council of 500, chosen from volunteers from each of the ten districts of the polis, helped the assembly sort out business. A smaller council of 50 men, whose membership changed 10 times a year, ran the day-to-day business of the city-state.

Athens was a *direct democracy*. That is, citizens took a direct part in government.

They discussed and voted on the issues for themselves. In court cases, citizens represented themselves and argued their cases before the jury. Citizens were also expected to serve as jurors and officeholders. Since the term of office was usually only one year, many citizens had the chance to serve their state.

Direct democracy did not work perfectly in Athens. The right to vote and take part in government was limited to a small, privileged group of citizens. Despite these restrictions, the Greeks had cause to be proud of their accomplishments in government. One Greek leader described how he saw the importance of Athens's democracy: "Our system of govenment is called a democracy because power is in the hands not of a minority but of the whole people."

Athens provided a model of government to the rest of Greece. It remains a model that is looked up to in many parts of the world today. For example, Athenian democracy inspired those who founded America's democracy as well as many other people around the world.

SECTION 2 REVIEW

Knowing Key Terms, People, and Places
1. Define: **a.** aristocracy **b.** tyrant **c.** helot **d.** citizen **e.** democracy
2. Identify: **a.** Lycurgus **b.** Draco **c.** Solon **d.** Cleisthenes **e.** Council of 500

Reviewing Main Ideas
3. What changes in Greek government occurred during the period of time when the nobles ruled?
4. How did the lives of women in Sparta differ from the lives of men?
5. What was Draco's code?
6. What were the main elements of Greek democracy?

Critical Thinking
Making Comparisons
7. In what ways were the governments of Athens and Sparta alike? In what ways were they different?

3 Wars Brought Changes to Ancient Greece

As you read, look for answers to these questions:

◆ How did the Greeks end the threat of conquest by Persia?
◆ Why did the city-states fight among themselves?
◆ Whose military conquests helped to spread Greek culture through Asia?

> **Key Terms:** marathon (defined on p. 103), infantry (p. 105), cavalry (p. 105), federation (p. 106)

Democracies must always be alert to challenges that come from within and from outside their countries. Beginning in the 400s B.C., democratic Athens, as well as the other Greek city-states, faced a series of such challenges.

Wars with Persia Threatened the Greek City-States

The first challenge to the city-states came from the mighty Persian Empire. In the 500s B.C., the Persians conquered the Greek colonies in Asia Minor. Sometime later, the Greek colonies rebelled against Persian rule. Persian armies quickly crushed the revolt, and the Persian emperor Darius I now looked hungrily beyond the Greek colonies to Greece itself.

In 492 B.C., Darius assembled a huge army and navy and moved toward Greece. By 490 B.C., the Persians had defeated several city-states and reached the Plains of Marathon, which were about 25 miles (40 kilometers) outside of Athens. The Athenian army, led by Miltiades (mil TY uh deez) moved out to stop the Persians.

Though badly outnumbered, the Greeks decided to charge the Persians. The fierceness of the attack shocked the Persians. Over 6,000 Persian lives were lost while the Greeks lost only 192. The crushing defeat convinced Darius to retreat to Persia.

A sad tale is told about the Greek victory at Marathon. The Greeks sent a runner from the battlefield to Athens with the news that they had won the battle. Upon reaching Athens, the runner cried "Nike! [NY kee]," the Greek word for victory. Then he tumbled to the ground, dead of exhaustion. Today, a 26-mile race is called a **marathon** in memory of that Greek runner.

Ten years after Darius retreated, the Persians tried once again to conquer Greece. This time Darius's son, King Xerxes (ZERK seez), commanded the Persian army and navy. In 480 B.C., the Persians attacked a small force of Spartans at Thermopylae (ther MAHP uh lee). Led by Leonidas (lee AHN uh duhs), the Spartans and soldiers from Thespiae heroically defended the narrow mountain pass. The Spartans fought bravely, but a Greek traitor showed the Persians a way to surround and defeat them. A generation after the battle Herodotus wrote:

> There was a bitter struggle over the body of Leonidas. Four times the Greeks drove the enemy off, and at last by their valor succeeded in dragging it away. . . . They withdrew into the narrow neck of the pass. . . . Here they resisted to the last, with their swords, if they had them, and if not, with their hands and teeth, until the Persians. . . . finally overwhelmed them.

Xerxes and his army moved on to defeat Athens and burn the city. While the Persian army looted Athens, the Persian navy attacked the Greek fleet at Salamis (SAL uh mis). The angry Greeks savagely attacked the Persian navy and destroyed most of their ships. Once again the Persians had to retreat to Asia, this time never to return.

Athens Entered a Golden Age

The Greek victory over the Persians was largely due to Athens. In the years after the Persian wars, Athens entered a period known as the Golden Age of Athens. It became a leader among the city-states.

Under their greatest leader, Pericles (PEHR uh kleez), the Athenians rebuilt their city after its destruction by the Persians. The Parthenon (PAHR thuh non) was built at this

Pericles' Funeral Oration

After a battle against Sparta in 431 B.C., the Greek leader Pericles gave an address in honor of those who had died in battle. His speech, as recorded by the historian Thucydides, summarized the most important values of the Athenians.

    •• But before I praise the dead, I should like to point out by what principles of action we rose to power, and under what institutions and through what manner of life our empire became great. . . .

    Our form of government does not enter into rivalry with the institutions of others. We do not copy our neighbors but are an example to them. It is true that we are called a democracy. . . . But while the law secures equal justice to all alike in their private disputes, the claim of excellence is also recognized; and when a citizen is in any way distinguished, he is preferred [sent] to the public service, not as a matter of privilege, but as the reward of merit. Neither is poverty a bar, but a man may benefit his country whatever be the obscurity of his condition. . . .

    An Athenian citizen does not neglect the state because he takes care of his own household; and even those of us who are engaged in business have a very fair idea of politics. We alone regard a man who takes no interest in public affairs, not as a harmless, but as a useless character. ••

1. According to Pericles, how does an individual become qualified to become a public servant?
2. How does the attitude of the Athenians toward politics differ from or resemble that of Americans today?

time, and many achievements were made in art and learning. These achievements will be discussed in more detail in the last section of this chapter.

Fearing another Persian invasion, the Athenians built strong walls around the city. Pericles also tried to unite the Greek city-states into an organization for defense. This alliance was called the Delian League. Members of the league contributed ships, money, and soldiers to protect Greece from attack. Athens, the richest and most powerful city-state, provided most of the money and soldiers to the league.

At first, the league worked well. As danger from the Persians passed, however, the city-states began to argue about the goals of the league. Athens, which paid the largest share, wanted the most power. It slowly turned the Delian League into an empire and ruled the other city-states as conquered cities.

Soon, war broke out. Sparta and other city-states that were not members of the league feared the growth of Athens's power. They formed their own league and attacked Athens in 431 B.C. This started the series of conflicts known as the Peloponnesian (PEHL uh puh NEE shun) Wars. In the end, Sparta defeated Athens, but the wars badly weakened both city-states.

Sparta tried to unify and rule Greece as Athens had done. The other city-states fought back, and further attempts at unity failed. With the defeat of Athens at the hands of Sparta, the Golden Age of Athens—and of Greece—ended.

Macedonia Conquered Greece and Lands Beyond

To the north of the Greeks lived the Macedonians (MAS uh DOH nee enz). They were distantly related to the Greeks, but their culture was not as advanced. After the Peloponnesian Wars, however, Macedonia had a more united government than Greece. Led by a strong king, Philip II, Macedonia became a dangerous neighbor.

Philip II of Macedonia, who lived between 382 B.C. and 336 B.C., believed he could conquer and unite the Greek city-states. In his youth, Philip had been a hostage in Thebes, then one of the strongest Greek city-states. There, Philip had learned to appreciate the Greek culture. He also learned how to build a strong army.

When Philip II came to power in Macedonia, he readied his army to conquer Greece. He turned his **infantry** (foot soldiers) and **cavalry** (soldiers mounted on horseback) into powerful fighting forces.

Philip slowly began to defeat the city-states of northern Greece. Demosthenes (deh MAHS thuh neez), an Athenian orator who feared Philip's steady advances, urged the city-states to unite against him. Demosthenes' philippics, or speeches, against Philip fell on deaf ears. In 338 B.C., Philip's armies overran Greece. All the city-states except Sparta came under his control. Philip then began to plan the conquest of Persia. Before he could put his plan into action, however, he died, the victim of an assassin in 336 B.C.

Philip's plans lived on through his son, who became known as Alexander the Great. As a boy, Alexander had been taught by the Greek teacher Aristotle to love culture and learning. Alexander also mastered military skills.

Only 21 when his father died, Alexander became ruler of Macedonia and Greece. Two years later, in 334 B.C., Alexander led 35,000 soldiers in an invasion of Persia. His army won victory after victory. By 331 B.C.,

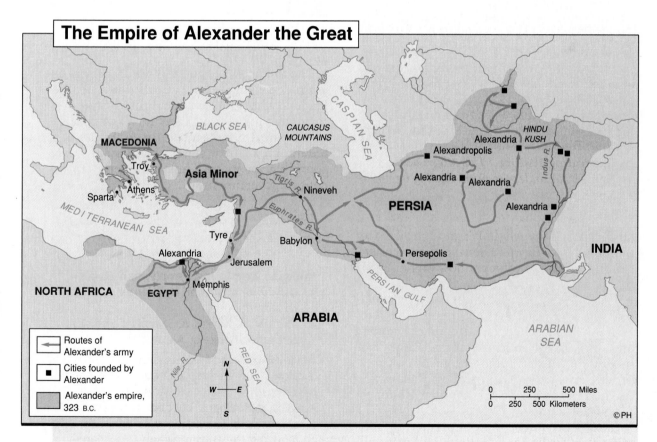

The Empire of Alexander the Great

Focus on Geography

Place As you study Alexander's empire, what clues might lead you to believe that Alexander founded cities along his route?

▲ **Illustrating History** *This Mogul artist painted Alexander the Great leading a battle.*

The Greeks Tried a New Experiment in Government

After Alexander's death, the Greek city-states began to fight against their new Macedonian ruler. They also continued to fight among themselves and remained relatively weak. By the 100s B.C., a new power, the Roman Empire, had defeated and absorbed the city-states. Yet before this happened, the city-states had begun an interesting experiment in government.

Several of the city-states joined in what was called the Achaean League. This was not a temporary association of city-states as the Delian League had been. It was, instead, a **federation,** a form of government in which smaller parts agree to give up some of their powers to a stronger central government. While each city-state in the Achaean League kept control of its own affairs, a central government had the power to tax and raise an army.

The Achaean League did not last long. Its main ideas, however, were known to the leaders who founded the United States. It may have influenced their ideas of government. The United States, for example, is a federation of fifty states. Each state is responsible for its own affairs under a strong central government.

he controlled the whole Persian Empire. He marched into Egypt. Then he turned east, gaining control of what are now Afghanistan and northern India.

Alexander's victories united the Eastern and Western worlds at that time under one king. As he marched, he founded new cities and spread Greek ideas to the East. The mixing of Eastern and Western cultures produced a new culture called *Hellenistic*. As you read earlier in this chapter, Hellenes is another name for Greeks.

Alexander might have conquered still more worlds, but he fell ill with a fever and died in Babylon in 323 B.C. at the age of 32. He had lived a short but brilliant life. After his death, the empire was divided into three parts, each ruled by one of Alexander's generals.

SECTION 3 REVIEW

Knowing Key Terms, People, and Places
1. Define: **a.** marathon **b.** infantry **c.** cavalry **d.** federation
2. Identify: **a.** Xerxes **b.** Salamis **c.** Pericles **d.** Demosthenes **e.** Alexander

Reviewing Main Ideas
3. How did Darius attempt to conquer Greece?
4. Why did Athens become the dominant city-state in Greece?
5. How did Hellenistic culture take shape?

Critical Thinking

Perceiving Cause and Effect
6. How did the defeat of Persia contribute to the growth of the Athenian Empire?

4 The Greeks Lived a Rich and Varied Life

As you read, look for answers to these questions:

◆ How did the Olympic Games begin?
◆ What kinds of products did Greek manufacturers produce?
◆ What roles were women expected to play in Greek society?

> **Key Terms:** oracle (defined on p. 108), metic (p. 109)

In the earlier sections of this chapter, you have seen how government in ancient Greece took shape and how wars changed Greek society. Now, you will take a closer look at the ways the Greeks followed their daily lives and made their livings.

Greeks Worshipped Many Gods

The Greeks were a religious people who worshipped many gods. Most of these gods represented the forces of nature. Stories of the gods and their deeds helped to explain winds, rains, storms, and births and deaths. Most of the great gods were thought to live on Mount Olympus, the highest peak in Greece. The chart on page 132 in Chapter 5 lists the names and responsibilities of the most important Greek gods.

The gods of the Greeks had human qualities. They argued, fell in love, and made mistakes, but they did all of these things on a grand scale. They did not set out strict moral rules for humans to follow.

The Greeks honored their gods in elaborate and varied rituals. They asked the gods for their help or tried to soothe them. Our modern Olympic Games have their roots in the Greek athletic games held every four years to honor Zeus. In early days, human sacrifices to the gods were common. Later, the Greeks substituted animals or food in their gifts to the gods.

The Greeks mixed superstition with their religion. They would never think of doing anything important without trying to learn whether or not the time chosen was a favorable one. To find out, Greeks consulted an

▼ **Illustrating History** *Greeks went to this shrine at Delphi to consult the oracle before making any important decisions concerning wars, treaties, or law making.*

▲ **Illustrating History** *City-states minted their own coins to use for trade. Athena is on one side of this coin, with her symbol, the owl, on the reverse.*

oracle, or a special priest whom the Greeks believed the gods spoke to through signs or omens. The most famous of the Greek oracles lived at Delphi. She gave information to various government leaders about the best time to pass laws, start wars, and make treaties. Such religious leaders had great influence on public policies throughout the Greek city-states.

Ancient Greeks Made Their Livings in Varied Ways

As in other places in the ancient world, poor farmers made up the largest group in Greek society. Unlike farmers in most other places, however, the poor farmers and peasants of Athens could own land if they were citizens. On their plots of land, farmers raised grains, figs, olives, and grapes, using crude tools and simple methods.

Many city-states could not grow enough food for their own needs. They had to buy food from other city-states and other countries. The shortage of basic food supplies led farmers in some areas to grow mostly grapes or olives. The wine and olive oil these crops produced could then be sold abroad, and the profits could be used to buy food supplies.

Business in ancient Greece centered around farming, manufacturing, and trading. Every city-state had its own system of coinage, weights and measures, and banking. Greece's many mountains made overland transportation expensive and often dangerous. Traders, therefore, usually conducted their business by sea. Their ships carried the products of Greek farms and shops all across the Mediterranean Sea.

Manufacturers turned out a whole range of goods for traders to carry abroad and merchants to sell in shops at home. Workers made weapons, harnesses for horses, clothing, and household utensils. Natural resources in Greece included silver, lead, zinc, iron, and a beautiful marble used in buildings and statues. There were few machines, but some factories and larger businesses did exist. One shield maker employed 120 slaves. Another mine owner used as many as 1,000 slaves. For the most part, however, businesses were small, and Greek stonecutters, shipbuilders, bakers, millers, potters, and butchers worked in small groups or by themselves.

Women's Lives Centered Around the Home

Generally, the Greeks expected women to be housekeepers, maintaining homes for their husbands and children. The Greek wife did not rule the household; her husband did. A wife did not even do the shopping. She made clothing and bedding for the family and prepared its meals.

The role of women varied among the city-states of ancient Greece. As you have read, women played important roles in the economic life of Sparta. This was not the case in Athens. There, women could not enter into contracts, buy or sell anything, borrow money, or sue in a court of law. When an Athenian woman's husband died, she did not inherit his property. Women wore veils at religious services. They spent most of their time in the women's quarters of the home.

By the middle of the fifth century B.C., Athenian women had begun to complain about their station in life. In Aristophanes' play *Lysistrata*, a female character asks, "What sensible thing are we women capable of doing? We do nothing but sit around." In 450 B.C., a woman named Aspasia (ahs PAY zhee uh), opened a school for young women that was well attended. Pericles and other important Athenian citizens are believed to have joined in discussions at her school. Gradually, the women of ancient Greece started to play more active parts in the culture of their communities.

Social Classes Divided Greek Society

As in Egypt, society in the various Greek city-states was divided into classes. At the top of the social ladder stood the citizens of the city-states. Just below them came the **metics** (MEH teeks), foreigners living in Greek city-states. The metics dominated the commercial life of the cities. For the most part, shopkeepers, workers, merchants, and bankers were not citizens of the city-states.

Most citizens considered it undignified to work for a living. As in Sparta, a large group of slaves did most of the work. These slaves made up about 35 percent of Athens's population. The percentage of slaves in other city-states was probably even greater. Most of the slaves were people who had been captured in wars with other city-states. Many had been teachers and professional people before they were captured. A few slaves either won or were granted their freedom. Those who became free often stayed on to work in the city-state.

The common people of ancient Greece lived simply. Clothing and shelter were plain, and people lived and entertained their guests in homes made of sun-dried brick. On the whole, the homes had little furni-

▲ **Illustrating History**   *A Greek warrior is shown with his shield and slaves.*

ture. Food, too, was simple; the Greek diet included cheese, fish, olives, and bread. Only rich Greeks ate meat. The Greeks also enjoyed such fruits as apples, pears, plums, and figs. They used honey to sweeten their food.

SECTION 4 REVIEW

Knowing Key Terms, People, and Places
1. Define: **a.** oracle **b.** metic
2. Identify: **a.** Mount Olympus **b.** Zeus **c.** Delphi **d.** Aspasia

Focus on Geography
3. Why did Greek traders prefer to ship goods by sea?

Reviewing Main Ideas
4. Describe the character of the Greek gods and tell how they influenced Greek life.
5. What roles did foreigners play in Athenian society?

Critical Thinking
Perceiving Cause and Effect
6. What impact would a crop failure have had on the economy of a Greek city-state?

5 Greek Culture Left Lasting Legacies

As you read, look for answers to these questions:

◆ What form of literature did the Greeks invent?
◆ Who were the Sophists?
◆ What contributions did Hellenistic scientists give to the world?

Key Terms: epic (defined on p. 111), philosopher (p. 112), Socratic method (p. 113)

Just as the Greeks' idea of democracy continues to influence the world, other parts of the Hellenic and Hellenistic cultures have also lasted to this day. People around the world still admire ancient Greek paintings and sculpture, and they still read Greek epics, poems, and plays. The deep questions asked by some Greek thinkers also continue to affect the way we look at the world around us.

Ancient Greece Set High Standards in Art and Literature

The Greeks produced many magnificent works of art, and Athens became the most beautiful city of the ancient world. Buildings dedicated to religion and art were clustered on the Acropolis (uh KRAHP uhl is), a hill in the center of Athens. The Parthenon, one of the most beautiful of these buildings, had splendidly painted sculptures and gleaming marble columns. These columns supported the roof and set a style of architecture that is still used today. Although in ruins, the Parthenon remains standing. The picture on page 95 shows it in the center.

LINKING PAST AND PRESENT

Standing the Test of Time

On the Acropolis, a rocky hill overlooking the city of Athens, Greece, stand the remains of some of the most beautiful buildings in the world. These temples were built in the fifth century B.C. to honor the goddess Athena. Finely constructed of gleaming white marble according to precise mathematical proportions, they represent the high point of Greek architecture.

Architects throughout the ages have used these temples as models for their own creations. The rows of evenly spaced columns are echoed in countless public buildings around the world. The United States Capitol is one such building.

1. What were two distinguishing features of Greek temples?
2. Why do you think Greek temples have had such a lasting influence on architectural styles?

▲ **Illustrating History** *Going to the theater was a favorite pastime for Greeks. The theaters were designed so that, even from the far seats, a whisper could be easily heard.*

Greek sculptors created many lasting works. The best-known artists, like Phidias (FIHD ee uhs) and Praxiteles (prak SIHT uh LEEZ), carved statues that have been preserved in museums around the world. These sculptures are fine examples of the simplicity and beauty of Greek art.

Among the Greek contributions to literature is the invention of drama. Revenge, death, politics, and religion were some of the subjects of Greek plays. The tragedies of Aeschylus (EHS kuh luhs) and the comedies of Aristophanes (AR uh STAHF uh NEEZ) drew large crowds who wept or laughed at the fates of the characters.

Greek plays were shown in open-air theaters where the audience sat on stone seats without backs. Although the seats were not comfortable, the theater was always crowded. The actors, who were always men, performed their roles wearing elaborate masks.

A chorus of actors commented on the actions of the main characters.

The power that language had to unite the Greek people is best shown by two great works of literature. Ever since the Achaeans seized Troy in about 1300 B.C., stories of the battles at that city had been passed down by word of mouth. Sometime during the 700s B.C., the tales were collected and woven together into two mighty **epics,** long poems that describe the deeds of heroes. According to tradition, a blind poet named Homer is the author of these epics that are called the *Iliad* and the *Odyssey.*

Every Greek knew the legend that served as background for the epics. Paris, a Trojan prince, had stolen the beautiful Helen from her husband, the Achaean king Menelaus (MEHN uh LAY us). In revenge, the Achaeans went to war with Troy. For 10 years the war dragged on. Then the Achaeans seemed to give up and sail away, leaving a huge wooden horse behind as an offering. The Trojans celebrated their victory and pulled the horse within the city walls. That night, Achaean soldiers who were hidden in the horse slipped out and opened the city gates for the returning Achaean army. By morning, the Achaeans had taken Troy.

The *Iliad* describes episodes from the tenth year of the war during which the great Achaean hero, Achilles (ah KIL eez), defeated the great Trojan hero, Hector. The *Odyssey* deals with events after the war. It tells of the Greek hero Odysseus (oh DIHS ee uhs) and his adventures on his 10-year journey home.

The *Iliad* and the *Odyssey* became more than stories to the ancient Greeks. The heroes in the tales became models that later Greeks tried to follow. The epics themselves helped to shape all Greek literature and thought. In fact, the impact of the poems on Greek civilization was so great that the years from 1100 B.C. to 700 B.C. are also known as the Homeric Age.

The Greeks Explored New Ways of Thinking About the World

Some Greek thinkers carefully studied the world around them. These thinkers were called **philosophers** from Greek words

---

BIOGRAPHY

Socrates

Socrates was astonished when he was declared the wisest man alive. Born in Athens in 469 B.C., Socrates knew the flaws in his thinking better than anyone. He believed it was his mission to expose the ignorance of others and thereby lead them to the truth. Socrates spent his life provoking people into questioning their beliefs. "The unexamined life is not worth living," he is reported to have said.

Socrates went about his mission in the streets, the marketplace, and the gymnasiums of Athens. He questioned all he met —politicians and poets, aristocrats and artists. Some brushed him off as a pesky busybody, but others admired him for his pursuit of knowledge. One of his admirers, Plato, hailed him as "the wisest, most just, and best man."

Eventually, Socrates' teachings, particularly his open mockery of those in power, got him into serious trouble. In 399 B.C., he was charged with corrupting the youth and showing disrespect for the religious traditions of Athens. Found guilty and sentenced to death, he rejected offers to help him escape. Instead, the 70-year-old philosopher met death calmly by drinking a cup of poison.

1. What do you think the phrase "the unexamined life is not worth living" means?
2. How did Socrates try to lead people to the truth?
3. Why do you suppose Socrates chose to die rather than escape from jail?

meaning lovers of wisdom. The philosophers believed that through their reasoning, people could understand how the world worked and how they should act in it.

Not all the Greek philosophers had noble goals. One group, the Sophists, worked to develop carefully reasoned cases so they could win political or legal arguments. The Sophists were more concerned with worldly success than with respect for tradition or moral issues. They stressed the art of public speaking. For a fee, they taught their methods to others.

Socrates. Other Greek thinkers cared more about the search for truth than about winning arguments. Socrates (SAHK rah teez) who lived from 469 B.C. to 399 B.C., wandered about Athens asking difficult and embarrassing questions of people. He did this to point out faults and evils in society. Because he left no writings of his own, what we have learned of him comes to us through the writings of his admiring pupil, Plato. Socrates believed that there was nothing else as useful as knowledge. He thought that if people had knowledge they could solve any problems they faced. Through his questions, Socrates hoped to help people focus their thinking clearly. This way of teaching, often used in schools today, is called the **Socratic method.**

Plato. Plato, who lived from 427 B.C. to 347 B.C., is best known for his book *The Republic,* a record of Socrates' conversations with other Athenians. *The Republic* outlines a perfect society in which philosophers would be the leaders because they were the wisest. Plato did not favor democracy. He thought that too often in a democracy unqualified people held important positions. He also feared that masses of people in a democracy would make incorrect or rash decisions.

In Plato's ideal society, each citizen would do the work that best suited his or her ability. The three classes of society would be the workers, the soldiers, and the ruling philosophers. Regarding education and opportunities for work, Plato believed that both women and men should be treated

▲ **Illustrating History** *A Roman mosaic shows Plato with some of his Greek students.*

equally. He also believed that there should be no individual wealth or privately owned property.

Aristotle. While Plato planned a perfect society, Aristotle, a student of Plato's, studied governments of the past. In his book *Politics,* he pointed out the advantages and disadvantages of various forms of government. He believed that the most stable government was one in which the actions and authority of one part of the government were checked and balanced by another. For example, the actions of a strong king might be reviewed by a democratically chosen assembly. A system of checks and balances is written into the United States Constitution. Whenever a president vetoes a bill that Congress has passed or the justices of the Supreme Court declare a law unconstitutional, they are "checking" the authority of another branch of government.

Aristotle was a scientist as well as a philosopher. He wrote about biology, physics, and botany, and he was one of the early scientists who believed that the earth was round.

Science. Other Greeks also made scientific contributions. Pythagoras (pih THAG er uhs) helped develop the ideas behind the study of geometry. Democritus (dih MAHK

113

ruh tuhs) first set forth the idea that all matter is made up of small moving atoms.

Medicine. Under Hippocrates (hih PAHK ruh TEEZ), who lived from 460 B.C. to 377 B.C., the study of medicine took its first steps toward becoming a science. Written records from the time show Hippocrates tried to diagnose and treat disease using scientific methods. Hippocrates said that all diseases have natural causes and were not caused by gods. He raised the medical profession to a higher standard by insisting on medical rules of conduct. One of these was that the doctor must not harm the patient. These rules now form the basis of the Hippocratic Oath, a pledge that doctors take upon graduating from medical school.

Hellenistic Culture Advanced Art and Science

Hellenistic culture showed the heavy influence of the ancient Middle Eastern world. The city of Alexandria in Egypt became the center of Hellenistic learning. Magnificent buildings and a tremendous library were built there. Other Hellenistic cities contained many dazzling sights. At Antioch, in Syria, streets were paved with stone and lighted with hundreds of torches. On the island of Rhodes, a 105 foot (31.5 meters) high statue of Apollo served as a beacon, guiding ships into the harbor. Art and architecture, however, do not tell the whole story of Hellenistic culture.

Scientists of the Hellenistic Age, which lasted from 323 B.C. to 30 B.C., developed a great deal of practical and useful knowledge. For example, Archimedes (AHR kuh MEE deez), probably the greatest of the ancient Greek scientists, contributed to the development of modern inventions like the steam engine and to the understanding of the mechanics of the lever and pulley. Using the lever and pulley, large, heavy objects could be moved. This discovery made it possible for all types of construction to proceed more easily and quickly. Talking about the lever, Archimedes once said, "Give me a place to stand, and I will move the world!"

Ptolemy (TAH luh mee), an Egyptian scholar, developed the theory that heavenly bodies revolve around the earth. We know today that he was wrong, but his theory was accepted as fact for over 1,500 years. Euclid (YOO klihd) advanced the study of geometry. The geographer Eratosthenes (EHR uh TAHS thuh NEEZ) estimated the size of the earth's circumference, within 195 miles (314 kilometers) of its actual size.

Hellenistic artists also created dazzling works. Sculptures created during the period remain among the most beautiful in the world. The statue of the goddess of love, the *Venus de Milo*, belongs to the Hellenistic period. The statue of Laocoön (lay AHK uh wahn) and his two sons struggling with two sea serpents is one of the great artistic creations of all time.

As you will read in the next chapter, by around 100 B.C., the Roman Empire had gained control of much of the Greek world. Yet it would be a mistake to think that Hellenic and Hellenistic cultures died. Hellenic and Hellenistic achievements continued to influence the Romans and had a lasting impact on cultures in many different parts of the world.

SECTION 5 REVIEW

Knowing Key Terms, People, and Places
1. Define: **a.** epic **b.** philosopher **c.** Socratic method
2. Identify: **a.** Parthenon **b.** Aeschylus **c.** Homer **d.** Sophists **e.** Archimedes

Reviewing Main Ideas
3. Describe Plato's idea of the ideal society.
4. What kind of government did Aristotle believe was the most stable?
5. How does work by Hellenistic scientists still influence the world?

Critical Thinking
Drawing Conclusions
6. Do you think Socrates would have approved of the Sophists? Explain your answer.

Expressing Ideas in Writing:
Paraphrasing and Summarizing

Paraphrasing and summarizing are skills that help you to understand and to remember a selection. Both skills require you to take the ideas of others and express them in your own words. You *paraphrase* ideas when you retell all the ideas and details in a selection. You *summarize* ideas when you tell only about the most important ideas and details.

Study the passage and its sample paraphrase and summary. Then practice the skills.

Original: In ancient Greece, athletic competitions, or games, were held to honor the gods. The games were meant to demonstrate human excellence, which the Greeks considered a worthy offering to the gods. At the games, an athlete either finished first or lost. Placing second was no better than finishing last.

Paraphrase: The idea of the ancient Greek games was to give a gift to the gods, and only the very best effort was a good enough gift. Therefore, the only person who really achieved anything important was the first-place winner. Everybody else was a loser, including the second and third-place finishers.

Summary: The ancient Greeks honored their gods with games. Only the person finishing first was successful.

1. **Paraphrase a passage by including all the author's ideas and details.** A paraphrase should not include any quotes from the original and should be similar in length. You may reorder the ideas found in the original, but your paraphrase should be just as detailed and descriptive. Write a paraphrase of paragraph 1.

2. **Summarize a passage by focusing on the author's most important ideas and details.** When summarizing, your aim is to express the main ideas and details as briefly as possible. The length of a summary is usually between one-fifth and one-third that of the original. Descriptive material and supporting details found in the original should be eliminated from your summary. Write a summary of paragraph 2.

3. **Check your work after you've finished writing.** (a) Have you included all the ideas and details from paragraph 1 in your paraphrase? (b) Have you included the main idea from paragraph 2 in your summary? (c) Are your paraphrase and summary written in your own words?

Paragraph 1

Despite frequent wars, the Greeks observed a sacred truce during the Olympic games. As the time for the Olympic games approached, city-states stopped fighting. The truce lasted for the duration of the festival and extended to athletes and spectators traveling to and from Olympia.

Paragraph 2

The greatest glory for an athlete was to win in the games held every four years at Olympia, a site sacred to the god Zeus. Athletes and spectators from all over the Greek world assembled at Olympia. An Olympic victory brought fame and honor to the athlete and his city. The winner wore a wreath of olive leaves from the sacred grove at Olympia. Upon his return home, he received a hero's welcome, and poets praised his success.

REVIEW

Section Summaries

Section 1 A New Civilization Emerged in Greece Invaders swept mainland Greece several times during ancient history. The mountainous geography of Greece divided the Dorians, who took control around 1200 B.C. and became known as the Hellenes, into separate communities. Each of these communities, or city-states, depended on the sea for food supplies and trading. The time between 1100 B.C. and 700 B.C. is called the Homeric Age.

Section 2 Greece Developed New Types of Government The power of kings was broken in the Greek city-states by wealthy nobles and strong leaders called tyrants. The tyrants, who were popular with the common people, often brought needed reforms. In Sparta, a military dictatorship was established. Athens, on the other hand, was the birthplace of the world's first democracy. Under the Athenian direct democracy, citizens participated in all aspects of their government.

Section 3 Wars Brought Changes to Ancient Greece In 480 B.C. the Greeks, led by Athens, defeated invading Persian forces. Athens then entered a Golden Age and became a leader among the city-states. The Spartans' fear of the increasing power of Athens led to the Peloponnesian Wars. Macedonians conquered and united the Greek city-states and spread Greek culture to the East. The city-states formed the Achaean League and experimented with the idea of a federation in which each city-state gave up some power to a stronger central government.

Section 4 The Greeks Lived a Rich and Varied Life The Greeks worshipped many gods, and their religion included many elements of superstition. Greeks made their living as farmers, traders, and manufacturers of various goods. Women's lives were focused on their homes and children. Greek society divided people into three social classes—citizens, metics, and slaves.

Section 5 Greek Culture Left Lasting Legacies The ancient Greeks set high standards in art and literature. Athens became the most beautiful city of the ancient world. The Greeks invented drama and produced great philosophers such as Socrates, Plato, and Aristotle. Scientists and mathematicians, like Hippocrates and Pythagoras, laid the foundations for our knowledge of these fields today. Hellenistic culture, which combined Greek and eastern cultures, also reached new heights in architecture, science, mathematics, and art.

Key Facts

1. Use each vocabulary word in a sentence.
   a. polis
   b. city-state
   c. monarchy
   d. aristocracy
   e. tyrant
   f. helot
   g. citizen
   h. democracy
   i. marathon
   j. infantry
   k. cavalry
   l. federation
   m. oracle
   n. metic
   o. epic
   p. philosopher
   q. Socratic method

2. Identify and briefly explain the importance of the following names, places, or events.
   a. Minoan culture
   b. Sparta
   c. Solon
   d. Salamis
   e. Hellenistic
   f. Delphi
   g. Homer
   h. *The Republic*

Main Ideas

1. Why was farming so difficult in ancient Greece?
2. Why did Greece enter a dark age when the Dorians took over the mainland?
3. How did Spartan men and women demonstrate their devotion to the city-state?
4. In what ways was the government of Athens a direct democracy?
5. How were the Greeks able to defeat Darius and his Persian army?
6. What caused the Peloponnesian Wars?
7. Identify three subjects of Greek dramas.

8. How were legends of the battles at Troy preserved by the Greeks?
9. Explain Plato's criticism of democracy.

Developing Skill in Reading History

Study the names in each set below. Then, write a sentence for each set describing what the items have in common.
1. Athens, Thebes, Corinth
2. Draco, Solon, Cleisthenes
3. citizens, metics, slaves
4. Pythagoras, Hippocrates, Aristotle

Using Social Studies Skills

1. **Evaluating Evidence** Evidence used by historians comes from written documents, eyewitness accounts, and artifacts. Which of these sources might a historian in ancient Greece have been able to use? Explain.
2. **Using Visual Evidence** The picture below is of Pericles, the great leader and statesman of Athens. Why do you think that the artist chose to show Pericles wearing a war helmet? What does this tell you about Greek society at that time?

Critical Thinking

1. **Identifying Assumptions** Why did Socrates believe in the power of knowledge?
2. **Recognizing Bias** How did the "perfect" society outlined in *The Republic* reflect Plato's criticism of democracy?
3. **Recognizing Ideologies** How were Socrates' views of society expressed in the questions he asked? What questions might have been most difficult or embarrassing for people to answer? Explain.

Focus on Writing

Developing Effective Paragraphs

A topic sentence expresses the main idea and defines the scope of a paragraph. A topic sentence should not be **too general,** covering more information than is in the paragraph, or **too narrow,** covering less information than is in the paragraph. Read the following paragraph and answer the questions below.

The coming of the Dorians greatly changed life in Greece. The Achaeans had united the land into a strong empire. But after the Dorian invasion, Greece once again became a divided country. Separated by Greece's mountain ranges, the Dorian tribes settled into different regions and developed independently.

1. What is the topic sentence?
2. What would be wrong with each of these substitute topic sentences?
   a. The Dorians were a group of people who lived in Greece.
   b. The Hellenic culture developed from a combination of Dorian and Achaean cultures.
   c. Under the Dorians, Greek life developed around city-states.
   d. The mountain ranges of Greece divided the country into several distinct regions and blocked foreign invasions.

Our Roman Heritage

(1000 B.C.-A.D. 476)

1 The Romans Formed a Republic

2 The Roman Republic Became an Empire

3 Rome Influenced Western Civilization

4 The Empire Declined and Split Apart

▲ **Illustrating History**
Octavian ruled over a time of peace and prosperity in the Roman Empire.

Octavian, the valiant general and ruler of Rome, swept into the great senate chamber. The year was 27 B.C., and the Roman republic had just recovered from many years of conflict and civil war. Before Octavian stood the senators of Rome, clad in the purple-bordered togas that reflected their high rank. The senators were expecting an announcement from this young man who had recently defeated his rivals for the throne and brought peace to Rome.

Humbly, Octavian told his audience that he planned to resign as sole ruler. But, this was nothing more than an empty gesture. Octavian had no intention of resigning, and the senators knew it. Octavian had his army standing by. A signal from Octavian would bring a terrible fury down upon the head of anyone who dared to cross him. The senators had a choice that was really no choice at all. They could either give Octavian the title he wanted or be shoved from power and possibly killed.

Their response was fast. The senators granted Octavian the title of *princeps,* or first citizen, and hailed him as *Augustus,* the "revered one." A power struggle had occurred without shedding a single drop of blood. For the citizens of Rome, Octavian's rise made a welcome change. As this chapter will show, from its earliest days, Roman history had been largely a cycle of warfare and internal struggle offset by rare periods of peace such as Octavian was now introducing to his people.

1000 B.C.	500 B.C.	B.C./A.D.	A.D. 500
	■ 800 B.C. Etruscans conquer Italy	■ 450 B.C. Romans adopt a code of laws	■ 44 B.C. Julius Caesar is assassinated ■ 31 B.C. Augustus becomes first Roman emperor	■ A.D. 476 Roman Empire falls

▲ **Illustrating History** *The Roman Forum, now in ruins, was the heart of ancient Rome and the place where the senators met.*

1 The Romans Formed a Republic

As you read, look for answers to these questions:

◆ How did geography affect the growth of Rome?
◆ What did the Romans learn from the Etruscans?
◆ How democratic was the Roman republic?

Key Terms: republic (defined on p. 121), patrician (p. 121), plebeian (p. 121), imperium (p. 121), consul (p. 121), veto (p. 121), tribune (p. 122)

Around 1000 B.C., the people who came to call themselves Romans lived in a cluster of small villages along the Tiber River in cen-

tral Italy. Over the next 500 years, the descendants of these people formed a republic and went on to conquer the whole of Italy. From Italy, the Romans spread out to form an empire that lasted for another 500 years and included most of the lands around the Mediterranean Sea. The capital of this empire was Rome, a city that still shows traces of its glorious past.

Rome Grew on the Banks of the Tiber

Between 800 B.C. and 750 B.C., a group of people from central Europe who were called Latins migrated to central Italy. There, they built farming settlements on the Latium Plain, which is south of the Tiber River. Around the middle of the eighth century B.C., the Latins united the other people who were living on the seven hills along the Tiber and formed the tiny city of Rome. Historians are not sure how this happened, but an ancient legend says that twin brothers founded the city.

119

▲ **Illustrating History** *An Etruscan artist sculpted this graceful dolphin.*

According to the legend, a Latin princess gave birth to twins, who were named Romulus and Remus. Their father was Mars, the god of war. The princess's uncle feared that the twins might someday challenge his authority as king. He therefore ordered the infants to be put in a basket and cast into the Tiber. Instead of sinking, the basket drifted ashore. There, it was found by a female wolf who nursed the boys as her own. When the boys grew up and discovered their origins, they killed their evil uncle. Then, they founded the city of Rome on the banks of the Tiber in 753 B.C.

The legend continues that Romulus traced the boundaries of the city with a plow and exclaimed: "Go, proclaim [that] it is heaven's will that my Rome shall be the capital of the world." As it turned out, Rome's geographic location proved favorable for growth, and in time Romulus' decree was fulfilled.

Geography Influenced Rome's Growth

The country now known as Italy is a boot-shaped peninsula that reaches into the central Mediterranean Sea. Although largely mountainous, it is blessed with a mild climate and a number of fertile river valleys and plains. In addition, Italy has many fine harbors with access to the Mediterranean Sea—the ancient world's highway for trade, communication, and invasion. As you can see from the map on page 121, Rome lies halfway down the west side of the peninsula. Its position near the mouth of the Tiber River gave it ready access to the Mediterranean. At the same time, the hills upon which Rome was built offered protection from attack. Rome's first settlers took advantage of their plains and valleys to raise cattle and grow crops. Eventually, they reached out to the Mediterranean to become a seafaring people as well.

The Etruscans Overpowered the Roman People

Although the Romans dated the founding of Rome as 753 B.C., the city may have existed long before then. Around 800 B.C., Rome fell under the control of a people from Asia Minor called the Etruscans (ih TRUHS kuhns). The Etruscan conquerors ruled nearly all of Italy.

The Etruscans were a highly civilized people. Archaeologists have discovered that the Etruscans were gifted in art, music, and dancing. They were also skilled metal workers, farmers, and architects, as well as avid traders and merchants.

From the Etruscans, the Romans learned how to construct buildings with arches, build aqueducts to carry water, use bronze, make better weapons, and build ships. In addition, the Etruscans taught the Romans the art of warfare. They also helped Rome to expand by draining the marshes around the city. The Etruscans showed the Romans how to raise grapes for wine-making and how to grow olive trees for olive oil.

The Romans Set Up a Republic

Under the Etruscans, kings ruled Rome and the rest of Italy. For two centuries, these rulers came from a family called Tarquin. Eventually, however, rivalries within the family led to struggles and weakened the power of the king. In 509 B.C., Tarquin the Proud murdered the king and declared himself tyrant. He was not able to keep power, however, and finally was overthrown by the Romans. The Roman people then declared their independence.

Free of monarchs, the Romans set up a new form of government, known as a republic. In a **republic**, elected representatives govern, as in the United States. Unlike the United States, however, Rome's elected leaders represented only one group of people, not the whole population. The representatives who governed came only from Rome's upper class. These wealthy landowners were called **patricians**, a word that comes from the Latin *patres*, or "fathers." Rome's **plebeians** (plih BEE uhnz), or common citizens, had only a limited say in government. Farmers, artisans, small merchants, and traders made up the plebeian class.

As a part of the republic, the Romans set up a legislature that included a senate and two assemblies. The members of the senate, or senators, were patricians who served for life. The senators proposed and passed all laws and ratified treaties. They also approved official appointments.

The Assembly of Centuries, also made up of patricians, directed military matters. The Assembly of Tribes, composed mainly of plebeians, represented the 35 tribes into which Roman citizens were divided. In theory, the assemblies represented all the people of Rome because their members were both patricians and plebeians. In practice, the patricians controlled the assemblies.

Even though the Romans had overthrown the king and set up a republic, they felt a need for a supreme authority, or what they called an **imperium.** (The word *imperial* comes from this Latin term.) The Romans placed the imperium in the hands of two consuls. A **consul** was an official, chosen from the patrician class, who carried out the laws of Rome. The consuls ruled for one year. In addition to helping to make and carry out laws, the consuls also commanded the army. Since each consul had the power to **veto,** or stop, the acts of the other, the two consuls had to agree with each other before they could act. (The word *veto* means "I forbid" in Latin.)

When quick decisions were needed in times of crisis, the senate could replace the consuls with a dictator for a six-month period. The dictator had full power to make decisions and guide the government through any emergency. He could not, however, change the basic laws of the republic.

The government of Rome was also served by *praetors* (PRAY tohrz), or judges, who played an important part in interpreting the laws of Rome. *Censors* counted the people of Rome and determined how much in taxes the people would pay. A person's tax was based on his or her wealth.

Throughout the early years of the republic, the plebeians struggled for a greater share in the government and greater social equality. Early in the republic, plebeians could not marry patricians and could not

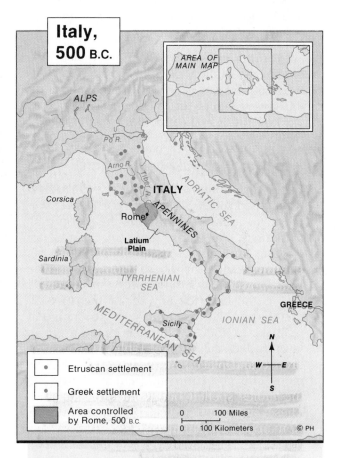

Italy, 500 B.C.

Focus on Geography

Location Find Rome on the map. Why was Rome in a good location to take over the Italian Peninsula?

121

▲ **Illustrating History**   *This carving shows a Roman market scene.*

hold important offices. They were also forbidden to conduct the religious rituals that were required of people who held offices in the government. Yet, plebeians paid taxes, worked for Rome, and more importantly, made up Rome's army.

Plebeians Won Additional Rights

In the fifth century B.C., after the plebeians threatened to refuse to fight for Rome, the patricians gave in to some of the plebeians' demands. Plebeians won the right to choose, through the Assembly of Tribes, 10 **tribunes** each year. These tribunes had unusual powers. By simply calling out "Veto," they could override any act or measure of the senate, the assemblies, or government officials. In 450 B.C., Rome adopted a set of laws called the Twelve Tables. Carved in bronze and placed in the Forum (the religious and governmental center of Rome), the tables spelled out Rome's basic laws. These laws covered nearly every aspect of Roman life, including wills, family law, property rights, court cases, and even the public behavior of citizens.

By 339 B.C., plebeians had won the right to marry patricians and hold the office of consul. They could also sit in the senate, and their assembly could pass laws without senate approval. However, in spite of these important reforms, Rome was still not a true democracy, since the new plebeian class guarded its power much as the patrician class had done earlier.

SECTION 1 REVIEW

Knowing Key Terms, People, and Places
1. Define: **a.** republic **b.** patrician **c.** plebeian **d.** imperium **e.** consul **f.** veto **g.** tribune
2. Identify: **a.** Tiber River **b.** Latins **c.** Romulus and Remus **d.** Etruscans **e.** Tarquin the Proud **f.** Twelve Tables **g.** Forum

Focus on Geography
3. How did geography aid the growth of Rome?

Reviewing Main Ideas
4. Why were the Etruscans important in the history of Rome?
5. What were the divisions of the Roman legislature?
6. Describe the Assembly of Tribes.

Critical Thinking
Identifying Central Issues
7. Why do you think that the patricians kept the plebeians from having an active role in government for so long?

2 The Roman Republic Became an Empire

As you read, look for answers to these questions:

◆ How did the Punic Wars both weaken and strengthen the republic?
◆ What reforms did the Gracchus brothers attempt?
◆ What were the accomplishments of Julius Caesar?
◆ How was the Roman Empire established?

Key Terms: phalanx (defined on p. 123), maniple (p. 123), gladiator (p. 126)

In order to protect themselves from invasion, Romans decided that they had to conquer or make allies of the other people on the peninsula. Thus from 450 B.C. to around 270 B.C., the Romans steadily extended their control over Italy. First, they took control of other cities and tribes. They also subdued the remaining Etruscans, whose city-states were already in decline. Finally, they turned south and conquered the Greek colonies at the foot of Italy. After this victory, Rome ruled all of Italy and was ready to conquer other lands.

The Roman Army Helped Build the Empire

The expansion of Rome was made possible in part by the courage and skill of its soldiers. Armed with the metal weapons they had been taught to make by the Etruscans, the Roman army became a match for any army in the Western World.

The Roman army was made up primarily of foot soldiers. In early times, soldiers were organized into groups of 8,000 called phalanxes (FAY langk sehs). A **phalanx** was a military formation that was made up of foot soldiers massed together with shields joined and spears overlapping. Later, the army did away with the phalanx and replaced it with a

▲ **Illustrating History** *Mars, the Roman god of war (shown at right), battles a centaur in this dramatic scene, painted on clay.*

simpler organization. It divided its forces into units of 3,600 men called legions. The legions in turn were divided into groups of 60 to 120 men called **maniples** (MAN uh puhlz), a term that means "handful." These units were more flexible in battle than the phalanxes.

Roman soldiers were tough, loyal, practical men who could survive long marches. They could handle just about any task, whether it was sewing their own clothes, repairing weapons, or building bridges. Furthermore, they took care to obey orders, because anyone who broke the rules was dealt with severely. One Greek historian, Polybius, described the fate of a Roman soldier who fell asleep while on duty: "A court-martial composed of all the tribunes at once meets to try him, and if he is found guilty he is punished. . . . The tribune takes a cudgel [club] and just touches the condemned man with it, after which all in the camp beat or stone him, in most cases [killing] him."

▲ **Illustrating History** *Two images document the 100 years of war between Carthage and Rome. At top is a carved war elephant such as Hannibal used to cross the Alps. The medieval plate below shows the Romans taking Carthage.*

Rome Became a World Power

After Rome took over all of Italy, it sent its mighty army to conquer the Mediterranean world—and more. Rome made its mark as a Mediterranean power in a series of wars with Carthage, the great trading center founded by the Phoenicians on the northern coast of Africa. These wars, known as the Punic Wars (*Punic* being the Latin word for Phoenicia), raged off and on between 264 B.C. and 146 B.C.

At the outset of the wars, Carthage controlled trading centers on the islands of Sardinia and Corsica as well as Sicily, and it dominated territories in northern Africa and present-day Spain. It was also the leading naval power in the Mediterranean. After over 100 years of fighting, Rome finally destroyed the power of Carthage—but not without suffering huge losses of its own.

The closest Rome came to defeat was in the Second Punic War, which was fought from 219 B.C. to 202 B.C. During this war, a brilliant Carthaginian general, Hannibal, gathered a mighty army that included elephants and crossed the Alps into northern Italy. For 15 years, Hannibal marched up and down the Italian peninsula, defeating the Romans. Because he was cut off from his lines of supply, however, he could never gain a decisive victory. Finally, Rome attacked Carthage, and Hannibal left Italy to defend the city.

The Third Punic War was the last and the most destructive of the wars. Fearing another invasion by Carthage, the Romans threw all their might into capturing that city, which they did in 146 B.C. To punish the Carthaginians, the Romans completely destroyed the city, sowed the fields with salt so that nothing would ever grow there again, and sold the people into slavery. Carthage then became the Roman province of Africa.

The Punic Wars are important for several reasons. They gave Rome control of the western Mediterranean, and they opened the way for Rome to exert its power over the eastern Mediterranean. During a break between the Punic Wars, Rome conquered lands that had been part of the empire of Alexander the Great. Rome, a republic, had defeated some of the world's great monarchies and dictatorships and had assured its supremacy in the Mediterranean.

Spain, which Rome won when it defeated Carthage, was the first Roman province in Europe. In later conquests, known as the Gallic Wars (58 B.C.–51 B.C.), Julius Caesar (SEE zahr), a dynamic Roman general, added Gaul (now France and Belgium) to the Roman lands. Caesar also invaded Britain and extended Rome's borders to the North Sea. (See the map on page 125.)

Conquest and Civil War Weakened Rome

Although the Punic and Gallic wars brought power and glory to Rome, they also created poverty and suffering among the common people and widened the gap between the rich and the poor. These conditions eventually weakened the republic.

Small farmers, the backbone of Roman agriculture, were particularly affected. Wealthy Romans bought up great amounts of land and turned them into large estates, squeezing out small, independent farmers. Tens of thousands of slaves were brought in from the provinces to work the estates, which lessened the need for the labor of free farmers. In addition, Rome began importing a number of cheap crops from its many provinces abroad, further hurting the position of the free farmers.

Displaced from the land, thousands of farmers drifted to the city of Rome, seeking work. Few jobs awaited them there, for the city had no large-scale industry. There were never enough jobs for the city poor because slaves did most of the work. Together, the farmers and laborers formed a huge mass of unhappy citizens.

In the senate, the patricians had gained more power during the wars of conquest. Corruption grew as the rich bought the votes of government officials who supported their interests. In the provinces, officials also helped themselves to tax money collected from the people.

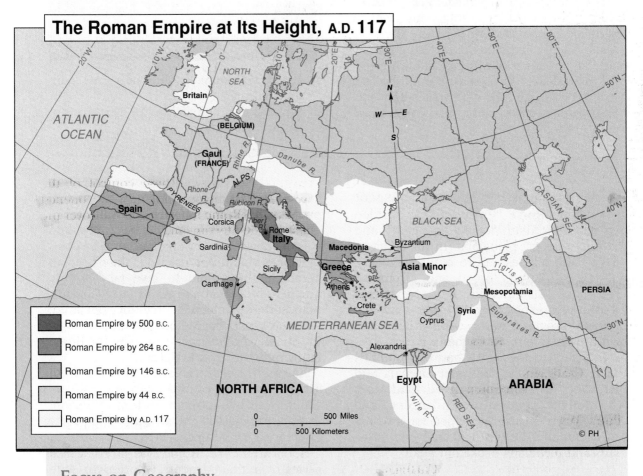

The Roman Empire at Its Height, A.D. 117

Roman Empire by 500 B.C.
Roman Empire by 264 B.C.
Roman Empire by 146 B.C.
Roman Empire by 44 B.C.
Roman Empire by A.D. 117

Focus on Geography

1. **Location** Study the map and the key. By A.D. 117, what westernmost regions did the Roman Empire include?
2. **Place** The higher the latitude, the colder the climate becomes. How would Britain's climate be different from Egypt's?

A Roman Banquet

In 45 B.C., the orator and philosopher Cicero entertained Julius Caesar at his country home. According to Cicero, Caesar and the other guests occupied four separate dining rooms and enjoyed an "elegant" meal in which they "lacked for nothing." Cicero's banquet, like the one shown at right, was the traditional way wealthy Romans entertained their guests.

After shedding their sandals, the diners relaxed on couches. Servants would set the delicacies on low tables before the guests. A truly luxurious dinner might include an appetizer of asparagus followed by a main dish such as roast parrot, boiled ostrich, or sea urchins with spices and honey. A dessert of exotic nuts, cakes, or fruit followed.

1. How did Romans traditionally entertain their guests?
2. Which foods enjoyed by the Romans do we still eat today?

As the gap between the rich and the poor grew wider, Rome became deeply divided between the luxury-loving patricians and the bitter, angry plebeians. In an effort to distract the masses and to buy their votes, politicians offered "bread and circuses." Free food distributed by the government filled the stomachs of the people while the circuses provided them with violent and brutal entertainment. Roman circuses featured fights to the death between animals (bears, lions, bulls), between animals and men, and between men called **gladiators** who fought with swords, daggers, and spears. These measures helped for a while, but eventually the old fight between patricians and plebeians broke out again.

Some Romans Attempted Reforms

In time, some Romans realized that the republic was in grave danger of collapse. A number of these people tried to reform the government.

The first of these reformers were two patrician brothers, Tiberius and Gaius Gracchus. Believing that Rome's basic problem was the condition of its farmers and landless plebeians, including soldiers, they tried to persuade the senate to give land to the landless. In a speech to the senate, Tiberius, who had been elected a tribune, declared: "Savage beasts have their places of refuge; but those who bear arms and die for Rome enjoy only the air and light."

Alarmed at such thinking, the senate put Tiberius and many of his followers to death. Gaius Gracchus took up his brother's fight, but he, too, gained the wrath of the senate and ended up killing himself.

Soon afterward, Rome was faced with a series of military leaders who fought each other for control of the empire. As soon as one became a hero through some great victory, he would try to become consul and even dictator. The last of these was a general named Sulla, who strengthened the powers of the senate and named himself dictator.

Julius Caesar Won Control of Rome

Although born to a noble family, Julius Caesar, who lived from 100 B.C. to 44 B.C., grew popular with the common people of Rome. To gain popularity, Caesar endeared himself to the masses by spending large sums of money in their behalf. He organized spectacular public games and gave gifts of food. When he married Cornelia, the daughter of the popular leader Cinna, he further strengthened his popularity. Through this marriage, however, Caesar also gained the hostility of Sulla, because Cinna was one of Sulla's enemies.

Sulla ordered Caesar to divorce his wife, which Caesar refused to do. He seemed marked for death but avoided capture by fleeing Rome and joining the Roman army in the Middle East. When Sulla died in 78 B.C., Caesar returned to Rome where his greatness as a speaker won him renewed fame.

The First Triumvirate. In 60 B.C., Caesar joined forces with two other ambitious politicians to form an alliance for political power called the First Triumvirate. One member of the Triumvirate was the military hero Pompey; the other, Crassus, was a military hero and the richest man in Rome. Jealousies among the three harmed their ability to rule effectively.

Caesar held the positions of consul and general in the First Triumvirate. His conquest of Gaul and his invasion of Britain in

▼ **Illustrating History** *Wealthy citizens of Rome lived in villas such as this. Often, the rich paid skilled artists to decorate their homes.*

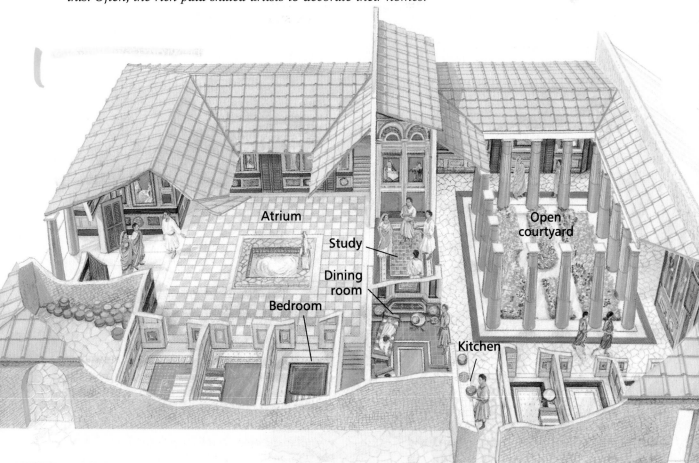

Atrium

Study

Dining room

Bedroom

Open courtyard

Kitchen

In their own words

Hortensia Defends Women

Following the death of Caesar in 44 B.C., Rome suffered through 15 years of civil war. The government needed money to pay for the war, so the leaders ordered 1,400 of the richest women in Rome to turn over their property to the government. The women refused. The following is an excerpt from a speech by one of these women, Hortensia.

"You have already deprived us of our fathers, our sons, our husbands, and our brothers, whom you accused of having wronged you. . . . But if we women have not voted any of you public enemies, have not torn down your houses, destroyed your army, or led another one against you; if we have not hindered you in obtaining offices and honors, why do we share the penalty when we did not share in the guilt?

Why should we pay taxes when we have no part in the honors, the commands, the state-craft, for which you contend [fight] against each other with such harmful results? 'Because this is a time of war,' do you say? When have there not been wars, and when have taxes ever been imposed on women, who are exempted [freed from] by their sex among all mankind? . . . Let war with the Gauls or the Parthians come, and we shall [respond with] zeal [enthusiasm] for the common safety; but for civil wars may we never . . . assist you against each other!**"**

1. Why did Hortensia believe that women should not have to pay taxes?
2. Does Hortensia claim that women should have equal rights with men? Explain.

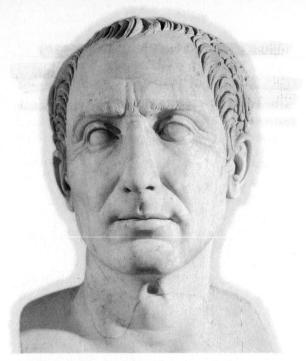

▲ **Illustrating History** *Julius Caesar ruled Rome as a dictator for five years.*

55 B.C. brought more territory under Roman rule. While in Gaul, he wrote *Commentaries on the Gallic Wars* in which he told the story of his military campaigns and victories. These stories spread far and wide, and Caesar became known as a brilliant military commander. His fame helped prepare the way for his return to Rome, where civil war had broken out.

While Caesar was winning victories in Gaul and building an army, Crassus was fighting in Persia. After Crassus was killed in battle in 53 B.C., Pompey ruled Rome almost as a dictator. Pompey felt that his powers were not safe as long as Caesar was in Gaul with an intensely loyal army supporting him. The senate ordered Caesar to resign and to disband his army. Instead, in 49 B.C., he crossed the Rubicon (ROO bik kahn) River and entered Italy.

The triumph of Caesar. During four years of bloody fighting, Caesar pursued and defeated his enemies. Finally, he entered Rome and became dictator. Pompey, who was defeated, managed to escape to Egypt, where he was murdered, thus ending the First Triumvirate.

Caesar ruled alone for only five years. In 44 B.C., he was assassinated by some aristocrats and former friends who feared that he might become king. On the Ides of March (March 15), his trusted friend Brutus and others stabbed and killed him.

Despite serving for only a brief time, Caesar tried to begin many reforms. He helped provide for the poor by redistributing land. He tried to set up a stable government by pardoning those aristocrats who had opposed him. By giving the people of the Roman provinces equal rights with the people of Rome, Caesar hoped to rebuild the republic. In addition, he did everything he could to make the senate representative of the entire republic.

Augustus Became Rome's First Emperor

Caesar's death led to another period of civil war. Caesar's grandnephew and adopted son, Octavian, and one of Caesar's generals and loyal followers, Mark Antony, hunted down and defeated in battle the men who had murdered Caesar. In the process, thousands of Romans suspected of being loyal to the assassins also were murdered.

Octavian and Mark Antony then divided up Rome's holdings. Octavian ruled the western part, and Antony ruled the eastern part. Octavian ruled from Rome, where he increased his popularity. Antony went to the province of Egypt. There, he enjoyed the luxuries of the court of Cleopatra, queen of Egypt, and plotted with her an invasion of the western empire.

Upon learning of these plans, the senate in Rome declared war on Antony and Cleopatra and chose Octavian to lead its forces. In a great naval battle at Actium off the coast of Greece in 31 B.C., Octavian defeated Antony and became the sole ruler, the first emperor, of Rome. From this time on, Rome was a monarchy.

Octavian, now called Augustus, or "revered one," ruled an empire united and at peace with itself. He worked hard to carry out many of Caesar's reforms. Augustus rebuilt highways, put up many public build-

▲ **Illustrating History** *Roman coins depicted emperors or mythological symbols.*

ings, collected taxes fairly, and made sure that laws were just. It has been said that Emperor Augustus "found Rome of brick and left it of marble."

During his reign, trade and commerce flourished, building increased, and there was widespread prosperity. Augustus' most notable achievement was the establishment of the period known as the *Pax Romana* (paks ROH MAHN ah), the 200 years of peace that began in 27 B.C.

3 Rome Influenced Western Civilization

As you read, look for answers to these questions:

- What were the basic principles of Roman law?
- Who were some of the greatest Roman writers?
- What practical gifts did Romans contribute to the Western world?
- How did Romans educate their children and practice religion?

Key Terms: Romance language (defined on p. 130), vernacular (p. 130)

In the course of building its empire, Rome spread its culture, language, law, and government to many parts of the world. The heritage of Rome can be seen today in art, architecture, languages, and legal institutions of the Western world.

Roman Laws Were a Model for World Laws

Law is perhaps Rome's greatest gift to the world. Based on the Twelve Tables, the code of laws that was described in Section 1, Roman law gradually expanded. When laws based on the Twelve Tables became out-of-date, Roman lawyers studied the laws passed by the senate and the decisions handed down by Roman judges. They also studied laws that were used in the lands Rome won through war. They tried to build fairness and justice into the law.

By our standards, many Roman laws were unfair. Slavery was legal and was practiced throughout the empire. An accused person was not given a jury trial, and judges often gave out overly harsh punishments. In any complaint against the government, the judges usually sided with the government, not the people.

On the other hand, Roman laws provided for new and better legal methods. People in lands ruled by Rome were allowed to obey their own laws. Roman citizens were all supposed to be treated equally, regardless of their position or wealth. However, the lower classes were often more cruelly treated.

Under Roman law, a citizen's life, property, and legal rights were assured. Today, the United States' laws concerning ownership of property and business contracts are based in large measure on Roman law. Above all, the Roman principle that a person is innocent until proven guilty is an important part of our legal system.

Language and Literature Were Lasting Roman Contributions

Latin, the language of the Romans, forms the basis for the modern-day **Romance languages**—French, Spanish, Italian, Romanian, and Portuguese. In fact, all of these languages are called Romance languages because they developed in areas that had once been part of the Roman Empire. Latin also contributed many words to English. It became the language of law, science, and medicine and of the Roman Catholic Church. Literary Latin, the form used in writing, as opposed to the **vernacular,** the everyday language spoken by the people, was kept and used through the centuries by the Church. Rome also gave us the Roman alphabet, which was used throughout later Western civilization.

Roman literature was strongly influenced by the Greeks. By the beginning of the second century B.C., however, Romans had developed their own style and had become very talented writers, especially of history and satire.

Among the greatest of Roman writers were Cicero and Lucretius, who made their contributions while Rome was still a republic. Virgil, Horace, Ovid, Seneca, and Tacitus gained fame later, during the period of the empire.

Cicero was a clever lawyer, politician, and orator whose speeches and other writings are still read by those who study Latin. Lucretius, a poet, wrote on philosophy and psychology. Virgil, who was the official poet of the Emperor Augustus, wrote the *Aeneid*, an epic that told of the great deeds of Rome. In his works, the satirist Horace urged the people of Rome to lead simple lives. Meanwhile Ovid, another poet, wrote of life's pleasures rather than of its simplicity. Seneca, a playwright, wrote tragedies about famous people. Tacitus, who is known as Rome's greatest historian, warned the Romans of the growing strength of the German peoples north of Rome's borders.

The Romans Valued Family Life, Religion, and Education

"It was Rome," says the historian Will Durant, "that raised the family to new heights in the ancient world." In the family structure, men were the head of the household and had the power of life or death over family members, although this power was rarely used. Women played important roles in rearing and educating children, in directing servants, and in budgeting the family's money. As an alternative to marriage, a Roman woman could choose to work.

BIOGRAPHY

Virgil

The year was 30 B.C. For the past seven years, the poet Virgil, shown in the medieval painting above, had been laboring over his four books of verse. At last they were finished. The Emperor Augustus had asked Virgil to write some poetry to encourage Romans to return to a peaceful life of farming after many years of civil war.

The four books were meant to give practical advice to farmers and to promote the value of country life.

Virgil was well qualified to carry out the assignment. He was both a poet and a farmer. Born in 70 B.C. in the rural north of Italy, he had grown up with a love of the land and a deep respect for those who tilled the soil. He seldom visited the bustling metropolis of Rome, preferring instead to write amid the peace of his farm near Naples.

Virgil was also a patriot who believed in the greatness Rome would achieve under Augustus. For 10 years, until his death in 19 B.C., he worked on his epic poem, the *Aeneid* (ih NEE uhd). Virgil's

pride and patriotism are reflected in this work. Although its twelve books relate the story of Rome's founding, the poem is much more than a tale of adventure. In the poem, Virgil praises Roman traditions and highlights the Roman ideals of devotion to family, loyalty to the state, and obedience to authority, as well as the classic Roman virtues of discipline and courage.

1. What was Virgil's purpose in writing the *Aeneid*?
2. How does the *Aeneid* reflect Roman ideals?
3. Why was Virgil capable of writing with feeling about both the city and the countryside of Italy?

Religion was an important part of every Roman's life. Romans worshipped many gods, many of whom were patterned after those of ancient Greece. For example, Jupiter, Rome's supreme god, was the same as Zeus, the supreme god of ancient Greece. The chart below lists the names of both the Greek and Roman gods.

The Romans thought their gods controlled the forces of nature, and they looked to the gods for signs of what would happen in the future. A streak of lightning or an unusually loud thunderclap might be taken as a sign that the gods were angry. These unfavorable omens were sometimes enough to postpone business deals or delay the outbreak of war. When the "signs" were favorable, people planned to make business deals and take action with confidence.

Roman religion encouraged worship of the emperor and patriotism. For their country, for their emperor, and for their gods, Romans were willing to serve in the Roman army and die on foreign soil.

Unless they were from the upper classes, most Romans received little education. In the Roman schools of the time, the chief aim was to teach boys and girls to obey. Study was limited to basic subjects such as reading, writing, and simple mathematical problems. Stories of Roman heroes were taught as examples to encourage the children to do brave deeds.

In the later republic and in the empire, Greek freemen and sometimes slaves opened schools. Students wrote on wax tablets with a stylus, and they studied Latin, Greek philosophy, and public speaking.

Rome Gave the World Practical Gifts

To be practical is to be concerned with everyday matters. While the Greeks often pondered the universe and the human spirit

▼ **Chart Skill** *What was the name of the Roman god of war?*

Greek and Roman Gods			
Greek	**Roman**	**Realm**	**Symbols**
Zeus	Jupiter (Jove)	King of the gods	Eagle, oak, thunderbolts
Poseidon	Neptune	God of sea	Spear
Phoebus Apollo	(Same)	God of sun, music, poetry	Lyre, arrows, sun chariot
Hermes	Mercury	Messenger of the gods	Winged cap, sandals, and staff
Ares	Mars	God of war	Sword, shield, dogs, vultures
Hephaestus	Vulcan	God of fire and of workers in metal	Anvil, forge
Hera	Juno	Queen of the gods	Pomegranate, peacock, cuckoo
Demeter	Ceres	Goddess of agriculture	Sheaf of wheat, poppies, horn of peace and plenty
Artemis	Diana	Goddess of moon and hunting	Crescent, stag, arrows
Pallas Athena	Minerva	Goddess of wisdom and war	Owl, shield, olive tree
Aphrodite	Venus	Goddess of love and beauty	Doves, sparrows
Hestia	Vesta	Goddess of hearth and home	Hearth fire
Hades Pluto	Dis	God of the underworld	Cypress, the spear

and enjoyed beauty for its own sake, the Romans concentrated on practical things that would make life more comfortable.

One of the practical wonders of the Roman world was the network of roads that bound the empire together. The Romans were superb engineers, and they built durable highways for moving their large military forces and for commerce and trade. The Appian Way, a 360-mile road (500 kilometers) of layered stone that stretched southward from Rome to the Adriatic Sea, is still in use today. Roman engineers also constructed dams, bridges, aqueducts, sewage systems, and public baths throughout the empire.

A Roman city usually spread out from a central forum, which was originally a marketplace but later became a place for public and religious buildings and shops. In Rome itself, the Forum Romanum, the oldest of the city's public squares, was the heart of the city. The Forum was said to be the burial site of the legendary Romulus. Temples, civic buildings, and the Roman senate stood in the Forum, and all roads from Rome started at the Forum.

As architects, the Romans built great public buildings. The Pantheon, a religious temple completed by Emperor Hadrian, who ruled from A.D. 117 to A.D. 138, is a fine example of Roman architecture. This circular building, with a dome measuring 142 feet (42.6 meters) across, still stands. The arch and dome are its distinctive features and make up Rome's unique contribution to architecture.

Few Roman buildings were used for religious purposes. Most were civic buildings and included libraries, theaters, and triumphal arches built to honor heroes or emperors. The Colosseum and the Circus Maximus were great arenas used for Roman entertainment. In the Colosseum, 50,000 spectators could watch the gladiators. The Circus Maximus was even larger. Here, some 260,000 could see the chariot races.

In science, Romans invented little that was new, but they made good use of what was already known. Pliny (PLIHN ee) the Elder proved that the world was round, but

▲ **Illustrating History** *The Colosseum, opened in* A.D. *80, was the site of great spectacles staged for the Roman public.*

he only confirmed a theory that had been known as early as 300 B.C. Surgery was done in ancient Rome, and operations were often successful. The removal of tonsils was not uncommon. Galen (GAY luhn), a Greek who lived in Rome, wrote an encyclopedia of medicine that included all the medical knowledge of the time.

SECTION 3 REVIEW

Knowing Key Terms, People, and Places
1. Define: **a.** Romance language **b.** vernacular
2. Identify: **a.** Cicero **b.** Virgil **c.** Tacitus **d.** Forum Romanum **e.** Pantheon **f.** Colosseum

Reviewing Main Ideas
3. Upon which three concepts of Roman law is our legal system based?
4. Why were Romans considered excellent engineers and city planners?
5. Name three Roman writers and describe the content of their works.
6. Describe Roman education and explain its basic purpose.

Critical Thinking
Making Comparisons
7. Compare the life of a woman in ancient Rome with the life of a woman in this country today.

The Glory of Rome

The art and architecture of Rome reflect how the ancient Romans saw themselves and their way of life. For example, the worship of ancestors was an important part of Roman life. Therefore, wealthy Roman citizens had lifelike images of themselves carved in stone so that their descendants would know what they had looked like. Most Roman portraits did not flatter their subjects by making them look better than they actually appeared. The portrait here shows a Roman matron in the prime of her life. Although we see only white marble now, portraits such as this one were once painted with appropriate skin, hair, and eye colors, which have since worn off. We also know that the Romans loved luxury and comfort. Their houses were painted richly and imaginatively. This *Garden Scene* covered the wall of a dining room and was meant to remind guests of the quiet pleasures of the country, even though the house was on a busy street in a large city. The art of Rome also reveals that the Romans were proud of their military strength. Roman emperors used public monuments, some of them quite large, to inform the public about important events during their reigns. The *Arch of Titus* is one such monument, commemorating the fall of Jerusalem to the emperor Titus in the year A.D. 70.

A Roman wall painting and a portrait bust are shown bottom right. Bottom left is the Arch of Titus.

4 The Empire Declined and Split Apart

As you read, look for answers to these questions:

◆ How did Emperor Augustus gather power for himself?
◆ What economic problems troubled the empire?
◆ How did the Roman army change under the empire?

Key Terms: princeps (defined on p. 135), despotism (p. 137), mercenary (p. 138)

Historians usually use the date A.D. 476 to mark the fall of the Roman Empire. In that year, the last emperor was removed from the throne. An empire does not fall, however, in one day or through a single event. Hundreds of years of slow decline led up to the final fall of the Roman Empire, and many factors played a part in it.

Good and Bad Emperors Ruled Rome

As you have read, Augustus was Rome's first emperor. Although Augustus, who liked to be known as the "Restorer of the Roman Republic," did much for Rome, he also gathered great authority for himself. A willing senate allowed him to be the head of state and the governor of several provinces. It also granted him the power of a tribune—a power he should not have had because he was a patrician. In addition, the senate named him **princeps,** or "first citizen," a title of great honor that allowed its holder to speak first in senate debates.

Augustus did not rule by law but rather by favoritism and by the prestige of his many offices. The historian Tacitus tells us that Augustus "first conciliated [won over] the army by gratuities [money], the populace by cheapened corn [grain], the world by the amenities [attractive features] of peace, then step by step began to make his ascent and to unite in his own person the functions of the senate, the magistracy [court system], and the legislature."

As well as giving cash payments to some soldiers, Augustus created a special palace guard, known as the Praetorian (pree TOH ree uhn) Guard. This force of 9,000 men policed the city of Rome and protected Augustus.

The authority that Augustus gathered did not end when he died but was passed down from emperor to emperor. If an emperor ruled well and wisely, he could bring peace and progress. If he did not, tyranny and conflict could result, and the citizens had no way to lessen his power.

Augustus named his stepson Tiberius as his successor. Tiberius's rule began in A.D. 14 and was marred by bloodshed and violence. Tiberius abused his powers and brutally disposed of anyone who opposed him.

▼ **Illustrating History** *The Praetorian Guard, shown in the marble relief below, included 9,000 of Augustus's soldiers.*

The emperor who followed Tiberius proved to be an even worse ruler. Caligula, a cruel, corrupt, and mentally unstable man, emptied the public treasury through extravagant spending. He declared himself a god and tried to have his horse made a senator. His conduct shocked even the Praetorian Guard, which assassinated him and many members of his family in A.D. 41.

The Praetorian Guard then decided to choose an emperor itself. Rampaging through the palace, they came upon Caligula's middle-aged, half-paralyzed uncle, Claudius, and named him ruler.

Surprisingly, Claudius proved to be an excellent ruler. Upon his death, however, disorder once again reigned in Rome when his stepson, Nero, came to the throne. Nero was a match for Caligula in cruelty and extravagance. He poisoned Claudius's son and murdered both his own mother and his wife. He spent most of his time staging plays and musical events. Any opposition to his strange deeds was quickly and cruelly put down. When the senate finally condemned Nero, he took his own life.

A year of chaos followed the death of Nero as four different army commanders from the provinces led their forces against one another in a battle for control. The general Vespasian emerged victorious and began his rule. To bring order to the empire, Vespasian imposed tight discipline on the army and on the provincial governments. He built new roads and forts that made the frontiers more safe, and he extended Roman citizenship to all provincial people who served in the army.

Vespasian was followed by his sons Titus and Domitian. Domitian returned to the excesses of Caligula and Nero, and the people of Rome lived in fear during all of his 15-year rule.

The next emperor, Nerva, a lawyer and respected citizen of Rome, was appointed by the senate. Although Nerva only reigned from A.D. 96 to A.D. 98, he was responsible for changing the system of hereditary succession to the throne. He started the tradition of the emperor adopting a qualified person as a son and training him for the job.

Nerva's reign began the ruling period that is known as the Five Good Emperors. Under these emperors—Nerva, Trajan, Hadrian, Antoninus Pius, and Marcus Aurelius—Rome enjoyed a long period of peace, and the empire reached its height. Their rule was marked by efficiency and prosperity.

Many historians consider Marcus Aurelius the greatest of the Five Good Emperors. He was respected and admired by nearly all Romans as well as the people of the provinces. His humanitarian approach to governing helped unify the empire. Although a scholarly, thoughtful man, Marcus Aurelius was forced to spend more and more time on military matters. He led his armies in many battles to protect the borders of the empire. They were in danger from groups along the borders in the north. This constant warfare strained the financial and human resources of the empire.

▼ **Illustrating History** *Nero, shown below, caused fear and confusion in Rome.*

The Empire Began Its Decline

At the death of Marcus Aurelius in A.D. 180, the empire began a period of long decline. A long line of emperors, many of them installed by the army, took their places on the imperial throne. The rise of each new emperor brought struggle and violence, much of it carried out by the army.

In the third and fourth centuries, two emperors attempted to enforce order and to halt the failing of the empire through **despotism,** government by a ruler with unlimited power. The first, Diocletian (DY uh KLEE shuhn), considered himself above all laws. He controlled business, industry, and agriculture. His successor, Constantine, became emperor in A.D. 324 and continued Diocletian's policies. If anything, Constantine's rule was even harsher as he repeatedly increased taxes to raise and supply his armies and allowed German tribesmen to enlist in the Roman army.

Germans Overthrew Rome's Last Emperor

Theodosius (THEE uh DOH shuhs), who lived from A.D. 347 to A.D. 395, was the last Roman emperor to rule over the entire empire before it was divided. Although some Germanic people had been allowed to settle within the empire earlier, most were prevented from doing so by the Roman army. This changed, however, when the fierce Huns from Asia swept into Europe and attacked the German tribes. To escape the Huns, the Visigoths (VIZ uh GOTHS), one of the German tribes, sought safety within the Roman Empire, and Theodosius reluctantly permitted them to enter. Once they settled in the empire, the Visigoths became powerful in the army. As the Visigoths gained power, the Romans began to regret their decision and sent an army against them. At the battle of Adrianople, however, the Visigoths defeated the Romans. The emperors who followed Theodosius could no longer control the Visigoths.

When Theodosius died in A.D. 395, the empire was divided into the Western Roman Empire and the Eastern Roman Empire. Each had a ruler of its own. Powerful German generals soon ruled the western part of the Roman Empire. In A.D. 410, the Visigoths pillaged Rome. Meanwhile, the Huns continued their attacks on Europe. Attila the Hun led an attack on Gaul in the western part of the empire. He was defeated at the battle of Chalons (shah LAWN) in

▼ **Illustrating History** *This French tapestry shows Pope Leo I (mounted at left) convincing Attila (on brown horse) not to sack Rome.*

A.D. 451. Attila later attacked Rome but was persuaded not to destroy it by Pope Leo I. Attila died two years later.

By A.D. 476 there was nothing left of Rome to "fall." In that year, Odoacer (OH doh AY suhr), of German birth, overthrew the last Roman emperor and proclaimed himself ruler of Rome. The empire in the west was gone. The eastern part lasted for another 1,000 years.

Many Factors Led to Rome's Fall

The reasons for the fall of Rome can be only summarized here. They extend far back into Roman history. The seeds of Rome's fall may have taken root as early as the first century B.C., when the army was used to fight a civil war rather than to unify the nation. The real decline began in the second century A.D., however, when men of questionable loyalty filled the ranks of the Roman army. These hired soldiers, called **mercenaries,** could not always be trusted to stand their ground when the battle seemed lost.

Economics also played a large part in the fall of Rome. The gap between the rich and the poor widened; paid laborers were replaced by slaves; and there were heavy, unfair taxes and high unemployment. Finally, huge estates were held by a few rich families, while the poor had no land at all. The consuls of Rome fought among themselves and gave little thought to the needs of the people.

As living costs increased, the ties of family life weakened. Raising a family became a heavy economic burden. The number of marriages fell, and the divorce rate soared. Crime, too, increased as more and more people lost their jobs and sank further into poverty.

As you have read, changes in government also caused problems for Rome. Except during the period of the Five Good Emperors, succession to the throne followed no orderly pattern. The death of each emperor seemed to be a signal for revolt and civil war. This was even more true when the generals of the army gained control of the state and sought to become rulers. Many of Rome's emperors were weak, so the nation and the conquered countries were not well governed.

The moral standards (values) of Rome declined. There was corruption and favoritism in government, luxurious living and idleness among the rich, limited education among the poor, and cruelty in the Colosseum and Circus Maximus. The once strong character of the Romans weakened.

Discontent increased due to Rome's failure to extend the privileges of full citizenship to people in the provinces and to give the people a voice in government. When it became clear that the power of Rome was declining, the provinces tried to take advantage of Rome's weaknesses to establish independent nations of their own. As the Roman Empire gradually fell apart, a new social order emerged from its ashes. This new social order would be greatly influenced by the rise of Christianity.

SECTION 4 REVIEW

Knowing Key Terms, People, and Places
1. Define: **a.** princeps **b.** despotism **c.** mercenary
2. Identify: **a.** Praetorian Guard **b.** Claudius **c.** Vespasian **d.** Hadrian

Reviewing Main Ideas
3. Why can the Emperor Augustus be considered a wise and shrewd ruler?
4. How did Roman economic policies encourage unemployment and add to the burden of the poor?
5. Describe the economic conditions that contributed to the decline of the Roman Empire.
6. List three ways in which Roman society declined under the empire.

Critical Thinking
Perceiving Cause and Effect
7. What conditions do you think might lead officials to abuse power?

Arranging events in chronological order can help you understand them. A time line helps you learn the order of events by visually presenting the events in the order that they occurred. Study the time line to the right. Then, practice reading and analyzing a time line by following these steps.

1. **Identify the time period covered by the time line.** Study the entire time line to learn the span of history it covers. Answer these questions: (a) What is the earliest date shown on the time line? (b) What is the latest event shown? (c) How many years are covered by this time line?

2. **Determine how the time line is divided.** Most time lines are divided into equal periods of years, decades, or centuries. Answer the following questions: (a) Into what period of years is this time line divided? (b) Was the Roman conquest of Italy completed before or after the year A.D. 1?

3. **Study the time line to see how events are related.** Use the time line to answer these questions. (a) How long did the Roman peace last? (b) What events occurred in 270 B.C. and 264 B.C.? How might the first event have helped to cause the second?

4. **Use the time line to help you draw conclusions about the period you are studying.** By analyzing the time line and the material in your textbook, you can draw conclusions about major events in Rome's history. Answer the following questions: (a) What were some major Roman concerns during the period from about 300 B.C. to about 100 B.C.? (b) Some dates in history signal a major change or development. What dates on this time line would you identify as most important? Why?

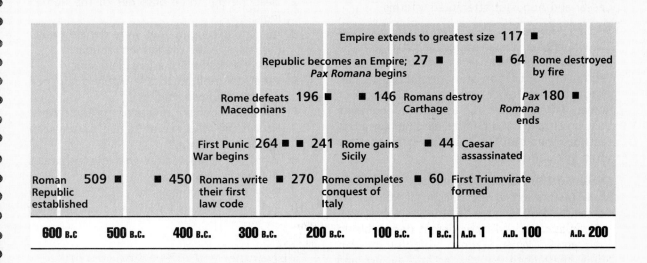

139

REVIEW

Section Summaries

Section 1 The Romans Formed a Republic Between 800 B.C. and 750 B.C., a group of people called the Latins migrated to central Italy and built farming communities south of the Tiber River. Access to the Mediterranean Sea gave the people many trading opportunities, while the hills offered protection from attack. Around 800 B.C. the Etruscans from Asia Minor conquered Rome and greatly influenced Roman culture. When the Etruscans were finally overthrown, the Romans set up a republican form of government. At first the patrician class controlled the government, but later the plebeians won more power.

Section 2 The Roman Republic Became an Empire The Romans began to conquer other Italian peoples and make allies for protection. Eventually Rome became a world power by conquering much of Europe and northern Africa. However, the years of fighting brought poverty and suffering to the Roman plebeians and widened the gap between rich and poor. The popular rulers Julius Caesar and Augustus attempted reforms.

Section 3 Rome Influenced Western Civilization The influence of Roman society and culture is still felt today. Roman law was a model for the world. Latin is the foundation of modern Romance languages such as French and Spanish. The work of Roman writers is still studied. Roman engineers built great roads and bridges, and Roman architects designed beautiful public buildings that are often imitated today.

Section 4 The Empire Declined and Split Apart Many factors led to the decline of Rome. The Roman system of government was slowly destroyed as cruel and incompetent rulers abused their power. When German Visigoths invaded Rome, the empire was divided into eastern and western halves. A poor economy, discontent among the social classes, and declining moral standards also contributed to Rome's decline. The Western Roman Empire ended in A.D. 476.

Key Facts

1. Use each vocabulary word in a sentence.
   - a. republic
   - b. patrician
   - c. plebeian
   - d. imperium
   - e. consul
   - f. veto
   - g. tribune
   - h. phalanx
   - i. maniple
   - j. gladiator
   - k. Romance language
   - l. vernacular
   - m. princeps
   - n. despotism
   - o. mercenary

2. Identify and briefly explain the importance of the following names, places, or events.
   - a. Etruscans
   - b. senate
   - c. Punic Wars
   - d. Pax Romana
   - e. Appian Way
   - f. Forum Romanum
   - g. Theodosius
   - h. Visigoths

Main Ideas

1. What historical evidence suggests that the Etruscans were highly civilized people?
2. Describe the three branches of the Roman legislature.
3. Identify two rights that were denied to all plebeians under the Roman republic.
4. Why was Rome not a true democracy?
5. What contributed to the highly disciplined nature of Roman soldiers?
6. List two important causes of the Punic Wars.
7. How is the influence of Roman culture seen in our world today?
8. What are three factors that made Marcus Aurelius a good emperor?
9. Why was the Roman Empire split in A.D. 395?
10. List some reasons for Rome's slow decline.

Developing Skill in Reading History

Each statement describes the effect of an action or event in Roman history. Read each statement carefully. Then, skim through the chapter to determine what was the cause of each effect. Finally, write a sentence explaining the relationship between the cause and the effect.

1. The Romans learned to build aqueducts, use bronze, and cultivate olive trees.
2. Hannibal was never able to gain a decisive victory against Roman forces.
3. France and Belgium became part of the Roman Empire.
4. Roman farmers and laborers were a giant mass of unemployed and unhappy citizens.
5. Octavian became the sole ruler and first emperor of Rome.

Using Social Studies Skills

1. **Making Generalizations** A variety of factors led to the decline of Rome. Which of these symptoms do you think might apply to our society today? What can people in the modern world learn from what happened in ancient Rome?
2. **Observing for Details** Carefully study the statue of the Emperor Claudius shown on this page. Make a list of the details that you notice in the statue. Which of these details do you think are especially important to understand-

ing the work? Are there any symbols that you would need to interpret before drawing conclusions about the statue?

Critical Thinking

1. **Determining Relevance** Why was the Mediterranean Sea thought of as the ancient world's highway for trade?
2. **Expressing Problems Clearly** What were the factors that made the First Triumvirate in Rome unsuccessful?
3. **Demonstrating Reasoned Judgment** What events during the rule of Augustus would lead people to say that he "found Rome of brick and left it of marble"?

Focus on Writing

Writing Paragraphs

Two critical elements of a paragraph are unity and coherence. **Unity** means that all of the sentences are closely related to the topic sentence and the main idea of the paragraph. **Coherence** means that all of the ideas in the paragraph are logically organized and clearly expressed. Other devices that help to hold a paragraph together are transitions (words such as *however* and *therefore)* and a strong concluding sentence.
Practice: Read the following paragraph:

Roman plebeians were unhappy. They had little money and no political power. Rome in A.D. 395 was not what it used to be! When Julius Caesar was in power, he had tried to help the poor. Many rulers after him didn't do so well. There were no moral standards. The Circus Maximus was an example. There were some good rulers, but they couldn't hold back the tide. The last emperor, Theodosius, died in A.D. 395. The Western Roman Empire fell in A.D. 476.

Does this paragraph have unity and coherence? Rewrite the paragraph, making sure that it has a clear topic sentence, a strong conclusion, and transitions where needed.

The Rise of Christendom

(4 B.C.-800)

1 **Christianity Began and Grew in Roman Times**

2 **Christianity Overcame Roman Persecution**

3 **Christianity Emerged as a Major Force**

▲ **Illustrating History** *This picture of Mary and Jesus was painted in a Roman catacomb in the early sixth century.*

The early Christians reached their favorite hiding place by traveling to the hills on the outskirts of Rome. They entered through damp, stone-lined stairways, their candles flickering in the dark. At the end of their journey, they were safe from Roman persecution.

The shadowy, underground caves the Christians relied on for safety were the catacombs. Catacombs were places where people buried their dead. The setting was frightening. At the foot of the stairways, visitors typically entered a large main room. Dim, mazelike corridors branched off from this central chamber. Graves enclosed by bricks or marble slabs were set into the walls. In this environment, Christians secretly carried on their religious services.

The Romans had built the catacombs and used them long before the birth of Jesus. Yet, it was the Christians who made them famous by using them as a refuge during the third and fourth centuries A.D. During this time, Roman leaders outlawed Christianity and persecuted many believers. But because Roman law regarded all burial places as sacred, small groups of Christians could enter the catacombs and practice their faith without fear.

Who were these early Christians and how did they become the victims of Roman persecution? In this chapter, you will read about the rise of Christendom.

4 B.C. / A.D.	A.D. 200	A.D. 400	A.D. 600

■ **A.D. 30**
The Romans
crucify Jesus

■ **A.D. 64**
The Romans condemn
Paul to death

A.D. 313 ■
Constantine grants
freedom of worship
to Christians

■ **A.D. 380**
Christianity becomes
the official religion
of the Roman Empire

■ **A.D. 520**
Benedict starts
the first monastery

▲ **Illustrating History** *Christians took refuge in catacombs to hold their services. A catacomb in modern-day Rome is shown above.*

1 Christianity Began and Grew in Roman Times

As you read, look for answers to these questions:

◆ How do we know about Jesus' life?
◆ How did Jesus relate his message to others?
◆ How did Christianity continue to spread after Jesus' death?

Key Terms: evangelist (defined on p. 144), disciple (p. 144), parable (p. 146), missionary (p. 147), epistle (p. 147)

In the first century A.D., Christians, or the followers of Jesus of Nazareth, numbered only a few. Hated and persecuted by Roman officials, this tiny religious movement seemed marked for destruction by the Roman Empire. As Rome's power declined, however, the Christian movement became stronger and stronger throughout parts of Europe, northern Africa, and the Middle East. In time, Christianity spread over the face of the earth and could claim more followers than any other single religion. Historians refer to the Christian world that arose from the ashes of the Roman Empire as Christendom.

The Gospels Are the Primary Sources of Jesus' Life

The story of Jesus' birth and the last few years of his life are well-known to most Christians. Since, however, Jesus himself wrote nothing and most of the Roman histories of the time do not refer to him, how have we learned about his life?

Most of what we know of the life of Jesus comes from four books in the New Testament of the Bible. These books are called

▲ **Illustrating History** *Jesus was born of Jewish parents in Judea and began to preach his message throughout Galilee after being baptized by John the Baptist. Jesus appears in this painting with two of his disciples.*

the Gospels. The word *gospel* means "good news" or "glad tidings" and refers to the religious message that Jesus taught to his followers. Four **evangelists,** or preachers, named Matthew, Mark, Luke, and John wrote the Gospels after Jesus' death.

From the Gospels, we learn that Jesus was born to Jewish parents, Mary and Joseph, in Bethlehem, a small village in the Palestinian province of Judea. Palestine, which then included parts of present-day Jordan and Israel, was an ancient country located along the eastern coast of the Mediterranean Sea. Historians date Jesus' birth at about 4 B.C.

When Jesus was about 30 years old, he was baptized in the Jordan River by his cousin, John the Baptist. John was a Jew who preached reform and repentance, which were symbolized by the act of being cleansed in the water of the river. Jesus' baptism was an important occasion because John hailed him as the long-awaited Messiah, or savior, who would free the Jews from foreign oppression.

The Greek word for messiah is *Christos*, hence Jesus was called Christ. After his baptism, Jesus began preaching. Soon, he attracted twelve close **disciples,** or followers, who traveled with him as he spread his message. These followers of Jesus are known as the apostles.

Jesus carried his message throughout Galilee (where northern Israel is today) and sometimes into Jerusalem, the religious center of Judaism. Wherever he went, enthusiastic crowds gathered to hear him. Sometimes, he spoke to small groups in synagogues, Jewish places of worship, or in people's homes. At other times, he spoke outdoors where thousands could gather to listen.

Many people found Jesus' popularity disturbing, and his message strange and potentially dangerous. Although the Roman government tolerated many religions, it required its subjects to worship the emperor as a god. Unlike the religions of the Roman Empire in which people worshipped many gods, the teachings of Jesus stated that there was only one God—the God of the Jewish tradition. These teachings clashed with the worship of the emperor and made Roman officials suspicious. They became even more suspicious of Jesus when some people began to call him "King of the Jews." Some even feared that Jesus might raise an army to try to topple the Roman Empire.

In about A.D. 30, Jesus led his disciples to Jerusalem for the annual celebration of the Jewish holiday known as Passover. After they had eaten their Passover meal, which later came to be known as the Last Supper, Judas Iscariot, one of Jesus' followers, helped the Roman authorities arrest Jesus. Jesus stood trial before Pontius Pilate, the Roman governor of Judea. Giving in to the demands of Jesus' angry accusers, Pilate charged Jesus with blasphemy, or contempt for the gods. He then sentenced Jesus to death by crucifixion, a common form of Roman punishment that consisted of being tied or nailed to a wooden cross and left to die. After only a few short years of preaching, Jesus died on a cross.

According to the Gospels of the apostles, however, Jesus rose from the dead and left the tomb in which his body had been laid. This event is known to Christians as the Resurrection. Forty days later, the Gospels say, Jesus ascended, or rose, into heaven. These events strengthened his followers' belief that Jesus was indeed the Son of God, the Messiah for whom the Jews had been

waiting many centuries. For these reasons, Jesus' crucifixion increased rather than decreased his following.

Jesus Preached a New Message

Much of what Jesus preached reflected the Jewish tradition in which he was born and raised. Like Jewish teachers, he preached that there was only one true God, the God of Israel. Jesus encouraged people to obey the Ten Commandments that were a part of Jewish law.

At the same time, Jesus added much that was new to the teachings of the Jews. He taught that God was the loving father of all people, not only Jews, and that all people

▼ **Chart Skill** *The Beatitudes are a section of Jesus' Sermon on the Mount. How might these lines have comforted his listeners?*

The Beatitudes

Blessed are the poor in spirit: for theirs is the kingdom of heaven.

Blessed are they that mourn: for they shall be comforted.

Blessed are the meek: for they shall inherit the earth.

Blessed are they which do hunger and thirst after righteousness: for they shall be filled.

Blessed are the merciful: for they shall obtain mercy.

Blessed are the pure in heart: for they shall see God.

Blessed are the peacemakers: for they shall be called the children of God.

Blessed are they which are persecuted for righteousness' sake: for theirs is the kingdom of heaven.

Blessed are ye, when men shall revile you, and persecute you, and shall say all manner of evil against you falsely, for my sake.

Rejoice, and be exceedingly glad: for great is your reward in heaven: for so persecuted they the prophets which were before you.

Paul of Tarsus

As a young man, Paul of Tarsus (see right) made no secret of his opposition to the fledgling Christian church. In fact, he actively persecuted Christians and sent many to prison. Paul was a devout Jew who had studied to be a rabbi. Then one day a few years after Jesus' crucifixion, Paul set out from Jerusalem on the road to Damascus, in Syria. Along the way, he had a vision of the crucified Christ. The experience changed his life. Not only did he embrace Christianity, but he also became the organizing genius of the new religion and one of its greatest teachers.

Born a few years after Jesus, Paul grew up in the community of Tarsus, in present-day Turkey. After his conversion, he chose to use his Roman name, Paulus, rather than using his Jewish name, Saul. He eventually came to be known as Paul the Apostle.

Paul spent 15 years traveling around the Middle East, spreading Jesus' message and reaching out to Jews and non-Jews alike. Everywhere he went, he held audiences spellbound. Paul also wrote several important letters home to his followers. These letters, called epistles, set guidelines for Christian behavior and eventually became

part of the New Testament. Paul is shown above in a sixteenth-century fresco.

1. What experience led Paul to accept Christianity?
2. How did Paul win people over to Christianity?
3. How has Paul's thinking survived to the current day?

---

were equal in God's sight. He promised that all who believed in him as the Messiah would enter the kingdom of heaven after they died. Jesus emphasized the brotherhood of all people—the highest and the lowest, the richest and the poorest—as children of God. To make his message understandable to uneducated people, Jesus often used **parables,** simple stories that taught moral lessons.

The Apostles Spread Jesus' Message

According to the Gospels, Jesus instructed his disciples to travel throughout the world and preach the gospel "to the whole creation." In the years after Jesus' death, his loyal apostles did what he had asked. They traveled throughout Palestine and into Syria, teaching Christian doctrines to all who would listen.

Of the eleven disciples, Peter had the most success. For more than 30 years, Peter diligently carried Jesus' message to the Jews of Palestine and converted many to the new religion. Eventually, however, he angered the Roman officials just as Jesus had. In an attempt to stop the spread of the new religion, Peter and other Christians were unfairly blamed for a devastating fire that swept through Rome. They were sentenced to death by the Emperor Nero. In the years to come, as the Roman Empire declined, Christians were persecuted repeatedly.

Paul Transformed Christianity into a Major Religion

Of all the members of the early Christian church, Paul of Tarsus became the most effective **missionary,** or person who works to teach and spread a particular religion. He was fluent in several languages, including Greek and Latin, which allowed him to spread his understanding of the Christian faith to many countries.

Paul separated Christianity from Judaism and gave structure and organization to the Christian faith. His **epistles,** or letters, eventually were made part of the New Testament. Because of his role in establishing a clear body of Christian beliefs, many authorities refer to Paul as the "second founder of Christianity."

During the course of Paul's missionary work, he attacked the Roman practice of worshipping the emperor as a god. He also criticized other Roman practices and beliefs, including the constant warfare and brutal gladiator shows. As a result, many of the people he tried to convert jeered or mocked him. He was imprisoned several times, and sometimes he was pelted with stones. Finally, in A.D. 64, he found himself among the many Christians whom the Emperor Nero condemned to death after the great fire in Rome.

Peter and Paul did not always agree on matters of Christian doctrine. Both men, however, made lasting contributions to the growth of Christianity and helped it to develop from a Jewish sect, or branch, into a full-fledged religion in its own right.

▲ **Illustrating History** *Paul was an important missionary of the early Christian church. His fluency in Hebrew, Latin, and Greek enabled him to win many converts. This twelfth-century enamel shows Paul, at left, preaching to Greeks and Jews.*

SECTION 1 REVIEW

Knowing Key Terms, People, and Places
1. Define: **a.** evangelist **b.** disciple **c.** parable **d.** missionary **e.** epistle
2. Identify: **a.** Christians **b.** Gospels **c.** apostles **d.** Last Supper **e.** Resurrection **f.** Peter **g.** Paul

Focus on Geography
3. In what part of the Roman Empire did Christianity originate and develop?

Reviewing Main Ideas
4. Why is Jesus called Christ?
5. How did the religious message that Jesus taught clash with the official Roman religion?
6. How was Jesus' message similiar to and yet different from the teachings of Judaism?

Critical Thinking
Perceiving Cause and Effect
7. Why do you think the worship of the emperor was important to the Roman Empire? How does this explain the Romans' hostility toward Christians?

2 Christianity Overcame Roman Persecution

As you read, look for answers to these questions:

◆ How were the early Christians treated in the Roman Empire before A.D. 313?
◆ What role did Constantine play in the history of Christianity?
◆ What factors helped Christianity to survive?

Key Terms: martyr (defined on p. 149)

Pontius Pilate and the Roman soldiers who carried out the order to crucify Jesus could never have imagined that, within a few hundred years, thousands of people throughout the Roman Empire would have declared

▼ **Illustrating History** *Peter was among those arrested and killed by the Romans. He is shown between two Roman soldiers in this sculpture.*

themselves the followers of Jesus Christ. As the Roman Empire declined and Christianity spread, a new world slowly emerged: the world of Christendom.

The Romans Persecuted Early Christians

As you read earlier, neither the crucifixion of Jesus nor the deaths of Peter and Paul could stop the growth of Christianity in the Roman Empire. As the map on page 150 shows, by A.D. 300 parts of Asia Minor and Greece, the eastern shore of the Mediterranean, and parts of northern Africa and western Europe were included in the expanding Christian world. Christianity continued to trouble Roman officials, who did not understand or like the new religion.

Because Christians refused to worship the emperor as a god, Roman officials began to view Christians as enemies of the state. In A.D. 64, the Emperor Nero began the first campaign to persecute Christians for their religious beliefs. Nero forced some Christians to fight wild animals in the colosseums to amuse the Roman mobs. Others he had soaked in oil and burned as torches. Still other Christians, including Peter and Paul, were crucified. These persecutions lasted for another 250 years in the Roman Empire.

The Romans' savage treatment of the Christians suggests that the issue of worshipping the emperor was not the only motivation for the persecutions. The power of the Roman Empire was beginning to crumble, and the Romans were looking for scapegoats to take the blame for this decline. They often blamed Christians for the political failures or military defeats of the empire. As Tertullian, a distinguished Roman convert to Christianity, wrote, "If the Tiber [River] reaches the walls, if the Nile [River] fails to rise to the fields, if the sky doesn't move, or the earth does, if there is famine or plague, the cry is at once, 'The Christians to the Lion!'"

Persecution was more intense during some periods than others. Emperor Marcus Aurelius, who ruled from A.D. 161 to A.D. 180 and was considered one of Rome's strongest rulers, persecuted Christians fiercely. He feared that people could not be Christians and loyal subjects of the emperor at the same time. Moreover, he resented the fact that Christians scorned military service.

The worst period of persecution came during the reign of Diocletian from A.D. 284 to A.D. 305. As an absolute monarch, Diocletian insisted that all people in the Roman Empire worship him as a god. Cruel punishments and sometimes death awaited those who refused. Diocletian outlawed Christian services, imprisoned the Christian clergy, and removed all Christians from public office. He also had the Scriptures, or Christian writings, burned, and ordered the razing of Christian churches.

The Roman Empire Eventually Tolerated and Accepted Christianity

Persecuting the Christians seemed to have exactly the opposite effect from what the Romans intended. Instead of viewing the martyrs, or people who had died for their faith, as criminals or revolutionaries, other Christians honored them. By honoring the martyrs, Christians drew attention to the unshakeable faith that their religion inspired. Many people were impressed by this show of faith and thus were attracted to Christianity. By the end of the third century, about 1 in 10 Romans had converted to Christianity.

Constantine. In A.D. 312, Constantine had an experience that profoundly affected his life and the course of Christian history. According to his writings, while preparing for battle, Constantine saw in the heavens a sign that told him to call upon the power of the Christian God. Constantine obeyed the sign and outfitted his soldiers with shields and banners bearing the Christian symbol of the cross. When his soldiers won the battle, which made him the Roman emperor, Constantine gave credit to the "God of the Christians" for the victory.

In the years that followed, the Emperor Constantine called often on the Christians for guidance. Although he continued to worship the pagan sun god as well, Constantine

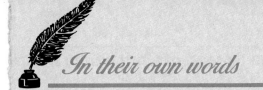

In their own words

The Persecution of a Christian Woman

When Perpetua of Carthage became a Christian in A.D. 203, she knew that she was risking her life. Perpetua's account of being persecuted was recorded by the writer Tertullian.

❝Because of his love for me [Perpetua], my father . . . tried to break down my faith.

'Father,' I said, 'do you see this vessel lying here, a waterpot, or whatever it is?'

'I see it,' he said.

'Can it be called by any other name than what it is?'

'No.'

'So neither can I call myself anything else than what I am, a Christian . . .'

After a few days we were cast into prison and I was terrified, for I had never known such darkness. What a day of horror! The stifling heat of the crowds there, the rough handling of the soldiers! Worst of all, I was tortured with anxiety for my baby. But then Tertius and Pomponius, the good deacons [leaders] who ministered to us, managed, at a price, to have us sent to better quarters of the prison for a few hours every day, and there I could [feed] my baby, already weak for want of food . . . I got leave to have my baby with me in the prison. Immediately, I regained my strength and stopped fretting [worrying] about the child, and the prison became a palace to me, and I would rather be here than anywhere else.❞

1. Why do you think Perpetua considered her prison cell a palace?
2. Do you think Tertullian is an accurate source? Explain.

149

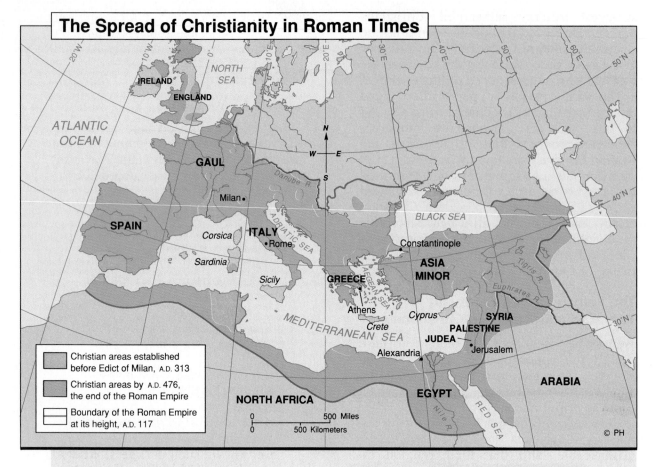

The Spread of Christianity in Roman Times

IRELAND
ENGLAND
NORTH SEA
ATLANTIC OCEAN
GAUL
Milan
SPAIN
Corsica
Sardinia
ITALY
Rome
Sicily
ADRIATIC SEA
Danube R.
BLACK SEA
Constantinople
ASIA MINOR
Tigris R.
Euphrates R.
GREECE
AEGEAN SEA
Athens
Crete
Cyprus
SYRIA
PALESTINE
JUDEA
Jerusalem
Alexandria
MEDITERRANEAN SEA
NORTH AFRICA
EGYPT
Nile R.
RED SEA
ARABIA

Christian areas established before Edict of Milan, A.D. 313

Christian areas by A.D. 476, the end of the Roman Empire

Boundary of the Roman Empire at its height, A.D. 117

0   500 Miles
0   500 Kilometers

© PH

Focus on Geography

Regions   Emperor Theodosius made Christianity the state religion and Christianity spread throughout the empire. By what year were parts of Ireland and England included in the Christian region?

considered himself a Christian. In A.D. 313, the year after his victory in battle, Constantine issued a statement extending complete freedom of worship to Christians. Known as the Edict of Milan, the statement proclaimed that "all who choose that religion [Christianity] are to be permitted to continue therein, without . . . hindrance [obstacles], and are not to be in any way troubled or molested."

The Edict of Milan marked a turning point in the history of Christianity. Persecution of Christians by the Roman government ended. Christians could now worship and spread their faith freely and openly, and in

the years ahead, the Christians did just that. Constantine himself was baptized a Christian shortly before his death in A.D. 337.

Theodosius.   Constantine put a temporary stop to any type of official religious persecution in the Roman Empire by making it legal to be a Christian. Another powerful emperor, Theodosius I, who ruled from A.D. 379 to A.D. 395, took Roman acceptance of Christianity a step further. He passed a law stating that everyone had to be a Christian.

In A.D. 380, Theodosius established Christianity as the official religion of the empire and made it unlawful to practice any other

150

religion. "It is our desire," Theodosius declared, "that all the various nations . . . should continue in the profession of that religion which was delivered to the Romans by the divine Apostle Peter. . . . We authorize the followers of this law to assume the title of Catholic Christians; but as for the others, since, in our judgment, they are foolish madmen, they will suffer in the first place the chastisement [criticism] of the divine condemnation, and in the second the punishment which our authority, in accordance with the will of Heaven, decrees." Unfortunately, this document opened the door to religious persecution. This time, however, it was the Christians who punished the non–Christians for their beliefs.

Christianity Had a Wide Appeal

Within the span of only a few hundred years, a small movement within the Jewish tradition spread rapidly as the map on page 150 shows. Eventually it would become one of the world's leading religions. This chain of events raises the question of how Christianity was able to attract so many devoted followers. The answers to this question are many.

First, the Christian message had a wide appeal. Christians welcomed converts from the peasantry as well as from the Roman army and the educated upper classes. It extended the hope of salvation to rich and poor alike in a time when life often was hard and brutal.

Second, although the early Christian movement took place during a period of peace in the Roman Empire, it was also a period of unrest. The state controlled all aspects of Roman life, including religion. Thus, many people were unhappy with Roman rule and particularly with the official religion, which they found meaningless. Many people hungered for a religion that would explain the meaning of life and offer moral guidance.

Before Jesus, the Jews had practiced a rich and satisfying religion that gave them a sense of their place in the universe and provided guidelines for their day-to-day behavior. The Jews, however, did not make an effort to convert non–Jews to their religion. Christians, by contrast, were constantly engaged in trying to convert others to their own faith.

Third, the Roman peace made communication and the exchange of ideas relatively easy. Rome's well-built and safe roads allowed Christian evangelists to carry their message throughout the empire.

Finally, the Christian message itself was perhaps the most essential element to the religion's success. Christians had an explanation for the suffering and evil in the world. They promised relief from this life's hardships and injustices in the next life. The Christian belief that each individual is responsible for making moral choices and for changing the world for the better inspired many people. Also, the Christian message of universal love and brotherhood won the hearts of many.

SECTION 2 REVIEW

Knowing Key Terms, People, and Places
1. Define: **a.** martyr
2. Identify: **a.** Tertullian **b.** Marcus Aurelius **c.** Diocletian **d.** Scriptures **e.** Constantine **f.** Edict of Milan

Reviewing Main Ideas
3. What were some of the reasons why the Roman government before Theodosius persecuted Christians?
4. How did Christians react to the martyrdom of their fellow believers?
5. What event in the life of Constantine made him decide to favor the Roman Christians?
6. What steps did Theodosius I take to promote the Christian religion?
7. Why did the Christian message appeal to such a wide audience?

Critical Thinking
Predicting Consequences
8. What changes would you expect to see in the Roman government, as well as in the Christian church itself, as a result of Rome's adoption of Christianity as its official religion?

151

3 Christianity Emerged as a Major Force

As you read, look for answers to these questions:

◆ What role did the Church play after the fall of the Roman Empire?
◆ How did monasteries preserve ancient learning?
◆ What lasting effects have Judaism and Christianity had on the development of Western culture?

Key Terms: orthodoxy (defined on p. 152), theology (p. 153), monastery (p. 154), hierarchy (p. 154)

Once Christians were free from the constant danger of being persecuted for their beliefs, church leaders could begin building the foundations for a stable religious organization. They needed to define the beliefs that would underlie all Church teachings. They also needed to establish a structure of authority in which each church official would have a definite role. In the fourth and fifth centuries, church leaders reached both those goals.

The Church Established a Common Body of Beliefs and Writings

At the time that Constantine became emperor of Rome, Christians agreed that Jesus was the Christ. They also agreed that he had been resurrected, or raised, from the dead. However, they disagreed on many other important matters concerning their religion. For nearly 300 years, Christians argued over what Jesus had taught. They also argued over whether or not Jesus had actually been a human being. They even argued over the way in which Christians should worship God. During the fourth and fifth centuries, Christian leaders finally began to take steps to settle these important disagreements among themselves.

One major issue that divided Christians early in the fourth century concerned the nature of Jesus and his relationship to God. Some Christians argued that Jesus, as the Son of God, must somehow inferior to or dependent on God. Other Christians argued that Jesus and God were, in all ways, equal and the same. In an attempt to get Christians to settle this debate once and for all, Constantine called the first ecumenical (meaning general or universal) council at Nicaea (ny SEE ah) near Constantinople in A.D. 325. After a long and heated debate, the council issued the Nicene Creed declaring that Jesus and God were of the same nature in every way.

The issuing of the Nicene Creed marked a crucial turning point in the history of the Church. For the first time, the leaders of a major religion had come together to debate and settle a religious issue. In so doing, the leaders demonstrated that the Church was to be an **orthodoxy.** Orthodoxy means that all the members of the Church had to follow the official teachings and practices of the Church. The council also began the process of planning how future church decisions were to be made.

Other important ecumenical meetings were called in the years that followed the Council of Nicaea. The Council of Chalcedon (KAL suh dahn), held in A.D. 451, declared that faithful Christians had to accept the teaching of the Church that Jesus was both fully human and fully divine at the same time.

Questions about the nature of Jesus were not the only sources of controversy in the early Church. For more than three centuries after Jesus' death, Christians argued over which of the many writings about Jesus and the Christian faith should be accepted. Eventually, an official list of Christian writing was established. Christians accepted the Jewish Scripture and referred to it as the Old Testament. They also organized the New Testament. This was made up of four accounts of Jesus' life, called the Gospels, some stories about how the apostles spread Jesus' message, twenty-one epistles written by Paul and others, and a book called the

Revelation of John. (A relevation is a revealing of divine truth.)

As the New Testament was being organized, a group of prominent leaders, later called the Church Fathers, wrote additional religious works that explained Christian **theology,** or beliefs about God. One scholar has called all of these writings "an ocean of commentary, persuasion, and teaching." Although not included in the New Testament, these works did become part of the body of important Christian writings.

One Church Father, Jerome, who lived from A.D. 340 to A.D. 420, translated the Old and New Testaments into Latin. Jerome's translation of the Bible became known as the Vulgate, or Bible in common use. The Vulgate made it possible for a large number of educated people throughout the Roman Empire to read the Christian message.

Of all the early Church Fathers, Augustine of Hippo, who lived from A.D. 354 to A.D. 430, was probably the most influential and best known. Augustine wrote several important books and an enormous number of letters on many topics, including morality, family life, and Church *dogma*, or the beliefs authorized by the Church.

Christian Ways of Worshipping Changed

The early Christian worship services were simple at first. They consisted of reciting prayers, reading from Christian writings, and singing hymns of praise. In addition, worshippers took part in a meal that symbolized the Last Supper of Jesus. Small numbers of Christians typically gathered for these services in private homes.

Gradually, the places of worship and the rituals themselves became more involved. Christians built impressive churches that were decorated with fine paintings and sculptures. Bishops wore elegant robes, read from beautifully bound Bibles, and preached to their congregations from gold-ornamented pulpits.

Some Christians banded together to lead lives of prayer, hard work, and charity.

▼ **Illustrating History** *This chapel in Ravenna, Italy, was built during the sixth century. St. Jerome is depicted at the upper right.*

These people, called monks or nuns, sought to preserve and spread the teachings of Christianity and to keep themselves free of sin by separating themselves from the rest of the world. The religious communities that they established throughout the Roman Empire were called **monasteries.**

One of the most famous monks was a man named Benedict, who lived from A.D. 480 to 543. He founded an order (distinct group) of monks known as the Benedictines in Italy. Benedictine monks were required to take a vow of absolute obedience to the abbot, the head of the monastery. They were not allowed to own any property—not even a book or a pen. They could not travel without permission, and their food and clothing were strictly regulated. They spent their

▼ **Illustrating History** *St. Benedict founded an order of monks devoted to a life of hard work and prayer. Here, he advises a fellow monk on a question of faith.*

time in study, prayer, and manual labor. The Benedictines worked from morning until night, for the Rule of St. Benedict stated, "Idleness is the enemy of the soul."

The Church Took on the Role of Government

By the time Theodosius made Christianity the official religion of the Roman Empire, the Church had already developed into a religious empire with considerable political power. The Church could now be called *catholic*, or universal, because it was a unified organization with a wide sphere of influence. The Church gradually had developed a **hierarchy,** that is, an organization of officials ranked in order of their power. Having a church hierarchy made it possible for decisions on all levels to be made and carried out. The councils of Nicaea and Chalcedon are two examples of meetings where important members of the church hierarchy gathered to resolve the theological issues.

The Church used the existing structure of the Roman Empire to establish its own hierarchy. Each important city in the empire had a bishop or a patriarch (respected church leader) who directed the affairs of the many smaller churches in the area. These smaller churches were run by prophets or teachers (eventually priests). In time, archbishops, who had their headquarters in the capital cities of the Roman provinces, presided over districts that were run by the bishops.

The bishop of Rome held the highest authority in the Church for two reasons. First, since Rome was the imperial capital of the Roman Empire, the bishop of Rome believed that he was entitled to be the highest authority. Second, a story from the New Testament said that Jesus had told Peter, "Thou art Peter and upon this rock I will build my church." Since Peter had been martyred in Rome, the bishop of that city claimed that Jesus had deliberately picked Rome as the foundation of the Church. This theory was not accepted by bishops in the

Eastern Roman Empire, however, so for many years Rome's power was shared with Constantinople. Nonetheless, the bishop of Rome took the title of pope, which means father.

After the fall of the Roman Empire, the Church played a major role in maintaining order in the Roman Empire. As the emperors lost power, the pope claimed political as well as spiritual authority. Christian laws and customs dominated people's lives as the Church assumed the role of government. The popes ruled as divine monarchs over all of Christendom, or the Christian world. During this period, the Church also spread Christianity to the peoples who invaded the empire, just as the conquests of Rome had helped to spread Roman culture in the preceding centuries. In this way, the Church became Rome's successor in political and spiritual power.

Monasteries Preserved Western Civilization

After the fall of Rome, religious orders such as the Benedictines and the Franciscans, founded by Francis of Assisi, performed a great service for future generations by preserving the knowledge and scholarship of ancient times. Monks and nuns copied classical Greek and Latin texts. Many of these valuable books might otherwise have been lost forever as a result of the chaos following the fall of Rome. It is through the painstaking work of these people that modern scholars have been able to learn about the philosophy of Plato and Aristotle and the history of the Roman Empire.

Besides preserving the great works of Western civilization for future scholars, religious orders also helped to spread knowledge among people living in their own time. Some religious orders established schools, usually for the children of nobles. Monks and nuns also experimented with new farming techniques and medical treatments (often involving the use of various herbs) that helped to improve the everyday lives of medieval people.

▲ **Illustrating History** *In a slow and painstaking process, monks copied ancient texts by hand and made them beautiful.*

Judeo-Christian Teachings Established a Lasting Heritage

The Judeo-Christian tradition refers to a body of common beliefs and values that have emerged from the combined influence of two major religions—Judaism and Christianity. The teachings of the Judeo-Christian tradition, however, have spread far beyond the realm of religion. Judeo-Christian values are found throughout Western culture and affect the thinking of those who are not Jews or Christians as well as those who are. For example, the idea that each human being is of value in himself or herself, apart from his or her relationship to a particular community, has roots in this tradition. Jesus taught that every person will be judged by God according to his or her own actions, not

155

Two Symbols of Religious Faith

How did early Christians recognize one another without giving away their identity to those outside their faith? In ancient Rome, they used a powerful symbol—the sign of the cross, made by a swift vertical and horizontal motion of the hand across the chest.

Until the early fourth century, most Christians feared punishment for displaying the cross too openly. Then, in A.D. 312, the Emperor Constantine declared himself a Christian. As a result, the cross soon became a popular image in Christian art (see right).

Less is known about the early history of the Jewish symbol, which is known as the Star of David (see left). This symbol dates back to 960 B.C. at least. Its use became widespread during the movement to create a Jewish nation in the late nineteenth century.

1. What did the sign of the cross represent to early Christians?
2. What was one result of Constantine's declaration of his belief in Christianity?

---

those of the person's ancestors. This idea underlies our modern views of justice.

Of course, many Judeo-Christian values are also found in other religions. For example, the emphasis on family life and respecting one's elders is found in many religions other than Judaism and Christianity. Similarly, the Judeo-Christian virtues of humility, charity, and honesty are common to many other religious faiths. Although other religions and philosophies share Judeo-Christian values, most of the basic values in our own culture have their roots somewhere in the Judeo-Christian tradition. That tradition lives on today and continues to influence Western thought, behavior, art, music, architecture, and politics.

In the next chapter you will read about the impact of the Church on the Byzantine Empire. You will also learn about the spreading influence of another of the world's major religions—Islam.

SECTION 3 REVIEW

Knowing Key Terms, People, and Places
1. Define: **a.** orthodoxy **b.** theology **c.** monastery **d.** hierarchy
2. Identify: **a.** Nicene Creed **b.** New Testament

Reviewing Main Ideas
3. Why did some men and women decide to live in religious orders?
4. What contribution did monasteries make to all future scholarship?
5. How are Judeo-Christian ideas reflected in modern culture?

Critical Thinking
Identifying Central Issues
6. Why would it be important for the church to set up a common body of beliefs and writings?

Locating and Gathering Information

Many good sources are available for locating and gathering information about historical topics. Some good sources include dictionaries, almanacs, encyclopedias, and periodical indexes. A card catalog is one of the most useful tools for locating and gathering information about a topic. The card catalog provides a complete listing of a library's resources.

Most card catalogs hold three separate cards for each book in the library. The author card is filed alphabetically according to the author's last name. The subject card is usually alphabetized within a general subject heading in the card catalog. The title card is arranged alphabetically according to the first word of the title, excluding *A, An,* and *The.* Each card shows the resource's call number, which classifies a book according to the Dewey Decimal System or to the Library of Congress System. You can use the call number to find where the book is located in the library.

Use the following steps to analyze how each card on the right might help you to locate and gather information.

1. **Study the cards to identify the information they provide.** The data shown on the cards are generally identical. Answer the following questions: (a) What is the title of the book? (b) Do the cards tell you whether or not the book is illustrated? (c) What is the book's call number?

2. **Use the cards to draw conclusions about the book's usefulness.** Notice that each card contains important information about the content of the book. Answer the following questions: (a) Would this book be a useful source of information about the early Christian church? (b) Do you think that this book describes the Christian church today?

3. **Analyze the purpose of the author, subject, and title cards in the card catalog.** Answer the following question: Why are there three separate cards for each book?

SUBJECT CARD

```
     CHRISTIANITY

270       Edwards, Otis Carl, 1928 -
Ed97   How it all began; origins of the
       Christian Church [by] O.C. Edwards,
       Jr.  New York, Seabury Press [1973]

           156 p.    illus.    22cm.

       "A Crossroad book."
       Bibliography:  p. 147-156.

           1.Christianity--Origin.  I.Title.
```

AUTHOR CARD

```
270    Edwards, Otis Carl,  1928 -
Ed97
       How it all began; origins of the
       Christian Church [by] O.C. Edwards,
       Jr.  New York, Seabury Press [1973]

           156 p.    illus.    22cm.

       "A Crossroad Book."
       Bibliography:  p. 147-156.

           1.Christianity  2.Church
       history--Primitive and early
       church  I.Title
```

TITLE CARD

```
       How it all began; origins of the
       Christian Church

270    Edwards, Otis Carl, 1928 -
Ed97   How it all began; origins of the
       Christian Church [by] O.C. Edwards,
       Jr.  New York, Seabury Press [1973]

           156 p.    illus.    22cm.

       "A Crossroad book."
       Bibliography:  p. 147-156.

           1.Christianity--Origin.  I.Title
```

REVIEW

Section Summaries

Section 1 Christianity Began and Grew in Roman Times Jesus of Nazareth spread his message throughout ancient Palestine. His followers believed that he was the Messiah of the Jewish people. Jesus attracted twelve close disciples who accompanied him on his travels. The Roman government was suspicious of Jesus' activities and disliked his teachings. He was accused of blasphemy and sentenced to be crucified. After his death, Jesus' followers continued to spread his ideas. Despite cruel persecution by the Roman government, Paul and Peter worked to establish Christianity as a religion separate from Judaism.

Section 2 Christianity Overcame Roman Persecution Christianity gained more and more followers as the Roman Empire declined. Emperors often blamed the Christians for problems in the empire and persecuted them. Christians were steadfast in their faith, however. Other people were inspired by their dedication and joined the new religion despite Roman oppression. In A.D. 313, Emperor Constantine made Christianity legal in the Roman Empire. Theodosius I later ordered all Romans to become Christians. The religion had a wide appeal because, in an age when life was hard, it offered hope of salvation, moral guidance, and universal brotherhood.

Section 3 Christianity Emerged as a Major Force Christians began to build a solid foundation for their church. Ecumenical meetings settled disagreements over Jesus' nature and his relationship to God. Christian writings were collected in the New Testament and translated into Latin, making it possible for many people to read Christ's message. Church leaders began to organize a church government with its own hierarchy and seats of authority in Rome and Constantinople. After the fall of Rome, the Church helped to keep order in the empire.

Key Facts

1. Use each vocabulary word in a sentence.
   a. evangelist   f. martyr
   b. disciple   g. orthodoxy
   c. parable   h. theology
   d. missionary   i. monastery
   e. epistle   j. hierarchy
2. Identify and briefly explain the importance of the following names, places, or events.
   a. Last Supper   d. Theodosius
   b. Paul   e. Nicene Creed
   c. Edict of Milan   f. Vulgate

Main Ideas

1. How did Jesus help uneducated people to understand his teachings?
2. How did the apostles help to spread Jesus' message after his death?
3. Why did Marcus Aurelius persecute the Christians? Did other emperors share his concerns? Explain.
4. How did the persecution of Christians have a different effect from what the Roman authorities intended?
5. Explain the significance of the Edict of Milan.
6. Why did the message of Christianity appeal to such a wide audience?
7. Once Christians were free from persecution, what were their most immediate needs?
8. How did the early church leaders settle disputes over religious issues?
9. How did Christians living in monasteries help to preserve ancient scholarship?

Developing Skill in Reading History

Analogies describe relationships. The analogy, *person : house :: bird : nest* means "person *is to* house *as* bird *is to* nest." The objects in both pairs have the same relationship to each other.

Use information from the chapter to complete the following analogies.

1. Matthew : evangelist :: Peter :_____.
   a. parable   **c.** gospel
   b. apostle   **d.** Jesus
   Explain the relationships in the analogy.
2. Diocletian : Christians :: Theodosius :_____.
   a. Romans   **c.** disciples
   b. orthodoxy   **d.** non–Christians
   Explain the relationships in the analogy.
3. Western Roman Empire : pope :: Eastern Roman Empire :_____.
   a. Paul   **c.** bishop of
   b. Augustine   Constantinople
                       d. apostle
   Explain the relationships in the analogy.

Using Social Studies Skills

1. **Forming Hypotheses** Read the following hypotheses. Then list two facts that would either support or disprove each.
   a. Some of the teachings of Jesus are not unique to the Christian religion.
   b. Early Christians were used as scapegoats by Roman emperors.
2. **Making Inferences** Study the Christian painting shown on the right. What inferences can you make from this painting about the way Christians thought about Jesus?

Critical Thinking

1. **Identifying Alternatives** The teachings of Jesus' apostles helped to spread Christianity. By what other methods did Christians spread their religious beliefs?
2. **Expressing Problems Clearly** How did Christianity continue Jewish traditions and how did it depart from them?
3. **Predicting Consequences** How would the growth of Christianity have been different if Jesus and his followers had not been persecuted by the Roman government?

Focus on Writing

Narrative Paragraphs

A **narrative paragraph** tells a story, either true or imaginary. When you write a narrative paragraph, you should focus on making the sequence of events clear to your readers. The topic sentence should set the scene of the story. Supporting details should be presented in chronological order and be closely related to the topic sentence. The **diction,** or the words you use, should be colorful—vivid action verbs, figures of speech, and sensory images.

Practice: Imagine that you are planning to write a narrative paragraph with the following topic sentence: "Early Christians were treated as scapegoats in the Roman Empire." Use information from the chapter to complete these prewriting activities:

1. List three specific events or facts that you would use to support the topic sentence.
2. List two vivid action verbs and one sensory image that you might use in your paragraph.

Geography in History

Geography, Grain, and Empire

The Greeks and Romans were not bold seafarers. It can be argued, of course, that to set sail on the open sea in small wooden ships without engines required some courage. The early sailors of the Mediterranean were careful. Their caution led them to make the most of the geographical features of the region. As Athens and Rome each came to power, they had to take regional geography into account to keep their empires.

High Lands, Rocky Shores

Mediterranean coasts are high and rocky and marked by thousands of bays and coves that make safe harbors for boats. Between the coves are promontories—ridges of land that jut out into the sea. Scattered across the open stretches of water are thousands of high, rocky islands.

In ancient times, sailors had no compasses to guide them, so they used landmarks by day or stars by night. They also knew places where they could cross the Mediterranean without losing sight of land.

Strong Winds

The sailing season lasted from about mid-March to mid-November. In the winter months, when the sea was considered too rough for sailing, trade, travel, and even warfare would stop. Sailors waited for the Etesian wind—a predictable wind that blows from the north during the summer.

This steady wind worked both for and against sailors. When sailing to Alexandria, Egypt, for grain, Roman ships had the wind at their backs. They might reach Alexandria in as little as 10 days. But, on the return voyage, they had to tack, or sail against the wind. It might take as many as 70 days before they reached Ostia, Rome's seaport.

Few Currents

The Mediterranean has little tidal action and few currents. However, the currents that do exist are quite strong. One current is created because the Black Sea is slightly higher than the Mediterranean. The current flows like a slow-motion, underwater waterfall through the Dardanelles, a strait leading into the Mediterranean from the Black Sea.

When Athens Ruled

Grain had to be brought from overseas because the Greeks' land was poor for farming. The Athenians built their empire by gradually taking command of the seas and thus controlling grain shipments. However, the Spartans challenged Athenian control in the Peloponnesian War.

The Athenians imported their grain from the shores of the Black Sea, taking advantage of the current that runs through the Dardanelles. In 405 B.C., after the war had been going on for 26 years, they sent their entire fleet of 180 ships to the Dardanelles to make sure the grain came through to Athens safely. But, the Spartans took control of the ships and stopped the grain from reaching the port in Athens. The Athenians were forced to surrender.

When Rome Ruled

In Rome, the emperors gave away 450,000 tons of grain every year. Such a great quantity could not be grown in the surrounding lands and had to be imported from Sicily and northern Africa. Because the sailing season was short, ships could only make one grain run a year. Emperor Augustus was the first to establish a regular grain fleet for this purpose, mostly to ensure that the people of Rome would not revolt against him.

Rome's need for grain became even more important in the centuries after A.D. 41. During this period, the position of emperor was often won by violence. Those who wanted to rule Rome soon learned that control of the empire meant control of the Mediterranean.

Focus on Geography

1. **Place** What features of the Mediterranean coast make it ideal for sailors?
2. **Location** Describe the route from Rome to one of the grain regions.
3. **Movement** In returning home after collecting grain, why couldn't the Greeks and Romans follow the same routes by which they had come?

Critical Thinking

Identifying Central Issues
4. Why was it vital for the Romans to extend their empire to include other lands around the Mediterranean?

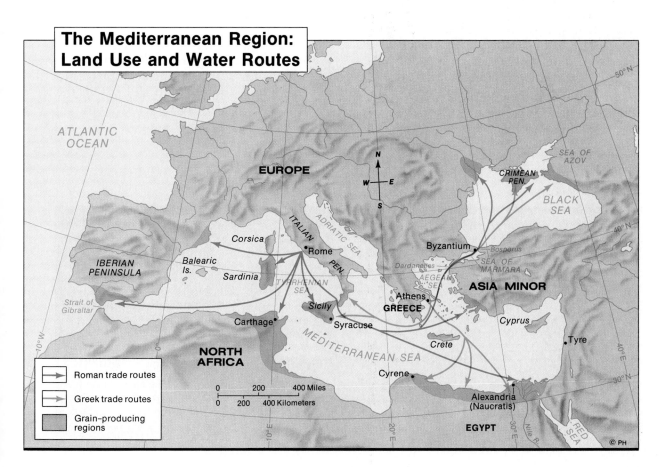

The Mediterranean Region: Land Use and Water Routes

Roman trade routes

Greek trade routes

Grain-producing regions

UNIT 1: Cradles of Civilization
(PREHISTORY–A.D. 500)

In 1954, archaeologists (AHR kee AHL uh jihsts)—scientists who study ancient people and civilizations—found a tomb that contained an ancient Egyptian funeral ship. It was about 4,600 years old. The archaeologists eagerly opened the tomb and were greeted by the aroma of cedar, the ship's wood. The tomb had been so well sealed that the original air had been trapped inside.

When archaeologists uncovered a similar funeral ship recently, they wanted to capture the air inside the tomb as well as preserve the condition of the ship. They concluded that the best way to accomplish their goal was to inspect the inside of the tomb without actually opening it. Workers used a highly advanced drill that could cut through the limestone tomb and still maintain an air-tight seal. Once the hole was drilled, a special camera, lights, and a video recorder were lowered into the tomb through the sealed opening around the hole. Pictures of the ship were studied on TV monitors and in still photographs. Finally, the scientists inserted small containers and captured their prize—a sample of 4,000 year-old air.

Archaeologists plan to open the tomb in the future when they have developed new techniques for studying ancient objects. In the meantime, the old ship still sits in the tomb where it has rested for more than 40 centuries.

▼ **Illustrating History**   *Below is an elaborately decorated Egyptian funeral ship made to guide the departed through the afterlife.*

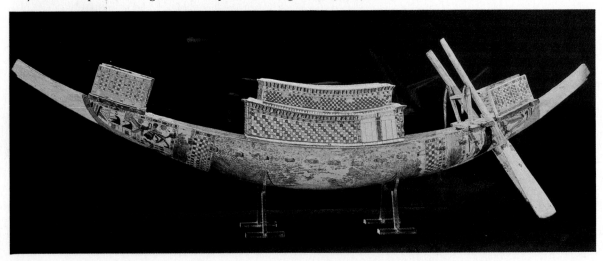

1 Early People

As you read, look for answers to these questions:

◆ What do we know about the Stone Age and the Bronze Age?
◆ What encourages the growth of a civilization?

Prehistory refers to that very long period before people invented writing. In fact, all human experience before about 5,000 years ago is prehistory. What we know about prehistory is the work of experts who have pieced together evidence of early people, such as bones, stone and metal tools, and crude pictures drawn in caves. Their work is not easy, however, and many questions are still unanswered.

Neanderthal People Lived in the Old Stone Age

Two million years ago, ice covered most of North America and much of Europe. The people who lived during this time, from 2 million B.C. to about 3500 B.C., used tools and weapons made of stone, so we call this period the Stone Age. One group of Stone Age people were Neanderthals (nee AN der THAWLZ). They were **nomads**—that is, they lived in small bands and moved from place to place in search of animals to hunt or food to gather. Neanderthals made simple tools and learned to control fire.

Neanderthal people were replaced by Cro-Magnon (kroh MAG nahn) people about 40,000 years ago. Slowly the Cro-Magnons refined their tools and made them more useful. They moved from caves and built their own shelters.

Farming Brought Important Changes

Sometime between 6000 B.C. and 3500 B.C., people made a new discovery that changed human lives forever. They learned to plant seeds and raise animals for food.

Farming brought about the *Neolithic revolution*. The food produced by farming allowed some people, for the first time, to spend substantial amounts of time at activities other than hunting or gathering food. Settlements grew, governments were established, and people developed new religious customs and ceremonies.

People Used Metals to Make New Tools

People started making metal tools sometime between 4000 B.C. and 3500 B.C. This new skill began a new age, which historians call the Bronze Age. The earliest bronze objects were found in the Middle East, where people learned how to get copper, tin, and other metals from the earth. Metal tools and weapons were much more effective than those made of stone.

Early Civilizations Took Root

When early people had mastered farming and had settled in communities, they began to think about how to improve their lives. They were becoming even more civilized. A **civilization** is an advanced society marked by the development and use of a written language, advances in the arts and sciences, and organized government.

In some places, farming communities gradually expanded into cities. For example, the first cities developed in river valleys in North Africa, the Middle East, and Asia. In early cities, government and religion laid down rules for living and working together.

REVIEW

1. Define: prehistory, nomad, civilization
2. Identify: Stone Age, Bronze Age
3. How do historians learn about early people?
4. How did Neanderthals get their food?
5. What changes were the result of farming?
6. Where did early cities develop?

2 In the Cradle of the Middle East

As you read, look for answers to these questions:

◆ How did geography help establish Egypt and Mesopotamia?
◆ What were the major contributions of these early civilizations?

Early civilizations were often the product of river valleys. This was true for Egypt and the civilizations of Mesopotamia (MESS uh puh TAY mee uh), where annual river flooding brought rich soil and water to the farmlands near the rivers.

A Civilization Grew in Egypt

Egyptian civilization, which lasted from 2780 B.C. to 1090 B.C., developed in the Nile River valley. Historians divide Egyptian history into three periods. The first is called the *Old Kingdom*, or the Age of Pyramids. The second is the *Middle Kingdom*, or the Age of Nobles, and the third period is the *New Kingdom*, or Age of Empire. Each period was ruled by one or more **dynasties**, in which political power was held and passed on within a single family. The **pharaoh** (FEHR oh), or ruler, held all governmental and religious authority in Egypt. All pharaohs were treated as gods and were considered immortal. To guard their spirits, the pharaohs ordered huge stone structures called pyramids to be built for their tombs.

The Egyptians applied the principles of mathematics and physics on a grand scale with their construction of the pyramids. They also invented a system of writing called **hieroglyphics** (HI er oh GLIHF iks), devised a sun calendar, and developed many new medicines.

Civilization Developed in Mesopotamia

Mesopotamia—which means the "land between the rivers"—is located between the Tigris and Euphrates rivers. Like the Egyptians, the people depended on annual river floods that made farming possible in their land. The rivers were also routes for transportation and communication. Unlike Egypt, the location of Mesopotamia made foreign invasion easy. Many different groups conquered this area—Sumerians, Hittites, Assyrians (uh SIHR ee uhnz), and Chaldeans (kal DEE uhnz)—and each group contributed to the development of the region's unique civilization.

The Babylonians ruled Mesopotamia from 2100 B.C. to 1100 B.C. Babylonians made great contributions to civilization. The first written code of law in history came from the Babylonian ruler Hammurabi (HAH moo RAH bee). Babylonians also made breakthroughs in arithmetic, astronomy, and writing—including an alphabet of more than 300 characters.

The Hebrews and Phoenicians Made Significant Contributions

The Hebrews were a nomadic people who settled in Palestine. Their religious belief of **monotheism** (MAHN uh thee ihzm) formed the basis of Judaism, Christianity, and Islam. In these religions, only one god is worshipped. The Hebrews also established a code of ethics, including the idea that no king or ruler is above the law.

The Phoenicians were merchants and traders who spread the gifts of other Middle Eastern civilizations from their ports on the Mediterranean Sea. One of their main contributions was the development of a 22-letter alphabet which is the forerunner of the alphabet we use today.

REVIEW

1. Define: dynasty, pharaoh, hieroglyphics, monotheism
2. Identify: Mesopotamia, Babylonians
3. What were two contributions of the Egyptians?
4. Who was Hammurabi?

3 Ancient India and China

As you read, look for answers to these questions:

◆ Where did civilization in India begin?
◆ What were some characteristics of the early civilizations of China?

Other civilizations, almost as old as Egypt and Mesopotamia, developed in river valleys of India and China.

Early Cities Grew in the Indus River Valley

Huge mountains isolate the **subcontinent** of India from the rest of Asia. The cities of Mohenjo-Daro (moh HEHN joh DAHR oh) and Harappa (huh RAP uh) developed in the valley along the Indus river. The cities were part of a rich, well-organized society that existed by 2500 B.C.

The Indo-Aryans (IN doh AR ee enz), a group from central Asia, conquered this advanced civilization around 2000 B.C. The Indo-Aryans established a rigid **caste** (kast) **system**—that is, a system that divided people into social groups from birth. The religious beliefs of the Indo-Aryans formed the basis of the Hindu (HIN doo) religion, the major religion in India today.

From 1500 B.C. to 1000 B.C., India was made up of many small kingdoms. Alexander the Great conquered northern India in 326 B.C. His rule provided the first link between Europe and India. Alexander ruled for only a few years. Then an Indian noble, Chandragupta Maurya (CHUN druh GUP tuh MAWR yah), united northern India and began its first dynasty. A golden age occurred 500 years later during the Gupta (GUP tuh) dynasty.

China Became a Great Empire

Like India, China is surrounded by barriers that once limited contact with outsiders. Many dynasties ruled in ancient China. In each dynasty art, writing, and learning

▲ **Illustrating History** *Siva, the Hindu god of both destruction and creativity, is shown in the sculpture above.*

flourished. Confucius was a great teacher during the early Zhou (joh) dynasty. He developed guides for both family life and government organization in China. His goal was to establish a stable, orderly society. His teachings remained a vital force throughout Chinese history.

Shi Huangdi (shee hwahng dee) became the first emperor of the Qin dynasty in 221 B.C. He tried to destroy the works of Confucius and other philosophers because he wanted to bring about change in China. He centralized political and military power and began building the Great Wall of China. Liu Bang (lyoo bahng) finally led a revolt against the unpopular Qin dynasty. Liu Bang became the first ruler of the Han dynasty and restored Confucian traditions.

REVIEW

1. Define: subcontinent, caste system
2. Identify: Mohenjo-Daro, Confucius
3. What contribution did the Indo-Aryans make to Indian life today?
4. What did Confucius teach?

Knowing Key Terms, People, and Places

1. Define: prehistory, nomad, civilization, dynasty, pharaoh, hieroglyphics, monotheism, subcontinent, caste system
2. Identify: Stone Age, Bronze Age, Mesopotamia, Babylonians, Mohenjo-Daro, Hindu religion, Confucius

Focus on Geography

3. Write the letter of each statement that tells why rivers were important to early civilizations.
   a. Rivers provided routes for transportation and communication.
   b. The high river banks were barriers that kept invading armies away.
   c. Rivers were a source of fresh water.
   d. Annual floods supplied new layers of fertile soil.
   e. Tourists were attracted by the many recreational activities available near rivers.
4. How has the geography of India kept it isolated from the rest of Asia for most of its history?

Reviewing Main Ideas

5. How do historians know about the groups that lived during prehistory?

6. In what ways did the Neolithic revolution change human life?
7. What part did religion play in Egyptian civilization?
8. Why was Mesopotamia the target of so many invasions?
9. What early civilization developed the first written code of laws?
10. Why was the invasion of Alexander the Great important to the development of civilization in India?
11. What was the major goal of Confucius's teaching?
12. Why are the early river civilizations called cradles of civilization?

Critical Thinking

13. **Making Comparisons** How were the early civilizations of Egypt, Mesopotamia, India, and China similar and different? Compare them in terms of geography and their contributions to civilization in general.
14. **Drawing Conclusions** Look at the photograph below of the pyramids. Name some of the skills and scientific knowledge you think the Egyptians needed to have to build such huge structures.

UNIT 2: Our Classical Heritage

(2000 B.C.–A.D. 476)

A woman leans over and turns a gold faucet. Water rushes out, filling her tub. Her husband is in another room reading. Their two children are playing in a pool in the backyard and a servant prepares the family's evening meal in the kitchen. The woman walks into the room where her husband is reading. They discuss the latest news from the Senate—what bills might pass, how individual senators will vote, and what certain groups hope to gain as a result of the possible legislation.

This isn't a scene from the present. It's a scene from ancient Rome in 27 B.C. The ancient Romans developed an elaborate civilization, which included, among other things, a form of self-government, great literature, a system of aqueducts with flowing water, and comfortable homes with many luxuries. The Roman civilization became a model for many civilizations that came later, including our own.

◀ **Illustrating History** *This portrait of a young couple from Pompeii (shown at left) and these coins (at right) provide a glimpse of everyday life in ancient Rome.*

167

4 The Gifts of Greece

As you read, look for answers to these questions:

◆ How did Greek civilization develop?
◆ How did people live in ancient Greece?

The people of ancient Greece were always willing to try new things. They experimented with democracy and accepted new ideas. They tried to separate science from superstition. As a result, they developed a civilization that is still admired today.

Greek Civilization Developed Slowly

The geography of Greece is partly responsible for the way that civilization developed there. The rugged interior mountains of Greece were difficult to cross and isolated the settlements that grew up along the coast. On the other hand, Greece has about 2,000 miles (3,202 kilometers) of coastline. Their access to the sea allowed the Greeks to trade with and learn about other civilizations.

Invaders swept through Greece several times during ancient history. The Minoans came from the island of Crete to establish an advanced civilization by 2000 B.C. They were followed by the Achaeans (ah KEE ehnz) 400 years later. The Achaeans were defeated by the Dorians (DOR ee uhnz) around 1200 B.C.

The Dorians founded many separate communities, or **city-states.** They were ruled by military leaders, who later became kings and who constantly fought with one another. However, the warring city-states did develop a common language and way of life. By 700 B.C., the Dorians became know as the Hellenes (HEL eenz), or Greeks.

Government Changed in the City-States

Each Greek city-state developed somewhat differently. For example, Sparta (SPAHR tah) was a military dictatorship. Spartans lived without luxuries and every male was raised to be a soldier. Athens (ATH enz), on the other hand, was the birthplace of **democracy**—a government in which citizens rule themselves. All free, male citizens, whether they owned land or not, could vote on laws and actively participate in the government of Athens.

The Greeks Fought Wars

The Greeks, led by Athens, defeated a Persian invasion in 480 B.C. The victory made Athens the leading Greek city-state and it entered a golden age. But the Spartans, fearing their loss of power, attacked Athens in 431 B.C. and began a series of wars known as the Peloponnesian (PEHL uh puh NEE shun) Wars, which Sparta finally won.

The Macedonians conquered and united the Greek city-states and spread Greek culture through a series of foreign wars. Under Alexander the Great, the Greeks conquered large parts of Europe, Asia, and Africa.

Greece Left a Lasting Legacy

The list of Greek achievements in architecture, literature, government, and philosophy is long. For example, Greek architecture, with its classic marble columns, is still copied today. The Greeks invented drama and wrote the first histories. They produced great **philosophers**—thinkers who carefully studied the world around them—such as Socrates (SAHK rah teez), Plato, and Aristotle, as well as many brilliant scientists and mathematicians.

REVIEW

1. Define: city-state, democracy, philosopher
2. Identify: Dorians, Peloponnesian Wars
3. What kind of government existed in Sparta? In Athens?
4. Name some contributions that ancient Greeks made to our world today.

5 Our Roman Heritage

As you read, look for answers to these questions:

◆ How did Rome become a world power?
◆ What factors caused the end of the Roman Empire?

Around 750 B.C., a group of people called Latins established the city of Rome south of the Tiber River in central Italy. Their descendants conquered all of Italy. From Italy, they acquired a huge empire that they ruled for more than 500 years.

Romans Formed a Republic

Between 800 B.C. and 500 B.C., the Romans were ruled by the Etruscans (ih TRUHS kuhns), a group from Asia Minor. Around 500 B.C., the Romans overthrew the Etruscan kings and set up a **republic**—a government in which elected representatives govern. Rome's republic, however, was not a true democracy because representatives were all **patricians**—members of the upper class. Rome's **plebeians** (plih BEE uhnz), or common citizens, had a very small voice in government.

The Republic Gained New Territory

From 450 B.C. to 270 B.C., the Romans conquered other Italian people. Rome then conquered much of Europe and northern Africa. In the Punic Wars, Rome defeated its leading rival, Carthage.

The years of fighting brought poverty and suffering to the Roman plebeians. A popular ruler, Julius Caesar, attempted to help the poor. After Caesar's death, however, Rome became a monarchy headed by an emperor.

The Empire Declined and Ended

The Roman Empire began its decline in the second century A.D. Some factors included cruel and incompetent rulers, the invasion of Rome by German Visigoths (VIZ uh

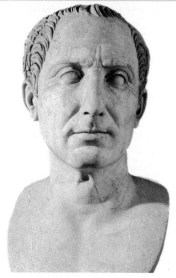

▲ **Illustrating History** *The bust above is of Julius Caesar, who ruled Rome as a dictator for five years.*

GOTHS), a poor economy, discontent among social classes, and declining moral standards. The Western Roman Empire ended in A.D. 476.

Romans Contributed to Western Civilization

Rome had a lasting influence on Western civilization. One contribution was the Roman system of law. Many of today's languages are based on Latin, and the works of Roman writers are still studied.

Roman engineers built great roads and bridges, and Roman architects designed beautiful public buildings that often are imitated today.

REVIEW

1. Define: republic, patricians, plebeians
2. Identify: Punic Wars, Julius Caesar
3. Why was the Roman republic not a true democracy?
4. Name three causes that contributed to the decline of Rome.

6 The Rise of Christendom

As you read, look for answers to these questions:

◆ How did Christianity develop to become the official religion of Rome?
◆ How did Christians build a stable religious organization?

In the first century A.D., Christians, or the followers of Jesus, were few. Despised and persecuted by Roman officials, this tiny religious movement seemed destined for destruction by the Roman Empire.

Romans Persecuted Christians

Jesus was a preacher in Palestine, a Roman colony whose people followed the religion of Judaism. His followers believed that Jesus was the Messiah of the Jewish people. Because the Messiah was supposed to deliver the Jews from foreign domination, the Roman government was suspicious of Jesus. In about A.D. 30, Jesus was accused of blasphemy and sentenced to death.

During his lifetime, Jesus attracted close **disciples,** or followers, who traveled with him. Jesus told them to spread his message throughout the world. After his death, the disciples worked to establish a Christian church. The two most effective disciples were Peter and Paul. Their message angered the Romans, and they were executed.

The Romans Embraced Christianity

Because Christians refused to worship the Roman emperor as a god, Romans viewed Christians as enemies of the state and persecuted them. But the execution of Jesus and his followers did not stop the growth of Christianity in the empire. Christians held to their faith, and others were drawn to Christianity by **martyrs**—people who died for their faith. The persecution of Christians finally ended when Emperor Constantine made their faith legal in A.D. 313. Emperor Theodosius I later ordered all Romans to become Christians.

Several reasons explain why Christianity appealed to Romans. First, Christianity offered hope of salvation in an age when life was hard and brutal. Second, people were upset with Roman rule and its old religion. Third, the well-built and safe Roman roads made it possible for Christians to spread their message. Finally, people were attracted by the Christian message itself, with its appeal of universal love and brotherhood.

The Christian Church Became a Major Force

Once free from persecution, Church leaders concentrated on building a stable religious organization. One of their goals was to define the beliefs that would underlie all Church teachings. Church leaders met and made major decisions about Christian **theology,** or beliefs about God.

A second goal of the Church was to establish a **hierarchy**—an organization of officials ranked in order of their power. The Church based its hierarchy on the existing structure of the Roman Empire. Each important city in the empire had a bishop or patriarch who ran the affairs of the churches in the area. All these bishops were under the authority of the bishop of Rome who held the highest rank in the Church. After the fall of Rome, this stable hierarchy played a major role in keeping order in the Roman Empire. The Church spread Christianity to invading groups of people and preserved the great works of Western civilization.

REVIEW

1. Define: disciple, martyr, theology, hierarchy
2. Identify: Peter and Paul, Constantine
3. What are three reasons why Christianity spread throughout the Roman Empire?
4. Describe the hierarchy of the early Christian church.

UNIT TWO REVIEW

Knowing Key Terms, People, and Places
Choose the best definition for each term.

1. republic
   a. a government in which all the citizens decide important issues
   b. a government ruled by a dictator
   c. a government in which elected representatives rule
2. hierarchy
   a. a structure of authority
   b. the beliefs of a church
   c. a democratic form of government

Identify the person, place, or group described below.

3. the Greek city-state that was ruled by a military dictatorship
   a. Athens
   b. Macedonia
   c. Sparta
4. the group that established Rome
   a. Etruscans
   b. Latins
   c. Visigoths
5. the Roman emperor who made Christianity legal in the Roman Empire
   a. Julius Caesar
   b. Theodosius I
   c. Constantine

Focus on Geography
6. What effect did the rugged mountains of Greece have on the growth of the settlements that developed along the Greek coast?

Reviewing Main Ideas
7. What were the series of wars known as the Peloponnesian Wars?
8. In what field of study did Socrates, Plato, and Aristotle make contributions?
9. What were the two major social classes in Rome?
10. How did the treatment of Christians change in the Roman Empire between the first and fourth centuries?
11. What were the major contributions of the Romans to Western civilization?

Critical Thinking
12. **Testing Conclusions** Evaluate the following opinion: "Christianity would never have become a major religion if it had not become the official religion of the Roman Empire."
13. **Formulating Questions** What questions would you ask a citizen of Athens about his city-state? State reasons why you would ask these questions.

Illustrating History ▶
Octavian and the senators met here at the Forum (now in ruins), the heart of the ancient city of Rome.

The Middle Ages

(A.D. 330–1453)

The Middle Ages are an important link between the ancient world and the modern world. As the Roman Empire fell, three civilizations rose to dominate the Middle Ages. Beginning around A.D. 300, the eastern part of the Roman Empire, known as Byzantium, rose to its height. Western Europe first declined and then gained strength as its people built a society that was based on trade and religious power. A third civilization grew from southwest Asia, home of a new religion called Islam. The map and the time line, linked by color, show where and when the three main civilizations of the Middle Ages developed.

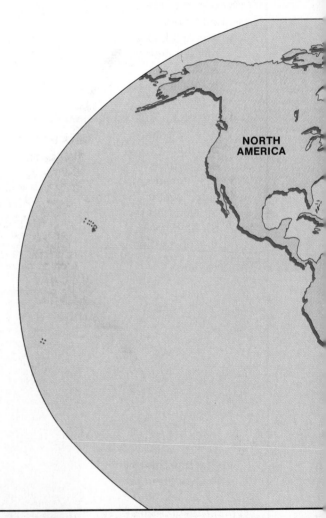

NORTH AMERICA

100	300	500	700

THE AGE OF BYZANTIUM 1 ■ A.D. 330 Constantinople becomes center of the Byzantine world   ■ A.D. 527 Justinian becomes emperor of Byzantium

MIDDLE AGES IN WESTERN EUROPE 2 ■ 570 Mohammed, founder of Islam, is born in Mecca

THE ISLAMIC WORLD 3 800 Charlemagne become Holy Roman Empere

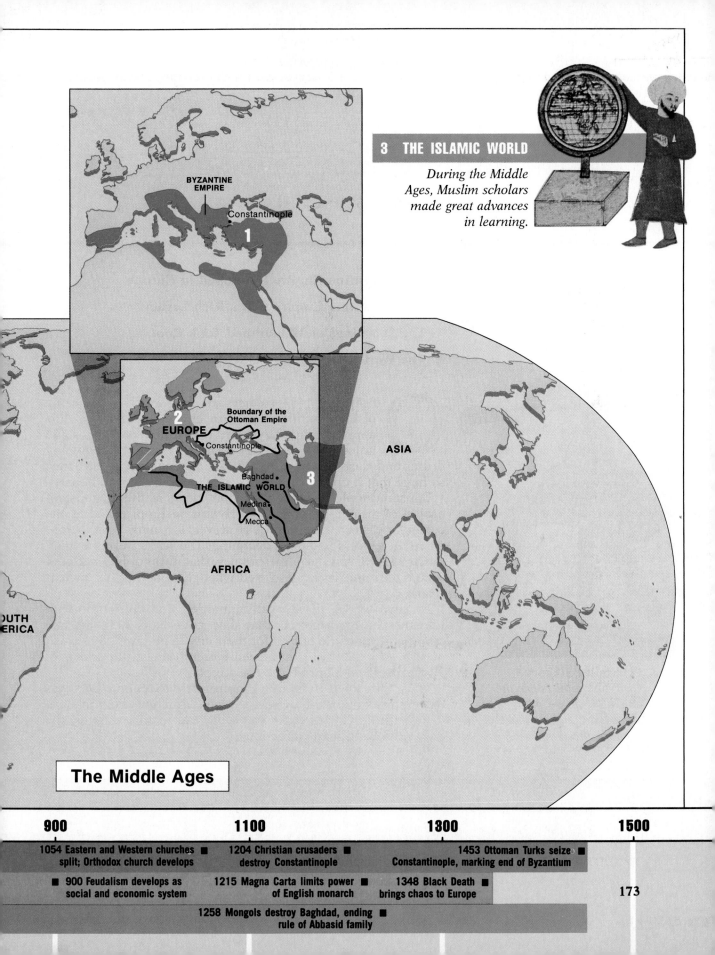

BYZANTINE EMPIRE

Constantinople

1

3 THE ISLAMIC WORLD

During the Middle Ages, Muslim scholars made great advances in learning.

Boundary of the
Ottoman Empire

2

EUROPE

Constantinople

Baghdad

THE ISLAMIC WORLD

3

Medina

Mecca

ASIA

AFRICA

**OUTH
ERICA**

The Middle Ages

900	1100	1300	1500

■ 1054 Eastern and Western churches
split; Orthodox church develops

■ 1204 Christian crusaders
destroy Constantinople

1453 Ottoman Turks seize ■
Constantinople, marking end of Byzantium

■ 900 Feudalism develops as
social and economic system

1215 Magna Carta limits power ■
of English monarch

1348 Black Death ■
brings chaos to Europe

1258 Mongols destroy Baghdad, ending ■
rule of Abbasid family

Byzantium and the Rise of Islam

(A.D. 330–1453)

▲ Illustrating History
Byzantine soldiers like the one in the above statue tried to defend Constantinople from the invading Turks.

1 **The Byzantine Empire Developed in Europe**

2 **The Byzantine Empire Left a Rich Legacy**

3 **The Teachings of Mohammed Took Root**

4 **The World of Islam Expanded**

On April 5, 1453, soldiers standing watch over the city of Constantinople saw an enormous cloud of dust approaching. They heard the rumble of wagons and horses, and soon they could make out the beating of drums and clashing of cymbals. It was the enemy Turkish army, so huge that it outnumbered the whole population of the city.

Constantinople had stood for 1,000 years as the magnificent capital of an empire called the Byzantine Empire and as the center of eastern Christianity. However, for many years before 1453, the empire had been declining. The Turks were the main enemy. The Byzantine emperor knew that it was only a matter of time before the Turks destroyed what remained of his ancient realm.

For two weeks, the Turks bombarded Constantinople with immense bronze cannons that shot stone balls weighing 600 pounds. The people prayed for their city to be saved, but it was no use. After the walls had been battered down, thousands of Turkish soldiers poured into the streets.

Thus, the fabled Byzantine Empire drew to an end. Why was this empire important in the first place? And how did it manage to last for 1,000 years? As you will read in this chapter, the answers lead in many directions.

A.D. 300	600	900	1200	1500

■ **A.D. 330**
Constantinople becomes the capital of the Byzantine Empire

■ **622**
Mohammed founds Muslim faith

■ **732**
Muslim armies are defeated at Tours, France

■ **1054**
Split between Orthodox and Roman churches occurs

■ **1453**
Constantinople falls into Turkish hands

▲ **Illustrating History** *This painting shows the Byzantine capital of Constantinople under attack by the Turkish army in 1453.*

1 The Byzantine Empire Developed in Europe

As you read, look for answers to these questions:

◆ How was the Byzantine Empire ruled and defended?
◆ How did the geography of Byzantium encourage its growth?
◆ How did the growth of the Christian church affect the Byzantine Empire?

Key Terms: schism (defined on p. 180)

The dramatic, final destruction of Constantinople that you have just read about ended this city's long, glorious history. During the Middle Ages, Constantinople was the capital of the flourishing Byzantine Empire. As the cultural and trading center of the world, its splendor eclipsed even that of Rome. In this chapter, you will learn about the Byzantine civilization and about the Muslim civilization that began to grow in the deserts of Arabia during the Middle Ages.

Constantine Began the Byzantine Empire

The Byzantine culture of southeastern Europe got its name from the ancient city of Byzantium, which, in turn, owed its name to its mythical founder, Byzas (BY zahs). It was founded in 667 B.C. In A.D. 330, a new city was built there by the Emperor Constantine, who renamed the city Constantinople (KHON stan tih NOH pul). It became the capital of the Eastern Roman Empire, which historians call the *Byzantine Empire*. From the fall of Rome in A.D. 476 until 1453, when the Turks captured Constantinople, this city was the nerve center of a great

175

▲ **Illustrating History** *This head of Emperor Constantine is from a colossus, or giant statue, in Rome.*

civilization and a great empire. While western Europe struggled for stability, the Byzantine Empire was flourishing.

The Geography of Constantinople Encouraged Growth

The ancient city of Constantinople is today the modern city of Istanbul (IHS tan bool). It is one of the most strategically located cities in the world. A careful study of the map on page 177 will show why Constantinople's location was important in ancient times. The city is surrounded on three sides by water, and the empire itself is located on both sides of the Bosporus (BOS poor uhs). It is at the entrance to the Sea of Marmara (MAHR ma ra). To the northeast lies the entrance to the Black Sea. To the southwest lie the Dardanelles (DAHR dah NELZ). These are *straits,* or narrow water passages, through which ships can enter the Aegean and from there go into the Mediterranean. The Dardanelles, the Sea of Marmara, and the Bosporus form a water passage that divides Europe from Asia.

The extent of the Byzantine Empire is difficult to define geographically. It alternately grew with conquest and shrank with defeat. Present-day Greece, Turkey, Bulgaria, Hungary, Yugoslavia, and Romania were all once part of the changing Byzantine Empire.

The Byzantine Rulers Had Absolute Power

Although the emperor of the Byzantine Empire was all-powerful, people did not worship him as a god. Instead, the emperor believed he was a servant of God and that God meant for him to be the ruler. The major emperors of the Byzantine Empire from A.D. 483 through 1025 were, in order, Justinian (jus TIN ee en), Heraclius (HEHR a KLEE uhs), Leo III, Basil I (BAZ il), and Basil II. Of these, Justinian was the most important, largely because of his contributions to law which you will read about later in this chapter. Justinian tried to reunite the Eastern Roman Empire with the Western Roman Empire. Although he was able to encourage trade between the two empires, he was unable to unite them. The Italian cities of Venice and Ravenna in the Western Empire became important trade centers, linking Byzantium with the West. Trade helped spread the culture of Byzantium to Italy and the rest of western Europe.

The Byzantine throne was not, by law, hereditary, although in many cases it was passed from father to son or daughter. A

▼ **Illustrating History** *The sixth-century mosaic below shows Emperor Justinian.*

future emperor was sometimes chosen by the reigning ruler with help from the army, the senate, the people, and the church. In the Byzantine Empire, the empress often held and exercised a great deal of power. As a symbol of this power, the portrait of the empress appeared on the coins of the realm. Sometimes, empresses ruled alone and exercised full power. The Empress Theodora was a constant, skillful, and cunning adviser to Emperor Justinian. Irene, the mother of Constantine VI, actually overthrew her son and ruled Byzantium alone as empress from 797 to 802.

Under Basil II, the Byzantine civilization reached its height. Maintaining a large empire required a strong military force and an effective group of administrators. The basileu (BAHZ ihl yoo), or king of kings, as the emperor of Byzantium was called, ruled absolutely. There was more wealth, pomp, and ceremony surrounding the emperor of Byzantium than the emperor of Rome. The enormous wealth, the many servants, the marble halls, and the gilded columns were used by Byzantine rulers to impress many visiting rulers from lesser states. These rulers were humbled even before they were presented to the Byzantine rulers.

Constantinople was the center of the Byzantine Empire. It was from there that the emperor ruled. The empire was divided into military districts. Each district was ruled by a general who was directly responsible to

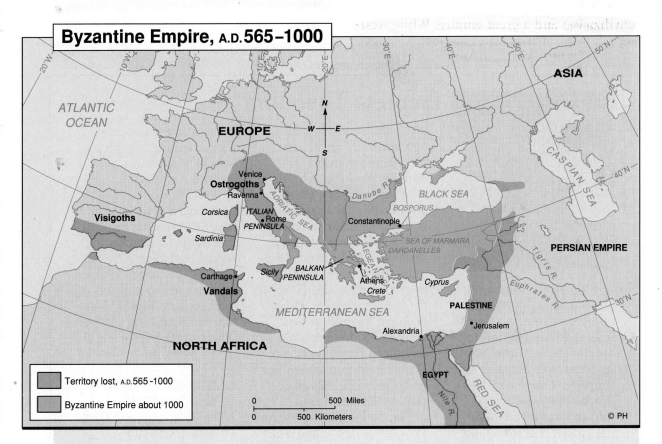

Byzantine Empire, A.D. 565–1000

Territory lost, A.D. 565–1000

Byzantine Empire about 1000

0   500 Miles
0   500 Kilometers

© PH

Focus on Geography

Place The Byzantine Empire reached its greatest size under Justinian. It was constantly threatened, however, by invading armies. What parts of the empire remained by about 1000?

the emperor. Soldiers in the district armies fought for the emperor and received the land on which they lived as payment. Because they were fighting for their own land or farms, they tended to be brave and loyal fighters.

Byzantine Military Power Defended the Empire

The skills of the army and navy were needed to defeat the many enemies who looked hungrily at the splendors and riches of the Byzantine Empire. The borders of the empire were constantly threatened. After Justinian's death in 565, the Lombards, the Avars, the Persians, and the Muslim Arabs tried to invade and conquer parts of the empire. The superior military strength of the Byzantines allowed them to remain in power until Constantinople finally fell to the Turks in 1453.

Because the Byzantines were nearly always at war, warfare became almost an art to them. Byzantine armies had capable military leaders and were ahead of their times in terms of fighting techniques. The music of military bands sent carefully trained and armed soldiers off to battle in high spirits. Mirrors were used to flash signals for attack or retreat. A medical corps was created to bring the wounded back from battle for the finest medical aid then available.

The Byzantine navy was no less renowned than the army. At one point, the navy launched 1,330 ships in a campaign against

BIOGRAPHY

Empress Theodora

In 532, all of Constantinople was in an uproar. People were rioting in the streets. Many wanted to overthrow the Emperor Justinian and his wife, the Empress Theodora. Justinian's advisers urged him to flee the city, but the steely Theodora told him that he had to stay and fight for his throne, even if he died in the attempt. "The imperial purple," she said, "is a glorious shroud." In the end, the emperor stood fast and crushed the rebellion.

Little is known about Theodora's background, but she was born around A.D. 500 and rose from a humble background. Her father may have been a bear-keeper at the Hippodrome. As a child, Theodora performed as an actress—a disreputable calling in those days. When Justinian chose her to be his wife, Byzantine nobles were shocked.

The Byzantine historian Procopius described Theodora as shifty and cruel. This was probably a biased view, but all historians agree that the empress was a woman of keen intelligence who sought power and destroyed anyone who blocked her path. Theodora had a gentler side, too. She tried to improve the status of women in Byzantine society by persuading Justinian to grant some rights to women.

Theodora died in 548. Her only existing portrait (above left) is in a mosaic in Ravenna, Italy.

1. Why did the nobles dislike Theodora?
2. In what way did Theodora try to help women in Byzantium?
3. How did she display courage during the rebellion of 532?

Crete. The navy used an ancient Greek device known as *Greek fire,* a combination of naphtha and sulphur, which could burn a ship on water. This device was an effective defense against those who tried to defeat Byzantium by sea power.

Religious and Political Differences Split Christianity

The strength of Byzantine emperors was reinforced by the support they received from the Byzantine church. The church was actually an arm of government and a willing supporter of the emperor. It was a political as well as a religious force.

Constantine was the first Christian emperor of the Roman Empire. Those who followed him as emperors of the Byzantine Empire were also Christians. Up to about the fifth century, the pope was looked upon as the head of all Christian churches. In the fifth century, however, a number of disagreements developed between the Eastern church and the Western church, which became known as the Roman Catholic church. The Eastern church gradually split into the Orthodox church and the Greek Orthodox church.

The first religious disagreement had to do with the nature of Jesus. Did he have one nature (divine) or two natures (human and divine)? The pope believed that Jesus had two natures. The *Monophysites,* who were influential in the churches of the East, believed Jesus had one nature (*mono,* or single). At the Council of Chalcedon (KAL SIH dahn) in A.D. 451, Pope Leo I decreed that Jesus, although one person, had two natures. This doctrine did not satisfy the religious leaders of the Eastern Orthodox church. Not only did they disagree with the doctrine, they also did not like the fact that the Roman pope had decided for them.

The second religious disagreement had to do with the question of whether or not images, or pictures and statues, were to be allowed in the church. The Eastern church opposed the use of images. The Western church believed that images were essential in helping people to imagine the divine. The

In their own words

Theodora Calls for Courage

In 532, a large-scale riot threatened to destroy Constantinople. Fearing for their lives, Emperor Justinian and his court considered fleeing the city. The following excerpt describes Empress Theodora's proud and courageous reaction to their fear. Her speech was recorded by the writer Procopius.

❝Now the emperor and his court were deliberating whether it would be better to remain or to flee in the ships. And many opinions were expressed on both sides. And the Empress Theodora also spoke as follows: 'As to the belief that a woman should not be daring among men or assert herself boldly, I consider the present crisis does not allow us to debate that. My opinion is that now is a poor time for flight, even though it bring safety. For any man who has seen the light of day will also die, but one who has been an emperor cannot endure to be a fugitive. If now you wish to go, Emperor, nothing prevents you. There is the sea, there are the steps to the boats. But take care that after you are safe, you do not find that you would gladly exchange that safety for death. For my part, I like the old saying that the empire is a fine burial cloth.' When the queen had spoken thus, all were filled with boldness and began to consider how they might defend themselves from their enemies.❞

1. Why does Theodora believe the emperor should remain in Constantinople?
2. What is meant by the old saying, "The empire is a fine burial cloth"? Why do you think Theodora mentions this saying in her speech?

controversy raged throughout the papacy of Leo III. Like the Monophysite controversy, it was never fully resolved, and it contributed to the permanent separation of the Eastern and Western churches in 1054.

This division, or **schism** (SIZ ehm), between the churches was political as well as religious. During the Middle Ages, the Roman Catholic church in the West was more powerful than the western monarchs. The patriarchs (PAY tree ARKS), or religious leaders of Constantinople, Alexandria, Antioch, and Jerusalem, were unwilling to recognize the power of the pope or the decision of Pope Leo I in the controversy over the nature of Jesus. They were also unwilling to recognize the decision of Leo III on the matter of the use of images in the church. In the East, the emperors of Byzantium dominated the Eastern church in a way that no emperor of the West could dominate the pope. The Byzantines were angry when the pope took it upon himself to preside over the coronation of Charlemagne as emperor of the Romans.

The schism between the Eastern Orthodox church and the Roman Catholic church goes on today. Throughout history, attempts to reconcile the views of these two churches have been unsuccessful.

Religion Influenced All of Byzantine Life

It is hard to appreciate the influence of religion in the lives of the Byzantines. From birth until death, church leaders were consulted for every important decision that had to be made. In political, artistic, and intellectual life, as well as people's personal lives, the role of the Eastern church was ever present. For men of high intelligence, a career in the church offered great opportunities for advancement.

All Byzantines were caught up in religious questions about the nature of the Trinity (the union of Father, Son, and Holy Spirit) and the relationship between the human and the divine. The quarrels that took place over these issues were not confined to religious or intellectual circles. These questions were discussed among the population as a whole. In fact, questions of religion dominated daily conversation.

SECTION 1 REVIEW

Knowing Key Terms, People, and Places
1. Define: **a.** schism
2. Identify: **a.** Constantinople **b.** Greek fire **c.** Monophysites

Focus on Geography
3. What bodies of water surrounded the ancient city of Byzantium?
4. How did the location of Byzantium affect its progress and wealth?

Reviewing Main Ideas
5. Describe the strength of the Byzantine army and navy.
6. What did the Council of Chalcedon decree?

Critical Thinking
Perceiving Cause and Effect
7. What effect did the schism in the Christian church have on the Byzantine Empire?

2 The Byzantine Empire Left a Rich Legacy

As you read, look for answers to these questions:

◆ Why was the trade economy of Byzantium so prosperous?
◆ What were the major contributions of the Byzantine Empire?
◆ Why did the Byzantine Empire fall?

Key Terms: guild (defined on p. 181)

During the height of the Byzantine Empire, its thriving economy led to increased trade and exploration. At the same time, the stability of the economy allowed people to devote time and energy to the advancement of education, law, art, and architecture. While the Roman tradition was the basis of many of the empire's achievements, a rich and unique Byzantine culture developed.

The Byzantine Economy Centered Around Trade

Most people in the Byzantine Empire farmed for a living. Trade, however, was more important. The wealthy merchants of the world and their goods found their way to Constantinople. At first, animal skins and furs, salt, wine, slaves, spices, and precious gems were common articles of trade.

Later, silk became a major item of Byzantine wealth. Around 550, the Byzantines learned the secret of making silk. For hundreds of years, only the Chinese had known how to do this. Legend has it that two monks brought silkworm eggs to Constantinople in the hollowed out parts of their walking sticks. From this unusual beginning, a great silk industry, controlled by the emperor, grew and prospered and added to the wealth of the Byzantine Empire.

In ancient Rome, trade was not a highly regarded activity. People of noble birth avoided business. In Constantinople, the opposite was true. The emperors and nobility

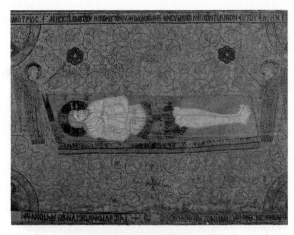

▲ **Illustrating History** *The much-admired art of Byzantine silk making is shown in this tapestry of the body of Jesus.*

of the Byzantine Empire were deeply concerned about the economy of the nation, and they encouraged business activities of all types. In fact, Justinian is credited with encouraging the journeys to China that led to the knowledge of silk making.

Constantinople was a city of trading and manufacturing. Cloth, jewelry, metal, and enamelware were made using the latest methods. It was in Constantinople that master builders of churches, palaces, and other great buildings learned their craft, as did decorative artists. Thus, the city of Constantinople became a commercial center for a rich variety of goods on their way to Asia and Europe.

Because of its vital role in the economy of the empire, the city of Constantinople was governed separately. It had a police force to catch criminals and courts of law to determine if they were guilty. Workers were organized into trade guilds. **Guilds** were organized groups of people in the same trade or craft who set rules to uphold standards and protect their members. Those merchants who tried to cheat buyers were punished by the guilds. The economic vitality of the Byzantine Empire was one reason for its long life. Because it was a dynamic and prosperous empire, it could support a huge government bureaucracy, an extravagant court, and costly wars.

Byzantium Contributed to Education, Law, Art, and Architecture

For many years, Latin was the language of the Byzantine government. It was then replaced by Greek. The great writings of Greece and Rome would have been lost forever if teachers, students, and monks in the Byzantine Empire had not copied them. Education was free and available to everyone in accordance with a church law that stated: "Knowledge is a gift of God, therefore it cannot be sold." Libraries and their books and schools and their teachers played leading roles in the growth of Byzantine culture. Many of the emperors were themselves learned, and universities supplied educated people for government service.

The missionaries Cyril and his brother Methodius knew the Slavic language and invented an alphabet that is still in use today by the Russians, Bulgarians, and Serbs. The brothers are sometimes called the "Apostles to the Slavs." (The Slavs were an Indo-European people who lived in the region around Kiev [KEE yef] in Russia.) The *Cyrillic* (suh RIHL ihk) *alphabet,* as it is called, played a significant role in bringing Christianity to those countries.

The Byzantines lived according to Roman law, which dominated people's everyday lives. Roman law also dominated the affairs of state. The Emperor Justinian is remembered mostly for having his lawyers organize and simplify the laws of ancient Rome. The *Corpus Juris Civilis* (KOR puhs joo rihs kih VIL is), a Latin title that means *Body of Civil Law,* was organized into four parts.

The first part, which was known as the *Code,* included all the laws created since Emperor Hadrian. The second part was the *Digest,* which contained the laws of the Roman republic as well as a summary of opinions of famous lawyers. The third part, the *Institutes,* was a general textbook on law. The laws created by Justinian were included in the *Novellae* (no WELL eye). While the first three volumes were written in Latin, this last volume was written in Greek. Eventually, Greek became the official language of the Byzantine Empire.

The Byzantines contributed a distinctive look to art and architecture. The church of St. Sophia was built in the sixth century and still stands today in all its beauty. The round dome of the church, which is characteristic of Roman architecture, was fitted to a square building. Interior columns, though borrowed from the Greeks, were modified to create a new type of column known as the Byzantine column. The architectural style of this church has influenced the art and architecture of other churches throughout the ages. With its mosaic inlays and marble veneers, or coverings, on the walls, St. Sophia was so colorful that one Byzantine historian said, "One would think we had come upon a meadow full of flowers in bloom. Who would not admire the purple tints of some and the green of others, the glowing red and glittering white, and those to which nature, like a painter, has marked with the strongest contrasts of color?"

The Byzantine Empire lasted for over 1,000 years. During most of that time, it was a model of prosperity and stability. Constantinople, as the center of the empire, became a blend of Roman, Christian, Greek, and Middle Eastern influences. One of the greatest contributions of the empire was that it preserved much of the heritage of many different people.

The Byzantine Empire Fell to the Turks

Although Byzantium was a continuation of the Roman Empire, it was a civilization with a character of its own. It also served as a cultural bridge between East and West.

Through its vast trade and many wars, Byzantine civilization spread to southern Italy, the Balkan countries, and western Russia. Constantinople preserved the learning of Greece and Rome and fought one invader after another. In so doing, it gave Europe the time it needed to develop. Constantinople was a major city when Paris and London were still small towns. Eventually, however, the Byzantine Empire collapsed.

There is no one explanation for the fall of the Byzantine Empire. Numerous wars made its enemies stronger and the empire

▲ **Illustrating History** *The Byzantine church of St. Sophia became an Ottoman mosque and is now a Turkish museum.*

weaker. Its church seemed more concerned about worldly power than about spiritual power. Its emperors gave the people little voice in the government and few opportunities to improve themselves.

The Byzantine Empire never recovered from two deadly blows that were struck against it. In 1204, the Christians from Europe traveled to Palestine to drive out the Seljuk Turks, who were said to have spoiled Christian holy places in Jerusalem. Envious of the wealth they saw in the Byzantine Empire, the warriors from Europe forgot who their enemies were and destroyed the city of Constantinople. The second and final blow occurred when the Ottoman Turks battered down the walls of Constantinople and captured the city in 1453. Most historians agree that this date also marks the fall of the Byzantine Empire.

Byzantine Civilization Influenced Russian Culture

Between 700 and 800, the Slavic peoples living to the north of Constantinople began a series of wars with the Byzantine Empire in an attempt to conquer lands around the Black Sea. By about 850, however, Byzantine missionaries had persuaded many Slavs to become Christians. Viking raiders then invaded Slavic territories and established the early Russian state. In about 988, the Russian ruler Prince Vladimir, who ruled from the city of Kiev, chose Byzantine Christianity as his kingdom's official religion. Thus, the pattern of Russian culture was determined for future centuries. Russian literature, art, laws, and customs were all shaped and influenced in some way by the Eastern Orthodox church and by the Byzantine civilization itself.

SECTION 2 REVIEW

Knowing Key Terms, People, and Places
1. Define: **a.** guild
2. Identify: **a.** Cyril and Methodius **b.** *Corpus Juris Civilis* **c.** Prince Vladimir

Reviewing Main Ideas
3. List five common articles that were traded in Constantinople.
4. How did teachers and monks help to preserve Byzantine culture?
5. Describe the architecture of St. Sophia.
6. What event and date marks the fall of Constantinople?

Critical Thinking
Drawing Conclusions
7. Why do you think that the Byzantine attitude toward trading was so different from that of Rome?

3 The Teachings of Mohammed Took Root

As you read, look for answers to these questions:

◆ How did the geographical conditions of the Arabian Peninsula affect the lives of the Bedouins?
◆ What did Mohammed teach?
◆ What do people of the Islam religion believe?

> **Key Terms:** oasis (defined on p. 185), mullah (p. 187), kismet (p. 187), jihad (p. 187)

During the Middle Ages, the Byzantine civilization shone brilliantly, but it did not shine alone. The civilization of the Muslim world was equally bright.

While eastern Europe was dominated by the Orthodox church and western Europe by the Roman Catholic church, the Middle East and northern Africa were dominated by the faith of Islam. The word Islam means surrender, that is, surrender to the will of God. Those who follow the teachings of Islam are called Muslims.

The Geography of the Desert Affected Arab Culture

The Arabian Peninsula, where the world of Islam began, is a large peninsula. (See the map on page 190.) Most of it is a vast desert that determined how its inhabitants lived.

The Bedouin (BED oo wihn) people were nomads living in the desert of the Arabian Peninsula. Descendants of these early Bedouins continue to live in the desert areas and are still referred to as Bedouins. With little rain and few, if any, rivers, the Bedouin had to develop a special way of life. That way

▼ **Illustrating History** *The Bedouins in this photograph still live as nomads.*

▲ **Illustrating History** *Above, Mohammed delivers his farewell sermon to his followers.*

of life often centered around areas that had permanent sources of underground water. Such a fertile area in the middle of a desert is called an **oasis.**

The dromedary, or one-humped camel, is a clumsy beast that is also known as the ship of the desert because it provides transportation over the vast expanses of sand. Because the dromedary can live and work for long periods of time without water, it made the life of the Bedouins easier.

The Bedouins lived in loose tribal association with other clans, and informal rules governed their relationships with one another and with other desert tribes. Because catching and punishing thieves and murderers was the responsibility of individual victims rather than a defined legal system, bitter feuds often developed among the tribes. This kind of life bred a fierce independence, a resistance to authority, and an ability to withstand hardship.

Two cities, 250 miles apart from each other, were to play important roles in the development of Islam. These cities—Mecca and Medina—owed their existence to their location in a semifertile strip of land near the Red Sea. To the Bedouins, Mecca was a holy city. Worship centered around the shrine called the Kaaba (KAH bah). In it were statues of male and female gods and a special black stone believed to be from heaven. Probably it was once a meteor.

The inhabitants of Mecca and Medina were part merchant, part nomad. Many Bedouins left the desert to live in the city for only a portion of the year. While there, they sought to earn their livings through trade. As their population grew, those Bedouins who remained in the desert had difficulty finding adequate food to feed their families. They were ready for a leader who would promise to improve their lives. The leader proved to be a holy man called Mohammed (moh HAHM ihd).

Mohammed Began the Muslim Faith

Mohammed, who lived from 570 to 632, was the prophet of a new faith. He was born in the holy city of Mecca in Arabia and, as an

185

adult, became a merchant. At the age of 25, he married a wealthy widow. As a merchant, Mohammed crossed the desert with caravans carrying goods to distant parts of the Arabian Peninsula. During the course of his journeys, he learned a lot about Greek culture as well as about Christian ideas and the Hebrew religion.

Mohammed was a thoughtful man who often liked to get away by himself to think about the world around him and his place in it. He often went into the desert alone to pray and to decide what he should do. By the time he was 40, he believed that he had been chosen by *Allah* to preach a new faith to the world. Allah is the Muslim name for God. Although Mohammed absorbed and accepted many of the ideas of the Jewish and Christian faiths, he believed that his revelations, which he said came from Allah, were the last true ones.

Mohammed was an eloquent speaker and freely shared his revelations. He taught that there is one God—Allah—and that one person—Mohammed—was his prophet. Just as other faiths do, Islam teaches kindness, humility, patience, and charity. The holy book of Islam is the Koran. Like the Old Testament and the Hebrew Talmud, the Koran is more than a collection of religious ideas. It contains rules of conduct, including rules on how to treat children, slaves, and animals. The Koran even became the basis for Islamic law and government.

The new religion was slow to gain popularity at first. There were many Arabs who would not accept Mohammed as a prophet of Allah. Instead, they preferred their own tribal gods. Since Arabs looked to Mecca as their holy city, Mohammed thought that Mecca would be a good place in which to spread his ideas. He thought that in this

LINKING PAST AND PRESENT

The Call to Prayer

As Mohammed began to win converts in the early seventh century, he wondered how he should summon them to prayer each day. Should he blow a trumpet like the Jews or ring bells like the Christians? Deciding to try something new, he had his slave, Bilal, stand on the roof of his mosque and call the Muslims together.

Bilal was the first muezzin (myu EZ ihn). The muezzin proclaims the call to prayer five times a day, crying out: "Allah is great. There is no God but Allah. Mohammed is the prophet of Allah. Come to prayer. Come to salvation. Allah is great. There is no God but Allah."

Today, the call of the muezzin (shown in photograph at right) can still be heard. But, in most places, his call is now recorded and broadcast from loudspeakers.

1. What does a muezzin do?
2. Why did Mohammed decide to use a muezzin?
3. How has the muezzin's job changed?

religious center the people would leave their tribal gods and follow him, but he was proven wrong.

In 622, Mohammed was driven out of Mecca and fled to the city of Medina. The flight from Mecca to Medina is called the *Hegira* (hih JY ruh). In Medina, among the Arabs of the desert, Mohammed began to win converts to his ideas. The year 622 was a turning point for the followers of the Muslim faith. In fact, followers of the Muslim faith count the year 622 as Year One.

Muslims Share Basic Beliefs

The Muslim faith imposes a number of obligations upon its faithful. Every Muslim must repeat the Muslim creed in Arabic: "There is no God but Allah, and Mohammed is His Prophet." It is the duty of every Muslim to pray five times daily. Muslims are required to fast from sunrise to sunset during the holy month of *Ramadan* (RAM uh DAHN). Ramadan is the ninth month in the Muslim year and the month in which Mohammed received his revelations. Every Muslim must make a pilgrimage to Mecca at least once during his or her lifetime. Finally, every devout Muslim must give charity (alms) to the poor. These five obligations of every faithful Muslim are called The Five Pillars of Islam.

The Kaaba is the center of worship in the holy city of Mecca. Any Muslim can lead people at prayer, but those who are highly educated in Muslim teachings and laws, called **mullahs** (MUL ahs), are treated with great respect and are considered holy. All worshippers are considered equal, however, and there is no organized clergy or order of priests.

Like Christians, Muslims believe in a Judgment Day. In the Muslim faith, however, whether or not one goes to paradise, or heaven, is predetermined, that is, determined beforehand by Allah. No amount of prayer or good works can change Allah's plan. Muslims believe in **kismet** (KIHZ met), or that one's time of death and one's fate in another world is predetermined. One

▲ **Illustrating History** *Shown above is a view of Mecca and its pilgrims as they appear today.*

sure way of getting into paradise, however, was to die in a **jihad** (jih HAHD), or a holy war, against non-Muslims. Because of this belief, Muslim fighters were courageous warriors. The deep faith and courage of the Muslims made possible the rapid expansion of Islam and the Muslim Empire as you will read in the next section.

187

In his teachings Mohammed sought to protect women. Thus, for example, Mohammed assured women the right to choose a marriage partner. They were also assured the right to inherit property. Although a man could easily divorce a woman, a contract agreed to in advance of a marriage set forth the conditions under which a divorce would be granted. It listed the rights to property a woman would have when the marriage ended. Mohammed did not require Muslim women to be veiled. This became a custom later, as the Muslim religion was influenced by the lands to which it spread. Some of the practices toward women in some modern Muslim countries are different from what Mohammed taught. As Elise Boulding noted in her book *The Underside of History,* "One could interpret the history of women in Islam as one long struggle on their part to maintain the rights enunciated [spelled out] by Mohammed."

▲ **Illustrating History** *Mohammed tried to improve the status of Muslim women, such as those shown in the painting above.*

Islam Improved the Status of Women

Arabs who were not Muslims could have as many wives as they could afford. In the Muslim faith, a man was permitted to have only four wives. The teachings of Mohammed limited the number of wives a man could have at one time. Mohammed sought to improve the role of the family, and at the same time, tried to strengthen the position of women in society.

4 The World of Islam Expanded

As you read, look for answers to these questions:

◆ How far did the world of Islam spread?
◆ How was the world of Islam ruled?
◆ What did the ancient Muslim culture add to civilization?

> **Key Terms:** caliph (defined on p. 190)

Many people accepted the teachings of Islam because they were clear and simple. They also were rooted in many of the traditional beliefs of Judaism and Christianity as well as in the beliefs of the Arabs. Mohammed had succeeded in establishing a religion that inspired its followers to the point of dying for its cause. He also preached the use of a jihad to spread his teachings.

The Islam World Grew Through Conquest

The conquests of Islam began when Mohammed's forces took the city of Medina and defeated the Bedouin tribes outside the city. Later, Mohammed conquered Mecca and made it the religious center of Islam. When Mohammed died in 632, he had conquered a large part of Arabia and had set an example for future jihads.

In a wave of conquest that swept across the Middle East and moved westward, Muslims conquered Arabia, Persia, Egypt, northern Africa, and the Iberian Peninsula (Portugal and Spain). The Muslims then crossed the Pyrenees Mountains and were about to conquer France and western Europe. They were stopped by Charles Martel at the Battle of Tours (toorz) in 732. As the map on page 190 shows, in a little over a hundred years from its birth in 622, the Muslim faith had spread across a part of Europe.

The Muslim drive westward carried Islam into northern Africa and Spain. In a drive eastward, the Muslims spread Islam just beyond the Indus River. Eventually, their influence was felt in the Malay Peninsula, Java, the Philippines, and even in China. By the middle of the eighth century, the Muslim Empire extended farther than the empires of Rome and Persia combined.

▼ **Illustrating History** *Both a palace and a fortress, the Alahambra was completed in 1354 by Muslims in Granada, Spain. It is a fine example of Islamic architecture.*

Powerful Caliphs Ruled Islam

After the death of Mohammed, the Muslim world was ruled by **caliphs** (KAY lihfs) who had total power except for the fact that they could not change religious teachings. The first four caliphs were elected by Arab leaders. These Caliphs were Abu-Bekr (ah BOO BEK ehr), Omar (OH mar), Othman (OTH mahn), and Ali (AH lee). These four are revered to this day in the Muslim faith. It was under Caliph Omar that the greatest of the jihads were carried out. Upon the death of Ali, however, the traditional way of choosing caliphs ended.

At that time, the leader of the Umayyads (oo MY adz), an Arab family, proclaimed himself as the caliph and established the *Umayyad Caliphate* with Damascus as its capital. With leadership passing from father to son, the Umayyad Caliphate lasted from 661 to 750. It was then overthrown by Abu al-Abbas (a BOOL a BAS), a descendant of one of Mohammed's uncles.

Under the *Abbasid* (uh BAS ihd) *Caliphate*, which Abu al-Abbas established, the Islamic Empire reached its peak. A new capital was established at Baghdad (BAG dad). Especially splendid was the Abbasid

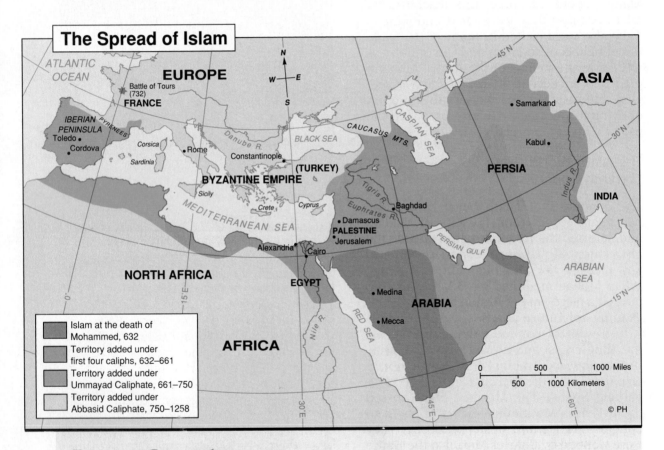

The Spread of Islam

Legend:
- Islam at the death of Mohammed, 632
- Territory added under first four caliphs, 632–661
- Territory added under Ummayad Caliphate, 661–750
- Territory added under Abbasid Caliphate, 750–1258

Focus on Geography

1. **Place** Muslims pray toward Mecca five times a day. In what direction would a Muslim in Toledo, Spain, face?
2. **Location** What direction is Medina from Mecca?
3. **Movement** What physical feature slowed the Umayyad caliphs as they tried to conquer France?

Great Religions of the World

Religion:	Hinduism	Buddhism	Judaism	Christianity	Islam
Founders:	No single founder	Buddha	Abraham	Jesus Christ	Mohammed
Symbols:	Sanskrit lettering for *om*	Meditating Buddha; wheel of life	Star of David	Cross	Crescent and star
Holy Books:	The Vedas	Four Noble Truths	The Torah	Holy Bible	Koran
Origins:	Prehistoric India	Northern India (500 B.C.)	Palestine (2000 B.C.)	Palestine (A.D. 30)	Arabia (A.D. 600)

▲ **Chart Skill** *Compare and contrast Hinduism and Christianity. What is similar about them? What is different?*

Caliphate of Harun Al-Rashid (hah ROON ahl rah SHEED). His heroic deeds are described in the stories called the *Arabian Nights*, which include the tales of "Aladdin and His Lamp" and "Ali Baba and the Forty Thieves." (According to legend, the narrator of these stories had to tell one story a night to the caliph for "a thousand and one nights" or be put to death.) The Abbasid Caliphate tried to kill all the princes of the overthrown Umayyads, but it failed. The grandson of the last Umayyad caliph escaped to Spain and established a separate and independent *Umayyad Caliphate of Cordova* (KOR doh vah). This caliphate lasted from 756 to 1036.

Although the two caliphates never recognized or acknowledged each other's authority, both Baghdad and Cordova became centers of power and prosperity. Two power centers, however, were not enough for rival claimants to the caliphates, and other centers of authority developed. One of these centers was located in Cairo, Egypt.

As a result of political disunity, the power of the caliphs declined and fell under the control of the Seljuk Turks. For over 200 years, the caliphs were largely subject to the rulers of Turkey.

Although the Muslims never achieved political unity after Mohammed's death, they were united by a common faith and a common language. All Muslims were required to know the Arabic language so they could read the Koran. Because all Muslims were required to make a pilgrimage to Mecca at least once in a lifetime, the city became a meeting ground for Muslims from many centers of the world. The Muslim world also was united by ties of trade and commerce. At a time when people in Western Europe were living on isolated manors, Muslim merchants were traveling to Africa, Asia, and Europe.

The Muslim Culture Influenced Civilization

As the Muslim religion spread, a Muslim culture began to develop. The scientific findings of the past were translated into Arabic. In fact, Arab textbooks on diseases were the best in their fields until the seventeenth century. Avicenna (AV ih SEHN uh), a tenth-century Arab physician and philosopher, is still famous for his written summary of all medical knowledge up to that time.

Arabs also made important contributions to astronomy and mathematics. Many of the caliphs who governed parts of the Arab world were eager to learn. They brought in scholars from all parts of the world. Educated Muslims, Greeks, and Jews contributed a great deal to Arab knowledge.

Since the Muslim faith does not allow human images to be created in artwork, the early Muslims did little in the way of painting or sculpturing. Allah, their God, was the one and only Creator of Life, so artistic depictions of anything lifelike was forbidden. They did, however, create exquisite carpets of geometric designs, and their architecture was magnificent. Their mosques (mosks), or churches, were often covered with intricate floral and geometric designs that represented the plan and beauty in Allah's laws. The Muslims also made notable contributions to literature. They read and translated the great books of Greece and Rome into Arabic. They share with the Byzantines the credit for preserving the learning of Greece and Rome. The *Arabian Nights* is the best-known work of Arab storytellers. Its stories of life and adventure have been translated into many languages.

The Muslim world prospered through trade and war. Baghdad (in what is present-day Iraq) and Cairo (in Egypt) became great cities. Trade and travel were carried on in nearly all parts of the known world. Silk fabrics and carpets were skillfully woven, and it was the Muslims who introduced cotton cloth to Europe. At Samarkand (SAM ehr KAND) and Baghdad, Muslims built factories for the manufacture of paper from rags. These cities with their shops, mosques, synagogues, churches, jails, cemeteries, orphanages, insane asylums, hospitals, schools, and colleges were among the most advanced in the world.

Contacts between Europeans and Muslims were few at first. The Christians and Muslims were religious rivals. For a while, Europeans doubted the worth of Muslim scholarship. Yet contact grew as Muslim learning spread from the great centers of Cordova and Toledo in Spain to the rest of western Europe. The two cultures also came into contact during the Crusades. As contacts grew, an appreciation of the contributions of Muslim civilization grew. Contacts between Europeans and Muslims were made in Jerusalem, Sicily, and southern Italy. Jewish scholars, some of whom knew Hebrew, Greek, and Latin as well as Arabic, played an important role in making translations of Greek and Latin classics available to scholarly Europeans.

The prosperity and growing culture of the world of Islam provided a stark contrast to western Europe after the fall of the Roman Empire. Gradually, as the Byzantine Empire faded and the Arab world divided into many rival caliphates, a new day began to dawn for Europe.

SECTION 4 REVIEW

Knowing Key Terms, People, and Places
1. Define: **a.** caliph

Reviewing Main Ideas
2. Describe the conquests of Islam by 732. What present-day countries were conquered by the Muslims?
3. What happened during the Abbasid Caliphate that led to the establishment of a separate caliphate at Cordova?
4. What were the main elements that united all Muslims?
5. Describe the Muslim contributions to literature and art.

Critical Thinking
Recognizing Bias
6. What bias made Europeans doubtful about the worth of Muslim civilization?

Reading Tables

Statistical tables present large amounts of data clearly and concisely. Historians use tables as a means of gathering data and illustrating trends.

The steps below will help you learn how to read and interpret data in a table.

1. **Determine the kinds of information shown in the table.** The title of the table and the labels for each vertical column and horizontal row tell you exactly what is presented. Answer these questions: (a) What is the table's title? (b) What time period is covered?

2. **Read the information in the table.** Note that membership in religious groups is given both in total number and in the percentage of all religious groups. Answer the following questions: (a) How many people were Muslims in 1930? in 1960? (b) What percentage of the population was Hindu in 1960? in 1988?

3. **Study the table to find relationships among the figures.** You can use the data in this table, for example, to compare membership in different religions or to trace changes in one religion over a period of time. Answer the following questions: (a) What was the world's largest religion in 1988? (b) Which religion showed the largest increase in its percentage of total world membership between 1930 and 1988? (c) Which religion gained the greatest number of members between 1930 and 1988?

4. **Use the data to draw conclusions.** Use your understanding of the data to reach conclusions about changes in religious membership between 1930 and 1988. Answer the following question: What two conclusions can you draw about changes in world religious membership since 1930?

Membership in Major World Religions* 1930–1988					
	1930		**1960**		**1988**
Buddhists	150	7.5%	150	5.4%	307	6.2%
Christians	682	34.1%	870	31.2%	1619	32.9%
Confucianists, Taoists	351	17.5%	350	12.5%	203	4.1%
Hindus	230	11.5%	329	11.8%	648	13.1%
Jews	16	.8%	12	.4%	18	.4%
Muslims	209	10.5%	429	15.4%	840	17.1%
Shintoists	25	1.2%	50	1.8%	4	.1%
Other or none	337	16.9%	602	21.5%	1284	26.1%
Total	2000	100.0%	2792	100.0%	4923	100.0%

*Estimated (members in millions)

REVIEW

Section Summaries

Section 1 The Byzantine Empire Developed in Europe Located at the water passage between the Mediterranean Sea and the Black Sea, Constantinople became the nerve center of a great civilization. The Byzantine Empire was a world leader in trade and culture and had a nearly invincible army and navy. All-powerful emperors such as Justinian were not regarded as gods but as servants of the Christian God. Religion dominated the political life of Byzantium. Disputes over religious issues ultimately led to a schism between the Roman Catholic church and the Eastern Orthodox church.

Section 2 The Byzantine Empire Left a Rich Legacy The strong, dynamic economy of the Byzantine Empire was one factor that allowed it to remain in power for such a long time. The emperors and the nobility encouraged and participated in the economy, which was centered in Constantinople. Justinian's *Corpus Juris Civilis* systematized the laws of the Byzantine Empire. The empire also made advances in language, art, and architecture. Eventually, after years of costly foreign wars, the empire weakened. In 1453, the Ottoman Turks captured Constantinople, and this date usually marks the fall of the Byzantine Empire.

Section 3 The Teachings of Mohammed Took Root The world of Islam began on the Arabian Peninsula, which was populated by a tribe of nomadic people called the Bedouin. The cities of Mecca and Medina were important centers of religious worship and trade for the Bedouins. Mohammed, who was born in the holy city of Mecca, believed that he had been chosen by Allah (God) to spread a new faith to the world. Although he was driven out of Mecca at first, in Medina, Mohammed won many converts to his religion, which was called Islam. Muslims believe that Mohammed was Allah's prophet, and they obey his laws concerning prayer, rituals, charity, the pilgrimage to Mecca, and family life.

Section 4 The World of Islam Expanded Since Islam glorified religious wars, the Muslim world grew in territory and influence through military conquests. Through a series of jihads, the Muslims conquered Arabia, Persia, Egypt, northern Africa, Spain, and Portugal. Although Arab scholarship was not respected by Europeans at first, its worth was finally recognized and its influence spread, especially in the field of medicine. Eventually, a lack of political unity caused the power of the caliphs to decline, but Muslims remained united by a common language, the pilgrimage to Mecca, and ties of commerce.

Key Facts

1. Use each vocabulary word in a sentence.
   a. schism
   b. guild
   c. oasis
   d. mullah
   e. kismet
   f. jihad
   g. caliph
2. Identify and briefly explain the importance of the following names, places, or events.
   a. Istanbul
   b. basileu
   c. Cyrillic alphabet
   d. church of St. Sophia
   e. Kaaba
   f. Mohammed
   g. Hegira
   h. *Arabian Nights*

Main Ideas

1. Describe the state of the Byzantine military.
2. What religious disputes led to the split between the Eastern and Western churches?
3. How did trade help the Byzantine Empire to survive for 10 centuries?
4. Identify three factors that contributed to the fall of the Byzantine Empire.
5. Describe the teachings of Mohammed.
6. How did the jihad contribute to the development of the Muslim Empire?
7. Identify three cities that became centers of Islamic authority.
8. Why does Muslim art consist mostly of elaborate carpets and mosques?

Developing Skill in Reading History

Read each of the statements below. Explain why you think each is a **fact** (a statement that can be proven true) or an **opinion** (a statement that represents a personal feeling or a subjective judgment).
1. The Muslim religion encourages violence.
2. The teachings of Islam are rooted in many traditional beliefs of Judaism and Christianity.
3. The pilgrimage to Mecca is not as important as the jihad in the Muslim faith.
4. Mohammed protected women because he liked them more than men.
5. Mullahs should be treated with great respect because they are holy.

Using Social Studies Skills

1. **Using Visual Evidence** Study the painting below. It is an official portrait of Jahangir holding a picture of his father, the Emperor Akbar. How might a historian know that the people in the painting are Muslim emperors? Are there any religious elements in the work? If so, explain what they might mean.

2. **Locating and Gathering Information** Select one of the Byzantine emperors mentioned in the chapter for a short report. Do some library research to gather information about the emperor. Then, select the information that you think is most important to include in your report.

Critical Thinking

1. **Making Comparisons** How did the Byzantine style of architecture differ from the Roman style of architecture?
2. **Identifying Central Issues** How was the conflict between the Western and Eastern churches in Europe both religious and political in nature?
3. **Predicting Consequences** What forms of art might have developed if Islam did not forbid images of living things?

Focus on Writing

Descriptive Paragraphs

A **descriptive paragraph** is one that describes a subject in detail. When you write a descriptive paragraph, you should try to give your readers a vivid impression of your subject. The topic sentence should introduce your subject. The rest of your paragraph should include many specific details. Also, the language you use should be colorful, including figures of speech and sensory images.

Practice: Select one of the following topics: Bedouin Life Style, Caliphs, The Hippodrome of Byzantium. Then, complete the following prewriting activities:

1. Write a topic sentence that tells the subject (or topic) of your paragraph.
2. List three specific details about the subject.
3. List one sensory image and one figure of speech that you might use in your paragraph.
4. Make an outline showing how you would organize your paragraph, including where your topic sentence would appear.

Western Europe: Foundations of the Middle Ages

(A.D. 500–1100)

1 **Europe Revived During the Early Middle Ages**

2 **The Feudal Pyramid Controlled Europe**

3 **The Church Was a Powerful Force**

▲ **Illustrating History** *Here, pages are shown serving their lords and ladies during a banquet on a medieval manor.*

I magine it is a cold morning in March, 1,000 years ago, just before dawn. You lift yourself off your mattress on the floor and help your European lord and lady prepare for the day.

After mass, a horn calls you to wash your hands before breakfast. The water in the bowl is half-frozen. You return with the family to the castle's main hall. Its few, high windows have been boarded up to keep out the cold. The rough-hewn plank table at the center of the room holds a meal of bread and ale. The lord's family sits at the table. You and the rest of the household stand while eating, or else squat on the dirty, straw-covered floor.

Because you know that your lord is anxious to get the day's business out of the way so he can go hunting, you eat quickly. Then you tell the lord that one of the villagers is waiting to file a complaint against a neighbor. Your lord boxes your ears for your trouble and then hears and settles the complaint. Finally, the lord and his men grab their weapons and head for the woods. You stay behind to do chores until dark.

Such was a servant's life in the rough-and-tumble Europe of the early Middle Ages (500–1000). Nowhere in Europe at that time, not even in a lord's castle, were there the refinements and splendor that marked China or Byzantium. Instead, as you will learn in this chapter, the average person was busy struggling to meet his or her most basic needs.

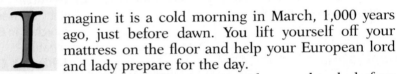

800	900	1000	1100

■ **800** Charlemagne heads Holy Roman Empire

■ **843** Treaty of Verdun divides Holy Roman Empire

■ **911** Vikings win Normandy from France

■ **1000** Leif Ericson lands in Newfoundland

1099 ■ Crusaders capture Jerusalem

▲ **Illustrating History**   *The Chateau de Chillon in Switzerland, like many medieval castles, was built next to water to protect it from invaders.*

1   Europe Revived During the Early Middle Ages

As you read, look for answers to these questions:

◆ How did the physical geography of Europe encourage progress?
◆ How did Germanic tribes end the failing Roman Empire?
◆ How did Viking invasions affect the early history of Europe?

Key Terms: mayor of the palace (defined on p. 198)

Daily life for people living in the Middle Ages was obviously not a life of luxury. As the Roman Empire declined, western Europe was cut off from the rich trade that the Byzantine Empire and Muslim world enjoyed. Cities declined, and the culture of the Roman Empire began to fade. During the early Middle Ages, from about A.D. 500 to 1100, however, western Europe gradually began to build its own civilization and culture, and faint outlines of today's nations began to emerge. Among the characteristics of a nation are established boundaries, a strong central government, and strong feelings of loyalty among the people. These qualities, especially in France and England, were just beginning to grow during the early Middle Ages.

Geography had endowed western Europe with rich farmlands, great forests, important waterways, and superior location. All of these factors combined to support development and progress. Due to these advantages, western Europe during the Middle Ages, the period between A.D. 500 and 1350, was better able to make a new beginning and to build a distinctive civilization.

Europe's Geography Set the Stage for Its History

Although Europe is the smallest continent except for Australia, its impact on history has been enormous. In fact, in some ways, Europe is not a continent at all. One glance at a world map will show you that Europe is really a peninsula of Asia that occupies only about one-fifteenth of the earth's surface. It is little more than one-fifth the size of Asia and less than one-third the size of Africa. Just where Asia ends and Europe begins has often been debated. Most people agree that the Ural Mountains, the Caspian Sea, and the Caucasus Mountains combine to form the dividing boundary line between Europe and Asia. (See the map on page 199.)

The Mediterranean Sea and the Strait of Gibraltar separate Europe from Africa. The North Sea, the Baltic Sea, and the immense Atlantic Ocean wash the northern and western shores of Europe. This long coastline with good harbors and many navigable rivers has always encouraged trade and commerce. While there are numerous mountains, most of these have important passes that have enabled the communities that are separated by the mountains to travel to and communicate with one another.

Barbarian Tribes Invaded Rome

As discussed in Chapter 5, for hundreds of years various German tribes had lived on or near the borders of the Roman Empire. Some of the tribes in the border areas were conquered and then made part of the Roman Empire. Others crossed over the borders into Rome peacefully, trying to secure better farmland for themselves and their followers. This peaceful and gradual migration and settlement of Germans in the Roman Empire became a wave and then a flood when the Huns from far-off China stormed across Siberia and into Europe.

During this time, the Visigoths crossed the Danube and asked for the protection of Rome. When they discovered that Rome was no longer in a position to help them, the Visigoths attacked the Romans. In A.D. 410, after they had plundered Rome, they expanded into southern France and then into Spain, where they set up a kingdom. In 711, the kingdom collapsed after the Muslims defeated the Visigoths in battle.

The Visigoths, however, were only one of many barbarian tribes. The Ostrogoths, the Vandals, the Burgundians, the Franks, the Slavs, the Goths, the Lombards, the Angles, and the Saxons were among the tribes that moved across Europe. The map on page 200 shows the kingdoms controlled by these tribes around A.D. 500. The most outstanding of these peoples were the Franks, from whom the nation of France gets its name.

The Franks Forged an Empire

The Franks established a mighty empire with a capital at Aix-la-Chapelle (aye lah shah PEL). Clovis (KLOH vis), the King of the Franks, became a Christian. His conversion made it possible for the king and the pope to work hand in hand. The pope needed the king's armies to protect church property and to help Christianity grow. The king needed the pope to encourage the people to obey him.

Unfortunately, the kings who followed Clovis were weaklings who preferred pleasure to the hard tasks of governing a new kingdom. They quarreled among themselves and allowed ambitious advisers to misguide them. Soon, the king's advisers, or **mayors of the palace,** as these people were called, had most of the power.

The most influential mayor was Charles Martel. His son, Pepin the Short, who ruled from 747 to 768, actually became king with the pope's help. In return for this help, Pepin gave land to the pope and agreed to protect the pope from any enemies. The land Pepin gave to the pope, combined with other lands near the city of Rome, became known as the Papal States. The gift gave the pope the status of a prince. The pope already had religious authority. The gift of land gave him political power as well. In return, Pepin and his son, Charlemagne (SHAR luh MAYN), built a great empire.

GEOGRAPHIC SETTING:
Europe

Key to colors
- Ice or snow
- Tundra
- Mixed forest
- Lightly forested or grasslands
- Desert, shrubs

BARENTS SEA
ARCTIC OCEAN
Iceland
GULF OF BOTHNIA
SCANDINAVIAN PENINSULA
60°N
URAL MTS.
GULF OF FINLAND
IRISH SEA
NORTH SEA
BALTIC SEA
50°N
Ireland
Great Britain
British Isles
Thames R.
Rhine R.
Elbe R.
Oder R.
Vistula R.
NORTH EUROPEAN PLAIN
Don R.
Volga R.
ATLANTIC OCEAN
ENGLISH CHANNEL
Seine R.
Loire R.
EUROPE
CARPATHIAN MTS.
Dnieper R.
Dniester R.
CASPIAN SEA
40°N
BAY OF BISCAY
ALPS
Po R.
CRIMEAN PENINSULA
CAUCASUS MTS.
IBERIAN PENINSULA
PYRENEES
Rhone R.
ADRIATIC SEA
Danube R.
BALKAN MOUNTAINS
BLACK SEA
Tagus R.
Corsica
APENNINES
BOSPORUS
Rome
Sardinia
ITALIAN PENINSULA
BALKAN PENINSULA
SEA OF MARMARA
Balearic Is.
TYRRHENIAN SEA
AEGEAN SEA
DARDENELLES
ASIA
Strait of Gibraltar
Sicily
IONIAN SEA
Malta
Tigris R.
Crete
Cyprus
Euphrates R.
30°N
MEDITERRANEAN SEA
AFRICA
0   500   1000 Miles
0   500   1000 Kilometers
N
W   E
S
Nile R.
RED SEA
20°N
0°E
10°E
20°E
30°E
40°E

© PH

Focus on Geography

1. **Interaction**   What is the name of the enormous fertile plain that Europeans have used for centuries as farm and pasture land to help feed their people?

2. **Regions**   The Italian Peninsula is separated from the fertile plains of northern Europe by what kind of region?

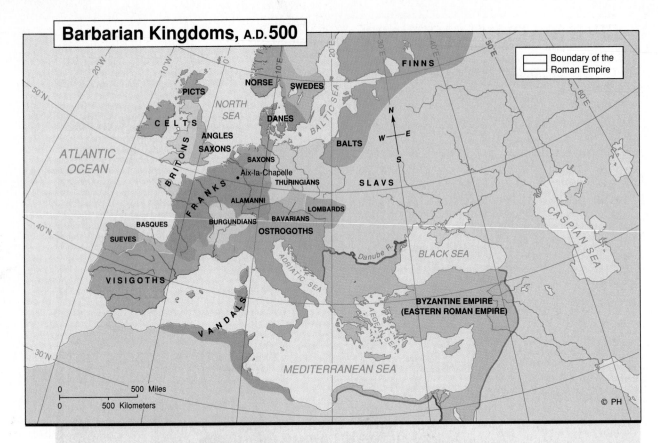

Barbarian Kingdoms, A.D. 500

FINNS

NORSE
SWEDES

PICTS

NORTH
SEA

CELTS

DANES

ANGLES

BALTS

SAXONS

ATLANTIC
OCEAN

BRITONS

SAXONS

Aix-la-Chapelle

THURINGIANS

SLAVS

FRANKS

ALAMANNI

LOMBARDS

BASQUES

BURGUNDIANS

BAVARIANS

OSTROGOTHS

SUEVES

Danube R.

BLACK SEA

CASPIAN SEA

VISIGOTHS

ADRIATIC SEA

VANDALS

AEGEAN SEA

BYZANTINE EMPIRE
(EASTERN ROMAN EMPIRE)

MEDITERRANEAN SEA

Boundary of the
Roman Empire

0   500 Miles
0   500 Kilometers

© PH

Focus on Geography

Interaction   When the barbarians invaded Europe, they swept from one region to another, which explains why some barbarian kingdoms are located on separate landmasses. Name two barbarian kingdoms that are separated by bodies of water.

Charlemagne Ruled Many Lands

Pepin's son, Charles the Great, or Charlemagne, who reigned from 768 to 814, ruled over the lands of present-day France, Belgium, the Netherlands, Austria, and Switzerland. He also controlled parts of Germany, Italy, Czechoslovakia, and Yugoslavia.

On Christmas Day in the year 800, Charlemagne was crowned and hailed as emperor by the pope. This event was important because it meant that Charlemagne accepted the pope as the spiritual ruler of the empire and the giver of power to the emperor. Later popes then could say that they were more powerful than kings. As spiritual leaders, the popes claimed the right to say who would become emperor. This claim led to endless fights between popes and kings over which of them had the higher authority.

Charlemagne and the kings who followed him said they had rebuilt the Roman Empire. They had not, of course, but the establishment of a European empire was a goal that kings would try again and again to achieve. What had been created, however, was the Holy Roman Empire. This empire was now a combination of the politics of the Roman Empire and the religion of the Christian church.

After Charlemagne died, none of his descendants was strong enough to hold his empire together. In 843, his three grandsons —Charles the Bald, Louis the German, and Lothar—divided the empire between themselves. They drew up the Treaty of Verdun, which described the boundaries of each of their kingdoms (see the map below).

One of Charlemagne's contributions was the advancement of learning during his reign. He insisted that the children of his nobles work hard in school. Under Alcuin (AL kwihn), an English scholar whom Charlemagne brought to France, the palace school flourished. In fact, Charlemagne himself became one of its students.

For nearly 200 years after Charlemagne's death, there were no strong kings in Europe. The violence and disorder that Charlemagne had stopped began again and grew worse.

Vikings Invaded the British Isles

One of the fiercest groups to attack Europe during the ninth and tenth centuries was the Vikings, or Northmen, who came from Norway, Sweden, and Denmark. These fierce warriors sailed the seas in small, well-built ships and raided the coasts of France and England. They landed in Iceland and Greenland and even reached America. Leif

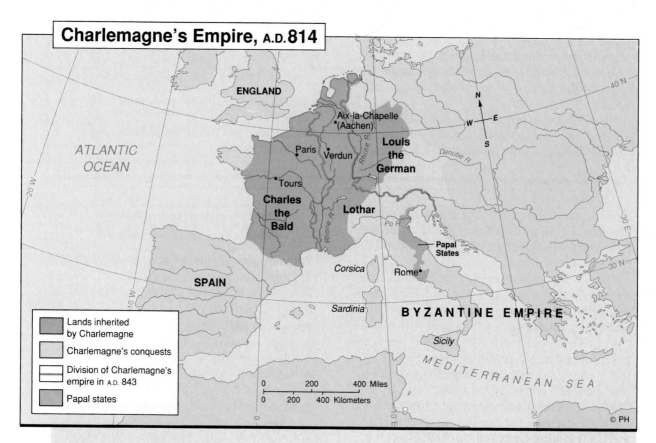

Charlemagne's Empire, A.D. 814

Legend:
- Lands inherited by Charlemagne
- Charlemagne's conquests
- Division of Charlemagne's empire in A.D. 843
- Papal states

0 200 400 Miles
0 200 400 Kilometers

Focus on Geography

1. **Location** Which of Charlemagne's grandsons could have enjoyed a view of the Danube River?
2. **Regions** Which grandson inherited the least amount of land that Charlemagne had conquered?

Charlemagne

Charlemagne, the first Christian emperor of western Europe, stood out in a crowd like a bright flag. Six feet, four inches tall, he towered over most people in his kingdom. The short white hair showing beneath his golden crown made his appearance all the more striking.

Born in 742, Charlemagne, shown right, became king of the Franks upon his brother's death in 771. A devout Christian, he aimed to unite the former Roman Empire under Christian rule. He did this by winning battles and steadily enlarging his empire. At the head of a large army, he drove the Muslims south to Barcelona, conquered most of western Europe, and forced the Germans to convert to Christianity.

But Charlemagne had another side. He had great intellectual curiosity and alertness. To encourage education, Charlemagne invited scholars from across Europe to his court. He commanded monasteries to set up schools and libraries. Charlemagne's revival of learning became the foundation for medieval civilization.

In 800, Pope Leo III crowned Charlemagne emperor of the Romans. When he died in 814, his vast empire was at peace, and he was the undisputed leader of all of Christendom.

1. In what ways did Charlemagne make a difference in the world?
2. What was his main goal? How did he accomplish it?

Ericson was one of the Vikings who probably journeyed to the New World centuries before the voyage of Christopher Columbus in 1492.

The Vikings who attacked the British Isles met resistance from the Angle, Saxon, and Jute tribes. These tribes not only fought the Northmen but also each other. Alfred the Great, who lived from 849 to 899, was the first English ruler to come close to achieving some kind of unity. He also protected his people from Northmen called the Danes. After his death, however, weak rulers were unable to resist the Danes, and in 1016, the Danish king Canute (kuh NOOT) defeated the Saxons and became king of England.

As the Danes conquered England, the Normans (another name for Northmen) conquered that part of France known as Normandy. It was from Normandy that William the Conqueror later attacked and conquered England in 1066.

SECTION 1 REVIEW

Knowing Key Terms, People, and Places
1. Define: **a.** mayor of the palace
2. Identify: **a.** Papal States **b.** Charlemagne **c.** Treaty of Verdun

Reviewing Main Ideas
3. Explain how King Clovis was able to establish an empire of Franks.
4. How did Pepin the Short enlist the help of a pope?
5. What lands did Charlemagne control as emperor?

Critical Thinking
Demonstrating Reasoned Judgment
6. Do you think that the struggle for power and control between the popes and kings was unavoidable? Explain the reasons for your answer.

2 The Feudal Pyramid Controlled Europe

As you read, look for answers to these questions:

◆ How did feudalism affect the lives of the people of medieval Europe?
◆ What were the roles of people at each level of the feudal pyramid?
◆ What was life like on a medieval manor?

Key Terms: serf (defined on p. 203), vassal (p. 203), feudalism (p. 203), freeman (p. 204), demesne (p. 204), fallow (p. 204), reeve (p. 206), tournament (p. 207), chivalry (p. 207)

If you could return to the European Middle Ages through a time machine, you would find that, in many ways, life resembled the game of chess. As in chess, kings and queens were important members of medieval society, but they were not necessarily the most powerful. Many of the bishops of the Church and nobles sought to check, or lessen, the power and prestige of a king. Lesser nobles served as knights, or armed warriors. The vast majority of the people were **serfs,** peasants who farmed and performed other duties for the lords. Like the pawns in a chess game, they had little power and little control over their own lives.

The Feudal Pyramid Controlled Medieval Europe

In the early Middle Ages, without a strong government or army, kings and queens were weak and had little power. Landowners were usually wealthy nobles who had managed to keep their lands, wealth, castles, and possibly some soldiers as the Roman Empire fell apart. These noblemen offered protection to less important landowners. In return, these landowners served the lord as **vassals** (VAS uhls), or lesser lords. In time, the relationship between a lord and his vassals became the center of the political, social, and eco-

nomic life of the Middle Ages. This relationship has been given the name **feudalism** (FYOOD uh LIZ uhm). For this reason, the Middle Ages in western Europe are often called the feudal period. It was, in many ways, similar to the feudal system that developed in China over a thousand years earlier, which was described in Chapter 3.

A feudal society can be pictured as a pyramid with a king or a queen at the top. Some monarchs were strong, while others held the title but lacked authority. Next in the pyramid came the lords and bishops, some of whom were powerful while others were relatively poor and powerless.

At the base of the pyramid were the serfs. Although they were not slaves because they could not be bought or sold, serfs and their children were bound to the land and owed certain duties to the lord who owned the land. Serfs worked the land for the lord in exchange for the produce that was left after the lord has taken a part of it for taxes. The serfs paid taxes to the lord in the form of food and work and in return obtained the privilege of using the lord's road, baking oven, gristmill, and wine press.

▼ **Illustrating History** *Vassals pledged loyalty and service to their lords.*

The Feudal Pyramid

King

Nobles

Lords

Lesser Lords

Knights

Peasants and Townspeople

▲ **Chart Skills** *What class in medieval society had direct power over the knights?*

There were some **freemen** in feudal society who were neither lords nor serfs. They were artisans and merchants who provided specialized services, such as carpentry, metal working, horseshoeing, or the buying and selling of goods. Although few in number, they increased as the Middle Ages came to an end.

Feudalism Provided a System of Government in Medieval Europe

Feudalism was a system of government in which a powerful noble commanded the obedience of less powerful nobles who became his vassals.

Although nobles held the lands and their authority in the monarch's name, the monarch had little power beyond his or her own land. In fact, many nobles were more powerful than monarchs, and the Church was more powerful than both.

Feudal nobles had their own courts from which they administered a rough form of justice. They collected their own taxes, and the more powerful nobles even minted their own coins. Feudal nobles expected certain duties from their vassals. These included ransom money if the nobleman was captured, money or land to help make a dowry

when a nobleman's daughter married, payment when a boy was knighted, and, when called upon, armed services in defense of the noble.

The importance of a noble depended upon the size of his estate or property, the strength of his castle, and the number of knights he could command in time of war.

The Manor Was the Center of the Feudal Economy

The manor, a lord's estate, was at the center of the feudal economy. In size, a typical manor consisted of 1,000 acres of land, and some lords controlled more than one manor. The manor, or estate, included a lord's castle, a church, several clusters of peasant huts, and the equipment needed to bake bread, make wine, and weave clothing. A manor was expected to be self-sufficient.

Farming. Feudalism was based on agriculture. The tools used were simple, and the farming methods were inefficient. The crude, horse-drawn plows that the serfs used were clumsy and slow, and they usually seeded the land by hand. Even so, serfs were expected to grow enough food to feed everyone who lived on the manor.

The best land, called the **demesne** (dih MAYN), belonged to the lord of the manor. Serfs worked strips of land scattered throughout the manor. In this way, it was thought, serfs would have an equal chance at good and poor land. These small strips of land were not easy to farm since it was hard to get from one strip to another. Although people did not know about fertilizers or about rotating crops to get the most from the soil, every year one-third of the land was left **fallow**, or untilled, to restore some fertility. After paying their feudal obligations to the lords, the serfs had little food, clothing, or time left for themselves.

Daily life. Most serfs lived in one-room, thatched cottages. These cottages were close to one another and shared a common green or lawn. Heat came from a fireplace in the middle of the room, and smoke escaped through a hole in the roof. Fires were

Woodland

Lord's house

Peasants' houses

Unplanted field

Church

Priest's house

Lord's kitchen

Blacksmith's shop

Pasture

Mill

Planted field

▲ **Illustrating History**   *A medieval manor had a church, a mill, an oven, and other facilities to provide for all the needs of its residents.*

a constant threat, and most communities lacked any way to fight them. On bitter cold days, families kept themselves and their cattle warm by bringing the animals into their cottages.

Women and men on the manor worked equally as hard. Families were large, and the first duty of the housewife was to feed, clothe, and raise the children. Like the men, however, they also did the heavy work in the field, where they planted and harvested grain, sheared sheep, and looked after chickens.

There was little trading during the feudal period. Money was scarce and travel was dangerous as well as difficult.

The castle. The manor was occupied by the lord, his serfs, and others who were dependent upon him for protection. The lord lived in a castle that was more a fort than a home. Because protection from enemies was the castle's main function, it was often built upon the highest point on the manor or was surrounded by a deep ditch, or moat, which was usually filled with

205

▲ **Illustrating History** *Medieval women, including wives of nobles, were responsible for making thread and weaving cloth.*

water. Entrance to the castle was across a drawbridge that could be raised or lowered as needed.

Most castles could be easily defended since the weapons used during an attack were no better than those used by the Roman armies. For example, there were battering rams and machines for hurling huge stones and iron bolts. A well-located castle could resist this type of attack. Often a foe simply tried to blockade the castle and starve those in it into surrendering. This type of attack, called a siege, could take months, especially if the food and water in the castle were plentiful.

During times of war, the lord and his family lived in a great central tower, called the keep. The castle walls were defended by knights who kept a lookout for enemies. Castles frequently had dark, dirty, damp dungeons, or prisons, where those captured in battle could be held for ransom.

Behind the walls of the castle could be found the great hall in which the lord and his family lived in times of peace. This room served as both a court, where justice was administered, and a dining room, where guests were entertained. Often, this room was used as a bedroom as well. When bedtime came, mattresses were brought in. Screens sometimes provided some privacy. There was an armory, a chapel, kitchens, laundry, stables, and places where the lord's attendants and servants could live.

Life in a castle was not comfortable or easy. For one thing, windows were few and small. Later in the Middle Ages, oiled paper or wooden shutters covered them to keep out some of the rain and cold. Light was provided by candles and by smoky torches. A wood fire in the center of the room provided heat, but during the extreme cold of winter, it offered little comfort. There was no chimney, but smoke could escape through a louver, or slatted opening, in the roof.

Life on a manor. A lord's life was not one of ease. From dawn to dusk and often beyond, his life was taken up with obligations to the lord above him and administrative responsibilities for managing his manor.

A staff of manorial officials helped him supervise the manor. The steward was the chief adviser to the lord and managed the manor when the lord was away in battle or visiting other manors. Often, the steward traveled to other manors in the service of the lord. The **reeve** was both a kind of foreman who supervised the work of the serfs and the spokesperson of the manor who reported the grievances of the serfs to the lords. The constable summoned the residents of the manor to meetings and was the chief law-enforcement officer for the entire community.

The lord's wife, the lady of the household, was generally as busy as he was. She was responsible for raising the children and supervising the servants. She supervised the baking of bread, the making of butter, and the salting down of meat for the winter. Another important duty was the planning and organizing of the spinning, weaving, and sewing that were needed to make the clothing for everyone in the household. The lady of the manor took charge of the manor when her husband went off to battle, and if he were captured, it often became her responsibility to raise the ransom that was demanded for his release.

While the lot of the serf was a hard one, the serf was often grateful for the lord's protection. The Church eased the burden of the serf with frequent holy days during which no work was permitted. One medieval churchman criticized the lords for abusing their serfs by saying, "Ye nobles are ravening wolves, you . . . live on the blood and sweat of the poor." Yet, at least until the thirteenth century, most peasants viewed their lords with a good deal of admiration and even affection.

Knights Prepared for Warfare

To be a knight, one had to be wellborn. Wellborn did not always mean rich. Instead, it meant one had to be born of a noble family. In addition, one had to go through a long and difficult period of training. At the age of 7, a boy became a page, or personal servant, in the castle of a prominent lord. When he was about 14, the boy became a squire and served his lord in every way. As a squire, he learned how to handle a sword, a bow and arrow, and a lance, and fought alongside his lord in battle.

Having gone through a long period of training, the squire then went through a ceremonial ordeal. He bathed, fasted, and spent a night in church praying and confessing his sins. The following day, he took part in an elaborate ceremony, the climax of which came when the lord rose and touched the candidate's shoulder three times with a sword and said, "I dub thee knight."

A knight's life was devoted to war and dangerous combat games that were known as **tournaments.** In tournaments, the knights showed off their skills and practiced for battle. Jousting, or tilting, in which a knight was supposed to unhorse his opponent with his lance, was the most popular contest. In other events, knights fought with battle axes. Participants in these contests were sometimes killed or maimed.

The knight rode off to war with the horse and rider both well protected in heavy suits of armor. The medieval knight was like a mobile fort. He rode on horseback although his retainers, or helpers, were often on foot. His weapons were his sword and lance. The object of knightly warfare was not so much to kill the enemy as it was to capture him and hold him for ransom. For example, when Henry I of England won all Normandy at the battle of Tinchebrai in 1106, 400 knights were captured, but not one of Henry's knights was killed. To be killed in battle was considered the only honorable way for a knight to die, so being captured was a disgrace that seemed worse than death.

In the feudal social system, the nobility were courted and entertained. Courtesy, or court manners, known as **chivalry,** (SHIV uhl ree), became highly developed. Knights were taught to be brave in war, gallant toward women of noble birth, and faithful to the Church. The ideals of bravery, courtesy, loyalty, and honor were not always lived up to. They did, however, provide a model for the ideals of chivalry and knighthood.

SECTION 2 REVIEW

Knowing Key Terms, People, and Places
1. Define: **a.** serf **b.** vassal **c.** feudalism **d.** freeman **e.** demesne **f.** fallow **g.** reeve **h.** tournament **i.** chivalry
2. Identify: **a.** steward **b.** constable

Reviewing Main Ideas
3. What obligations did feudal nobles expect from their vassals?
4. Describe the levels of the feudal pyramid.
5. What land and other possessions were included in a manor?
6. What was the role of a knight?

Critical Thinking
Predicting Consequences
7. The serfs supplied the most important product in medieval society—its food. Do you think that they realized the power they possessed? Do you think they could have improved their lives if they had asked for more privileges in exchange for farming? Explain your answers.

3 The Church Was a Powerful Force

As you read, look for answers to these questions:

◆ How much power did the Church have in medieval Europe?
◆ How did the Church influence the medieval economy and government?
◆ What was the basic struggle between monarchs and popes?

> **Key Terms:** excommunicate (defined on p. 208), heresy (p. 208), usury (p. 208), tithe (p. 208), Crusade (p. 209), ghetto (p. 211)

During the Middle Ages, church and state were not separate as they are in the United States today. In medieval Europe, the Church had great power and influence. Church and government worked hand in hand to direct people's lives, and they were expected to cooperate with each other.

Medieval People Sought Salvation in the Church

People in the Middle Ages believed that God had the answers to their problems. For example, they believed that God took an active part in their lives by curing the sick, bringing rain, and causing earthquakes.

During the Middle Ages people were looking for meaning in lives that were short and often brutal. Because people looked to the Church to provide this meaning, the Church had great power. To punish an extremely sinful act, the Church **excommunicated** (EKS kuh MYOO nuh KAYT ed), or cut off, people from its protection. One example of an act serious enough to deserve excommunication was heresy (HEHR ih see). **Heresy** involved holding beliefs that did not agree with those of the Church. Excommunicated people could not receive spiritual blessings from priests. They could not marry, and

they could not receive the Church's last rites, or blessings, when they died. Through its power of excommunication, the Church controlled the upper and lower classes.

The Church Was an Important Part of the Medieval Economy

The Church made vital contributions to the feudal economy. Farming was the most important way of making a living during the Middle Ages. As the monks farmed church property, they found better ways of growing crops and looking after livestock. They taught these new methods to other farmers so everyone could benefit.

The Church often regulated the activities of those engaged in business. For example, it forbade **usury**, the practice of charging interest on money that had been lent to another person. It urged merchants and artisans to charge a just, or fair, price for goods.

The Church Played a Central Role in Medieval Government

In a real sense, the Church was itself a government. It was stronger than any monarch or any noble and was usually able to tell the monarchs and nobles what to do. As a government, it had the power to tax. This tax, known as a **tithe** (tyth), amounted to one-tenth of one's income, and every church member was expected to pay it. Through tithing, the Church got the money to do its work and became the world's greatest single landowner. The pope ruled the Papal States in central Italy, where he was head of a government as well as head of the Church. Because of its power, wealth, and lands, the Church was envied by monarchs and nobles alike.

Today, you expect your government to administer justice, to establish courts of law, to provide for education, and to look after the sick, the hungry, and the needy. In medieval days, the Church provided most of these services.

Because of its great influence, the Church could make and unmake monarchs. The land and titles necessary for a monarch to rule were held only with the consent of the

A Monk's Life

When a young man entered a monastery in the early Middle Ages, he knew he was giving up a lot. From then on, he could own nothing. Furthermore, he would have no control over his time. On the other hand, he believed the rewards for this self-denial were great: a chance to enter the kingdom of heaven.

A monk's life was hard and tedious. The wake-up bells rang at 3 A.M. Monks commonly spent a long day in prayer, reading, meditation, and chores according to the strict schedule of their religious order. After a simple evening meal of bread, meatless stew, and a cup of wine, a monk would thank God for having survived another day—and then turn in early. Tomorrow's schedule would be just the same.

1. What did monks give up when they entered a monastery?
2. How did they spend their days?

---

pope. Therefore, conflict as well as cooperation between pope and monarch was a part of medieval life.

Monarchs and Popes Cooperated in the Crusades

In 1095, Pope Urban II called upon the monarchs, their nobles, and their people to help the Church by driving the Muslims out of Palestine. The pope urged war against the Muslims because, he said, they were interfering with the right of Christians to worship in Jerusalem. These Muslims were Seljuk Turks who had recently adopted Islam as their religion. The Turks were making trips to the Holy City of Jerusalem unsafe, and they were threatening the Eastern Orthodox Church in the Byzantine Empire. The series of holy wars the Christians organized to drive the Muslims out of this region were called the **Crusades.**

Four major Crusades were undertaken, but they failed to recapture the Holy Land. The First Crusade, which lasted from 1096 to 1099, was the most successful. As a result, Jerusalem was temporarily recaptured from the Muslims. The Crusaders then set up four Crusader states: Edessa, Antioch, Tripoli, and Jerusalem. (See the map on p. 210.) Some of the Crusaders adopted local customs and grew more tolerant of the Jewish and Muslim people who were now their neighbors. The Second Crusade started in answer to calls for help from the Crusader states when Edessa fell to the Turks in 1144. That Crusade ended in 1149.

In 1187, the Muslim warrior Saladin (SAL uh dihn) recaptured Jerusalem, and a call for a Third Crusade was sounded. This Crusade is famous in history because three great, rival kings took part in it. Even so, the Third Crusade failed. Emperor Frederick Barbarossa (BAR buh RAHS uh) from the Holy Roman Empire drowned on the way. Philip Augustus of France got tired of fighting and went home. Richard the Lion-Hearted of England fought bravely and well, but he finally returned to England without having recaptured the Holy Land.

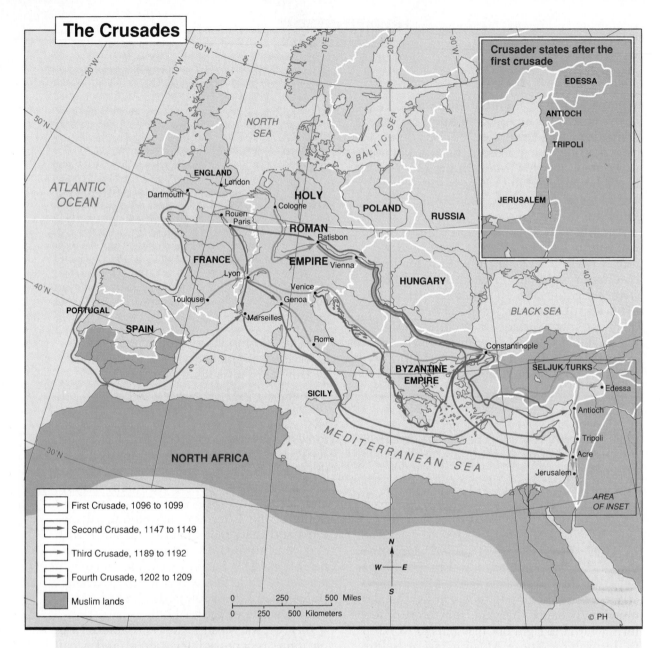

The Crusades

Crusader states after the first crusade

EDESSA

ANTIOCH

TRIPOLI

JERUSALEM

NORTH SEA

ATLANTIC OCEAN

BALTIC SEA

ENGLAND
London
Dartmouth
Cologne
HOLY
Rouen
Paris
ROMAN
Ratisbon
POLAND
RUSSIA
FRANCE
Vienna
EMPIRE
Lyon
HUNGARY
Venice
Genoa
BLACK SEA
Toulouse
PORTUGAL
Marseilles
SPAIN
Rome
Constantinople
BYZANTINE
EMPIRE
SELJUK TURKS
Edessa
SICILY
Antioch
NORTH AFRICA
Tripoli
Acre
MEDITERRANEAN SEA
Jerusalem

AREA OF INSET

First Crusade, 1096 to 1099
Second Crusade, 1147 to 1149
Third Crusade, 1189 to 1192
Fourth Crusade, 1202 to 1209
Muslim lands

| 0 | 250 | 500 Miles |
| 0 | 250 | 500 Kilometers |

N
W — E
S

© PH

Focus on Geography

Regions After the first Crusade, the Crusaders established four states along the eastern coast of the Mediterranean. Unprotected by any landforms, the states soon fell to the Muslims, starting the second and third Crusades. Which states were held by the Crusaders?

In the Fourth Crusade, the crusaders forgot that their enemies were Muslims. Political and financial reasons caused them to plunder the wealth of their fellow Christians in Constantinople in 1204. As discussed in Chapter 7, this was one of the blows that shattered the Byzantine Empire. Other Crusades were attempted, but they too were unsuccessful. One of them was undertaken by children. It was a dismal failure; many children died, and others were sold into slavery. It showed, however, the tremendous religious faith of the people.

As the Crusaders made their way east, they often attacked Jews, spreading terror throughout the sections of the cities in which Jews lived. These sections were called **ghettos** (GET ohz). Many Jews were killed and saw their homes burned to the ground and their possessions stolen.

The Crusades Brought Changes

The Crusades increased the status of the pope, increased contact between western Europe and the Middle East, and contributed to the growth of trade and business. Necessities and luxuries, such as sugar, rice, lemons, cotton, and precious gems, were introduced into western Europe. As trade increased, money, banking, and credit, long frowned upon by the Church, became necessary to carry on business.

The Crusades also contributed to the growth of towns. Goods and services were needed to support large troop movements. As a result, people left the land for towns where there were better opportunities.

To some extent, the Crusades also brought about an increase in the power of the monarchs over the nobles. The monarchs were able to strengthen their taxing power to raise money for the Crusades. When the Crusades ended, the power to tax remained in the hands of the monarchs. The establishment of town life and the growth in the power of the monarchs were forces that led to the decline of the feudal period.

Monarchs and Popes Fought for Power and Wealth

Because the Church was powerful, monarchs envied it. Because there was no separation of church and state, the powers of the monarch and those of the pope were often in conflict.

During the Middle Ages, almost the only people who were well educated were bishops, monks, and abbots. For this reason,

In their own words

Letters from Home

In 1382, at age 22, Margherita Datini decided to learn to read and write. She wanted to be able to correspond with her husband, Francesco, without the aid of a servant. Francesco was a medieval merchant who was frequently away from their home in Prato, Italy, on business trips. In the following excerpts from two letters, Margherita complains about his absences.

❝As for your staying away till Thursday, you can do as you please as master, a fine office, but to be used with discretion; . . . I am fully disposed [willing] to live together as long as God wills it. . . . I do not see the necessity of your sending a message to me every Wednesday to say that you will be here on Sunday, since every Friday you repent [ask forgiveness]. It would be sufficient to let me know Saturday afternoon so that I could lay in supplies; at least we would fare well on Sunday. I have found companions in my female friends; sad would be the woman who had to depend on you!

. . . You say, always sermonizing, that we will have a fine life, and every month and every week will be the one [when it will begin]. You have told me this for ten years, and today it seems more timely than ever to reply: it is your fault [that it has not started]. . . .

If you delay so much, you will never seize this 'fine life'. . . .❞

1. What words or phrases in the excerpts indicate that Margherita is angry at her husband?
2. Why are the letters between Margherita and Francesco likely to be more open and honest than many letters written during this period?

211

monarchs often appointed bishops to help them run their governments. Like the feudal lords, the bishops were vassals of the monarch; and as vassals, they swore to support the monarch. As bishops, however, they were also subject to the commands of the Church.

Since a bishop was an official of the Church, the pope claimed the power to appoint him and to inherit his land when he died. Since a bishop was also a vassal of the monarch, the monarch also claimed the right to inherit the vassal's land. These issues led to a test of strength between monarch and pope.

Henry IV Lost, Then Won, His Fight With Pope Gregory VII

In 1075, under Pope Gregory VII, the conflict between monarch and pope came to a head. Gregory was determined that the pope would be obeyed. He also insisted that only the pope, and not the monarch, had the power to appoint bishops.

The argument over who would appoint bishops angered the Holy Roman Emperor Henry IV, who lived from 1050 to 1106. When he refused to obey the pope, a struggle for control followed, and Gregory excommunicated Henry.

Henry nearly lost his kingdom. He seemed to be no match for Pope Gregory. Henry decided to make a pilgrimage to Canossa (kuh NOSS uh) in northern Italy to plead for the pope's forgiveness. In 1077, in the cold of winter and dressed in rags amid a snowstorm, he stood waiting for three days for the pope to appear. Finally, the pope gave in and removed the sentence of excommunication. Henry's pilgrimage to Canossa served to illustrate the vast powers of the pope.

In the dispute between Henry and the pope, the pope had won the first round, but the argument was not over. Henry returned to his country where he behaved as before. Again, he was excommunicated. This time Henry marched against Rome and defeated Gregory in 1081. Gregory died in 1085, but other popes continued the struggle.

In 1122, under Henry V, a compromise between the pope and the king was worked out. The *Concordat* (khon KOR daht) *of Worms* (vohrms) decreed that the pope and the king would share the loyalty of bishops and other church officials. On behalf of the king, the bishops were responsible for affairs of state. On behalf of the pope, the bishops were responsible for the affairs of God. The king gave the bishop lands, and the pope appointed the bishop and gave him religious authority.

The results of the quarrels between monarch and pope show the comparative power of each. As monarchs grew stronger, they became more sure of their own authority. They were less willing to give the pope a share of it.

As the small, enclosed world of the manor began to expand and people began to move to the towns to find a better life, the feudal period came to a close. The larger world, rediscovered through the Crusades, encouraged trade and travel. All of these developments led to even more progress and to the flowering of medieval society, which will be described in the next chapter.

SECTION 3 REVIEW

Knowing Key Terms, People, and Places
1. Define: **a.** excommunicate **b.** heresy
   c. usury **d.** tithe **e.** Crusade **f.** ghetto
2. Identify: **a.** Saladin **b.** Concordat of Worms

Reviewing Main Ideas
3. What was the major purpose of the four Crusades?
4. How did the Crusades affect trade and commerce?
5. How did the balance of power between the Church and the monarchs shift after 1122?

Critical Thinking
Drawing Conclusions
6. Do you think that the influence of the Church in medieval Europe was more good than bad? Explain your answer.

Distinguishing Fact from Opinion

When reading social studies materials, you read both facts and opinions. As you know, an opinion is a point of view that is not necessarily true. Authors have different opinions that they may express as they describe people and events in history. To determine the soundness of an author's ideas, you need to be able to distinguish between the author's opinions and the historical facts.

The ability to separate facts and opinions helps you to reach your own conclusions about different issues and historical events. To practice this skill, follow these steps.

1. **Determine which statements are based on facts.** Remember that a fact can be proven by checking other sources. Read statements 1 through 8 below. Answer the following questions: (a) Which statements are based solely upon facts? (b) List two sources you could use to check these statements to make sure they are true.

2. **Determine which statements are opinions.** An opinion states a person's belief or feeling about a subject. It usually cannot be proven. Statements of opinion are often signaled by words or phrases such as *I believe, extraordinary, worst,* or *outstanding.* Study statements 1 through 8 again. Answer the following questions: (a) Which of the statements express opinions? (b) What words or phrases in the statements signal that they are opinions? (c) Do any statements contain both facts and opinions? Which ones?

3. **Separate facts and opinions when you read.** Generally, an opinion is more reliable when an author gives facts to support it. Answer the following questions: (a) What opinions are expressed in the paragraph? (b) What facts does the author use to support each opinion? (c) Do you think that the author has done a good job of supporting the opinions? Explain your answer.

Statements

(1) In 768 Pepin's son, Charles, became king of the Franks.
(2) Charles, or Charlemagne, was an extraordinary human being.
(3) He was a very capable general.
(4) He defeated the Lombards in Italy and the Muslims in northern Spain.
(5) Charlemagne was an effective and energetic ruler.
(6) He used traveling representatives to supervise the conduct of local officials.
(7) Charlemagne, who was very religious, had a chapel built at his capital, Aachen.
(8) The crowning of Charlemagne in 800 was a pivotal event in the history of the Middle Ages.

Paragraph

Charlemagne placed great value on education. It is said that he slept with a pen and paper under his pillow. He brought scholars to live at his court. They studied Roman authors and wrote histories, poems and works of philosophy. At the palace school, directed by Alcuin, subjects such as grammar, philosophy, and mathematics were taught. Charlemagne issued regulations regarding religious education and ordered monasteries to establish schools and libraries. His actions in support of education strengthened medieval civilization.

REVIEW

Section Summaries

Section 1 Europe Revived During the Early Middle Ages The decline of the Roman Empire isolated western Europe from former trade contacts. However, the geography and resources of this small continent helped it to survive and build a distinctive civilization. Many barbarian tribes moved across Europe. The Franks established a Christian empire under King Clovis. A series of weak rulers followed Clovis until kings Pepin and Charlemagne, who attempted to rebuild the Roman Empire. During the ninth and tenth centuries, fierce Vikings from Norway, Sweden, and Denmark attacked Europe.

Section 2 The Feudal Pyramid Controlled Europe Feudal society was arranged in a pyramid of power and privilege. Kings and queens were at the top of the feudal pyramid, but they were not always the most powerful. Nobles, who owned land, and church officials, who had religious power, were at the next level. The nobility provided the king with military protection. At the bottom of the pyramid were serfs, peasants who worked the land for their noble lords. Feudalism became the government of medieval Europe, and the manor was the center of the economy. A code of manners known as chivalry developed, and nobles tried to live up to its high moral ideals.

Section 3 The Church Was a Powerful Force As the power of monarchs increased, conflicts between kings and popes (such as that between Henry IV and Pope Gregory VII) became more frequent. Medieval people believed that the Church could determine whether or not they would go to heaven. Because they were afraid they would be excommunicated, people were often afraid to support a monarch in conflict with the pope. The Church regulated business activities, collected tithes, and had law courts. Beginning in the 1000s, popes and monarchs cooperated in a series of Crusades to free Palestine from the Muslims. The Crusades spurred the growth of European civilization.

Key Facts

1. Use each vocabulary word in a sentence.

   a. mayor of the palace
   b. serf
   c. vassal
   d. feudalism
   e. freeman
   f. demesne
   g. fallow
   h. reeve
   i. tournament
   j. chivalry
   k. excommunicate
   l. heresy
   m. usury
   n. tithe
   o. Crusade
   p. ghetto

2. Identify and briefly explain the importance of the following names, places, or events.

   a. Ural Mountains
   b. Franks
   c. Charlemagne
   d. Vikings
   e. Pope Urban II
   f. Pope Gregory VII
   g. Henry IV

Main Ideas

1. Why were the resources of Europe especially important after the fall of the Roman Empire?
2. How did the conversion of King Clovis to Christianity help him to maintain his empire?
3. How did Charlemagne encourage learning in his empire?
4. Who were the Vikings?
5. Describe the structure of the feudal pyramid.
6. List three privileges that serfs received in exchange for their labor.
7. In what ways did the Church function like a government?
8. What did Pope Urban II want to accomplish through the Crusades?
9. What were three results of the Crusades?

Developing Skill in Reading History

Read each of the following statements and decide whether it is based on fact or opinion. Explain your answers.

1. Europe would have collapsed entirely after the fall of the Roman Empire if the continent had not had such rich farmland.
2. The Visigoths were only one of many barbarian tribes that raided Europe during the early Middle Ages.
3. The work done by women living on feudal manors was much harder than the men's work.
4. The Church gained too much power during the Middle Ages.
5. The Crusades were aimed at driving the Muslims from Palestine.

Using Social Studies Skills

1. **Interpreting Art** Study the medieval painting shown below. Then, answer the following questions:
   a. How does the painting depict women?
   b. How does the painting depict men?
   c. What event is taking place in the painting?
   d. What does the action of the painting suggest about the relationship between men and women in the Middle Ages?
   e. What code of values is represented by this painting?

2. **Writing Historical Fiction** Imagine that you are one of the men or women in the painting. Write an account of what this person might be thinking as the action takes place. Or, write a story that explains how the event in the painting came about.

Critical Thinking

1. **Recognizing Ideologies** How did the teachings of the Church give meaning to people's often short and brutal lives during the Middle Ages?
2. **Determining Relevance** How did the division of power between church officials and nobles in medieval Europe prevent the rise of an all-powerful ruler?
3. **Predicting Consequences** If a medieval knight were transplanted into twentieth-century America, which of his chivalrous values might he need to change, and why would he need to?

Focus on Writing

Writing Different Types of Paragraphs

Recall that a **narrative paragraph** tells a story, whether true or imaginary, and that a **descriptive paragraph** explains or describes something. Read each of the topic sentences listed below:
   a. Monarchs envied the power that the Church had attained during the Middle Ages.
   b. A medieval castle lacked the modern conveniences that we rely on today.
Now answer the following questions:
1. Which topic sentence would be appropriate for use in a narrative paragraph? Why?
2. Which topic sentence could be used in a descriptive paragraph? Explain.
3. List three facts that could be used to support each topic sentence.
4. Select one of the topic sentences and write a paragraph based on it. Use the facts that you listed in the previous question.

The Flowering of Medieval Society

(1050–1350)

1 **Towns Grew as Trade and Commerce Revived**

2 **Medieval Learning and Culture Flourished**

3 **Democracy and Capitalism Emerged**

▲ **Illustrating History** *This detail from an illuminated manuscript shows a medieval fair. Once religious in nature, the fairs grew more commercial during the Middle Ages.*

Cartloads of grain rumbled toward the cathedral of Chartres (SHART re) in France, where a crowd of merchants had already spread their wares. Fuel, vegetables, and meat were on sale in the streets adjoining the southern flank of the cathedral, and textiles were at the northern end. Unemployed masons and carpenters could be seen milling around inside the church, waiting for someone to hire them. The year was 1200, and the scene taking place was one of the great fairs of medieval Europe.

The great fairs of medieval Europe were typical of a trend away from sacred aims. Held four times a year at strategic locations along overland routes, the great fairs of Europe had grown increasingly commercial in purpose and international in scope. Wool merchants from Flanders rubbed elbows with Italian bankers or peddlers from the Middle East or Africa.

The great fairs generally lasted seven weeks. The first week was used to set up stalls and unload merchandise. The next four weeks were filled with buying and selling, and the final two weeks were devoted to settling accounts. Our modern notion of credit arose from the commerce of these medieval fairs. Merchants began to exchange notes promising each other payment at the next season's fair. By the thirteenth century, the great fairs were functioning as Europe's central bank.

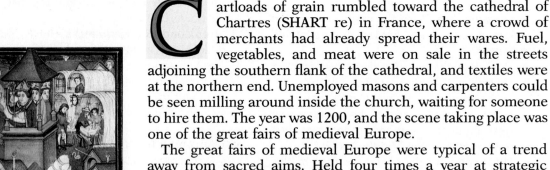

1200	1250	1300	1350
■ **1215** King John signs the Magna Carta	**1280s** ■ Hanseatic League controls European trade	■ **1295** King Edward holds English Model Parliament	**1350** ■ The Black Death strikes

▲ **Illustrating History** *The cathedral at Chartres is a fine example of medieval architecture. Chartres was also the site of a medieval fair.*

1 Towns Grew as Trade and Commerce Revived

As you read, look for answers to these questions:

◆ What factors contributed to increased trade and commerce?
◆ How did the growth of towns cause changes in society?
◆ What was the role of the medieval guild?
◆ What role did women have in medieval society?

> **Key Terms:** journeyman (defined on p. 220)

As you read in Chapter 8, after the fall of the Roman Empire, many cities declined. As a result, during the early Middle Ages, the manor, and not the town, was the center of community life in Europe. In the later Middle Ages when trade and commerce grew quickly, town life began to flourish again.

Trade and Commerce Grew

Although Byzantine and Muslim traders did a flourishing business in eastern Europe and the Middle East, trade in western Europe suffered during the early Middle Ages for a number of reasons. One reason was the lack of a strong central government to enforce laws and protect private property. Thieves made the transportation of goods risky and expensive. Roads were poor, and using the best roads was costly because tolls were collected at frequent intervals by feudal nobles. Many merchants could not afford to pay the high tolls. During the feudal period, therefore, trade and commerce could not move freely throughout western Europe.

Another obstacle to trade in feudal times was the lack of a sound money system.

217

Feudal banks were not as numerous or as able to serve the needs of the merchants as were the banks of ancient Rome. Barter, the exchange of goods and/or services for other goods and services was frequent. The unwillingness of the Church to allow profit-making or moneylending was another obstacle in the growth of medieval trade.

The Crusades and trade. The Crusades, which were discussed earlier in Chapter 8, encouraged the growth of trade and commerce by introducing the Crusaders to the products of distant lands, such as sugar, silk, and precious spices. In time, the luxuries of the East became necessities to Europeans, and merchants tried to supply the needed goods. The Italian cities of Genoa, Venice, Milan, Florence, and Pisa, which were near the Mediterranean Sea, became leading centers for world trade. These cities specialized in luxury goods. Trade in northern Europe was based on more ordinary but necessary goods, such as fish, furs, skins, and leather.

▼ **Illustrating History** *The wealthy hunters in this tapestry enjoyed luxuries, such as rich clothing, from Europe's growing trade.*

Since overland travel was dangerous, sea travel became highly developed as stronger and larger ships, which could travel farther and faster than earlier ships, were built. The merchants' desire for more trade also encouraged the exploration and colonization of the New World. Improved methods of coining money, new banking techniques, and the weighing and measuring of goods all contributed to a revival of trade.

Population growth. The growth in population at this time also contributed to the growth in trade and commerce. More people had to be fed and clothed. To feed and clothe more people, it became necessary to send farm goods and other goods from one part of Europe to another. Serfs who fled to the towns could find jobs in commerce and in the crafts. For example, a person might work making shoes or baking bread. Any products that they made were then sold rather than bartered, and the money received was used to buy the food that grew on manorial lands. Since the oldest son inherited the manor from his father, younger sons often left the manor to establish new lives for themselves in the towns, where trade and commerce provided many new opportunities to make a living.

Towns Gradually Replaced the Manor

As trade and commerce grew, the manor began to change. In fact, the self-sufficient feudal manor was often the beginning of a town. As the manors became more and more crowded, tradespeople and farmers moved outside the manor walls, and these settlements grew until they became small towns. For example, if the lord's castle was located near a strategic position, such as a bend in the river, merchants might stop there to rest. Sometimes, the manor would become the site of local fairs where people gathered to exchange goods. Sometimes, a monastery became the site of a town. Merchants and tradespeople settled nearby to supply the needs of the many pilgrims, or religious people, who made the journey to the monastery.

The growth of leagues. As trade increased in the later feudal period, around 1300, towns grew in number and size. As towns increased in population, the townspeople grew to dislike the rule of the noble or monastery, and they sought to govern and tax themselves. Gradually, the citizens of a town began to administer justice, coin money, build streets, and erect town halls without asking the consent of the noble or monastery.

Sometimes, towns joined together to form leagues—organizations that promoted trade and secured protection from thieves and pirates. The cities of Italy and those of northern Europe worked with merchants to form several important and powerful leagues. An example of such a union to defend trading interests was the Hanseatic (HAN see AT ik) League in northern Europe, which was formed in the late 1200s. Made up of more than 50 cities at its height, the Hanseatic League dominated trading in the

▲ **Illustrating History** *Coining money increased with trade. King Henry III of England is shown here.*

North and Baltic seas. In particular, the ships of the league controlled the profitable wool trade between England and Flanders.

DAILY LIFE

"Do-It-Yourself" Services

In twelfth-century England, townspeople tossing buckets of water onto a blaze in a panic might succeed in snuffing out a fire. These bucket brigades, however, were a long way from the professional fire-fighting teams we know today.

As European towns grew, they offered their residents little in the way of police or fire protection—or simple sanitation, for that matter. In twelfth-century England, some police duties were carried out by groups of neighbors, called *tithings*, who agreed to monitor one another's conduct.

By the fourteenth century, builders had learned how to install cesspools, drainage pipes, and latrines. Even so, many people remained ignorant of plumbing and its purposes. They demonstrated their scorn

of local efforts at regulation by pitching their waste water and sewage directly onto city streets.

1. What was one way twelfth-century England provided police services?
2. Before modern-day fire-fighting teams came along, how did people in a town put out fires?

Opposition to towns. Feudal lords viewed the growth of towns with alarm. They realized that the growth of trade meant that a town could become wealthier than a manor and that the merchants who lived in towns could become richer than the feudal lords. The wealth of the feudal lords was in land, but the wealth of the townspeople was in money, goods, and services. As townspeople traded and produced more manufactured goods, their wealth increased, and their living conditions improved. This progress contrasted sharply with life on the lord's manor. There, people labored to supply only the needs of the manor. Little opportunity existed for the people living on the manor to improve their own living conditions.

Monarchs had power over the nobles, and the two were often in conflict. As towns became wealthier, monarchs who wished to strengthen their positions gave them certain rights and privileges and, in return, received money. Sometimes, the monarch relieved the townspeople of their feudal obligations to the noble. Taxes, paid in money rather than in the form of work or goods, gave people more time to work for themselves and monarchs more power. With the money they collected from towns, some monarchs were able to hire soldiers of their own and no longer had to depend on the feudal obligations of their vassals. Once monarchs no longer had to rely on their vassals, they could extend their power and authority.

Towns and new opportunities. Realizing the opportunities that towns offered, serfs and their families began to move away from their manors. In a town, it was possible for a serf to climb from a low level in society to a higher one. Wealth, not birth, made the difference in a town. Although it was a difficult process, people who once were serfs could become rich, and highly regarded members of their towns. Serfs who ran away and were not caught for one year often won their freedom, escaped their feudal obligations, and achieved personal success. The medieval expression, "The city air makes free" certainly was applicable to the life of the serf.

▲ **Illustrating History** *Each medieval craft had its own guild. Above is the banner of the United Boot and Shoemakers Guild.*

Guilds Controlled Business Life

Many of those who moved to towns joined guilds. Medieval guilds were associations of people in the same craft or trade who set rules to uphold standards and protect members. Craft and merchant guilds controlled the prices and the quality of products made and sold in the towns. The craft guilds were made up of male and female artisans, or craftspeople, in the various trades. Thus, a medieval town might have guilds of stone masons, weavers, clockmakers, butchers, tanners, shoemakers, bakers, and lacemakers. Guilds regulated business dealings and provided a system through which a person could learn a trade. Someone who wished to be a weaver, for example, would begin as an apprentice (beginner) and gradually rise to the rank of **journeyman,** meaning a person who has learned the trade. After passing a difficult test, he or she became a master artisan. The guilds determined the wages of apprentices and guarded the trade secrets that were peculiar to the guild's individual crafts.

The cost of an object depended on the guild, and guilds usually tried to charge a just price. That is, they tried to charge a price that they and the Church believed to be fair to the consumer. Since the guilds controlled prices, there was little or no price competition, and a shopper looking for a pair of shoes could hardly expect to get a bargain. There was no oversupply of goods because most products were made as they were needed.

The guilds tried to discourage too many people from entering crafts. To limit the number of apprentices, guild masters made entrance examinations difficult. As time went on, it became almost impossible for a newcomer to enter a guild unless his or her father or mother had been a member.

Craft and Merchant Guilds Had Different Purposes

Craft guilds controlled the making of products, but merchant guilds controlled their sale. Because of their important position between maker and buyer, the merchant guilds became more powerful than the craft guilds. In Italy, where Venice became the center of trade in luxury goods, the merchant guilds were particularly important. Venice led other cities in trading along the Mediterranean Sea.

Because of their wealth, the merchant guilds played a prominent role in local government. They urged cities to improve sewers and sanitary facilities. They also tried to establish and maintain a system of weights and measures that could be used by everyone in the town. Sometimes, they would join together to provide police protection or to force a noble to do away with tolls. Each guild had its own town hall and possessed the power to punish members who did not follow directions.

Guilds tried to look after the welfare of their members by providing old-age benefits, fire and theft insurance, and by building hospitals and orphanages. Today, many of the social duties of guilds are still carried out by fraternal organizations. For example, the Masons of today owe their origins to the craft guilds of medieval days.

▼ **Chart Skill** *Which guilds were more involved in public affairs?*

Medieval Guilds		
	Merchant Guilds	**Craft Guilds**
Purpose:	To control the sale of products	To control the making of products
Members:	Merchants or traders	Artisans or craftspeople in various trades
Functions:	Restricted activities of foreign merchants	Set wages earned and hours worked by artisans
	Settled disputes among members in own courts	Set standards of quality and just prices for goods
	Encouraged improvement of sewers and sanitation	Guarded secrets of various trades
	Established weights and measures for towns	Prevented competition in the trades
	Provided police protection	Provided old-age benefits, fire and theft insurance
	Tried to abolish road tolls	Provided money to needy members
		Sponsored entertainment on religious feast days; contributed to building churches

Medieval Europe Was a Man's Society but Some Women Achieved Much

To the Church of medieval Europe, women were inferior to men. They were, in the Church's view, "a necessary evil, a natural temptation, a desirable calamity, a domestic peril, a deadly fascination, a painted ill." According to the Church, man, not woman, was made in the image of God. As the great theologian Thomas Aquinas (uh KWI nuhs) once wrote, "The woman is subject to the man on account of the weakness of her nature, both of mind and of body."

Although the Church and society as a whole gave women a second-class position, marriages were important. Men and women were expected to marry when they were quite young. Among the nobility, marriage contracts (written agreements to marry) were extremely important. They could be used to seal treaties or to establish alliances.

BIOGRAPHY

Eleanor of Aquitaine

Born in France in 1122, Eleanor of Aquitaine spent her childhood at play in a court filled with poetry and music. Her father, the duke of Aquitaine, ruled French lands larger than those of the French king, which made Eleanor's marriage to Louis VII at age 15 a natural step. When their marriage failed to produce a son, however, the pope dissolved it. In 1152, Eleanor wed Henry Plantagenet, who was destined to become king of England.

Henry was constantly unfaithful and the marriage grew stormy. After Eleanor unsuccessfully plotted Henry's overthrow in 1173, she became her husband's prisoner for 16 years.

When Henry died in 1189, Eleanor's favorite son Richard the Lion-Hearted took the throne. While Richard was away fighting a Crusade, Eleanor ruled England with a firm but fair hand. A master of diplomacy, Eleanor worked to increase her son's popularity. She freed political prisoners and ended some taxes on the abbeys. After Richard was captured and held for ransom, Eleanor successfully raised the money to free him. She remained a force in European politics, arranging dynastic marriages to increase the wealth and power of her children. She died in 1204 at 82, at the height of her power.

1. What was the basis of Eleanor's father's wealth?
2. What advantages do you suppose Henry Plantagenet saw in marrying Eleanor?
3. How did Eleanor show a mastery of politics?

According to church law, it was the duty of the husband to protect the wife, and the duty of the wife to obey her husband. Wife beating, which was common, was not a crime under church or civil law. Women could not testify or give evidence in a court of law, nor could they take part in government, although some noble women did. No woman could become a licensed physician, but some woman practiced medicine despite the law.

Women worked in the fields and cared for their families. A woman needed to know how to cook, bake, mend clothing, make soap and candles, brew beer, and mix medicines. Although not allowed to participate in government, women could join guilds. In the towns, women did most of the spinning and weaving in the textile guilds. In fact, there were often as many women as men in the guilds because women were encouraged to help their husbands at their crafts. Several guilds devoted to the manufacture of women's clothing were made up entirely of women. Even when they were members of a guild, however, women usually received lower wages than men, and in guilds made up of both men and women, it was rare for a woman to become a master.

Education was not considered particularly important for a woman. Some noblewomen learned to read, write, and play musical instruments, activities sometimes considered beneath the dignity of warrior knights. With men often away at war, upper-class women frequently had to manage the family estate, which required hard work and skill. Women often joined in pilgrimages to holy places, and some shared with men the difficulties and the dangers of the Crusades.

The life of a medieval woman was a difficult one. Even noblewomen toiled long hours, caring for home and family. Church and civil laws kept all women in a lesser position than men. Education included practical skills such as weaving, and with some exceptions, most women could not read or write. Although chivalry had improved the protection of women, their lives during the Middle Ages remained limited and harsh.

▲ **Illustrating History** *This painting shows medieval farm laborers in France.*

SECTION 1 REVIEW

Knowing Key Terms, People, and Places
1. Define: **a.** journeyman
2. Identify: **a.** Hanseatic League

Reviewing Main Ideas
3. What advantages did life in a town offer to a serf?
4. Why did feudal lords oppose the growth of towns?
5. Explain how a person became a master artisan through the guilds.
6. How did the merchant guilds attempt to improve local government?

Critical Thinking
Recognizing Bias
7. What bias existed against women during the Middle Ages?

223

2 Medieval Learning and Culture Flourished

As you read, look for answers to these questions:

◆ How did learning advance during the Middle Ages?
◆ What types of literature arose in the Middle Ages?
◆ How did art and architecture reflect the faith of the medieval people?
◆ How did medieval philosophy clash with the Church's teachings?

> **Key Terms:** alchemy (defined on p. 225), troubadour (p. 226), scholasticism (p. 228)

Some people think of the Middle Ages as a time during which little happened. While the Middle Ages may not have been as rich in achievements as other periods, it was a time of significant advancement. Progress was made in education, philosophy, literature, art, and architecture. Although less spectacular, progress was also made in science.

Medieval Universities Became Centers for Study, Teaching, and Research

Education during much of the Middle Ages was centered around the Church. Because the priests and bishops of the Church were able to read and write at a time when most other people could not, they were educators and preservers of culture. Monks carefully copied the great books of the ancient world and kept historical records called chronicles. Church schools grew up around parish churches and monasteries. Thus, the Church maintained a high degree of learning that could then be passed on to others.

Since education was mostly in the hands of the Church, the chance to learn was free for those who could take advantage of it. However, many parents in those days needed their children as workers or failed to realize the importance of education. Many did not let their children take advantage of the schooling the Church offered.

Gradually the desire for education grew, and the Church founded many universities. Although the teachers were often religious leaders, they taught subjects other than religion. Students wishing to become doctors or lawyers studied medicine and law, as well as religion. Universities began at London, Paris, Salerno, Padua, Salamanca, and Bologna. During the late Middle Ages, other universities emerged that had little connection with the Church.

Student life. In many ways, university student life was different from student life today. In southern Europe, for example, students ran the universities and formed student guilds. Students helped to establish the rules they needed and decided which teachers should be hired. In the early universities, teachers received their pay directly from the students. If a teacher's lecture was too long or too boring, students would leave the room.

▼ **Illustrating History** *As today, students in medieval times took breaks from their studies. The students pictured below are playing a game that looks similar to the modern game of baseball.*

The scarcity of books was the major roadblock to the advancement of learning in the Middle Ages. Since printing was not invented until the 1400s, most of the teaching was done by reading orally from the few books that were available. The books that were available had been copied by hand on parchment and were often handsomely illustrated. Even the simplest of them was expensive. It is estimated that an ordinary volume cost the equivalent of several hundred dollars. In the households of the wealthy, books were precious objects to be handed down from generation to generation.

Scientific knowledge. In the field of science, the scholars of the Middle Ages were followers of the early Greeks, Aristotle, Galen, and Ptolemy. Roger Bacon, one of the most famous of the medieval scientists, used observation and experimentation in chemistry. Because of his significant contribution to the scientific method of study, Bacon is now called the founder of experimental science.

In spite of the growing emphasis on observation and interpretation, however, medieval scientists often returned to magic and alchemy. Through **alchemy,** an early form of chemistry, scientists tried to change metals into gold and to find ways to lengthen human life. The attempt to change ordinary metals to gold was useless, and it delayed the development of the science of chemistry.

As science in the Middle Ages became more mature, there was less emphasis on magic and alchemy and more emphasis on observation and experimentation and conclusions based on them. Instead of accepting the traditional explanations of the past, scientists actually began to prove or disprove their theories, using the emerging scientific method. Although the scientific method had not yet fully developed, there were a number of useful advances. Among other things, the scientists and mathematicians of the Middle Ages adopted the Arabic numbering system from the Middle East. Mirrors, lenses, and clocks were among the practical medieval inventions.

In their own words

A Student's Letter Home

As you write letters, you may be preparing documents for some future historian. Personal letters are an excellent source of information about the everyday problems faced by people in history. The following excerpt was written by a university student to his father during the medieval period.

❝Well-beloved father, I have not a penny nor can I get any save through you, for all things at the University are so dear; nor can I study in my Code or Digest [textbooks], for they are all tattered. Moreover, I owe ten crowns due to the Provost [university official], and can find no man to lend them to me: I send you word of greetings and of money.

The Student hath need of many things if he will profit here; his father and his kin [relatives] must needs supply him freely, that he be not compelled to pawn his books, but have ready money in his purse, with gowns and furs and decent clothing, or he will be damned for a beggar; wherefore, that men may not take me for a beast, I send you word of greetings and of money.

Wines are dear, and hostels [inns], and other good things; I owe . . . and am hard bested to free myself from such snares. Dear father, deign [stoop] to help me! I fear to be excommunicated. . . . wherefore, grant my supplication [plea], for I send you word of greetings and of money.❞

1. What phrase does the student repeat three times in the letter? Why?
2. What precautions should historians take if they use this letter as a guide to discovering how expensive items were in the medieval period?

▲ **Illustrating History** *Medieval astronomers used astrolabes to study the stars.*

Medieval Literature Was Read, Recited, and Sung

During the Middle Ages, when chivalry was an ideal, epics were an important part of the literature. As you read in Chapter 4, an epic is a long poem telling of a hero's or heroine's brave deeds. One of the earliest epics, was written in the 700s. *Beowulf* tells of the hero Beowulf's battles with wicked people and ferocious animals. Other epics of this period that have survived are the stories of King Arthur and the Knights of the Round Table. The French contributed the *Song of Roland*, the story of Charlemagne's heroic commander who died bravely in battle. This early literature became the source for later poetry and music.

In this age of chivalry, the idea of romantic love played as crucial a role in the epic as bravery. Stories of romance were often sung by wandering **troubadours** or minstrels—poet-musicians—who traveled from castle to castle singing songs of love and adventure, such as the tales of Robin Hood, and telling of the charms of fair ladies.

Not all the stories of this time were about heroic deeds or undying love. A fable is a story that teaches a lesson. In medieval days, stories about Reynard the Fox were the best-known fables. In these stories, the animals take on human qualities. One story tells of a fox who outwits a crow by flattering him into singing so he will open his mouth and drop a bunch of grapes. The lesson, of course, is that human vanity, or excessive pride in oneself, can make us forget good judgment. Even today, those who read the stories cannot help laughing at the foolish ways in which people behave, especially when they are pointed out to them by the actions of the animals in the fables.

The Church used drama as a means of telling people what it expected of them. Plays based on stories from the Bible were called *mystery plays;* those based on religious events not in the Bible were called *miracle plays;* those that tried to show the continuing struggle between good and evil were called *morality plays*. The theme of the plays was that it paid to be good.

Medieval Art and Architecture Were Expressions of Faith

The Middle Ages were an age of faith, and the medieval cathedral was an expression of that faith. The building of a cathedral was a community affair. The community in which it was built paid for the cathedral and often supplied the laborers and artisans needed for its construction.

Architecture. Architecture was the greatest of the medieval arts. The Gothic style, as it is now called, used tall spires, pointed arches, flying buttresses (stone or brick supports on buildings), stained glass windows, and carved statues to express its faith. By using the flying buttress, medieval builders were able to make high roofs and thin walls. The Cathedral of Notre Dame and the Cathedral of Chartres are among the finest examples of Gothic architecture.

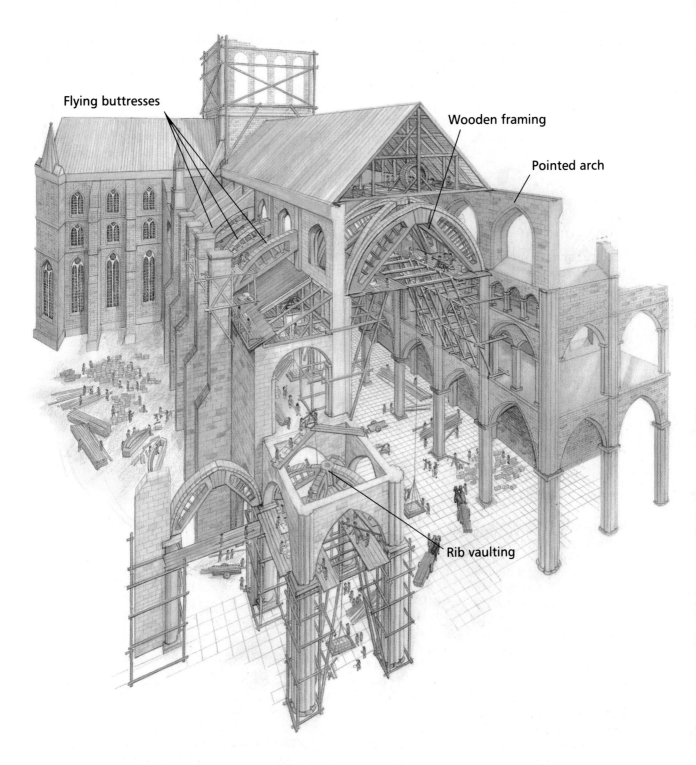

Flying buttresses

Wooden framing

Pointed arch

Rib vaulting

▲ **Illustrating History** *Built as expressions of religious faith, medieval cathedrals often took decades to complete. The cathedral shown above is an example of the Gothic style of architecture. Among the most notable features of Gothic architecture are vaulted ceilings, pointed arches, and flying buttresses.*

Sculpture. Important as the Gothic cathedrals were, there were still many other artistic expressions of faith. They may be found in thousands of images of Jesus and Mary and the apostles and the saints. Sculpture took the form of carved stone reliefs rather than free-standing statues. Reliefs are raised figures and forms that stand out from the flat surface to which they are attached. These stone reliefs, sometimes in the form of grotesque gargoyles, were meant to enrich the worship service and to humble the devout before God.

Art and music. Painting, although not as important as architecture, was also used to express faith. The Italian painter Giotto, who lived from 1276 to 1337, used light, shadow, and perspective in new ways to make his subjects appear more alive and began the artistic changes that characterize the Renaissance. Medieval music was written to involve the worshippers in prayer and to help establish a harmonious relationship with God. The Gregorian chant with its austere, somber tones provided a background against which the psalms might be said. Church music developed great hymns to God that were simple at first and grew more complex as the Middle Ages wore on.

Medieval Philosophy Tried to Prove Faith With Reason

Scholasticism (skuh LAS tih SIZ uhm) was the philosophy that dominated the medieval period. According to scholasticism, faith could be achieved through logical reasoning. In fact, the scholastic method was similar to the method used in the study of geometry. Geometry tries to prove theorems, or principles, in a number of logical steps. It is necessary to write down what is given, to state what has to be proven, and to list the steps of the actual proof. In medieval times, this type of formal logic was used to try to prove difficult questions of faith.

One famous scholastic teacher was Peter Abelard (AB uh lard). His unhappy love affair with the brilliant and beautiful Heloise (EL oh EEZ) first got him into difficulty with the Church. More troubles beset him when he wrote his well-known book *Sic et Non,* or *Yes and No,* in which he claimed the Bible could be interpreted in many ways. The idea shocked many church leaders, who believed that there was only one correct way to interpret the Bible. Although Abelard was unpopular with church leaders, he was so respected by his students that they flocked to his lectures. The attendance at his lectures was so large that he is said to be responsible for starting the University of Paris.

Thomas Aquinas was another famous scholastic teacher. Aquinas is best known for his book *Summa Theologica* in which he tried to show that Christian teachings did not disagree with reason. According to him, if there were disagreements between Christian teachings and reason, then the method of reasoning must be wrong. Aquinas offered logical proof of the existence of God, of life after death, and of the authority of the Church. Aquinas was probably the greatest of all the scholastic philosophers.

SECTION 2 REVIEW

Knowing Key Terms, People, and Places
1. Define: **a.** alchemy **b.** troubadour **c.** scholasticism
2. Identify: **a.** *Beowulf* **b.** morality plays **c.** Peter Abelard **d.** Thomas Aquinas

Reviewing Main Ideas
3. Why didn't many children of the Middle Ages get an education?
4. Explain the high value placed on books during the Middle Ages.
5. Describe four characteristics of the Gothic style of architecture.

Critical Thinking
Making Comparisons
6. Compare the role of a medieval university student with your role as a high-school student. Explain why you would or would not want similiar responsibilities.

The Majestic Cathedrals of Medieval Europe

If one wishes to study the art of the Middle Ages, one need look no further than the Chartres cathedral in northern France, near Paris. Its doors, or portals, are richly decorated with sculpture; its many tall windows of stained glass fill the interior with softly glowing colors; and the immense, soaring spaces lead one's eyes toward the sky. Since most of the medieval public could not read, pictures and sculptures could be used to teach the Christian faith more effectively than the written word.

Therefore, every sculpted figure or stained-glass image was meant to remind the viewer of a story or person from the Christian texts. For example, the Jamb Statues at Chartres portray several saints. Even the building itself was intended to suggest the splendors of heaven. Large medieval churches took decades or, in some cases, even centuries to build. When they were finished, they amazed humble pilgrims with their elaborate decorations. The ornate stone work in the interior of Chartres is shown here; an exterior view is shown on page 217.

Below right is the interior of Chartres cathedral. Several Jamb Statues are shown below left.

3 Democracy and Capitalism Emerged

As you read, look for answers to these questions:

◆ How did the ideas of the medieval period lay the foundations of democracy?
◆ How did the change to a money economy lead to the end of feudalism?
◆ What events and factors contributed to end of the Middle Ages?

Key Terms: capitalism (defined on p. 231)

Democracy as we know it did not exist in the Middle Ages, nor did modern economic systems. Nevertheless, some elements that make both democracy and current economic systems possible have their roots in the Middle Ages.

Democracy Had Roots in the Medieval Period

Although democracy in its modern sense did not exist in the Middle Ages, a number of circumstances contributed to its growth.

The feudal system. The feudal system of government was one in which no one person had all the power. While vassals owed obligations to the king, the king owed obligations to his vassals. Both the king and his vassals, in turn, owed obligations to the Church. The king who sought to ignore his obligations could not hope to hold his throne for long, and anyone who disobeyed the Church risked excommunication. Just as each group in the feudal pyramid owed obligations, so each group had some freedom as well. This idea of mutual obligation can be found more clearly defined in our democracy, which depends largely on maintaining a balance of power among competing groups.

Church teachings. Our Declaration of Independence declares, as a "self-evident truth" that "all men are created equal." It goes on to declare that people have "certain inalienable rights," including "life, liberty, and the pursuit of happiness." Where did these ideas come from? The teachings of the Church that all are equal before God introduced the idea of equality between people. If human beings were equal before God, did it not then follow that people should work toward equality or at least to improve their lives as best they could here on earth? This

▼ **Illustrating History** *Toward the end of the Middle Ages, many medieval cities became bustling centers of business and trade. Below is a painting of the Italian city of Siena by Lorenzetti.*

view encouraged medieval rulers to be responsible for the well-being of those they ruled. In the eighteenth century, European thinkers again spoke of these ideas. Important Americans then read these ideas and included them in the Declaration of Independence and the U.S. Constitution.

The Magna Carta and the Model Parliament. In 1215, King John of England was forced to sign the Magna Carta, which spelled out some of the limits of the king's power. In 1295, Edward I convened the Model Parliament, which was the basis for the current Parliament of England. Combined with the canon law of the Church, these two events helped to establish a system of justice that included a jury system so that those accused could be judged by ordinary men and women. They also encouraged the idea of *habeas corpus,* a legal writ that protects a person against illegal imprisonment. These practices were later incorporated into those societies that sought fair and democratic procedures.

Capitalism Emerged During the Middle Ages

Like democracy, the modern economic system of capitalism has its root in the Middle Ages. Free enterprise, or **capitalism,** can be defined as an economic system based on private ownership of the means of producing goods and services. Capitalism involves profit and usually competition.

Toward the end of the Middle Ages, as the towns grew and the manors declined, an economy based on money replaced an economy based on land. As a result, the buying and selling of goods and services became important in determining prices and the quality or quantity of what was sold.

As the economy changed, serfdom began to disappear. While not slaves, serfs could not leave the land and owed obligations to a lord. By the end of the fourteenth century, however, many serfs paid rent. As the self-sufficient economy of the manor changed to a money economy, the serf's obligations were converted to a money payment.

This change was both good and bad for serfs. It was good because they no longer were required to work for the lord or to share what they harvested. On the other hand, if they could not sell what they grew and were unable to pay the rent, they could be thrown off the farm altogether. When this happened, rent-paying farmers became farm laborers. The fourteenth century was marked by numerous peasant uprisings. These uprising demonstrated that the medieval practices and customs could no longer meet the needs of the people.

The nobility, too, was having economic troubles. As the costs of serving a lord increased, many nobles found they could no longer support an army of knights. Many could not even raise money for dowries so that their daughters could marry. Some tried to make good marriages to maintain their accustomed ways. For the most part, however, nobles found that they had to tie their fortunes to a king and become part of the royal court. In this way, monarchies were strengthened, and national governments replaced feudal arrangements.

As the economy of the Middle Ages expanded, some of the church-imposed rules on how business should be conducted clashed with the needs of the times. To meet these needs, the Church reluctantly eased the restrictions on charging interest for loans. The idea of the "just price" also had to give way to the idea of a fair profit, the financial gain received through doing business.

While some guilds lasted for many more decades, by the end of the fourteenth century craft guilds no longer could provide the goods a growing economy required. People who once would have sought to become masters in their crafts found their paths to advancement blocked. The result was that many people became wage workers in the cities. As such, they were subject to problems of earning enough for themselves and their families. Unemployment was frequent, and finding a place to live and enough to eat made life harsh for many people.

What was happening to the medieval way of life was the beginning of capitalism. The traditional feudal obligations were breaking down and a money economy was growing. The clash between feudalism and a money economy tore the fabric of feudal society.

Unlike land, money could be carried from one place to another. It could be banked or loaned or used to pay for luxuries, such as cloth, spices, perfumes, and jewels, or necessities, such as grain or herring. The self-sufficient community of the medieval manor had little desire and less ability to produce new luxuries or even necessities. When these became available, capitalists found ways to provide them and so challenged the existing economic system. In the process of doing so, they helped bring the Middle Ages to an end.

Many Factors Contributed to the Waning of the Middle Ages

The Middle Ages waned because of the problems that developed within it. An economy based on land clashed with an economy based on money. In government, monarchs sought to increase their powers at the expense of their vassals. By the end of the fourteenth century, the Middle Ages were drawing to an end as feudal society either disappeared or changed beyond recognition. Just as Rome did not crumble at once, so the waning of the Middle Ages took place slowly. Two developments, however, hastened the end of the Middle Ages.

The Black Death. In 1348, the Black Death, which we now know was bubonic plague, struck Europe. The plague began in Asia and was brought to Europe in the holds of ships that were havens for flea-infested rats. The fleas carried the disease to humans who then suffered fever and swelling of the lymph glands and developed spots of blood that turned black under the skin. Before the plague ended, between one-third and one-half of the population of Europe had died.

As a result of the plague, lands went untended and workshops were deserted. Food production fell, and famine soon followed. Economic chaos became the rule since the plague made worse an economy that was already reeling. So many people died that there were too few people to farm and produce needed goods. Uprisings among peasants and townspeople became frequent.

The Peasants' Rebellion. One of the more serious uprisings was the Peasants' Rebellion of 1381 under England's King Richard II. Angry over newly imposed taxes that they could not pay, peasants and townspeople, under the leadership of a tradesman named Wat Tyler, burned tax rolls and manorial records. They killed unpopular officials, marched on London, burned the palace of the Duke of Lancaster, and murdered the chancellor and treasurer of England.

Leaders of the rebellion were able to force King Richard to end serfdom and manorial dues. Although the king forgot his promises when Wat Tyler was killed, serfdom was clearly doomed. Feudalism, too, would soon end, as monarchs recognized that a feudal system could not govern in the kind of Europe that was emerging.

Meanwhile, the world beyond Europe was continuing to advance. The civilizations in India and Southeast Asia were ready to begin their golden ages of change and progress as you will learn in the next chapter.

SECTION 3 REVIEW

Knowing Key Terms, People, and Places
1. Define: **a.** capitalism
2. Identify: **a.** *habeas corpus* **b.** Black Death **c.** Peasants' Rebellion

Reviewing Main Ideas
3. How did the doctrine of the medieval church provide some of the basic ideas of democracy?
4. Explain how the change to a money economy was both good and bad for the serfs.
5. What happened to the craft guilds as the Middle Ages ended? Why did this occur?

Critical Thinking
Demonstrating Reasoned Judgment
6. If the Black Death had never occurred, do you think that the feudal system would have continued? Explain your answer.

SKILLS NOTEBOOK

Analyzing Information: Evaluating Evidence

Many different types of accounts provide you with information about a historical period, a development, or an event. For example, your history text provides you with one type of information; primary source materials, such as diaries, provide you with another type of information. Works of fiction may be useful as sources of historical knowledge.

When you read a source of information, you must analyze and evaluate the source carefully to determine its value and accuracy. Use the following steps to evaluate the excerpt below.

1. **Identify the nature of the document.** Look at the subject of the document, the date the document was written, and any other general information you can discover by skimming the document. Answer the following questions: (a) What type of document is it? (b) Who wrote it? (c) Where do you think the author got her information about her subject?

2. **Decide how reliable and accurate the document is.** Answer the following questions: (a) What conclusions are drawn in the document? (b) What factual information does the document present to support its conclusions? (c) Is the information in the document consistent with what you already know about the subject? Give an example.

3. **Study the document to learn more about a historical period or event?** Use the information in the paragraphs to help you answer the following questions: (a) What were two dangers faced by townspeople? (b) How many people might have lived in a town of average size? (c) What were the largest cities in medieval Europe? (d) What information does the document give about the factors that helped to speed the growth of towns and cities?

In their heyday, medieval towns had little of the charm that now enchants the 20th century. Within their encircling walls, space was a luxury for the few. Jam-packed wooden houses, each a potential tinderbox, sought extra room through upper stories jutting out over the street. The streets themselves were mere alleys, 6 to 10 feet across. Sewers were open and sanitation scant. . . . Except when [a town dweller] raised his eyes to the Gothic grace of town belfry or church spire, signs of filth and disease assailed him everywhere. . . .

Many of Europe's renowned cities, among them Hamburg, Frankfurt, Innsbruck, Bruges, Ghent, Oxford and Cambridge, started from scratch during the latter half of the Middle Ages, while urban centers already in existence, such as London, Paris, Venice, Genoa, Milan and Florence, mushroomed astonishingly. An ordinary town might have 2,500 inhabitants, a sizable town, 20,000. London and Genoa boasted 50,000 each; the largest, Paris, Venice and Milan, had more than 100,000 each.

Excerpt from: Anne Fremantle, *Age of Faith*, Time-Life Books, Age of Faith Series (New York: Time, Inc., 1965), pp. 71, 75.

REVIEW

Section Summaries

Section 1 Towns Grew as Trade and Commerce Revived The self-sufficient feudal manor was often the beginning of a medieval town, as it became a busy center for trade. Many serfs were able to escape their feudal obligations and become prosperous by working as artisans or merchants in the new towns. Craft and merchant guilds controlled the business life of a town. They set guidelines for who would be able to join the guilds, how products would be made, and what prices would be charged. The lack of a strong central government in western Europe was an obstacle to trade. Church teachings kept medieval women in a second-class position, but some women were able to join guilds, become educated, and greatly influence their husbands.

Section 2 Medieval Learning and Culture Flourished The Middle Ages were a time of significant advancements. The Church fostered the growth of universities. Books were scarce, so teaching was done by reading aloud. Science moved from the pursuit of magic and alchemy to the methods of observation and experimentation. Literature was dominated by epics, fables, and religious plays. With the birth of scholasticism, logic was used to prove religious truths. Art, architecture, and music were explored as means of religious expression.

Section 3 Democracy and Capitalism Emerged The feudal system and Christian teachings provided the foundations for democracy. Toward the end of the Middle Ages an economy based on money began to replace feudalism, which was based on land. Serfs were no longer tied to the land, but they lost the security of the feudal system. Europe's changing economy caused problems for the nobles, who were trying to stay independent of kings, and for the Church, which had tried to regulate business. The Middle Ages declined because of economic and political tensions that gradually changed the structure of European life.

Key Facts

1. Use each vocabulary word in a sentence.
   a. journeyman   d. scholasticism
   b. alchemy   e. capitalism
   c. troubadour
2. Identify and briefly explain the importance of the following names, places, or events.
   a. Hanseatic League   e. *Beowulf*
   b. barter   f. Thomas Aquinas
   c. master artisan   g. Black Death
   d. Roger Bacon   h. Wat Tyler

Main Ideas

1. Identify two factors that contributed to the growth of trade during the Middle Ages.
2. How did the growth of towns affect the power of feudal lords?
3. List three functions of the medieval guilds.
4. What role did merchant guilds play in the government?
5. How were medieval universities different from modern universities?
6. How did the methods of science change during the Middle Ages?
7. What was the focus of most medieval art?
8. How did the growth of capitalism change the economy of medieval Europe?
9. How did changes in the economy and the government bring about the decline of the Middle Ages?

Developing Skill in Reading History

An **inference** is a logical conclusion based on facts. When you make an inference, you must read between the lines, or draw a conclusion that goes beyond what is explicitly stated in a text. Chapter 9 states that the medieval Church made use of drama to show its members what was expected of them. Find the passage in the chapter that discusses this issue and answer the following questions:

1. What are three expectations that the Church might have had for its members during the Middle Ages?
2. Explain the inferences that you had to make in order to answer question 1. What was your evidence for these inferences?

Using Social Studies Skills

1. **Interpreting Evidence** The flying buttress was an advancement in architecture because it allowed people to build cathedrals with very high ceilings. Study the interior of the Gothic cathedral shown on this page. Then answer the following questions:
   a. What emotional effect might you feel as you entered a building like this one?
   b. Based on what you have learned in the chapter about the purpose behind medieval art and architecture, why do you think it was important for the Church to build cathedrals like this one?

2. **Imagining Historical Events** Pretend that you are a medieval peasant and that you have just returned from your first visit to a Gothic cathedral like the one shown on this page. Write an account of how you might describe your experience to your family, including what most impressed you and how the experience has changed your feelings about the Church.

Critical Thinking

1. **Determining Relevance** How did population growth in medieval Europe contribute to a growth in trade and commerce?
2. **Making Comparisons** How did the use of observation and experimentation depart from early scientific methods?
3. **Formulating Questions** Create a list of questions that a craft guild would need to ask when it was trying to establish prices for its goods.

Focus on Writing

Persuasive Paragraph

A **persuasive paragraph** is one that attempts to persuade an audience to take action or to accept a certain idea, belief, or position. The *topic sentence* tells what action or idea will be promoted in the paragraph. *Supporting details* give strong reasons why the audience should go along with the action or idea. The *language* used in a persuasive paragraph should create a tone that is rational and, in some cases, emotionally powerful or inspiring.

Practice: Use the following topic to plan a persuasive paragraph: "Women as Second-Class Citizens in the Middle Ages." Complete the following prewriting activities:

1. Write a topic sentence that tells the position that you intend to support.
2. List three arguments that you would use to support your topic sentence.
3. In what order would you present your arguments? Explain why.

Geography in History

The Black Death and Population Change

Spreading across a sea of humanity, disease ravaged Europe during the Middle Ages (see page 232). The death knell rang daily as thousands lost their lives every day.

Before the Black Death Struck

Four factors are used to measure population change in an area—births, deaths, and the departure and arrival of new people. From 950 to 1250, the number of people in Europe more than tripled, from 25 million to over 75 million. Several factors contributed to this boom. Agriculture had been improved, and food production quadrupled. A worldwide warm spell between about 800 and 1200 made land more productive. Wars were fewer and less destructive.

However, even before the Black Death struck, too many mouths hungered for food. The "Little Ice Age" ended warmer temperatures. After 1300, cold, wet weather rotted crops and brought famine.

However, the birthrate—the annual number of births per 1,000 people—stayed high. Deaths due to hunger were made up by new births. But, population gains were soon stopped by one of the worst enemies the human race had ever faced—the Black Death.

The Death Arrives

Late in the year 1347, something merciless arrived in Europe. Nearly a century before, when Mongol warriors raided China, their swift horses had carried it back to Mongolia. Decades later, it began to spread along the Silk Road, a trade route to the Black Sea. Devastation came in the form of a flea and what the flea carried—bacteria.

Several conditions made the spread of these bacteria possible. The flea that brought them lived on the common black rat. Ships sailing from the Mediterranean to northern Europe carried these rats into every harbor. Finally, the plague spread rapidly in Europe because of the dense population there.

The Death Spreads

The plague spread west from Constantinople, gradually turning north. From Sicily, it infected France and crossed the English Channel. Finally, it turned east again, toward Scandinavia and Russia. It killed about 90 percent of the people it affected.

The exact drop in population caused by the Black Death is not known. Good records were not always kept, but it can be guessed that about one-third of the population of Europe died—about 25 million people. Losses were about 50 percent in cities. Even rural areas lost about 30 percent of their population. Italy and southern France lost the most people.

The Death Returns

Human population groups tend to recover quickly, and in the years after 1350, birthrates were high.

Still, the plague was not over. It returned in 1361, particularly affecting the young, since they had not been exposed to it before.

Over the next century it returned every 5 to 12 years. Although these later plagues killed fewer people, they prevented any population growth. Between 1349 and 1450, the population decreased by 50 percent.

Other Effects

After 1500, attacks of the plague lessened. By then, however, the plague had caused lasting changes. For instance, between 1350 and 1500, about 1,300 villages in England were abandoned. Some of those spared by the plague fled to the cities, and others moved into farming areas.

The Black Death had ended population growth and caused tremendous suffering. But, in less than a century, the population would grow back to its previous size.

Focus on Geography

1. **Interaction** What effect did the warm spell between 800 and 1200 have on the population of Europe?

2. **Movement** What type of movement brought the plague to the European population centers?

3. **Regions** What regions of Europe were most and least affected by the plague?

Critical Thinking

Predicting Consequences
4. What effect would the loss of young people, rather than old, have on the growth of population?

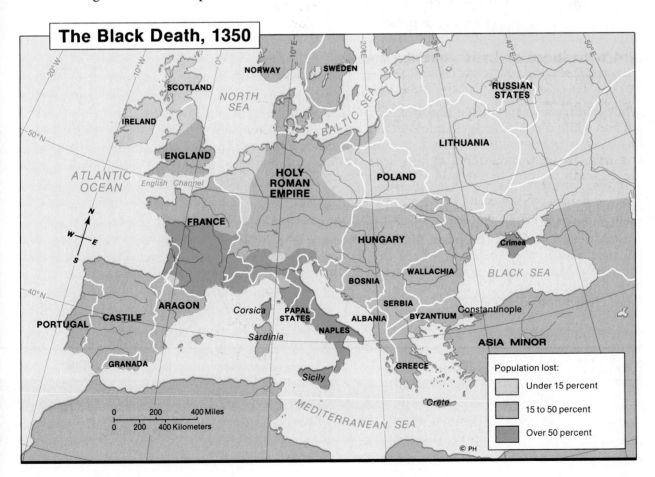

The Black Death, 1350

Population lost:
- Under 15 percent
- 15 to 50 percent
- Over 50 percent

© PH

UNIT
4

The World Beyond Europe

(600 B.C.–A.D. 1700)

Chapters

While civilizations in Greece and Rome rose and fell and while the Middle Ages unfolded in Europe, history was being made in Africa, the Americas, and Asia. In India, great civilizations lasted from the eleventh century to the mid-1700s. Southeast Asian kingdoms helped shaped the land of today. In China, four major dynasties ruled from 618 to 1644. Civilizations also flourished in Africa, where the West African kingdoms of Ghana, Mali, and Songhai rose, and in the Americas, where the Aztecs, Incas, and Mayas built empires. The map and the time line, linked by color, show where and when these civilizations developed.

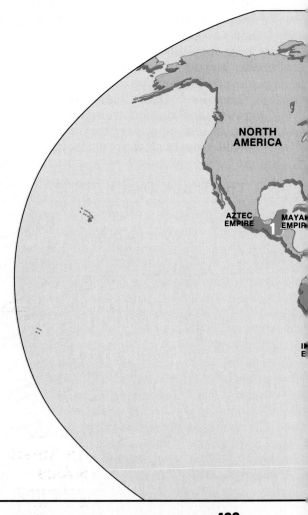

NORTH AMERICA

AZTEC EMPIRE

MAYAN EMPIRE

800 B.C.	400 B.C.	B.C. / A.D.	A.D. 400

■ A.D. 300 Mayan civilization enters a golden age

■ 600 B.C. The Phoenicians trade with coastal African towns

A.D. 395 Ethiopians ■ adopt Christianity

CHINA, JAPAN, AND KOREA

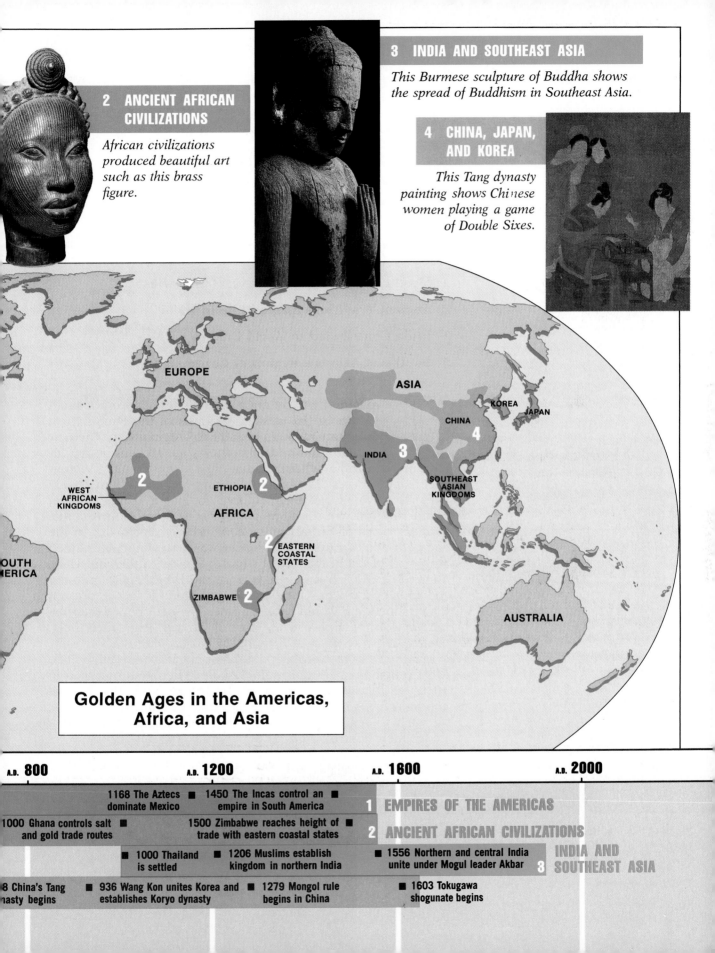

2 ANCIENT AFRICAN CIVILIZATIONS

African civilizations produced beautiful art such as this brass figure.

3 INDIA AND SOUTHEAST ASIA

This Burmese sculpture of Buddha shows the spread of Buddhism in Southeast Asia.

4 CHINA, JAPAN, AND KOREA

This Tang dynasty painting shows Chinese women playing a game of Double Sixes.

EUROPE

ASIA

KOREA

JAPAN

CHINA

4

INDIA

3

SOUTHEAST ASIAN KINGDOMS

WEST AFRICAN KINGDOMS

ETHIOPIA **2**

2

AFRICA

2 EASTERN COASTAL STATES

ZIMBABWE **2**

AUSTRALIA

SOUTH AMERICA

Golden Ages in the Americas, Africa, and Asia

A.D. **800**   A.D. **1200**   A.D. **1600**   A.D. **2000**

1168 The Aztecs ■ dominate Mexico   1450 The Incas control an ■ empire in South America   **1 EMPIRES OF THE AMERICAS**

1000 Ghana controls salt ■ and gold trade routes   1500 Zimbabwe reaches height of ■ trade with eastern coastal states   **2 ANCIENT AFRICAN CIVILIZATIONS**

■ 1000 Thailand is settled   ■ 1206 Muslims establish kingdom in northern India   ■ 1556 Northern and central India unite under Mogul leader Akbar   **3 INDIA AND SOUTHEAST ASIA**

8 China's Tang nasty begins   ■ 936 Wang Kon unites Korea and establishes Koryo dynasty   ■ 1279 Mongol rule begins in China   ■ 1603 Tokugawa shogunate begins

The Splendor of India and Southeast Asia

(1000–1700)

1 **Muslims Ruled India for Several Centuries**

2 **Ancient Traditions Shaped Life in India**

3 **India Contributed to World Culture**

4 **Southeast Asia is a Region of Contrasts**

▲ **Illustrating History** *Muslims used the Hindu Kush Mountains as a base from which to launch regular raids into India in the early eleventh century.*

Imagine that you are a Muslim soldier from a small village in the western foothills of the Hindu Kush mountain range in present-day Afghanistan. The year is 1024. You and 30,000 of your Muslim comrades have invaded India, where you have just scored a major victory over Hindu forces. The bloody fighting has cost about 50,000 lives. Now you have been ordered to loot a Hindu temple. Tomorrow you will round up your prisoners and return home.

These types of brutal raids occurred like clockwork in the early eleventh century. Their leader was a Muslim ruler named Mahmud, based in the city of Ghazni. Between 1000 and 1026, Mahmud led 17 separate raids from the Hindu Kush onto the Indian subcontinent. Once he had gathered his loot and taken his prisoners, he would return home. The prisoners were then put to work as slaves in the city of Ghazni. With their help, Ghazni began to grow as a center of Islamic culture.

Mahmud's raids were the first major clashes between the two great religions of Hinduism and Islam. When Mahmud died in 1030, his followers lost most of the Indian lands that he had conquered. Even so, some Muslims stayed on in India. In time, as you will see in this chapter, they united the subcontinent under their control.

1000	1200	1400	1600

■ **1008** Muslims conquer India

■ **1150** Khmers build Angkor Wat temple

■ **1287** Mongols control Burma

■ **1398** Tamerlane destroys the Indian capital of Delhi

■ **1524** Mogul dynasty begins in India

▲ **Illustrating History** *The clothing worn by the soldiers in this richly colored painting is evidence of Muslim influence on Indian culture.*

1 Muslims Ruled India for Several Centuries

As you read, look for answers to these questions:

◆ What people invaded and conquered India about 1000?
◆ Who were the Mogul leaders who ruled India for nearly 200 years?
◆ Why is Akbar considered one of the world's great rulers?

> **Key Terms:** sultan (defined on p. 241), sultanate (p. 242), civil service (p. 242)

Founded by the prophet Mohammed, the religion of Islam began in Arabia in the seventh century and quickly spread to other parts of the world. Its followers conquered lands to both the east and the west of Arabia.

As discussed in Chapter 7, in western Europe, the invasion of Spain by the Muslims was stopped at the battle of Tours, France, in 732. In the East, however, Persia and much of western Asia became part of the Islamic Empire. In this way, the influence of Muslim culture was felt in the civilization of India.

Muslim Leaders Invaded India

From their lands in western Asia, Muslim military leaders began to invade India. (For a better understanding of their invasion routes, review the geographic setting map of Asia in Chapter 3.) At first, they were successful only along the western coast of the country. Around the year 1000, however, an ambitious Muslim leader named Mahmud of Ghazni became **sultan,** or ruler, of a small state on India's northwest frontier (in present-day Afghanistan). His ruthless soldiers swept across the border of India, looted gold and jewels from Hindu temples, and took Indians home as slaves. For the next 25 years, Mahmud of Ghazni periodically raided northern India and terrorized the Indian people living there.

Other Muslim rulers observed Mahmud's success, and saw a chance to fight for both wealth and Allah. About 1206, Sultan Aibak Kutb-ud-din (KUHTB uhd DIHN) established a kingdom, or **sultanate,** in northern India. Its capital was the city of Delhi (DELL ee). Hundreds of thousands of Indians were killed as the Delhi sultanate conquered most of the lands between the Indus and the Ganges rivers. For several hundred years after the sultanate was established, the Muslim conquerors followed a policy of cruelty toward the Hindu population.

In the late 1300s, a new and even more ruthless conqueror ended the Muslim sultanate. Tamerlane (TAM ur lane) was a Mongol warrior who came from Asiatic Russia. He and his conquering horsemen swept across Asia, looting and killing. Although Tamerlane was a Muslim, it did not stop him from attacking Delhi. In 1398, the city was destroyed. Thousands of people—both Hindu and Muslim—were killed.

Mogul Rulers Led a Rich and Powerful Empire

The final conqueror of the sultanate of Delhi was Babur, the founder of a line of Mongol, or Mogul (MOH gull), rulers. Mogul is another version of the word Mongol. Babur was a descendant of Tamerlane. Babur ruled northern India for only a few years before he died in 1530. The Mogul dynasty he established, however, was to have great power and lasting influence.

The next great Mogul ruler was Babur's grandson Akbar, who became one of the great monarchs in history. His reign covered the last half of the 1500s, which is about the same period as the reigns of Philip II of Spain and Elizabeth I of England.

Akbar became emperor in 1556 at the age of 13. He ruled for nearly 50 years. Early in his reign, he expanded the Mogul Empire to include all of northern and central India.

Creating an empire is one thing, but ruling it well is another. Akbar proved equal to the task. Although his word was absolute, he appointed intelligent advisers and followed their advice. Trained officials of the **civil service,** a body of employees trained in government administration, helped to make his reign smooth and effective. Taxes were heavy but fair, and the empire grew rich. Although Akbar had a lavish court, he spent his money carefully. As emperor, Akbar spent much of his time as a judge.

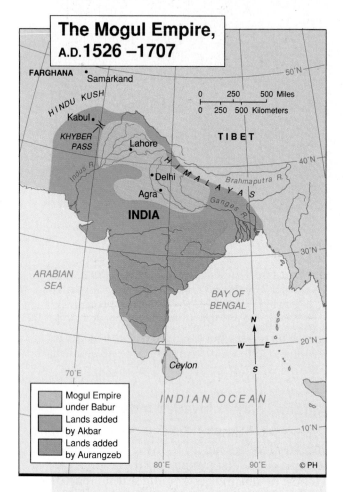

The Mogul Empire, A.D. 1526–1707

FARGHANA
Samarkand
HINDU KUSH
Kabul
KHYBER PASS
Lahore
TIBET
Indus R.
Delhi
HIMALAYAS
Brahmaputra R.
Agra
Ganges R.
INDIA
ARABIAN SEA
BAY OF BENGAL
Ceylon
INDIAN OCEAN

0   250   500 Miles
0   250   500 Kilometers

50°N
40°N
30°N
20°N
10°N
70°E   80°E   90°E

N W E S

© PH

Mogul Empire under Babur
Lands added by Akbar
Lands added by Aurangzeb

Focus on Geography

1. **Location** Use the scale to measure the greatest extent of the Mogul Empire from east to west. About how many miles did it extend?
2. **Regions** Look back at the map on page 70. In physical terms, describe the region added by Aurangzeb.

Akbar the Great

According to one story, Akbar the Great, the Mogul emperor of India (shown at right), challenged an unconquered Hindu ruler by asking, "Well, Rao Surjan, what is to be done?" The ruler's reply is not known. He did, however, hand over his land to Akbar. What Akbar could not gain through battle, he won quietly with a smile.

Akbar became emperor in 1556 at the age of 13. He was determined to expand Mogul rule, but he was more than just a conqueror. He organized India into a nation of provinces and townships. He built roads and minted new coins. He planted shade trees that still stand today. Akbar slept only three hours a night, and every minute of his day was put to use.

Akbar earned a reputation for religious tolerance. At the age of 18, he had set out alone into the desert to think and pray. He heard a voice urging him to seek spiritual truth, and this is what he did for the rest of his life. He invited Taoist monks, Confucian scholars, and Catholic priests to mingle in his court. He lifted the taxes that Muslims had imposed on Hindus for centuries, which eased many of the hard feelings between the two groups.

Under Akbar's rule, the Mogul Empire reached its height. When he died in 1605, he was known as the "lord of the age."

1. How did Akbar improve India?
2. How did Akbar treat non-Muslims?

He listened to the complaints of his people and tried to make fair decisions.

Unlike most Muslim rulers, Akbar was tolerant of other religions and ways of life. He gave Hindus full freedom to practice their faith and no longer forced them to pay special taxes. When Europeans brought Christianity to India, Akbar was a sympathetic listener. He had the New Testament translated and invited Jesuit missionaries to come to his court at Delhi. As the historian Will Durant has noted in *The Story of Civilization: Our Oriental Heritage*, "While Catholics were murdering Protestants in France, and Protestants . . . were murdering Catholics in England, and the Inquisition was killing and robbing Jews in Spain, Akbar . . . issued edicts of tolerance for every . . . creed." Akbar's fairness and tolerance did not go unnoticed. He was deeply loved by his people.

The Mogul Empire Declined After Akbar

Akbar, emperor of India, died in 1605. The emperors who followed him were not as strong, but they did follow his tolerant policies. Like Akbar, they encouraged art, architecture, and literature in the Mogul style. Shah Jahan (juh HAHN), Akbar's grandson, constructed the beautiful Taj Mahal as a tomb for his much-loved wife, Mumtaz Mahal. Under Shah Jahan, the Mogul empire reached its height. (See the map on page 242.) Its fall, however, came soon after.

The Taj Mahal

Twenty thousand laborers worked day and night for 22 years in the mid-1600s to build a great tomb for the wife of the Mogul emperor, Shah Jahan. The white marble structure, named the Taj Mahal, arose on the outskirts of the city of Agra, in northwestern India.

Today, the Taj Mahal (shown right) is still regarded as one of the world's most beautiful buildings. Yet, air pollution from a nearby oil refinery may threaten its future. If this facility someday switches to high-sulfur crude oil, it will emit fumes containing sulfuric acid. Scientists warn that these fumes could erode the Taj Mahal's delicate marble surface and destroy the beauty of this exquisite monument that has endured for 350 years.

1. Why was the Taj Mahal built?
2. What danger is modern technology posing to the Taj Mahal?

In 1658, Shah Jahan was forced from the throne by Aurangzeb (AH rung zehb), his son, the last great Mogul emperor. Once he had seized the throne, Aurangzeb proved to be a strict Muslim who was intolerant of other faiths. Hindu temples were destroyed, and Hindus again had to pay special taxes.

During the reign of Aurangzeb, the Mogul Empire began to fall apart. His intolerance of Hindus led them to form kingdoms of their own that Aurangzeb was unable to conquer. He lost the support of the rajputs, Hindu warrior princes who protected the northwest frontier. Other Muslim princes, recognizing the weakness of the central government, began to build up their own power. In a few years, Aurangzeb had destroyed the unity that had taken centuries to build. It was not long after the death of Aurangzeb that India was again split into many small kingdoms and princely states. When European traders arrived, India was too divided to resist their influence.

SECTION 1 REVIEW

Knowing Key Terms, People, and Places
1. Define: **a.** sultan **b.** sultanate **c.** civil service
2. Identify: **a.** Mahmud of Ghazni **b.** Delhi sultanate **c.** Tamerlane **d.** Babur **e.** Akbar **f.** Shah Jahan **g.** Aurangzeb

Reviewing Main Ideas
3. Explain who the Moguls were and the part they played in India's history.
4. Why is Akbar considered a great ruler?
5. How did Aurangzeb's policies weaken India?

Critical Thinking
Identifying Central Issues
6. Compare the reigns of Akbar and Aurangzeb. What was the main way in which they differed? What were the consequences of this difference?

2 Ancient Traditions Shaped Life in India

As you read, look for answers to these questions:

◆ What three factors had the most influence on everyday life in India?
◆ How did the caste system affect people's lives?
◆ How did most people make a living in India?

Key Terms: suttee (defined on p. 246), purdah (p. 246)

Even under the rule of Muslim conquerors and Mogul emperors, most people in India followed the traditional Hindu way of living. The family, the caste system, and the village formed a circle within which the ordinary person lived his or her life.

The Family Was the Center of Indian Life

The family in India extended beyond a mother, father, and children to include grandparents and married children with their own families. Brothers, sisters, uncles, aunts, cousins, and grandchildren shared adjoining rooms or houses. The family also included slaves. Within the family, the father was the head of the household and its unquestioned leader.

For the family to prosper, all its members had to work. Women prepared food, cared for children, and ran the household. Men worked in the fields or at their trades. People usually wove their own cloth and made their own clothing. Food had to be saved for times when there might be famine.

Children were important to a family because they could help to support the family by working with the adults in the fields, farming, or learning the family business or trade. This was especially important when parents could no longer work. Children also could ensure that the souls of their dead parents would rest in peace through proper and frequent prayer. Therefore, children could help their parents both in this world and the next.

Property belonged to the head of the family. When the head of the family died, each son was entitled to a share of the property. Each unmarried daughter was also entitled to a share, which became part of her dowry, the property and money she would take with her when she married.

Indian Women Had Little Freedom

The Vedic Age, named after the prayers and holy songs of Hinduism, lasted from 1500 B.C. to 1000 B.C. During this era, women in India enjoyed more freedom than in later periods of Indian history. They often took part in religious ceremonies, celebrations, and dances. They could study philosophy and remarry if their husbands died.

Traditionally, marriages were arranged by the couple's families. Choosing your own marriage partner was considered slightly immoral. Indian women thought it was more honorable for a wife to be bought with gold or other valuable property. Polygamy (puh LIG ah mee), the practice in which a man has a number of wives, was common.

▼ **Illustrating History** *Many Indian families still follow ancient traditions. Below, a woman spins thread for clothing.*

▲ **Illustrating History** *This young bride from the Indian state of Rajasthan is dressed for a traditional wedding.*

Polyandry (PAHL ee AN dree), a woman's marriage to several husbands, was not unknown. It was the man, however, who had property rights and who could sell his wives and children as he wished, according to an ancient code.

The *Code of Manu*, an ancient book in Sanskrit, the written language of India, was a kind of guide to proper behavior in each caste. It said that the mother of many children was to be honored. Men could not strike or beat their wives. Women in wealthy families were to have gold jewelry and be dressed attractively to display the wealth of the household. The ideal wife devoted herself entirely to her husband, serving him faithfully and courageously until she died.

After about 500 B.C., for reasons that remain unclear to historians, Indian women lost many of their rights. Women were discouraged from studying or following intellectual pursuits. Child marriages, arranged by the parents, became the usual rule. A young bride left her own home to live with her husband's family, learn its ways, and obey the older women of her new family.

The future of the woman whose husband died was a tragic one. She was expected to die in the funeral fire that burned his body. This practice was called **suttee** (SU tee). Women who chose not to practice suttee became the lowest members of the family. Such a woman shaved her head, gave up all pleasure, and was expected to pray constantly. She prepared the food but ate last and then had only the leftover scraps.

In post–Vedic India, women's freedom declined even more. During this period, the practice of **purdah** (PUR dah), which means "curtain," grew. Women wore heavy veils in public. Only at home, where they could be seen by no men except their husbands and sons, could they go unveiled.

Caste Ruled Everyday Life

Next to the Hindu family, caste was most important in deciding people's everyday activities and relationships. The caste system, which was discussed in Chapter 3, had strict rules about food, dress, social behavior, and most details of daily life. People stayed in the caste in which they were born for their entire lives. Members of one caste were prohibited from associating with members of another caste. There was no idea of moving up from a lower caste to a higher one by any means.

When the caste system first began, people belonged to four main castes. Over time, however, hundreds of castes developed, each one based mainly on occupation. For example, there were castes of farmers, carpenters, merchants, herders, metalworkers, and barbers. The lowliest tasks, such as tanning leather or cleaning streets, were performed by the untouchables. They were considered so lowly that they had no caste at all.

By contrast, the upper class (the Brahmins, or priestly caste) were entitled to many privileges. In return, they prayed for the souls of others. The Brahmins were usually the only people who could read and write. Because they did not willingly share this knowledge with others, the Brahmins grew rich and powerful. Although invaders came and went throughout the history of India, the Brahmins continued to maintain their high social position.

Few Changes Took Place in Village Life

Along with family and caste, village traditions also influenced the lives of ordinary people in India. Life in the villages changed little over the centuries. Even though different rulers came to power, the capital of India was far away, and people were mostly concerned with what went on in their own villages.

The most prominent person in the village was the headman, who was appointed by the prince or lord on whose land the village stood. The job of headman was an important one that often was handed down in a family from generation to generation. The headman represented the voice of a local but powerful ruler whose orders the headman had to follow. He was helped by a council with whom he talked over the village problems.

The headman's biggest responsibility was to get the villagers to work together for the common good. Sharing work was necessary because a village received little outside help. Villagers had to work together to irrigate the farmland, to share and save water, and to use food carefully. Failure to cooperate might mean starvation in the year ahead.

Although village life stayed much the same over the years, the villagers themselves were affected by wars and political changes. Heavy taxation was one important way in which the government touched village life. Sometimes, the taxes could amount to as much as one-half a farmer's crop. Trade between villages and cities was also taxed. The government even charged money to use the roads.

Indians Were Farmers and Traders

Most Indian villagers made their living by growing vegetables, fruits, rice, and cotton. Because many Hindus did not eat meat, farm products were important, but many

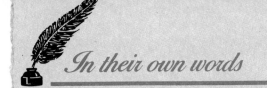

In their own words

The Nature of India's Society

The caste system in India remained strong even after Muslim rulers replaced Hindu rulers. The following excerpt is by Abul Fazl, an Indian writer who lived during the Mogul era. He compares each of four major castes to a part of the physical world.

**❝The people of the world may be divided into four classes:

1. *Warriors,* who in the political body have the nature of fire. Their flames . . . [burn] the straw and rubbish of rebellion and strife, but kindle also the lamp of rest in this world of disturbances.

2. *Artificers* [craftworkers] *and merchants,* who hold the place of air. From their labors and travels, God's gifts become universal, and the breeze of contentment nourishes the rose-tree of life.

3. *The learned,* such as the philosopher, the physician, the arithmetician, the geometrician, the astronomer, who resemble water. From their pen and their wisdom, a river rises in the drought of the world, and the garden of the creation receives from their irrigating powers a peculiar freshness.

4. *Husbandmen and laborers,* who may be compared to earth. By their exertions, the staple of life is brought to perfection, and strength and happiness flow from their work.

It is therefore obligatory for a king to put each of these in its proper place, and by uniting personal ability with due respect for others, to cause the world to flourish.❞

1. What are the four castes of people, according to Fazl?
2. Explain how Fazl makes the division of people into castes appear to be natural.

▲ **Illustrating History** *Above is a merchant selling dyes at a market in Mysore.*

things made farming difficult. Rainfall was unpredictable. Tools were simple. Because it was the custom for a father to divide the land among his sons, family lands grew smaller and smaller after several generations. In time, each family had only a small piece of land on which to grow food.

In some parts of India, trade was as important as farming. Cotton, grown in India from the earliest times, was an important item of trade in the Deccan Plateau. Products from all over India and from other countries as well were traded in the bazaar, or market. People used gold, silver, and copper coins to buy the goods they needed.

In ancient times, India traded with Sumer, Babylonia, China, Greece, and Rome. During the Middle Ages, products of India were sent to Europe through the Italian cities of Genoa, Venice, and Milan. India was one source for the spices, such as cloves and ginger, that Europeans wanted and needed.

SECTION 2 REVIEW

Knowing Key Terms, People, and Places
1. Define: **a.** suttee **b.** purdah
2. Identify: **a.** Brahmans **b.** headman **c.** Deccan Plateau

Reviewing Main Ideas
3. Describe the traditional Hindu family.
4. How did women's lives in India change from the Vedic Age to the Muslim period?
5. How did the caste system affect the lives of Indian people?
6. What were the two main ways in which the people of India made a living?

Critical Thinking
Identifying Assumptions
7. Marriages were arranged by parents in traditional Indian families. What assumptions about family life did this custom show?

248

3 India Contributed to World Culture

As you read, look for answers to these questions:

◆ What were some important discoveries made by mathematicians in ancient India?
◆ Why are the numerals 1, 2, 3, and so on called Arabic numerals?
◆ In what fields of science did Indians make outstanding discoveries?
◆ What was the inspiration for most Indian literature?

> **Key Terms:** Arabic numeral (defined on p. 249)

Beginning in what is known as the Golden Age of the Gupta rulers, which lasted from A.D. 320 to 535, science, mathematics, and literature were highly developed in India. Students studied in universities, and hospitals cared for people who were sick. Scientists made discoveries in medical science, mathematics, and astronomy. Religious writing, poetry, fables, and plays were all part of Indian literature. During this time, India made many contributions to the world.

Indians Were Able Scientists and Mathematicians

The so-called **Arabic numerals** (1, 2, 3, and so on) that we use today are actually one of India's greatest gifts to the Western world. These numerals were used as early as the reign of Asoka the Great in 265 B.C., hundreds of years before Muslim scholars used them. We know them as Arabic numerals because Europeans learned about them from the Arabs. In fact, the Pythagorean theorem, a key discovery in the field of geometry, is said to have been developed by an Indian mathematician. However, it has been named after Pythagoras, a Greek mathematician, because it came to Europe by way of Greece.

One great Indian mathematician was Aryabhata (AHR yah BUT ah), who lived in the sixth century A.D. He worked out a decimal system and taught about the rotation of the earth on its axis. Aryabhata's teachings spread from India to China, Arabia, and the rest of the world.

In chemistry and technology, Indian scientists were also far ahead of Europeans. At the time of Alexander the Great's invasion of India in 326 B.C., Indian metalworkers already knew how to make steel. A ball of steel was given to Alexander as a gift worthy of a conqueror. The Indians also were far ahead of Europeans in ways of making soap, dyeing cloth, tanning leather, blowing glass, and mixing cement.

▼ **Chart Skill** *During what period did the persecution of Hindus in India end?*

Major Events in India 1000–1707		
1000		Mahmud of Ghazni begins Muslim conquest of India.
1206–1398	Delhi sultanate	Lands between Indus and Ganges rivers are conquered by Muslims. Hindus are persecuted.
1495–1707	Mogul Empire	Three major rulers of India are Babur, Akbar, and Shah Jahan.
1556–1605		Akbar is emperor of India. He expands empire to include all of northern and central India. Akbar extends religious toleration to all faiths.
1658		Aurangzeb seizes throne of India from his father (Shah Jahan).
1707		Aurangzeb, the last of the Mogul rulers, dies. India is weak and divided.

▲ Illustrating History *This painting shows an educated Indian princess writing a letter.*

In the field of medicine, Indian doctors explained the system of circulation about 100 or more years before the English scientist William Harvey described it in the seventeenth century. In time, Indian doctors won great fame for their skill and knowledge in medicine.

Religion Influenced Learning and Culture

Two of the world's major religions—Hinduism and Buddhism—began in ancient India. For thousands of years, many people in India have tried to understand the meaning of life. During the ancient Hindu period, there were many branches of philosophy. Students, eager to question, to debate, and to learn, sat before philosopher-teachers. Learning was important as early as the reign of Asoka the Great. Many people could read, and Indian universities grew famous.

Although India developed great oral literature, the development of writing itself was slow. India's earliest literature, the Vedas, consisted of religious songs and poems that were passed down by priests who had memorized them word for word.

Two great epics appeared later in the Vedic Age. The *Mahabharata* (muh HAH BAH ruh tuh) is an epic retelling of the legends of ancient heroes and gods. It was handed down orally for hundreds of years before it was written down. Through the years, its original 9,000 verses were expanded to 100,000. Some people consider it one of the greatest poems ever written. A part of the *Mahabharata* is known as the Bhagavad-Gita (BUHG uh vuhd GEE tuh), which means "Song of the Lord." It is in the form of a conversation, or dialogue, between a warrior and the god Krishna. For Hindus, the Bhagavad-Gita is a holy book, just as the Bible is a holy book for Christians. The other epic, the *Ramayana,* is an adventure story that serves to illustrate many of the ideas and virtues that Hindus admire.

The *Panchatantra* (PAHN chuh TUN druh), written about A.D. 500, is one of the earliest collections of Indian fables. A fable is a short tale that tries to teach a lesson. In fables, animals talk and act like people in order to teach a lesson about human life. Each fable in the *Panchatantra* illustrates a principle of politics or ethical behavior. Among other things, it explains how to win allies, how to prevent the loss of what one has, and how to avoid hasty action.

Many other forms of Indian culture were based on religion. Songs, dances, and music in India were mostly religious in nature. The ancient instruments would look and sound strange to you. Indian painting would also seem different to you. The most popular forms of painting were miniatures and illustrated manuscripts. Architecture and sculpture were also influenced by religion. Hindu temples were elaborately carved with the images of many gods.

Indian civilization changed greatly over the centuries. Changes began when the West first demanded admission to the empire of India. You will see in Chapter 16 and in later chapters how India's splendor fared during the Age of Discovery and modern times.

SECTION 3 REVIEW

Knowing Key Terms, People, and Places
1. Define: **a.** Arabic numeral
2. Identify: **a.** Bhagavad-Gita **b.** *Ramayana*

Reviewing Main Ideas
3. What achievements were made in ancient India in mathematics and science technology?
4. What two major world religions began in ancient India?
5. How has Hinduism influenced the development of literature in India?

Critical Thinking
Recognizing Bias
6. Why do you think Europeans and Americans might expect an idea in geometry (such as the Pythagorean theorem) to come from ancient Greece rather than ancient India?

▲ **Illustrating History** *Above, the Hindu god Krishna plays the flute for a dancer.*

4 Southeast Asia Is a Region of Contrasts

As you read, look for answers to these questions:

◆ What kinds of landscapes and climates are found in Southeast Asia?
◆ From what countries did people migrate to settle in Southeast Asia?
◆ What religion influenced the cultures of Southeast Asia?
◆ Why were the Khmers important in the history of Southeast Asia?

Key Terms: archipelago (defined on p. 252), monsoon (p. 253)

Since ancient times, Southeast Asia has been one of the world's great geographic crossroads. Over the centuries, people from many countries and cultures have met here to trade goods. Often, their cultures and ways of life have mixed and blended together to form new, unique cultures.

Geography Influenced the Region's History

Modern Southeast Asia includes countries both on the mainland and on great chains of islands, called **archipelagoes** (AHR kih PELL uh GOHS). While some of these countries have new political systems, most have histories that go back thousands of years. Countries on the mainland of Asia include Thailand (TYE land), Burma, Vietnam, Laos (LAH ohs), Kampuchea (Cambodia), and part of Malaysia. Singapore is a small island country near the mainland. Two other countries, the Philippines and Indonesia, are located on two large groups of islands.

If you turn to the map on page 254, you can see how the geography of Southeast Asia influenced the region's development. The ocean has been a highway for trade for thousands of years, but it also has kept apart the people of Southeast Asia. Great distances separate some parts of the island nations. Rugged mountains and dense jungles form other barriers on individual islands.

The Republic of the Philippines, for instance, includes 6 main islands and more than 7,000 smaller ones. The distance from north to south in the Philippines is 1,100 miles (1,760 kilometers). Similarly, Indonesia contains 5 large islands and thousands of smaller ones. Some 3,000 miles (4,800 kilometers)—about the distance from California to New York—separates one tip of Indonesia from the other.

As in other parts of the world, river valleys have been important in the history of Southeast Asia. In Burma, for example, most people live in the valley of the Irrawaddy River. Because the river is navigable for about 600 miles (960 kilometers) inland, the Irrawaddy is important for trade as well as agriculture. In Vietnam, the Mekong River and its delta are known as the "rice bowl" for the entire region.

Except in the mountains, nearly all of Southeast Asia has a tropical climate. Heavy

▼ **Illustrating History** *The Irrawaddy River is the main waterway in Burma.*

seasonal rains, called **monsoons,** bring a wet season to different areas at different times. Burma and the Malay Peninsula get rain from the month of May to October. In Indochina, the rains come in October and last until January. During the monsoon season, rivers often overflow, flooding fields, roads, and villages. Travel becomes dangerous and difficult at this time.

Different Groups Settled Southeast Asia

A rich variety of people whose ancestors migrated from China, India, or Tibet long ago live in the countries of Southeast Asia. Historians think that over hundreds of years various groups of people from the northern regions crossed the mountains and traveled down the rivers. Gradually, they settled throughout Southeast Asia and then moved onto the nearby islands. They brought with them different languages, religions, and cultural traditions.

Some of the most important of these migrating people were the Khmers (kmehrz), Thais (tyz), Mons, Burmese, and Malays. In some places, the newcomers mixed with, or drove away, the Negritos who already lived there. In addition to the traditions the newcomers brought with them, these regions were influenced by the cultures of nearby India and China. Hindu religion and culture were important in Southeast Asia from earliest times. Buddhist missionaries arrived from India in the third century B.C. Later, Arab traders brought the religion of Islam to Southeast Asia, where it became important, particularly in Malaya and Indonesia, by about 1300.

Many Rulers and Kingdoms Existed in Early Southeast Asia

The variety of peoples and cultures that mingled in Southeast Asia have given the region a complex history. This section gives only highlights of some major areas.

Burma. Burma, the country closest to India, was the gateway through which many people migrated to Southeast Asia. Many

▲ **Illustrating History** *Above is a Burmese sculpture of Buddha from the Pagan period.*

crossed the Mangin Range and then traveled southward through the valley of the Irrawaddy River. Traders traveling overland between China and India also passed through Burma. As a result, Burma was the first part of Southeast Asia to accept the Buddhist faith brought from India.

The first important culture in Burma was that of the Mons, a group who came into the region in the third century B.C. They gave Burma a rich, distinctive culture that included a system of writing and Buddhism.

253

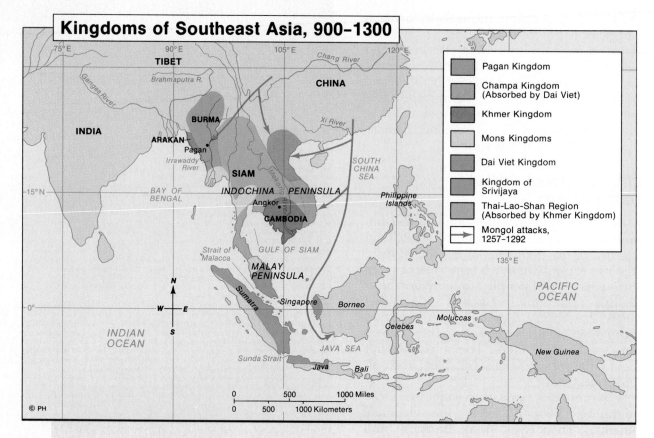

Kingdoms of Southeast Asia, 900–1300

Legend:
- Pagan Kingdom
- Champa Kingdom (Absorbed by Dai Viet)
- Khmer Kingdom
- Mons Kingdoms
- Dai Viet Kingdom
- Kingdom of Srivijaya
- Thai-Lao-Shan Region (Absorbed by Khmer Kingdom)
- Mongol attacks, 1257–1292

Focus on Geography

Place   A series of kingdoms ruled Southeast Asia between 900 and 1200. Find the Champa Kingdom on the map. Name the kingdom that absorbed it.

In the eleventh century, Anawratha, the first real ruler of Burma, seized power. During his reign, from 1044 to 1077, he unified the country and created a strong kingdom. His capital was the walled city of Pagan (PAY gun). This city became famous for its beautiful temples and statues and for the Buddhist scholars who taught there.

In 1287, the Mongol conqueror Kublai Khan destroyed the city of Pagan. The kingdom fell, and for the next 400 years Burma was split into many small territories.

Thailand. Thailand, once called Siam, was settled about 1000 by Thai people from northern China. The Thais mixed with many people from India who already lived in this area. By about the fourteenth century, the Thais had established the kingdom of Siam. The kingdom was often at war with its neighbor, Burma. Unlike other countries in Southeast Asia, Siam kept its independence even when European nations began to take colonies in Asia.

To Americans, the best-known ruler of Siam is King Mongkut, or Rama IV. He ruled from 1851 to 1868 (about the same time that Abraham Lincoln was president). Mongkut was interested in European ideas and in improving the lives of his people. He invited European teachers and specialists to Siam. One of them, an Englishwoman who taught the king's children, wrote a book on which the musical *The King and I* was based.

Indochina. A number of different groups of people settled in Laos, Vietnam, and Kampuchea, the countries that make up the Indochina Peninsula. The Lao people are related to the Thais. Many Vietnamese are descended from the ancient Annamese people, who came from China. The ancestors of the modern Kampuchean people were the Khmers. For centuries, the Khmers were the most powerful people in the region of Southeast Asia.

By about the first century A.D., the Khmer people had established a small state called Funan. It was strongly influenced by Indian culture and by both Hindu and Buddhist traditions. The rich Khmer rulers dominated most of Indochina for hundreds of years, until their final defeat in the 1400s. At its height, their kingdom included the lands of present-day Thailand, Kampuchea, South Vietnam, and into Laos.

Beginning in the 800s, the kings of the powerful Khmer dynasty built the city of Angkor as their capital. Although Angkor was later abandoned and overtaken by the jungle, the city once had great temples, palaces, and waterways. The most famous temple, Angkor Wat, was built in the 1100s.

▼ **Illustrating History** *This drawing shows the magnificent Angkor Wat as an artist believed it looked in the twelfth century. Today, the temple is in ruins.*

Indonesia and Malaysia. The nation of Indonesia includes the islands of Sumatra, Java, Bali, and most of the island of Borneo. These are the islands that were once called the East Indies. They have been important trade centers for hundreds of years. Malaysia occupies both the long, spoon-shaped Malay Peninsula and the northern part of the island of Borneo.

Hindu culture, brought from India by traders, was the most important early influence on what are now Indonesia and Malaysia. Over time, however, despite this major influence, two distinct cultures, Malay and Javanese, developed. Sumatra and Borneo were centers for the Malay people. By about the seventh century A.D., the Malay kingdom of Shrivijaya (shriv ih JY ah) was the most powerful in the region.

A different culture developed on the islands of Java and Bali, where the people also followed Hindu traditions in religion, art, and literature. In the 1200s, the Javanese overthrew the Malay kingdom of Shrivijaya and established their own empire on the islands of Indonesia.

At about the same time, Arab Muslim traders began to set up trading kingdoms in Indonesia. By the fifteenth century, Islam had become a major religion in Malaysia and Indonesia.

The Philippines. The islands of the Philippines were settled late when the last waves of migration occurred from the mainland of Asia. As a result, Chinese traders and the kingdoms of Indonesia did not greatly influence the people of the Philippines. The residents were mostly farmers and hunters who lived in large family groups and worshipped nature spirits. They did not organize a central government or build great cities, palaces, or temples.

Unlike the rest of Southeast Asia, the people of the islands did not adopt either Hinduism or Buddhism as their religion. When Islam was introduced in the fifteenth century, it spread rapidly, and several sultanates were set up. The arrival of European explorers in the 1500s brought further drastic changes. During this time, the Spanish occupied and colonized the islands, naming them after their king, Philip II.

European Traders and Explorers Caused Great Changes

For centuries, the people of Southeast Asia had traded among themselves and with India, China, and the Muslim world. Their wealth and their rich natural resources —especially rare spices—soon became well known in Europe.

The desire for gold and spices brought more European explorers to Southeast Asia in the 1500s and 1600s. Soon, European nations were setting up colonies and establishing rule over the once independent kingdoms of Southeast Asia. These European explorers brought important cultural changes, including Christianity.

SECTION 4 REVIEW

Knowing Key Terms, People, and Places
1. Define: **a.** archipelago **b.** monsoon
2. Identify: **a.** Indochina **b.** Irrawaddy River **c.** Malay Peninsula **d.** Mongkut

Focus on Geography
3. Describe the geographical factors that influenced the settlement of Southeast Asia.

Reviewing Main Ideas
4. Describe the pattern by which people migrated and settled in Southeast Asia.
5. What two countries had the greatest influence on cultures in Southeast Asia?

Critical Thinking
Perceiving Cause and Effect
6. The Philippines were the last part of Southeast Asia to be settled by people from the Asian mainland. How did this affect the development of religion, government, and culture on the islands up to the time of the Europeans' arrival?

Reading Bar and Circle Graphs

Bar and circle graphs are useful ways to present information visually and to condense large amounts of data. Graphs also allow you to see the relationships among two or more sets of data. A bar graph shows changes over time, or trends. A circle graph shows the relationship among various parts of a whole.

Use the following steps to read and analyze the bar and circle graphs shown below.

1. **Identify the kind of information presented in the graph.** Answer the following questions about the graphs below: (a) What subject does the bar graph portray? (b) What do the numbers on the vertical axis (the left side) of the bar graph represent? (c) What do the numbers on the horizontal axis (along the bottom) of the bar graph represent? (d) What does the entire circle represent in the circle graph? (e) What does the key in the circle graph tell you?

2. **Practice reading the information shown in the graphs.** Answer these questions: (a) What percentage of the world's population lived on the Indian subcontinent in 1650? Which graph did you use to find this data? (b) What was the population of the Indian subcontinent in 1600? Which graph shows this? (c) Which graph shows population trends?

3. **Look for relationships among the data.** Answer these questions: (a) How much did the population of the Indian subcontinent grow from 1000 to 1800? (b) Which two continents had about the same population in 1650?

4. **Use the graphs to draw conclusions.** Answer the following questions: (a) Estimate the population of India in 1850. Which graph did you use for your estimate? (b) Estimate the total world population in 1650. Why do you need to use both graphs for this estimate?

Population of Indian Subcontinent During Years 1000–1800

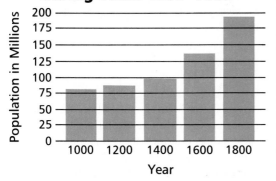

Sources: Colin McEvedy and Richard Jones, *Atlas of World Population History* (London: Penguin Books, Ltd., 1978), pp. 182–85. Mark S. Hoffman, ed., *The World Almanac and Book of Facts: 1987 Edition* (New York: Pharos Books, Inc., 1986), pp. 501, 544

World Population Distribution, 1650

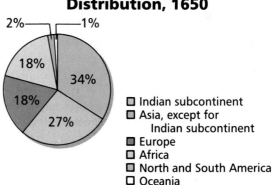

Sources: Colin McEvedy and Richard Jones, *Atlas of World Population History* (London: Penguin Books, Ltd., 1978), pp. 182–85. Mark S. Hoffman, ed., *The World Almanac and Book of Facts: 1987 Edition* (New York: Pharos Books, Inc., 1986), pp. 501, 544

REVIEW

Section Summaries

Section 1 Muslims Ruled India for Several Centuries The first major Muslim conquest in India came around 1000 when Mahmud of Ghazni became sultan of a small state in the northwest of the country. Babur established the Mogul dynasty, and his grandson, Akbar, became a great ruler. Akbar was tolerant of all religions, including Islam, Hinduism, and Christianity. Aurangzeb became the last Mogul ruler in 1648. His strict Muslim beliefs destroyed the unity of the empire, leaving it open to European conquest.

Section 2 Ancient Traditions Shaped Life in India The basic social unit in India was the extended family. Hindu tradition determined the role that each family member played, and each person did his or her share of work. In the post-Vedic era, women lost many of the freedoms that they had enjoyed for centuries. The caste system was the next level of social organization, and it dictated how people from each class could interact. Within a village, the headman was the highest authority. He organized the work done by the villagers, most of whom were farmers or traders.

Section 3 India Contributed to World Culture Indian mathematicians and scientists gave the world many gifts. They invented Arabic numerals and explained the circulation of blood. Indian technology and medicine was also highly advanced. India's two major religions, Hinduism and Buddhism, inspired both literature and art. Vedas, epics, and Indian fables are among the great literary contributions. Brightly colored miniature paintings, illustrated Hindu manuscripts, and sculptures of gods are typical of Indian art.

Section 4 Southeast Asia Is a Region of Contrasts Modern Southeast Asia has countries both on the mainland and on chains of islands. A rich variety of people live in this area, having migrated from China, India, or Tibet. Burma, which is closest to India, was the gateway to Southeast Asia. Thailand was settled by people from northern China and remained independent even when European nations began to colonize the area. Indochina is peopled by a number of different groups related to the Thais, Chinese, and Khmers. Indonesia and Malaysia were influenced by India's Hindu culture. The Philippines were the last islands to be settled and were strongly influenced by Islam. The arrival of Europeans bent on trading in the Far East made permanent changes in this region.

Key Facts

1. Use each vocabulary word in a sentence.
   a. sultan
   b. sultanate
   c. civil service
   d. suttee
   e. purdah
   f. Arabic numeral
   g. archipelago
   h. monsoon
2. Identify and briefly explain the importance of the following names, places, or events.
   a. Akbar
   b. Taj Mahal
   c. civil service
   d. *Code of Manu*
   e. Sanskrit
   f. *Bhagavad-Gita*
   g. King Mongkut
   h. Khmers

Main Ideas

1. How did Islam spread to India?
2. How did the Muslim ruler Akbar demonstrate tolerance for other religions?
3. Why were children especially important to Hindu families?
4. Who was the headman in a Hindu village?
5. In what academic areas were the Indians advanced?
6. Describe the geography of Southeast Asia.
7. What groups of people settled in Southeast Asia?
8. Why did Europeans become interested in Southeast Asia in the 1500s and 1600s?

Developing Skill in Reading History

Use this quotation from the chapter to answer the questions below: "While Catholics were murdering Protestants in France, and Protestants . . . were murdering Catholics in England, and the Inquisition was killing and robbing Jews in Spain, Akbar issued edicts of tolerance for every . . . creed."

1. According to the quotation, what European nations practiced religious intolerance?
   a. all of them
   b. France and Rome
   c. France, England, and Spain
2. One nation that practiced religious tolerance at this time was
   a. Burma
   b. India
   c. Southeast Asia
3. What is the main idea of this quotation?
   a. Akbar was an unusual ruler in that he showed religious tolerance in the sixteenth century.
   b. Indian people are more tolerant of religious diversity than English people.
   c. Religion only causes strife among people.

Using Social Studies Skills

1. **Using Visual Evidence** Historians know that Babur was a great military leader. What else can you conclude about him from the painting below left, which shows him dictating his memoirs?
2. **Understanding Art** In general, what can art tell us about the history and culture of a civilization? Pick some examples of artwork from the chapter to support your answer.

Critical Thinking

1. **Making Comparisons** How did the rule of Akbar compare with other Muslim rulers of India?
2. **Identifying Assumptions** What assumptions were made about women in Indian society? Give evidence from the chapter to support your conclusions.
3. **Predicting Consequences** How do you think Southeast Asia would have developed if Europeans had never arrived?

Focus on Writing

Expository Paragraphs

An **expository paragraph** is one in which you explain or teach something to your readers. The most important thing to remember about expository writing is that it must be clear. The topic sentence should tell what you intend to discuss. Supporting details should all help to explain your topic, and you should define any terms that your readers may not already know.

Practice: Plan an expository paragraph on the following topic: Indians Were Capable Scientists and Mathematicians. Complete these prewriting activities:

1. Write a topic sentence.
2. List three supporting facts or ideas.
3. Define or explain one technical term.
4. Make an outline for your paragraph that shows how you will organize your writing.

Golden Ages in China, Japan, and Korea

(618–1644)

1 **China Entered a Golden Age**

2 **Chinese Culture Is Based on Tradition**

3 **Korea Created a Distinctive Heritage**

4 **Japan's Unique Civilization Emerged**

The emperor Yang Ti was worried. Revolts had been spreading through northern China, forcing him to move his court to the more tranquil south. And now, most maddening of all, a fortuneteller had predicted that his kingdom would be overthrown by a man named Li. The emperor did not know what to do. Li was one of the most common names in China, and his enemy might be anyone.

A rumor began to spread across China that the anxious emperor intended to have every official and army officer named Li put to death. A bold general named Li Yuan decided to thwart the plan. He marched with his troops to the court and seized the throne. Yang Ti was murdered in his own bathhouse.

With the death of Yang Ti in 618, another of China's many dynasties came to an abrupt end. Perhaps this was just as well for the people of Yang Ti's immense realm. Historians have regarded this emperor as a tyrant who enslaved hundreds of thousands of peasants and taxed his people cruelly to finance wars against other countries. When Li Yuan came to power, he took the name Taizong and launched the Tang dynasty—one of the longest and most glorious dynasties in China's history. As you will read in this chapter, the Tang dynasty gave China a golden age and influenced the cultures of Japan and Korea.

▲ **Illustrating History** *This ferocious marble lion is an example of the art of China's prosperous Tang dynasty.*

600	900	1200	1500

■ **600s**
Tang dynasty
rules China;
Buddhism grows
in Japan

■ **900s**
Koryo dynasty
rules Korea

■ **1100s**
Japan
unites
under
Shoguns

■ **1200s**
Japan
defeats
Mongols

■ **1300s**
Mongols
withdraw
from China
and Korea

▲ **Illustrating History** *Taizong (at right), the founder of the Tang dynasty, was one of its most important emperors.*

1 China Entered a Golden Age

As you read, look for answers to these questions:

◆ Why is the Tang dynasty considered a golden age?
◆ Who were the first foreigners to rule China?
◆ How did Ming rulers isolate China from the world?

> **Key Terms:** tribute (defined on p. 265)

Long before Yang Ti was emperor, the Han dynasty ruled China. As you read in Chapter 3, China became a great empire during nearly 400 years of Han rule. When that empire fell, centuries of chaos resulted.

Gradually, other strong dynasties reunited China, rebuilt the empire, and led the country into another golden age.

Troubles Followed the Fall of the Han Dynasty

Invasions by nomadic, barbarian peoples brought chaos to Asia and Europe for about 200 years in the period A.D. 200 to A.D. 400. As you read in Chapter 5, Germans fleeing the Huns were one cause for the fall of Rome. In a similar way, invasions by the Tartars (a people related to the Huns) threw northern China into disorder after the fall of the Han dynasty in A.D. 220. Northern China was not protected by mountains as was southern China, and invaders were able to enter the region through the Gobi Desert. Chaos lasted for over 300 years as the Chinese fought among themselves and against invaders. No one dynasty was strong enough to bring order to the country.

In many ways, China was hurt less by invasions than was Europe. Invaders who tried to conquer China were themselves usually conquered by Chinese culture. Most of these invaders adopted Chinese ways, learned the language, and became part of the culture of the country they had invaded. Buddhism, which had almost died out in India, grew strong in China. To escape the threat of invasion, millions of Chinese people moved away from the northern borders to the south, where many new cities and centers of culture grew up.

In 589, the Sui (swee) dynasty gained control of China. The two emperors of this dynasty ruled harshly but accomplished a great deal in the 30 years of their rule. Roads and canals were built, food was stored to try to prevent famine, and the Great Wall was rebuilt. The most important accomplishment of this dynasty, however, was the reuniting of China. Still, the harshness of the Sui dynasty eventually led to its overthrow. Two greater dynasties followed—the Tang, from 618 to 907, and the Song, from 960 to 1279.

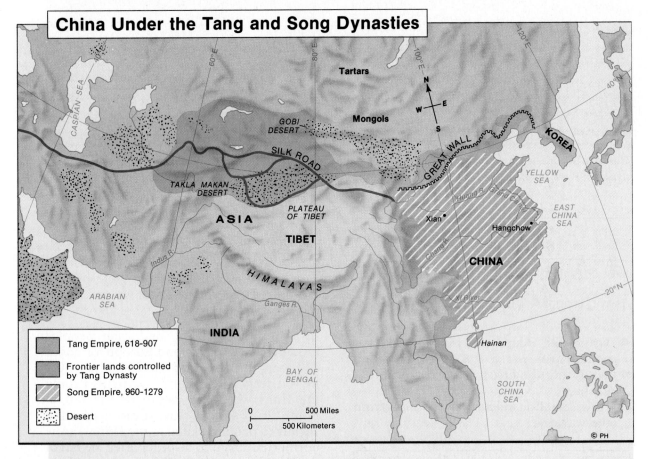

China Under the Tang and Song Dynasties

Tang Empire, 618-907

Frontier lands controlled by Tang Dynasty

Song Empire, 960-1279

Desert

0   500 Miles
0   500 Kilometers

Focus on Geography

1. **Interaction**   One of the Sui rulers masterminded the building of the Grand Canal. What two rivers does the canal connect?
2. **Movement**   Along the Chang River, southern China was more fertile than northern China. How do you think the canal might have helped?

Chinese Dynasties 589–1644		
589–616	Sui dynasty	Chinese build roads and rebuild Great Wall; China is reunited
618–907	Tang dynasty	Golden age begins; government is stable; trade prospers; examinations on Confucian teachings determine jobs
960–1279	Song dynasty	China continues to prosper; Song leaders move south to escape invaders
1279–1368	Yuan dynasty	Emperors trade with Europe and India; Marco Polo visits; Kublai Khan sets up efficient tax collection
1368–1644	Ming dynasty	Rule of Chinese is restored; Chinese sponsor voyages of exploration

▲ **Chart Skill** *What dynasty reunited China?*

China Reached New Heights Under Tang and Song Rulers

Under the Tang, a long golden age began for China. The country developed a stable government and a rich culture. Trade prospered. Ambassadors from Byzantium, Muslim lands, and India came to China.

Tang China was the greatest empire in the world at that time. (The map on page 262 shows the extent of the Tang empire.) A strict system of examinations, based on the teachings of Confucius, weeded out all but the best civil service, or government, workers. People in other Asian countries admired and imitated Tang art, architecture, and poetry. They traded their goods for China's rich silks and fine porcelains.

The center of this brilliant society was the beautiful capital city, Xian (SHEE AN). About 1 million people lived there in Tang times. Xian was made up of three major cities. The imperial court was in the Palace City, while officials lived in the Imperial City. Merchants and craftspeople lived in the Outer City. Foreign visitors from the rest of Asia and the Muslim world came to Xian to trade in the marketplaces and enjoy the temples, parks, and flower gardens.

One of the greatest rulers of the Tang family was Taizong (TY DZOHNG), who ruled from 627 to 650. Although he started his rule badly by murdering his brothers to gain power, he ended his rule in glory by turning to the ways of peace. From 712 to 756, during the reign of Xuan Zong, China grew wealthier than ever before.

The Tang dynasty ended around 907, after a period of rebellion that was followed by years of chaos and unrest. When the Song kings began their dynasty, around 960, China continued to prosper, although not quite as much as it had under the Tangs. During the Song dynasty, invaders again attacked northern China. By the 1200s, China faced invasion from the dreaded Mongols. The leader of these fierce, hard-riding warriors was Temujin, known as Genghis (GEHNG gihs) Khan, or "lord of the world." He united the wild tribes of Mongols and led them across the Gobi Desert to conquer most of northern Asia. Upon his death in 1227, his sons and grandsons continued to conquer. The greatest of these descendants was his grandson Kublai (KOO bly) Khan.

▼ **Illustrating History** *Below is Kublai Khan, first ruler of China's Yuan dynasty.*

Mongol Conquerors Ruled China for 100 Years

Kublai Khan established his capital at Beijing, and his forces wiped out the last of the Song defenders. He then created the Yuan (yoo AHN) dynasty, which was China's first dynasty of foreign rulers. The Yuan dynasty ruled China from 1279 to 1368. We know more about this period in China than many others because Kublai Khan, who was known as the "Great Khan," encouraged trade with Europe and India. Marco Polo, a young Venetian merchant, came to China about 1275 and worked for Kublai Khan. The map on this page shows his travels. Returning to Europe, Polo wrote a book about his adventures. Polo's book told of the great summer and winter palaces, Kublai Khan's magnificent court, and the efficient systems for tax collection and mail delivery that the Great Khan had established. His

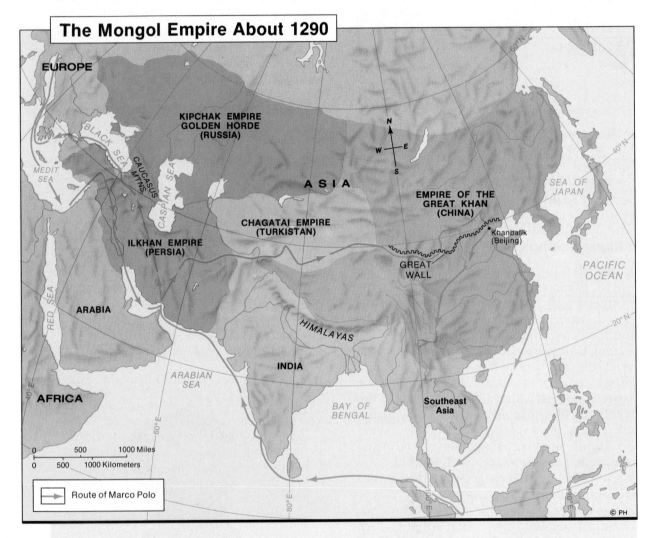

The Mongol Empire About 1290

Route of Marco Polo

Focus on Geography

Regions By the middle of the thirteenth century, four khans ruled over the Mongol Empire. Three of them were lesser khans who served the Great Khan. Over what three regions did lesser khans rule?

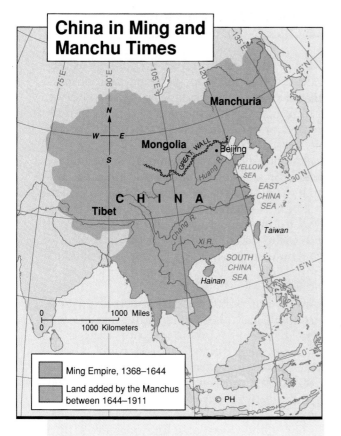

China in Ming and Manchu Times

Ming Empire, 1368–1644

Land added by the Manchus between 1644–1911

© PH

Focus on Geography

Regions What three regions did the Manchus control?

new capital was greater than any city in Europe. Its splendors were so great that most Europeans did not believe Marco Polo's tales.

The Mongol rulers were one of the few groups of foreigners who did not acquire Chinese ways. They even practiced a different form of Buddhism. Over time, rebellions broke out in many parts of China. One rebel leader, a Buddhist monk called Hong Wu (hoong WOO), led an army that drove the Mongols from China. He began the Ming dynasty, which lasted from 1368 to 1644.

The Ming Dynasty Enriched China

In Chinese, *Ming* means "glorious." While the Ming dynasty did not equal the glory of the Han, Tang, or Song dynasties, it did

restore China's pride. Other countries of East Asia were forced to pay money and goods as **tribute** to the Ming rulers in return for protection. In this period of wealth and prosperity, art and architecture flourished.

Beginning about 1405, Chinese ships sailed to unknown parts of Asia and Africa. Then, Ming rulers deliberately began to isolate their country from change. For reasons that are not clear, the ruling powers began to emphasize tradition and the greatness of the Chinese past and made little preparation for the future. Nonetheless, it was during the Ming period that European traders started coming to China.

In the 1600s, rebellions broke out against the Ming rulers. Once again, nomadic people from Manchuria in the north moved into China. These people, known as Manchus, set up their own dynasty. It was the last dynasty of imperial China and ruled until 1911. (See the map on this page.) The story of its rule is told in Chapter 24.

SECTION 1 REVIEW

Knowing Key Terms, People, and Places
1. Define: **a.** tribute
2. Identify: **a.** Tang dynasty **b.** Song dynasty **c.** Mongols **d.** Genghis Khan **e.** Kublai Khan **f.** Ming dynasty

Focus on Geography
3. Why was the northern border of China easily invaded?

Reviewing Main Ideas
4. Why is the era of the Tang and Song dynasties considered a golden age?
5. What benefits did Mongol rule bring to China?
6. What changes occurred in Chinese policy during the Ming dynasty?

Critical Thinking
Demonstrating Reasoned Judgment
7. What do you think was the main cause for the Ming rulers' emphasis on old traditions and past greatness?

2 Chinese Culture Is Based on Tradition

As you read, look for answers to these questions:

◆ What was the traditional Chinese family like?
◆ How did people in ancient China make a living?
◆ What achievements did the Chinese make in art, literature, and science?

Key Terms: dialect (defined on p. 269)

Because of the teachings of Confucius and other Chinese thinkers, the people of China, like their rulers, often resisted change. As a result, some ancient Chinese traditions and customs lasted well into modern times. But the Chinese did not only look backward. While preserving their heritage, they also created brilliant literature, beautiful works of art, and ingenious scientific inventions.

▼ **Illustrating History** *Shown below is a family portrait of the Ming dynasty, which ruled China from 1368 to 1644.*

Family Life Was the Basis of Chinese Society

Even more than in India, the family was the hub of Chinese life. In fact, the family, rather than the individual, was the center of Chinese society. Confucius, a great Chinese philosopher of the fifth century B.C., recognized this and created a series of rules about behavior among family members. He taught that children had to obey their parents, and that a wife had to obey and honor her husband. Among siblings, a younger child had to obey and respect an older one. People often called each other by their family position, such as "Elder Sister" or "Second Son," rather than by personal names.

The family in China included cousins, uncles, and aunts as well as children and grandchildren. Members of the family who had died were worshipped, not as gods or divine beings, but as honored, often powerful, spirits. Just as a father carried out the correct ceremonies for his dead parents, his children were expected to carry out the correct ceremonies for him after his death.

The father was absolute master of the Chinese household. Although women in Chinese society usually were treated with indifference, the mother of many sons was often honored. Parents usually arranged marriages for their children while they were still young. After marriage, a wife was expected to live with her husband's family and learn its ways.

Nobles, high officials, and rich merchants lived in far more comfort and luxury than ordinary people. Still, family ties were as much the center of life for the rich as for the common people. Honoring the spirits of dead ancestors also played a vital part in the lives of well-to-do families. They could afford to build elaborate altars to offer prayers for dead relatives. Since much of the wealth they enjoyed was inherited, it seemed natural to pray for those ancestors who had founded the family fortune.

While the ideas of Confucius were basic to Chinese society, family life, and government, most Chinese also followed Buddhism or Taoism. You read about some of the central ideas and beliefs of Buddhism and Taoism in Chapter 3. For the most part, the Chinese were tolerant of other religions and saw no conflicts between them. They celebrated many different festivals with ceremonies drawn from several faiths and prayers to different gods.

Besides festivals, the theater was a popular form of entertainment, especially for people in cities. Actors dressed in elegant costumes sang, danced, and acted out stories before audiences. The audiences had to watch the actors closely because no scenery or stage props were used. Instead, actors used certain movements to indicate when they were entering a room, climbing stairs, or crossing a river.

Crafts Were Important to China's Economy

Families in China worked together to make a living. The peasant class was the largest class of society. Most peasants farmed land that belonged to a prince or noble. Other peasants lived and worked on patches of land that were often too small to provide the family with what it needed. Peasants grew vegetables, cotton (for clothing), rice, and tea. They raised chickens, pigs, ducks, and geese. Although peasants often faced starvation, the teachings of Chinese philosophers encouraged them to accept things as they were. As one proverb said, "All that a man needs . . . is a hat and a bowl of rice."

Although farming was the major work of most peasants, several specialized skills became important industries in ancient China. Many Chinese made a living by breeding silkworms and weaving silk textiles. As early as 300 B.C., there were guilds of silkweavers, glassblowers, and papermakers. As you learned in Chapter 7, guilds were groups of people in the same craft or trade who set rules to uphold standards, protect members, and set prices. Chinese workers had organized guilds hundreds of years before they were known in Europe.

You may call your dinner plates and cups "china" without realizing that the country of China was the first to make this beautiful and useful product. The making of pottery

In their own words

Preparing for Ancestor Worship

Ssu-ma Kuang was a government official during the Song Dynasty. He wrote a widely read book on the proper etiquette for weddings, funerals, and other ceremonies. In the following selection, he describes some of the duties required on the day before the actual ceremony honoring a family's ancestors.

❝On the day before the ceremony, the master organizes all the male members of the family and the assistants to dust and sweep the place where the sacrifice will be held, to wash and clean the utensils and containers, and to arrange the furniture. The places for the departed ancestors are so arranged that each husband and wife are side by side, arranged according to proper ranking from west to east, and all facing south. The mistress of the house supervises the women of the household in cleaning the cooking utensils and preparing the food, which should include five kinds of vegetables and five kinds of fruits and not more than fifteen dishes of the following sorts: red stew, roast meat, fried meat, ribs, boiled white meat, dried meat, ground meat, special meats other than pork or lamb, foods made of flour. (If the family is poor, or if certain items cannot be obtained, then merely include several items from each category, that is, vegetable, fruit, meat, flour-foods, and rice-foods.)❞

1. Who is responsible for cleaning the room and the utensils that will be used in the ceremony?
2. What suggests that this advice is written for wealthy families?

▲ **Illustrating History** *Chinese festivals, such as the one pictured above, were times of celebration and religious ceremonies.*

and porcelain was not only a major industry but also a fine art in China. China's soil was rich in the clay used in pottery making. The Chinese were so skillful that they became world famous in this industry. Today, people still treasure beautiful vases and statues made long ago by Chinese artisans.

The Chinese also were active merchants and traders. Merchants did business with the peoples of the Byzantine Empire and, later, the Muslim world, including the Malay Peninsula, India, and Persia. To these people, the Chinese sold porcelain, paper, silk, tea, and gunpowder. In return, they bought peanuts, glass, tobacco, and opium. Merchants who needed money could borrow from bankers whose systems of finance, coinage, and paper money helped the Chinese do business with far-off places. Crops and handicrafts were carried from one location to another on the backs of unskilled laborers called coolies or were moved by boat on China's many canals.

Chinese aristocrats looked down on people who worked at any trade. Members of the upper class relied on favors from the imperial court, rents collected from their tenant farmers, and profits from the products of their lands. To show their distaste for work, the wealthy wore elegant silk gowns and let their fingernails grow long.

Scholarship Was a Way to Success

Education and a knowledge of the Chinese classics were valued highly in China. Scholars were highly respected for only they could hold government jobs. It was the ambition of most families, rich and poor alike, to have a son who could pass the test for government service. For a poor family, a government position was a source of pride and a step up the social ladder. A family member with a government job could help make the family rich or influential.

To pass the examination for government service, candidates had to memorize the teachings of Confucius. Only the most brilliant scholars could memorize and understand these teachings. Students sometimes studied for years, taking the examinations several times in an attempt to pass them.

Although the tests were open to rich and poor, the rich were more likely to pass because they had more opportunity to get an education.

The higher the grades, the better the jobs available to scholars who passed the examinations. Students who failed the government examinations sometimes took easier examinations to enter military service. For those who failed to pass either test, the door to advancement in government was closed.

The emphasis on memorizing Confucius's teachings meant that new knowledge and ideas were not thought valuable. Scholars who were successful formed a new aristocracy. They did not use their education to create new knowledge or improve people's working and living conditions.

The Chinese Language Produced Great Literature

One challenge for Chinese students who wished to be scholars was the difficulty of the Chinese language. The Chinese language is not written with an alphabet. Instead, it has thousands of characters. Each character is a different symbol, or set of lines that represents a thing or an idea, not a letter or sound. A page of Chinese writing is made up of these individual characters. They are written from the top to the bottom of the page rather than from left to right.

The meaning of each of the thousands of different characters used in Chinese writing varies with its use in a particular sentence. Even the meaning of a spoken word depends on the tone that is used when it is pronounced.

Spoken Chinese has many **dialects** (DY uh LEKTS) or different ways of pronunciation. Some of these are understood by only a few people. The written language, however, can be read by many people throughout Asia who do not understand each other's spoken language. In fact, the Chinese language is probably used by more people than any other language.

Written literature and poetry began early in Chinese history. By the time of the Tang dynasty, poets were greatly admired and given influential positions. Du Fu and Li Bo were two well-known poets of the period. The following lines from a poem by Du Fu express sadness over the fact that war had taken the lives of many young men:

> If I had only known how sad is the
> fate of boys
> I would have had my children all girls. . . .
> Boys are only born to be buried
> beneath tall grass.
> Still the bones of the war dead of long
> ago are beside
> the Blue Sea when you pass.

The interest in books and written literature stimulated several inventions. About the year A.D. 150, the Chinese discovered how to make paper from scraps of cotton or linen. The paper was used for painting, writing, and paper money. Because paper was invented and used at such an early date, China had books early in its history. By 700, block printing (the use of blocks engraved with letters and then coated with ink and pressed on paper) was well on its way to becoming a highly developed craft in China. The demand for religious books and textbooks for government examinations further encouraged this development. The world's oldest printed book, dated 868, was found in China. Scholarly books, histories, and novels all became popular during this time.

The Chinese Were Inventors and Artists

The invention of paper and printing shows that the Chinese were a practical, inventive people. Chinese sailors were using a magnetic compass at least as early as 1100, and as early as 600, the Chinese knew about and used gunpowder. For centuries, however, gunpowder was used for fireworks, not for firearms. Not until the thirteenth and fourteenth centuries was gunpowder used to fire weapons.

Like chemists in medieval Europe, Chinese chemists practiced alchemy, but they also failed in their attempts to make gold out of less valuable metals. They did, however, make other useful discoveries, including

▲ **Illustrating History** *Chinese artists were skilled in many mediums. Above are examples of porcelain and landscape painting.*

the techniques of porcelain making and the use of lacquers and enamels.

The Chinese admired beauty as well as knowledge. Practical objects, such as furniture and clothing, became objects of beauty. Lovely bronze cups were made for religious purposes. Delicate jade was carved into fantastic figures. As in other periods, Chinese artisans of the Tang and Song dynasties made fine jewelry and porcelain. Architecture, too, became a fine art. Elaborate temples and pagodas built of wood developed during this period. Although many of the original buildings are gone, they set the style for later buildings.

Under the Song dynasty, Chinese painting reached its peak. The paintings showed insects, fish, birds, flowers, or the hills, waters, deserts, and mountains of China. These subjects reflected the beauty and order of nature taught by Confucius. These paintings were not made to be hung permanently on walls. Instead, they were designed to be rolled or unrolled like a scroll and viewed when the owner wished.

Knowing Key Terms, Peoples, and Places
1. Define: **a.** dialect
2. Identify: **a.** Du Fu **b.** Li Bo

Reviewing Main Ideas
3. How did Confucius's idea about relationships apply to Chinese family life?
4. What kinds of entertainment did Chinese people enjoy?
5. What skilled crafts became valuable in China's economy?
6. How could being a good scholar help an individual and his family in China?

Critical Thinking

Drawing Conclusions
7. The government examinations for China emphasized memorizing the writings of Confucius. What effects do you think this would have on the government itself? (Refer to Chapter 3 to review the basic philosophy of Confucius.)

3 Korea Created a Distinctive Heritage

As you read, look for answers to these questions:

◆ What is the land of Korea like?
◆ What were the three kingdoms?
◆ What dynasty drove out the Mongols in 1392 and ruled Korea for nearly 600 years?
◆ What country had the greatest influence on Korea's government and culture?

Key Terms: turtle ship (defined on p. 272), movable type (p. 273)

The splendor of China's empire made it natural that other countries in East Asia would admire and imitate many elements of its culture and government. Korea and Japan were two countries that borrowed much from China. In this section, you will read about Korea, one of the oldest nations in the world. The final section of this chapter will discuss the history of Japan.

Geography Made Korea Vulnerable

Korea is a beautiful peninsula that extends 600 miles (966 kilometers) into the Yellow Sea off northern Asia. It is separated from the islands of Japan by only a few miles of ocean and from China by rugged mountains and the Yalu River. Korea shares most of its northern boundary with Manchuria in China and the rest with Siberia. Mountains run down the center of the peninsula, which is about the size of the state of Minnesota. Refer to the map on this page to locate Korea and Japan.

Korea's climate varies from region to region. Southern Korea has moist, hot summers and moderate winters. Mountainous Korea, which is farther from the ocean, has long, harsh winters and cool summers. All of Korea has enough rainfall for farming.

In the past, the Korean peninsula has acted as a bridge by which people and ideas

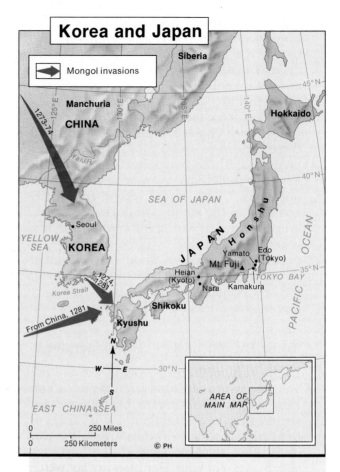

Korea and Japan

→ Mongol invasions

Focus on Geography

1. **Location** What is the shortest distance between Korea and Japan?
2. **Place** Name the four islands that make up Japan.

could move from the continent of Asia to Japan. Although Korea's location tempted would-be invaders from both China and Japan, its mountainous geography encouraged isolation and the growth of a unique national culture.

The Three Kingdoms Ruled Early Korea

Korea's history, like that of many countries, begins with a legend. According to legend, Tangun, "the grandson of Heaven," founded Choson, the first kingdom in Korea, in 2333 B.C. Of course, this date comes only from legend. Historians do know, however, that Choson existed as early as the third century B.C. In 108 B.C., the soldiers of China's Han dynasty conquered the kingdom of Choson and set up colonies.

Meanwhile, Koreans in other parts of the peninsula were building small, independent states with Chinese support. By A.D. 400, three kingdoms ruled most of the Korean peninsula. These kingdoms were known as Koguryo (KOH GOO ryuh), which was on the border of China, and Paekche (pi CHEE) and Silla in the south. Although these three kingdoms ruled Korea for several hundred years, the influence of Chinese culture remained strong. When Buddhism was introduced from China, most Koreans accepted the new religion and, through trade, passed it and other ideas on to Japan.

Korea Fought to Remain Independent

In the early 600s, emperors of the Sui and Tang dynasties of China tried again to conquer Korea. The Koreans fought hard and successfully to defend their walled cities on the Chinese border. The Empress Wu Hou of the Tang dynasty decided to try an invasion by sea, not land. Her plan worked. After the coastal kingdom of Silla was conquered, it helped China to defeat the other two kingdoms. Once they were defeated, Silla took over the whole Korean peninsula and paid tribute to China.

Unlike China, Korea was governed by several wealthy families rather than by scholars and officials loyal to the emperor. Eventually, the country was divided by fighting among local rulers. Bandits and pirates also troubled the people of Korea.

In 936 (after the fall of China's Tang dynasty), a general named Wang Kon (wang GON) reunited Korea and created an independent kingdom. He named his dynasty Koryo after the old kingdom of Koguryo. It ruled for more than 450 years, giving its name to Korea. In the 1200s, however, the Mongol conquerors who had swept across Asia overcame Korea's defenders. The Mongols dominated Koryo rulers for the last 100 years of the dynasty.

The Yi Dynasty Ruled for More Than 500 Years

In 1392, General Yi T'aejo (YEE dye joh) led the Korean people in a revolt against the Mongols and became a national hero. He also led his troops against the pirates of Japan who were raiding the coasts of Korea and plundering Korean ships. Once the Mongols were defeated, Yi declared himself king, won support among the people, and began a new Korean dynasty. Known as the Yi dynasty, it lasted from 1392 to 1910.

Yi was a hard-working ruler who was determined to make Korea a strong nation. He began by building a new capital city at Seoul (sohl). He also took some land away from the aristocrats and distributed it to the people, improved the government, and saw to it that Korea was ruled wisely.

During most of the Yi dynasty, Korea had close ties with Ming China. By the 1500s, however, Japan was becoming powerful. Japanese pirates again raided the coasts of Korea and plundered Korean ships. In 1592, an ambitious Japanese military leader, Hideyoshi (hee duh yoh shee), made a serious and nearly successful attempt to conquer Korea. In this war, the Japanese used firearms for the first time in their history. Although the Ming dynasty in China sent help to the Koreans, the Korean navy was able to meet the Japanese challenge with a new weapon—ships protected by plates of iron armor. These ships, known as **turtle ships,** held off the Japanese.

Unfortunately, Korea's victory over the Japanese invasion exhausted the country. The war caused great destruction and a deep fear of foreigners. Korea withdrew from contact with foreign nations. Traders and other outsiders were turned away, and for many years, Korea was known as the Hermit Kingdom.

Korean Culture Was Unique and Inventive

Daily life in Korea centered on the family. The father was the head of the family, and his word was law. Women left the house only at a certain time each day, usually early in the evening. For the most part, men and women lived separate lives. As in other parts of Asia, most people in Korea depended on farming for a living.

As you have read, Korea was greatly influenced by China. From the Chinese, the Koreans learned the teachings of Buddha and Confucius. Like the Chinese, the Koreans thought that books and learning were an important part of life. Schools were based on Confucian ideas, and Korean scholars had to be able to read and pass examinations in the Chinese language. Although movable type for printing was probably invented in China, the Koreans in the 1400s were the first to use it widely for printing large books. **Movable type** consists of separate pieces of metal that can be used again and again. Each piece of type prints an individual letter or character. Using this invention, the Koreans were able to dramatically increase the number of books they produced. At about the same time, a scholarly ruler of the Yi dynasty invented an alphabet to use in writing the Korean language instead of Chinese characters. In the arts, Koreans were particularly skilled in painting and in the creation of special types of pottery.

The Koreans made several important advances in technology. Besides the use of movable type and the invention of ironclad ships, Koreans are credited with inventing the spinning wheel, the observation balloon, and an instrument to measure rainfall.

To promote scholarship, a royal college of literature was established in 1420. Korean scholars compiled a 112 volume encyclopedia. The Yi Palace Orchestra was founded 500 years ago to perform Korean music.

Korea is famous for its wise sayings, or proverbs. Some of these sayings are similiar to proverbs of other countries. Do you know what they mean?

- Don't draw a sword to kill a mosquito.
- You cannot sit in the valley and see the new moon set.
- It is useless to pour instruction into a sow's ear.
- It is foolish to mourn over a broken vase.

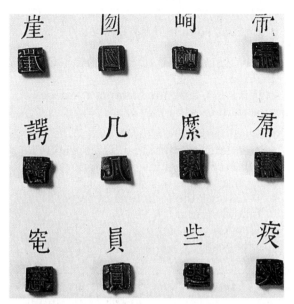

▲ **Illustrating History** *The Koreans used movable type, shown above, to produce books.*

SECTION 3 REVIEW

Knowing Key Terms, People, and Places
1. Define: **a.** turtle ship **b.** movable type
2. Identify: **a.** Koguryo **b.** Paekche **c.** Silla **d.** Empress Wu Hou **e.** Wang Kon **f.** Koryo **g.** Yi T'aejo **h.** Seoul

Focus on Geography
3. How did geography affect Korea's history and culture?

Reviewing Main Ideas
4. What part did Wang Kon play in the history of Korea?
5. What changes did the Yi dynasty bring to Korea?
6. Why was Korea given the name the Hermit Kingdom?

Critical Thinking
Predicting Consequences
7. If a small and fairly isolated country like Korea has a large, powerful empire like China as a neighbor, what predictions might you make about the history of the smaller country? Which of your predictions are true for Korea? Which are not?

4 Japan's Unique Civilization Emerged

As you read, look for answers to these questions:

◆ What is the most important characteristic of Japan's geography?
◆ What two religions were important in Japan?
◆ What was the structure of Japan's feudal system?
◆ How did the samurai code affect the Japanese?

> **Key Terms:** clan (defined on p. 274), kami (p. 274), daimyo (p. 276), samurai (p. 276), ronin (p. 276), shogun (p. 276), bushido (p. 277)

According to legend, the goddess Izanami looked on from the Floating Bridge of Heaven as her husband Izangi plunged a jeweled spear into the ocean. Lifting it, he let the sparkling drops fall. These drops of water became the islands of Japan. Although this story is a myth, Japan's island location is its single most important geographic characteristic. It played an important part in the country's history.

Geography Influenced Japanese History

Japan is made up of four large islands. The northernmost island is Hokkaido (hoh KY doh). The largest island, where Tokyo, the capital of the country, is located, is Honshu. The remaining large islands to the south are Shikoku (SHEE koh KOO) and Kyushu (KYOO shoo). Like Great Britain, Japan is an island nation near a major continent. As in Great Britain, no part of Japan is far from the sea, and as it developed, it too became a seagoing nation.

Unlike Great Britain, however, Japan is in a part of the world where volcanoes and earthquakes occur frequently. Much of its land is made up of rugged, volcanic mountains. The most famous mountain is the 12,000 (3.7 kilometers) foot Mount Fuji, which is 60 (96.6 kilometers) miles west of Tokyo. This mountain has been considered sacred since ancient times when the Japanese worshipped all natural objects that inspired awe or fear. Thousands of Japanese people continue to make religious pilgrimages there.

Yamato Rulers Unified Early Japan

Historians are not sure of the ancestry of the Japanese people. It seems likely that over many years different groups of people migrated to the islands from Asia, often by way of the Korean peninsula. Historians believe this because the Japanese and Korean languages are related to the languages spoken in northern Asia but are not at all like Chinese. One group of early people, the Ainu, did not mix with the others and developed their own unique language. A few thousand Ainu people still live on the northern island of Hokkaido.

By about A.D. 200, the Japanese people were living in **clans,** or communities based on family ties. Each clan was divided into groups of farmers, craftworkers, fishers, and other workers who owed their loyalty to the clan and its leaders. Clan leaders, who could be either men or women, were also religious leaders. They led the members of the clan and surrounding community in worshipping nature spirits, or **kami** (KAH mee). These spirits might be seen in a mountain or waterfall or be represented by a jewel or bronze mirror. This belief in nature spirits became the basis of the religion known as Shinto.

Over the next 200 years, one clan finally united the country. Its leaders used a combination of diplomacy and force to unite the clans around the area of Yamato in western Honshu. The Yamato clan leaders were acknowledged as rulers and as descendants of the sun goddess. In Japanese mythology, the first Yamato emperor was Jimmu, "Divine Warrior," whose reign began in 660 B.C. Actually, the Yamato rulers came to power about A.D. 400.

A Crane's Meaning

In Japan, origami, the art of paper folding, has been practiced for centuries. The oldest known books on origami are devoted to the making of one shape—that of the crane. The Japanese regard this graceful bird as a symbol of long life and good fortune. (See the picture at right.)

Today in Japan, people also recognize the crane as a symbol of peace. The crane came to be known as a peace symbol after the Japanese city of Hiroshima was destroyed by an atomic bomb in 1945. One of its victims, a 12-year-old girl, lay in a hospital with radiation poisoning. She believed that if she could fold 1,000 cranes she would bring world peace. She died before she reached her goal. Today in Hiroshima, there is a statue of a little girl

holding an origami crane. The statue is decorated with paper cranes sent in by children from all over the world.

1. What is origami?
2. What is the original meaning of the crane symbol?
3. How did the crane come to be a symbol of peace?

The Japanese Borrowed Political and Religious Ideas from China

Not surprisingly, the Japanese people admired China's splendor and began to borrow ideas from its culture. Prince Shotoku (SHOH tuh koo), for example, was a scholar who encouraged Buddhism and other ideas from China. In 607, Shotoku began to send ambassadors and students from Japan to China. He urged the Japanese people to study Chinese history and art, as well as Confucian ethics and political theory.

Under the leadership of Shotoku, Buddhism grew to be an important part of Japanese life. Buddhist priests and scholars came from China, and huge statues of the Buddha were built along with temples and monasteries. Although many people adopted Buddhism as their religion, they also continued to practice Shinto.

The Japanese did not copy Chinese ideas. Instead, they adapted Chinese institutions to their own society. In doing so, they made these institutions uniquely Japanese.

Japan's political development is one example of how the Japanese changed ideas they borrowed. Leaders like Prince Shotoku wanted to give Japan a strong central government similar to that of the Tang dynasty in China, in which the emperor had absolute power. In 646, a series of laws, known as the Taika (tah ee kah) Reforms, tried to make the emperor stronger. These laws gave the government control over taxes and all land.

At the same time, the leaders of clans and powerful families in Japan, unlike those in China, did not give up all their power. Instead, they became a class of nobles who had great influence at the emperor's court. Sometimes, they competed with the imperial family for official positions and power. One important family clan was the Soga. Another was the Fujiwara (foo jee wah rah), which became powerful in the late 600s. Over time, some of these families gained even more power than the emperor.

In 710, a beautiful new capital city was built at Nara. Modeled after the Chinese capital at Xian, Nara was a political and a religious center. A gigantic bronze and gold statue of Buddha was built for the royal temple. This impressive statue, one sign of the influence Buddhist leaders had, can still be seen today. In 794, a new capital was established at Heian (HAY ahn), which is now called Kyoto. The city remained the capital of Japan until 1868.

The Heian period, which lasted from 794 to 1182, was a time of rapid growth for Japan. The aristocratic men and women of the Heian court lived elegantly. They developed distinctive styles in literature and art that influenced later Japanese culture.

A Feudal Society Developed in Japan

By about the twelfth century, the power of the central government—the emperor and the aristocratic court families—had declined. Military families and landowners who lived far from the capital gradually gained power. Over the years, these families had built up private armies for local defense or police forces. Gradually, a system of feudalism, much like that in medieval Europe, developed. The emperor was the chief lord to whom the great lords and landowners, called **daimyo** (DY myoh), owed loyalty. Lesser vassals and warriors, called **samurai** (SAH muh rye), owed loyalty to their daimyo. Warriors who had no overlord to serve were called **ronin** (ROH nin). These warriors could be hired by other nobles. Peasants, workers, merchants, and other ordinary Japanese people served their local lords, much as in the time of the clans.

In time, two warrior clans, the Taira (tah ee rah) and the Minamoto (mee nuh moh toh), became the main rivals for power. Civil war broke out in 1180. In 1192, the Minamoto clan defeated the Taira, and Yoritomo Minamoto set up his own government at the town of Kamakura. Because the emperor was believed to be descended from the sun goddess, he was too respected to be overthrown. Instead, he became a revered, shadowy, powerless figure. Yoritomo gained the title and power as supreme military leader, or **shogun** (SHOH GUHN). For the next 600 years, Japan was led by three different governments, called shogunates. Each one was headed by the all-powerful shoguns.

About a hundred years after Yoritomo set up the Kamakura shogunate, Japan faced its most serious threat from the outside world. In 1281, Kublai Khan, the Mongol conqueror of China, tried to invade Japan. Although several earlier invasions had failed, Kublai Khan put together a huge invasion force. Some 3,500 ships and more than 100,000 Chinese and Korean soldiers set out for Japan. A violent storm destroyed the Mongol fleet, drowning more than half of the invasion force. The Japanese gave credit to the kami and called the storm *kamikaze*, or "divine wind."

The Feudal System Changed Under Later Shoguns

The second family of shoguns came to power in 1338 and ruled until 1567. This period, known as the Ashikaga (ah shee kah gah) period, was a troubled time in Japan. The shoguns' governments were weak, and military lords and their samurai were often at war with each other. As in medieval Europe, however, towns and trade developed in spite of the warfare.

It was late in this period that the first European explorers and Christian missionaries arrived in Japan. As the government grew weaker, several powerful generals tried to unite the country again under one strong leader. About 1580, Hideyoshi came to power. Because he was ugly to look at, his subjects called him "monkey face" (when they felt it safe to do so).

Ambitious almost to the point of insanity, Hideyoshi tried to conquer both Korea and China. His two invasions failed. Next, he tried to strengthen Japan by weakening the power of the daimyo and banishing the missionaries who had arrived in 1549.

War broke out when Hideyoshi died in 1598. The victor, Tokugawa Iyeyasu (ee yeh yah soo), established Japan's third and last shogunate in 1603. He moved the capital to Edo (modern Tokyo). The Tokugawa shogunate, which governed from this city until 1868, soon imposed isolation on Japan. Japanese people could not leave the country, and almost no foreigners could enter the country, although a few Dutch traders were allowed to visit the port city of Nagasaki. This isolation was not broken until Commodore Perry led a fleet of American ships into Tokyo Bay in 1853. Despite Japan's isolation, Japanese society and culture continued to grow and prosper in the Tokugawa period.

Japanese Society Followed the Samurai Code

Like the code of chivalry in medieval Europe, the ideals and goals of the samurai became important in feudal Japan. Loyalty to one's lord and personal bravery were the most important things for a samurai. In

▼ **Illustrating History** *Yoritomo Minamoto became Japan's first shogun in 1192. Japan's governments were headed by shoguns, supreme military leaders, for the next 600 years.*

many cases, loyalty to one's lord was considered more important than family loyalty or even loyalty to the emperor. In China, by contrast, no loyalties were more important than those to the family.

In Japan, the samurai code was known as **bushido,** or "the way of the warrior." Like the knights of medieval Europe, the samurai and their brave deeds were the subjects of exciting stories and novels. Merchants and middle-class townspeople also tried to follow the samurai ideals of loyalty, bravery, and discipline.

Elaborate, formal manners and courtesies became part of the samurai tradition. People bowed to show respect when they met or when they entered or left a room. Even a simple daily routine such as serving tea became formalized and involved a careful, precise ceremony.

For Japanese women, the way of the warrior limited the privileges and freedoms they had had earlier. In early Japan, women had been clan leaders and religious leaders. In the early feudal period, women of the samurai class were expected to be loyal and brave. Some had political power. As the feudal period went on, however, women came to be considered inferior. In the upper classes, which included the samurai and wealthy merchants, women had no freedoms outside the home. Respectable women did not go out except on family occasions. At home, men had complete power over their families. To show their low status, women bowed to their husbands when they either entered or left a room. They served meals in silence.

In one important way, Japanese women had an advantage over most women in Asia or in medieval Europe. In the towns and cities of Japan, women of samurai and merchant families were educated. They learned to read and write and could enjoy the books written during the Tokugawa period.

Many Japanese, of course, were not part of the samurai way of life. As in most of the countries of East Asia, most people were farmers. Many farmers did not own the land they worked. As in medieval Europe, they had to give much of what they grew to the lord of the land. The most important food

277

Lady Murasaki

The graceful life of the imperial Japanese court at Kyoto crept by at a snail's pace. Between elaborate rituals, there were many idle hours. A young woman, recently widowed and now a lady-in-waiting to the empress, used her free time to begin a long narrative called *The Tale of Genji* (GEN gee). Eventually the tale would be recognized as one of the greatest works of Japanese literature—and the world's first true novel. (Shown right, a scene from it.)

Not much is known about this author, not even her name. She was born about 978, died some time after 1025, and has been referred to as Lady Murasaki in honor of one of her fictional characters. Her novel describes the adventures of Prince Genji and his kin.

Lady Murasaki left behind a revealing diary. It tells us that she was a Buddhist who, while fascinated by the elegance and style of the imperial court, believed that none of it really mattered in the end.

1. Who was Lady Murasaki?
2. What is the importance of *The Tale of Genji?*

---

was rice. Fishing was another major industry. In fact, fish and rice made up the basic diet of most Japanese people.

Literature and Religion Flourished in Feudal Japan

Much of Japanese literature and art follows a style older than the samurai way of life in feudal times. The court at Heian was a place where noble women played important roles in shaping Japanese culture. One outstanding contribution to Japanese culture—and world literature—was made by the Lady Murasaki Shikibu, a member of the powerful Fujiwara family. At Heian, while an attendant to the empress, she wrote tales about the adventures of Genji, a handsome prince. *The Tale of Genji* was written about 1000. While their lords were writing in Chinese, Lady Murasaki and other noblewomen wrote in Japanese. By doing this, they contributed to the development of Japanese literature and language.

SECTION 4 REVIEW

Knowing Key Terms, People, and Places
1. Define: **a.** clan **b.** kami **c.** daimyo
   d. samurai **e.** ronin **f.** shogun **g.** bushido
2. Identify: **a.** Yamato **b.** Shotoku **c.** Heian
   d. Yoritomo Minamoto **e.** Tokugawa Ieyasu

Focus on Geography
3. How has the geography of Japan forced its people to look outward for resources?

Reviewing Main Ideas
4. How was society organized at the time the Yamato rulers unified Japan?
5. What kind of government ruled Japan between 1192 and 1868?

Critical Thinking
Drawing Conclusions
6. Why do you think that Buddhism was adaptable to so many cultures, including those of China, Japan, and Korea?

Analyzing Primary Sources

Historians use primary and secondary sources in studying the past. A *secondary source* is an account written some time after an event. A *primary source* is information produced during or soon after the event, usually by someone who participated in or observed the event. Examples of primary sources are letters, government documents, and eyewitness accounts.

Primary sources can convey a strong sense of an event or historical period. But, if the writer is personally involved in the event, the account may be biased or false. For that reason, you must analyze primary sources when they are used to determine their reliability.

In the box below is some advice given by General Yu-wu-lun to Li-lu-ku in the late fourth century A.D. As you have learned in this chapter, the Chinese were fighting among themselves and against invaders at this time, and no one dynasty was strong enough to bring order. Read the passage and practice analyzing primary sources by following the steps below.

1. **Identify the nature of the document.** Answer the following questions: (a) What type of document does it seem to be? (b) What is the position of the person being addressed? (c) What is the main idea being expressed in the document?

2. **Decide how reliable the source is.** Answer the following questions: (a) What is the writer's relationship to the person he is addressing? What does the word "we" suggest about this relationship? (b) What does the writer think should be done about people who do not accept the present ruler? What does this tell you about the writer? (c) Would you say that this is a reliable source? Give reasons for your answer.

3. **Study the source to learn more about the time in which it was written.** Answer the following questions: (a) According to the writer, how secure is the power of the person he is addressing? (b) What kinds of work produce valuable resources and wealth for the empire? (c) Does the writer believe the ruler will be able to defeat his enemies in war? (d) Does war seem to have been a common event in his experience, or does it sound as if war happened rarely in those times?

Our former rulers in ancient times did not have any special clothing, and they wandered around the country, which then had no cities. In this way, they were able to split the empire down the middle and conquer various regions. You have now taken over the dignified office of emperor, and are acting according to the wishes of Heaven. But the paradise in which we now live cannot last from generation to generation. Our storehouses, which are bursting with grain and silks, will arouse the greed of our enemies. We should send Chinese people to live in the walled cities and assign them to agriculture and the raising of silkworms, so that they may supply us with the resources we need for our army and our government. We should practice the arts of war ourselves, so we will be able to kill those who do not accept our rule. With well-prepared plans, we will be able to put down any rebellions to the east or the west. If there is an enemy who is stronger than we are, we will be able to escape his attack by running away.

REVIEW

Section Summaries

Section 1 China Entered a Golden Age After the fall of the Han dynasty, invasions by various barbarian tribes kept China in chaos for 300 years. China became brilliant and prosperous again during the Tang and Song dynasties. However, in the 1200s Genghis Khan led the Mongols to conquer most of northern Asia, and the Mongols ruled China for 100 years. It was during this period that Marco Polo visited China and wrote about the culture he observed. Finally, the Buddhist monk Hong Wu lead a rebellion that drove the Mongols out. In 1368, Hong Wu began the Ming dynasty, which would isolate China from the rest of the world.

Section 2 Chinese Culture Is Based on Tradition The basic unit of Chinese society was the family. Confucius laid down many rules of behavior between family members that created a rigid hierarchy. Guilds of silkweavers, glassblowers, and papermakers existed in China as early as 300 B.C. (long before they were known in Europe), and Chinese merchants traded in the Byzantine and Muslim empires. Chinese scholars were highly respected and could hold government positions after passing exams based on Confucian ideas. The Chinese made great achievements in written literature, book printing, navigation, porcelain making, art, and architecture.

Section 3 Korea Created a Distinctive Heritage Korea's location between China and Japan made the country vulnerable to attacks by its East Asian neighbors. By A.D. 400, three kingdoms ruled Korea: Koguryo, Paekche, and Silla. The Chinese and the Mongols both tried to conquer Korea and were successful for short periods. Eventually both the Chinese and the Mongols were driven out. The successful revolt against the Mongols was led by Yi T'aejo, who founded the Yi dynasty in 1392. Although Korea was heavily influenced by China—especially by the ideas of Confucius and Buddha—Korean culture was unique and inventive.

Section 4 Japan's Unique Civilization Emerged Japan is a small island nation with limited natural resources. Therefore, its people learned to use the sea and to farm efficiently. Around A.D. 400, the Yamato rulers united the ancient Japanese clans. Japan adapted many political and religious ideas from China, including Buddhism. As the power of emperors declined in the 1100s, a system of feudalism developed. The Tokugawa shogunate, which began in 1603, isolated Japan. Like European chivalry, the Japanese samurai code promoted loyalty, bravery, and discipline.

Key Facts

1. Use each vocabulary word in a sentence.
   a. tribute
   b. dialect
   c. turtle ship
   d. movable type
   e. clan
   f. kami
   g. daimyo
   h. samurai
   i. ronin
   j. shogun
   k. bushido
2. Identify and briefly explain the importance of the following names, places, or events.
   a. Tang dynasty
   b. Xian
   c. Kublai Khan
   d. Choson
   e. Yi dynasty
   f. Prince Shotoku

Main Ideas

1. List three achievements of the Sui dynasty.
2. Why is the Tang dynasty considered a "golden age" in Chinese history?
3. Describe the Chinese tradition of ancestor worship.
4. How were Chinese aristocrats able to support themselves without working?
5. List three ways in which Korea's history was affected by foreigners.
6. List three Korean inventions.
7. How has Japan's geography influenced the nation's history?
8. State one significant detail about the rule of each of Japan's three shogunates.

Developing Skill in Reading History

Read each of the following Korean proverbs. Then match it to the more familiar saying listed below that has approximately the same meaning. Finally, for each proverb, think of a real-life situation to which it would apply.

_____1. Don't draw a sword to kill a mosquito.
_____2. It is useless to pour instruction into a sow's ear.
_____3. It is foolish to mourn over a broken vase.

A. Don't cry over spilled milk.
B. Don't make a mountain out of a mole hill.
C. You can't teach an old dog new tricks.

Using Social Studies Skills

1. **Understanding Cultural Values** The samurai code developed as part of the feudal system in Japan, but gradually it spread through the entire culture. As you have read, the Japanese male warrior was glorified in popular tales of adventure. How did each of the following developments result from the way samurai warriors were presented in literature?
   a. Elaborate, formal manners became a part of Japanese tradition.
   b. Limits were placed on the privileges and freedom of women.
2. **Using Visual Evidence** Study the painting of the Japanese samurai shown in the next column. How does the painting reflect the values of the samurai code?

Critical Thinking

1. **Testing Conclusions** Cite evidence to show how the Japanese adapted the Chinese form of government to fit their purposes.
2. **Making Comparisons** In what ways is Korean culture similar to Japanese culture? How is it different?
3. **Expressing Problems Clearly** How did the teachings of Confucius help to preserve a peasant class in China?

Focus on Writing

Overcoming Writer's Block

Writers often complain of something they call **writer's block.** However, anyone who has written even a simple shopping list has probably suffered from it. Writer's block happens when you want to write something but cannot seem to come up with any good ideas. Some useful approaches to getting started on a writing project and overcoming writer's block include:

- Brainstorming to collect all the ideas you can think of in three minutes
- Looking for ideas in your own environment or experience, such as a magazine or your family
- Sharing your ideas with someone else to see if he or she can help you to develop them

Practice: Reread the Japanese myth that explains the country's origin at the beginning of Section 4 of this chapter. What other mythical stories might explain Japan's existence? Use your "getting started" techniques to think of three alternatives to Japan's creation story.

Civilizations of Latin America and Africa

(500 B.C.–1550)

1 Early Civilizations Grew in the Americas

2 Ancient Africa Was a Land of Great Variety

3 African Culture Gave Gifts to the World

▲ **Illustrating History** *The Inca emperor Atahualpa fell to the Spanish in 1532.*

S weat soaked his face as Hiram Bingham crossed a shaky bridge of ropes and logs, deep in the Peruvian jungle. The year was 1911. Below, the churning waters of the Urubamba River roared across jagged rocks. The stifling heat and lush vegetation on every side reminded Bingham of his home in Hawaii. Yet, when he glanced up, he saw the great snow peaks of the Andes Mountains looming more than two miles overhead.

Bingham had come to the Andes to search for a fabled "lost city," today known as Machu Picchu (MAH choo PEEK choo). Legends told of an Incan prince who led his people to safety in 1537 when Spanish invaders swept over the Inca Empire and pillaged its treasure. These tales said the prince had built a hidden fortress high in the jungle, but not even natives of Peru had ever found its exact location.

Now Bingham was beginning to climb a mountain that towered above the Urubamba. Part way up, he discovered stone terraces crowding the flanks of the mountain. He pushed still higher. At the top, half buried by trees and vines, lay something more. "I suddenly found myself in a maze of beautiful granite houses!" the explorer later recalled. The stones all around him were so expertly cut that Bingham suspected the truth immediately. He had discovered the lost city of Machu Picchu.

500 B.C.	A.D. 200	900	1600°

| ■ 600 B.C. Phoenicians sail around the African coast | ■ 203 B.C. Hannibal defeated by Roman armies | ■ A.D. 395 Ethiopia adopts Christianity; Mayas control central America | 1000 ■ Aztecs overthrow Mayas 1076 ■ Muslims enter Ghana | ■ 1200 Mali controls gold and salt trades | ■ 1450 Incas rule Pacific Coast |

▲ **Illustrating History** *Above is a photograph of the "maze of beautiful granite houses" of Machu Picchu, an Inca city lost for nearly 400 years.*

1 Early Civilizations Grew in the Americas

As you read, look for answers to these questions:

◆ Where did the first settlers in the Americas come from?
◆ What people set the pattern for civilizations in Central America?
◆ How have we learned about the early Latin American civilizations?

Key Terms: glyph (defined on p. 284), quipu (p. 289)

Discoveries such as that of Machu Picchu reveal that long before any European explorers arrived in the Americas, several groups of people there already had developed ad-

vanced civilizations. The earliest of these civilizations was in Central America. Advanced civilizations also developed along the west coast of South America, in present-day Colombia, Ecuador, Peru, and Chile.

Migrating Peoples from Asia Settled in the Americas

Most of the land in the Western Hemisphere lies on two huge continents—North and South America. These continents are connected by a land bridge known as Central America. The Americas were settled slowly over thousands of years, beginning probably during the last Ice Ages.

As you can see from the map on page 287, the peoples who migrated to the lands of North and South America came from Asia across the Bering Strait. Some of them settled in the cold lands of the Arctic. Most, however, traveled farther south to what are now Canada and the United States. Others moved still farther, spreading out through Mexico and South America. These migrations probably ended by 500 B.C.

Some civilizations in the Americas never developed past the Stone Age. Other people in the Americas, however, developed governments, studied science, and created beautiful works of art. The best-known of these civilizations were located in Mexico and in Central and South America. This region is also called Latin America because the modern languages spoken there —Spanish and Portuguese—are based on Latin. Many people in this region, however, also speak older Indian languages.

The Geography of Latin America Varies Widely

Geographically, Latin America is surprisingly large. From the Rio Grande, Mexico's northern border, to Cape Horn, at the bottom tip of South America, is a distance of over 10,000 miles (16,093 kilometers). It takes longer to fly from New York to most places in South America than it does to fly to western Europe. Buenos Aires, the capital of Argentina, is farther from Chicago than Moscow, the capital of the Soviet Union.

In many ways, the climate of Latin America, which varies greatly throughout, has kept the region from developing. Many Latin American countries lie in the tropics, where the heat and humidity make living difficult. The rain-forest region of the Amazon River basin in Brazil is a particularly harsh and dangerous place to live.

In extreme contrast to the tropical rain forests of the Amazon, other parts of Latin America have cold deserts and dry, rugged mountains. (See the map on page 285.) The Atacama (AH tah KAH mah) Desert of southern Peru and northern Chile is mostly barren and unable to support life. The Andes mountain range runs about 4,000 miles (6,440 kilometers) north to south along the western coast of South America. The Andes are a formidable barrier to transportation and communication. The southernmost parts of Latin America are close to the Antarctic and are thus very cold.

Mayan Civilization Developed in Mexico

The civilizations that grew up in Mexico and Central America were alike in many ways. They had similar systems of picture writing, or **glyphs** (glifs). They built pyramids, studied the stars, and were skillful in measuring time. The earliest of these people were the Olmecs (OHL meks) who lived in parts of Mexico. By about 100 B.C., the Olmecs' civilization had disappeared, but later people were influenced by it. (See map on page 287.)

One of the best known of the later civilizations in Central America was that of the Mayas. What we know about the Mayas comes from archaeology and from the records left by conquering Spanish explorers. Mayan civilization probably began around 2000 B.C. Scholars who have just begun to translate the glyphs of Mayan picture writing have learned that the Mayas did not have a central ruler or government but lived in numerous small communities. These communities were united by a common culture, tradition, trade, and language.

The center of the Mayan civilization was Mexico's Yucatán (YOO kuh TAHN) peninsula. Here, the people built towns with pyramids in the center as places of worship. Smaller than Egyptian pyramids, the Mayan pyramids had sides like steps. The remains of some pyramids can be seen at Tikal (tih KAHL) and at Chichén Itzá (chee CHENH eet SAH). By studying the pyramids, archaeologists and historians have learned a great deal about Mayan civilization.

Although many of the Mayas were farmers who grew maize (corn) and other crops, others sailed the sea for adventure and for trade. Sailing around the Caribbean and along the Gulf coasts, the Mayas were the most successful merchants and traders in America before Columbus's arrival. They traded feathers woven into cloaks, salt, dried fish, cotton, honey, beans, and chocolate. Merchants occupied a high place in Mayan society and were allowed special privileges. For example, even though they often became rich, merchants did not have to pay taxes.

GEOGRAPHIC SETTING:
The Americas

ARCTIC OCEAN

Greenland

Bering
Sea

Bering
Strait

BROOKS RANGE

Yukon R.

ALASKA RANGE

Mackenzie

Baffin
Island

ALASKA
PEN.

GULF OF
ALASKA

COAST MTS.

ROCKY MTS.

HUDSON
BAY

Saskatchewan

Lake
Winnipeg

NORTH
AMERICA

GREAT LAKES

Newfoundland

CASCADE RA.

Columbia R.

COAST RANGES

SIERRA NEVADA

Snake R.

Great
Salt
Lake

GREAT
BASIN

GREAT PLAINS

Platte R.

Missouri R.

CENTRAL
PLAINS

Arkansas R.

Ohio R.

APPALACHIAN MTS.

Bermuda
Is.

ATLANTIC
OCEAN

GRAND
CANYON

Colorado
R.

Red R.

COASTAL PLAIN

Rio Grande

FLORIDA
PEN.

BAJA
PENINSULA

SIERRA MADRE WEST

SIERRA MADRE EAST

GULF OF
CALIFORNIA

GULF OF
MEXICO

Bahama
Is.

WEST   INDIES

Cuba

YUCATAN
PEN.

GREATER ANTILLES

Hispaniola

Puerto
Rico

Jamaica

LESSER
ANTILLES

PACIFIC
OCEAN

CENTRAL
AMERICA

ISTHMUS OF
TEHUANTEPEC

CARIBBEAN SEA

ISTHMUS
OF PANAMA

Magdalena R.

Orinoco R.

GUIANA HIGHLANDS

Galapagos
Islands

Amazon R.

AMAZON BASIN

Sao Francisco

SOUTH
AMERICA

BRAZILIAN
HIGHLANDS

Machu
Picchu

ANDES

Lake
Titicaca

ATACAMA
DESERT

MOUNTAINS

PAMPAS

Parana R.

Iguacu Falls

Colorado R.

Rio de
la Plata

PATAGONIA

Strait
of Magellan

Tierra del
Fuego

Falkland
Islands

CAPE
HORN

© PH

Key to colors

Ice or snow

Tundra

Mixed forest

Lightly forested
or grasslands

Desert, shrubs

N
W   E
S

0   1000   2000 Miles
0   1000   2000 Kilometers

60°N

40°N

20°N

0°

20°S

40°S

140°W

120°W

100°W

80°W

60°W

40°W

20°W

Focus on Geography

Interaction   The Incas settled in the western part of South America
at about 10°S latitude and 75°W longitude. What landform is found
in that area?

One of the great puzzles in history is how the Mayan civilization disappeared. The Mayan pyramids stand in the midst of the jungle, but there is no evidence to explain why the civilization vanished. There is no record of defeat in war nor of destruction by a natural disaster. By 1000, Mayan civilization was already in decline. When the Spanish arrived in the 1500s, the Mayas were so weak that they were simply pushed aside rather than conquered. Some of their culture, however, has survived. Descendants of the Mayas still live in Central America and follow many ancient traditions.

The Aztec Civilization Was Rooted in Religion and War

When the Europeans first arrived in central Mexico, the Aztecs were ruling the area shown on the map on page 287. We have been able to learn about Aztecs from some of the Spanish explorers who wrote descriptions of the people they found. We have also learned about Aztec civilization from the ruins of their stone and stucco buildings, from their calendar and writing samples, and from their pottery and other beautiful works of art.

The Aztecs were a warlike people with a strong king who ruled a large empire. The Aztec throne was not hereditary; instead, the king was picked for his bravery or great wisdom. As ruler, he was a religious leader, a politician, and a god to be worshipped.

The Aztecs were skilled in technology. They worked with copper and tin and learned to combine the two to make bronze, which was used for tools, weapons, and works of art. They also made pottery and wove delicate fabrics from cotton. Ingenious systems for bringing water to their cities and crops allowed Aztec farmers to grow foods that are still widely used today, such as corn and tomatoes. The Aztec calendar and system of numbers were similar to those of the Mayas and the Olmecs.

In the Aztec religion the sun, moon, stars, and fire were gods. The chief god was Huitzilopochtli (WEE tsee loh POHCH tlee), the god of war, to whom the Aztecs sacrificed human beings. This sacrifice of human life was a part of Aztec civilization. Each year, hundreds of prisoners of war were led up the great stone steps of an altar where they were killed. Their still-beating hearts were removed as offerings to the god of war. One reason the Aztecs went to war so often was to have prisoners to sacrifice to Huitzilopochtli.

Montezuma, king of the Aztecs. From about the late 1100s to 1521, the Aztecs dominated what is now Mexico. In 1521, they were conquered by the Spanish explorer Cortes. The Aztec ruler at this time was Montezuma (MAHN tuh ZOO muh), the ninth and last Aztec ruler. He had been chosen as king in 1503 by a group of leading priests and nobles.

Although he was king, Montezuma was not from the class from which rulers were usually chosen. For this reason, he prepared himself to rule. He learned to read the glyphs, and he studied Aztec fighting techniques. He also studied religious ceremonies and learned how to carry out the commands of the Aztec gods.

Aztec daily life. From their study of Aztec civilization, archaeologists have learned some of the details of daily life. They believe that for most Aztecs, the day began as early as 4:00 A.M., when they were awakened by priests who blew shell trumpets. Farmers probably went to their fields, and others began their work of building or working at crafts. In the capital at Tenochtitlán (tay NOCH tee TLAHN), the ruler Montezuma arose early to hold religious ceremonies. Because Aztec cities had water systems, people probably took steam baths and washed before beginning their working day.

Since the Aztecs were constantly at war, it was important to have a steady supply of new soldiers. As a result, children were highly regarded, and so were women who had many children. Children were also well cared for. People made offerings to the gods in hopes that their child would be born under a lucky sign. A child's name was thought to be very important to his or her future, so parents asked the priests' advice before choosing it.

Some Early Civilizations of the Americas

ASIA

Bering Strait

LAND BRIDGE

SIERRA NEVADA

ROCKY MOUNTAINS

Rio Grande

NORTH AMERICA

Great Lakes

Mississippi River

PACIFIC OCEAN

YUCATÁN PENINSULA

Tenochtitlán •

• Chichén Itzá

• Tikal

CENTRAL AMERICA

ISTHMUS OF PANAMA

ATLANTIC OCEAN

Amazon River

ANDES MOUNTAINS

SOUTH AMERICA

• Machu Picchu

Cuzco •

Lake Titicaca

Equator

CAPE HORN

© PH

60°N
40°N
20°N
0°
20°S
40°S

140°W 120°W 100°W 80°W 60°W 40°W 20°W 0°

N
W — E
S

Legend:
- Ice sheet about 20,000 B.C.
- Ancient migration routes
- Olmec civilization about 500 B.C.
- Mayan civilization about A.D. 900
- Aztec civilization about A.D. 1500
- Inca civilization about A.D. 1500

0   500   1000 Miles
0 500 1000 Kilometers

Focus on Geography

1. **Location** Which two Mayan cities are on the Yucatán Peninsula?
2. **Movement** Describe the ancient migration routes in North and South America in terms of the continents' physical features.

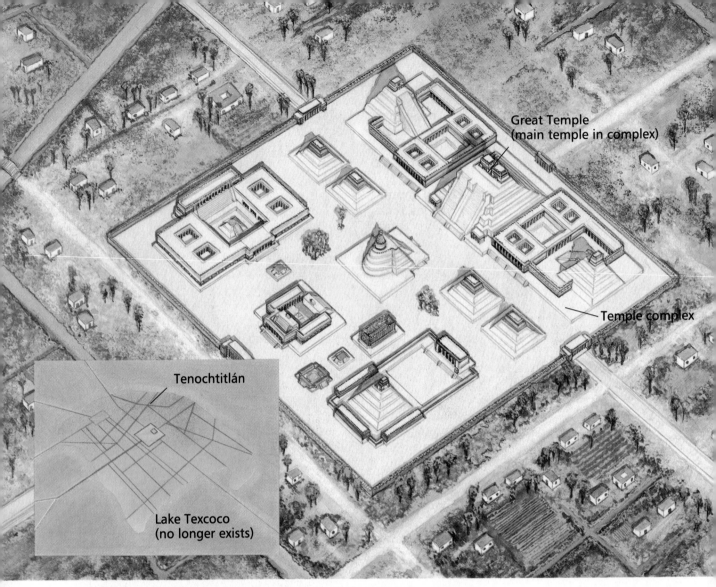

Great Temple
(main temple in complex)

Temple complex

Tenochtitlán

Lake Texcoco
(no longer exists)

▲ **Illustrating History** *Shown above is the Aztec capital, Tenochtitlán. From this city, Montezuma, the Aztec king, ruled a mighty empire.*

Unlike many early civilizations, the Aztec civilization allowed people to rise from one class to a higher class. Excellence in anything—farming, hunting, fighting, or even trading—could help a person move up the social ladder. Schooling was available for each social class. Boys learned the arts of war and the myths and legends of their people. Some attempt was made to determine a child's aptitude. Was it for fighting, for making gold jewelry, or for entering the priesthood? Girls were not as well educated. For the most part, they were expected to be good homemakers and mothers.

The Inca Empire Was Large and Highly Controlled

The Inca Empire was the other major power in Latin America when the Spanish arrived. The Incas ruled all the lands of the Andes from southern Colombia to southern Chile. The center of the empire was the magnificent capital of Cuzco (KOOS koh) in Peru. In 1532, when the Spanish arrived, the emperor was Atahualpa (AH tuh WAHL puh).

The Inca Empire had a highly organized social and political structure. The emperor, called the *Inca*, was regarded as a god who was descended from the sun god. The empire was governed through officials appointed by the Inca. Often these officials were members of the royal family. The entire population was closely supervised and expected to be loyal to the Inca. Every person had to work at least part of the time on projects for the state.

In order to farm the dry, rugged mountain lands, the Incas used irrigation and terracing. Terracing involves farming on flat platforms of earth like steps to make use of hilly land. They domesticated two mountain animals, the llama (LAH mah) and the alpaca (al PACK uh), as farm animals.

The Inca was considered the owner of all land. He and his officials planned what crops would be grown and how they would be distributed. The average farm family had to live on what they were permitted to keep for themselves after harvest. The state stored extra grain, which was made available to needy people in times of famine. Those who could not work because they were too old, too young, too sick, or physically handicapped were assured of food.

The Incas did not develop a written language. They kept records and sent messages by means of the **quipu** (KEE poo), a cord or string with knots that stood for quantities of grain, numbers of soldiers, or other amounts. All parts of the huge empire were connected to the capital, Cuzco, by well-planned roads. Runners carried messages from place to place. Only official travelers and royal messengers could use the roads.

Inca Life Was Hard but Secure

Inca rule was strict, and Inca farmers worked long and hard cultivating the emperor's land. As in the Aztec culture, children were important. They were precious to the state as well as to their parents. Parents educated their young children. In his early teens, a boy of an upper class made a pilgrimage to Cuzco. A llama was sacrificed, and a dab of its blood was smeared on the boy's face as a sign that he was becoming an adult. Young men were trained to be soldiers or to help administer the empire.

Class divisions in Inca society were fairly strict. Men and women usually remained in the classes into which they were born because there was little movement among social classes. Women did have a chance of moving into a higher class through marriage. If a woman were attractive or especially good at weaving, cooking, or spinning, she might be taken to Cuzco to learn additional skills. At the royal court, she might marry a nobleman. Then, she and her children would be in the noble class.

The Incas were less warlike than the Aztecs. Human sacrifices were not performed. Religious practices were kept simple. Prayers to the gods were accompanied by offerings of the first harvests of the fields. On great occasions of state, the official priesthood took part.

The life of the ordinary Inca man or woman was hard. The Incas, however, like people in medieval Europe, did not expect that it could be any other way.

SECTION 1 REVIEW

Knowing Key Terms, People, and Places
1. Define: **a.** glyph **b.** quipu
2. Identify: **a.** Latin America **b.** Olmecs **c.** Mayas **d.** Yucatán Peninsula **e.** Aztecs **f.** Montezuma **g.** Tenochtitlán **h.** Incas **i.** Atahualpa

Reviewing Main Ideas
3. How and by whom were the continents of North and South America settled?
4. What early civilization set the pattern for other civilizations in Central America?
5. What were some achievements of the Mayas?
6. What was daily life like in (a) Aztec society (b) Inca society?

Critical Thinking
Making Comparisons
7. How were the civilizations of the Aztecs and the Incas alike or different in terms of (a) government (b) social class structure?

2 Ancient Africa Was a Land of Great Variety

As you read, look for answers to these questions:

◆ What different kinds of landscapes are found on the African continent?
◆ What are some ways that historians have learned about the history of early African cultures?
◆ What great trading empires grew up in western Africa?
◆ What kind of civilizations developed in eastern Africa?

Key Terms: sub-Saharan (defined on p. 290), savanna (p. 290)

Africa is a huge continent of many countries and many different groups of people. It is three times the size of Europe and nearly four times the size of the United States. Geography and culture have combined to make Africa a continent of great diversity. As you will learn in this section, the history of Africa dates back thousands of years.

The African Continent Was Geographically Diverse

The two major geographic divisions of the African continent are northern Africa and sub–Saharan Africa. Northern Africa, including Egypt, has long been part of the Muslim world, and its history is linked with the history of the Middle East. Sub–Saharan Africa is all the rest of the continent south of the Sahara. It includes the regions commonly called western Africa, eastern Africa, central Africa and southern Africa. Today, every geographical region of the continent has been further subdivided into many different nations. All have separate histories, distinctive cultural characteristics, and different geographical features.

Most of the land of Africa is a series of rolling plateaus. At the edges of the plateaus are narrow coastal plains. A number of great rivers—including the Zambezi and Congo, today known as the Zaire—begin in the central African plateau. They flow to the oceans through wide valleys or basins. At the edge of the plateau region, many rivers drop sharply over cliffs to form spectacular waterfalls.

The equator crosses central Africa, which means that much of the continent is in the tropics. Because of heavy rainfall, a band of tropical rain forest covers the continent from the "bulge" of western Africa to the interior. By contrast, other parts of Africa are deserts. The huge Sahara lies in the north. The Namib Desert and the Kalahari Desert are located in southern Africa.

Many people think rain forests and deserts are typical African landscapes. In fact, the broad grasslands to the north and south of the rain forests are much more characteristic. These rolling **savannas,** or grasslands with shrubs and small trees, cover about 40 percent of Africa. (See the map on page 291.) They are home to the great herds of wild animals for which Africa is famous. Farther from the equator, temperatures become less tropical and more moderate.

In eastern Africa, volcanic activity and movement of the earth's crust have created the Great Rift Valley, a region that is unique in Africa. Its spectacular scenery includes huge lakes and some of the longest and deepest valleys in the world. Africa's two tallest mountains rise above the Great Rift Valley. They are Mount Kilimanjaro and Mount Kenya.

Early African History Was Unwritten

Almost none of the early peoples of sub–Saharan Africa developed a written language. Thus, historians, archaeologists, and anthropologists have had to use other methods to discover the histories of the ancient kingdoms, empires, and people of Africa. One method has been to visit the modern peoples and listen to the stories the tribal elders tell. These stories have been passed down from generation to generation for thousands of years. Often, the stories describe earthquakes, floods, or eclipses of the

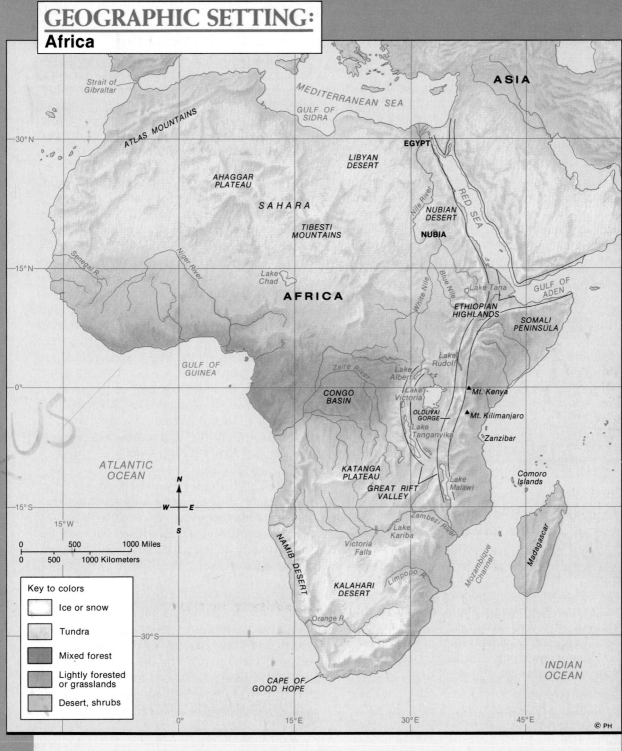

GEOGRAPHIC SETTING:
Africa

Strait of Gibraltar

MEDITERRANEAN SEA

ASIA

GULF OF SIDRA

ATLAS MOUNTAINS

30°N

EGYPT

LIBYAN DESERT

AHAGGAR PLATEAU

SAHARA

Nile River

RED SEA

NUBIAN DESERT

TIBESTI MOUNTAINS

NUBIA

Senegal R.

Niger River

Lake Chad

15°N

AFRICA

White Nile

Blue Nile

Lake Tana

GULF OF ADEN

ETHIOPIAN HIGHLANDS

SOMALI PENINSULA

GULF OF GUINEA

Zaire River

Lake Albert

Lake Rudolf

0°

CONGO BASIN

Lake Victoria

▲ Mt. Kenya

OLDUVAI GORGE

▲ Mt. Kilimanjaro

Lake Tanganyika

Zanzibar

ATLANTIC OCEAN

N
W — E
S

KATANGA PLATEAU

Comoro Islands

GREAT RIFT VALLEY

Lake Malawi

15°S

15°W

0   500   1000 Miles
0   500   1000 Kilometers

NAMIB DESERT

Zambezi River

Lake Kariba

Victoria Falls

Limpopo R.

Mozambique Channel

Madagascar

Key to colors

Ice or snow

Tundra

Mixed forest

Lightly forested or grasslands

Desert, shrubs

30°S

KALAHARI DESERT

Orange R.

CAPE OF GOOD HOPE

INDIAN OCEAN

0°   15°E   30°E   45°E

© PH

Focus on Geography

Location   What lake is located between two branches of the Great Rift Valley?

sun or moon. Sometimes, scholars are able to determine the approximate date on which these natural disturbances occurred. They then compare the legends with events found in the records of ancient Egypt, Greece, or Rome or in the writings of European or Arabic traders and adventurers. In this way, scholars can determine relative times and even pinpoint important dates.

Historians know that the Kushites of Nubia, a land on the Nile River, briefly conquered and ruled Egypt between about 730 B.C. and 670 B.C. Later, the Kushites learned how to work with iron ore, a rare skill in ancient times. Their technology and success in trading kept the Kushite kingdom rich and powerful until about A.D. 300.

After Carthage was defeated in the Punic Wars, its outposts in northern Africa were taken into the Roman Empire as a province. This province was given the name *Africa*. As more of the continent was discovered and explored, the name *Africa* was applied to an even greater area. In time, it came to mean the entire continent. From bases in northern Africa, the Romans traded with some countries south of the Sahara. Although they crossed the Sahara or traded along the coasts for gold and ivory, they rarely traveled to sub–Saharan Africa.

Except for conducting business in coastal trading towns, Africans had few contacts with other peoples. Foreigners were ignorant of what the African continent really looked like. Greek geographers could only guess at the shape and size of Africa. On a map made by one Greek geographer, for example, most of sub–Saharan Africa did not exist. On the other hand, Ptolemy's map showed Africa to be larger than it actually was. These early maps were used much later by Europeans when they began their explorations into the interior of Africa.

Western African Empires Were Built on Trade

Rich African kingdoms, shown on the map on page 295, grew in the savanna region of western Africa. They were built along the trade routes across the Sahara.

Ghana.   *Ghana* was the title of the ruler of the first trading kingdom to gain power over a large part of western Africa. Ghana also was the name given to the land he ruled. The kingdom's power reached its peak by the eleventh century when it had complete control over the trade routes between the salt mines in the Sahara and the gold mines on its own southern borders. During the reign of Tenkamenin (tehn kuh MEHN ihn), the kingdom became a highly developed state with a monarchy similar to the monarchies that ruled in Europe at a later time.

In 1076 (ten years after William the Conqueror had conquered England), Tenkamenin's empire fell. The Almoravids (ahl MOH rah vihdz), a Muslim group who had been living northwest of Ghana, invaded the kingdom. Although their reign did not last long, Ghana never recovered. Rival chiefs were eager to make themselves monarchs of a great land. As a result, tribal warfare interfered with rebuilding the kingdom, and Ghana began to decline.

Today, Ghana is the name of the western African country located on the Gulf of Guinea (GIHN ee). When it became an independent nation in 1957, it took the name of the ancient trading kingdom.

Mali.   The history of western Africa from the decline of Ghana in the eleventh century to the arrival of Europeans during the fifteenth century involves the rivalry of the two Muslim nations that succeeded Ghana. These nations were Mali, which arose first, and Songhai (SONG ay).

The kingdoms of Ghana and Mali depended on their control of the salt and gold trade for wealth and power. Rivalry for the control of trade routes meant that fighting often broke out on Mali's borders as rival African kingdoms and Arab rulers tried to take control of the trade routes. By the thirteenth century, Mali had taken over Ghana.

Mali's most famous ruler, Mansa Musa, was a devout Muslim. His elaborate pilgrimage to Mecca in 1324 made other nations aware of Mali's fabulous wealth. Traveling with hundreds of servants in a caravan laden with gold and ivory, Mansa Musa gave these riches to people as he journeyed through Cairo and on to Mecca. At home, he encouraged Muslim scholarship. The Mali city of Timbuktu became a great center of culture and commerce.

Mansa Musa's empire was as large as all of western Europe, which at the time was still in the feudal era. The European monarchs could make their power felt only over a small area. In contrast to the chaos and war in Europe, Mansa Musa's realm was orderly and stable.

Songhai. The Songhai were an African people displeased at living under Mali's rule. In 1468, they captured Timbuktu. In 1492, the year Columbus discovered America, a general named Askia Mohammed took the throne of Songhai. He ruled until 1529 and was known as Askia the Great.

Under Askia's leadership, the Songhai Empire reached its height. It stretched

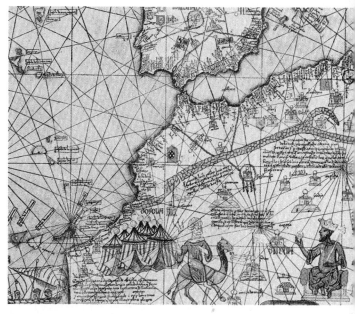

▲ **Illustrating History** *This Spanish map of Africa shows Mansa Musa on the right, holding a scepter and a gold nugget.*

DAILY LIFE

Salt: Worth Its Weight in Gold

In the fiercely hot lands of sub-Saharan Africa, people lose great amounts of salt through perspiration. To survive, they must continually replenish this lost salt. The kingdoms of ancient sub-Sarahan Africa had almost no natural deposits of this precious mineral. These kingdoms did, however, have gold mines.

For hundreds of years, African kings south of the Sahara traded gold for salt with other nations in the Sahara. A traveler in the sixteenth century, Leo Africanus, described the lives of some Saharan salt miners: "These workmen . . . are distant from all inhabited places almost 20 days' journey, [and] oftentimes they perish for lack of food."

Camel caravans, like the one at left, carried the salt in solid slabs across the Sahara. Salt traders usually sold their cargo on the simplest possible terms. Equal weights of salt were exchanged for gold.

1. Why was salt precious in sub-Saharan Africa?
2. What determines how much people will pay for goods?

1,500 miles (3,218 kilometers) from east to west. Timbuktu, still its chief city, had a fine mosque and a great school at which students studied the Muslim Koran. The city again prospered as a trading center. Outside traders sought the tin and leather goods of Songhai. From as far north as Morocco, great caravans crossed the Sahara on camels and exchanged goods, gold, and slaves. In time, rivalry for power, civil war, and invasions from northern Africa led to the decline of the kingdom of Songhai. No major new kingdom arose in western Africa.

Smaller Kingdoms Prospered in Eastern Africa

Across the continent, in eastern Africa, many different cultures and states developed. Two of the most important of these states were Ethiopia (EE thee OH pee uh) and Zimbabwe (zihm BAH bweh). They thrived between 1000 and 1500.

Ethiopia. Ethiopia is one of the world's oldest nations. Known as Axum in ancient times, its history can be dated from at least 1000 B.C. The Queen of Sheba, whose visit to King Solomon of Israel is described in the Bible, probably came from Ethiopia. As far back as the sixth century B.C., the Hebrews sought refuge in Ethiopia when Babylonians overran their country. About A.D. 395, the Ethiopians adopted Christianity. The Ethiopian Christian Church of today still follows an old form of Christian beliefs and rituals. The Muslim faith also was popular, and today one-third of Ethiopia is Muslim.

BIOGRAPHY

Askia the Great

The year was 1492, the year that Columbus discovered America. In the West African empire of Songhai, the aging Sunni Ali died, leaving the throne to his son, Bara. Out of the ranks of Songhai's army rose a challenger to Bara's rule—a 50-year-old general named Mohammed Toure.

Mohammed, a devoted Muslim, had long been offended that Bara and his father allowed the traditional African religions to be practiced side by side with Islam. He insisted that Bara declare Islam the kingdom's sole religion. When Bara refused, Mohammed prepared for war. In 1493, Mohammed and his army defeated Bara. Mohammed established himself as Askia (or general) of all Songhai.

Askia wasted no time in making Islam the empire's official religion. He built many mosques and Islamic centers of learning. He also instituted Islamic law throughout the empire. Askia strengthened Songhai's government in its chief city, Gao (above right) and set up departments of finance, farming, and justice. He also formed Africa's first professional army—a cavalry of about 4,000 men. By the end of Askia's reign in 1528, Songhai

was the richest and most powerful kingdom in Africa. Askia the Great died in 1538.

1. How did Askia become ruler of Songhai?
2. What role did religion play in Askia's life?
3. What were some of Askia's achievements?

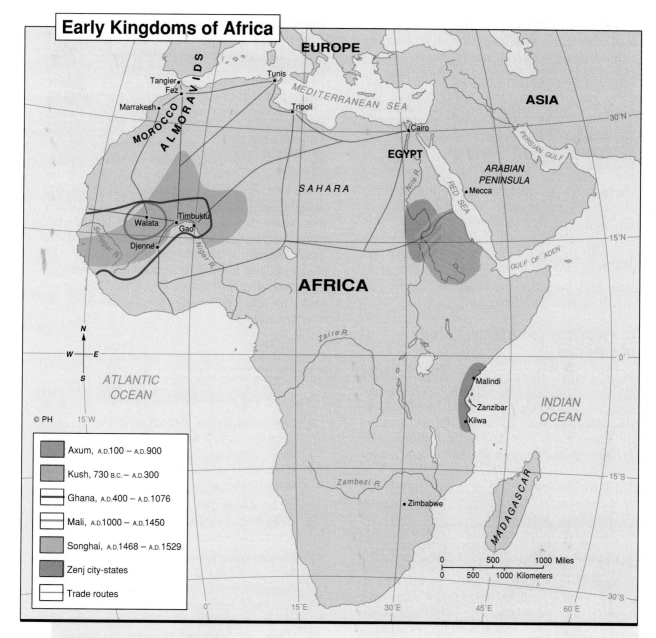

Early Kingdoms of Africa

EUROPE

MEDITERRANEAN SEA

ASIA

Tangier
Fez
Marrakesh
MOROCCO ALMORAVIDS
Tunis
Tripoli

Cairo

EGYPT

SAHARA

Nile R.

ARABIAN
PENINSULA
Mecca

RED SEA

PERSIAN GULF

30°N

Walata
Timbuktu
Gao
Djenné

Senegal R.
Niger R.

15°N

GULF OF ADEN

AFRICA

Zaire R.

N
W — E
S

ATLANTIC
OCEAN

0°

Malindi
Zanzibar
Kilwa

INDIAN
OCEAN

© PH   15°W

Zambezi R.

Zimbabwe

MADAGASCAR

15°S

	Axum, A.D.100 – A.D.900
	Kush, 730 B.C. – A.D.300
	Ghana, A.D.400 – A.D.1076
	Mali, A.D.1000 – A.D.1450
	Songhai, A.D.1468 – A.D.1529
	Zenj city-states
	Trade routes

0   500   1000 Miles
0   500   1000 Kilometers

30°S

0°   15°E   30°E   45°E   60°E

Focus on Geography

1. **Place**   What two kingdoms shared the same general region in northeastern Africa?
2. **Regions**   Most trade routes passed through what kind of region?

Zimbabwe.   Many of the African peoples who settled in southern Africa were part of a huge group who spoke Bantu languages. Some of them are thought to have built the mysterious city of stone known as Great Zimbabwe. Discovered by explorers in 1871, the stone structures of Zimbabwe are believed to have been built during either the

295

fourteenth or fifteenth century. The buildings were decorated in gold, which probably came from the rich mines nearby.

Eastern coastal city-states. A lively trade grew up between eastern Africa and the Arabs. Numerous Arab outposts along the coast grew into separate, prosperous city-states. Kilwa, Zanzibar, and Malindi were the most famous city-states along the coastal area from the Zambezi (zahm BEE zee) River north to what is today Somalia. Each city-state was responsible for its own economy and its own defense. In these city-states, a mix of Bantu and Arabic languages and cultures developed. The language that developed is known as Swahili (swah HEE lee). This language became the language of much of eastern Africa.

Islam Influenced African Culture and Politics

Along with their goods, Arab traders brought the religion of Islam to Africa and sought converts long before Christian missionaries arrived. Although Greek traders did bring early Christianity to Ethiopia, the religion's success was the exception rather than the rule.

Islam, however, had a great impact on sub–Saharan Africa. It brought a religious unity to the region and exposed the people of Africa to a culture and a civilization that they quickly adapted to their own needs. Islamic learning provided a written language, Arabic, that Africans could use to carry on trade and to write down their own history and traditions. The adoption of an Islamic system of law allowed sub–Saharan Africans to govern trade and commerce and to build a political organization.

Because Islam was a religion that permitted adaptations according to the traditions and customs of the people, the Islamic faith in sub–Saharan Africa became quite different from what it was in Cairo or Baghdad. Even so, it never totally replaced the traditional religions of the Africans who, like the people of Japan, believed in the worship of spirits found in nature.

The Kingdoms of Africa Declined

There were many reasons why the great kingdoms of Africa did not last. One was that they were large and sparsely inhabited, which made them difficult to defend against attackers. Moreover, the kingdoms of Ghana, Mali, and Songhai all had poorly defined borders. Because of this, they were fair game for those who desired their wealth.

Finally, each kingdom was made up of many different peoples. Groups or families who were unwilling to be ruled by others formed kingdoms of their own. In time, these kingdoms grew powerful enough to challenge the large kingdoms. Often, people living within the borders of a kingdom were eager to rebel or to ally themselves with a new conqueror.

SECTION 2 REVIEW

Knowing Key Terms, People, and Places
1. Define: **a.** sub-Saharan **b.** savanna
2. Identify: **a.** Sahara **b.** Great Rift Valley **c.** Kushites **d.** Ghana **e.** Mali **f.** Mansa Musa **g.** Timbuktu

Focus on Geography
3. What kind of landscape is most characteristic of the African continent?

Reviewing Main Ideas
4. Why do historians depend on outside sources for most early African history?
5. What was the basis for the great empires of western Africa?
6. What two cultures blended in eastern Africa?

Critical Thinking
Distinguishing False from Accurate Images
7. Most people still think of early Africa as a continent that was mostly jungle, with people living in primitive villages. In what ways is this picture incorrect? Why do you think people have this image of Africa?

The Religious Art of Africa and Latin America

Many African rulers were also the high priests of their local religions, and sometimes they were worshipped as gods themselves. In the city of Ife, a large religious center in southwest Nigeria, the priest-king was called an *oni*. This portrait head, which wears a crown, was originally mounted on a body made of wood that was dressed in priestly garments. In this way, the oni could participate in religious ceremonies even after his death. Religious services were an important part of life in many African cultures, and all classes of people were expected to join in.

Ritual and ceremony were also important to the ancient Indian cultures of Central and South America. The figure of the Corn God, from the Zapotec culture of central Mexico, is actually a hollow vase. Figures such as these were placed in both temples and tombs and contained offerings for the god shown on each vase. Another work of art that was also used in rituals is the Portrait Vase, made by artisans of the Moche culture in Peru. Jars such as this, representing the deceased and containing offerings, were buried with the dead as part of the rituals of burial. You may remember from Chapter 2 that the ancient Egyptians had similar beliefs concerning the afterlife, and they also buried many beautiful works of art with their dead.

Below left is the Zapotec Corn God. At right is the Ife portrait head, and in the center is the Portrait Vase.

3 African Culture Gave Gifts to the World

As you read, look for answers to these questions:

◆ Why was storytelling important in early Africa?
◆ What forms of art were most highly developed in western Africa?
◆ What influence did African culture have on Western music?

Key Terms: griot (defined on p. 298), mimicry (p. 300), pantomime (p. 300)

The variety of people and cultures in early Africa produced an equal variety of art styles and forms. Over the centuries, these styles and forms have had a great impact on world culture.

▼ **Illustrating History** *Picasso imitated African masks in this modern painting.*

Storytellers Preserved Myth and History

Because African languages were unwritten for thousands of years, many African peoples developed a strong oral tradition of storytelling and history. African literature grew out of folklore, including myths, riddles, proverbs, and tales that were passed down from generation to generation. Songs and chants were often accompanied by music, dance, and responses in unison by the listeners. Professional storytellers, who were known as **griots** (GREE ohts), went through a long period of training and preparation. Griots were supposed to have faultless memories. It was their responsibility to learn all the history and favorite stories of their people and to repeat them from memory without error.

After many Africans adopted Islam, they began to use the Arabic language. They then developed a written literature using Arabic. Literature flourished throughout the area, especially in eastern Africa where poetry and histories were written.

African Artists Were Skilled Sculptors

In art, Africa's traditions go back many thousands of years. Some ancient people of Africa, such as the Egyptians and Kushites, worked in stone. South of the Sahara, artists worked mainly in wood. Because stone endures and wood does not, much more art from northern Africa has survived.

Nonetheless, sub–Saharan Africa's greatest contribution to art probably has been in sculpture and in masks made of wood and ivory. Some of the continent's richest and most original works of art come from western Africa and central Africa. Much of this art was made for religious purposes. Wooden sculptures were often decorated with shells, feathers, beads, and ivory. Some of them were colorfully painted.

Artists in the region of Nigeria became famous for their elegant and expressive statues cast in bronze. The area of Benin (beh NEEN), in southwest Nigeria, was the center of bronze art. The portrait busts from this area made of ivory or bronze are highly prized today. The Benin artists used a method of casting in bronze that has never been fully understood. Artists of the Asante (ah SHAHN tee) people of western Africa made small bronze weights used to measure gold.

African figures often had religious significance. In Nigeria, art expressed not only religious themes but the power of the kingdom as well. In African sculpture, the shape of the human body was often distorted. For example, the body, eyes, neck, and shape of the head were often out of proportion. The freedom to show distortion encouraged originality of expression. In the twentieth century, the African art forms influenced the work of such European artists as Pablo Picasso and Amedeo Modigliani.

▼ **Illustrating History** *This African sculpture depicts a man playing a flute. Note that the size of the man's feet are distorted in comparison with his body.*

African Proverbs

Proverbs express the "common sense" of a culture. Hence, they can tell historians what ideas were widely held in a culture. The following proverbs are from the Yoruba and Fulani cultures of western Africa.

Yoruba Proverbs

❝He fled from the sword and hid in the scabbard [a case to hold a sword].

Peace is the father of friendship. Wrangling is the father of fighting.

One here, two there, [so gathers] a vast multitude.

The young cannot teach tradition to the old.

One who does not understand the yellow palm-bird says the yellow palm-bird is noisy.❞

Fulani Wisdom

❝The ant-eater's grief is not the monkey's.

Whoever cooks the food of malice [anger], remnants will stick to his pocket.

Alive he was insufficient, dead he is missed.

An enemy slaughters, a friend distributes.

If you want to hear the news of the heart, ask the face.

It is not his deserts that a man gets but his destiny.

He who rides the horse of greed at a gallop will pull it up at the door of shame.❞

1. What is the meaning of the proverb, "The ant-eater's grief is not the monkey's"? Which proverb is similar to the English proverb, "Out of the frying pan and into the fire"?
2. Would any of these proverbs be unsuitable for your society? Explain.

299

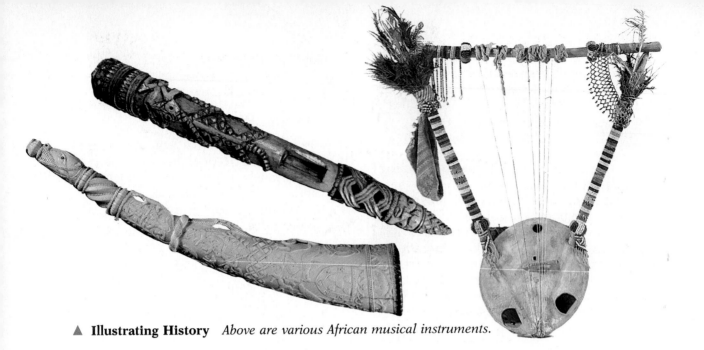

▲ **Illustrating History** *Above are various African musical instruments.*

African Music Had Great Influence

It has been said that there are as many forms of African music as there are African languages. Drums, bells, whistles, rattles, and xylophones were among the musical instruments of ancient Africa. The one-string bow and the many-stringed harp were also important instruments.

The people of Africa had songs about planting, harvesting, fishing, and fighting. Percussion instruments—drums of various kinds—were particularly important. The best drummers were chosen to accompany ceremonies at religious festivals. Tribes also used the beat of the drum to send messages to one another.

In addition, drums provided the beat for dances, which have always been important in African culture. There were dances of joy and dances of sadness. There were war dances, and there were peace dances. There were dances for religious observances and for the sheer pleasure of dancing. Participants were professional dancers, warriors going off to battle, or priests leading a religious ritual. The arts of **mimicry** (MIHM ik ree) and **pantomime** (PAHN tuh MYME) played a large part in African dance. In mimicry, the performer imitates the sounds of birds and animals. In pantomime, the actor shows the actions of animals or folk-tale characters without using words.

Many forms of Western music and dance have some roots in African music and musical traditions. This is particularly evident in the rhythms and harmonies of jazz, gospel songs, and the blues.

SECTION 3 REVIEW °

Knowing Key Terms, People, and Places
1. Define: **a.** griot **b.** mimicry **c.** pantomime
2. Identify: **a.** Benin **b.** Ashanti

Reviewing Main Ideas
3. Why was storytelling important as an African art form?
4. What kind of art work made the region of Benin famous?
5. In what ways did African music influence Western music?

Critical Thinking

Perceiving Cause and Effect
6. Most of sub–Saharan Africa did not have written language until late in its history. What effect would this have on the kind of arts that African people developed?

Perceiving Cause and Effect

History is more than a list of events; it is a study of the relationships between events. One of the most basic relationships between events is when one event—an effect—is the direct result of another event—a cause. Follow these steps to practice identifying statements that tell about cause and effect.

1. **Be able to identify the two parts of a cause-effect relationship.** Because a cause is an event or action that brings about an effect, the cause must occur before the effect. Nevertheless, because one event happened before another event does not automatically mean the first caused the second. Bear in mind, too, that an author may discuss two related events without suggesting that one caused the other. Authors usually indicate a cause-effect relationship by using words such as *so, thus, because,* and *as a result.* Read statements 1 through 4 below and answer the following questions: (a) Which statements are cause-effect statements? (b) Identify the cause and the effect in each cause-effect statement. (c) Which word or words signal the cause-effect relationship?

2. **Remember that an event can have more than one cause and more than one effect.** Several causes can combine to create one effect, just as one cause can bring about several effects. Read statement 5 in the box below and answer the following question: What are the causes and the effects presented in the statement?

3. **An event can be both a cause and an effect.** Causes and effects can form a chain of events that extend over a period of time. You can diagram such a chain of events as follows: The Aztecs were constantly at war → they needed a steady supply of new soldiers → they regarded children highly. The middle part of the chain was an effect of the first part, but then became a cause that led to the third. Read statement 6 below. Draw a diagram of its causes and effects, using an arrow to point from each cause to its effect.

Statements

1. Because the king of Kush was tempted by Egypt's riches, he invaded the country.

2. About 80 years after the Kushites invaded Egypt, the Assyrians also invaded Egypt.

3. The Assyrians had iron weapons; the Kushites learned to smelt iron, too.

4. The city's ability to control the trade of its region was due to its strategic location.

5. Because European trade was expanding and African trade routes shifted from the Sahara to the coast, the Saharan grasslands declined in importance, coastal communities became more powerful, and contact with Europeans increased.

6. In several African kingdoms, gold and the control of trade produced great wealth. With this wealth, the rulers built up their military might. Thus, each kingdom was able to conquer neighboring areas and demand tribute from these subject areas. The demands for tribute caused unrest among the conquered areas, and eventually the unrest led to the conquered areas breaking free.

REVIEW

Section Summaries

Section 1 Early Civilizations Grew in the Americas Several groups of people in the Americas developed advanced civilizations long before European explorers arrived. These people had migrated to North and South America by a land bridge from Asia thousands of years earlier. The oldest civilization, the Olmecs, disappeared around 100 B.C. The Mayas, who lived in Central America, built great pyramids, farmed, and traded in the Caribbean. Their civilization began to decline around 1000 and was very weak by the 1500s. The Aztecs, warlike people who had a technologically advanced society, ruled Mexico at the time when the Europeans arrived. The Inca Empire stretched along the west coast of South America. The Incas had highly organized social and political systems.

Section 2 Ancient Africa Was a Land of Great Variety The huge continent of Africa is divided geographically into northern Africa and sub-Saharan Africa (the region south of the Sahara). Although many people associate Africa with either rain forests or deserts, in fact the savanna, or grassland, is a more typical African landscape. Early African history was not written down but was preserved in oral traditions. During the late Middle Ages, the trading empires of Ghana, Mali, and Songhai grew in western Africa. In eastern Africa, the trading states of Ethiopia and Zimbabwe also prospered. Islam spread throughout Africa and had a great influence on African culture and politics.

Section 3 African Culture Gave Gifts to the World Professional storytellers preserved African myths and history in oral traditions. African artists were skilled sculptors, working in stone, wood, ivory, and bronze to create highly original figures that often had religious meaning. African musical traditions form the basis of much of the music that we enjoy today. Percussion instruments were particularly important in Africa's music.

Key Facts

1. Use each vocabulary word in a sentence.
   - **a.** glyph
   - **b.** quipu
   - **c.** sub-Saharan
   - **d.** savanna
   - **e.** griot
   - **f.** mimicry
   - **g.** pantomime
2. Identify and briefly explain the importance of the following names, places, or events.
   - **a.** Bering Strait
   - **b.** Yucatán Peninsula
   - **c.** Montezuma
   - **d.** Tenochtitlán
   - **e.** Mali
   - **f.** Swahili

Main Ideas

1. How did prehistoric settlers arrive in North and South America?
2. Name three types of climates that can be found in Latin America.
3. List three items that the Mayas were known for trading. With whom did they trade?
4. List three Aztec technological achievements.
5. What is the most typical kind of landscape on the African continent?
6. In what ways were the kingdoms of Ghana and Mali dependent on salt and gold?
7. How did Islam benefit sub-Saharan Africa?
8. What brought about the decline of the African kingdoms?
9. How were drums used by the African people?

Developing Skill in Reading History

Read each of the following section subheadings and decide what information you would expect to find under the heading.
1. **The Aztec Civilization Was Rooted in Religion and War**
   - **a.** How the Aztecs related to other groups of people and what gods they worshipped
   - **b.** The many technological achievements of the Aztecs
   - **c.** The relationship between men and women in Aztec society

2. **The African Continent Was Geographically Diverse**
   a. The variety of languages spoken in Africa
   b. The different types of landscapes found in all parts of Africa
   c. The influence of African music on Western music
3. **Early African History Was Unwritten**
   a. The development of the Roman alphabet
   b. The size of various African kingdoms
   c. The oral traditions of African people

Using Social Studies Skills

Observing for Detail Clothes were a way of showing an Aztec's rank. The best warriors, for example, wore jaguar skins or eagle feathers. Ordinary citizens wore plain, undyed cloth. Low-level government officials wore clothing edged with a dyed border. Military commanders wore bright colors. Look at the pictures below, which were drawn to look like Aztec glyphs. Which do you think represents a jaguar warrior? Look at the figure on the right. What detail tells you that this figure represents a low-level government official?

Aztec Costumes

Critical Thinking

1. **Distinguishing False from Accurate Images** The Aztecs have been labeled as a warlike people. Is this an accurate image of the Aztec civilization?
2. **Testing Conclusions** Evaluate the following statement: African griots had to be extremely intelligent.
3. **Demonstrating Reasoned Judgment** Which of the reasons presented in this chapter to explain the decline of African kingdoms do you think best explains what happened? Explain your answer.

Focus on Writing

Writing an Introduction

An essay has three main parts: the introduction, the body, and the conclusion. The **introduction** may take any of several forms. It may give the main idea of the essay in a general way. Or, an introduction may tell an interesting story that makes the reader want to find out more about the subject of the essay. Another kind of introduction grabs the attention of the reader with a startling statement.

Example: Each section in this chapter is similar to an essay in that it begins with a brief introduction. Section 3 begins with the following sentence: ''The variety of people and cultures in early Africa produced an equal variety of art styles and forms.'' This sentence tells the reader what the main idea of the section will be. It is broad and general, because specific facts will be given in the body paragraphs that follow it.

Practice: Pretend that you are going to write an essay entitled ''African Sounds Hit the Pop Charts.'' In the essay, you will discuss the influence of African music on current popular music. Write an introduction for the essay using one of the techniques described above: general introduction, interesting story, or startling statement. Share your introduction with your classmates to see how they approached the assignment.

Geography in History

Dreams and Voyages: How Three Religions Spread

One night in A.D. 65, Ming Di, the Chinese emperor, dreamed that a powerful god ruled over the lands to the west. When he awoke, he sent an official to find this god. His messenger returned from India with stories of Buddha.

How did the great religions of Buddhism, Islam, and Hinduism spread across Asia? The answer lies not in legend, but in landforms—landforms that acted as barriers and bodies of water that connected people.

Buddhism Circles Asia

Buddhism began in what is now Nepal. Nepal lies at the base of the Himalayas, a great wall of mountains that shield the Tibetan plateau from the outside world. Probably carried by missionaries, Buddhism skirted the western edge of this natural barrier. Before the first century B.C., Buddhism was adopted by the nomadic tribes of the Tarim basin. Over time, Buddhist cities grew up in Central Asia and served as stepping stones for Buddhism to move on to northern China.

At the time, China was in a period of disorder. One foreign tribe after another invaded the north, driven by hunger during dry spells. Refugees—some of them Buddhists—moved south. In the wetter lands of the Chang River, the invaders' horsemen could not pursue the refugees. Brought by the refugees, Buddhism gradually became a popular religion.

Monks carried Buddhism north into neighboring Korea. In the fifth century, Buddhism went on to Japan and flowered into several forms.

During all these centuries of travel, however, Buddhism had circled but never entered the great Tibetan plateau. Then, in the seventh century, a Tibetan king married two women, one from China and one from Nepal. Both Buddhists, the women persuaded the king to bring their religion to Tibet.

Islam from Out of the Desert

While Buddhism was growing in Tibet, another religion was spreading in the Middle East. By 600, the people of the Arabian Peninsula were crowded. They were looking for new land.

In 633, armies of fierce nomads, carrying the sword of Islam, galloped east toward Persia, north toward the Fertile Crescent, and west toward Egypt. They fought well in the desert, and the Muslim conquest was swift. In five years, all of Palestine and Syria had fallen. Another five years brought them the rich grain lands of Egypt, and by 644, Islam had conquered Persia.

Only natural barriers stopped or slowed the march of Islam. One barrier was the Atlantic Ocean. Another was the Pyrenees Mountains, which kept the Muslims from conquering France. The Arab Muslims also failed to conquer India.

Later, Islam was carried by merchants who took the religion both into the Tarim basin and to the shores of Indonesia. It did not pierce far into China because that nation was once again isolated behind its natural defenses of desert and mountain.

Hinduism Sails Eastward

Hinduism did not become as popular outside of its homeland as either Buddhism or Islam. Hinduism is tied to India. There, the Ganges and other sacred rivers form a key part of its worship.

Hinduism did spread, however, not by land, but by sea. Sometime after the second century A.D., Hindu princes sailed to the east, searching for what traders called "a land of gold." In what is now Kampuchea, Malaysia, Vietnam, and Indonesia, Hindu princes built kingdoms. Some of these Indian "colonies" lasted 1,000 years. In them, the Hindu religion grew far from the sacred Ganges River.

Focus on Geography

1. **Location** Study the map on page 262. What was the human-made barrier Buddhism crossed to enter China?

2. **Interaction** Why did foreign tribes invade northern China?

3. **Regions** What prevented Islam from spreading into China?

Critical Thinking

Identifying Central Issues
4. Why did Islam spread more rapidly than Buddhism?

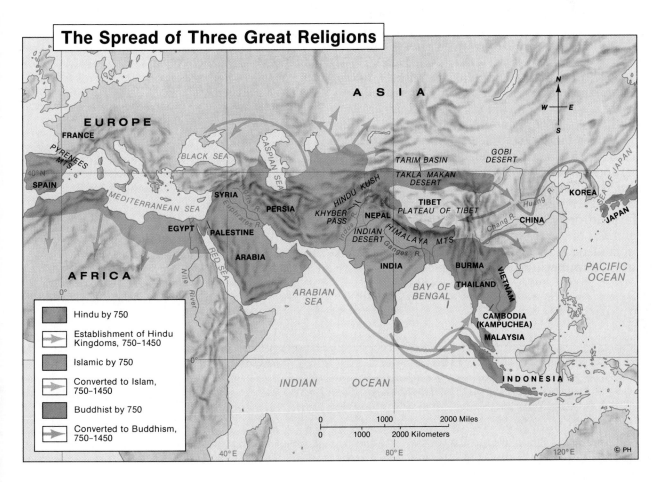

The Spread of Three Great Religions

Hindu by 750

Establishment of Hindu Kingdoms, 750–1450

Islamic by 750

Converted to Islam, 750–1450

Buddhist by 750

Converted to Buddhism, 750–1450

0   1000   2000 Miles
0   1000   2000 Kilometers

© PH

UNIT
5

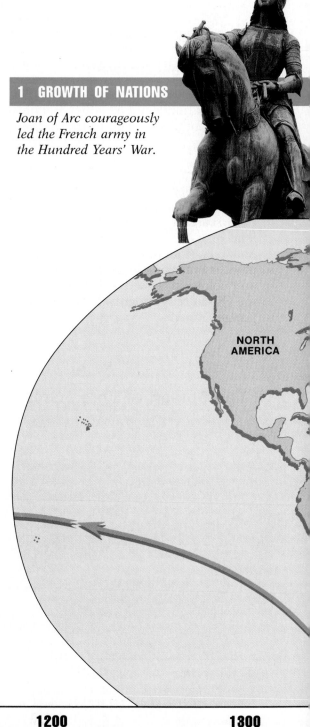

1 GROWTH OF NATIONS

Joan of Arc courageously led the French army in the Hundred Years' War.

Journey Into Modern Times

(1000–1750)

After a visit to Italy in the early 1500s, a scholar from northern Europe exclaimed: "Immortal God, what a day I see dawning!" Great changes were taking place throughout much of Europe at that time. In this unit, you will learn about three periods of change known as the Renaissance, the Reformation, and the Age of Discovery. You will also learn about the development of nations, in which kingdoms and empires gave way to unified nation-states. Many historians believe these four periods mark the beginning of modern times. The map and the time line, linked by color, show where and when this journey into modern times took place.

NORTH
AMERICA

1000	1100	1200	1300

■ **1066** William the Conqueror invades
England

1302 Philip the Fair of France calls ■
first meeting of Estates-General

THE RENAISSANCE 2

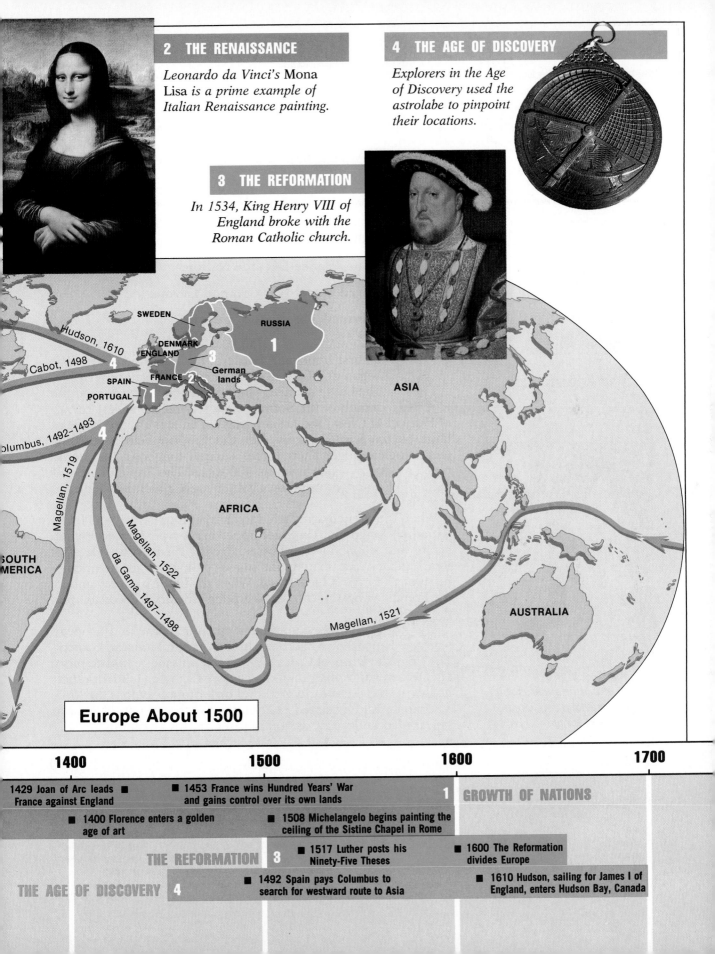

2 THE RENAISSANCE

Leonardo da Vinci's Mona Lisa *is a prime example of Italian Renaissance painting.*

4 THE AGE OF DISCOVERY

Explorers in the Age of Discovery used the astrolabe to pinpoint their locations.

3 THE REFORMATION

In 1534, King Henry VIII of England broke with the Roman Catholic church.

Hudson, 1610

Cabot, 1498

Columbus, 1492–1493

Magellan, 1519

Magellan, 1522

da Gama 1497–1498

Magellan, 1521

SWEDEN

DENMARK
ENGLAND

FRANCE

SPAIN

PORTUGAL

German
lands

RUSSIA
1

3

2

1

ASIA

AFRICA

SOUTH
AMERICA

AUSTRALIA

Europe About 1500

1400	1500	1600	1700

1429 Joan of Arc leads ■
France against England

■ 1453 France wins Hundred Years' War
and gains control over its own lands

1 GROWTH OF NATIONS

■ 1400 Florence enters a golden
age of art

■ 1508 Michelangelo begins painting the
ceiling of the Sistine Chapel in Rome

THE REFORMATION **3**

■ 1517 Luther posts his
Ninety-Five Theses

■ 1600 The Reformation
divides Europe

THE AGE OF DISCOVERY **4**

■ 1492 Spain pays Columbus to
search for westward route to Asia

■ 1610 Hudson, sailing for James I of
England, enters Hudson Bay, Canada

The Growth of Nations

(1000–1600)

1 **Nation-Building Began in Medieval Europe**

2 **England and France Became Nations**

3 **The Hundred Years' War Gripped Europe**

4 **Nations Formed Throughout Europe**

▲ **Illustrating History** *Even a suit of armor such as this would not have protected a knight from longbow arrows.*

The first important battle of the Hundred Years' War began at 5:00 P.M. on a Saturday afternoon in 1346. The battle occurred in the level countryside near the mouth of the Somme River in the northwest corner of France. At Crécy, the French massed an army about twice as large as the English army, but the English held a startling technological edge. Their forces carried longbows that could reach an enemy as far away as 400 yards. The French had only their old-fashioned crossbows, which were much less effective at a distance.

When the French army tried to charge, English archers let fly with their longbows. The steel-tipped arrows penetrated French armor and stabbed at the horses, driving them wild with pain. Rearing back and turning, the horses galloped into the oncoming French forces. Chaos ruled. When the battle of Crécy ended, the French army, the "flower of French chivalry," lay dead upon the battlefield.

The battle of Crécy marked a turning point in European warfare. Knighthood had been based on hand-to-hand combat. The English victory at Crécy showed that missiles could be more effective in battle than men. As armored knights fell from their horses, so too did the old medieval order topple before the force of change. And a related phenomenon—the growth of nations —was also underway, as you will see in this chapter.

1100	1250	1400	1550

■ **1066** William the Conqueror becomes king of England

■ **1185** Portugal unites as a nation

■ **1337** England and France begin Hundred Years' War

■ **1485** Henry Tudor wins the English crown

■ **1492** Muslims and Jews leave Spain

▲ **Illustrating History** *The English army's use of deadly longbows in the Hundred Years' War marked the beginning of modern warfare.*

1 Nation-Building Began in Medieval Europe

As you read, look for answers to these questions:

◆ What are the characteristics of a nation?
◆ How did geography influence the growth of nations?
◆ What steps did some medieval monarchs take to build their nations?

Key Terms: nationalism (defined on p. 309), sovereignty (p. 310), middle class (p. 312)

The desire to form a nation, or **nationalism,** has been a powerful force in history. The process of nation-building began as early as the eleventh century when England became a nation, and it is still going on today. In the twentieth century, hundreds of new nations have been formed in all parts of the world. Some of the nations formed since 1900 include Yugoslavia, Pakistan, Indonesia, Ghana, and Zimbabwe. In the 1980s, Israel was still struggling to establish firmly its status as a nation.

In ancient times, as you have read, people lived in tribes, city-states, empires, and other kinds of organized societies. The idea of a nation, however, had not yet developed. Even when Charlemagne was crowned emperor in 800, there were no nations in Europe. During the centuries following Charlemagne's rule, many Europeans began to feel that certain groups of people belonged together under smaller, separate governments. These feelings gradually led to the development of nations. By the late Middle Ages, when feudalism had all but disappeared in Europe, several strong nations existed, and others were rapidly developing.

309

Nations Share Important Characteristics

Nations have certain things in common. These include: land with definite boundaries, people and other resources, a shared language and culture, and government. Without any one of these characteristics, a nation probably could not exist for long.

Geography. A nation must, of course, have land—the geographic area where a people live. Boundaries set off the land of one nation from the land of another. Boundaries may be natural features, such as rivers, oceans, or mountains, or they may be artificial borders that neighboring nations have agreed upon.

Geographic boundaries can play an important role in helping or hurting the growth of nations. Rivers, oceans, and mountains can unite people by separating or isolating them from others. England, for example, became a nation relatively early because it was part of an island. Miles of water separated England from the European

▼ **Illustrating History** *The Alps in southern Europe separate Switzerland from France, Italy, and Austria.*

continent and the people living there. France, Spain, and Portugal also became countries fairly early because their geography set them apart. Natural features protected them from outsiders and gave the people a sense of having many things in common. On the other hand, the lack of geographic boundaries slowed the growth of nations in other parts of Europe.

People and resources. If a nation is to prosper, it must have a population and natural resources. Good land for farming is important, along with energy sources such as coal or oil. It is not necessary for every nation to have all the resources it needs or wants. To survive, however, a nation needs a reasonable amount of natural resources on which to build its economy, develop trade with other nations, and provide its people with a decent standard of living. Sometimes a population that is inventive, industrious, and hard-working is a human resource that can help a nation overcome its lack of natural resources.

Language and culture. Two important characteristics of a nation are language and culture. As you read earlier, most of medieval western Europe once had been part of the Roman Empire, and most Europeans were Christians who had been influenced by Roman language and culture. At the same time, however, they had never completely lost the traditions of their own people. In different regions, local languages developed out of the Latin of the Roman Empire. As these languages developed, nations grew with them. Latin-based languages, such as French, Spanish, Portuguese, and Italian, encouraged individuals who spoke the same or similar languages to think of themselves as a people.

Government. To build a nation, there must be a government. This can be, for example, a monarchy or a republic. Any national government must have the power and authority to do as it wishes within its borders. This important characteristic of a nation is called **sovereignty** (SOV er uhn

TEE). It means that a nation, through its government, has the power to set its policies and make decisions that affect its people freely and independently.

The European nations that gradually developed toward the end of the eleventh century were governed by strong rulers. Five centuries later, Thomas Hobbes, a famous English political thinker, would say that the growth of a system of government based on powerful monarchs was the most important development in the history of humankind. Hobbes, who lived during the 1600s, believed that without strong nations and rulers to keep order, the lives of most people would be "solitary, poor, nasty, brutish, and short." The system of nations that Hobbes praised so much first began to develop in western Europe toward the end of the eleventh century.

▼ **Illustrating History** *Below is a cover illustration from Hobbes's* Leviathan, *in which he described how the forming of nations had affected people's lives.*

In their own words

A Female Law Professor

Christine de Pizan's father was the astrologer for King Charles V of France in the late 1300s. With the support of her father, she became one of the best-educated women in Europe. As an adult, de Pizan wrote several books, including *The Book of the City of Ladies.* This book describes the achievements of women throughout European history and argues in favor of sexual equality. In the following excerpt, she tells the story of Novella, another well-educated woman.

❝Giovanni Andrea, a solemn law professor in Bologna [a city in Italy] not quite sixty years ago, was not of the opinion that it was bad for women to be educated. He had a fair and good daughter, named Novella, who was educated in the law to such an advanced degree that when he was occupied by some task . . . he would send Novella, his daughter, in his place to lecture to the students from his chair. And to prevent her beauty from distracting the concentration of her audience, she had a little curtain drawn in front of her. In this manner, she could on occasion supplement and lighten her father's occupation. . . .

Thus, not all men (and especially the wisest) share the opinion that it is bad for women to be educated. But it is very true that many foolish men have claimed this because it displeased them that women knew more than they did.❞

1. Who supported de Pizan and Novella in their desire to learn?
2. What does the story of Novella and the curtain show about men's view of women in medieval Bologna?

Strong Monarchs Directed the Growth of European Nations

From the eleventh to the fifteenth century, strong monarchs directed the growth of European nations. The people as a whole had little real influence on their nation's growth. Their feelings of loyalty and patriotism usually were directed to their ruler, their city, such as Florence (in Italy), or their province, such as Burgundy (in France). The idea of loyalty to a nation or to a monarch who ruled an entire nation would come later.

Early in the Middle Ages, as you read in Chapter 8, monarchs were not always as powerful as the feudal lords who were their vassals. A monarch at this time had to ask his vassals to provide the knights and foot soldiers he needed for fighting wars, and so he was dependent on their favors to preserve his own power. As towns and commerce grew and a middle class developed, this situation changed. As its name suggests, the **middle class** was made up of those people between the upper class of nobles and the peasants or serfs. This class included wealthy merchants and skilled craftspeople. Monarchs gave the middle class special privileges and rights in exchange for the taxes they paid and loans they would make to a monarch. Loans and taxes allowed monarchs to pay for soldiers and equipment directly, rather than relying on their vassals.

The growth of nations began when monarchs became strong enough to unify and control the land occupied by their vassals. Some monarchs also acquired territory through marriage. That is, a king might marry the daughter of a wealthy nobleman who would give him land as part of the marriage agreement. In time, a unified area large enough to be called a nation came into being. Loyalty to ruler and to nation slowly followed.

The rise of nations had a number of consequences. Some monarchs took their job of providing for the welfare of their people seriously. Others merely tried to increase their own power, wealth, and prestige by waging wars against other nations. As nations became larger, wars were conducted on a much larger scale than ever before. A strong monarch could command thousands of soldiers, vast amounts of resources, and the loyalty of the nation's people as well. In some ways, war became a national obsession. It is small wonder that Thomas Hobbes chose the term leviathan as the title for his book about monarchs and nations. The word *leviathan* means a legendary monster that devours all creatures foolish or unlucky enough to come within its reach.

England and France were among the earliest nations to be formed in Europe. Both had favorable geography, important natural resources, a language and heritage shared by most of their people, and strong monarchs on their thrones. In the next section, you will read how England and France became modern nations.

SECTION 1 REVIEW

Knowing Key Terms, People, and Places
1. Define: **a.** nationalism **b.** sovereignty **c.** middle class
2. Identify: **a.** Thomas Hobbes

Focus on Geography
3. How can geographic boundaries affect the growth of nations?

Reviewing Main Ideas
4. In addition to geography, what important characteristics do nations have?
5. Why are natural resources important to the growth of a nation?
6. How did the rise of nations affect the conduct of wars?

Critical Thinking
Identifying Central Issues
7. Most European nations developed under the leadership of strong rulers or monarchs, with no ideas of democratic government. What problems can you see in trying to form a nation in a democratic way?

2 England and France Became Nations

As you read, look for answers to these questions:

- How did geography influence England's development as a nation?
- When and where did the system of trial by jury begin?
- What was the Magna Carta?
- How did France become a nation?

Key Terms: grand jury (defined on p. 314), petit jury (p. 314), common law (p. 314), burgess (p. 315), estate (p. 316)

The small town of Bayeux (bay YOO) in France draws thousands of tourists every year to see a famous tapestry, or embroidered picture, known as the Bayeux tapestry. Many yards long, the tapestry shows how William the Conqueror crossed the English Channel from Normandy, France, and conquered England in 1066. This event is known as the Norman Conquest.

The Norman Conquest Started England Toward Nationhood

The English were one of the first groups of people in Europe to form a nation of their own. As you read in the first section, geography played an important part in the development of England as a nation. The English Channel separated the island of Britain from the continent of Europe. Thus, the people of England could avoid the wars in Europe and develop a sense of their own identity. Although England had been invaded and settled by several different groups of people, most of the people on the island lived in a fairly small area, spoke similar languages, and shared a common history.

Anglo-Saxon rulers had made a start toward unifying England. Like other monarchs of the time, however, they had to depend on the loyalty of the earls and nobles who controlled most of the land. When the Anglo-Saxon king known as Edward the Confessor died in 1066, there were several rivals for the English throne. The Anglo-Saxons chose Harold, a powerful noble who was Edward's brother-in-law. In France, however, William of Normandy, a cousin of Edward, also claimed the throne.

The Norman Conquest. In the fall of 1066, William and an army of 5,000 Normans sailed from France across the English Channel and landed in England. At the same time, the king of Norway and an army of Vikings invaded England. King Harold and the Saxons fought off the Viking invaders and faced the Normans. At the Battle of Hastings, Harold was killed and the Anglo-Saxons were defeated. William, now known as William the Conqueror, declared himself king of England and set up a strong, efficient government. William had taken the first steps toward making England a nation.

Henry II. The kings who followed William were also strong, able rulers. William's great-grandson Henry II, who ruled from 1154 to 1189, for example, strengthened the English legal system by establishing royal courts of law throughout the country. This

▼ **Illustrating History** *The Battle of Hastings is shown in the Bayeux tapestry.*

meant that all people would be judged by the same laws everywhere in England, instead of by the local laws of each region.

Under Henry's system, there were two kinds of juries. A **grand jury** reported the names of those accused of committing crimes to judges who were appointed by the king. A **petit** (PEH tee) **jury,** made up of twelve men, then discussed what they knew about the crime. The king's judges based their decisions on the customs of the people. The body of law that developed from their decisions was called **common law.** For common law and for the jury system, the English and Americans both are indebted to Henry II. Common law is the basis of most of our laws today.

Henry II tried to do even more. He wanted the monarchy to have more control over church officials. In particular, he wanted the members of clergy who were accused of crimes to be tried in the royal courts, not in separate church courts. This plan of Henry's led to serious disagreements with the Church.

Henry appointed Thomas à Becket, his close friend and adviser, to be Archbishop of Canterbury as a reward for his loyal and devoted service. After Thomas became archbishop, however, he opposed Henry's attempts to limit the power of the Church. Furious at what he saw as disobedience, the hot-tempered king supposedly exclaimed, "Will no one rid me of this obstinate [stubborn] priest?" Henry was shocked when four of his loyal knights, thinking to obey him, assassinated Archbishop Thomas in 1170, while he was at prayer.

People were horrified by the killing. Threatened with excommunication, King Henry sought out the assassins and apologized to Pope Alexander. Thomas à Becket, who was seen as a martyr, was quickly made a saint by the Church. His tomb at Canterbury became England's favorite place for pilgrims to visit. In 1174, Henry himself became a pilgrim as public penance for Becket's death. Henry walked the last three miles to the tomb barefoot, his feet bleeding, while monks beat him. At the tomb of his friend, the king begged forgiveness. It would

be centuries before the clergy were brought under royal laws, so Henry was at the mercy of the Church officials who blamed him for Saint Thomas's death.

The Church was not the only challenge to Henry's authority. His wife, Eleanor of Aquitaine (AH kwih TAYN), was an independent, spirited noblewoman who owned huge estates in France. In 1173, Eleanor encouraged her sons Richard and John to rebel against their father. Henry had Eleanor put in prison, but the rebellions continued. Cursing his disloyal sons, Henry II died in 1189. His son Richard I, known as Richard the Lion-Hearted, became king but spent nearly his entire 10-year reign away from England either on the Crusades or at war in France.

The Magna Carta. The death of Richard the Lion-Hearted in 1199 brought his brother John to the throne of England. John was a weak, unpopular ruler who lost most of England's lands in France and quarreled with the pope and the English feudal lords. As conditions grew worse in England, the feudal lords who had lands and soldiers united to make the king agree to certain limits on royal power.

This agreement was written down in the Great Charter, or Magna Carta, which John signed in 1215. The Magna Carta stated that no free person could be punished or put into prison without a trial by jury or according to "the law of the land." Another section declared: "To no man will we sell or deny, or delay justice or right." The document also said that the king could not tax people without the consent of the Great Council. The Great Council, which had been begun by William the Conqueror, was made up of prominent nobles and church officials who advised the monarch.

The Magna Carta established several basic rights that we take for granted in modern democratic governments. These rights were limited and did not apply to everyone. At the time, many English people were landless serfs who were bound to the nobles' lands. The rights in the Magna Carta did not apply to these people. Only those people who were free—townspeople, clergy, peasants—claimed the rights in the Magna Carta.

For all its limits, the Magna Carta was a political milestone. It showed for the first time that a monarch's power could be limited by law. Gradually, the principles of the Magna Carta were applied to a greater number of people and became part of the basic rights of the English. Its ideas and words later influenced American government as well.

Parliament. Soon after the Norman Conquest, William I called together a group of nobles and clergy. This group, which eventually became known as the Great Council, acted as his advisers. The Magna Carta gave the council the right to approve—not just advise on—certain royal decisions. Gradually, townspeople and knights were invited to council meetings. The council came to be known as Parliament (PAR luh ment), a word that means a meeting for discussion.

On the principle, "Let that which toucheth all be approved by all," King Edward I, who ruled from 1272 to 1307, regularly called meetings of Parliament. He saw it as a good way to keep in touch with all his subjects and gain their support. The meeting in 1295 has been called the Model Parliament because it represented most of the people. It was made up of important clergy, nobles, knights, and townspeople, or **burgesses** (BUR jess ez). Everyone met in one room, where royal officials and great lords talked and the knights and burgesses listened. Over time, the two groups divided. Eventually, the House of Lords (nobles and clergy) and the House of Commons (knights and burgesses) met separately.

The year 1066—the Norman Conquest—is the date usually given for the beginning of England as a nation. By the end of the thirteenth century, England had a strong monarch, a united country, and the beginnings of representative government.

[handwritten annotation: Citizen of a burrow or town that served in PARLIAMENT]

▼ **Chart Skill** *Who were Eleanor of Aquitaine's two husbands? What was the name of Philip IV's daughter, and whom did she marry?*

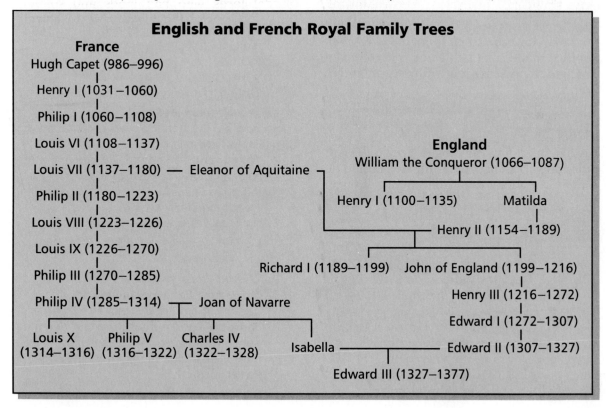

English and French Royal Family Trees

France
Hugh Capet (986–996)
Henry I (1031–1060)
Philip I (1060–1108)
Louis VI (1108–1137)
Louis VII (1137–1180) — Eleanor of Aquitaine
Philip II (1180–1223)
Louis VIII (1223–1226)
Louis IX (1226–1270)
Philip III (1270–1285)
Philip IV (1285–1314) — Joan of Navarre
Louis X (1314–1316)   Philip V (1316–1322)   Charles IV (1322–1328)

England
William the Conqueror (1066–1087)
Henry I (1100–1135)   Matilda
Henry II (1154–1189)
Richard I (1189–1199)   John of England (1199–1216)
Henry III (1216–1272)
Edward I (1272–1307)
Isabella ———— Edward II (1307–1327)
Edward III (1327–1377)

Monarchs Remained Powerful as France Became a Nation

France became a nation more slowly than England and followed a different pattern. Like the rest of western Europe, France was involved in local wars and, because of its location, could be invaded more easily than the island of Britain. During the ninth century, France had been part of the territories of Charlemagne. Charlemagne, however, thought in terms of an empire, not a nation, and after his death, the empire had fallen apart. In 843, as you read in Chapter 8, his grandsons divided the empire into three parts. For the next century, weak kings and strong feudal lords kept France split into small territories that were ruled by dukes and counts.

In 987, Hugh Capet (KAY piht), the Count of Paris, was chosen king by other French lords. Although Capet began a line of kings that lasted for 350 years, at the time of his selection many feudal lords were far more powerful than he. For years, the French kings tried to add to the land they ruled. Their rivals were the lords who ruled Normandy, Burgundy, and Aquitaine. In addition, marriages between French and English nobility made it possible for the rulers of England to possess great amounts of land in France.

When Philip Augustus became king in 1180, he actually governed only a small portion of land around Paris. Many of his vassals, including the king of England, were more powerful than he. Philip decided to do something about this difference in power. He encouraged the sons of Henry II of England to rebel against Henry. In 1202, only three years after John, Henry's youngest son, became king of England, Philip boldly took John's French lands away from him along with the lands of French nobles. To gain support against the nobles, the king granted favors to the middle-class townspeople. By extending his authority over a greater territory, weakening the power of the lords, and winning the help of the middle classes, King Philip Augustus greatly strengthened the French monarchy.

Another strong king who helped France to become a nation was Philip the Fair, who reigned from 1285 to 1314. He, too, tried to increase the king's authority over both feudal lords and church officials. To win his people's backing, Philip called a meeting of clergy, nobles, and townspeople in 1302. This meeting became known as the Estates-General because it represented the three **estates,** or classes, of French society.

The Estates-General never became as powerful as the English Parliament. It met only when the king called upon it and could not limit the king's power. It was, however, a start toward representative government, and it weakened the feudal system. A strong monarch, weaker feudal lords, and the development of an Estates-General encouraged greater loyalty to the French government and helped it develop as a nation.

SECTION 2 REVIEW

Knowing Key Terms, People, and Places
1. Define: **a.** grand jury **b.** petit jury **c.** common law **d.** burgess **e.** estate
2. Identify: **a.** William the Conqueror **b.** Henry II **c.** Thomas à Becket **d.** Magna Carta **e.** Parliament **f.** Estates-General

Reviewing Main Ideas
3. How did the creation of royal courts make English law fairer?
4. What event marked the real beginning of England's development as a nation?
5. What did Philip Augustus do to make the French monarchy stronger?
6. How was the Estates-General in France different from Parliament in England?

Critical Thinking
Perceiving Cause and Effect
7. The Magna Carta was unusual for its time because it limited the monarch's powers and gave English people certain definite rights. How do you think this might have influenced the development of the English Parliament?

3 The Hundred Years' War Gripped Europe

As you read, look for answers to these questions:

◆ Why did the king of England try to claim the throne of France as well?
◆ How did new weapons change the course of the Hundred Years' War?
◆ Why was Joan of Arc important to the people of France?
◆ What was the outcome of the Wars of the Roses?

Key Terms: dauphin (defined on p. 319)

As England and France became strong, unified nations, they became rivals. Between 1337 and 1453, the two countries fought a long series of wars that we now call the Hundred Years' War. This struggle had important results for both countries. Oddly enough, the country that won the major battles lost the war; and the country that lost the war was better off than the country that won. In many ways, the Hundred Years' War marked the start of a new type of war. Gunpowder and other new weapons were used in European warfare for the first time.

French and English Kings Fought for Territory and Trade

For many years, the ruler of England held land in France and therefore was a vassal of the French king. As feelings of nationalism grew, the English came to resent these ties to the French king. Hostility between France and England also grew over the rich wool trade of Flanders, which both nations wanted to control. (Flanders lay along the northern coastline of France in a location that made trade with England easy.) France also helped Scotland in its quarrels with England, which irritated the English.

When the king of France, Charles IV, died in 1328, there was no direct heir in the line of kings started by Hugh Capet. A cousin, Philip of Valois (val WAH), was crowned king, but the English quickly challenged his right to the throne. Edward III, who was the king of England at this time, thought it was time for a showdown with France. Edward thought he had a better claim to the French throne because he was the nephew of Charles IV. (Edward's mother was the sister of the late French king.) However, just as the English did not want a French king, so the French did not want a king who was English. This dispute led Edward to invade France in 1337. Edward's invasion of France marked the beginning of the Hundred Years' War.

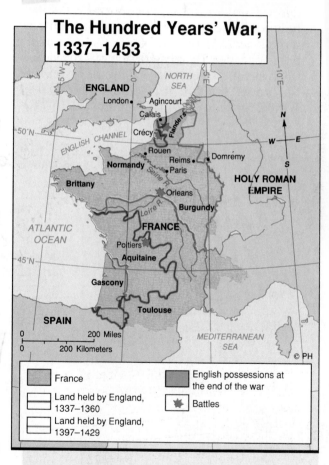

The Hundred Years' War, 1337–1453

- France
- Land held by England, 1337–1360
- Land held by England, 1397–1429
- English possessions at the end of the war
- ★ Battles

Focus on Geography

Regions Describe the region in France that was held by England at the end of the war.

317

New Weapons Were Used in the Hundred Years' War

The opposing English and French armies were equipped quite differently. The English army was made up mainly of foot soldiers, each of whom carried a longbow and a supply of arrows. The French army was made up of knights on horseback, armed with lances and swords. The knights wore heavy suits of armor. Coats of metal protected their horses.

At the great battles of the Hundred Years' War, such as the battle of Crécy (KRAY see) in 1346, the English soldiers proved that the days of armored knights and hand-to-hand fighting were over. Arrows shot with a longbow could cover great distances, reach their targets accurately, and pierce the armor of horse or rider. Deadly showers of arrows, as thick as rain, struck terror into the hearts of the bravest knights. In addition, their heavy armor made it hard for knights to move.

Once they were forced off their horses, they could neither fight effectively nor run swiftly enough to escape.

The new weapons called for a new kind of warfare. Later in the war, gunpowder was used for the first time to load small cannons. The use of gunpowder also brought about great changes in how warfare was conducted. In a sense, the Hundred Years' War was the first modern war.

All the land battles of the Hundred Years' War were fought in France. Although knights and lords fought the battles, it was the French peasants' farms, crops, and homes that were destroyed. Even with this destruction, the feudal lords demanded taxes from the peasants to pay for the war. As the war continued, famine spread, and hatred grew between lord and peasant.

In 1358, there was a peasant uprising known as the *Jacquerie* (zhahk eh REE). Desperate peasants revolted, killed their lords, and burned their castles. Many people

---

DAILY LIFE

Iron-Fisted Warriors

From the 1300s to the 1500s, many European warriors became knights in shining armor—plate armor, that is. The man pictured at left is making a coat of chain mail, flexible armor of joined metal links. As the Middle Ages wore on, chain mail was reinforced with metal plates, until knights were completely encased in plate metal.

Each iron suit weighed between 55 and 65 pounds (25 and 30 kilograms). Armor was expensive. One suit could cost as much as a small farm. Thus, families passed these uniforms down from one generation to the next.

Despite appearances, the armor was not necessarily cumbersome. Wearing armor, a knight could lie down, get up, climb stairs, and leap into a horse's saddle without using stirrups. But, the armor was uncomfortable in extreme heat or cold and dangerously heavy for a knight who landed in deep water and tried to swim.

1. Why was armor passed from father to son?
2. How would you compare medieval armor to bulletproof vests and similar devices today?

Joan of Arc

She came from a small village in northeastern France. She did not live beyond her teens. Yet Joan of Arc, a simple peasant girl, became a heroine of epic proportions.

Born about 1412, Joan (shown right) grew up in the countryside of Lorraine. When she was 12 years old, she began to see visions that urged her to deepen her faith. Then, in 1428, Joan's visions instructed her to help her country.

In those days, France was led by a dauphin named Charles VII, and English and French forces were locked in the Hundred Years' War. Joan went to the dauphin and persuaded him to let her break the English siege of Orléans. Next, she wanted to lead a march on the town of Reims, where Charles could be crowned king of France.

Joan accomplished both missions, but in 1430 she was captured by the Burgundians and sold to the English as a prisoner, Joan was brought to Rouen in 1431 and convicted of being a witch. Unwilling to renounce her visions, as the English wished, Joan of Arc was burned at the stake. Her brief life became a symbol of heroism to the French.

1. What did Joan's visions instruct her to do?
2. What was the significance of her actions to those around her?

---

died before the uprising was finally put down. Although the Jacquerie failed, its challenge to the power of feudal nobles showed that feudalism was on its way out.

Joan of Arc Led the French to Victory in Battle

In 1428, defeat seemed near for France. The English were laying siege to the French city of Orléans (or lay AHN), and it looked as if France would be defeated. Then, in an unlikely chain of events, France's situation changed, partly because of a seventeen-year-old peasant girl—Joan of Arc.

Joan claimed that she had received messages from God in the form of dreams or visions, telling her she must save France. Her faith convinced the **dauphin** (DAW fihn), the title of the eldest son and heir of the king of France. The dauphin, who would become Charles VII, agreed to let Joan try to save Orleans and unite France.

Mounted on a fine horse and dressed in a suit of shining armor, Joan led a French army toward Orléans. Inspired by Joan, the tired French soldiers defeated the English. By 1429, the English troops were finally driven from the city of Orléans, and Charles VII was crowned in the cathedral at Reims (reems).

Joan led the French in other battles but won no more victories. In 1430, she was captured by the people of Burgundy. These people were loyal to the English and turned Joan over to them. In May 1431, church officials in the city of Rouen (roo AHN) convicted her of witchcraft and burned her at the stake. In her short lifetime, Joan of Arc, "the Maid of Orléans," had united the French people. By 1453, the English held only one French city, the port of Calais (kah LAY), as shown on the map on page 317. Thus, France came out the winner of the Hundred Years' War.

319

Civil War Broke Out in England

After the English lost the Hundred Years' War and most of their land in France, they began to concentrate on uniting their nation. England had not suffered the destruction France had, but unrest and discontent had spread throughout the country. Rival branches of the royal family tried to gain control of the English throne, bringing about a series of civil wars that lasted from 1455 to 1485. These are known as the Wars of the Roses. During the civil wars, the English people supported either the House of Lancaster, whose symbol was a red rose, or the House of York, whose symbol was a white rose. The outcome of these wars had a great effect on England's history.

The Wars of the Roses gave England a new family of rulers, the Tudors (TOO durz). Henry Tudor, a member of the House of Lancaster, defeated King Richard III of the House of York in 1485. Henry then took the throne as King Henry VII of England. The Wars of the Roses also helped bring the end of feudalism in England. The bloody battles killed hundreds of noblemen and wiped out some families altogether, thus lessening the strength of the nobles.

To unite England, Henry VII married Elizabeth of York. The Tudor family ruled England until 1603, giving the nation a number of strong rulers, including Henry VIII and his daughter, Elizabeth I. These rulers broke with the Roman Catholic church, encouraged trade, and supported explorers who extended the boundaries of the known world.

Feudalism Came to an End in France

By winning the Hundred Years' War, France rid itself of a foreign power that had occupied its land for many years. Charles VII began to show greater strength as king. In 1438, he issued a decree that took power away from the Church and reduced the influence of the pope. In 1440, he got the Estates-General to agree to a land tax. The land tax increased the king's income and made him stronger. He could now hire a small but efficient standing army of his own, instead of relying on soldiers provided by the nobles. Charles's son, Louis XI, who became king in 1461, further strengthened the French monarchy by eliminating its greatest opponent—the Duke of Burgundy.

When the wealthy landowner Charles the Bold became Duke of Burgundy in 1467, he was the leader of the feudal lords of France. For himself, he wanted Burgundy to be an independent kingdom. Louis XI, who was called "the Spider" because of his clever plotting, encouraged rebellions in Burgundy. He then convinced both the Swiss and the Holy Roman Emperor that the Duke of Burgundy was a threat to them. In 1477, the Swiss defeated Burgundy, and Charles the Bold was killed. Louis then claimed much of the Duchy (DUTCH ee) of Burgundy for the French throne. Through his plotting, he had not only gained some rich land but also eliminated his main enemy, thus strengthening the power of the French monarch and uniting the French nation even more.

SECTION 3 REVIEW

Knowing Key Terms, People, and Places
1. Define: **a.** dauphin
2. Identify: **a.** Philip of Valois **b.** Edward III **c.** Orleans **d.** Henry Tudor (Henry VII) **e.** Charles VII

Reviewing Main Ideas
3. What was the issue that started the Hundred Years' War?
4. Explain how the armies and equipment of France differed from those of England in the Hundred Years' War.
5. Why is Joan of Arc important in French history?
6. What were the results of the Wars of the Roses?

Critical Thinking
Expressing Problems Clearly
7. Explain why the Duke of Burgundy was a threat to the French monarch and to the unity of the French nation.

4 Nations Formed Throughout Europe

As you read, look for answers to these questions:

◆ Who were the rulers of Spain in the early Middle Ages?
◆ How did the Mongols change the course of Russian history?
◆ What kept Italy from becoming a nation?

Key Terms: czar (defined on p. 322), autocrat (p. 322), neutrality (p. 323)

During the Hundred Years' War, feudalism declined and France and England took giant steps forward toward becoming strong nations. Although they were leaders, France and England were only two of many countries developing in Europe in this period. This section looks at how some other European nations grew.

Two Nations Developed on the Iberian Peninsula

The two countries of Spain and Portugal occupy the Iberian Peninsula. During the eighth century, much of the peninsula had been conquered by a group of Muslims who

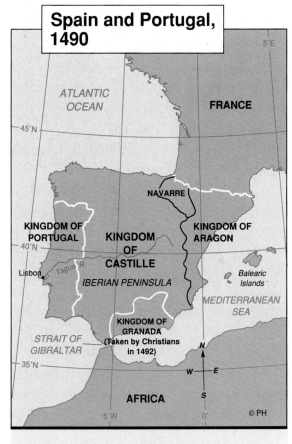

Spain and Portugal, 1200

- Christian lands
- Muslim lands

0   100   200 Miles
0   100   200 Kilometers

AREA OF MAIN MAP

Spain and Portugal, 1490

Focus on Geography

Regions By what date did the Muslims lose complete control of their territory in Spain and Portugal?

were known as Moors. Moorish civilization was superior to that of most European countries at that time, but Europeans still saw the Moors as foreigners and enemies.

Under Moorish rule, earlier settlers in Spain retreated to small Christian kingdoms in the northern part of the Iberian Peninsula. These Christian kingdoms soon began a long fight—known as the Reconquest—to drive out the Moors. In 1147, Alfonso I, Count of Portugal, took the city of Lisbon from the Moors and extended his lands to the Tagus River, which cuts through central Portugal. By the time Alfonso died in 1185, the kingdom of Portugal was established as a new nation.

In the rest of the peninsula, the Reconquest and the establishment of Spain as a nation took longer. In about 1200, there were four Spanish Christian kingdoms: Navarre (nah VAHR), Leon (ley OHN), Castile (kah STEEL), and Aragon (AHR ah gon). These kingdoms are shown on the map on page 321. Castile and Aragon were by far the strongest, and Castile soon absorbed Leon. In 1469, Ferdinand of Aragon and Isabella of Castile married and united their kingdoms. By this time, the Moors held only the small kingdom of Granada on the Mediterranean coast. Ferdinand and Isabella together governed an area that included most of the future nation of Spain.

As in France and England, a strong monarchy developed in Spain. The rulers brought local nobles under control and won the loyalty of the people. Townspeople and others came together to form an assembly called the Cortes (KOR tihz), which was similar to the Parliament in England and the Estates-General in France.

Russia Followed a Different Path to Nationhood

France, Spain, and most of western Europe were once part of the Roman Empire and were greatly influenced by its language and culture. Eastern Europe, however, was not greatly influenced by the Roman Empire, and different cultures developed. Strong kingdoms and states grew in Hungary, Po-

land, and along the Baltic Sea. The one that eventually would become the largest and strongest nation was Russia. The map on page 323 shows the growth of Russia.

In the ninth century, a band of Danish and Swedish raiders set up a small kingdom around the city of Kiev. Their legendary leader was a man named Rurik. These people, called *Rus*, at first raided other settlements. Over time, they became river traders, carrying goods to Constantinople. From their name comes the word Russia.

In 1237, invading Mongols destroyed Kiev and conquered other Russian towns. The Mongols ruled for more than 200 years, leaving Russia as much an Asian country as a European one. During the fourteenth century, the princes of Moscow, or Muscovy (MUSS koh vee), tired of paying tribute to the Mongols, began to unify nearby lands and people. Finally, the leader of the Muscovy princes, Ivan the Great, declared Moscow's independence from Mongol rule and began to build the Russian nation.

In 1472, Ivan the Great married a Byzantine princess. Even though Constantinople had fallen to the Turks in 1453, thus ending the Byzantine Empire, Ivan claimed that he had a right to the power of the Byzantines and ancient Rome. The princes of Moscow were to be called **czar** (zar) from the word *caesar*, meaning "emperor."

Russia expanded quickly, and its borders soon were extended to Siberia and the Caspian Sea. Under Ivan IV, known as Ivan the Terrible, Russia became a country in which the wishes of the czar were the law of the land. In no other country was the monarch such a complete **autocrat**, a ruler with total power. In 1613, the Romanov family became the rulers of Russia and remained so until the Russian revolution in 1917.

Smaller Nations Developed in Western Europe

The Swiss, the Dutch, and the Scandinavians were also forming nations at the same time as their more powerful neighbors. Although they never dominated western Europe, they played major roles in history.

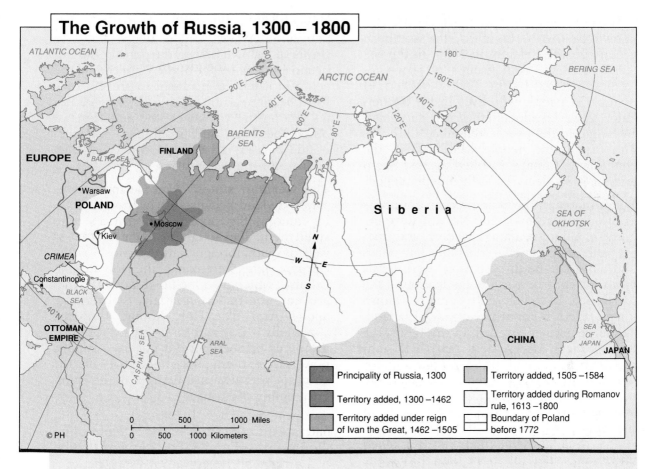

The Growth of Russia, 1300 – 1800

Legend:
- Principality of Russia, 1300
- Territory added, 1300 –1462
- Territory added under reign of Ivan the Great, 1462 –1505
- Territory added, 1505 –1584
- Territory added during Romanov rule, 1613 –1800
- Boundary of Poland before 1772

© PH

Focus on Geography

Movement Land-locked Russia was anxious to have ports. In 1772, Russia gained part of Poland. What sea did Russia gain access to as a result?

Switzerland. In 1291, the people of the Swiss cantons, or states, united as the Swiss Confederation in order to resist rule by the Hapsburgs of Austria. Even though their location in the Alps helped to protect them from invasions, the Swiss had to resist many foreign rulers who wanted to occupy their small nation.

By the 1400s, the strong Swiss army was feared by larger nations. They defeated the Duke of Burgundy in the 1470s and, in 1499, won their independence from the Holy Roman Empire and the Emperor Maximilian. In 1515, however, the Swiss suffered serious losses in a battle with France. From then on the Swiss chose **neutrality,** the policy of a nation not participating directly or indirectly in a war between other nations.

The Netherlands. Bordering on the North Sea were a group of provinces that had been a part of Charlemagne's empire. Because of their flat terrain, these provinces were often called the Low Countries, or the Netherlands. After Charlemagne's death, these provinces came under the rule of more powerful neighbors—France, then Burgundy, then the Hapsburgs of Austria. The province of Flanders in particular was desired for its prospering cloth trade.

323

The northern group of provinces are still known as the Netherlands; the southern group became Belgium in 1830. In the sixteenth century, both groups of provinces were controlled by the Catholic rulers of Spain. The people who lived in the Netherlands, however, adopted the Protestant faith. In Belgium, the people remained Catholic. The Dutch (the people who lived in the Netherlands) finally revolted against Spain and, in 1581, declared their independence.

Scandinavia. The Scandinavian countries of Sweden, Denmark, and Norway were the home of Viking seafarers, raiders, and traders. Although they shared similar languages and cultures, the three nations were fierce rivals for control over the lands around the North Sea. In the eleventh century, Danish kings ruled Denmark, Norway, England, and large parts of Sweden. In the 1380s, the Danish queen Margrethe I (mar GRET teh) managed to unite all of Scandinavia under her rule. In 1397, Margrethe had her nephew crowned as king of Sweden, Denmark, and Norway, and of their possessions in Iceland and Finland.

The Scandinavian nations remained under one ruler for more than 100 years. Finally, the Swedes, seeking independence, rebelled against the Danish king, Christian II, and broke away. In 1523, the Swedish leader Gustavus Vasa became King Gustav I and began to build Sweden into a powerful nation.

Germany and Italy Remained Divided

Neither Germany nor Italy became unified as nations until the later 1800s. While the names *Germany* and *Italy* were used during the Middle Ages, they were really only geographic terms to indicate an area made up of independent states that were somewhat similar in culture and language. Some of these states were small; others large and powerful.

Italy. The Italian peninsula was divided among a number of prominent city-states and the Papal States, which were lands belonging to the pope. The Papal States lay between northern and southern Italy. To preserve his own power, the pope could use his position as leader of the Church and the central location of his lands to prevent Italy from becoming united. In addition, jealousies among the city-states, the ambitions of other countries, and geographic and economic barriers all combined to keep Italy divided for many centuries.

The German states. The German states stayed divided because of rivalry and fighting among the nobles and princes who ruled them. They fought with one another as well as with foreign nations. Most of the German states were part of the Holy Roman Empire, which also included lands in what are now the nations of Italy, Switzerland, and Austria. The Holy Roman Emperor —actually a German king—was chosen by the other princes but did not exercise any power over them. After about 1440, the emperor was always a member of the Hapsburg family of Austria.

SECTION 4 REVIEW

Knowing Key Terms, People, and Places
1. Define: **a.** czar **b.** autocrat **c.** neutrality
2. Identify: **a.** Ferdinand of Aragon **b.** Isabella of Castile **c.** Ivan the Great **d.** Ivan the Terrible

Reviewing Main Ideas
3. What common enemy helped to unite Spain as a nation?
4. What nations were founded by the Vikings?
5. What kept Italy and Germany from becoming nations during the Middle Ages?

Critical Thinking
Testing Conclusions
6. Considering Switzerland's location in Europe, explain why the nation's decision to remain neutral may have helped it to stay independent.

Writing Effective Paragraphs

There are many different ways to write an effective paragraph. However, all well-written paragraphs have three essential characteristics. The first of these characteristics is unity; that is, an effective paragraph is a group of sentences that develop one main idea. That main idea may be stated in a topic sentence, or it may only be implied. In either case, every sentence in the paragraph will support the main idea.

A second characteristic of effective paragraphs is adequate development. This means that the main idea is explained well enough so that the reader can understand it. It may also mean that enough details or examples are included to make the main idea believable.

A third characteristic of effective paragraphs is coherence. This means that the paragraph hangs together well; it reads smoothly and the points it makes are clear.

Use the following steps to write an effective paragraph.

1. **Decide on the main idea you want to express. Write this idea as a topic sentence.** Look back at section 2 of this chapter. Write a topic sentence that will answer the following question: What was the main purpose of the Magna Carta?

2. **Select details to explain or support the main idea adequately.** For this paragraph, you will need to select details that explain or give examples of how the Magna Carta did what your topic sentence says it did.

3. **Choose a reasonable order in which to present the topic sentence and the supporting sentences.** Do you want the topic sentence to come first or last? Can you use some principle for ordering the supporting sentences? Writers may use time order, space order, or order of importance. If no clear principle seems appropriate for ordering a paragraph's sentences, you must use your own judgment about the order that makes the paragraph clear and smooth. Write a draft of your paragraph using the order you have chosen.

4. **Read your draft paragraph and revise as needed to make it clear and easy to read.** Transition words—such as *first, next, finally, also, however, nevertheless, because,* and *therefore*—can be especially helpful. Does your paragraph need more transition words? Should any sentences be shorter or longer? Make any changes on your draft and write a final version of your paragraph.

An Effective Paragraph Has

Unity
- There is one main idea.
- All details support the main idea.

Adequate Development
- Main idea is explained clearly.
- Details or examples make the main idea believable.

Coherence
- Sentences are arranged in a reasonable order.
- Careful wording makes ideas come across clearly and smoothly.

REVIEW

Section Summaries

Section 1 Nation-Building Began in Medieval Europe The idea of forming nations first appeared during the Middle Ages. Prior to the eleventh century, Europeans lived in tribes, city-states, and empires. Any nation must have certain characteristics, including geographic boundaries, people and other resources, common language and culture, and a central government. Between the eleventh and fifteenth centuries, strong monarchs slowly took over the power of the noble class and unified the lands and people in areas large enough to be called nations.

Section 2 England and France Became Nations The geographic isolation of England allowed its people to avoid Europe's wars and to develop their own identity. Anglo-Saxon rulers began the unification of England, but it was the Norman Conquest that provided a strong central government. Henry II strengthened the English legal system during his rule. He was succeeded by his sons Richard I and John. Nobles forced King John to sign the Magna Carta, which ensured the nobles' basic rights and gave Parliament the power to approve certain royal decisions. In France, weak kings kept the country divided until Hugh Capet became king. Later Capet monarchs increased their power over larger territories and created the Estates-General to advise the king.

Section 3 The Hundred Years' War Gripped Europe As England and France each gained strength and unity, they became rivals for land and trading advantages. Between 1337 and 1453 they fought a long series of wars called the Hundred Years' War. The English armies used a new weapon—the longbow—and later gunpowder was introduced. Fighting took place mainly in France, destroying the peasants' land and homes. A devout peasant girl, Joan of Arc, led the French to victory at Orléans. The English returned home to face a civil war that helped to end feudalism and brought the Tudors to the throne. Feudalism also declined in France as a result of war.

Section 4 Nations Formed Throughout Europe Two nations developed on the Iberian Peninsula: Portugal and Spain. The marriage of Isabella and Ferdinand in 1469 united Spain under one monarchy. An assembly called the Cortés, which was similar to the English Parliament, was formed in Spain. Mongol conquerors controlled Russia until Ivan the Great declared Russia's independence in the late 1400s. Russia expanded quickly to Siberia and the Caspian Sea, and the czar became an absolute ruler. In western Europe, Switzerland, the Netherlands, Sweden, Italy, and Germany all had developed as independent nations by the late 1800s.

Key Facts

1. Use each vocabulary word in a sentence.
   a. nationalism   g. burgess
   b. sovereignty   h. estate
   c. middle class   i. dauphin
   d. grand jury   j. czar
   e. petit jury   k. autocrat
   f. common law   l. neutrality
2. Identify and briefly explain the importance of the following names, places, or events.
   a. Battle of Hastings   d. Philip the Fair
   b. Eleanor of Aquitaine   e. Cortés
   c. Parliament   f. Ivan IV

Main Ideas

1. List two types of national boundaries.
2. List the three functions of natural resources.
3. What did King Henry II of England achieve?
4. Why was the Magna Carta significant?
5. What advantage did England have over France at the beginning of the Hundred Years' War?
6. What effect did the war have on France's peasant population?
7. What events led to the end of feudalism in France?
8. Why did Russia develop much more slowly than western European nations?

Developing Skill in Reading History

When you read history, it is important to relate what you are reading to other events and ideas that you already know about. For each of the events listed below, tell what other events or ideas are related to it.

1. An army of Normans invaded England in 1066.
2. King John signed the Magna Carta in 1215.
3. French peasants staged an uprising known as the Jacquerie in 1358.
4. Feudalism declined in France.
5. Ferdinand of Aragon and Isabella of Castile were married in 1469.

Using Social Studies Skills

1. **Using Visual Evidence** Study the art below, which shows Ivan the Terrible of Russia. What significant change did the rule of Ivan the Terrible represent in Russian history?
2. **Recognizing Parallels** What parallels do you see between the use of new weapons in the Hundred Years' War and the nuclear arms race in the twentieth century?

Critical Thinking

1. **Checking Consistency** You have read that the winner of the major battles lost the Hundred Years' War, and that the loser was better off than the winner. Explain why these statements are consistent.
2. **Testing Conclusions** "Regional disputes in Italy and Germany were the main factor preventing their unification as nations." Explain why you would agree or disagree with this statement.
3. **Predicting Consequences** Would a document like the Magna Carta ever have been signed if King John had not been such a weak and unpopular leader?

Focus on Writing

Interpreting Essay Questions

Before attempting to answer an essay question, it is important to determine what the question is really asking you to do. There are several common types of essay questions. Each type of question contains **instruction words** that tell the writer what he or she is expected to do in answering the question. Listed below are several instruction words and a brief description of what each instruction word asks you to do.

- **Compare:** Tell what is similar between two things, people, or events
- **Contrast:** Tell what is different between two things, people, or events
- **Define:** Tell exactly what is meant by a particular word, phrase, or idea

Practice: Read each question below and briefly describe how you would answer the question.

1. Contrast the establishment of Russia as a nation with the formation of the nations in western Europe.
2. Compare how England become a nation with the way in which France became a nation.
3. Define the purpose of the English Parliament under the Magna Carta.
4. Compare and contrast the reasons for the decline of feudalism in France and England.

The Renaissance

(1300–1600)

1 **Modern Times Began with the Renaissance**

2 **The Renaissance Flourished in Cities**

3 **Artists Expressed the Renaissance Spirit**

4 **Science Advanced in the Renaissance**

▲ **Illustrating History** *This detail from a larger painting depicts Lorenzo de' Medici.*

On Easter Sunday, 1478, the great cathedral of Florence teemed with worshippers. Among them, Lorenzo and Giuliano, members of the powerful Medici family and rulers of Florence, knelt in prayer before the altar. Standing nearby, glancing at each other nervously, three men awaited the moment when they would carry out a horrible plot—to murder Lorenzo and his brother and seize power for themselves.

At a signal from their leader, the plotters fell upon their victims. Giuliano died beneath a rain of dagger blows. Lorenzo managed to wrestle free of his attackers and run screaming through the huge bronze doors of the cathedral. Outside, an enraged mob quickly grabbed the conspirators and put them to death.

In the end, the murderous plot failed. Not only did Lorenzo survive the assassination attempt, but he tightened his control over Florence and carried forward the family tradition of encouraging learning and the arts. Scholars thronged his palace, and artists flocked to the city, drawn both by Lorenzo's generosity in supporting their work and his genuine appreciation of their talent. Under his leadership, Florence secured its place as Italy's cultural capital. In this chapter, you will learn how Lorenzo de' Medici and others helped spread and deepen the glory of Renaissance culture.

1300	1400	1500	1600

■ 1300
Renaissance begins in Italy; Dante writes *The Divine Comedy*

1434 ■
Medici family controls Florence

■ 1450
Gutenberg invents movable type

■1513
Machiavelli writes "The Prince"

■ 1543
Copernicus publishes works on astronomy

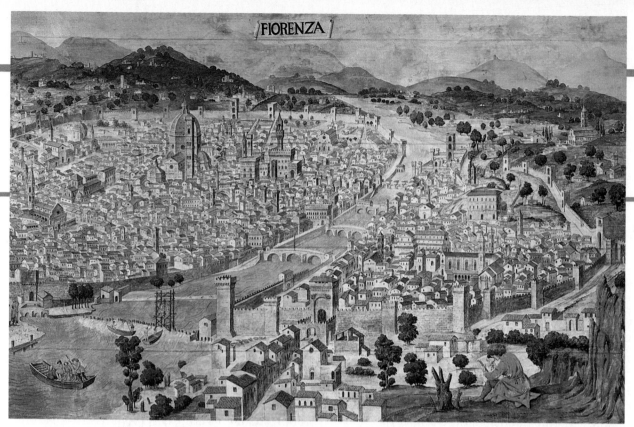

▲ **Illustrating History** *This painting shows Renaissance Florence at its peak. On the left is the cathedral where the Medicis were attacked.*

1 Modern Times Began with the Renaissance

As you read, look for answers to these questions:

◆ Why is this period in history described by a term that means "rebirth"?
◆ What was the main interest of people in Renaissance times?
◆ Why did the Renaissance begin in Italy?
◆ How did the Latin of Rome influence people's everyday speech?

> **Key Terms:** Renaissance (defined on p. 329), humanism (p. 330)

To many people, living in the modern world means having skyscrapers, superhighways, television, space travel, microwaves, and computers. Being modern, however, means much more than having advanced technology. It means a way of thinking in which people believe that their own efforts, education, and imagination can improve the quality of their lives. This was not the way most medieval people thought.

Our modern attitude dates back to the Renaissance (REHN uh sahns), which encouraged a more advanced way of looking at the world.

The Renaissance View of Life Differed from the Medieval View

The **Renaissance** was a major cultural movement that began in Italy and then spread to England, France, Germany, and the Netherlands. The word Renaissance comes from a Latin word that means rebirth. This "rebirth" of ideas did not occur all at once, of course. Like every new age, it began slowly, gained force, and then ended gradually. Specifically, the Renaissance began about 1300 and ended about 1600. However, in a very real way, the light of learning and the beauty of the Renaissance have never ended. The gifts of this exciting age live on in art, literature, science, and education. Most historians agree that the Renaissance marked the dawn of what we call modern history.

The central ideas of the Renaissance were different from those of the Middle Ages. In the Middle Ages, the major focus was on the study of God and the importance of earning salvation after death. While these ideas remained important, the Renaissance focused more on the study of humanity than on religion. This does not mean that people turned away from religion but rather that they looked for more of a balance in their lives. Instead of believing that society was evil, which medieval philosophy had taught, Renaissance thinkers believed that the individual could improve society. An optimistic belief in the talents and strength of each person marked the Renaissance.

▼ **Illustrating History** *Plato and Aristotle dominate Raphael's* School of Athens.

The focus on humanity that occurred during the Renaissance is called **humanism.** The humanists were no longer willing to accept knowledge and beliefs without questioning them. Instead, they turned to the thinking of ancient Greeks and Romans like Plato, Socrates, and Aristotle. As a movement, humanism emphasized the beauty and goodness of people and the world. It also stressed the accomplishments of people in all cultures, particularly those of ancient Greece and Rome. This way of thinking encouraged the people of the Renaissance to believe in themselves, to dare to try, and to accomplish great things.

One of the most important Renaissance thinkers was Erasmus (ih RASS mus), a Dutch teacher who became a great humanist. In his book, *The Praise of Folly*, published in 1509, he poked fun at the privileged position of the nobles. Although Erasmus criticized the Church, he did not believe in breaking away from it. Erasmus urged people to try to improve their lives by following Christian principles.

Another leading humanist, and a close friend of Erasmus, was the English statesman, Sir Thomas More, an adviser to King Henry VIII. Sir Thomas More coined the word *utopia* for his book, *Utopia*, published in 1516. In it he described a perfect society based on reason.

The Renaissance Began in Italy

Why did the Renaissance begin in Italy and not somewhere else? There are several reasons that Italy became the birthplace of the Renaissance. These reasons include the geography as well as the economic, political, and cultural conditions in Italy at the time the Renaissance began.

Trade and contact with other cultures. Looking at a map of the trade routes that existed at the beginning of the Renaissance, it is easy to see that the seaports of Italy were vital to the distribution of goods from around the world. Whether Italian merchants traveled over land or by sea to buy goods in Asia and the Middle East, they brought the goods back to seaports in Italy such as Venice or Genoa. From there, the goods could be sold and distributed to the people in northern Europe.

Because of Italy's prime location for trade, its merchants came into close contact with many other cultures. As their world expanded through trade, they came to appreciate the ideas and accomplishments of other peoples. These cultural contacts contributed to the birth of the Renaissance.

Wealth of powerful merchants. As trade flourished, the merchants of Italy made huge fortunes for themselves. These fortunes allowed them to devote money, time, and energy to other activities, such as the development of the arts. Wealthy families began to sponsor artists, writers, and philosophers. They also paid for the construction of many impressive statues, monuments, and buildings. Thus, the wealth of the merchants contributed to the growth of the Renaissance itself.

Conditions in the city-states. Another reason that the Renaissance began in Italy has to do with the city-states there. The city-states, shown on the map on page 331, competed for wealth, power, and glory. The competition between them encouraged people to try new forms of government, new ways of doing business, and new forms of art. At a time when wars slowed the growth of the developing nations in northern Europe, enough freedom existed in the Italian city-states to encourage a thirst for learning. The small city-states were not strong enough to conquer each other or carry on large-scale wars. These developments further explain why the Renaissance began in Italy.

The heritage of ancient Rome. Still another reason for the birth of the Renaissance in Italy was that Italy was the home of ancient Rome. Scholars came to Italy from all over Europe to study the famous writings of the past and to see remains of ancient buildings. Italy was also the center of the Church, which had preserved the writings of the past and used its wealth to promote painting, learning, and writing.

Changes Took Place in Literature, Art, and Architecture

The humanistic ideas of the Renaissance influenced the literature, art, and architecture of the time. In each of these areas, the old, narrow methods gave way to more modern methods that reflected the Renaissance spirit. Individual writers and artists expressed themselves with a new, more creative freedom that allowed them to portray life, people, and nature more realistically.

Literature in the vernacular. In the early medieval period, educated people spoke and wrote mostly in Latin rather than the

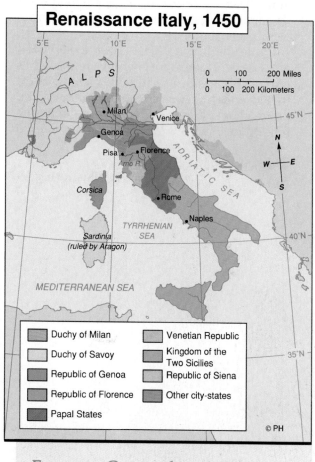

Renaissance Italy, 1450

Legend:
- Duchy of Milan
- Duchy of Savoy
- Republic of Genoa
- Republic of Florence
- Papal States
- Venetian Republic
- Kingdom of the Two Sicilies
- Republic of Siena
- Other city-states

© PH

Focus on Geography

1. **Location** In what state is Rome located?
2. **Regions** A mountainous region is located north of what states?

language used by the common people around them who could neither write nor read. In different parts of Europe where the Roman Empire had ruled, Latin dialects, or spoken versions of Latin, changed to become people's everyday spoken languages. These special forms of Latin are known today as Romance languages. They formed the basis of the French, Spanish, Italian, Portuguese, and Romanian spoken today.

During the late Middle Ages and the Renaissance, some writers began to write in everyday, or common, languages rather than in Latin. These languages are known as the vernacular. As you read in Chapter 5, vernacular is the native language of a region. Dante, Petrarch, and Chaucer are three writers of the Renaissance who wrote in the vernacular.

Dante Alighieri (DAHN tay ah lee GYEHR ee) was an Italian poet who is regarded as one of the greatest writers in history. Born in Florence, he was active in military and political activities there. As a young man, he fell in love with a young woman named Beatrice. Although he saw her only a few times before she died, she became the inspiration for many of his literary works. His *Divine Comedy* is a beautiful epic that describes an imaginary trip through heaven and hell. Beatrice appears in the poem as Dante's guide after he has finally found his way to heaven.

The Divine Comedy depicts the political and spiritual life of the Middle Ages and the journey of the individual toward God. Dante used real people as characters in the poem, which examines many of the concerns and issues of the Renaissance age. In addition to encouraging other writers to use the vernacular, Dante's work bridged the old world of the Middle Ages and the new world of the Renaissance.

Because of his political pursuits, Dante was exiled from his beloved Florence during a civil war. He spent the next 20 years before his death in 1321, hoping he would be able to return. He thought that the success of *The Divine Comedy* might earn his pardon, but it did not, and he died in exile.

▼ **Illustrating History** *Below are a painting of Dante at work and an illustration from* The Divine Comedy *in which Beatrice guides Dante.*

Petrarch (PEE trahrk), born in 1304, was another Italian Renaissance writer who expressed the ideas of humanism in his works. He wrote about love, nature, and human life in a style that imitated the classical Roman writers, Cicero and Virgil. Like Dante, his love of a young woman who died provided the spiritual and literary inspiration for many of his poems. Her name was Laura.

In England, other writers were producing brilliant works in their own vernacular. One of these was the master storyteller, Geoffrey Chaucer, who wrote *The Canterbury Tales* late in the fourteenth century. Through the stories told by its colorful characters, this poem reveals a great deal about the customs and attitudes of fourteenth-century English life. The characters are people from different walks of life who are traveling on horseback from London to the shrine of Thomas à Becket at Canterbury. To pass the time, each person tells either a humorous or a serious story. As they journey, Chaucer's characters reveal their thoughts on such issues as love, marriage, and religion.

Toward the end of the Renaissance, late in the sixteenth century, William Shakespeare built upon the foundation of earlier English writers such as Chaucer to create a lasting literary legacy of poetry and plays. Shakespeare is regarded as the world's greatest playwright because of his truly human characters who come to life in his comedies, tragedies, and historical plays. Shakespeare's works continue to be universally appreciated because of the basic truths of human nature they reveal.

New styles in art. Just as the literature of the Renaissance told the story of real life, so did its art. The glory of nature and the human body came alive at the hands of gifted painters. The duller medieval paintings of ideal men and women gave way to the modern, vibrant, true-to-life colors and rounded forms of the Renaissance. Painters studied the anatomy of the human body in order to paint realistically. Although religious subjects continued to be painted, Renaissance paintings also included portraits of contemporary people and vivid scenes of city life. Many Renaissance artists also portrayed scenes from classical Greece and Rome in their work.

Renaissance painters also developed new methods of painting. They experimented with new color combinations and learned to use line, light, and shadow to show realism. Unlike medieval paintings, Renaissance paintings showed dimension and depth, so that people felt as if they were looking into a painting and seeing objects from a distance. This method is called *perspective*.

One of the earliest Renaissance painters who successfully used the new techniques was Giotto di Bondone. He was the first to paint frescoes, which are paintings done on wet plaster. As he painted religious scenes on church walls, Giotto made the figures seem alive by giving them depth and roundness. Among the most famous works of Italian art are the frescoes of biblical scenes that Giotto painted in the Scrovegni Chapel in Padua, Italy. Because he was a pioneer in breaking away from the medieval style, the artist Giotto is credited with charting the future course of painting in Europe.

Sculpture, too, experienced a revival during the Renaissance. Sculptors returned to crafting single, free-standing pieces like those of Roman times. Donatello (DOHN uh TELL oh), who lived in Florence, was a noted sculptor of the early 1400s. His bronze statue, entitled *David*, is one of the earliest free-standing figures of the Renaissance. Donatello is also famous for his magnificent statue of a Venetian general on horseback, entitled *Gattamelata*. These and all of his works reflect the realism and energy of the Renaissance.

Renaissance architecture. Renaissance architects turned away from the huge medieval cathedrals that emphasized the majesty of God. Instead, they designed smaller buildings to focus on people's talents and achievements. Greek and Roman buildings served as models for the works of these architects.

Lorenzo Ghiberti (gih BAYR tee), the teacher of Donatello, and Filippo Brunelleschi (broo nuh LES kee) were two talented

▲ **Illustrating History** *The architect Brunelleschi designed both of the structures shown above: the dome of Florence Cathedral (top) and the Pozzi Chapel.*

artists who lived early in the fifteenth century in Florence. Ghiberti and Brunelleschi were actually rivals in a sculpting competition that Ghiberti won. As a result of the competition, Ghiberti earned the job of working on the doors of the baptistery of San Giovanni in Florence. People still come from all over the world to see the intricate bronze sculpting on the north and east doors, which took Ghiberti over forty years to complete.

Brunelleschi also won fame as an architect. He was one of the first Renaissance architects to revive the arches, columns, and other features that marked classical Greek and Roman buildings. One of his most famous buildings is the beautifully proportioned Pozzi Chapel in Florence, Italy. You will learn more about the Renaissance glory of Florence in the next section of this chapter.

SECTION 1 REVIEW

Knowing Key Terms, People, and Places
1. Define: **a.** Renaissance **b.** humanism
2. Identify: **a.** Erasmus **b.** Dante **c.** Giotto **d.** Ghiberti

Focus on Geography
3. How did the location of Italy help to make it the birthplace of the Renaissance?

Reviewing Main Ideas
4. How did some people's attitudes toward life on earth change during the period of the Renaissance?
5. Describe at least three reasons, in addition to location, why the Renaissance began in Italy.
6. Name two writers who used the vernacular as the language in which they wrote.

Critical Thinking
Predicting Consequences
7. In the Middle Ages, only the clergy and a few educated people could read and write in Latin. What effects, do you think, did writing books in everyday language have on literacy and education?

2 The Renaissance Flourished in Cities

As you read, look for answers to these questions:

◆ Why did finance and banking develop during the Renaissance?
◆ In what ways were both Florence and Venice typical of the spirit of the Renaissance?
◆ How did Venice become so prosperous as a trade center?

Key Terms: patron (defined on p. 336), galley (p. 337)

During the Renaissance, as in ancient times, cities were the centers of civilization, growth, and change. Thus, the Renaissance began in Italy where the largest cities in western Europe existed. Two rich cities that typified the Renaissance spirit were Florence and Venice.

Banking and Finance Advanced During the Renaissance

One of the major changes that took place in the Renaissance was a growth in finance and banking systems. As you read in Chapter 9, the Church did not allow moneylending and charging interest on borrowed money. Although these practices were regarded with suspicion during the Renaissance, people came to realize that they were necessary for trade, commerce, and manufacturing. Rulers, popes, and merchants needed money to finance their activities.

The Italians were the bankers of the Renaissance. Banks grew in number and wealth and performed many functions. They loaned money and helped to change money from one currency to another. Without such services, trade could not go on between different countries. Much of the wealth of both Florence and Venice was due to their thriving banking systems, which allowed business to flourish.

Florence Was a Center of Renaissance Culture

The city of Florence was, and remains, the "flower" of the Italian Renaissance. Except for Venice, Florence was the richest city-state in Italy. Trade flourished, as did the production of fine goods. Silks, tapestries, and jewelry made in Florence brought high prices throughout Europe.

Banking thrived in Florence. In the 1400s, however, as the city continued to prosper, it became the scene of political plotting. A number of banking families tried to win control of the city. Out of this struggle, the Medici (MEH dih chee) family rose to power. The Medici family had made a huge fortune through trade and banking.

Lorenzo (loh REN zo) the Magnificent was the most famous of the Medici. He was probably the richest man in Florence and perhaps in all of Italy. Lorenzo was a Renaissance ruler who possessed great talent and abilities. At times, he was ruthless and cunning. He avoided the assassination attempt

▼ **Chart Skill** *When was the most woolen cloth produced in Florence?*

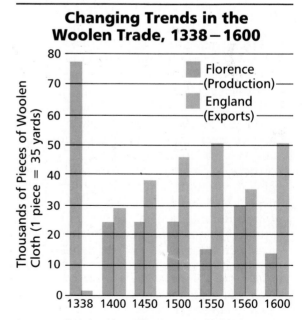

Changing Trends in the Woolen Trade, 1338–1600

Florence (Production)
England (Exports)

Thousands of Pieces of Woolen Cloth (1 piece = 35 yards)

1338 1400 1450 1500 1550 1560 1600

Sources: *Before the Industrial Revolution*, C. M. Cipolla; *Economy of Early Renaissance Europe*, H.A. Miskimin

335

Advice to Rulers on Honesty

Niccolo Machiavelli became famous by writing down what many people already believed. Machiavelli argued that the rules of individual morality should not apply to politicians. In the following excerpt from *The Prince*, Machiavelli advises political leaders on telling the truth.

"Everyone realizes how laudable [praiseworthy] it is for a prince to keep his word and to live by honesty, not cunning. Nevertheless, we see from contemporary experience that those princes who have done great deeds have held their word in little esteem [honor]; they have known how to bewilder men's wits through cunning, and in the end have gotten the better of those who relied on sincerity. . . . a prudent ruler cannot and should not respect his word, when such respect works to his disadvantage and when the reasons for which he made his promise no longer exist. If all men were good, this precept [rule] would be invalid; but since they are bad and do not respect their own word, you need not respect your word either. . . . I could give countless . . . examples, proving how many peace treaties and promises have been made null and void by the dishonesty of princes. . . . a prince must know how to whitewash these attributes perfectly, to be a liar and a hypocrite: men are . . . so bound to the needs of the moment that the deceiver will always find someone who will let himself be deceived."

1. According to Machiavelli, when should a ruler lie?
2. How would the ancient Greeks have responded to the ideas of Machiavelli?

in which his brother was killed and used his influence to have his son made a cardinal of the Church at the age of 14. He kept the support of the people by holding balls, carnivals, and festivals.

Lorenzo was also a generous **patron,** or sponsor, of arts and learning. A talented poet and classical scholar himself, he supported the development of the Italian language and made Florence a center for artists. He spent huge sums of money to buy ancient Greek and Roman manuscripts, and he personally sponsored many great Italian artists, such as Donatello. During Lorenzo's rule, Florence became a magnificent city filled with beautiful buildings, paintings, and statues.

Encouraged by the Medici family, Giovanni Pico della Mirandola was an outstanding Florentine scholar and writer who lived toward the end of the fifteenth century. Pico della Mirandola became a model for future humanist scholars. He studied and read ancient languages and, in his writings, tried to bring together the great ideas of Judaism, Christianity, and Islam, as well as the teachings of Plato and Aristotle. Although he was unsuccessful in this effort, his attempt to accomplish this goal helps us understand the nature of Renaissance learning.

The power of the Medici family in Florence can be seen in the political rivalries, plots, and intrigues that surrounded them. One Florentine court official who lost his job as a result of political scheming was Niccolo Machiavelli (mak ya VELL ee), who lived from 1469 to 1527. Machiavelli, who was accused of plotting against the Medici family, was imprisoned briefly and then retired to his country estate. Bitter about his treatment at the hands of the Medicis, he wrote a book called *The Prince*. In this book, he stated that a ruler was not bound by any consideration of right and wrong when governing. Machiavelli also claimed that the ends justified the means and maintained that violence and trickery could be excused if they kept the ruler in power. Since then, the word *Machiavellian* has been used to describe any deceitful ruler scheming for power and personal gain.

Venice Was a Leader in Renaissance Commerce

Venice was built on islands on the coast of the Adriatic Sea. Its streets were canals, lined with palazzos, or palaces of rich nobles. The city-state was a republic headed by a doge (dozh), or duke. The Council of Ten, a council made up of wealthy and important families, chose the doge. The government used its wealth to build the Grand Canal —the "main street"—the doge's palace, and the Church of St. Mark.

The great schools of Venetian painting included the artists Titian (TISH un) and Tintoretto (teen toh RET toh). Both of these artists represented the new style and lavish use of color that marked Renaissance painting. Titian is especially noted for his color techniques. Tintoretto, once a pupil of Titian's, is noted for his highly dramatic lighting effects. Both artists gave deep humanity and emotional expression to the figures they painted.

Venice's government and culture rested on its great wealth, which came from trade. Because of the city's location, Venetian merchants controlled trade between Europe, the Middle East, and Asia. If Florence represented Renaissance culture, then Venice represented Renaissance commerce.

The economy of many Italian cities flourished during the Crusades. Although Genoa, Pisa, Milan, and Florence all profited, Venice, known as the "Queen of the Adriatic," prospered more than the others. Venetian ships, or **galleys,** were the envy of the world. Fleets of these vessels carried wines, spices, and other products to many places, including Flanders, London, and Lebanon. These vessels made regular trade possible between Italy and northern Europe because water routes were safer than overland routes.

Venice's industry also was central to the economic life of southern Europe. In markets throughout Europe, the Middle East, and Asia, people eagerly bought fine cloth, glass, and leather goods made in Venice.

The importance of Venice as a trading community began to decline in the fifteenth century. New routes to Asia gradually broke

▲ **Illustrating History** *The painting above shows Renaissance Venice, with its busy canals full of gondolas, or canalboats.*

the Venetians' monopoly on trade. The discovery of the New World made the Atlantic more important than the Mediterranean as a commercial waterway. Gradually, Venice's dominance as a commercial center faded, and other European cities took over as centers of business and trade.

SECTION 2 REVIEW

Reviewing Key Terms, People, and Places
1. Define: **a.** patron **b.** galley
2. Identify: **a.** Florence **b.** Venice **c.** Medici **d.** Lorenzo the Magnificent

Focus on Geography
3. How did the locations of Florence and Venice contribute to their wealth?

Reviewing Main Ideas
4. According to Machiavelli, what was a ruler's principal goal?
5. How was the city-state of Venice ruled?

Critical Thinking
Predicting Consequences
6. What do you think would happen today if world leaders followed the ideas found in *The Prince?*

3 Artists Expressed the Renaissance Spirit

As you read, look for answers to these questions:

◆ What does it mean to be a "Renaissance man"?
◆ What different careers did Leonardo da Vinci follow?
◆ What contributions did women make to the art of the Renaissance?

Key Terms: basilica (defined on p. 340)

It is important to understand that the Renaissance was mostly an upper-class movement. Only the nobility and the rich merchant families could buy paintings, order

▼ **Illustrating History** *The* Mona Lisa's *mysterious smile still fascinates people.*

statues, and support the work of artists. Still, the Renaissance gave talented people from every class of society a chance to succeed. Many geniuses emerged in art, literature, and science. A simple listing of them, however, does not convey the restless spirit, the inquiring mind, and the ability to do many things well that marked so many Renaissance men and women.

To be called a "Renaissance man" was to be complimented for one's ability to do, understand, and have an interest in many things. Many of the great Renaissance figures were writers as well as painters, sculptors as well as scientists, poets as well as politicians. Two major examples of the "Renaissance man" are Leonardo da Vinci and Michelangelo.

Leonardo da Vinci Symbolized the Spirit of the Renaissance

No one is more typical of the spirit of the Renaissance than Leonardo da Vinci (dah VEEN chee). Although Leonardo is best known as a painter, few of his paintings have survived. The *Last Supper* and the *Mona Lisa* are probably the most famous of his works.

Leonardo was also a sculptor, a scientist, an engineer, and an inventor. He did all of these things equally well. His drawings of the human form were used by medical students in their studies. He made detailed drawings of growing plants, birds in flight, and animals and insects in motion. Leonardo was active in every science and wanted to test everything by experience rather than accept what others had found.

As an inventor, Leonardo was a genius whose ideas were many years ahead of his time. He is credited with having made a thread-cutting machine and an improved water wheel. He made designs for military fortifications, a machine gun, and other weapons. Fascinated with the idea of flight, he made many drawings and models of flying machines.

Leonardo was aware of his many talents. When he felt sure that his work would be better appreciated in Milan rather than in Florence, he applied for a job to Duke

Restoring a Renaissance Treasure

On a platform facing the wall on which Leonardo da Vinci painted his masterpiece, *The Last Supper* (shown at right), a woman works at cleaning and scraping away centuries of grime, mold, glue, and excess paint. First, she examines the wall through a microscope. Next, she applies specially developed solvents to the surface of the painting. Stripping away a layer at a time, it will take her a week to clean an area the size of a postage stamp.

Leonardo's original brilliant colors, darkened by six earlier restorations, are beginning to shine again. So, too, are many of his exquisite details that were covered by later painters. Once the job is complete, viewers will be able to see the painting just as it looked the day Leonardo laid down his brush in 1497.

1. What does the current restoration of *The Last Supper* reveal about Leonardo's painting?
2. Why is it important to restore such a painting?

Lodovico Sforza (SFOR tsah), ruler of Milan, who was looking for a military engineer, an architect, a sculptor, and a painter. Leonardo felt qualified to offer himself for these positions. In a famous letter to the duke, who later hired him, he wrote, with pride:

Most illustrious Lord . . . I have plans for bridges, very light and strong and suitable for carrying very easily . . . When a place is besieged I know how to cut off water from the trenches, and how to construct an infinite number of . . . scaling ladders . . . . I have plans for making cannon . . . And if it should happen that the engagement battle is at sea, I have plans for constructing many engines suitable for attack or defense, and ships which can resist fire . . . . In time of peace I can give you as complete satisfaction as anyone else in architecture . . . . Also I can sculpture in marble, bronze, or clay, and also painting . . . .

Leonardo's last patron was King Francis I of France, who admired him greatly and gave him a home in France. The king's interest in art and architecture helped spread Renaissance ideas in France. While doing many things well was characteristic of many people of the Renaissance, Leonardo still remains amazing for his versatility.

Michelangelo Was a Symbol of Renaissance Artistry

The other towering figure of the Renaissance is Michelangelo Buonarroti (BWOH nahr ROH tee). Like many other geniuses of the time, he came from the city of Florence. In the household of Lorenzo de' Medici, his first patron, Michelangelo came under the influence of the humanists. They encouraged him in carving such famous marble sculptures as *Bacchus* and the *Pieta* (pyay TAH). *Bacchus* shows the young god of wine and worldly pleasure nibbling on grapes.

339

▲ **Illustrating History**   *Above is a view of the Sistine Chapel ceiling. At left is another work by Michelangelo, the* Pieta, *which depicts Jesus in the arms of his mother, Mary.*

The *Pieta* represents Mary holding the body of her son Jesus after the crucifixion. Among Michelangelo's other great sculptures are the larger-than-life marble statues, *David* and *Moses*. They are considered works of genius for both their spiritual strength and their accurate portrayal of the structure of the human body.

Also famous as a painter, Michelangelo is especially well known for the huge paintings of biblical scenes on the ceiling of the Sistine Chapel in the Vatican in Rome. The sponsor of the work was Pope Julius II, who prodded Michelangelo to finish the task so that he could show off the chapel.

Michelangelo, however, was as strong-willed and stubborn as the pope and would not be hurried. He began the ceiling work with other artists to help him but later worked all alone lying on his back on a scaffold. His progress was slow and painful, but he produced a work of art that remains one of the glories of the Western world. From time to time, the ceiling is carefully cleaned so that its original beauty can be preserved and enjoyed by the crowds of tourists who continue to visit the Sistine Chapel each year.

Michelangelo was also the architect of St. Peter's Basilica in Rome. A **basilica** is a Christian church with a rectangular building and a domed ceiling at one end. He began work on the project in 1546 at the age of 70. Although he died before the church was completed, his design was followed for its most famous feature, the great dome that rises 435 feet (130 meters) above the floor.

In an age when rich people dressed with elegance and flair, Michelangelo lived with few comforts. He came from a noble family and usually had enough money to live comfortably, but he chose to live in a poor part of town. He gave most of his earnings to less successful relatives. Michelangelo's strong character made him a loner who often complained about his health and wrote poems about art and love. He once wrote: "My children will be the works I leave behind. For even if they will be of little value, they will last for a while." Both his works and his forceful personality made him a major artist in a brilliantly creative period.

Raphael (RAH fee ehl) was another Renaissance painter who lived about the same time as Leonardo and Michelangelo. He worked mainly in Rome, where he painted a famous group of rooms in the Vatican for Pope Julius II. Raphael was known for his lifelike portraits, gentle madonnas, and scenes of classical Greece. One of his most famous paintings, entitled *School of Athens*, shows Plato, Aristotle, and other Greek philosophers gathered in a great hall.

Women Contributed to the Renaissance

It was more difficult for women than men to achieve great things during the Renaissance. Even so, many women played an active part in the Renaissance, in spite of the fact that they had less chance to gain an education or develop creative talents.

Women of the upper classes, particularly in Italy, knew Latin, wrote sonnets, and became patrons of the arts. Some women supported the work of great Renaissance artists. For instance, Leonardo was only one of the artists who worked for the Duchess Beatrice d'Este at the court of Milan. Her sister, Isabella d'Este, became even more famous. You can read a short biography of Isabella d'Este on this page. Because of the political power she possessed and her contributions in other areas, Isabella d'Este can be included in the category of the Renaissance person.

Some women were artists. During her long career, Sofonisba Anguissola (ahng GWEE shoh lah) of Cremona was in demand

---

BIOGRAPHY

Isabella d'Este

When the Marquis of Mantua, Italy, was suddenly jailed by the Venetians in 1494, someone had to take over his job. So during his long imprisonment, his quick-witted wife, Isabella d'Este, (shown above) kept the Mantuan state together.

Isabella d'Este was born in 1474, the eldest daughter in the Este family, one of Italy's oldest ruling clans. At age 15, she married the 24-year-old marquis,

Francesco Gonzago. Isabella soon gained fame across Italy as a steadfast patron of the arts and an expert in statecraft.

When her husband died in 1519, Isabella once more displayed her skill at governing. Serving as regent for her son, she maintained a delicate balance among the great powers that divided Italy. In an age of striking personalities, Isabella d'Este stands out as a woman who made an art of her every act. She died in 1539 at age 64.

1. In what way did Isabella d'Este win a reputation?
2. What was Isabella d'Este's political position after her husband's death?

all over Europe as a portrait painter. Michelangelo helped her get started as an artist, and for a time, she was court painter in Spain. As a tribute to her talent, Pope Pius IV asked her to send him a portrait of the queen of Spain. Sophonisba Anguissola was one of the first women artists to achieve international fame. At least 50 of her paintings remain in art collections throughout the world.

The Renaissance brought opportunities for women in other European countries. In Spain, Queen Isabella, who ruled from 1474 to 1504, was a learned woman who encouraged scholarship among the women of her court. Beatriz Galindo (gah LEEN do) founded schools, hospitals, and convents all over Spain. At the age of 25, Olivia Sabuco (sah BOO koh) de Nantes wrote a 70-volume series of books on the subjects of biology, psychology, anthropology, medicine, and agriculture.

In France, Marie de Jars de Gournay (GOOR NAY), a fine scholar and a writer, was another important Renaissance woman. Her books on education and public affairs were dedicated to King Henry IV and his wife, Marie de' Medici, who were her patrons. Her books, including her translations of Virgil, Ovid, and Tacitus, were widely read. She was one of the few Renaissance women who actually made a living from her writings. An early supporter of women's equality, de Jars de Gournay attacked a society in which it was difficult for women to receive recognition for their achievements. She noted in one of her works: "Lucky are you, reader, if you happen not to be of that sex to whom it is forbidden all good things; to whom liberty is denied; to whom almost all virtues are denied; lucky are you if you are one of those who can be wise without its being a crime."

This quotation illustrates the difficulties faced by talented women during the Renaissance. Schooling for them was possible only if men permitted it and encouraged them. In most countries, permission was rarely given and then usually only to upper-class women. In Italy and Spain, for example, women of the upper classes could some-times attend universities, but this was an unusual event. In general, only the most determined and talented women even tried to practice their art professionally, and they had to deal with the disapproval of many people.

Renaissance Art Influenced Other Europeans

Diplomats and scholars who visited Italy were impressed with the beauty and craftsmanship they saw in the Renaissance art. They returned to their homes, praising the art of Italy. From the late 1400s to the early 1500s, invading armies from France, Germany, and Spain returned home with glowing reports of Italian art and culture. As a result, imitations of Italian art began to appear in other parts of Europe. These other countries, however, did not have the wealth of classical art that Italy had. Flemish painters of the Renaissance, for example, painted realistic human figures, but these figures did not have either the rounded quality or emotion of Italian art.

SECTION 3 REVIEW

Knowing Key Terms, People, and Places
1. Define: **a.** basilica
2. Identify: **a.** Leonardo da Vinci **b.** Michelangelo Buonarroti **c.** Raphael

Reviewing Main Ideas
3. How does Leonardo da Vinci represent the term "Renaissance man"?
4. Describe how Michelangelo painted the ceiling of the Sistine Chapel.
5. What were the contributions of Marie de Jars de Gournay?
6. What were some obstacles faced by women artists in the Renaissance?

Critical Thinking
Demonstrating Reasoned Judgment
7. Why do you think that powerful, wealthy Renaissance rulers were so willing to encourage the arts? Do you think they had selfish reasons? Explain your answer.

The Rebirth of the Individual in Art

In contrast to the art of the Middle Ages, the art of the Renaissance celebrated individuals and individual achievement. Donatello's statue of Erasmo di Narni, called *Gattamelata*, depicts an Italian mercenary—a soldier for hire—who, through his own ambition and courage, rose above poverty and low birth to a position of great wealth and power. The painter Raphael shows us, in the portrait of his friend *Baldassare Castiglione*, the ideal Renaissance person: intelligent, polite, well-dressed, sincere. The Renaissance introduced the individual personality in the realm of art, as you can easily see in *Castiglione*. The Christian religion continued to be an inspiration for Renaissance artists, however. Many Renaissance works portrayed scenes or people from the Bible, as in Leonardo da Vinci's *Virgin and Child with St. Anne*. Mary, in the center, reaches forward to pick up her son, the young Jesus, as he plays with a lamb. Tender family scenes such as this were very popular during the time of the Renaissance.

Below are these striking pieces of Renaissance art. Left, the painting Virgin and Child with St. Anne; *center, the statue* Gattamelata; *right, the portrait* Castiglione.

343

4 Science Advanced in the Renaissance

As you read, look for answers to these questions:

◆ Why was the invention of the printing press an important development?
◆ How did northern Europe prosper from the Renaissance?

> **Key Terms:** printing press (defined on p. 344)

Many people think of the Renaissance as only a movement in art, architecture, and literature. Along with artistic genius, however, there were also advances in technology, science, and business. In technology, the most important advance was the development of printing.

▼ **Illustrating History** *The printing press spread Renaissance ideas to many people.*

Printing Helped Spread New Knowledge

The Chinese had invented printing using wood blocks carved with a whole page of written characters. The Koreans developed a printing system using movable type.

In Germany about 1450, the printer Johann Gutenberg (GOO tehn burg) developed a new printing method that worked for the alphabets used in European languages. He cut out each letter from a separate piece of wood. The letters could be put together in words fixed to a slotted board. The printer could then spread thick ink over the page of wooden type and use a **printing press** to press sheets of paper firmly against the letters. When the printing process was finished, the letters could be separated and rearranged to form another page. Gutenberg soon invented a method to cast letters and decorations in metal. He also designed a better printing press. The printing press, together with a method for making cheap paper, encouraged the spread of learning.

Modern science also had its beginnings in the curiosity and new ideas of the Renaissance spirit. For example, Leonardo da Vinci's anatomical drawings of the human body provided a better understanding of how the body worked and how blood circulated. In medicine, a Flemish physician named Vesalius (vih SAY lee uhs), who lived from 1514 to 1564, wrote *The Structure of the Human Body*. It contained the most accurate illustrations of the human body available up to that time.

A Polish astronomer, Nicolaus Copernicus (ko PUR nih kus), who lived from 1473 to 1543, made a discovery that would change people's thinking about the universe. From observing the skies, Copernicus concluded that the sun, not the earth, was the center of the universe. This upset the theory of the Greek scientist Ptolemy, which scientists had believed for centuries. According to Ptolemy, the earth was at the center of the universe with the sun, moon, and planets moving around it. Copernicus, however, observed that the earth made a circular path about the sun. (We now know that the path is an oval.) The findings of Copernicus helped prepare the way for greater advances in astronomy in the seventeenth century.

Although Renaissance science laid the foundation for modern science, it had its limitations. Renaissance scientists still looked with reverence on the learning of Greece and Rome. The humanists believed that little of scientific value could be discovered beyond what Greek and Roman scientists had already described. Many Renaissance scientists were reluctant to risk the criticism that their new theories would draw from the Church and the scholars of the day. For these reasons, scientific studies advanced slowly.

Copernicus, for example, worked on his theories for about 30 years but did not publish them until 1543, the year of his death. (His book was one of the first scientific works to be printed using the new technology.) Similarly, Leonardo da Vinci kept notes on subjects and scientific observations that interested him, but he did not publish his observations. He kept his notebooks private, using a kind of "mirror writing."

Northern Europe Prospered from the Renaissance

In northern Europe, the "rebirth" of the Renaissance period brought changes and discoveries in industry and business. Valuable minerals were found in mountain areas, and new industries such as mining and metalworking began to appear. Improvements in metalworking also encouraged the new printing industry. Trade and towns flourished along the great Rhine River, which linked northern Europe and its resources with the sea. New technologies gave the northern nations ways to develop well-armed ships and to better equip their soldiers.

In Spain, Portugal, northern Europe, and England, it was the rulers of nations, rather than the princes of city-states, who supported and encouraged Renaissance artists and writers. These monarchs also benefited from their nations' economic progress and

were able to speed the decline of the old feudal system. Once-powerful nobles had to accept positions as diplomats or as officers in the military.

With the new prosperity, finance and banking became highly sophisticated. The center of northern Europe's financial Renaissance was the city of Antwerp in Belgium. The world's oldest stock exchange was founded there in 1460. Lyons, in France, and Amsterdam, in the Netherlands, were among the rival cities that financed the growth of wealth in Europe.

One of the great international bankers of the northern Renaissance was Jacob Fugger, (FOOG uhr), known as "Jacob the

▼ **Illustrating History** *The painting below shows the city of Antwerp, the heart of northern Europe's commercial Renaissance.*

▲ **Illustrating History** *The Flemish artist Brueghel captured a scene from everyday life in his painting* The Peasants' Wedding.

Rich." At the height of their wealth, the Fugger family of Germany owned silver, copper, and mercury mines. Jacob Fugger lent vast sums of money to the Holy Roman Emperor Maximilian I, leaving the emperor and other Hapsburgs obligated to the Fugger family. Jacob Fugger also raised money to influence the electors who chose Charles V (Maximilian's grandson) as emperor in 1519. As a reward, the emperor gave the Fuggers titles of nobility and land along with the right to coin money for the empire.

As the Renaissance continued, artists from northern Europe traveled to Italy to study under the great Italian masters. Many of these students made contributions of their own. Using oil paints, for example, was a technique credited to the Flemish painter Jan van Eyck, who painted portraits and religious themes in the early 1400s.

The events and modern thinking that marked the Renaissance in Europe contributed to both the Protestant Reformation and the Age of Discovery. You will read about these developments in world history in the next two chapters.

The many pictures in this textbook—including paintings, drawings, and photographs—provide valuable clues to the past. They can show what people and places in history looked like. They also offer visual evidence concerning the people, places, and events discussed in the text.

As you study the illustrations throughout this text, remember that artists and photographers, like other observers, have points of view. Therefore, you must analyze their pictures carefully.

Follow the steps given here and use the picture below to practice analyzing visual evidence.

1. **Study the illustration and decide what you are seeing.** Be sure to read the caption if one is provided, and look at the overall picture and its details. Answer the following questions: (a) What is the painting's title? (b) When was it painted and by whom? (c) The person third from the right in the painting is receiving a document. Is this person of high or low rank? Cite evidence for your answer.

2. **Analyze the reliability of the visual evidence.** The artist who created this painting may have held a certain bias. Answer the following questions: (a) What do you think was the artist's opinion of Venice and its leaders? (b) What evidence can you cite that indicates the artist's opinion or point of view? (c) How reliable a representation of the real event would you judge this painting to be?

3. **Study the illustration to learn more about the time, the people, or the event that it depicts.** Use the painting below and the information in your textbook to draw conclusions about life in Venice during the Renaissance. Answer the following questions: (a) What can you learn about the manner in which wealthy Venetians lived by studying the people in the background? (b) Give four facts you could learn about Venice if this painting were your only source of information.

▼ Arrival of the Ambassadors, *painted around the year 1498 by Vittore Carpaccio. The artist has portrayed a party of diplomats being received with ceremony by the leaders of Renaissance Venice.*

REVIEW

Section Summaries

Section 1 Modern Times Began with the Renaissance The Renaissance moved the focus of people's thoughts from achieving religious salvation to admiring the accomplishments of people in all cultures. Italy was the birthplace of the Renaissance because of its location, wealth, and Roman heritage. Humanistic ideas of this period influenced the literature, art, and architecture of the time. Writers began to use the vernacular and to write about such topics as love, nature, and human experience. Art celebrated nature and the human body, and experimented with color and perspective.

Section 2 The Renaissance Flourished in Cities The Renaissance began in wealthy Italian cities. Florence and Venice especially typified the Renaissance spirit. Finance and banking became crucial to trade during the Renaissance. In Florence, the Medici family gained money and power through trade and banking, and they became great patrons of art and learning. Venice was a center of Renaissance commerce, controlling trade between Europe, the Middle East, and Asia. Venice was also noted for the great Venetian schools of painting.

Section 3 Artists Expressed the Renaissance Spirit The term "Renaissance man" means a person who is able to do, understand, and be interested in many things. Leonardo da Vinci and Michelangelo are two prime examples. Da Vinci was a sculptor, painter, scientist, engineer, and inventor. Michelangelo was a sculptor, painter, poet, and architect. St. Peter's Basilica is Michelangelo's most famous building. Women also contributed to the Renaissance, although it was more difficult for them to receive educations. Ultimately, the work of Italian artists influenced other Europeans.

Section 4 Science Advanced in the Renaissance Johann Gutenberg's printing press helped to spread learning in the Renaissance. Modern science was born of the curiosity of Renaissance people. Anatomical studies and drawings of the human body brought a greater understanding of its functions. The period also brought changes and discoveries in industry and business. Banking became highly sophisticated. Artists from northern Europe began to travel to Italy to study under the Italian masters. Renaissance thinking contributed to the Protestant Reformation and the Age of Discovery.

Key Facts

1. Use each vocabulary word in a sentence.
   a. Renaissance
   b. humanism
   c. patron
   d. galley
   e. basilica
   f. printing press
2. Identify and briefly explain the importance of the following names, places, or events.
   a. *Utopia*
   b. Geoffrey Chaucer
   c. William Shakespeare
   d. Lorenzo Ghiberti
   e. Medici family
   f. *The Prince*
   g. Leonardo da Vinci
   h. Sistine Chapel
   i. Jacob Fugger

Main Ideas

1. How did the Renaissance reflect a general feeling of optimism?
2. How did Italy's role as a trading nation give rise to the Renaissance?
3. In what ways did Dante's *Divine Comedy* reflect the concerns of his age?
4. Describe three ways in which Lorenzo de' Medici was a patron of the arts and learning.
5. What caused the decline of Venice as a commercial center?
6. In what ways does Leonardo da Vinci deserve to be called a "Renaissance man"?
7. Describe the life of Michelangelo Buonarroti.
8. How were Renaissance scientists influenced by the ancient Greeks and Romans?
9. Identify three centers of banking and finance during this age.

Developing Skill in Reading History

A statement may be either general or specific. A **general statement** covers a broad subject but does not give any details about it. A **specific statement** is narrow and provides details about a certain subject. Read each of the following statements and decide whether it is general or specific. Be prepared to explain your answers.

1. The Renaissance was a major cultural movement that began in Italy.
2. Instead of believing that society was evil, which medieval philosophy had taught, Renaissance thinkers believed that the individual could reform or improve society.
3. French, Spanish, Italian, Portuguese, and Romanian are modern Romance languages.
4. Pope Pius IV asked Sofonisba Anguissola to send him a portrait of the queen of Spain.
5. The printing press was important to learning.

Using Social Studies Skills

1. **Using Visual Evidence** Study the painting below. What is the subject of the painting?

How can you tell that the painting was done during the Renaissance? How would this work have been different if it had been done by a medieval artist?

2. **Researching** Select one of the Renaissance artists mentioned in the chapter and do some research to learn more about the person's life. Try to answer this question: What were the major influences in this person's life and art?

Critical Thinking

1. **Perceiving Cause and Effect** About 100 years after the invention of the printing press, the Church issued the *Index of Forbidden Books*. How might these two events have been related?
2. **Recognizing Ideologies** Unlike men, women were not encouraged to contribute to the Renaissance. How might this have led to the growth of feminist thought?
3. **Predicting Consequences** Knowing that Renaissance ideas led to major changes in science, literature, and art, how would you expect people to begin to change the way they viewed the Church?

Focus on Writing

Interpreting Essay Questions

In order to answer an essay question, you must understand what the instruction word is telling you to do. Listed below are some of the most common instruction words and the type of answer each requires.

- **Discuss:** Tell the significance of a person, idea, or event, whether actual or imaginary
- **Describe:** Write a full account of what happened
- **Explain:** Tell how or why an action or event affects something else

Practice: Re-read the Critical Thinking questions that follow each section in this chapter. Tell which type of response each one of these questions calls for.

The Reformation

(1500–1650)

1 **Problems Within the Church Brought Reform**

2 **The Reformation Led to Protestant Churches**

3 **Reforms Changed Thought and Culture**

▲ **Illustrating History** *This painting of Sir Thomas More shows the luxurious life style More enjoyed as lord chancellor, before his quarrel with King Henry VIII landed him in prison.*

From a narrow slit in his cell in the Tower of London, the prisoner could see the monks going bravely to their deaths. Sir Thomas More, former lord chancellor to King Henry VIII, knew that the same fate awaited him if he did not swear an oath acknowledging the king, rather than the pope, as the supreme head of the Church of England. Although More had served the king faithfully, his conscience would not allow him to swear this oath. His wife called him a fool for abandoning his comfortable London home "to be shut up among mice and rats."

More was permitted visitors and granted the use of pen, paper, and books at the start of his imprisonment. He even enjoyed the company of his personal servant while in jail. The books and writing materials were taken from him when he stubbornly refused to swear the oath. His own servant was then replaced by another who could neither read nor write. More was reduced to scratching messages to his beloved daughter with a piece of charcoal.

Finally, the king's patience ran out. On July 7, 1535, More was taken from his cell and beheaded. True to his convictions to the end, he died "the king's good servant, but God's first." More's dilemma symbolized the growing strain between political and religious beliefs in sixteenth-century Europe. This strain contributed to the drive for religious reform that swept across Europe during the Reformation.

1500	1550	1600	1650

1517 ■
Martin Luther
issues
95 Theses

■ **1534**
Henry VIII
starts Church
of England

■ **1563**
Calvin rules
Geneva as a
theocracy

■ **1598**
Edict of Nantes
recognizes
religious
freedom

1648 ■
Thirty Years'
War ends

▲ **Illustrating History** *The photograph above shows the famous Tower of London, the prison where Thomas More was held before his execution.*

1 Problems Within the Church Brought Reform

As you read, look for answers to these questions:

◆ What did the term *protestant* originally mean?
◆ What role did the Roman Catholic church play in medieval Europe?
◆ Who were some early thinkers who urged reforms in the Church?

Key Terms: sacrament (defined on p. 352), indulgence (p. 352)

Every civilization develops some kind of religious belief. In some civilizations, religion has been the major focus. Religion has inspired art, literature, and architecture. It has also provided a moral guide for living. Because religion has always been a powerful part of civilization, we can understand why the Protestant Reformation was such a revolutionary event in history.

The Reformation Included Both Reform and Revolution

During the Middle Ages, all Christians in western Europe belonged to the same church. They considered the pope in Rome to be God's representative on earth. Therefore, they dutifully obeyed his wishes, which were handed down through bishops and local parish priests. By the 1500s, the Church was more than 1,500 years old. It was, by that time, the oldest and best established institution in the whole Western world. With age and growth, it had become so rich and powerful that it was feared by monarchs and commoners alike. During the 1500s, however, a new religious movement

▲ **Illustrating History** *The dome of St. Peter's Church dominates Rome's Vatican City, the spiritual heart of the Catholic church.*

known as the Reformation changed the way many people thought about religion and the Church's authority.

This change usually is called the Protestant Reformation. The term *protestant* means people who protest against or are opposed to something. Those who protested against the Church were called Protestants. The change was called a "reformation" because it began as a movement to make the Church better, or to reform it. Some people saw the movement as a revolt against the established authority and named the change "the Protestant Revolt." Whether a reformation or a revolt, the religious changes of the 1500s had far-reaching results.

Life Centered on the Church

The Protestant Reformation began as an attack on the evils that had come into the Church. Before the Reformation began, the Church had held Western civilization together after the end of the Roman Empire. In fact, the Church had acted as a government that taxed and a court that administered justice. It controlled the lives of the lowliest peasant and the proudest monarch.

During the Middle Ages, as you have read, the Church carried on Rome's civilizing mission. Monks copied and preserved the great literary works of Greece and Rome.

Monasteries offered schooling for boys, while convents offered education for girls. Monasteries farmed the land and grew valuable crops. The Church and its monasteries and convents provided services such as hospitals and food for the poor.

For over 1,000 years, the Church trained Europe's diplomats, judges, and other leaders. The Latin language, which the Church preserved, served to unify Europe, and this unity was reinforced by the beliefs that European Christians shared.

The main beliefs of the Church included belief in the Trinity (the unity of the Father, the Son, and the Holy Spirit) and in the divinity of Jesus. Christians also believed that the Church could free them of their sins so they could achieve salvation in the next world. Only the Church had the authority to administer sacraments. These **sacraments** are solemn ceremonies that give spiritual grace to those who receive them.

During the Middle Ages, one of the ways a person could be freed from some or all of his or her sins was to be granted by the Church an **indulgence,** or pardon. Usually, to obtain an indulgence, the person had to undertake a crusade or pilgrimage, say certain prayers, or even contribute money to the Church. As time went on, however, some members of the clergy simply sold indulgences. The widespread sale of indulgences was the immediate cause of the Protestant Reformation. The real causes of that event were deeper and more serious.

Dissenting Ideas Challenged the Church

Today, people are used to a variety of religions and religious ideas. This was not true in medieval western Europe. While some Jews lived in Europe, most people were members of the Church. Even within the Church, however, disagreements occurred. As you read in Chapter 8, a disagreement with the official teachings of the Church was called a heresy.

The Albigensians. In the eleventh century, near Albi in southern France, a group of Christians established their own church with its own priests and bishops. The Albigensians (al bih JENTZ ee unz) believed that history was a struggle between the forces of good (light) and the forces of evil (darkness). They saw the Jehovah of the Old Testament as the God of evil; Satan, they believed, created man and earth. Since life was basically evil, devout Albigensians often fasted until they starved to death. They denied the sacraments and opposed what they believed to be the worldliness of the priests of the Church in Rome.

The Church considered the doctrines of the Albigensians heresy. In 1208, Pope Innocent III proclaimed a crusade against them. The Albigensians were finally defeated in a series of wars, but they did not entirely disappear for 100 years. Moreover, some of their ideas lingered on to form the basis of other challenges to the Church.

The Waldensians. A more long-lasting challenge to the Church came from the Waldensians, followers of Peter Waldo, a traveling French preacher who died about 1217. The Waldensians believed that the Bible was the sole rule of life. They rejected the papacy, indulgences, purgatory (a place where those who have died suffer for their sins in order to reach heaven), and the Mass. They also believed that preaching should not be limited to priests alone. The Walden-

sians were declared heretics by the Church in 1215, but branches of the group took part in the Reformation and have continued to modern times.

Wycliffe. John Wycliffe (WIK lif), who lived during the 1300s, helped to launch the Protestant Reformation. He was a scholar at Oxford University in England, where he taught that people needed only the Bible, not priests, for salvation. He preached against the worship of saints and criticized the worldly riches of the clergy.

Wycliffe translated the Bible into English. His followers, who were called Poor Preachers, preached in the vernacular so that his message could be understood by all. Although Wycliffe was declared a heretic by the Church, and some heretics were put to death, Wycliffe died peacefully in retirement. His body was not allowed to rest in peace, however. Thirty years later, it was dug up and burned by his opponents.

Wycliffe's influence can be seen clearly in the ideas that are central to Protestantism. In his own day, his ideas also influenced a

▼ **Illustrating History** *Below is a colored engraving of Bible scholar John Wycliffe.*

revolutionary group called the Lollards. This group attacked the luxurious ways in which the highest ranks of the clergy lived, and they urged social reform to raise the standard of living for other people. They opposed all war and sought to improve the living conditions of the poor.

John Huss.   At the University of Prague in Bohemia (now part of Czechoslovakia), Wycliffe's ideas were well received by John Huss, another distinguished university scholar. Although he was a priest, Huss fearlessly attacked the wealth of the Church and some practices, such as the sale of indulgences. In 1415, Huss was condemned as a heretic and burned at the stake. He died heroically and became a martyr whose ideas lived on through the reform efforts of his followers.

The Church Faced Many Internal Divisions

The strong Church of the early Middle Ages was much weaker by the fifteenth century. Groups of heretics demanded reforms and changes in the Church's teachings. Kings and popes vied for power and fought over how to divide money paid to the Church. As nations developed under the control of strong monarchs, new national rivalries influenced relationships with the pope. The Church itself was no longer unified.

The Avignon popes.   The French monarch Philip IV, known as Philip the Fair, provides a classic example of conflict between church and state. Philip wanted to tax the castles and lands owned by the Church in order to use the money he collected for the defense of his kingdom. The Church, however, claimed that he could not tax these lands. To gain support for his efforts, he called a meeting of what would become the Estates-General in 1302. This meeting gave him official support for his ideas.

In 1305, Philip arranged the election of a French archbishop as the new pope. As if to emphasize the superiority of the kingdom of France over the Church, the new pope, Clement V, settled in Avignon (a vee NYON) in southern France. The papacy remained in France, not Rome, for the next 70 years, from 1307 to 1377. This period is sometimes called the Babylonian Captivity, referring to the biblical account of the Hebrews' captivity. During this period, all the popes were French and were controlled by the French monarch. This clearly was an embarrassment for the Church. To make matters even worse, soon there was a quarrel within the papacy itself.

The Great Schism.   In 1377, Pope Gregory XI left Avignon to move back to Rome. When Gregory died in 1378, the question arose whether the new pope should be French or Italian. The Italian people demanded an Italian pope. Once Pope Urban VI was selected, however, his conduct irritated the cardinals. Although mild-tempered before his selection, as pope he turned harsh and severe. Some of the cardinals held meetings outside Rome and elected another pope, Clement VII, who then returned to Avignon. The Church now had two popes, one in Rome and the other in Avignon, and

▼ **Illustrating History**   *This engraving shows the palace of the popes at Avignon.*

each claimed to be the rightful pope. The Great Schism (SIZ um), or split, as this episode is called, lasted from 1378 to 1417 and seriously weakened the Church.

To end the schism, the Church called a council in 1414 in Constance, Germany. After meeting for four years, the council finally elected a new pope who, they declared, would head the Church from Rome. Although the council members knew that reforms were needed, they were unable to bring them about. It was this same council that condemned John Huss to be burned at the stake for heresy.

By the time the schism had ended and the pope had returned to Rome, the Church could no longer command the total and undivided loyalty of all Christians in the Western world.

The Sale of Indulgences Brought New Challenges to the Church

By 1500, then, the Church had already faced numerous challenges from those who sought to change its teachings. The power of the papacy itself was weakened by strong monarchs and internal quarrels. In addition, with riches, age, and power had come certain abuses. Some bishops and priests were more concerned with worldly affairs than with affairs of the spirit. The Church had taught that prayer and repentance would open the gates of heaven to sinners. By 1500, however, the sale of indulgences made forgiveness more a matter of money than of good works. The large sums of money raised by selling indulgences went to the pope in Rome.

In 1514, Pope Leo X needed money to rebuild St. Peter's Basilica in Rome. He hoped to raise the money through the sale of many indulgences. Johann Tetzel, an ambitious Dominican monk, traveled around northern Germany urging people to buy indulgences and thus be forgiven for their sins. The Dominican monk arrived with all the fanfare of a circus coming to town. He set up a pulpit on the outskirts of the city of Wittenberg in eastern Germany and, in a carnival atmosphere, sold indulgences. "So

soon as the coin in the coffer [treasury] rings," declared Tetzel, "the soul from purgatory springs." In his great enthusiasm, Tetzel declared that if one gave generously enough, one's future sins would also be forgiven. In saying this, Tetzel strayed far from traditional teachings of the Church.

The sale of indulgences annoyed the German princes, some of whom objected to seeing so much money leaving their lands for Rome. They were further angered when they learned that some of the money would be going to the Fugger banking family, who had loaned huge sums to the ruling family of Prussia, one of the German states. The ruling family had needed the money to buy a post as bishop for a member of the family.

Tetzel also aroused the anger of a local monk named Martin Luther, who taught at Wittenberg. Luther's attack on the sale of indulgences and other abuses was to lead to a confrontation with the Church and trigger the Reformation.

SECTION 1 REVIEW

Knowing Key Terms, People, and Places
1. Define: **a.** sacrament **b.** indulgence
2. Identify: **a.** John Wycliffe **b.** John Huss **c.** Philip the Fair **d.** Babylonian Captivity

Reviewing Main Ideas
3. In what ways was the Church important to ordinary people in medieval western Europe?
4. How did Wycliffe and Huss challenge the Church?
5. What caused the Great Schism?
6. Explain why the Church had two popes between 1378 and 1417.

Critical Thinking
Recognizing Bias
7. What groups of people might be likely to use the term "Protestant Revolt" rather than the term "Protestant Reformation"? Do you think that any bias is obvious in the choice of the term "Protestant Revolt"? Explain your answer.

2 The Reformation Led to Protestant Churches

As you read, look for answers to these questions:

◆ What teachings of the Church did Martin Luther challenge?
◆ How did John Calvin's reforms differ from Luther's ideas?
◆ What changes occurred in religion in England?
◆ How did the Roman Catholic church try to stop the spread of Protestantism?

> **Key Terms:** theses (defined on p. 356), papal bull (p. 357), recant (p. 357), theocracy (p. 359)

Two outstanding leaders of the Reformation were Martin Luther, who lived from 1483 to 1546, and John Calvin, who lived from 1509 to 1564. Luther and Calvin protested against some of the traditional practices of the Church. Their views on many issues were so different from those of the Church that their followers formed new religious groups. These became some of today's Protestant churches.

Martin Luther Questioned Church Teachings and Practices

As discussed in the preceding section, Martin Luther was a German monk who taught theology at the University of Wittenberg. He taught, fasted, and prayed with deep feeling. Despite his religious life, Luther's mind and soul were troubled.

From his study of the Bible, Luther had come to believe that faith in God, along with God's grace, was all that a person needed to be saved. "The just shall live by faith," St. Paul had written. If that was so, Luther argued, one could not buy his or her way into heaven by purchasing indulgences or even by doing good works. Going even further, Luther concluded that if faith alone could bring salvation, then the services of the Church and the pope were not necessary. He felt that faithful believers could interpret the Bible without the aid of priests.

Like Erasmus, the great Renaissance scholar who was discussed in Chapter 14, Luther's original goal was to reform the Church. On October 31, 1517, Luther nailed a list of **theses** (THEE seez), or arguments, to the door of the Wittenberg church. These were known as the Ninety-Five Theses. Each one spoke out against indulgences and other Church abuses.

In days when there were no newspapers, posting a notice on the church door was the usual way of advertising one's ideas. In this way, Luther publicly invited scholars to debate his views. At the time, he had no idea or wish that the debate would divide the Church. "One should help and cling to the Church," he wrote, "for conditions will not be improved by separation."

The new printing presses quickly spread Luther's ideas throughout Europe, generating a great deal of controversy. Luther wrote to German princes, urging them to free their states from the Church's political influence. Luther also urged the princes to resist

▼ **Illustrating History** *Martin Luther was the determined leader of the Reformation.*

Erasmus

Erasmus (shown above) was born in Holland around 1469. After several unhappy years in a monastery, he became a wandering scholar. His travels in France, Italy, and England brought him into contact with John Colet and Thomas More, two of England's leading thinkers.

During this period Erasmus completed his famous book, *The Praise of Folly*, and began a translation of the Greek New Testament. In these and other works, Erasmus exposed the flaws of the Roman Catholic church and society as a whole. His work thus inspired the Reformation.

When Martin Luther nailed his theses to the Wittenberg church doors in 1517, a storm of religious controversy began to crackle across the European continent. Erasmus was caught in the middle. He was finally forced to denounce Luther publicly in order to prevent the Catholic church from crumbling. Until his death in 1536, Erasmus tried to make peace between the warring Protestant and Catholic camps.

1. What other scholars influenced Erasmus?
2. How did Erasmus inspire the Reformation?

---

the papacy as a foreign power. He said that money going to the pope could be better used to help the poor.

Many Germans agreed with Luther. Even the German princes were quick to adopt Luther's ideas. Some responded favorably because they genuinely believed in what he said. Others used Luther's beliefs as a way to take over the Church's lands and wealth and to escape the Church's political influence.

The Church Excommunicated Luther

As Luther continued to attack the Church's authority, a split between Luther and the Church became unavoidable. Sales of indulgences had already declined, and Pope Leo X feared there would be a further loss in funds. In 1520, he issued a **papal bull**, or decree, against Luther. The pope ordered Luther to **recant**—to take back what he said—or face excommunication. Determined to resist, Luther publicly burned the papal bull in a bonfire set by cheering university students. The pope then declared Luther a heretic and excommunicated him.

After this event, Luther was summoned before a meeting of the Diet, the assembly of the Holy Roman Empire, which was meeting at Worms (VOHRMZ) in 1521. The pope had excommunicated him from the Church. The Diet, headed by the new emperor, Charles V, now would decide whether he was a political outlaw as well.

The Diet's speakers asked Luther if he would recant, but he again responded that he could not act against his own conscience. He declared: "I cannot . . . go against my conscience. Here I stand. I cannot do otherwise. God help me." From Luther's answers, it became evident that he could not stay within the Church. The Diet declared him an outlaw. This meant that his books were to be burned and he was not entitled to protection by the princes. Even so, many princes continued to shelter and protect him.

357

Justification by Faith

Martin Luther criticized the Roman Catholic church for overemphasizing the importance of what people did and underemphasizing the value of what they believed. In the following passage from *A Treatise on Christian Liberty,* Luther states his views on how Christians are justified in going to heaven after they die.

❝What can it profit the soul if the body fare well, be free and active, eat, drink, and do as it pleases? For in these things even the most godless slaves of all the vices [sins] fare well. On the other hand, how will ill health or imprisonment or hunger or thirst or any other external misfortune hurt the soul? With these things even the most godly men are afflicted [suffer], and those [men] because of a clear conscience are most free. None of these things touch either the liberty or the bondage of the soul. The soul receives no benefit if the body is adorned [dressed] with the sacred robes of the priesthood, or dwells in sacred places, or is occupied with sacred duties, or prays, fasts. . . . The Word of God cannot be received and cherished by any works whatever, but only by faith. Hence it is clear that, as the soul needs only the Word for its life and righteousness, so it is justified by faith alone and not by any works. . . . Wherefore it ought to be the first concern of every Christian to lay aside all trust in works, and more and more to strengthen faith alone.❞

1. How does Luther believe Christians become justified in going to heaven?
2. Explain what Luther means by "works."

Luther's Followers Began a New Church

Gradually, a new worship service, following Luther's ideas (and often using hymns he wrote), developed. Of the traditional sacraments, Luther's followers practiced only baptism, communion, and penance. Luther also eliminated the leadership structure of the Roman Catholic church from his new church and allowed clergy to marry.

Luther translated the New Testament into German and later wrote a worship service in German. By doing so, he helped to develop German, rather than Latin, as a written language. Luther was successful where other reformers failed because his views were timely. Princes and ordinary people alike were ready to establish their freedom from Rome.

Luther also was violently opposed to Jews and to any Christians who did not interpret the Bible as he did. His opposition, however, did not prevent the growth of other Protestant faiths. Lutheranism was the name given to the Protestant faith founded by Martin Luther. It spread from the German states to the Scandinavian countries and to some parts of central Europe.

In 1546, shortly after Luther's death, war broke out in the German states between the German Protestant princes, on the one hand, and Emperor Charles V and his Roman Catholic supporters on the other. The war ended in 1555 with the Peace of Augsburg, which declared that the religion of the prince would be the religion of the people in his state. Although the peace treaty did not take into account the wishes of the people, it did recognize the idea that different religious beliefs were possible. Most of the northern German states became Protestant while the southern states stayed Catholic.

John Calvin Established Another Protestant Church

Just as Germany became the birthplace of Lutheranism, so did Switzerland become the birthplace of Calvinism, the second major new church of the Reformation. The Swiss people, like the Germans, were unhappy with many practices of the Roman Catholic church and were ready to hear some new ideas about their religion.

Ulrich Zwingli (ZWIHN glee) of the Swiss city of Zurich was the first to seek reform. Zwingli was eager to free Zurich and other Swiss cities from the control of the Roman Catholic church. He knew the teachings of Luther but did not agree with all of them. In 1519, he began his own movement for reform. When war broke out in 1531 between the Catholic Swiss cantons (Swiss states) and the Protestant city of Zurich, Zwingli was killed in battle. A few years later, however, another Swiss city became a center for Protestant reform under the powerful leadership of John Calvin.

Calvin, a French theology student, went to Switzerland in 1534 to avoid being persecuted for his Protestant beliefs. Moving to Geneva, he made the city a model of his teachings and practices. Calvin made his views known in a famous work, *Institutes of the Christian Religion,* which was published in 1536. It is one of the great books of the Protestant faith. Calvin and his followers believed that only the people whom God had chosen would be saved. Neither good works nor faith could change God's plans. Calvinists were taught that they must lead God-fearing lives since they could not know whether they were saved or doomed.

Calvin's ideas appealed to many people. He departed even further from traditional Catholic doctrine than did Luther. Calvin rejected the ceremonies and ritual of the Catholic church entirely. He believed that church buildings should be without decorations to permit direct communication between the worshippers and God. For 23 years, Calvin ruled Geneva. It became a **theocracy** (thee OCK rah see), a government shaped by religion.

Under Calvin, Geneva became a city where merriment and pleasure were viewed as sinful. Calvin and his followers frowned on luxury, idleness, games, and dancing. They watched and supervised people's behavior. No one really knew who was assured of salvation. Therefore, it was only wise to behave as if one was of "the elect of God."

▲ **Illustrating History** *John Calvin molded Geneva according to his Protestant beliefs.*

Everyone in Geneva was expected to work hard because the "devil waits for idle hands."

Despite these stern ideas, Calvin's teachings spread to other countries. In France, the followers of Calvin were called Huguenots (HYOO guh nots) and in England they were called Puritans. A Scottish reformer, John Knox, who studied in Geneva, made Calvin's ideas the basis for the Presbyterian church in Scotland. Other churches that followed the practice of Calvinism were founded in Hungary, Bohemia, Netherlands, and elsewhere.

England Broke with Rome

In England, too, a movement against the Catholic church had begun. The English no longer wanted the pope to interfere in national affairs, nor did they want to pay church taxes. They also disliked foreigners in

England's church offices. In the 1300s, John Wycliffe had attacked the wealth and power of the clergy. Thomas More and Erasmus had also urged reform. Lutheranism spread to England via merchants, wandering scholars, and literature.

Thus, when Henry VIII began to rebel against the pope, he had the support of the people. Henry had a number of reasons for rebelling against the Catholic church. No male heir to the throne had been born to Henry and his Spanish queen, Catherine of Aragon. In hopes of an heir, Henry asked the pope to end his marriage so that he could marry the younger Anne Boleyn (BOOHL ihn). Catherine bitterly opposed the idea and called for help from her nephew, the Holy Roman Emperor Charles V. Not wanting to offend the emperor, the pope refused Henry's request.

Despite the pope's opposition, Henry was determined to marry Anne Boleyn, and the English Parliament was willing to support his break with Rome. The vast lands belonging to the Roman Catholic church would then come under government control, and the influence of the pope would be lessened in England. In 1534, Parliament passed the Act of Supremacy, which established the Church of England with Henry, not the pope, as its head.

The Church of England, called the Anglican church, differed little from the Roman Catholic church in doctrine. It did not, however, acknowledge the pope as its leader. Opposition to the newly established Church of England from those who preferred the Catholic church continued throughout Henry's reign. However, by the reign of his daughter, Elizabeth I, the Anglican church was firmly established.

The Catholic Church Made Its Own Reforms

Wise Catholic church leaders now realized that the time had come for the Roman Catholic church to take the reform movement into its own hands. They began what is known as the Catholic Reformation, or Counter-Reformation. Many efforts were made in Spain, Italy, and Rome to reform the Catholic church. The Council of Trent, which began to meet in Italy in 1545, made a number of important reforms that strengthened the Catholic church and helped prevent further losses to Protestantism. The council met over a period of 18 years during which it restated the main teachings of the Catholic church, issued a new edition of the Bible, and improved the way that priests were trained. A powerful missionary order, the Society of Jesus, or Jesuits (JEHZ yoo wihtz), was established to improve Catholic education and win converts in far-off places of the world.

Because of the Counter-Reformation, the Catholic church changed some of its practices. The worst abuses, such as the sale of indulgences, were abolished. The Inquisition (in kwih ZISH un), a special court that had been established in the thirteenth century to try and to punish heretics, was strengthened. In many Catholic countries, people's fear of the Inquisition was used to discourage the growth of Protestantism.

3 Reforms Changed Thought and Culture

As you read, look for answers to these questions:

◆ Did the Reformation bring freedom of religion to Europe?
◆ How did religious differences lead to the Thirty Years' War?
◆ What is the "Protestant ethic"?
◆ How did the Reformation affect business and labor?

Key Terms: religious toleration (defined on p. 362)

In the fifteenth century, maps of the world often showed vast, unknown spaces that carried warning labels of "Here be dragons." When Luther was born, the belief in dragons and other demons was still real. The fear of hell dominated the lives of ordinary men and women in Europe. Superstition, though frowned upon by the Roman Catholic church, was widespread. People feared the "wrath of God," which they thought was displayed in thunder and lightning, in plagues and disease, and in other dreadful events. It was an angry God that ruled the world, people thought. To satisfy God, the devout had to flog themselves or starve themselves to make up for their sins. Children had to be severely punished to prevent them from sinning unknowingly. Heretics were cruelly burned at the stake.

In this setting, the Reformation brought about widespread changes, not only in religious thought, but also in politics, society, and economics. Along with the Renaissance, the Reformation helped to change the continent of Europe from a medieval society to a modern one.

The Reformation Changed Religious Ideas

The influence of religion remained strong even after the Reformation. However, people began to believe more in themselves and view the world with greater optimism. Instead of accepting a negative view of human nature and the world, they began to believe more strongly in their ability to accomplish good things with God's help. This change in religious attitudes, combined with the humanism of the Renaissance, led to a new age of achievement.

By the close of the sixteenth century, the Reformation was nearly over. Subsequently, Christendom was officially divided into the Protestant and Roman Catholic religions. Nearly half of Europe—the northern half—had become Protestant. Most of the German states and Switzerland, Norway, Sweden, Denmark, the Netherlands, England, Wales, and Scotland were no longer Catholic countries. (See the map on page 362.) Although there were many branches of

▼ **Chart Skill** *What events may have caused Martin Luther to be excommunicated?*

Major Events of the Reformation

Germany:

1517	Martin Luther nails his 95 Theses to the door of Wittenberg Church
1520	Pope Leo X issues papal bull against Martin Luther
1521	Martin Luther excommunicated and establishes own church

England:

1521	Henry VIII attacks Luther
1533	Henry VIII appoints his own Archbishop of Canterbury Archbishop of Canterbury dissolves first marriage of Henry VIII
1534	Act of Supremacy makes Henry VIII head of the Anglican church

Switzerland:

1536	Calvin publishes *Institutes of the Christian Religion*

Italy:

1545	Council of Trent begins

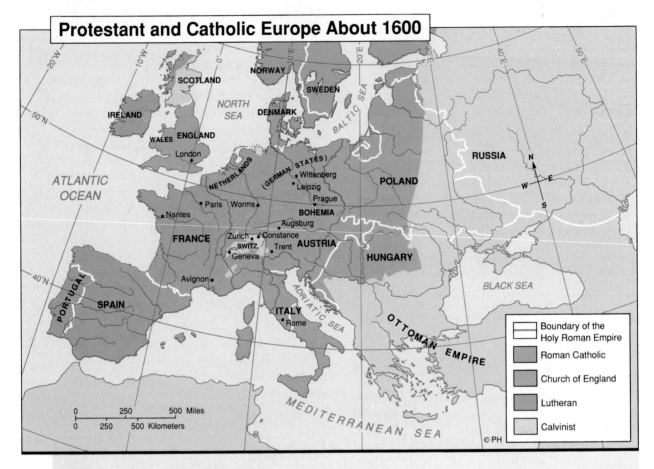

Protestant and Catholic Europe About 1600

SCOTLAND
NORWAY
SWEDEN
IRELAND
NORTH SEA
DENMARK
BALTIC SEA
WALES ENGLAND
• London
ATLANTIC OCEAN
NETHERLANDS
(GERMAN STATES)
• Wittenberg
• Leipzig
• Prague
RUSSIA
POLAND
• Paris Worms•
BOHEMIA
• Nantes
• Augsburg
FRANCE
Zurich • Constance
SWITZ. • Trent AUSTRIA
• Geneva
HUNGARY
• Avignon
BLACK SEA
PORTUGAL
SPAIN
ITALY
• Rome
ADRIATIC SEA
OTTOMAN EMPIRE
MEDITERRANEAN SEA

0   250   500 Miles
0   250   500 Kilometers

Legend:
- Boundary of the Holy Roman Empire
- Roman Catholic
- Church of England
- Lutheran
- Calvinist

© PH

Focus on Geography

Regions   Throughout Europe, there were always some people who practiced religions other than what was common to a region. Many Protestants lived in France; many Catholics lived in England. Where was Protestantism stronger, in Leipzig or in Prague?

Protestantism, they all shared common disagreements with Catholicism. For Protestants, (1) the authority of the Bible replaced the authority of the pope and other clergy; (2) the monastic system, belief in purgatory, the worship of saints and the sale of indulgences, as well as most of the sacraments were not valid; and (3) their churches became more democratic than the Roman Catholic church since most Protestant leaders did not encourage a sharp separation between the minister and the congregation. The congregation, in some churches, made up the governing body.

The Reformation Unleashed Religious Wars

Even with the Reformation, there was little **religious toleration,** or acceptance of the fact that different religions could have different beliefs. Luther represented this lack of religious toleration well with the words: "He who does not receive my doctrine cannot be saved."

Each new religion sought to enlist the power of the state or nation to enforce its religious beliefs, to persecute those who disagreed, and to spread a particular faith to other peoples in Europe and throughout the world. The result was a long series of bitter religious wars that lasted until the middle of the seventeenth century. There were political as well as religious reasons for these wars. They began, however, mostly because Protestants and Catholics believed not only that they had the only true faith but also that they had a duty to spread the truth as they understood it.

The Huguenots. While France's rulers remained Catholic, many noble and wealthy middle-class French families became Huguenots, or French Protestants. In 1562, their rivalries led to bloody civil war that went on for some 30 years. One dramatic incident of the war came in August 1572, when prominent Huguenots attending the wedding of their leader, Henry of Navarre, were ambushed and killed by mobs of Parisians. In the riots that followed throughout France, thousands more were killed. The event became known as the St. Bartholomew's Day Massacre.

Henry of Navarre, although Protestant, was also heir to the French throne. In order to unite the nation when he became king in 1589, Henry became a Roman Catholic. In an unusual move, Henry issued the Edict of Nantes in 1598, which ordered religious toleration in France and gave the Huguenots their full civil rights. This policy was unusual because it officially allowed two forms of Christianity in one country.

The Thirty Years' War. A few years later, the religious war known as the Thirty Years' War tore Germany apart. The war started in 1618 in Bohemia, where the martyred John Huss was still remembered. Czech and German Protestants rebelled against their rulers, the Catholic Hapsburgs, and sought the right to establish their own churches.

▌DAILY LIFE▐

The Unsafe Road

Leaving home wasn't very safe in the sixteenth century. "None goeth unarmed in public," wrote one man. "Each hath his sword by his side for any chance emergency." Travelers like those shown at right were in constant danger from roving gangs of bandits. Made up of unemployed soldiers and peasants who had been forced off their land, these gangs would rob and sometimes kill travelers they met.

Roads were thick with mud and led to crowded, filthy inns. Life was so rough for travelers in general that the English word "travel" was originally the same as "travail," or hard labor.

1. Why was travel dangerous in the sixteenth century?
2. Why did Europeans think of travel as hard labor?

Eventually, most nations of Europe became involved in the conflict for political, as well as religious, reasons. The first round of the war was won by the Catholics. Led by the king of Denmark, the Protestants returned to battle and were again defeated. In 1630, the Protestants, now led by King Gustavus Adolphus of Sweden, won important victories. The Swedish king was a brilliant general who was known as the "Lion of the North." His death in battle took the joy out of their victory, but the Protestant side was strengthened. It gained even more when Catholic France, under the leadership of Cardinal Richelieu (RIHSH uh loo), joined them. As the chief minister of France, Richelieu decided to back the Protestant side in order to strengthen the power of his king and country. His decision showed the war had shifted from religion to politics, for France hoped to replace the Hapsburgs as the greatest power in Europe. With France's help, the Protestants won.

In 1648, the Thirty Years' War ended with the Peace of Westphalia. According to the terms of the peace treaty, German princes could decide whether or not the people in their states would be Catholic, Lutheran, or Calvinist. Switzerland and the Netherlands were assured of their independence. Germany remained divided and would take almost 200 years to recover from the war.

Protestantism Changed Ideas About Work and Business

Both Luther and Calvin glorified the dignity of work. The growth of Protestant faiths encouraged the idea of individualism and indirectly encouraged competition in the marketplace. Unlike Catholics, Protestants no longer frowned on profit or lending money at interest. Since worldly success was considered a sign of God's favor, competition flourished. Individuals were encouraged to provide new goods and services through hard work.

On the other hand, this system allowed workers to be driven mercilessly. Women and children were often forced to labor for long hours for low pay. The many holy days that the Catholic church observed, often with feasts and celebrations, were dropped. In some Calvinist churches, even Christmas was abandoned as a holiday. While Sunday was retained as the Sabbath day and devoted to church-going, for most workers, the work week was long and exhausting.

The Protestant Reformation did not directly give birth to what we today know as capitalism. The beginnings of capitalistic ideas occurred in the Middle Ages and would develop further in the Age of Discovery. Nevertheless, what has been called the "Protestant ethic" of hard work, little extravagance, and careful saving did begin with the stern Protestant reformers of the sixteenth century. In this way, the Protestant Reformation did encourage the underlying ideas of capitalism.

SECTION 3 REVIEW

Knowing Key Terms, People, and Places
1. Define: **a.** religious toleration
2. Identify: **a.** Huguenots **b.** Henry of Navarre **c.** St. Bartholomew's Day Massacre **d.** Edict of Nantes **e.** Thirty Years' War

Focus on Geography
3. In general, how was Europe geographically divided between Catholic lands and Protestant lands?

Reviewing Main Ideas
4. What were the three common disagreements between the Protestant churches and the Roman Catholic church?
5. What were the terms of the Peace of Westphalia?
6. How did the "Protestant ethic" help the development of capitalism?

Critical Thinking
Demonstrating Reasoned Judgment
7. Think of arguments on both sides of this statement: The Reformation could not have failed.

Reading Line Graphs

A line graph is a useful way to present a large quantity of statistical data easily and clearly. Historians often use line graphs to illustrate evidence of trends or patterns that have developed over time.

Use the following steps to read and interpret the line graph below.

1. **Identify the type of information presented on the graph.** The graph title and the key indicate the meaning of the lines on the graph. Answer the following questions: (a) What period of time does the graph describe? (b) How many different categories are represented in the key? (c) What do the numbers on the vertical axis represent?

2. **Read the data shown on the graph.** Study the graph's axes carefully. Answer the follow-

ing questions: (a) What is the largest population in millions that can be shown on the graph? (b) What year represents the midpoint of the period covered by the graph? (c) What was the approximate population of Spain in 1200? (d) What country or group of countries had the largest population between 1050 and 1500?

3. **Study the data shown in the graph to look for relationships or draw conclusions about a topic.** Use the graph and the information in your textbook to understand population trends in European history. Answer the following questions: (a) In general, how did the population of western Europe change between 1000 and 1500? (b) What might have caused the population decline that took place between about 1350 and 1450?

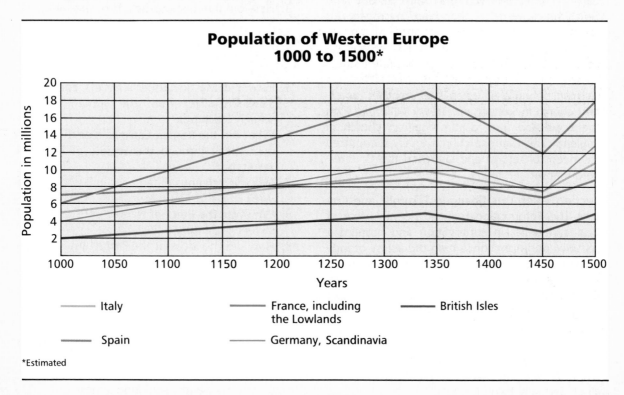

Population of Western Europe 1000 to 1500*

Key:
— Italy
— France, including the Lowlands
— British Isles
— Spain
— Germany, Scandinavia

*Estimated

REVIEW

Section Summaries

Section 1 Problems Within the Church Brought Reform The Protestant Reformation was both a reform movement and a revolution. The sale of indulgences by some members of the clergy, especially Johann Tetzel, was an immediate cause, but various heresies challenged deeper issues of faith. Heretics were condemned by the Roman Catholic church and sometimes persecuted. Kings and popes fought for power, which began to weaken the unity of the Catholic church. The Great Schism was a period during which two popes—one in Rome and one in Avignon—both claimed authority. A council was called to decide the matter in 1414.

Section 2 The Reformation Led to Protestant Churches Two outstanding leaders of the Protestant Reformation were Martin Luther and John Calvin. Luther believed that faith in God and God's grace were all that were necessary for salvation—not indulgences and some of the sacraments of the Catholic church. Luther was excommunicated, but his followers founded a new church, and Luther translated the Bible into German. John Calvin established another Protestant church in Switzerland. Henry VIII broke with the pope and formed the Anglican church in England. The Catholic church finally recognized the need for reform and launched the Counter-Reformation.

Section 3 Reforms Changed Thought and Culture The Reformation reduced people's fear of God and belief in superstition and brought a sense of optimism concerning the ability of individuals to achieve great things. Protestants respected hard work and success in business ventures. Therefore, Protestant ideas encouraged the growth of capitalism. The Reformation also affected politics, unleashing various religious wars. The Thirty Years' War was fought between German princes, who wanted to set up their own churches, and the Hapsburg rulers, who wanted all of Germany to be Catholic.

Key Facts

1. Use each vocabulary word in a sentence.
   - **a.** sacrament
   - **b.** indulgence
   - **c.** theses
   - **d.** papal bull
   - **e.** recant
   - **f.** theocracy
   - **g.** religious toleration
2. Identify and briefly explain the importance of the following names, places, or events.
   - **a.** John Wycliffe
   - **b.** John Huss
   - **c.** Great Schism
   - **d.** Johann Tetzel
   - **e.** Martin Luther
   - **f.** Ninety-Five Theses
   - **g.** Anglican church
   - **h.** Thirty Years' War

Main Ideas

1. What is the origin of the term "Protestant Reformation"?
2. What was the most immediate cause of the Protestant Reformation?
3. How did the religious beliefs of the Albigensians differ from the beliefs of the Roman Catholic church?
4. Name several factors that weakened the unity of the Roman Catholic church.
5. How did Martin Luther's beliefs concerning salvation differ from the Roman Catholic church teachings?
6. What did the Roman Catholic church hope to accomplish through the Society of Jesus, or Jesuits?
7. Why did religious differences in Europe end in war?
8. Why was the Edict of Nantes unusual for the sixteenth century?
9. How did the ideas of the Protestant Reformation promote capitalism?

Developing Skill in Reading History

Identify the information that you would expect to find under the following headings.
1. Dissenting Ideas Challenged the Church
   - **a.** Church leaders sold indulgences.

   b. Waldensians believed that the Bible alone was the rule of life.

   c. People in the Middle Ages feared God's wrath.

2. John Calvin Established Another Protestant Church

   a. The Protestant Reformation began as an attack on the evils of the Catholic church.

   b. Calvin rejected the symbols and ceremonies of the Catholic church.

   c. Luther practiced religious intolerance.

3. The Catholic Church Made Its Own Reforms

   a. The Council of Trent met to reform and strengthen the Catholic church.

   b. The growth of Protestant faiths meant that they would have to compete for survival.

   c. Martin Luther questioned the teachings of the Catholic church.

Using Social Studies Skills

1. Using Visual Evidence Study the woodcut from the Reformation below, which shows members of a Protestant sect holding a religious service. Why do you think these people might have chosen a boat as a place to worship? What does the art reveal about their commitment to their faith?

2. Making Connections How could the growth of the printing press have contributed to the Protestant Reformation?

Critical Thinking

1. Identifying Central Issues Although a variety of theologians presented their views on religious doctrine, what beliefs did all the Protestant sects hold in common?

2. Determining Relevance Luther's message came at a time when many people were ready to cut their ties with the Roman Catholic church. How important to you think timing was to the overall success of the Protestant Reformation?

3. Checking Consistency The Protestant Reformation challenged the Catholic church's authority to interpret Christian teachings. At the same time, this movement promoted its own brand of religious intolerance. How could this contradiction be explained?

Focus on Writing

Organizing an Essay

After determining what a particular essay question is asking you to do, your next step is to gather information and plan how you will organize it in your essay.

Practice: Select one of the essay questions listed below.

1. How did the reasons for Henry VIII's break with the Catholic church differ from those of Calvin and Luther?

2. Why was Luther saved from death while Huss was not?

3. What were the significant results of the Protestant Reformation?

Now follow these steps to organize your essay:

a. Brainstorm to gather a list of ideas that would help to answer the question.

b. Identify the four most important points in your list.

c. Determine the order in which you would discuss these points and explain why.

The Age of Discovery

(1450–1700)

1 **Many Factors Fostered an Age of Discovery**

2 **Portugal and Spain Led in Exploration**

3 **Other Nations Established Empires**

4 **The Age of Discovery Brought Many Changes**

I n many ways, horizons broadened as the Reformation spread throughout Europe. In addition to changing their views about religion, people began to look beyond the shores of their continent. Led by Portugal and Spain, European explorers set out across the oceans in search of new lands. Fifteenth and sixteenth-century explorers endured terrible conditions in order to push back the limits of the known world.

Except for officers, everyone aboard ship lived on the open deck. For those who sailed south, the intense tropical heat caused food to rot within a few days. Lice and maggots swarmed over the ship's interior. Even a strong stomach could be unsettled by the filth of life at sea, as well as by the ship's constant pitching and rolling.

Diets at sea were wretchedly poor. Usually, the sailors ate nothing but dried meat, as tough as shoe leather, and flat bread crawling with bugs. Any fresh food quickly vanished. Sailors drank wine almost constantly to relieve the boredom of life at sea. Alcohol also helped to deaden the pain of disease. As you read this chapter, you will learn why so many explorers risked their lives to make dangerous voyages to new lands. You will also learn how the Age of Discovery changed the way people saw the world.

▲ **Illustrating History** *This instrument, the astrolabe, was used to calculate the exact latitude of one's ship.*

1450	1500	1550	1600	1650

1488 Dias sails around the Cape of Good Hope

1492 Columbus lands in America

1521 Cortes conquers Aztecs

1534 Cartier discovers the St. Lawrence River

1535 Pizarro defeats the Incas

1607 England settles Jamestown, Virginia

▲ **Illustrating History** *Portuguese sailing ships were able to survive the rough seas and high winds of ocean travel.*

1 Many Factors Fostered an Age of Discovery

As you read, look for answers to these questions:

◆ How did most Europeans see the world in the fifteenth century?
◆ What did explorers expect to find on their voyages?
◆ How did "glory, gold, and God" motivate the explorers?

Key Terms: interdependent (defined on p. 369), maritime (p. 371), scurvy (p. 371)

Today, with satellites, supersonic flight, and worldwide telephone service, many people think of the world as "small." What is more, we recognize that continents and countries are **interdependent.** In other words, continents and countries need each other for trade, protection, and natural resources. During the Middle Ages, however, ideas such as these would have sounded strange. The world that the average person knew was seldom larger than the village in which he or she was born. Except for traveling traders, news from the outside world rarely came to the community. To travel to a distant town was, for the ordinary man or woman, rare. For the most part, each community tried to be self-sufficient, providing at least the food, clothing, and shelter people needed to survive.

Although Europe, Africa, and Asia had some contact with each other through trade, these contacts meant little to the average European person. The continents of North and South America were, at this time, worlds of their own, with their own unique cultures and civilizations. Their inhabitants had little or no contact with people of other

369

continents. This situation would change beginning about 1450 during a time that is now known as the Age of Discovery.

The Age of Discovery is when Europeans developed a greater awareness of the world outside Europe. It sprang in part from the new spirit and curiosity of the Renaissance and in part from other factors that will be discussed in the following sections.

Explorers Risked Their Lives for Glory, Gold, and God

The Age of Discovery, which began in the fifteenth century, may be thought of as a time of the systematic discovery of new lands as well as new routes and new ways to reach known lands more easily. Although the motives of any individual or nation are difficult to untangle, the motives of the European explorers often are summed up as "glory, gold, and God."

Glory. The astronauts who first landed on the moon in 1969 earned lasting fame and glory. In much the same way, the explorers who ventured out in search of India or sailed around Africa or stumbled upon the New World did so for the sheer joy of being the first to find and conquer new lands. In doing so, they also achieved lasting fame and glory.

They did not win their glory easily. Some explorers never returned from their search. All knew they were taking risks. They had to learn to deal with winds that might send their ships in directions they preferred not to go. The seas often could be violent, and waves and icebergs could destroy even the best-built vessel.

Moreover, the explorers of the fifteenth and sixteenth centuries did not know what they might find in lands beyond the seas. In fact, the first travelers did not know if they would find any land at all. Although intelligent and educated Europeans believed the world was round, that idea had not been proven through experience. Many a sailor who risked his life in a frail craft must have wondered whether or not his ship would fall off the edge of a saucer-shaped world.

Gold. Simple greed may have driven many of the explorers to risk their lives. The search for gold or wealth was a powerful magnet that drew people of all nations. For the most part, however, the voyages during the Age of Discovery were sponsored by countries that needed metal, spices, and other forms of wealth. Many Europeans wanted to find a new route to Asia to acquire these goods and avoid paying the fees of the Italian merchants. Italy had almost complete control of the Mediterranean ports before the Age of Discovery. Gold and silver were also needed for the growing economies that were now based on money. Neither the gold mines of Ireland nor the silver mines of Germany could supply all the gold and silver needed to coin money.

In an age in which there was no refrigeration, spices were not luxury goods but necessities. Since certain foods, such as meats, spoiled when they were not kept cold, people needed spices to preserve food they ate. The spices of Asia, as well as its gold and silver, were important factors in luring seafarers to risk hazardous journeys on uncharted seas.

God. Finally, but no less important, many Europeans believed that God required them to convert the non–Christians they encountered on their voyages to Christianity. Columbus, for example, was aware that if the Spanish monarchs were to support voyages of exploration, he would have to produce spices and precious metals. Nevertheless, he spoke from the heart when he wrote to the king of Spain, "What I conceive to be the principal wish of our most serene King . . . [is] the conversion of these people to the holy faith of Christ."

Better Ships Reduced the Dangers of Ocean Voyages

By the fifteenth century, it had become safer for ships to travel out of sight of land. The magnetic compass had been available to European sailors as a navigation aid on the open seas for some time. In fact, navigators now had an instrument that could help them pinpoint latitude. In addition, ships were built better and could withstand heavy seas and high winds. Europeans first used the lateen sail about this time, making it possible for their stronger ships to sail against the wind. Finally, among navigators, there was a greater confidence that the world was round and that there was little danger of falling off the edge.

Consequently, European sailing vessels of the fifteenth century could go almost everywhere and still find their way home. Moreover, European ships could be armed with cannons to defend themselves or to attack other vessels.

In addition to better ships, many European nations had good sailors. Over time, a **maritime,** or sea-going, tradition had grown up in Europe. Even so, the life of a sailor was a dangerous one. One estimate suggests that during the Age of Discovery, a sailor had a 50-50 chance of surviving his adventures.

Most of the deaths did not come from mishaps at sea but from illness brought by poor eating, especially a lack of fresh fruits and vegetables. Many died of **scurvy,** a disease caused by a lack of vitamin C. According to the detailed account of one sick sailor: "It rotted all my gums which gave out a black and putrid blood. My thighs and lower legs were black and gangrenous, and I was forced to use my knife each day to cut into my flesh in order to release this black and foul blood. . . . Many of our people died of it everyday." Despite the dangers, a ship's captain usually could find men who were willing to make the journey.

India, China, and the Arab empires were all wealthy countries in the fifteenth century. Why, then, did they not explore and "discover" Europe? For one reason, they did not believe there was anything on that continent that they wanted. Their own cultures seemed to them to be far superior, and they already possessed great riches. Furthermore, by the fifteenth century, Asians had little if any interest in converting Christians to other faiths. As a result, they had none of the motivations to explore other continents that the Europeans had.

▲ **Illustrating History** *This painting by Jan Vermeer,* The Geographer, *captures the spirit of the Age of Discovery.*

SECTION 1 REVIEW

Knowing Key Terms, People, and Places
1. Define: **a.** interdependent **b.** maritime **c.** scurvy

Focus on Geography
2. Why do you think that Europe developed a maritime tradition?

Reviewing Main Ideas
3. How did the Age of Discovery change ordinary European people's view of the world around them?
4. How were spices necessary in everyday life in the fifteenth century?
5. Explain what is meant by "glory, gold, and God."

Critical Thinking
Making Comparisons
6. How is twentieth-century space travel like and unlike the voyages of discovery in the fifteenth and sixteenth centuries?

2 Portugal and Spain Led in Exploration

As you read, look for answers to these questions:

◆ How did the voyages of Columbus encourage future exploration?
◆ How did the Spanish conquer lands in the Americas?
◆ How were colonies in Spanish America organized?

Key Terms: caravel (defined on p. 373), circumnavigate (p. 376), conquistador (p. 377), viceroy (p. 379)

Europe's expansion overseas began about the middle of the fifteenth century. In an incredibly short period of time, only about 250 years, curious European explorers had discovered almost every region of the earth. (See the map on pages 374–375.) Some parts, such as the interiors of Africa and Australia, remained to be explored. Even today, some areas are still largely unexplored. But, by 1700, as the Age of Discovery was ending, the size, shape and nature of the world were known. It was discovered, for example, that the world was not one great land area, but rather one great ocean. All the oceans and seas flowed into one another.

The Age of Discovery proved that with patience, courage, money, and technological skill, people could investigate any part of the world. During the fifteenth century, Portugal and Spain became the leaders in reaching new lands and in finding new routes to old lands.

Columbus Was a Hero of the Age of Discovery

Although Italian by birth, Christopher Columbus gained fame as an explorer while serving the government of Spain. As a youth, Columbus helped in his father's tavern, serving food and wine to sailors in the Italian port city of Genoa. He heard their tall tales about reaching the Barbary Coast of northern Africa and sailing to the fantastic, mythical, island of Atlantis. These stories stirred the imagination of Columbus, and he longed to see the world for himself. Probably he went to sea while he was still a teenager.

In 1476, Columbus was shipwrecked off the coast of Portugal. He swam ashore and settled there. A few years later, he fell in love with a young, wealthy woman from a prominent Portuguese family. Columbus's father-in-law knew the sea well. Like many educated people at the time, he believed that the world was round, not flat. In his library, he had many books that seemed to prove this theory, although the calculations of the earth's size were much too small. From these books and from talks with mapmakers and adventurous sailors, Columbus began to believe that one could reach the rich lands of Asia by sailing west.

To carry out his dream of finding a new route to the Indies, Columbus needed sailors, money, and ships. For six years, he sought help from influential friends and the rulers of Portugal and Spain. He may even have gone to England and France. His plans were costly, however, and he was asking for great personal rewards and profits as well. As a result, he was refused everywhere. Finally, early in 1492, friends at the court of Spain persuaded King Ferdinand and Queen Isabella to sponsor Columbus. Ferdinand and Isabella agreed to pay for a small fleet of three ships.

In October 1492, after sailing westward for more than two months, Columbus landed on an island in the Caribbean Sea between North and South America. Believing this island and those nearby were Japan and the East Indies, he sailed around Jamaica, Cuba, Haiti, and other islands. Today, these islands are called the West Indies.

Columbus eventually made three more voyages to the Caribbean. He established colonies there, but he was a failure as their governor. Columbus died in 1506, still thinking he had reached Asia but frustrated at not finding much of the gold of stories and legends.

▲ **Illustrating History** *Christopher Columbus (see inset) addressed Ferdinand and Isabella at the Spanish royal court in 1492.*

Columbus's Vision Began a New Era

Although Columbus failed to achieve his own dreams, his voyages began a new period in history. In a biography of Columbus entitled *Admiral of the Ocean Sea*, Samuel Eliot Morison, a historian and experienced sailor, actually traced the route Columbus took to the New World. In judging Columbus's role in the Age of Discovery, Morison noted, "He [Columbus] . . . had done more to direct the course of history than any individual since Augustus Caesar."

In 1986, faded documents found in a Spanish archive gave a vivid picture of what it was like to venture over unknown seas in Columbus's times. Although the *Santa Maria* was his flagship on the first voyage, the *Niña* was Columbus's favorite vessel. The *Niña* was a **caravel** (KAHR uh VEL), a small, fast sailing ship. It was about 67 feet long (20.4 meters) with a beam width of 21 feet (6.4 meters). Many pleasure yachts are much larger. The *Niña* made several voyages to the Americas. For different voyages, it was outfitted differently, sometimes with two masts, sometimes with four.

The crew of the *Niña* included farmers, a miner, a priest, an archer skilled with the crossbow, and several convicted murderers. The crew ate on deck in the shade of the square sails. Their food consisted of biscuits, fatback pork, and beans seasoned heavily with garlic. They cooked their meals in large copper kettles over fires kindled with vine shoots and fed with olive wood. Below deck, they stored tons of wheat, casks of wine and olive oil, cheese, vinegar, salt pork, and sardines.

The voyage was perilous, and the sailors grew worried as they sailed further from home. Other explorers who had attempted such voyages had never been seen again. Since the only "engines" were the ship's sails, the winds, or lack of them, were treacherous. Columbus, however, had gauged the direction of the winds correctly, and they pushed his ship steadily westward, away from Spain. In fact, Columbus changed the records to make the nervous crew believe they were closer to home.

Although the magnetic compass told them they were on course, Columbus and his men began to doubt that they would ever

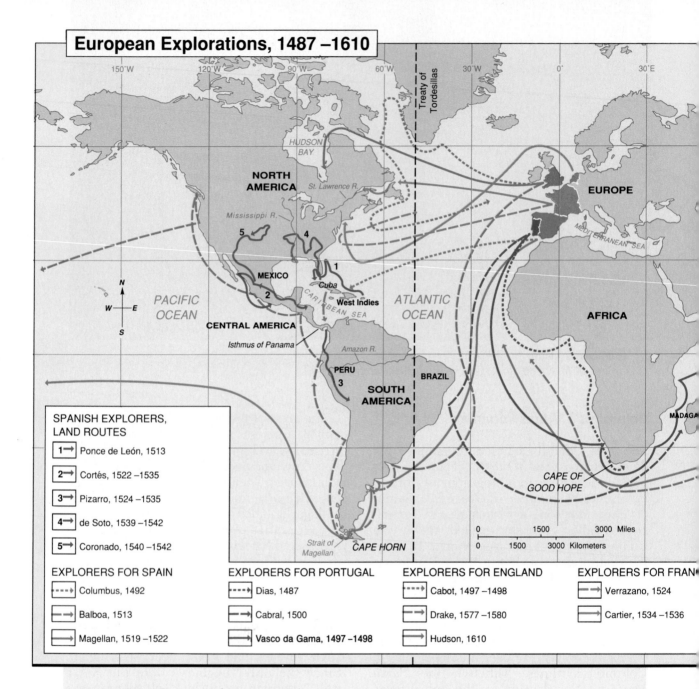

European Explorations, 1487 –1610

150°W 120°W 90°W 60°W Treaty of Tordesillas 30°W 0° 30°E

HUDSON BAY

NORTH AMERICA

St. Lawrence R.

Mississippi R.

EUROPE

MEDITERRANEAN SEA

5

4

N
W — E
S

PACIFIC OCEAN

MEXICO

Cuba

1

West Indies

2

CARIBBEAN SEA

ATLANTIC OCEAN

AFRICA

CENTRAL AMERICA

Isthmus of Panama

Amazon R.

PERU

3

BRAZIL

SOUTH AMERICA

MADAGA

CAPE OF GOOD HOPE

| 0 | 1500 | 3000 Miles |
| 0 | 1500 | 3000 Kilometers |

Strait of Magellan CAPE HORN

SPANISH EXPLORERS, LAND ROUTES

1 →	Ponce de León, 1513
2 →	Cortés, 1522 –1535
3 →	Pizarro, 1524 –1535
4 →	de Soto, 1539 –1542
5 →	Coronado, 1540 –1542

EXPLORERS FOR SPAIN

- Columbus, 1492
- Balboa, 1513
- Magellan, 1519 –1522

EXPLORERS FOR PORTUGAL

- Dias, 1487
- Cabral, 1500
- **Vasco da Gama, 1497 –1498**

EXPLORERS FOR ENGLAND

- Cabot, 1497 –1498
- Drake, 1577 –1580
- Hudson, 1610

EXPLORERS FOR FRAN⦿

- Verrazano, 1524
- Cartier, 1534 –1536

Focus on Geography

1. **Location**   Where did Cortés spend most of his 13 years in the New World?
2. **Movement**   What country sent the most explorers to the New World?
3. **Interaction**   Which explorer sailed the closest to the western coast of Africa? Which two explorers sailed all the way across the Indian Ocean?

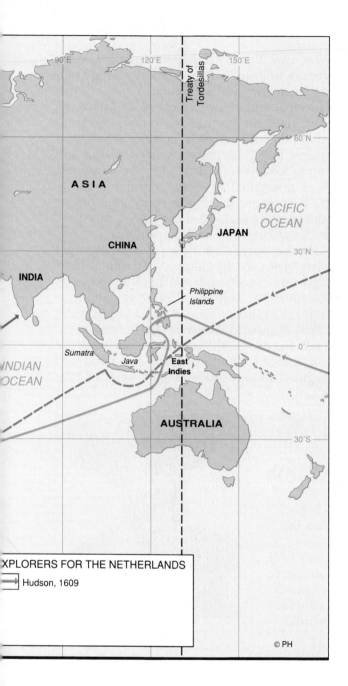

Illustrating History *Portugal's Prince Henry the Navigator encouraged voyages of exploration during the fifteenth century.*

Despite Columbus's achievements, the New World was not named after him. It was named after Amerigo Vespucci (ah may REE goh veh SPOO chee) who, after the voyage of Columbus, probably explored much of the coast of South America and identified it as a new continent that was not attached to Asia. In 1507, a mapmaker honored Vespucci by naming the new continent *America.* Nonetheless, for most people, the hero of the discovery of the Americas remains Christopher Columbus.

Portuguese Sailors Found New Routes to Asia

Columbus's ambitions owed much to the years he lived in Portugal. Early in the fifteenth century, Portugal's Prince Henry the Navigator set up a school to teach navigation, map making, and other skills of seamanship, which allowed Portugal's sailors to be among the first to brave unknown seas. Under Prince Henry's direction, Portuguese ships and sailors explored the west coast of Africa. Portuguese sea captains were the first to find an all-water route from

reach land. Slowly, they began to spot signs of land, including sea birds and leaves in the water. Then, before dawn on October 12, 1492, shouts of "Tierra! Tierra!" ("Land! Land!") told the weary sailors that a lookout on the *Pinta* had spotted land at last. Unlike many before them, Columbus and his men had overcome the perils of fifteenth-century ocean voyages.

Europe to the continent of Asia. Others sailed boldly westward across the Atlantic Ocean.

In 1488, Bartholomeu Dias (DEE ahz), a Portuguese navigator, sailed around the Cape of Good Hope, at the southern tip of Africa. Following this discovery, another Portuguese captain, Vasco da Gama (VASS koh dah GAHM ah), extended the ocean trip around the southern tip of Africa. After making stops in the Muslim states in eastern Africa, he reached India in 1498.

In 1522, the crew of the Spanish ship *Victoria* were the first to **circumnavigate**, or sail completely around, the world. They were the only survivors of the fleet of Ferdinand Magellan (mah JEHL ahn), the Portuguese explorer who crossed the Atlantic and rounded the southern tip of South America. Magellan himself was killed in a battle in the Philippines, but the historic trip revealed that a huge ocean, the Pacific, separated the Americas and Asia.

The Portuguese Built a World Empire

Wherever the Portuguese explorers went, traders followed. These traders set up trading posts in India, China, Japan, South America, and along the coasts of Africa. In each place the Portuguese settled, they traded goods such as guns, cotton fabrics, and knives for gold, silver, spices, silks, and other luxuries. When they encountered local resistance or competition for trade, the Portuguese used their ships' cannons to take over the area. In some places, however, the local rulers welcomed traders.

By the early 1500s, Spain and Portugal were in a race to claim all the lands their explorers discovered and develop overseas colonies. To avoid conflict, they called on Pope Alexander VI to divide the non–Christian world between their two countries. He drew an imaginary line from the North Pole to the South Pole at a point 100 leagues (about 300 miles) west of the

BIOGRAPHY

Vasco da Gama

Vasco da Gama (shown at right) was the brilliant navigator and fearless sea captain who opened the first all-water trade route between Europe and Asia. He was also ruthless and often cruel in fighting for the glory of Portugal.

Da Gama was born in 1469 to wealthy parents. At some point in his early life, he mastered sailing and mathematics. In 1497, the king of Portugal gave da Gama command of four ships to find a sea route to India. The king wanted to break the monopoly of

Arab merchants in the spice trade between Europe and Asia.

Da Gama's journey took almost a year. After his return, Portugal sent more ships to India. Portuguese traders arrived in India only to be killed by Arab merchants. In a spirit of revenge, the king gave da Gama a fleet of 21 ships and sent him back to India in 1502. Da Gama attacked the Arabs without mercy.

In 1524, da Gama was named Portuguese viceroy, or governor, of India and sent back for the third

time. Soon after arriving, however, he became ill and died. He is remembered as a key explorer of the Age of Discovery.

1. What was the purpose of Vasco da Gama's first voyage to India?
2. What was the purpose of his second voyage?

Azores, islands in the Atlantic. The lands to the west of this line were to be Spanish. The lands to the east were to be Portuguese. The settlement did not satisfy the Portuguese king, who threatened war. In 1494, in a separate agreement called the Treaty of Tordesillas, Spain and Portugal moved the imaginary line drawn by the pope. The line they agreed upon was farther west (about 46° west longitude). As a result of their agreement, the Portuguese could claim and keep Brazil, while Spain took the rest of South America. Brazil's language and customs remain Portuguese to this day.

The Spanish Conquered and Colonized the Americas

Spain won its empire in the New World through the brutal military conquests of the **conquistadors** (kon KEES tah dorz), the Spanish conquerors. Wearing shining armor, mounted on horses, and armed with guns, the Spanish soldiers seemed like gods to many of the Indians of Central and South America.

Spain's first colonies were on the Caribbean islands. In 1511, Cuba was settled. Under the able management of Diego Velasquez (vuh LAHS kehs), the colony prospered and became a jumping-off point for further discovery and exploration in the New World. In 1513, Vasco Núñez de Balboa (bal BOH ah) crossed the Isthmus of Panama and reached the Pacific Ocean. During these same years, Ponce de Leon (PAWN thay deh lay OHN), discovered and named the Florida peninsula, where he later tried unsuccessfully to build a colony. In 1517, Francisco de Cordova discovered the Mayan civilization on the Mexican mainland. Two years later, Hernán Cortés (kohr TEZ) made his way to central Mexico, where he found the wealthy Aztec Empire the Spanish had been seeking. In 1565, the Spanish established the city of St. Augustine on the northeast coast of what is now Florida. It is the oldest city in the United States.

Cortés and the Aztecs. Cortés was a conquistador who took Mexico by military force. His soldiers willingly followed him to

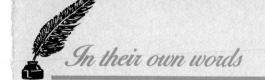

In their own words

Famine on Magellan's Voyage

Antonio Pigafetta kept a diary while sailing with Magellan on the first voyage around the world. Magellan thought that the world was much smaller than it actually is. Hence, he underestimated the width of the Pacific Ocean. In this excerpt, Pigafetta describes the Pacific voyage.

"They sailed out from this strait into the Pacific Sea on the 28th of November in the year 1520, and they were three months and twenty days without eating anything [fresh food], and they ate biscuit, and when there was no more of that they ate the crumbs which were full of maggots [insect larvae] and smelled strongly of [mice and rats]. They drank yellow water, already several days putrid [spoiled]. And they ate some of the hides that were on the largest shroud [rope] to keep it from breaking and that were very much toughened by the sun, rain and winds. And they softened them in the sea for four or five days, and then they put them in a pot over the fire and ate them and also much sawdust. A mouse would bring half a ducat [a gold coin] or a ducat. The gums of some of the men swelled over their upper and lower teeth, so that they could not eat and so died. And nineteen men died from that sickness [beri beri] . . . and twenty-five or thirty were so sick that they could not help with arm or limb. And others (but only a small number) were by the grace of God spared any sickness.**"**

1. How long did the crew go without eating any fresh food?
2. What kinds of things did the men have to eat?

▲ **Illustrating History** *Balboa (left) claimed the Pacific Ocean for Spain; Coronado (center, right) explored the American southwest.*

Mexico, where some met fame and fortune and some met death. With 11 ships, a few horses, and 600 soldiers armed with guns and cannons, Cortés set out from Cuba for Mexico. He landed on the coast of what is now Veracruz. As described in Chapter 12, Mexico was ruled by the Aztecs, who had built a rich but warlike culture. Cortés headed inland toward the Aztec capital, Tenochtitlán (tay NOCH tee TLAHN).

Cortés met large numbers of Indians who were loyal to Montezuma, the Aztec ruler. Some Indians, however, had suffered at the hands of Montezuma and were willing to join with the Spanish against him. When Cortés and his followers first reached the capital, Montezuma thought they were messengers from the gods and gave them rich gifts. This only proved to Cortés that the Aztecs had gold and other treasures. Within two years, the Aztecs were defeated, Monte-

zuma was dead, and Tenochtitlán was burned. Mexico City was built in its place, and Mexico became a colony of Spain.

Pizarro and the Incas. The other great Indian empire also fell to Spanish conquistadors. In 1531, Francisco Pizarro (pih ZAHR oh) discovered the rich Inca Empire in Peru. Their lands were, for a time, the richest in South America. Although Pizarro could neither read nor write, he was both determined and brutal. Upon hearing news of a great people and great wealth, Pizarro tried to get soldiers and ships together to conquer the Incas. Eventually, he received permission and money from Emperor Charles V of Spain and set sail for Peru.

Although Atahualpa (AH tah WALL pah), the trusting Inca king, seemed eager to please Pizarro when he arrived, the Spanish cruelly slaughtered Atahualpa's people and captured the king. To ransom their ruler, the Incas were ordered to fill a room with gold and treasure. Even though the treasure's value has been estimated at 5 million dollars, it was not enough to prevent the murder of the Inca king.

Spanish America. Success made the Spanish bold. They sought more gold and more colonies. Hernando de Soto, for example, left Cuba with a great number of men and horses and a good supply of food. He explored the lands in what is now the southern United States, between Georgia and Oklahoma. He died a disappointed man, for he found no gold. In 1540, Francisco Coronado (KOH roh NAH do) traveled from Mexico to try his luck in what is now the American southwest. With a group larger than de Soto's, he sought the great riches of El Dorado, a legendary city of gold. No matter how far he traveled, however, he never found El Dorado. Although he discovered more than he realized at the time, Coronado died heartbroken.

The Spanish empire in South America was ruled by **viceroys,** governors sent from Spain as agents of the monarch. In all things and in every way, the colonies of Spain existed only for making Spain rich. The once proud and highly advanced Aztec and Inca civilizations were destroyed, and the Indians of the Americas were given a place on the lowest rung of the social ladder. Many were enslaved by the Spanish.

Missionaries tried to teach Christianity to the native peoples. At least one Catholic priest, Bartolomé de Las Casas (lahs KAH sahs), fought for the Indians' rights, and laws were passed in Spain protecting these rights. More often than not, however, these laws were not obeyed by the Spanish conquistadors. Encouraged by its conquest of South America, Spain moved to establish colonies in the rest of the New World. Some of the Spanish, as well as Portuguese, colonies were hundreds of years old by the time the English first established their colonies in North America at Jamestown and Plymouth. The English colonies will be discussed in the next section.

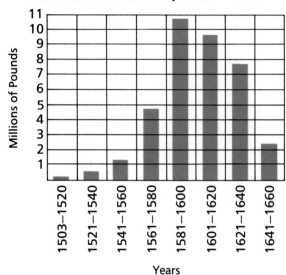

Spanish Silver and Gold From the Americas, 1503–1660

Source: Earle J. Hamilton, *American Treasure and the Price Revolution in Spain, 1501–1650.*

▲ **Chart Skill** *When did the flow of gold and silver into Spain reach its peak?*

SECTION 2 REVIEW

Knowing Key Terms, People, and Places
1. Define: **a.** caravel **b.** circumnavigate **c.** conquistador **d.** viceroy
2. Identify: **a.** Columbus **b.** Henry the Navigator **c.** Dias **d.** da Gama **e.** Magellan

Focus on Geography
3. What new knowledge of geography came from Magellan's voyage?

Reviewing Main Ideas
4. What did Columbus believe he had found in his voyages?
5. How did Spain conquer territory in the New World?

Critical Thinking

Recognizing Bias
6. What do you think was the attitude of the Spanish conquistadors toward the culture of the Indians they conquered in Mexico and Peru?

3 Other Nations Established Empires

As you read, look for answers to these questions:

◆ What nations dominated the easy routes to the New World and Asia?
◆ Why did explorers seek a northwest passage?
◆ What American lands did the Dutch and French claim?
◆ How did the English establish their empire?

Key Terms: northwest passage (defined on p. 380), privateer (p. 381)

In 1527, an English merchant wrote in some dismay, "There is no way [left] to discover. . . . For out of Spain they have discovered all the Indies and seas occidental [western], and out of Portugal all the Indies and seas oriental [eastern]." The merchant's words reflected the disappointment felt by many nations of northern Europe—particularly Holland, England, and France in the early 1500s. Those nations feared that Spain and Portugal had such a head start in discovering and claiming new lands that they could not possibly catch up.

Explorers Sought a Northwest Passage to Asia

The goal of the countries of northern Europe was similiar to that of Spain and Portugal—namely to find an all-water route to Asia. As Portugal and Spain had already laid claim to the southern routes, the countries of northern Europe would have to try to find a way by the far more hazardous northern routes. Some ships tried to go eastward through the icy seas north of Europe, but most searched for a **northwest passage**, a water route from Europe, around or through North America to Asia. The northern countries were not successful in their search for a northwest passage, but in the process of exploring, they stumbled upon vast lands that would become important in the world's history.

John Cabot. In 1497, in the hope of finding the elusive northwest passage to Asia, Henry VII of England sponsored the voyage of John Cabot, an Italian navigator. (Cabot's name was originally Caboto.) As captain of the ship *Matthew,* Cabot left England with every expectation of success.

It is not entirely clear where Cabot landed, but it was probably Nova Scotia in present-day Canada. Although the Vikings, led by Leif Ericson, probably reached this area long before, Cabot's voyage gave England its first important claim to the New World.

Giovanni da Verrazano. Giovanni da Verrazano (VEHR rah TSAH noh), an Italian navigator working for France, also sought an all-water route to China. In his unsuccessful quest, he explored the east coast of North America. In 1524, he led his ship into what is now New York harbor.

Jacques Cartier. Jacques Cartier (kar TYAY), also sailing for France, discovered the St. Lawrence River in 1534 and established France's claims to eastern North America, an area he called New France. French and English claims would later conflict and eventually lead to war.

Henry Hudson. Later explorers continued to search for a northwest route to China. Henry Hudson, an Englishman, first sailed for the Dutch and then the English. He discovered Delaware Bay and explored what is now the Hudson River as far as present-day Albany, New York. In 1610, while exploring the coast of Canada, Hudson entered what is now the Hudson Bay. He thought that he had entered the Pacific and was baffled by the thickening ice.

Trapped by the ice, Hudson had to spend the winter in the bay area of what is now the province of Ontario, Canada. When the ice melted and the ship was free, Hudson announced his intention of exploring further. His crew, hostile and hungry, mutinied. Hudson, his son, and five loyal sailors were lowered into an open boat, towed through the ice floes, and cut loose. He was never heard from again.

The explorers of northern routes never found gold, and they never found a northern route to Asia. They did, however, lay claims to vast lands and opened up trading routes for furs, whale, cod, seal, and walrus tusks.

The Dutch and French Gained Empires on Three Continents

Following explorations by Hudson and others, the Netherlands founded trading colonies in North America. (See the map on pages 382–383.) Dutch possessions included a settlement at New York which they called New Netherland. The Dutch also bought present-day Manhattan Island from the Indians. By 1664, however, the Dutch had been slowly pushed out of the New World by the English.

In Asia, the Dutch East India Company, established in 1602, built up a rich trade. It occupied what came to be called the Dutch East Indies. These islands, which include Java and Sumatra, remained under Dutch control until the early 1940s. In Africa, too, the Dutch began a settlement at Cape Colony, now known as South Africa. Dutch farmers, known as Boers (bohrz), moved to the colony. Their descendants still live in the Republic of South Africa.

The French built a large number of trading posts in what is now Canada and the Mississippi River valley. Furs were the chief source of wealth and one of the chief items of trade for French North America. Today, Montreal, in the province of Quebec, is a thriving French-speaking city.

France later extended its empire to western and central Africa and to the island of Madagascar. While France lost most of its empire in the New World to Britain, its empire in Africa and Asia grew. France held on to these parts of its empire until the middle of the twentieth century.

▲ **Illustrating History** *This engraving shows Cabot off the Canadian coast in 1497.*

England's Empire Grew in America and India

The English were latecomers to the Age of Discovery and made relatively few voyages of exploration. Instead, English sea raiders, or **privateers,** attacked the Spanish treasure ships. The gold and silver that were being taken from colonies in the Americas to Spain went to England instead. Two English sailors, John Hawkins and Sir Francis Drake, became famous for raiding these Spanish ships with the approval of England's Queen Elizabeth I. In 1577, after seizing Spanish treasure off the coast of Peru, Drake took his ship westward across the Pacific and started the second successful round-the-world voyage.

North America. In 1607, the first permanent English settlement in the New World was made at Jamestown in the colony of Virginia. Over the next 50 years, the English would establish 12 more colonies in North

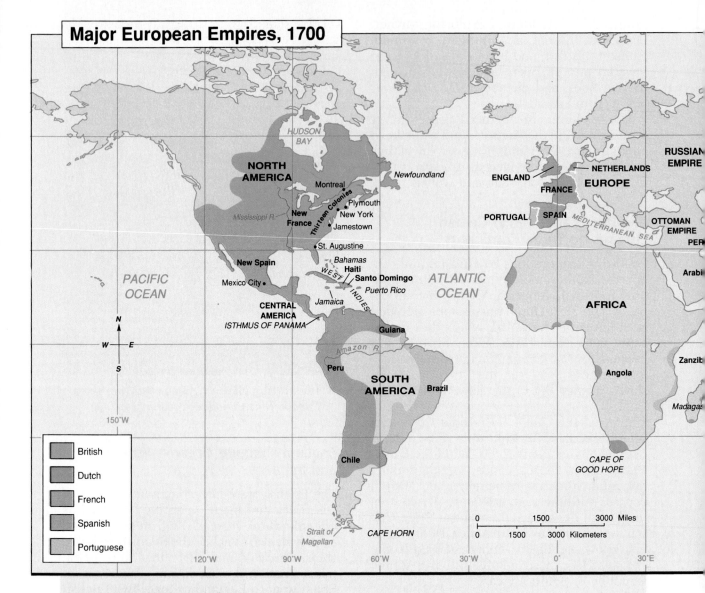

Major European Empires, 1700

HUDSON BAY

NORTH AMERICA

Montreal

Newfoundland

Plymouth

New France

New York

Mississippi R.

Jamestown

Thirteen Colonies

St. Augustine

PACIFIC OCEAN

New Spain

Bahamas

Haiti

WEST

Santo Domingo

Puerto Rico

ATLANTIC OCEAN

Mexico City

Jamaica

INDIES

CENTRAL AMERICA

ISTHMUS OF PANAMA

Guiana

N

W—E

S

Amazon R.

Peru

SOUTH AMERICA

Brazil

150°W

Chile

ENGLAND

NETHERLANDS

FRANCE

EUROPE

PORTUGAL

SPAIN

MEDITERRANEAN SEA

RUSSIAN EMPIRE

OTTOMAN EMPIRE

PER

Arabi

AFRICA

Zanzib

Angola

Madagas

CAPE OF GOOD HOPE

	British
	Dutch
	French
	Spanish
	Portuguese

Strait of Magellan

CAPE HORN

| 0 | | 1500 | | 3000 Miles |
| 0 | 1500 | | 3000 Kilometers | |

120°W   90°W   60°W   30°W   0°   30°E

Focus on Geography

1. **Interaction** Do you think it was easier for Europeans to maintain their empires in the New World or in Asia? Explain.
2. **Regions** What European country had the largest empire with colonies all over the world?

America. The English settlers who came to live in the New World wanted to make a fresh start and have the chance to make a good living. Many wanted to be free from Europe's religious persecution. They brought with them the seeds of democracy, which grew and developed throughout the 13 colonies. The House of Burgesses, for instance, founded in Virginia in the early 1600s, was the first example of representative government in the New World. Other colonies also developed legislative bodies.

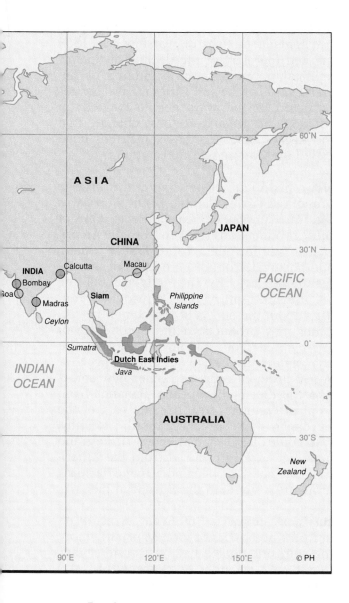

get rich quickly and then enjoy their wealth back home. The French and Spanish settlers were under the direct control of both their government and their church, that is, the Roman Catholic church. The English settlers, however, enjoyed more freedom from government restrictions.

India. In India, the British East India Company gradually pushed out the Portuguese, Dutch, and French who had set up trading posts there. In time, India came almost completely under British rule and remained so until after 1947. By the seventeenth century, the English were well on their way toward the establishment of the largest colonial empire in the world.

Although these early legislatures were controlled by the privileged few, they served as the foundation for our current democratic system of government.

The Spanish, French, and English settlers in North America differed in several ways. English settlers in the New World, whether looking for a good living or seeking religious freedom, came with the desire to establish permanent homes. For the most part, the Spanish and the French came for the riches to be earned by finding gold or by participating in the fur trade. They hoped to

SECTION 3 REVIEW

Knowing Key Terms, People, and Places
1. Define: **a.** northwest passage **b.** privateer
2. Identify: **a.** Cabot **b.** Verrazano **c.** Cartier **d.** St. Lawrence River **e.** Henry Hudson **f.** New Netherland **g.** Cape Colony **h.** Sir Francis Drake

Focus on Geography
3. What parts of North America did Henry Hudson explore?
4. In what parts of the world did the French and Dutch claim colonial territories?

Reviewing Main Ideas
5. How did Spain and Portugal's control over southern ocean routes affect the explorers from northern European countries?
6. How did the English benefit from Spain's colonies in South America?

Critical Thinking
Testing Conclusions
7. The English merchant quoted at the beginning of this section worried that England would never have an empire, yet Britain eventually had the largest empire of all. Do you think that England's late start may actually have helped it obtain its empire? Explain your answer.

4 The Age of Discovery Brought Many Changes

As you read, look for answers to these questions:

◆ How did trade and travel change as a result of the Age of Discovery?
◆ What changes in economic systems resulted from the Age of Discovery?
◆ What problems were caused by the Age of Discovery?

> **Key Terms:** entrepreneur (defined on p. 384), joint-stock company (p. 384), mercantilism (p. 385)

The daring voyages of the Age of Discovery changed forever the way Europeans looked at the rest of the world. It also brought changes in where and how people traveled. For centuries, trade and power had been centered in the Mediterranean Sea. Now the Atlantic Ocean was the main route for commerce. Similarly, explorers of old traveled by foot or on camels or horses to reach remote parts of the world. Marco Polo, for example, had traveled over land most of the way from Venice to China. With the Age of Discovery, the routes of explorers would be over the oceans.

The ability of mariners to sail out of sight of land and to find the way back home was a notable technological advance. Because western Europe conquered the seas, it dominated and unified the world. As you will read in this section, Europeans found that the Age of Discovery brought mainly beneficial results. These gains, however, also brought some problems, especially in other parts of the world.

The Age of Discovery Led to a Revolution in Trade and Commerce

As sea routes shifted from the south to the north, England, France, and the Netherlands became the leading nations in trade. Italy, Spain, and Portugal became less im-

portant. England's naval defeat of the Spanish Armada (a fleet of warships) in 1588 marked the start of the decline of Spain's political power and the beginning of England's rule of the sea. Other major changes occurred in the ways people carried on business. So great were these changes that the Age of Discovery has sometimes been called the Commercial Revolution.

New products. One important change brought about by the Age of Discovery was the introduction of new products. One of these products was tobacco from the Americas. It was introduced into France, Spain, and Portugal around the middle of the sixteenth century. By the early part of the seventeenth century, there already was concern about the effects of tobacco on health. Other new products included coffee from Turkey, tea from China, and cocoa and chocolate from South America. The New World brought sugar and other new spices into the diet of Europeans. Bananas from tropical countries also became part of the European diet, especially for the wealthy, who could afford such luxuries. Turkeys and potatoes were introduced from the Americas, and potatoes became a major farming crop and a staple in the European diet.

Business changes. Overseas projects required a great deal of money, usually more than any one person had. As a result, many merchants became **entrepreneurs** (AHN truh pruh NOORS), people who risked beginning their own businesses to make profits. As entrepreneurs, the merchants had to find new ways of bringing together the savings of many people in order to finance their business dealings. Selling shares of stock was one method of raising money and soon became common practice. The businesses that were formed when people bought shares of stock were called **joint-stock companies**. People could risk their money in a joint-stock company in hopes that the company would bring them a profit. Since they invested only a part of the huge expenses involved, people also risked less if the company failed. On the other hand, if the company succeeded, they could share in profits over a long period of time. The joint-stock company became the chief way in which business dealings in the New World were organized and financed.

Economic changes. Changes in business methods and organization led to the growth of capitalism as the main economic institution of modern times. As described in Chapter 9, capitalism is an economic system based on competition, private property, the investment of money for profit, and freedom from government interference. It is based on pooling of money from many people who invest in commercial activities in order to make a profit. As capitalism grew, a moderately wealthy group of people arose and gradually gained political and economic power. Their power was based on profits made from business rather than from owning land. In European society, the growth of this "middle class" marked a dramatic change. As the wealth of this new class grew,

the people who belonged to it questioned the rights of kings and the hereditary power of the aristocrats.

Another change in economic thinking came with the growth of overseas empires. European monarchs and their advisers believed that colonies existed for the exclusive benefit of the parent countries. The colonies had to do what they were told to do by the parent, or controlling, country. From this view, the theory known as mercantilism (MER kun til izm) developed. In practice, **mercantilism** meant that the people in the colonies were supposed to produce raw materials for the parent country and then provide a market for the products it manufactured from the materials. Since wealth was as important as power, a parent country tried to get as much gold and silver as possible. To do so, it needed to sell its manufactured products to foreign countries. It also needed to discourage its colonies from buying foreign goods. The parent country could do this by taxing the goods

---

┤ DAILY LIFE ├

A New Food for Europe

In the sixteenth century, vegetables from the New World began to appear in Europe. They included corn, tomatoes, and squash, but the most important were potatoes. To poor Europeans especially, potatoes proved a blessing. In the past, their diets had been meager and lacking in nutrition, they had often gone hungry.

Voyagers brought potatoes to Europe from South America around 1530. The new vegetable was quickly recognized as a cheap and filling food. Unlike other crops, potatoes could thrive in poor soil. Growing them did not require expensive animals or equipment. And, they went a long way: one plant alone could provide a meal for a large family. Since then, the potato has been one of Europe's main food crops.

1. Why were potatoes easy to grow?
2. Why were potatoes inexpensive to grow?

---

coming into the
tries or even by
trade with other

How best to
tice was a source
colonists deeply
tions and the ta

The Age of Di
Varied Problem

While some pe
greatly from th
sion, exploratio
caused great pr
ments took mor
were new caus
Each nation trie
or to take rich
tions. Because
wealth, power,
of the newly fou
treated. Wealth
second, especia

There, greed
ers enslaved pe
Thousands of I

▼ **Illustrating H**
slaves are bro

REVIEW

Section Summaries

Section 1 Many Factors Fostered an Age of Discovery The Age of Discovery was a time when the people of Europe developed a greater awareness of the world around them. European explorers searched out new lands as well as new routes to lands that were already known. The desire to gain glory, to find gold and other riches, and to serve God were strong motivations for early explorers, even though voyages were dangerous. Improved navigational equipment and sailing vessels made exploration easier.

Section 2 Portugal and Spain Led in Exploration Christopher Columbus, sailing for Spain and looking for a western route to Asia, reached the islands of the Caribbean in 1492. Prince Henry the Navigator encouraged Portuguese sailors to explore the west coast of Africa, and in 1488, Bartholomeu Dias sailed around the Cape of Good Hope. Portugal built an empire with trading posts in Asia and colonies in South America. Spanish conquistadors conquered the Aztec and Inca empires in the Americas.

Section 3 Other Nations Established Empires Northern European countries also wanted to find an all-water route to Asia. Most ships looked for a northwest passage around or through America. Henry VII of England sponsored John Cabot's voyage to find a route to China. Later explorers continued the search but ended up exploring North America. The Dutch and French gained empires in North America, Asia, and Africa. England's empire grew in America and India. By the seventeenth century, the English had begun establishing the largest colonial empire in the world.

Section 4 The Age of Discovery Brought Many Changes The Age of Discovery changed forever the way Europeans looked at the rest of the world. It also led to a revolution in trade and commerce. New products were introduced to Europe from the Americas. Capitalism grew as entrepreneurs used money from investors to start joint-stock companies. Mercantilism created inflation in Europe and angered the colonists. Since colonies were profitable, some European nations went to war over them.

Key Facts

1. Use each vocabulary word in a sentence.
   a. interdependent
   b. maritime
   c. scurvy
   d. caravel
   e. circumnavigate
   f. conquistador
   g. viceroy
   h. northwest passage
   i. privateer
   j. entrepreneur
   k. joint-stock company
   l. mercantilism
2. Identify and briefly explain the importance of the following names, places, or events.
   a. Columbus
   b. West Indies
   c. Magellan
   d. Cortés
   e. Hudson
   f. Boers

Main Ideas

1. How did "glory, gold, and God" motivate European explorers?
2. Name and describe two technological advances that aided explorers during the Age of Discovery.
3. Why did India, China, and the Arab empires not attempt to explore other parts of the world?
4. Identify three Portuguese sailors and their contributions to the Age of Discovery.
5. How did the Treaty of Tordesillas affect the growth of Spain and Portugal's empires?
6. In what ways did French settlement in North America differ from English settlement?
7. What were the advantages of investing in a joint-stock company?
8. How did the Age of Discovery affect the native peoples of the Americas?

Developing Skill in Reading History

For each of the events below, tell what other event caused it.

1. By the fifteenth century, people could travel in ships far from shore in reasonable safety.
2. Christopher Columbus developed an interest in sailing.
3. Pope Alexander VI divided the non–Christian world between Spain and Portugal.
4. Henry VII sponsored John Cabot's voyage.
5. England controlled the seas.

Using Social Studies Skills

1. **Using Visual Evidence** Study the painting below, which shows Hernán Cortés meeting with Aztec Indians. What seems to be the Aztecs' attitude toward Cortés? Why did Cortés destroy the Aztec empire rather than working together with its people?
2. **Understanding Historical Perspective** Imagine that you have never seen a map of the world. Based only on what you have actually seen with your own eyes—oceans, rivers, hills, mountains, and so on—create a "map of the world" according to your own travels.

Critical Thinking

1. **Perceiving Cause and Effect** The explorations of the Age of Discovery, aside from charting unknown lands and seas, enabled an exchange of plants and animals between the Old and New worlds. How did this exchange affect the variety of food that was available to Europeans?
2. **Demonstrating Reasoned Judgment** The three major motivations for exploration were "glory, gold, and God." Which, if any, of these do you think was the strongest motivating force? Explain your answer.
3. **Determining Relevance** How important do you think the discoveries of the European explorers were to the growth of capitalism? Explain your answer.

Focus on Writing

Proofreading

The final, crucial step in writing a paragraph or an essay is **proofreading.** Proofreading means checking that your essay accomplishes its purpose, is clearly written, and is free from errors in grammar, punctuation, and spelling. Ask yourself the following questions when you proofread your own writing:

1. Does the essay answer the question or completely cover my topic?
2. Is there a clear topic sentence with enough supporting information? Is the supporting information clearly written?
3. Does the writing flow well, so that my paragraph or essay is easy to read and understand? Have someone read your work to help you make certain.
4. Are there any mistakes in grammar, punctuation, or spelling? Check a dictionary for any words that you are unsure of.

Practice: Write a short paragraph that answers one of the Critical Thinking questions in this chapter review. Then, proofread your paragraph using the guidelines listed above. Rewrite your paragraph in its final form.

The Age of Absolutism

(1500–1750)

1 **Spain and England Had Absolute Monarchs**

2 **An Absolute Monarchy Ruled France**

3 **Monarchs Ruled Russia, Prussia, and Austria**

4 **Other Countries Fought Absolutism**

Louis XIV became king of France in 1643, when he was 4 years old. By 1661, he was Europe's most powerful ruler. Louis was determined to own the finest palace on the continent—a marvel that would stun everyone who saw it with the range of his glory. He succeeded. With its gigantic halls, polished mirrored walls, lush tapestries, and blazing chandeliers, his palace at Versailles (ver SY) became one of the great palaces of the world.

A park containing 1,400 fountains surrounded the palace. The king liked to see the fountains all in motion at once. The task of supplying the fountains with water constantly challenged the royal engineers. They came up with a plan for bringing water in from several miles away. Louis demanded that the plan be carried out at once. Thousands of peasants were forced to dig at a furious pace, night and day. Many died. One court observer noted that the workers' deaths were so frequent that every night she saw bodies being carted away for secret burial.

The king had no interest in the suffering of those beneath him. As the ruler of France, he had complete control over his people. Louis was not the only monarch in Europe who had such power. In this chapter, you will read about other monarchs who, like Louis, ruled European countries between 1500 and 1750. You will learn why these rulers came to have so much power and how they used it to run their governments.

▲ **Illustrating History** *For this portrait, the vain Louis XIV of France posed in his richest, most impressive royal garments.*

1500	1600	1700	1800
■ 1478 Spanish Inquisition begins	1588 ■ England defeats Spanish Armada	· 1643 ■ Louis XIV becomes king of France 1689 ■ Peter the Great becomes ruler of Russia	■ 1713 Treaty of Utrecht restores European balance of power ■ 1795 Russia, Prussia, and Austria partition Poland

▲ **Illustrating History** *The above painting shows the dazzling Palace of Versailles, the exciting center of French culture under Louis XIV.*

1 Spain and England Had Absolute Monarchs

As you read, look for answers to these questions:

◆ Why was Charles V an especially important figure in sixteenth-century European affairs?
◆ Why was Charles V unable to keep Spain powerful?
◆ How did Philip II contribute to Spain's decline?
◆ Which members of the Tudor dynasty were effective rulers of England and why?

Key Terms: absolutism (defined on p. 391), divine right (p. 391), balance of power (p. 392)

If you have read *Alice in Wonderland* by Lewis Carroll, you may remember that at Alice's first meeting with the Queen of Hearts, the queen shouts, "Off with her head!" The king and queen in Alice's adventure are part of a dream, but the enormous power of rulers in the seventeenth and eighteenth centuries was very real to the people of Europe. The complete, or absolute, control of a monarch over his or her people is called **absolutism.** This form of government gives its name to the period in history known as the Age of Absolutism, which lasted from 1500 to 1750.

Today, Americans have grown accustomed to the idea that government should be based on the will of the people. During the Age of Absolutism, however, the monarchs of Europe claimed that they ruled by the will of God, or by **divine right.** Louis XIV of France, for example, said, "God has set me up that I may serve as an exemplar [example] to others."

391

Because monarchs were the source of all political power during the Age of Absolutism, they were flattered and admired by those who wished royal favor or wanted a share in their power. Monarchs set the fashion in clothes, the taste in music and books, and the nation's moral code and social patterns. How well the nation was governed depended solely on the talent of the monarch and the monarch's chosen advisers. The common people could only hope for the best.

Charles V Was Absolute Monarch of Spain

Charles V, who ruled the Holy Roman Empire from 1516 to 1556, is a good example of an absolute monarch. He controlled more lands than any other ruler since the reign of Charlemagne, and he had enough titles to cover the space on this page. To describe how he came to have all those titles would take a book in itself.

As a member of the Hapsburg family of Austria, Charles V was also Charles I of Spain, ruler of Spain's lands overseas, king of the Netherlands, and king of part of Italy. A combination of luck and skill was responsible for his gaining so much power at one time. To begin with, he inherited much of his land and power from his grandparents, Ferdinand and Isabella, and from the powerful Hapsburg family who ruled Austria. With his fingers in so many different political pies, Charles V played an important role in the affairs of Europe.

Keeping himself in the center of the European stage, however, was not easy. Two other powerful kings, Henry VIII of England and Francis I of France, wanted to share the stage with him. Shakespeare wrote, "Uneasy lies the head that wears a crown." Certainly, Charles, as well as many other monarchs, had uneasy times.

War between Charles V and Francis I for supremacy in Europe was almost constant. Even when Francis I died, the fighting continued. The wars only came to an end when Charles V finally gave up the struggle for power and retired to a monastery. At that point, Charles V left his German lands to his brother Ferdinand and his Spanish lands to his son, Philip II.

The wars between France and Spain had ended in a draw. The draw was a good outcome for Henry VIII of England, who would have been in a bad position if either Francis or Charles had won control of Europe. It was England's plan to stop any one power from dominating Europe. This is known as keeping the **balance of power.**

Spain Lost Its Power

The reign of Charles V was, in many ways, a glorious one for the king and for Spain, but not long after his death, Spain began to decline. Why? As Holy Roman Emperor as well as king of Spain and king of the Netherlands, Charles was the most powerful monarch in Europe, but one ruler could not successfully govern all these countries at once. What was good for Spain often was bad for the Netherlands. What was right to do as Holy Roman Emperor often was wrong to do as king of Spain or king of the Netherlands.

As Holy Roman Emperor, Charles V had tried to unify his empire and protect the Roman Catholic church from Martin Luther's attacks. Since he failed to defeat France after many years of fighting, he could not unify his empire. Luther's influence continued to spread even though Charles V ordered him to stop his attacks. Charles's rule as Holy Roman Emperor was, for the most part, unsuccessful, and he ended his reign a disappointed man.

Spain's economic decline was largely the result of its dependence on riches seized in the New World. Spanish conquistadors stole gold and silver from the Aztecs and the Incas and sent the wealth back to Spain. While much of this wealth was used to finance wars, a large amount of gold and silver still found its way into the Spanish economy. The increase in gold and silver caused inflation. People in other countries could not afford to buy Spanish goods, which were expensive. The Spanish themselves were forced to spend much of their money in foreign markets, and so the wealth flowed out of Spain even more quickly than it poured in. When the New World stopped being a source of precious metals for Spain, the nation was plunged into poverty.

Philip II Furthered the Decline of Spain

As discussed above, Charles V divided his empire in 1556 and left the rule of Spain and the Netherlands to his son, Philip II, who ruled from 1556 to 1598. While Philip had a smaller kingdom to rule than his father, he also had less ability as a monarch and often misused his absolute power. Philip II believed that God expected him to save the Roman Catholic church from Protestantism and to make Spain the strongest country in Europe. In an attempt to create religious unity in Spain, he drove out or destroyed all those who were not Catholics. He proposed to stamp out heresy, or opposition to beliefs of a particular religion, by bringing back the Inquisition. The Inquisition, as you read in Chapter 15, was a court of law that tried and punished people who were not Catholics or who worked against the Roman Catholic church. Actually, the Spanish Inquisition, which began in 1478, was much bloodier than the original Inquisition, established by the Roman Catholic church in the Middle Ages. At the height of the Spanish Inquisition under Philip, the death penalty was common. Jews and converts to the Jewish religion, for example, were particularly persecuted.

Philip's plan to make Spain a stronger nation, however, was not successful. He tried to centralize power by filling government offices with people who were responsible to and depended on him alone. However, he was not always capable of making sound decisions or choosing competent people, and so Spain suffered. Furthermore, the flow of gold and silver from the New World began to slow down, and Philip did not know how to encourage economic growth in the country. Frustrated by the economic situation in Spain, Philip turned toward the Netherlands, where the economy was flourishing.

▲ **Illustrating History** *This Flemish tapestry shows Charles V of Spain engaged in the Battle of Tunis.*

In the Netherlands, Philip treated the people so harshly that they rebelled. A Spanish army led by the cruel Duke of Alva attempted to put down the Protestant Dutch rebellion, but the Dutch, led by William the Silent, were able to defeat the Spanish forces. Philip II lost the better part of his Netherlands possessions, which became the Dutch Republic in 1581.

To make up for his losses in the Netherlands, Philip conquered Portugal. Sixty years later, Portugal too broke away from Spanish rule. In 1588, Philip II sent his Armada (a fleet of warships) against England, only to suffer a stunning defeat by the British navy. By this time, it was clear that Spain was no longer the dominant power in Europe that it had been under Charles V.

Absolutism Was Harmful to Spain

Charles V and Philip II tried to do what they thought was right, but neither king was able to solve the problems he faced. For success, an absolute government depends on the leadership of one person. When the monarch was able, absolutism sometimes succeeded for short periods of time. When the monarch made too many mistakes, government failed, and the people suffered. This explains why Spanish glory faded so quickly in spite of all the wealth it gained from its New World colonies.

The first cracks in Spain's power were seen when parts of the empire began to throw off Spanish control. This shrinking of the Spanish empire was to continue throughout much of Spain's history. Religious intolerance also added to Spain's decline. Spanish rulers encouraged the persecution of people, such as the Moors and the Jews, who might have helped Spain become rich. When these people were driven out of the country, Spain fell to second place in the commercial and political affairs of Europe.

Absolutism Grew Under the Tudors in England

As you read in Chapter 13, a new family of rulers began in England when the Tudors were victorious in the Wars of the Roses. In 1485, an act of Parliament declared Henry Tudor, known as Henry VII, king of England. He was followed by his son Henry VIII, who ruled from 1509 to 1547. After the brief reigns of Edward VI and Mary Tudor, Elizabeth I ruled England as the last Tudor until 1603.

Henry VIII. Under the able Henry VII, England began to expand overseas and to grow in wealth and strength. During the reign of Henry VIII, England broke with the Roman Catholic church. Henry VIII, who was extravagant and strong-willed, also used his diplomatic skills to maintain the balance of power in Europe. When Henry VIII died, there was some confusion about who would follow him. His son Edward VI, who became king when he was 10 years old, died when he was 16 years old. He was followed by his older sister Mary Tudor, who was a devout Roman Catholic.

Mary Tudor. For a time during Mary's rule, which lasted from 1553 to 1558, the Roman Catholic church was again the leading church in England. Mary married Philip II of Spain. Under his influence, Mary persecuted heretics and non–Catholics and earned the title "Bloody Mary." When Mary finally died in 1558, Elizabeth became queen. The last surviving child of Henry VIII, Elizabeth I proved to be the strongest of the Tudor monarchs.

Elizabeth I. Elizabeth I wanted a national church that was free of Rome but subject to the crown. She tried to steer a course between Catholicism and Protestantism, but this plan dissatisfied many people. Although she restored the Anglican church (the Protestant Church of England), many Puritans left England because the church was "too Catholic" to suit them. The attempt to find a middle ground between Protestantism and Catholicism caused Elizabeth many problems throughout her reign.

One of the most serious of these problems was Mary Stuart. During Elizabeth's reign, Mary Stuart, a great-granddaughter of Henry VII, ruled Scotland. Since Mary was Catholic and had been married to the Catholic heir to the French throne, she tried to advance Catholicism in Scotland, which was chiefly Protestant. While Mary tried to prevent the spread of Protestantism in her country, Elizabeth allied herself with the Calvinist (Protestant) party in Scotland. Mary, known as Mary, Queen of Scots, was ultimately unsuccessful. She lost the support of the Scottish people and was forced to give up the throne in 1567. When this happened, she fled Scotland and sought refuge in England.

In England, Mary Stuart was a threat to Elizabeth I. As the great-granddaughter of Henry VII, Mary could say that she had a claim to the English throne. As a strong Catholic, she opposed Elizabeth's attempt to promote Anglicanism. In 1587, Elizabeth I had Mary Stuart executed on the grounds that she had conspired with Philip II of Spain against England.

The Spanish Armada of 1588. To restore Catholicism to England and stop the growing power of England, Philip II launched an enormous fleet of ships, the Armada, to invade England. Spain had long been a dominant military power on the seas. This time, however, bad weather and poor planning helped to doom the attack. A great naval battle raged. The smaller, speedier English ships soundly defeated the Spanish Armada and forced them to escape to the North Sea. Violent storms in the North Sea destroyed many of the fleeing Spanish ships and scattered the rest. The English nicknamed the stormy wind "the Protestant wind." Thus, at a critical crossroads in European history, England won a crucial naval battle with Spain. After this, Spain declined further, and under Elizabeth's rule, England became a leading power in Europe.

During Elizabeth's reign, England became a great seagoing nation. Improvements in the construction and handling of ships gave England a superior navy. Under the leadership of the sea adventurers Sir Francis Drake and John Hawkins, England began to build an empire by exploring and conquering lands beyond Europe.

Elizabethan culture. English culture, especially literature, flourished under Queen Elizabeth. The term *Elizabethan* is given to the entire period and style. William Shakespeare, who was discussed in Chapter 14, was the leading poet and dramatist of this period. The Elizabethan theater became world famous, but to a modern theatergoer, it might seem strange. The stage had no curtain and little scenery. Men and boys did all of the acting, even the roles of women.

▼ **Illustrating History** *The plays of Elizabethan dramatist William Shakespeare were performed at the Globe Theatre, shown below.*

▲ **Illustrating History** *Elizabeth I, at right, used her diplomatic skills to make Parliament (building left) grant her wishes.*

The Tudors Worked With Parliament

Among England's gifts to the world are its models of great lawmaking bodies such as Parliament and its democratic traditions such as trial by jury. Under the Tudors, these expressions of democracy did not die, but they were used to serve the monarch.

Elizabeth I was one of England's most popular and powerful monarchs. Even so, her power was never as absolute as that of the kings of Spain. Elizabeth I, like her father and grandfather, knew how to get her way with Parliament. She did not abolish Parliament but instead used it to serve her own purposes. Although this practice did not encourage democracy, the people nevertheless loved and respected Elizabeth.

The Tudors did not follow the theory of divine right, but they did rule as absolute monarchs. Although they may have twisted the meaning of democracy to suit their own needs, Parliament gained power under them, and the democratic traditions such as trial by jury also expanded. As you will read in Chapter 18, the Stuarts, who followed the Tudors as English monarchs, were unable to match the Tudors' skill in negotiating with Parliament.

2 An Absolute Monarchy Ruled France

As you read, look for answers to these questions:

◆ What French rulers made France ready for the absolutism of Louis XIV?
◆ What was the policy of Louis XIV concerning the expansion of French borders?
◆ How did the French economy operate under Louis XIV?
◆ What mistakes did Louis XIV make during his reign?

Key Terms: revenue (defined on p. 397), tariff (p. 399)

Absolutism and the divine right of kings was perhaps best exemplified in the reign of Louis XIV of France, who ruled for 72 years, from 1643 to 1715. The magnificence of Louis's reign would not have been possible, however, if previous rulers had not laid the groundwork for him.

France Was Made Ready for Absolutism

Henry of Navarre came to the throne of France as Henry IV in 1589 as a result of a series of religious wars. Henry was Huguenot, or French Calvinist, and many French Catholics did not wish to see a Protestant on the throne of France. To keep peace, to get on with the business of governing, and to rebuild the nation that had been torn by war, Henry became a Catholic.

Henry IV ruled wisely and well. With the aid of his brilliant adviser Maximilien Sully, he cut government expenses, created new sources of **revenue** or government income, and rebuilt bridges, roads, and canals. Henry wanted the French people to develop their businesses, industry, and trade. Under Henry, the silk textile industry, for which France became world famous, was born. Henry was also responsible for the Edict of Nantes in 1598, which you read about in Chapter 15. Under this law, Protestants were given the right to worship freely and to hold public office.

Henry IV was truly interested in the welfare of the people. He is supposed to have remarked that every peasant should have a chicken in the pot on Sunday. Despite Henry's popularity and political skills, he did have at least one enemy. As he was about to go to war against the Hapsburg rulers of Austria in 1610, he was assassinated.

Cardinal Richelieu. On the death of Henry IV, his young son, Louis XIII, became king. Since Louis was too young to rule, his mother, Marie de' Medici (duh MED ih chee), ruled in his place. She ruled badly, and France was weakened through her mistakes. It was not until Cardinal Richelieu (RIHSH uh loo), regional head of the Catholic church, was given permission to govern by Louis XIII that France regained its prominence in Europe.

▼ **Illustrating History** *Cardinal Richelieu ruled France for the young King Louis XIII.*

Louis XIII let Richelieu rule France as chief minister from 1624 to his death in 1642. Richelieu, who was popular with no one, including the king, ruled forcefully. He wanted the crown to have absolute control of France, and he wanted France to be the strongest nation in Europe. Unfortunately, his way was not always the best way for the French people. Unlike Henry IV who had cared for his subjects, Richelieu referred to the French people as mules that had to be driven.

To drive the "mules," Richelieu placed his trust in new government officers called the *intendants* (in TEN dunts). These local government officials were loyal bureaucrats who served as Richelieu's eyes and ears as well as his tax collectors. It was their job to report disloyal people who might undermine the king's power. *The Three Musketeers*, an exciting book by Alexandre Dumas, tells of the struggle between Richelieu and his enemies.

Cardinal Mazarin. The 4-year-old boy who became the new king of France after the death of Louis XIII was destined to have a long and glorious reign. His title was Louis XIV, but since a 4-year-old child can hardly be expected to rule, both Louis and France were fortunate in finding a new and extremely capable minister, Cardinal Jules Mazarin (mah zah RAHN).

Although not quite the equal of Richelieu in cunning, Mazarin was able to rule France within the centralized system that Richelieu had established. Mazarin led France successfully through the remaining years of the Thirty Years' War. By the time of his death, Mazarin had made France the foremost country in Europe. It was indeed a nation fit for a king, and Louis XIV, now 23 years old, was ready to take over the leadership of this nation. He was known as the Sun King because he was thought to be as important to France as the sun is to the world.

Louis XIV Exemplified Absolutism

From 1661, when Mazarin died, to 1715, Louis XIV was the absolute ruler of France. During that time, he was the most influen-tial king on the European continent. Because other European kings modelled their courts and their nations after Louis's, one can learn a great deal about absolutism by studying his reign.

Louis XIV was ambitious and wanted to expand the area that he ruled. To satisfy his ambition, he waged war during much of his reign—in America as well as in Europe, on land as well as on sea. Beginning in 1667 and continuing for the next forty years, Louis made war on his European neighbors. He hoped to push the borders of France to the Pyrenees, the Mediterranean Sea, the Atlantic Ocean, the English Channel, the Alps, and the Rhine River. Although he looked upon these physical features as the natural and rightful borders of France, he was not successful in his attempts to expand the country.

One such attempt, known as the War of the Spanish Succession, which lasted from 1701 to 1714, was fought over the inheritance of Spain. Charles II of Spain had made a will in which he gave his lands to Louis's grandson, Philip of Anjou. This gift pleased Louis but worried the other European kings who did not like to see the crown of Spain and the crown of France in the same family. England especially did not like to see the balance of power upset, and so France and England went to war.

The results of this bloody conflict were disappointing for Louis XIV, since France lost much more than it gained. The Treaty of Utrecht (YOO trekt), which ended the war in 1713, gave Nova Scotia, Newfoundland, land in the Hudson Bay region of Canada, and islands in the Caribbean Sea to England. England also gained Gibraltar—the gateway to the Mediterranean Sea. Although Louis's grandson was allowed to keep the title to the throne of Spain, the crowns of the two countries were never united.

Colbert and the French economy. Louis XIV relied on wise advisers. Among the most influential of his advisers was Jean Baptiste Colbert (kawl BAYR), Louis's minister of finance. Colbert introduced a budget system and encouraged the growth of

Mailing a Letter in Eighteenth-Century England

Between 1680 and 1780, England developed a fast, efficient postal system. At first, the state postal system was so slow and expensive that most people used privately owned operations like the London Penny Post. Begun in 1680, the Penny Post delivered letters anywhere in London for a penny. (See photo right.) It used postmarks and promised delivery within one hour.

Outside of London, boys, known as post-boys, carried the mail on horseback. They were slow and often were attacked by highway robbers. In 1780, the government introduced special postal stagecoaches. These were speedy, safe, and economical.

1. What modern practice was introduced by the London Penny Post?
2. Why do you think the post-boy system was unreliable?
3. Why were coaches an improvement?

French industry. He improved manufacturing, especially the manufacturing of luxury items such as silk and fine glass. He also supervised a number of public projects, which helped to increase employment throughout France.

Colbert was responsible for bringing mercantilism into France. According to the mercantile philosophy, the wealth of a country was measured by the amount of gold and silver that it had. Mercantilism also taught that high **tariffs** (taxes on goods coming into a country) helped to make a nation rich. These tariffs made foreign goods more expensive than goods produced in the home country. This encouraged people to buy more domestic products—products made within the country. Modern economists see many flaws in the mercantilist system. Nevertheless, under Colbert's direction France did become the leading European nation in industry and trade.

French culture under Louis XIV.   Just as Henry IV, Richelieu, and Mazarin had set the political stage for absolutism, so too, certain French writers set the stage for the growth of French culture. In his influential books, *Gargantua* (gahr GAHN choo uh) and *Pantagruel* (pahn TAHG roo EL), Rabelais (RAH BLAY), who lived from 1494 to 1553, wrote that life was meant to be enjoyed. Montaigne (mohn TEN yuh), who is today considered the inventor of the informal essay, wrote a series of brilliant essays in which he expressed his own deepest thoughts about life. In 1635, Richelieu established the French Academy to encourage French writing. Some years later, Colbert established the French Academy of Science to encourage the growth of science.

It was under Louis XIV that a great age in French literature was born. Great tragedies were written by Corneille (kohr NAY yuh), and great comedies were written by Moliere (mole YAHR). Racine (rah SEEN) is still considered one of France's greatest dramatists. The fables of La Fontaine (LAH fohn TAYN) and the teachings of the Duc de la Rochefoucauld (duh lah ROSHE foo KO) in a book of maxims are prized to this day.

Louis XIV Made Many Mistakes

Louis XIV is supposed to have said, "L'état c'est moi"—"I am the state." By this, he meant that he could do whatever he wished without the people's consent. He thought that the nation and the people lived for the monarch. Did Louis use his great power wisely? For the most part, the answer is no.

Under Louis XIV, France rejected the Edict of Nantes and drove the Huguenots out of the country. Driving out the Huguenots proved to be nearly as harmful to France as the expulsion of the Moors and Jews from Spain was to that country. The Huguenots were hard-working people who had helped to make the country prosperous.

Louis XIV left a heavy financial burden for others to pay after he died. The extravagant life style that he and the members of his court enjoyed was part of the reason for this. Large sums of money, as well as years of labor, were invested in building the court at Versailles. The fountains, buildings, and gardens of the Versailles court were incredibly lavish and beautiful. At a time when bread was scarce for many of his subjects, Louis XIV was hosting huge banquets and parties in magnificent ballrooms. The American writer Mark Twain who visited the restored court at Versailles in the late 1800s, gives us some idea of its glories. He wrote: "You gaze, and stare, and try to understand that it is real, that it is on earth, that it is not the Garden of Eden [heaven] . . ." All of this splendor, however, bled the French treasury and planted the seeds of unrest that led to revolution.

Louis also devoted more time and money to war than to peace. Unfortunately, the results of his military adventures did little to improve France. A wise monarch was needed to undo the mistakes of Louis XIV. Unfortunately, those who followed Louis were not wise. Under Louis XV, France lost control of Canada. During the reign of Louis XVI, the French Revolution took place.

Absolutism Differed in France and England

As you have read, both France and England had absolute monarchies. In England, however, age-old traditions and institutions helped to check the power of the monarchy. For example, the English monarchy had to work with Parliament to accomplish its goals. From the time of the Magna Carta, discussed in Chapter 13, the English had held the belief that government should protect certain liberties and that the power to govern came from the consent of the governed. Thus, over time, England's monarchy evolved into a limited monarchy. Without the political institutions or the philosophy of England, other European countries, especially Russia, Prussia, and Austria, developed absolute monarchies. Absolutism in these monarchies is described in the next section.

SECTION 2 REVIEW

Knowing Key Terms, People, and Places
1. Define: **a.** revenue **b.** tariff
2. Identify: **a.** Henry IV **b.** Cardinal Richelieu **c.** Louis XIV **d.** Treaty of Utrecht

Focus on Geography
3. What did Louis XIV consider to be France's natural borders?

Reviewing Main Ideas
4. Describe the reign of Henry IV.
5. How successful was Louis XIV in expanding France's borders?
6. How did Louis XIV hurt the French nation?

Critical Thinking
Formulating Questions
7. Write five specific questions that would lead to the answer of this complex question: How did the reign of Louis XIV affect the future of the French nation?

3 Monarchs Ruled Russia, Prussia, and Austria

As you read, look for answers to these questions:

◆ How did the rule of Peter the Great change Russia?
◆ What kind of ruler was Frederick the Great?
◆ How did absolutism grow and develop in Austria?

Key Terms: diplomatic revolution (defined on p. 404)

The foundations of modern Russia were laid by Peter the Great, who ruled from 1689 to 1725. While Louis XIV was declaring "I am the state," Peter was the czar of Russia. Peter was determined that Russia would catch up with the countries of western Europe, both in culture and in power. Peter's reign was characterized by an intense effort to modernize and westernize his country. His reign also was marked by almost constant warfare with other countries.

Peter Tried to Modernize Russia

In 1696, Peter the Great left Russia and traveled throughout Europe in disguise. He visited several famous capitals, where he learned much about western European civilization. Although Peter was interested in many fields, he was particularly fascinated by European ships. In the Netherlands and England, he actually worked in shipyards and learned how to build ships. He would have stayed in Europe longer, but a peasant uprising in Russia made it necessary for him to return home in 1698. Peter put down the uprising forcefully, thus further securing his absolute power and preventing any opposition to his rule.

Peter then hurriedly put his new knowledge to use. He ordered his people to wear European-style clothes and commanded the men to shorten their beards. Although many

Russian nobles objected to this sudden break with tradition, Peter stood firm. The czar also saw to it that schools and hospitals were built, and he established a new capital at St. Petersburg, now known as Leningrad. In his determination to modernize his country, Peter sent Russians to other countries to study and established a Russian Academy of Science.

Under the rule of Peter the Great, Russia became a powerful country, but it still had few ports, or, as Peter called them, "windows to the west." Ports, Peter believed, would allow trade to move between Russia and western Europe. With the object of getting a port in northern Europe, Peter declared war on Charles XII of Sweden. The gallant and intelligent Charles was defeated. Peter won his window on the Baltic Sea, and Sweden never again became a major power.

Absolutism Continued Under Catherine

Peter's death brought to the throne several weak rulers. In 1762, however, Catherine II, known as Catherine the Great, came to the

▼ **Illustrating History** *Peter the Great introduced European customs to Russia.*

Catherine the Great

Early one morning in 1762, the woman who would later be known as Catherine the Great was shaken awake by her friend, Prince Orlov. He said, "It is time to get up; everything is prepared for proclaiming you."

Catherine, shown at left, was not surprised. By her order, Emperor Peter III, her husband, had been removed from the throne. She would take his place. As empress, she ruled from 1762 to 1796.

Under Catherine's command, schools were built, freedom of religion was enlarged, and public health measures were created. But, most of these acts benefited only the Russian nobles. Millions of serfs still struggled for life's most basic needs.

Catherine's greatest achievement was to expand the Russian Empire. She acquired most of Poland and vast lands along the Black Sea. By the time she died in 1796, she was known as Catherine the Great.

1. Which group of people benefited from Catherine's rule? Why do you think this was so?
2. Why was she known as Catherine the Great?

---

throne. Catherine meant well and wanted to give her people privileges that they had not enjoyed before, but her good intentions were never carried out. Instead, she spent time and effort in expanding Russia. To this end, she took part in several divisions of Poland.

Poland had been a large and powerful nation in the 1400s and 1500s. During the 1600s and 1700s, however, the government of Poland became increasingly disorganized as Polish nobles ruled like feudal lords instead of uniting behind their kings. Poland's weakened condition left the door open for Catherine to move in and gain more land for Russia. In 1772, three nations—Russia, Prussia, and Austria—divided Poland, taking parts of the country for their own nations. This first partition was followed by two more—one in 1793 and the last in 1795. Poland eventually disappeared from the map of Europe and did not appear again until 1919, after World War I.

A war with Turkey gave Russia a window on the Black Sea. This window was the land area called the Crimea. By controlling this area, Russia finally gained an ice-free port in southern Europe.

Absolutism Was Harmful to Russia

Nowhere in Europe did absolutism last as long or become as complete as it did in Russia. Strong-willed rulers such as Peter and Catherine were determined to have their way. A Parliament and an Estates-General had been formed in England and France, and the American Revolution had brought independence to America. Russia, however, did not have any of the traditions or institutions that would have modified absolutism. Russian rulers, therefore, had no check on their royal powers.

To the monarchs of Europe, Russia may have seemed more Asiatic than European, but Peter and Catherine were determined to make Russia a European power. As a result, Russia became deeply involved in European affairs. Because Russia wanted to find new, ice-free ports, it often clashed with the countries of Europe.

Absolutism Developed in Prussia

As absolutism developed in western Europe and Russia, so too did it develop in Prussia, one of the many small states that once made up the Holy Roman Empire. Today, Prussia is part of modern-day Germany.

Prussia. During the seventeenth century, the little state of Brandenburg in northern Germany grew and became the important state of Prussia. Frederick William of Hohenzollern, known as the Great Elector, started Prussia on the road it followed for many years. He built a strong army, a stable government, and a sound economy. His grandson, Frederick William I, who was the elector from 1713 to 1740, continued in his footsteps by building the army and the treasury and by expanding the size of Prussia.

Frederick the Great. Under Frederick the Great, who ruled from 1740 to 1786, Prussia became a strong nation. As a youth, Frederick liked philosophy, music, and poetry. From his father, he learned about armies, war, and power. In fact, Frederick served in almost every department of the kingdom. He learned from experience about the inner workings of government and the job of being a king.

It was through a series of wars that Frederick added to Prussia's power and to his own prestige. Allied with Spain and France, Prussia made war on Austria, Britain, and the Netherlands. The war, known as the War of the Austrian Succession, lasted from 1740 to 1748. Although Prussia gained territory from Austria's new empress, Maria Theresa, peace was not achieved. The Seven Years' War, which lasted from 1756 to 1763, soon followed.

The Seven Years' War seemed like another inning in the game the monarchs of Europe were playing. The game was the same as it had been in many other wars; only the sides

▼ **Illustrating History** *Apart from being a powerful ruler, Frederick the Great (shown below center) had a strong interest in philosophy, poetry, and music.*

Maria Theresa Takes Charge

Maria Theresa became ruler of the Hapsburg lands at age 23. Immediately, war broke out with France. During this conflict, the young empress quickly established her authority over the family empire, which included Austria, Hungary, and Bohemia. In a letter to her minister in Bohemia, Chancellor Kinsky, she reacts to the French conquest of Prague in Bohemia.

❝So Prague is lost, and perhaps even worse will follow unless we can secure three months supplies. It is out of the question for Austria to supply them, and it is doubtful even if Hungary will be able to do so.

Here then, Kinsky, we find ourselves at the sticking point where only courage can save the country [Bohemia] and the Queen, for without the country I should indeed be a poor princess. My own resolve is taken: to stake everything, win or lose, on saving Bohemia; and it is with this in view that you should work and lay your plans. It may involve destruction and desolation which twenty years will be insufficient to restore; but I must hold the country and the soil, and for this all my armies, all the Hungarians, shall die before I surrender an inch of it. . . . You will say that I am cruel; that is true. But I know that all the cruelties I commit today to hold the country I shall one day be in a position to make good a hundredfold. . . . But for the present I close my heart to pity.❞

1. Whose lives did Maria Theresa pledge in order to keep Bohemia under Hapsburg control?
2. Summarize the main goal of Maria Theresa, as expressed in this letter.

were different. Whereas Britain and Prussia had been on opposite sides during the Austrian War of Succession, now they were on the same side. The desire to maintain the balance of power and the outbreak of war between France and Britain in the New World drove Prussia and Britain together. At the same time, fear of the growing Prussian strength drew France and Austria together. Such a shift in loyalties between countries is called a **diplomatic revolution.** It is marked by a great change in the way nations bargain or deal with one another. The search for power, glory, and land in the New World, as well as in the Old World, was one reason for the diplomatic revolution in 1756. As a result of the Seven Years' War, Prussia increased in size and still kept Silesia. The fact that Prussia also took part in the division of Poland only added to Frederick's fame.

Although Frederick's ability in war was great, he was equally great in peace. He looked upon himself as "the first servant of the state," and as such, he was up early and worked late. The pleasures found at the French palace at Versailles were not for him. Instead, he devoted himself to building schools and hospitals, giving land and seed to the poor, and trying to repair the damage caused by the war. Frederick was truly interested in the welfare of the people. He tolerated nearly all religions and expected each to give something to the glory of the country. He also tried to see to it that the law was fair to rich and poor alike.

Absolutism Was Harmful to Prussia

As great as the Hohenzollerns' vision for Prussia had been, their influence was, in the long run, harmful to their country. As in Russia, there were no democratic institutions in Prussia to check the absolute powers of the Hohenzollern monarchs. Because they had never experienced a different political tradition, the German people rarely questioned authority and rarely asked to take part in the government. Although Prussia's early kings were able, they never gave the German people the opportunity to govern themselves. When it became necessary for the Germans to do so, it was difficult for them because they were accustomed to absolute monarchs.

Absolutism Grew in Austria

To the Hohenzollerns of seventeenth- and eighteenth-century Prussia, absolute power was a fairly new development. To the Hapsburgs of Austria, however, it was already quite old. While the absolute power of the Hohenzollerns was growing, that of the Hapsburgs was declining.

In 1273, Rudolf of Hapsburg was elected Holy Roman Emperor. This election added to the fame and fortune of the Hapsburg family. Gradually, from control over a small area in Switzerland, the Hapsburgs came to rule all of Austria. Through marriage, the influence of the family spread to still other lands, including Spain, the Netherlands, Hungary, and Bohemia.

Maria Theresa. When Charles VI died in 1740, his Hapsburg lands, including Austria, Hungary, and northern Italy, went to his young daughter, Maria Theresa, who ruled from 1740 to 1780. She was an intelligent woman and worked hard as empress of Austria. Under her father, Austria had fallen upon difficult days. The army had not been paid, and the king had had difficulty in ruling the territories of his empire. Furthermore, the rise of the Hohenzollerns in Germany had challenged Austria's power.

Maria Theresa wanted to strengthen Austria. To do this, she decided to copy Prussia, which she disliked although she admired its government. Maria Theresa increased taxes and pressed the nobles to pay their fair share. In 1772, she took part in the division of Poland and added to her lands.

Joseph II. Her son, Joseph II, who was emperor of Austria from 1780 to 1790, tried hard to improve conditions for his people. While the other absolute monarchs struggled to make themselves more powerful, Joseph worked to give his people the freedom he thought they wanted. He tolerated all religions and freed the Jews from the restrictions and discriminations that they experienced in most other European countries. He built schools and encouraged learning. Unlike the schools in other countries, these schools were not only for the rich, but also for the poor. Joseph abolished the death penalty for certain crimes, freed the serfs, and canceled many of their feudal obligations.

Unfortunately, Joseph's good deeds were not appreciated. The nobles did not like to see their ancient feudal rights taken away. The peasants were discontented because Joseph seemed to interfere with their age-old habits. Joseph also was unsuccessful in war and lost out in diplomatic dealings with other countries.

The rulers of Austria controlled many lands made of people of many nationalities. The Austrian monarchs, though absolute, were never able to unite their nation. By the early 1800s, the proud but empty title of Holy Roman Emperor had vanished.

SECTION 3 REVIEW

Knowing Key Terms, People, and Places
1. Define: **a.** diplomatic revolution
2. Identify: **a.** Peter the Great **b.** "windows to the west" **c.** Hohenzollerns **d.** the Great Elector **e.** Frederick the Great

Reviewing Main Ideas
3. What steps did Peter the Great take to modernize Russia?
4. What did Frederick the Great of Prussia accomplish during his reign?
5. In what ways did Joseph II of Austria try to improve conditions for his people?

Critical Thinking
Identifying Assumptions
6. Catherine the Great, Frederick the Great, and Joseph II considered themselves "enlightened" rulers because they felt a responsibility to take care of their people, and yet they did not give up their absolute power. What did these people and their supporters take for granted about the relationship between a government and the people governed?

405

4 Other Countries Fought Absolutism

As you read, look for answers to these questions:

◆ How did the Swiss avoid falling under the control of an absolute ruler?
◆ How did William the Silent prevent Philip II from taking control of the Netherlands?
◆ Why did many religious dissenters flock to the Netherlands in the seventeenth and eighteenth centuries?
◆ What were the benefits and drawbacks of absolutism?

Key Terms: canton (defined on p. 406), stadholder (p. 407)

Switzerland and the Netherlands (Holland, Belgium, and Flanders) were among the first countries to free themselves from the oppression of absolutism. They did not necessarily intend to establish democracies, but having overthrown absolute rulers, they showed that a nation can flourish without a hereditary monarchy and without the absolute rule of a king or queen.

Switzerland Freed Itself from Hapsburg Absolutism

In 58 B.C., the people known as the Helvetii (hel VEE shee eye) were conquered by Julius Caesar during the Gallic Wars. Under Roman rule the people flourished, but with the fall of Rome, many people sought to dominate the lands in which the Helvetii lived. Luckily for the Helvetii, the mountains surrounding the region made conquest difficult.

By the eleventh century, Helvetii, now known as Switzerland, had become part of the Holy Roman Empire, and by the thirteenth century, it had fallen under Hapsburg rule. However, as described in Chapter 13, in 1291, when the absolute Hapsburg rulers sought to assert their authority over

the Swiss, the legendary hero William Tell led the three communities, called **cantons,** of Schwyz, Uri, and Underwalden in a successful revolt against the Hapsburgs.

By the fifteenth century, the Swiss had established themselves as a formidable military power. Impressed by their success, other cantons joined the original group, and the country of Switzerland was born. In 1515, however, the French finally defeated the Swiss. As a result of this defeat, the Swiss pursued a policy of independence and neutrality in foreign wars. It is a policy that Switzerland has followed even to the present. Swiss soldiers, however, were fine fighters, and they continued to serve other European nations. Even after Switzerland itself no longer took part in the wars of Europe, many European nations eagerly sought its mercenaries, or professional soldiers, for their armies.

Since there was no one person to act as a monarch or central ruler in Switzerland, each canton made its own laws and elected a common body of officials to act as a central government. A weak central government, called the Swiss Confederation, held together this group of small, self-governing communities. Switzerland remained neutral in the Thirty Years' War, and in 1648 with the Peace of Westphalia, which ended the war, the countries of Europe recognized the independence of Switzerland.

Although Switzerland did not have an absolute monarch, the country was not really a democracy. Instead, it was a community of business people among whom the wealthiest and most prominent held political power. Even so, the fact that a nation could prosper without an absolute ruler was a lesson that others in Europe would eventually learn.

Holland Freed Itself From the Absolutism of Philip II

As you read in the first section of this chapter, the Netherlands were brought under the rule of Philip II, the son of Charles V. Philip II opposed the Protestant Dutch rebellion and attempted to end it.

The hero and liberator of the Netherlands during the rebellion was William the Silent. In 1574, Spanish troops blockaded the city of Leyden (LYDE 'n), cutting off supplies. To stay alive, the people of the city were forced to eat rats and cats. In an effort to lift the seige, William the Silent broke the dikes that held back the ocean. By flooding the land where the Spanish soldiers were stationed, William could unleash the small, agile Dutch ships, known as "Beggars of the Sea," to rescue the city. The Spanish were forced to flee, but the cost in lives of the people of Leyden was high. As a reward for their heroism, the citizens of the city were offered a choice between freedom from taxes or the establishment of a university. They wisely chose the university.

In 1581, the Dutch Republic officially known as the United Provinces was formed. It was made up of the Protestant northern provinces of the Netherlands, including the important province of Holland. William became the republic's **stadholder,** or ruler. Although William was killed by an assassin three years later, the survival of the republic was assured. The Peace of Westphalia in 1648 recognized the independence of the Dutch republic as well as that of Switzerland. The southern provinces (what is now Belgium) remained under Philip's rule.

As in the case of Switzerland, the Dutch did not set out to establish a democracy, nor did they particularly plan to show that a country could survive without an absolute monarch. Nevertheless, the Netherlands became a prosperous example of these ideas and developed a formidable overseas empire. While absolute rulers throughout Europe were persecuting Jews and other people because of their religious beliefs, the Netherlands became a haven for religious dissenters and an inspiring model of religious tolerance.

Absolutism Had Both Benefits and Hazards

Absolutism as a form of government offered the European people several benefits over feudalism. For example, it brought people together to form nations, to create national

▼ **Illustrating History** *William the Silent, shown on horseback in the painting below, freed the Netherlands from Spanish rule.*

Absolutism vs. Democracy	
Absolutism	**Democracy**
Monarch has absolute power	Government is based on will of the people
Monarch combines political and religious power through divine right	Separation between church and state
Rulers selected by family line	Leaders selected by popular vote
Subjects must accept and obey authority of monarch	Citizens have the right to question or criticize government
Government exists for its own sake; people exist to serve monarch	Government exists to serve the people

▲ **Chart Skill** *How do absolutism and democracy compare on the issue of free speech?*

laws, and to build national armies. A strong, central government could collect taxes from many people and build the nation's trade and industry. People learned that there is strength in numbers, especially when one strong and intelligent person leads a large group.

Nevertheless, absolutism deserves more criticism than praise. Perhaps absolutism's greatest evil was the tendency of monarchs to wage costly wars that claimed many lives. Wars were fought over religion, power, prestige, and land in both the New World and in the Old World. In order to support these wars, the monarchs taxed the peasants heavily. The poorest people often paid the heaviest taxes to support the unnecessary wars that they had not chosen to enter. These same people also had to pay for the court life of an idle and privileged nobility.

Absolutism did not provide stable and lasting governments. Absolutism depends upon the ability of one person, the ruler. When a competent monarch died, the government often fell into weaker hands, and whatever progress had been made was lost. This happened when the government of Spain passed from Charles V to Philip II.

The humanistic ideas of the Renaissance and the philosophy of the Enlightenment, which are discussed in Chapter 18, helped to pave the way for the rejection of absolutism. Writers and philosophers taught that government had a responsibility to take care of the people. Even rulers such as Catherine of Russia, Frederick of Prussia, and Joseph II of Austria came to believe that they had responsibilities toward the people. These rulers are sometimes called *enlightened despots,* meaning rulers who want to use their power to improve the lives of their people. Frederick the Great even called himself the first servant of the state. But, the rulers were still despots because they would not give up their power or the idea that they ruled by the will of God. Yet, the enlightened despots did show more concern for the welfare of ordinary people.

SECTION 4 REVIEW

Knowing Key Terms, People, and Places
1. Define: **a.** canton **b.** stadholder
2. Identify: **a.** William Tell **b.** Swiss Confederation **c.** Peace of Westphalia **d.** William the Silent

Focus on Geography
3. How did the geography of the Netherlands help William the Silent to defeat the Spanish?

Reviewing Main Ideas
4. How did the Swiss free themselves from Hapsburg rule?
5. How were the Dutch treated under Philip II of Spain?
6. Describe the Dutch Republic in 1581.

Critical Thinking
Recognizing Bias
7. What form of bias or prejudice led Philip II to persecute the people who were living in the Netherlands?

An outline is a plan for organizing the main points and details of an essay in a clear and logical order. Once you have made an outline, you can use it as a guide for writing an essay.

Below are several statements about King Louis XIV. Follow the steps to write an outline that uses these statements. Your outline should have a form similar to that shown in the box.

1. **Group related ideas together.** Study the statements about Louis XIV. Answer these questions: (a) What generalizations could you make about Louis XIV, based on these statements? (b) Which statements are examples, or evidence, of each generalization?

2. **Decide which generalizations you want to include as main points of your essay.** Answer the following questions: (a) Which of the generalizations you made seem most interesting or important? List them as your main points. (b) What statement could you make about Louis XIV that would tie all these generalizations together? Make this the major argument or statement of your essay.

3. **Choose an order in which to present the main points.** Think about the central idea of the essay as it is expressed in its major statement. Once you have done this, answer the following question: How can I organize the main points in a way that best supports that statement?

4. **Write a concluding statement.** Answer the following question: What summary can you make or what conclusion can you draw from this essay?

Essay Outline

Major argument or statement

I. First main point
  A. Example or evidence
  B. Example or evidence

    1. Detail about B.
    2. Detail about B.

II. Second main point

  A. Example or evidence
  B. Example or evidence
  C. Example or evidence

1) Louis XIV encouraged the production of literature and art.
2) He believed he could do whatever he wanted without the people's approval.
3) He chose wise advisers who helped industry develop.
4) Because he wanted to expand the territory he ruled, he often waged war.
5) He reigned from 1643 to 1715.
6) Other European monarchs imitated his model of absolute monarchy.
7) He left France in debt when he died, especially because he spent so much on war.
8) He was not an "enlightened despot."

REVIEW

Section Summaries

Section 1 Spain and England Had Absolute Monarchs Powerful monarchs ruled much of Europe from 1500 to 1750. Charles V ruled the Holy Roman Empire and, as Charles I, also ruled Spain. Charles had a larger empire than any ruler since Charlemagne. A long war with France made it impossible for either France or Spain to dominate Europe. In spite of Charles's power, he could never unite his empire or stop the spread of Protestantism. After Charles's death, Spain declined politically and economically. Meanwhile, England, under the Tudors, became Europe's leading power.

Section 2 An Absolute Monarchy Ruled France In France, events set the stage for Louis XIV to become the best example of absolutism and divine right of kings. From 1624 to 1642 Cardinal Richelieu, ruling for the young Louis XIII, governed France forcefully. Under Richelieu and his successor, Cardinal Mazarin, France became Europe's strongest nation. Louis XIV came to the throne believing that he could use France's wealth and power any way he wanted. He lived in great splendor and fought unsuccessful wars. His many mistakes left a great financial burden on the French kings who followed.

Section 3 Monarchs Ruled Russia, Prussia, and Austria In Russia, rulers had no check on their absolute powers. Peter the Great launched an energetic effort to modernize and westernize Russia. Through warfare, he expanded Russia and won new ports. Catherine the Great continued the policy of expansion. In Prussia, absolutism grew with the power of the Hohenzollern family. Hohenzollern rulers built and maintained a strong army, a stable government, and a healthy economy. As in Russia, however, no democratic traditions developed. In Austria, Maria Theresa tried to copy the model of Prussia, yet she could not unite her nation.

Section 4 Other Countries Fought Absolutism The Swiss had overthrown their Hapsburg rulers in 1291. From then on, a weak central government held together a group of self-governing communities. Even so, Switzerland became strong and prosperous. Similarly, Holland freed itself from the absolutist ruler Philip II and, soon after, set up a republic. In general, however, absolutism helped some rulers form nations, yet it brought war, hardship, and unstable rule.

Key Facts

1. Use each vocabulary word in a sentence.
   a. absolutism
   b. divine right
   c. balance of power
   d. revenue
   e. tariff
   f. diplomatic revolution
   g. canton
   h. stadholder
2. Identify and briefly explain the importance of the following names, places, and events.
   a. Charles V
   b. Spanish Inquisition
   c. Henry VIII
   d. Elizabeth I
   e. Cardinal Richelieu
   f. Louis XIV
   g. Peter the Great
   h. Hohenzollerns
   i. the Hapsburgs
   j. Maria Theresa

Main Ideas

1. What was the result of the war between Charles V and Francis I?
2. List two important developments in England under the rule of Elizabeth I.
3. Did Louis XIV use his power wisely? Explain your answer.
4. What changes did Peter the Great and Catherine the Great bring to Russia?
5. How did Frederick the Great make Prussia a powerful nation?
6. How did Switzerland become free of the absolutism of Hapsburg rule?
7. List three facts about the Dutch Republic.

Developing Skill in Reading History

Study the sentences below. Each is a topic sentence for one of the paragraphs on pages 392–394. Review the paragraphs. Then, write two details that support each topic sentence. Notice that the first answer has been started for you.

1. Spain's economic decline was largely the result of its dependence on riches seized in the New World.
   a. The sudden increase in gold and silver caused inflation in Spain.
   b. _____

2. While Philip had a smaller kingdom to rule than his father, he also had less ability as a monarch and often misused his absolute power.
3. Philip's plan to make Spain a stronger nation, however, was not successful.
4. In the Netherlands, Philip treated people so harshly that they rebelled.
5. By this time, it was clear that Spain was no longer the dominant power in Europe that it had been under Charles V.
6. A new family of rulers began in England when the Tudors were victorious in the Wars of the Roses.

Using Social Studies Skills

Analyzing Visual Evidence Study the painting of Louis XIV on this page. In what ways does the painting reinforce what you learned about him?

Critical Thinking

1. **Analyzing Primary Sources** French Bishop Jacques Bossuet, who lived during the 1600s, declared, "the royal throne is not the throne of a man, but the throne of God . . ." Explain what Bishop Bossuet meant.
2. **Formulating Questions** Not all absolutist rulers were the same. Make up three to five

questions that will help you decide whether each absolutist monarch in this chapter was a "good" or "bad" leader.

3. **Predicting Consequences** How do you think Spain's fate might have been different if the Spanish had traded goods for Aztec and Inca gold and silver instead of stealing these precious metals?

Focus on Writing

Making an Outline
When you plan an essay, you must first organize your ideas in an outline. Your outline divides the essay into main ideas, subtopics, and supporting details. Write an outline for an essay on "The Benefits and Hazards of Absolutism." Use the following main ideas for your outline.
   I. Definition of Absolutism
   II. Benefits
   III. Hazards
   IV. Conclusions

Geography in History

The New World Becomes the Old World

When European explorers were sent to the New World (see page 368), they made the Americas a part of the territory they controlled. The first Europeans and the later settlers who were descended from them did not just gain political control of the New World. They also changed its ecology—the whole system of relationships between living things and the environment.

Invasion

When the Europeans came, they brought many common types of plants and animals. They had no understanding, however, of the tremendous effect their "baggage" would have on the land.

One example can be seen in the grasslands of the South American pampas, or plains. Before Europeans came, the pampas were covered with a type of grass called needlegrass. Europeans turned their cattle loose on the almost empty pampas in the early 1500s. The cattle multiplied from 12 or so to about 48 million by 1780. The number of horses also grew until there were vast herds.

When these animals trampled and ate the native grasses, they left large areas open for new weeds to grow. Foreign plants, such as white clover and red-stemmed filaree, moved in. By the 1900s, 75 percent of the plants growing on the pampas were of European origin.

Physical Changes Across the Continents

The change across the Americas was astonishing. Plants brought by Europeans spread far in advance of the first explorers, their seeds carried by winds, birds, and insects.

The honeybee, another European import, also came before the settlers and helped to pollinate new plants. Apparently, native Americans came to dread the arrival of the honeybee. They knew it meant that the Europeans would not be far behind.

When plant and animal populations change, the whole ecological system changes. Soil is affected. Also, different plants use and give off different amounts of oxygen and water. In some areas where the Europeans cleared the native vegetation and planted vast plantations of a single crop, the local climate may even have changed.

Changes in the Human World

The Mound Builders were native Americans with large populations all across the central part of North America before 1500. By the time European settlers began pushing into this area, the cities of the Mound Builders were deserted and overgrown. Experts believe that European diseases were brought to the Mound Builders from Mexico or through trade with settlers on the coast. The spread of disease in advance of explorers also explains why it was so easy for Cortés to conquer Mexico and for Pizarro to conquer Peru. Smallpox had already cleared the path, devastating the native populations in these places.

The Europeans succeeded in establishing a "new Europe" in the Americas. Their success was greatest in the temperate climate regions. North of Mexico and south of southern Brazil, people of European descent make up over 80 percent of the population. They speak languages and practice religions brought to the continents by the first Europeans.

The change in tropical climate regions was less complete. The European staple crops—grain, for instance—did not grow well in the hot, wet climate. Cattle and horses took generations to adjust to the hot climate. To this day the tropical regions of the Americas are peopled mostly by those of African or native American descent. Only the country of Chile remains non-European in makeup because its rugged terrain attracted few immigrants.

Focus on Geography

1. **Location** Between what two latitudes was it most difficult for the new plants to thrive?

2. **Interaction** Describe the changes that occurred in the pampas after the Europeans arrived.

3. **Regions** What regions of the Americas have an ecology that is most like the ecology of Europe?

Critical Thinking

Identifying Central Issues

4. Why do you think people, plants, and animals from the Americas did not take over Europe?

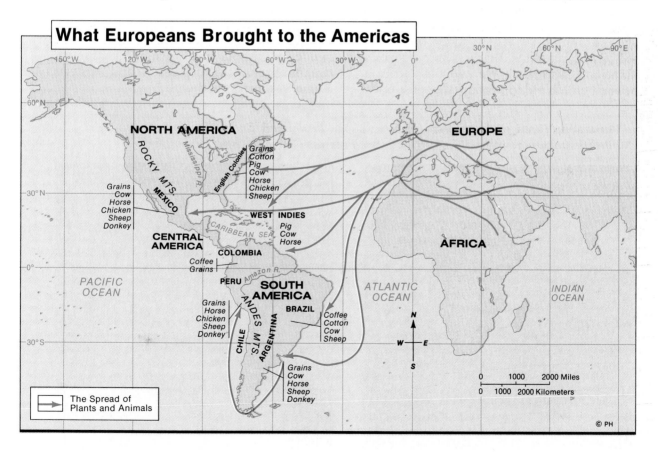

What Europeans Brought to the Americas

The Spread of Plants and Animals

© PH

UNIT 3: The Middle Ages

(A.D. 330–1453)

It was the night of November 14, 565. The 83-year-old emperor—the "emperor who never sleeps"—was, as usual, working by candlelight in his room in the Great Palace of Constantine, in what is today known as the city of Istanbul, Turkey. The emperor's name was Justinian I. He had risen from a peasant childhood to become the most powerful ruler of his day and had ruled the mighty Byzantine Empire for nearly 40 years. Justinian, with the help of the Empress Theodora, had begun to rebuild the power and grandeur of imperial Rome. They had recaptured much of the land lost by earlier, weaker emperors. Once again, the Mediterranean Sea was a "Roman lake."

Many people could not remember a time when Justinian had not ruled. He seemed indestructible. So did the empire that he had rebuilt and ruled so well for so long. But Justinian's reign—far from being the rebirth of Roman power—actually marked its end. Late that night, the great emperor died suddenly without any warning. Justinian's dream of reuniting the Eastern and Western Roman empires died with him.

▼ **Illustrating History** *The mosaic art below shows Justinian (left), who ruled Byzantium from A.D. 527 to 565, and the Empress Theodora (right).*

7 Byzantium and the Rise of Islam

As you read, look for answers to these questions:

◆ In what ways did Byzantium build upon the Roman legacy?
◆ Who was Mohammed and how did his ideas affect Arab culture?

The Byzantine Empire, with its splendid capital of Constantinople (KHON stan tih NOH pul), dominated many aspects of life in eastern Europe after the fall of the Western Roman Empire in A.D. 476. At the same time, the new religion of Islam unified the people of the Arabian Peninsula.

Byzantium Emerged as a Mighty Empire

Constantinople lay astride the Bosporus (BOS poor uhs), the water passage that separates Asia and Europe. Its location made Constantinople a center of trade and transportation.

Byzantine Rulers Extended the Empire

Able rulers, such as Leo III and Basil (BAZ il) II, extended Byzantine power. The emperor Justinian fought to restore the Roman Empire and organized Roman law into a single, simplified form. Imperial conquests and the need to defend their empire from its many enemies led the Byzantines to build a great military organization in the Roman tradition.

Christianity flourished throughout the empire. Religious leaders called patriarchs served as the heads of the Byzantine church. Religious thought dominated Byzantine intellectual and artistic life.

Mohammed Founded a New Religious Empire

The nomadic Arab people of the Arabian Peninsula—called Bedouins (BED oo wihnz)—had lived for centuries in a loosely organized tribal society. During the seventh century, the teachings of Mohammed (moh HAHM ihd) spread throughout the peninsula. Mohammed believed that he had been chosen by *Allah*—the single, all-powerful God—to serve as a prophet and to bring the Arabs together under a new faith known as Islam.

By his death in 632, Mohammed had unified much of Arabia under his leadership. The followers of Islam, who were known as Muslims, quickly began to push into the Byzantine lands of Asia and Africa. By the early 900s, they had moved into Europe and had conquered parts of Italy and Spain.

Muslim Beliefs Attracted Many Followers

The attraction of Islam served to unify the Arab people into a closely knit community of faithful followers in the years after Mohammed's death. Muslim religious leaders called **mullahs** (MUL ahs) helped to spread the prophet's teachings.

During the mid-600s, the growing Muslim empire came under the rule of political and religious leaders called **caliphs** (KAY lihfs). Under these leaders, Muslim influence expanded through **jihads** (jih HAHDZ)—holy wars against non-Muslims.

In the eleventh century, the Muslim Seljuks of Turkey won control of much of the Muslim world. The Seljuks eventually conquered the Byzantine lands in eastern Europe. In 1453, the Turks brought about the end of the Byzantine Empire by conquering the city of Constantinople.

REVIEW

1. Define: mullah, caliph, jihad
2. Identify: the Bosporus, Justinian, Mohammed
3. Name two ways that Constantinople's location shaped its development.
4. Describe the importance of the mullahs.

8 Western Europe: Foundations of the Middle Ages

As you read, look for answers to these questions:

◆ How did Germanic culture influence European civilization?
◆ What role did the Church play in medieval European life?

By about A.D. 500, Germanic people had settled throughout western Europe. One Germanic group, the Franks, built a powerful kingdom in the area of modern France. By about 800, the Frankish ruler Charlemagne (SHAR luh MAYN) had joined with the Roman Catholic church to establish the Holy Roman Empire. The alliance of Church and empire allowed the Church to control Europe's politics and trade.

European society during the Middle Ages was shaped by the concept of **feudalism** (FYOOD uh LIZ uhm). Powerful lords provided land and protection to lesser nobles, called **vassals** (VAS uhls), who pledged loyalty and service in return. **Serfs,** who farmed the nobles' land, made up Europe's largest social class. Most Europeans lived on large, self-sufficient farms called **manors.**

The Crusades Challenged Muslim Control

After the eleventh century, a series of **crusades**—wars to end Muslim control of the Holy Land—brought Europeans into contact with new people. This encouraged the growth of trade and communication.

REVIEW

1. Define: feudalism, vassal, serf, manor, crusade
2. Identify: the Franks, Charlemagne
3. What were the effects of the crusades?

9 The Flowering of Medieval Society

As you read, look for answers to these questions:

◆ What were the causes of urban growth?
◆ How did religion affect learning in medieval Europe?

European society became increasingly sophisticated during the late Middle Ages. Towns developed as trade and commerce revived, and learning and culture began to flourish again.

As trade and commerce grew, the manor began to fade as the basic unit of Europe's economy. The manors of the early Middle Ages had been self-sufficient farming villages. The growth of trade made towns the new centers of economic activity. Skilled workers in towns organized into craft associations called **guilds.**

Religious thought provided the basis of learning in the Middle Ages. Philosophers, such as Thomas Aquinas and Peter Abelard, developed the ideas known as **scholasticism** (skuh LAS tih SIZ uhm), which used logic to prove the existence of God. Art and architecture, too, drew inspiration from religious themes.

Toward the end of the Middle Ages, an economy based on money began to replace the feudal economy, which was based on land. The nobles gradually lost power to kings, and the Church lost much of its control over everyday life. Changing institutions, wars, and disasters such as the Black Death signalled the end of the Middle Ages in Europe.

REVIEW

1. Define: guild, scholasticism.
2. Identify: Thomas Aquinas.
3. How did increased trade affect town life during the Middle Ages?

UNIT THREE REVIEW

Knowing Key Terms, People, and Places
1. Define: mullah, caliph, jihad, feudalism, vassal, serf, manor, crusade, guild, scholasticism
2. Identify: Constantinople, Islam, Bedouin, Allah, Baghdad, Holy Roman Empire

Focus on Geography
3. Compare the map of Charlemagne's empire below with the map of Europe today on page 788 of your textbook. What modern European nations did Charlemagne control?

Reviewing Main Ideas
4. Why was Constantinople's geographic location significant?
5. What ideas dominated intellectual and artistic life in the Byzantine Empire?

6. In what way did the social organization of the Bedouin people change as a result of the teachings of Mohammed?
7. How did the alliance between the Roman Catholic church and the Holy Roman Empire influence political development in medieval Europe?

Critical Thinking
8. **Making Comparisons** Compare the Islamic Empire founded by Mohammed with the Holy Roman Empire of Charlemagne. What role did religion play in the establishment of each empire?
9. **Determining Relevance** What was the significance of Constantinople's geographic location for the city's commercial success?

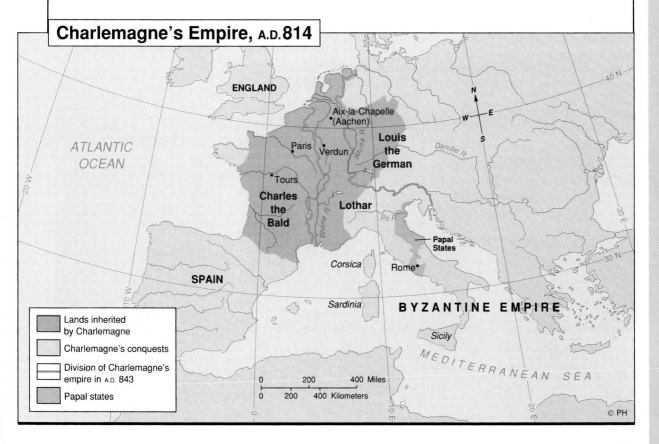

Charlemagne's Empire, A.D. 814

- Lands inherited by Charlemagne
- Charlemagne's conquests
- Division of Charlemagne's empire in A.D. 843
- Papal states

ENGLAND

ATLANTIC OCEAN

Aix-la-Chapelle (Aachen)

Paris • Verdun

Louis the German

Tours •

Charles the Bald

Lothar

Danube R.

Po R.

Papal States

Corsica

Rome •

SPAIN

Sardinia

BYZANTINE EMPIRE

Sicily

MEDITERRANEAN SEA

0   200   400 Miles
0   200   400 Kilometers

© PH

UNIT 4: The World Beyond Europe

(600 B.C.–1700)

He was Shah Jahan, the Mogul emperor of India. She was Mumtaz Mahal, "the chosen one of the palace," his constant companion since the two of them were married 20 years earlier. On this day in 1631, the emperor was awaiting news of his wife, who was about to give birth to a child. When the messenger entered and gave Shah Jahan the news, his world was crushed. His wife had died in childbirth.

The emperor called together architects from India, Persia, Turkey, and beyond to plan a memorial for his deceased wife, Mumtaz Mahal. It became know as the Taj Mahal, the most elaborate tomb the world has ever seen. It took more than 20,000 workmen 22 years to build at the cost of 40 million rupees. But when it was finished, Shah Jahan had accomplished his goal. The world would never forget the name of his beloved wife.

▼ **Illustrating History** *Below is a picture of the Taj Mahal, built in loving memory of Mumtaz Mahal by her husband, Shah Jahan.*

10 The Splendor of India and Southeast Asia

As you read, look for answers to these questions:

◆ How did Indians live under their Muslim conquerors?
◆ What groups of people shaped the cultures of Southeast Asia?

India is an ancient civilization, as old as those of Mesopotamia. Although India was conquered several times, its people kept their own distinct culture.

Muslims Conquered India

The first major Muslim conquest in India came around 1000 when a Muslim named Mahmud became **sultan,** or ruler, of Ghazni, a small state in the northwest of the country. His ruthless soldiers swept across the border of India, looting gold and jewels from Hindu temples, and taking Indians back to the Middle East as slaves.

The major conqueror of India, Babur, was a Muslim from Asiatic Russia. He founded the Mogul (MOH gull) dynasty in 1524. His grandson, Akbar, became ruler in 1556, at the age of 13. Akbar was tolerant of all religions, named good advisers, and started a **civil service**—a body of employees trained in government administration.

Aurangzeb (AH rung zehb) became the last Mogul ruler in 1658. His strict Muslim beliefs and intolerant treatment of the Hindus destroyed the unity of the empire, leaving it open to conquest when European traders arrived.

Traditional Hindu Life Continued Under Muslim Rule

The basic social unit in India, according to Hindu tradition, was the extended family. Next to the family, the caste system was most important in deciding people's everyday activities and relationships. The caste system dictated how people from each class behaved. People were born into a caste and stayed there for life. The highest caste was the Brahmins, who were usually the only people who could read and write.

India Contributed to World Culture

Indian mathematicians and scientists gave the world many gifts. They invented the number symbols we use today called **Arabic numerals.** As early as 326 B.C., when Alexander the Great invaded India, Indian metalworkers were making steel.

India's two major religions, Hinduism and Buddhism, inspired both literature and art. Religious songs and poems, called Vedas, as well as epics and Indian fables are among the great literary contributions. Brightly colored miniature paintings, illustrated Hindu manuscripts, and sculptures of gods are typical of Indian art.

Southeast Asian Cultures Developed

Modern Southeast Asia has countries both on the mainland and on chains of islands, called **archipelagoes** (AHR kih PELL uh gohs). The countries of the mainland are Burma, Thailand, Vietnam, Kampuchea and Laos. The island nations include the Philippines, Indonesia, and Malaysia.

A rich variety of people live in this area who have migrated from China, India, or Tibet. They have brought with them different languages, religions, and cultural traditions. Often, these cultures and ways of life have mixed and blended together.

REVIEW

1. Define: sultan, civil service, Arabic numeral, archipelago
2. Identify: Akbar, Brahmins
3. How did the religion of India's rulers differ from that of most people?
4. From what areas did the people who settled Southeast Asia come?

11 Golden Ages in China, Japan, and Korea

As you read, look for answers to these questions:

◆ How do traditions affect the culture of China?
◆ What are some unique aspects of Korean and Japanese culture?

When Charlemagne was at his peak in Europe in 800, the Tangs were ruling China. As great as Charlemagne was, China's power, cultural achievement, and wealth were far greater than anything Charlemagne could dream of or ever hope to accomplish.

China Entered a New Golden Age

China's first Golden Age occurred during the Han dynasty. But, when this empire fell in A.D. 220, centuries of disorder resulted. During this time, the Chinese fought among themselves and against invaders.

In 618, the Tang dynasty began and China entered a new Golden Age. Tang China was the greatest empire in the world at its time. The Song dynasty, which began around 960, continued China's Golden Age. It was destroyed by a Mongol invasion in the 1200s.

The Mongol rulers, especially Kublai (KOO bly) Khan, proved to be able rulers. To the Chinese, however, the Mongols were foreigners. Eventually, rebellions broke out that toppled the Mongols and established the Ming dynasty in 1368.

Chinese Culture Followed Many Traditions

Even more than in India, the family was the hub of Chinese life. In fact, the Chinese extended family, rather than the individual, was the center of Chinese society. Family members followed strict rules about obedience: children obeyed parents, wives obeyed husbands, and younger children obeyed older ones in a family.

Education was highly valued in China. Scholars were respected, and passing a civil service examination could improve social position. One challenge for Chinese students was the difficulty of the Chinese language. The written language has thousands of characters, and spoken Chinese has many **dialects** (DY uh LEKTS)—different ways of pronouncing words.

Korea and Japan Created Unique Cultures

Korea and Japan borrowed and learned much from China. Despite the influence of China, however, Korea and Japan retained their own heritage and maintained their political independence.

Korea's location has tempted invaders from China and Japan. However, its mountainous geography encouraged isolation and the development of a unique national culture. Korea was defeated by China's Han dynasty, by the Tang dynasty, and by the Mongols. However, the Koreans were able to regain their independence each time.

The Koreans greatly valued scholarship and invention. In the 1400s, Korean people were the first to use **movable type**—separate pieces of metal that can be used again—to print large numbers of books.

Japan developed a feudal system similar to Europe's in which powerful landowners controlled peasants and warriors called **samurai** (SAH mah rye). During this period, Japan developed the samurai code—"the way of the warrior." Under this code, loyalty to the lord was more important than loyalty to the family or to the emperor.

REVIEW

1. Define: dialect, movable type, samurai
2. Identify: Kublai Khan, samurai code
3. Name two important traditions in China.
4. What is one important invention developed in Korea?

12 Civilizations of Latin America and Africa

As you read, look for answers to these questions:

◆ What were some of the achievements of pre-Columbian American cultures?
◆ What civilizations developed in Africa?

When Europeans arrived in South America and Africa, they set up colonies to serve European interests. In the process, they destroyed many advanced civilizations. People today have developed a new appreciation of the achievements of these early American and African civilizations.

Civilizations Developed in the Americas

Many pre-Columbian cultures, or cultures that existed in the Americas before Columbus's voyages, developed in Mexico and Central America. They had similar systems of picture writing called **glyphs** (glifs), built pyramids, and studied the stars. One of the best known of these cultures is the Mayas. Mayan civilization may have developed as early as 2000 B.C., and it lasted until the Spanish came in the 1500s.

The Aztecs were a warlike people ruled by a strong king. The king ruled a large empire that was centered in Tenochtitlán (tay NOCH tee TLAHN), or present-day Mexico City. The Aztecs were skilled in technology, farming, astronomy, and mathematics.

The Inca Empire lay in the Andes Mountains, extending from southern Colombia to southern Chile in South America. They had a highly organized society that was ruled by an emperor called the Inca. In order to farm the dry, rugged mountain lands, the Incas developed irrigation and terracing.

Many African Civilizations Developed

Many mighty African kingdoms rose and fell. These included the western African kingdom of Ghana, which reached the

▲ **Illustrating History** *The picture above shows an Aztec calendar covered with intricate symbols and designs.*

height of its ancient glory during the reign of Tenkamenin (tehn kuh MEHN ihn). The people of Mali, too, developed strong traditions under their king Mansa Musa. All the western African kingdoms were built along the trade routes that crossed the Sahara to the Mediterranean Sea.

Important cultures developed in eastern Africa also. Great Zimbabwe (zihm BAH bweh), an old city of stone elaborately decorated in gold, provides evidence of one East African culture. Along the coast, such city-states as Zanzibar, Kilwa, and Malinda developed a culture and language known as Swahili (swah HEE lee).

REVIEW

1. Define: glyph
2. Identify: Tenochtitlán, Great Zimbabwe
3. Name three advanced civilizations that existed in pre-Columbian America.
4. How was the development of western African kingdoms affected by trade?

Knowing Key Terms, People, and Places
Choose the best definition for each term.

1. sultan
   a. a ruler in India
   b. a ruler in China
   c. a ruler in Japan
2. samurai
   a. a Japanese warrior
   b. Chinese pottery
   c. Korean printing press
3. glyph
   a. a number symbol
   b. picture writing
   c. a form of literature

Identify the person, place, or group described below.

4. highest level in Indian caste system
   a. sultan
   b. Veda
   c. Brahmin
5. pre-Columbian civilization whose capital was Tenochtitlán
   a. Aztec
   b. Inca
   c. Maya
6. Mongol ruler of China
   a. Akbar
   b. Manchu
   c. Kublai Khan
7. kingdom in western Africa
   a. Ghana
   b. Great Zimbabwe
   c. Zanzibar

Focus on Geography

8. What aspect of Korea's geography favored the development of its unique culture?
9. What techniques did the Incas develop in order to farm the hillsides of the Andes Mountains?

Reviewing Main Ideas

10. In general, how did the Muslim rulers of India treat their Hindu subjects?

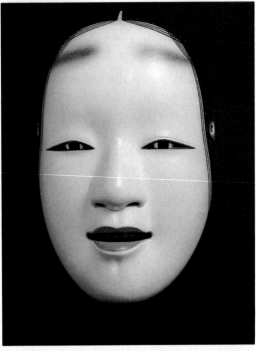

▲ **Illustrating History** *Above is a Japanese character mask used in drama. The first of these* Noh *masks were made during the eighteenth century.*

11. During what two dynasties did China enjoy a new Golden Age?
12. Why is the political and economic system of Japan referred to as a feudal system?
13. What was the name of the pre-Columbian civilization located in Central America and Mexico?

Critical Thinking

14. **Drawing Conclusions** Why do you think that people of the lower castes in India generally did not learn to read or write?

UNIT 5: The Journey into Modern Times

(1000–1750)

It was the late 1400s, and a young sailor named Christopher Columbus was visiting Venice, the most important city in the world. Venice was an unlikely city to be the world's leading economic and political power and the center of Renaissance art and learning. It lay on about 120 islands in the Adriatic Sea, and, instead of streets, it had canals. Because the islands were unsuitable for farming, they weren't even inhabited during the height of the Roman Empire. But Venetians now controlled trade in the eastern Mediterranean Sea, and their ships carried almost all the goods that reached Europe from Asia.

As Columbus left the city, he couldn't possibly realize that his future travels would lead to the city's decline. For when Columbus and other explorers discovered new ocean routes, Venice lost its position as the major trading center of the world. The nations with ports on the Atlantic Ocean would soon replace Venice and the other Italian city-states as the dominant players in world affairs.

▼ **Illustrating History**   *This painting shows the city of Florence in Italy at the height of the Renaissance.*

13 The Growth of Nations

As you read, look for answers to these questions:

◆ How did England and France become nations?
◆ What other nations developed in Europe during the Middle Ages?

One of the most important developments of modern world history was the rise of nation-states. A nation-state can provide protection for its people, raise money, and improve the way people live.

Nations Shared Important Characteristics

The desire to form a nation, or **nationalism,** has been a powerful force in history. The process of nation-building began as early as the eleventh century and is still going on today.

Nations have certain things in common. One characteristic is land with definite boundaries, which can unite a people by separating them from others. A second feature of a nation is its people and resources, which provide labor and raw materials upon which to build an economy. Third, a nation needs a shared language and culture. Finally, a nation must have a government. Whatever form the government takes, the nation must have the power and authority to set policies and make decisions for itself. This important characteristic of a nation is called **sovereignty** (SOV er uhn TEE).

Nation-Building Began in England and France

Although England was invaded and settled by several different groups of people, most of them lived in a fairly small area, spoke similar languages, and shared a similar culture. Nation-building began when the Normans, who were French, invaded England in 1066 and set up a strong monarchy.

Under the Normans, England developed a set of laws to govern the nation. Much of this law was **common law,** or law based on the customs of the people. In 1215, King John signed the Magna Carta. This document placed limits on the monarch's power and gave some fundamental rights to the people, such as the right to be tried by a jury.

France became a nation more slowly than England, partly because of its geography. France was not isolated by water as England was, and its boundaries continually changed as a result of local wars. Strong kings, however, eventually extended their authority over greater territory. They weakened the power of the feudal lords and won the loyalty of the people.

As England and France became strong, unified nations, they also became rivals. Between 1337 and 1453, the two countries fought a long series of wars that we now call the Hundred Years' War. The war marked the end of feudalism, and each nation set about the task of unifying its people.

Other Nations Developed in Europe

Feudalism declined elsewhere in Europe as England and France fought. In Spain and Portugal, strong monarchs drove out foreign invaders, united the people, and developed national loyalties. Russia, even though it controlled a large area, developed slowly. The Netherlands, Switzerland, and the Scandinavian nations also developed gradually. Germany and Italy remained divided, however, and did not become nations until the nineteenth century.

REVIEW

1. Define: nationalism, sovereignty, common law
2. Identify: Normans, Magna Carta
3. What are four characteristics that nations have in common?
4. What was a major result of the Hundred Years' War?

14 The Renaissance

As you read, look for answers to these questions:

◆ How did people's view of the world change during the Renaissance?
◆ What were some of the major achievements of the Renaissance?

The **Renaissance** (REHN uh sahns) was a major cultural movement that began in Italy and then spread throughout Europe, including England, France, Germany, and the Netherlands. The word *renaissance* comes from a Latin word that means rebirth.

The ideas of the Renaissance focused more on the study of humanity than on religion. The focus on humanity that oc-curred during the Renaissance is called **humanism.** Humanism influenced the literature, art, and architecture. For example, writers began to write in the languages used by common people, rather than Latin. Writers also turned away from religious ideas and focused on real-life themes such as love and marriage.

The Renaissance Flourished in Italy

The Renaissance began in Italy where the largest cities in western Europe existed. It thrived especially in the cities of Venice and Florence, where wealthy bankers and merchants acted as sponsors, or **patrons,** of arts and learning.

Two great figures of the Renaissance were Leonardo da Vinci (dah VEEN chee) and Michelangelo. Leonardo was a painter, sculptor, engineer, scientist, and inventor. Michelangelo's patron was the Roman Catholic pope, and most of his paintings and sculptures had religious themes. He also designed St. Peter's Basilica in Rome.

Modern Science Began in the Renaissance

Modern science also had its beginnings in the curiosity and new ideas of the Renaissance. Johann Gutenburg (GOO tehn burg) invented the printing press and Nicolaus Copernicus (ko PUR nih kus) concluded that the sun was the center of the universe. But Renaissance science had its limitations. For example, scientists still felt that little knowledge could be added beyond what the Greeks and Romans had discovered.

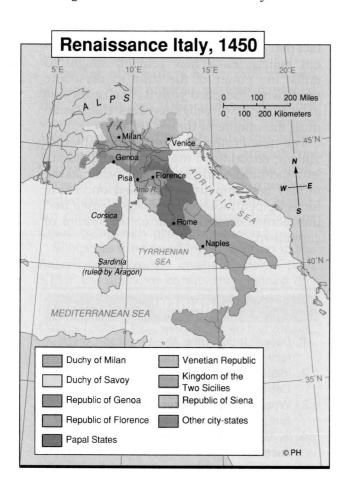

Renaissance Italy, 1450

Duchy of Milan
Duchy of Savoy
Republic of Genoa
Republic of Florence
Papal States
Venetian Republic
Kingdom of the Two Sicilies
Republic of Siena
Other city-states

© PH

REVIEW

1. Define: Renaissance, humanism, patron
2. Identify: Venice, Leonardo da Vinci, Johann Gutenburg
3. How did the ideas of the Renaissance affect literature?
4. Why did science develop slowly during the Renaissance?

17 The Age of Absolutism

As you read, look for answers to these questions:

◆ What were some of the powers of absolute monarchs?
◆ How did people in some countries fight absolutism?

The complete, or absolute, control of a monarch over his or her people is called **absolutism,** and this form of government gives its name to the period in history known as the Age of Absolutism. During the Age of Absolutism, the monarchs of Europe claimed that they ruled by the will of God, or by **divine right.**

Absolute Monarchs Ruled Most of Europe

The Spanish monarch, Charles V, was one of the most powerful monarchs in Europe. He was king of Spain, emperor of the Holy Roman Empire, king of the Netherlands, and king of part of Italy. When his son, Philip II, was defeated by England in the battle that destroyed his Armada, the Spanish empire began to decline.

In England, Henry VIII was later followed by Elizabeth I, probably England's most popular ruler. She was an absolute monarch, and, like her father, she knew how to get her way with Parliament. Under Elizabeth I's reign, England became a major seagoing nation. Also during the Elizabethan period, great works of English literature were written by authors such as the poet and playwright William Shakespeare.

The height of absolutism and its classic example was the reign of Louis XIV of France. Louis built a palace at Versailles (ver SY), that had 1,300 rooms. He said, "I am the state," thus indicating his absolute authority. Other absolute monarchs in Europe were Peter the Great and Catherine the Great of Russia, and the Prussian monarch, Frederick the Great.

Absolutism Helped and Hurt Civilization

During the Age of Absolutism, many good things were done for the people and nations of Europe. Absolutism was a better form of government than feudalism for most people. Absolute rulers held nations together, and they built trade and industry. Absolute rulers also encouraged the growth of literature and science.

However, despite these good things, absolutism probably did not serve civilization very well. Absolute rulers made wars that cost many lives. In order to fight the wars, the monarchs taxed the peasants heavily. The people also had to pay for the court life of an idle and privileged nobility while suffering in poverty themselves.

Switzerland and the Netherlands Fought Absolutism

Switzerland and the Netherlands were among the first countries to free themselves from the oppression of absolutism and establish democracies. They showed that a nation can flourish without a hereditary monarchy and without the absolute rule of a king or queen.

Switzerland freed itself from monarchies in the early 1300s and maintained its independence with a strong army. The Netherlands was under the control of Philip II of Spain until 1581. In that year, the Protestant northern provinces, under the leadership of William the Silent, broke away from Spain. These northern provinces then formed an independent nation.

REVIEW

1. Define: absolutism, divine right
2. Identify: Charles V, Louis XIV
3. What event began the decline of the Spanish monarchy?
4. What were three ways that absolutism hurt Western civilization?

UNIT FIVE REVIEW

Knowing Key Terms, People, and Places
Choose the best definition for each term.

1. sovereignty
   a. a government shaped by religion
   b. the ability of a country to demand the loyalty of its people
   c. the power and authority of a nation to set policies and make decisions independently

2. indulgence
   a. a pardon granted by the Church for sins
   b. an argument against the abuses of the Church
   c. an act that bars a person from membership in the Church

3. patron
   a. a person who helps pay for the arts and learning
   b. a person who develops new ideas for inventions
   c. a person who creates works of art

4. entrepreneur
   a. a person who tries to convert others to his or her faith
   b. a person who risks opening his or her own business to make a profit
   c. a person who seeks adventure for the fame he or she will receive

5. Identify: Elizabeth I, Magna Carta, Martin Luther, Michelangelo, Florence, Geneva

Focus on Geography
6. What aspect of England's geography helped it in the process of nation-building?
7. How did the development of ocean trade routes shift trading centers from Italy to Europe's Atlantic coast?

Reviewing Main Ideas
8. What event led to the establishment of a strong monarchy in England?
9. What two major European national groups did not form nations until the nineteenth century?

▲ **Illustrating History** *For this portrait, the vain Louis XIV posed in his richest royal garments.*

10. How is the Renaissance related to humanism?
11. Name two great artists of the Italian Renaissance.
12. What did the Ninety-Five Theses of Martin Luther argue against?
13. Why did the Reformation help to start wars in Europe?
14. Which European nation was the first to found colonies in the Americas?
15. What were some benefits of absolutism for the people of Europe?

Critical Thinking
16. **Demonstrating Reasoned Judgment** The great expansion of business, trade, and finance closely followed the Renaissance and Reformation movements. Do you think that these events are related? Explain your answer.
17. **Identifying Central Issues** Why was the defeat of the Spanish Armada an important event?

UNIT
6

An Age of Revolution

(1600–1848)

Chapters

"Liberty, Equality, Fraternity," was the battle cry on French streets when angry citizens stormed public buildings in a revolt against absolute rule. This was the beginning of the Age of Revolution that swept Europe and the Americas. These political revolutions were accompanied by a revolution in thought, known as the Age of Reason. Some changes were peaceful; others were violent. But, a common thread was the speed at which change took place during this period. The map and the time line, linked by color, show where and when the Age of Revolution and the Age of Reason took place.

1 AGE OF REVOLUTION

At right is a poster promoting the French Revolution; Simon Bolivar, far right, led revolutions in Latin America.

UNITÉ
INDIVISIBILITÉ
DE LA
RÉPUBLIQUE
LIBERTÉ
ÉGALITÉ
FRATERNITÉ
OU LA
MORT

NORTH
AMERICA   AMER
COLO

MEXICO
1

CENTRAL
AMERICA

VENEZ

COLO

1550	1600	1650

AGE OF REVOLUTION 1

1689 The Bill of Rights restor
order in England without bloodsh

AGE OF REASON 2

■ 1610 The invention of the microscope
advances scientific study

■ 1665 Isaac Newton
theory of gravitation

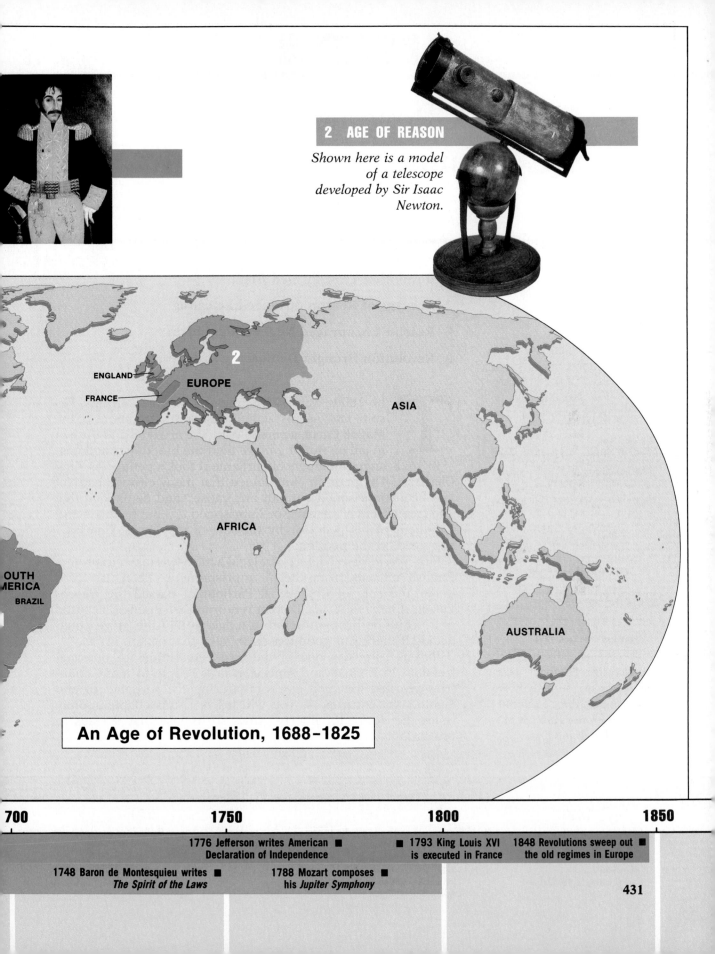

2 AGE OF REASON

Shown here is a model of a telescope developed by Sir Isaac Newton.

ENGLAND

EUROPE

FRANCE

ASIA

AFRICA

SOUTH AMERICA

BRAZIL

AUSTRALIA

An Age of Revolution, 1688–1825

700   1750   1800   1850

1776 Jefferson writes American ■
Declaration of Independence

■ 1793 King Louis XVI
is executed in France

1848 Revolutions sweep out ■
the old regimes in Europe

1748 Baron de Montesquieu writes ■
The Spirit of the Laws

1788 Mozart composes ■
his *Jupiter Symphony*

A Revolution in Government and Thought

(1600–1800)

1 **Revolution Transformed England**

2 **The Age of Reason Advanced Learning**

3 **Reason Encouraged New Political Ideas**

4 **Revolution Brought Democracy to America**

AREOPAGITICA;

A

SPEECH

OF

M*r*. *JOHN MILTON*

For the Liberty of VNLICENC'D PRINTING,

To the PARLAMENT of ENGLAND.

Τὸνδ'ἀμείβετ' ἔπειτα, οι πεδίφ μάλς
Χρηςὸ τι διλόμ' οἱ μέσῳ ἔχθειτε, ὑγαν.
Καὶ ἰαυθ' ὁ χρεζων, λαμνωςι λδ', ὁ μὲ θέλων,
Σιγῷ, τι τέτων ἐςι ἰνδικώτερον πόλι;
. Euripid. Hicetid.

*This is true Liberty when free born men
Having to advise the public may speak free,
Which he who can, and will, deferv's high praise,
Who neither can nor will, may hold his peace;
What can be jufter in a State then this?*
Euripid. Hicetid.

LONDON,
'Printed' in the Yeare, 1644.

▲ **Illustrating History** *This pamphlet was written by the English poet John Milton in 1644 to protest Parliament's censorship of the press.*

The 1600s were risky times for English citizens. Despite laws against it, and despite the traditions of the Magna Carta, a person could be arrested and thrown in jail on nothing more than the hint of wrongdoing.

In 1628, angry members of Parliament took a petition to King Charles I. The petition complained that many citizens had "of late been imprisoned without any cause" and demanded that "no freeman may be taken or imprisoned . . . but by the lawful judgment of his peers or by the law of the land." Charles I shrugged off the petition.

Fifty years passed before any legal action was taken to protect English citizens from illegal imprisonment. Then, in 1679, under the rule of Charles II, Parliament passed the *Habeas Corpus Amendment Act*. The act required that a person accused of a crime be brought before a judge so that the judge could decide if there was good reason to keep that person in jail.

Habeas corpus is one of the basic guarantees of personal freedom in English and American law. People in many countries yearned for such freedoms during the seventeenth and eighteenth centuries. As you will learn in this chapter, sometimes the desire for liberty grows so intense that it leads to revolution.

1650	1700	1750	1800

■ **1642**
English Civil War breaks out

■ **1649**
Cromwell rules England

■ **1687**
Newton's *Principia* starts the Enlightenment

■ **1689**
Glorious Revolution produces the English Bill of Rights

■ **1726**
Jonathan Swift writes *Gulliver's Travels*

■ **1776**
America issues the Declaration of Independence

▲ **Illustrating History** *Above is a colored engraving of King Charles II entering London in 1660 amid cheers from the English people.*

1 Revolution Transformed England

As you read, look for answers to these questions:

◆ How did the rule of the Stuarts lead to civil war in England?
◆ What were the results of the civil war in England?
◆ What happened during the Glorious Revolution?

Key Terms: limited monarchy (defined on p. 436), right of petition (p. 437)

When Elizabeth, the last of the Tudor rulers of England, died in 1603, she left no direct heir. The English throne passed to the Stuarts, the ruling family of Scotland. When King James VI of Scotland, a cousin of Elizabeth's, was crowned James I of England in 1603, a dramatic change in English politics began to take place.

Under the Stuart rulers, the confidence of the English people was shaken, since the new dynasty ignored or tried to abolish the institutions of Parliament, jury trial, and common law. These changes led England from the restrictions of a monarchy to a revolution that established some firm, democratic institutions in that country.

Religious and Parliamentary Leaders Fought with James I

Unlike the Tudors, who had known how to deal with Parliament, James I could not get along with the members of Parliament. James believed that he ruled by divine right. To the English, however, the divine right of kings and queens was an unwelcome concept. James's lack of common sense and

433

lack of tact made his reign a failure. His quarrels with Parliament centered around three main issues: religion, money, and foreign policy.

Religion. Throughout his 22-year reign, James opposed the Puritans, even when Parliament was sympathetic to their cause. His negative attitude was hard for the Puritans to accept because Elizabeth had at least tolerated them. The Puritans wanted to purify the Anglican church by following the teachings of John Calvin. They believed church services should be simple, and they wanted to organize the church on a democratic basis. James was determined that the Puritans should follow the Anglican church, which he was head of, so he denied their wishes. To obtain religious freedom, some Puritans eventually left England and settled in America. These people became known as the Pilgrims.

Money and foreign policy. Financial problems proved to be as troublesome to James as religious ones. Parliament controlled the "purse strings," or money, and James was always in need of money. He was waging war against Spain as well as living a luxurious life at his court. Often, the members of Parliament were unwilling to let James have the money he needed because they did not agree with his policies, especially the religious ones. When Parliament did not give James the money he needed, he sent its members home. Relations between James I and Parliament grew worse each year, and James's son, Charles I, would pay for his father's mistakes.

Charles I Continued the Battle with Parliament

In 1625, James I died, and his son, Charles I, became king. Charles did not forget how badly Parliament had treated his father, nor did he ever learn how to get along with or without Parliament.

When Parliament refused to give Charles the money he needed to govern and to fight foreign wars, Charles tried to rule without Parliament. As his father had done, Charles sold titles of nobility, gave special privileges

to business owners who could pay for them, and taxed cities that had not been taxed before. He forced people to make loans to the government—loans that were never repaid. These activities further angered the people and Parliament.

Petition of Right. Even using illegal means, Charles I was unable to raise enough money and finally had to go to Parliament to ask for more money. At that point, Parliament made Charles sign an agreement stating that he would no longer force people to pay taxes or to make loans without first consulting Parliament. Charles also was forced to do away with special courts, such as the Court of Star Chamber, that had imprisoned people unjustly. He had to agree not to make arrests without giving reasons and that soldiers would no longer be housed in people's homes if they were not welcome. These new rules were included in an act entitled the Petition of Right, which Parliament forced the reluctant Charles I to sign in 1628.

Unfortunately, after signing the Petition of Right, Charles I decided to break the agreement and rule without Parliament. From 1629 to 1640, he was able to do so, but his religious policies finally led to increasing trouble with Scotland.

Religious war with Scotland. Following in his father's footsteps, Charles continued to force the English to worship in the Anglican church. Large numbers of Puritans continued to leave England for America. In 1638, Charles tried to force the practices of the Anglican church on Scotland. The angered Scots raised an army and invaded England in protest. Charles again needed money for a war, so he summoned Parliament. Once again, Parliament, which had some powerful Puritan members who did not support the Anglican church, refused him the money, and Charles dismissed the assembly angrily.

The Scots forced Charles I to pay them to leave the country. To do so, the king was forced to call still another Parliament to get the money. The awkward position in which the king found himself ultimately would bring about his downfall.

▲ **Illustrating History** *This painting shows Charles I being led to his execution in 1649. He was condemned to death by Cromwell's court.*

The Long Parliament Limited Charles I

The new Parliament was made up mostly of Charles's enemies. It is known as the Long Parliament because it was in session for 13 years, from 1640 to 1653.

Once called into session, the Long Parliament proceeded to pass laws limiting the monarch's powers. The Triennial Act required Parliament to be called into session at least once every three years. Once again, the Court of Star Chamber was abolished, as was the Court of High Commission, which had dealt with church matters.

The Long Parliament also declared that Parliament could not be dismissed without its own consent and that Parliament must agree to all taxes to be imposed upon the people. Charles I signed most of these laws reluctantly, but he finally decided that Parliament was going too far. Fearing for his life, he went in person to try to arrest five of the leading members of the House of Commons. When he got there, however, they had already fled. When Charles demanded to know where they were, the Speaker (presiding officer) of Parliament declared, "I have neither eyes nor tongue to speak in this place but as this House is pleased to direct me." Thus, king and Parliament were embarked on a course of unavoidable confrontation. Civil war began.

The Cavaliers and the Roundheads Clashed In Civil War

The civil war in England, which lasted from 1642 to 1649, was fought between the Cavaliers (those who supported the king) and the Roundheads (those who supported Parliament). The Cavaliers, who wore long curls, were made up of aristocrats, Catholics, Anglicans, and landholders, for the most part. The Roundheads, who cut their hair short, included, for the most part, the middle class, merchants, and Puritans.

At first, the king's soldiers had the advantage of experience and organization. But, Oliver Cromwell, the leader of the Roundheads, soon organized the disorganized forces of the Roundheads. Under his leadership, the so-called New Model Army marched off to battle singing hymns and quoting scripture. With improved organization and a cause in which they strongly believed, the New Model Army defeated the Cavaliers at Marston Moor in northern England in 1644 and again at Naseby (NAYZ bee) in central England in 1645.

In the meantime, Charles I had surrendered to the Scots, who promptly turned him over to the Roundheads. The Roundheads set up a special court, tried the king, and sentenced him to death. Charles was beheaded on January 30, 1649.

435

Cromwell Established the Commonwealth

The Long Parliament dissolved the monarchy and established a republic, or commonwealth. Oliver Cromwell, the Puritan leader of the Roundheads, became a ruthless military dictator.

Under Cromwell, Puritanism was the main religious faith of England, and Puritans tried to force their ways on everyone. Since the Puritans frowned on dancing, games, and the theater, these forms of entertainment were made illegal. By the time Cromwell died, the English had become tired of his military dictatorship and strict ways. A so-called Convention Parliament restored the Stuarts to the English throne in 1660 by inviting Charles II, the son of Charles I, to return to England from exile in France.

▼ **Illustrating History** *In this painting, Oliver Cromwell is shown dissolving the Commonwealth Parliament in 1653.*

Charles II Was Restored to the Throne

The return of the Stuarts to the English throne is known as the Restoration. The English were happy to have a king once more, but their rejoicing would not last long. Charles II intended to rule as much as possible without Parliament.

Charles II was often able to get along without Parliament because Louis XIV of France gave him money. When it was necessary, Charles looked to a group of friends in Parliament, known as *Tories*, who favored the monarchy. Those who opposed the monarchy became known as *Whigs*. The division between Whigs and Tories marked the beginning of a two-party system.

In contrast to its somber mood under the Puritan dictatorship of Cromwell, England was a festive country, at least for the wealthy, under Charles II. When Charles II died in 1685 and was succeeded by his brother, James II, the happy times ended.

James II Gave Up the Throne in the Glorious Revolution

The reign of James II was brief and unpopular. His conversion to Catholicism upset the English, who were concerned when he placed Catholics in high government positions. When his queen gave birth to a son, Parliament and the people of England realized that another Catholic would follow James to the throne. To prevent this from happening, leaders in Parliament invited William III of Orange (Holland) and his wife, Mary Stuart (a daughter of James II), to become king and queen of England. William welcomed the opportunity. He disliked James II because James had been a friend of Louis XIV, who was trying to destroy Holland. As king of England, William believed that he would be able to save Holland.

William III landed in England on November 5, 1688, fully expecting to fight a civil war. But, James II had fled to France. A bloodless revolution, called the Glorious Revolution, had taken place.

The result of the Glorious Revolution was a limited monarchy in England. **A limited monarchy** is a monarchy that restricts the powers of the ruler in some way. Parliament had learned its lesson in trying to deal with absolute monarchs. Therefore, before William and Mary could become king and queen, they had to agree that they would not do certain things. In order to check their power, they had to agree to a bill of rights, which made the laws of Parliament supreme in England. Parliament had to be called into session each year, and only Parliament could levy taxes.

The English people also were given the **right of petition;** that is, they could make a formal request, or petition, to the monarch to correct abuses. A standing army in peacetime, which the English feared could be used against citizens, was declared illegal. A Toleration Act, passed in 1689, gave Puritans the right to have their own churches. The Act of Settlement, passed in 1701, gave only those of the Protestant faith the right to rule England.

Mary's sister, Anne, followed William and Mary to the throne. In 1707, during Queen Anne's reign, the Act of Union was passed under which England and Wales were united with Scotland to form one nation, Great Britain. From this time forward, the history of England became the history of Great Britain, and the British Parliament ruled both these countries. When Anne died in 1714 without an heir, the English turned to George I of Hanover, who was the great-grandson of James I.

The Glorious Revolution Was a Victory for Democracy

As a result of its struggles, Great Britain had made a number of advances along the road to democracy. The monarch's power was limited. Kings and queens could no longer make or veto laws, levy taxes, or keep an army without Parliament's consent. The law courts of Great Britain were free of royal influence, since no one could be put into prison without a fair and speedy trial by a jury of peers, or equals.

A two-party system developed in England. The prime minister was no longer the king's favorite, but was instead the majority party

In their own words

Effects of the London Fire

Samuel Pepys was an important British naval administrator in the mid–1600s. Today, though, he is remembered for his detailed diary. The following excerpt is from September 5, 1666, three days after the beginning of a tremendous fire that ravaged London.

"Walked into Moorefields (our feet ready to burn, walking through the town among the hot coals) and find that full of people, and poor wretches carrying their goods there, and everybody keeping his goods together by themselves (and a great blessing it is to them that it is fair weather for them to keep abroad night and day); drank there, and paid twopence for a plain penny loaf. Thence homeward, having passed through Cheapside and Newgate market, all burned—and seen Anthony Joyce's house in fire. And took up (which I keep by me) a piece of glass of Mercer's chapel in the street, where much more was, so melted and buckled with the heat of the fire, like parchment. I also did see a poor cat taken out a hole in the chimney joining to the wall of the Exchange, with the hair all burned off the body and yet alive. So home at night and find there good hopes of saving our office. . . . But it is a strange thing to see how long this time did look since Sunday, having been always full of variety of actions, and little sleep, that it looked like a week or more. And I had forgot almost the day of the week.**"**

1. Why were the people Pepys saw carrying their goods with them?
2. Describe what happened to the windows of Mercer's chapel.

From Rulers to Celebrities

The role of the monarch in Britain today is vastly different from that of the past. Like her famous ancestor Charles I, Queen Elizabeth II is head of state. Unlike him, however, she does not rule. She may enter Parliament with great fanfare to deliver a speech, but she must be invited to do so. She cannot participate in Britain's political affairs in any way.

The queen has often been called a figurehead. In fact, she and the royal family are much more. To the majority of Britons, the royal family offers a source of stability and a link to the past. Elizabeth II's ancestors were absolute rulers. Today, she and the royal family are celebrities, as is shown by the magazine covers at left.

1. What is the role of England's monarch today?
2. Do you think the people of Britain will ever decide not to have a monarchy? Explain.

---

leader in the House of Commons. The House of Commons itself became more powerful and more directly reflected the will of the people.

Even with all the changes, Parliament was not a truly democratic body because the wealthy people, or aristocrats, controlled it. Freedom of speech and freedom of the press were not well established. Intolerance of Catholics and Jews continued, and punishments for crimes remained cruel.

Nevertheless, by 1688, England had taken a big step toward democratic government. The concept that there was a body of law—a constitution—that even the king could not alter without approval was perhaps the most important achievement. Government by the consent of the governed and limited in power by law would become the rallying cry for other revolutions, notably those in America and in France.

Knowing Key Terms, People, and Places
1. Define: **a.** limited monarchy **b.** right of petition
2. Identify: **a.** James I **b.** Long Parliament **c.** Oliver Cromwell **d.** the Restoration

Reviewing Main Ideas
3. Why was James I unable to deal effectively with Parliament?
4. What were conditions in England like during the military dictatorship of Cromwell?
5. In what way was the Glorious Revolution a victory for democracy in England?

Critical Thinking
Demonstrating Reasoned Judgment
6. Why do you think Cromwell insisted that everyone in England follow Puritanism?

2 The Age of Reason Advanced Learning

As you read, look for answers to these questions:

◆ How did the scientific method change the way people thought about the world?
◆ How did the study of medicine change during the Age of Reason?
◆ What developments were made in literature and art during the Enlightenment?

Key Terms: scientific method (defined on p. 439), novel (p. 441)

▲ **Illustrating History** *This colored engraving shows Galileo using his telescope to make a calculation.*

The Age of Reason is also known as the Enlightenment. It began roughly with the publication of *Principia* by Sir Isaac Newton in 1687 and ended with the outbreak of the French Revolution in 1789. It is called the Enlightenment because scientists, writers, philosophers, and artists sought to enlighten or free people from ignorance. During this period, people learned how the laws of nature and the laws of government could be used to better the human condition.

In many ways, the Age of Reason was a continuation of the Renaissance. While many of the creative activities of the Renaissance took place in Italy, much of the great work of the Enlightenment was done in northern Europe and later in America.

The Scientific Method Was Born

In high-school science laboratories today, students observe their experiments carefully and write down exactly what they see. After noting the facts, students interpret their observations and form conclusions. These steps make up the **scientific method.** For this method, science is indebted to Francis Bacon, an Englishman who lived from 1561 to 1626. Bacon believed that scientific progress would have to be based on the scientific method.

The use of the scientific method was not widespread early in the seventeenth century. However, the invention of the telescope in 1608 and the microscope in 1610 made scientific observation somewhat easier, and the use of the scientific method became more widespread.

The Scientific Method Led to New Discoveries

Using the scientific method, scholars began to make exact measurements and observations that they could then apply to all of the sciences. This led to giant strides in science in the fields of astronomy, mathematics, and medicine. New knowledge began to replace incorrect ideas of the past.

Astronomy and mathematics. As you read in Chapter 14, in the sixteenth century Nicolaus Copernicus claimed that the sun was the center of the universe and that the earth and other planets moved around it. At the time this fact had not yet been proven, and few people believed him. The accepted theory was that the earth was the center of the universe. The Italian scientist Galileo (GAL uh LEE oh), who lived from 1564 to 1642, put his faith in experimentation and

Aphra Behn

"The plays she [sells] she never made," remarks a character in an English play of the 1600s. The words suggest that a woman could not possibly write a play on her own. At the time, most people believed that only men were fit to be writers. In spite of this belief, Aphra Behn (shown at right) became the first woman in England to make her living as a playwright, poet, and novelist. There was "no reason," she insisted, "why women should not write as well as men."

Aphra Behn was born in 1640 and married a London merchant in 1658. When her husband died, she was poverty-stricken and thrown into jail for debt. Determined to escape the grimness of prison life, Behn picked up a quill and set to work.

Behn's writings reflected her heartfelt concern over the plight of women, as well as many other injustices that marked the society of her time. Her play, *The Rover,* featured an independent, adventurous woman struggling against the unbending conventions of her day. Her best-known novel, *Oroonoko,* tells of a black prince enslaved by whites. In this novel, she condemned slavery.

Aphra Behn died in 1689. Only recently has the work of England's first woman playwright been recognized.

1. Why did Aphra Behn turn to writing as a career?
2. What obstacles stood in the way of Aphra Behn's success?
3. How do her writings reflect the social concerns she had?

---

observation. Using the scientific method as he studied the movement of the solar system through a telescope, Galileo became convinced that the Copernican theory of the universe was right.

At first, people would not accept Galileo's ideas. He was called before the Inquisition for heresy, because at that time the Roman Catholic church believed the earth was at the center of the universe. The Inquisition forced Galileo to say that his observations were untrue.

Using mathematics, the German astronomer Johannes Kepler (KEP lur) further improved on the work of Copernicus and discovered that the orbit, or path, of the earth around the sun was oval-shaped and not circular as people had believed.

The importance of mathematics in the scientific method was further demonstrated by the seventeenth-century French philosopher and mathematician René Descartes (day KAHRT). All things in nature, Descartes claimed, could be shown to have a mathematical basis. He used the laws of geometry to describe the motion of physical objects.

Another great thinker, the Englishman Sir Isaac Newton, pushed open the door to our understanding of the world and the universe even further. His curiosity led him to formulate Newton's laws of gravity, which explain why apples and everything else fall down and partially explain the universe as a whole. Why do the planets move as they do? What keeps them from hitting one another?

How can people walk on a spinning earth? What keeps the planets from falling down? These are among the questions that Newton answered many years ago. Even when travel through space becomes frequent, Newton will continue to stand among the heroes of science who made it possible.

Medicine. As doctors became willing to use the scientific method, medicine improved in the seventeenth and eighteenth centuries. By performing experiments on the bodies of animals and humans, the English physician William Harvey discovered that the heart pumps the blood through the veins and arteries of the human body. Careful observation allowed doctors to become more expert in diagnosing different types of sickness. They began to measure blood pressure and to use stethoscopes in physical examinations.

By improving the microscope, the Dutch naturalist Anton van Leeuwenhoek (LAY vuhn HOOK) was able to see bacteria. Later scientists saw a connection between some of these organisms and human illnesses.

The Enlightenment Inspired Great Writers

The Age of Reason also encouraged creative expression in literature. Stories of this age became part of the world's great literature. Writers described what they saw or how they felt in new forms of writing. The novel was one such form. A **novel** is a long story with a complex plot and human characters. In a novel, a writer not only tells a story but also often criticizes the way real people behave. For example, *Gulliver's Travels*, written in 1726 by Jonathan Swift, amuses readers but also points out the silly behavior of people and the foolish causes of war.

In German writing, the works of Johann Friedrich von Schiller (SHIL ur) and Johann Wolfgang von Goethe (GUR tuh) stand out. In Schiller's *Wilhelm Tell*, written in 1804, the author describes Tell's eager search for liberty. Goethe's *Faust*, written in 1808, tells the story of a man who sells his soul to the devil in exchange for knowledge and pleasure. This familiar plot has formed the basis of many stories.

Art, Architecture, and Music Flourished

During the seventeenth and eighteenth centuries, private homes and public buildings, as well as churches, became works of art. Christopher Wren of England was a leading architect of the period. After a great fire destroyed much of London in 1666, Christopher Wren was the major contributor to its rebuilding. The Cathedral of St. Paul and many smaller churches are his most lasting gifts to architecture. The steeples found on many New England churches reflect Wren's influence.

In painting, as in other artistic fields, Renaissance influences continued. The works of the Flemish artist Rubens (ROO buhnz) and the Dutch artist Rembrandt (REM brant) are characteristic of the paintings of the period. The subjects vary from landscapes to sacred subjects.

Opera, which combined the talents of singers, musicians, and actors, was a new form of musical expression. Claudio Monteverdi (MAWN tuh VAYR dee) was the first great figure in the development of opera. Among the great composers of the age were George Frederick Handel (HAN duhl) and Johann Sebastian Bach (bahk) of Germany, and Wolfgang Amadeus Mozart (MOHT sahrt) of Austria.

SECTION 2 REVIEW

Knowing Key Terms, People, and Places
1. Define: **a.** scientific method **b.** novel
2. Identify: **a.** Francis Bacon **b.** Galileo **c.** Newton **d.** Wren

Reviewing Main Ideas
3. Why was the development of the scientific method such an important event?
4. Why was Galileo forced to deny his conclusions about the solar system?
5. What did Sir Isaac Newton contribute?

Critical Thinking
Predicting Consequences
6. Would you expect the scientific ideas of the Age of Reason to have any effect on religion in Europe? Explain your answer.

3 Reason Encouraged New Political Ideas

As you read, look for answers to these questions:

◆ How did the Age of Reason affect the way people thought about the purpose and function of a government?
◆ How did the political philosophers contribute to the improvement of society?
◆ What role did women play in the Age of Reason?

Key Terms: philosophe (defined on p. 442), laissez faire (p. 443), salon (p. 443)

During the Age of Reason, new ideas offered possibilities for a better life. Old-fashioned ways of thinking and doing things were changing. Changes and new ideas make people think and ask questions. If these new ideas in mathematics and science were true, was it still true that monarchs ruled by the will of God? Was it reasonable for the poor to pay higher taxes than the rich? If permanent laws controlled nature, were not laws to control government also possible? Did it always have to be that some people were rich and others poor? These were the kinds of questions intelligent people started to ask themselves. Thought led to talk, and talk to action.

The ideas of the Age of Reason spread throughout Europe rapidly. For one thing, people were ready to hear new ideas and eager to debate and discuss them because they realized that social and economic conditions needed to be improved. As the number of people who could read and write increased during the 1700s, there was a wider audience for the enlightened ideas of the day. More journals, newspapers, and reports were published, and public lectures that spread new ideas became common. Increased travel spread new philosophies as

people met and discussed their points of view. People who could not travel from country to country carried on conversations and debates in the streets, at home, or in coffee houses. Nothing could stop the bright new dawn of the Age of Reason.

Political Philosophy Encouraged Change in Government

The thought, the talk, and the writing of the Age of Reason was, for the most part, the work of a group of philosophers. Today, the word *intellectual* would be used to describe the philosophers. Many of the philosophers of the eighteenth century were French, and the term **philosophes** (fee law ZAWFS) was used to identify them. Their writings and ideas were greatly influenced by the writings of the English philosopher John Locke. Locke believed that a government should exist only with the consent of the people. This idea grew out of his experiences with the Glorious Revolution of 1688.

Voltaire, Montesquieu, and Rousseau were the greatest of the philosophes. They disagreed in many ways, but they did agree on one thing—that society could be better than it was.

Voltaire. Voltaire (vohl TAYR), who lived from 1694 to 1778, was a French philosopher and writer who questioned accepted beliefs and criticized the actions of many prominent people. He wanted freedom of thought and freedom of religion. He especially criticized the Roman Catholic church because he felt that it discouraged freedom of thought. His book, called *Letters on the English,* actually criticized the French. By using the term *English,* he tried to make the title seem harmless to government leaders. At a time when freedom of speech and the press did not exist in France, Voltaire preached tolerance in religion and politics. Surprisingly, he was popular at the courts of such absolute rulers as Frederick of Prussia and Catherine of Russia.

Montesquieu. Another French writer, Baron de Montesquieu (MAHN tuhs KYOO), wrote a book that influenced government.

The Spirit of the Laws, written in 1748, praised the government of England because it was democratic. Montesquieu urged that the three branches of the government—the law-enforcing, the law-making, and the law-interpreting—be kept separate so that one could act as a check on the other. Montesquieu's book influenced the writers of the Constitution of the United States, as you will read later in this chapter.

Rousseau. Jean Jacques Rousseau (roo SOH) believed that people were basically good and that society corrupted them. According to Rousseau, people had been happier in the distant past because they were closer to nature. When people found they needed laws to live by, they established governments and gave to governments the right to rule. In 1762, Rousseau expressed his ideas in a book called *The Social Contract*. Rousseau reasoned that since people —not God—give governments the right to rule, people can take power away from governments when they rule unwisely. These thoughts were expanded upon by Thomas Jefferson when he wrote the Declaration of Independence.

Reason Influenced Economic Theories

Writers in the field of economics also demanded more freedom. Perhaps no one had more influence than Adam Smith, author of a book in 1776 entitled *The Wealth of Nations*. Smith criticized mercantilism and wrote that businesses would be better off if they were not closely controlled by the government. He preferred the idea of **laissez faire** (LES ay FAYR), a French term meaning that government should keep its hands off business. Smith also wanted the government to provide a sound currency and an army to protect property. He felt that competition and the laws of supply and demand would be enough to control wages, prices, and profits.

Both *The Wealth of Nations* and the American Declaration of Independence were written in 1776. The first asked for economic independence; the second asked for political independence.

▲ **Illustrating History** *This oil painting depicts the French philosopher Rousseau.*

An Encyclopedia of Knowledge Stirred New Ideas

The Encyclopedists were a group of French philosophers. Led by Denis Diderot (DEE duh ROH), philosophers, including Rousseau, Montesquieu, and Voltaire, wrote articles for a new encyclopedia. This encyclopedia would contain many of the new ideas that were to pave the way for a change from absolutism to democracy. The encyclopedia they compiled contained the latest in scientific information. There were also articles opposing slavery, cruel punishments, unfair taxation, and religious intolerance.

Government and religious leaders in France banned the encyclopedia because it criticized religious persecution, but the book was widely read by learned people everywhere. In fact, because of their advanced thinking, the lives of the writers of the encyclopedia were often in danger. Ideas were gradually changing, but not without resistance.

Women Contributed to the Age of Reason

Not all of the philosophes were men. Several women hosted **salons,** or regular gatherings of distinguished guests, including writers, artists, poets, and essayists of both sexes.

▲ **Illustrating History** *The Paris salon of Princess de Conti, shown in this painting, featured glittering guests and stimulating conversation.*

These people met to talk freely about their ideas, and they made many contributions to the Age of Reason. At first, wealthy women hosted most salons. Later in the 1700s, however, middle-class women also held salons. In the drawing rooms of their hostesses, many geniuses sharpened their wits by trying out new ideas in politics and science.

Among the great salons of the day was the salon of Marie-Therese Geoffrin (zhaw FRAN) of France. Voltaire was one great philosophe who attended her salon frequently. Two other French women, Marie du Deffand (doo deh FAWN) and Julie de Lespinasse (duh LES pee NAHS), also hosted famous salons.

The salons kept alive the ideas of the Age of Reason. What philosophes wrote could be burned, and often it was. What they said in the salons of France, Prussia, Austria, England, and elsewhere, however, could not be silenced. Their ideas were passed on by others in a revolutionary fire that was to sweep America and Europe.

SECTION 3 REVIEW

Knowing Key Terms, People, and Places
1. Define: **a.** philosophe **b.** laissez faire **c.** salon
2. Identify: **a.** Voltaire **b.** Locke **c.** *The Spirit of the Laws* **d.** Encyclopedists

Reviewing Main Ideas
3. What ideas of Montesquieu influenced the organization of the government of the United States?
4. What ideas about government did Rousseau express in *The Social Contract?*
5. Describe the economic ideas Adam Smith set forth in *The Wealth of Nations.*
6. What purposes did the salons serve in eighteenth-century France?

Critical Thinking
Demonstrating Reasoned Judgment
7. Why do you think that the lives of the Encyclopedists were often in danger?

4 Revolution Brought Democracy to America

As you read, look for answers to these questions:

◆ Why did the American colonies decide to fight for their independence from England?
◆ What ideas fueled the American quest for freedom?
◆ How did the Constitution make democracy possible?

> **Key Terms:** minuteman (defined on p. 446), redcoat (p. 446)

While new ideas about government, business, and society were developing in Europe, important changes were also taking place in America. The people of the American colonies believed that the democratic advances of the Glorious Revolution in England should be shared with the British colonies. When the colonies thought they were being treated less democratically than the people at home, they rebelled.

The Causes of the American Revolution Were Many

The American nation began its life as a "child" of England. Although immigrants from many other nations helped to settle the colonies, the English language and style of life remained the major influences on colonial America. In 1607, English colonists settled in Jamestown, Virginia, and in 1620, the Pilgrims (British Puritans) settled in the Massachusetts Bay area. Before leaving their ship, the *Mayflower*, the Pilgrims adopted the Mayflower Compact, under which they agreed to enact laws for the welfare of the colony. The basis of government in their new world would be the will of the colonists, not the will of the English crown. By 1733, 13 colonies extended along the eastern coast of North America.

Results of the French and Indian War. Once the colonies were firmly established, they found themselves embroiled in Europe's problems. In the French and Indian War, which was the American phase of Europe's Seven Years' War, the colonists joined with the British to defeat the French in North America. The results of the war, which lasted from 1755 to 1763, eventually fueled the revolutionary fire in the American colonies. By the terms of the Treaty of Paris, the British added Canada and all French territory east of the Mississippi River (except New Orleans) to their empire.

Because George III and his ministers believed that they had saved the American colonies from French rule, it seemed reasonable to them that the colonies should contribute generously to paying the debt the war had created. The colonists, on the other hand, believed that without their military aid, England would have lost the war to France. They believed the British should be grateful to them. This difference in perspective helped to prepare the way for revolution and independence.

Taxation without representation. Since the colonists had no elected representatives in the Parliament, they had no part in deciding what taxes they would pay. The colonists called this "taxation without representation." They felt that they were not being treated fairly, and they expressed their outrage in many ways. The colonists refused to buy British goods, for example, and protested each new tax. By 1773, the taxes on tea had caused protests by colonists. A group of Bostonians, disguised as Indians, boarded British ships and dumped bales of tea into Boston Harbor. The Boston Tea Party, as this event was called, was viewed by the colonists as an act of heroism. The British, however, viewed it as an act of treachery.

The Intolerable Acts and the Quebec Act. To punish the colonies, Parliament passed a series of laws that the colonists called the Intolerable Acts. The port of Boston was closed until the tea was paid for, and a military government was forced on the Massachusetts colony. The final straw to the colonists was Parliament's passage of the Quebec Act. By this act, Parliament established a permanent government for the colony of Quebec. What angered the colonists most was that this area included the land between the Ohio River and the Mississippi River. To the colonists, this suggested that Parliament was limiting their ability to move westward.

As tensions built in the colonies, many wise leaders in Parliament sought compromise. These compromises were never reached, however, and the angry colonists prepared to revolt. In 1775, fighting broke out between the Americans and British in Massachusetts. In the towns of Lexington and Concord, the **minutemen** (citizens who had volunteered to be ready to fight at a minute's notice) and the **redcoats,** the British troops, fired the first shots of the American Revolution. The war would last for six years.

The Colonies Declared Independence and Defeated Great Britian

By the second year of the American Revolution, Americans were ready for separation from England no matter what the cost. Many Americans, such as Thomas Paine, had ideas similar to those of the European philosophers who were helping to prepare the way for change in Europe. In a pamphlet entitled *Common Sense,* Paine helped to convince the colonists to separate from Britain. He showed that independence was a reasonable thing to demand. After the battles of Lexington and Concord, Paine said that it was not right to work for a settlement with Britain. Instead, as he stated, "The blood of the slain, the weeping voice of nature cries, ''TIS TIME TO PART.'"

Many people in the colonies took Paine's words to heart. His ideas inspired American leaders to declare that the colonies should be independent from Great Britain. Thomas Jefferson, the brilliant statesman from Virginia, drafted the Declaration of Independence in July, 1776. In it, he described the revolutionary ideals of the day, including the concepts that all people are created

equal and that they are born with certain rights. To protect these rights, they set up governments based on the consent of the governed. When a government does not protect these rights, the people may change that government.

Five years after the signing of the Declaration of Independence, the Americans won a decisive victory. In 1781, with help from France, George Washington defeated the British at Yorktown, Virginia. In a peace treaty, England acknowledged the independence of the United States. The map on page 447 shows the United States in 1783.

American Leaders Wrote the Constitution of the United States

George Washington and other leaders proposed the creation of a new constitution. In 1787, leaders of the 13 former colonies met in Philadelphia and, during a long, hot summer, wrote the Constitution of the United States of America.

The final document was by no means perfect. Its greatest imperfection was its compromise over slavery. Luther Martin of Delaware had declared at the convention, "A nation that has appealed to God to grant it freedom should not fail to take the first step toward granting the Africans their freedom too." But this did not happen, and slaves were denied rights as citizens.

Nevertheless, despite this and other faults, the American Constitution was later described by the nineteenth-century British statesman William E. Gladstone as "the most wonderful work ever struck off at a given time by the brain and purpose of man." The Constitution has lasted to the present day and has influenced constitutions around the world. The fact that the Constitution has been amended only 26 times in about 200 years shows the remarkable stability of the document.

The Constitution Established a Democratic Government

Although the American Constitution has influenced thinkers around the globe, it is important to remember that it was influenced by the ideas of many European and

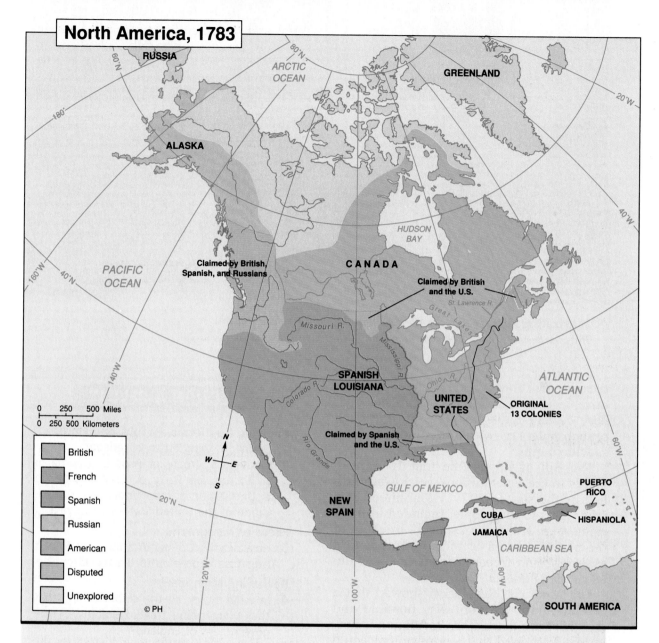

North America, 1783

RUSSIA

ARCTIC OCEAN

GREENLAND

ALASKA

Claimed by British, Spanish, and Russians

CANADA

HUDSON BAY

Claimed by British and the U.S.

St. Lawrence R.

PACIFIC OCEAN

Great Lakes

Missouri R.

Mississippi R.

ATLANTIC OCEAN

SPANISH LOUISIANA

Colorado R.

Ohio R.

UNITED STATES

ORIGINAL 13 COLONIES

Claimed by Spanish and the U.S.

Rio Grande

N W E S

British
French
Spanish
Russian
American
Disputed
Unexplored

0   250   500 Miles
0   250 500 Kilometers

GULF OF MEXICO

NEW SPAIN

PUERTO RICO

CUBA

HISPANIOLA

JAMAICA

CARIBBEAN SEA

SOUTH AMERICA

© PH

Focus on Geography

Regions   The map shows the boundaries of the United States in 1783. Use the map and the key to describe the territory that made up the newly formed United States in 1783.

American writers. Among these writers are Locke, Montesquieu, Paine, and Jefferson. When the Americans formed their new government, they separated it into three branches, as Montesquieu had envisioned. Each branch would check, or restrain, and balance the others so that no one branch could become too powerful. According to

447

▲ **Illustrating History** *In the above engraving, the Declaration of Independence is read to an enthusiastic Philadelphia crowd in 1776.*

the system of checks and balances, the executive, legislative, and judicial branches each have certain duties to perform, and each branch must stay within the limits of these specific duties.

The Bill of Rights (the first 10 amendments to the Constitution, which were ratified by the states in 1791) guaranteed specific rights to the people. Included in these rights were freedom of speech, freedom of the press, freedom of religion, freedom of assembly, and freedom from cruel or unusual punishments.

The American Revolution showed that a revolution for freedom was possible and that there are times when revolution is necessary. It showed that a government could work without a monarch. These lessons were not lost on the people and nations of Europe. The shots that were fired at Lexington and Concord were heard in Paris, where a more terrible revolution was about to break out. The French Revolution was next in the series of explosive events that marked the beginning of Europe's march toward political freedom. The ideas of the American and French revolutions would continue to inspire worldwide political change in the nineteenth and twentieth centuries.

SECTION 4 REVIEW

Knowing Key Terms, People, and Places
1. Define: **a.** minuteman **b.** redcoat
2. Identify: **a.** Treaty of Paris **b.** George III **c.** Boston Tea Party **d.** *Common Sense* **e.** Declaration of Independence **f.** Constitution of the United States of America

Focus on Geography
3. How did the Quebec Act threaten to halt American expansion to the west?

Reviewing Main Ideas
4. In what ways did the colonists feel that they were being treated unfairly by the government of England?
5. What rights did the Declaration of Independence proclaim for all Americans?
6. Describe the Bill of Rights and list five of the specific rights it guarantees.

Critical Thinking
Making Comparisons
7. Compare and contrast the concept of government expressed in the Declaration of Independence with the concept of government demonstrated by the Restoration in England in the seventeenth century.

SKILLS NOTEBOOK

Drawing Conclusions

As you study history—or any other subject—you can learn more than facts and other people's ideas. You also can draw conclusions. This means you can figure out things that are suggested but not stated directly. It means you can go beyond what is presented in the text and form new insights. Use the following steps to practice drawing conclusions.

1. **Study the facts and ideas that the author presents.** Learning the facts presented by the author is the first step toward forming your own conclusions. Read the two passages below and answer these questions: (a) What was the central idea of Puritanism? (b) Under what king and queen did Spanish expansion begin?

2. **Make a summary statement as a conclusion about a group of details.** A statement that summarizes the major points of a passage is one type of conclusion. Answer the following questions: (a) For passage A, what can you conclude about the Pilgrims' decision to settle in the New World? Was it a result of disappointment after many years of struggle? Or, was it the impulsive act of an enthusiastic new religious movement? (b) For passage B, what can you conclude about how Charles came to rule such a large territory?

3. **Think whether you can come to a conclusion that is suggested by what is stated.** Answer the following questions: (a) Given what you read in passage A, can you conclude that the Puritans were strongly united in their beliefs, or did they sometimes disagree with each other? (b) Given what you read in passage B, what conclusion can you draw about the connection between family relationships and political power in Europe during this period?

Passage A

Puritan religious beliefs were first expressed in England in the late 1500s. Puritanism centered around the idea that religious belief, worship, and organization should be as simple as possible. Puritans objected to the elegant priestly clothes, complicated ceremonies, and ornate buildings of the Church of England.

Although some Puritan ideas were adopted by the Church of England, most Puritans remained unhappy. They began disagreeing among themselves. Some were inclined to go along with Anglican practices, while others insisted on the need for change. A few small groups broke away completely from the church. Among these were the Pilgrims who eventually sailed the Atlantic in 1620.

Passage B

The Spanish dynasty came to rule an enormous territory. Its expansion began in 1479, when Ferdinand and Isabella married and joined their kingdoms of Aragon and Castile. Their daughter, Joanna, later married Philip, one of the Hapsburg family who ruled central Europe. Joanna and Philip had a son, Charles. From the Spanish side of his family, Charles inherited the Spanish kingdom as well as possessions in the New World and in Italy. From the Hapsburg side, Charles inherited family lands in central Europe. Charles's grandmother also left him domains in Burgundy, Luxembourg, and the Netherlands. By the time he was 19, Charles was ruling more territory than any ruler had controlled for centuries.

REVIEW

Section Summaries

Section 1 Revolution Transformed England The Stuarts were harsh rulers, often ignoring Parliament, trial by jury, and the common law. James I constantly quarrelled with Parliament, which often refused to pay for James's wars and for his luxurious life. Charles I had similar conflicts. When he called Parliament in 1628 to get funds, he was forced to sign the Petition of Right, granting important reforms. Yet, Charles continued to rule unfairly. Finally, he was driven from office by civil war. England became a commonwealth, but the new leader, Oliver Cromwell, was a dictator. After Cromwell's death, the monarchy was restored. Eventually, however, the Glorious Revolution allowed Parliament to place limits on the monarch's power. In this bloodless revolution, Parliament replaced James II with William of Orange and Mary Stuart. The new rulers signed the Bill of Rights, making Parliament supreme in England.

Section 2 The Age of Reason Advanced Learning The Age of Reason, also called the Enlightenment, began in the 1680s and was a time of great progress in science, art, and literature. Thinkers, writers, artists, and scientists worked to free people from ignorance and to improve the human condition. Scientists used the careful steps of the scientific method to advance their knowledge of astronomy, mathematics, and medicine. The Enlightenment also encouraged great writing, beautiful music, and magnificent art and architecture.

Section 3 Reason Encouraged New Political Ideas The Age of Reason spurred people to ask questions about their governments and their economic systems. Many new ideas were directed toward improving people's lives. Thinkers like the French philosophes encouraged revolutionary changes in government. Adam Smith recommended economic change—an end to government control of business. One group of French thinkers even wrote an encyclopedia explaining many of the new ideas that were paving the way toward greater political, economic, and religious freedom. Women in the Age of Reason discussed ideas with men in intellectual gatherings called salons.

Section 4 Revolution Brought Democracy to America The American colonists felt they were being governed unfairly by Britain. They were taxed heavily without representation, in part because King George believed that the colonists should pay most of the debt created by the French and Indian War. Other laws limited their ability to move west. The colonists' complaints brought a revolution and a Declaration of Independence, both based on Enlightenment ideas about government. The Americans won their revolution. They created a strong central government in which power would be shared among three branches and the rights of citizens would be recognized. The new democracy provided a model for the rest of the world.

Key Facts

1. Use each vocabulary word in a sentence.
   a. limited monarchy
   b. right of petition
   c. scientific method
   d. novel
   e. philosophe
   f. laissez faire
   g. salon
   h. minuteman
   i. redcoat
2. Identify and briefly explain the importance of the following names, places, or events.
   a. James I
   b. Charles I
   c. England's civil war
   d. The Glorious Revolution
   e. Rousseau
   f. Adam Smith
   g. Boston Tea Party
   h. Thomas Jefferson

Main Ideas

1. List four actions by Charles I that helped bring on England's civil war.

2. What was the commonwealth and how did it bring about the Restoration?
3. List three events that were part of the Glorious Revolution.
4. Tell of one Enlightenment advance in each of these fields: astronomy, mathematics, medicine, literature, and music.
5. Give a brief summary of the basic beliefs of each of these thinkers: Voltaire, Montesquieu, Rousseau, and Adam Smith.
6. List three causes and three results of the American Revolution.

Developing Skill in Reading History

Each of the following statements was made by an American revolutionary leader. Explain what effect each quotation was intended to have on its audience. Then paraphrase each quotation, or restate it using your own words.
1. "There are no differences between Virginians, Pennsylvanians, New Yorkers, and New Englanders. I am not a Virginian but an American."
2. "The blood of the slain, the weeping voice of nature cries, ''TIS TIME TO PART.'"
3. "These are times that try men's souls. The summer soldier and the sunshine patriot will, in this crisis, shrink from the service of their country; but he that stands it now deserves the love and thanks of man and woman."

Using Social Studies Skills

1. **Making Generalizations** The Enlightenment thinker Jean Jacques Rousseau believed that people were basically good and that society made them do bad things. Do you agree or disagree? Give examples from your own experiences to support your answer.
2. **Making Inferences** The painting in the next column shows a meeting of philosophes at a salon. What inferences can you make from the painting about what these great French thinkers were like?

Critical Thinking

1. **Making Comparisons** In what ways did the Glorious Revolution differ from the American Revolution?
2. **Determining Relevance** How did Enlightenment ideas influence the American Revolution and the new government? Discuss at least three Enlightenment ideas.
3. **Drawing Conclusions** Explain the following statement: "The harsher a monarch ruled, the more determined Parliament became to fight for greater democracy."

Focus on Writing

Planning a Research Paper

Plan a research paper about one topic from this chapter. Some possible topics might be:
· The Glorious Revolution
· The discoveries of Sir Isaac Newton
· The paintings of Rubens and Rembrandt
· Why many Puritans left England
To write such a paper, you will need to consult many books. Do some library research to compile a beginning list of sources for your research paper. Since you may add or drop sources as you continue your research and writing, this type of list is called a **working bibliography.**

The French Revolution and Napoleon

(1789–1815)

1 **The Old Regime Abused the French**

2 **The Revolutionaries Ended Absolute Rule**

3 **Terror and Warfare Swept France**

4 **Napoleon Rose to Power in France**

▲ **Illustrating History** *Above, Marie Antoinette is shown in mourning for her husband, Louis XVI, who was guillotined in January 1793.*

Dawn was breaking on October 6, 1789, when a ragged mob of men and women, armed with muskets, swords, and pikes, swarmed through the royal palace of Versailles. Rushing up the steps to Queen Marie Antoinette's private apartments, they killed two guards who tried to stop them. A third guard escaped to sound the alarm. The queen had just enough time to slip a petticoat over her nightgown before racing down the hall to warn the king.

As she pounded frantically on his apartment door, the mob raged through her rooms, stabbing her bed and ransacking cupboards. From below the palace windows came the cry, "The Queen to the balcony!" Pale with fear, the queen faced the mob pointing muskets up at her. There was silence. And then, surprisingly, the crowd shouted, "Long live the Queen!"

The royal family was then forced into a carriage bound for a prison in Paris. Working women and fishmongers surrounded the carriage, yelling insults. One thousand years of French monarchy was drawing to a close, and a revolution was just beginning. As you read this chapter, you will learn about the French Revolution that began on that October morning—its causes, its violent course, and its lasting effects.

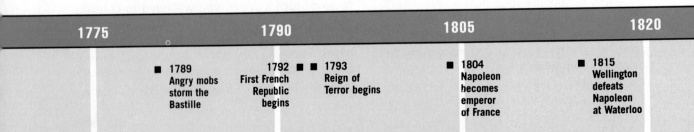

1775	1790	1805	1820

■ **1789** Angry mobs storm the Bastille

1792 First French Republic begins

■ ■ **1793** Reign of Terror begins

■ **1804** Napoleon becomes emperor of France

■ **1815** Wellington defeats Napoleon at Waterloo

▲ **Illustrating History** *Angry mobs, like the one pictured in the painting above, were a common sight in Paris in 1789.*

1 The Old Regime Abused the French

As you read, look for answers to these questions.

◆ What was France like under the Old Regime?

◆ How did the new ideas of the Enlightenment add to the discontent of the French people?

> **Key Terms:** bourgeoisie (defined on p. 454)

"It was the best of times, it was the worst of times. . . ." So begins Charles Dickens's novel, *A Tale of Two Cities*, which was based on the French Revolution. The two cities were London and Paris, the hearts of two great nations and the seats of two strong governments. For the privileged classes of these two cities, in Dickens's view, it was the best of times. For the great majority of citizens who lived in poverty, however, it was probably the worst of times. Thus, during the late 1700s, both of these cities became the centers of revolution.

France Under the Old Regime Had Changed Little

If a French family of the Middle Ages had been transported to the France of 1789, it would have found conditions unchanged in many ways. Society was still divided into privileged and unprivileged classes. Unfair taxation, under which the poor paid more than the rich, still existed, and highway tolls still interfered with travel.

The form of government and the way society was organized before the French Revolution are known as the Old Regime.

Government and society under the Old Regime had many features that had not changed since feudal days. Perhaps the most outstanding feature of the Old Regime was the absolute power of the monarch. The misuse of that power angered the poor.

In 1789, the power of governing was in the hands of a well-meaning but feeble king, Louis XVI, who ruled from 1774 to 1792. He had inherited many problems from his father, Louis XV, who was said to have noted that after his reign there would be a flood of troubles, and he was certainly right. The wife of Louis XVI was Marie Antoinette (AN twuh NET), who was Austrian by birth. The thoughtlessness and extravagance of the queen frequently angered the French people.

Three Classes Emerged During the Old Regime

Under the Old Regime, the French people were divided into three social classes, or estates. The first estate, made up of religious leaders and members of the clergy, repre-

▼ **Illustrating History** *The artist Louis Le Nain used oil paints for this painting of a French peasant family around 1642.*

sented less than 1 percent of the 25 million French people. This small minority, however, owned or controlled one-fifth of the land. Members of the first estate enjoyed special rights and were free from the burden of taxes.

The second estate, made up of the nobles, included less than 2 percent of the population, but it, too, had many privileges and owned much land. Today, people with high incomes pay more taxes than those who earn less, but this was not true during the Old Regime in France. The nobles paid few or no taxes and retained many feudal privileges. They also held the best political offices and had a great deal of influence with the monarch.

Among members of the first and second estates were many poor and well-meaning people. Parish priests, for example, served the religious needs of their people but received few rewards. Furthermore, there were many nobles who knew that the privileges they had were unfair. In fact, some of the thoughtful people among the nobles and the clergy felt these privileges should be ended.

More than 24 million people—95 percent of the population—belonged to the third estate. This group included serfs who were still bound to the soil, members of the middle class, or **bourgeoisie** (BOOR zhwah ZEE), and many peasants. Servants, skilled and unskilled workers, doctors, lawyers, teachers, storekeepers, and laborers made up the third estate.

These people were the backbone of the country, but they had few privileges. They also had a very limited voice in the Estates-General, a kind of lawmaking group without much democratic influence. Like French society, it was made up of three estates, known as the First Estate, the Second Estate, and the Third Estate. In the Estates-General, voting was done separately by estate, and each estate had only one vote. Because the First Estate and Second Estate always banded together to overrule any laws that would help the middle and lower classes, the Third Estate had almost no voice in government.

Many Factors Led to Revolution in France

The government and society of France under the Old Regime were little different from those in other European countries with the exception of Great Britain. Why then did revolution on the European continent come first to France?

As discussed in Chapter 18, France was the home of Voltaire, Rousseau, and others who taught that freedom of thought and action is a basic human right. Revolution came first to France because the middle and lower classes there were not oppressed as severely as they were in other countries. Historically, revolution often occurs not when conditions are the worst, but when they are beginning to improve. When people see that there is the possibility of change, they begin to expect even better conditions. The underprivileged in France came to realize that their lives could be better than they were under the Old Regime. As the middle class grew and became wealthy, it demanded a voice in the government. Finally, Louis XVI himself, a weak monarch who was unable or unwilling to tackle the problems of his country, added to the causes of the revolution.

Both fundamental and immediate causes brought about revolution in France. A fundamental cause is one that has roots in the past. Under the Old Regime, there were many feudal laws and customs that were not in step with Enlightenment thinking. At the same time, the attitudes of the people toward government and social relations were changing. These were among the fundamental causes of the revolution.

An immediate cause is one that directly leads to action. In the case of the French Revolution, this cause was the need for money to pay the costs of running the government and supporting a costly court. The income of the French nation was less than the amount spent each year. The government's debt was so great that the interest on it was the nation's greatest single expense. Louis XVI simply did not know how to save France from financial collapse.

Although Louis XIV had warned those who followed him not to spend too much money or to fight costly wars, the monarchs who followed him did not take his advice. Instead, they followed his bad example. Since they were less skilled in governing than he, the results were disastrous for France. Furthermore, France could not afford the aid it gave to America during the American Revolution. Its loans to America contributed to its bankruptcy.

Louis XVI and Marie Antoinette might have held off bankruptcy and saved the monarchy if they had listened to their finance ministers, Jacques Necker (NEK ur) and Robert Turgot (toor GOH). However, the monarchy and the nobility would not do what was needed to save France or themselves. They refused to lower expenses, and they would not allow themselves to be taxed. When Turgot and Necker suggested these measures, they were dismissed by the king. The stubbornness of the monarch and the nobility made disaster almost inevitable.

SECTION 1 REVIEW

Knowing Key Terms, People, and Places
1. Define: **a.** bourgeoisie
2. Identify: **a.** Louis XVI **b.** Marie Antoinette **c.** Estates-General **d.** Necker and Turgot

Reviewing Main Ideas
3. Why were Louis XVI and Marie Antoinette not popular with the French people?
4. How was French society organized under the Old Regime?
5. How did the ideas of the Enlightenment inspire the French people to revolt?
6. What were some of the fundamental and immediate causes of the French Revolution?

Critical Thinking
Expressing Problems Clearly
7. Imagine that someone has asked you to explain the causes of the French Revolution. Make an outline showing how you would answer this question.

2 The Revolutionaries Ended Absolute Rule

As you read, look for answers to these questions:

◆ What were Louis XVI's goals when he called together the Estates-General? What were the goals of the Third Estate members?
◆ Why was the National Assembly originally set up? How did its goals change with time?
◆ What did the National Assembly accomplish?

> **Key Terms:** cahier (defined on p. 456)

French bankruptcy made Louis XVI desperate. He decided to call a meeting of the Estates-General, hoping that this body would have some ideas for solving the crisis. However, Louis was not prepared for the reaction his decision would cause. The meeting of the Estates-General gave people their long-awaited voice in the government. They were eager to make the most of this meeting, which they saw as a golden opportunity. The king needed money, and he would need their help to get it. They hoped that he would be willing to give them something in return.

The Third Estate Desired Changes in Government

In the Estates-General, the Third Estate thought that they could work out a deal with the monarchy to secure more rights for their class. After all, wasn't this the way the English Parliament became strong under Charles I? Didn't the philosophers tell them that governments are to be run by the people? Didn't the American Declaration of Independence state that when government destroys the people's rights, it should be changed? With these thoughts to guide them, various groups met in large and small cities early in 1789. They drew up lists of the peoples' grievances, complaints, and criticisms and put them in books that were known as **cahiers** (kah YAYS).

Although the cahiers expressed some of the new, democratic ideas of the day, for the most part, they did not demand extreme changes in the government. They did not suggest that the monarch should be executed or leave the throne. Instead, they asked only that special privileges of the nobles be abolished, that taxes be fair for all the people, and that the Estates-General meet more often to discuss government affairs. In the cahiers, the people asked that the government allow freedom of speech and press and leave business alone.

The Estates-General Became the National Assembly

When the Estates-General met in 1789, the First and Second Estates had 300 members each. The Third Estate had about 600. As you read in the first section, voting was not done by individuals but by entire estates, and each estate had one vote. The First and Second Estates usually voted against the wishes of the Third Estate. So the Third Estate was usually outvoted two to one.

This method of voting struck hard at the hopes that the members of the Third Estate had brought to Paris. However, they were determined not to go away empty-handed. They declared themselves to be the National Assembly for all of France, and they invited members of the other estates to join them.

Because the meeting hall of the Estates-General was closed to them, the members of the Third Estate met on an indoor tennis court and swore that they would not disband until they had given France a constitution. Only when they had gained a constitution would they give their attention to the king's money problems. This agreement, which is known as the Tennis Court Oath of June 20, 1789, was a significant step in the French Revolution. It showed that the three estates could unite, at least for a time, against the crown. But, Louis XVI would not listen to their demands for a constitution. Instead, he threatened to send them home.

By the time Louis XVI had decided to listen to the Third Estate, it was too late. The French Revolution had begun. The attempt by the Third Estate to establish a constitution was cheered by the people of Paris. To show their support, angry mobs attacked the Bastille (bas TEEL), an old fortress used as a prison and a symbol of the Old Regime. This action, which was taken on July 14, 1789, is still remembered by the French, who celebrate Bastille Day as a national holiday.

The Women of Paris Led an Angry March on Versailles

While mobs in Paris stormed the Bastille, riots were breaking out in the countryside. Economic depression, as well as revolution, gripped the country. Unemployment was widespread; troops seemed to be everywhere. The people were afraid and uneasy. A rumor that the queen had told the people to eat cake if they had no bread, aroused the women of Paris to action. In the rain, they marched 20 miles from Paris to the palace at Versailles in early October of 1789, as you read in the introduction to this chapter. They wanted to force "the baker, the baker's wife, and the baker's little boy"—that is, the king and queen and their son—to return to Paris with them and to provide them with more grain. Madelaine Chabray (shah BRAY), a 17-year-old unemployed sculptor who sold flowers for a living, led the march. She was successful in getting the king to distribute grain, which she hoped would relieve starvation in France.

To prevent violence, the king returned to Paris wearing the tricolor (red, white, and blue) ribbon that had become a revolutionary symbol. Thus, led by a band of angry women, the French people had made great strides in their move toward revolution.

The National Assembly Made Important Reforms

At the National Assembly, which met from 1789 to 1791, important work was being done. On August 4, 1789, a noble suggested that the members of the First and Second

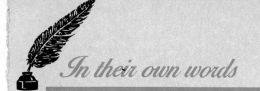

In their own words

Storming the Bastille

M. Keversau, a French lawyer, participated in the capture of the Bastille on July 14, 1789. The taking of this prison by a group of citizens was the symbolic start of the French Revolution. In the following excerpt, Keversau tells what happened after the crowd entered the prison.

❝Those who came in first treated the conquered enemy humanely and embraced the staff officers to show there was no ill-feeling. But a few soldiers posted on the platforms and unaware that the fortress had surrendered discharged their muskets, whereupon the people, transported with rage, threw themselves on the [soldiers] and used them with the utmost violence. . . . All the officers were seized and their quarters were invaded by the mob, who smashed the furniture, the doors, and the windows. In the general turmoil the people in the courtyard fired on those who were in the private quarters and on the platforms. Several were killed. . . .

In the intoxication [joy] of victory the unfortunate inmates of the . . . Bastille had been forgotten. All the keys had been carried off in triumph and it was necessary to force the doors of the cells. Seven prisoners were found and brought to the Palais Royal. These poor fellows were in transports of pleasure and could scarcely realize they were not dreaming.❞

1. What evidence suggests that the people who took the Bastille did not originally intend to kill the guards?
2. How many prisoners were released from the Bastille?

457

▲ **Illustrating History** *This colorful, nineteenth-century etching shows a mob of Parisians storming the Bastille on July 14, 1789.*

Estates should give up their special privileges. The members of the Third Estate cheered with delight. This suggestion marked the beginning of reforms and the opportunity for which the Third Estate had been waiting. The assembly also discussed having nobles pay more taxes and abolishing ancient feudal privileges.

During August, the Third Estate also introduced the Declaration of the Rights of Man. This proclamation repeated some of the new ideas of the time, such as "Men are born and remain free and equal in rights." It also defended the rights of liberty, ownership of property, and resistance to oppression. All citizens were to have a voice in the government, to be equal before the law, and to be protected against unfair arrest. These were happy days for the people, who seemed to be getting exactly what they wanted.

The period of happiness for the people ended quickly, however. Many women in France were bitterly disappointed with the results of the National Assembly. While the Declaration of the Rights of Man was being written and adopted, the assembly rejected a declaration on the rights of women. The gathering even prohibited women from holding any kind of meeting in the future. Women tried to resist this act of the National Assembly, but they were unsuccessful. Many women, as well as men, felt that it was improper for women to take an active role in the political life of the nation. Furthermore, the Third Estate, which controlled the National Assembly, consisted of three major groups that did not always share the same goals.

The bourgeoisie, the middle class, wanted to control the government. The second group, the peasants, wanted to own land. The third group, city workers, wanted liberty, better wages and working conditions, and more extreme reforms. The conflicting interests and goals of these groups undermined the unity of the National Assembly.

458

Ultimately, however, the demands of each of these groups were at least partially met as a result of the French Revolution.

The Assembly Tried to Solve the Financial Woes of France

The resolutions of August 4 and the Declaration of the Rights of Man did not solve the financial problems of France. The king needed money, and good ideas alone did not supply the money he needed. It was one thing to say that all should be taxed according to their ability to pay, but it took time to collect the money. In the meantime, how were the financial problems to be solved?

The National Assembly decided that one answer was to make the Catholic church give up its lands, which were worth a great deal. Against the value of these lands, the National Assembly printed assignats (AS ig NATS), or paper money. The money was to be used to pay the nation's debts, and the land was to be sold at low prices to the French peasants. In this way, the assembly believed, two problems would be solved at one time. The national government would have money to pay its debts, and the peasants would have the opportunity to become landowners.

Unfortunately, the new financial program backfired when more paper money was printed than the Catholic church lands were worth. As a result, the prices of food, clothing, and shelter rose so high that the people could not pay for the things they needed. Church officials were angry at losing their lands, and people were angry that they could not satisfy the basic needs of life.

The National Assembly Wrote a Constitution for France

In the famous Tennis Court Oath, the members of the National Assembly had sworn to give France a constitution. After two years of discussions, the Constitution of 1791 was adopted. It allowed the king to keep his throne as long as the rules of limited monarchy were observed. Under the Constitution of 1791, French rulers would be limited to those activities approved by the representatives of the French people.

The National Assembly then divided France into 83 departments, or local districts, and created a one-house lawmaking body to be elected by the people. The right to vote was limited to people who could pay taxes. This voting restriction did not agree with the Declaration of the Rights of Man, which said that all citizens had a right to take part in government.

The National Assembly also granted freedom to all religious groups. The assembly wanted to weaken the power of the Roman Catholic church and had done so, in part, by

▼ **Chart Skill** *How long after the Tennis Court Oath was Louis XVI executed?*

Major Events of the French Revolution	
1789–1791	National Assembly meets
June 20, 1789	Tennis Court Oath: National Assembly vows to gain a French constitution
July 14, 1789	Bastille Day: angry mob storms and captures Bastille
August 1789	National Assembly resolves that nobles and clergy will give up special privileges
	Third Estate introduces Declaration of the Rights of Man
1790	Civil Constitution of the Clergy places clergy under government control
1791	National Assembly adopts Constitution of 1791 and divides France into 83 departments
September 1792	National Convention replaces National Assembly
1792–1795	First Republic rules France
January 1793	Louis XVI is sent to the guillotine
1793–1795	Reign of Terror: National Convention appoints Committee of Public Safety

taking church lands. The assembly also passed an act, known as the Civil Constitution of the Clergy, that placed the priests and other officials of the church under state control. In the opinion of many French people, however, this act went too far. They remembered the good work of the parish priests, and they had no wish to see the priests become salaried servants of the government. Many people who had supported the ideas of the revolution now turned against them.

The middle class, who now controlled the National Assembly, were using the new French constitution to further their own ends. Only the middle class and the peasants who had bought the church lands had gained from the new government. The city workers and the laboring classes had gained little so far. They had a right to be disappointed. In their eyes, the revolution had not gone far enough, and they intended to push it further.

The Limited Monarchy Failed

The new limited monarchy failed because it was not supported. The lawmaking body provided for in the constitution met for less than a year. During this time, there were bitter arguments between those who felt

▼ **Illustrating History** *This painting shows a meeting of a patriotic women's club during the French Revolution.*

that the revolution had not gone far enough (the workers) and those who felt that the revolution had gone too far (the nobles and bourgeoisie). The bourgeoisie and the workers could not agree on what changes were necessary for France. The majority of the old Third Estate did not know exactly what they wanted. They were usually unable to make up their minds whether to support the limited monarchy or to encourage further revolution.

Often, a few people who know what they want can sway the opinions of many who do not. The workers, who were few in number, were supported by Jacobin (JAK uh bin) clubs. These were clubs usually made up of Parisian laborers who felt that the revolution had been betrayed by the French nobles now living in other countries. The Parisian laborers also felt they had been betrayed by the king who, unable to accept a limited monarchy, had been caught trying to leave the country. The Jacobins believed that France was surrounded by enemies who were trying to return the king to power. Although they were in the minority, the Jacobins forced the majority to declare war on Austria and Prussia. They took advantage of opportunities to remove the king and abolish the National Assembly. The undecided majority of the Third Estate accepted what the Jacobins wanted. The assembly was replaced by the National Convention, which would form the First Republic.

The First French Republic Governed France

The National Convention, which represented the working people, governed the First Republic from 1792 to 1795. Although France was fighting a war, Georges Jacques Danton (dahn TOHN), one of the leaders of the revolution, demanded that the working people demonstrate "boldness, more boldness, always boldness." Groups of Parisians took his advice and began a wave of killings in the city that spread to the country. People who were not in favor of carrying on with the violent activities of the revolution were looked upon by others as enemies.

Revolutionary Pastimes

Just as in more peaceful times, people of revolutionary France tried to amuse themselves. They played cards and other games, enjoying many of the same pastimes that are still with us today.

The game of solitaire, for example, is said to have been invented by a French nobleman sentenced to solitary confinement in the Bastille. To pass the time, he cut a series of holes in a board, filling all but the center hole with wooden pegs. Then, he shifted and removed the pegs so that the last peg landed in the center hole.

People who fled France to escape imprisonment, called emigrés, were among those who used a toy that is still popular today. Ivory yo-yos, first used by both the ancient Chinese and the Greeks, became so popular with French emigrés that they were mockingly called *l'emigrettes*.

1. How did the game of solitaire originate?
2. Why were yo-yos nicknamed "l'emigrettes"?

France became a nation torn by conflicts. The National Convention was trying to keep order in France and, at the same time, defend the country from foreign invasions. The French were fighting against a foreign enemy—Austria—for the ideals of liberty, equality, and fraternity. They marched to the tune of a new hymn that became the French national anthem, *La Marseillaise* (lah MAHR say YEZ).

Those who favored extreme measures were in control of the National Convention. On January 15, 1793, King Louis XVI, now known as Citizen Louis Capet, was declared guilty of treason and condemned to the guillotine (GIHL uh TEEN). He was executed within a week.

Most members of the National Convention did not like what was being done, but they could not stop it. Armed Parisians forced their way into the National Convention, where they arrested and put to death many of those who opposed the extreme measures. The Reign of Terror had begun.

SECTION 2 REVIEW

Knowing Key Terms, People, and Places
1. Define: **a.** cahier
2. Identify: **a.** National Assembly **b.** Tennis Court Oath **c.** Bastille **d.** Declaration of the Rights of Man **e.** First Republic.

Reviewing Main Ideas
3. What opportunities did the members of the Third Estate see when Louis XVI called a meeting of the Estates-General?
4. Why was the National Assembly formed?
5. Why were the city workers disappointed in the results of the National Assembly?
6. Who controlled the First Republic of France?

Critical Thinking
Testing Conclusions
7. How accurate is the following statement: "The French Revolution was the result of high prices and hard times"?

3 Terror and Warfare Swept France

As you read, look for answers to these questions:

◆ How was France governed under the Committee of Public Safety?
◆ What role did women play in the French Revolution?
◆ What reforms did the National Convention make in France?
◆ What kind of government emerged after the Reign of Terror had ended?

Key Terms: *pain d'égalité* (defined on p. 464).

Killing without reason is usually a sign of weakness, not of strength. This was true of France during the Reign of Terror. Rioting and war, disagreement over the kind of government to have, a lack of leadership,

▼ **Illustrating History** *This* Portrait of Robespierre *was painted by an unknown artist around the year 1790.*

unemployment, high prices, and food shortages weakened France. Without help from other nations, France was at war with the countries of Europe. It also was trying to keep the progress that had been made in the revolution.

A Reign of Terror Seized France

The National Convention created a new constitution that gave all men the right to vote and again gave all lawmaking power to a single legislative body. However, it did not follow its constitution. Instead, the National Convention appointed a committee of 12 men, known as the Committee of Public Safety, to rule France during the years following the revolution.

The Committee of Public Safety, which had unlimited power, was headed by Maximilien de Robespierre (roh behs PEEAYR). The committee paid no attention to the democratic constitution. It arrested and put to death anyone who was even suspected of not agreeing with the revolutionary ideas of the National Convention. Danton, an early leader of the revolution, lost his life. Later, the queen, Marie Antoinette, was also beheaded. Thousands of people were executed in the name of the republic. Some were real enemies, but many others were not.

Before the Reign of Terror had finished, Robespierre himself was executed. Upon the death of Robespierre, those who favored less extreme measures finally won control of France.

Women Played an Active Role in the French Revolution

Many women took part in the French Revolution. Among these women were shopkeepers, fish vendors, launderers, tailors, journalists, and actors. Between 1725 and 1783, there were frequent riots for bread in the streets of Paris and elsewhere. French women took part in these riots and learned about revolutionary tactics as they fought.

Madame de Condorcet (duh kawn dor SAY) and her husband championed the cause of equal rights for women. Condorcet himself spoke out strongly for the political rights of women in the National Assembly. He was eventually executed during the Reign of Terror.

Madame Manon Roland (roh LAWN) was also actively involved in the revolution during its early days. As a member of the upper middle class she sought to establish a limited monarchy, not a republic. Those who favored a limited monarchy felt that she was not doing enough to make such a government possible. Those who favored a republic thought that she was doing too much to encourage a limited monarchy. She was despised by both groups. In the end, she too died in the Reign of Terror.

It is important to note that although women took part in the French Revolution, their role was limited. Public opinion did not support them, and most women were not ready to take bold political action. The process of thinking through the role of women in government, in society, and in the economic life of the community was a long and slow one. That process, however, did begin in France during the time of the French Revolution.

The National Convention Adopted Many Reforms

The National Convention should be remembered for more than violence. It attempted to change all parts of French life. The National Convention even adopted a new calendar. September 22, 1792, the first day of the new government, became the first day of the new year in the new calendar. The

▲ **Illustrating History** *Marie Antoinette approaches the guillotine in this etching.*

National Convention also changed the names of the months that had been in use.

The National Convention made other changes. Under the orders of the National Convention, men had to wear long pants rather than knee breeches, and women had to wear simple dresses. People were forbidden to use expensive white flour and instead had to eat **pain d'égalité** (pan day GAHL ee TAY) or "equality bread," made from whole wheat flour. The words *Monsieur* and *Madame* were replaced by the French word meaning "Citizen." These changes were made in an attempt to create more equality among French people.

The convention made more lasting reforms as well. It adopted the metric system of weights and measures, based on units of ten, which was considered a more rational system than the English and American system of pounds and inches. It also abolished imprisonment for debt and slavery in the French colonies. The convention even planned a national system of education.

Another Constitution Followed the Reign of Terror

Following the Reign of Terror, the people of France wanted peace. The National Convention dismissed the Committee of Public Safety and adopted the Constitution of 1795.

This constitution was less democratic than the one produced by the National Assembly. The new government included a two-house lawmaking body and a five-person law-enforcing body known as the Directory. This type of government was a far cry from the high ideals that the National Assembly had formed in 1791.

It is said that two heads are better than one. Perhaps the members of the National Convention thought that five heads would be better than two. Unfortunately, the five members of the Directory, which lasted from 1795 to 1799, did not have the answers to the problems that plagued France. These problems included finding money to run the government, ending the foreign war with victory, and providing law and order for the country. With little success, the Directory worked to solve these problems until 1799.

The Directory was not equal to the difficult task it faced. The dissatisfied people of France were looking for a strong leader who could promise them peace, glory, and lasting victory. Such a leader soon appeared. His name was Napoleon Bonaparte.

SECTION 3 REVIEW

Knowing Key Terms, People, and Places
1. Define: **a.** *pain d'égalité*
2. Identify: **a.** Committee of Public Safety **b.** Robespierre **c.** Directory

Reviewing Main Ideas
3. How did the Committee of Public Safety control France?
4. What reforms did the National Convention introduce?
5. How did the Constitution of 1795 and the Directory set the stage for Napoleon?

Critical Thinking
Checking Consistency
6. The slogan of the French Revolution called for liberty, equality, and brotherhood. Were the methods of Robespierre and his followers consistent with these ideals? Why or why not?

Art in the Age of Revolution

The art of the revolutionary period is marked by extremes, from very intimate, human portrayals to scenes of brutality and inhumanity. Elisabeth Louise Vigée-Lebrun was a successful and popular painter in pre-revolutionary France and a favorite of Queen Marie Antoinette. Although a celebrity, she chose a quiet, personal moment with her daughter in which to record her own image. By contrast, Francisco Goya's *Third of May, 1808* portrays the violence of revolution and war. In his painting, Goya shows how Spanish peasants, suspected of resisting the French invaders, are rounded up and shot, regardless of their guilt or innocence. If you look at the faces of the peasants in the work, it will become obvious that Goya's sympathies lie with his fellow Spaniards: the men are portrayed as innocent but heroic victims. We can think of this painting as the first artistic representation of modern warfare.

(Below) Francisco Goya's Third of May, 1808; *(Right) Elisabeth Vigée-Lebrun's portrait of herself and her daughter.*

Seperate Test

4 Napoleon Rose to Power in France

As you read, look for answers to these questions:

◆ What kind of man was Napoleon Bonaparte?
◆ How did Napoleon rise to power in France?
◆ What changes did Napoleon make in France?
◆ How was Napoleon finally defeated?

> **Key Terms:** coup d'état (defined on p. 467), dictator (p. 467), plebiscite (p. 467)

Over 200,000 books and many shorter works have been written about Napoleon. In fact, some historians have devoted their lives to studying what Napoleon did and how he did it. Even so, there is no agreement as to whether France and Europe were better off or worse off as a result of his rule. What is clear, however, is that the world was dominated by his personality when he was in power, perhaps in a way no person had ever dominated it before or has since.

Napoleon Was a Child of the Revolution

Napoleon Bonaparte was born in 1769 in Corsica, an island off the coast of Italy. Three months before he was born, the island became a French possession. When he was 5 years old, Napoleon was sent to a school for girls in hopes that he would become less stubborn and easier to handle. This was not to be the case, however. Napoleon, who was the second of eight Bonaparte children, was a strong-willed, obstinate, and often disagreeable child.

Napoleon's parents then sent him to a Jesuit school where his older brother was a student. The young Napoleon apparently liked this school, because when he became emperor, he awarded his reading teacher

20,000 francs as a token of his gratitude for what he had learned. As a student, Napoleon read all kinds of books. When he finally received a scholarship to a French military academy and later to the Military College of France, his love of reading allowed him to stay near the top of his class.

Napoleon rose quickly from poverty to power and then fell from power almost as quickly. During his career, he fascinated those who came into contact with him. He was short, slightly below average height, but stocky and hearty. His energy was unfailing, and his subordinates often could not keep up with the exhausting pace he set.

It is said of Napoleon that his most powerful tool for commanding the respect and obedience of others was his eyes. A cardinal who was negotiating with him admitted to wearing a huge pair of green eyeglasses to soften the intense glare of Napoleon's eyes. And one of Napoleon's generals confessed, "I am ready to tremble like a child when I am in his presence, and he could make me go through the eye of a needle to throw myself into the fire." Such was the man who was to set France right side up and turn Europe upside down.

Napoleon's Rise to Power Was Rapid

As a young man, Napoleon supported the French Revolution and fought against the foreign enemies of France as an officer in the army. He was noticed by the Directory when he saved the National Convention from an attack by a Parisian mob. Using what was called a "whiff of grapeshot" (artillery fire), Napoleon held back the mob. As a reward for his bravery and loyalty, he was made a general and given command of the French armies in northern Italy. There, he defeated the Austrians, who controlled the region. Later, Napoleon went to Egypt and unsuccessfully attempted to destroy the British trade route to the Middle East and India. Hearing that there was unrest at home, Napoleon returned to France and soon took control of the country. The map on page 468 shows the extent of the empire he established in Europe.

With the help of his brother and two members of the Directory, he successfully forced the Directory from power. A revolution of this kind, in which the government is suddenly changed or overthrown by a small group of people, is known as a **coup d'état** (KOO day TAH). Napoleon quickly issued a new constitution in which power was given to the first consul of a three-person consulate (KAHN suh let). The new constitution was acceptable to the people mainly because its author was so popular. Napoleon then became first consul and ruler of France.

Napoleon Made Lasting Changes in France

By 1802, Napoleon had brought victory to France and peace to Europe. During this interval of peace, he made a number of lasting reforms in France.

First, Napoleon turned his attention to the problem of establishing a strong central government. So effectively did he gather all power into the hands of the national government that even today France is largely ruled from Paris as Napoleon had planned. To help centralize power, Napoleon established the Napoleonic code of law. The code also included many democratic principles, such as religious tolerance, trial by jury, the abolition of serfdom, and fair legal methods.

To strengthen the government further, Napoleon established the University of France. This was not a college but rather an office responsible for overseeing the schools of France. In this way, Napoleon made sure that the schools taught what he wanted. In doing this, Napoleon set a pattern that would be imitated by many dictators in modern times. A **dictator** is any ruler with absolute power and authority, especially one whose rule is harsh and cruel.

The age-old problem of money also needed solutions. Napoleon organized the Bank of France, which provided a basis for an economic system that could help France to prosper. He also collected taxes efficiently and controlled government spending. Business and trade were encouraged.

▲ **Illustrating History** *This dramatic painting shows Napoleon on horseback.*

The French Revolution had left Catholic church officials unhappy. Their lands had been taken away, and they had been forced to accept the Civil Constitution of the Clergy. To regain the confidence and support of church leaders, Napoleon made an agreement with the pope. This agreement made Catholicism the official religion of France again. In exchange, the pope gave up all claims to the lands taken from the Catholic church by the National Assembly.

To make France more beautiful, Napoleon undertook many public works, improved the roads, dug canals, and deepened harbors. He tried to enlist the support of prominent people for these jobs. To get their support, he established the Legion of Honor, which, to this day, honors people who have made outstanding contributions to France.

Because of his successes at home and abroad, the people were ready to give Napoleon whatever he wanted. He wanted to be first consul for life, which would amount to a dictatorship. In 1802, the French agreed by plebiscite (PLEHB uh SYT). A **plebiscite**

467

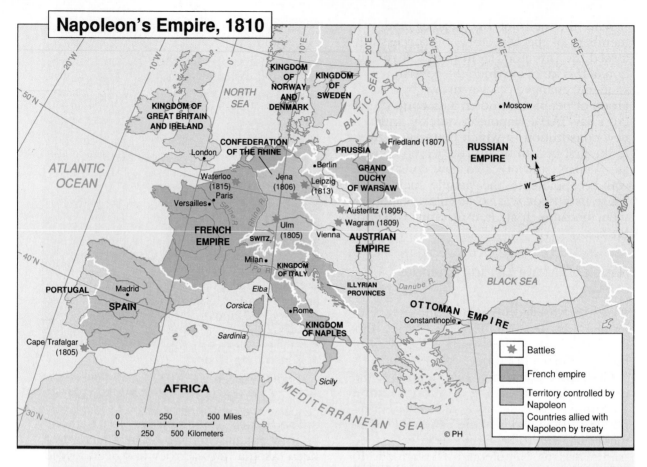

Napoleon's Empire, 1810

KINGDOM OF NORWAY AND DENMARK
KINGDOM OF SWEDEN
KINGDOM OF GREAT BRITAIN AND IRELAND
NORTH SEA
BALTIC SEA
•Moscow
Friedland (1807)
RUSSIAN EMPIRE
London•
CONFEDERATION OF THE RHINE
PRUSSIA
•Berlin
GRAND DUCHY OF WARSAW
ATLANTIC OCEAN
Waterloo (1815)
Jena (1806)
Leipzig (1813)
Paris•
Versailles•
Austerlitz (1805)
Wagram (1809)
FRENCH EMPIRE
SWITZ.
Ulm (1805)
Vienna•
AUSTRIAN EMPIRE
Milan•
Po R.
KINGDOM OF ITALY
ILLYRIAN PROVINCES
Danube R.
BLACK SEA
PORTUGAL
Madrid•
SPAIN
Elba
Corsica
•Rome
OTTOMAN EMPIRE
Constantinople•
Cape Trafalgar (1805)
Sardinia
KINGDOM OF NAPLES
AFRICA
Sicily
MEDITERRANEAN SEA

0   250   500 Miles
0 250 500 Kilometers
© PH

N
W — E
S

Legend:
✴ Battles
French empire
Territory controlled by Napoleon
Countries allied with Napoleon by treaty

Focus on Geography

1. **Location**   You will read about Napoleon's march into Russia on page 469. How far is it from Paris to Moscow?
2. **Interaction**   In fighting the British on land, Napoleon usually was the victor. What sea battle did France lose to the British?

is a vote of the people by direct ballot on a political issue. When Napoleon later wanted to name himself emperor, the people again agreed by plebiscite. By 1804, Napoleon, emperor of France, was looking for new worlds to conquer.

Napoleon Brought War to Europe

Napoleon once said, "My power would fall if I did not support it with more victories." He felt he needed victories abroad to continue to remind the people of his greatness. In 1803, Napoleon began a war with Great Britain. Later, most of the nations of Europe, as well as Russia and the United States, became involved in the war. On land, Napoleon was usually successful against the British, but on the sea, the brilliant strategy of the British admiral Horatio Nelson defeated Napoleon. Admiral Nelson's naval victory over the combined French and Spanish fleets at Cape Trafalgar is one of history's most famous battles. It proved that Great Britain controlled the seas.

On land, the battles at Austerlitz and Wagram in Austria, and those at Jena and Friedland in Prussia were key victories for

Napoleon. Over time, Napoleon became the most feared person in Europe, and France became the most powerful nation on the continent.

To keep France in its powerful position, Napoleon tried to reorganize Europe. He united German states into the Confederation of the Rhine and placed his relatives on many of the European thrones. He also made an alliance for mutual protection with Alexander I of Russia. By 1807, the continent of Europe was in Napoleon's palm, but Great Britain remained a thorn in his side.

Europe United Against Napoleon

When he failed to defeat Great Britain by military means, Napoleon decided he would crush what he called the "nation of shopkeepers" in another way. He would keep Great Britain from trading on the continent of Europe. In his Berlin Decree and his Milan Decree, Napoleon ordered the countries under his control to stop trading with Britain. This move, which isolated Britain economically from the European continent, was called the Continental System.

Great Britain struck back with the Orders in Council, which ordered neutral nations not to trade with France. The Orders in Council were more effective than the Berlin and Milan decrees because Great Britain controlled the seas, which were crucial to commerce.

The defeat of Napoleon. Napoleon finally began to suffer defeat when his country went to war with Russia. Alexander I decided to break his alliance with Napoleon. This brought about a war with Russia in which Napoleon met his first serious defeat. The climate of Russia contributed to it. When Napoleon invaded Russia, his troops had to fight in the bitter cold, as well as ice and snow, which they had not had to do before. The Russians shot at the French troops from behind trees and burned Russian cities before the French armies could take them.

Other geographic factors aided the Russians. The vast size of the country actually helped to defeat the French. At the start of the war, the Russians forced the French to chase them for 500 miles (1,800 kilometers) into Russia before a battle occurred near Moscow. Although the French won that battle, they had to retreat because Moscow was in flames. Alexander had decided to destroy the city rather than to surrender it to Napoleon. Stranded far from home with little food, the French army began its retreat. The distance, however, was too great for the weakened French troops. Many froze, starved to death, or were killed.

The defeat of Napoleon's army in Russia brought a reaction from other European countries. It encouraged the nations that Napoleon had defeated to try for victory. In 1813 at the battle of Leipzig in eastern Germany, these nations combined to inflict another serious defeat on Napoleon. After this battle, Napoleon was forced to give up his title of emperor, and he was sent to live on the tiny island of Elba in the Mediterranean Sea.

Once Napoleon was defeated, the monarchs of Europe were restored to power and peace was established. Louis XVIII, one of the younger brothers of Louis XVI, became king of France. Europe heaved a sigh of relief at the restoration of the Bourbon kings to the throne of France. It seemed that the Napoleonic menace had been removed forever. Luckily for France, a generous peace settlement was made. A brilliant gathering of foreign ministers met at the Congress of Vienna for the purpose of restoring order throughout Europe. You will read about the Congress of Vienna in the next chapter.

In the midst of the Congress of Vienna, however, news came that Napoleon had escaped from Elba and, with 1,500 men, was marching on Paris. On March 20, 1815, Napoleon reentered Paris, and it seemed as if a new Napoleonic era had begun. Austria, Prussia, Russia, and Britain combined forces once again to stop Napoleon. One million men, led by the Duke of Wellington, managed to defeat the French general. On June 18, 1815, Wellington's troops defeated Napoleon at Waterloo in Belgium. Napoleon surrendered to the British. This time Napoleon was sent as a prisoner of war to the

▲ **Illustrating History** *The oil painting above captures a moment during the crucial Battle of Waterloo, where Napoleon met his final defeat.*

lonely British island of St. Helena in the southern Atlantic Ocean off the western coast of Africa. He died there in 1821.

France after Napoleon. Under Napoleon, France failed to gain one of the most important features of democracy—political freedom. The French Revolution had destroyed the power of absolute monarchs in France, but Napoleon brought absolutism back as emperor. The French Revolution separated church and state, but Napoleon joined them again. The French Revolution established free speech and freedom of the press, but Napoleon took them away.

The democratic values of the French Revolution were only temporarily destroyed by Napoleon. The ideas behind the democratic reforms lived on in the minds of the French people to gather new strength after Napoleon was destroyed. Probably without knowing it or even caring, Napoleon planted the seeds of revolution in other countries. In the soil of Europe and Latin America, these seeds took root—some grew strong, while others were crushed. The struggle for democracy went on long after Napoleon.

SECTION 4 REVIEW

Knowing Key Terms, People, and Places
1. Define: **a.** coup d'état **b.** dictator **c.** plebiscite
2. Identify: **a.** Napoleon **b.** first consul **c.** Napoleonic code of law **d.** Continental System **e.** Waterloo

Focus on Geography
3. How did the geography of Russia help to defeat Napoleon?

Reviewing Main Ideas
4. How did Napoleon's personality help him to gain power?
5. What reforms did Napoleon bring to France?
6. Describe how specific European nations united to defeat Napoleon.

Critical Thinking
Identifying Central Issues
7. List and explain three major factors that allowed Napoleon Bonaparte to rise to the position of emperor of France.

Comparing Two Points of View

Eyewitness accounts of the same event can differ greatly in their descriptions and conclusions. For example, the observers may disagree over the causes or the effects of the event. Or they may each hold a *bias*—a prejudice or a personal slant—toward the event. You can better understand the event if you carefully evaluate the different accounts.

The two documents below are eyewitness accounts of the same event. Use the following steps to read and analyze the documents.

1. **Carefully study each account to gain an overall sense of the event they describe.** Determine the source of each account. Answer the following questions: (a) What event do the accounts describe? (b) What is the source of Account 1? Of Account 2?

2. **Compare the documents to identify their similarities and differences.** Determine how the documents support or contradict one another. Answer the following questions: (a) What are three points on which both accounts agree? (b) What are two points on which the accounts disagree? (c) What points are noted in one account but not in the other?

3. **Evaluate the validity of the accounts.** Study the backgrounds of the authors and the language they use to determine if they have a bias or an opinion toward the event. Answer the following questions: (a) Do you think the authors might be biased? Explain. (b) Do both accounts seem equally factual and objective? Which would you use as historical evidence? Explain.

Account 1: Lieutenant Deflue, a foreign officer in the Bastille's garrison

. . . . Then M. de Launcey [governor of the Bastille] . . . wrote a note in which he warned the [attackers] that . . . if they would not [surrender], he would blow up the fort, the garrison and the entire neighborhood. . . . I went to the gate and passed the note through . . . but it had no effect. . . . I was waiting for the governor to keep his word and blow up the fortress, but greatly to my surprise I saw four [of our soldiers] go up to the bridges, open and lower them. Then the crowd rushed in. They immediately disarmed us and seized hold of us, each of us being given a guard. They went into all the apartments and rifled everything, taking possession of weapons, throwing papers and records out of the windows. . . .

Account 2: Paris newspaper article, July 17, 1789

. . . . The enemy produced a document which they thrust through the opening of the drawbridge. . . . It contained the words: *We will blow up the garrison and the entire neighborhood, unless you accept our capitulation.* Meanwhile the firing went on. The cannon balls hurled against the drawbridge finally broke one of its chains. The enemy saw that the bridge was about to fall, and realizing that there was no hope, lowered the small drawbridge. . . . Three men . . . then leapt on to the bridge and fearlessly demanded that the last gate should be opened. The enemy obeyed. Our men sought to force an entrance [but] the garrison defended itself. We slaughtered all who opposed our progress . . . The people rushed on . . . [and] forced their way in everywhere. . . .

REVIEW

Section Summaries

Section 1 The Old Regime Abused the French
Under the Old Regime in France there were two privileged classes. The first estate, or religious leaders and clergy, and the second estate, made up of the nobles. Together these two estates made up less than three percent of the population. Yet they owned much of the land and paid few or no taxes. Most taxes came from the third estate—serfs, peasants, servants, workers, and middle-class people. However, the third estate had little say in France's lawmaking body, the Estates-General. Thus, after years of economic problems, France was ripe for a revolution.

Section 2 The Revolutionaries Ended Absolute Rule In need of more money, Louis XVI convened the Estates-General. The Third Estate hoped to win new rights at this meeting. When the king refused, they declared themselves the National Assembly. Meanwhile, revolution gripped France as angry mobs ran through Paris and Versailles. As the assembly argued about how to solve the nation's problems, a group called the Jacobins took over. They set up a republic and encouraged the mobs to terrorize the nation. The Jacobins had the king executed.

Section 3 Terror and Warfare Swept France A Reign of Terror swept through France. The National Convention wrote a democratic constitution, but the Committee of Public Safety now ruled with no concern for democracy. Many citizens were excuted. Finally, less extreme leaders took power, and the Reign of Terror ended. The National Convention appointed a Directory of five leaders who tried unsuccessfully to solve France's problems.

Section 4 Napoleon Rose to Power in France As unrest grew in France, an ambitious general named Napoleon Bonaparte overthrew the Directory. Napoleon made himself France's ruler, or first consul. The new ruler strengthened the government and the economy. He also made many democratic reforms. By 1804, Napoleon was France's emperor. Trying to spread his empire, Napoleon went to war against his European neighbors. Only the combined armies of European nations were finally able to drive Napoleon from power. After Napoleon's defeat, Europe's foreign ministers met to restore order to Europe and to bring back the monarchy in France.

Key Facts

1. Use each vocabulary word in a sentence.
   a. bourgeoisie
   b. cahier
   c. *pain d'égalité*
   d. coup d'état
   e. dictator
   f. plebescite
2. Identify and briefly explain the importance of the following names, places, or events.
   a. Louis XVI
   b. Marie Antoinette
   c. the Bastille
   d. Georges Jacques Danton
   e. the Reign of Terror
   f. Napoleon Bonaparte
   g. the Orders in Council
   h. the Battle of Liepzig
   i. the Congress of Vienna

Main Ideas

1. Explain how the Third Estate became France's National Assembly.
2. List the steps by which the Jacobins led France into the Reign of Terror.
3. Describe the way in which France was ruled by the Committee of Public Safety.
4. List the important steps that were involved in Napoleon's rapid rise to power and his eventual exile.

Developing Skill in Reading History

Select the best ending for each sentence.
1. One reason why revolution on the European continent came to France first was that

a. France was the home of great thinkers who had written about freedom and human rights.

b. France's peasants were the most severely oppressed in Europe.

c. France was ruled by Napoleon.

2. When Louis XVI convened the Estates-General, the Third Estate at first

a. called for immediate revolution.

b. hoped to work out a deal for more rights.

c. called for the king's execution.

Using Social Studies Skills

Drawing a Political Cartoon A political cartoon is a valuable tool for influencing people's opinions. Imagine that you are a political cartoonist during the years covered in this chapter. Draw a political cartoon to illustrate *one* of the following points. Try to think of a good caption for your cartoon.

1. Louis XVI lived in splendor while most of the French people suffered.

2. The National Assembly met on a tennis court and vowed to write a constitution for France.

Critical Thinking

1. **Identifying Central Issues** What do the Third Estate, the angry mobs in Paris, and the Jacobins all have in common?

2. **Comparing Two Points of View** When Louis XVI called the Estates-General, the Third Estate drew up a list of grievances and presented their demands to the king. Imagine that you are a member of the Third Estate. Write a short note to the king, explaining why he should consider these demands. Then, imagine that you are the king. Write a short note explaining why you are rejecting the demands.

3. **Distinguishing Between False and Accurate Images** Study the Jacobin poster on this page. The words on the poster mean "Unity and Indivisibility of the Republic; Liberty, Equality,

and Fraternity [Brotherhood]—or Death." What kind of image do you think this poster presents of the Jacobins? Is it an accurate image? Explain.

Focus on Writing

Preparing Answers to Essay Exam Questions

Answer the numbered questions below about one of the following essay exam questions.

· Discuss the role of women in the French Revolution.

· Compare and contrast Louis XVI and Napoleon.

· Describe the Reign of Terror.

· Tell how Napoleon rose from army officer to emperor.

1. What pieces of information should you include in your answer?

2. What would be a good topic sentence for your answer?

3. What would be a logical order in which to present the ideas from question 2?

The Congress of Vienna and Its Aftermath

(1814–1848)

1 The Congress of Vienna Restructured Europe

2 Europe and Latin America Sought Freedom

3 Revolutions Continued in Europe

▲ **Illustrating History** *Above is a chalk drawing of Prince Metternich of Austria, whose ideas shaped the Congress of Vienna.*

S omeone once wrote of one of history's most famous generals, Napoleon Bonaparte, "I have never seen a man with so much . . . restless perseverance." Even imprisoned on the island of Elba, near Corsica in the Mediterranean Sea, Napoleon cast a long shadow across the face of Europe.

He remained very much in the thoughts of Europe's monarchs as they gathered in the Austrian capital in the early winter of 1814. These rulers had come to the Congress of Vienna to rebuild Europe after years of Napoleonic rule. Under the guidance of Austria's minister of foreign affairs, Prince Metternich, they had cleverly planned to protect the great powers.

At 6:00 A.M. on March 7, a servant brought word to Metternich's bedside that Napoleon had escaped from Elba. This was a nightmare come true. The news threw the diplomats attending the Congress into panic and gloom. According to one observer, "a thousand candles seemed in a single instant to have been extinguished." But, the darkness did not last long.

Napoleon's crushing defeat at Waterloo came just 11 days after diplomats at the Congress of Vienna had signed their final act establishing a new balance of power on the continent. A long period of European peace—which was to last without a full-scale war until 1870—had begun.

1815	1825	1835	1845

■ **1814** Congress of Vienna opens

1825 ■ Latin America wins independence from colonial powers

1829 ■ Greece wins independence from Ottoman Turks

■ **1830** Revolution breaks out in France

■ **1836** Texas declares its independence from Mexico

1848 ■ Revolution returns in France and spreads to other nations

▲ **Illustrating History**   *European leaders gathered in 1814 at the Congress of Vienna. Talleyrand of France is seated second from the right.*

1 The Congress of Vienna Restructured Europe

As you read, look for answers to these questions:

◆ What was the Congress of Vienna?
◆ Who were the leading figures at the congress, and what did each hope to achieve?
◆ How successful were the efforts of the congress?

Key Terms: liberalism (defined on p. 475), conservatism (p. 476)

Had you received an invitation to the Congress of Vienna in 1814, you would have been honored. Such an invitation meant that you were at, or very near the top of,

the social and political ladder of early nineteenth-century Europe. At the Congress of Vienna you would have met kings and queens, dukes and duchesses, lords and ladies, princes and counts, and many foreign diplomats. But, while the Congress of Vienna was certainly an important social and diplomatic event, its main goals were to bring an end to the Napoleonic Wars and secure peace in Europe. In order to understand the results of the congress, you need to understand the political forces of the early nineteenth century in Europe, which were at work at the Congress.

New Political Philosophies Emerged

Two opposing political philosophies greatly influenced events in the 1800s. These were liberalism and conservatism. **Liberalism,** in general, is a philosophy that supports guarantees for individual freedom, political change, and social reform. Liberals at the

475

time of the Congress of Vienna supported the ideas of the Enlightenment and the French Revolution. Throughout the 1800s, liberals supported freedom of speech, freedom of the press, and freedom of religion.

Conservatism, on the other hand, is a philosophy that supports the traditional political and social order and resists changes that threaten that way of life. In the early 1800s, conservatives condemned the French Revolution because it upset the traditional way of governing by the monarchy and the nobility.

Nationalism also became a more powerful force in Europe during the nineteenth century. As discussed in Chapter 13, nationalism had begun as the desire to form a nation. In the 1800s, however, the concept of nationalism grew to mean not only love of country but also pride in a common cultural heritage regardless of political boundaries. Liberals, at that time, usually supported nationalism because it united people in a common cause, such as freeing their countries from foreign control. Conservatives usually feared nationalism because it threatened to upset the traditional political order.

It is important to understand that there were more conservatives than liberals at the Congress of Vienna in 1814. This fact would strongly influence the results of the work of the congress.

The "Big Four" Sought to Redraw the Map of Europe

Fox hunts during the day, dances at night, and parties in between took up the time of many delegates to the almost year-long Congress of Vienna. Delegates who found time for serious work were determined to redraw the map of Europe. Among these delegates was Prince Klemens von Metternich (MET ur nik), the Austrian minister of foreign affairs who hosted the congress. Russia had an influential voice at the congress in the person of Czar Alexander I. Great Britain had sent both the Duke of Wellington, the war hero who had defeated Napoleon, and Lord Castlereagh (KASS uhl RAY), Britain's foreign minister, to the congress. Representing France was Charles de Talleyrand (TAL ee RAND), the country's leading policymaker and diplomat.

Prince Metternich was a German-born aristocrat whose family moved to Vienna after the wars of the French Revolution had left them penniless. Metternich's handsome looks and charming personality won the affection of the wealthy Countess Eleonore von Kaunitz, whom he married in 1793. Through his marriage Metternich gained not only wealth and land but also access to the highest social and political circles in Austria. His political career advanced and as foreign minister and later chancellor of Austria, Metternich served his adopted country for 40 years. Metternich was the driving force behind the Congress of Vienna as well as one of its most glittering stars. Politically, he was a conservative who opposed liberalism and nationalism.

Alexander I of Russia was both vain and idealistic. His vanity was shown in his love of handsome uniforms, which he had specially tailored. His idealism took the form of religious enthusiasm. By 1814, he was spending hours each day in prayer. Alexander brought to the Congress of Vienna a vision of international relations based on the Christian values of charity and justice.

Viscount Castlereagh, the British foreign minister, shared Prince Metternich's conservative outlook in that he was opposed to changes that would shake the order and balance of European politics. At the Congress of Vienna, Castlereagh wanted to prevent anything like the French Revolution or the Napoleonic Wars from happening in the future. The way to achieve this, he believed, was to restore the balance of power in Europe. Once the balance of power was restored, no nation could become either too strong or too weak.

Charles de Talleyrand had the most difficult job of all at the congress. It was in his country that the French Revolution had taken place, and it was his country that had been at war with Europe for nearly 25 years. France was the villain at the Congress of Vienna, and Talleyrand had to see his nation was not punished too severely.

A Revolution in Style

High fashion influences many people, but what are the factors shaping high fashion? In nineteenth-century Europe, the answer had to do with politics.

The eighteenth century had been known for its colorful style. The picture of the man and woman to the right is taken from an eighteenth-century French fashion magazine. Women favored fancy dresses and frills. Men wore wigs, waistcoats, and buckles on their shoes. The French Revolution, with its emphasis on equality, swept these styles aside. In nineteenth-century Europe, many men wore simple coats and dark-colored pants. Women also chose to wear darker shades.

1. What were eighteenth-century styles like?
2. How did dress styles in the nineteenth century differ from those in the eighteenth century?

The Congress of Vienna Sought to Turn Back the Political Clock

The "Big Four"—Castlereagh, Metternich, Alexander I, and Talleyrand—wanted to turn back the political clock of European history. They wanted to return power to the rulers whose families had been removed from the throne by Napoleon.

The return to monarchies. The Bourbons, represented by Louis XVIII, had already been restored to the French throne. The French king was no longer an absolute monarch, however. In 1814, Louis XVIII issued a constitution that established a two-house legislature, or lawmaking body. Although France had the most liberal monarchy in all of Europe, liberals still criticized the constitution for limiting the right to vote to wealthy citizens.

In Prussia, Austria, Spain, and some of the smaller states of the Italian peninsula, absolute rulers were returned to the thrones that Napoleon had taken from them. The "Big Four" at the Congress of Vienna hoped to return the rest of the European governments and political boundaries to what they had been before 1789. In their attempt to reverse the course of history, however, the four delegates were not always successful. For example, royal families in many of the smaller German states never regained the thrones they had lost.

The struggle for new boundaries. As it tried to reestablish former monarchs in Europe, the Congress of Vienna also sought to repay each country for the lands it had lost to Napoleon. However, greed, rather than justice, usually guided the thinking of the delegates. Each delegate tried to acquire as much land as possible for his own country, while Talleyrand of France tried to surrender as little as possible. Due to his great

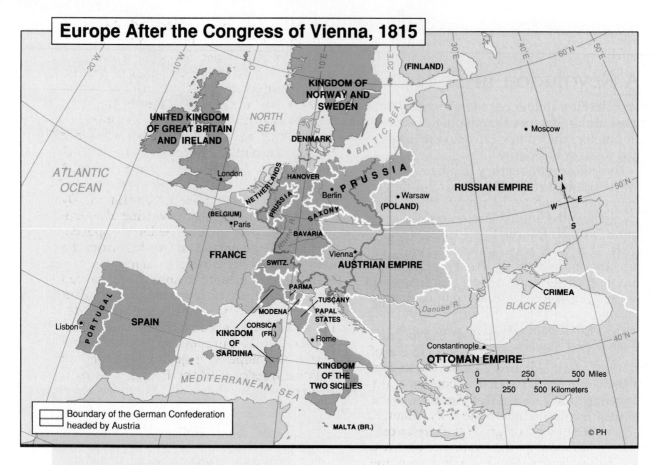

Europe After the Congress of Vienna, 1815

Boundary of the German Confederation headed by Austria

Focus on Geography

Regions One goal of the Congress of Vienna was to restore the map of Europe to what it had been before Napoleon established his empire. However, some countries won additional lands for themselves. What territories did Russia gain?

diplomatic skills, Talleyrand was largely successful. In the end, France was reduced only to the size it had been in 1790. This was mild punishment indeed for the nation that had plunged much of the continent of Europe into war.

In remaking the map of Europe, as the map above shows, the leaders at the congress paid little attention to the wishes of the people who would have to live within the new boundaries. Russia was awarded Finland and part of Poland. Norway was taken from Denmark and handed to Sweden. Austria lost Belgium to the Netherlands but

gained some territory in northern Italy. Great Britain got the islands of Malta and Ceylon and the land at the southern point of Africa, called the Cape of Good Hope. Finally, a German confederation of 39 states was formed, ending the Holy Roman Empire.

The Metternich system. The conservative political policies of the Austrian foreign minister Prince Metternich are referred to as the Metternich system. This system, including the return to absolute rule, tried to enforce the decisions of the Congress of Vienna. Specifically, it intended to prevent

France from starting other wars. The Congress of Vienna thought it had reached its goal by making Europe similar to what it had been before 1789. However, the system was only partially successful in returning the map of Europe to what it had been before the Napoleonic Wars.

The Quadruple Alliance and the Holy Alliance.

To protect the settlement at Vienna, the leaders of Great Britain, Prussia, Russia, and Austria signed an agreement known as the Quadruple Alliance. The four nations agreed to act as the "fire department" of Europe. That is, they agreed to use their armies to put out the flames of revolution wherever they burned. The signers also agreed to meet from time to time to see what needed to be done to hold back the tide of change.

The idealistic Alexander I of Russia tried to do even more to control the course of history in Europe. He devised a plan known as the Holy Alliance and encouraged the delegates to the Congress of Vienna to agree to its terms. According to the Holy Alliance, nations would let God guide their relations, and they would help one another to ensure a peaceful world for all. Although most of the countries at the Congress of Vienna joined the Holy Alliance, they did not really believe that it could be carried out.

The Congress of Vienna Achieved Stability at the Price of Liberty

In some ways, the Congress of Vienna did its work well. The chief delegates had come to redraw the map of Europe, which they did. They had come to build a peaceful and stable Europe, which they also did. In the years following the congress, several revolutions broke out that threatened to upset the Metternich system. There was no world war, however, for 100 years, until 1914 when World War I began.

Other accomplishments may also be credited to the Congress of Vienna. Switzerland was enlarged and its neutrality was guaranteed when the larger nations agreed not to send troops across its borders. Travel on the Rhine River was opened to all countries.

The delegates also condemned the slave trade in which African blacks were captured and sold in North and South America.

The diplomats at the Congress of Vienna were cautious people who had seen the violence of the French Revolution and hoped to avoid revolutions in the future. To do so, they tried to kill the spirit of the French Revolution, and they nearly succeeded. But, that spirit died hard. "Liberty, equality, and fraternity" were the goals of the leaders of the French Revolution. By liberty, they had meant the writing of constitutions that guaranteed freedom of speech, freedom of the press, and freedom from the heavy hands of absolute monarchs. By equality, they meant the abolition of special class privileges. By fraternity, they meant the unity of the people in wanting a better life and a free government. With the fading of these ideals, European nations lost their immediate hope of enjoying the kind of political freedom that the United States had secured.

SECTION 1 REVIEW

Knowing Key Terms, People, and Places
1. Define: **a.** liberalism **b.** conservatism
2. Identify: **a.** Congress of Vienna **b.** Metternich **c.** Alexander I **d.** Castlereagh

Focus on Geography
3. In what specific ways did the Congress of Vienna redraw the political boundaries of Europe?

Reviewing Main Ideas
4. What were the main goals of the Congress of Vienna?
5. How did the congress "turn back the clock" of European history?

Critical Thinking

Perceiving Cause and Effect
6. How might the Metternich system have contributed to the revolutions that occurred throughout Europe after the Congress of Vienna?

2 Europe and Latin America Sought Freedom

As you read, look for answers to these questions:

◆ What revolutions in Europe followed the Congress of Vienna?
◆ What factors led to discontent and revolution in Spain and Portugal's Latin American colonies?
◆ Who were the central figures in Latin America's fight for freedom?
◆ What were some of the results of Latin America's wars of independence?

Key Terms: encomienda (defined on p. 481), asiento (p. 481), creole (p. 481), mestizo (p. 481)

Observing the political climate of his day, Metternich said, "When France sneezes, Europe catches cold." In other words, what happened in France influenced most of the other countries in Europe. The leaders of the Congress of Vienna viewed the French Revolution as a dangerous illness. In spite of their efforts to combat the disease, the fever of revolution continued to spread to other parts of Europe and to the European colonies in Latin America.

Revolutions Swept Europe and Russia

Soon after the Congress of Vienna ended, revolutions broke out in Spain, Portugal, Naples (later Italy), and Russia. In the first three countries, the forces of revolution had made temporary gains when the Quadruple Alliance (with France replacing Great Britain, which opposed intervention and left the alliance) sent troops to squash the revolutions. The well-organized military troops of the Quadruple Alliance easily defeated the disorganized, rioting mobs of revolutionaries in Spain, Portugal, and Naples.

In Russia, when Czar Alexander I died suddenly in 1825, a brief period of confusion followed. As the debate over which of his sons would take over the throne raged, a group of army officers, known as the Northern Society, staged a revolt in St. Petersburg on December 26, 1825. Nicholas I, quickly put in place as the new czar, ruthlessly put down the uprising, which was known as the Decembrist Revolt. The Decembrist Revolt failed to win greater freedom for the Russian people. It also convinced Nicholas I to rule the country sternly.

When other European countries aided the Greeks in their fight for independence from the Turks, the Metternich system was shaken. Beginning in 1821, this fierce, eight-year struggle between Muslim Turkey and Christian Greece aroused the interest of the world. The Greeks finally did defeat the Turks with help from Great Britain, France, and Russia.

Spain and Portugal Ruled Their Empires with a Heavy Hand

The kings of Spain and Portugal were absolute rulers in the New World, just as they were in Europe. In Spain, the Royal and Supreme Council of the Indies ruled the Spanish colonies in the Americas. It was this group, made up of nobles who were responsible to the king alone, that was in charge of colonial life.

Establishing full control was no easy matter. It was especially difficult to control the area of the Caribbean known in history as the Spanish Main, which was short for Spanish Mainland. This area included the northern coast of South America and the islands there. Until the eighteenth century, the Spanish Main was subject to frequent raids by Dutch, French, and British pirates.

Spanish colonial rule. After finally suppressing foreign piracy, the council expanded its control over Latin America. It established strong viceroyalties, shown on the map on page 483, each of which was headed by a viceroy who was the king's representative. The viceroy had absolute power that he exercised from an elaborately maintained court. He administered colonial activities, chose colonial officials, and controlled colonial justice.

The Portuguese colonial empire. The Portuguese system of ruling its empire was similar to that of Spain. Portugal regulated the trade and economy of Brazil closely. Although the viceroyalty of Brazil had a structure similar to that of the Spanish viceroyalties, the administration of Brazil from Portugal was more flexible. Under the Portuguese system, many local matters were left in the hands of the colonists.

The Spanish and Portuguese systems of governing their colonial empires presented many problems. For one thing, the New World was so far from home that good laws written in Spain and Portugal were not always carried out in the Americas. Able and willing viceroys and officials were hard to find and to keep in the colonies. Neither the Indians nor the colonial-born Spanish or Portuguese people were given a chance to rule themselves. This closely supervised control by the parent countries became a source of friction between the colonies and their parent countries.

Forced Labor Existed in Latin America

At first, the Spanish made slaves of the Indians in their colonies. The fact that slavery did not become worse was due, in part, to the good work of Bartolomé de Las Casas. Las Casas, a Spanish missionary who converted many Indians to Christianity, taught about the evils of slavery. In response, the Spanish government made the Indians serfs who were as bound to the land as were the serfs of medieval Europe. This system of labor was called the **encomienda** (ehn koh mee EHN dah). The Indian serfs worked for a Spanish noble, whom they depended on for a minimum of food, clothing, and shelter. In time, this system of forced labor was made illegal.

The **asiento** (ah see EN toh) was a special trading privilege granted by the king. The asiento gave a person or a group of persons the right to sell a certain number of slaves in the New World. Taking blacks from Africa against their will, bringing them to the New World, and selling them became a profitable business for Europeans.

▲ **Illustrating History** *The Spanish and Portuguese conquerors enslaved Indians in their New World colonies. The painting above shows Indians doing forced labor for a wealthy landowner.*

Europeans Became Wealthy at the Expense of Latin American Peasants

The search for gold and silver at first lured many adventurers to the New World. These people wanted the colonies' riches and were not interested in agriculture. In time, however, farming increased, and sugar cane, grapes, oranges, rice, and native products such as corn and potatoes were grown. As agriculture increased, a plantation system developed.

The social structure of the Latin American colonies clearly reflected the Europeans' unfair treatment of the native inhabitants. The officials who came from Spain to rule were at the top of the social ladder. Below them were **creoles** (KREE ohlz), persons of Spanish descent who were born in the colonies. Below the Spanish and creoles were the **mestizos** (mee STEE zohs), or children of marriages between the Spanish and Indians. Although they soon became the largest group in terms of population, the mestizos had the lowest social standing.

Latin America Fought for Independence

In spite of the poor treatment of many of the people there, the fight for independence in Latin America took a long time to begin. Spain and Portugal ruled with an iron hand for about 300 years. The people of Latin America, who had never tasted freedom, were not certain it was worth the struggle. In any war for independence, the support and enthusiasm of the people are essential to achieving success.

In Latin America, it was difficult for revolutionary leaders to get full support from their own people. Many racial groups did not get along with one another. Some people felt they would be merely exchanging masters, and so they saw no point in fighting. Among the whites, those who came from Spain opposed independence. The creoles, however, called loudly for it. Because the lower classes in Latin America often were uneducated, few people could read or understand the reasoning behind the revolutionary movement.

The desire for independence, however, was eventually planted in a soil of aggravating conditions. The colonists of Latin America had at least as many complaints as the colonists of North America. They could point to a long history of unfair treatment and unfair taxes. While the wealthy did not have to pay many of these taxes, the poor paid heavily. The Spanish and Portuguese colonists also wanted more freedom to trade and laws that would attract more settlers. Moved by the new ideas of the English, American, and French revolutions, the Latin American colonies finally revolted.

Mexican and Central American independence movements. In Mexico, the Catholic priests Miguel Hidalgo (ee DAHL goh) and José Morelos (maw RAY laws) led the fight for independence. In the course of the struggle, both men were captured and killed, but not before Morelos declared Mexican independence in 1813.

After Morelos' death, the fight to gain Mexican independence was continued by Agustin de Iturbidé (day EE tur BEE day), a Spanish soldier who deserted when he saw a chance for fame and fortune by joining the revolutionary forces. Although his fight against Spain succeeded and he became emperor of Mexico in February 1821, Iturbidé's rule was unpopular. In 1823, he was forced to resign. A convention then drew up a new constitution that established Mexico as a republic with a president and a congress made up of two houses. Following Mexico's example, the countries of Central America also declared their independence from Spain, and in 1823, they formed the United Provinces of Central America.

The fight for independence continued in South America under the leadership of Francisco Miranda (mee RAHN duh). A Venezuelan creole who had taken part in the French Revolutoin, Miranda fought to free what is now known as Venezuela. Many of his ideas came from some of the most important people of the day, including Alexander Hamilton, James Madison, and Thomas Jefferson in the United States as well as Catherine the Great of Russia. Both of Miranda's attempts at revolution failed, however, and a defeated Miranda died in 1816 in a Spanish prison.

Simón Bolívar and other independence fighters. Miranda's ideas were adopted by Simón Bolívar (baw LEE vahr), who had helped Miranda in his second try at revolution in Venezuela. Over time, Bolívar became the hero of Latin America's fight for independence. First, he succeeded in achieving freedom from the Viceroyalty of New Granada. Then, in 1819, he defeated the Spanish forces in Colombia and liberated that country. The newly liberated country named Bolívar president of the Republic of Great Colombia, which included the countries that are now known as Colombia, Venezuela, Ecuador, and Panama.

In 1822, Antonio José de Sucre (day SOO kray), a follower of Bolívar, led the battle that freed Ecuador. Another revolutionary leader, José de San Martin (day sahn mahr TEEN), freed parts of Peru and Argentina. Bernardo O'Higgins is the hero of Chile's struggle for independence. As a result of his efforts for independence, the Spanish were

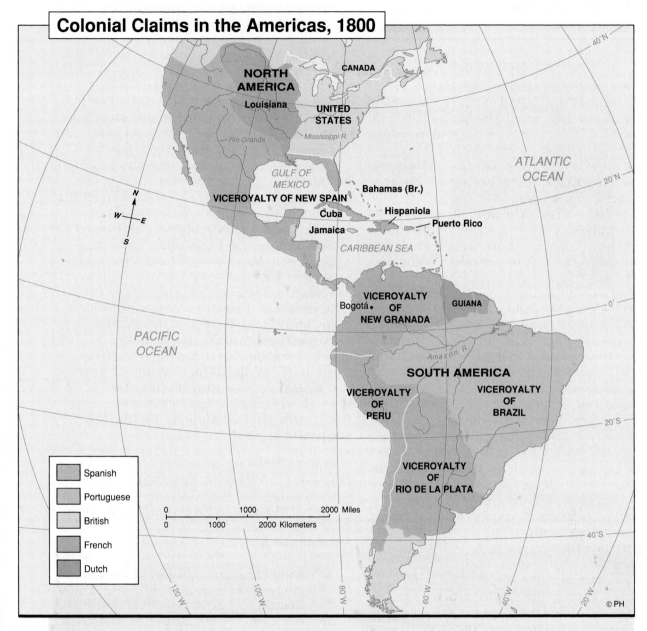

Colonial Claims in the Americas, 1800

NORTH AMERICA

CANADA

Louisiana

UNITED STATES

Rio Grande

Mississippi R.

ATLANTIC OCEAN

40°N

20°N

GULF OF MEXICO

VICEROYALTY OF NEW SPAIN

Bahamas (Br.)

Cuba

Hispaniola

Jamaica

Puerto Rico

CARIBBEAN SEA

N
W — E
S

VICEROYALTY OF NEW GRANADA

Bogotá

GUIANA

0°

PACIFIC OCEAN

Amazon R.

SOUTH AMERICA

VICEROYALTY OF PERU

VICEROYALTY OF BRAZIL

20°S

VICEROYALTY OF RIO DE LA PLATA

Spanish
Portuguese
British
French
Dutch

| 0 | | 1000 | | 2000 Miles |
| 0 | 1000 | | 2000 Kilometers | |

120°W 100°W 80°W 60°W 40°W 20°W

40°S

© PH

Focus on Geography

1. **Place** What powers controlled South America in 1800?
2. **Movement** In 1783, Spain controlled the land west of the Mississippi. By 1800, what territory in North America had it lost?

defeated in 1818. Later disputes over the reforms he wished to make caused O'Higgins to be eventually ousted from his position of power in Chile.

Brazil's peaceful revolution. The independence movement in Brazil took a different and somewhat more peaceful course. The coming of Napoleon's army to Portugal

Simón Bolívar

Hosts and hostesses who cared about their dinner plates needed to think twice before inviting Simón Bolívar, shown above, over for a meal. After eating, Bolívar liked to climb onto the table and deliver a speech. As he walked from one end of the table to the other, he often sent dishes and glassware crashing to the floor. The subject of Bolívar's after-dinner speeches? His dream of freeing South America from Spain's colonial rule.

Bolívar had been born of wealthy parents in Caracas, Venezuela, in 1783. His parents died before he was 10 years old. At 16, Bolívar traveled to Europe, which was then caught up in the whirlwind of the French Revolution. He was inspired by books on freedom and independence written by such thinkers as Locke and Voltaire.

After returning home, Bolívar became a leader of revolution in his own hemisphere. Again and again, he led his army against the Spanish royalists in Caracas. Bolívar's brilliant military tactics ended with victory over the Spanish and his triumphal entry into Caracas in 1819.

Bolívar went on to free Upper Peru (now Bolivia) from Spanish control. As a result, he became known throughout South America as "The Liberator." Bolívar retired to an estate in Colombia, where he died of tuberculosis in 1830.

1. What was the guiding passion in Simón Bolívar's life?
2. How did the thinking of Enlightenment writers affect Simón Bolívar?
3. How was he regarded by most South Americans?

---

forced King John VI to flee to his colony of Brazil. While in Brazil, King John declared the colony to be his kingdom and did much to improve conditions. The Brazilians, however, were displeased with him. He favored members of the royal family and put Portuguese nobles, not Brazilians, into high offices. After Napoleon was defeated in Europe, the people of Brazil demanded that John VI return to Portugal. A revolutionary army finally forced him to leave Brazil on April 26, 1821.

Although he returned to Portugal, John VI left his son Dom Pedro I in charge of Brazil. The Brazilian parliament then demanded complete separation from Portugal, and some members of the government were eager to drive Pedro from Brazil. Determined to stay, Pedro declared, "I remain." That day, January 9, 1822, has been known to Brazilians ever since as "I Remain Day." In September, Pedro proclaimed Brazil independent of Portugal. In October 1822, Dom Pedro became the constitutional emperor of an independent nation.

New Nations Emerged from the Latin American Wars of Independence

The wars for independence in Latin America were over by 1825. Some of the countries that emerged were larger than they are today. For example, Mexico once held the lands of the southwestern United States, and the Republic of Colombia included Venezuela, Ecuador, and Colombia. These nations were divided into a number of smaller ones. In time, the Latin American countries of the present day were formed.

The Monroe Doctrine and Latin America.
Like Great Britain, which enjoyed a rich trade with the new nations of Latin America, the United States thought that it would be to its advantage to support the new nations of Latin America. In a speech in 1823, President James Monroe warned Europe to stay out of the Western Hemisphere. This warning to the European nations came to be called the Monroe Doctrine. No European nation immediately challenged its authority. European nations that might have been tempted to interfere in Latin America knew that British naval forces stood ready to challenge them if they tried.

Mexico under Santa Anna.
In Mexico, the imperial government of Iturbidé fell in 1823. The kind of government that would replace it was in question. After a period of violence and disorder, the revolutionary general Antonio López de Santa Anna (SAN tuh AN uh) gained control of the government as president. Santa Anna controlled Mexico until 1855.

In 1836, when Texas declared itself independent from Mexico, Santa Anna lost a sizable territory that later became one of the American states. In 1847, the United States Army defeated Santa Anna in the Mexican War. As a result of that war, Mexico was forced to give up most of what is now California, Utah, Nevada, Arizona, Colorado, New Mexico, and Wyoming.

Dictatorship in Argentina.
Argentina's history has been marked by military dictatorships and revolutions. For several years, from 1829 to 1852, Argentina was ruled by a dictator, Juan de Rosas (day RAW sus). Although discontented groups drove him out and wrote a constitution similar to that of the United States, it did not work well in Argentina. The government remained largely in the hands of big landowners and cattle ranchers who had control of the politics of the nation.

Pedro II and Brazil.
Brazil, which had established a constitutional monarchy, faced new problems when Pedro I tried to get more power than the constitution gave him. He was forced from the throne in 1831, and the government was left in the hands of his 5-year-old son who became emperor in 1840. Under Pedro II's long and happy reign, Brazil made great progress. Even so, there was a large, influential group that wanted no emperor at all. In 1889, Pedro II was driven from the throne. Two years later, in 1891, Brazil became a republic.

Stability in Chile.
O'Higgins, the liberator of Chile, ruled from 1818 to 1823 as a dictator. He made so many enemies that a revolt forced him to resign. One weak government after another tried to maintain law and order, but each was unable to do so. Finally, in 1833, a group of business leaders, religious leaders, and landowners, led by Diego Portales (port TAL es), wrote a new constitution. Thus, earlier than most countries of Latin America, Chile developed a stable, if not always democratic, system of government.

SECTION 2 REVIEW

Knowing Key Terms, People, and Places
1. Define: **a.** encomienda **b.** asiento **c.** creole **d.** mestizo
2. Identify: **a.** Decembrist Revolt **b.** Agustin de Iturbidé **c.** Simón Bolívar **d.** "I Remain Day" **e.** Monroe Doctrine **f.** Santa Anna

Reviewing Main Ideas
3. What did the Greek war of independence reveal about the Metternich system?
4. Describe the social structure in the Latin American colonies.

Critical Thinking
Identifying Alternatives
5. What alternatives did Nicholas I have in dealing with the Decembrist Revolt? How might Russian history have been different if he had chosen a different course of action?

3 Revolutions Continued in Europe

As you read, look for answers to these questions:

◆ What kind of government did the citizens of Belgium establish after they drove out the Dutch?
◆ How did the French people continue to press for a freer government?
◆ What happened to the Metternich system and the old regimes by the middle of the nineteenth century?

Key Terms: abdicate (defined on p. 487)

Although the revolutions of the 1820s had not been entirely successful in Europe, the dream of a freer and more democratic society remained. Revolts continued across the European continent, and many met with considerable success. Once again, one of the central characters in the drama of revolution was France. Belgium was also the scene of a revolution aimed at gaining independence and freedom.

Democracy Triumphed in Belgium

The fever of revolution began to spread again in Europe. The Congress of Vienna had joined the Netherlands and Belgium. In August and September of 1830, the Belgians rebelled and drove out the Dutch. A limited monarchy was established in Belgium, and Britain and France agreed to support the neutrality and independence of the country. Austria, Prussia, and Russia eventually added their support. The success of the Belgian revolution widened the growing crack in the Metternich system, which did not last long after this time.

Revolution Began in France

When Louis XVIII of France died, Charles X took his place. He tried to rule as an absolute monarch. Although he had the sup-port of the nobility, Charles's attempt to return to the old ways of absolutism was a mistake. For example, Charles tried to increase the power of the clergy and control the freedom of the press. The French, however, remembered the ideals of their revolution and remembered how to deal with a king whose policies they opposed.

In 1830, when Charles X tried to dissolve the Chamber of Deputies, the French people revolted. They put up barricades, behind which they could fight the army and the police if these forces came to the defense of the monarch. Their preparations were unnecessary. Neither the army nor the police would have fired on the people with whom they sympathized. Without bloodshed, the rioters captured the city hall of Paris and prepared to take over the government of France.

Limited monarchy in France. Charles X began to worry. He recalled the beheading of Louis XVI and did not want to face the guillotine himself. Therefore, he fled to England for safety. Because those who fought in the revolution of 1830 could not agree on whether to have a republic or a monarchy, the Chamber of Deputies decided on a limited monarch. But who would be king? The chamber chose Louis Philippe, Duke of Orleans and a cousin of Charles. The duke had been living in Paris as a member of the upper middle class. He seemed to be a man who would not seek absolute power.

The return of revolutions. Revolutionary fever was again high, because people were disappointed with Louis Philippe. Although he had begun by showing concern for the people, as the years went by, he became more interested in the affairs of the nobility. He became more and more a servant of the rich and a master of the poor. When depression and hunger came to France, as they did in 1848, people blamed Louis Philippe.

The French, particularly the Parisians, were used to revolution. Up went the barricades in 1848. This time the fighting was more serious than the rioting of 1830. Many people were killed and injured. Louis Philippe, like Charles X, had no wish to lose his head. He hastily packed his things and **abdicated,** or abandoned the throne, heading for the safety of England.

With the monarch gone, the people were undecided about the kind of government to have. For three days in June of 1848, France was torn by class war as the middle class and the working class fought one another for control of the government. This period became known as the Terrible June Days. The middle class ultimately won, and its leaders fiercely subdued their opposition.

The return of the Bonapartes. A new national assembly was formed. Under the new constitution, all men had the right to vote. France was to have a one-house lawmaking body and an elected president. But, who was going to be the new president? When the votes were counted, the president-elect was Louis Napoleon Bonaparte, a nephew of the great Napoleon. The people who had voted for Louis Napoleon hoped that he would perform the same magic for France that his uncle had. Not long before, the body of Napoleon had been brought home from St. Helena and placed in an expensive tomb. It had been built to remind the French people of the glory that Napoleon had brought to their nation. The election offered further proof that the name of Napoleon still inspired respect and admiration among the French.

For three years, Louis Napoleon governed as the first and only president of the Second French Republic. Although he arrested his enemies, dissolved the legislature, and asked the people to approve his acts, his name continued to have magic in the minds of many. The French agreed to Louis Napoleon's request to change the Second French Republic to the Second French Empire with Louis Napoleon as emperor. As emperor, he governed the Second French Empire until its downfall in 1871.

Revolutions Swept Europe in 1848

The fires of revolution and the move toward democracy swept other European countries in addition to France. In Germany, the revolutions that swept Europe in 1848 failed. As

In their own words

Revolution in Berlin

In 1848, public demonstrations shook Europe. In Berlin, a large crowd gathered to demand democratic reforms from King Frederick Wilhelm IV. When soldiers fired two shots into the crowd, the peaceful scene changed. The following excerpt is by one member of the crowd.

❝At one moment everybody was rejoicing and shouting 'Hurrah!' and a few minutes later all was changed to yells of rage and cries for revenge. In one hour the appearance of the city was entirely different. . . . As if by magic, barricades arose. At every street corner people gathered, young and old, of high and low degree, to build barricades. Stalls, carriages, omnibuses [large carriages], cabs, heavy transport wagons, postal and brewery carts, and scaffolding poles were collected by thousands of hands in all parts of the city. Even women and children took part; the unity which prevailed in building was marvelous. All were equal: two men would be seen dragging a beam, one a workman with a torn shirt and the other a well-dressed gentleman. The chief materials of the barricades nearly everywhere were torn-up pavements, stone flags, beams, and the many boards and planks lying across the gutters, or carriages, carts, etc., which were upset. Beds, sacks of flour, and furniture were brought out of the houses; everyone gave willingly what he had; gates, doors, fences, palings [fence boards], hooks, bars, etc.❞

1. Why did people begin to erect barricades?
2. Did two gunshots cause the Berlin uprising in 1848? Explain.

they had been in Paris, barricades were erected in Berlin, and many people were killed in the rioting that followed. Even so, the rioters fought their way into the king's palace and forced a frightened King Frederick to call a meeting. The purpose of this meeting was to write a democratic constitution for Germany that would serve as the basis for a new system of government.

The meeting to draft a constitution was held in Frankfurt, but King Frederick changed his mind before the Frankfurt Assembly could complete its work. Months of talk, differences of opinion, and unwillingness to compromise gave the king time to think over his situation. When a fair constitution that united Germany and made the king a limited monarch was finally written, King Frederick turned it down. He believed that he was king by divine right and he would not accept a crown offered by the people. Since there was no united revolutionary group to come to its rescue, the constitution that had been born at Frankfurt died in infancy. The failure of the Frankfurt Assembly to establish the constitutional monarchy was a setback for the unification and democratization (making democratic) of Germany. It would be many years before Germany achieved those goals and become a unified nation.

In Vienna, Austria, the barricades also were up, and blood was spilled in the rioting. Metternich was forced to resign and had to leave the country. Afraid of what the angry mobs might do if they got their hands on him, Metternich changed his name and hid in a laundry wagon to cross the Austrian border. Having escaped from Austria, he finally found a safe haven in England.

The Hungarians fought for independence from the Austrian Empire under Louis Kossuth (KOS ooth), but the effort was only partly successful. A constitution granting freedom of speech, freedom of press, and freedom of religion was written as a result of the revolution. The Hungarians also were guaranteed a lawmaking body of their own. In 1849, however, Russian troops finally came to the aid of the Austrian Empire, and the Austrians successfully put down the Hungarian revolt.

The Old Regimes Finally Ended Despite the Failures of the 1848 Revolutions

The year 1848 was a year of revolution on the continent of Europe. Everywhere, the forces of democracy fought slow, uphill battles. Nevertheless, the revolutions showed that democratic ideas would not easily die. The revolutions of 1848 also taught that careful planning was necessary for a revolution to succeed. Too often, the people who fought for freedom also fought among themselves about their goals.

Europe, nevertheless, was free from the old regimes of autocratic rule. Metternich was overthrown, and his system of absolutism fell with him. Political action, the speaker's platform, and the ballot box became the means to achieve greater democratic reforms in Europe.

The desire for freedom was the main force behind democratic reforms in Europe. In the next chapter, you will learn about the role that nationalism played in European affairs. You will see that the force of nationalism sometimes worked for and sometimes against the development of democracy.

SECTION 3 REVIEW

Knowing Key Terms, People, and Places
1. Define: **a.** abdicate
2. Identify: **a.** Charles X **b.** Louis Philippe **c.** Terrible June Days **d.** King Frederick

Reviewing Main Ideas
3. How did Louis Philippe become king of France?
4. Explain why the Frankfurt Assembly was unsuccessful.
5. Did the 1848 revolutions immediately bring democracy to Europe?

Critical Thinking
Demonstrating Reasoned Judgment
6. Do you think that the nineteenth-century revolutionary spirit played a major role or only a minor role in causing the downfall of the old regimes? Support your answer with a logical argument and facts.

Using Maps to Make Comparisons

Maps can be a useful tool for making comparisons. You can use a single map or two maps with common elements to make comparisons.

Use the following steps to make comparisons on the map below.

1. **Determine the general information provided by the map.** Read the title, label, and key to see what information they provide. Answer these questions: (a) What political event is illustrated? (b) What is the time period (c) What does the heavy line represent?

2. **Look for comparisons that are shown on the map.** The map below can be used to compare the boundaries of Europe before and after the Congress of Vienna. Answer the following questions: (a) How does the map indicate countries that were absorbed by other nations? (b) What formerly independent kingdom east of the German Confederation was absorbed by the Russian Empire? (c) What nation immediately northeast of France did the Congress of Vienna unite with Holland?

3. **Use the comparisons shown on the map to draw conclusions.** The Congress of Vienna reorganized Europe after the defeat of Napoleon. You can draw conclusions about the new boundaries based on the map's comparisons. Answer these questions. (a) Which countries gained the most? (b) Would you say the changes resulting from the Congress of Vienna were extensive? Give supporting facts to explain your answer.

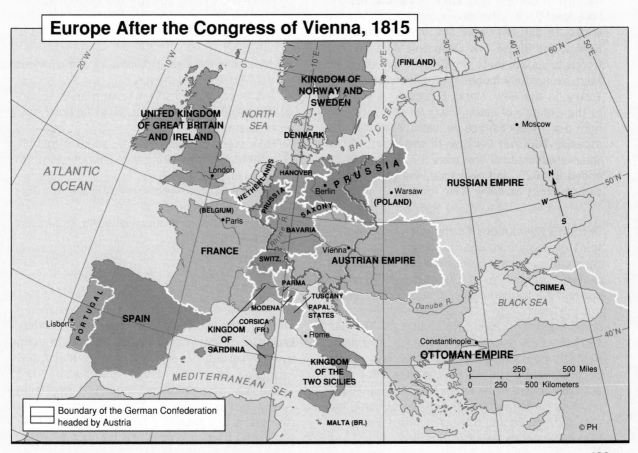

Europe After the Congress of Vienna, 1815

REVIEW

Section Summaries

Section 1 The Congress of Vienna Restructured Europe The Congress of Vienna was both a social event and a meeting to end the Napoleonic Wars and secure peace in Europe. The "Big Four" —Castlereagh, Metternich, Alexander I, and Talleyrand—wanted to return European borders to what they had been before 1789 and to restore monarchs to power. Delegates tried to get or keep as much land as possible for their own countries. The work accomplished by the Congress of Vienna, known as the Metternich system, was meant to preserve traditional governments. The Quadruple Alliance was formed to protect Europe from future revolutions.

Section 2 Europe and Latin America Sought Freedom Soon after the Congress of Vienna ended, revolutions broke out in Spain, Portugal, Naples, and Russia. The Quadruple Alliance sent troops to squash these revolutions. Greece, however, successfully fought for independence from Turkey. In the New World, Europeans prospered at the expense of Latin American peasants. The fight for independence in Latin America was especially difficult because of the strict rule of Spain and Portugal. The wars for independence ended in 1825, and over time, the Latin American countries of today were formed.

Section 3 Revolutions Continued in Europe The spirit of revolution and the desire for a more democratic society continued in nineteenth-century Europe. In 1830, Belgium revolted against the Netherlands and successfully drove out the Dutch. Also in 1830, the French staged a revolt that led to Charles X's abdication. The year 1848 marked revolutions in France, Germany, Austria, and Hungary. Louis Napoleon Bonaparte became president of the Second French Republic, but later he was made emperor. Little immediate progress came from the revolutions of 1848, but they did free Europe from absolutism and prove that democratic ideals had not died.

Key Facts

1. Use each vocabulary word in a sentence.
   - **a.** liberalism
   - **b.** conservatism
   - **c.** encomienda
   - **d.** asiento
   - **e.** creole
   - **f.** mestizo
   - **g.** abdicate
2. Identify and briefly explain the importance of the following names, places, or events.
   - **a.** "Big Four"
   - **b.** Metternich system
   - **c.** Quadruple Alliance
   - **d.** Decembrist revolt
   - **e.** Agustin de Iturbidé
   - **f.** Simón Bolívar
   - **g.** Monroe Doctrine
   - **h.** Louis Napoleon

Main Ideas

1. Who were the leading figures at the Congress of Vienna? What country did each individual represent?
2. What was the Metternich system intended to achieve?
3. What did the Greek revolution prove about the Metternich system?
4. List three problems that arose from the Spanish and Portuguese systems of colonial government.
5. How were the native Latin American people treated by their European conquerers from Spain and Portugal?
6. How did Louis Napoleon Bonaparte become emperor of France?
7. What did the revolutions of 1848 accomplish throughout Europe?

Developing Skill in Reading History

An important part of learning history is understanding how various events relate to each other. Each set of statements below includes a main event, an event that explains why the main event happened, and an event that tells how the main event was accomplished. Label the events in each set as either **what** (the main event), **why** (the event that caused the main event), or **how** (the event that accomplished the main event).

1. **a.** Protestant Holland and Catholic Belgium were joined by the Congress of Vienna.
   b. The Belgians established an independent limited monarchy in 1830.
   c. The Belgians successfully drove out the Dutch.
2. **a.** By 1825, the former colonies in Latin America had established their independence from European powers.
   b. The colonists of Latin America fought bloody wars with their European rulers.
   c. Latin Americans were treated unfairly by Spain and Portugal.

Using Social Studies Skills

1. **Using Visual Evidence** Study the symbolic painting on this page, which shows Father Hidalgo crowning Mexico. Why does Mexico have chains around her ankles? What country do you think the man under Hidalgo's feet symbolizes? What event is symbolized in the breaking of the chains?
2. **Understanding Historical Problems** Imagine that you are a Latin American revolutionary leader in the 1800s and that you need to explain to the peasants of your country why

independence from Spain or Portugal would be a good thing. How could you make an uneducated person understand this?

Critical Thinking

1. **Making Comparisons** In what ways was the Holy Alliance different from the Quadruple Alliance?
2. **Drawing Conclusions** It was difficult for Latin American peasants to understand why fighting for independence was important. What can you conclude about the importance of education in a democracy?
3. **Recognizing Ideologies** How was the conservative philosophy of the "Big Four" reflected in the Metternich system?

Focus on Writing

Documenting Source Materials

When you write a research paper, you must give information about the sources from which you gathered facts, quotations, and so on. **Informal citations** list the source in parentheses within the text of the paper. **Footnotes** give the source at the bottom of the page, with a number that matches the source to the fact or quotation.

Sample Informal Citation:
(Frank J. Sorauf, *Party Politics in America,* 221)

Sample Footnote:
[1]Frank J. Sorauf, *Party Politics in America* (Boston: Little, Brown and Company, 1976), p. 221.

Practice: Using the card catalog at a library, find a book about the Congress of Vienna or one of its leaders. Then, write both an informal citation and a footnote for the book using the author's name, the title of the book, the place where the book was published, the publishing company, the date of publication, and a specific page number from the book.

Geography in History

Climate as Enemy: Napoleon in Russia

On June 24, 1812, Napoleon led the greatest army ever assembled, 450,000 soldiers, over the Niemen River into Russia. Six months later, this army retreated over the same river into Poland, a weak and beaten column of 5,000 men. This tremendous loss had occurred despite Napoleon's victories in almost every battle he had fought (see page 467). What, then, had defeated the greatest general in history? "It's the winter that has been our undoing," Napoleon said as he made his way back to Paris. "We are victims of the climate."

The region of Russia that Napoleon invaded has a continental climate. Continental climates usually are found in higher latitudes in the interiors of continents, far from large bodies of water that make the temperature milder. Temperatures in these climates tend to be extreme—hot in the summer and very cold in the winter.

Summer Heat and Midnight Sun

From the beginning of the invasion, Russia's continental climate took its toll on the French forces. In early July, there were biting frosts by night as well as piercing rains. New recruits died by the thousands. Then, hot weather set in. Carrying 75-pound packs, the soldiers began to fall, sharing the same fate as their overloaded horses. Through August and September, the army pressed on. Before reaching Smolensk, 200,000 men had died.

Although the Russians burned most of Moscow soon after Napoleon reached it, there was enough food in Moscow to last six months. However, the troops raided the city and quickly devoured its luxuries.

Napoleon himself gave no orders to prepare for the coming cold. One of his aides, General Caulaincourt, insisted that: "Every man must have a sheepskin, stout fur-lined gloves, a cap with ear-tabs, warm boot-socks, heavy boots to keep his feet from getting frost-bitten. You lack all this. Not a single calkin [spike] has been forged to rough-shoe the horses."

"We have not had autumn yet," replied Napoleon. "We shall have plenty of fine days before winter sets in." He dismissed Caulaincourt's warnings as "fairy tales."

All the same, Napoleon soon knew he was in trouble. The Russians knew it, too. When he made a peace offer after staying in Moscow for a month, the czar calmly replied, "Now is the moment my campaign opens." While Napoleon had wasted his time, the Russian army had moved to the south of Moscow, blocking his way to the rich Ukraine region. In retreat, Napoleon would have to go back through land the Russians had burned and abandoned.

The Killing Winter

On October 19, Napoleon left Moscow. Heavy rain and chilly nights were the first signs of winter. The horses began to die from tiredness and the cold. "The zigzag road was a sheet of ice on which even men on foot could hardly stand upright," Caulaincourt remembered later. Frostbite stopped soldiers who were otherwise healthy. The cold, wrote a survivor, "strewed the roads of Russia with our fingers and toes."

The first snow fell on November 3. Soon, the French were struggling through snow six feet deep. By night, the troops packed themselves so tightly around bonfires that many were suffocated by the smoke. Sentries froze to death standing at their posts.

After a perilous crossing of the Berezina River, Napoleon left his army to fend for itself. The temperature fell to a paralyzing -22°F. Before Napoleon had gone eight miles, half of his guard of 100 horsemen had fallen by the side of the road. The winter Napoleon had once called a fairy tale would claim nearly 25,000 more soldiers before the army reached the Niemen River.

Focus on Geography

1. **Place** Look at the map below. Describe what the climate is like in western Russia.

2. **Location** Look at the map below. How far is Moscow from the Niemen River?

3. **Movement** What was it about Napoleon's route that ensured that his men would suffer hunger?

Critical Thinking

Predicting Consequences

4. How might Napoleon have reacted if the autumn of 1812 had been cooler, and what results might this have had?

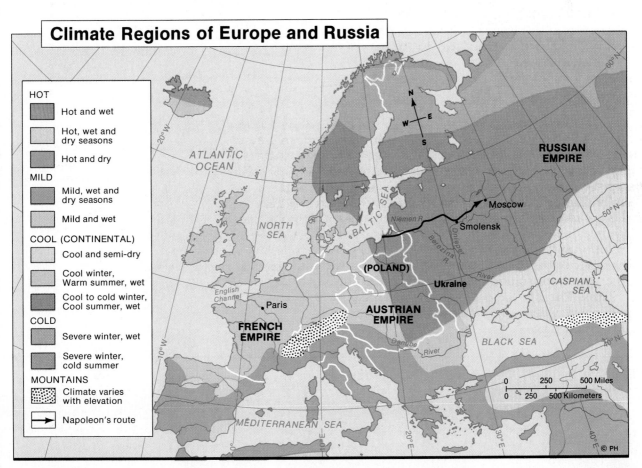

Climate Regions of Europe and Russia

HOT
- Hot and wet
- Hot, wet and dry seasons
- Hot and dry

MILD
- Mild, wet and dry seasons
- Mild and wet

COOL (CONTINENTAL)
- Cool and semi-dry
- Cool winter, Warm summer, wet
- Cool to cold winter, Cool summer, wet

COLD
- Severe winter, wet
- Severe winter, cold summer

MOUNTAINS
- Climate varies with elevation
- Napoleon's route

The Dominance of Europe

(1700–1914)

Chapters

In the years between 1700 and 1914, Europe dominated much of the world scene. European powers entered a period of empire-building in Africa and Asia; England began a revolution in agriculture and industry; and some countries such as Germany and Italy became unified nations. As the Industrial Revolution spread from England to the rest of Great Britain and to the United States, Britain led the way in the search for solutions to economic and social problems. The map and the time line, linked by color, show where and when the dominance of Europe took place.

1 INDUSTRIAL REVOLUTION

Early steam locomotives like this one helped to carry England into the Industrial Revolution.

NORTH AMERICA

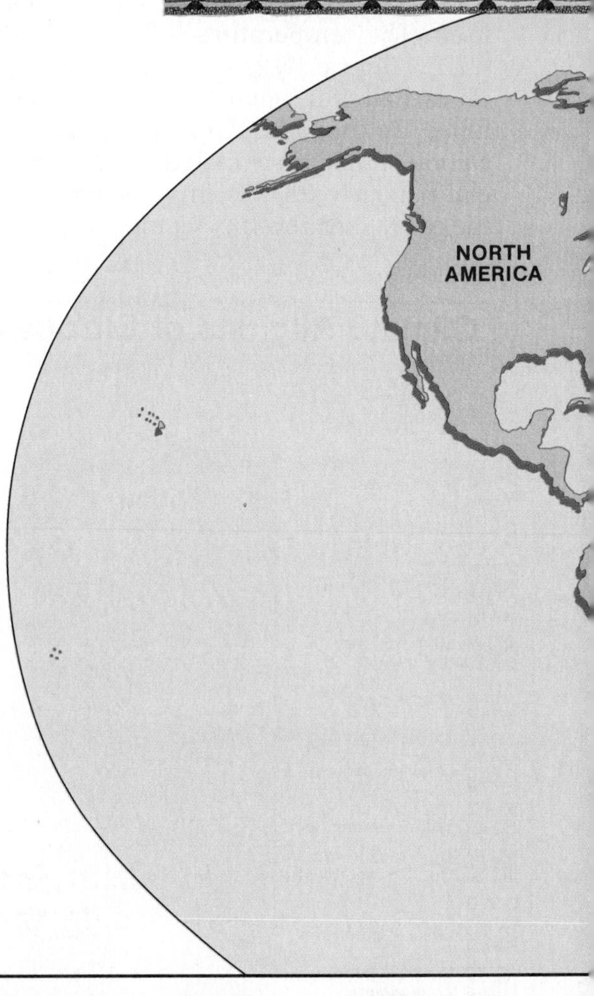

1700   1750   1800

■ 1733 John Kay speeds weaving process with invention of flying shuttle

■ 1800s Advances in mi increase output of coa

1824 Great Brita legalizes labor unio

■ 1757 Great Britain becomes a major imperial power in India

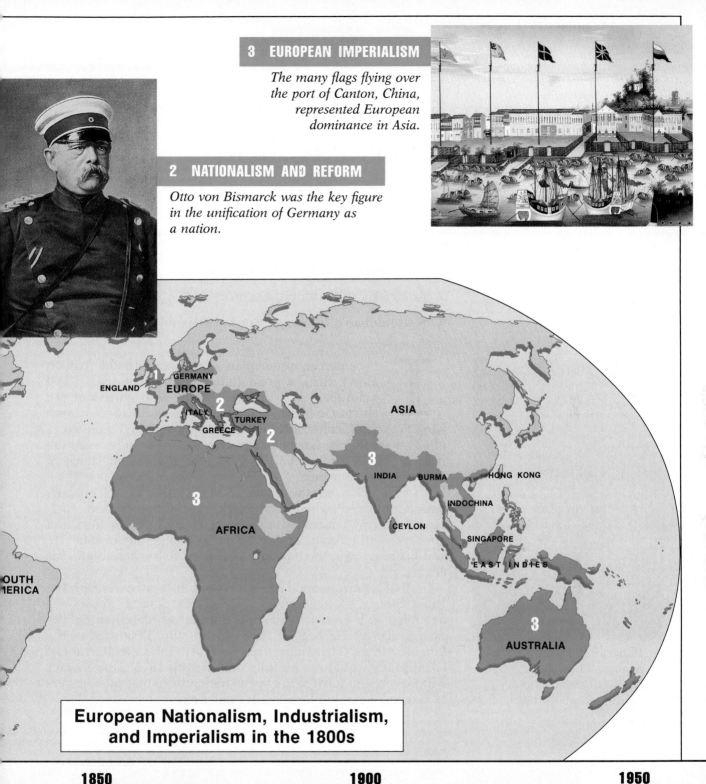

The many flags flying over the port of Canton, China, represented European dominance in Asia.

2 NATIONALISM AND REFORM

Otto von Bismarck was the key figure in the unification of Germany as a nation.

ENGLAND GERMANY EUROPE
ITALY TURKEY
GREECE
ASIA
INDIA BURMA HONG KONG
INDOCHINA
CEYLON
SINGAPORE
EAST INDIES
AFRICA
SOUTH AMERICA
AUSTRALIA

European Nationalism, Industrialism, and Imperialism in the 1800s

1850	1900	1950

■ 1856 Henry Bessemer improves method of steel production **1 INDUSTRIAL REVOLUTION**

1871 Italy is a united nation ■ and Bismarck unites Germany   ■ 1884 All men get right to vote in Britain **2 NATIONALISM AND REFORM**

■ 1853 Perry arrives in Tokyo Bay, ending Japan's isolation   ■ 1878 Belgium takes control of the Congo in Africa **3 EUROPEAN IMPERIALISM**

495

Nationalism: New European Nations Are Born

(1848–1914)

1 **Italy and Germany Became Nations**

2 **Austrian and Ottoman Empires Broke Apart**

3 **Nationalism's Influence Spread Beyond Europe**

▲ **Illustrating History** *The painting above shows Garibaldi prepared to do battle for a united Italy.*

It seemed an insane plan. Giuseppe Garibaldi (GAR uh BAWL dee), a great Italian leader, collected 1,000 volunteers and provided them with guns and red shirts. On May 5, 1860, this force set sail to overthrow King Francis II, ruler of Naples and Sicily and the commander of 124,000 soldiers. Garibaldi's goal was to unite Italy under the rule of Victor Emmanuel, the king of the Italian states of Piedmont and Sardinia.

After landing on the coast of Sicily, Garibaldi's soldiers marched inland. Their first battle was a tough one. King Francis's army controlled a steep, terraced hill, but Garibaldi attacked with ferocity, crying "Here we make Italy or die!" He and his army won the day, and new recruits rushed to join his efforts.

Garibaldi next planned to march on Rome and overthrow the Papal States. Victor Emmanuel had his doubts. Rome was defended by a French army, and Emmanuel feared an embarrassing defeat. He begged Garibaldi to stop. Disgusted at the king's caution, Garibaldi retired to a farm on a Mediterranean island. Italy would not be fully united until 1870. This chapter will explore the spirit of European nationalism that such leaders as Garibaldi carried forward in their lives.

1850	1870	1890	1910

■ **1856** Treaty of Paris ends the Crimean War

■ **1861** The American Civil War begins

■ **1867** Britain grants Canada self-rule

■ **1870** Rome becomes capital of a united Italy

■ **1871** William I becomes emperor of new German Empire

■ **1901** Australia becomes independent under the British crown

▲ **Illustrating History**   *This painting conveys the fierce intensity of the battle as Garibaldi's soldiers claimed Sicily in May of 1860.*

1 Italy and Germany Became Nations

As you read, look for answers to these questions:

◆ How did Italy become a nation?
◆ How did Germany become a nation?
◆ What role did Bismarck play in the unification of Germany?

Key Terms: confederation (defined on p. 500), suffrage (p. 501)

The desire of a group of people to form a nation is called nationalism. As you read in Chapter 13, people who want to form a nation generally share a common language and literature, have similar customs and beliefs, and share economic and political interests. These elements act as the cement that holds a nation together. Sometimes, nationalism makes one nation out of many, as it did during the nineteenth century in Italy and Germany. In other cases, nationalism results in the division of one nation into many smaller nations, as it did in Austria-Hungary and Turkey.

Italy Faced Barriers to Unification

When Prince Metternich of Austria called Italy a "geographic expression," he meant that Italy could not properly be termed a nation because of its many individual states. In 1815, Italy was made up of nine states, the largest of which was the kingdom of Sardinia. The northern provinces of Venetia and Lombardy belonged to Austria, and the pope ruled the Papal States in central Italy. The rest of Italy was ruled by a number of foreign princes who were under the control of the Austrian Empire.

There were many obstacles to Italian unification. Among them was the geography of Italy. The Apennine Mountains separate

497

Mazzini's Nationalism

Today in the United States, young people are taught to love their nation. Yet, the nationalism that is common today sounded radical when declared by Joseph Mazzini and others in the 1800s. In the middle of the last century, many Europeans felt loyalty to their city or region, but not to their nation. They were no more loyal to their nations than people today are loyal to their continents. The following excerpt is from a speech Mazzini gave at Milan, Italy in 1848.

"Love your country. Your country is the land where your parents sleep, where is spoken that language in which the chosen of your heart blushing whispered the first word of love; it is the home that God has given you, that by striving to perfect yourselves therein, you may prepare to ascend [rise] to Him. It is your name, your glory, your sign among the people. Give to it your thoughts, your counsels, your blood. Raise it up, great and beautiful as it was foretold by our great men. And see that you leave it uncontaminated by any trace of falsehood or of servitude; unprofaned by dismemberment [division]. Let it be one, as the thought of God. You are twenty-five millions of men, endowed with active, splendid faculties; possessing a tradition of glory the envy of the nations of Europe; an immense future is before you; you lift your eyes to the loveliest heaven, and around you smiles the loveliest land in Europe. . . ."

1. What two values does Mazzini link when he says, "your country is the land where your parents sleep"?
2. Explain how this appeal could apply to any nationality.

Italy into east and west, and the Po River divides northern Italy from the southern peninsula. Nationalism was slow in coming to Italy for other reasons as well. First, the pope wanted control of the Papal States. Second, the other states could not agree on who should lead the nation. Third, many European countries did not want a strong Italy that could interfere with their plans for expansion.

Diplomacy and War Unified Italy

Despite obstacles, Italy's history encouraged nationalism. Italy had been the birthplace of the Renaissance, and Italians were proud of their people's contributions. Italian unification, or joining together, centered around three men: Giuseppe Mazzini (maht TSEE nee), Count Cavour (kah VOOR), and Giuseppe Garibaldi.

Mazzini, the prophet of Italian unification, was a young man who was violently in favor of a united Italy. Mazzini had been a member of the Carbonari (CAHR buh NAHR ee), a secret group that used violence to obtain what it wanted. The Carbonari tried to unite Italy by force but failed. After its failure, Mazzini tried other ways to build a united Italy, which were also unsuccessful. Still, Mazzini's work was not a loss. He prepared the way for Cavour, who took more practical steps.

Cavour, sometimes called the architect of Italian unification, was the prime minister of the kingdom of Sardinia. Italy's greatest obstacle to unification was Austria, which controlled many of the Italian states. Cavour knew that Sardinia needed outside help to defeat Austria. He joined Britain and France against Russia in the Crimean War. Then, he made an agreement with France that France would help Sardinia if there were a war with Austria. The Austro-Sardinia War followed the agreement. The forces of France and Sardinia defeated Austria, and Lombardy (an Italian city-state) was united with the kingdom of Sardinia in the agreement with Austria at the war's end. The addition of Lombardy encouraged a number of smaller Italian city states to revolt against Austria and to join Sardinia.

In 1860, the fiery leader, Giuseppe Garibaldi, invaded the Kingdom of the Two Sicilies (southern Italy and the island of Sicily) and won Sicily for Italy. Garibaldi urged the Sicilian people to join the kingdom of Sardinia under the leadership of Victor Emmanuel. At this point, with the exception of Venetia and Rome, unification was almost complete.

Italy United

In 1860, in widespread elections, Italians strongly supported a united nation. In 1861, representatives of the city-states formed a parliament and established the kingdom of Italy under Victor Emmanuel II. Finally, in 1870, the people of Rome voted to join the new nation of Italy, and Rome became the capital of a fully united Italy. (See the map on page 499.)

The papacy remained opposed to Italian unification, however, and it was not until 1929 that the papacy and the Italian government reached an agreement. In the agreement, the pope became ruler of a tiny area known as Vatican City. The Catholic church was paid back to compensate for the loss of the Papal States.

Germany Faced Obstacles to Unification

Germany's prospects for becoming a unified nation were not bright. Most of Germany's European neighbors were against the idea of a united Germany, and many of the rulers of the smaller German states felt that their power would decline if Germany were united. The Thirty Years' War in the early 1600s had set Protestants and Catholics against one another. Economic differences between the industrial states of the west and the agricultural states of the east also stood in the way of German unification.

Other Factors Encouraged Unification

Despite these obstacles, there were signs that pointed in the direction of a united Germany. Many German teachers, writers, and philosophers taught that Germany was destined to become a great nation. History

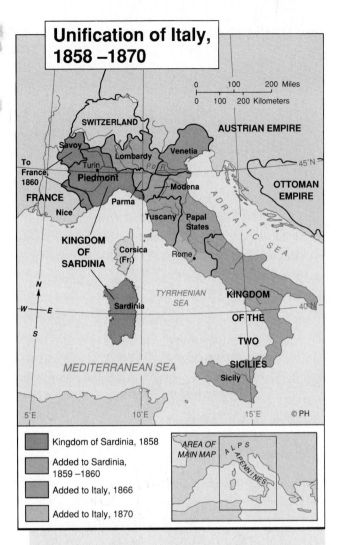

Unification of Italy, 1858–1870

- Kingdom of Sardinia, 1858
- Added to Sardinia, 1859–1860
- Added to Italy, 1866
- Added to Italy, 1870

Focus on Geography

Regions By 1860, most Italian states had joined with the kingdom of Sardinia. In 1861, Sardinia declared itself to be the Kingdom of Italy. What region was added to the kingdom of Italy in 1866?

already had moved Germany toward unification. Napoleon had combined the German states into a loose union called the Confederation of the Rhine. The Napoleonic code had helped to destroy what was left of feudalism by encouraging uniform laws. As you read in Chapter 20, the Congress of Vienna had also encouraged unity by forming a new German confederation.

499

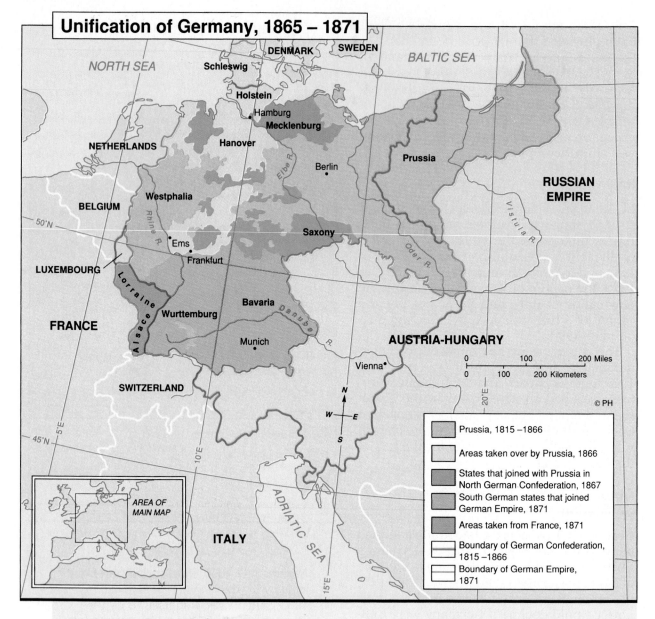

Unification of Germany, 1865 – 1871

NORTH SEA

DENMARK

SWEDEN

BALTIC SEA

Schleswig

Holstein

Hamburg

Mecklenburg

NETHERLANDS

Hanover

Elbe R.

Berlin

Prussia

RUSSIAN EMPIRE

BELGIUM

Westphalia

Rhine R.

50°N

Ems

Frankfurt

Saxony

Oder R.

Vistula R.

LUXEMBOURG

Lorraine

FRANCE

Alsace

Wurttemburg

Bavaria

Danube R.

Munich

AUSTRIA-HUNGARY

Vienna

SWITZERLAND

45°N

5°E

10°E

N
W — E
S

20°E

© PH

| | 0 | 100 | 200 Miles |
| | 0 | 100 | 200 Kilometers |

AREA OF MAIN MAP

15°E

ADRIATIC SEA

ITALY

Legend:

- Prussia, 1815 –1866
- Areas taken over by Prussia, 1866
- States that joined with Prussia in North German Confederation, 1867
- South German states that joined German Empire, 1871
- Areas taken from France, 1871
- Boundary of German Confederation, 1815 –1866
- Boundary of German Empire, 1871

Focus on Geography

1. **Location** Which was larger, the German Confederation or the new German Empire?
2. **Movement** What state led the drive for German unification?

A **confederation** is a loose association of states in which each state is practically independent and the central government has limited powers. In the German Confed- eration, because each state had its own government, it was difficult for one state to do business with another. To increase trade, the German states set up a tariff union,

500

called the Zollverein (TSAWL fur YN), in the middle of the nineteenth century. The Zollverein states agreed not to place taxes on goods coming from other member states. This trade agreement showed the financial benefits of a united Germany.

Bismarck United Germany

Prussia led the move toward German unification, and Prussia was led by Otto von Bismarck (BIZ mark). Bismarck, a wealthy landowner who trusted neither the people nor a system of democracy, became the central figure in Germany's unification. As chief minister of Prussia under King William I, Bismarck soon made his theories of government clear. He said, "Not by speeches and resolutions of majorities are the great questions of time decided upon—but by blood and iron."

Bismarck proved his point, and the strength of Prussia, by winning a series of wars. The Danish War of 1864, the Austro-Prussian War of 1866, and the Franco-Prussian War, which lasted from 1870 to 1871, all helped to unify Germany. In the first war, Prussia joined with Austria and easily defeated Denmark. Then, Prussia and Austria went to war with each other, as Bismarck had planned. Prussia won this war, which is known as the Austro-Prussian War, in seven weeks and removed Austria as an obstacle to German unification. After Austria's defeat, the North German Confederation was created, with Prussia as its leading state.

Bismarck knew that a war with France would not only help unification but would be popular with the German people, which would encourage other states to join the North German Confederation. Bismarck waited for a chance to fight France. His opportunity arrived in the form of a telegram sent by William I of Prussia from the city of Ems. Bismarck read the telegram, changed its wording to create trouble, and had it printed in the newspapers. The *Ems Dispatch*, as this message is called, brought about a war between France and Prussia

known as the Franco-Prussian War. Prussia was ready for war; France was not. Prussia gained the French provinces of Alsace and Lorraine, thus completing the unification of Germany. The southern German states had joined the North German Confederation to fight their common enemy, France. In the palace of Versailles, in 1871, the German Empire was proclaimed with William I of Prussia as emperor. (See the map on page 500).

The government of Germany was a federal union of states with the king of Prussia as the nation's ruler. A two-house legislature made the laws, but power was not divided fairly between the houses. The upper house, appointed by the states, held most of the power. The lower house was chosen by voters. **Suffrage** is the right to vote. In Germany, the 400 members of the lower house of the legislature were chosen by *universal male suffrage*—the right of all men to vote. The lower house had, however, only a small voice in government.

SECTION 1 REVIEW

Knowing Key Terms, People, and Places
1. Define: **a.** confederation **b.** suffrage
2. Identify: **a.** Cavour **b.** Zollverein
   c. Bismarck **d.** Ems Dispatch

Focus on Geography
3. In what specific ways did the geography of Italy discourage unity?

Reviewing Main Ideas
4. What was Garibaldi's role in Italy's movement toward becoming a nation?
5. How did the nation of Italy finally achieve unification?
6. What hurdles discouraged the unification of Germany?

Critical Thinking
Identifying Central Issues
7. Why did neighboring countries of both Italy and Germany oppose unification?

2 Austrian and Ottoman Empires Broke Apart

As you read, look for answers to these questions:

◆ What did nationalism mean to the peoples of the Austrian Empire, especially the Hungarians?
◆ What role did nationalism play in the downfall of the Ottoman Empire?
◆ What were some of the results of the Crimean War?
◆ What happened to the Turkish Empire as a result of the Russo-Turkish War?

> **Key Terms:** nationality (defined on p. 502)

You have seen that the spirit of nationalism in Italy and in Germany served as a cement to bind people into nations. In Austria and in Turkey, nationalism acted as a hammer that broke these two empires apart. In this section, you will see how growing feelings of national pride led to the disintegration of the mighty Austrian and Ottoman empires.

Nationalism Divided the Austrian Empire

Bismarck did not want Austria as a part of a united Germany because Austria was a country made up of many nationalities. A **nationality** is a group of people who share common history, customs, beliefs, and language but do not necessarily have a country of their own. The Austrian Empire ruled over groups of Germans, Hungarians, Italians, Russians, Poles, Czechs, Croats, and Slovenes. Each group was proud of its heritage and humiliated by Austrian rule. Inspired by the spirit of nationalism that was sweeping over Europe, these people wanted to govern themselves.

Austria had been defeated twice, first by Sardinia and later by Prussia. These defeats encouraged the various nationalities in the weakened empire to ask for a greater voice in government and for independence. The Hungarians were the most numerous and influential people in the empire. They demanded, and were given, a large measure of independence. In 1867, Austria and Hungary agreed to establish the dual monarchy of Austria-Hungary. The agreement was called the *Ausgleich* (OUS glyk).

The term *Ausgleich* is a German word that means compromise. The agreement of 1867 was a compromise between the wishes of Austria and the aims of Hungary. According to the agreement, each country was to have its own language and its own government. Under the dual monarchy, Emperor Franz Joseph of Austria was to be king of Hungary as well. Foreign affairs, war, and money matters were to be governed by Austria. In domestic matters (those inside each country), however, the separate peoples of Austria and Hungary would govern themselves.

Austria and Hungary each had its own parliament to pass domestic laws. Each country treated its people as it wished. The Hungarians, who had fought for their own rights when ruled by others, were not willing to give these rights to the people they ruled. Hungarian children were favored in the schools. The Hungarian language was

▼ **Graph Skill** *According to the graph, what was Europe's population in 1850?*

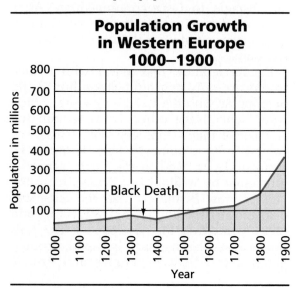

Population Growth in Western Europe 1000–1900

Population in millions (y-axis: 100, 200, 300, 400, 500, 600, 700, 800)

Black Death

Year (x-axis: 1000, 1100, 1200, 1300, 1400, 1500, 1600, 1700, 1800, 1900)

Waltz Fever

In the 1830s, the people of Vienna flocked to the dance halls where Johann Strauss the Elder (The Waltz King) conducted his powerful orchestra. Hundreds of people would dance, almost in a frenzy, until the early hours of the morning. Waltzing went on wherever the Viennese gathered.

"The garden is illuminated by a thousand lamps . . . people are seated at innumerable tables eating and drinking, chattering, laughing and listening. In their midst is the orchestra . . ." wrote one visitor to an outdoor park in Vienna. The first few notes of a well-known melody would always bring thunderous applause.

1. Who was known as The Waltz King?
2. Where in Vienna was the waltz performed?

---

used in the press, though there were other languages spoken in the country. Both Austria and Hungary were made up of different peoples with different customs. As you will read in Chapter 25, the discontent of the people ruled by Austria and Hungary was to be a cause of World War I.

Nationalism Broke Up the Ottoman Empire

Turkish rule in Europe extended as far as the city of Vienna, which the Turks had nearly captured in 1683. The Turks ruled many peoples, including Arabs, Egyptians, Albanians, Slavs, Romanians, Bulgarians, and Greeks. The rulers of Turkey were Muslim. By contrast, the countries of the Balkan Peninsula were, for the most part, Christian and belonged to the Greek Orthodox church. (See the map on page 504.)

The "sick man" of Europe. During the nineteenth century, Turkey had many domestic and foreign problems. As the Ottoman Empire declined, Nicholas I of Russia described it as the "sick man" of Europe. He was especially eager to hasten its death. In particular, Russia was eager to get control of Istanbul. Great Britain, however, wanted to keep the Ottoman Empire alive. The business people of Great Britain felt that their trade with the countries of the Mediterranean region would suffer if Istanbul were under Russian rule. The British also feared that Russian control of Istanbul would threaten British control of India. Most importantly, since the failure of Napoleon's invasion of Russia in 1812, the leaders of Great Britain and France were afraid of Russia. These countries saw Russia as unconquerable, and they feared both its size and its strength.

The first nationalities to take advantage of Turkey's weakness were the Greeks. They succeeded in gaining their independence from Turkey in 1829. As Turkey weakened still further, Russia and France tried to annex Turkish provinces.

The Crimean War. In 1853, Great Britain tried to stop the Russians from breaking up the Ottoman Empire. British troops were sent to the Crimea, a peninsula in the Black Sea. Between 1853 and 1856, the British, French, Sardinians, and Turks fought against Russia. Russia lost and in 1856, diplomats from Great Britain, France, and Russia met in Paris to work out a treaty. The lasting results of the Treaty of Paris, however, were not territorial. Rather they were in its attempt to limit the violence of war and to protect the rights of neutral parties.

Although these ideals have been violated often, the Treaty of Paris was the first attempt to limit the cruelty of war.

The Russo-Turkish War. Russia tried again to get control of Istanbul in the Russo-Turkish War of 1877 and 1878. Russia easily defeated Turkey, but at the Congress of Berlin, which ended the war, Bismarck claimed he wanted to be sure that Turkey was treated fairly. Actually, his plan was to prevent Russia from enjoying her victory and taking over the Balkan countries of Montenegro, Romania, and Serbia. These

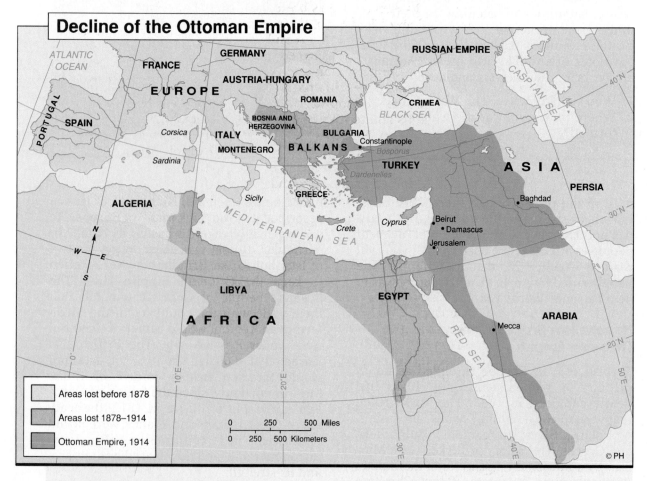

Decline of the Ottoman Empire

Areas lost before 1878
Areas lost 1878–1914
Ottoman Empire, 1914

Focus on Geography

1. **Place** Why was it so important to Russia to gain control of Constantinople?
2. **Regions** When did the Ottoman Empire lose Algeria and the Crimea?

Mustapha Kemal Atatürk

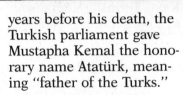

Mustapha Kemal, shown at right, was a proud Turkish nationalist. At the same time, he was ashamed of his government's weakness and the backwardness of his people. He believed that in order to survive as a nation, Turkey had to modernize. And, he succeeded in bringing about this dramatic change.

Mustapha was born in Greece in 1881. As a young man, he attended military school, where he excelled in his studies. A math teacher gave him the nickname *Kemal*, meaning "perfection." As an officer in the Ottoman army,

Mustapha Kemal joined the Young Turks, a nationalist movement that wanted Turkey to adopt a European political system and way of life.

Kemal overthrew the sultan and set up the Turkish republic in 1923. He then served as president of Turkey until his death in 1938. A forceful leader, he transformed the country at an astonishing pace. He urged women to stop wearing veils and to take part in politics. He replaced Turkey's Arabic alphabet with the Roman alphabet. He improved education and promoted industry. Five

years before his death, the Turkish parliament gave Mustapha Kemal the honorary name Atatürk, meaning "father of the Turks."

1. What did Mustapha Kemal believe his country needed?
2. How did he go about making changes?
3. Name several of his reforms.

countries gained complete independence. Bulgaria remained partly under the Ottoman Empire, and the island of Cyprus, which had belonged to Turkey, was given to Great Britain. Russia gained only a province on the Black Sea. The former territory of Turkey was protected by the major European powers. The breakup of the Ottoman Empire continued into the early 1900s and through World War I.

The Armenian massacres. Like the Jews in Russia who suffered through pogroms (government-ordered attacks in which Jews were killed and their towns and businesses destroyed), ethnic groups in the Ottoman Empire also faced persecution. In 1894, for example, the Ottoman Turks attempted to destroy the Armenians living in the empire. Lasting through World War I, great massacres killed about 1,800,000 Armenians.

SECTION 2 REVIEW

Knowing Key Terms, People, and Places
1. Define: **a.** nationality
2. Identify: **a.** dual monarchy **b.** Nicholas I **c.** Treaty of Paris **d.** Congress of Berlin

Focus on Geography
3. Why would the Dardanelles be so crucial?

Reviewing Main Ideas
4. How did nationalism affect Austria?
5. Why did France enter the Crimean War?
6. What did the Treaty of Paris do?

Critical Thinking
Drawing Conclusions
7. "Nations are more stable political entities than vast empires." Do you agree? What do you think makes it true or false?

3 Nationalism's Influence Spread Beyond Europe

As you read, look for answers to these questions:

◆ What issues were behind the United States Civil War?
◆ How did Canada become a British colony?
◆ How did Australia and New Zealand develop into self-governing nations?

Key Terms: federalism (defined on p. 506), secede (p. 506)

Europe was not the only continent that felt the effects of the nationalist spirit of the nineteenth century. In the United States, Canada, Australia, and New Zealand, people were thinking about and fighting over the issues of nationalism. It is not always obvious how groups of people should divide themselves into nations and then govern themselves. The American Civil War is an example of the great tragedy that can result when people disagree strongly enough to fight over their ideas of nationalism.

The Civil War Proved That the United States Were One Nation

The type of government that was established under the United States Constitution is known as federalism. **Federalism** is a system of government in which power is divided among national and state governments. In the United States, the central government was given the right to tax, to raise an army, and to enforce the country's laws. The states then agreed to subordinate, or lessen, their powers in relation to those of the federal government.

As time went on, people questioned the powers of the national government. An early test of the federal union occurred when the farmers of Pennsylvania rose in rebellion against the right of the government to tax them. Later, Virginia and Kentucky questioned the right of the government to pass certain laws. In 1814, during the War of 1812, the New England states threatened to **secede,** or formally withdraw, from the nation. In 1828, South Carolina questioned the right of the federal government to enforce taxes that the state did not approve.

Over time, the industrial northern states and the agricultural southern states disagreed on many economic and social issues. Slavery was the major issue. The northern states did not favor slavery, while the southern states felt they needed slavery to maintain their agricultural growth. Arguments also arose over whether new states to the west would be admitted to the union as slave or free states. There were many other disagreements, such as the southerners' objections to the high tariffs that northerners wanted placed on foreign goods coming into the United States. Northern industries produced many goods, and they wanted to protect themselves from foreign competition. Southerners resented paying higher prices caused by the tariffs. These are some of the major issues that divided the northern and southern states and brought the nation to the brink of war.

In 1861, the southern states denied the right of the government to limit slavery, and the Civil War between the northern states and the southern states began. On the surface, it was a war over the question of slavery. However, it was also a war over the question of what powers the central government could exercise over individual states. On November 19, 1863, following the Union (northern) army's victory at Gettysburg, President Abraham Lincoln delivered his famous Gettysburg Address. The following lines from his speech show that Lincoln believed the war was a test of whether or not a united nation could last:

Four score and seven years ago our fathers brought forth on this continent a new nation conceived in liberty and dedicated to the proposition that all men are created equal. Now we are engaged in a great civil war, testing whether that nation or any nation so conceived and so dedicated can long endure.

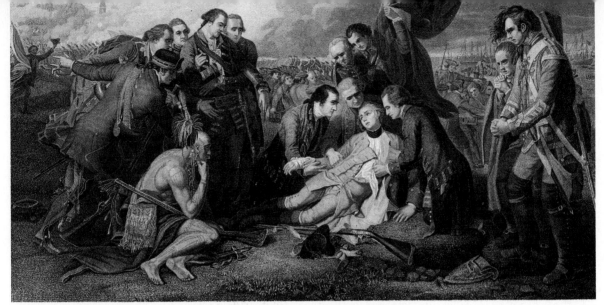

▲ **Illustrating History** *This painting glorifies the death of a British general, James Wolfe, during the French and Indian War.*

The disastrous Civil War ended in 1865. The United States, born in liberty in 1776, had been rededicated as a solid union of states. Although the healing process was long and difficult, the United States had managed to survive as a nation.

The British Colony of Canada Avoided Conflict with French Canadians

In 1713, Nova Scotia and the lands around the Hudson Bay were won by Great Britain after war with France. Some 50 years later, as a result of the French and Indian War, which ended in 1763, all of Canada was in the hands of the British. After their victory over the French, the British began to trade with Canada and to settle there. The French settlers were already in Lower Canada, or present-day Quebec. The British settled farther west in Upper Canada, or present-day Ontario.

By the time the British began to settle in 1763, however, the French had already established their own way of life. They had their own language and their own laws, and they were Roman Catholics. Many of the British authorities felt that the French Canadians should be made to give up their ways and accept British ways. This question was debated until 1774, when the British came to a decision.

In the Quebec Act of 1774, the French Canadians were given the right to worship in the Catholic church. They were allowed to follow their own laws and language. To satisfy the French, the Province of Quebec was increased in size to include lands around the Ohio River.

The Quebec Act of 1774 was not popular in the American colonies. The Americans were already angry with Great Britain for many reasons. Now, they were further irritated because some of their western lands had been taken from them. Although the British held on to Canada, it was partly because of the Quebec Act that the British lost their American colonies.

Canada Won Self-Government

By 1837, Canada had many complaints of its own against Great Britain. Canadians wanted to govern themselves. At the very least, they wanted a greater voice in their government. Led by William Mackenzie and Louis Joseph Papineau (pah pee NOH), a revolution seemed to be on the way. However, instead of fighting a war to gain independence, Canada became independent gradually without violence.

Remembering the loss of their 13 colonies after the American Revolution, the British decided not to take any chances. In 1839,

507

they issued the Durham Report, which recommended that Upper and Lower Canada be united and that Canadians be given some control over their domestic affairs. The Union Act of 1840 did unite Upper and Lower Canada.

In 1867, Britain passed the North American Act, which united nearly all of Canada and formed the Dominion of Canada. (At that time, dominions were countries of the British Commonwealth of Nations.) Gradually, the government of Canada was given the right to make its own laws. In foreign affairs, however, Great Britain spoke for Canada. While glad that they were now self-governing, the Canadians held closely to their British ties because they feared the growing power of the United States. They did not wish to be taken over by their southern neighbor. In time, however, Canada began to act and speak independently of Great Britain, even in foreign affairs.

Australia and New Zealand Won Self-Government

At about the same time that gold was discovered in California in 1848, gold was also discovered in Australia. The Australian gold rush that followed helped open the doors to settlement. By 1875, most of Australia had been explored, but little of it had been judged fit for settlement. The central and western parts of the country were desert. The better areas did attract British settlers who made Australia a vigorous colony.

In time, the first colony of New South Wales in southeast Australia was joined by other colonies in southern, western, and northern Australia, Queensland, Victoria, and the nearby island of Tasmania. As early as the 1850s, some people believed that these colonies should be united to form an Australian nation. This idea was not to occur for about 40 years. By 1860, however, nearly all of the separate colonies had won a measure of self-government.

In 1897, a constitution for all of Australia was created. Under the constitution, the six Australian states and Tasmania were united under a central government. This constitu-

tion was approved by the British Parliament in 1900. On January 1, 1901, the Commonwealth of Australia came into being.

New Zealand, 1,200 miles (1,932 kilometers) to the east of Australia, became a part of the British Empire in 1839. The native New Zealanders, called Maoris (MOU reez), fought against the British, but these uprisings were put down. Later, the Maoris were given equal status with the rest of the population. In 1907, New Zealand became a dominion in the British Empire.

Nationalism has been, and continues to be, a powerful force in history. The desire of people to form their own nations and to control their destinies continues to burn brightly. Like the nations in the nineteenth century, the nations that struggle to emerge today rarely do so without conflict.

Drawing inferences means reading between the lines, that is, forming conclusions that are not stated directly but are suggested by other facts. Inferences may be limited and describe only specific people, places, or things. If you read about Napoleon's goals for conquering Europe, you can easily infer that ruling only one country did not satisfy him.

Inferences may also be general statements about how some aspect of reality tends to operate. Inferences such as these can help illuminate the past. They can also be used to predict what is likely to happen in the future if certain conditions exist. This is the idea behind the statement: "Those who do not learn from the past are doomed to repeat it."

Use the following steps to practice drawing inferences from the things you read.

1. **Find the main idea of a sentence, paragraph, or longer passage.** Read the paragraph below. Answer the following question: How can you summarize briefly the main idea that is contained in the last sentence of the paragraph?

2. **Think about other facts you know about the same subject, either stated or unstated.** Answer the following questions: (a) Which social group was more likely to travel and have contact with the world outside its own community—the upper class or the masses of ordinary people? (b) What historical developments led to increased contact with the larger world and increased travel?

3. **Think about the main idea and the other facts you know about the subject. Decide whether these facts together suggest more facts or conclusions about the subject.** Using the answers you gave in Steps 1 and 2, answer the following questions: (a) What inference can you draw about the masses of ordinary people and the rise of national feelings? (b) What inference can you draw as to which historical developments contributed to the growth of national feelings?

Toward the end of the Middle Ages, nationalist feelings began developing in many countries throughout Europe. Why did this not happen sooner? Because until that time, most people were unable to think beyond their own communities. In fact, most people never went outside the communities in which they were born, since travel was difficult and limited. Communication, too, was limited. It was not easy for people to find out about life beyond their own communities. As a result, any feelings of belonging to a nation were weak and limited throughout the Middle Ages. Of course, if a nation was attacked, soldiers went to war to defend it. But, they were loyal to the noblemen under whom they fought, rather than to a king they might never have seen. Gradually, however, through increased contact with outsiders and more travel, people from the upper classes began developing a sense that they belonged not just to a local community, but to a larger nation.

REVIEW

Section Summaries

Section 1 Italy and Germany Became Nations
The nationalists who hoped to unify Italy faced geographical and political obstacles. Success came, however, through the efforts of Giuseppe Mazzini, Count Cavour, and Giuseppe Garibaldi. Opposition from neighboring nations and hostility among German states blocked German unification. Germans had always believed, however, that their nation would become great. Napoleon's conquest had united Germans into a confederation. Unification was left up to Prussia's chief minister, Otto von Bismarck, who built up Germany's prestige and gained more land. In 1871, Germany became an empire, led by William I of Prussia.

Section 2 Austrian and Ottoman Empires Broke Apart The many nationalities ruled by the Austrian Empire wanted to govern themselves. As wars weakened Austria, these nationalities demanded their rights. Finally, Hungary won the right to govern itself in domestic affairs as part of the Dual Monarchy. Yet discontent remained in the empire. The Ottoman Turks also ruled a crumbling empire that governed many nationalities. In 1829, Greece won its independence. After the Russo-Turkish War, the weakened empire granted independence to a number of its other lands. Then, in 1923, the empire ended, as Turkey declared itself a republic.

Section 3 Nationalism's Influence Spread Beyond Europe The American Civil War questioned the power of the central government over the states. The war proved the United States was a solid national union. In Canada, by 1837, English and French Canadians wanted to govern their own country. Britain avoided a revolution and gave Canada more and more freedom. Canada had won self-government by 1867 and the right to conduct its own foreign affairs by 1931. Britain also granted independence to Australia in 1901 and gave self-rule to New Zealand in 1907.

Key Facts

1. Use each vocabulary word in a sentence.
   a. confederation
   b. suffrage
   c. nationality
   d. federalism
   e. secede
2. Identify and briefly explain the importance of the following names, places or events.
   a. Apennine Mountains
   b. Giuseppe Mazzini
   c. Count Cavour
   d. Giuseppe Garibaldi
   e. Otto von Bismarck
   f. Franco-Prussian War
   g. Crimean War
   h. Atatürk
   i. Gettysburg Address
   j. Durham Report

Main Ideas

1. Beginning with the Crimean War, list the steps in the unification of Italy.
2. List the wars that helped Bismarck create a strong and unified Germany.
3. Why did many groups in the Austrian Empire want to govern themselves?
4. How did Montenegro, Romania, and Serbia win their independence from the Ottoman Empire?
5. What did the Civil War prove about the United States?
6. How did Australia and New Zealand win the right to govern themselves?

Developing Skill in Reading History

Based on your reading of this chapter, place the three events of each group in the proper chronological order.

A. _____ Italy became a kingdom.
_____ The Carbonari attempted a revolution.
_____ Garibaldi won Sicily for Italy.

B. _____ Greece won its independence.
_____ Atatürk declared the Turkish republic.
_____ The Congress of Berlin ended the Russo-Turkish War.

C. _____ The American Civil War began.
_____ The United States Constitution was drawn up.
_____ Lincoln gave his Gettysburg Address.

D. _____ Bismarck told his people of the Ems Dispatch.
_____ The German empire was proclaimed, with William I as its emperor.
_____ Prussia won the Franco-Prussian War.

E. _____ Gold was discovered in Australia.
_____ New Zealand gained self-rule.
_____ Australia won its independence.

Using Social Studies Skills

Using Maps to Make Comparisons Review the two maps in the chapter that show the unification of Italy and of Germany. Then, use the information on the maps to complete the chart below on a separate sheet of paper.

Critical Thinking

1. **Perceiving Cause and Effect** What was the immediate effect of the call for revolution in Canada during the 1830s?
2. **Drawing Inferences** How might Bismarck have responded to the following statement? "Diplomacy is always the best way to achieve unification."
3. **Identifying Alternatives** Using the more successful nations as models, explain some ways in which the Austrians and the Ottomans might have kept their empires both strong and unified.

Focus on Writing

Prewriting

Plan a paragraph on one of the following topics, or choose a topic of your own from the chapter. Then answer the questions that follow.
· Defining Nationalism
· How War Brings Unification
· The Civil War vs. the Constitution
· The *Ems* Incident: A Brilliant Trick
· Garibaldi's Contribution to Italy

1. Who will be your audience? (Make up a possible audience if you need to.)
2. What will be the main idea of your paragraph? That is, what do you want to explain to your audience?
3. What is your purpose—to inform, explain, describe, or narrate?
4. What will be your topic sentence?
5. What ideas in your paragraph will support your topic sentence?

Italy and Germany		
	Italy	**Germany**
Period of unification		
Some major parts of the nation		East Prussia, West Prussia, Bavaria, Saxony
Length of nation in miles at longest point		
Bordering lands	Switzerland, France, Austrian Empire	

People, Money, and Machines

(1750–1900)

1 **Revolutions in Industry and Agriculture Began**

2 **Society Faced Complex Problems**

3 **Culture Reflected the Spirit of the Times**

▲ **Illustrating History** *The victim of the first railway accident, William Huskisson, was a former member of the British Parliament.*

The steam locomotive *Northumbrian* came clanking along the new rails between Liverpool and Manchester, England, on September 15, 1830. Sadly, this exciting day was to have a tragic conclusion.

Puffing away at a top speed of 24 miles (nearly 40 kilometers) per hour, the caravan of eight trains in a row thrilled an estimated 1 million onlookers. The trains stopped briefly to take on water at a point 17 miles (28 kilometers) from Liverpool. William Huskisson, a politician, was among those passengers who dismounted for a look around.

After a few minutes, everyone began climbing back aboard. Suddenly, a passenger heard a second train bearing down on the spot where Huskisson stood and yelled at Huskisson to get inside. For whatever reason, Huskisson did not heed the warning. The train struck him. He fell onto the tracks and was struck again. "Where is Mrs. Huskisson?" he gasped. "I have met my death. God forgive me." Huskisson died later that evening.

Despite this tragic episode, the trains kept on running. By 1850, Britain had 6,000 miles (about 10,620 kilometers) of track, and the number more than doubled in the next two decades. Railways became the most visible sign of the Industrial Revolution that was transforming Europe and America. That transformation is the subject of this chapter.

1750	1800	1850	1900

1764 ■
James Hargreaves invents the spinning jenny

1793 ■
Eli Whitney invents the cotton gin

■ **1800**
Robert Owen starts a utopian community in Scotland

1848 ■
Karl Marx publishes *The Communist Manifesto*

■ **1859**
Charles Darwin writes *On the Origin of Species*

▲ **Illustrating History** *Railroads like the Liverpool and Manchester Railway in England, above, made transporting goods more efficient.*

1 Revolutions in Industry and Agriculture Began

As you read, look for answers to these questions:

◆ Why did the Industrial Revolution and Agricultural Revolution occur?
◆ Why did the revolutions in industry and agriculture start in England?
◆ What were the major inventions that made the Industrial Revolution and Agricultural Revolution possible?

Key Terms: domestic system (defined on p. 514), factory system (p. 514)

Revolution may be defined as drastic or complete change. Previous chapters have discussed the English, American, and French revolutions in which great changes occurred in governments. In England, an absolute monarchy became a limited, constitutional monarchy; in America, colonies became an independent nation; and in France, a kingdom became a republic.

The Industrial Revolution was a different kind of change. First of all, it involved the economy rather than the government. That is, it changed how goods were produced and how people earned their living. Second, it was a slow, not a sudden, change. People knew the American and French revolutions were happening, but they probably were not aware that the Industrial Revolution was going on at the same time.

Between 1750 and 1850, Great Britain was the home of the Industrial Revolution and the Agricultural Revolution. However, the Industrial Revolution was not limited to Great Britain. It took place in many European countries and the United States. It spread to other parts of the world as well.

513

The Industrial Revolution Had Roots Far in the Past

During the Middle Ages, work was done by hand in small shops under the direction of craft guilds. With the discovery of the New World, however, wealth grew, commerce increased, and there was a greater demand for goods. With this increased demand for goods, entrepreneurs, or business people who were willing to take risks to find new ways to make and sell things, arose. These people created the domestic system for the production of goods. Under the **domestic system,** entrepreneurs used their own money to buy raw materials, which they gave to their workers. Their workers would then turn the raw materials into finished products at home, using simple machines, such as spinning wheels or hand-operated looms. Before long, however, even the domestic system could not keep up with the demand for manufactured goods.

The need to produce goods on a large scale prompted the invention of many new machines that used new sources of power. Because the machines were too expensive to be owned by a worker and too big to be kept in a home, the domestic system could not make use of these inventions. The new, power-driven machines also did not call for much skill, so many unskilled workers could be hired. The new steam-powered machines and the large numbers of unskilled workers were housed in large buildings called factories. This change from the domestic system to the **factory system**, and all the effects that followed, has been called the Industrial Revolution.

England Was the Birthplace of the Industrial Revolution

England was the birthplace of the Industrial Revolution for a number of reasons. First, there was a plentiful supply of labor for new factories. Second, England had a wealthy class of entrepreneurs who used their money to invest in new businesses and inventions. England was also blessed with good harbors, natural resources, and a favorable climate. The damp climate was good for the textile industry because without moisture in the air, cotton threads broke quite easily.

In addition to these resources, England had skilled workers who learned how to operate and repair the new machines. England also had large numbers of unskilled workers who wanted to work in factories rather than on farms. Small farmers, who were unable to compete with large-scale farming, joined the labor force needed by the Industrial Revolution.

Manufactured goods sell best in areas where many people have the money to buy them. England's large population provided a good market for textiles, furniture, household utensils, saddles, coaches, and farm implements. In addition to the demand for goods within the country, England had many colonies where people were willing to buy goods manufactured in England.

In the early stages of the Industrial Revolution, the new machines used water as their source of power. Water wheels, which were turned by running water from creeks and rivers, supplied the power for the machines. By the first part of the nineteenth century, however, steam engines were used to supply the energy for machines. Coal, which was used to produce steam, was so plentiful in England and so important to England's wealth that it was called black gold. Iron ore was another important natural resource for the Industrial Revolution, and England had a good supply of iron ore as shown on the map on page 516.

Textile industry inventions. In the eighteenth century, two inventions revolutionized the textile industry. In 1733, John Kay invented a *flying shuttle,* which dramatically increased the speed of weaving. In 1764, James Hargreaves (hahr GREEVZ) invented the *spinning jenny,* which increased the speed of spinning yarn. Unlike the spinning wheel, which could spin only a single thread at a time, the spinning jenny produced many threads at one time. These two inventions greatly increased the amount of material that could be produced. Then, in 1769, Richard Arkwright invented the *water* *frame.* The water frame used water power to drive a spinning machine. The new machine spun thread faster than any other machine. In 1779, Samuel Crompton invented the *spinning mule,* which was a combination of the spinning jenny and the water frame. The spinning mule streamlined the production of thread and yarn even further. The *power loom,* invented by Edmund Cartwright in 1785 to weave yarns into cloth, was also driven by water power. As the time needed to produce cotton textiles lessened, the demand for them increased. In 1793, an American, Eli Whitney, invented the cotton gin, a machine that could quickly separate the seeds from raw cotton.

Most of the new spinning and weaving machines used water power, but in 1769, James Watt improved on earlier steam engines. By the beginning of the nineteenth century, the steam engine was running looms for the manufacture of cloth. This meant that the production of cloth could be increased.

Breakthroughs in coal mining. Just as important as the inventions in the textile industry were the inventions in the coal mining industry. The mining of coal was a dangerous job. Coal gas inside a dark mine could explode when exposed to open flame, but the miners needed light to work. Sir Humphrey Davy's *safety lamp,* invented in 1816, allowed miners to see where they were going while keeping them safe from explosions since the flame of the lamp was enclosed. Engineers learned how to provide for air in deep mine tunnels and how to strengthen the tunnel walls. These improvements increased mining safety and also increased the output of coal. Although coal mining remained a dangerous job, coal was the base upon which the Industrial Revolution rested.

Iron and steel industry. Inventions also furthered the growth of the iron industry. When iron comes from the ground, it has many impurities that must be removed in a blast furnace. Soon, however, an even stronger material was needed for construction, and steel came into widespread use.

▲ **Illustrating History** *The invention of new spinning and weaving machinery revolutionized the textile industry.*

By 1800, the manufacture of steel was possible, but its production was so expensive that for the first half of the nineteenth century, steel was scarce. In 1856, Henry Bessemer invented a process that could change iron into steel by removing more of the impurities found in iron. Soon steel took the place of iron as the most important product of the Industrial Revolution. The *open-hearth* process, which used a better furnace and could make more types of steel than the Bessemer process, was a later improvement in the making of steel.

A new mobility. Industrial growth cannot take place unless it is possible to move people and materials quickly and cheaply over long distances. The need to move things from place to place resulted in many changes in transportation and communication. Great steps were made in land transportation. John McAdam, a Scot, improved roads by using crushed stone, which made them passable in rainy weather. Most of today's roads are still called "macadam" after this inventive man.

The inventions of steam-powered trains and boats were equally important. In 1807, Robert Fulton demonstrated that steam

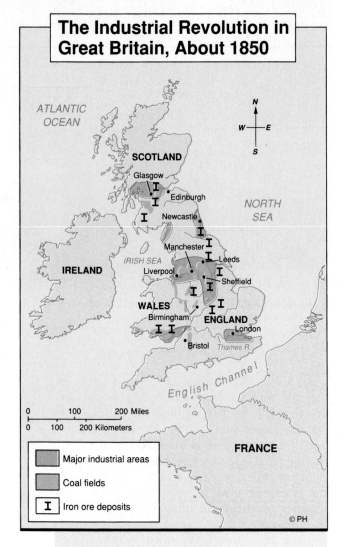

The Industrial Revolution in Great Britain, About 1850

Focus on Geography

Regions What statement can you make about the location of coal regions and industrial areas?

Legend:
- Major industrial areas
- Coal fields
- I Iron ore deposits

A Revolution in Agriculture Began

The Agricultural Revolution contributed to and accompanied the Industrial Revolution. Although their tools had improved since the days of the feudal manor, eighteenth-century English farmers still worked separate strips of land in a number of fields. They also shared common lands to feed their livestock and woodlands for timber to heat their homes. The *open field system,* as this system of common land was called, was good for small farmers who grew food for their own use. It was not good if large amounts of food were to be grown inexpensively and sold to people living in cities or even in other countries. If farming was to be made more efficient, the open field system would have to change.

The enclosure movement. The *enclosure movement,* which took place between the sixteenth and eighteenth centuries in England, combined, or enclosed, lands that had been scattered in several fields into a single farm under a single ownership. Lands that were held in common, such as pastures and woodland, were also consolidated, or enclosed. Between 1702 and 1797, Parliament passed thousands of laws encouraging the enclosure of millions of acres of farmland. Landowners then rented fields to farmers who lived on the land and worked it.

Although land that had been consolidated could be used more efficiently and productively, every enclosure act of Parliament drove out some poor farmers who had worked the smaller plots under the old system. Often these farmers left the land, headed for the city, and became skilled or unskilled workers in the factories that developed during the Industrial Revolution.

New farming techniques. The search for better farming techniques led to an agricultural revolution in England, which slowly spread to many other countries. One of the earliest changes occurred in the eighteenth century. During the seventeenth century, the usual way of planting was simply to scatter the seeds by hand. Many of the seeds did not grow into plants. In 1701, however,

could be used to power ships when his steamboat, the *Clermont,* made its famous trip up the Hudson. By 1820, horse-drawn rail cars were common in England. Then, in 1829, George Stephenson invented a steam locomotive. In 1840, the first transoceanic crossing under steam power took place. By 1860, the days of sailing vessels and horse-drawn vehicles were numbered. Steam power had taken the lead.

Industrial Growth in Great Britain

Pig Iron Production 1788–1910
(Thousands of tons)

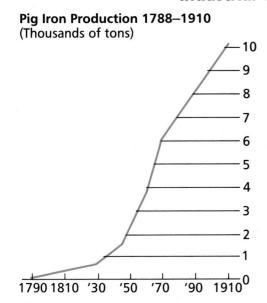

Miles of Railroad Track 1825–1910

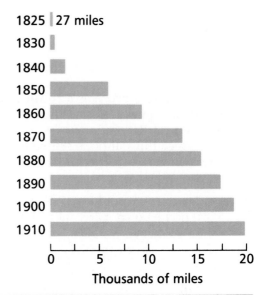

Thousands of miles

▲ **Graph Skill** *The production of pig iron (crude iron from the blast furnace) increased as railroads grew. How much was produced in 1890?*

Jethro Tull invented a drill for planting seeds in straight rows. This invention increased the crops and the food supplies.

In about the middle of the 1700s, Viscount Townshend told farmers that they should periodically change the kind of crops grown in the same soil. *Crop rotation,* as this method is called, makes it possible for the soil to retain valuable minerals and stay fertile longer. At about the same time, Robert Bakewell taught farmers how to breed and raise more productive cattle.

Many improvements also were made in farm machinery. As steel became more common, steel plows took the place of wooden ones. The *reaper,* invented in 1834 by Cyrus McCormick, made it possible to cut grain more rapidly than with a hand scythe. The reaper cut and tied the grain into bundles. The *thresher* was a stationary machine designed to strip the grain from the stems. The new inventions, together with the use of natural and chemical fertilizers, were major developments of the Agricultural Revolution.

SECTION 1 REVIEW

Knowing Key Terms, People, and Places
1. Define: **a.** domestic system **b.** factory system
2. Identify: **a.** spinning jenny **b.** Eli Whitney **c.** enclosure movement

Focus on Geography
3. How did the geography of England encourage the growth of industry?

Reviewing Main Ideas
4. How did new inventions improve transportation and provide a new mobility? Explain with examples.
5. What agricultural changes caused rural workers to migrate to urban areas during the late 1700s and early 1800s?

Critical Thinking

Perceiving Cause and Effect
6. Why was the Agricultural Revolution so devastating to small farm owners? Explain your answer with logical reasons.

2 Society Faced Complex Problems

As you read, look for answers to these questions:

◆ How did the English class system change?
◆ What problems arose as a result of the Industrial Revolution and the Agricultural Revolution?
◆ What were the solutions reformers proposed for social problems?

> **Key Terms:** corporation (defined on p. 518), dividend (p. 518), labor union (p. 523), socialism (p. 523), communism (p. 524), anarchism (p. 524)

By the turn of a switch, a home can be lighted. With the turn of a key, an automobile can be started. Modern forms of energy and power may not seem unusual to you because you see them every day. Yet, not many years ago, heating, lighting, or cooling a home or office was a difficult task. It was not long ago that human and animal muscle was the main source of power. Railroads, automobiles, and airplanes were unknown.

Today, the Industrial Revolution is still going on. As science and technology are applied to new activities, there are new revolutions in transportation, communications, and manufacturing. We travel and transport goods with jets that fly faster than the speed of sound. We communicate with satellites, and we manufacture products with the help of computers and robots. These advances are among the long-term results of the Industrial and Agricultural revolutions. As you will read, however, these revolutions also brought many problems.

The Industrial Revolution Brought Dramatic Changes

The Industrial Revolution brought about sweeping changes in society. One change was the creation of new forms of business as a result of the increased production of goods. The wealth these new businesses produced caused another major change—the rapid growth of the middle class and the breakdown of the old class system.

The growth of capitalism. As you read in Chapter 9, capitalism is an economic system based on private ownership of the means of producing goods and services. As the Industrial Revolution moved ahead, capital, or money for investment, was no longer created only by agriculture. Under the new businesses, labor and trade became the primary vehicles for the creation of capital. The most important new form of business organization was the corporation. A **corporation** is a business organized by people who are given permission by the government to sell to the public certificates of ownership, or shares of stock, in that corporation. The sale of stock gives the purchaser part ownership in the corporation. In this way, the corporation can raise more money than a single individual may be able to put into a business.

Why are people willing to buy the shares of corporation stock? As you read in Chapter 16, people invest their money in hopes that the corporation will make a profit. If the corporation does make a profit, it pays a **dividend,** or a share of its profits, to each of the stockholders. If the business does very well, the stock shares may increase in value. Thus, people who are not wealthy can own a share in a business and get some of the rewards. At the same time, the stockholder shares the risk of a loss. If the company does not make a profit, the stockholder may receive no dividend and the value of the stock may drop. The corporation is a widely used form of business organization.

The end of the old class system. Before the Industrial Revolution, the English population was divided into fixed classes. There was a small upper class (the very wealthy), a small middle class (the moderately wealthy), and a large lower class (the poor). The Industrial Revolution made possible the rise of a powerful middle class that owed its position in society, not to birth, but to its ability to gain wealth. Once ability rather

The Telephone, Then and Now

A platinum needle, a dish of water, a length of wire, and a reed receiver were the major materials used in Alexander Graham Bell's first telephone in 1875. In fact, Bell's early experiments did not grow much more complex than this. In making long-distance calls, for instance, he merely connected his new device with existing telegraph lines.

These days, the phone system is a large, sophisticated business. Telephones interact with computers, report emergencies on their own, and function cordlessly. Telephone calls can be sent by satellite or through a light-wave cable, a system that transmits crystal-clear calls on pulses of light.

1. Name three materials used in the first phone.
2. How have phones been put to more complex uses?

than birth was the key to financial success, it became possible for poor but ambitious people to become wealthy.

The wealthiest members of the growing middle class were the owners of factories, mines, and small businesses, as well as bankers and merchants. Professional people, such as doctors, and workers, such as business clerks, completed the ranks of the middle class.

As the Industrial Revolution progressed, society allowed the middle class to rise to important positions previously held only by the upper class. Indeed, many wealthy middle-class people could play the role of the aristocrat. They acted that role in their social behavior and in their purchase of huge estates and other extravagant items. With their rise in society, the middle class began to experience increased political and economic power.

The members of the new entrepreneurial middle class were usually self-made, hard-working, and proud of their positions in society. Factory owners and merchants were convinced that they contributed far more to society than landowners who lived off their lands. At the same time, however, these entrepreneurs regarded the poor as lazy and in need of guidance. The new middle class came to believe they were performing a public service by employing people who would otherwise live lazy, immoral lives. The new industrialists did not want government to interfere with the ways they ran their businesses. They really believed that *patronage*, the power to appoint people to office and grant political favors, made things work better. They made money, produced goods that improved life for everyone, and kept the poor employed, saving them from idleness and starvation. In other words, the new entrepreneurs were convinced that the future prosperity of Great Britain was safe in their hands if they were left alone.

The philosophy of laissez faire. Those who believed that the government should not control the economy were followers of the philosophy of laissez faire. As you learned in Chapter 18, this is the term used to describe the belief that the government should keep "hands off" business. This philosophy is the opposite of the philosophy of mercantilism in which the government regulates the economy to enrich the nation.

In his 1776 book, *The Wealth of Nations*, Adam Smith said that a government should only "protect society from violence. . . . protect society from injustice, and maintain certain public works." According to Smith, a free market was guided by an "invisible hand." That is, if each person pursued his or her own self-interest, the common interests of all would be met. Many factory owners, landowners, and merchants felt that the ideas of Adam Smith were right.

Some business people felt that the theory that government should not interfere with business meant that business people did not have to clean up the wastes their factories created or provide safe working conditions or shorter hours or better wages for their workers. The theory of laissez faire claimed that if industry were left to itself, competition among businesses would lead to improvements for the workers and consumers, as well as for the owners.

The writings of other thinkers at the time supported this belief. The writer Thomas Malthus said that the population would grow faster than the ability of industry and agriculture to provide the food, clothing, and shelter that people needed. Malthus recommended letting nature take care of itself. Overpopulation would be kept in check by nature. Wars, diseases, and famines would keep down the birthrate. Malthus also advised people to marry late and thus have fewer children.

Another writer, David Ricardo, said that the wages paid to workers depended upon the demand for workers. If workers were needed, wages would rise. If workers were not needed, wages would fall. Ricardo felt that nothing should, or could, be done about this process. He called the process the *iron law of wages.*

These writers were satisfied that total wealth was increasing as a result of the Industrial Revolution. They were less concerned that the new wealth was not evenly distributed among people. Competition in industry would, they felt, lead to better products, lower prices, higher wages, and an improvement in the quality of life for all people. Many writers and thinkers were interested only in the growth of national wealth.

The Agricultural and the Industrial Revolutions Caused Problems

The social changes that occurred during the Agricultural Revolution and the Industrial Revolution caused many problems. The middle class had become powerful, but they had done so by using the workers of the lower class. The middle class now had economic power and high hopes that they could gain political power. The workers, on the other hand, often felt hopeless.

Farming difficulties. The development of farm machines and the enclosure acts of Parliament had done away with the common lands, the lands farmers could use to pasture cows and sheep or to cut trees for firewood. Farmers could not afford to buy the new farm machines, and they could not compete with those farmers who did use machines. Small farmers found themselves caught in a difficult position. To survive the competition, these people had to do one of three things: (1) keep their farms and work harder to produce a small income; (2) give up their farms and become poorly paid farm workers; or (3) go to the city in search of factory jobs.

Farm machinery made it possible to grow food in large quantities at low prices in many parts of the world. Because English landlords wanted to get high prices for their grains (rye, barley, oats), they tried to keep cheaper foreign grain from coming into

England. Since these landowners had a great deal of influence in Parliament, they were able to persuade Parliament to pass the *Corn Laws*. These laws taxed grain that came from other countries. (All grains in England are called corn.)

The Corn Laws made the prices of bread and cereals unnecessarily high. Although the laws were good for the landlords, they were bad for workers and factory owners. Factory owners liked cheap grains because then they did not have to pay high salaries to their workers. In 1846, when the factory owners had become more powerful than the landowners, the Corn Laws were dropped.

Poor working conditions. Wages, hours, and working conditions concerned the workers of the Industrial Revolution. During the early period of the Industrial Revolution, wages were so low that a factory worker could not support a family. Women and children worked alongside men in the factories, trying to make a living. Working hours were long—14 to 16 hours a day. Factories were unhealthy, dirty places with little light or air circulation. Since machines were expensive and labor was cheap, the machines were often more carefully protected than the people who ran them. Most factories had no safety devices. Often, the work was dangerous, and accidents were frequent when unskilled workers came in contact with the machines. This was particularly true when workers became tired and careless from the long hours. Through fines or beatings, factory owners could punish those who failed to keep up with the work.

To make matters worse, employment depended on the demand for whatever the factories made. Because sickness was frequent, workers could not always count on a full week's pay. Not only did workers lose wages when they were sick, but in some cases they paid fines for being absent. A worker might escape paying a fine for an absence if he or she could find a substitute.

As new machines replaced people in the factories, unemployment increased. Workers who lost their jobs found it difficult to learn a new trade. Workers often started

In their own words

A Childhood in an English Factory

Adults used to the independence of farming did not like the working conditions of factory jobs. Hence, factory owners often hired children. This excerpt is from testimony given by a parent to an 1832 committee investigating child factory labor.

Question: At what time . . . in the brisk time [busy season], did your girls go to the mills?

Answer: In the brisk time, for about six weeks, they have gone at three o'clock in the morning and ended at ten or nearly half-past, at night. . . .

Question: What intervals were allowed for rest or refreshment?

Answer: Breakfast a quarter of an hour, and dinner half an hour, and drinking a quarter of an hour. . . .

Question: Had you not great difficulty in awakening your children . . . ?

Answer: Yes, in the early time we had to take them up asleep and shake them . . . before we could get them off to work; but not so in the common hours. . . .

Question: The common [regular] hours of labor were from six in the morning till half-past eight at night?

Answer: Yes. . . .

Question: Did this excessive term of labor occasion much cruelty also?

Answer: Yes, with being so very fatigued, the strap was frequently used. . . .

Question: Have any of your children been strapped?

Answer: Yes, every one.

1. How long was the work day during the busy season at the factory?
2. How important was educating children during the Industrial Revolution?

521

riots against the introduction of machines that could be used to reduce the need for human labor.

Poor living conditions. While factory conditions were bad with low pay, long hours, and poor working conditions, conditions were not much better in the homes. Cities were growing rapidly. Often, buildings were built faster than the streets or water and sewerage systems that were needed for them. In every large industrial city, workers lived in wretched slums. Whole families often occupied one room that was too hot in summer and too cold in winter. The stuffy and unsanitary living quarters were breeding places for crime and disease. When industrialism began in earnest, the government did nothing about improving the living conditions of the working classes. Thus, the improvements the Industrial Revolution brought came only with great hardship and suffering.

Reformers' Solutions Ranged from Peaceful to Violent

Some people believed that the government had to do something to improve the lives of poor people. They believed the Industrial Revolution had to be brought under some form of government control or else its shortcomings would ruin the lives of people who could not help themselves.

The poor conditions and frustrations of the workers caught the attention of various reformers and began many new political

---

BIOGRAPHY

Elizabeth Gaskell

Whether dusting a bookcase or stirring a kettle on the stove, Elizabeth Gaskell, shown above, had the sort of steadiness expected of a minister's wife in Victorian England. She cheerfully managed to keep house, raise four children, and run several charities. As a writer, however, she often at-tacked the very life that she led.

Elizabeth Cleghorn Stevenson was born the daughter of a clergyman in 1810 in London. She grew into a woman of great beauty. She was of medium height and had blue eyes and brown hair. Three years after her father's death in 1829, she married William Gaskell and settled in Manchester, where she lived a happy family life.

Then misfortune struck. In 1845, her son William died of scarlet fever. Overwhelmed by grief, Gaskell turned to writing. Her first book, *Mary Barton*, told of a working-class Manchester family torn by class hatred. Gaskell's story was one of the first to tell of the distress suffered by the urban poor and the indifference of the Victorian middle classes to their problems.

The book was a success, and Gaskell continued writing. In 1865, she died of a heart attack suffered at her country home. By that time, she was famous for her books.

1. How did Elizabeth Gaskell resist her middle-class Victorian life?
2. What was the significance of Gaskell's writing?
3. Why might writing act as therapy for a grieving person?

movements. The union movement and the liberal, socialist, communist, anarchist, and utopian philosophies were all different attempts to solve the problems of society. The solutions suggested by these political philosophies ranged from peaceful to violent.

The union movement. Workers of the early 1800s tried to improve their situations by forming labor unions. A **labor union** is an organized group of workers who represent the interests and demands of the workers in a particular industry. For example, a union of factory workers might bargain with the owner of the factory for better working conditions and better wages. If these demands are refused, union members may strike, or refuse to work. As a result of the union movement, and the efforts of many reformers, some changes were made.

By 1819, the hiring of children under the age of 10 became illegal. In 1824, labor unions finally became legal. Before that time, people who joined unions often lost their jobs and sometimes were put in jail. Even though labor unions became legal, the right to strike still had not been won. New laws, however, somewhat improved working conditions. In 1841, Parliament reduced the length of the work day for children to 10 hours. Later, Parliament passed laws that regulated health and safety conditions for English workers. In 1871, the Trades Union Act assured that union members would not be punished for striking.

The liberal response. English liberals believed in worker organization and the freedom of the press. They criticized religion for not encouraging the poor to be more demanding and less resigned to their plight. Liberals wanted to bring about change within the law by peaceful means. They urged free public education in the belief that literate workers could bring about changes by themselves. While the bloodshed of the French Revolution had horrified them, these liberals were passionately in favor of change within the existing political system.

John Stuart Mill was a noted English philosopher and a liberal. In 1859, Mill wrote an essay, entitled *On Liberty*, that be-

▲ **Illustrating History** *This painting of coal miners shows the poor working conditions reformers tried to improve.*

came the inspiration for the liberal movement. He was also a strong supporter of women's rights. In 1869, he wrote *On the Subjection of Women* in which he pointed out that women had been put in an unfavorable legal and social position throughout history by men.

Jeremy Bentham was another English philosopher who influenced the call for social reform. Along with Mill, he believed in capitalism and in keeping industry in private hands. According to Bentham, government should step in only to correct abuses. His philosophy held that the greatest happiness of the greatest number of people is the fundamental principle of morality. Along with Mill, therefore, Bentham supported the union movement and the peaceful improvement of working conditions.

The socialist movement. Socialism was another "ism" that emerged in response to industrialization. **Socialism** is an economic and political system in which society as a whole, rather than individuals, owns all property and operates all businesses. Thus, believers in socialism are opposed to the basic ideas of capitalism. Followers of socialism were outraged by what they felt were the economic inequities of the Industrial Revolution. They urged workers to unite against employers who paid them low wages and

523

▲ **Illustrating History** *This English cartoon of 1843 contrasts the lives of the rich with those of the coal mine workers.*

Marx thought of history as a struggle between the rich and the poor. In the industrial age, the struggle was between owners and workers. From his reading and understanding of history, Marx believed that the workers were bound to win this fight. In the *Communist Manifesto*, Marx called capitalism an alien monster that would destroy society. Marx and his followers were successful in organizing political groups in many countries.

The ideas of Marx have influenced both followers of communism and followers of socialism. Communists teach the use of revolution to gain their goals. Socialists maintain that their goals can be reached through orderly, democratic processes. Communists want the government to own all industries. Socialists would have the government own just the large industries.

could hire or fire them at will. Socialists told workers that they, too, were entitled to the benefits the new industrialist/merchant class enjoyed. Socialists encouraged workers in their attempts to form labor unions.

Marx and communism. Some followers of socialism saw the evils in the industrial society and wanted to do something about them at once. They felt that the workers themselves could take steps to get a share of industrial profits. In its complete rejection of capitalism, **communism** is an extreme form of socialism in which there is collective (centralized state) ownership of all land and all the means of production. Under communism, all individuals are expected to contribute to society according to their abilities and receive from society according to their needs.

The most prominent person who felt this way was Karl Marx, who lived from 1818 to 1883. In his pamphlet, *Communist Manifesto*, and in his three-volume study, *Das Kapital* (dahs KAHP e tahl), Marx outlined his beliefs. There are two basic ideas found in the writings of Karl Marx. The first is that history is decided by how people make a living, that is, by economics. The second is the idea of *class struggle*.

Anarchists and violent reform. Anarchists were among the other groups who wanted to make conditions better for workers. Marx had insisted that the workers were bound to win in the struggle between workers and capitalist owners. The struggle, Marx felt, would be long. Anarchists believed that capitalism had to be overthrown quickly and violently. **Anarchism** was an attempt to overthrow capitalism by force and to do away with government altogether. The two most famous nineteenth-century anarchists were Pierre Joseph Proudhon (proo DOHN), a Frenchman, and Mikhail Bakunin (ba KOO nin), a Russian. Neither anarchism nor communism was in favor of private property. Anarchists, however, were opposed to any kind of government at all. Government, anarchists felt, prevented workers from having a better life. Bakunin went to jail many times for taking part in violent attempts to overthrow the government of Russia.

The utopian socialists. While there were people who thought that improvement for the workers was hopeless, there were others who thought that society could attain perfection. *Utopia*, as you know, was an imaginary place where perfect government, perfect law, and a perfect economy existed. In such a community, extremes of wealth and poverty did not exist, and people were supposed to be happy.

Those who believed in these ideas were called *utopian socialists*. They were utopian because they believed that perfection was possible on earth. They were socialists because they wanted the factories, farms, railroads, and mines to be owned and run by government for the benefit of all people. They believed that wealth should be shared.

Robert Owen, a wealthy manufacturer and a successful entrepreneur, was one of the early utopian socialists. At New Lanark, Scotland, he built an industrial community that paid high profits to the owners and high wages to the workers. He reduced working hours, raised wages, and improved working conditions. He made it possible for workers to get a better education and would not hire any children under the age of 10. These reforms were very much ahead of the times in those days. Owen's humanitarianism proved that you did not have to be cruel and uncaring to show a profit.

When the New Lanark community grew rich, Owen tried to build another utopian society in New Harmony, Indiana, in the United States. Although this one failed, Owen spent the rest of his life trying to convince others that his social experiments were worthwhile. In 1841, followers of Owen made another unsuccessful attempt to establish a cooperative community in Massachusetts. The community of Brook Farm tried to carry out some of the ideas of a utopian community.

Although they may have differed on how to approach and solve problems, all of the people who wanted to reform English life and improve the conditions of the poor shared an important quality called humanitarianism. That is, they all agreed on the need to abolish workhouses, to prohibit the use of orphanages as a labor supply for factories, to correct the inhumane treatment of the mentally ill in insane asylums, and to make other changes in society. These ideas spread to other countries and influenced some American slave owners who began to doubt the morality of their actions.

▲ **Illustrating History** *Karl Marx, shown above, was the founder of modern socialism and communism.*

SECTION 2 REVIEW

Knowing Key Terms, People, and Places
1. Define: **a.** corporation **b.** dividend **c.** labor union **d.** socialism **e.** communism **f.** anarchism
2. Identify: **a.** Malthus **b.** Corn Laws **c.** Marx **d.** class struggle

Reviewing Main Ideas
3. Explain how the Industrial Revolution brought about the rise of the middle class.
4. Why did the philosophy of laissez faire appeal to the new middle class?
5. Why were working conditions so harsh at the beginning of the Industrial Revolution in England?

Critical Thinking
Drawing Conclusions
6. New social conditions and political ideas change the ways people think about themselves and others. How do you think the Industrial and Agricultural revolutions changed the way the English working-class people felt about themselves? Explain with logical examples.

Reflections of Industry in Art

Few artists of the nineteenth century went unaffected by the changes of the Industrial Revolution. Some enthusiastically accepted the new machines and materials, while others refused to acknowledge them. Two artists who embraced the achievements of modern industry were Claude Monet and Joseph Paxton. Monet, a French painter, was almost as happy to paint locomotives in their train sheds as he was to paint flowers in a field. As shown by his *Gare Saint-Lazare in Paris,* below on the left, he was fascinated by the great clouds of steam and smoke that the engines produced. Paxton took advantage of the cheap iron and glass of England's early industrial age to build the *Crystal Palace* for the British World Exhibition of 1851. Visitors at the fair were astonished at the enormous open spaces and the light, airy feeling they produced. Paxton was the first to use industrial materials to create such an artistic effect.

(Left) Claude Monet's Gare Saint-Lazare in Paris; *(Below) the Crystal Palace*

3 Culture Reflected the Spirit of the Times

As you read, look for answers to these questions:

◆ How did scientific discoveries create new possibilities?
◆ Who were the leading figures of Darwinism and Social Darwinism?
◆ Why was the nineteenth century so rich in creative expression?

Key Terms: atom (defined on p. 527), evolution (p. 527), romanticism (p. 528), realism (p. 528)

The achievements resulting from the Industrial Revolution spilled over into all other areas of nineteenth-century society. Most men and women were confident that having made so much progress, further advances were bound to occur. New discoveries in science happened almost daily and were important enough to be reported in the many newspapers of the day. Inspired by what they read, people thought about new ideas and pondered such fundamental questions as how the earth was formed and when life first appeared on it. In the mid-nineteenth century, these important topics were widely discussed.

New Scientific Discoveries Expanded the Limits of the Possible

Chemistry and physics were among the first fields to take major steps forward. John Dalton, an English chemist, discovered that elements are made up of tiny particles called **atoms.** He said that elements were the basic building blocks of matter. Dalton's work led to further developments in physics and chemistry. Only during the twentieth century have scientists learned how to split the atom and put its energy to work.

Throughout history, people have been interested in the earth's relation to the sun and to the other planets in the solar system.

They have wondered about the age of the earth. Sir Charles Lyell (LY el), a British geologist, offered one of the early theories about the earth's age. In 1830, he wrote a book in which he said that the face of the earth is changing all the time. Earthquakes, rivers, winds, and rains produce constant changes on the face of the earth and help to explain why the earth looks the way it does. These changes take place over thousands of years. From this observation, Lyell reasoned that the earth is many millions of years old.

Charles Darwin Changed the Way People Thought

If the earth is millions of years old, when did living things first appear? When did men and women first appear? Some scientists are still not sure of the answers to these questions. However, the ideas of Charles Darwin, an English naturalist who lived from 1809 to 1882, are accepted by many scientists. Darwin's book, *On the Origin of Species,* which was published in 1859, described his theory of evolution. It is one of the most important books ever written. Darwin said that all forms of life, including human life, began from simple forms millions of years ago. He called the slow process of change from simple forms to complex forms **evolution.** In the process of evolution, some forms of life die. The forms that are best fitted to their environment live. This part of the process of evolution is called survival of the fittest. Darwin pointed out that life is a constant struggle between the strong and the weak. This struggle, he said, will always continue.

Darwin's views had an enormous impact on the nineteenth century. Their influence was felt not only in science but also in attitudes toward the relations among human beings as well. If nature was a biological struggle for the survival of the fittest, surely there was also a social struggle in which the able survived and the less able fell by the way and failed.

Herbert Spencer, a prominent British philosopher, took Darwin's theory and applied it to groups of people and to whole nations. History, he claimed, was a struggle among

527

▲ **Illustrating History** *The controversy created by the ideas of Charles Darwin, above, has lasted for over a century.*

individuals, and only the most fit would survive. This view is sometimes called *Social Darwinism.* In the nineteenth century, Spencer's ideas allowed the rich to justify the wealth they had accumulated. At the same time, it encouraged a disregard for the needs of the poor and the weak. Among nations, Social Darwinism invited warfare because war was believed to be the ultimate test for determining who was fit to survive and who was not.

Romanticism and Realism Influenced the Arts in the 1800s

As the Industrial Revolution increased the wealth of the middle class, more people could afford the time and the money to enjoy the arts. Books, paintings, and music reflected a wider variety of creative expression. As class boundaries changed and industrialism progressed, the life of the individual became important in every form of creative expression. The ideas of romanticism and realism provided contrasting views.

Romanticism was a movement of the eighteenth and early nineteenth centuries that emphasized feeling and emotion, freedom of individual expression, and a love of nature, beauty, and liberty. Nationalism was another popular romantic theme. Romantics were fascinated with the past and especially with the Middle Ages.

Realism provided a sharp contrast with the ideas of the romantics. Followers of **realism,** whether they were painters or writers, believed that life should be portrayed as it really is, with both its ugly and beautiful aspects. Realists viewed nature as a force people often had to deal with, rather than as just a source of beauty.

Both romanticism and realism affected life during the 1800s. Literature, art, and music reflected both of these movements. As the nineteenth century drew to a close, realism became even more influential.

Literature Grew in the Nineteenth Century

During the 1800s, as more people were educated, the audience for books grew. Romanticism influenced much of the literature of the times. Short stories and poetry were popular with many readers. The romantic poems of Wordsworth, Byron, Keats, and Shelley were well known. These English poets were moved by the great events that touched their lives, including the French Revolution and the fight for Greek independence. Their feelings for these events found expression in their works. *Prometheus Unbound,* by Percy Bysshe Shelley, is a good example of this. William Wordsworth was another English poet of distinction. He wrote of the natural beauty that surrounded him. Both Shelley and Wordsworth wrote also about the sad state of the poor and the effect of the pursuit of wealth on society. In his poem *The World,* Wordsworth expresses his feelings as he writes, "The world is too much with us; late and soon/Getting and spending, we lay waste our powers. . . ."

Charles Dickens was one of the most important novelists of nineteenth-century England. His stories reflected the turn toward realism in literature, because he wrote about many of the reforms needed in society. As a child, Dickens himself had experienced poverty, and he wrote novels such as *Hard Times, David Copperfield,* and *Oliver Twist* to expose the hardships endured by orphans, child laborers, and the poor. Dickens also showed that poverty and cruelty often result in crime and delinquency.

As the century advanced, realism began to replace romanticism in literature. Victor Hugo wrote *Les Misérables,* a novel about the suffering of humanity, which was a bestseller. Hugo's importance in the nineteenth-century literature of realism was matched by Alexandre Dumas (doo MAH), Guy de Maupassant (de MOH peh sahn), and Honoré de Balzac (BAHL zak). Émile Zola (ZOH lah) was another literary giant. He was a newspaperman as well as a novelist. His celebrated newspaper article, "J'Accuse," helped reopen the Dreyfus Affair, which you will read about in Chapter 23.

Russian writers expanded the tradition of realism. *Crime and Punishment* by Fyodor Dostoevski (dos toh YEFF skee) and *War and Peace* by Leo Tolstoy (TOHL stoy) are among Russia's literary gifts to the world.

Music Developed in the Nineteenth Century

Many nineteenth-century composers wrote music in the romantic tradition. This music expressed strong emotions and freedom from the strict form of earlier music. Toward the end of the century, some composers broke away from romantic tradition and created new trends in music.

Because of the development of new instruments and techniques, some sounds could be more richly expressed. Also, because more people had the time to listen to good music, the number of orchestras and outstanding musicians increased.

One great European composer of the nineteenth century was Ludwig van Beethoven (BAY toh vehn), a German composer.

Beethoven wrote nine symphonies after developing a hearing problem that led to complete deafness. His Third Symphony praises freedom and liberty. The Sixth Symphony praises the beauties of nature—both romantic themes. All of Beethoven's music represents the move away from the classical forms of the 1700s. Beethoven's works also represent the move toward the less-structured, emotional themes of romanticism in the 1800s.

Other leaders of the romantic movement in music included Franz Schubert of Austria and Robert Schumann of Germany. Their songs and symphonies are lyrical melodies about love and other romantic themes. Among the brilliant pianists and composers of this musical period were Frederic Chopin (SHOH pahn) of Poland and Pyotr Tchaikovsky (chy KOF skee) of Russia. The stirring nationalistic story of the defeat of Napoleon and his troops in Russia is told in Tchaikovsky's famous *1812 Overture.*

Nineteenth-Century Artists Developed New Forms

Early in the 1800s, art, in the form of painting, sculpture, and architecture, reflected romantic themes. Artists developed more emotional styles and painted with new boldness and imagination. The French painter Eugene Delacroix (DELL a crwah) painted canvasses and murals in rich and lively colors. Many of his paintings are on display in Paris and in the library of Luxembourg. Honoré Daumier (doh MYAH), a cartoonist by profession, ridiculed middle-class life in his cartoons.

In the late 1800s, one group of painters turned from both romanticism and realism and began their own trend. The French are known for the Impressionist school of painting. These artists painted their impressions of what they saw around them. Edouard Manet (mah NAY), Pierre Renoir (rehn WAHR), Claude Monet (moh NAY), and Paul Cézanne (say ZAHN) were among the most famous of these painters. Rosa Bonheur (boh NURE) was a French painter whose pictures of horses and animal life brought her widespread fame.

Architecture Changed with New Technology

It is in architecture that the marriage of art and industry can best be seen. Industry developed new materials and used old materials in new ways. Iron and steel made it possible to build taller buildings. In the romantic tradition, the styles of Greek and Roman buildings were copied for structures such as libraries, railroad stations and other public buildings.

Steel, iron, brick, glass, and stone were used as construction materials in homes, schools, hospitals, libraries, and hotels. Louis Sullivan and Frank Lloyd Wright were pioneers in modern nineteenth and twentieth-century American architecture. They said that a good building design did not depend on decoration. Rather, a build-ing's location and purpose should determine its shape and the materials used to build it. If these were properly balanced, a beautiful building would be the result. The skyscrapers with which you are familiar are the result of this thinking in design.

The nineteenth century was one in which industrial and agricultural advances occurred almost daily. Scientific achievements and new forms of creative expression reflected these rapid changes. Many people were caught up in the excitement of the century and sought opportunities to express themselves and to have a say in the directions their community and their country were moving. It was inevitable, in such an environment, that the demand for democratic reform would grow.

▼ **Illustrating History** *The buildings of architect Louis Sullivan, like the one below, reflect his intent to have outward form reflect function, or use.*

Analyzing Statistics

Statistics provide us with useful information about historical trends. The patterns suggested by statistics, however, must be carefully analyzed, and their sources evaluated for reliability. The statistics also need to be verified by other forms of historical evidence.

Use the following steps to read and interpret the statistical data below.

1. **Determine the source of the statistics and decide if the source is reliable.** If a statistical source is reliable, the data will probably be a good source of historical information. Answer the following questions: (a) What is the source of the statistics below? (b) In your opinion, is the source reliable? (c) Based upon the source, can the data be used as historical evidence?

2. **Study the statistics to determine what information they provide.** Statistical data are often accompanied by explanatory material. Answer the following questions: (a) What do the data show? (b) What period of time does the data cover? (c) How does the explanatory note help organize the statistics?

3. **Analyze the data to determine historical trends or patterns that it may explain.** You may be able to use statistical data to draw conclusions. Answer the following questions: (a) In what way did the value of U.S. exports change between 1825 and 1840? Was the rate of change steady or uneven? (b) Was the U.S. balance of trade generally favorable or unfavorable between 1825 and 1840? (c) Use what you have learned in Chapter 22 to explain the trend shown by the statistics.

Value of United States Exports and Imports 1825–1840 (In millions of dollars)					
Year	Exports	Imports	Year	Exports	Imports
1825	100	96	1833	90	108
1826	78	85	1834	104	127
1827	82	79	1835	122	150
1828	72	89	1836	129	190
1829	72	74	1837	117	141
1830	74	71	1838	108	114
1831	81	103	1839	121	162
1832	87	101	1840	132	107

Source: U.S. Department of Commerce, Bureau of the Census

Notes:
1. *Trade Surplus* — When the annual value of goods sold to foreign countries (exports) is greater than the value of goods purchased from them (imports). This is a *favorable* balance of trade.
2. *Trade Deficit* — When the annual value of goods sold to foreign countries (exports) is less than the value of goods purchased from them (imports). This is an *unfavorable* balance of trade.

REVIEW

Section Summaries

Section 1 Revolutions in Industry and Agriculture Began As the demand for goods grew, business people needed faster methods of production. They found these methods through power-driven machines, which they brought together in factories. For many reasons, including its labor supply and natural resources, England was the birthplace of the Industrial Revolution. A series of inventions in England and America also helped speed up this revolution. Meanwhile, the growth of large-scale farms put many small farmers out of business, sending them to work in the new factories.

Section 2 Society Faced Complex Problems As the Industrial Revolution progressed, labor and trade replaced farming as the main creators of capital (money for investment). The corporation became the most important form of business. Successful business people made up a growing middle class and soon gained more power than the landowning aristocrats. As industry increased the nation's wealth, writers and business people urged that government leave businesses alone. Yet, the Industrial and Agricultural revolutions brought problems, also. Small farmers had difficulty staying in business. In cities, factory workers faced horrible working conditions and living conditions. Government did nothing to stop these hardships. Various groups arose, however, that believed that something should be done.

Section 3 Culture Reflected the Spirit of the Times Along with the great progress in industry came new ideas and discoveries in many other fields. Scientists learned about atoms and also studied the age of the earth. Darwin introduced the idea of evolution, and Herbert Spencer applied Darwin's ideas to society. Romanticism and realism became important movements in the arts. Poets wrote of nature and beauty, while some novelists described deep suffering. Music evolved, with new instruments and great composers. Many artistis painted romantic themes, while the Impressionists began their own trend. Architecture benefitted from the great advances of industry.

Key Facts

1. Use each vocabulary word in a sentence.
   - **a.** domestic system
   - **b.** factory system
   - **c.** corporation
   - **d.** dividend
   - **e.** labor union
   - **f.** socialism
   - **g.** communism
   - **h.** anarchism
   - **i.** atom
   - **j.** evolution
   - **k.** romanticism
   - **l.** realism
2. Identify and briefly explain the importance of the following names, places, or events.
   - **a.** Eli Whitney
   - **b.** Henry Bessemer
   - **c.** Robert Fulton
   - **d.** Cyrus McCormick
   - **e.** Thomas Malthus
   - **f.** Karl Marx
   - **g.** Charles Darwin
   - **h.** Charles Dickens
   - **i.** Ludwig van Beethoven
   - **j.** Eugene Delacroix

Main Ideas

1. List the conditions that made England the ideal place for the Industrial Revolution to begin.
2. List five important inventions of the Industrial Revolution.
3. What changes made up England's Agricultural Revolution?
4. What was life like for factory workers in the early days of the Industrial Revolution?
5. List five groups that proposed solutions to the problems of workers.
6. List three important scientific ideas of the nineteenth century.
7. Name one major nineteenth-century figure in each of these fields: literature, music, painting, architecture.

Developing Skill in Reading History

Study the names in each set below. Then write a sentence for each set describing what its three members have in common.
1. flying shuttle, spinning jenny, power loom
2. Adam Smith, Thomas Malthus, David Ricardo
3. John Stuart Mill, Karl Marx, Robert Owen
4. Victor Hugo, Fyodor Dostoevski, Leo Tolstoy

Using Social Studies Skills

Analyzing Statistics Read the following selection from *The Economic History of Europe* by Shepard Clough and Charles Cole. Then choose the correct answer for each question that follows.

From 1727 to 1845 there were 1,385 enclosure acts. . . . From 1700 to 1845 about 14,000,000 acres were enclosed—a quarter of the arable land in the country. In 1873, it is believed, 2,250 persons owned about half the land of England. . . .

1. The main idea of this selection is that, in England,
   a. agricultural prices rose.
   b. land was combined into large holdings.
   c. the free market affected agricultural changes.
2. The 1,385 enclosures mentioned took place over a period of
   a. 118 years.   b. 100 years.   c. 88 years.

Critical Thinking

1. **Drawing Inferences** Study the drawing at right of a London street scene during the 1800s. What can you infer about life among London's poor people then?
2. **Comparing Points of View** What was the basic disagreement between Adam Smith and John Stuart Mill?
3. **Determining Relevance** Evaluate the following statement. "Quite often, one major invention will lead directly to another, and that one to still another."

Focus on Writing

Writing a Narrative Paragraph

When you write a narrative paragraph, be sure to make the **sequence of events** clear. Read the following brief paragraph from Leo Tolstoy's novel, *War and Peace*. Then, list in chronological order each event the author describes.

All were silent. Tushin appeared in the doorway. He timidly made his way out from behind the generals that had crowded into the hut. Embarrassed as always at the sight of his superior officers, he did not notice the staff of the banner and stumbled over it. Several of the officers laughed.

Now, plan and write a narrative paragraph of your own.

The Age of Democratic Reform

(1815–1914)

▲ **Illustrating History**
During the early 1800s, the life of a worker was difficult and dangerous. Above, a woman from England breaks up iron ore.

1 Great Britain Reformed Its Government

2 France Became a Republic

3 Science and Education Improved Society

I t was hard work and often dangerous. The hours were long—generally 12 to 14 hours a day, 6 days a week. And the pay? Just a few cents an hour. Yet, no one complained, because the boss could always find another worker to take his or her place. This was the plight of millions of workers, many of them women and children, who toiled in the British mines and factories of the early 1800s.

Few factory or mine owners at the time gave much thought to the safety or well-being of their workers. Fire was a constant threat in the factories, as was becoming injured from unsafe machinery or being beaten by an angry foreman. Sickness was widespread. Factories could be cold, drafty places in winter and hot as ovens in summer. Conditions in the mines were even worse. There, women and children, harnessed like dogs, dragged heavy loads in and out of narrow tunnels.

The worker's life during the birth of the Industrial Revolution in England was so bleak that it could not continue without some basic changes. Eventually, reformers began asking for laws to improve the lives of British workers. The spirit of revolution in England also argued for making the politics of the nation more democratic. As you will see in this chapter, one result of factory life was a stronger middle class and a desire among workers to gain influence where it mattered—in Parliament.

1820	1870	1920

■ **1832**
British Parliament passes the Reform Bill

■ **1848**
Louis Napoleon rules Second French Republic; American suffragist movement begins

■ **1871**
Third French Republic begins

1895 ■
France imprisons Alfred Dreyfus

1921 ■
Ireland divides into Ulster and Irish Free State

▲ **Illustrating History** *This painting by John Ferguson Weir dramatizes the forging of a steel shaft by workers in a nineteenth-century factory.*

1 Great Britain Reformed Its Government

As you read, look for answers to these questions:

◆ How did the Reform Bill of 1832 bring democratic changes to Great Britain?
◆ What reforms improved the relationship between Ireland and Great Britain?
◆ What progress did women make in their struggle for equal rights?

> **Key Terms:** borough (defined on p. 536), absentee landlord (p. 538), home rule (p. 539), suffragist (p. 539)

During the revolutions of 1820, 1830, and 1848, people in many European countries tried to make their governments more dem-ocratic. They wanted the secret ballot, the right to read books and newspapers without censorship, the right to assemble, and the right to be represented by elected officials. These advances were slow in coming, but during the nineteenth century, new political reforms strengthened democracy in Great Britain and France. In this section, you will read about reforms in Great Britain. In the next section, you will read about reforms in France.

Great Britain Needed Political Reform

In the 1780s and early 1800s, democracy still had a long way to go in Great Britain. For the most part, only the rich could afford to serve as unpaid members of Parliament. Although members of the House of Com-mons were elected, members of the House of Lords were born to their posts. Further-more, only members of the Anglican church could serve in Parliament.

535

In order to vote, people had to own a certain amount of land. Thus, most people could not vote, and without the secret ballot, many people who could vote were afraid to vote for their choices. They were afraid their choices would displease their employers, who could fire them.

Representation in the House of Commons was based on voting districts that were called **boroughs** (BUHR ohz). The number of representatives from each borough had not changed in years, even when population had changed. With the coming of the Industrial Revolution, new cities, such as Leeds and Manchester, grew, but they were not represented by members in the House of Commons. Other districts that became smaller or disappeared altogether kept their representation in Parliament even though they no longer needed funding. These districts were called *rotten boroughs*.

Sometimes, a rich landlord, rather than the people who lived in a particular district, chose a representative. Because the landowner was said to have the district in his pocket, the name *pocket borough* was used to describe this kind of situation. Pocket and rotten boroughs made it possible for rich people to control Parliament.

Some People Recognized Threats to the Democratic System

Because a number of groups in England were calling for change, the news of riots and violence in France caused many people to fear that a revolution might happen in England. In some factories, desperate, displaced workers, known as *Luddites*, destroyed textile machines. (The term *Luddites* came from Lud, the family name of a man who first smashed factory equipment in protest.) The Luddites led an angry crowd of followers to London in 1816. The largest mass gathering occurred when about 60,000 workers gathered in protest at St. Peter's Field, near Manchester. Soldiers and police attacked the crowd and killed 11 protesters. In mocking reference to Britain's triumph at Waterloo, this event became known as the Peterloo Massacre.

With unrest growing in Britain, people who wanted changes were able to gather support for reforms. Liberal Tories, like the foreign minister George Canning, began to respond to the new industrialists. First, the bans were lifted on exporting skilled workers and new technology to foreign countries. Second, the Catholic Emancipation Act of 1829 lifted the ban on the participation of Catholics in most public offices and, at the same time, weakened the supremacy of the Church of England. Finally, the laws that made hundreds of crimes punishable by hanging were changed. It was no longer legal, for example, to hang people who stole food to feed their hungry families.

The Reform Bill of 1832 Was a Bold Democratic Advance

Public pressure and the resignations of several prime ministers finally forced the House of Lords and the king to pass the Reform Bill of 1832. Because the Reform Bill of 1832 met some of the demands of the middle and working classes, it marked a giant step in the growth of democracy in Britain.

The Reform Bill of 1832 took away from the nobles the power to run the government. It lowered the property qualifications for voting and so extended the right to vote to wealthy members of the middle class. These new voters included merchants, traders, bankers, factory owners, and mill owners. The Reform Bill of 1832 also did away with many of the rotten boroughs and gave the new industrial cities representatives in Parliament. With the passage of the Reform Bill of 1832, the leaders of industry became more important than the large landowners and nobles. This, in itself, was a great change. People in the cities became as influential as people in the country.

Because of the nonviolent way in which the Reform Bill of 1832 was passed, some historians say that England became more democratic by *evolution* rather than by *revolution*. In other words, Britain became more democratic through gradual change rather than quick, violent change.

Queen Victoria

Early on the morning of June 20, 1837, 18-year-old Victoria received some disturbing news. Her uncle, King William IV, had died in the night. Because he had no children, Victoria would now succeed him. All her life, she had prepared for this moment.

Three years after she was crowned, Victoria (shown right) married her cousin Albert, a German prince. The prince was a great help to Victoria, both as a political adviser and in the rearing of their nine children. After Albert's death in 1861, Victoria wore nothing but black for many years.

Victoria proved to be an effective ruler, with the aid of her capable prime ministers. Britain had carved out a vast colonial empire that made it the richest country on earth. At least one-fourth of the world's people bowed to Queen Victoria as their monarch. Through her steady leadership and concern for the public welfare, she restored the prestige of the throne and won the admiration of her subjects.

Queen Victoria's 63-year reign was the longest of any British ruler in history. She headed the British Empire at the height of its power and influence. Victoria so dominated the times in which she lived that the period of her reign is known as the Victorian Age. She died in 1901.

1. Why did Victoria succeed her uncle as Britain's monarch?
2. How was her marriage to Prince Albert significant?
3. What personal traits did Victoria bring to the challenge of her role as queen?

The Reform Bill of 1832 still left many people without the right to vote. Also, with industrial leaders controlling Parliament, many factory workers feared that future laws would favor owners. Thus, workers united to press for further changes. Under Queen Victoria, who took the throne in 1837, many of these changes would occur.

The Chartists Represented Workers

The workers outlined their demands in a petition known as a *charter*, or guarantee of right. The Chartists, as those who signed the charter were called, demanded that all men be given the right to vote and that voting be done by secret ballot. They wanted annual meetings of Parliament, salaries for members of Parliament (so poor people could serve), and the elimination of property qualifications for membership in Parliament.

These demands were not easily won. Parliament turned down the Chartist petitions again and again. By 1848, however, when there was real danger that England would face the same type of violence that was going on in France, the Chartists presented a so-called monster petition, which they claimed had over 5 million signatures. Although closer examination of the petition revealed about 2 million signatures, the demands of the Chartists were finally turned

Pankhurst Disappoints Her Father

Emmeline Pankhurst, the leader of British suffragists, claimed that her commitment stemmed from her childhood. In the following excerpt, she recalls an event from her childhood that shaped her personality.

❝My childhood was protected by love and a comfortable home. Yet, while still a very young child, I began . . . to feel that there was something lacking, even in my own home, some false conception of family relations, some incomplete deal. . . .

The answer to these puzzling questions came to me unexpectedly one night when I lay in my little bed waiting for sleep to overtake me. It was a custom of my father and mother to make the round of our bedrooms every night before going themselves to bed. When they entered my room that night I was still awake, but for some reason I chose to feign [fake] slumber. My father bent over me, shielding the candle flame with his big hand [and] I heard him say, somewhat sadly, 'What a pity she wasn't born a lad.'

My first hot impulse was to sit up in bed and protest that I didn't want to be a boy, but I lay still and heard my parents' footsteps pass on toward the next child's bed. I thought about my father's remark for many days afterward, but I think I never decided that I regretted my sex.❞

1. Explain how this incident could have strengthened Pankhurst's commitment to equality for women.
2. What can this story tell historians about the attitudes of English men and women who supported women's suffrage in the 1800s?

into law. These reforms became a standard for workers in other countries who wanted democratic reform.

More People Gained the Right to Vote in Britain

In mid-nineteenth century Britain, two major political parties, Conservative (Tory) and Liberal, were heirs to the old Tory-Whig system that you read about in Chapter 18. Landowners, clergy, and the military usually backed the Conservatives. Most industrialists, merchants, and secular, or nonreligious, groups supported the Liberals.

Both Conservatives and Liberals claimed credit for extending the right to vote. In 1867, the Conservatives, under Benjamin Disraeli (dihz RAY lee), passed a law that reduced the voting restrictions on city workers and allowed them to vote. In 1872, the Liberal party passed the secret ballot law, which made it possible to vote as one wished without fear or threat of losing one's job. In 1884, led by William Gladstone, the Liberal party further extended the right to vote. By 1918, all men had gained the right to vote, and so had women over 30. Ten years later, after a difficult struggle, all women over 21 had won the right to vote.

Britain Reformed Relations with Ireland

Relations between England and Ireland had been troubled for centuries. During the twelfth century, the English had invaded Ireland, and for hundreds of years thereafter, the Irish suffered under the heavy hand of English rule. Religious, economic, and political differences sowed the seeds of hatred between the two nations. As a result of the Reformation, England became officially Protestant, while Ireland remained Catholic. Until 1793, Catholics in England could not even vote for members of Parliament, and English Catholics were not allowed to hold public office until 1829.

To make matters worse, most of the land in Ireland was owned by wealthy English absentee landlords. **Absentee landlords** are owners of property who do not live on the property or care about it except as a source of rent. British absentee landlords sent harsh rent collectors to gather rents from their already poor Irish tenants. Starvation was sometimes widespread. In 1848, as a result of the failure of the potato crop, famine caused many Irish to emigrate to America to find better living conditions.

In matters of government, Ireland was ruled entirely from Great Britain. The Act of Union in 1801 dissolved the Irish Parliament, and the Irish had to send representatives to the British Parliament instead. In Parliament, however, Irish representatives had few chances to improve their people's conditions because they were outvoted by British members.

Because of these problems, the Irish decided to fight for laws that would help them. In 1869, when William Gladstone was prime minister of Great Britain, Parliament passed a law by which the Anglican Church of Ireland was no longer the official, or established, church of Ireland. As a result of this new law, Irish Catholics no longer had to pay taxes that supported the Anglican Church of Ireland.

In response to the demand by the Irish for more self-government, Gladstone supported, without success, a number of parliamentary bills that would have given the Irish **home rule,** the power to make their own laws on domestic affairs. Even in 1914, partly because of World War I, a bill for Irish home rule did not become law.

Sinn Fein and the Irish Free State. The delay in home rule made Irish nationalists angry and impatient. Sinn Fein (SHIN FAYN), which means "we ourselves," was an Irish nationalist movement begun in the late 1800s. By 1914, Sinn Fein had grown in numbers and political strength under the leadership of Eamon De Valera. The Sinn Fein took matters into its own hands and decided to fight for full independence, not just home rule. The methods of the Sinn Fein were violent, but they resulted in the creation of the Irish Free State, a self-governing dominion, in 1921. Some 28 years later, Ireland became the Republic of Ireland and left the Commonwealth.

British Women Won the Right to Vote

Political reforms in Great Britain also focused on voting rights for women. In the early 1900s, the suffragist movement in England grew stronger as more women demanded the right to vote. **Suffragists** were those people who worked toward winning the right to vote for others, especially women. Suffragists spoke on street corners, held parades and demonstrations, and attended sessions of Parliament. Finally, the government began to listen and extended limited voting rights in 1918 to women over 30 years of age. In 1928, as you have read, women in Great Britain were given the same voting rights as men.

SECTION 1 REVIEW

Knowing Key Terms, People, and Places
1. Define: **a.** borough **b.** absentee landlord **c.** home rule **d.** suffragist
2. Identify: **a.** Luddites **b.** Catholic Emancipation Act **c.** Chartists **d.** Sinn Fein

Reviewing Main Ideas
3. Who gained the most from the passage of the Reform Bill of 1832? Who lost the most?
4. How did the issues of religion and land ownership cause problems between England and Ireland?
5. Describe the suffragist movement in Great Britain in the early 1900s.

Critical Thinking
Analyzing Information
6. Nineteenth-century reforms in Great Britain are often described as evolutionary rather than revolutionary. Do you agree or disagree? Support your argument with clear examples from Great Britain's process of reform.

2 France Became a Republic

As you read, look for answers to these questions:

◆ Why was Louis Napoleon an unpopular leader?
◆ What events led to the Third French Republic?
◆ What was the significance of the Dreyfus Affair?

Key Terms: anti-Semitism (defined on p. 542)

When Louis Philippe was driven from office in 1848, Louis Napoleon was elected president of the Second French Republic. Louis Napoleon was the nephew of the great Napoleon Bonaparte. Louis Napoleon hoped to destroy the Second Republic and set himself up as Napoleon III, emperor of France. It was Louis Napoleon's dream to become as great as his uncle had been. Skillfully, Louis Napoleon sought help from both the aristocracy and the middle class. He won the support of ordinary men when he introduced universal male suffrage in France.

Louis Napoleon Changed the Republic into an Empire

As his uncle had done before him, Louis Napoleon asked the people of France to extend his term of office and to give him more power. This the people did, but Louis Napoleon was not satisfied. In 1852, in another vote, the voters of France made Louis Napoleon emperor. He was given the title Napoleon III, thereby falsely suggesting that he was the grandson of Napoleon I. Thus, Louis Napoleon turned the Second French Republic into an empire under his rule.

Napoleon III did not have an easy time as emperor. He faced too much opposition. Monarchists, or those who favor a monarchy, sought to seize power from him. The middle class felt that his policies should favor business and independent farmers, since these groups had supported his desire to be emperor. Catholics wanted him to work for the interests of the Catholic church. Napoleon tried to satisfy everyone and ended up satisfying no one. He did, however, begin projects to beautify Paris and, in doing so, offered employment to many workers. To encourage French industry, he built railroads and imposed tariffs on products coming into France. These changes, however, were little comfort to the people of France.

As emperor, Napoleon III destroyed democracy because there was no effective legislature to check his powers. There was no free press, and criticism of the emperor was forbidden. Those believed to be against the emperor could be imprisoned or even forced to leave the country. Under these conditions, the people grew restless, and some began to regret the decision to make Louis Napoleon emperor.

Louis Napoleon Tried to Expand the Second Empire

To keep the support of the French people, Louis Napoleon tried to restore France to its former glory in Europe. He took part in the Crimean War in which France and England fought Russia. As discussed earlier, that war was known best for its waste of lives. Napoleon III then turned to other countries to expand France's power.

In 1863, while the United States was fighting the Civil War, Napoleon III forced the president of Mexico, Benito Juárez (WHAR ehz), from office. Napoleon III then placed Maximilian of Austria and his Spanish-born wife, Carlotta, on the throne of Mexico.

When the Civil War ended, the United States immediately applied the principles of the Monroe Doctrine to the situation. The Monroe Doctrine, which had been issued by President Monroe in 1823, declared that the Americas were no longer open to European colonization and conquest. In support of the Monroe Doctrine, the United States sent troops to the Mexican border. Juárez was encouraged to overthrow Maximilian, and

▲ **Illustrating History** *In the above painting, Emperor Louis Napoleon (center) surveys a battle during the Franco-Prussian War.*

the United States threatened to invade Mexico. Maximilian, thoroughly disliked by Mexicans, was captured and killed. Juárez was reelected president of Mexico, and he served in that office from 1867 to 1872. When his actions in Mexico had been challenged, Napoleon III had not dared to send troops.

In other attempts to increase his empire, Napoleon III strengthened French rule in Algeria and established French control in Laos, Cambodia, and Vietnam. In 1859, Napoleon III began the construction of the Suez Canal. As discussed in Chapter 21, Napoleon III made his greatest mistake when he let himself be lured into the Franco-Prussian War by Bismarck. France's defeat led to the end of Napoleon III and the Second French Empire and the beginning of the Third French Republic.

Problems Plagued the Third French Republic

The Third French Republic began under unfavorable conditions. After France's defeat in the Franco-Prussian War, a new National Assembly was elected. Its first duty was to negotiate a peace treaty with Germany. Under the terms of the treaty, France was forced to give Germany an area known as Alsace-Lorraine, which included the province of Alsace and part of the province of Lorraine. It also had to pay Germany 1 billion dollars for war damages, and until the money was paid, the Germans would occupy France. The harshness of the treaty angered the French, who deeply resented the loss of Alsace-Lorraine.

In Paris, radicals working for fundamental social and economic changes were furious over the National Assembly's acceptance of the peace treaty. Because a majority of the National Assembly was monarchist, the radicals also feared the revival of a monarchy in France. In March 1871, they rose in revolt and set up a government called the Paris Commune.

Leaders of the Paris Commune demanded reforms such as lower prices, higher wages, and better working conditions. Although these demands were fairly moderate, the National Assembly sent troops to crush the commune. In a week-long battle, over 20,000 French men and women died. The uprising and its suppression created bitter

541

▲ **Illustrating History** *Alfred Dreyfus, falsely accused of stealing war secrets, was expelled from France's army in 1895.*

divisions between monarchists and republicans. These divisions threatened the stability of the Third Republic.

From time to time, there were other incidents that threatened to replace the Third Republic with a monarchy. For example, at one point, a flamboyant French general, Georges Boulanger (boo lahn ZHAY), tried to overthrow the Third Republic for the royalists.

A major scandal, known as the Dreyfus Affair, proved even more embarrassing to the Third Republic than Boulanger's attempt to overthrow the government. Someone was stealing secrets from the French war office and selling them to the Germans. Captain Alfred Dreyfus (DRAY fuhs), a Jew, was falsely accused. Captain Dreyfus was courtmartialed and found guilty, despite the fact that much of the evidence had been forged. On January 5, 1895, Captain Dreyfus was humiliated and degraded before a "guard of dishonor" in a ceremony at the École Militaire, the French military academy. His medals and ribbons were torn from his sleeve and tunic one by one, and his sword was broken. On January 17, 1895, Dreyfus was sent to prison on Devil's Island, a penal colony off the coast of French Guiana near South America.

While Dreyfus was on Devil's Island, there were those in France who sought justice for him. They did not want to see the Third Republic tarnished with the charge of **anti-Semitism,** or hatred of Jews. Further evidence made it clear that Dreyfus was innocent. The prominent French writer Émile Zola wrote a scathing article, entitled "J'Accuse," on the Dreyfus Affair. As a result, Zola himself was imprisoned for a year on the charge of libel, or writing falsely about someone. He had accused the General Staff of the French army of "illegalities, frauds, and judicial crimes." Zola's accusations and his own trial for libel seared the conscience of the French people.

Ferdinand Esterhazy, a French army officer, was charged with the crime, but at his trial, his fellow officers had him acquitted. In 1899, however, as the tide turned against him, he fled to England and confessed that he had stolen the military secrets and sold them to the Germans to pay his debts. Even with this confession, it was not until July 21, 1906, that Dreyfus was reinstated in the army. That justice was finally achieved in the Dreyfus case strengthened the parties that sought to secure republicanism in France.

SECTION 2 REVIEW

Knowing Key Terms, People, and Places
1. Define: **a.** anti-Semitism
2. Identify: **a.** Juárez **b.** Paris Commune **c.** Dreyfus

Reviewing Main Ideas
3. What events led to the downfall of the Second French Republic?
4. Explain why Louis Napoleon's empire failed.
5. How did the Dreyfus Affair reflect the weaknesses of the Third French Republic?

Critical Thinking
Making Comparisons
6. Compare the way political change occurred in England and France during the 1800s.

3 Science and Education Improved Society

As you read, look for answers to these questions:

◆ Why did living conditions improve for many people in the nineteenth century?
◆ What were the major advances in health and education of the nineteenth century?
◆ How did women gain rights in education?

Key Terms: immunization (defined on p. 544), pasteurization (p. 544)

If you had lived in Europe during the middle of the nineteenth century, you might have taken a trip to the Crystal Palace in London. The Crystal Palace, an engineering marvel of iron and glass, was opened to the public in May 1851. Thousands of visitors came to see the "Works of Industry of All Nations." The Crystal Palace was really a modern-day world's fair. It showed that nations were seeking a better world in the industrial age. The Industrial Revolution and the growth of democracy brought about a new period of improved living conditions for many people.

Population Increased and Cities Grew

After 1650, the world's population began to increase rapidly for many reasons. Medical advances made over the centuries helped people to live longer. In Europe, at least, improved housing and sewage disposal made it possible for people to live with less fear of plagues. In the nineteenth century, the Agricultural Revolution made growing more and better food possible, and improved methods of transportation allowed the food to be distributed more widely.

Along with the growth in population occurred the growth of cities. The expansion of industry and the development of railroads, which could serve the cities' needs, made this growth possible. Up to 1800, most people lived on farms or in rural areas. During the nineteenth century, this began to change rapidly. By 1851, more than half the people of Great Britain—50.8 percent—were living in urban, or city, areas. The growth of cities took place faster in Great Britain than in France or Germany.

Health Conditions Improved in the Nineteenth Century

With all its problems, the Industrial Revolution still opened the way to a cleaner and healthier life. Shipping food by railroads, roads, and steamships made it possible for many people to eat fresh meat and fruit for the first time. Improved farm machinery increased the amount of food that could be grown. Public sewerage and sanitary facilities made homes and cities cleaner places in which to live. As a result, people were healthier and lived longer. Fewer children

▼ **Graph Skill** *How many more years could a person born in 1910 expect to live than a person who was born in 1810?*

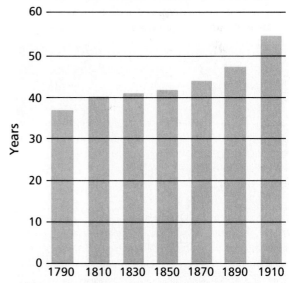

Life Expectancy (at birth) 1790–1910 in Northern and Western Europe

Sources: *Population and History*, E. A. Wrigley; *Before the Industrial Revolution*, C. M. Cipolla

died at birth or during infancy, and there were fewer epidemics of disease. Population grew due to the decrease in both disease and the death rate. Several major medical advances and discoveries helped to make this possible.

Edward Jenner, an English medical doctor, noticed that smallpox rarely occurred among milkmaids. This led to his discovery of the use of the cowpox virus as a vaccine to prevent smallpox. Before 1800, almost no family escaped smallpox. Jenner's vaccination showed that the disease could be prevented. When a patient is vaccinated, a small dose of a virus is given. By building up resistance, the body can fight off smallpox. The process of building up resistance to a disease is called **immunization.**

Today, adults and children are made immune to many diseases by vaccination. In Jenner's day, most people were afraid of being vaccinated. Not until the king and queen of England urged vaccination did it become common. From England, smallpox vaccine and the knowledge of vaccination spread to other parts of the world.

Louis Pasteur (pass TUHR), a French chemist and pioneer in medicine, found that bacteria caused many diseases. Bacteria are

▼ **Illustrating History** *Marie Curie, the chemist who discovered radium, won two Nobel prizes for her work.*

tiny living creatures that cannot be seen with the naked eye. Pasteur said that bacteria turned milk sour and made humans and animals ill. **Pasteurization,** a method of treating foods, especially milk, to make them safe for human consumption, kills bacteria through heat. Pasteur also showed people how to save farm animals from certain diseases and how to treat rabies.

Joseph Lister, an English surgeon, used Pasteur's discovery of bacteria to save his patients. Lister's patients did not get infections after operations because Lister used carbolic acid to keep his medical instruments and the wounds of his patients clean and free of bacteria. Dr. Lister became known as the founder of antiseptic surgery.

Others also took advantage of the pioneering work done by Pasteur. In 1876, Robert Koch, a German doctor, found that specific bacteria caused specific diseases. Koch identified the bacteria that caused anthrax, tuberculosis, cholera, and other diseases. In 1905, he was awarded the Nobel Prize for his work in developing a test to determine if a person has tuberculosis.

Marie Curie (KOO REE), a French chemist and physicist, made outstanding contributions to the field of medicine. She is best known for her work with radioactivity, including the discovery of radium. She was awarded two Nobel Prizes for her work.

Free Education Advanced

Up to the nineteenth century, there was little attempt on the part of governments to educate their people. As the right to vote was given to more people, it became obvious that the right to vote by itself was useless. In order for voters to make reasonable choices when it came to voting and to other decisions in their lives, illiteracy and ignorance had to be wiped out.

In Europe, education was readily available for the rich. For the most part, however, Europeans were slow to accept the idea that all people should be sent to school. In England, the first gift of public money for free schooling was made in 1832. It was not until 1870 that a national system of free

Playing to Learn

Imagine that it is a Monday morning in 1837. As you walk along a street in the German city of Blankenburg, you hear young voices coming from an old building. You stop to peek in a window. There, in a large, open room, groups of 3- to 7-year-olds are happily playing. "Why aren't these children in school?" you ask a passerby. "Oh, but they are," is the response. "They are in kindergarten."

In 1837, kindergarten, which means garden of children, was a new concept in education. At kindergarten, young children learned not through reading and writing, but through activities such as playing and drawing. (See photo at right.) The idea quickly spread across Germany and beyond. Within a few years, American children, too, were attending these "gardens."

1. What does the word *kindergarten* mean in English?
2. In what way was kindergarten a new idea in early childhood education?

public schools was born. Soon, all children from the ages of 5 to 14 were required by law to attend school. In France, the Ferry Laws of the 1880s provided free, compulsory education. In England, France, Germany, Belgium, the Netherlands, and the Scandinavian countries, free education gained a firm foothold in the late nineteenth century.

One of the outstanding figures in nineteenth-century education was Swiss educational reformer Johann Pestalozzi (PEHS tuh LOHT see). He taught that the ills of society could be improved through education. He also improved methods of teaching reading, writing, and arithmetic. Pestalozzi thought the teacher-pupil relationship should be one of love. This idea shocked many people because, in those days, teachers were expected to be harsh.

Johann Herbart, a German thinker and educator, learned from Pestalozzi and improved upon his methods. Herbart believed that a teacher should try to hold the attention of students through interesting subjects rather than through beatings. He felt that schools should develop good character traits among students.

Another German educator, Friedrich Froebel (FROO behl) may be looked upon as the founder of the kindergarten system. In kindergarten, children were taught through play that prepared them to learn the skills of reading and writing in higher grades.

Maria Montessori (MOHN tuh SOH ree), who lived from 1870 to 1952, was the first Italian woman to become a doctor. She earned fame, however, as a teacher who developed new ways of teaching very young children. Her ideas attracted a wide audience, and her methods are still widely used in Europe and the United States

America Pioneered Public Education

Thomas Jefferson once stated that if people expect to be ignorant and free in a state of civilization, they expect what has never been and never will be. For democracy to work well, people need education.

In the United States, the idea of free public education was adopted early in some parts of the country. This education was training in reading, writing, arithmetic, and religion. Nevertheless, education was open to all and free. In 1821, the first public high school in the United States was opened in Boston, Massachusetts. In 1837, Massachusetts organized the first state Board of Education. By 1860, most of the northern and western states had free public schooling.

John Dewey, an American who lived from 1859 to 1952, was one of the greatest of the educational pioneers. He developed the belief that students learn best by doing. He believed there should be close ties between the home, the school, and the neighborhood. He also believed that schools should teach students how to solve life's problems. Dewey's ideas have influenced education in nearly every country in the world.

Women Moved Toward Equality in Education

In America, Elizabeth Cady Stanton, who lived from 1815 to 1902, took the lead in fighting for the rights of women. She organized the first women's rights meetings. At the Seneca Falls Convention, which met in New York in 1848, women took a strong stand against the tyranny of men. The convention marked the beginning of the American suffragist movement. By 1919, women in the United States had won the right to vote and had opened at least some doors to educational opportunities.

Among the first victories of women in their struggles for equal rights was their admission to colleges and universities. In the United States, in 1833, Oberlin College admitted women as well as men. In 1836, Mount Holyoke College in Massachusetts became the first college for women in America. In 1847, Elizabeth Blackwell was admitted to the study of medicine in the United States. In Geneva, New York, the first women's medical college opened in 1865.

In Europe, the admission of women to higher education was somewhat slower. The University of Zurich, Switzerland, was one of the first to admit women. In 1866, the University of Paris admitted women and men students on an equal basis, as did Italian universities. In 1869, however, there were riots in Edinburgh, Scotland, when a small group of women was admitted to the study of medicine. Even as late as 1880, it was difficult for women to be admitted to many colleges and universities. It was not until 1919, for example, that England allowed women to become lawyers.

SECTION 3 REVIEW

Knowing Key Terms, People, and Places
1. Define: **a.** immunization **b.** pasteurization
2. Identify: **a.** Jenner **b.** Lister **c.** Pestalozzi **d.** Dewey

Focus on Geography
3. Explain how the shift of population from the country to the cities was a direct result of the Industrial Revolution.

Reviewing Main Ideas
4. How did Pasteur contribute to the improvement of health conditions?
5. How did the nature of the teacher-pupil relationship change because of educators such as Pestalozzi and Herbart?
6. What did Jefferson say about the need for education, and how was this reflected in public education in America?

Critical Thinking
Perceiving Cause and Effect
7. What do you think were the factors that caused such resistance to women receiving equal rights in voting and education?

Supporting Opinions with Facts

As we think or learn about issues, we form opinions about them. If we share our opinions with others, we need to support those opinions with facts. Use the following steps to practice supporting opinions with facts.

1. **Clarify your opinion on the subject.** Read the passage below about Robert Owen. Answer the following questions: (a) Do you agree with any of these opinions about Owen? If so, choose one you want to support with facts.
   1. *He was a dedicated person with ideas that still make sense.*
   2. *He had worthwhile goals, but he was unrealistic.*
   3. *His goals sounded good, but they would have had undesirable results.*

(b) If you don't agree with any of these opinions, what is your opinion of Owen?

2. **Decide which facts support your opinion.** Reread the passage and answer the following question: Which facts support your opinion of Owen?

3. **Determine whether you need more facts to support your opinion. If so, decide which questions those facts should answer.** Answer the following questions: (a) Does the passage provide you with enough facts to make a strong argument for your opinion? (b) If not, what else do you need to know that would strengthen your argument? Where might you look for this information?

Robert Owen, who lived from 1771 to 1858, was born to an ordinary family. At age 9, he left school to go to work as a cotton spinner. He rose to become part owner and head of an important cotton mill when he was only 20. During these years, Owen saw how factory workers—including children—were slaves to machines, subject to unhealthy conditions, long working hours, and low pay. Determined to establish justice, Owen reorganized his mill to be a model community. He paid the workers high wages and reduced their working hours. He built housing and company stores where workers could buy their necessities at low prices. Instead of putting children to work, he built schools for them to attend.

Owen tried to interest the British government in setting up "villages of cooperation." These communities would be part agricultural and part industrial, and people in them could produce everything they needed to live. But the government was not interested. In 1825, Owen went to America, where he set up a small cooperative community called New Harmony. There, everyone worked equally and shared equally in the profits. But, in two years, New Harmony failed, and Owen returned to England.

Owen continued campaigning for laws to protect workers and began working for the labor union movement. In 1833, he organized a union encompassing many industries and attracted more than 500,000 members. This giant union tried to reorganize British industry into cooperatives along the lines of New Harmony. But, the government and manufacturers resisted, and by 1834, the union had collapsed.

REVIEW

Section Summaries

Section 1 Great Britain Reformed Its Government Even in the early 1800s, rich and powerful landowners continued to control Britain's government. Some groups, like the Luddites, demanded change. Slowly, Parliament granted reforms. Although the Reform Bill of 1832 gave greater political power and representation to the middle class, Britain's workers still pressed for change. The Chartists demanded greater power for workers, including universal male suffrage and the secret ballot. Eventually, such demands became law. The vote was extended further, and by ·1928, all women over 21 could cast their ballots in Britain. Britain even worked to improve troubled relations with Ireland, granting self-government to the Irish Free State.

Section 2 France Became a Republic Louis Napoleon was president of the Second French Republic, but he persuaded voters to make him emperor. He became known as Napoleon III. Facing opposition from many sectors of French society, Napoleon III destroyed democracy and allowed no opposition. He hoped to win support by restoring French glory. Yet, he wasted French lives in the Crimean War and tried unsuccessfully to control Mexico. France's loss in the Franco-Prussian War ended his rule and brought in the Third French Republic. The Third Republic also had problems. It was forced to accept a harsh settlement to end the Franco-Prussian War. At home, the Third Republic violently crushed the Paris Commune, a group of radicals demanding change. The Republic also faced charges of anti-Semitism over the Dreyfus Affair.

Section 3 Science and Education Improved Society In spite of its problems, the Industrial Revolution improved living conditions for many people. Beginning around 1650, world population began to grow and great cities developed.

Better housing and sewerage lessened the chances of epidemics, and improved farming methods and transportation brought people more food. Health conditions improved as doctors learned to prevent or cure a number of diseases. Free public education also grew, in both Europe and America. In addition, women won the right to attend colleges and universities.

Key Facts

1. Use each vocabulary word in a sentence.
   a. borough
   b. absentee landlord
   c. home rule
   d. suffragist
   e. anti-Semitism
   f. immunization
   g. pasteurization
2. Identify and briefly explain the importance of the following names, places, or events.
   a. Reform Bill of 1832
   b. Benjamin Disraeli
   c. William Gladstone
   d. Sinn Fein
   e. Louis Napoleon
   f. Alfred Dreyfus
   g. Crystal Palace
   h. Louis Pasteur
   i. Marie Curie
   j. Maria Montessori
   k. John Dewey
   l. Elizabeth Cady Stanton

Main Ideas

1. List at least four reasons that explain why rich landowners were able to control Britain's government in the early 1800s.
2. Why was the Reform Bill of 1832 important to the advance of British democracy?
3. List the steps that the British government took in granting greater voting rights between 1867 and 1928.
4. Why did the Irish resent British rule?
5. What war ended the reign of Napoleon III?
6. What were the major problems of the Third French Republic?
7. List four important medical advances of the nineteenth century.

Developing Skill in Reading History

Read the following sentences and choose the best definition for each word in italics.

1. Some historians say that England became more democratic by *evolution* rather than by revolution.
   a. a gradual process of change
   b. quick, violent change
   c. orders of the monarch
2. In 1848, famine caused many Irish to *emigrate* to America to find better living conditions.
   a. borrow new ideas
   b. ask for financial aid
   c. leave one's native country
3. Captain Dreyfus was *courtmartialed* and found guilty of stealing military secrets.
   a. caught committing a crime
   b. tried in a military court
   c. put in prison
4. Today, adults and children are made immune to many diseases by *vaccination.*
   a. killing bacteria with heat
   b. cleaning medical instruments with acid
   c. giving the patient a small dose of the virus

Using Social Studies Skills

Understanding Chronological Order The time line below shows some important events from Chapter 23. Redraw the time line on a sheet of paper and add at least five more events from the chapter in their proper places.

Critical Thinking

1. **Supporting Opinions with Facts** Give two facts to support this conclusion: "During the 1800s, many people in Britain and France were restless for reform."
2. **Formulating Questions** Create a list of questions that a historian might ask to decide whether a certain nation in the 1800s was progressing toward democracy.
3. **Drawing Conclusions** Thomas Jefferson believed people could not be both free and ignorant in a civilization. In other words, a democracy needs educated citizens. Is this belief still true today? Explain.

Focus on Writing

Paraphrasing

When you **paraphrase,** you present a writer's (or speaker's) material in your own words. Your paraphrase should be approximately the same length as the original. In your paraphrase, provide the main idea of the original and all important **supporting details.** You should also try to keep the author's **tone,** or attitude, in mind. In addition, you should try to **simplify the wording** of the original whenever necessary. Write a paraphrase of the final paragraph in this chapter. The paragraph, which is on page 546, begins: "In Europe, the admission of women to higher education was somewhat slower. . . ."

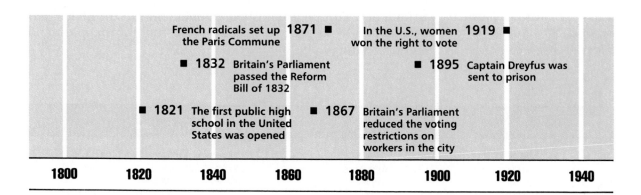

French radicals set up **1871** ■ the Paris Commune				In the U.S., women **1919** ■ won the right to vote			
■ **1832** Britain's Parliament passed the Reform Bill of 1832				■ **1895** Captain Dreyfus was sent to prison			
■ **1821** The first public high school in the United States was opened				■ **1867** Britain's Parliament reduced the voting restrictions on workers in the city			
1800	**1820**	**1840**	**1860**	**1880**	**1900**	**1920**	**1940**

Imperialism in Africa and Asia

(1700–1914)

1 Europeans Divided Africa into Colonies

2 British Imperialism Dominated India

3 European Imperialism Extended to Asia

I n 1900, a poster appeared on a wall in the Chinese city of Beijing. Those who pressed near to read the text found this message: "The rain does not fall. The ground has dried up. . . . The gods are angry, and the immortals vexed. . . . If you want to drive away the devils, it will not take much effort. Pull up the railway lines! Smash the great steamships!"

Anger at foreigners living in China had been building among the Chinese for some time. Beginning in 1899, groups of Chinese rebels calling themselves the Righteous and Harmonious Fists—known as Boxers by Westerners—attacked railroads, factories, shops, and Christian churches. To the Boxers, these symbolized the Western presence in China.

The Boxers wanted all foreign elements expelled from their country. In Beijing, the Boxers burned buildings and killed more than 240 foreigners. Finally, the foreign powers under attack—Britain, the United States, Japan, France, Russia, and Germany—sent a combined army to defeat the Boxers.

This clash, known to historians as the Boxer Rebellion, illustrates the conflict between new ideas and a traditional culture. Such conflict was only one dimension of imperialism at the turn of the century. In this chapter, you will learn how Great Britain and Europe established colonial empires in Africa and Asia, and the impact imperialism had on the peoples and cultures of these continents.

▲ **Illustrating History** *The Boxers formed a secret society of Chinese soldiers that tried, but failed, to rid China of foreigners.*

1775	1825	1875	1925

■ **1784**
India Act
expands
British
control
of India

1842 ■
Britain
controls
Hong Kong

1882 ■
Britain
occupies
Egypt

■ **1885**
Indian
National
Congress
forms

■ **1899**
Boer War
begins

■ **1910**
Japan occupies
Korea

▲ **Illustrating History** *The Boxer Rebellion in China in 1900 was a violent reaction against foreigners and the effects of imperialism.*

1 Europeans Divided Africa into Colonies

As you read, look for answers to these questions:

◆ Why was Africa so necessary to European interests?
◆ What was the impact of colonialism on Africa?
◆ How did imperialism affect relations between the European powers?

Key Terms: imperialism (defined on p. 551), paternalism (p. 554), assimilation (p. 554)

This is the first chapter in this book on **imperialism,** which is the domination of the political, economic, and cultural life of one country or region by another country. It is not, however, the first time you have read about it. Imperialism was at work when Egypt conquered its neighbors, when Alexander the Great conquered northern India, when Rome overpowered Carthage, and when Genghis Khan overran China.

During the Age of Discovery, which lasted from the fifteenth century to the seventeenth century, imperialism took the form of finding new lands, making converts to Christianity, and searching for precious metals. The old imperialism, as this is called, is sometimes called the search for gold, God, and glory.

There were several reasons for the new imperialism. Nationalism sparked the desire to build overseas empires. The new imperialism was also a result of the Industrial Revolution. With the production of more goods, nations looked for sources for raw materials from which to manufacture goods and for places to sell the goods they made.

551

Arrival of a White Man

In the late 1800s, Christian missionaries spread throughout Africa. They were the first whites many Africans had ever seen. The following excerpt describes the first visit by a missionary to a village in West Africa. The writer, Prince Modupe, was a young boy in the village.

"Everyone was abuzz about the expected arrival of the white man with the powerful juju [magic]. If his magic was more powerful than ours, then we must have it. That was Grandfather's decree. Grandfather wanted our people to have the best of everything. . . . There were a few other white, or nearly white things in our lives—cotton, white chickens, white cola [a bean], grubs [insect larvae] in rotten stumps, white ants. These seemed natural and everyday enough but a white human was beyond simple imagining.

As I listened to the wild speculation among the villagers, the image which formed in my mind was that of a white ant or a termite queen. . . .

Finally, the white man arrived. My first sight of him was a delightful relief. He did not appear to have demon quality and although his belly was large, it was not out of proportion to his head like the termite queen's. The only part of him that was much out of scale was his feet which were encased in leather."

1. Why did Modupe's grandfather want to meet the missionary?
2. What does this excerpt suggest about the attitude of Modupe's people toward European culture?

Cotton, coal, iron ore, oil, copper, rubber, tin, and uranium were among the raw materials sought and found in the lands beyond the European peninsula. Other reasons for the spread of imperialism were religious and humanitarian. Some Europeans and Christian missionaries were convinced that they could bring a better civilization to what they considered uncivilized areas.

As imperialism grew, Europe, the smallest of the continents, spread its cultures to nearly every part of the globe, as the map on pages 564 and 565 shows. A few Europeans ruled many of the world's people. Whether that rule was good or bad is something that you will have to judge as you read.

Geography Was a Factor in African Imperialism

During the Age of Discovery, Europeans rounded the southern tip of Africa, named it the Cape of Good Hope, and discovered an all-water route to India. Although northern Africa was well known to Europeans, southern Africa and the interior of Africa remained mysteries to them. So deep was European ignorance about Africa's interior that myths about the land and its people were widespread. Among the more famous myths was that of Prester John, whom Europeans believed ruled a vast African kingdom and was a model of what a good Christian king should be. The search for the legendary kingdom of Prester John encouraged exploration in the interior of Africa.

However, Africa was not easily explored. For one thing, while the part of Africa that bordered the Mediterranean Sea was familiar to Europeans, the Sahara Desert remained a formidable barrier that only the bravest of explorers would dare to cross. Moreover, much of Africa is located in the equatorial regions, tropical areas, where Europeans often caught tropical diseases and died.

Where the climate was attractive, for example, around the Cape of Good Hope, Dutch and, later, English settlers came to find new opportunities. The English and the Dutch would eventually clash with one another and with the Africans who lived there.

The Cape of Good Hope was a base from which the English tried to protect their interests in India. Because Africa had few good harbors, sending ships with colonists to settle and cargoes to trade was no easy task. The African rivers, the Nile, Congo, Zambezi, and Niger, offered the best hope for opening the interior of Africa to Europeans. The interior of Africa is a plateau. Because of the sharp drops at the edges of the plateaus, the rivers of Africa are subject to falls and rapids that make transportation and travel along the rivers extremely difficult. Nevertheless, finding the source of these rivers was the basis for the exploration of Africa. Exploring the interior of Africa depended on how far into the interior the rivers were navigable.

Africa Was Systematically Explored

It was not until the eighteenth century that Europeans, including the British, French, Belgians, Dutch, Scots, and Germans, began to explore the interior of Africa. Among the early European explorers of Africa was a Scot named James Bruce, who was one of many who looked for the source of the White Nile River. Later, African adventurers used his notes of his journey as a guide.

Alexandrine Tinne (tihn), a Dutch explorer, chose to devote her wealth and energy to geographic discovery in sub-Saharan Africa. She explored Central Africa, including the Nubian desert, and moved on to Khartoum in the Sudan. Later, she explored the unknown regions of the Nile.

The world learned about southern Africa largely through the work of David Livingstone and Henry M. Stanley. Livingstone was a Scottish doctor and missionary who went to Africa in 1840 to convert the Africans to Christianity. After returning to England briefly in 1864, Livingstone went back to Africa and remained there as an explorer as well as a preacher. Livingstone also wrote articles on the evils of slavery and helped to change opinions in England. As discussed in Chapter 16, many Africans were sent to the New World as slaves. (See the chart on page 555.)

Stanley traveled to Africa to find Dr. Livingstone at a time when many people feared that the doctor had died. Their famous

▼ **Illustrating History** *This colored engraving, done in 1872, shows the famous meeting of Stanley and Livingstone in Africa.*

meeting in November of 1871 is described with emotion by Stanley in his journal. Part of his account reads:

I . . . would have embraced him, only he, being an Englishmen, I did not know how he would receive me; so I did what moral cowardice and false pride suggested was the best thing —walked deliberately to him, took off my hat and said: "Dr. Livingstone, I presume." "Yes," says he, with a kind smile, lifting his cap slightly. I replace my hat on my head, and he puts on his cap and we both grasp hands and I then say aloud: "I thank God, Doctor, I have been permitted to see you!" He answered, "I feel thankful that I am here to welcome you!"

The explorations of Livingstone and Stanley widened world knowledge of Africa. The big nations of Europe, eager for new markets for their goods and new sources for raw materials, recklessly scrambled for African colonies. Germany, Italy, Belgium, England, and France, all joined the rush to claim colonies. The map on pages 564–565 shows the parts of Africa that had been claimed by European nations by 1914. By that time, 90 percent of Africa was controlled by foreign countries.

European Governments Controlled Their Colonies

There were two types of colonial governments used in Africa by the Europeans. These were *direct rule* and *indirect rule.*

Direct rule meant that the European nation controlled all levels of government. Direct rule reflected **paternalism,** meaning that the ruling European country felt itself superior to its colony and played a "parental" role that included strict control over all areas of life in the colony. Most of the nations that used direct rule followed a policy of **assimilation.** Under this policy, colonies were to be absorbed culturally and politically into the ruling nation.

Great Britain was the only European nation to exercise indirect rule in its colonies. Indirect rule allowed local rulers who were loyal to Britain to keep some limited power.

Their power, however, did not have any real impact on government decisions. A British governor and a council of advisers who made the laws ruled each colony.

European colonial rule upset traditional ways. As European language, culture, religion, and dress became symbols of "superiority," people in the colonized countries lost some of their own rich traditions and customs.

Life in the villages changed, for example, as some people left to become migrant workers for their European rulers. As you will read, greed led to even harsher abuses in the colonies as imperialism spread.

British Influence in Africa Grew

British imperialists at home dreamed of an "Africa British from the Cape to Cairo." Colonizers like Cecil Rhodes encouraged their ambitions. In South Africa, Rhodes, a British businessman, dreamed of building a railroad from the southern tip of Africa to Egypt, a Cape-to-Cairo railroad.

The Dutch had settled at Cape Colony as early as 1652. In 1815, however, the Congress of Vienna gave Cape Colony to the British. The Dutch farmers in South Africa who opposed British rule left Cape Colony in 1836. The Boers, as these farmers were called, traveled northward out of Cape Colony in ox-drawn wagons much like those used by the pioneers in the United States. This long journey was called the *Great Trek.* Once they had settled, the Boers established two independent Boer republics, known as the Transvaal and the Orange Free State. Here, they lived peacefully until the 1880s when gold and diamonds were discovered.

At that point, Cecil Rhodes, then prime minister of Cape Colony, decided to push for British control of all of South Africa, including the rich Boer republics. As tensions increased, the British made it clear that they intended to use their superior strength to overpower the weaker Boers.

The Boer War, which began in 1899, was won by the British. For three years, the Boers fought fiercely to protect what was theirs. Many Boers died in prison camps. Finally, the defeated people were forced to

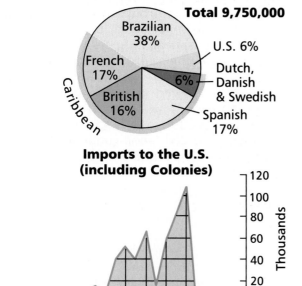

The Slave Trade
Imports to the New World, 1500–1870

Total 9,750,000

Brazilian 38%

U.S. 6%

French 17%

Dutch, Danish & Swedish 6%

British 16%

Caribbean

Spanish 17%

Imports to the U.S. (including Colonies)

Thousands

120
100
80
60
40
20
10

1620–'30   1701–'10   '21–'30   '61–'70   1801–'10   '41–'50

Source: *Time on the Cross (The Economics of American Slavery)* R.W. Fogel and S.L. Engerman

▲ **Chart Skill** *From 1500 to 1870, what percentage of Africans were imported as slaves to the country of Brazil?*

accept British rule. In 1910, the two countries of Transvaal and Orange Free State were joined with two other English colonies to form the Union of South Africa. Later, the Union of South Africa joined the British Commonwealth of Nations.

Britain Gained Control of the Suez Canal

During the nineteenth century, much of northern Africa was ruled by the Ottoman Turks. As you read in Chapter 21, the declining Ottoman Empire was nicknamed "the sick man of Europe." The rival powers of Europe were quite willing to nudge the weakened Ottomans out of northern Africa.

Until a French company completed the Suez Canal in 1869, most Europeans were not interested in Egypt. Once the Suez Canal was completed, however, the Mediterranean Sea, the Red Sea, and the Indian Ocean were connected, creating an important route between Europe and Asia. At first, Egyptians controlled the canal. However, years of wasteful spending caught up with Egypt's leaders and made it necessary to sell part of the canal for extra revenue, or income. In 1875, the Egyptian government sold shares of Suez Canal stock to Britain.

British control of Egypt. Although the revenue raised from the sale of Suez Canal stock helped for a while, Egypt's weak government was soon hopelessly in debt again. Britain used the situation to summon military forces to Egypt. In 1882, Britain occupied Egypt.

Once the Suez Canal was opened, the traveling distance between India and Europe was shortened. The canal made possible the shorter all-water route to the East that Europeans had been seeking for more than 300 years. This route became known as the *British lifeline*. Britain depended on it for the defense of its empire as well as its prosperity at home. Along this route, Britain owned strategic lands, including the Straits of Gibraltar. From the straits, Britain could attack any vessels that threatened its empire. Over this route traveled the raw materials needed by Britain's factories as well as goods manufactured in Britain. These goods were then sold in India and other countries of the East.

Under British control, Egypt paid off its foreign debts and built a dam at Aswan on the upper Nile. The dam improved agricultural production by supplying water for irrigation. However, Egyptian nationalists resented foreign control and particularly criticized the British for not paying attention to education and industry in Egypt.

The British in the Sudan. The British thought that they could control Egypt and the Suez Canal only if they also controlled the headwaters of the Nile in the Sudan. Not suprisingly, the Sudan did not want to be occupied by Britain and its old enemy, Egypt. For 16 years, Sudanese nationalists resisted British and Egyptian attempts to occupy their country. In one famous battle in 1885, the Sudanese army trapped and massacred the British and Egyptian forces in the capital city of Khartoum. Finally, in 1898, a combined force of British and Egyptian soldiers conquered the Sudan.

Meanwhile, French forces had reached the Sudan, and in what became known as the Fashoda Incident, British and French forces came face to face at Fashoda, nearly starting a full-fledged war. However, the crisis in France over the Dreyfus Affair, which was discussed in Chapter 23, forced the French to withdraw.

The French and British continued to be jealous of each other's influence in northern Africa. However, as the clouds of World War I approached, the two nations settled their differences.

Other Powers Gained Control in Africa

France controlled the northern and western areas of Africa. As early as 1830, the French had occupied Algeria. Later, French influence spread to Tunisia, Morocco, French West Africa, and French Equatorial Africa.

The Belgians gained control of a large part of the interior of Africa called the Congo. In 1878, King Leopold II of Belgium formed a company that used the natural resources of the Congo to make profits. When it was discovered how cruelly it had treated the Congolese people, the company was deprived of its rights and the Congo became a Belgian colony called the Belgian Congo.

Germany and Italy were among the last of the European nations to join the race for colonies in Africa. In 1912, after failing to conquer Ethiopia, Italy declared war on Turkey and seized Tripoli. During the years before 1914, Germany tried to get African colonies by befriending Turkey rather than by attacking that weakened empire.

Europeans Treated Africans Harshly

The Europeans treated the Africans harshly. African rulers were often cheated out of their wealth in minerals, farmlands, and other natural resources, such as rubber, by the Europeans. Many groups of Africans fought the European colonizers. The Zulu, for example, fought the Boers for years until the British stepped in and defeated the Zulu. Although African groups tried to hold off the forces of imperialism, in the end they lost to the Europeans' superior weapons.

European imperialists often forced the African peoples to work under inhuman conditions. Forced to work long hours, many Africans were beaten if they did not work hard enough to satisfy their European managers. Forced labor continued to exist in much of Africa until World War I.

After World War II, the cry to improve the workers' lives grew so loud that it could not be ignored. By this time, however, European efforts to provide better government, schools, hospitals, roads, and more healthful diets all came too late. One by one, the colonies overthrew their foreign governments and became independent nations.

SECTION 1 REVIEW

Knowing Key Terms, People, and Places
1. Define: **a.** imperialism **b.** paternalism **c.** assimilation
2. Identify: **a.** Cape of Good Hope **b.** David Livingstone and Henry Stanley **c.** Cecil Rhodes **d.** Boers **e.** Fashoda Incident

Focus on Geography
3. Why was Africa such a challenge to the first white explorers?

Reviewing Main Ideas
4. In what specific ways did the Suez Canal change trade routes in the nineteenth century? Explain why the British fiercely protected the canal.
5. Did imperialism improve or worsen living conditions for the Africans? Explain your answer with specific examples.

Critical Thinking
Recognizing Bias
6. What bias does the imperialist policy of "paternalism" represent?

2 British Imperialism Dominated India

As you read, look for answers to these questions:

◆ What was the British East India Company?
◆ Why did imperialism lead to revolt?
◆ How did imperialism change India?

Key Terms: sepoy (defined on p. 558)

Although most nations really wanted the wealth the colonies could bring them, some Europeans persuaded themselves that it was their duty to bring the knowledge of medicine, science, technology, and sanitation to those they believed to be "uncivilized." This attitude of superiority paved the way for discord between the ruler and the ruled. There may be no better place to explore the problems this attitude created than in the British conquest of India.

The British Won Control of India

For hundreds of years, strangers had invaded India. Most of them came from the northeast through the Khyber Pass and other mountain passes. In 1498, however, Vasco da Gama and his Portuguese ships rounded Africa and dropped anchor near the city of Calicut on the west coast of India. Britain's grip on India was based on its control of these two invasion routes.

To keep control of India, British settlers would have to get used to a new climate and learn how to rule a people quite different from themselves. In fact, fewer than 200,000 English men and women ruled hundreds of millions of Indians.

In the 1700s, as the once-powerful Mogul Empire collapsed, Britain and France both looked ambitiously toward India. The trading companies of these countries, along with those of other countries, competed for control of the profitable business in Indian goods such as silk, sugar, and cotton cloth.

The British East India Company was founded in 1600 by London merchants as a trading exchange for Indian goods. Making profits was not easy to do. For one thing, India was a long way from England. For another, since India was broken up into small, independent states, the company had to do business with many Indian princes. Sometimes, these princes would not give the company what it wanted. Without government control, the East India Company took it upon itself to do what it thought best. If the company wanted to increase its land holdings, it took over new land. If it decided to increase taxes or make war, it did these things, too. By taking these actions, the British East India Company slowly became the government of India. As the power of the company grew, it ran up against the growing power of the French.

The British and French were rivals all over the world. In a series of wars sometimes known as the Second Hundred Years' War, the British and French fought one

▼ **Illustrating History** *Britain's military strength in India is reflected in this painting of British troops at Red Fort.*

another for power in Europe, in the New World, and in India. The English were victorious over their French rivals in these wars, especially in India.

Robert Clive, a former clerk of the East India Company, organized the private army that finally drove the French out of India in 1757. As a result of this victory, rule by the East India Company was firmly established in eastern India.

The British East India Company Ruled India

By 1774, Warren Hastings had become governor of India. He tried to reform the government created by the East India Company, hoping to make it more efficient. He also wanted the Indian people treated more fairly. Hastings was responsible for a law that stopped the directors of the company from receiving gifts from princes and from carrying on private trade. Through these reforms, Hastings annoyed many prominent people. The British government ordered him to return home, where he was tried and found innocent of the charges against him.

When Great Britain lost its thirteen colonies in America, it tightened its grip on its colonies in India. A new law, called the *India Act*, gave the British government a greater voice in the affairs of India. Before the India Act, the East India Company was the final authority in India. That authority, without fear of having to answer for its actions, had often been harsh and unfair to the people of India.

Lord Cornwallis, who had been defeated by George Washington at the Battle of Yorktown, was appointed governor of India from 1786 to 1793 and again in 1805. He was the first governor to serve under the India Act. Under Cornwallis and the new law, the Indian people were more fairly treated. There was some consideration given to their welfare and interest. Despite Cornwallis's efforts, there were many wars with different groups of Indian people. Since the British were always victorious, their influence in India grew. Slowly, Great Britain gained control of the entire country.

Britain Gained Complete Control of India

By 1857, there was little question that the British had won India. They had done so because they had sent governors to India, and used Indian soldiers, known as **sepoys** (SEE poys), in their armies. These sepoys proved their loyalty to Great Britain.

In 1857, however, the great Sepoy Mutiny took place. This marked a turning point in Britain's relations with India. As British influence spread in India, the Hindus and the Muslims grew uneasy. Their traditional way of life was changing as the British pushed for adoption of European customs. For example, suttee, the practice of burning a widow on her dead husband's funeral pyre, had been made illegal by the British. The British also ignored part of the caste system in India as they created new jobs. Many of the new jobs in factories, offices, and on ships did not please the Indian people. In some areas, peasants were forced to pay high taxes, and small landowners were denied their traditional hereditary rights to their land. These were some of the causes for revolt.

The immediate cause of the Sepoy Mutiny was rooted in religious beliefs. The British had given the sepoys a new type of bullet, which had to be bitten before it could be used. A rumor spread that the grease on the bullet came from a pig or cow. If the grease came from a pig, the religious beliefs of the Muslims were violated because practicing Muslims are not permitted to eat pork. If it came from a cow, the religious beliefs of the Hindus were violated because the cow was a sacred animal to Hindus. Mutiny broke out among the sepoys, and the fighting spread to many parts of India. Although the mutiny was stopped after several months of fighting, ill feelings among Muslims, Hindus, and the English increased.

The Sepoy Mutiny awoke Parliament to its responsibility. The rule of an empire could not be left to a trading company. In 1858, Parliament ended the powers of the East India Company in India. In 1877, Queen Victoria became Empress of India.

When Cultures Clash

Imagine if someone decided to turn the Lincoln Memorial in Washington, D.C., into a video arcade. Americans would be horrified. Yet, this resembles the neglect of a sacred monument in India under British rule. (See photo at right.)

You have read how Shah Jahan built the Taj Mahal as a memorial and tomb for his beloved wife. During the late 1800s, the Taj Mahal became a favorite site among the British for open-air balls and dances. Party-goers often arrived with hammers and chisels in hand, prepared to chip off souvenirs. Mosques on either side of the Taj Mahal were turned into honeymoon cottages for rent. Not all who showed disrespect for the Taj Mahal were British. Indians sometimes held fairs and picnics at the Taj Mahal. In time, however, appreciation took the place of neglect. Led by a British lord, work began in the early 1900s to restore the Taj Mahal to the improved condition it is in today.

1. How was the Taj Mahal treated by the British?
2. Why do you suppose that the British showed so little respect for the Taj Mahal?

British Rule Helped and Hurt India

The British could point to many improvements in India. They built new roads, railroads, schools, and hospitals. They improved the postal system and constructed telephone and telegraph lines. However, the benefits that the British brought to India were not without a price. This price was high enough to make the Indian people question the values of European civilization.

Under the East India Company, taxes were so heavy that people tried to flee to those parts of India that were not under control of the company. Will Durant, an American historian, has this to say about the rule of the East India Company over the people of India, "They had been accustomed to live under tyranny, but never under tyranny like this."

Under the British crown, or government, the people of India fared slightly better, but their problems continued to mount. Although the British built and ran schools, soon there were too many educated Indians for whom there was no work. Unemployment brought discontent to the educated class. This discontent and the other problems created by colonial rule finally led to open revolt.

The new schools in India were modeled after those in Britain. The subjects taught were important to the British, but they were not as meaningful to most Indians. Subjects included British history and language, science, and arithmetic. Schools taught the culture of Britain, not the culture of India. There were many Indians who felt that their own culture was disappearing under the British system of education. English, the

▲ **Illustrating History** *In this painting, Indians escort an important British official with great style and ceremony.*

language of the schools, also became the language used by Indian government officials and the educated classes. Their use of English set them apart from their fellow Indians and aroused growing resentment against them.

The economic policies of the British also brought many negative results. The British encouraged Indian farmers to switch from growing food to growing cotton. This helped the British, who turned the cotton into cloth and sold it back to the Indians. The Indians, however, suffered because their food supply could not keep pace with their population. Many famines swept India. In fact, it is estimated that between 1800 and 1900 over 30 million Indians died of starvation. Changes in the economy also led to the loss of small local handicraft industries in India because Britain imported and used its own manufactured goods.

The British who came to India tried to do what they thought was right in managing Indian affairs, but they did not mix with the Indian people. In their daily lives they sought the company of other English people and did not learn Indian customs. This, too, caused ill feeling. Most English people in India made the Indians feel that they were inferior. The British lived well, while most of the Indians lived in poverty. The British were Christians; the Indians were Muslims or Hindus. The British were the rulers; the Indians were the ruled. The British were the

owners; the Indians were the servants. The Indians could not help resenting the differences between themselves and the British and the ways the British tried to devalue the ancient Indian cultures.

SECTION 2 REVIEW

Knowing Key Terms, People, and Places
1. Define: **a.** sepoy
2. Identify: **a.** British East India Company **b.** Robert Clive **c.** Warren Hastings **d.** Sepoy Mutiny

Focus on Geography
3. Identify India's two invasion routes and explain why they were so important to Britain.

Reviewing Main Ideas
4. How did the British East India Company act like a government?
5. What was the attitude of the British toward the Indian people and how did this affect relations between them?

Critical Thinking
Predicting Consequences
6. Britain was proud enough to call India her "crown jewel." But, Indian nationalists thought otherwise. Show how and why revolt against imperialism was inevitable in India.

560

3 European Imperialism Extended to Asia

As you read, look for answers to these questions:

◆ Why was China so isolated until the nineteenth century?
◆ How did imperialism break down Chinese isolation?
◆ How did China and Japan differ in their attitudes to the West?

Key Terms: extraterritoriality (defined on p. 562)

Marco Polo's journey in 1225 marked the beginning of foreign visits to China. The Portuguese, Dutch, French, and English were later joined by the Russians, Germans, Americans, and Japanese. By 1644, the Europeans were knocking at the doors of China, but the Chinese did not allow them to enter. From the fourteenth century to the seventeenth century, the Ming dynasty successfully fought European advances. Under the Manchus, however, the Chinese were less successful in holding back the foreigners. The European invasion that started as a trickle soon became a flood.

Geography Was a Factor in European Imperialism in China

China, like India, is a land with a vast population and a long history. Because of its size, it was never really possible to conquer the country. Moreover, by the time Europeans became interested in China, the United States had become a factor in competition for influence in China. It was not in the interest of the United States to allow China to be conquered by any one nation, because this might end or restrict trade.

While China had a civilization centuries old, its natural resources, including coal, iron, copper, and other metals, remained undeveloped. It was then, as it remains today, an enormous country that made up nearly one-fourth of the Asian land mass. Greater China is larger than the continental United States and Mexico. Yet, most of its people live on the coast. Its huge population was the target of Europeans who thirsted after the market that so many millions of people would create.

Europeans Gained a Foothold in China

Europe wanted a great deal from China, including silks, porcelain, tea, and spices. There was nothing, however, that China wanted from Europe. The goods of Europe, including coal, road rails, pig lead, firewood, ironware, and tin trays, were not attractive to the Chinese. Nevertheless, Europe kept trying to develop trade relations. In time, China signed a series of formal treaties and trade agreements.

The British took the lead in bringing about changes. More Chinese seaports were opened for trade with Britain. While the British wanted to be treated as equals by the Chinese, they also wanted to be tried under their own laws rather than Chinese law if they were accused of crimes in China.

What the British were determined to have, other European countries also wanted. To them, these demands seemed reasonable. To the Chinese, they could not be granted without "loss of face," or loss of honor or self-respect. The British, however, were determined to have their way in China. The First Opium War, which lasted from 1830 to 1842, was a struggle to decide whether the British would have their way.

The Opium Wars Forced China to Trade

Opium is a habit-forming drug. In the nineteenth century, opium was grown in poppy fields in India and then used by the British to trade with the Chinese. The Manchu emperor had ordered the opium trade stopped. Foreign and Chinese merchants alike ignored the emperor's ruling.

Lin Ze Xu (lihn tseh shoo), the Chinese governor-general at Canton, was determined to carry out the emperor's wishes. To do so, Lin Ze Xu destroyed the foreign opium. Thousands of chests of the narcotic were burned in Canton in 1839.

Unfortunately, Lin was not speaking for the Chinese who wanted opium and for the British who were determined to sell it. The British government became involved in the matter, and British warships were sent to Canton and Nanking. War broke out between China and Britain.

In 1842, the British won the First Opium War. The Treaty of Nanking, which ended the war, gave the island of Hong Kong to Great Britain and forced the Chinese to open more ports for trade. The Chinese also granted **extraterritoriality,** the right of a British citizen accused of a crime to be tried under British law, not Chinese law. The first Opium War was followed by a Second Opium War, which lasted from 1856 to 1860 with similar results. Still more ports were opened to European trade and it became legal to import opium into China.

The Opium Wars were a turning point in Chinese history. They proved that China was no match for the modern power of Europe. The foreigners, having won many privileges, would try to win even more.

The Manchu Dynasty Resisted Change

China's defeats meant that the emperor and the Chinese people had "lost face," or honor, and some Chinese were determined to do something about it. At the same time, China's problems were growing worse. The people of China needed a leader to show them how to solve their problems.

The Taiping Rebellion. Hong Xiu Chuan (hung shu chwan) proved to be such a leader. Believing he was related to Jesus, Hong gathered an army of followers. From 1850 to 1864, they made many successful attacks against the Chinese government. Once the government was overthrown, Hong planned to set up a new dynasty to be known as Taiping (ty ping), or Great Peace. Eventually, Hong and his followers were defeated by the armies of the Manchu.

The Taiping Rebellion started a debate in China. Some Chinese demanded that China adopt Western ways, while others demanded that China resist change. The emperor did not know which side to support.

From 1861 to 1908, China was governed by Empress Ci Xi (TSHER shee). In the years after the Taiping Rebellion, Ci Xi usually sided with the people who wanted to resist change. Because of Ci Xi's unwillingness to accept change, China had to wait many years before reforms were made.

Foreign Powers Mistreated China

In spite of some efforts to modernize, China remained a sleeping giant that was easy to attack. In 1895, Japan defeated China in the Sino-Japanese War. As a result of this war, China gave Formosa, known today as Taiwan (TY WAHN), to Japan. Because China was easily defeated by Japan, other nations felt that they too could defeat China.

Because Russia, Germany, Great Britain, France, and Portugal had helped to arrange the peace with Japan, they expected payment from China. These countries persuaded the Chinese to grant long-term leases on the various ports in which they alone had the right to do business. Getting these leases was a first step toward the actual division of China by some of the great powers. Because the great powers had planned the division of China without consulting the United States, the United States opposed the division of China and the plan failed.

As a result of its victory in the Spanish-American War, the United States took over the Philippines from Spain and became a power in the East. In 1899, to prevent the division of China, John Hay, the American secretary of state, proposed what came to be known as the Open Door Policy. This policy tried to make the European powers agree to leave China open to the trade of all nations. Although Great Britain encouraged the Open Door Policy, other nations only mildly supported it. In 1941, America was forced to fight with Japan, in part, over the ideas in the Open Door Policy.

The Boxer Rebellion Weakened China

During the debate over the need for reform, a Chinese author wrote a book called *Learn*. In it, he suggested that China could learn something from Western ideas. Emperor

Ci Xi

Ci Xi (TSEHR shee), the Dowager Empress of China, shown at right, once said, "I have often thought that I am the cleverest woman who ever lived and that others cannot compare with me . . . I have 400 million people all dependent on my judgment." Ci Xi was clever. And through her cleverness, she became the most powerful woman in China in the late 1800s.

Born in 1835, Ci Xi arrived at the emperor's court when she was 16. She soon rose to power as the mother of the emperor's only son. When the emperor died, she put her son on the throne. Her intelligence and strong personality gave her control over the weak emperors who came to power, including her son and her nephew. For nearly 50 years, Ci Xi ruled China from behind the scenes.

Ci Xi was an unwilling reformer. At first, she did not encourage social and political changes. But, she came to realize that without change, China might be completely taken over by foreign powers. She began by modernizing China's civil service and removing many Europeans from high office. She also opened schools to girls and abolished the binding of girls' feet.

The Dowager Empress died in 1908. Three years after her death, the Chinese monarchy came to an end.

1. How did Ci Xi rise to a position of power?
2. What reforms did Ci Xi begin?

Kuang Hsu seemed to favor reform and issued orders that ended some outworn Chinese customs. He also thought that the Confucian examinations for civil service should be stopped and that schools and railroads should be built. He began to strengthen the army and navy. Although Emperor Kuang Hsu tried to make reforms, Empress Ci Xi, did not want China to change.

The people who favored the empress's position were called the Boxers. Encouraged by her, they blamed China's difficulties on the presence of foreigners. In a violent uprising that promised "death to the foreigners," the Boxers tried to rid China of its "foreign devils." Over 240 foreigners were slaughtered.

The Boxer Rebellion, which took place from 1900 to 1903, angered the British, French, Germans, and Americans. These countries sent troops to China to put down the rebellion. The Boxers were defeated, but China was forced to pay for the ill-planned rebellion, and the emperor and empress were forced to flee. China had to agree to Western terms for peace. The terms included payment for war costs, lowering of tariffs, and protection of diplomats.

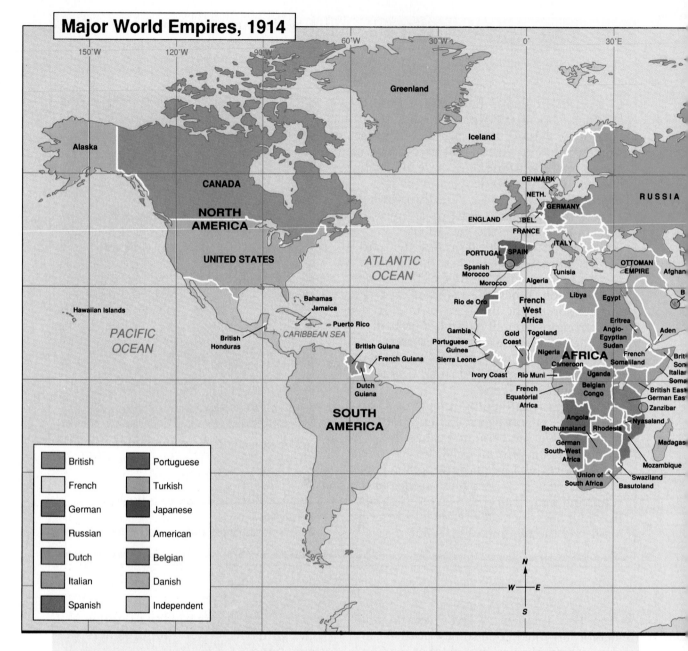

Major World Empires, 1914

Focus on Geography

1. **Location** On what two islands was the Danish empire located?
2. **Place** What European power ruled most of India?
3. **Regions** What European power controlled the largest region in Africa?

China's punishment for the Boxer Rebellion was severe. The fact that China was not further divided at this time was due to America's insistence upon the Open Door Policy. The United States used the money it received from the Chinese government for war damages to pay for the education of Chinese youths living in the United States.

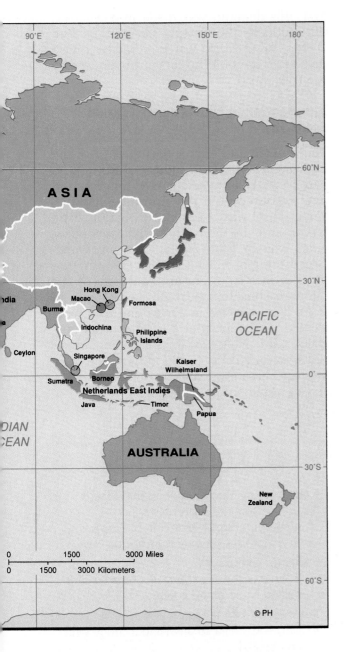

asking that American sailors be protected when lost at sea or shipwrecked. He also requested that one or two ports be opened for trade. In 1857, Townsend Harris became United States consul general in Japan. He persuaded the Japanese to open more ports to American trade. Again, foreigners received the privilege of extraterritoriality.

Japan and Korea Were Forced to End Their Isolation

The arrival of foreigners in Japan touched off a disagreement between those Japanese who favored learning Western ways and those who wanted to follow traditional ways. After a struggle, the side that felt that Japan should be agreeable to Western diplomats and their ideas was successful. Soon, the government under a military leader, called the shogun, ended. Emperor Mutsuhito (moo tsoo hee toh) became the ruler of Japan in fact as well as in name. After 700 years, the old feudal military government had ended and, while China was still debating whether or not to keep Westerners out, Japan chose the West as its model to copy.

On the farms and in the cities important changes were beginning to take place. The Japanese were quick to buy and use the machines the West had to sell. New factories went up, seemingly overnight. Ships flying Japanese flags crossed the seas. During this period, the needs of the economy and the needs of the army were uppermost in the minds of Japanese leaders as they rebuilt their nation. It would not be long before a strong Japan would challenge China, Russia, and the United States.

The West had little to do with Korea until the nineteenth century, when it tried to open Korea to trade. British, French, Russian, and American efforts failed, but the efforts of Japan were successful. Three times Japan tried to bring Korea under its rule. The Sino-Japanese War was one attempt, and the Russo-Japanese War was another. Finally, on August 22, 1910, the Japanese took over Korea. The Koreans called this day of their defeat "National Humiliation Day."

European Powers Extended Their Control in Asia

Commodore Perry's arrival in Japan in 1853 marks the beginning of the end of ancient Japan and Korea. Japan was another country in which change was discouraged, but it soon became eager to adopt Western ways. In the eyes of the Japanese, Perry's steamships were objects of wonder. Perry presented a letter from the American president

Although Japan built industry, railroads, highways, and farms, it gave the Koreans little voice in their government and little freedom. Japanese became the language of the schools. The Koreans kept hoping that one day they would become independent again. During the years between World War I and World War II, the Koreans worked hard to make their dreams of independence come true. In 1945, when World War II ended, Korea finally became independent.

Europeans Came to Dominate Southeast Asia

The Malay Peninsula is about the same size as Florida and occupies a very important geographical position. The shortest water route from Europe to the Far East passes the southern end of the Malay Peninsula.

In 1819, Britain gained the port of Singapore at the southern end of the Malay Peninsula. Because they possessed this small island city, the British were able to hold on to the Malay Peninsula until well into the twentieth century.

In the struggle to gain empires, the Dutch proved to be the strongest in the East Indies. The Dutch East India Company, like the British East India Company, was for a time the government of the East Indies. Over time, the Dutch East India Company became more interested in making profits than in looking after the welfare of the people it ruled. In 1798, the Dutch government took over the East Indies from the East India Company. In 1811, however, as a result of the Napoleonic Wars, the East Indies were temporarily given to the British. When the wars with Napoleon were over, they were returned to the Dutch.

The Dutch government encouraged private business firms to develop tea, tin, and rubber industries in the East Indies. These industries became vital to the East Indies, to the Dutch, and to the people of the world. While they brought the Dutch great wealth, only some of it was used to improve living conditions on the islands. These improvements came too late and were too few. The island people demanded independence. At

first, this demand was made in a whisper, but gradually the whisper became a shout. By the end of World War II, it had become a demand that could no longer be ignored by the free world.

Independence Movements Gained Strength

The nineteenth century was the age of the new imperialism. The Industrial Revolution had created the need for new markets and new resources for the European powers. Imperialism was also fueled by nationalistic fervor and the conviction that the European way of life was best for everyone. Greed brought out fierce rivalries between the European powers and was one of the main reasons for the outbreak of war in 1914. The colonies in Africa and Asia were treated insensitively at best and often governed with cruelty. At the same time, imperialism brought European ideas to the colonies and created a sense of national pride among some colonial peoples.

SECTION 3 REVIEW

Knowing Key Terms, People, and Places
1. Define: **a.** extraterritoriality
2. Identify: **a.** Boxer Rebellion **b.** Empress Ci Xi **c.** Korea's National Humiliation Day

Focus on Geography
3. Why was the mainland of China so difficult to explore and conquer?

Reviewing Main Ideas
4. Why was China so unwilling to trade with Europeans?
5. How did Britain, and the other European powers, break down Chinese resistance?

Critical Thinking
Making Comparisons
6. Compare the different ways in which China and Japan dealt with European interference in their internal affairs. How did these differences affect the subsequent histories of China and Japan?

SKILLS NOTEBOOK
Recognizing Bias

When you study history or any other social science, it is important to be on guard for signs of bias in what you read. *Bias* is a general term meaning an unfair or one-sided presentation of an issue, event, or person. A piece of writing may be biased because it appeals only to readers' emotions and not to their reason. It may be biased because it offers only a partial view of its subject, while suggesting it is a full view. Or it may be biased because it implies—but does not state openly—things that are not valid.

The following questions will help you determine if something you read is biased. Follow these steps to see if each of the six statements in the box below is biased.

1. **Does the statement have connotations, either positive or negative, that may be unjustified?** It is not necessarily wrong for writing to contain connotations. The question is whether they are justified or backed up by evidence. Answer the following question: What words or phrases in Statement 5 have negative connotations?

2. **Does the statement present only one side of an issue, while suggesting it is a full view?** Answer this question: Which statement—4 or 6—presents only one side of an issue?

3. **Does the statement consist mostly of opinions with little supporting evidence?** Answer this question: Which statement contains mostly opinions?

4. **Does the statement contain hidden assumptions, or implied beliefs, that are not justified?** Answer this question: What are the hidden assumptions in Statements 1 and 4?

5. **Determine if the statement is free of bias.** Which two statements below are mostly free of bias?

Statement

1. Because India had little culture of its own, the English colonizers rarely doubted that they were right in trying to dominate all aspects of Indian life.

2. The British were wrong to resist Indian attempts to become independent. The Indians were brave and right to insist they had a right to be free of British domination.

3. Westerners were eager to have Chinese silk, pottery, and tea. But China was not interested in anything that Westerners could offer in exchange—except silver.

4. How can we criticize imperialism and argue that it is unjust? It is as old as human history; it has taken place on every continent on earth. Westerners have ruled Easterners, and vice versa. Northerners have ruled Southerners, and vice versa. Is it then not foolish moralism, blind to human reality, to insist that imperialism should be wiped out?

5. In the late nineteenth century, as the Chinese empire reeled from years of rebellions and a lost war, several Western nations rushed in like hungry jackals, eager to snatch any valuable morsel they could find to keep for themselves.

6. National rivalry was an important factor in the growth of imperialism. When one imperialist country acquired a new colony, the other colonizing countries were spurred on to do the same thing.

REVIEW

Section Summaries

Section 1 Europeans Divided Africa into Colonies As a result of the Industrial Revolution, a new imperialism developed among European powers, sparked by the nationalist desire to build empires and by the need for raw materials. Africa was a major focus of this new imperialism. A scramble for colonies came with knowledge of Africa. Europeans faced heat, disease, and geographical barriers to explore this vast continent. By 1914, most of the continent was under foreign rule. Britain gained control of southern Africa, Egypt, and the Sudan. France, Belgium, Germany, and Italy controlled other parts of Africa. In pursuit of the continent's valuable resources, the Europeans treated their African subjects harshly. As a result, Africans began to demand freedom.

Section 2 British Imperialism Dominated India Britain won control of India through the British East India Company. This group of merchants did whatever it wanted in order to do business in India. The company took over lands, made war, and collected taxes. Soon the company's private army drove the French out. The British East India Company thus became the true government of most of India. The company ruled harshly and for its own profit, ignoring the welfare of the Indian people. When Britain lost the American colonies, however, the British government decided to take more control of India. After a number of battles with Indian groups, Britain ruled all of India by 1857. That year, a rebellion in India, called the Sepoy Mutiny, created a lasting bitterness between the Indians and the British. Yet, there were benefits to British rule, such as railroads, schools, and hospitals. These benefits, however, did not outweigh the destruction of India's way of life and of its economy.

Section 3 European Imperialism Extended to Asia Searching the world for raw materials and new markets, the industrial powers looked to China's undeveloped resources and its enormous population. Yet the Chinese were not interested in trading with the Europeans. Through victories in the Opium Wars, however, the British won sweeping trade privileges in China. Later, other European nations and Japan also gained such privileges. All of these powerful nations were ready to divide China among themselves. The United States recommended the Open Door Policy, leaving China open to trade with all nations. China's bitterness over foreign control was reflected in the Boxer Rebellion. During the same period, industrial powers opened other parts of Asia to trade. The United States forced Japan to open its ports, and Japan later did the same to Korea. The British and Dutch gained control of vital lands in Southeast Asia.

Key Facts

1. Use each vocabulary word in a sentence.
   - **a.** imperialism
   - **b.** paternalism
   - **c.** assimilation
   - **d.** sepoy
   - **e.** extraterritoriality
2. Identify and briefly explain the importance of the following names, places, and events.
   - **a.** Cape of Good Hope
   - **b.** Alexandrine Tinne
   - **c.** David Livingstone
   - **d.** Cecil Rhodes
   - **e.** Cape Colony
   - **f.** Suez Canal
   - **g.** Khyber Pass
   - **h.** Robert Clive
   - **i.** Sepoy Mutiny
   - **j.** Opium Wars
   - **k.** Empress Ci Xi
   - **l.** Boxer Rebellion
   - **m.** Emperor Mutsuhito
   - **n.** Singapore

Main Ideas

1. List three reasons for the new imperialism.
2. List three geographical features that were important in the exploration of Africa. Explain why each was important.
3. How were the British able to gain control of South Africa and Egypt?
4. How did Britain gain control of India?
5. How were China, Japan, and Korea forcibly opened to trade?

6. Name two Southeast Asian lands that were taken over by European nations.

Developing Skills in Reading History

Select the best ending for each sentence.

1. In Britain's colonies, the system of *indirect rule* gave local leaders
  a. a powerful say in government decisions.
  b. little impact on government decisions.
  c. complete control over their own regions.

2. After the Sepoy Mutiny, Britain decided that India should be
  a. ruled by the British government.
  b. ruled by the British East India Company.
  c. slowly granted its independence.

Using Social Studies Skills

Analyzing Political Cartoons Study the political cartoon shown below. Then answer the following questions.

1. What events or developments does the cartoon depict?

2. What symbols does the cartoonist use? What do these symbols mean?

3. What *opinion* do you think this cartoon expresses? Use specific items from the cartoon to support your answer.

Critical Thinking

1. Identifying Central Issues What route became known as *the British lifeline?* What did this name mean?

2. Making Comparisons In what ways was the U.S. attitude toward China similar to the attitude of the European powers? In what way was the attitude of the U.S. different? How can you explain these differences in these attitudes?

3. Recognizing Bias Some Europeans justified imperialism by saying that it was their duty to "civilize" people in other parts of the world. How might a person in India or Africa react to this idea?

Focus on Writing

Summarizing

Like a paraphrase, a **summary** presents a writer's (or speaker's) material in your own words. The summary, however, is shorter than the paraphrase—usually about one-third the size of the original. Many of the steps in writing a summary are the same as those used to write a paraphrase. For example, you should determine and express the piece's *main idea* and *important points* in your summary. You should also *express the tone* of the original and *simplify the language.* Yet, to make the summary brief enough, you should *eliminate unnecessary details,* such as anecdotes and extra examples. Write a summary of the material under the heading "Europeans Came to Dominate Southeast Asia" (found on page 566).

Geography in History

Ancient Origins of the Industrial Revolution

The Industrial Revolution of Europe and the United States (see page 512) was powered by water that fell down ancient hills and by coal dug out of ancient mountains. The location of water power and coal influenced where towns would grow into great cities, and where entirely new cities would spring up.

A Collision

Most scientists believe that about 500 million years ago, the continents, adrift on separate crusts of the earth, began to close together to form one vast continent. When they collided, they were in the tropical regions near the equator, far from their present latitudes. In the hot, humid environment, huge plants grew—some over 100 feet high—the first of their size to grow on earth. For as long as 450,000 years, these lush, fernlike trees grew, died, fell, and rotted away in the steaming swamps. Peat, a layer of decayed plant matter, grew 1,500 feet thick in some places.

The meeting of the continents was a violent event. Along the line where they collided, the Appalachian Mountains in North America and the hills of Great Britain and Scandinavia buckled skyward. The intense heat and pressure inside the folding earth squeezed the peat into hard anthracite coal. Other swamplands that escaped this crushing force were turned into a softer coal, called bituminous.

Coal and Cities

Gradually, most scientists believe, the continents began to drift apart. For 300 million years they inched away from one another. Long after the continents split, humans began to populate the planet.

To human beings living in the 1700s, the ancient earth changes acquired new importance. In Great Britain, many of the forests had been used to build and heat houses and to fire the furnaces that made iron. Faced with running out of wood, iron manufacturers of the early 1700s found a way to use coal as a fuel. Great Britain, located where those prehistoric swamps had rotted and hardened, had plenty of coal.

Factories grew up near the coal fields. Some cities were already prosperous. Manchester, for example, had plentiful water power in its nearby hills. Others, such as Leeds and Sheffield, became industrial centers after coal became important.

By the 1850s, half of Great Britain's population lived in the industrial towns and cities. Similar city growth took place on the continent of Europe somewhat later. Near the Ruhr district of Germany, for instance, cities like Düsseldorf and Essen drew hundreds of thousands of workers from the countryside to work in new industries founded on coal.

The Appalachians

On the other side of the Atlantic, the young United States depended at first on another source of power created by the collision of the continents. Water falling on the Appalachians tumbled down its foothills and from there plunged to the coastal plain. Cities along the line where the water fell used water power to drive machines.

When the United States entered the Coal Age, its miners turned to the anthracite of the Appalachians. Just west of the mountains were wide beds of bituminous coal. As had happened in England, industry soon followed. New centers of manufacturing grew up in cities like Pittsburgh, Pennsylvania, and Youngstown, Ohio, which were located near the coal fields.

Whether in New England or Old England, whether in Birmingham, Alabama, or Birmingham, Warwickshire, the gritty plumes that poured from the smokestacks of these industrial cities had something in common. That smoky residue had all once been trees growing in a single belt of tropical forest beneath an equatorial sun.

Focus on Geography

1. **Place** Describe the location of North America and Europe 500 million years ago that made possible the formation of coal.

2. **Location** What is the present latitude of New York? Of Manchester?

3. **Movement** Why did English workers move to cities such as Sheffield?

Critical Thinking

Predicting Consequences

4. If coal had formed in Great Britain but not in the eastern United States, how might the history of the United States have been different?

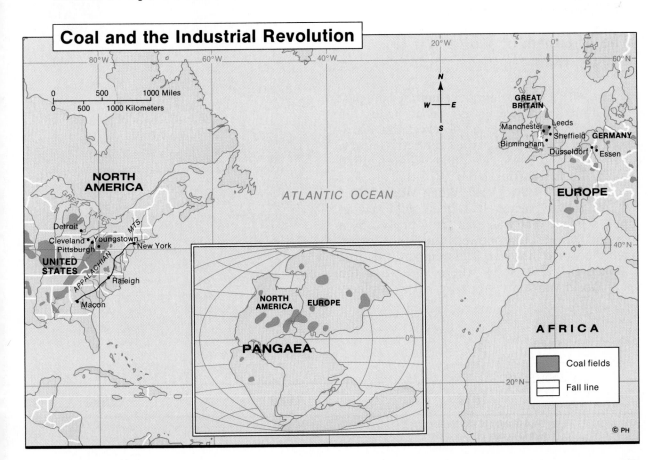

Coal and the Industrial Revolution

UNIT

8

The World in Crisis

(1914–1960)

The phrase, "Those who cannot remember the past are condemned to repeat it," is used to justify the study of history, and no period deserves this warning more than the first half of the twentieth century. Between 1900 and 1945, two great wars engulfed the world, the first lasting from 1914 to 1919 and the second from 1939 to 1945. When World War I ended, an uneasy peace had been achieved in Europe—a peace that was eventually broken by a new brand of absolute power that once again plunged the world into war. The map and the time line, linked by color, show where and when the crises of World War I and World War II took place.

1   WW I AND THE RISE OF DICTATORSHIPS

This recruiting poster encouraged Britons to join the fighting in World War I.

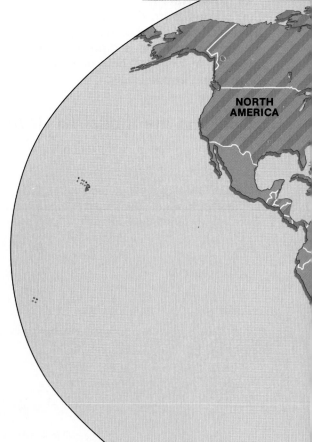

NORTH
AMERICA

1900

1910

1920

1930

1914 Murder of Austria-Hungary's ■
archduke sets off World War I

■ 1917 Bolsheviks take
control of Russia

1933 Hitler and his Nazi ■
party control Germany

2   WW II AND ITS AFTERMATH

*Fighter planes shaped the combat in World War II
(above). Churchill, Roosevelt, and Stalin met
at Yalta at the end of the war (right).*

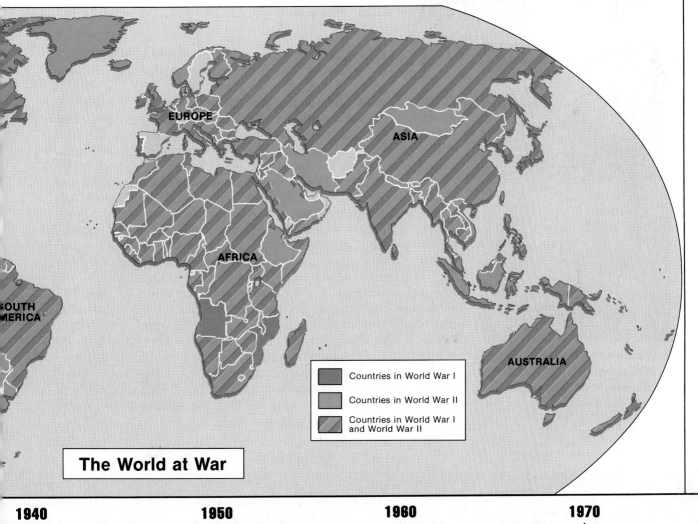

EUROPE

ASIA

AFRICA

SOUTH
AMERICA

AUSTRALIA

	Countries in World War I
	Countries in World War II
	Countries in World War I and World War II

The World at War

1 WORLD WAR I AND THE RISE OF DICTATORSHIPS

■ **1939 Hitler invades**   ■ **1945 War ends in Allied victory;**
Poland; WWII begins   **Allies divide East and West Germany**

2 WORLD WAR II AND ITS AFTERMATH

World War I and Its Aftermath

(1914–1937)

Tensions and Crises Led to War in Europe

2 World War I Was Set on Land and Sea

3 War Brought an End to Mighty Empires

4 The Postwar World Searched for Peace

▲ **Illustrating History**
Thousands of Allied soldiers like the one shown above lost their lives in the Battle of the Somme.

The soldiers who fought in the Battle of the Somme during World War I were the unlucky ones. In four years of slow, bloody trench warfare, this battle in 1916 ranks as perhaps the most horrible. The British attacked the Germans at a point where the German army had built its strongest defenses, along the Somme River in France.

For an entire week, British artillery pounded the German trenches, covering the landscape with craters for 25 miles. The object was to break down the German defenses. But, unknown to the British, the Germans had reinforced bunkers 40 feet deep, which enabled them to survive the heaviest bombardment. On July 1, thinking they had weakened the Germans, British soldiers climbed out of their trenches and advanced slowly. The Germans mowed them down. In 24 hours, a total of 20,000 British soldiers were killed and 20,000 wounded.

Fighting continued at the Somme for four more months. The Germans used poison gas and flamethrowers, and the British sent their new tanks churning through the mud. Each army suffered 450,000 casualties. But the British and French could not defeat the Germans, and the Germans could not advance. Neither side gained any advantage. What kind of war was it that would sacrifice so many lives for nothing? This chapter will explore the causes, the course, and the aftermath of World War I.

1914	1916	1918	1920

■ **1914** World War I begins

■ **1915** Republic of China forms

■ **1916** Battle of the Somme is fought

1918 ■ America enters the war; Germany and Russia sign the Treaty of Brest-Litovsk

1919 ■ India Act gives India limited self-rule

1920 ■ Treaty of Versailles ends World War I; League of Nations begins

▲ **Illustrating History** *This haunting painting of German soldiers in the trenches wearing gas masks reflects the horror of war.*

1 Tensions and Crises Led to War in Europe

As you read, look for answers to these questions:

◆ What was the alliance system in Europe?
◆ Why was Germany's prosperity a factor in starting World War I?
◆ How did nationalism in Serbia help trigger World War I?

> **Key Terms:** alliance (defined on p. 576), entente (p. 576), militarism (p. 576)

In her book *The Guns of August*, the historian Barbara Tuchman gives a vivid description of a way of life that still existed at the beginning of the twentieth century:

So gorgeous was the spectacle on the May morning of 1910 when nine kings rode in the funeral of Edward VII of England that the crowd, waiting in hushed and black-clad awe, could not keep back the gasps of admiration. In scarlet and blue and green and purple three by three the sovereigns rode through the palace gates, with plumed helmets, gold braid, crimson sashes, and jewelled orders flashing in the sun. . . .

A new century had begun a decade earlier, but the assembled royalty could not know that the twentieth century would not be theirs. In a few years, most of them would lose their thrones, and some would lose their lives. All of them, along with their millions of subjects, would face a vastly different world, which the outbreak of World War I would set in motion. The map of Europe before World War I (see page 577)

575

would be a very different one when the battles of the war were over and various nations had lost or gained territories.

Military Alliances Created Suspicion

World War I started for many reasons. The buildup toward war started when the countries of the world decided that their safety depended on large armies and navies. Britain insisted on being the "mistress of the seas." Germany became a "nation at arms," where members of the military enjoyed great power and glory.

Military strength was not enough. To protect themselves from attack, European nations also tried making **alliances,** or agreements, with nations that shared their goals. In 1882, Bismarck formed an alliance with Austria-Hungary and Italy, which was called the Triple Alliance. The three nations in the alliance agreed to come to one another's aid if one was attacked. This agreement would play a central role in the events leading to World War I.

France also decided to look for friends. First, it made a military agreement with Russia in 1893. In 1907, Great Britain joined Russia and France to form an alliance that was known as the Triple Entente (ahn TAHNT). An **entente** is an understanding or agreement between nations. Under the terms of the entente, these nations promised to help one another if one of them was attacked by Germany.

These two alliances partly determined the opposing sides in World War I. However, Italy, a member of the Triple Alliance, did not live up to its agreement with Germany and Austria-Hungary. Instead, because of a secret agreement with the Triple Entente, Italy joined with Great Britain and France when war broke out.

Many of the smaller countries of Europe were also tangled in secret agreements. Thus, fear and mutual suspicions among countries created a climate for war.

Nationalism and imperialism. Because Germany, Italy, and Japan were late in becoming industrialized nations, they were trying to make up for lost time. Japan was trying to become a dominant power in Asia. Germany and Italy wanted to become dominant in European affairs and in building colonial empires.

The growth of Germany, in particular, upset the balance of power among the European nations. Germany hoped to equal—or outdo—Great Britain in power and wealth. Germany's growing economic power, along with its military might, made other nations uneasy.

World nations also competed for colonies. At first, the race was largely between France and Great Britain. Soon, however, Germany entered the competition. This led to problems between France and Germany over Morocco in northern Africa and over areas of the Middle East and Asia. In addition, Japan was increasing its pressure on China, hoping to acquire more wealth.

Nationalism was still another factor that helped to bring on World War I. While Germany and France disputed control of Morocco, Austria-Hungary and Russia argued over the Balkans, the mountainous region north and east of Greece. Russia felt that it should protect the Slavic peoples who lived there, whom it saw as "little brothers" with languages and customs similar to its own. Thus, Russia decided to help Serbia to get a needed seaport. Austria-Hungary, however, opposed Serbian expansion, and bad feelings grew between Serbia and Austria-Hungary.

Further tensions. Nationalism, imperialism, militarism, secret agreements, and international lawlessness are all terms used to sum up the causes of World War I. Nationalism helped cause World War I by arousing the patriotic feelings of those people who for years had been ruled by others. Imperialism helped cause the war by pushing the major European nations into the race for colonies. **Militarism** led to war by glorifying war as heroic, encouraging arms-building, and preparing people and equipment for battle. As a result, Europe became a "powder keg," waiting for the spark that would make it explode.

Europe Before World War I, 1914

Triple Alliance
Triple Entente
Balkan countries

Focus on Geography

Location The map shows the countries in the Triple Alliance and the Triple Entente in 1914. In that year, France, Russia, and Great Britain made up the Triple Entente. Which of these nations shared a boundary with Germany?

Crises in Morocco Brought War Nearer

Both France and Germany wanted Morocco in northern Africa. French soldiers were stationed in the neighboring colony of Algeria, and France wanted to join Morocco to its Algerian lands. Germany, fearing this move, waited for the chance to stop it.

In 1905, the German emperor declared that the sultan of Morocco must remain an independent ruler. France did not like to be threatened in this way, and the possibility of war loomed until an international meeting was called about the crisis.

The powerful world nations met in 1906 at Algeciras, Spain. They agreed that Morocco was to be independent but that France could have police power there. At this conference, Austria-Hungary supported Germany. Great Britain, Russia, and Italy sided with France.

In 1911, France sent an army to Fez, Morocco's chief city. The Germans answered the challenge by sending a warship to the Moroccan port city of Agadir, and preparations for war began. Great Britain and Italy again came to the support of France, and Germany backed down. This Moroccan crisis became known as the "Agadir Affair."

War was avoided again, but the nations of the world could hear Germany's threats. Morocco was made a protectorate of France, but Germany was given a strip of land in the French Congo as compensation.

Unrest Grew in the Balkans

Northern Africa was not the only place where trouble was brewing. In the small Balkan states of southeastern Europe, crises arose that brought Russia and Austria-Hungary near war. (See the map on this page.) The main cause was intense nationalism among the Slavic peoples both inside and outside Austria-Hungary.

In 1908, Austria-Hungary tried to add the states of Bosnia (BAHZ nee uh) and Herzegovina (hehr tsuh guh VEE nah) to its own territory. Because nationalism was strong among the Slavs there, they violently opposed the efforts of Austria-Hungary. Russia came to the help of Serbia; Germany came to the help of Austria-Hungary. Again, fighting did not break out because the Serbians gave in.

In 1912 and 1913, two wars were fought in the Balkans in which Serbia tried to get outlets to the Adriatic Sea. In the first Balkan war, an alliance of Bulgaria, Serbia, Greece, and the small state of Montenegro defeated Turkey.

Although they had won, the Balkan states disagreed among themselves over territory. In the second Balkan war, Serbia and Greece defeated their former ally Bulgaria.

Again, Austria-Hungary prevented Serbia from getting territory on the coast. World war did not follow only because Serbia again backed down.

An Assassination Turned Tensions into War

Eventually, a crisis came from which no nation would back down. Each little war and crisis of the late 1800s and early 1900s added to a climate that was ripe for the outbreak of a major war.

On June 28, 1914, the Archduke Francis Ferdinand, who would have been the next king of Austria-Hungary, was shot and killed in Sarajevo (sah ruh YAY voh), a city in Bosnia (now part of Yugoslavia).

Because the assassin had been a Serbian nationalist, Austria-Hungary's leaders decided to make war on Serbia. Austria-Hungary asked Germany for help, and Serbia looked to Russia. When Serbia refused to accept harsh penalties for the crime, Austria-Hungary declared war on Serbia.

The nations of Europe quickly began to take sides. Counting on help from France, Russia supported Serbia and went to war against Austria-Hungary. Germany, in turn, declared war on Russia. France, Russia's ally, called up its army and sent help, but no one knew what Great Britain would do. The British minister of foreign affairs tried to work for peace but was unsuccessful.

Germany next marched into neutral Belgium, which Britain was pledged to protect. Great Britain therefore joined Russia and France, and World War I was on. Nations fell into line beside their allies, except Italy, which deserted the Triple Alliance and joined Great Britain and France. Although most of the war was fought in Europe, it involved other nations as well, including Japan and Turkey. In 1917, the United States went to the aid of Great Britain and France.

The Opposing Sides Were Equally Matched

In World War I, the Allies fought the Central Powers. The major Allies were Russia, France, Great Britain, Italy, and, later, the United States. The largest Central Powers were Germany, Austria-Hungary, Turkey, and Bulgaria.

The Central Powers had many advantages and had reason to hope for victory. The German army was the best trained in the world. The German navy was also strong. The nations of the Central Powers were geographically close to each other and so could work together easily.

The Allies had more resources and more money to spend on the war effort. The British navy, the best in the world, gave the Allies command of the seas. Supremacy on the sea meant that they could stop ships going to Germany or to German allies. The naval blockade, or attempts to cut off supplies to the enemy, that the Allies put into effect early in the war helped them win. The French army was the best on the Allies' side. The Russian army, though large, was weak and badly equipped. The Allies had no unified military command and not until later in the war were they really united.

SECTION 1 REVIEW

Knowing Key Terms, People, and Places
1. Define: **a.** alliance **b.** entente **c.** militarism
2. Identify: **a.** Triple Alliance **b.** Triple Entente **c.** Balkans **d.** Archduke Francis Ferdinand **e.** Central Powers

Focus on Geography
3. Use the map on page 577 to explain why the Balkans caused trouble between Russia and Austria-Hungary.

Reviewing Main Ideas
4. What leader organized the Triple Alliance, and what countries did it include?
5. Explain how nationalism and militarism were both causes of World War I.
6. What event actually triggered the war?

Critical Thinking
Identifying Assumptions
7. Why do you think the nations of Europe in the early 1900s felt they needed to make defensive alliances?

578

2 World War I Was Set on Land and Sea

As you read, look for answers to these questions:

◆ How was World War I different from earlier wars?
◆ What were the Western and Eastern Fronts?
◆ Why did the United States become involved in World War I?
◆ What were the results of World War I?

> **Key Terms:** propaganda (defined on p. 579), armistice (p. 584), reparation (p. 585)

World War I was not only a world war but a *total war.* Both sides called on the farm, the factory, and the science laboratory for products to help fight and win the war. All the inventions of the Industrial Revolution were turned to wartime uses.

War Efforts Depended on the Home Front

In former wars—except for the wars that grew out of the French Revolution—the fighting was done by professional soldiers. World War I was different because the armies of all the nations were made up of ordinary citizens, most of whom had been drafted. The success and outcome of the war depended largely on public loyalty. Because of this change in warfare, propaganda became an important weapon for both the Central and Allied powers.

Propaganda is a technique for influencing people's minds and shaping public opinion. More than in any earlier war, the news media were used to spread propaganda to win World War I. From 1914 through 1918, news media included newspapers, magazines, telephone, telegraph, cable, and even early radio. The Allied governments were the more successful in controlling and using news media. Propaganda convinced the

British and American people that the Germans were demons who were committing brutal crimes. Although some of these stories were true, it is important to realize that propaganda was used to whip up hatred for the enemy.

Economic resources were as important as military resources in determining the outcome of World War I. Industries speeded up production, and on both sides, the economies of countries came under the control of their governments.

As people began to dig in for a long war, managing their nations' transportation systems became crucial. Railroads were essential to shift armies and equipment from one front to another. Food and fuel were also strictly controlled during the war. A rationing system allowed people only a certain amount of food and fuel each month.

Paying for the war was a severe problem for every nation. Only two methods were available—taxation and borrowing. Because no country could have paid for the war through taxation alone, they had to borrow money. Selling war bonds and issuing paper money through the central banks of a country were the major ways that

▼ **Illustrating History** *In this painting of aerial combat in World War I, a French plane shoots down a German plane.*

Posters and Propaganda

To wage a war successfully, a country needs the support of its people. To win public support for their cause during World War I, most governments relied heavily on propaganda—a systematic campaign to influence peoples' minds and shape public opinion. Posters were used to encourage citizens to enlist in military service, to work for the war effort, and to make sacrifices. One British poster tried to shame men who had not joined the armed forces. It pictured a little girl asking her father, "Daddy, what did YOU do in the Great War?"

Posters such as the one at right were also used to build up hatred of the enemy. The Allies portrayed Germans as "Huns," the barbarians of medieval times. On German posters, the Russians were shown as savages unleashed by the Allies.

1. What were the goals of propaganda in World War I?
2. What were some techniques used to achieve these ends?

countries borrowed during World War I. In the course of the war, however, some governments printed too much paper money, causing excessively high prices, or inflation.

Another problem faced by the warring countries was how to replace the men who left the factories and farms for military service. To replace them, women in many places did all types of work. In addition, machines were developed to replace the workers who went to war.

German Attack Plans Failed on the Western Front

Germany's plans to win the war called for the quick defeat of France on its Western Front, before Russian troops could gather on the so-called Eastern Front. The German army went quickly through Belgium in an effort to encircle Paris. For a time it looked as though they would succeed, but in September 1914, the French, under General Joffre (ZHOF ruh), successfully defeated the Germans in the first battle of the Marne, and the Germans never took Paris. They tried to capture French seaports, but the British stopped them at Ypres (EE preh).

By the end of 1914, the Western Front had been stabilized. This battle area formed a line running about 600 miles from the North Sea to the Swiss frontier. The commanders on both sides dug deep trenches along the Western Front, where soldiers lived and fought. Both sides in World War I tried to kill as many enemy soldiers as they could by sending their own troops recklessly against the enemy. Thus, the casualties in trench warfare were greater than ever before seen in wartime.

On the Eastern Front, the German armies met the Russians at Tannenberg Forest in August 1914 and defeated them. (See the map on page 583.) This victory made the Germans decide to try to knock Russia out of the war. While the Russians fought gallantly, they were badly led and lacked food, supplies, and equipment. To help the

Russians, the British and French fought their way to the Dardanelles and captured Istanbul (Constantinople). In the eight-month battle of Gallipoli (guh LIP uh lee), the Allies tried to control the Dardanelles and open the Black Sea routes, but the campaign was a humiliating disaster. More than 145,000 men were killed and wounded, and Russia never provided the expected military help. Nevertheless, the German plan to knock Russia out of the war was not easy to achieve.

In 1915, French and British soldiers were defending the Western Front when the Germans tried to take the fortress of Verdun (vehr DUN). The battle of Verdun, which began in February 1916, lasted for nearly six months. Half a million men died. The French, under General Henri Philippe Pétain (pay TAN), were determined to defeat the Germans. Pétain promised, "They shall not pass," and he kept his word. In July of 1916, the French and British took the offensive at the battle of the Somme, where the British used tanks for the first time. After months of fighting, only a few thousand yards of ground had been gained.

The year 1917 was a turning point in the war for the Allies. In March 1917, the Allies suffered a blow when Russia made a separate armistice and left the war. The Allies were given a lift, however, when the United States entered the war that year. The United States's entry on the Allied side on April 6, 1917, made victory certain. An American army led by General John J. Pershing landed in France in 1918 to take part in the historic second battle of the Marne, Château-Thierry, and Saint-Mihiel. The Central Powers began to give up one by one.

Great Britain Dominated the War at Sea

The Central Powers were successful at first in fighting on land; the Allies were successful at first in fighting at sea. The Allies were able to capture, sink, or drive into port all ships flying enemy flags. Great Britain declared all enemy territory in a state of blockade and began to stop foreign ships at sea, seizing war materials as illegal shipments.

In their own words

The Crowded Trenches of War

August Hopp was a 23-year-old theology student fighting in World War I. Like many soldiers, Hopp was shocked by the brutality of war. In this letter from the front, he describes a typical, gruesome skirmish in the trenches. Hopp died 17 days after writing this letter.

"At last came the order: 'The Company will at once relieve a Company of the 154th in the recaptured trench.' . . . in these trenches one saw death in a hundredfold frightful forms. Right at the entrance lay one of the 130th, leaning against the breastwork [a low wall], as if he had dropped asleep as he fell, a little bloody hole in his forehead, cold and stark. And then we forced ourselves along . . . through the trench, on the bottom of which were stagnating pools of blood in which lay, in wildest confusion, corpses of Germans and French, almost blocking the way every few steps, so that one had to clamber [climb] over the heaped-up bodies, constantly finding one's hands and face in contact with ghastly, bleeding wounds. . . . The ground looked as if there had been an earthquake; the trench was here and there a chaos of earth, stones, tree-trunks and corpses, and the nearer we got to the left wing the more ghastly it became, the thicker and thicker lay the bodies, and the more the bullets whistled.**"**

1. What was the goal of the activity described by Hopp?
2. This excerpt does not tell for which country Hopp was fighting. Why might this information be unimportant to a historian?

When Britain increased the list of goods it considered illegal, the United States joined other neutral countries in protesting this British action.

The British blockade became so tight that Germany decided to fight back. Its main weapon was its submarines, or U-boats. The Germans declared the seas around the British Isles a war zone and claimed the right to attack Allied merchant ships without warning. On May 7, 1915, a U-boat torpedoed the British passenger liner *Lusitania* and over 1,200 lives were lost, including 100 Americans. This incident and other submarine attacks on civilian ships enraged world public opinion against Germany and helped to draw the United States into the war.

In general, the Germans sought to avoid a major fight with the powerful British navy. In May 1916, at the Battle of Jutland in the North Sea, the British were almost success- ful in destroying the bulk of the German fleet. Both sides claimed victory. The Germans said they had inflicted greater losses, while the British claimed they had driven the German fleet away. For the rest of the war, however, the British were not challenged directly at sea by the Germans.

Communist Leaders Took Russia Out of the War

Russia's entry into the war meant that Germany had to fight a two-front war, against France on the west and Russia on the east. On the Western Front, Germany met stalemate and then defeat. Germany was far more successful on the Eastern Front, where it defeated the Russians. Russia's defeat was made easier by a revolution that broke out in Russia in 1917, bringing the Communists to power.

BIOGRAPHY

Henri Philippe Pétain

In 1916, the French showered praise and war medals on Henri Philippe Pétain (shown on the right). Thirty years later, he stood condemned as a traitor to France.

Pétain was born in France in 1856. He began a military career and eventually reached the rank of general. After some early success commanding troops during World War I, Pétain was put in charge of the fortress of Verdun. From February to July of 1916, the Germans attacked relentlessly. When the situation seemed hopeless, Pétain calmly told his troops: "They shall not pass." The Germans abandoned their attack, and Pétain was made a Marshal of France.

In 1940, the Germans again invaded France, but this time the French resistance collapsed within a few weeks. Pétain was called out of retirement to head a new wartime government. Sympathetic to the Nazis, he stunned those loyal to France by agreeing to help the Germans. His government helped Germany persecute French Jews and sent French workers to German factories. When the Allies liberated France toward the end of World War II, Pétain was put on

trial for treason and found guilty. Disgraced and hated by many, he died in prison in 1951.

1. Why did Pétain become a national hero?
2. Why was the German assault on Verdun a failure?
3. Why was Pétain called a traitor after World War II?

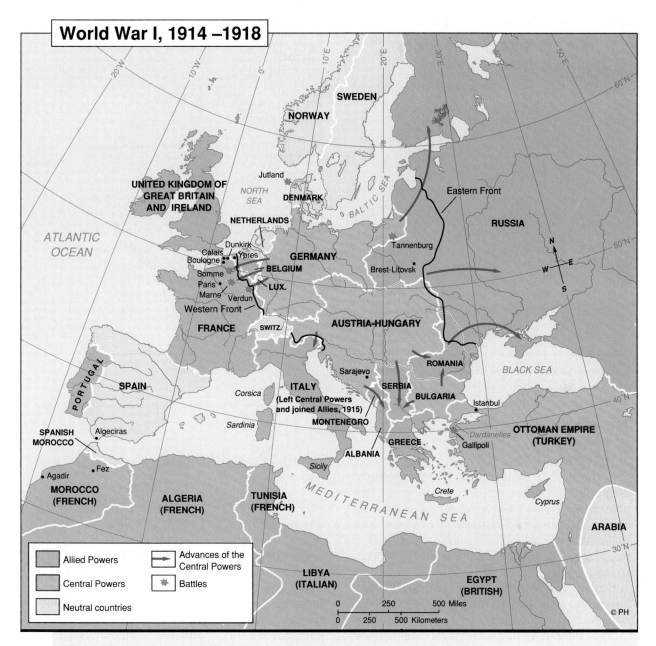

World War I, 1914–1918

SWEDEN

NORWAY

Jutland

NORTH SEA

BALTIC SEA

UNITED KINGDOM OF GREAT BRITAIN AND IRELAND

DENMARK

NETHERLANDS

Eastern Front

RUSSIA

Tannenburg

ATLANTIC OCEAN

Dunkirk
Calais
Ypres
Boulogne
BELGIUM
Somme
Paris
Marne
Verdun
Western Front
LUX.

GERMANY

Brest-Litovsk

FRANCE

SWITZ.

AUSTRIA-HUNGARY

PORTUGAL

SPAIN

Corsica

ITALY
(Left Central Powers and joined Allies, 1915)

Sardinia

MONTENEGRO

Sarajevo

SERBIA

ROMANIA

BLACK SEA

BULGARIA

Istanbul

SPANISH MOROCCO

Algeciras

Agadir
Fez

GREECE

ALBANIA

Dardanelles
Gallipoli

OTTOMAN EMPIRE (TURKEY)

Sicily

Crete

Cyprus

MOROCCO (FRENCH)

ALGERIA (FRENCH)

TUNISIA (FRENCH)

MEDITERRANEAN SEA

ARABIA

LIBYA (ITALIAN)

EGYPT (BRITISH)

	Allied Powers
	Central Powers
	Neutral countries

→ Advances of the Central Powers

★ Battles

0   250   500 Miles
0   250   500 Kilometers

© PH

Focus on Geography

Interaction Which covered more territory—the Eastern Front or the Western Front? For both Allied and Central Powers, why was the Eastern Front a more difficult place to fight than the Western Front?

The Russian people wanted peace, and under the leadership of V. I. Lenin, Russia left the war. It signed a harsh separate peace treaty with Germany in 1918, which took away rich land and much of Russia's industry and resources.

The United States Entered World War I on the Allied Side

Running for a second term, United States President Woodrow Wilson promised not to involve America in the European war, and

583

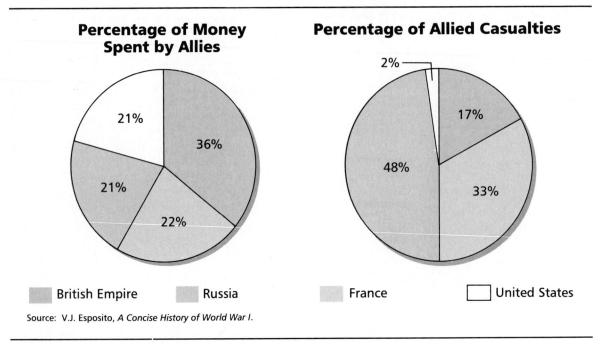

Percentage of Money Spent by Allies

- 36%
- 22%
- 21%
- 21%

Percentage of Allied Casualties

- 2%
- 17%
- 48%
- 33%

Legend: ■ British Empire ■ Russia ■ France ☐ United States

Source: V.J. Esposito, *A Concise History of World War I.*

▲ **Graph Skill** *This graph shows war costs for the Allies in terms of both money and lives lost. Which Allied country suffered the most casualties?*

he was reelected in 1916. As months passed and the Allied cause became increasingly desperate, Wilson felt unable to keep his promise. Wilson thought that the United States should help France and England "to make the world safe for democracy." The people of the United States began to think so, too.

Both the Allied and the Central Powers looked to the United States as a neutral nation that could supply them with the things they needed. American businesses were eager to trade and believed they could sell anything, except weapons of war, to either side. The British, as well as the Germans, however, were determined that the other side should not get the things it needed. This was the reason for stopping and searching American ships.

The American entry into World War I was a sign that the world was getting smaller. It was no longer possible not to be concerned about events in far-off places. The arrival of American troops in France early in 1918 changed the course of the war and helped to make the Allied victory possible.

World War I Was Costly for Both Sides

On November 11, 1918, the Allies and Germany agreed to an **armistice,** a temporary agreement to stop fighting. Later, it would be replaced by a peace treaty, which outlined the conditions for permanent settlement and peace. Although Germany and its friends were defeated, World War I was costly for winner and loser alike. Before World War I ended, more than 30 nations had become involved. No part of the earth was unaffected by it. Eight million soldiers died, and nearly three times as many were wounded, gassed, blinded, crippled, or paralyzed. Many civilians also perished. At one point, the war was costing $10 million an hour. By November 1918, the total cost was about $186 billion.

New weapons, such as poison gas, submarines, tanks, and airplanes, were used in World War I. When the war ended in

November 1918, a long, cold, hungry winter lay ahead for many people. These conditions made time ripe for change.

"Big Four" Leaders Decided Terms for Peace

The representatives of the victorious nations met at Versailles in France. Known as the Big Four, they were Woodrow Wilson of the United States, Georges Clemenceau (KLEHM uhn SOH) of France, David Lloyd George of England, and Vitorio Orlando of Italy. They hoped to write a treaty that would make a peaceful future possible.

One peace plan came from President Woodrow Wilson, who wanted "peace without victory." The Fourteen Points is the name given to the program that he hoped would bring peace and future security to the nations of the world. These were high goals—too high to be acceptable to most nations.

The Big Four wrote the Versailles Treaty without consulting the defeated countries. The Central Powers found it extremely difficult to accept the terms of this treaty. The Germans did not want to give back to France the province of Alsace-Lorraine. They were stunned by the part of the treaty that blamed Germany for starting the war and ordered it to make **reparations**, or payments for war damages, to the countries it had fought.

Similar terms were used in making separate treaties with other countries. By these treaties, Austria, Hungary, Bulgaria, and the Ottoman Empire lost large parts of their former land areas. National groups in the former empire of Austria-Hungary now formed the new nations of Czechoslovakia and Yugoslavia. The Ottoman Empire lost all its possessions in the Middle East, keeping only Turkey.

Overall, the Versailles Treaty was a disappointment to President Wilson because only a few of the Fourteen Points found their way into the treaty. However, the treaty did call for the establishment of the League of Nations, whose work was to try to keep the peace in Europe.

▲ **Illustrating History** *Seated from left to right are the Big Four: Orlando of Italy, Lloyd George of Great Britain, Clemenceau of France, and Wilson of the United States.*

Even though the league was Wilson's idea, the United States Senate did not feel that it was wise for the country to take part in world affairs. As a result, the United States never signed the Versailles Treaty and never joined the league. The League of Nations brought new hope to the world of the 1920s, but what kind of world was it?

SECTION 2 REVIEW

Knowing Key Terms, People, and Places
1. Define: **a.** propaganda **b.** armistice **c.** reparations
2. Identify: **a.** Western Front **b.** Verdun **c.** Versailles Treaty **d.** Fourteen Points

Reviewing Main Ideas
3. What was Germany's battle plan on the Western Front early in the war?
4. What two important events in 1917 changed the course of the war?

Critical Thinking
Determining Relevance
5. Between 1914 and 1918, there were new communications media like early radio, newspapers, and magazines. How did this relate to the greater use of propaganda in the war?

3 War Brought an End to Mighty Empires

As you read, look for answers to these questions:

◆ Who led India's movement for independence?
◆ How did China become a republic?
◆ What nations were established in the Middle East after World War I?

Key Terms: boycott (defined on p. 586), civil disobedience (p. 586), protectorate (p. 588)

The issue of self-government for national groups had been one cause of World War I. This issue still remained important, not only in Europe but also in colonies in Asia and the Middle East. Many territories that the major powers had acquired as colonies during the previous centuries now wanted to govern themselves.

Indian Leaders Worked for Independence

By the early 1900s, Indian nationalists began calling for an end to British rule. At the end of World War I, an English-educated lawyer named Mohandas K. Gandhi, who lived from 1869 to 1948, became the leader of the Indian nationalist movement. Indians had been loyal to Britain during the war. Now, they expected more self-government. Some dissatisfied nationalist leaders encouraged strikes and riots, but Gandhi disagreed with these leaders.

Gandhi urged people to **boycott,** or refuse to buy, British goods, to make simple clothing for themselves, to pay no taxes, and to refuse to serve in the British army. If they were arrested, they were not to fight back but to let themselves be taken to jail. Soon, Gandhi said, the jails would become overcrowded, and the British would have to set the Indians free. These methods of nonviolent resistance to government action are called **civil disobedience.** Gandhi believed they would make it impossible for the British to continue to rule India.

In April 1919, in Amritsar (ahm RIHT sihr), several hundred Indians were killed and hundreds more wounded when British troops fired on the crowd at a peaceful political demonstration. Gandhi urged peaceful resistance in response to the massacre. Some Indians fought back, however, and bloody rioting followed. Gandhi called off his campaign and took the blame for the violence. In 1922, he went to prison, where he remained for two years. When he was released, he became an even greater hero. People called him Mahatma, or "Great Soul," and followed wherever he led. In 1929, the British arrested Gandhi again, because his renewed campaign of civil disobedience was drawing world sympathy.

In the 1930s, another outstanding Indian leader, Jawaharlal Nehru (juh WAH huhr lahl NAY roo), began to work alongside Gandhi. More conferences with the British led to the Government of India Act of 1935, which established provinces governed entirely by Indians and gave the Indian legislature more power.

Imperial China Became a Republic

China's Boxer Rebellion, which lasted from 1900 to 1903, was one sign of growing nationalism and unhappiness with Manchu rule. Attempts to form a constitutional government failed, and by 1911, the time to overthrow the Manchu dynasty had come. The leader who would guide the Chinese revolution was Sun Yat-sen. When rebellion broke out in China in 1911, Sun Yat-sen assumed leadership. He became the first president of the Republic of China.

Sun Yat-sen turned over the presidency to a strong army general, Yuan Shi Kai (yoo ahn shee KY), in 1912. In order to be sure his voice would be heard in Yuan's government, Sun Yat-sen formed the Nationalist People's party, better known as the Kuomintang (kwoh min DAHNG). Yuan, however, had ambitions of becoming emperor. Yuan's failure, combined with rebellions and civil war in China, brought his death in

1916. Yuan's death left China more divided than ever. Civil war raged in China between 1920 and 1926, and the government had no real power.

Meanwhile, Sun Yat-sen spent his time trying to rebuild the Kuomintang. Under his leadership the Kuomintang pledged itself to fight for the removal of foreigners from China, to build democracy, and to raise living standards. The people supported the Kuomintang, which had its first National Congress in Canton in 1924.

The next year, however, Sun Yat-sen died. In the fight for power that followed the death of Sun, one of his followers, Chiang Kai-shek (CHANG ky SHEK), became leader of the Kuomintang.

Chiang's first task as Kuomintang leader was to unite the nation under democratic leadership. Chiang tried to unite China by military force, marching from his base at Canton in the south to the capital at Beijing. In 1928, after three years of fighting, the new Nationalist government set up a capital at Nanking. Under Chiang, China was united. Foreign nations gave up special rights and privileges and gradually abandoned extraterritoriality. Modern machines and factories began to manufacture goods, and modern cities with business centers grew. A middle class began to emerge.

The new government also had drawbacks. Although Chiang was expected to give China a democratic government, in actuality he set up a dictatorship in which the Kuomintang was the only party. Chiang promised more democracy, but many people thought he was too slow in making changes. Many peasants and poor people began to find the Chinese Communists' program for governing China more appealing.

Japan Gained New Power in Asia

The strongest, most modern nation in Asia was China's neighbor, Japan. Industrialized at home, Japan began expanding overseas. It had won wars against China and Russia, and it controlled Formosa and Korea. Even though Japan played a small role in World War I, it was awarded the Pacific island colonies that had belonged to Germany.

▲ **Illustrating History** *Some of his disciples accompany Gandhi, second from right, as he walks to a meeting in July, 1937.*

During the 1930s, Japanese military experts thought that an answer to economic problems was to expand into China. In 1931, Japan took over Manchuria in northern China and set up the independent state of Manchukuo. The Chinese boy emperor Pu Yi, now a man, became ruler. As a puppet controlled by Japan, Pu Yi had no real power of his own.

Japan's armies next sought to capture all of China. The Chinese Nationalists and the Chinese Communists united to resist the Japanese invasion. China appealed to the League of Nations for help against Japan. The league condemned the Japanese attacks but did not provide China with weapons or supplies.

Nationalist Movements Began in Southeast Asia

All of Southeast Asia had been taken over by European powers during the age of imperialism. Now, the peoples of Burma, Indochina, and Indonesia sought independence from colonial empires.

In 1937, Britain granted Burma the beginnings of self-government and democracy. Indian and Chinese business people in the country, however, continued to control economic profits. This led to a demand that all foreigners leave Burma so the Burmese could run their country.

People in the French colony of Indochina (Laos, Vietnam, and Cambodia) also were beginning to demand self-rule. The French had built air fields and a naval base at Saigon, but the people began to think about becoming independent of French rule.

At the end of World War I, the Dutch government of Indonesia set up the People's Council, an assembly of Indonesians, Asians, and Dutch settlers. But, the Dutch governor-general still ran the country. In 1927, a National Indonesian Party was created, led by Sukarno (soo KAHR noh).

Oil Brought New Interest in the Middle East

After World War I, the Arab countries of southwestern Asia became very important. They were vital for their large deposits of oil, which were necessary to the economies of industrialized countries. The Arabs expected to become independent after World War I because of the help they had given the Allies. Instead, Britain and France took temporary control of these countries through the League of Nations.

Iraq. In response to Iraq's demands for independence, the British, in 1922, called upon Faisal (FY sul), an Arab prince, to be king. Baghdad became the capital of Iraq and the center for the British, French, and American oil companies.

Iran. Russia and Great Britain had long competed for control of Persia, now known as Iran. Not only did Persia have oil, but it was strategically located between southern Russia and British India. When Russia fell to Communist rule during World War I, Great Britain tried to keep its control of the vast Anglo-Iranian Oil Company. In 1925, in an elaborate ceremony, a military man, Reza Khan, took control as shah, or king, of Persia. He urged modernization and invited foreign investments. In 1935, by royal decree, the ancient name of Persia was changed to Iran.

Saudi Arabia. On the Arabian Peninsula, an Arab tribesman named Ibn Saud conquered and united the holy cities of Islam along the Red Sea. In 1932, he established the kingdom of Saudi Arabia. In 1933, American companies agreed to develop the region's oil.

Egypt. In Egypt, the desire to throw off British influence grew after World War I. None was more aggressive in demanding the end to British influence than the Wafd political party. The Wafd party stood for Egyptian independence and extensive social and economic reforms. Before World War I, Britain, with Egyptian help, completed the conquest of the Sudan, which was jointly ruled as Anglo-Egyptian Sudan. During World War I, Great Britain made Egypt a British **protectorate,** a country with limited self-government under the control of a stronger country. After the war, in 1922, the Wafd party was successful in winning independence for Egypt, and the country was ruled by King Faud I. In 1936, the British agreed to withdraw their troops.

SECTION 3 REVIEW

Knowing Key Terms, People, and Places
1. Define: **a.** boycott **b.** civil disobedience **c.** protectorate
2. Identify: **a.** Gandhi **b.** Sun Yat-sen **c.** Chiang Kai-shek

Focus on Geography
3. How did natural resources and geographic location make Persia (now Iran) especially important to Russia and Great Britain?

Reviewing Main Ideas
4. Explain why Gandhi felt that civil disobedience would end British rule in India.
5. What changes took place in China once it was united under Chiang Kai-shek?

Critical Thinking

Perceiving Cause and Effect
6. Do you think that China's long history as a great empire hurt Sun Yat-sen's efforts to build a democracy?

New Directions in Art

World War I radically changed the way many people looked at life. Feelings of security, confidence, and optimism were replaced by the sense that life was confusing and painful and that people simply could not solve many of the problems that faced them. It was during this time that abstract art appeared. Abstract art does not seek to present an idealized vision of things in the real world. By using only colors, lines, and shapes, it suggests that reality may take many forms, and it challenges each person to interpret the art in his or her own way. Vassily Kandinsky, a Russian painter, was the first to paint in this style. In *Violet-Orange, October 1935*, the colors, forms, and lines of the picture are pleasing, but do not show objects realistically. Abstract art such as Kandinsky's was not the only form in which artists expressed the emotions brought forth by World War I, however. Many artists in the years following the war painfully remembered the destruction of families that had taken place, and they turned to family themes in their art. In *Mother and Child*, the Yugoslav sculptor Ivan Mestrovich depicts the loving, intimate bond between parent and child. The work reflects the fear of separation and loss that always accompanies war.

The more traditional art, Mother and Child, *at left, contrasts with the abstract work,* Violet-Orange, October 1935 *at right.*

589

4 The Postwar World Searched for Peace

As you read, look for answers to these questions:

◆ How old is the idea of having an international organization to keep peace?
◆ What peace efforts were made around 1900?
◆ In what ways was the League of Nations a success?

Key Terms: mandate system (defined on p. 591)

Peace has been a goal that wise men and women everywhere and in all eras have tried to reach. People realized that the dream of world peace needed organization. The League of Nations was an attempt to provide this organization after World War I.

World Leaders Tried to Establish Peace

The League of Nations was not the first organized effort to support and maintain world peace. For example, following the Napoleonic Wars in Europe in the nineteenth century, Czar Alexander I of Russia formed what he called a Holy Alliance. Members of this alliance agreed to let justice and Christian charity govern them in their relations with one another. Although several European rulers signed this agreement, few took it seriously.

After 1850, a number of organizations worked to establish a world in which wars would be unnecessary. Leaders met to agree on the rights of neutral nations, or those not taking part in wars. A further step in decreasing the brutality of war was the formation of the International Red Cross in 1864. Leaders of many countries agreed to let Red Cross workers give medical help to all those wounded in war.

In 1899, as war clouds began to gather, Czar Nicholas II of Russia asked for a meeting, which was held at the Hague (hayg),

capital of the Netherlands. At this peace conference, 26 nations met to talk about reducing the dangers of war. One plan they approved was the establishment of an international court of arbitration. Nations could bring their disagreements to a panel of judges in the hope of having them settled peacefully and fairly. An American, Andrew Carnegie, built a beautiful building in which the court met. Alfred Nobel, the Swedish chemist who invented dynamite, offered a yearly prize to the person who had done most in the cause of peace. Unfortunately, the court had no power to enforce its decisions. In 1907, a second peace conference was held at the Hague, but little came of this effort. The people "prayed for peace and prepared for war." Unchecked national tensions would eventually lead to World War I.

A League of Nations Was Organized to Prevent Wars

At the end of World War I, the map of Europe was redrawn as shown on the map on page 591. There were many who felt the time was ripe to prepare for future peace. Let us build, they said, an organization to forestall future wars by overseeing those nations of the world that are eager to fight. Their hopes rested on the League of Nations, suggested by American President Woodrow Wilson. The basis of the League of Nations was a covenant, or agreement, in which nations pledged to avoid war and deal frankly with one another.

Membership in the League of Nations grew from 29 nations in the beginning to a maximum of 62, each of which had one vote in the league's assembly. This body could investigate and discuss disputes and vote on admitting states into the league.

Whatever real power existed in this new international organization belonged to the league council, made up of permanent and nonpermanent members. The council met at least once a year and dealt with any matter affecting world peace. The chief meeting place of the league was in Geneva, Switzerland. The league also set up the permanent Court of International Justice, or World Court, made up of 15 judges who

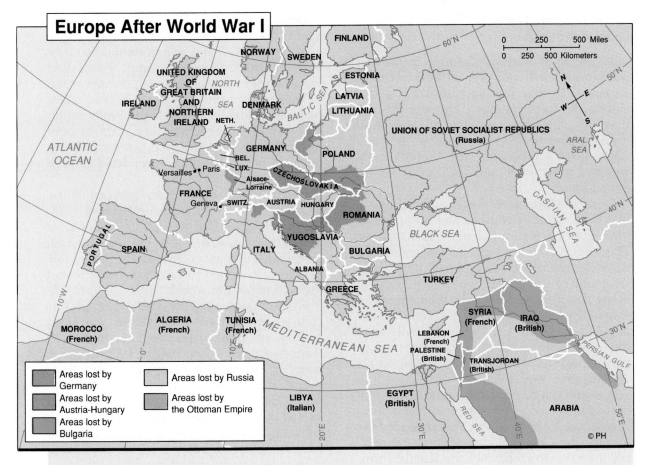

Europe After World War I

Focus on Geography

1. **Place** Study the key and the map. What four countries gained the land lost by Austria-Hungary as a result of World War I?
2. **Regions** Which country lost the most land after World War I —Russia or Germany?

Key:
- Areas lost by Germany
- Areas lost by Austria-Hungary
- Areas lost by Bulgaria
- Areas lost by Russia
- Areas lost by the Ottoman Empire

were chosen by the council and assembly for nine-year terms. The World Court met regularly at The Hague and handed down decisions on cases. The judges could be chosen from any nation, whether or not it was a member of the league. A number of Americans served as judges on the World Court, even though the United States was not a member of the league.

Because imperialism had been an important cause of war, the League of Nations was faced with the problem of what to do with the colonies taken from the defeated na-tions. Its answer to this problem was a mandate system. By a **mandate system,** a big nation was placed in charge of one or more colonies until such colonies could rule themselves.

The League of Nations tried to get at the causes of war. Many people felt that better working and living conditions would make war less likely to occur. League workers studied labor and living conditions all over the world. They also studied health conditions the world over, cared for refugees, and sought to abolish slavery.

Large Nations Failed to Support League Actions

The League of Nations was able to prevent war among small nations a number of times. However, it was not able to keep peace among the large nations. Why was this so? Certainly, the league was less effective than it might have been in dealing with international disputes, because the United States was not a member and the Soviet Union joined late.

More important, however, was the fact that the League of Nations had no power to force member nations to obey its decisions. The league could not punish aggressive nations by military action, and members could drop out of the league when they wanted. Many countries did not take their membership in the league seriously, nor did they live up to its high ideals. Germany, Italy, and Japan were among those who did not honor their promises. Their violations helped set the stage for World War II.

It would not be fair to leave the discussion of the League of Nations on a note of failure. In a sense, it was a pioneer that prepared the way for the United Nations, whose organizers learned from some of the league's mistakes. The United Nations owes much to the league. Some United Nations agencies, such as the International Labor Organization, were once part of the league. The Court of International Justice met until the International Court of Justice was ready to take over in 1946. Much of the work done by special committees of the league has been used by the United Nations as it tries to build a world free from war.

Peace Efforts Were Made

Because the League of Nations was often ineffective, the nations of the world looked for other ways in which to solve the problems of world peace. A race for military superiority had been one cause of World War I. During this postwar period, the league, therefore, tried to limit the production of land and sea weapons, such as airplanes and battleships. Most of these efforts, however, were not successful.

After World War I, the big world powers again tried to take over parts of China. Since conflict over China was a potential cause of war, the United States, England, France, and Japan eventually agreed to respect each other's trade rights in that area. This agreement was short-lived, and in the 1930s, Japan grew more imperialistic and tried to conquer China. The Chinese suffered much because the world did not try hard enough to stop Japan.

Germany still made many nations in the world uneasy. In the Locarno Pacts of 1925, Germany agreed to accept its boundaries with France and Belgium and to settle future disputes peacefully. At the time, this agreement seemed to satisfy the people and the nations of the world.

For a time during the 1920s, the air was cleared of thoughts and talk of war. This feeling of hope came partly from the Kellogg-Briand Peace Pact of 1928. It made war "as an instrument of national policy" illegal. It called upon all nations to agree to settle disputes peacefully. The pact was signed by most of the countries of the world. Germany, Japan, Italy, and Russia were soon to ignore it, however, with tragic consequences for the entire world.

SECTION 4 REVIEW

Knowing Key Terms, People, and Places
1. Define: **a.** mandate system
2. Identify: **a.** The Hague **b.** League of Nations **c.** Court of International Justice

Reviewing Main Ideas
3. How was the League of Nations organized?
4. What factors weakened the League of Nations?

Critical Thinking

Demonstrating Reasoned Judgment
5. Can you think of ways that the League of Nations could have been more successful? Present arguments, including possible contributions of the United States.

Propaganda is an intentional slanting of the truth about people or events to further one's own cause or to damage an opposing cause.

During the course of World War I, both sides used propaganda extensively. Study the following guidelines and then apply them to the examples from World War I that are printed below.

1. **Identify propaganda that uses facts.** A fact is a statement that can be proven true. Answer this question: Which examples include facts in some way?

2. **Identify propaganda that uses lies or distortions.** Propagandists frequently lie; they make statements they know are false, or they twist the truth so that the facts are lost. Some think that if people hear a lie often enough, the people will eventually believe the lie. Answer this question: Which examples use lies or obvious distortions of the truth?

3. **Analyze the appeal to emotion.** Many propagandists appeal to emotions, such as patriotism, pride, anger, and disgust. They hope these emotions will cause people to take some action. Answer this question: Which examples appeal to emotions?

4. **Reach conclusions.** Which three examples of propaganda do you think were the most effective? Give reasons for your answers.

Examples of World War I Propaganda

1. The British displayed fake diaries—supposedly from German soldiers—that said bodies were being melted down to obtain fat for cooking.
2. The German government claimed that the British blockade was a horrible crime against the women and children of Germany. It also claimed that the blockade was having no effect upon Germany.
3. The Austrian government told its soldiers that Austria had no responsibility for starting the war.
4. Germans were told that the French were fighting to regain lands lost in 1870. Other reasons why the French were fighting were not mentioned.
5. Both sides printed fake newspapers, filled with lies, and distributed them behind enemy lines.
6. The British published a book in the United States in which 60 prominent Americans, including two ex-presidents, urged the country to join in the war.

7. The British released a movie entitled *Once a Hun, Always a Hun.*
8. A French pamphlet said: "The struggle against Germany is that of civilization itself against barbarism."
9. The British released a report listing supposed German war crimes. Although only a few facts were proven, all were widely accepted because many well-known scholars signed the report.
10. Americans were told that they were fighting "the war to end all wars."
11. The Germans published a picture in occupied areas of France showing a German soldier feeding a French child.
12. German propaganda sometimes referred to the Allies as the "All-Lies."
13. Copies of letters written by Germans in British prisoner-of-war camps were dropped to Germans in the trenches. Quotes were selected out of context to give a favorable view of the camps.

REVIEW

Section Summaries

Section 1 Tensions and Crises Led to War in Europe During the early years of the 1900s, nations built up their armies and navies and made alliances for protection. Tensions increased as industrialized nations competed for wealth and for colonies. These tensions finally erupted into war when an Austrian archduke was assassinated in the Balkans. World War I saw the Allies (Russia, France, Great Britain, and later, the United States) battle the Central Powers (Germany, Austria, Turkey, and Bulgaria).

Section 2 World War I Was Set on Land and Sea World War I was a *total war,* fought mostly by ordinary citizens. The war depended not only on soldiers but also on those at home who ran the factories, farms, and railroads to keep supplies coming. Nations struggled to pay for the war. On the battlefield, Germany hoped to win quickly, but the French held them off. Casualties in the war's battles were more numerous than in any previous war. In 1917, Russia left the war. In that same year, the United States entered on the side of the Allies. Although Germany won many important battles, by 1918, the tide had turned and the Allies won the war. The Allies imposed harsh treaties on Germany and the other Central Powers. In hopes of preventing wars in the future, the League of Nations was established, but the United States did not join.

Section 3 War Brought an End to Mighty Empires After World War I, many former colonies demanded freedom. Britain gradually changed its empire to a commonwealth of self-governing nations. India's independence movement did not reach its goal until after World War II. China became an independent republic, but by 1928, its leader was a dictator. The powerful nation of Japan was determined to take over more and more of China. In Southeast Asia, former colonies called for freedom. In the oil-rich Middle East, nations gained their independence.

Section 4 The Postwar World Searched for Peace After World War I, the nations of the world sought a way to maintain peace. Their hopes rested on the League of Nations. Members of the league pledged to avoid war and deal frankly with one another. The league handled matters affecting world peace, but it could not force nations to accept its decisions. Some powerful nations ignored the league.

Key Facts

1. Use each vocabulary word in a sentence.
   a. alliance
   b. entente
   c. militarism
   d. propaganda
   e. armistice
   f. reparation
   g. boycott
   h. civil disobedience
   i. protectorate
   j. mandate system
2. Identify and briefly explain the importance of the following names, places, or events.
   a. the Balkans
   b. John J. Pershing
   c. Woodrow Wilson
   d. Georges Clemenceau
   e. Versailles Treaty
   f. Kellogg-Briand Pact

Main Ideas

1. Militarism was one of the conditions in Europe that brought on World War I. List four other conditions that helped cause the war.
2. What steps led from the killing of Archduke Francis Ferdinand to the outbreak of the war?
3. In what ways were the people who remained at home during the fighting important to victory in World War I?
4. Why was 1917 a turning point of World War I?
5. In the years just after World War I, how did Britain's relations change with India, Burma, and Egypt?
6. Why did Japan try to take over China?
7. What were the goals of the League of Nations? Was the league successful? Explain.

Developing Skill in Reading History

Match the correct person with each event on the numbered list below.

a. Ibn Saud   **d.** Mohandas K. Gandhi
b. Chiang Kai-shek   **e.** Woodrow Wilson
c. General Pershing **f.** Sukarno

_____**1.** nonviolent resistance to British rule
_____**2.** the American landing at France
_____**3.** the presentation of the Fourteen Points to assure world peace
_____**4.** the uniting of China
_____**5.** the establishment of the National Indonesian party
_____**6.** the establishment of the kingdom of Saudi Arabia

Using Social Studies Skills

1. **Analyzing a Primary Source** Review the "In Their Own Words" letter on page 581. Then, write a one- or two-sentence summary of it, including your impressions.
2. **Identify Propaganda** Review the explanation of *propaganda* on page 579. Is the poster at right propaganda? Explain.

Critical Thinking

1. **Making Comparisons** What did the leaders Sun Yat-sen and Mohandas Gandhi have in common? In what central way were their struggles different?
2. **Recognizing Bias** The Versailles Treaty blamed Germany for starting World War I. The treaty also required Germany to pay reparations. Why do you think the Germans were stunned by these provisions of the treaty?
3. **Demonstrating Reasoned Judgment** Based on what you have learned in this chapter, what advice would you give the president before the next summit meeting with the leader of the Soviet Union?

FOOD WILL WIN THE WAR
You came here seeking Freedom
You must now help to preserve it
WHEAT is needed for the allies
Waste nothing
UNITED STATES FOOD ADMINISTRATION

Focus on Writing

Writing a Descriptive Paragraph
A descriptive paragraph should give a vivid impression of a scene. The paragraph's topic sentence should present a dominant impression. Supporting sentences should include as many details as possible. Language should be colorful. Read Barbara Tuchman's descriptive paragraph on page 575. Then, answer the questions.
1. What is the topic sentence?
2. What are three specific details that support the topic sentence?
3. What are three examples of sensory impressions in the paragraph?
4. What, in your opinion, is the paragraph's most striking example of colorful language?
Now, using Tuchman's paragraph as a model, write a descriptive paragraph of your own.

The Rise of Dictatorships

(1917–1939)

1 Russia Became a Communist Dictatorship

2 Fascist Dictators Took Over Italy and Germany

3 Other Countries Fell to Dictators

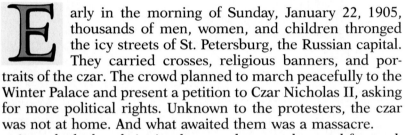

▲ **Illustrating History** *Czar Nicholas II, above, ordered the "Bloody Sunday" massacre in 1905 that killed about 1,000 people.*

Early in the morning of Sunday, January 22, 1905, thousands of men, women, and children thronged the icy streets of St. Petersburg, the Russian capital. They carried crosses, religious banners, and portraits of the czar. The crowd planned to march peacefully to the Winter Palace and present a petition to Czar Nicholas II, asking for more political rights. Unknown to the protesters, the czar was not at home. And what awaited them was a massacre.

Arms locked and singing hymns, the crowd surged forward. They soon reached barricades, and soldiers ordered them to go home. When the crowd refused, cavalry and armed police charged their ranks, firing guns and swinging sabres. Soon, hundreds of marchers lay dead on the snowy pavement.

This massacre, which came to be known as "Bloody Sunday," deeply shocked the Russian people. They had long regarded the czar as their protector. Now, it was clear that asking politely for change would not work. They would have to take matters into their own hands. All across Russia, factory workers went out on strike. Peasants in the countryside began seizing land.

The events that would hit a fever pitch in 1917 were receiving a "dress rehearsal." In this chapter, you will examine both the reasons for and the results of the Russian Revolution. You will also learn about events in Germany, Italy, and other European countries, where old systems of government were overthrown.

1915	1922	1929	1936
1917 ■ Bolsheviks control Russia	**1921** ■ Lenin tries new economic policy in Russia	■ **1928** Stalin begins forced collectivization of agriculture	■ **1933** Hitler becomes Fascist dictator of Germany
	■ **1922** Mussolini becomes Fascist dictator of Italy		■ **1936** Civil war breaks out in Spain

▲ **Illustrating History** *This painting shows the massacre of unarmed Russian protesters at the czar's Winter Palace.*

1 Russia Became a Communist Dictatorship

As you read, look for answers to these questions:

◆ What groups of Russians were unhappy with the czar's rule?
◆ What reforms were promised by the Communist government after the revolution in Russia?
◆ How was Lenin important in creating the modern Soviet Union?
◆ How did Stalin take and keep control in the Soviet Union?

Key Terms: underground (defined on p. 598), provisional government (p. 599), soviet (p. 599), proletariat (p. 599), gulag (p. 602)

Like the revolutions in England, America, and France, the Russian Revolution of 1917 marked a turning point in world history. Unlike the earlier revolutions, however, this revolution did not result in freedom and democracy. Under the czars, Russia had no tradition of liberty or individual rights, and those who did support such democratic ideas were too few to influence this large country. Although the Russian Revolution ended the autocratic rule of the czars, it brought new dictators to power.

Russian Czars Resisted Change and Reform

By 1917, Russia was one of the few places in Europe where the old regime continued. Russian czars ruled as absolute monarchs. The Russian people were unequally divided between the privileged and unprivileged classes. As in other European countries that had lived under the old regime, the link between the monarchy and the church was strong. The Russian Orthodox church had vast wealth and power and great influence in government. Millions of Russians were serfs who worked the land without pay. Under an unfair system, the poor paid more taxes than did the rich.

During the nineteenth century, many Russians observed the events in Western Europe and wanted to bring about reform or change in their own country. It was difficult for these people to pass their ideas on because newspapers and magazines opposing the Russian government or suggesting even the mildest reforms were not allowed. In addition, few Russian people could read or write. Despite these difficulties, Alexander II, who became czar in 1855, began to make some changes. Hoping to be regarded as a forward-looking ruler, he allowed some self-government in local community assemblies, jury trials, and improvements in education for villagers. Although he freed the serfs in 1861, he did not give them land of their own, so discontent was widespread.

▼ **Illustrating History** *Below, a Russian peasant sows seeds. Food shortages were one cause of the Russian Revolution.*

In 1881, Alexander II was assassinated in a terrorist bombing. This event caused the czars who followed Alexander to fear constantly for their lives, and they were thus unwilling to grant any freedoms or reforms. Secret and illegal, or **underground**, movements to overthrow the czars grew.

Czar Nicholas II, who came to the throne in 1895, was a weak ruler. Many Russians began to realize that their government was weak when Russia lost to Japan in the Russo-Japanese War, which lasted from 1904 to 1905. To some, this defeat also proved that the government was weak enough for a revolution to succeed.

Strikes and revolts became common among Russian soldiers and sailors. In January 1905, Father Gapon, a Russian revolutionary who had been educated for the priesthood, led a group of workers to the czar's palace with a petition asking for reforms. Soldiers fired on the group, and hundreds of Russians were killed on what became known as "Bloody Sunday."

The events of 1905 frightened the czar and his ministers enough to make them realize they would have to make changes. Nicholas II granted the people a representative lawmaking body known as the Duma (DOO mah), but he did not let it make laws. When the Duma did something he did not like, the czar would dismiss it.

Revolutionaries Overthrew the Czar's Government

By 1914, the Russians' complaints against their government had increased. The people had little freedom and still lived under feudal conditions. They did not have much land, and food was often scarce. Industry was growing, but the middle class remained small, and workers were discontented. The government of Nicholas II was weak, corrupt, and inefficient.

Russia's entry in World War I made these problems worse. The soldiers were brave, but under Czar Nicholas's government, they were poorly fed, poorly clothed, poorly armed, and poorly led. The railroads could not bring war supplies to the soldiers on time. On the home front, prices were high. Workers and peasants alike could not buy the food and goods they needed with their small wages.

Nicholas decided that his presence on the battle front might help the spirit of his soldiers. Although he was not a soldier, he insisted on taking charge of his armies. The results, however, proved disastrous, and his absence from the capital at Petrograd (formerly St. Petersburg) only made matters worse at home.

On his return, the czar sought advice from Gregory Rasputin (ras PYOO tin), an evil-minded adviser and monk who had had great influence on Czarina Alexandra while Nicholas was away. Only Rasputin seemed able to help the czarina's son, who suffered from hemophilia (HEE muh FIHL ee uh), a disease in which the blood does not clot properly. Because of this, Rasputin gained the czarina's trust, and she began to rely on Rasputin's advice in other matters. Rasputin was feared and hated by the nobles at court. In 1916, as they became aware that Rasputin's power and influence were growing with the czar as well as the czarina, a group of nobles murdered Rasputin.

In March 1917, riot, revolt, and strikes broke out in Petrograd, and the troops mutinied, signaling the end of the old regime in Russia. The Duma took power into its own hands, arrested the czar, and insisted that he resign. Czar Nicholas II was the last of the Romanov dynasty, which had ruled in Russia for 300 years. As the Romanov dynasty came to an end, several groups competed for control of Russia.

When the czar resigned, a **provisional government,** or temporary government, was formed. A popular revolutionary leader, Alexander Kerensky (kuh REN skee), became its head. Although he promised civil rights and far-reaching reforms, Kerensky wanted to continue the war and keep Russia on the side of the Allies. He lost the support of the extreme revolutionaries and was unable to give the people at home what they wanted. By the fall of 1917, one of the things the Russian people wanted most was an end to war.

The provisional government's main rival for control of Russia was a **soviet,** or council, of workers and soldiers that had been formed in Petrograd. At first, the provisional government and the soviet worked together. Then, the Bolsheviks, a more radical revolutionary group led by Lenin, took over the Petrograd soviet. More soviets, representing peasants and workers, formed in other parts of Russia.

Communists Under Lenin Gained Power in Russia

Nikolai Lenin, whose real name was Vladimir Ilyich Ulyanov, had been preparing for revolution for 20 years. Born in 1870, he studied the works of Karl Marx and became a revolutionary while still a teenager. Lenin believed that the time would come when the working class, or **proletariat,** would overthrow the capitalists and replace them as the world's rulers. He also believed that such a revolution would be led by a few disciplined and dedicated leaders who would overthrow the government. From the 1890s onward, Lenin organized and trained his Bolsheviks, the most extreme of several groups who followed Marx's ideas.

Lenin was jailed and exiled many times for his views and revolutionary activities. When Russia entered World War I, Lenin was living in Switzerland. He was preparing to return home when the revolutions in Russia began. In the spring of 1917, after Lenin promised the Germans that he would take Russia out of World War I, the Germans sent him home in a sealed railway car that carried him across the borders of Germany and into Russia. A hero's welcome—prepared by the members of the soviet—awaited Lenin in Russia.

Lenin's ideas were too extreme for some members of the soviet, but he convinced the majority to follow him. As the Bolsheviks, now called Communists, gained in strength, the people followed. The Bolsheviks used terror and a secret police, which Lenin organized, to take control of Russia. In November 1917, the Bolsheviks seized the capital of Russia, Petrograd. Kerensky, who

▲ Illustrating History *Above, Lenin is declaring the power of his new Soviet government to a crowd in 1917.*

had led the provisional government, fled the country, but other members of the government were arrested. The control of the revolution and of Russia had been captured by a well-organized, disciplined, and aggressive minority of the people.

"Peace, Land, and Bread" were the things the Communists promised the people. Peace, land, and bread were the things the war-weary Russian people wanted. This simple slogan appealed to the Russian people and explains a great deal about the rise of the Communists.

Lenin's new government was not strong, however, and he knew that he must end the war quickly. In 1918, Russia signed the Treaty of Brest-Litovsk with Germany. It was a harsh treaty that took Russia out of the war but gave up important Russian territory to Germany.

Meanwhile, civil war continued to rage throughout Russia. Communist forces in the civil war were called "Reds" because the color red had long been associated with revolutionary Socialists. The opposing group, called "Whites," included army officers, nobles, peasants, and people from the middle class. The Bolsheviks' well-trained

Red Army, led by Leon Trotsky (TROT skee), defeated the White Army of those loyal to the czar. In his fight for the control of Russia, Lenin also used his secret police, who became more feared even than the secret police of the czars. Aristocrats and political enemies of the Bolsheviks were killed or sent to prison camps. In July 1918, revolutionaries killed the czar and czarina and their children at a country house where they had been imprisoned.

Lenin quickly tried to introduce communism into Russia. The Russian Orthodox church, a strong supporter of the czar's rule, was all but destroyed, and the new government discouraged religious worship. The government took over factories and industry. Private business was abolished, and small farms were joined together to form government-owned farms. Lenin hoped that through government ownership of property, the classless society of Marxist communism would be established quickly. He moved too swiftly, however, and the results were disastrous for Russia.

In 1919, the Russian nation faced starvation. The Communist drive to place all land under government ownership reduced the amount of food farmers were able to grow. Industrial production dropped sharply. Many people died from shortages of food, fuel, and medical supplies. Lenin realized that Russia needed time to build the kind of government and economy he wanted. He decided it would be wise to move more slowly toward his goals. In 1921, under the New Economic Policy, known as the NEP, Lenin returned some farms and factories to private owners. This temporary measure helped somewhat, but as soon as it seemed possible, farms and factories were placed under government ownership again.

By 1924, when Lenin died, the Communist government was in complete control of Russia. A new government organization, formed in 1922, set up separate republics for each major population group in the country, such as the Ukrainians and the Georgians. Each republic had its own government controlled by the Communist party. Because the national government represented all the republics, the country was called the Union of Soviet Socialist Republics (USSR), or the Soviet Union.

Stalin Imposed Brutal Dictatorship on the Soviet People

When Lenin died, Soviet leaders were divided over questions of power and policy. One question was how fast the Soviet Union should be converted into a Communist state following the teachings of Marx. Another question was whether communism should be an international movement, as Lenin had planned. Leon Trotsky, who had organized the Red Army, was Lenin's choice to suc-

ceed him as head of the Communist party. Trotsky, however, lost a fierce power struggle to Joseph Stalin, a ruthless, dedicated Communist. Stalin, who had served the revolution from the beginning, was to hold the Union of Soviet Socialist Republics in his grip for an entire generation and profoundly influence the country's direction.

Stalin swept away all his opponents and gave his own answers to both of the early policy questions. He decided communism should be imposed on Russia quickly and ruthlessly. He also decided that the Soviet Union should first become a strong, model Communist state before its ideas were spread to other countries.

BIOGRAPHY

Joseph Stalin

Shortly before his death in 1924, V.I. Lenin wrote that Joseph Stalin should be removed as secretary general of the Communist party because of his ruthlessness. Lenin was right to distrust Stalin. Once in

power, Stalin, shown at left, became one of the most feared figures in history.

Born in a small village in southwestern Russia in 1879, Stalin was the son of a shoemaker. His mother worked as a washerwoman. At school, young Stalin was expelled for his radical ideas, and thereafter became a revolutionary. He was arrested and exiled several times. Released from prison in Siberia after the czar's fall in 1917, Stalin played a minor role in the October Revolution that brought the Bolsheviks to power.

After Lenin's death, Stalin swept his rivals aside. He made himself dictator in 1929 and set out to

transform the Soviet Union into a strong, modern nation. He built up heavy industry and collectivized farming. Trusting no one, Stalin established a police system more terrible than that of the czars. Millions of people were executed or shipped off to labor camps. Stalin was planning to remove, or purge, other Communist party leaders when he died in 1953.

1. What were two things that Stalin achieved during his rule of the Soviet Union?
2. Why was he so feared by the Soviet people?
3. Can harsh measures such as Stalin's ever be justified by the desire to improve a society?

Stalin looked to Russian history for a model to follow. He found it in the work of Czar Peter the Great, who had tried to impose western ways on Russia. Determined to modernize Russia within his lifetime, Peter had ordered modernization in Russian industry and society. Taking power into his own hands, Peter had also set up a huge bureaucracy of officials who carried out his harsh ideas and orders. This is what Stalin did in the 1920s and 1930s to impose his ideas on the Soviet Union.

Under Stalin, agriculture was seen as less important than the speedy development of industry. The five-year plans for the Soviet economy emphasized heavy industry. To produce food for factory workers, Stalin terrorized the peasants. He forced them to give up what land they had and to form collective farms. Workers on a collective farm lived and worked on land owned by the collective. Forced collectivization, however, once again made serfs of the peasants, who had been freed from serfdom only 70 years before. Well-to-do farmers, along with those who resisted, were shot or imprisoned. In sullen rebellion, the peasants slaughtered their own livestock rather than work on the collective. The winter of 1932 brought the worst famine in Russia's history. Millions starved to death as scarce grain was taken for export. According to recent estimates, forced collectivization was responsible for the deaths of 5 to 10 million people.

In Russia's still underdeveloped industries, huge state monopolies called ministries tried to increase the production of iron, coal, steel, oil, and other basic resources. Many industrial workers were forced to work in certain industries and in distant places. Those who would not submit were tortured, imprisoned, or sent to forced-labor camps, known as **gulags,** in Siberia and elsewhere. One famous prisoner was the Soviet writer Alexander I. Solzhenitsyn (SOHL zhuh NEET sihn), who was imprisoned and sentenced to eight years of forced labor for criticizing "the man with the mustache [Stalin]" in a letter to a friend. Only in 1956, after many years in labor camps, was he freed.

Many loyal Russian Communists bitterly opposed both Stalin's idea of communism and his methods. They agreed that communism should be established in Russia before becoming an international movement, but they did not agree with Stalin's haste and violence. Stalin wiped out his critics by eliminating his enemies. Though many had worked loyally with Stalin at first, if they criticized him later they were framed and tried publicly in "show trials." After being forced to confess their own "crimes," they were shot.

Fifty years later, in 1988, the Supreme Court of the USSR declared the show trials to have been frame-ups. The new Soviet leaders were developing ideas of greater freedom in the economy and in daily life. We will look at developments in the modern Soviet Union in a later chapter.

2 Fascist Dictators Took Over Italy and Germany

As you read, look for answers to these questions:

◆ How did Mussolini and the Fascists gain support in Italy after World War I?
◆ What troubles weakened Germany's democratic postwar government?
◆ What were Adolf Hitler's goals?
◆ What happened to the Jewish people of Europe under Hitler's rule?

Key Terms: fascism (defined on p. 603), corporate state (p. 604), scapegoat (p. 607), genocide (p. 607)

While both Mussolini in Italy and Hitler in Germany were dictatorial tyrants, it was Hitler who came to dominate Germany and the world from 1935 to 1945. It was Mussolini, however, who was Hitler's teacher and who first imposed a Fascist dictatorship on the people of Italy.

Mussolini Promised Italy a Return to Power

Even after Italy was unified in the nineteenth century, the country's experience with democracy caused problems and made its government unstable. Although Italy was a victorious nation in World War I, the war taxed its resources heavily. The Treaty of Versailles gave Italy little in repayment, and its postwar problems were grave. It was unable to reorganize its industry or put its soldiers back to work. Farm production fell, workers rioted, and farmers demanded land of their own. Some Italians saw communism as an answer. Many felt a sense of disgrace because Italy was not playing an influential role in world affairs.

Benito Mussolini (moos soh LEE nee), born in 1883, became a Socialist journalist and wrote articles favoring the overthrow of capitalism. When World War I began, he urged Italy to join the war on the side of the Allies. After the war, his Socialist views began to change, and he wrote about Italy's need to become a great nation.

In 1919, Mussolini organized the Fascist (FASH ist) party, which undertook the task of restoring Italy to a glorious position in the world. The Fascist party urged its members to obey the rules of party discipline and to fight all those who had different ideas. As their symbol, the Fascists chose an ancient Roman emblem of power, a battle-ax that was wrapped in reeds and was known as a *fasces* (FASS eez). As a political philosophy, **fascism** calls for glorification of the state, a single-party system with a strong ruler, and aggressive nationalism. Fascism promised jobs to the unemployed, land to the peasants, and protection from communism to business owners. Workers and property owners alike thought they could find something of value in fascism.

Soon, Mussolini felt strong enough to challenge the government. In October 1922, his followers began the March on Rome. From all parts of Italy, Fascists began to make their way to Rome, and civil war seemed near. King Victor Emmanuel III gave in to the threat and appointed Mussolini as premier. Soon the Fascists controlled the Italian legislature. Democracy, which the patriots of Italy had worked so hard to build, fell. Dictatorship took its place.

Fascists Took Control in Italy

In a short time, Italy became a dictatorship under the direction and control of the Fascist party and of its leader, Mussolini. The press was censored, and personal rights crushed. The Fascists outlawed rival political parties and restricted voting rights. Mussolini held all the power, controlling both king and government. School children were taught to believe, obey, and fight. The Italian people were told that they were better than other nations and should build up their military strength in order to defeat the "corrupt democracies."

Mussolini was not satisfied with complete control over Italy's political life. He wanted control over social and industrial life as well. He wanted to combine politics with the economy by creating the **corporate state**. Mussolini organized industrial units called "corporations." Owners, workers, and Fascist party members were to decide together what products factories would manufacture and what profits would be made. Labor unions were not allowed, and strikes were forbidden. Although there were also some restrictions on owners, Italian business prospered under the corporate state.

For a time, fascism seemed to be successful. There were many employers in other countries who envied a nation free of strikes and labor troubles. Mussolini was proud of the efficiency he brought to the government and boasted that the trains, which were often late under the democratic government, now ran on time. In 1929, he made peace with the Roman Catholic church by signing a treaty that recognized the pope as ruler of Vatican City and made Catholicism the official religion of the nation.

For the first 10 years or so of Fascist rule, everything seemed to go well. The second 10 years were to prove stormy. Success encouraged Mussolini, but his ambition was to prove a bad thing for Italy and for the world as well.

Conditions in German Society Opened the Door to Dictatorship

In order to understand Hitler's dramatic rise to power and the lack of success of democracy in Germany after World War I, it is necessary to understand what life was like in Germany at that time. For one thing, German national pride had been deeply wounded. The legacy of the Versailles Treaty would be difficult to erase. Not only had Germany been blamed for the war, but it also had been deprived of its overseas colonies. In addition, Germany was forbidden to maintain any military forces in its western Rhineland.

Economic conditions in Germany were also at a low point. The burden of paying huge sums to other nations for war damages weighed heavily on a poor economy. Inflation made life very difficult during the early 1920s in Germany, and the Great Depression followed, continuing to cripple the economic system. Against this backdrop, the Weimar Republic, established in 1919, was struggling to survive.

The Weimar Republic had been instituted only two days before World War I ended. Government under the republic had a constitution and an elected legislature. From the start, the democratic Weimar Republic faced political opposition. Many Germans felt betrayed by those representatives of the republic who had signed the hated Versailles Treaty. As social conditions worsened, the republic became increasingly threatened.

▼ **Graph Skill** *Why do you think the unemployment rate in Germany declined so rapidly in the late 1930s?*

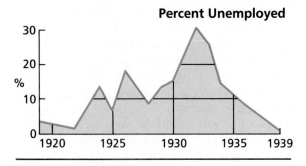

The German Economy 1919–1939

Cost of Living   1929 = 100

Percent Unemployed

When Cabbage Cost Millions

Runaway inflation was a severe problem in Germany in the years after World War I. Between 1914 and 1923, the value of the German mark fell from 4.2 marks for 1 dollar to 4.2 *trillion*. Paper money became almost worthless. (See picture at right.) It was said that "the price of a meal often increased between soup [the first course] and nuts [the last course]."

Middle class families lost their savings overnight. They had to wait in long lines at soup kitchens, or send their children out to beg or steal food. Workers rushed to buy food and clothing as soon as they were paid but still couldn't keep pace with sky-rocketing prices. Inflation was the new enemy.

1. How did inflation affect the Germans?
2. Is inflation still a problem today?

Hitler's Nazis Brought Fascism to Germany

In the midst of Germany's unrest, new political parties appeared. One was a violently nationalistic group called the National Socialist party, commonly known as "Nazi," a short form of its German name. With Adolf Hitler as its leader, this party soon gained many members who believed it could offer a program to save the country.

Adolf Hitler, born in Austria in 1889, believed himself destined to lead Germany to greatness. While he was in prison for a Nazi attempt to overthrow the Weimar Republic in 1923, he wrote the book *Mein Kampf* (mine KAHMF), meaning "My Struggle." The book expresses some of Hitler's chief ideas—his passionate German nationalism, his hatred of the Jews, and his ideas about a super race of people.

From Italian fascism, Hitler learned how to draw people to his ideas through fiery speeches. He also could see the importance and popular appeal of a uniformed, disciplined political party. The Nazi party that Hitler led drew support from those who wished to see a greater Germany. It was also supported by those who wished to avenge Germany's defeat in World War I. People who feared communism, workers who wanted jobs, soldiers who wanted uniforms, and officers who wanted promotion could be found in the Nazi party. Many were flattered when Hitler referred to them as a "master race."

The Nazis Gained Followers in Postwar Germany

By 1923, Nazi party membership had risen from about 6,000 people two years earlier to about 50,000 people. The desperate need for any improvement in Germany's postwar economic conditions provided the major reason for this sharp increase. Realizing this, Hitler raged against the Weimar Republic, blaming it for Germany's woes.

605

Revolts against the Weimar Republic became frequent. Many people feared that Marxist Communists would take over the country. Hitler appeared to be offering the Germans a return to extreme nationalism. His emotional speaking style and fanatical belief in his own causes swept many Germans into the swelling ranks of the Nazi party. Historian Alan Bullock described Hitler's effect on the crowds:

> Hitler's gestures and the emotional character of his speaking, lashing himself up to a pitch of near-hysteria in which he would scream and spit out his resentment, had the same effect on an audience, so that men groaned or hissed and women sobbed involuntarily, caught up in the spell of hatred and exaltation, from which all restraint had been removed.

By 1932, although Hitler's Nazi party was not in the majority, it was the largest single party in the Reichstag (RIKES tahg), the legislature of the Weimar Republic. Field Marshal von Hindenburg, a hero of World War I, was president of the Weimar Republic. Real power, however, was in the hands of a chancellor, who had the support of a majority of the Reichstag. Because no party leader except Hitler could command such a majority, Hindenburg was forced to ask him to be chancellor. As chancellor, Hitler dissolved the Reichstag and, in 1933, called for a new election.

Before the election, Hitler and the Nazis used every tactic, from propaganda to violence, to make sure that they would win. They succeeded in winning enough votes to give Hitler power. The Reichstag adjourned, leaving Hitler supreme in Germany. His goal, however, was to become supreme in all of Europe.

Hitler Became Dictator of Germany

Hitler quickly made sure of his control as dictator of Germany. The Nazi party became the only legal party in Germany. An elite group, known as the Storm Troopers, or Brown Shirts, went about destroying anyone who opposed the party. The Nazis held mass meetings in which thousands cheered Hitler as Der Führer (FYOO rur), or leader, and hailed the idea of a greater Germany. Books disagreeing with Nazi ideas were burned. A secret police force, the Gestapo (geh STAH poh), was organized to enforce the party's ideas. Many great German writers, such as Thomas Mann, fled to the United States. Many German Jews, including the brilliant scientist Albert Einstein, left Germany, fearing the growing power of the Nazis. They emigrated to other countries, including the United States.

Hitler relied heavily on propaganda to persuade people to believe in his domestic and foreign goals. He held that if a "big lie" was told often enough, people would believe it. That is, he said, even the most distorted interpretations of history would be believed if they were repeated often in speeches and books and on the radio. Textbooks were rewritten, and teachers were told what to teach. Hitler used radio as a tool to tell the Germans whom to believe, what to expect, and how to behave.

▼ **Illustrating History** *Adolf Hitler, shown below, became chancellor of Germany in 1933 and quickly consolidated his power.*

Once he was in power, Hitler prepared for war. The Treaty of Versailles limited the size of the German army, but Hitler believed he could violate the treaty because it was a "blot on German honor." German industry began war production. When important business people had first supported Hitler, they had hoped he would be their puppet. Soon, he controlled industry as well as government. While many business people wished they could do away with this monster, it was too late.

Hitler Persecuted Religious Groups

Hitler's belief in a "master race" and his hatred of Jews led eventually to the deaths of 6 million Jews, both in Germany and in the lands he conquered. He was determined not only to drive the Jews out of Germany but also to wipe them out as a people. Hitler had Jews rounded up and shipped to concentration camps where they were killed immediately or imprisoned and systematically murdered. Torture, medical experiments, and the gas chamber were used in an effort to exterminate all Jews. The *New York Times* quoted an eyewitness to these atrocities: "He saw his family battered to death with Nazi rifle butts and he saw countless other Jewish men, women, and children shot, clubbed, drowned, gassed, burned, and turned into fertilizer and laundry soap."

In the minds of many Germans, the Jewish people were being punished for causing Germany's economic troubles. Although this was irrational, the Jews became the scapegoats for the problems in German society. A **scapegoat** is a person, group, or thing that is wrongfully blamed for the mistakes or crimes of others. One of Hitler's lieutenants, Adolf Eichmann (IKE mahn), was given the responsibility of providing a "final solution to the Jewish question." For Hitler, this phrase meant that the Jews were to be destroyed as a people.

Today, people often use the word *holocaust* to describe the Nazi's destruction of European Jews. The world had never seen such inhuman and barbaric methods of killing and torture as Hitler devised. The enormity of his crime was beyond any description. A new word, **genocide** (JEN uh side), was coined to describe such a deliberate attempt to wipe out an entire religious or racial group.

Under the Nazis, other groups were persecuted as well. Slavs, gypsies, political prisoners, and the disabled were often killed in the same manner as were the Jews. Protestant and Catholic clergy suffered for protesting inhumane behavior. For example, Pastor Martin Niemöller, a German Lutheran, was arrested and sent to a concentration camp for opposing Hitler. Priests found it difficult and at times impossible to hold church services or to perform the rites of the Roman Catholic church. Many of them were arrested for what Hitler called "meddling in political affairs." Increasingly, Christianity itself came under attack since it taught kindness, mercy, humility, and self-sacrifice—virtues scorned by the Nazis.

SECTION 2 REVIEW

Knowing Key Terms, People, and Places
1. Define: **a.** fascism **b.** corporate state **c.** scapegoat **d.** genocide
2. Identify: **a.** Benito Mussolini **b.** Weimar Republic **c.** National Socialist party **d.** *Mein Kampf* **e.** Gestapo

Reviewing Main Ideas
3. What conditions in postwar Italy led the Italians to follow the Fascist party?
4. Explain how Mussolini used feelings of nationalism to gain support.
5. After Hitler became chancellor, how did he gain total power?
6. What did Hitler see as the "final solution" to the question of the Jews in Europe?

Critical Thinking
Making Comparisons
7. Even though Germany and Italy had been on opposite sides in World War I, what similar problems did they face after the war that made it easy for dictators to take power?

607

3 Other Countries Fell to Dictators

As you read, look for answers to these questions:

◆ What were the opposing sides in the Spanish Civil War?
◆ Why did the new European democracies face postwar problems?
◆ What are some characteristics of totalitarian governments?
◆ Why are totalitarian governments dangerous enemies to have?

Key Terms: totalitarian government (defined on p. 609)

In the smaller countries of Europe, democracy, fascism, and communism waged a three-cornered fight for power during the 1920s and 1930s. Those governments with strong democratic traditions, such as those of the Netherlands, Belgium, Norway, Denmark, and Sweden, were able to resist fascism and communism. Other countries were less successful.

Fascists Overthrow the New Spanish Republic

At the end of World War I, Spain was a backward, poverty-stricken monarchy. In 1931, Spain's king left the country and was not allowed to return. In new elections, the people established a republic. The new Spanish government tried many reforms, but many people wanted to go back to the old ways and old privileges of the monarchy. The wealthy wanted to hold onto their property. Military officers and the clergy wanted to keep their special privileges. These groups turned to a Fascist group of army officers led by General Francisco Franco.

In 1936, these conflicts led to the Spanish Civil War, which has been called a "dress rehearsal" for World War II. The Fascist countries of Italy and Germany supported Franco and his rebels, while Russia supported the Loyalists, those who fought for the Spanish republic. The democratic countries might have supported the Loyalists, too, but fear of being on the same side as the Communists kept them from doing so. Many individuals, however, went to Spain on their own to join the International Brigade, which fought for the Spanish republic.

With outside help, Franco defeated the Loyalists, and in 1938, he became a dictator of Spain. As *El Caudillo,* "the Leader," Franco ruled Spain until his death in 1975. He was succeeded by Prince Juan Carlos of Bourbon, the heir of the former ruling family. In 1969, Franco had named Juan Carlos to be king and head of state after his death.

Fascists Gained Power in Eastern Europe

Several of the new nations established at the end of World War I were not yet strong enough to resist being taken over by dictators, most of whom followed Hitler. In Hungary, there was much poverty and unrest

▼ **Illustrating History** *Francisco Franco, shown below, became the Fascist dictator of Spain after the Spanish Civil War.*

because of the harsh terms of the Versailles Treaty at the end of World War I. Monarchists, Communists, and Fascists all tried to rule, but the Fascists under Admiral Nicholas Horthy (HOHR tee) won out in 1919. Horthy eventually became a puppet ruler controlled by Hitler.

In Poland, a similar fight for control took place between Communists and Fascists. Hitler tried to make Poland a German puppet state, and this struggle was a contributing cause of World War II. Dictators gained power also in Austria, Romania, Greece, and other European countries.

Both Fascists and Communists Ruled Totalitarian States

Twentieth-century dictatorships, whether Communist or Fascist, have tended to be totalitarian governments. In a **totalitarian government,** one leader, or party, becomes the symbol of power and prestige. Such a leader has nearly unlimited power, for the leader's party has total political control. In all totalitarian governments, the leader relies heavily on propaganda and control of the press and radio to bend the people to his or her will. Propaganda takes advantage of ignorance, distorts the truth, and paints exaggerated pictures of the leader's virtues and greatness. In Stalin's regime, for instance, the so-called cult of personality portrayed him as superhuman.

In all totalitarian governments, those who do not bend readily to the demands of the leader or the government are killed or imprisoned. To stamp out opposition, spies report any suspicious people to the government, and secret police carry out arrests and punishments without legal protection or fair trials. Individual rights disappear. Totalitarianism depends on military force, exaggerated feelings of nationalism, and war as a means of achieving power.

Totalitarian governments have certain weaknesses. When the all-powerful leader makes bad decisions, those mistakes are costly to the nation and its people. For example, Hitler's mistakes caused great suffering for the country of Germany and the

In their own words

Hitler's View of History

Adolf Hitler, like other totalitarian leaders, based decisions on exaggerated feelings of nationalism. In this excerpt from a 1926 speech, Hitler explains one of the lessons that he believed history taught.

••The fundamental motif [theme] through all the centuries has been the principle that force and power are the determining factors. All development is struggle. Only force rules. Force is the first law. . . . Only through struggle have states and the world become great. If one should ask whether this struggle is gruesome, then the only answer could be: For the weak, yes, for humanity as a whole, no.

World history proves that in the struggle between nations, that race has always won out whose drive for self-preservation was the more pronounced, the stronger. . . . Unfortunately, the contemporary world stresses internationalism instead of the innate values of race, democracy and the majority instead of the worth of a great leader. Instead of everlasting struggle, the world preaches cowardly pacifism, and everlasting peace. These three things, considered in the light of their ultimate consequences, are the causes of the downfall of all humanity. The practical result of conciliation [peace] among nations is the renunciation [denial] of a people's own strength and their voluntary enslavement.**••**

1. According to Hitler, what two factors determine events in history?
2. What phrase indicates that Hitler believed in sacrificing some people in order that others may prosper?

609

▲ **Illustrating History** *This well-known photograph by Robert Capa captures a Spanish Loyalist soldier at the moment of death as he is struck by a Fascist bullet during the Spanish Civil War.*

German people. Totalitarianism seems to encourage conspiracy, since no one can be sure of another's trust or loyalty. No one knows when he or she will be the next person to be reported to the secret police. As a result, totalitarian governments, despite their boasts, often are inefficient. Moreover, totalitarian governments use war in order to demand a great many sacrifices from their people. This, in itself, eventually creates discontent.

Although fascism and communism are both based on the concept of totalitarian government, there are differences between them. Fascism is highly nationalistic. Communism teaches the need for international or worldwide revolution. Under fascism, private profit and ownership continue to exist, although they are under the direct control of the government. Communism abolishes private profit and private ownership except on a small scale. Fascism glorifies the state. Communism, on the other hand, claims that after worldwide revolution has been accomplished, "the state will wither away."

Totalitarian governments can be formidable enemies. In times of war, they are able to move quickly, take chances, and risk lives as no democracy would dare. As a result, World War II lasted six years before a final Allied victory was achieved. The causes, events, and results of World War II are the subject of the next chapter.

SECTION 3 REVIEW

Knowing Key Terms, People, and Places
1. Define: totalitarian government
2. Identify: **a.** Spanish Civil War **b.** Spanish republic **c.** Loyalists **d.** International Brigade **e.** Francisco Franco

Reviewing Main Ideas
3. What kind of government did Franco and the Spanish Fascists want? What countries backed them?
4. Why didn't European democracies aid the new Spanish republic?
5. What happened to many of the new European democracies established after World War I?
6. What are some characteristics of totalitarian governments?

Critical Thinking
Recognizing Ideologies
7. By refusing to help the Spanish republic, the United States and European democracies essentially supported Franco and the Fascists. Why, do you suppose, did they adopt this policy?

Translating Information: Analyzing Political Cartoons in Writing

Political cartoons are visual evidence that can tell you a great deal about issues or events. Many political cartoons use humor or satire to express a point in a powerful, interesting way. Political cartoons usually express their creators' points of view. For this reason, newspapers usually place them on the editorial pages where opinions about many subjects appear.

Use the following steps to interpret the political cartoon below.

1. **Examine the cartoon carefully to determine its message or its point of view.** Use the cartoon's title or its captions or labels to gather further information about its main idea. Remember that effective cartoons express a single idea clearly and simply. Answer the following questions: (a) What is the cartoon's title? (b) How do the labels of the lesser figures help to identify the cartoon's time frame? (c) What is the general topic of the cartoon?

2. **Analyze any symbols used in the cartoon.** A symbol is something that represents something else. A dove, for example, often symbolizes peace. Evaluate the cartoon's symbols for positive or negative meaning. Answer the following questions: (a) What does the central figure in the cartoon symbolize? (b) What concept is symbolized by the dark figure in the cloud? (c) Why do you think that the cartoonist makes the surrounding figures so small?

3. **Analyze the meaning of the cartoon.** Use your knowledge of Chapter 26 and your understanding of the cartoon to determine the artist's message. Answer the following questions: (a) What is the meaning of the title? (b) Why is the central figure portrayed as asleep? (c) What is the cartoonist's attitude toward this issue?

Daniel Bishop, *St. Louis Star-Times*

REVIEW

Section Summaries

Section 1 Russia Became a Communist Dictatorship During the late 1800s Russia was still ruled by an absolutist czar. This old regime way of life brought hardship to most Russians. Secret movements to overthrow rule by a czar grew. The badly run government of Czar Nicholas II was further weakened by World War I, and revolutionary groups overthrew the czar in 1917. The group that finally gained power was the Bolsheviks, or Communists, led by Lenin. They took Russia out of the war and worked to build a Communist nation. Lenin was succeeded by Stalin, a ruthless dictator who killed and imprisoned millions in his attempt to industrialize and to build communism.

Section 2 Fascist Dictators Took Over Italy and Germany Italy had great problems after World War I. Workers needed jobs; farmers wanted more land. Benito Mussolini organized the Fascist party, promising to return order and glory to Italy. His promises appealed to Italians, and by 1922, Mussolini was the nation's dictator. For 10 years, Fascist rule seemed successful. Businesses prospered, workers had jobs, and marshes were drained to create more farmland. Yet, the next 10 years would bring troubles because of Mussolini's great ambitions. German Fascist leader Adolf Hitler started the National Socialist party, or Nazis, in hopes of solving Germany's problems and ending its humiliation from the loss in World War I. Hitler gained support among the German people and became Germany's dictator in 1933. Hitler silenced all opponents, and his secret police forced Nazi ideas on all Germans. Hitler began preparing for another world war. He also began an inhuman program aimed at exterminating, or murdering, Europe's Jews.

Section 3 Other Countries Fell to Dictators Spain ended its monarchy and established a republic in 1931. In a civil war, however, Italy and Germany helped Spain's Fascist forces overthrow the republic. Fascist dictator Francisco Franco came to power. Fascist dictators also took control of a number of nations in eastern Europe. These new dictatorships, like most others of the twentieth century, were totalitarian governments. In a totalitarian government an all-powerful leader allows no opposition. Individual rights disappear, and war becomes a major way of reaching goals.

Key Facts

1. Use each vocabulary word in a sentence.
   a. underground
   b. provisional government
   c. soviet
   d. proletariat
   e. gulag
   f. fascism
   g. corporate state
   h. scapegoat
   i. genocide
   j. totalitarian government
2. Identify and briefly explain the importance of the following names, places, or events.
   a. Czar Alexander II
   b. Czar Nicholas II
   c. "Bloody Sunday"
   d. Lenin
   e. Joseph Stalin
   f. Benito Mussolini
   g. Adolf Hitler
   h. the holocaust
   i. Francisco Franco
   j. Nicholas Horthy

Main Ideas

1. What was life like for most people in Russia under the czars?
2. How were the Communists able to take over Russia?
3. Why did many Italians find Mussolini's Fascist party so appealing?
4. List the steps in 1932 and 1933 that allowed Hitler to become Germany's dictator.
5. Who were the two opposing forces in the Spanish Civil War? What kind of government did each side want?
6. List at least three characteristics of a totalitarian government.

Developing Skill in Reading History

As discussed earlier, analogies describe relationships. For example, a possible analogy from this chapter would be Hitler:Germany::Mussolini:Italy (Hitler is to Germany as Mussolini is to Italy). The elements in both pairs have the same relationship to each other. Use information from the chapter to complete the following analogies from the choices provided below. Then explain the relationships in each analogy.

1. Hitler:fascism::Lenin:_____
- **a.** democracy
- **c.** monarchy
- **b.** communism
- **d.** Old Regime

2. Italy:Mussolini::Spain:_____
- **a.** Horthy
- **c.** Franco
- **b.** the Loyalists
- **d.** King Alfonso

3. Hitler:concentration camps::Stalin:_____
- **a.** gulags
- **c.** persecution
- **b.** secret police
- **d.** Gestapo

Using Social Studies Skills

1. Analyzing Political Cartoons Study the political cartoon below. The figure on the left represents Adolf Hitler. What is the cartoonist saying about Hitler? What symbols does the cartoonist use?

EUROPE IS ALSO PAVED WITH GOOD INTENTIONS

2. Forming Hypotheses Read the following hypotheses. Then list two facts that would either support or disprove each.
- **a.** Forced collectivization is a good way to produce enough food in an emergency.
- **b.** Fascist dictators rely on terror to maintain their rule.
- **c.** Fascists gain support through overblown promises of glory and greatness for the nation.

Critical Thinking

1. Determining Relevance How did the Treaty of Versailles, which ended World War I, contribute to Hitler's rise to power?

2. Distinguishing Fact from Opinion Is the following statement a fact or an opinion? "Franco would not have won the Spanish Civil War if the world's democratic nations had supported the Loyalist forces."

3. Recognizing Ideologies What were Lenin's basic political views? How did his actions reflect these views?

Focus on Writing

Writing Expository Paragraphs

As you have learned, an *expository paragraph* is one that explains or teaches. In such a paragraph, you should focus on expressing everything as clearly as possible. Your *topic sentence* should be a direct factual statement. Your *support* should be strong and clear. Your *language* should be understandable, and all special terms should be defined. Plan and write an expository paragraph on one of the following topics or on a topic of your own choice from the chapter.
- **a.** The Appeal of Fascism in Germany and Italy
- **b.** Stalin: Rule by Terror
- **c.** Twentieth-Century Dictatorships
- **d.** The Weaknesses Found in Totalitarian Governments

World War II

(1936–1945)

1 **Unchecked Aggression Grew into Total War**

2 **Germany and Its Allies Scored Early Victories**

3 **The Allies Triumphed in Europe and Asia**

4 **World Nations United to Prevent Future Wars**

▲ **Illustrating History**
A smiling Prime Minister Neville Chamberlain is shown above on his return to England after negotiating with Adolf Hitler.

On September 30, 1938, Britain's prime minister, Neville Chamberlain, stepped down from the plane that had just brought him to London from Munich, Germany. He held a declaration of peace that he had signed with Adolf Hitler of Germany. Chamberlain read the document to the officials who had come to greet him. The declaration promised that Germany and Britain would work together to bring peace to Europe. Chamberlain then drove through cheering crowds to his office. There, he stepped to the window and, waving the paper, proclaimed to the crowd, "I believe it is peace in our time."

Chamberlain felt sure that the declaration of peace would last. In exchange for giving in to Hitler's demand for certain parts of the small country of Czechoslovakia, Hitler promised to halt his expansion. Unfortunately, the deal was fake.

Six months later, heavily armed German troops marched into Czechoslovakia and claimed the entire nation for their own. Poland fell to Germany in September 1939. A shaken man, Chamberlain then declared Britain at war with Germany. The world was gradually waking up to the terrible threat it faced in Adolf Hitler. In this chapter, you will learn about the rise of aggression in Europe, and the global war that followed.

1930	1935	1940	1945
■ 1930 Worldwide depression begins	1935 ■ Italy occupies Ethiopia; Nuremberg Laws attack German Jews	1938 ■ Germany occupies Austria; Munich Conference meets	■ 1939 World War II begins
		1941 ■ Germany invades Russia; Japan attacks Pearl Harbor	1945 ■ Germany surrenders; United States drops atomic bombs and Japan surrenders

▲ **Illustrating History** *The photograph above shows the advancing German army as it attacked Yugoslavia in April of 1941.*

1 Unchecked Aggression Grew into Total War

As you read, look for answers to these questions:

◆ How did America's postwar prosperity end in 1929?
◆ How did Germany, Italy, and Japan become allies?
◆ What were Adolf Hitler's ambitions in Europe?
◆ Why did the democratic nations allow Hitler to have his way?

Key Terms: isolationism (defined on p. 616), axis (p. 616), buffer zone (p. 617), annexation (p. 617), appeasement (p. 617), nonaggression pact (p. 618)

For many Americans, the years after World War I were exciting and prosperous. American businesses were growing, and factories were providing employment while modern production methods supplied the growing demand for cars, radios, and other goods. Foreign countries paid billions of dollars for American products. As President Calvin Coolidge put it, "The business of America is business." Population grew in the early 1920s, and people experienced greater wealth. The prosperity of the 1920s, however, could not last. This was true because of conditions both at home and in other parts of the world.

Postwar Prosperity Gave Way to Worldwide Depression

If Americans seemed to be interested only in their own affairs, it was because the horrors of World War I made them want to turn their backs on Europe and the rest of

615

the world. Now, the American mood was one of **isolationism**, a wish to stay out of international affairs.

Economic problems at home. By 1928, American farmers were suffering economically, since neither Europe nor America could buy all the food they produced. European farmers had recovered from World War I and were supplying their own crops. In cities, workers were earning high wages, but they could not keep up with prices that were rising at a faster rate than their earnings. Banks failed as companies and farmers failed to pay back loans.

Millions of Americans, confident that the economy was healthy, put all their money into buying stocks, the value of which kept soaring. Then, in October 1929, stock prices began to drop and kept going down until the stock market "crashed." Many people lost their savings, businesses closed down, and jobs were hard to find. The Great Depression had begun.

The depression of the 1930s abruptly awoke Americans to hard times. After his election in 1932, President Franklin D. Roosevelt began a program of recovery and relief through government intervention. It became increasingly clear that the economic crisis of the 1930s was worldwide.

Economic problems abroad. The nations of Europe were trying to recover from World War I. Their problems included restoring industry, creating jobs, rebuilding destroyed cities, and paying back their war debts. For most nations, these debts were staggering. The Allies insisted that defeated Germany pay for the damages caused by the war—more than 30 billion dollars. The United States wanted the Allies to pay back the money they had borrowed. When Germany could not pay for the war damages, the Allies could not pay their war debts either. All these nations angrily resented demands for payment. The Allies became even angrier as the interest on those tremendous loans mounted up.

The United States also withdrew foreign investments as it struggled with its own depression. Thus, many European factories and businesses failed, causing hardship and unemployment abroad. The Allies were thus even less likely to pay their war debts.

Much of Europe Was Politically Unstable

In addition to financial problems, other problems plagued postwar Europe. The Versailles Treaty, which was supposed to create a stable peace, actually contained some of the seeds of its own undoing. As peace settlements of World War I erased some old borders and created new ones, shaky political situations arose. Most of the new nations, were fighting an uphill battle to make their democratic governments work. The peoples of eastern Europe did not have strong democratic traditions because they had been ruled differently for years. In short, the Versailles Treaty had called for political change without providing a plan to accomplish that change.

Because of the widespread unrest, the period between World War I and World War II has often been called the "long armistice." This 20-year period of peace was only temporary, and many people expected another world war.

Nationalism and Militarism Gained Strength

After World War I, some leaders tried to safeguard peace through treaties and agreements. In the 1930s, with the rise of dictatorships, these agreements began to fail.

The alliance of Japan, Germany, and Italy. In 1934, Germany started to rearm in violation of the Versailles Treaty. A year later, Japan began to rebuild its navy in violation of the Washington Agreement of 1922, which limited the number of naval vessels that a nation could have. In 1936, Hitler and Mussolini made an **axis,** or an alliance, to encourage their common purposes. In an alliance known as the Rome-Berlin Axis, they agreed to help one another in their drive for power and conquest. In 1940, Japan's leaders joined this alliance, forming the Rome-Berlin-Tokyo Axis.

Nationalism in Japan, Germany, and Italy. As in World War I, extreme nationalism played a part in bringing on World War II. Worship of the emperor in Japan and idolization of Hitler and Mussolini in Europe encouraged the growth of an extreme and dangerous form of patriotism.

Imperialism, which is closely tied to extreme nationalism, was also a cause of the war. The grab for new lands contributed to instability in many parts of the world.

Militarism in Japan. You read in Chapter 25 that, although Japan was a member of the League of Nations, it still made war on China. In 1931, Japan took over Manchuria and set up the state of Manchukuo with the Chinese emperor Pu Yi as puppet ruler. With the vast resources of Manchuria, Japan built factories whose products fed the Japanese war machine. China and the Chinese people, already divided by civil war, were exploited for the benefit of Japan.

The League of Nations condemned Japan's action and urged Japan to withdraw its troops from China. Japan refused and, in 1933, quit the league. This was a sign that the League of Nations was not able to stop a strong country.

Militarism in Germany. Observing that the League of Nations had not been able to stop Japan, Hitler felt safe in violating international law. In October 1933, he withdrew Germany from the League of Nations. In 1936, he sent his troops into the Rhineland. This area between France and Germany was supposed to be a **buffer zone,** a neutral area that separates nations. The league was unable to to stop Hitler. In 1938, Hitler sent his troops into Austria. The *Anschluss* (AHN shluss), as the **annexation,** or takeover, of Austria was called, was in violation of the Versailles Treaty.

Militarism in Italy. Fascist Italy felt that it too should grab new territory as soon as possible. In 1935, Mussolini sent his new Italian army into Ethiopia, an ancient, independent nation in Africa, which he wanted as a colony. The League of Nations was unable to stop Mussolini's "adventure."

▲ **Illustrating History** *This photograph of Pu Yi was taken in 1934, just before he was crowned emperor of Manchuria.*

Failure to Stop Dictators Led to War

Although leaders in the democracies watched events in China, Europe, and Africa with growing concern, they felt the best action was inaction. For example, leaders of the large nations thought that if they gave in a little to Germany's demands for more territory, perhaps Germany would be satisfied. This policy of giving in to a strong power in hopes of avoiding trouble is called **appeasement.** The democracies were not ready for war, did not want war, and hoped that they would not have to fight. Their economic problems due to the depression also discouraged entry into another war. Thus, the United States turned its back on Europe's political problems to avoid being involved in another war.

Not long after occupying the Rhineland and taking over Austria, Hitler announced that he had only "one last demand" to make. He wanted the Sudetenland (soo DAY tun land), an area of Czechoslovakia bordering Germany where many Czechs of German

▲ **Illustrating History** *The Munich Conference brought together (from left) British Prime Minister Neville Chamberlain, French Premier Edouard Daladier, German Dictator Adolf Hitler, and Italian Dictator Benito Mussolini.*

An Attack on Poland Leads to War

By now the Soviet dictator Joseph Stalin was dealing with both sides of the European conflict. In August 1939, the Soviet Union and Nazi Germany surprised the world by signing a **nonaggression pact.** This was an agreement not to go to war with each other. Stalin knew the Soviet Union was not ready for war. Hitler hoped to avoid the mistakes of World War I, in which Germany had had to fight on both the eastern and western fronts. The Nazi-Soviet pact of 1939 gave Germany a quiet eastern border.

Feeling secure in eastern Europe, Hitler invaded Poland on September 1, 1939. He believed that England and France would go along with him again, but this time he was wrong. On September 3, 1939, England and France declared war on Germany. World War II had begun. However, Hitler had grown strong. It took a long and costly war to defeat him.

descent lived. Czechoslovakia prepared for war, but it was no match for Germany's military power. In 1935, England, France, and the Soviet Union had agreed by treaty to help Czechoslovakia. Now, Czechoslovakia looked to England and France for help.

In 1938, Prime Minister Neville Chamberlain of England, Premier Edouard Daladier (dah lah DYAY) of France, and Mussolini of Italy met with Hitler in the German city of Munich. At Munich, the democracies again gave in to Hitler's demands and allowed Germany to annex the Sudetenland. The name of "Munich" came to stand for appeasement and humiliation.

In 1938, the Sudetenland became part of Germany. Within the same year Hitler broke his promise, took most of the rest of Czechoslovakia, and in effect, erased that country from the map.

Following in Hitler's path of broken promises, Italy grabbed Albania, on the seacoast of the Balkan Peninsula in April of 1939. The countries of England and France, now really worried, looked for the first time to the Soviet Union as an ally.

618

2 Germany and Its Allies Scored Early Victories

As you read, look for answers to these questions:

◆ How did Hitler use the blitzkrieg to take over most of Europe?
◆ How did Germany and the Soviet Union become enemies instead of allies?
◆ What brought the United States into World War II?

> **Key Terms:** blitzkrieg (defined on p. 619), collaborate (p. 620), lend-lease (p. 622), embargo (p. 622)

German military leaders had been getting ready for this war for a long time. They had developed a new method of fighting known as **blitzkrieg** (BLITZ kreeg), which means "lightning war." It was a sudden, swift, overpowering attack that used airplanes to bomb cities and to machine gun soldiers and civilians. Then, German ground forces would rush into battle.

Dictators Quickly Conquered Most of Europe

Blitzkrieg tactics made Germany successful during the early years of the war because they caught other nations unprepared. Within a week, the Germans had conquered most of Poland. The German army then marched east, the Russian army marched west, and they divided Poland between them. Poland, like Czechoslovakia, disappeared from the map of Europe.

Although still Hitler's ally on paper, the Soviet Union took steps to protect itself from a possible German attack. Stalin correctly realized that he and Hitler were truly enemies and that a German attack was a distinct possibility. Thus, the Soviet Union took advantage of its success in Poland and moved to conquer Estonia, Latvia, and Lithuania in 1939 and 1940. Finally, the Soviet Union attacked and conquered Finland.

DAILY LIFE

The London Blitz

Winston Churchill once declared proudly that "London can take it." During the winter of 1940, London did. The air-raid sirens wailed almost nightly as waves of German bombers attacked (or "blitzed") the city. (See right.) Londoners huddled in basements or backyard shelters. Fire engines and ambulances raced through the streets.

For children, the bombings could be thrilling. "My parents were scared, but to me it was all exciting and sort of a game," one 7-year-old boy later recalled. "You'd go down [into the shelter] and have secret meetings and take candy and chocolate."

1. What was the blitz of London?
2. How did Londoners deal with the blitz?

Hitler's armies advanced into Denmark, Norway, the Netherlands, Belgium, and Luxembourg. By 1940, all these nations had fallen under Nazi rule. Germany was now ready for its old enemy, France.

France Fell to the Nazis

From 1930 to 1934, France had been building a line of forts along its eastern border. Known as the Maginot (MAH jih NOH) line, it was the key to France's defense against invasion. When the Nazi armies suddenly began to move into France, however, they went around the northern end of the Maginot Line. In June of 1940, German troops marched, unopposed, into Paris.

A few days before the invasion, Italy had also declared war on France and England and invaded southern France. Hitler was elated when, on June 22, 1940, France signed an armistice at Compiegne, in the same railway car and in the same place where Germany had surrendered to France in 1918 at the end of World War I.

According to the terms of the armistice, Nazi forces would occupy most of France. French resources and factories were to be placed at the disposal of Germany. A government that agreed to **collaborate** with, or cooperate with, the Nazis was set up under French Marshal Henri Philippe Pétain.

A few brave French leaders flew to England, where they set up a "Free French" government. Led by General Charles de Gaulle (duh GAHL), the French organized an underground movement, the Resistance. It carried out secret missions against the Germans.

Hitler Attacked Britain and the Soviet Union

After the French were defeated, Britain stood alone against Germany. In August 1940, Hitler launched an attack, which is now known as the Battle of Britain. Hundreds of planes from the Nazi air force, the *Luftwaffe* (LOOFT vah fuh), made countless bombing raids over London and other English cities. For the many months of the "blitz," English families spent hours at a time in hurriedly built air raid shelters.

Despite the danger and destruction, Hitler could not defeat Britain. The British people courageously faced the worst that Hitler could deal out, inspired by the rousing speeches of their prime minister, Winston Churchill. The Royal Air Force, known as the RAF, fought back valiantly. It destroyed many of Hitler's bombers and so much of his invasion fleet that he gave up his plan to invade Britain. At sea, British ships torpedoed and sank the German battleship *Bismarck* in May 1941.

By 1941, it appeared that the war would last longer than Hitler had expected. Hitler realized he would need more resources such as oil for his war machinery and wheat for his troops. Hitler, therefore, attacked the Soviet Union, a nation rich in these and other resources.

On June 22, 1941, using his well-known blitzkrieg methods, Hitler invaded the Soviet Union. This attack was a costly mistake, because he began a two-front war. Now he would be battling England and France to the west and the Soviet Union to the east. Stalin's unprepared Soviet armies fell back in a retreat that drew the Germans farther into the Soviet Union. Furthermore, having Hitler as a common enemy made the Soviet Union and England allies.

Hitler Brought Terror to European Peoples

Since he had come to power, Hitler had planned the destruction of all European Jews. He sought to accomplish this terrible goal through the horrors that occurred during the holocaust. The Nazis set up concentration camps in Germany and in the countries Germany conquered. Railroad freight cars brought to the camps Jews, Germans who disagreed with Nazi activities, and millions of Russians, Poles, and other peoples whom Hitler considered "inferior" to his "master race." In the camps, these prisoners were forced into slave labor for the large German corporations that made German war materials. Slave laborers worked with little food or medical attention until they died of exhaustion or starvation or were executed.

Anne Frank

In Amsterdam, Holland, shortly after World War II, people looking through the rubble of an old office building found some handwritten notebooks. They turned out to be the writings of a young Jewish girl named Anne Frank, pictured here.

From 1942 until 1944, Anne had hidden from the Nazis with her family and another family in a secret attic in that build-ing. During the two years of hiding, Anne wrote what it was like to live concealed from the world. She expressed the conflicts and crises all young people share and told of her plans and dreams for the future. "I want to go on living even after my death!" Anne wrote. "And therefore I am grateful to God for giving me this gift, this possibility of developing myself and of writing, of expressing all that is in me."

Anne Frank did not sur-vive World War II. The Nazis discovered her and her family and sent them to a concentration camp. She died in the camp at the age of 15. But Anne Frank's wish to live after her death was fulfilled through her notebooks. Published in 1947, these notebooks have become the world-famous *The Diary of a Young Girl*. Her diary has been read by some 60 million people. The site of her hiding place in Am-sterdam is now the Anne Frank Museum, visited by thousands of people each year. Close by the muse-um stands a statue dedi-cated to her memory.

1. Why did Anne Frank and her family have to hide from the Nazis?
2. What did Frank write about in her note-books?
3. Why can we say that she lives on after her death?

Six million Jews died in the holocaust—about two-thirds of the prewar Jewish popu-lation of Europe. Millions of other people also died in Nazi death camps.

No hiding place. It is not easy to under-stand why so many Jews were unable to escape. Many Jews who tried to escape found their way blocked by countries that were unwilling to accept them. Others were betrayed by anti-Semites or for money. Some Jews found homes in Palestine. As the war went on, more escape routes closed.

Throughout Europe, in the Netherlands, Denmark, and other countries, there were some brave individuals and families who tried to protect their Jewish friends and help them to escape the Nazis. In Germany, some people had the courage to come to the rescue of Jews. One was Oscar Schindler, a German Catholic businessman who had an armaments factory. When Jews were sent to him as workers, he saw to it that they were fed, clothed, and given medical attention. Between 1943 and 1945, he saved over 1,500 Jews. When Schindler died in Germany in 1974, he was honored in Jerusalem by more than 400 Jews whose lives he had saved.

The Swedish diplomat Raoul Wallenberg also saved many Jews. In 1944, at the re-quest of the U.S. War Refugee Board, Wallenberg went to Budapest, Hungary, where he provided passports and "safe houses" to Jews and helped them to escape.

▲ **Illustrating History** *These concentration camp victims were photographed at Auschwitz, one of Hitler's death camps.*

The United States Gave Help to Great Britain

At first, the United States tried to stay out of World War II. Soon, however, the United States realized the danger that Hitler posed. Congress passed laws so that American businesses could sell England and France the war materials they needed.

In March 1941, Congress passed a law allowing President Roosevelt to lend or lease military equipment to England and its allies. Under this **lend-lease** agreement, those nations could pay for the equipment after the war. American aid helped Britain carry on when it needed food and supplies.

By August 1941, Churchill and Roosevelt knew that they would soon be fighting allies. The two leaders drew up the Atlantic Charter, which promised that neither Great Britain nor the United States wanted to gain territory as a result of world war. It stated that the United States and Britain believed people should be able to choose the kinds of government they wished.

Japanese Attack Brought America into the War

While Hitler was grabbing more and more land in Europe, Japan was doing the same in Asia. In 1940, Japan prepared to overrun the rich islands of the Dutch East Indies. Since 1898 America had followed the "Open Door" policy, which gave all nations the right to trade equally in China and the Far East. Americans were unwilling to let Japan change this policy. In 1940, America stopped exporting gasoline and metal to Japan in an attempt to stop the Japanese by hurting their economy. A restriction of trade is called an **embargo.** Late in 1941, Japan sent a special ambassador to the United States to discuss the embargo and other problems with President Roosevelt.

Then, the Japanese shocked the United States with a surprise attack. On December 7, 1941, Japanese planes bombed the naval base at Pearl Harbor in Hawaii. The attack sank or badly damaged 13 ships, destroyed about 170 planes, and killed many Americans.

The next day, December 8, 1941, President Roosevelt labeled December 7 as "a day which will live in infamy." He asked Congress for a declaration of war against Japan, and Congress quickly granted his request. On December 11, Germany and Italy declared war on the United States, and the United States declared war on them.

SECTION 2 REVIEW

Knowing Key Terms, People, and Places
1. Define: **a.** blitzkrieg **b.** collaborate **c.** lend-lease **d.** embargo
2. Identify: **a.** Maginot Line **b.** Battle of Britain **c.** Winston Churchill **d.** holocaust

Reviewing Main Ideas
3. How did mistakes made by French military leaders let Hitler conquer France?
4. What were Hitler's plans for peoples who he did not think were part of the "master race"?

Critical Thinking
Drawing Conclusions
5. If the Japanese had not bombed Pearl Harbor, would the United States have entered World War II? Explain.

3 The Allies Triumphed in Europe and Asia

As you read, look for answers to these questions:

◆ How did war begin in the Far East?
◆ What events marked the turning point of the war for the Allies?
◆ What events brought an end to the war with Japan?

Key Terms: theater of war (defined on p. 623)

Once Japan and the United States went to war, World War II was truly worldwide. It was fought in four main areas, or **theaters of war:** Europe, North Africa, Asia, and the Pacific Islands. The United States and its friends soon called themselves the Allies. Many of the Latin American countries agreed with the ideas of the Atlantic Charter and declared that they would cut off relations with the Axis nations.

Axis Victories Continued

The early years of the war were discouraging for the Allies. Japanese aggression on United States and British possessions opened the far eastern theater of war. Within a few days of the Pearl Harbor attack, Japanese forces captured Guam (gwahm) and the Wake Islands. The Japanese took the British port of Hong Kong and invaded British Malaya in Southeast Asia. Then, in early 1942, the Philippines and the Dutch East Indies fell to the Japanese. Although the Soviet troops fought well for over a year, the Nazis had advanced as far as Stalingrad by September.

In North Africa, German General Erwin Rommel, known as "the Desert Fox," reached Egypt in 1942. He threatened the Suez Canal and the British naval base at Alexandria. For a time, it seemed that the military successes of Japan and Germany might bring an Axis victory.

1942 Was the Allies' Turning Point

With lend-lease, the United States became the "arsenal of democracy," providing the Allies with weapons, fuel, and food.

Victories in the Pacific. In 1942, American aid and military strength began to help the Allies. For example, American fliers led by Colonel James Doolittle made a surprise air attack on Tokyo. Then, at the Battle of the Coral Sea (see the map on page 625) between Australia and New Guinea, American naval strength stopped the threat of a Japanese invasion of Australia. Still another major naval defeat for the Japanese was a sea-and-air battle at Midway Island in June 1942. Three months later, the United States Marines captured Japanese airfields on Guadalcanal in the Solomon Islands.

Victories in North Africa and Europe. The progress of the war in Europe and Africa is shown on the map on page 624. In North Africa, British Field Marshal Bernard Montgomery resisted Rommel's desert troops and drove the Germans out of Egypt. Allied forces under American General Dwight D. Eisenhower completed the German defeat in North Africa. The Allies then crossed the Mediterranean to the island of Sicily and launched an invasion on the mainland of Italy.

In Europe, the Soviet armies, aided by a bitterly cold winter, made a heroic stand at Stalingrad and stopped the Nazi advance. While all this was going on, the Soviet Union wanted Britain and the United States to attack the Germans from the west. The Allies agreed, but it took a long time to get ready. In the meantime, Allied planes made a series of round-the-clock bombings of German factories and cities, which resulted in high death tolls. The raids did not do much to halt Germany's ability to manufacture weapons, but they made the German people realize how terrible war could be and what Hitler had caused.

D-Day. With Germany weakening, the Allies made plans for a massive invasion of Europe. On June 6, 1944, called "D-Day," British, American, Canadian, and Free

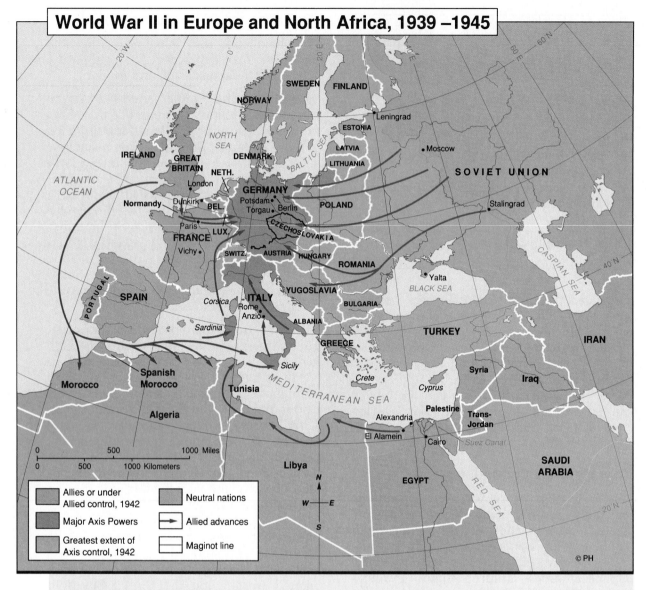

World War II in Europe and North Africa, 1939 –1945

Map labels: SWEDEN, NORWAY, FINLAND, Leningrad, ESTONIA, Moscow, IRELAND, GREAT BRITAIN, DENMARK, NORTH SEA, LATVIA, LITHUANIA, SOVIET UNION, BALTIC SEA, London, NETH., GERMANY, POLAND, ATLANTIC OCEAN, Normandy, Dunkirk, BEL., Potsdam, Berlin, Stalingrad, Paris, LUX., Torgau, CZECHOSLOVAKIA, FRANCE, Vichy, SWITZ., AUSTRIA, HUNGARY, ROMANIA, Yalta, CASPIAN SEA, PORTUGAL, SPAIN, Corsica, ITALY, YUGOSLAVIA, BLACK SEA, Rome, Anzio, BULGARIA, Sardinia, ALBANIA, TURKEY, IRAN, GREECE, Crete, Syria, Iraq, Morocco, Spanish Morocco, Sicily, Cyprus, Tunisia, MEDITERRANEAN SEA, Palestine, Trans-Jordan, Algeria, Alexandria, El Alamein, Cairo, Suez Canal, SAUDI ARABIA, Libya, EGYPT, RED SEA

Scale: 0 – 500 – 1000 Miles; 0 – 500 – 1000 Kilometers

Compass: N, W–E, S

Legend:
- Allies or under Allied control, 1942
- Major Axis Powers
- Greatest extent of Axis control, 1942
- Neutral nations
- Allied advances
- Maginot line

© PH

Focus on Geography

1. **Movement** By 1942, the Axis powers had gotten within how many miles of Moscow?
2. **Regions** What are the two countries that formed the major Axis powers?

French troops invaded the French region of Normandy. Commanded by General Eisenhower, the Allies began the offensive that took them across France to Germany and final victory. During the remaining months of 1944, Allied soldiers liberated Paris and reached the German border.

The Germans made their last counteroffensive in Belgium in December 1944. In what is known as the Battle of the Bulge, at the frightful cost of more than 76,000 men, the Allied forces finally won. The Allies were assured of success on both the western and the eastern fronts. Both the Soviet and

624

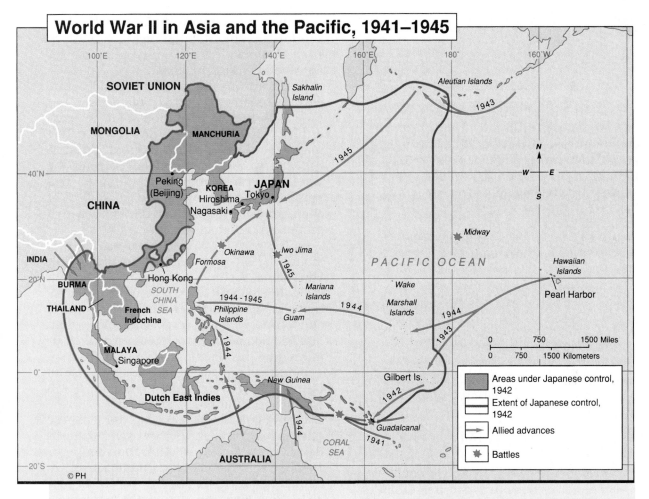

World War II in Asia and the Pacific, 1941–1945

Focus on Geography

1. **Location** Due south from Tokyo, Japanese control stretched how many miles at its peak in 1942?
2. **Movement** What were the main objectives of the Allies, judging from the directions of their advances?

American armies moved across Germany, meeting at Torgau on April 25, 1945. The end of Nazi Germany was in sight.

The War Ended in Europe and in Asia

The war ended in 1945, and three wartime leaders died that same year. With victory in sight, President Franklin D. Roosevelt died suddenly on April 12, 1945. He was listed as a war victim. In Italy, Benito Mussolini's anti-Fascist captors shot him without a formal trial in April 1945.

Hitler passed his last days hidden in a bombproof shelter. Germany's Third Reich was near collapse. On April 30, 1945, as the Soviet army was entering Berlin, Hitler killed himself. The fighting ended in Italy on the same day. On May 8, 1945, President Truman proclaimed victory in Europe. The day is known as V-E Day.

The Japanese were near defeat when the war ended in Europe. American General Douglas MacArthur captured the Philippines in October 1944. Moving north toward Japan, United States Marines captured

625

Effects of the Atomic Bomb

Before the United States dropped the first atomic bomb on Japan, scientists could only speculate about the effects of the bomb. After Japan surrendered, the United States tried to evaluate the damage that had actually been done by this terrifying new weapon. The following excerpt is from a 1947 United States government study of the impact of the atomic bomb on Hiroshima.

❝At about 0815 [8:15 A.M.] there was a blinding flash. Some describe it as brighter than the sun. . . . Following the flash there was a blast of heat and wind. The large majority of people within 3,000 feet of ground zero [where the bomb was dropped] were killed immediately. . . . Persons in the open were burned on exposed surfaces, and within 3,000–5,000 feet, many were burned to death while others received serious burns through their clothes. In many instances clothing burst into spontaneous flame and had to be beaten out. Thousands of people were pinned beneath collapsed buildings or injured by flying debris [rubble].

Shortly after the blast, fires began to spring up over the city. Those who were able made a mass exodus [departure] from the city into the outlying hills. . . . Pandemonium [wild confusion] reigned as the uninjured and slightly injured fled the city in fearful panic.**❞**

1. According to this report, what happened to people within 3,000 feet of the center of the explosion?
2. What does this report suggest about the psychological effect of the bomb on the people of Japan?

the island of Okinawa in June 1945, after several months of bitter fighting. Eastern front commanders continued planning for an Allied invasion of Japan.

By any means, the invasion would not be easy. Estimates of United States casualties ranged as high as 1 million soldiers. Such estimates must have been on President Truman's mind when he made the decision to use a new weapon developed during the war—an atomic bomb. According to Truman, the bomb offered the possibility of ending the war quickly and decisively with a minimum of loss of life.

As the map on page 625 shows, the first atomic bomb was dropped on the city of Hiroshima, Japan, on August 6, 1945. With many times the force of the most powerful bomb known until that time, it destroyed life and property on a vast scale. More than 160,000 people in Hiroshima were killed or injured by this one bomb.

In spite of the horror of Hiroshima, Japan refused to give in. Another atomic bomb was dropped on the Japanese city of Nagasaki on August 9. The next day, the Japanese offered to surrender. Victory over Japan was declared on August 14, 1945, and Emperor Hirohito told the people of their defeat. On September 2, 1945, aboard the U.S.S. *Missouri,* the Japanese signed the agreement ending the war. American troops occupied Japan, and World War II was over.

Allied Leaders Made Plans for Peace

The meeting between Roosevelt and Churchill that produced the Atlantic Charter was followed by other conferences among the leaders of the Allied nations. One of the big problems in the conferences was the mutual distrust between the Soviet Union and the other Allies.

Nevertheless, meetings involving the Big Three Allied leaders—Winston Churchill, Franklin D. Roosevelt, and Joseph Stalin—had taken place at several points during the course of the war. In February of 1945, these leaders met at Yalta in southern Russia to make plans to end the war and to discuss the future of eastern Europe.

▲ **Illustrating History** *Thousands of New Yorkers poured into the streets to celebrate Germany's surrender on May 7, 1945.*

Initial plans to form the United Nations were made. It was agreed that free elections would be held in the eastern European countries. Poland was to be given German land in the west in exchange for Polish land to be taken in the east by Russia. Germany itself was to be divided into American, British, French, and Soviet military zones. The Allies also agreed that trials of Nazi war criminals would take place. Although the Allied leaders disagreed on some points, they all shared the common goal of ending every trace of Nazism.

In July 1945, the Allied leaders met for a final conference in Potsdam, Germany. They agreed on the peace settlement with Germany and drew up plans for Japan's surrender and occupation.

At Potsdam, Truman hinted to Stalin that America had an atomic bomb. Some historians think that this was Truman's way of trying to gain the upper hand with the Soviets. They maintain that Truman dropped the atomic bombs partly as a warning to the Soviets. According to one author, "Very few turning points of history can be specified precisely . . . when Rome began to decline . . . when the Renaissance began . . . [but] here is one turning point that can be dated with extraordinary precision: the twentieth-century nuclear arms race began . . . 7:30 P.M., on July 24, 1945 [at Potsdam]."

SECTION 3 REVIEW

Knowing Key Terms, People, and Places
1. Define: **a.** theater of war
2. Identify: **a.** Philippines **b.** Rommel **c.** D-Day **d.** Battle of the Bulge **e.** Hiroshima **f.** Yalta Conference

Focus on Geography
3. In what two ways was control of North Africa important in World War II? Use the map to help you explain.

Reviewing Main Ideas
4. What were some of the early Axis victories in 1941 and 1942?
5. What were the main topics at the conferences among Allied leaders?

Critical Thinking
Perceiving Cause and Effect
6. Explain the quotation on this page about the beginning of the nuclear arms race. Why can this turning point be "dated with extraordinary precision"?

627

4 World Nations United to Prevent Future Wars

As you read, look for answers to these questions:

- What was the aim of the United Nations?
- What powers does the United Nations General Assembly have?
- How can one nation's veto stop United Nations action?
- What is the job of the United Nations secretary-general?

Key Terms: veto power (defined on p. 629), trust territory (p. 630)

During World War II, there were high hopes that people could create a new international organization that would be strong enough to prevent war. The United Nations was the result. Just as they had joined in a common effort to win the war, the Allied nations met in April 1945 and worked out a plan called the Charter of the United Nations. In June 1945, 50 nations signed the charter to preserve peace.

The United Nations Charter Stated Its Aims

The preamble to the United Nations Charter contains the aims and purposes of the organization. It states in part:

We the people of the United Nations, determined
TO SAVE succeeding generations from the scourge of war, . . .
TO REAFFIRM FAITH in fundamental human rights, . . .
TO ESTABLISH conditions under which justice and respect for the obligations arising from . . . international law can be maintained, . . .
TO PROMOTE social progress . . . and for these ends
TO PRACTICE tolerance . . .
TO UNITE our strength to maintain international peace . . .
TO ENSURE . . . that armed force shall not be used, save in the common interest . . .
TO EMPLOY international machinery for the promotion of economic and social advancement of peoples,

have resolved to combine our efforts to accomplish these aims.

The Work of the United Nations Was Divided Among Different Parts

To carry out its plans and reach its goals, the United Nations set up various bodies and organizations, each with specific jobs. The United Nations originally had six main parts: the General Assembly, the Security Council, the Economic and Social Council, the Secretariat, The International Court of Justice, and the Trusteeship Council.

General Assembly. In the General Assembly, each member nation has one vote. The General Assembly meets once a year and can be called into a special meeting when necessary. It is in the General Assembly that problems of the world may be brought into the open. Here, member nations can freely discuss world problems in hopes of finding solutions. The General Assembly cannot pass laws, but it can make decisions about what action the nations should take.

With the recommendation of the Security Council, the General Assembly chooses the secretary-general of the United Nations, the United Nations' chief administrator. It also decides on the admission of new members and chooses the nonpermanent members of the Security Council. A two-thirds vote is needed to decide important matters, such as sending troops to troubled areas.

Security Council. The Security Council has 15 member nations. Five of these nations are permanent members—the United States, the Soviet Union, France, Great Britain, and the People's Republic of China. The other 10 member nations on the Security Council are elected every two years by the General Assembly.

The council meets regularly. Because its members can be called together quickly, it is always in a position to take up world problems when they arise. The Security Council's main job is to keep peace. It looks into problems that may cause wars and urges nations to settle their differences. The council has the authority to use armed forces to protect member nations. A Military Staff Committee, which works at the direction of the Security Council, has the job of directing troops in an emergency. An Atomic Energy Commission is responsible for international control of atomic energy.

In order to know how the United Nations works, it is necessary to understand the voting method of the Security Council. In most cases, the vote of any 9 of the 15 members is enough to carry a decision. On important questions, however, every one of the permanent members must agree. If any permanent member votes "No," the council cannot take action. This is the well-known **veto power,** which belongs to all of the permanent members on the council.

Sometimes a question that has been vetoed by one member of the Security Council can be turned over to the General Assembly in which there is no veto. By a two-thirds vote, the General Assembly can urge members to take the step that was vetoed in the Security Council. This mechanism serves as a check on the veto power of the permanent nations of the Security Council.

Economic and Social Council. Another body in the United Nations, the Economic and Social Council, includes 54 nations elected by the General Assembly for three-year terms. Since hunger, sickness, and poverty are among the underlying causes of war, this branch of the United Nations studies these problems. The United Nations tries to eliminate the reasons for which wars have been fought. It does this by studying ways of improving people's health and their working and living conditions.

One of the most significant bodies of the Economic and Social Council is the Commission on Human Rights. Its Universal Declaration of Human Rights states that all

▲ **Illustrating History** *Delegates from many countries meet to discuss issues at the United Nations Building in New York.*

human beings are entitled to certain rights, including the right to choose their government and to enjoy a good standard of living.

Secretariat. The Secretariat does the necessary day-to-day work of running the United Nations. The Secretariat's staff members keep records, distribute information, and do hundreds of other tasks. The head of the Secretariat is called the secretary-general. He or she is chosen by the General Assembly for five years and may be reelected. The first United Nations secretary-general was Trygve Lie (LEE) of Norway. He was followed in 1953 by Dag Hammarskjold (HAHM ahr SHULD) of Sweden, who was killed in a plane crash in 1961. His successors were U Thant of Burma, followed by Kurt Waldheim (VAHLT HYM) of Austria in 1971, and then Javier Perez de Cuellar (KWAY YAHR) of Peru in 1981.

The secretary-general is a highly qualified diplomat who can have much influence on world affairs. The secretary-general spends much time traveling from one trouble spot to another, hoping to get the nations of the world to solve their problems without using force. He or she lives in an apartment on the grounds of the United Nations territory in

New York City but is really a citizen of the world. The secretary-general cannot be a citizen of any of the permanent nations in the Security Council.

The United Nations buildings and land in New York City belong to no country. The United Nations' special police officers and workers come from all parts of the world and, like the secretary-general, must think like citizens of the world. For these people, the interests of the United Nations are supposed to come before the interests of any one country.

International Court of Justice. The International Court of Justice, or World Court, has 15 judges. While the General Assembly and Security Council meet in New York, the World Court meets at the Hague in the Netherlands. The judges are chosen by the General Assembly and Security Council for a term of nine years. No nation can have more than one judge at a time on the bench of the court.

The International Court of Justice tries to settle disagreements among nations on the basis of international law. A nation can be a member of the court without being a member of the United Nations. Furthermore, all nations who signed the Court Statute are subject to its decisions. The court also gives opinions on cases put before it by organizations of the United Nations.

Trusteeship Council. The Trusteeship Council of the United Nations was set up to look after the interests of lands placed under its trusteeship system. These former colonies, taken from defeated nations after World War II, are called **trust territories.** They were given to certain United Nations members to hold in trust until the colony could rule itself. The council was once a major body of the United Nations, but by the 1980s, most trust territories had become independent.

Other Agencies. Many other United Nations agencies work in specialized fields, such as health, finance, and education. They include UNICEF (the United Nations Children's Fund), the World Health Organization (WHO), and the World Bank.

A number of points should be kept in mind about the United Nations. It is not a government or a confederation of nations. The United Nations has no power to tell its members what to do. Each nation retains the right to do as it wishes because the government of each nation is completely independent. The idea is that member nations are interested in world peace and progress. They have, therefore, volunteered to support the plans and ideas of the United Nations Charter.

The United Nations was founded in 1945. Since that time, it has gained much experience by facing many problems. How successful has the United Nations been? It is not easy to keep score. Much of the work of the United Nations deals with problems of improving education, health, and living conditions. These jobs do not often make headlines. In the long run, however, they are most important because they are directed at trying to solve the underlying causes of war. As you study the postwar world in the next unit, you will be able to judge how successful the United Nations has been.

The history of our world has been shaped, in part, by decisions and by the actions that followed them. Reaching a decision involves a series of steps, and understanding the decision-making process allows you to evaluate the judgments made by historical figures.

Use the following steps to study the decision-making process and to evaluate the decision described below.

1. **Determine what decision is to be made and where to locate the information needed to reach it.** Unless there is a clear and accurate understanding of what needs to be decided, the decision itself may be flawed. Answer the following questions: (a) According to the excerpt below, what decision did President Truman have to make? (b) What steps did the president take to gather the information needed to make his decision?

2. **Before reaching a final decision, determine the available options and the consequences of each.** Remember that some choices may not be immediately apparent. Answer the following questions: (a) List three possible decisions relative to using the atomic bomb that President Truman might have made. (b) List one positive and one negative result of each of these decisions.

3. **Analyze the decision.** Determine its probable effects and evaluate its impact upon events. Answer the following questions: (a) What decision did President Truman actually make? (b) Based upon your understanding of Chapter 27, what were the effects of this decision? (c) How would you evaluate the president's decision based on the information given? Give reasons for your answer.

I . . . set up a committee of top men and . . . asked them to study with great care the implications the [use of the atomic bomb] might have for us . . .

It was their recommendation that the bomb be used against the enemy as soon as it could be done. They recommended further that it should be used without specific warning, and against a target that would clearly show its devastating strength. . . .

It was their conclusion that no technical demonstration they might propose, such as [exploding the bomb] over a deserted island, would be likely to bring the war to an end. . . .

The final decision of where and when to use the bomb was up to me. Let there be no mistake about it. I regarded the bomb as a military weapon, and never had any doubt that it should be used.

In deciding to use this bomb I wanted to make sure that it would be used as a weapon of war in a manner prescribed by the laws of war. That meant that I wanted it dropped on a military target.—Excerpt from the *Memoirs* of President Harry S. Truman

REVIEW

Section Summaries

Section 1 Unchecked Aggression Grew into Total War As the depression spread around the world, Americans began to realize that they could not remain isolated from the problems of other nations. Financial and political problems faced Europe as a result of the war and the need to rebuild. Some nations turned to dictators to solve their problems. The dictators hoped to strengthen their nations through conquest. Germany, Italy, and Japan formed a strong alliance. All three began invading neighboring lands. The League of Nations seemed unable to stop them and the democratic nations refused to intervene. Finally, when German troops stormed into Poland, Britain and France declared war.

Section 2 Germany and Its Allies Scored Early Victories Germany quickly conquered much of Europe. When France fell, Britain stood alone against the Axis powers. The Nazi air force began bombing raids on Britain, but Hitler could not defeat the British. In search of more resources, Hitler invaded his ally, the Soviet Union, creating a two-front war for Germany. Meanwhile, Hitler continued his policy of exterminating, or murdering, the Jews. As the war went on, the United States began to end its neutrality and supply equipment to Britain. Finally, a Japanese attack on the American fleet at Pearl Harbor brought the United States into the war in 1941.

Section 3 The Allies Triumphed in Europe and Asia Axis victories continued in 1941 and 1942. The year 1942 was a turning point, however, as U.S. forces bombed Tokyo and won important victories in the Pacific. The Allies also turned the tide in the Soviet Union and North Africa. Next, Allied forces took Italy and, in late 1944, landed at Normandy to begin their victorious drive toward Germany to end the war in Europe. The United States next used a fearsome new weapon, the atomic bomb, on two Japanese cities, forcing Japan to surrender. As the war ended, Allied leaders made plans for the postwar world.

Section 4 World Nations United to Prevent Future Wars in 1945 the Allied powers formed the United Nations in hopes of preventing future wars. The bodies of the United Nations include the General Assembly, the Security Council, the Economic and Social Council, the Secretariat, the World Court, and many other groups and agencies that address specific problems.

Key Facts

1. Use each vocabulary word in a sentence.
   - **a.** isolationism
   - **b.** axis
   - **c.** buffer zone
   - **d.** annexation
   - **e.** appeasement
   - **f.** nonaggression pact
   - **g.** blitzkrieg
   - **h.** collaborate
   - **i.** lend-lease
   - **j.** embargo
   - **k.** theater of war
   - **l.** veto power
   - **m.** trust territory
2. Identify and briefly explain the importance of the following names, places, or events.
   - **a.** Manchukuo
   - **b.** Ethiopia
   - **c.** Sudetenland
   - **d.** Battle of Britain
   - **e.** Pearl Harbor
   - **f.** Normandy
   - **g.** Hiroshima
   - **h.** Yalta

Main Ideas

1. What were the major problems of the European nations in the years following World War I?
2. How did Germany, Japan, and Italy violate international law?
3. List Germany's conquests from the beginning of the war to June 1940.
4. Describe the conflict between Japan and the United States that eventually brought the United States into the war.
5. Why was 1942 a turning point in the war?
6. What was D-Day?
7. How did the United States force the Japanese to surrender?
8. List the original six main parts of the United Nations and the function of each.

Developing Skill in Reading History

Use this quotation from the chapter to answer the questions below: "The Swedish diplomat Raoul Wallenberg also saved many Jews. In 1944, at the request of the U.S. War Refugee Board, Wallenberg went to Budapest, Hungary, where he provided passports and 'safe houses' to Jews and helped them to escape."

1. The quotation indicates that "safe houses" were
   a. camps
   b. hiding places
   c. railroad stations
2. Which would be the *best* topic sentence for a paragraph that included this quotation?
   a. Throughout Europe, there were some brave individuals and families who tried to protect Jews and help them to escape from the Nazis.
   b. The Nazis had a specific program to destroy the Jews.

Using Social Studies Skills

Using Visual Evidence How can photography help us understand more about a specific period of history? Use the photograph on this page and some photographs from the chapter to support your answer.

Critical Thinking

1. **Making Comparisons** How did the Axis powers differ from the Allies?
2. **Formulating Questions** Imagine that you are a judge on the United Nations' World Court. Two nations come to the court with a dispute over an area of land that each claims. Think of three important questions you will need to ask the disputing nations.
3. **Making Decisions** President Truman had to make one of the most important decisions in history over whether to drop atomic bombs on Japan to end the war. Create two lists that

the president might have made to help make his decision. Title one list "Reasons For." Title the second "Reasons Against."

Focus on Writing

Writing Persuasive Paragraphs

In a persuasive paragraph, you try to convince the audience that your opinion is correct. The *topic sentence* should present your opinion. The *support* should be strong and clear and cover opposing arguments. The *language* should be reasonable. It should not offend or insult. Imagine that you are living during the years covered by this chapter. Write a "letter to the editor" of your local newspaper on one of the following topics.
   a. 1938: Why Neville Chamberlain should (or should not) have stood up to Hitler at the meeting in Munich
   b. 1940: Why the United States should enter the war or remain neutral
   c. 1945: Why the United States should (or should not) join the United Nations

The Aftermath of World War II

(1945–1960)

1 **Two World Powers Emerged**

2 **Europe Recovered from the War**

3 **Nations Formed in Asia, Middle East, and Africa**

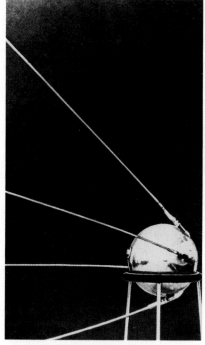

▲ **Illustrating History** *Above is a picture of the Soviet satellite, Sputnik, which extended the cold war into space in 1957.*

The time: October 4, 1957. The place: a grassy plain in southwestern Russia. A group of Soviet scientists intently watch a nearby launching pad, where a huge rocket hisses and steams. When the countdown finishes, the rocket roars aloft carrying a shiny sphere about twice the size of a basketball. Called Sputnik, this is the first artificial satellite ever to orbit the earth. The Soviet triumph begins a new era in human history—the Space Age.

News of Sputnik simply stuns the United States. Many Americans are amazed that the Soviets have raced ahead of the United States in the area of space exploration. One senator calls the launch "a devastating blow to U.S. scientific, industrial, and technological prestige." Other Americans worry about the possibility of a Soviet nuclear attack from space.

This was America in 1957. The rivalry between the United States and the Soviet Union made Americans nervous about the latest Soviet achievement. America had fought a "cold war" with the Russians on the political, military, and economic fronts. Now, space was the new battlefield. As you will learn in this chapter, the reaction to Sputnik grew out of cold war tension and distrust dating back more than a decade.

1945	1950	1955	1960

■ **1945**
Britain chooses socialism; De Gaulle leads France

■ **1947**
Marshall Plan aids Europe; independence divides India

■ **1949**
NATO joins Western nations; Communists rule China

1955 ■
Warsaw Pact joins Eastern European nations

■ **1956**
Soviets invade Hungary

■ **1957**
European Common Market begins

1961 ■
East Germany builds the Berlin wall

▲ **Illustrating History** *President Dwight Eisenhower (center) hosted Soviet leader Khrushchev (right) in 1959 during the cold war.*

1 Two World Powers Emerged

As you read, look for answers to these questions:

◆ What led to the cold war?
◆ What were the main goals of the Truman Doctrine and Marshall Plan?
◆ How did the Soviet satellite states respond to Russian domination?

> **Key Terms:** expansionism (defined on p. 635), cold war (p. 636), satellite country (p. 636)

In March 1946, in a speech made at Westminster College in Fulton, Missouri, British Prime Minister Winston Churchill stated:

"From Stettin in the Baltic to Trieste in the Adriatic, an *iron curtain* has descended across the Continent." Churchill went on to say that on one side of that curtain, now known as Eastern Europe, was the Soviet Union and the Communist-dominated countries. On the other side, now known as Western Europe, were the democratic nations allied to the United States. Churchill urged that Great Britain and America work together against Soviet **expansionism,** or the drive to increase territory.

World War II had made uneasy partners of the Communist and non-Communist countries. They had joined forces for one reason —to defeat Adolf Hitler. Even so, few people expected the wartime alliance between the Communist and non-Communist countries to break down quite as quickly as it did. The truth of Churchill's warning became evident, however, as increasing postwar tensions dissolved the wartime alliance.

635

The Cold War Was a War of Ideas

A **cold war,** a condition of tension and hostility without armed conflict, began shortly after World War II ended. The Soviet Union and other Communist countries of Eastern Europe were on one side in the cold war. The United States, Great Britain, France, and other nations of Western Europe were allied on the opposite side.

The cold war, then, represented a battle between opposing ideas and political systems. The basic ideas of democracy and capitalism clashed with those of communism and socialism. The cold war was fought with brain power, propaganda, and money, instead of tanks and guns.

The cold war was fought by scientists as well as politicians. Eventually, for example, the Soviet Union and the United States competed to lead in space explorations and experimentation. In this area of the cold war, the battlefields were the classrooms and laboratories of both countries.

The immediate cause of the cold war was the Soviet Union's effort to expand its territory. In order to expand, the Soviet Union was setting up Communist governments under Soviet control. The non-Communist countries, mostly allied with the United States, watched with growing mistrust. They believed that any expansion of communism had to be stopped. They felt that unless the spread of communism was stopped, both democracy and capitalism would fall.

The Soviet Movement to Expand Created Conflict

During World War II, the Nazi armies had caused serious damage to the Soviet Union. Soviet losses amounted to about 20 million dead, more than the total losses of all the other Allies combined. Property damage amounted to many billions of dollars. These great losses contributed to the Soviet feeling that they should gain the most at the end of the war.

As the war drew to an end, Soviet troops moved into Czechoslovakia, Hungary, Romania, and Bulgaria. As Churchill predicted, these countries—as well as Poland, Yugoslavia, and Albania—became **satellite countries** of the Soviet Union, that is, they were controlled by the Soviets and were independent in name only. Their original postwar governments, made up of both Communists and non-Communists, were changed. Stalin gradually forced all non-Communists out of the governments and took tight control of them. By 1948, the governments of all the Eastern European countries were brought under Communist control. These Communist countries of Eastern Europe came to be referred to as the "Soviet bloc."

Other Communist moves increased world tension. Turkey grew suspicious when the Soviet Union cancelled a friendship agreement with that country. In Greece, the Communists waged a civil war against the government, and in Southeast Asia, Communist forces took territory from the French. Then, in 1948 and 1949, the eyes of the world focused on postwar Germany where a dramatic cold war event took place.

Postwar Germany Became a Divided Land

Under the Allied occupation, high-ranking German Nazis were tried for their war crimes by a military court. The military court proceedings were called the *Nuremberg trials.* The Nazi leaders were found guilty of breaking world peace and committing horrible crimes against humanity. Eleven former high-ranking Nazis were condemned to death. Others were given prison sentences.

The Yalta agreement of 1945 gave the Soviet Union, France, Great Britain, and the United States the right to govern Germany on a temporary basis. In 1949, France, Great Britain, and the United States set up the German Federal Republic, or West Germany. Konrad Adenauer was the first chancellor of the German Federal Republic, and Bonn was named the capital of this new state. East Germany, officially known as the German Democratic Republic, was controlled by the Soviet Union.

Berlin, the capital of prewar Germany, was a special problem. Located entirely within East Germany, Berlin was divided among the Allies, with the Soviet Union in control of East Berlin and the Western powers in control of West Berlin. In time, East Berlin became the capital of the German Democratic Republic, and West Berlin became a state within the German Federal Republic. Ever since, relations between the Soviet Union and the West have been troubled over the division of Berlin.

The Berlin airlift. In June 1948, in Berlin, the cold war became dangerously heated. The Soviets strongly objected to the formation of the German Federal Republic, fearing that Germany might become strong enough to reunify and threaten Soviet power. In an attempt to force the Western powers to turn Berlin over to them, the Soviets blockaded the city. They stopped the transportation of goods and people between West Berlin and East Germany.

President Truman immediately ordered an American airlift of large cargo planes carrying food and other supplies into West Berlin. Throughout the following winter, bundles of coal were also airlifted to West Berlin to be used for heating. The Soviets finally stopped their blockade in May 1949. Although the threat of actual fighting was avoided, the Berlin airlift was not forgotten. The stage had been set for many more years

BIOGRAPHY

Harry S Truman

Born May 8, 1884, Harry Truman (seen at right) seemed an unlikely future president. Withdrawn and severely nearsighted as a child, Truman was kept from enjoying the activities of other boys. It was not until he served as a captain in World War I and then ran a men's clothing store in Kansas City that he developed the outgoing personality that made him a popular politician.

Truman faced many hard choices when he became president in April 1945. First, he had to make the painful decision to drop the atomic bomb on the Japanese city of Hiroshima. Then, because he believed the Soviets should not build an empire as the Japanese and Germans had during the 1930s, he had to choose a foreign policy. When the Soviets tested his policy by imposing a blockade on Berlin, Truman flew supplies into the city and thus broke the Soviet blockade.

Truman maintained that the cold war was the most important issue of his presidency. He said, "I have hardly had a day in office that has not been dominated by this all-embracing struggle—this conflict between those who love freedom and those who would lead the world back into slavery and darkness." He died in 1972.

1. What was Truman's childhood like?
2. How did Truman prevent the Soviets from building an empire after World War II?
3. Was Truman right to risk a new world war by confronting the Soviets as he did? Support your opinion.

of cold war. In the meantime, America was establishing a foreign policy to react to what it saw as the growing Soviet threat.

America Responded to Increased World Tensions

After making the critical decision to drop the atomic bomb on Japan at the end of World War II, President Truman faced the problems of the cold war. Truman realized that the cold war had to be fought with money, not guns. That is, he understood that communism would win in those countries where devastation was the greatest and where hopes for improvement were the lowest, unless the Communist threat could be weakened by the West.

Containment and the Truman Doctrine. To control Soviet expansion, the United States began an unstated policy of containment. The goal of this policy was to contain, or hold, the Soviets within their current boundaries. Political, economic, and, if needed, military pressures were used to accomplish this goal.

The first test of the containment policy came in Greece and Turkey in 1947. In March, the Truman Doctrine was established as the formal statement on the policy of containment. Under this doctrine, Congress approved 400 million dollars in economic and military aid to Greece and Turkey. This money enabled the Greek government to defeat the Communists and the Turks to resist Soviet pressure.

The Marshall Plan. The Marshall Plan, named after George Marshall, the distinguished U.S. secretary of state and former chief of staff during World War II, gave aid to 16 European countries trying to recover from the effects of the war. The plan was proposed in June of 1947. Even countries in Eastern Europe were eligible for Marshall Plan aid, but the Soviet Union would not allow them to apply for it. The United States gave financial aid to nations it considered at risk of giving in to communism. Between 1948 and 1952, about 12 billion dollars of aid were given. As a result, Western Europe was able to resist the threat of communism.

Military Alliances Divided Europe

In 1949, Western European leaders were successful in forming an organization that united their countries for military protection. This was the North Atlantic Treaty Organization or NATO. Its original members were Great Britain, France, Belgium, Luxembourg, the Netherlands, Denmark, Iceland, Italy, Norway, Portugal, and two non-European nations—Canada and the United States. Later, West Germany, Greece, Spain, and Turkey joined NATO. Each member of the group promises to come to the aid of the others in case of military attack.

Lined up against NATO are the countries of Eastern Europe. In 1955, the Soviet Union signed an agreement, known as the Warsaw Pact, with its satellite nations. This pact is the Soviet Union's answer to NATO, and the members are Bulgaria, Czechoslovakia, East Germany, Hungary, Poland, Romania, and the Soviet Union. Albania joined but later withdrew. The map on page 639 shows Warsaw Pact countries in 1955.

These two military alliances, NATO and the Warsaw Pact, clearly drew the lines between the Soviet Union and the United States. They demonstrated that each side intended to back up its members with military force if necessary.

Soviet Aggression Continued in Europe

In spite of alliances and efforts by the West, Soviet communism continued to control countries, often with cruelty and force. Events in Yugoslavia, Poland, and Hungary showed the world that not all Eastern European countries accepted Soviet domination.

Yugoslavia. Yugoslavia under its dictator, Marshal Tito, developed an amazing amount of independence within the Soviet sphere of influence. Tito, though never weakening his Communist views, defied Stalin and rebuilt Yugoslavia with some Western assistance. In 1948, Stalin expelled Yugoslavia from the Soviet bloc. Within the country, Tito allowed more private enterprise and civil rights than were allowed in neighboring satellite states. The Soviet Union was forced reluctantly to accept "Titoism."

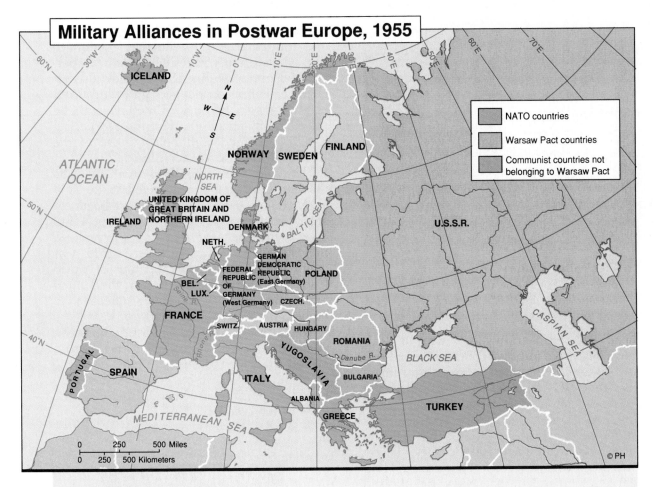

Military Alliances in Postwar Europe, 1955

NATO countries

Warsaw Pact countries

Communist countries not belonging to Warsaw Pact

ATLANTIC OCEAN

ICELAND

NORWAY   SWEDEN   FINLAND

NORTH SEA

UNITED KINGDOM OF GREAT BRITAIN AND NORTHERN IRELAND

IRELAND

DENMARK

BALTIC SEA

U.S.S.R.

NETH.

FEDERAL REPUBLIC OF GERMANY (West Germany)

GERMAN DEMOCRATIC REPUBLIC (East Germany)

POLAND

BEL.

LUX.

CZECH.

FRANCE

SWITZ.   AUSTRIA   HUNGARY

ROMANIA

CASPIAN SEA

YUGOSLAVIA

Danube R.

BLACK SEA

PORTUGAL

SPAIN

ITALY

BULGARIA

ALBANIA

GREECE

TURKEY

MEDITERRANEAN SEA

0   250   500 Miles
0   250   500 Kilometers

© PH

Focus on Geography

1. **Place**   What communist country did not belong to the Warsaw Pact?
2. **Regions**   Before World War II, Germany was a unified nation. What happened to Germany after the war, in terms of both political status and military alliance?

Poland.   When Stalin died in 1953, Nikita Khrushchev (KROOS chehv) became the new head of the Communist party and premier of the Soviet Union. Soon afterwards, Poland tried to break free of Soviet control.

In 1956, Polish workers rioted in an attempt to gain better working conditions and higher pay. The Communist leader Wladyslaw Gomulka (VLAH dee slah guh MOOL kuh) became the head of the Polish government. He was an anti-Stalinist who had served time in prison during Stalin's rule. He allowed Polish workers to improve labor conditions and brought about other social and economic reforms. When he broke up the secret police and continued other reforms, Khrushchev threatened to send in troops and remove Gomulka from power. This did not happen, however, and eventually Khrushchev accepted Poland under Gomulka's rule.

Hungary.   Influenced by Poland's success, Hungary attempted its own revolt, but this time Soviet communism showed its teeth. When Imre Nagy (NAH djuh) became the

639

▲ **Illustrating History** *Hungarians protesting Soviet rule destroyed a statue of Stalin during their 1956 uprising.*

head of the Hungarian government in 1953, he promised to improve conditions by allowing greater freedom in business and farming. In 1956, he pulled Hungary out of the Warsaw Pact. This alarmed the leaders of the Soviet Union, and they removed Nagy as prime minister. In the fall of 1956, fighting broke out in Hungary, and the Soviet Union was faced with a widespread uprising. Hungarians demanded that Nagy be allowed back as head of their government and that Soviet troops be withdrawn. Instead, the Soviet Union sent more troops into Hungary. Thousands of Hungarians were killed in bloody street fighting. Many were captured and sent to labor camps while others fled to the West.

Tragically, the Hungarian freedom fight was lost. Nagy was later arrested and executed. Janos Kadar, a Hungarian willing to be a Soviet puppet ruler, replaced Nagy. The Soviet brutality in Hungary shocked the world and was condemned by the United Nations, but Russian troops remained in Hungary.

The Cold War Continued Under Khrushchev

Throughout the 1950s, and until his rule ended in 1964, Khrushchev "de-Stalinized" the Soviet Union through various reforms.

He eased conditions in some labor camps and granted greater intellectual freedom to some artists and writers who had been persecuted under Stalin. Khrushchev also focused attention on needed agricultural improvements in the Soviet Union. Overall, he raised the living standard for the people, but it still remained well below those of the United States and Western Europe.

The cold war actually appeared to be thawing as Khrushchev traveled to the United States in 1959. World leaders began to speak openly about the need for peaceful co-existence because many people realized the destruction that another world war would bring. A summit meeting of world leaders from the Soviet Union, the United States, Britain, and France was scheduled to be held in Paris in May 1960.

The summit plans collapsed, however, when the Soviet Union captured an unarmed American U-2 plane that was flying over the Soviet Union. Khrushchev cancelled the summit and brought an end to the thaw in the cold war.

SECTION 1 REVIEW

Knowing Key Terms, People, and Places
1. Define: **a.** expansionism **b.** cold war **c.** satellite country
2. Identify: **a.** Soviet bloc **b.** Nuremberg trials **c.** NATO **d.** Warsaw Pact

Focus on Geography
3. How was the city of Berlin divided after World War II?

Reviewing Main Ideas
4. What were the opposing political ideas of the two sides in the cold war?
5. How did the policy of containment and the Marshall Plan seek to end the spread of communism?

Critical Thinking
Making Comparisons
6. Compare the results of the struggles against Soviet domination in postwar Poland and Hungary.

2 Europe Recovered from the War

As you read, look for answers to these questions:

◆ How did European nations move toward postwar recovery?
◆ What economic and political changes occurred in Europe after World War II?
◆ What was the purpose of the Common Market?

Key Terms: nationalization (defined on p. 641)

Western Europe lay in ruins when World War II ended. Recovery seemed to be a long way off. Nevertheless, the most remarkable thing about Europe in the years immediately after 1945 was that it did indeed manage to recover.

Postwar Britain Underwent Social Change

The Britain that emerged from World War II bore little resemblance to the prewar nation. The country had been bombed without mercy by the Germans. In the cities, whole blocks lay in shambles. The war had cut Britain off from its colonies that helped supply needed raw materials, and there were shortages of food and clothing for a number of years after the war. Yet, Britain did not realize that its role in world affairs had changed until several years after the fighting had stopped.

Labour party solutions. Britain's government had the task of rebuilding the nation. Political parties offered varied solutions. Although Winston Churchill had masterminded Britain's military and homefront strategies during the war, his Conservative party was defeated by the Labour party in the election of 1945. The Labour party came into power because many people in Britain believed that it was more likely than the Conservative party to raise living standards and improve access to health and education for a greater number of people.

Nationalization. Under the leadership of the Labour party, the government became the owner of the Bank of England, the coal mines, the railroads, and the iron and steel industries. The taking over of industry by government is called **nationalization.** For most people, nationalization meant few changes in their daily lives. They went to work as usual; they were paid in the same way, and their employers also remained the same.

It was thought that under nationalization, British industry would function more efficiently. This proved not to be the case because Britain had fallen behind in plant modernization, and nationalization did little to speed up the modernization process. Strong labor unions fought hard and successfully for better wages and working conditions for employees.

Health care changes. In addition to nationalizing some industries, the Labour party started a National Health Service. Under this plan, which is called socialized medicine in the United States, the government pays doctors and dentists for treating patients. The British refer to this plan as "cradle to the grave" security, because every citizen is guaranteed health care throughout his or her entire life.

The loss of the empire. In the postwar years, Britain's empire gradually broke up. Most British possessions became independent between 1947 and 1965. When they gained independence, many former colonies joined the British Commonwealth of Nations, which had been established in 1931. Commonwealth countries shared trade advantages and met to discuss common problems.

Canada, New Zealand, and Australia had won their independence in 1931 and were the original members of the Commonwealth. Many of the new nations you will read about in the third section of this chapter were former parts of the British Empire.

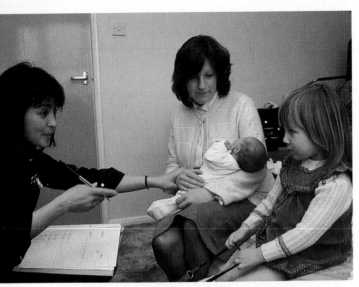

▲ **Illustrating History** *Britain's Labour party began the National Health Service. Through taxation, the National Health Service of Great Britain continues to provide health care for all British citizens, such as the children above.*

De Gaulle Sought to Restore French Pride and Prosperity

Five years of war and enemy occupation left their mark on France. About 1,800 cities, some quite large, needed to be rebuilt. Inefficient factory methods and out-of-date machinery pushed the prices of goods and services sky high. As a result, France, as well as Britain, was unable to compete in the world market. Collecting taxes and holding onto the French empire drained the already low resources of postwar France.

As the government of Britain had done, France nationalized some important industries. Wages for workers were improved, and most French people were protected against sickness, accident, and loss of jobs. However, the real hero of French recovery and of the reestablishment of French prestige was Charles de Gaulle.

After the Allied victory in 1945, de Gaulle returned to France, received a hero's welcome, and was elected president of the Fourth French Republic. As a leader of the French Resistance during World War II, de Gaulle had made many contributions to French morale and pride. Because of his imperial and stubborn nature, however, he quickly lost his popularity and stayed in office for only one year.

In 1958, however, de Gaulle was called back to power when France became deeply divided over the demands of one of its colonies for independence. A new constitution established the Fifth French Republic and de Gaulle was elected its first president. He was given the powers he wanted to provide greater prosperity at home and prestige abroad.

De Gaulle often took independent positions in his efforts to restore France as a world leader. He urged the country to develop its own atomic weapons. In 1966, he withdrew French troops from the NATO command. Although other Western nations did not approve, de Gaulle also opened discussions between France and the Soviet Union. Before his death in 1970, de Gaulle had surprised most people with his careful handling of the colonial crisis and his strong role in the restoration of French pride during the postwar era.

Germany Struggled Toward Recovery

The postwar division of Germany into two nations has greatly influenced the lives of the German people. In East Germany, for example, the Soviets drained much of the country's resources and industries, thus making economic recovery slow. While most people in West Germany worked in manufacturing, most people in East Germany were farmers. To this day, dominance of the Soviet Union is evident in every detail of life in East Germany.

The economic recovery. After the war, in West Germany the economy made a dramatic recovery. Certainly, the funds provided by the Marshall Plan helped, but the West German political leaders also were determined to improve the economy. Private investment was encouraged, and modern factories produced improved goods. By the late 1950s, as you will read in Chapter 29, the West German people were enjoying a high standard of living, especially in comparison to the standard of living experienced by the people of East Germany.

The Berlin Wall. The better living conditions in West Germany led many East Germans to move to West Germany. In the summer of 1961, the East German government stopped East Germans from going to West Berlin by building a concrete wall between East and West Berlin. This wall, topped with barbed wire and guarded by armed soldiers, is known as the Berlin Wall.

Until 1989, most East Germans who wanted to leave had to sneak across the West German border. Many escapees have been shot while trying to climb over the Berlin Wall. In order to leave in secret, these people had to abandon homes, possessions, and even family members. But in 1989, as part of many historic events that astonished the entire world, the East German government opened its borders and people tore down parts of the Wall. For the first time since 1961, East Germans were free to cross over their country's borders.

Recovery Was Slow in Other European Countries

Many other European countries were struggling to emerge from the terrible conditions the war had created. Italy, Greece, Turkey, Spain, and Portugal all faced economic and political postwar problems.

Italy. Italy had to recover not only from war but also from the political disorder left from Mussolini and the Fascists. A new Italian republic was formed in 1946, and one government followed another almost yearly. Economic progress was slower in Italy because of the country's lack of industry. Although the Marshall Plan helped, a shaky economy added to political instability. During the 1950s and 1960s, the Communist party in Italy continued to challenge Italy's major political party for power.

Greece and Turkey. The postwar period was also a difficult time for Greece and Turkey. During World War II, Greece was occupied by German, Italian, and Bulgarian troops. In 1944, the invading forces left Greece and, with the aid of the Truman Doctrine, the Communist forces inside the country were defeated.

Between 1947 and 1949, and again with the support of the Truman Doctrine, other Communist uprisings in Greece were put down. In 1967, a military dictatorship took power after sending King Constantine into exile. The democratic process was finally restored when Greece overthrew the military government in 1974.

Greece and Turkey were also at odds over the island of Cyprus, which is home to both Greeks and Turks. Cyprus, which became a British colony in 1914, was in turmoil after World War II, when its Greek majority urged union with Greece. Britain did not want to give up its eastern Mediterranean military bases on Cyprus and fought the independence movement. A republican form of government, in which all citizens were promised a role, was worked out in 1959.

Spain. During World War II, Spain was a neutral country, even though its dictator, Francisco Franco, openly sided with the Axis Powers. Because of its postwar Fascist government, Spain was excluded from the United Nations until 1955.

Portugal. Portugal was also neutral during World War II. The Portuguese dictator, Antonio Salazar, was sympathetic to the Fascists, but air bases were given to the Allies during the war. Portugal, as well as Spain, did not become a member of the United Nations until 1955. Attempts to democratize the country were unsuccessful until illness at last forced Salazar from office in 1968.

The European Countries Sought Cooperation

The cold war and the growth of the Soviet Union and the United States as superpowers forced the countries of Western Europe to unite for security and for economic development. Both the United States and the United Nations encouraged them to organize for their own benefit. As you learned earlier, the

In their own words

Eleanor Roosevelt at the United Nations

Eleanor Roosevelt, the wife of President Franklin D. Roosevelt, was active in social reform movements. When the United Nations was being organized, she was part of the United States delegation. Below, she describes how she felt as a woman in a diplomatic world dominated by men.

❝During the entire London session of the Assembly I walked on eggs. I knew that as the only woman on the delegation I was not very welcome. Moreover, if I failed to be a useful member, it would not be considered merely that I as an individual had failed, but that all women had failed, and there would be little chance for others to serve in the near future.

I tried to think of small ways in which I might be more helpful. There were not too many women on the other delegations, and as soon as I got to know some of them I invited them all to tea in my sitting room at the hotel. . . . The talk was partly just social but as we became better acquainted we also talked about the problems on which we were working in the various committees. . . . I discovered that in such informal sessions we sometimes made more progress in reaching an understanding on some question before the United Nations than we had been able to achieve in the formal work of our committees.❞

1. According to Roosevelt, how did the male delegates react to her being there?
2. What problem is caused for historians when groups meet informally to solve problems?

Marshall Plan encouraged cooperation by requiring that the countries of Western Europe get together to decide what help they could give one another. Sixteen nations met at Paris, France, and established the *Organization of European Economic Cooperation* (OEEC) to carry out the Marshall Plan. The establishment of the OEEC was a significant step toward economic cooperation among the nations of Europe.

In 1957, the leaders of Belgium, the Netherlands, Luxembourg, France, Italy, and West Germany met to plan the European Economic Community or Common Market. These founding countries agreed to allow goods to move freely without tariffs among the member nations. On the other hand, they agreed to tax the goods of nations that were not members. Thus, the goods of the Common Market members would be cheaper for members and made membership attractive to countries that were not part of the initial group. Britain was among the other Western European countries that later joined in this effort to strengthen European economic unity.

SECTION 2 REVIEW

Knowing Key Terms, People, and Places
1. Define: **a.** nationalization
2. Identify: **a.** National Health Service **b.** Charles de Gaulle **c.** Berlin Wall **d.** Common Market

Focus on Geography
3. Explain the strategic importance of Cyprus to Britain.

Reviewing Main Ideas
4. What did the Labour party do to strengthen postwar Britain?
5. Why was postwar recovery slow in Italy and Greece?

Critical Thinking
Drawing Conclusions
6. How can a healthy economy help a nation to avoid domination by another nation?

3 Nations Formed in Asia, Middle East, and Africa

As you read, look for answers to these questions:

◆ Why did Indian independence lead to Hindu and Muslim states?
◆ How did the United States and the United Nations become involved in Korea?
◆ How did Israel become a nation?

> **Key Terms:** zionism (defined on p. 648)

World War II brought to an end the age of European dominance. Colonial armies returned home angry and frustrated. With no mass support and no democratic institutions in the colonies, the imperialistic empires were mostly glitter and little substance. It became clear that a few people, backed by war-tired nations, could no longer hold onto the colonies.

The people of Asia and Africa felt that they had helped the Allies to win the war, and that the war had been fought for freedom from tyranny. Therefore, they wanted freedom and independence for their own nations. To gain their independence, they waged successful struggles against their former colonial masters.

Indonesia, after four years of fighting, became independent of the Netherlands in 1949. Under an act passed by the United States Congress in 1934, the Philippines became independent of the United States in 1946. Malaysia became independent of Britain in 1957. However, the struggle for freedom in India is the best example of postwar independence movements. It is a story of hope, courage, and hardships.

India and Pakistan Became Independent

As you have read, Mohandas Gandhi continued to be a leading force for change in India after World War I. Between 1935 and 1945,

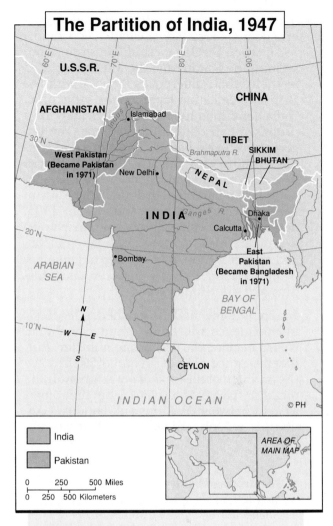

The Partition of India, 1947

India

Pakistan

0   250   500 Miles
0 250 500 Kilometers

Focus on Geography

Movement Once India was divided, thousands of Muslims moved out of India. To what newly established country did they go?

continuing the tactics of nonviolent resistance to British rule, he was joined by a growing class of educated Indians. As you read in Chapter 25, the most important of these people was Jawaharlal Nehru, who became Gandhi's friend and follower.

Problems between Muslims and Hindus. In the early days of World War II, a conflict grew between the Hindus and the Muslims about who should lead the movement for

645

independence and how India should be governed once independence had been won. In 1941, when the Japanese threat grew more serious, the Hindus and the Muslims agreed to shelve their differences to work with the British in defeating Japan. At the same time, India continued to press Great Britain for a promise of absolute independence. The lingering problems between Muslims and Hindus in India were the last stumbling blocks to complete independence.

Under Mohammed Ali Jinnah, the Muslim League, which had been founded in 1906, demanded the establishment of Pakistan as a separate Muslim state. As time went on, and as victory for Indian independence appeared closer, hostility between the Muslims and the Hindus grew.

Independence and bloodshed. In 1947, independence was finally granted to India. Nehru became the first prime minister. But, independence did not, in and of itself, solve the problem of the kind of government India ought to have or the relationship that ought to exist between Muslims and Hindus. Gandhi yearned for a united India. This was not

to be, and Gandhi bitterly agreed to the establishment of a separate Muslim state, known as Pakistan. Muslims were concentrated in two different regions of India. Thus, Pakistan itself was divided into East and West Pakistan, 1,000 miles apart, as shown on the map on page 645.

Bloodshed followed. The end result was division into a mostly Hindu India and a mostly Muslim Pakistan.

The Communists Won Control of China

When the Communists were defeated by Chiang Kai-shek in 1928, they faced a setback, but they were not discouraged. For a time, they tried to regain their strength in southeastern China, but they were pushed out by Chiang Kai-shek and his armies. Later, from southeastern China, the Communists, under the leadership of Mao Zedong, made what they called the Long March. Traveling several hundred miles out of their way to avoid Chiang's armies, they made their way to Shensi province in northern China. There, they established a stronghold, studied communism, and prepared themselves to take power. It was among the masses, particularly the peasants, that the Communists gained their strength.

Defeat of the Kuomintang. From 1945 until 1949, China was torn by civil war, which ended when Chiang Kai-shek and the Nationalist party were defeated by Mao Zedong and the Communists. Chiang and his forces, who had been strongly supported by the United States, were driven from the mainland of China to the island of Taiwan (then called Formosa), where the *Republic of China* was set up. In October 1949, the Communist government, which called itself the *People's Republic of China*, was established on the mainland.

War Came to Korea

Korea, which had been annexed by Japan in 1910, became independent when Japan was defeated in 1945. The Soviet Union insisted that Korea be divided along 38° North Latitude, also known as the 38th parallel. (See

▼ **Illustrating History** *Below, Chairman Mao (on horse) moves his army toward Shensi during the Long March in 1947.*

the map on this page.) United States troops remained in the south, and Soviet troops remained in the north. Both countries were to withdraw their troops as soon as Korea was able to rule itself. However, what began as a temporary division of Korea proved to be a permanent one.

The Republic of Korea was founded in the south in 1948, and a Communist People's Republic was formed in the north. The troops of both nations were to remain under the supervision of the United Nations until a government for Korea could be established. The Soviets, however, established a permanent Communist government in the north. In South Korea, Syngman Rhee (sing muhn REE) became president, and American troops left Korea in 1949.

Communist attacks on South Korea. In June 1950, well-armed Communist troops of North Korea suddenly attacked South Korea. President Truman ordered American aircraft and soldiers to the scene with the approval of the Security Council of the United Nations. The United Nations urged its members to supply more troops and asked President Truman to name Douglas MacArthur as supreme commander of the troops. While most of the troops were from South Korea and the United States, some 14 other nations provided troops for this "police action" against North Korea. The United States also provided most of the money and materials. The significance of the Korean War was that, for the first time, an international United Nations army tried to stop one nation from attacking another.

Victories under MacArthur. The Communists almost defeated South Korea. That they were not able to do so was a tribute to the skillful leadership of General MacArthur. Although the United Nations forces drove the North Koreans back to the 38th parallel, MacArthur was not satisfied. He wanted to drive the Communists back to the Yalu River, which separates Korea from mainland China. He was even prepared to go beyond that point, because China was supplying the Korean Communists with weapons. When MacArthur brought his troops to

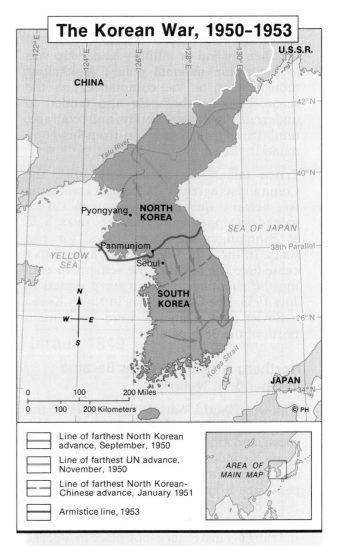

The Korean War, 1950–1953

	Line of farthest North Korean advance, September, 1950
	Line of farthest UN advance, November, 1950
	Line of farthest North Korean–Chinese advance, January 1951
	Armistice line, 1953

AREA OF MAIN MAP

Focus on Geography

Movement The Korean War was a series of advances and retreats. How far into South Korea had the North Koreans advanced in 1950?

the Chinese border of North Korea, he was met by an attack of 200,000 Chinese Communist troops. This massive force drove the United Nations forces back and the war dragged on.

Truman and MacArthur. President Truman feared that MacArthur's actions would result in a war not only with China but also

647

Old Name for a New Nation

In 1947, black nationalists in the British colony of the Gold Coast met to discuss ways to win independence. A question arose. What should the new nation be called? The area had been known as the "Gold Coast" ever since Portuguese explorers arrived there in the late 1400s. To the nationalists, this name symbolized 500 years of European domination.

One leader suggested the name Ghana, after the kingdom that had flourished in Africa before 1200. The idea was a winner. "We take pride in the name," explained Kwame Nkrumah, the colony's first premier, "not out of romanticism but as an inspiration for the future." In 1957, the name Gold Coast was changed to Ghana. Ghana's flag is shown at right.

1. Why did the nationalists prefer the name "Ghana" to "Gold Coast"?
2. Why do people consider their nation's name an important matter?

Bernadotte of Sweden and Dr. Ralph Bunche of the United States. However, Bernadotte was assassinated, and Bunche negotiated the armistice between the Arabs and the Israelis, thus earning a Nobel Peace Prize. In 1949, Israel became a member of the United Nations.

As a result of the 1948 Arab-Israeli War, Israel extended its land beyond the borders that had been set by the United Nations. The city of Jerusalem remained divided between Jews and Arabs. Jordan was to control the Old City of Jerusalem. The New City of Jerusalem was to be controlled by Israel. The Gaza Strip, an area along the Mediterranean, was given to Egypt. After the war, the Arab states refused to recognize the existence of Israel and were determined to make all of Palestine an Arab state once again. More bloodshed and millions of displaced people resulted from the modern division of Palestine. In Chapter 31, you will read about continuing peace efforts in the Middle East.

SECTION 3 REVIEW

Knowing Key Terms, People, and Places
1. Define: **a.** zionism
2. Identify: **a.** Jawaharlal Nehru **b.** Mao Zedong **c.** Douglas MacArthur **d.** Algeria

Focus on Geography
3. Explain how independence changed the politics and culture of India and Pakistan.

Reviewing Main Ideas
4. Describe the events that led to the formation of the People's Republic of China in October of 1949.
5. When and how was the Jewish state of Israel established?

Critical Thinking
Analyzing Information
6. Why was United Nations intervention in Korea a unique historic event? What was the "classic conflict" between President Truman and General MacArthur?

Analyzing Conflicting Interpretations

Two historians considering the same event can reach very different conclusions because they interpret the event differently. Thus, you will need to build your skill in analyzing conflicting interpretations to reach your own conclusions.

Use the following steps to analyze the conflicting interpretations given below.

1. **Study both interpretations to fully understand their respective arguments.** Answer the following questions: (a) What did Hayes see as the main goal of the USSR after World War II? (b) List three facts that are given to support his position. (c) What is given as the main goal of the United States in the quotation from Rose?

2. **Compare the two interpretations and analyze their different viewpoints.** Answer the following questions: (a) On what point do the two interpretations agree? (b) What does each author identify as the main cause of the cold war?

3. **Determine which interpretation is more accurate.** Use the excerpts themselves and your understanding of attitudes at the time when each was written to evaluate the respective interpretations. Answer the following questions: (a) Which interpretation would you judge more accurate based upon the supporting reasons each gives? Explain. (b) With which author would you agree? Explain.

Carlton J.H. Hayes, 1958

Following World War II, the United States was not only the foremost world power in material respects, but . . . it was the leading champion of liberal democracy, national self-determination, and international cooperation through the United Nations.

. . . By the end of 1946 it was becoming quite obvious that the Soviet dictatorship attached quite different meanings to "democracy," "free elections," and "self-determination" from those usual in the United States, and that . . . it was aggressively seeking to transform as much of Europe as possible into a Communist empire dependent on Moscow. It was retaining armies at wartime strength, and using them to impose satellite communist regimes on country after country in east-central Europe. At the same time it was also fostering subversive Communist movements in the West . . .

Lisle A. Rose, 1973

The drama of the cold war . . . has tended to obscure what is truly the central fact of our time—America's indisputable possession of the balance of global power. . . .

[Some historians] have argued . . . that aggressive American plans to shape the postwar international economic structure along the lines of free trade and capitalistic supremacy led to attempts to create a global American empire and this, in turn, caused the . . . cold war between East and West. . . .

Washington's decision to retain the atomic monopoly [after 1945] and then, after the Russian [development of nuclear weapons] to maintain nuclear supremacy, has been the salient [leading] factor defining America's global pre-eminence.

REVIEW

Section Summaries

Section 1 Two World Powers Emerged After World War II suspicion and mistrust brought about a *cold war* between the Soviet Union and the United States. This was a war of brain power, aid, and propaganda, rather than shooting. The Soviet Union swiftly gained control of Eastern Europe. In 1949, the nations of Western Europe formed NATO as protection against the Soviets. In response, the Soviets formed the Warsaw Pact.

Section 2 Europe Recovered from the War In Britain, the Labour party made sweeping changes. While nationalization of industries failed to increase efficiency, other Labour party measures helped raise living standards and improved health care and education. The French government also worked to improve living conditions, and French pride was restored by the skillful leadership of Charles de Gaulle. Germany was divided. The Soviet Union controlled East Germany, while the Allies occupied West Germany. In other Western European nations, recovery was slow and political instability remained a concern. For greater economic development and security, the nations of Western Europe formed a number of cooperative organizations such as the Common Market.

Section 3 New Nations Formed in Asia, Middle East, and Africa Nations in Asia, Africa, and the Middle East began demanding freedom and independence. In India, for example, Gandhi's movement won independence from Britain by 1947. In China, Mao Zedong's Communists won control. After World War II the Soviets and Americans divided Korea into two parts. A bitter war between United Nations and Communist forces ended in a standoff, and Korea remained divided. Former colonies in northern Africa and Sub-Saharan Africa won their independence. In the Middle East, the United Nations helped establish the nation of Israel in spite of Arab resistance.

Key Facts

1. Use each vocabulary word in a sentence.
   a. expansionism
   b. cold war
   c. satellite countries
   d. nationalization
   e. zionism
2. Identify and briefly explain the importance of the following names, places, and events.
   a. the Nuremburg Trials
   b. Marshal Tito
   c. Charles de Gaulle
   d. West Germany
   e. East Germany
   f. Mohandas Gandhi
   g. The People's Republic of China
   h. Algeria
   i. Kenya
   j. Palestine
   k. Israel

Main Ideas

1. In the years after World War II, what did President Truman do to deal with the cold war?
2. Give three examples of Soviet satellite countries that resisted complete domination by the Soviet Union.
3. In what ways did Britain and France change in the years after the war?
4. How did the country of Germany become divided after World War II?
5. List two examples of cooperation among Western European nations in the years after World War II.
6. What problems accompanied India's independence in 1947?
7. Who were the opposing sides in the Korean "police action?"
8. List five African nations that won their independence between 1945 and 1961.
9. Why did the Arabs and Israelis fight each other in 1948?

Developing Skill in Reading History

Read the following sentences, and choose the best definition for each word in italics.

1. When Nagy promised the Hungarians more freedom, the Soviet Union *deposed* him as prime minister and expelled him from the Communist party.
   a. promoted   b. got rid of   c. elected
2. Hungarians demanded that Nagy be *reinstated* and that Soviet troops be withdrawn.
   a. put back in power   c. exiled
   b. imprisoned
3. Nagy was replaced by Janos Kadar, a Hungarian willing to be a Soviet *puppet ruler*.
   a. strong leader
   b. leader controlled by others
   c. absolute monarch

Using Social Studies Skills

1. **Analyzing Conflicting Interpretations** In reading history, you learn of many conflicts. In this chapter, for example, you read about the conflict over Korea between President Truman and General MacArthur. Read each statement below and tell whether it expresses Truman's side of the conflict or MacArthur's.
   a. We should have a full-scale war with China.
   b. Civilian leadership must decide national policy.
   c. Military commanders know the best actions to take in a war, since they are on the scene.
2. **Analyzing Visual Evidence** Look at the photograph of the Berlin Wall (above). List the important details in the picture. What overall impression do these details give you?

Critical Thinking

1. **Perceiving Cause and Effect** List one cause for each of the following effects.
   a. the Berlin Wall   c. the Korean War
   b. the Marshall Plan   d. the Long March
2. **Recognizing Bias** How did the Arab nations feel about the establishment of Israel in 1948? How did their actions reflect their opinion? What were the results?

3. **Demonstrating Reasoned Judgment** What changes in the postwar world caused one observer to say, "Britain has lost an empire and has not found a role?"

Focus on Writing

Writing Unified Paragraphs

A paragraph has **unity** if all of its sentences are closely related to the topic sentence. Read the paragraph below. Find the sentence that is *not* closely related to the topic sentence.

Under Allied occupation, important German Nazis were tried for their war crimes in a Four Power military court. In addition, the city of Berlin was divided. The military court proceedings were called the *Nuremberg Trials*. The Nazi leaders were found guilty of breaking world peace and committing horrible crimes against humanity. Eleven former high-ranking Nazis were condemned to death. Others were given prison sentences.

Geography in History

The Island War

The Pacific Ocean is vast—some 70,000,000 square miles in size. Scattered across it are thousands of islands. It was this region that the Japanese, too crowded in their own island region, hoped to make their empire. When the United States and its allies went to war against the Japanese in 1941 (see page 622), they found they had to deal with the vast size and numerous islands of the Pacific before they could even reach the enemy.

Distances and Resources

As an island nation, Japan's resources were limited. Oil had to be brought about 2,500 miles from the captured Dutch East Indies. Aluminum for aircraft, iron ore to make ships, rubber for tires—these were only a few of the dozens of items Japan had to import.

The United States, on the other hand, had almost endless resources within its own borders. Its problem was transporting them to the area of the fighting. From San Francisco to Brisbane, Australia, is a distance of 7,000 miles, which takes a ship 28 days. It was another 1,500 miles from Brisbane to Guadalcanal, the site of the first major U.S.–Japanese battle of World War II.

Island Hopping

By 1942, the Japanese were building an airfield at Guadalcanal to attack the American supply routes to Australia. A similar Japanese airfield was already in operation at Rabaul on the island of New Britain.

The United States Army commander, General Douglas MacArthur, and his navy counterpart, Admiral Chester Nimitz, came up with a new tactic, well-suited to Pacific geography, called "island hopping." Why attack an enemy base when it could be surrounded, and its supplies cut off? In Operation CARTWHEEL, U.S. naval forces moved up the Solomon Island chain from Guadalcanal toward Rabaul. With the other islands now in Allied hands, Rabaul itself became unimportant.

Fueling Up

In their island-hopping campaign, U.S. forces faced supply problems themselves. MacArthur had no good ports on the north coast of New Guinea. Small boats had to ferry supplies in from freighters offshore. Sometimes as many as 140 ships would be anchored for a month, waiting to be unloaded.

The enormous aircraft carriers used large quantities of fuel. To supply them, huge tankers protected by destroyers would sail to the combat zone.

The Japanese had not planned as well. They had fewer freighters than the Allies and had never developed a system to protect their supply lines. American submarines could destroy Japanese tankers from the occupied Dutch East Indies or Japanese supply ships sailing to isolated outposts.

By late 1944, Japan's imports had fallen 40 percent. East Indies' oil could not reach Japan, and the Japanese fleet had to stay close to the Singapore refineries. Japanese submarines supplied troops left behind on places like Truk and Rabaul.

The Air Arm Reaches Out

Beginning in February 1945, the U.S. long-range bombing of Japan began to show results. Oil refineries were struck, and production dropped 83 percent. What was worse for the Japanese, the bombers dropped floating mines in the waters between Honshu and Shikoku islands, Japan's last protected waterway. Shipping fell by about 80 percent in a few months.

After atomic bombs were dropped on Hiroshima and Nagasaki, Japan surrendered. It had built an empire to gain resources it didn't have. With its surrender, Japan bowed to the superior resources of the United States, and its skill in using the geography of the Pacific.

Focus on Geography

1. **Location** Look at the map below. Where did the Allied advance go in relation to Japan and Singapore?

2. **Movement** Why did the Japanese want to expand into the Pacific region?

3. **Regions** What advantage did the United States have over Japan?

Critical Thinking

Predicting Consequences

4. What effect do you think the Japanese use of submarines to supply isolated outposts had on the outcome of war?

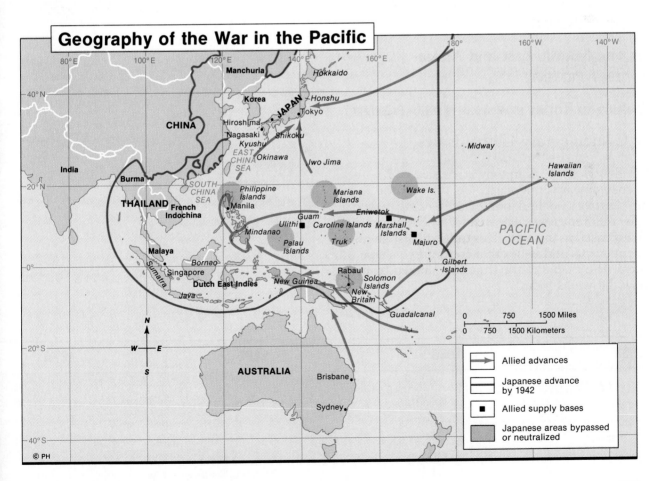

Geography of the War in the Pacific

UNIT

9

The World Today

(1960–Present)

1 THE WESTERN HEMISPHERE

The modern artist Diego Rivera created this mural of the Mexican Revolution.

Chapters

President John F. Kennedy once said, "The mere absence of war is not peace." As we near the end of the century, we find ourselves seeking peace in many different ways. The results of that search will be discussed in this unit. This unit will also focus on recent events and issues that continue to shape our world. The map and the time line, linked by color, show the world today.

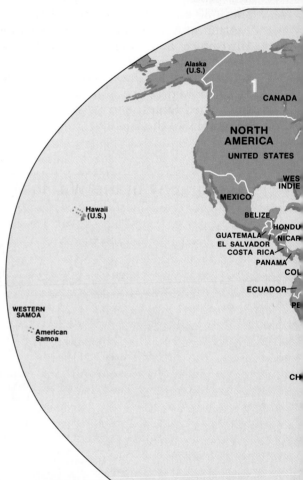

1955	**1960**	**1965**	**1970**

THE WESTERN HEMISPHERE **1**   ■ **1961 United States invades Cuba at the Bay of Pigs**   **1969 American astronauts ■ land on the moon**

EUROPE AND THE SOVIET UNION **2**   **1969 Willy Brandt becomes ■ chancellor of West Germany**

AFRICA AND THE MIDDLE EAST **3**   **1969 Qaddafi overthrows ■ Libyan monarchy**

ASIA **4**   ■ **1964 United States expands its military presence in South Vietnam**

656

2 EUROPE AND THE SOVIET UNION

Gorbachev and Thatcher worked to improve Soviet-European relations.

4 ASIA

In 1986, Corazon Aquino was elected president of the Philippines.

3 AFRICA AND THE MIDDLE EAST

Archbishop Desmond Tutu is leading the fight to end apartheid in South Africa.

Greenland (Den.)

ICELAND

NORWAY SWEDEN FINLAND

UNITED KINGDOM DEN. NETH.

IRELAND BEL. W. E. POLAND

FRANCE LUX. GER. GER. CZECH.

SWITZ. AUST. HUNGARY

EUROPE

PORTUGAL ITALY BULGARIA

SPAIN GREECE TURKEY

Azores (Port.) ALBANIA CYPRUS SYRIA

MALTA LEBANON

Canary Is. (Spain) TUNISIA ISRAEL IRAQ IRAN

MOROCCO JORDAN

WESTERN SAHARA ALGERIA LIBYA EGYPT KUWAIT BAHRAIN PAKISTAN

SAUDI ARABIA QATAR

MAURITANIA UNITED ARAB EMIRATES

OMAN INDIA

CAPE VERDE SENEGAL MALI NIGER CHAD SUDAN

GAMBIA BURKINA FASO BENIN YEMEN P.D.R. OF YEMEN

GUINEA-BISSAU GUINEA NIGERIA DJIBOUTI

SIERRA LEONE CENTRAL AFRICAN REPUBLIC ETHIOPIA

LIBERIA TOGO CAMEROON

IVORY COAST GHANA EQUATORIAL GUINEA SOMALIA

SÃO TOMÉ AND PRÍNCIPE GABON CONGO UGANDA KENYA

ZAIRE RWANDA BURUNDI

AFRICA

TANZANIA

COMOROS

ANGOLA ZAMBIA MOZAMBIQUE

MALAWI

NAMIBIA ZIMBABWE MADAGASCAR MAURITIUS

BOTSWANA

SWAZILAND

SOUTH AFRICA LESOTHO

UNION OF SOVIET SOCIALIST REPUBLICS **2**

MONGOLIA

ASIA **4**

AFGHANISTAN CHINA NO. KOREA

SO. KOREA JAPAN

NEPAL BHUTAN

BANGLADESH

BURMA LAOS TAIWAN

THAILAND VIETNAM

SRI LANKA KAMPUCHEA PHILIPPINES

SINGAPORE BRUNEI

MALAYSIA KIRIBATI

INDONESIA

PAPUA NEW GUINEA SOLOMON IS.

AUSTRALIA VANUATU FIJI

New Caledonia (Fr.)

NEW ZEALAND

EZUELA

GUYANA SURINAME French Guiana

SOUTH AMERICA

BRAZIL

BOLIVIA

PARAGUAY

URUGUAY

ARGENTINA

Falkland Is. (Br.)

The World Today

1975	1980	1985	1990

■ **1973 Allende's government in Chile is overthrown**

■ **1978 United States agrees to give up Panama Canal by 2000**

■ **1983 Argentina elects a democratic government**

■ **1986 Oscar Arias Sanchez becomes president of Costa Rica**

■ **1979 Margaret Thatcher becomes prime minister of Great Britain**

■ **1982 Britain and Argentina fight over Falkland Islands**

■ **1988 Soviet Armenia and Baltic states demand more political freedom**

■ **1979 Islamic fundamentalists overthrow shah of Iran**

■ **1980 Iran and Iraq go to war**

■ **1988 Ethiopia and the Sudan are immersed in civil wars**

■ **1975 Kampuchea falls under the control of the Khmer Rouge**

■ **1979 The United States recognizes the People's Republic of China**

■ **1986 Corazon Aquino is elected president of the Philippines**

Europe
and the Soviet Union Today

(1960–PRESENT)

▲ **Illustrating History** *In a gesture of unity, a joyous West Berliner hands a flower to an East German soldier atop the Berlin Wall, no longer a barrier between East and West.*

1 Western Europe Worked for a Stable Society

2 The Soviet Union Made Drastic Reforms

3 Changes Swept Eastern Europe

At the stroke of midnight on November 9, 1989, in Berlin, a great roar filled the air. The crowd of Germans that had gathered on both sides of the Berlin Wall began pouring through its gates. West Berliners helped East Berliners over the top of the jagged barrier which had cut their city in half for 28 years. In the past, many people had been shot and killed while trying to escape the Communist sector. Now, in an effort to appease its protesting citizens, the East German government opened the wall, allowing East Berliners to cross easily and safely to the West. "I just can't believe it!" cried a young woman as she crossed into West Berlin. "I don't feel like I'm in prison anymore!" shouted another member of the crowd.

In their haste to break down the hated symbol, Berliners used whatever tools they had at hand. The *chink-chink* of hammers and chisels rang through the night. Aided by crowbars, ropes, and chains, those who had lived so long in the wall's shadow toppled large sections of the concrete-and-steel barrier. Some Berliners celebrated atop the wall, dancing and blowing horns. Others gripped their friends and relatives in tears of joy. Within the next 48 hours, nearly two million East Germans visited the West. In this chapter, you will read about the many other dramatic changes that are transforming the face of Europe and the Soviet Union.

1960	1970	1980	1990

1968 ■ Soviet Union invades Czechoslovakia

■ **1970** West Germany signs treaty with the Soviet Union

■ **1974** Democracy returns to Greece

1981 ■ Solidarity gains strength in Poland

1985 ■ Gorbachev heads the Soviet Union

■ **1987** European Community begins plans for union

▲ **Illustrating History** *Exuberant East and West Berliners come together at the Berlin Wall to celebrate East Germany's newfound freedom.*

1 Western Europe Worked for a Stable Society

As you read, look for answers to these questions:

◆ How has Margaret Thatcher managed England's economy?
◆ Why did Charles de Gaulle step down as president of France?
◆ What was the purpose of *Ostpolitik?*
◆ What goal does the European Community hope to achieve by 1992?

Key Terms: referendum (defined on p. 660)

The nations of Europe have a long history of wars on their continent. This area of the world has been a testing ground for a wide variety of ideas about government. In mod-

ern times, these countries still seek long-term solutions to political and economic problems. European governments are eager to ensure peace and stability.

British Conservatives Gained Power

In the past few decades, control of the English government has passed several times between the Conservative party and the Labour party. The Conservatives usually seek to solve problems with traditional methods that do not involve government intervention in the economy. The Labour party, on the other hand, supports many Socialist policies. These policies would bring the economy of England under tighter government control and would tend to benefit Britain's working class.

The fight for control of Parliament. The British Labour party regained power in Parliament in 1964, after 13 years of control by the Conservatives. Harold Wilson became

659

the new prime minister. In 1970, Edward Heath, the leader of the Conservative party, became prime minister. He served until 1974, when Harold Wilson defeated him to become prime minister once again. Between 1974 and 1979, the major problems faced by Wilson's Labour government were inflation and continuing unrest and violence in Northern Ireland.

Margaret Thatcher. In 1979, the Conservative party took control again, and Margaret Thatcher was elected Britain's first woman prime minister. She rejected the Labour party's idea of "cradle to grave security," or socialized welfare programs. Instead, Thatcher supported private enterprise, or less government control.

Thatcher's solution to the economic problems of her country had three main parts. First, she wanted to return industries, such as electrical utilities, to private ownership. Second, she wanted to cut government spending, in part by ending expensive social programs. Third, she tried to decrease the power of England's labor unions. In some areas, Thatcher's policies greatly improved Britain's economy. Although unemployment remained high, for example, inflation fell significantly.

Thatcher's popularity increased during a brief war with Argentina in 1982. This war was fought over the Falkland Islands, which lie off the coast of South America. England defeated Argentina easily. In 1987, Thatcher became the first British prime minister in 160 years to be elected for a third consecutive term. However, dissatisfied members of the British Labour party formed the Social Democratic party in 1982.

French Leaders Restored National Prosperity

Several strong leaders have worked to restore France to a state of prosperity and national pride since the 1960s. These leaders are Charles de Gaulle, Georges Pompidou, (zhorzh pohn pee DOO) Valéry Giscard d'Estaing (vah lay REE zhees KAHR des TAN), and François Mitterrand (frahn SWAH mee tehr AHN).

Charles de Gaulle. Charles de Gaulle was elected president of France in 1958. As part of his independent course, De Gaulle withdrew French troops from NATO in 1966. In 1968, there were widespread riots, strikes, student protests, and demands for government reform in France. In response, de Gaulle began a program of economic and social reforms. Although he had won the election of 1968 easily, de Gaulle insisted on a **referendum,** a vote by the people, to measure their support of his new reform plan. He said that unless the people approved the program, he would leave office. The voters defeated the referendum, and an era of French government ended.

Georges Pompidou and Valéry Giscard d'Estaing. Georges Pompidou replaced de Gaulle and continued de Gaulle's plans to restore France to prominence in Europe. Pompidou, however, was more concerned with domestic affairs than de Gaulle had been. Pompidou tried to raise the French standard of living by improving French industry. When Pompidou died in 1974, Valéry Giscard d'Estaing was elected president. D'Estaing raised minimum wages and increased employee benefits. However, his government did not fulfill all the promises of social reform that his party had made, and d'Estaing's popularity declined.

François Mitterrand. On May 10, 1981, François Mitterrand was elected president of France. Mitterrand was a Socialist, and under his direction five major industries were nationalized, along with most private banks. In 1982, the minimum wage was again raised, and French workers received longer vacations and a reduced work week. To fight growing inflation, Mitterrand raised taxes, a move that was unpopular. However, Mitterrand also reaffirmed the French commitment to NATO.

West Germany Became an Economic Force

The so-called West German miracle refers to West Germany's economic recovery after World War II. During World War II, much of

Margaret Thatcher

"Maggie Is Our Man" read the poster held by a group of smiling London women. The year was 1983, and Margaret Thatcher (shown right), Britain's first woman prime minister, was running for reelection.

Margaret Thatcher was born in 1925, the daughter of a small-town grocer. After graduating from Oxford University, she tried twice for a seat in the House of Commons. She also met and married a businessman named Dennis Thatcher. In 1959, she ran again for the House of Commons and won. Thatcher became known as a forceful leader of the Conservative party. She became prime minister in 1979.

When she took office, Britain's economy was in a serious slump. Thatcher restored a spirit of competition and stressed traditional values of hard work and thrift. Even when her policies caused problems, Thatcher refused to compromise. Her swift military defense of the Falkland Islands when they came under attack from Argentina in 1982

impressed many Britons. They overwhelmingly reelected her in 1983.

1. What economic policies did Thatcher stress?
2. Why did Thatcher win in 1983?

Germany's industry had been completely destroyed. This fact actually worked in West Germany's favor after the war, however, because new facilities were built with the latest technological equipment. Gradually, the United States, Great Britain, and France withdrew control over West Germany's economy, provided economic aid, and decreased West Germany's war debt. The West German gross national product, that is, the total value of all goods and services produced in the country in one year, rose from 23 billion dollars in 1950 to 103 billion dollars in 1964.

Willy Brandt. In 1969, Willy Brandt became chancellor of West Germany. His main goal in foreign policy was to create better relations between West Germany and East Germany. He called his plan *Ostpolitik*, or Eastern policy. The policy acknowledged the fact that East and West Germany would not soon be reunited.

In 1970, as part of Brandt's *Ostpolitik*, West Germany and the Soviet Union signed a treaty in which the two nations agreed to accept the existing borders in Europe and never to use force to try to change them. West Germany signed similar agreements with Poland, East Germany, and Czechoslovakia. For his work in improving East-West relations, Brandt was awarded the Nobel Peace Prize in 1971.

Continuing internal problems. Even with good leaders, however, there were still serious problems in West Germany. From time to time, extremist, neo-Nazi groups threatened West Germany's stability. Some business and political leaders became targets of terrorism by these extremist groups. In 1982, Helmut Kohl became chancellor, and he faced economic challenges such as inflation and growing unemployment. In spite of these problems, West Germany continued to make economic progress.

Other European Nations Fought for Stability

England, France, and Germany were not the only nations in Europe that struggled for economic and political stability. Ireland, Italy, Spain, Portugal, Greece, and Turkey were among those other countries that looked for new ways to organize their domestic and foreign affairs.

Ireland's internal strife. When the Republic of Ireland was formed in 1949, the six Protestant counties of Ulster, which made up Northern Ireland, remained under British rule. In 1969, Catholics living in Ulster demanded a greater voice in politics and equal opportunity in housing and employment. The Catholic minority, sometimes called Republicans, insisted that Ulster should be part of Ireland, which is mostly Catholic. The Protestants, sometimes called Loyalists because of their loyalty to Britain, believed that Ulster should remain part of the United Kingdom. Fighting broke out between Catholics and Protestants, and the British troops that had been sent to restore order only increased the violence.

In 1972, Britain dissolved the parliament of Northern Ireland and tried to rule Ulster directly. The Irish Republican Army, called the IRA, was enraged by this move and began a series of terrorist attacks.

In 1985, the Hillsborough Agreement gave the Republic of Ireland a voice in governing Northern Ireland. However, few people in Ulster were satisfied with this compromise. In 15 years of fighting, over 2,000 people had been killed in the dispute over Northern Ireland.

Poverty and discontent in Italy. Although politically unstable, Italy made good economic progress in the postwar years. In part, its recovery was made possible by its membership in the Common Market. However, Italy's people were divided economically. Southern Italy was largely agricultural and remained poor even though land was given to small farmers after World War II. Northern Italy was more industrialized and therefore richer than the south.

Terrorism, both domestic and international, added to Italy's problems. In May 1978, the former premier of Italy, Aldo Moro, was kidnapped and killed by an Italian terrorist group known as the Red Brigade. In October 1985, Middle Eastern terrorists hijacked the Italian cruise ship *Achille Lauro* and killed an American Jewish passenger. Italy was finally able to gain more control over terrorism, however, and looked forward to unity and peace within the European community.

Spain's fight for democracy. After Francisco Franco died in 1975, Prince Juan Carlos became a constitutional monarch in Spain. Free elections were held, and moderate parties were elected to the Cortes, the Spanish legislature.

In recent years, Spain has rapidly become more industrialized. However, it continues to have problems with groups, such as the Basques and Catalans, that seek self-rule and sometimes resort to terrorism to promote their causes.

Democracy in Portugal. In 1974, a military group seized control of Portugal and forced its dictator into exile without violence. In 1976, a new constitution was written for Portugal, and free elections were held. The moderate Socialist party gained a majority of the votes, but in recent years, the Socialist government of Portugal has been weakened because it has been forced to work together with various other political groups. Nevertheless, after generations of dictatorship, Portugal—a member of the Common Market—has a promising future.

Conflicts in Greece and Turkey. When the military dictatorship in Greece fell apart in 1974, a civilian government took power. In 1981, Andreas Papandreou (pah PAHN DRAY oo) became president. As president, however, he did not fulfill his campaign promises to end Greek participation in NATO and in the Common Market.

The postwar years have brought conflict to Turkey as well. A series of governments were unable to solve its basic political and economic problems. Industrial production

Europe Today

Common Market countries

⊛ Capital cities

Focus on Geography

Regions The map uses green to show Common Market countries.
Look back at the map on page 639 and use the key to locate Warsaw
Pact countries. What can you say about the military alliances of the
countries that are not in the Common Market?

in Turkey is low, unemployment has stayed
high, and high prices have kept most Turkish
people relatively poor.

The European Community Sought Unity

The nations of Western Europe are not the
superpowers that they once were. Therefore, in order to have a stronger voice in

world affairs, these nations have considered
the possibility of uniting to form a "Europe
without frontiers."

Expansion of the Common Market. As
discussed earlier, the Common Market, or
European Economic Community, was established in 1957 with six member nations.
The map on this page shows the other countries that joined the market as the benefits of

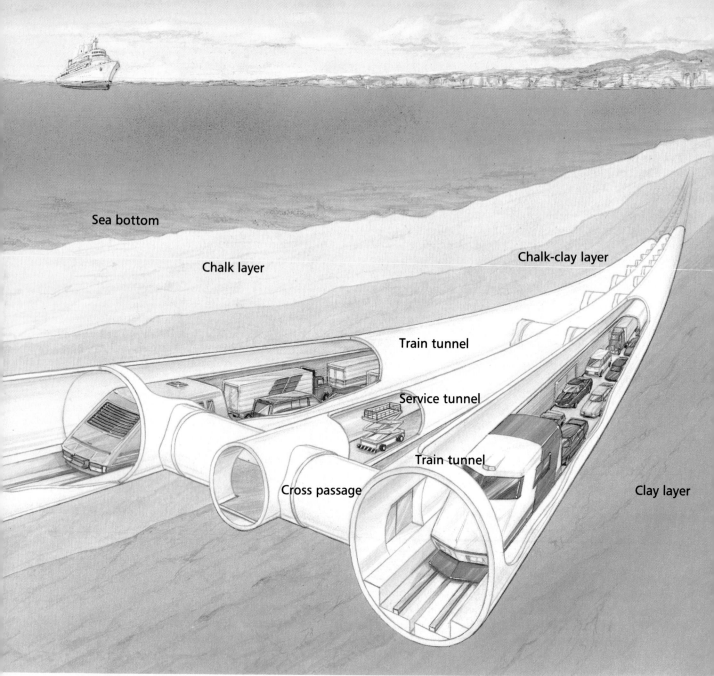

Labels on image: Sea bottom · Chalk layer · Chalk-clay layer · Train tunnel · Service tunnel · Train tunnel · Cross passage · Clay layer

▲ **Illustrating History** *The "Chunnel" between England and France, pictured above, symbolizes the dream of a European community.*

working together became clear. Since 1973, Great Britain, Ireland, Denmark, Greece, Spain, and Portugal, have become members.

Economic unity in 1992. In 1987, the members of the Common Market agreed that, by 1992, they would try to create a system in which there would be no trade barriers among member nations. Under the system, known as the European Community, people and goods would travel across borders without the usual security checks or tariffs. In other words, people should be able to travel from France to Portugal as

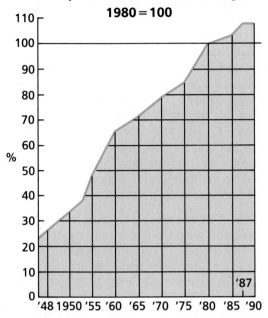

Trend of Industrial Production, 1948–1987
(European Economic Community)
1980 = 100

▲ **Graph Skill** *By how much did industrial production increase from 1965 to 1985?*

easily as they would from Louisiana to Nebraska, if political and economic differences can be worked out among the members.

If the Common Market achieves its goals, the 12 countries of the European Community could become a collective superpower. The new superpower would have 320 million people and a gross national product of over 4.6 trillion dollars. It would control 20 percent of the world's trade. What Charlemagne and Napoleon failed to do by force of arms, the countries of the European Community may be able to achieve through economic unity.

The first European parliament. In June 1979, in an historic vote, the people of the Common Market nations elected members of the first European parliament. The parliament met in Strasbourg, France, in July 1979. For the first time, representatives of West Germany, Great Britain, Italy, France, the Netherlands, Greece, Belgium, Denmark, Ireland, Luxembourg, Portugal, and Spain held a forum to discuss mutually important issues.

The Chunnel. In the early 1800s, the English Channel saved England from invasion by the forces of Napoleon. Today, Britain and France are building a tunnel under the English Channel. The 22-mile (35 kilometers) tunnel, nicknamed the "Chunnel," will connect England and France for the first time in history. As a member of the French legislature said of the Chunnel effort:

> When the engineers from the two sides meet in the middle of the Channel, under these waters bloodied by so much combat, the cordial [friendly] handshake they will exchange will do more than all the diplomatic instruments to seal a sincere alliance between the two peoples.

That handshake between countries is expected to take place in 1993.

SECTION 1 REVIEW

Knowing Key Terms, People, and Places
1. Define: **a.** referendum
2. Identify: **a.** Margaret Thatcher **b.** Falkland Islands **c.** François Mitterrand **d.** Irish Republican Army **e.** European Community

Focus on Geography
3. Why is the standard of living lower in southern part of Italy than it is in the northern part of the country?

Reviewing Main Ideas
4. Why was Willy Brandt awarded a Nobel Peace Prize in 1971?
5. What are some of the advantages of a unified European Community?

Critical Thinking
Making Comparisons
6. Compare the domestic policies of British Prime Minister Margaret Thatcher with those of French President François Mitterrand.

665

2 The Soviet Union Made Drastic Reforms

As you read, look for answers to these questions:

◆ How is Mikhail Gorbachev different from previous Soviet leaders?
◆ How has *glasnost* affected Jews in the Soviet Union?
◆ Why do some Soviet workers fear *perestroika*?

Key Terms: dissident (defined on p. 666), *glasnost* (p. 666), *perestroika* (p. 668)

Many people living in Communist countries no longer believe that communism can bring about a just, prosperous society. Unfortunately, there is nothing democratic in the histories, traditions, or experiences of either the Soviet Union or the nations of Eastern Europe. However, signs of change are beginning to appear in the Soviet bloc. These changes are the result of new ideas about government from Soviet leaders.

Soviet Leaders Followed Different Policies

Over the past few decades, the Soviet leaders who have come to power have had different ideas and policies. Each leader has left a distinctive mark in Soviet history.

Leonid Brezhnev. In October 1964, political rivals forced Nikita Khrushchev from power. One of the main reasons for Khrushchev's fall was his failure to increase Soviet food production. Leonid Brezhnev (LEE uh nid BREZH nev) replaced Khrushchev as the general secretary of the Communist party. In 1977, Brezhnev also became president of the Supreme Soviet, the legislature of the Soviet Union.

Freedom under Brezhnev. The limited freedoms that Khrushchev had allowed were ended under Brezhnev. **Dissidents,** people who opposed the policies of the Soviet government, were often sentenced to terms in labor camps or mental hospitals.

One outstanding dissident was Alexander Solzhenitsyn (SOHL zhuh NEET sihn), a Russian writer who spent years in a Soviet labor camp for the crime of saying something against Stalin. In 1970, Solzhenitsyn won the Nobel Prize for literature. His book *One Day in the Life of Ivan Denisovich* described his own prison experiences. In 1973, he published the first volume of *The Gulag Archipelago*, in which he described slave labor camps in the Soviet Union. Soviet leaders were furious, and Solzhenitsyn was exiled from the Soviet Union in 1974. He moved to the United States.

Mikhail Gorbachev. When Brezhnev died in 1982, he was replaced by Yuri Andropov (ahn DROH pov). The ailing Andropov died soon after his selection. Another elderly leader, Konstantin Chernenko (cher NEHN koh), replaced him. Chernenko also died within a short time. In March 1985, Mikhail Gorbachev (mee KAYL GOR buh CHEV) became the general secretary of the Communist party.

Gorbachev was ready to tackle the Soviet Union's serious problems, including the day-to-day hardships of Soviet life. Most of the manufacturing in the Soviet Union was planned by a central agency for heavy industry or for military supplies. Thus, the troubled economy produced few consumer goods and forced the Soviet people to wait in long lines to get food, clothing, and everyday necessities. It was clear to Gorbachev that the central planning of the economy was not working. He also saw that the Soviet Union would have to reduce military spending and spend more on consumer goods and services.

Glasnost Meant Greater Political Freedom

Part of Gorbachev's plan to improve Soviet life involved a policy of *glasnost* (GLAHS NOHST), which means "openness." Under *glasnost*, Russians were able to speak out more honestly about what they thought of

Fast Food Hits Moscow

Cooperative business ventures with the West are changing life in the Soviet Union. When the first McDonald's was preparing to open in Moscow in early 1990 (the picture shows the building site), more than 25,000 local job seekers applied for work beneath the golden arches. A thousand applicants showed up the first day in hopes of landing one of the 630 available crew spots.

The restaurant in Pushkin Square, a joint venture between the Canadian branch of the American fast-food chain and Soviet officials, is the biggest McDonald's in the world. It has a total of 900 seats and serves about 15,000 customers a day.

1. Why did so many Soviets apply for work at the McDonald's in Moscow?
2. What special problems might a new company encounter in the course of doing business in the Soviet Union?

---

the Soviet government. Writers, artists, and film makers expressed themselves more creatively, and young people listened to music that was once forbidden.

Political dissidents. Gorbachev extended his policy of *glasnost* to include the release of some Soviet dissidents. One outspoken dissident was Andrei Sakharov (SAK uh rov). Sakharov, the inventor of the Soviet hydrogen bomb, spoke out for nuclear disarmament and won the Nobel Peace Prize in 1975. Because the Soviet government saw Sakharov as a threat, he was sent into internal exile, that is, exile within the Soviet Union, in the remote city of Gorki. As a result of the new openness, Gorbachev allowed Sakharov to come out of exile and return to Moscow in 1987. Sakharov died in 1989 after being elected to the Congress of People's Deputies.

Russian Jews. Soviet Jews have had a particularly difficult time in this country, which has a long tradition of anti-Semitism. In 1979, in hopes of gaining a more favorable trade status with the United States, the Soviets granted the American request that more Jews be allowed to leave the country. Fifty thousand Jews emigrated in that year. Unfortunately, the number of Jews permitted to leave varies with Soviet-American relations. In 1984, only 896 Jews were able to leave. Since 1985, however, *glasnost* has increasingly loosened restrictions on Jewish emigration from the Soviet Union.

Glasnost has its limits, however. In 1986, for example, the American journalist Nicholas Danilov was arrested and jailed in Moscow for several weeks when he was accused of being a spy. The American government had to negotiate carefully to have him released.

667

Gorbachev Calls for Reform

Mikhail Gorbachev represented a new generation of Soviet leaders when he rose to power in 1985. He was approximately 20 years younger than the three leaders who had preceded him. Gorbachev advocated a series of reforms to restructure the economy to make it more efficient. This program is called *perestroika*. In the following excerpt, he describes the goals of *perestroika*.

❝Today our main job is to lift the individual spiritually, respecting his inner world and giving him moral strength. We are seeking to make the whole intellectual potential of society and all the potentialities of culture work to mold a socially active person, spiritually rich, just and conscientious. An individual must know and feel that his contribution is needed, that his dignity is not being infringed upon, that he is being treated with trust and respect. When an individual sees all this, he is capable of accomplishing much. . . .

There are quite a few people who have adapted the existing laws and practices to their own selfish interests. They give little to society, but nevertheless managed to get from it all that is possible and what even seems impossible; they have lived on unearned incomes.

The policy of restructuring puts everything in its place. We are fully restoring the principle of socialism: 'From each according to his ability, to each according to his work.❞

1. What is the main goal of *perestroika*?
2. Explain who have "lived on unearned incomes."

Perestroika Brought Economic Reforms

Aware that the Soviet Union was lagging far behind the United States in economic production, Gorbachev saw the need for bold steps to improve the Soviet economy. Gorbachev's policy for economic reform was called ***perestroika*** (PEHR uh STROY kuh), which basically means less government control.

Fewer government controls. Gorbachev hoped that loosening the government's grip on the Soviet economy would help it to become healthier. Gorbachev wanted to shift the Soviet Union from "an overly centralized command [directed by the government] system of management to a democratic system based mainly on economic methods." In other words, Gorbachev wanted the government to play a smaller role in deciding how the economy would run.

More responsibility for workers. In order for *perestroika* to work, managers in Soviet factories would have to learn to make more decisions for themselves. Wages were to depend more heavily on the amount and quality of the work done by each worker.

To encourage Soviet farmers to increase their production, farmers were given the chance to sell their surplus, or extra, products for personal profit in a free marketplace. Such a marketplace offered a higher price than the state paid for the farmers' products. Gorbachev also wanted to end the system of collective farming. He proposed leasing land to farmers for periods of 50 years. Farmers would then take greater personal interest in improving the soil on their land, thus increasing the amounts of wheat and other crops that they could grow.

Problems with *perestroika*. Gorbachev's economic reforms went too far for some people and not far enough for others. Because they were used to depending completely on the authority of the state, factory managers were reluctant to make decisions and to take personal responsibility for them. Workers worried about the idea of being paid according to amount and quality of work. They feared that they could be forced to work harder or be exploited. Thousands of government officials feared losing their jobs. Some of the higher officials felt that *perestroika* betrayed Communist ideals.

Gorbachev, however, wanted to move even faster. He removed from power those members of the Communist party who did not support his reform. At a 1988 meeting of the Politburo, the executive committee of the Communist party, Gorbachev became president of the Soviet Union while keeping his position as general secretary. Gorbachev stilled shared power with 12 other members of the Politburo, but he had control of the Soviet government. As long as Gorbachev stays in power, the effects of *glasnost* and *perestroika* should continue to be felt throughout the Soviet Union.

Soviet Republics Voiced Their Complaints

Since the end of World War II, the countries west of the Iron Curtain have enjoyed the longest period without war in history. While Western European nations look with hope toward a European Community in 1992, old rivalries are surfacing once again in Eastern Europe. Many of these rivalries are centuries old and have simmered just below the surface for decades, but *glasnost* and *perestroika* are causing them to boil over.

The Baltic states. As you read earlier, Stalin and the Soviet leaders who followed him kept a tight lid on the 20 nationalities and 200 or more ethnic groups in Eastern Europe. The philosophies of Marxism and Leninism taught that the time for nationalism had passed and that communism alone could unify all of these different groups. This theory did not prove true, however. The Baltic countries of Latvia, Lithuania, and Estonia gradually began to express their wish for freedom from their Soviet masters. Gorbachev responded favorably to these demands, and as a result of *glasnost*, the nationalist movements in the Baltic states moved forward peacefully. In 1990, Lithuania enacted legislation permitting a plebiscite on full independence for Lithuania.

Armenia and Azerbaijan. In the Soviet republics of Armenia and Azerbaijan (AH zer by JAHN), however, the situation was more threatening. The people of Armenia, who were Christians, wanted control over the territory of Nagorno-Karabakh, which was populated mostly by Armenians but was part of the Muslim Azerbaijan. Gorbachev cracked down hard on the Armenians' demands, fearing too much Armenian independence. Also, the Soviet Union needed to strengthen its ties with its Muslim population. Tension increased, and in 1988, Soviet troops put down an attack by 1,500 Azerbaijanis on the Armenians living in Baku, the capital of Azerbaijan. A devastating earthquake that same month diverted attention to relief efforts. Conflict erupted again in January 1990, when Azerbaijanis attacked an Armenian village and Communist troops were sent in to restore order.

Glasnost has provided an outlet for people in Soviet republics, such as Armenia and Azerbaijan, to voice their complaints. Even as the Soviets have allowed increased freedom, however, the people of the republics have demanded release from oppression of Soviet domination.

SECTION 2 REVIEW

Knowing Key Terms, People, and Places
1. Define: **a.** dissident **b.** *glasnost*
   c. *perestroika*
2. Identify: **a.** Leonid Brezhnev **b.** Mikhail Gorbachev **c.** Alexander Solzhenitsyn
   d. Andrei Sakharov **e.** Azerbaijan

Reviewing Main Ideas
3. Describe the political policies of Leonid Brezhnev.
4. What different groups did *glasnost* especially benefit?
5. Why did some people in the Soviet Union oppose *perestroika*?

Critical Thinking
Predicting Consequences
6. How might *glasnost* and *perestroika* threaten the stability of the Soviet Union?

3 Changes Swept Eastern Europe

As you read, look for answers to these questions:

◆ How did *glasnost* and *perestroika* encourage sweeping changes in Eastern Europe?
◆ What changes have occurred in Soviet nations?
◆ How have East-West relations changed?

Key Terms: censorship (defined on p. 670), mixed economy (p. 671)

You have just read about the effect that *glasnost* and *perestroika* had on the Soviet republics. In this section, you will learn how Gorbachev's new openness spread to the Soviet satellite nations in Eastern Europe. You will also see how Gorbachev's policies affected relations between the Soviet Union and Western nations.

East Germany's Borders Opened

In January 1989, the Berlin Wall still stood as a continuing symbol of tensions between East and West. In February of that year a 20-year-old man was shot trying to escape across the Berlin Wall. Few people could predict that he would be the last person killed in this way.

In September 1989, Hungary opened its border with Austria. This made it possible for East Germans, who were sheltered in the West German Embassy in Budapest, the capital of Hungary, to flee to West Germany. What was first a trickle became a flood of East German refugees who had at long last found a new route around the Berlin Wall.

In October, as the government of East Germany celebrated its fortieth anniversary, there were massive protests against the Communist leadership. By the end of October, Erich Honecker was ousted as leader of the Communist Party. In an attempt to halt the protests and retain some vestiges of its former power, a new Communist government opened the Berlin Wall in November. The joy of Berliners at this turn of events was overwhelming as they danced and celebrated upon this once threatening symbol of oppression.

Pressures for greater democracy grew as the spirit of *glasnost* swept the country. Free elections were to be held in the spring of 1990. With the opening of the border between East and West Germany, new trade and cultural relations between East and West Germans rapidly developed, suggesting that reunification into one Germany may be a real possibility.

Poland Formed a New Government

Although Poland was controlled by Communists, the Roman Catholic Church had great influence on the lives of the people. In 1978, Polish Catholics rejoiced when a Polish-born cardinal became Pope John Paul II. Despite this encouraging sign that Poland's future held much promise, there would be a long struggle before that promise could be kept.

Labor unrest. In August 1980, after two months of strikes and demonstrations, the Polish government caved in and gave workers the right to strike and form independent labor unions. This was the first time such a right was granted by a country behind the iron curtain. The strikes were led by Lech Walesa (lek vah LEHN sah), an electrician, who became leader of Solidarity.

Solidarity. By 1981, 9.5 million workers belonged to Solidarity, the new trade union. In December 1981, Solidarity proposed a national referendum to set up a non-Communist government. Fearing that the Soviet Union would send troops to Poland, the Polish government declared a state of martial law and introduced strict **censorship,** a system of controlling public information and free speech. Most travel was banned and workers were forced at gunpoint to remain on their jobs. Lech Walesa was imprisoned along with other union officials. Martial law ended in 1982.

Economic conditions in Poland remained critical, with housing shortages, poor health care, and a lack of consumer goods. Solidarity sought reform programs, and by 1988, the union began negotiating with the government.

In June 1989, the Poles held free elections and Solidarity won an overwhelming victory. In August, Tadeusz Mazowiecki (tah DAY oosh mah zoh vee ET skee), a colleague of Walesa, became Prime Minister, while Jaruzelski was president. While Communists still held important posts, they could no longer dictate Poland's future. The new government sought to improve living standards by attempting to swiftly adopt a market economy.

Other Satellite Nations Moved Toward Freedom

The rest of the Communist nations soon began their own moves toward freedom. Dramatic events unfolded in many nations of Eastern Europe including Yugoslavia, Hungary, Czechoslovakia, and Romania.

Yugoslavia. Marshal Tito governed the many different nationalities in Yugoslavia by the sheer force of his personality and also because he was thought of as the founding father of the nation. When Tito died, however, the new constitution of 1974 divided Yugoslavia into six republics and two self-governing provinces that had almost complete veto power over decisions made by the central government.

Traditional hostilities among the various ethnic groups threatened the unity and stability of the nation. As the decade of the 1990s opened, Yugoslavia remained threatened with an eroding economy as well as political disunity. Moves toward democratic reform began, however. The Yugoslavian republic of Slovenia planned to hold its first free Western-style elections in 1990.

Hungary. Even though Soviet troops ruthlessly put down the Hungarian revolution of 1956, Hungary was allowed to keep a surprising degree of economic independence. As a result, Hungary developed a **mixed economy,** combining government controls and free trade. Hungary's capital, Budapest, became one of the most brilliant cities of the Eastern bloc and offered many consumer

▲ **Illustrating History** *Millions of Czechs took to the streets in November 1989 to peacefully demonstrate for democracy.*

goods unknown in other Soviet states. Even so, in 1988, 10,000 people demonstrated for greater freedom.

Because Hungarian Communist reformers did not go far enough, further demonstrations and unrest led to the toppling of the Communists in Hungary. New parties were formed and plans were made for free elections in early 1990.

Czechoslovakia. In January 1968, Alexander Dubcek (DOOB chek) became first secretary of the Czech Communist party. He tried to loosen the postwar restrictions on Czechoslovakia and to steer the country toward a more democratic system.

This period of relaxation, known as the Prague Spring, ended in August 1968, when the Soviet Union invaded Czechoslovakia with hundreds of thousands of Russian and Warsaw Pact troops. Dubcek was forced from office and replaced by Gustav Husak.

671

▲ **Illustrating History** *Bush and Gorbachev meet at the 1989 Malta Summit to discuss a new era in U.S.-Soviet relations.*

Throughout the 1970s and 1980s, pressure for reform mounted and by 1989 could no longer be resisted. The entire government resigned and new leaders came into power. In the new government, Alexander Dubcek became the new Chairman of the Czechoslovak parliament. An active opponent of Communism and a talented playwright, Vaclav Havel, became the new President. Free elections were planned for 1990.

Romania. The rapid changes toward democracy in Eastern Europe were especially noteworthy because they were made without widespread violence. Romania, long under the heel of President Nicolae Ceausescu (chow SHEHS koo) and his wife Elena, proved to be the exception.

The Ceausescus and their children lived lavishly in a grand palace while the common people of their country starved. In late 1989, popular demonstrations against Ceausescu grew violent and the dictator and his wife tried to flee the country. The Ceausescus were captured, secretly put on trial, found guilty of many cruelties, and both executed on December 25, 1989. After a period of turmoil and further killing by government forces, those loyal to Ceausescu were captured, tried and punished.

The Ceausescu regime shattered the economy of Romania. There are shortages of food and medicine. But the Communist monopoly of power has been ended and free elections were promised for 1990.

East and West Grew Closer

The political changes that swept Eastern Europe and the Soviet Union won the approval of the West. Gorbachev was hailed as the force behind these changes that appeared to mark the end of the cold war. Further easing of old tensions occurred at the Malta Summit in 1989 as Bush and Gorbachev discussed arms reduction.

Many issues remained that would affect the futures of the formerly Communist nations. Most of them struggled to stabilize their political and economic systems. Just how much financial help the West would provide was a key question to be answered. New questions also surfaced about the future balance of world trade. With freedom came new optimism, however, and most political experts agreed that a new era in closer East–West relations had begun.

SECTION 3 REVIEW

Knowing Key Terms, People, and Places
1. Define: **a.** censorship **b.** mixed economy
2. Identify: **a.** Pope John Paul II **b.** Lech Walesa **c.** Budapest **d.** the Prague Spring **e.** Nicolae Ceausescu

Reviewing Main Ideas
3. What factors led to the development of Yugoslavia's instability?
4. What rights has the labor movement in Poland won?
5. How did the Soviet Union end Czechoslovakia's Prague Spring?

Critical Thinking
Distinguishing False from Accurate Images
6. "Under *glasnost* the countries of Eastern Europe have become just like Western nations." Explain why you do or do not think that this statement gives an accurate picture of Eastern Europe today.

As we lead our everyday lives, many things happen that we have already experienced, and that we understand. If something happens that we haven't experienced before, most of us try to figure out what accounts for it. Our minds produce possible explanations, called *hypotheses,* of how this event or situation came to be.

A hypothesis may not always be *correct.* But it should be a *possible* explanation that *may* be true. In some cases we can test a hypothesis through experiments, as scientists do. In other cases, we must simply wait and collect more experiences that will suggest whether or not a hypothesis is true.

When you study history, you should form hypotheses about the events you study. Through hypotheses, you can suggest possible explanations for these events. In other words, a hypothesis can provide a basis for further investigation or argument. Use the following steps to practice forming hypotheses.

1. **State clearly the event or condition you want to explain.** Read the passage below and answer the following question: What is the main trend that the passage describes? Make this trend the event about which you will form hypotheses.
2. **Gather information about the event or condition and list all facts related to it that may have helped cause it.** Answer the following questions: (a) What facts are mentioned in the passage that relate to the event it describes? (b) Do you know any other facts that are not mentioned in the passage but that may have helped cause that event?
3. **For each fact you listed above, make a hypothesis—a statement suggesting a possible connection between the fact and the event you wish to explain.** Do this by answering the following question about each fact: Does this fact suggest a possible explanation for the event?

The European Community has been a long time in the making. For centuries, many leaders had spoken in favor of a unified Europe. Little came of the idea, however, until after World War II. In 1945, a French statesman named Jean Monnet argued in favor of uniting the economic interests of all free European countries. Such a move, he argued, would help prevent future wars. In 1951, a concrete step in this direction was made. Six countries, France, West Germany, Italy, Belgium, the Netherlands, and Luxembourg, agreed to cooperate over the production of coal and steel. These products would be freely traded between countries without the barriers that formerly existed. Coal and steel workers could take jobs in any member country, no matter what nationality they were. This agreement was called the European Coal and Steel Community.

The success of this community led its members to expand cooperation to a new realm —nuclear energy. In 1957, they agreed to work together to develop nuclear power and other peaceful uses of atomic energy. With this agreement, the European Atomic Energy Community was established.

Since the 1950s, the member countries of the European community have experienced rapid economic growth. Average income per person has risen dramatically, as have trade and the total value of goods and services produced.

REVIEW

Section Summaries

Section 1 Western Europe Worked for a Stable Society Margaret Thatcher, a member of the Conservative party, became Britain's prime minister in 1979. Thatcher wanted less government control in the economy. In France, Charles de Gaulle left office in 1968 when he lost public support. In the 1980s, Socialist President François Mitterrand nationalized some industries and strengthened France's support of NATO. West Germany developed a strong economy and came to accept the long-term division of Germany. Italy's major problems were poverty and terrorism. During the 1970s, Spain and Portugal both became democracies. The European Community hopes to achieve economic unity by the year 1992.

Section 2 The Soviet Union Made Drastic Reforms Soviet leader Leonid Brezhnev limited freedom in the Soviet Union severely. In 1985, Mikhail Gorbachev came to power and proposed the policies of *glasnost,* which means openness, and *perestroika,* which means less government control over the economy. Some political dissidents were released from prison, more Jews were allowed to emigrate, and factory workers took on more responsibility. *Glasnost* also led to changes in the Baltic states and in Armenia and Azerbaijan, as citizens moved toward self-government.

Section 3 Changes Swept Eastern Europe The Berlin Wall, communism's most visible symbol, was opened by the end of 1989 and the Communist government of Erich Honecker was replaced. Free elections in East Germany are slated for the spring of 1990. In Poland, *Solidarity,* led by Lech Walesa, helped bring reforms to Poland. Poles held their first free elections in 1989. In addition, pressures for democratic reforms have mounted in Hungary, Yugoslavia, and Czechoslovakia. The execution of Romania's dictatorial President Ceausescu and subsequent violence ended the Communist monopoly of power there.

Key Facts

1. Use each vocabulary word in a sentence.
   - **a.** referendum
   - **b.** dissident
   - **c.** *glasnost*
   - **d.** *perestroika*
   - **e.** censorship
   - **f.** mixed economy
2. Identify and briefly explain the importance of the following names, places, or events.
   - **a.** Margaret Thatcher
   - **b.** Northern Ireland
   - **c.** François Mitterrand
   - **d.** Willy Brandt
   - **e.** European Community
   - **f.** Leonid Brezhnev
   - **g.** Mikhail Gorbachev
   - **h.** Andrei Sakharov
   - **i.** Azerbaijan
   - **j.** Lech Walesa

Main Ideas

1. How did Margaret Thatcher reverse the economic policies of the Labour government?
2. How was *Ostpolitik* a major change for West Germany?
3. How is Italy divided economically; and what are its major concerns?
4. What did Spain and Portugal have in common?
5. List five actual and planned steps toward Western European unity since 1957.
6. In what ways did the Soviet Union change after Mikhail Gorbachev came to power?
7. Name one major problem in each of the following nations: Yugoslavia, Poland, Hungary, and Czechoslovakia.
8. How has Gorbachev's new openness affected United States-Soviet relations?

Developing Skill in Reading History

When you read history, you should pay attention to new terms that you come across in the text. Often these terms are not defined explicitly, but you can understand what they mean from the **context** in which they appear. Context means the information surrounding the term plus the way in which the term is used. Using clues from the context of the chapter, briefly explain each of the following terms in your own words.

1. neo-Nazi groups (page 661)
2. equal opportunity (page 662)
3. dissolved the parliament (page 662)
4. collective superpower (page 665)
5. consumer goods (page 666)
6. internal exile (page 667)
7. martial law (page 670)
8. Prague Spring (page 671)

Using Social Studies Skills

1. **Forming Hypotheses** Read the following hypotheses. Then list two facts that would support or disprove each.
    a. The Soviet Union went through great changes during Gorbachev's first few years in power.
    b. Economic cooperation will build a healthy economy in Western Europe.
    c. Yugoslavia needs another leader like Marshal Tito.
    d. It is unlikely that Solidarity will keep alive hopes for freedom in Poland.
2. **Analyzing Political Cartoons** Study the political cartoon at right. What is the cartoonist saying about the possibilities for United States-Soviet relations? What symbols does the cartoon use? What do you think the caption means?

Critical Thinking

1. **Perceiving Cause and Effect** How did France's problems in 1968 lead to the political defeat of Charles de Gaulle?
2. **Identifying Alternatives** Through *glasnost* and *perestroika,* Gorbachev planned to give more freedom to the people of the Soviet Union and Eastern Europe. Yet, what methods have these people themselves used to demand more freedom?
3. **Predicting Consequences** How might the situation in Ireland be different if Northern Ireland had become part of the Irish Republic in 1949?

THE ODD COUPLE

Focus on Writing

Writing a Coherent Paragraph

A coherent paragraph is one that sticks together and makes sense. One essential element of a coherent paragraph is a **logical order**. Four possible ways to organize the information in a paragraph are: **chronological order** (according to the times when events took place), **spatial order** (according to space, or location), **order of importance** (from least to most or most to least important), and **comparison and contrast** (telling how two things are similar and then how they are different).

Practice: Choose the best logical order for a paragraph on each topic below. Explain each of your choices.

1. Gorbachev's program of perestroika
2. The events of the Prague Spring
3. The first view of the Falkland Islands from a British battleship
4. The new democracies of Spain and Portugal

675

The Western Hemisphere Today

(1960–PRESENT)

1 **The United States Faced a Changing World**

2 **Canada Sought an Independent Course**

3 **Latin America Faced Many Challenges**

▲ **Illustrating History**
President John F. Kennedy, above, inspired enthusiasm and patriotic spirit in many Americans, including Peace Corps volunteers.

L ate on an October night in 1960, students at the University of Michigan held a torchlight rally to welcome presidential candidate John F. Kennedy. When he spoke, the candidate suggested that young Americans might dedicate part of their lives to serving their country by helping less fortunate people in other nations—in Asia, Africa, Latin America, and elsewhere. Would they be interested in this? The students responded enthusiastically.

John Kennedy was elected as the youngest president in our nation's history the following month. He remained committed to a program staffed by young people in a mood to help others. "We have in this country," he said, "an immense reservoir of dedicated men and women willing to devote their energies and time and toil to the cause of world peace and human progress." The program became known as the Peace Corps. At first carried forward by high-school and college graduates, the corps has since expanded to include people of all ages and from all walks of life.

Kennedy's program is still dedicated to helping poor people in countries around the world. The Peace Corps offers a good example of the great optimism of the American nation during the early 1960s. Charmed by the good looks and vitality of their new president, Americans were confident that they could achieve anything they wanted. As you will see in this chapter, their innocence did not last long.

1960	1970	1980	1990

1962 ■
Soviet Union removes missiles from Cuba

■ **1964**
United States passes the Civil Rights Act

1974 ■
President Richard Nixon resigns

1979 ■
Sandinistas control Nicaragua

1985 ■
Brazil becomes a democracy

1987 ■
United States ratifies INF treaty; Canada supports free-trade

■ **1988**
Chile votes against dictator Pinochet

▲ **Illustrating History** *The Peace Corps tries to improve the lives of people in the developing nations. This volunteer teaches in Costa Rica.*

1 The United States Faced a Changing World

As you read, look for answers to these questions:

- How did unrest mark the 1960s in the United States?
- What problems occurred in the 1970s in the United States?
- How did political policies and arms control agreements mark the 1980s?

> **Key Terms:** discrimination (defined on p. 678), arms limitation (p. 680)

The enthusiasm aroused by the election of John Fitzgerald Kennedy was summarized in a poem about Camelot, home of the legendary King Arthur and his knights of the Round Table. Alfred, Lord Tennyson, the poet, wrote: "The city is built/To music, therefore never built at all,/And therefore built forever." It was hoped that under the young, new president from Massachusetts, the nation would hear a new music and gladly march to it.

The 1960s Were Years of Unrest

The 1960s began as a time of vigor and hope for the future under President Kennedy. But, the Kennedy administration and the dream of Camelot ended when their leader was assassinated. A war in Vietnam and a political scandal called Watergate further eroded the optimism of the early 1960s.

Kennedy's brief administration. John F. Kennedy won the 1960 election over Richard Nixon. In his inaugural address, Kennedy said, "Let us begin anew, remembering on both sides [American and Soviet], that civility is not a sign of weakness, and sincerity is always subject to proof."

677

In June 1961, in Vienna, Austria, Kennedy met with Soviet leader Nikita Khrushchev. Khrushchev warned that he had not given up his plan to place Berlin under East German control. Kennedy warned that the United States would not sacrifice the freedom of the West Berlin people. During his administration, Kennedy also made Khrushchev back down on missiles in Cuba, as you will learn later in this chapter.

Congress considered Kennedy's bill to end **discrimination** (showing preference for one person over another based on race or religion). Although he did not live to sign it, the Civil Rights Act of 1964 was Kennedy's legacy. President Kennedy created the Peace Corps. In this organization, Americans volunteered to help people in less developed countries to improve their industry, agriculture, and education. Peace Corps workers taught in Peru, dug wells in Ethiopia, and built clinics in Colombia.

On November 22, 1963, Kennedy was assassinated in Dallas, Texas. Although uncertainty still surrounds the circumstances of his murder, it is likely that a bullet from Lee Harvey Oswald's rifle ended his life.

Johnson and an unpopular war. Vice President Lyndon Johnson became president and continued Kennedy's civil rights program. However, Johnson was more often criticized for the war in Vietnam than praised for his domestic programs.

Protest over the Vietnam War swelled in the late 1960s as casualties grew and the war seemed no closer to an end. Mass demonstrations and student strikes in protest of the war became common. Sure that the Vietnam issue would defeat him, Johnson decided not to run in the 1968 election.

In 1968, two other American leaders were assassinated. Reverend Martin Luther King, Jr. was killed in Memphis, Tennessee. King had led black Americans' fight against segregation. In the same year, Senator Robert F. Kennedy, brother of John F. Kennedy and attorney-general during the Kennedy era, was shot and killed in Los Angeles.

Nixon's election. In 1968, Richard Nixon again ran for president and defeated Hubert Humphrey. Nixon was largely concerned with foreign policy. He gradually decreased American troops in Vietnam and replaced them with South Vietnamese troops. In January 1973, a cease-fire was finally declared. Perhaps Nixon's most notable achievement was improving relations with the People's Republic of China.

Political Corruption and Economic Problems Marked the 1970s

During the 1970s, the United States suffered through several humiliating events. One event was the resignation of a president. Also, the taking of American hostages by Iran frustrated and angered the nation. Problems at home included inflation, unemployment, and energy shortages.

Watergate. During Nixon's second term in office, a grand jury found that Vice President Spiro Agnew had accepted money from companies seeking government contracts. Agnew resigned in 1973 and was replaced by Gerald Ford. Less than a year later, Nixon himself was toppled by scandal.

In 1972, burglars had broken into the headquarters of the Democratic party in the Watergate building in Washington, D.C. Nixon tried to deny any role in the Watergate event or in the cover-up that followed. The testimony of top aides and Nixon's own tapes of White House conversations, however, proved otherwise. In August 1974, Richard Nixon became the first United States president forced to resign from office. Gerald Ford became president. In 1976, Ford lost the presidency to Jimmy Carter, the former Democratic governor of Georgia.

Carter's administration. President Carter became chief executive during a period of high unemployment and discontent. Carter's most notable achievement was the role he played in helping Egypt and Israel to reach the peace agreement known as the Camp David Agreement, which will be discussed in Chapter 31.

Carter's administration ended in 1981, after four years of rising inflation and energy shortages. Carter had supported the shah

▲ **Illustrating History** *Senator Samuel Ervin of North Carolina (center) served as chairman at the Watergate hearings in 1974.*

of Iran, who allowed the United States to buy oil from his country. When the shah fell from power, Americans lost an important ally in the Middle East, and oil prices rose as supplies got scarce.

When the exiled shah of Iran was brought to the United States for medical treatment, a group of Iranians seized the United States embassy in Tehran. Demanding that the shah be returned to Iran, the Iranians held more than 60 American hostages for over a year. Carter tried to get the hostages released, but this did not occur until President Reagan's first term in office.

Ronald Reagan Began New Policies in the 1980s

President Carter lost the election in 1980 to former California governor Ronald Reagan. Reagan offered tax cuts, fewer social programs, and a defense buildup. He promised to balance the federal budget, but was unable to do so. Inflation dropped but unemployment rose. By 1984, the economy had improved, and Reagan was overwhelmingly reelected over Democrat Walter Mondale.

Reagan negotiated arms reductions with the Soviets. He sent aircraft carriers into the Persian Gulf to ensure the flow of oil, which was threatened in the Iran-Iraq War. Reagan also fought Communist movements in Central America.

President Reagan had high hopes for his Strategic Defense Initiative (SDI), sometimes called "Star Wars." This plan would put a protective shield into orbit to deflect incoming missiles. It requires highly sophisticated technology. Some scientists doubt that all the knowledge needed for SDI to work can be achieved any time soon.

In 1986, the Reagan administration became entangled in the Iran-Contra controversy. There appeared to be an agreement to sell arms to Iran in exchange for American hostages. The money from the sale was to be used to aid the Contras in Nicaragua. The Contras are the forces fighting against the Communist Sandinista regime in Nicaragua. President Reagan denied these charges, but the Iran-Contra affair caused many to doubt the honesty of his administration.

The Threat of Nuclear War Led to Arms Control Agreement

People began to realize that if nuclear war came, the resulting world would not be a place in which anyone would wish to live, even if parts of it survived. In such circumstances, what was the best way to ensure peace? One way was by **arms limitations,** or agreements among nations to limit how many nuclear weapons are produced.

Nuclear Test Ban Treaty. In 1963, the United States, Great Britain, and the Soviet Union signed a limited nuclear test ban treaty. They agreed to halt all tests of nuclear bombs, except those held underground.

SALT talks. In 1972, Congress ratified a treaty that limited the United States and the Soviet Union to two defensive missile sites each. This treaty grew out of the Strategic Arms Limitations Talks, known as SALT I. In 1979, the United States and the Soviet Union signed a second treaty, called SALT II. SALT II, signed by President Carter and Leonid Brezhnev, limited the amount and types of nuclear weapons that the United States and the Soviet Union could make.

The INF Treaty. In Washington, D.C., in December of 1987, an important meeting occurred between Gorbachev and Reagan. At that meeting, the two leaders signed the Intermediate-Range Nuclear Forces Test Ban Treaty, called INF. According to its terms, the two nations agreed to ban an entire class, or type, of nuclear arms. After much debate, the treaty was approved by the United States Senate.

In June 1988, President Reagan visited Gorbachev in Moscow. There, they began talks on limiting both strategic nuclear weapons and conventional weapons.

Malta Summit. In a shipboard meeting off the coast of Malta in December 1989, President Bush and Gorbachev declared their commitment to reducing conventional forces and strategic nuclear arms.

The Space Program Recovered and Advanced

In 1962, John Glenn became the first American to orbit the earth. In 1969, American astronaut Neil Armstrong became the first human to walk on the moon.

In 1981, the United States launched the first reusable spacecraft, a space shuttle called Columbia. Shuttles can be used to launch weather satellites, telecommunications satellites, and even spy satellites.

Public enthusiasm for the space program was intense when the shuttle Challenger was launched in January 1986. Tragically, Challenger exploded just after takeoff and all seven crewmembers perished. In September 1988, the space shuttle Discovery was launched into orbit, and the American space program seemed back on track.

SECTION 1 REVIEW

Knowing Key Terms, People, and Places
1. Define: **a.** discrimination **b.** arms limitation
2. Identify: **a.** Peace Corps **b.** Martin Luther King, Jr. **c.** Jimmy Carter **d.** INF Treaty

Reviewing Main Ideas
3. How did Lyndon Johnson become president in 1963? Was he a popular president? Explain.
4. Why did Watergate force President Nixon to resign?
5. Why have arms reductions talks been so important in the 1970s and 1980s?

Critical Thinking
Demonstrating Reasoned Judgment
6. The 1960s began with "Camelot," and the 1980s drew to a close with "Star Wars." Explain why these two ideas are used to describe historical events.

Contemporary Images

One characteristic of contemporary art is that it frequently uses the "commonplace" or "ordinary" as its theme. In this way, artists hope to speak to a greater number of people. Romare Bearden, a well-known black American painter, creates for the viewer the experience of urban life by arranging fragments of photographs of people against a backdrop of buildings, sidewalks, and walls in *Sunday After Sermon*. Bearden's picture is not of a particular street or place but is a collection of images that might be found in any city. Another way in which modern art can reach large audiences is in the architecture of public buildings. Public museums are an ever-growing source of popular entertainment and education. One of the most visited is the East Wing of the National Museum in Washington, D.C. Designed by the Chinese-American architect I. M. Pei, the structure has an enormous glass-covered lobby and unexpected sharp angles that are as interesting to visitors as the art that it houses.

The spirit of contemporary art is reflected below in the architecture of the National Museum's East Wing on the left and in Sunday After Sermon *on the right.*

2 Canada Sought an Independent Course

As you read, look for answers to these questions:

◆ How are the economies of Canada and the United States related?
◆ Why do some Canadians want more economic independence from the United States?

> **Key Terms:** vote of confidence (defined on p. 683)

As discussed in Chapter 21, Canada won self-government as a British dominion in 1867 without going through a revolution. After World War I, in which the Canadian army and navy served, the cry for greater freedom in foreign and domestic affairs grew louder. Canada became a separate member of the League of Nations and signed its own peace treaty with Germany. In 1931, after a series of conferences in which the commonwealth dominions discussed their problems with the British government, the English Parliament passed the Statute of Westminster. This law created the Commonwealth of Nations and gave Canada as well as the other dominions equality and independence under the symbolic protection of the British crown.

Canada's Geography Was Critical to Its History

If you study a world map carefully, you will see that one of the great land masses of the world is the country of Canada. It is the world's second largest nation. Furthermore, if you have a map with the North Pole at its center, you will see that Canada and the Soviet Union are neighbors and share the Polar Sea. By airplane, a polar route is often the shortest distance between two points, and so, a good deal of international travel may go over or near Canada.

Canada and the United States share a border of 3,223 miles (5,159 kilometers), the longest undefended border in the world. They share also the Great Lakes and the St. Lawrence Seaway, which the two countries developed as partners. During World War II, Canada and the United States formed a permanent joint defense board to protect the Atlantic and Pacific coasts. This joint effort resulted in a radar network called the Distant Early Warning System, or DEW Line, which stretches across northern Canada to detect hostile planes. Because they are neighbors, it is essential for the two countries to work together in war. Canada and America were allies during World War I, World War II, and the Korean War.

The two countries have also worked together to build the Alaskan Highway and are trading partners as well. Paper, newsprint, lumber, nickel, asbestos, iron ore, machinery, and petroleum are only a few of the products the United States buys from Canada.

Canada Established Its Own Government

Perhaps because of its size, the government of Canada became a confederacy. This means that Canada's provinces have substantial authority to rule themselves and are far more self-governing than are the American states. While the French-speaking city of Montreal is Canada's second largest city, the central government is located in the English-speaking city of Ottawa, in the province of Ontario. The other Canadian provinces are Newfoundland, Nova Scotia, New Brunswick, Prince Edward Island, Quebec, Manitoba, Saskatchewan, Alberta, and British Columbia. There are two territories, the Northwest and the Yukon territories.

The Canadian prime minister and the cabinet members are members of the House of Commons, the highest government authority in Canada. Its members are elected by the Canadian people. The symbolic head of Canada is the British monarch, who is represented by a governor-general; however,

▲ **Illustrating History** *The children above, residents of the Canadian province of Quebec, are marching in support of French nationalism.*

Queen Elizabeth II has no real power. In 1982, Canada severed all legal ties with Britain by obtaining the right to amend its own constitution.

French Nationalists. For 12 years after World War II, Canadian politics were dominated by the Liberal party. This party sought to establish good relationships with the large French community of Canada. But, there was frequent friction between the English and French-speaking communities.

In the 1960s, the French Canadians in Quebec felt that they did not have a fair share of political or economic power in their own country. French Canadians also felt that their language and culture were losing deserved respect. They organized a movement to separate Quebec from Canada and become an independent state.

Special privileges were granted to Quebec under Prime Minister Pearson to try to appease the French Canadians. In 1969, under Prime Minister Trudeau, the Canadian parliament passed a law that made both French and English the official languages of Canada. Disagreements and some violence occurred, but when the issue of a separate Quebec came to a vote in 1980, 60 percent of voters rejected the idea. The Meech Lake Agreement, which was signed on June 3, 1987, provides constitutional protection for Quebec's French language and culture.

Relations with the United States were especially friendly under Prime Minister Lester Pearson. He was followed in 1968 by Pierre Trudeau, a popular leader who served until 1979, when he was defeated by Joe Clark. However, Trudeau was returned to power in 1980 when Clark failed to receive a vote of confidence in the House of Commons. A **vote of confidence** is a vote taken within a parliamentary body to show that the majority of legislators supports a particular leader. Some people saw Trudeau's election as a symbol of Canada's political maturity, because he was the country's first French-Canadian prime minister. During Trudeau's administration, Canada's ethnic divisions became less bitter.

683

▲ **Illustrating History** *Supporters helped to reelect Mulroney despite much Canadian opposition to his free-trade policy.*

Canadians Debate Economic Ties with the United States

According to many Canadians, the United States has invested too heavily in Canada. Canadians want to work toward more control of their own economy, rather than depending on the United States. Presently, Canada's economy is vulnerable to conditions in the United States. Furthermore, the United States receives much of the profit from Canadian industries because it has controlling interests in many of them. These facts have led to disagreements among Canadians over the extent of trade Canada should conduct with the United States.

Free-trade agreement. In September of 1984, Conservative Brian Mulroney won a landslide victory at the polls. In 1987, Mulroney and President Reagan agreed to eliminate all tariffs, or taxes, over a 10-year period on goods coming into each other's countries. Barriers to investment were to be lowered, and the two nations would agree to curbs on trade in agriculture, energy, and services. The United States approved this so-called free-trade agreement with Canada, but the Canadian Liberal opposition did not share Mulroney's enthusiasm for the agreement. In fact, the promotion of free-trade with the United States lessened Mulroney's popularity with the Canadian public just before the November 1988 election.

1988 election results. Although Mulroney won the election, many Canadians worry about the effect of the free-trade agreement he supports. As in Britain, Canadians enjoy socialized medicine and generous retirement and unemployment benefits. Liberal Canadians have argued that their hard-earned "cradle-to-grave" security will be destroyed by closer economic ties to the United States. A report on this subject in the Boston Globe on November 3, 1988 stated:

> Almost 60% of Canadians oppose the [free-trade] agreement because they fear it will give the United States control of the Canadian economy, making Canada a 51st state.

SECTION 2 REVIEW

Knowing Key Terms, People, and Places
1. Define: **a.** vote of confidence
2. Identify: **a.** DEW Line **b.** Mulroney **c.** free-trade agreement

Focus on Geography
3. Besides a common border, what natural resources do Canada and the United States share?

Reviewing Main Ideas
4. Why did French Canadians seek to separate Quebec from Canada?

Critical Thinking
Identifying Central Issues
5. The continuing fear that Canada would become a "51st state" was a central issue in the 1988 Canadian elections. Discuss the main reason for this concern.

3 Latin America Faced Many Challenges

As you read, look for answers to these questions:

◆ What social and economic problems face Latin American countries?
◆ Why has it been so difficult to achieve democracy in Latin America?
◆ Why has the United States continued to be involved in Latin America?

Key Terms: land reform (defined on p. 685)

Since gaining their independence, the countries of Latin America have struggled with serious economic and political problems. Social justice, more equal land distribution, and a better life for the poor are major goals. Results have been mixed, but efforts continue. The map on page 689 shows the political systems of these countries.

Mexico Moved Toward Stability

After the Mexican Revolution, which occurred early in the twentieth century, the government of Mexico took steps toward managing its own future. Under a program of **land reform,** many large estates owned by wealthy people were divided up, and the land was given to peasants. The government took charge of Mexico's oil industry. The growing tourist industry also helped the economy. By the mid-1970s, the Mexican economy was booming.

The downturn came when oil prices declined in the 1980s. Mounting debts to foreign banks created a steady economic crisis. In October 1988, the United States agreed to a loan of 3.5 billion dollars to help Mexico weather its financial crisis.

Politically, the one-party governments of Mexico have been stable. The country is not a democracy as we understand it, but Mexico has enjoyed greater stability than many of its Latin American neighbors.

Castro Led a Communist Revolution in Cuba

In January 1959, Fidel Castro became premier of Cuba. Shortly afterward, Cuba became a Communist dictatorship. Land reform broke up many large sugar plantations. At the same time, agriculture and other private businesses were nationalized. Education was improved, but shortages of food and consumer goods made life hard.

Relations Worsened Between Cuba and the United States

Castro seized property owned by the United States in Cuba. In addition, Castro became friendly with the Soviet Union, which wanted a Communist ally close to the United States. (Cuba is only 90 miles [144 kilometers] from Florida.) As cold war tensions built, conflict between Cuba and the United States increased.

Bay of Pigs. In 1961, about 1,400 Cuban exiles, with help from the United States government, tried to overthrow Castro by invading Cuba. Cuban troops were waiting for their landing at the Bay of Pigs on Cuba's south coast, and most of the invaders were either killed or imprisoned. This event, which was known as the Bay of Pigs incident, brought the United States close to war with both Cuba and the Soviet Union.

The Cuban missile crisis. In October of 1962, United States intelligence agencies learned that the Soviet Union was building missile bases in Cuba. President Kennedy ordered a naval blockade of Cuba to keep Russian supply ships from reaching Cuban ports. Kennedy also demanded that the Soviet missiles already in Cuba be removed. Armed conflict seemed unavoidable. Finally, Khrushchev ordered the Soviet ships steaming toward Cuba to turn back. The Soviet missile bases were removed, and war was avoided.

Relations have not improved much between Cuba and the United States, although limited diplomatic relations were restored in 1977. Castro has encouraged revolutionary movements in other Latin American

Pollution in Mexico City

Cars, trucks, and buses roar past, spewing out their fumes. "I've been here 29 years, but it was never like this," grumbles a woman in front of her shop. "By the end of the day, my eyes are watering." This shopkeeper lives in Mexico City, Mexico, home of about 35,000 factories, 2 million vehicles, and perhaps the world's worst pollution. (See photo at right.)

Limiting the use of cars in Mexico City is difficult. Public transportation is poor, and people need to get around. What's the greatest single problem Mexico City faces? Growth. The current population is 20 million. Experts say that by the year 2000, some 30 million people may be living in Mexico City.

1. How has Mexico City become polluted?
2. What measures can you suggest that might help the pollution problem in Mexico City?

---

countries, which has created more tension. However, Castro has allowed thousands of Cubans who disagree with his policies to leave Cuba. Many have moved to the United States and other countries.

Puerto Rico Maintained Close Ties with the United States

At one time, Puerto Rico was called the "poorhouse of the Caribbean." As governor of Puerto Rico between 1948 and 1964, Luis Munoz Marin raised living standards. In "Operation Bootstrap," industry and business were attracted to the island. Jobs and educational opportunities improved.

In 1952, Puerto Rico voted to become an "associated free state" of the United States. The Commonwealth of Puerto Rico writes its own constitution and controls its own internal affairs. Although the people of Puerto Rico are citizens of the United States, they cannot vote in American presidential elections and are not represented in Congress. Puerto Rico is still divided between those who want closer ties to the

United States through statehood and those who want to retain commonwealth status.

Conflict Shook Central America

Much of Central America today is torn by violent conflict. Without modern machinery and farming methods, poor people in rural areas can barely supply themselves and their families with food. In sharp contrast, the wealthy own much of the land and control the industries. Most of the wealthy also support the military rulers who do little or nothing to improve conditions for the poor.

El Salvador. As in many South American nations, a series of military dictators have ruled El Salvador. Corrupt elections in the 1960s and 1970s placed military men in power. Violence increased in the late 1970s in opposition to the election of Carlos Romero. He was removed from office in 1979.

In 1984, after years of violence and bloodshed, José Napoleon Duarte (D'WAHR tay) was elected president of El Salvador. The United States supported Duarte in return for promises of reform. Even so, El Salvador still faces many problems.

Nicaragua. Anastasio Somoza (soh MOH sah) became president of Nicaragua in 1936. After his assassination in 1956, two of his sons acted as dictators. Opposition to the Somozas was led by Marxist guerillas called the Sandinista National Liberation Front. The Sandinistas overthrew the Somozas in 1979. Since then, Nicaragua has been governed by the Sandinistas with support from Cuba and the Soviet Union.

The Sandinistas, led by Daniel Ortega (or TAY gah), set up programs for economic and social reform but were accused by the United States of spreading revolution in Latin America. Fearing the Sandinistas would encourage communism through revolution, President Reagan supported the rebel group in Nicaragua, the Contras.

On March 23, 1988, with encouragement from Cardinal Obando y Bravo (oh BAHN doh ee BRAHV oh) and Costa Rican President Oscar Arias Sanchez, the Contras and the Sandinistas signed a cease-fire. President Arias's work to bring peace to the region earned him a Nobel Peace Prize. At the start of the 1990s, however, lasting peace has not been accomplished.

Costa Rica. Costa Rica provides a dramatic contrast to the violence and unrest in other Central American nations. Costa Rica has a stable, democratic government. The standard of living is quite high. Over 90 percent of the people in Costa Rica can read and write. The government provides public health care as well as education.

Panama. At the turn of the century, the United States was given the permanent right to use the Panama Canal, which was built with American money. The canal allowed ships to sail from the Atlantic Ocean to the Pacific Ocean without going all the way around South America. Panamanian nationalists soon resented their arrangement with the United States. In 1978, the United States finally approved a treaty that will hand over the canal to Panama in the year 2000.

In December 1989, President Bush ordered a military invasion of Panama which accomplished its mission of overthrowing

In their own words

A Woman Fights for Freedom

Poverty in Central America affects women as well as men. The following excerpt tells how one Guatemalan woman got involved in a revolutionary movement trying to bring justice and prosperity to her country.

❝I began working for the revolution some time ago. . . . I went to work in a factory again, and there, convinced that I should stay, joined a union. I have girlfriends who say I am crazy, that I shouldn't get involved in these things, that all I am going to get in return is unemployment or death. But I feel even braver when they tell me that I am going to end up dead. Also, it makes me want to know things I haven't known before.

I have had a lot of serious problems, but I have never been afraid. They have taken away my job. . . . I think about my son. But he tells me: 'If my mother dies, I will stay with the compañeros [comrades]. . . .' The compañeros are from the sindicato [union]. Therefore, thinking about the welfare of my child has not kept me from organizing. Sooner or later we all have to die. It might be in some accident. My little boy already is aware of everything, and I have taught him how one survives here. He already pays attention to the movements of the police . . . and advises us of them.**❞**

1. What did this woman's friends believe she would get for her collaboration with the revolutionary movement?
2. What does the woman say that implies that she and her son are suspicious of the police?

687

the government of military strongman General Manuel Noriega. Just prior to the invasion, Panama Defense Forces (PDF) had killed a U.S. serviceman and threatened other U.S. citizens in Panama. Noriega sought asylum, then surrendered to U.S. authorities who took him to the United States where he faced drug charges.

South America Made Some Economic and Political Gains

South America has struggled since the mid-1900s with serious economic and political problems. In recent decades, however, some South American countries have developed industrial economies, and some have replaced dictatorships with more democratic governments. (See the map on page 689.)

Argentina. Foremost in Argentina's history of military dictators was Juan Peron who ruled from 1946 until 1955, then again from 1973 to his death in 1974.

In late 1982, the military government tried to take over the Falkland Islands, which Britain controlled. A brief war resulted in a victory for Britain and the fall of the military government in Argentina.

In free elections, Raul Alfonsin (rah OOL al fohn SEEN) became president in 1983. Alfonsin was determined to govern as a democratic leader and has punished many of the former military rulers.

Brazil Turned Back to Democracy

Between 1956 and 1964, Brazil, Latin America's largest nation, was a democracy. Then, a military dictatorship ruled Brazil from 1964 to 1985. Injustice in the form of censorship and political oppression marked those years. At the same time, Brazil became the most highly industrialized country in Latin America.

In 1985, the military rulers agreed to free elections and a return to civilian rule. The elected rulers faced a massive foreign debt of over 100 billion dollars. Brazil's cities are overcrowded and lack opportunities for the poor. Overpopulation and poverty are also major problems.

Dictatorship in Chile Began to Unravel

Chile had a long tradition of democratic rule before the Marxist candidate Salvador Allende (ah YEHN day) was elected president in 1970. Allende tried to rid Chile's economy of United States involvement. Allende's government took over copper mines owned by American businesses, as well as many large farms and factories. His policies, however, angered the wealthy class, who helped to end Allende's democratically elected government in 1973.

Chile's next leader, President Augusto Pinochet (PEE noh SHAY), led a harsh military dictatorship. Torture, murder and imprisonment of so-called enemies of the state

▼ **Chart Skill**   *The chart below shows illiteracy rates in Mexico and Central America. As of 1985, which country had the highest illiteracy rate?*

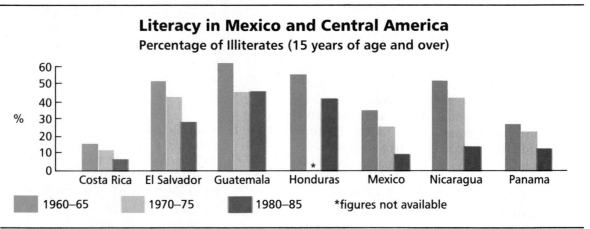

Literacy in Mexico and Central America
Percentage of Illiterates (15 years of age and over)

■ 1960–65   ■ 1970–75   ■ 1980–85   *figures not available

Political Systems in Latin America Today

UNITED STATES

ATLANTIC OCEAN

GULF OF CALIFORNIA

GULF OF MEXICO

BAHAMAS

HAITI
1986 –Present

MEXICO

CUBA

DOMINICAN REPUBLIC

PUERTO RICO (U.S.)

BELIZE

HONDURAS

JAMAICA

GUATEMALA
1982 –1985

NICARAGUA
1979 –Present

CARIBBEAN SEA

EL SALVADOR

COSTA RICA

VENEZUELA

GUYANA

SURINAM
1976 –1986

FRENCH GUIANA (Fr.)

ISTHMUS OF PANAMA

PANAMA
1987 –Present

COLOMBIA

PACIFIC OCEAN

Amazon River

ECUADOR
1972 –1979

PERU
1968 –1980

BRAZIL
1964 –1985

BOLIVIA
1971 –1978
1980 –1982

PARAGUAY
1965 –1986

CHILE
1973 –1988

ARGENTINA
1976 –1983

URUGUAY
1973 –1985

0   1000   2000 Miles

0   1000   2000 Kilometers

Communist states, elections but no free choice

Autocratic governments with or without some popular representation

Democratic elections with choice of parties

Under military rule during dates shown or overthrown by force

Source: Atlas of the World Today, 1988.

© PH

Focus on Geography

1. **Place**   What kind of government do most of these countries have?

2. **Movement**   What has happened to many of the democratic governments of Latin America in the last two decades?

were widespread. Thousands of dissidents, or people who opposed the government, died or simply disappeared. Censorship in all forms was the order of the day.

Public pressure forced Pinochet to hold a plebiscite, or direct vote, to determine pub-

lic opinion on the question of whether or not he should remain in power. Four million Chilean people voted for the removal of Pinochet by 1990. Although Pinochet is legally bound to abide by the plebiscite, there may well be a power struggle.

Oscar Arias Sanchez

The citizens of San José, Costa Rica, proudly gathered around President Oscar Arias Sanchez (shown at right) as he accepted their congratulations. "This is the happiest day of my life," he declared. Arias had just received the 1987 Nobel Peace Prize for his plan to bring peace to war-torn Central America.

Born in 1941, Arias Sanchez grew up determined to serve his country. As a young man, Arias spent time studying in England. During those years, he has said, "I learned to look at things from a dif-

ferent perspective than that of a superpower."

When he ran for president of Costa Rica in 1986, his campaign theme was "Peace with Arias." After winning the election, Arias convinced the leaders of four other Central American nations—El Salvador, Guatemala, Honduras, and Nicaragua —to meet with him in Guatemala. They signed the "Arias Plan," calling for the nations of the region to solve their own problems without outside interference. Arias himself admits, however, that problems remain. "No

human work is perfect," he has said. "But now the ball is in the court of the Central Americans."

1. Why did Oscar Arias Sanchez receive the Nobel Peace Prize?
2. What does "the ball is in the court of the Central Americans" mean?

Latin America Continues to Face Great Challenges

Several organizations have been established to help stabilize Latin America. In 1948, the Organization of American States (OAS) was formed to maintain the independence of the members and to keep peace among them. The Alliance for Progress was established in 1961 under President Kennedy. This organization extends loans and other economic aid to needy countries of North, South, and Central America.

United States aid to Latin America is awarded carefully. The poor human rights records of many Latin American countries, the lack of control of the illegal drug trade, and the massive foreign debts are all serious problems that need attention and solutions in the future.

Identifying Assumptions: Reading Newspaper Editorials

Newspaper editorials can be excellent sources of information about public attitudes toward historical events. Editorials, however, present points of view, not facts. To examine the validity of an editorial's point of view you must be able to identify and evaluate its assumptions. The assumptions are the ideas that the editorial takes for granted without offering additional facts to support them.

Use the following steps to analyze the assumptions contained in the editorial below.

1. **Read the editorial carefully to focus on its topic and its approach.** Identify the subject with which the editorial is concerned. Answer the following questions: (a) With what subject does the editorial below deal? (b) According to the writers of the editorial, what is the purpose of the proposed law? (c) According

to the people who wrote the bill, what is the purpose of the proposed law?
2. **Define the author's point of view.** Determine if the author is for or against the subject. Note that the author's point of view is expressed early in the editorial. Answer the following questions: (a) What is the author's purpose in writing the editorial? (b) Why does the author support or oppose the proposed law? (c) Is the author's view stated clearly? If so, quote the author's opinion.
3. **Determine the assumptions upon which the author's view is based and decide if they are valid.** Decide if the author's assumptions are supported by factual evidence. Answer the following questions: (a) What major facts does the editorial take for granted? (b) How could you find out if these assumptions of the author are valid?

The Washington Post
Washington, D.C., November 13, 1977

The Humphrey-Hawkins employment bill, as it emerges from the latest compromise, amounts to a get-well card for the American economy. To the unemployment rate, the bill would offer best wishes for a speedy recovery; to the inflation rate, it would extend every hope for a rapid return to health. The bill is full of nice thoughts. But its practical effect, in behalf of people who need jobs, would be zero. That's why the bill ought not to be passed. It is wrong for the U.S. government to make public promises that it knows very well it cannot fulfill.

. . . The main point of the bill, in its present form, is to set a 4 percent unemployment rate as a goal to be achieved over five years. How? The bill doesn't say. Why 4 percent? Because, until recently, that was the conventional def-

inition of full employment. It was the level below which the rate could not be pushed without a surge of wage inflation, as employers bid against each other for scarce manpower. Unfortunately, that threshold has shifted upward in recent years. In terms of inflationary risk, an unemployment rate of 5 or even 5.5 percent is the equivalent of 4 percent in the 1950s.

If there were a way to reduce unemployment by merely passing a bill, every American would have a moral duty to support that bill. But a bill setting an illusory goal for unemployment isn't going to help. . . . The remedy for unemployment is the slow, difficult, tedious process of lifting the pace of economic growth. That's doing it the hard way, but there isn't any other way.

REVIEW

Section Summaries

Section 1 The United States Faced a Changing World The optimism of the early 1960s ended with the assassination of President John F. Kennedy and the Vietnam War. The war was enough to topple Lyndon Johnson from the presidency in spite of his many domestic programs. The assassinations of Martin Luther King, Jr. and Robert Kennedy saddened the nation. President Richard Nixon improved relations with China, yet the Watergate affair forced his resignation. President Jimmy Carter faced severe economic problems. Ronald Reagan's presidency seemed to bring back a spirit of optimism. The economy showed signs of revival, and, like Reagan, President Bush continues to discuss arms limitations with the Soviets.

Section 2 Canada Sought an Independent Course Canada, the world's second largest nation in area, has a long history of friendship and cooperation with the United States. Canada differs from the United States in many ways, though. Its government is a confederacy, in which the provinces have substantial self-rule. Government leaders are members of the House of Commons. Canada's leaders have enacted many important social programs and have faced the crucial issue of conflict between the nation's French-speaking and English-speaking populations. In 1968, Canada elected French-Canadian Pierre Trudeau as prime minister. Trudeau served for over 15 years. In 1984, Brian Mulroney became prime minister and signed a free-trade agreement with the United States.

Section 3 Latin America Faced Many Challenges The countries of Latin America have struggled with social, political, and economic problems for many years. The United States has helped Mexico by lending it billions of dollars. Cuba under Castro became a Communist nation. Its relations with the United States remain unfriendly. The small nation of El Salvador struggles to maintain democracy. Meanwhile, the United States is divided over whether to support the Contras. With its crucial canal and the recent ousting of Noriega, Panama remains an important nation. Argentina and Brazil have both built democracies after years of military rule, while Chile is struggling toward democracy. American foreign aid is distributed carefully to Latin America. Poor human rights records, illegal drug trade, and massive foreign debt are problems that many nations in Latin America still face.

Key Facts

1. Use each vocabulary word in a sentence.
   a. discrimination   c. vote of confidence
   b. arms limitations   d. land reform
2. Identify and briefly explain the importance of the following names, places or events.
   a. John F. Kennedy   h. DEW Line
   b. Nikita Khrushchev   i. Quebec
   c. Lyndon Johnson   j. Pierre Trudeau
   d. Martin Luther King, Jr.   k. Fidel Castro
                        l. Nicaragua
   e. Richard Nixon   m. Panama Canal
   f. Ronald Reagan   n. Juan Peron
   g. SALT II   o. Augusto Pinochet

Main Ideas

1. What were considered to be the major accomplishments of Presidents Johnson, Nixon, Carter, and Reagan?
2. What steps were taken to reduce the arms race between 1963 and 1988?
3. List some examples of friendly relations between Canada and the United States.
4. Describe the government of Costa Rica.

Developing Skill in Reading History

Each chapter in your book has been divided into sections. Review the three section titles for this chapter. Now think of a new title for each section. Explain why you think your new titles are appropriate.

Using Social Studies Skills

Identifying Assumptions: Reading Newspaper Editorials Read this excerpt from a newspaper editorial. Then, choose the correct answer for each question. (The editorial, written by Charles Krauthammer, appeared in the *Chicago Sun-Times* on Tuesday, December 1, 1987.)

The Reagan administration's change of heart regarding the evils of the Soviet Empire is well advertised. Buried in the pre-summit enthusiasm, however is an even more remarkable about-face: the Reagan administration's bailout of the United Nations.

The United Nations is facing financial calamity. Two weeks ago, Secretary General Javier Perez de Cuellar declared that the UN would be unable to meet its payroll unless it received at least $87 million from the United States. The Reagan administration has now promised the money. . . .

1. This editorial is about
   a. the United Nations.
   b. the Soviet Union.
   c. Latin America.
2. Javier Perez de Cuellar is the
   a. president of Argentina.
   b. leader of Cuba.
   c. secretary-general of the United Nations.
3. The term bailout in this context means
   a. giving needed money.
   b. changing your mind.
   c. refusing to pay a bill.

Critical Thinking

1. **Distinguishing Fact from Opinion** The Boston Globe reported that according to opinion polls, "almost 60% of Canadians oppose the [free trade] agreement. . . ." Is this a fact or an opinion?
2. **Expressing Problems Clearly** Write a few sentences that clearly summarize the major problems of Latin America today.
3. **Checking Consistency** In 1983, President Reagan called the Soviet Union "the focus of evil in the modern world." Based on later actions, do you think he changed his mind? Explain.

Focus on Writing

Selecting a Topic
There are a number of ways to choose a topic. Think of a topic from this chapter that you would like to report on. Try each of the following methods to help you make your choice.
1. Brainstorm (let your mind run free) to create a list of possible topics. You may brainstorm alone, with a classmate, or in a group.
2. Skim the chapter rapidly, jotting down topics of interest.
3. Use your imagination to ask creative questions about what you have learned. For example: "What would the world be like if there were no nuclear weapons?" Such questions can result in interesting reports.
4. Look at the photograph below. Write down any topic or topics it brings to mind.

The Middle East and Africa

(1960–Present)

▲ **Illustrating History**
During the Camp David negotiations, Egyptian President Anwar Sadat (left) and Israeli Prime Minister Menachem Begin share a private moment.

On the afternoon of September 5, 1978, two helicopters landed separately at Camp David, the sprawling presidential retreat set in the Maryland mountains. The first carried President Anwar Sadat of Egypt. Two hours later, Menachem Begin, prime minister of Israel, also arrived. Both leaders were there at the urging of President Jimmy Carter. By bringing them together, Carter hoped to settle the age-old conflict between Arabs and Jews in the Middle East.

Sadat and Begin each greeted Carter warmly, but neither met the other that first day. When they did meet, on the second day, discussions were tense. On the third day, the exchanges between Sadat and Begin were so heated that they broke off direct negotiations. Instead, President Carter shuttled back and forth between the two men in their cabins, acting as a mediator. After 13 days of meetings, an agreement was reached. Issues addressed in the agreement included Israeli security, Palestinian rights, and handling of the territories occupied by Israel since the 1967 Six-Day War.

Were the Camp David Accords a turning point in the Middle East? In 1979, both Egypt and Israel ratified a peace treaty based on the accords. The settlement, though fragile, laid new foundations for further negotiations. As you read this chapter, you will learn how conflict arose in the Middle East and how people are working today to bring peace to the region.

1960	1970	1980	1990

■ **1960**
Oil nations form OPEC; South Africa bans African National Congress

■ **1967**
Israel begins Six-Day war; civil war begins in Nigeria

■ **1973**
Oil embargo begins

■ **1978**
Israel and Egypt sign Camp David Agreement

■ **1980**
Zimbabwe becomes independent; Iran-Iraq war starts

■ **1987**
West Bank rioting breaks out; anti-apartheid protests continue in South Africa

▲ **Illustrating History** *President Sadat (left), President Carter (center), and Prime Minister Begin celebrate the Camp David Accords.*

1 Old Rivalries Prevented Middle East Peace

As you read, look for answers to these questions:

◆ How have natural resources made the Middle East important to the world?
◆ What Middle Eastern leaders worked to achieve peace in 1978?
◆ What groups fought over Lebanon?
◆ Why was the Ayatollah Khomeini able to gain power in Iran?

Key Terms: ayatollah (defined on p. 699)

The history of the Middle East in the late twentieth century has been a history of conflicts—over religion, nationalism, and oil. When the Jewish state of Israel was established in 1948, it became the focus for the hostility of the region's mainly Muslim Arab nations. Religious difference among the Muslims themselves, combined with nationalist movements, also played a role in Middle East conflicts. World nations became involved because troubles in the Middle East disrupted vital oil supplies.

Resources Shaped the Modern Middle East

The Middle East is an area defined as much by language and culture as by geography. Fifteen countries make up the Middle East. There are 12 Arab nations. Turkey and Iran are Muslim nations, but their people are not Arab in origin. Most of Israel's people are Jews.

Islam is the chief religion of the Middle East, and Arabic is the region's major language. Hebrew is the principal language of the Jewish state of Israel, while most Iranians speak the Persian language of Farsi.

695

Although in ancient times, this area included the Fertile Crescent, desert is the most common geographic feature. There are also high plateaus and desolate mountains. Although food can be grown mainly in the river valleys or coastal areas, the people of the Middle East cannot raise enough food to feed themselves.

Oil. While fertile land is scarce, the Middle East has the world's largest reserves of oil. When automobiles, airplanes, and industry created an immense world demand for oil, these reserves suddenly became valuable.

In 1960, oil-producing nations formed the Organization of Petroleum Exporting Countries, or OPEC. Its members included nations from the Middle East, Africa, and South America. The purpose of OPEC is to control the supply of oil and so try to keep world oil prices high.

The Suez Canal. Another important area resource is the Suez Canal, which connects the Mediterranean Sea and the Red Sea. The canal, controlled by Egypt, is a major link in the East-West overseas trade route and thus vitally important to the region. Huge quantities of food, petroleum, and other essential goods pass through the canal.

Conflicts Continued Between Israelis and Arabs

During the mid-1960s new tensions grew between Israel and its Arab neighbors. In 1967, President Nasser of Egypt took steps to stop Israeli shipping in the Red Sea and to blockade the vital Israeli Red Sea port of Eilat, through which much of Israel's trade with Africa and Asia and most of its petroleum supplies passed.

Suddenly, Israel struck back. On June 5, 1967, Israeli jets made surprise air attacks that caught the Egyptian air force on the ground and destroyed it. The Israelis also attacked Syria and Jordan and quickly destroyed the armies of both countries. In the process, Israel captured huge areas of territory along its eastern and northern borders, as well as the Arab-held portion of Jerusalem and the West Bank of the Jordan River.

By June 12, the Israelis had achieved a decisive victory on all fronts. Two Israeli leaders—Yizhak Rabin (rah BEEN) and Moshe Dayan (dah YAHN)—emerged as heroes of the lightning Six-Day War.

Despite world hopes for peace, another major Arab-Israeli war began in October of 1973, just as Israelis were celebrating the holy day of Yom Kippur. Egypt and Syria

▼ **Graph Skill** *In what year did oil production peak? During what period did oil prices increase at the fastest rate?*

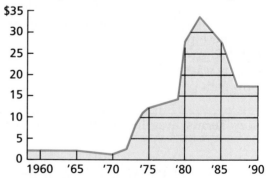

Middle East Oil Production and Prices, 1960–1987

Production—Billions of Barrels per Year

Year	
1960	
1965	
1970	
1974	
1975	
1977	
1980	
1985	
1987	

0 1 2 3 4 5 6 7 8 9 10

Sources: International Petroleum Annual; World Crude Oil Production Annual; CIA, International Energy Statistical Review

Price per Barrel (Saudi Arabian Light)

Source: Petroleum Intelligence Weekly (est.)

An Ancient Custom

Islam's holy book, the Koran, urges women to "reveal not" by covering their heads and veiling their faces. In Arab lands the custom may have begun as women imitated the wives of the prophet Mohammed, who asked his wives to veil themselves in public. As shown in the picture, it is still the custom in parts of the Islamic world.

In Saudi Arabia, for example, most women still wear veils. Many see them as a sign of tradition, not as a sign of oppression. One Saudi woman who is a student in England still practices the Arab custom when she's at home. "I'm a Saudi woman," she says simply. "I like my veil."

1. How did the custom of wearing veils begin?
2. How do most Saudi women view the custom?
3. Do you think Saudi women will ever give up their veils? Explain your answer.

attacked Israel on two fronts and won initial victories. After much fighting and loss of life, however, Israel's troops began to win. They regained lost territory and once again destroyed the forces of Egypt and Syria. The maps on page 698 show the changes in Israel between 1967 and 1982.

During the fighting, the Arabs tried to isolate Israel by using their control of oil supplies as a political weapon. Countries that had backed Israel thought twice before giving that country aid and losing their oil supply. As a result, Israel found itself almost alone, with only the United States as a reliable ally.

Israel and Egypt Wanted Peace

For both Arabs and Israelis, the wars were costly in money and lives. Egyptian president Anwar Sadat, who had succeeded Nasser in 1970, called for a peace with Israel. In 1977, Sadat made a historic visit to Jerusalem and, in a speech to the Israeli parliament, urged that the two nations make peace. Other Arab nations were outraged.

In September 1978, Sadat, Prime Minister Menachem Begin of Israel, and U.S. President Jimmy Carter met at Camp David, Maryland. In a long meeting, they hammered out the basis for a future agreement between Israel and Egypt. For their efforts to achieve peace, Sadat and Begin were given the Nobel Peace Prize in 1978.

In October 1981, however, President Sadat was assassinated by Muslim fanatics who opposed his attempts to modernize Egypt and make peace with Israel. The new president of Egypt, Hosni Mubarak, continued to defend the Camp David treaty and to follow Sadat's policies. He also ended Egypt's isolation from the Arab world.

Israel, 1967

SYRIA
LEBANON
Golan Heights
MEDITERRANEAN SEA
West Bank
Jerusalem · Jordan R.
Gaza Strip
DEAD SEA
EGYPT
· Cairo
Suez Canal
JORDAN
SINAI PENINSULA · Eilat
GULF OF SUEZ
GULF OF AQABA
SAUDI ARABIA
Nile R.

0   100 Miles
0   100 Kilometers
· Sharm-al-Sheikh

Israel
Territories occupied by Israel after the Six-Day War
RED SEA
© PH

Israel Today

SYRIA
LEBANON
Golan Heights
MEDITERRANEAN SEA
West Bank
Jerusalem · Jordan R.
Gaza Strip
DEAD SEA
EGYPT
· Cairo
Suez Canal
JORDAN
SINAI PENINSULA · Eilat
GULF OF SUEZ
GULF OF AQABA
SAUDI ARABIA
Nile R.

0   100 Miles
0   100 Kilometers
· Sharm-al-Sheikh

Israel
Territories occupied by Israel, 1982 to present
RED SEA
© PH

Focus on Geography

1. **Location**   Where is Eilat located, and why is it in a critical location?
2. **Regions**   What territories did Israel gain after the Six-Day War?

Palestinians Demanded Their Own State

As discussed in Chapter 28, when Israel was formed out of part of Palestine, many Palestinians became homeless. As a result of the first Arab-Israeli War in 1948, about 900,000 Palestinians fled Israel. They were forced to settle in refugee camps in Lebanon, Syria, Jordan, Gaza, and the West Bank of the Jordan River, which was, at that time, a part of Jordan.

The PLO.   In 1964, the Palestine Liberation Organization, called the PLO, was formed. Led by Yasir Arafat (YAH sir AH rah faht), the PLO uses terrorist tactics, including raids against Israeli settlements, to draw international attention to its demands. In 1972, for example, PLO terrorists killed Israeli athletes who were participating in the Olympic Games in Munich, West Germany.

The West Bank became the scene of continuing conflict between Israelis and Palestinians. Israel, which had taken the West Bank in the Six-Day War, considered the territory strategically important and encouraged permanent settlement there. The Palestinians who lived on the West Bank, however, were bitter about losing more land and being ruled by the Israelis.

West Bank unrest.   The West Bank situation exploded in 1988. Rock-throwing Palestinian youths on the West Bank began widespread rioting, termed an *intifada* (Arabic for "uprising"), against Israeli troops.

Meanwhile, Arafat and the PLO leadership began to move toward more moderate methods to gain the acceptance of other nations. Arafat stated that, in return for Israel's acceptance of the Palestinians' right to a state in the occupied territories, the PLO would agree to Israel's right to exist. In November 1988, the Palestine National Council, or the PNC, declared an independent Palestinian state. The PNC is the political wing of the PLO and represents millions of exiled Palestinians.

Religious Violence Shattered Lebanon

By the 1970s, several religious groups in Lebanon, including Christians and Muslims, were struggling for political power. Although the Muslims were Lebanon's largest group, they were split among at least three rival factions.

Violent civil war began in 1975. It involved not only the Lebanese Christians and the Muslims but also troops from neighboring Syria and PLO factions living in Lebanon. Several Arab countries supported the Muslim groups, and Israel aided the Christians. The Palestine Liberation Organization, with help from Syria, used southern Lebanon as a base for terrorist attacks on Israel. In 1982, Israeli forces invaded Lebanon and drove out Arafat and the PLO at the cost of thousands of deaths and injuries. Contributing to the disorder in Lebanon were the frequent kidnappings of innocent people by various extremist groups.

Muslim Fundamentalists Controlled Iran

Another Middle Eastern trouble spot was Iran, once called Persia. Mohammed Reza Pahlavi became shah of Iran in 1941. By the 1960s, the shah's program to make Iran a modern nation was underway. It included land reform, more social and political rights for women, and new farming methods. Those who watched closely, however, knew that the benefits of modernization were not reaching the majority of the population. Frustrated, the Iranian opposition groups turned to the **ayatollahs,** or Muslim holy men, to lead the resistance against the shah.

The Ayatollah Khomeini (koh MAY nee) had been exiled by the shah. He became the leader in exile of the Shiites (SHEE ites), the branch of Islam to which most Iranians belong. Early in 1979, the shah was overthrown by Khomeini and his followers, and a Muslim fundamentalist government was established. A Muslim fundamentalist government rules by traditional Islamic law. In November 1979, Iranian militants stormed the United States embassy in Teheran, Iran, and took 52 Americans as hostages. The American hostages remained in Iranian captivity until they were finally released on January 20, 1981.

From the earliest days of his regime, the Ayatollah Khomeini imposed strict Islamic law on the people of Iran. The return to older ways affected the women of Iran in particular. They had not obtained equality under the shah's rule but had gained many new freedoms. New Islamic legislation took away many of these rights.

Iran and Iraq Went to War

On September 4, 1980, war broke out between Iran and Iraq. Border disputes between Iran and Iraq played a part. So did rivalry between Khomeini and Iraqi President Saddam Hussein for leadership among Arab countries. Iraq had superior weapons against Iran's larger army. Other nations became worried when the war began to disrupt oil shipping in the Persian Gulf in 1984. Violence in the gulf continued until August 1988, when the United Nations negotiated a cease-fire. In 1989, the Ayatollah Khomeini died.

SECTION 1 REVIEW

Reviewing Key Terms, People, and Places
1. Define: **a.** ayatollah
2. Identify: **a.** Nasser **b.** West Bank **c.** Anwar Sadat

Focus on Geography
3. Why was Egypt's blockade of the port of Eilat in 1967 so serious for Israel's trade?

Reviewing Main Ideas
4. For what achievement were Sadat and Begin given the Nobel Peace Prize?
5. What changes did the rule of the Ayatollah Khomeini bring in Iran?

Critical Thinking
Recognizing Ideologies
6. What was the purpose behind the use of terrorist tactics by the PLO? Why did the PLO begin to move away from terrorism during the mid-1980s?

2 Conflicts Disrupted Northern Africa

As you read, look for answers to these questions:

◆ What were Qaddafi's aims for Libya?
◆ What were his methods?
◆ Why did several countries try to claim the western Sahara?
◆ What caused a drop in the standard of living in Algeria?

Key Terms: pan-Arabism (defined on p. 700)

The troubled politics of the Middle East often involved the nations of northwestern Africa, a region that has long been part of the Muslim world. These countries, populated by many different races, were all once colonies of European powers. As a group, Algeria, Tunisia, Libya, and Morocco are sometimes called the Arab West. Like their neighbor Egypt, these newer nations are closely linked with the Middle East by their Arabic language and culture and by the religion of Islam. The income received from oil exports is important in many of their economies. Major oil fields are shown on the map on page 701.

Libya Turned to Terrorism

The former French colonies of Tunisia, Morocco, and Algeria gained their independence in the 1950s and 1960s. Libya, the other country on the northern coast of Africa, was taken from Italy after World War II. Ninety percent of Libya is desert. A small, fertile area along the Mediterranean coast is used for growing fruit.

Until large oil reserves were discovered in 1959, Libya was one of the poorest Arab countries. It depended heavily on economic aid from the United States and Britain. The newly discovered oil brought huge amounts of cash into the country and became the basis of Libya's economy. Today 80 percent

of Libya's income and 99 percent of its exports come from oil. Some of this money has been used to improve farmland and make Libya more self-sufficient.

In 1969, a 27-year old military leader, Colonel Muammar el-Qaddafi (guht DAW fee), overthrew the monarchy. Under Qaddafi's leadership, Libya took over Libyan oil holdings from foreign companies.

In affairs of the Muslim world, Qaddafi was an extreme Arab nationalist with a deep hatred for Israel. Qaddafi saw himself as the leader of **pan-Arabism.** This is the movement dedicated to uniting the Muslim peoples in a common language, Arabic, and one religion and political system, Islam. Qaddafi tried to establish a Saharan confederation made up of Mauritania, Morocco, and Algeria, as well as the former territory of Spanish Sahara. He also once tried to unite Egypt and Libya. In the early 1980s, Qaddafi sought to annex the neighboring country of Chad. A minority of Chadians supported Qaddafi's extremist Islamic aims, rebelled against the government, and invited Libya to invade the war-torn country. Libyan forces, armed by the Soviets, attacked Chad's army. France supported Chad's government and

▼ **Illustrating History** *Muammar Qaddafi became the leader of Arab unity in Libya.*

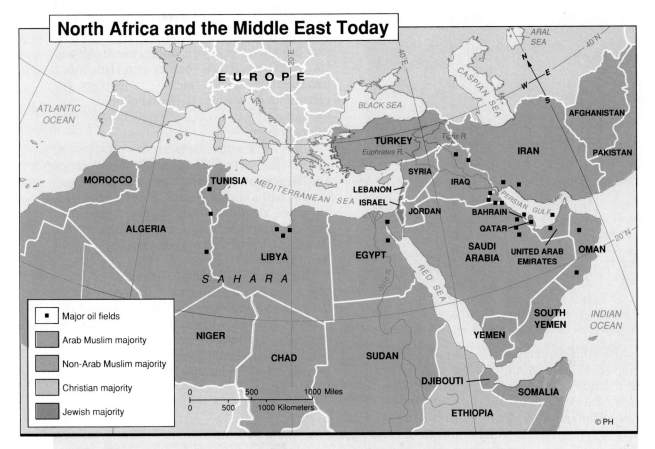

North Africa and the Middle East Today

Legend:
- ■ Major oil fields
- Arab Muslim majority
- Non-Arab Muslim majority
- Christian majority
- Jewish majority

Focus on Geography

1. **Place**   The map shows the countries of North Africa and the Middle East. What is the one Jewish country in the Middle East?
2. **Regions**   In what region are most of the oil fields located?

by 1987, Qaddafi and his troops had been turned back and the Libyan threat to Chad ended.

Under Qaddafi, Libya became a center for international terrorism. For example, Qaddafi praised the 1985 attacks in the Vienna and Rome airports that killed 20 people. The United States blamed him for the 1986 terrorist attack on a Berlin disco in which an American soldier was killed. In retaliation, United States war planes attacked Libyan cities and military bases near Tripoli and Benghazi. The world's democracies joined with the United States in condemning Libya as a terrorist nation.

Several Nations Claimed the Western Sahara

Political stability in northern Africa was also endangered by a dispute over the mineral-rich area of the western Sahara, once called Spanish Sahara.

Morocco.   In 1975, thousands of people from Morocco occupied territory across the border in Spanish Sahara. Spain gave up its claims, and the land was divided between Mauritania and Morocco. Mauritania withdrew a few years later, and a movement for independence developed in the western Sahara. Algeria backed this movement, known

▲ **Illustrating History** *Students seeking reforms rioted in Algeria in 1988.*

as the Polisario Front. However, the conflict caused trouble among all the countries of the Arab West. Algerian president Chadli Benjedid decided to end the costly war and establish friendlier relations with King Hassan of Morocco. Eventually, the United Nations and the Organization for African Unity, or OAU, worked out a settlement that Morocco and the Polisario Front accepted in August 1988. It brought a cease-fire in the western Sahara.

Algeria. The settlement did not bring peace in Algeria, however. Algerians' standard of living had been badly hurt by falling oil prices, inflation, and food and housing shortages. In the fall of 1988, Algerian students and youths rioted, demanding reforms in education and the economy. Several hundred people were reported killed when soldiers attacked the crowds. President Benjedid promised the people changes and proposed a free market economy.

Tunisia Followed a Moderate Course

When Tunisia became a republic in 1957, Habib Bourguiba (bohr GEE bah), who had led the fight for independence for 20 years, became its first president. The Tunisians

continued to reelect the popular leader, and in 1975 he was named president for life. Tunisia was considered the most modern and advanced country in northern Africa. Under Bourguiba, it took a peaceful, more pro-Western course than its neighbors. Investments encouraged modernization, and foreign tourists brought more money into the economy.

Bourguiba even supported negotiations, rather than war, between the Arab states and Israel, and he kept ties with the United States when other Arab nations did not. Tunisia's location among larger, more militant Arab states, particularly Libya, sometimes made it hard for the country to remain moderate.

The aging Bourguiba was removed from office peacefully in 1987. The new president, Zine el-Abidine Ben Ali, promised the country more political freedoms and democracy. He took legal action to control Islamic fundamentalists. Ben Ali continued Tunisia's good relations with France and the United States.

SECTION 2 REVIEW

Reviewing Key Terms, People, and Places
1. Define: **a.** pan-Arabism
2. Identify: **a.** Muammar el-Qaddafi **b.** western Sahara **c.** Polisario Front **d.** Habib Bourguiba

Reviewing Main Ideas
3. What methods did Qaddafi use to promote his goals?
4. What made the western Sahara a valuable possession?
5. How did Tunisia's policies differ from those of other northern African countries?

Critical Thinking
Expressing Problems Clearly
6. The countries of northern Africa were part of the Ottoman Empire and then colonies of different European powers. What problems might their history have caused them as independent nations?

3 Sub-Saharan Africa Faced Challenges

As you read, look for answers to these questions:

◆ What economic problems troubled countries in sub-Saharan Africa?
◆ What are the causes of starvation in Ethiopia?
◆ How was Biafra formed?
◆ How did black Rhodesians win political rights?

Key Terms: tribalism (defined on p. 704)

Sub-Saharan Africa—the part of Africa south of the Sahara Desert—developed separately from the nations of the desert and the Mediterranean coast. There is great variety among the nations in this huge region. They include the tropical lands of western Africa, the vast central savannas, and the fertile highlands of eastern Africa.

Nearly all the countries of sub-Saharan Africa are former colonies that moved toward independence after World War II. Along with their own unique cultures, colonial history and geography played a role in how each nation developed. Politically, strong African nationalist leaders tended to establish one-man rule. Economically, many new African nations plunged deeply into debt because of slow economic growth. Weak economies meant hardship, hunger, and poverty for many people.

An Ancient Nation Struggled to Survive

Ethiopia is located in the region known as the Horn of Africa, across the Red Sea from Saudi Arabia and Yemen. Ethiopia is one of the oldest nations in Africa, but by the late 1980s, it was one of the world's poorest countries, facing many grave crises.

Famine and drought have become Ethiopia's greatest problems. In 1974, Emperor Haile Selassie (HY lee sihl LAH see) was pushed from power by army officers who promised to improve food distribution and bring about land and economic reforms. Progress was halted by fighting inside and outside the country. With aid from the Soviet Union, the new government won a war with neighboring Somalia, but civil war continued with the province of Eritrea.

Neither the government nor help from world nations seemed able to improve the situation for millions of starving Ethiopians. In 1984, nearly 1 million Ethiopians died of starvation or disease in refugee camps. Another famine period began in 1987. World nations sent aid, but the civil war kept food from reaching those who needed it.

Independence Challenged Eastern African States

Elsewhere in eastern Africa, former colonies coped in different ways with the challenges of independence. The most successful was Kenya, a model for stability in the region.

Kenya. In 1963, Kenya became a sovereign republic. Jomo Kenyatta (JOH moh kehn YAHT uh), a nationalist leader, became president and carried out a policy known as *Harambee,* which means "Let us all pull together." Kenyatta restored stability to the country. When he died in 1978, Daniel arap Moi became president of Kenya. Under his leadership, Kenya continued to be regarded as a model African nation.

Uganda. Uganda, which gained independence in 1962, came under the harsh dictatorship of Idi Amin Dada (EE dee ah MEEN dah dah), who ruled by terror and torture. In 1980, invading troops from Tanzania helped rebel Ugandans overthrow Idi Amin, but Uganda remained in turmoil. Rival military leaders combined to fight for control of the government.

Tanzania. Tanzania was formed in 1964 with the merger of former Tanganyika (on the mainland) and the island of Zanzibar. Its leader and first president, Julius K. Nyerere (nyuh RAIR aay), followed a Socialist economic program for the development of the new nation. The government organized co-operative farms and nationalized banks and many industries. By 1987, the country was shifting toward a freer economy.

Internal Strife Slowed Nigeria's Progress

Nigeria is a large country on the coast of western Africa, more than twice the size of California. Nigeria became independent in 1960 and in 1963 joined the British Commonwealth of Nations. Nigeria's constitution assured personal liberties and set up a federation of four self-governing regions. Nigeria's problems have come partly from conflicts among tribes. Tribal loyalties, or **tribalism**, hurt national unity.

Conflict between Nigeria's Ibo (EE boh) tribe and the Hausa (HOW zah) people of the north erupted into a tragic civil war in 1967. The Christian Ibos declared their independence from Nigeria and set up the new nation of Biafra (bee AHF rah). In the civil war that followed, 2 million people —soldiers and civilians—lost their lives, many through starvation. The Biafran cause was lost when the Ibos were defeated by the Hausa in 1970.

Despite the fact that it has been ruled by military governments for most of its history, Nigeria allowed its people more freedoms during the 1980s. Due to a drop in oil revenues, Nigeria, a major petroleum producer, has suffered economic setbacks in recent years.

Zaire Was Unprepared for Independence

When Zaire (zah EER), once known as the Belgian Congo, won independence from Belgium in June 1960, chaos followed. Belgian colonial administrators had severely restricted the opportunities for blacks. Most businesses were owned by white Belgians, and there were few educational opportunities for native Congolese. Another serious grievance was that the native Africans were not allowed to vote.

By 1960, these grievances led to a clamor for independence. Belgium, realizing that nationalism could not be put off indefinitely,

704

gave in. The Congolese, however, lacking education and governmental skills or experience, were unable to immediately establish an effectively united government.

The rich mining province of Katanga broke away from the rest of the Congo to set up an independent government led by Moise Tshombe (SHOM beh). This government lasted until 1963. After the collapse of the Katanga rebellion in 1963, Zaire became a nation.

In 1971, Zaire changed its name from the Belgian Congo to the Republic of Zaire and tried to eliminate memories of Belgian rule. In 1972, people were required to adopt African names. Foreign-owned businesses were forced to sell to citizens of Zaire. But when these practices hurt the economy, the government backed down and allowed many foreign business owners to return to Zaire.

Under President Mobutu Sese Seko, Zaire achieved a period of stability. Katanga was not yet fully a part of the nation, however, and Zaire remained a troubled land.

Ghana and Zimbabwe Took Different Routes to Independence

Although the nations of Ghana and Zimbabwe are both former British colonies, their experiences with independence offer a study in contrasts. Modern Ghana was one of the first European colonies in Africa to receive its independence following World War II. Zimbabwe (zim BAHB way) did not finally gain independence until 1980, more than 20 years later. The map on page 705 shows when the nations of Africa became independent.

Ghana. Kwame Nkrumah, who became Ghana's first premier, was hailed as a great hero. He built schools, hospitals, aluminum and hydroelectric plants and a university. He improved education so more people could read and write. In the process of building his country, Nkrumah also plunged it into debt. The democracy he had promised turned into a one-man rule. In 1962, Nkrumah was voted president for life. In 1964, he was granted dictatorial powers. Only one political party was allowed, and opponents were jailed or killed.

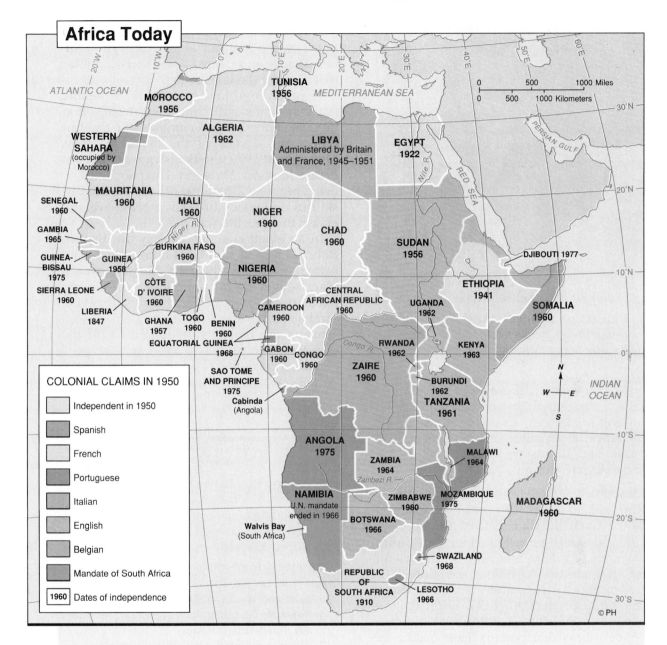

Africa Today

COLONIAL CLAIMS IN 1950

- Independent in 1950
- Spanish
- French
- Portuguese
- Italian
- English
- Belgian
- Mandate of South Africa
- 1960 Dates of independence

MOROCCO 1956
TUNISIA 1956
WESTERN SAHARA (occupied by Morocco)
ALGERIA 1962
LIBYA Administered by Britain and France, 1945–1951
EGYPT 1922
MAURITANIA 1960
SENEGAL 1960
GAMBIA 1965
GUINEA-BISSAU 1975
GUINEA 1958
SIERRA LEONE 1960
LIBERIA 1847
MALI 1960
BURKINA FASO 1960
NIGER 1960
CHAD 1960
SUDAN 1956
DJIBOUTI 1977
CÔTE D'IVOIRE 1960
GHANA 1957
TOGO 1960
BENIN 1960
NIGERIA 1960
CAMEROON 1960
CENTRAL AFRICAN REPUBLIC 1960
ETHIOPIA 1941
UGANDA 1962
SOMALIA 1960
EQUATORIAL GUINEA 1968
GABON 1960
CONGO 1960
ZAIRE 1960
RWANDA 1962
KENYA 1963
SAO TOME AND PRINCIPE 1975
Cabinda (Angola)
BURUNDI 1962
TANZANIA 1961
ANGOLA 1975
ZAMBIA 1964
MALAWI 1964
MOZAMBIQUE 1975
MADAGASCAR 1960
NAMIBIA U.N. mandate ended in 1966
ZIMBABWE 1980
Walvis Bay (South Africa)
BOTSWANA 1966
SWAZILAND 1968
REPUBLIC OF SOUTH AFRICA 1910
LESOTHO 1966

ATLANTIC OCEAN
MEDITERRANEAN SEA
Nile R.
RED SEA
PERSIAN GULF
Niger R.
Congo R.
Zambezi R.
INDIAN OCEAN

0   500   1000 Miles
0   500   1000 Kilometers

© PH

Focus on Geography

1. **Place** What was the first country in Africa to win its independence?
2. **Interaction** Find the Central African Republic and Nigeria. Which of these countries could have a deep-sea fishing industry?

Nkrumah was overthrown in a military coup in 1966. A succession of military coups and a brief period of civilian rule followed. Flight Lieutenant Jerry Rawlings became dictator of Ghana in 1981.

What happened in Ghana was typical of many new African nations. Independence led to the hope of democracy, but political and tribal rivalries, fanned by extremes of wealth and poverty, resulted in one-person,

705

▲ **Illustrating History** *Nkrumah, Ghana's first premier, speaks to a child. His rule brought both advances and debt.*

one-party rule. As in parts of Europe in the 1930s, instead of regular elections determining leadership, heads of state became dictators. This pattern has been difficult to break, and it presents a major challenge in sub-Saharan Africa today.

Zimbabwe. Zimbabwe, once known as Rhodesia, took much longer to win independence than did Ghana. On November 11, 1965, its white prime minister, Ian Smith, declared Rhodesia independent of Britain. Smith intended to follow the pattern of nearby South Africa, where a white minority ruled a huge black majority. Great Britain, however, refused to give Rhodesia independence unless that country gave blacks the right to vote and recognized black majority rule. Instead of using force, Britain refused to sell Rhodesia needed oil and gasoline. Backed by the United Nations, many other countries followed Britain's example.

By the election of 1979, black Rhodesians had gained the right to vote. In the new government of Rhodesia, now called Zimbabwe-Rhodesia, black candidates won two-thirds of the elected cabinet posts. The most powerful posts were still held by whites, however. Bishop Abel T. Muzorewa,

a moderate black leader, replaced Ian Smith as the prime minister and head of the cabinet. Blacks and whites voted separately for members of the legislature.

Violence continued because many people felt that whites still controlled the election process, and the government still did not reflect the wishes of the black majority. Throughout 1979, the British government of Prime Minister Margaret Thatcher tried to bring peace to Zimbabwe-Rhodesia. Finally, skillful diplomacy brought a cease-fire and ended the guerilla war.

In an election supervised by the British, Robert Mugabe (mu GAH beh) was elected prime minister. Although Mugabe was a Marxist, he followed a moderate course and tried to establish political unity. In 1980, Zimbabwe became an independent nation. Mugabe was reelected in 1985. In 1987 the country's two parties merged, and Mugabe became "executive president."

SECTION 3 REVIEW

Reviewing Key Terms, People, and Places
1. Define: **a.** tribalism
2. Identify: **a.** Horn of Africa **b.** Jomo Kenyatta **c.** Biafra **d.** Mobutu Sese Seko **e.** Robert Mugabe

Reviewing Main Ideas
3. What caused the civil war between the Ibos and Hausa in Nigeria?
4. How did Belgian colonial rule hurt Zaire as an independent nation?
5. What problems slowed the coming of independence in Rhodesia/Zimbabwe?

Critical Thinking
Identifying Assumptions
6. Governments dominated by one political party are not unusual in the world, but most Americans automatically assume they are oppressive and dictatorial. Why might a one-party system develop in a new country? Why might such a system not be oppressive?

4 Racial Conflicts Split South Africa

As you read, look for answers to these questions:

◆ What geographical advantages does South Africa have among African nations?
◆ How has apartheid affected black South Africans?
◆ What groups fought over Namibia?

> **Key Terms:** apartheid (defined on p. 707), Bantustan (p. 707), sanction (p. 708)

The Republic of South Africa is different in many ways from the other countries in sub-Saharan Africa. Economically, it is a rich, modern nation with good agricultural land and highly developed industry. As you have read, the black majority in other sub-Saharan African countries now have equal political rights and majority rule, but, in the Republic of South Africa, the white minority still keeps tight control. The results have been violence and tragedy.

Located south of the Tropic of Capricorn, South Africa attracted European colonists because of its temperate climate. South Africa is best known for its rich reserves of diamonds and gold, but it also has minerals vital for industry, such as manganese, asbestos, antimony, vanadium, and tungsten. While agriculture is less valuable than mining, the country grows corn, wheat, and sugar cane.

South Africa Adopted Strict Racial Laws

Although only 18 percent of the people of South Africa are white, strict laws kept this white minority in power. White South Africans are either Afrikaners, who are descendants of the early Dutch, or Boer settlers, or descendents of British settlers. Whites control the country's economy and government.

Historically, race relations have always been a source of conflict, even in early meetings between British and Dutch settlers. Many laws were passed that limited freedom of movement and economic opportunity for black South Africans. In 1948, when the Afrikaner Daniel Malan became prime minister, the country officially adopted a policy of strict racial separation known as **apartheid** (ah PART hite).

The purpose of apartheid was to make sure that whites would always be dominant. Laws divided the nonwhite peoples into three groups: African blacks, or "Bantus"; Asians, who are mostly Indians; and Coloreds, or people of mixed ancestry. Each group lived separately on lands reserved for them and followed laws that limited their rights and their chances for education. Blacks in particular had to carry passports and work permits to travel outside of their homes. Without them, they could not even enter white areas.

Under a later Afrikaner prime minister, Dr. Hendrik Verwoerd, the blacks were pushed into so-called "homelands," or **Bantustans,** which were large-scale reserves. Blacks would live in compounds but be available to travel into South Africa to work as servants, miners, cleaners, or at other menial jobs. South Africa declared the "homelands" independent states.

Opposition from the United Nations, unfavorable opinion in the international community, and mounting violence within the country had little effect on South Africa's apartheid policy. Rather than give up apartheid, South Africa declared itself a republic and left the British Commonwealth of Nations in 1961. Three branches of the Dutch Reformed church also gave up membership in the world Council of Churches rather than abandon apartheid.

Many People Protested Against Apartheid

In 1948, the year that apartheid was put into practice, a white South African, Alan Paton, wrote *Cry, the Beloved Country*. In this novel he expressed his dismay and sadness over

Albert Luthuli's Nobel Prize Acceptance Speech

Albert John Luthuli entered South African politics when he joined the African National Congress in 1946. He advocated nonviolent resistance to apartheid, which led the government to ban him from publishing and confine him to his home village of Groutville. Luthuli persevered, however, and in 1960 he was awarded the Nobel Peace Prize. The following is from his acceptance speech.

❝In a strife-torn world, tottering on the brink of complete destruction by man-made nuclear weapons, a free and independent Africa is in the making. . . . Acting in concert with other nations, she is man's last hope for a mediator between the East and West, and is qualified to demand the great powers to 'turn the swords into ploughshares' because two-thirds of mankind is hungry and illiterate; to engage human energy, human skill and human talent in the service of peace, for the alternative is unthinkable— war, destruction and desolation; and to build a world community which will stand as a lasting monument to the millions of men and women . . . who have given their lives that we may live in happiness and peace.

Africa's qualification for this noble task is incontestable, for her own fight has never been and is not now a fight for conquest of land, for accumulation of wealth or domination of peoples, but for the recognition and preservation of the rights of man and the establishment of a truly free world for a free people.❞

1. Why does Luthuli say people should devote their energy to peace?
2. Why does he say that Africa's struggle is unique in history?

the apartheid path his "beloved country" had chosen. For his efforts, Paton was placed under house arrest. Soon, arrests and persecution became common for all —black or white—who protested apartheid.

As time went on, more South Africans joined the protest against apartheid. One prominent leader of the protest movement was Albert John Luthuli (luh TOO lee). A leader in fighting for the rights of black South Africans, Luthuli was president of the black political party, the African National Congress, in the 1950s. He preached nonviolence and encouraged civil disobedience. For his anti-apartheid activities, the government arrested him and restricted where he could travel. In 1960, Luthuli was the first African to be awarded the Nobel Peace Prize. "I think as an African," he once said, "I act as an African, and as an African I worship the God whose children we all are."

Black leaders continued to risk imprisonment and their lives in the fight against apartheid. Also in 1960, Nelson Mandela, another leader of the African National Congress, was imprisoned after his political party was declared illegal. His wife, Winnie Mandela, took up the struggle against apartheid and kept her husband's 28-year imprisonment a public affair. Under guard, Nelson Mandela was transferred to a hospital for medical treatment in 1988. He then was kept in a minimum security prison.

Another leader who preached nonviolence was Archbishop Desmond Tutu, an Anglican clergyman, who was awarded the Nobel Peace Prize in 1984. Archbishop Tutu called for Western nations to apply **sanctions,** that is, refusing to trade with or invest in a country, until apartheid was ended.

Protests Became Violent

In 1960, hundreds of blacks deliberately left their passes behind to protest pass laws, and staged a massive demonstration at Sharpeville, 20 miles from Johannesburg. Police with tanks and machine guns fired into the crowds, killing 69 and wounding about 200. Worldwide protests followed. A 1976 riot at Soweto, a suburb of Johannesburg, only

Archbishop Desmond Tutu

"We are winning! Justice is going to win!" cried the Reverend Desmond Tutu when he received word he had been awarded the Nobel Peace Prize in 1984. The Anglican bishop of Johannesburg, South Africa (the only black ever to hold that position), Tutu won the award for his role as "a unifying leader . . . in the campaign to resolve the problem of apartheid in South Africa."

Tutu (shown on the right) was born in South Africa in 1931. Because he was a sickly baby, his grandmother gave him the middle name of "Mpilo," which means "life." Years later, Tutu told a reporter, "That was my first com-

mitment to faith." His faith has proven to be the guiding force throughout a life devoted to social change. Tutu has committed himself to the belief that apartheid in South Africa can end through nonviolent struggle.

Using sermons, lectures, and writings, Archbishop Tutu has brought worldwide attention to his government's treatment of South Africa's blacks. He has organized black protests and urged nationwide school boycotts. He has headed the movement to get other nations to limit their trade with South Africa to force his government to make changes. Despite constant threats of arrest, Tutu has

continued to press his demands.

1. Why did Desmond Tutu receive the Nobel Peace Prize?
2. How has Desmond Tutu fought apartheid in South Africa?
3. Why do you think the South African government has not jailed Tutu?

brought more arrests. Violent encounters between the South African government and anti-apartheid forces got worse in the 1980s. In 1985, under a "state of emergency" law, more troops and police were used against demonstrators and more people were killed.

In 1984, Prime Minister Pieter William Botha (BOE tah) became president under a new constitution that gave him greater powers. It also gave Asians and "Coloreds" some representation in parliament but continued to exclude the black majority. Botha offered blacks an advisory role in government, and laws were changed to make travel less difficult. However, violence continued to mount on both sides. In 1986, South African forces moved to strike at guerilla bases of the

African National Congress in Zimbabwe, Botswana, and Zambia. Some white South Africans joined extremist or neo-Nazi groups. Others were determined not to bargain with black leaders.

Other factors also were working against apartheid and for the black majority. In the larger cities, blacks and whites were mingling despite traditions and apartheid laws. In 1988, P.W. Botha announced that interracial neighborhoods could remain in larger cities. This, in effect, meant that the government was forced to make some changes for the black majority in the country that whites had wanted for themselves. The events in South Africa led to international protests against apartheid. Also, the United States,

▲ **Illustrating History** *Under apartheid, public facilities such as these steps located in Port Elizabeth, South Africa, are divided by skin color.*

along with many other countries, withdrew investments in South Africa and restricted trade with that nation to a minimum.

Namibia Wanted Independence from South Africa

South Africa's racial policies and its actions in the neighboring territory of Namibia brought international disapproval. This rich land came under South African control after World War I and has been trying to gain independence.

Guerilla war. Instead of preparing Namibia for independence, South Africa placed its own laws, including apartheid, over the territory. Other African nations charged that South Africa had exploited Namibia and built military bases there. In 1970, the United Nations General Assembly declared that South Africa held this area illegally, and the International Court of Justice agreed. Despite a United Nations resolution, South Africa delayed granting independence. Instead, white voters in Namibia approved a plan for a multiracial government that would lead the way to independence. The South West Africa People's Organization, or SWAPO, opposed the plan, however, and began a guerilla war for independence.

Angola. The presence of Cuban troops in nearby Angola complicated Namibian politics. Along with Portugal's other African colonies, Angola became independent in 1975. Unprepared for self-government, Angola was soon taken over by a Marxist group backed by troops sent by Fidel Castro. Still another guerilla group, known as UNITA, or National Union for Total Independence of Angola, opposed the government. Its leader, who had American support, was Jonas Savimbi. Border skirmishes among Cubans, South Africans, and two guerilla groups added to the unrest in Angola and Namibia.

In 1988, representatives of South Africa, Angola, and Cuba met to resolve problems. One was timing the withdrawal of South African and Cuban troops. Another was putting into action a 1978 United Nations resolution calling for supervised elections in Namibia. The United States attended some meetings, and the Soviet Union pressured Angola and Cuba to cooperate. Neither SWAPO or UNITA took part, however.

SECTION 4 REVIEW

Reviewing Key Terms, People, and Places
1. Define: **a.** apartheid **b.** Bantustan **c.** sanction
2. Identify: **a.** Hendrik Verwoerd **b.** Alan Paton **c.** Albert John Luthuli **d.** Archbishop Desmond Tutu **e.** P.W. Botha **f.** Jonas Savimbi

Focus on Geography
3. How did climate and resources make South Africa prosperous?

Reviewing Main Ideas
4. What racial divisions exist legally in South Africa? What limits did apartheid put on the freedom of black South Africans?
5. What were the issues in Namibia?

Critical Thinking
Recognizing Ideologies
6. What do South Africa's laws regarding apartheid show about the attitudes white South Africans have toward black South Africans?

Solving problems requires a thoughtful step-by-step approach. You must go through each step carefully to come up with the best solution.

Read the description of Nation X. Then study and apply the five problem-solving steps that are explained below.

1. **Identify the problem.** You must have a clear understanding of exactly what the problem is before you attempt to solve it. Answer the following questions: (a) What is a major industrial problem faced by Nation X? (b) Name one of Nation X's main agricultural problems.

2. **Discover the causes of the problem.** Understanding the causes of a problem helps you find its solution. Answer the following questions: (a) What are two causes of Nation X's industrial problems? (b) What are two causes of Nation X's agricultural problems?

3. **Propose possible solutions.** Begin by brainstorming possible answers. This means that you want to list every possible solution, no matter how unusual or seemingly ridiculous. Answer the following questions: (a) What are two possible things that Nation X can do to solve its major industrial problem? (b) What are two possible solutions to Nation X's main agricultural problem?

4. **Predict the consequences of each solution.** Think of the good effects and bad effects that each solution might have. Consider such factors as cost, time, ease of application, and acceptability to others. Answer the following questions: (a) Predict the effects of each of your proposed solutions for the industrial problems. (b) List some effects for each of your solutions to the agricultural problems.

5. **Solve the problem by choosing the best solution.** Select the solution that seems to be the best for solving the industrial problem and the one that seems to be best for the agricultural problem. Explain your choices.

Nation X

Nation X is a small nation of 3.2 million people that is located on the west coast of Africa. It has several good ports and an acceptable road and railroad system.

Industry: Good mineral deposits are located in the country, but currently there is only a small, outdated steel industry. The country has a declining standard of living and increasing unemployment, but the capital and technical expertise needed for industrialization are lacking. Two large foreign companies want to develop industries, but many citizens of Nation X fear that these powerful companies would control their government.

Agriculture: Currently, 80 percent of the people earn a living in agriculture, The only important cash crop is cacao, and income shifts widely, based on world demand for chocolate. Because of irregular rainfall, a growing desert region in the northwest, and a decaying irrigation system, grain production has been falling since 1975. Experts project that the country will have to import 12 percent of its grain in the coming year.

REVIEW

Section Summaries

Section 1 Old Rivalries Prevented Middle East Peace Disagreements stemming from religion, nationalism, and oil production have led to conflict in the Middle East. Since 1948, Arabs and Israelis have fought three wars. By the late 1970s, Egypt and Israel began working out a peace agreement. Palestinians, however, continued to seek a homeland. In Lebanon, a violent civil war involved Lebanese, Christians, and Muslims, as well as the Palestinians, other Arab groups, and Israeli forces. In Iran, religious fundamentalists overthrew the shah and set up a strict Islamic state. Shortly afterward, Iran's new leaders faced a long war with Iraq.

Section 2 Conflicts Disrupted Northern Africa Northern Africa's nations were linked to the Arab world by language, culture, and the Islamic religion. Oil-rich Libya was led by Muammar el-Qaddafi, who hated Israel and the West and supported Arab unity. Qaddafi allowed Libya to become a center of world terrorism. Morocco and Algeria became involved in disputes over the western Sahara. Algeria remained troubled by domestic problems, such as a low standard of living. The modern, pro-Western nation of Tunisia, however, had a strong economy.

Section 3 Sub-Saharan Africa Faced Challenges Ethiopia was plagued by civil war and famine. Kenya, however, became a model of stability and prosperity. Uganda's government remained unstable, even after the overthrow of a harsh dictator. In Tanzania, a Socialist economy began a shift toward more freedom. Nigeria was torn by tribal conflicts. In Zaire, a rebellion in Katanga collapsed, and the nation began to move toward stability. Ghana went through a series of dictatorships, while Zimbabwe's agricultural success strengthened its economy.

Section 4 Racial Conflicts Split South Africa In rich, industrialized South Africa, a white minority kept tight control of the government. Laws greatly limited the freedom of South Africa's black people as part of a policy called *apartheid.* International disapproval had little effect on these racial policies. South African forces violently put down protests and attacked rebels. South Africa also tried to extend apartheid to Namibia. The United Nations demanded independence for Namibia, but independence did not come quickly enough for rebels who began a guerilla war. Unrest in Angola created even more problems for this troubled region.

Key Facts

1. Use each vocabulary word in a sentence.
   a. ayatollah
   b. pan-Arabism
   c. tribalism
   d. apartheid
   e. Bantustan
   f. sanction
2. Identify and briefly explain the importance of the following names, places, or events.
   a. Nasser
   b. the West Bank
   c. the Yom Kippur War
   d. Menachem Begin
   e. Anwar Sadat
   f. Yasir Arafat
   g. Ayatollah Khomeini
   h. the Persian Gulf
   i. the Arab West
   j. Muammar el-Qaddafi
   k. sub-Saharan Africa
   l. Jomo Kenyatta
   m. Nelson Mandela
   n. Pieter Botha

Main Ideas

1. What were the results of the Arab-Israeli wars of 1967 and 1973?
2. How did so many Palestinian people become refugees?
3. What groups were involved in Lebanon's civil war?
4. Tell what kind of leader each of the following was: Qaddafi, Benjedid, Bourguiba.
5. Which sub-Saharan nation faced famine and civil war? Which had an agricultural miracle?
6. List some ways the white minority has worked to remain dominant in South Africa.

Developing Skill in Reading History

As you know, analogies describe relationships. One analogy from this chapter would be the following. Sadat:Egypt::Begin:Israel. (Sadat is to Egypt as Begin is to Israel.) The elements in both pairs have the same relationship to each other. Use information from the chapter to complete the following analogies. Then, explain the relationship in each analogy.

1. Israel:Hebrew::Iran:_____
   a. Farsi   c. Jewish
   b. Arabic   d. Islamic
2. Tunisia:northern Africa::Kenya:_____
   a. sub-Saharan Africa   c. South Africa
   b. the western Sahara   d. the Middle East
3. 1960:Sharpeville::_____:Soweto
   a. 1948   c. 1980
   b. 1976   d. 1986

Using Social Studies Skills

Reading Maps Study the maps of Israel on page 698. Then, use the information on the maps to write a brief report about the changes in Israel's boundaries between 1967 and 1982. In your report, be sure to mention neighboring nations and important bodies of water. Also mention one fact you learned by using the map scale.

Critical Thinking

1. **Making Comparisons** How did life in Iran change after Islamic fundamentalists overthrew the shah?
2. **Perceiving Cause and Effect** Use information from this chapter and, on a separate sheet of paper, complete the cause-and-effect chart below.
3. **Solving Problems** Brainstorm to create a list of actions that might help solve one of the following problems.
   a. the need for a Palestinian homeland
   b. the famine in Ethiopia
   c. the apartheid system in South Africa

Focus on Writing

Writing a Persuasive Paragraph

As you know, a **persuasive paragraph** attempts to persuade an audience to take action or to accept a certain idea, belief, or position. Skim the chapter and choose an appropriate topic for a persuasive paragraph. Then, complete the following prewriting activities.

1. Tell what position you intend to support.
2. Write a topic sentence for your paragraph.
3. List three arguments that you will use to support your position.

Cause	Effect
1. Nasser blockaded the port of Eilat.	
2.	Libyan troops withdrew from Chad.
3. Tanzanian troops helped Ugandan rebels.	
4. The African National Congress was declared illegal.	

Asia in Today's World

(1960–PRESENT)

1 **Japan and Korea Developed Rapidly**

2 **China Reentered World Affairs**

3 **Southeast Asia Faced Major Challenges**

4 **South Asia Made Slow but Steady Progress**

▲ **Illustrating History** *The above photograph shows Japanese workers building cars in an assembly line at a Mazda automobile factory in Hiroshima.*

I t is 8:20 A.M. in Japan. Wearing jackets displaying the company trademark, workers at the Kyoto Ceramics Company gather for calisthenics, followed by a reading from a book of advice written by the company president. Meanwhile, workers at all the factories of the Matsushita (mat soo SHEE tah) Electric Company are beginning the day by singing the company song: "For the building of a new Japan/Let's put our strength and mind together/Harmony and sincerity!/Matsushita Electric!"

In Japan, such intense company spirit grows from the moment a worker joins a firm. Newcomers are welcomed with a special ceremony, then trained at the company's expense. Workers may live in dormitories. They can join company-sponsored sports teams. In fact, their entire social life usually centers around the company. As one worker said, "Here, if you change your factory, you have to change your friends."

Workers are well rewarded for being loyal employees. They can expect promotion based on age and length of service—even retraining for a new job, if necessary. What's more, they are guaranteed lifelong employment. Little wonder, then, that a Japanese worker's voice rings with pride when he says, "I'm Arai, of Matsushita!" In this chapter, you will see how its spirited workforce has enabled Japan to rise to the top of the industrial world since World War II. You will also learn about the recent history of China, India, and other Asian countries.

1960	1970	1980	1990

1966 ■
Cultural Revolution begins in China; Indira Gandhi leads India

1972 ■
Bangladesh becomes independent; United States returns Okinawa to Japan

1976 ■
Vietnam establishes a socialist republic

1981 ■
Deng Xiaoping leads China

1986 ■
Corazon Aquino becomes president of the Philippines

■ **1988**
Pakistan elects Benazir Bhutto; Soviet troops withdraw from Afghanistan

▲ **Illustrating History** *Workers in the Matsushita Electric Company, each proudly wearing the company uniform, exercise together daily.*

1 Japan and Korea Developed Rapidly

As you read, look for answers to these questions:

◆ What factors helped Japan to develop industrially?
◆ What problems existed in South Korea from the 1960s to the present?
◆ How did South Koreans achieve a democratic election in 1987?

Key Terms: stereotype (defined on p. 715)

Often, people's impressions of other lands are little more than **stereotypes,** or fixed, generalized ideas that ignore facts about individual situations. The "Made in Japan" label once made people think of cheap products that were poorly made. The long running television show "M*A*S*H" formed many people's views of South Korea. Today, however, these stereotypes are fading. The quality of Japanese and Korean products in the West illustrate their remarkable industrial progress.

Japan Rose from the Ashes

After the atomic bomb was dropped on Hiroshima and Nagasaki in August 1945, Japan surrendered unconditionally to the United States. The occupation of Japan by Allied forces (almost all of them American) marked a new beginning for Japan. With the help of its American conquerors, the nation became an industrial giant.

At first, the American occupation was expected to last a long time, but its goals were achieved much sooner than originally planned. The Japanese cooperated with the

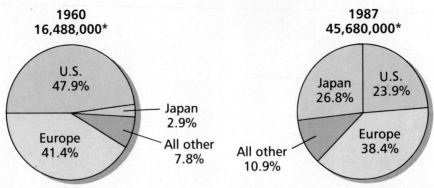

Motor Vehicle Production

1960
16,488,000*

U.S. 47.9%
Europe 41.4%
Japan 2.9%
All other 7.8%

1987
45,680,000*

Japan 26.8%
U.S. 23.9%
Europe 38.4%
All other 10.9%

Source: Motor Vehicle Manufacturers Association of the U.S.

*Total number of motor vehicles produced

▲ **Graph Skill** *Which country had the largest increase in automobile production from 1960 to 1987? Which had the sharpest decrease?*

American authorities in Japan. The country was also successful in ratifying a new, democratic constitution.

Six years after Japan's surrender, the American occupation ended with a peace treaty signed by Japan, the United States, and 47 other nations. By 1954, most American troops occupying Japan had left, and in 1956, Japan was admitted to the United Nations.

Japan Wanted Independence from the United States

In 1960, President Eisenhower planned a good will trip to Japan. He hoped that Japan would sign a treaty to strengthen the alliance between itself and the United States. However, rioting by young Japanese Socialists and university students forced Eisenhower to cancel his trip. Despite the riots, the treaty was approved, and Japanese-American relations passed their first test.

In May 1972, the United States returned Okinawa to Japan. The United States had occupied this important island since World War II, when conquering it had cost many American lives. The growing national pride in Japan, however, made the return of Okinawa a good diplomatic move.

Low Military Spending Helped Japan to Become an Industrial Giant

What Japan had sought by military conquest, it would achieve through military defeat. According to Japan's postwar constitution, the country's military is limited to defensive purposes only. As a result, Japan spends only 1 percent of its gross national product on the military. With so little of its budget tied up in military spending, Japan has been able to concentrate its resources on economic development. As a result, Japan's industry has progressed at an astounding rate. Japan has become a formidable competitor of the United States in the markets for automobiles, televisions, VCRs, computers, stereo equipment, and other products. Japan's products are found in markets all over the globe, and the standard of living of its people rivals that of the United States.

South Korea Suffered some Growing Pains

With the grand ceremonies and outpourings of national pride, the Summer Olympic Games of 1988 were a vivid symbol of South Korea's progress since the Korean War.

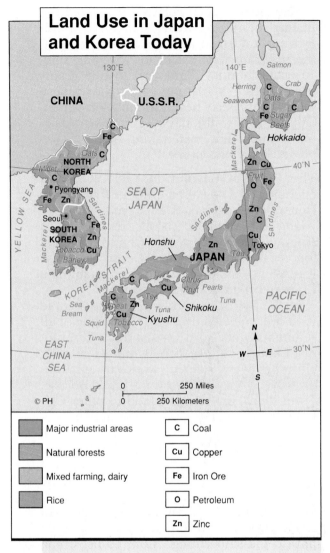

Land Use in Japan and Korea Today

Focus on Geography

1. **Place** What is the one crop in the Koreas that seems to be grown more than any other?
2. **Interaction** What one crop is harvested from the ocean near Japan?

During the past three decades, South Korea has made great economic progress.

At the end of the Korean War, South Korea remained a troubled land. Between 1960 and 1987, student protests, harsh lead-ership, and violent takeovers of the government went hand in hand with Korea's rapid industrialization. These developments caused much unrest.

In 1987, the Korean people felt the time had come for genuine democracy. Protesting students, supported by a growing middle class, forced President Chun's government to hold its first free election in 20 years. Roh Tae Woo had to run for office rather than merely accept Chun's appointment, and he was elected president of Korea.

The economies of both Japan and Korea depend on the use of their resources and land, as shown on the map on this page. In 1988, the year of the Olympics, South Korea had a 10 billion dollar trade surplus, and the gross national product was $3,000 for each of its 42 million people. Even so, South Korea still has a long way to go toward stability. Undoubtedly, the biggest problem President Roh faces is the question of reuniting North and South Korea. North Korea is a Communist state under the rule of Kim Il Sung. The two nations have attempted to discuss unification several times, in 1972, in 1985, and again in 1988.

SECTION 1 REVIEW

Knowing Key Terms, People, and Places
1. Define: **a.** stereotype
2. Identify: **a.** Hiroshima **b.** Roh Tae Woo

Reviewing Main Ideas
3. How has the constitutional limit on military spending boosted Japan's economy?
4. How did Korea's first free election in 20 years come about?

Critical Thinking
Determining Relevance
5. Both Japan and South Korea have flourished economically since gaining more freedom. How do you think a country's form of government is related to its economic growth?

717

2 China Reentered World Affairs

As you read, look for answers to these questions:

◆ What was the idea behind the Great Leap Forward?
◆ How did the Cultural Revolution in China come about?
◆ How has China changed since the death of Mao Zedong?
◆ How did the Republic of China (Taiwan) lose its claim on the Chinese mainland?

Key Terms: commune (defined on p. 718), indoctrinate (p. 718)

In 1956, Mao Zedong, the founder of the People's Republic of China, decided to allow the Chinese people more freedom of speech. Mao, however, had unleashed more than he realized. People began to criticize the government openly. Freedom to speak out was once again restricted, and Mao was free to impose further changes on China.

Between 1958 and 1960, China, under Mao, tried to catch up economically with the United States and the Soviet Union. To do so, China needed to modernize its production of agricultural and industrial goods.

Economic Experiments Failed

During the 1960s, Mao tried to transform the Chinese economy and culture to fit his image of the ideal Communist society.

Great Leap Forward. In a program called the *Great Leap Forward*, Mao organized China's farms and factories into **communes**, or strictly organized communities. The state-controlled communes had economic and political goals. Economically, the communes were supposed to help China produce more and better goods. Politically, the communes were designed to watch over their members and to **indoctrinate**, or instruct, members in Communist thought.

Mao's Great Leap Forward was a failure. Instead of raising living standards or improving industrial and agricultural output, the program brought chaos and hardship. To avoid famine, China had to buy grains from abroad. Moderates within the Chinese Communist party began to question whether Mao's revolutionary spirit was really more important than taking steps to improve China's economy.

The Cultural Revolution. In 1966, Mao encouraged a so-called *Cultural Revolution*. During this period, Mao urged bands of young Communists, mostly teenagers, to stop any resistance to the Communist zeal for revolution. The Red Guard, as these youths were known, wanted to establish a Chinese brand of communism.

In Beijing, thousands of young people took over the city, trying to rid Beijing of all remnants of Western ways and pre-Communist Chinese culture. Streets were renamed; churches were robbed; works of art were destroyed. A reign of terror gripped Beijing. From there, the terror spread to other Chinese cities. In 1969, when the activities of the Red Guard appeared to be hurting him, Mao stopped the Cultural Revolution.

Mao's Cultural Revolution was an indirect attack on the Soviet Union. Mao felt that the Soviet Union had abandoned its revolutionary ways since the Communist Revolution of 1917. He was determined that China would not do the same thing. Communist China and the Soviet Union thus became bitter enemies. It was not until 1988 that a thaw in their relationship began.

China Became Involved in Global Affairs

In April 1971, the U.S. table tennis team was allowed to visit the People's Republic of China. The match was a sign that relations between the United States and China might be easing a little.

Nixon's visit to China. President Nixon visited China in February 1972, after the United States withdrew its opposition to admitting the People's Republic of China to the United Nations. During his visit, Nixon met with Chairman Mao and Premier Zhou Enlai (JOH en LY). It was a highly publicized trip that marked the beginning of friendlier and more normal diplomatic relations between the two countries.

The Four Modernizations. In 1976, both Zhou Enlai and Mao Zedong died. At this time, Mao's widow and three associates tried to take power. This "Gang of Four," as they were called, failed in their attempt to seize control and were arrested. While the "Gang of Four" had planned to continue Mao's policies, the new group of moderates who took power wanted to modernize China more quickly. The "Four Modernizations," as their program was called, were these: (1) developing better relations with Japan and the West and obtaining loans from the World Bank and the International Monetary Fund; (2) increasing the flexibility for industry to produce the goods that people needed and developing "Special Economic Zones" to attract investments by foreign entrepreneurs; (3) restructuring the educational system; and (4) encouraging cultural exchanges. Under the leadership of Deng Xiaoping (shyow ping), who became chairman of the Communist party's Affairs Council in 1981, this program was zealously pursued.

In January 1979, President Carter extended full recognition to the People's Republic of China. While many Americans applauded the move, others strongly opposed it. They did not favor supporting a Communist government, and they saw it as hurting the Chinese in Taiwan, whom the United States had supported for years.

War with Vietnam. In February 1979, China declared war on Vietnam. There were several reasons for this war. One reason was that Deng Xiaoping felt that Vietnam was growing too close to the Soviet Union politically. Another was that Vietnam had defeated Pol Pot, the leader of Kampuchea (formerly known as Cambodia) who was supported by the Chinese. The war between China and Vietnam had no clear winner, but it did show that China was willing to challenge the influence of the Soviet Union in other Asian nations.

In their own words

Repeating the Long March

During the Cultural Revolution, many young Chinese walked from their villages to Beijing. These young activists wanted to remind people of the famous Long March led by Mao Zedong over 30 years earlier. As they passed through villages, they gave lectures and stage plays to educate people about Mao. The following excerpt describes the march.

❝Our long march team was made up of eight boys and three girls averaging eighteen years of age. . . . After forty-four days of walking we had covered a thousand kilometers [about 600 miles] and arrived in Beijing to be alongside our beloved leader Chairman Mao. . . .

To make a start is always difficult. The first day we walked twenty-seven kilometers [about 16 miles]. Many of our schoolmates suffered swollen feet and had to clench their teeth with each step they took. Even when we stopped and rested, our backs and feet really ached. A few of us debated about going back home. . . . It was a crucial moment. To solve the problem, we studied a passage in [Mao's] works. . . .

'How shall we wage revolution if we can't even pass this first test?' we asked ourselves. 'No! We must keep on. To go forward means victory!' In this way we applied Mao Zedong's ideas and prevailed over the vacillating muck [uncertainty] in our minds. We all became more confident than ever.❞

1. Summarize how the marchers felt at the end of the first day.
2. What insights into the youth who were involved in the Cultural Revolution does this excerpt provide historians?

China in the 1980s. Through its policy of freer trade with Western nations, China has been able to import new technology. Recognizing the failure of strict Communist economic policies, the Chinese government now allows farmers to sell part of what they produce for personal profit in the free market. China has also encouraged tourism, and in joint economic ventures with America and other Western countries, China has built modern hotels and factories. In 1984, President Reagan visited China and saw evidence of these more flexible economic policies and practices.

Totalitarian political policies, however, remain. In the spring of 1989, Chinese students staged peaceful pro-democracy demonstrations in Beijing's Tiananmen Square. The world watched in horror as the Chinese government brutally massacred demonstrators and later denied the killings.

Taiwan Remained Prosperous Despite Diplomatic Blows

As discussed in Chapter 28, when the Chinese Communists defeated the Kuomintang in 1949, 2 million Chinese nationalists, led

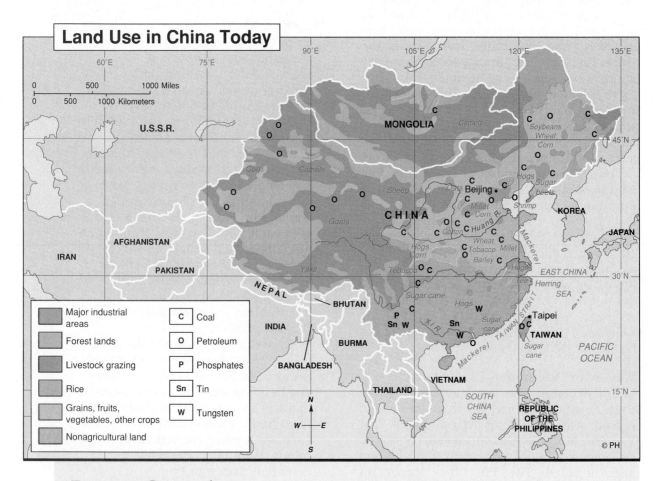

Focus on Geography

Interaction As you can see from the map, rice is grown in the southern part of China, where the climate is warm to hot. In northern China, the climate is too cool for raising rice. What crop is raised there instead?

China's No Longer Forbidden City

In the middle of Beijing stands a magnificent monument to China's past—the Imperial Palace, or Forbidden City. (See the photograph at right.) In this 250-acre walled complex, a sequence of 24 Ming and Qing emperors lived in luxury until 1911. The emperors rarely left the Forbidden City, and ordinary citizens needed special permission to enter the grounds.

Today, however, anyone can visit the site. An estimated 10,000 Chinese and foreign visitors do so daily. They come to marvel at the yellow-roofed palaces, vast courtyards, and lavish gardens. They stand in awe before the splendid Dragon Throne in the Hall of Supreme Harmony from which the emperor ruled his realm with unquestioned authority.

1. Why was the Imperial Palace called the Forbidden City?
2. Why do people continue to visit the Forbidden City today?

---

by General Chiang Kai-shek, fled to the island of Taiwan. There, they established the Republic of China. The Taiwanese hoped that at some point they would be able to overthrow the Communists and restore their rule over all of China, but this hope has since vanished. The United States had supported Taiwan; and during the United Nations debates on the admission of the People's Republic of China in 1972, the United States hoped that both the Republic of China and the People's Republic of China would be accepted as members. The United Nations, however, voted to admit only the People's Republic of China.

When the United States extended full recognition to the People's Republic of China, it had to give up diplomatic recognition of Taiwan. This was a bitter moment for the people and government of Taiwan. However, although the United States removed its troops from the island, the Taiwanese and Americans continued their business relationships much as they had before.

SECTION 2 REVIEW

Knowing Key Terms, People, and Places
1. Define: **a.** commune **b.** indoctrinate
2. Identify: **a.** Great Leap Forward **b.** Cultural Revolution **c.** Red Guard **d.** Gang of Four

Reviewing Main Ideas
3. What was the purpose of Mao's program called the Great Leap Forward? Did it accomplish this purpose?
4. What was the significance of President Nixon's 1972 visit to China?
5. How did the United States weaken Taiwan's claim to mainland China?

Critical Thinking
Checking Consistency
6. In 1976, the Gang of Four failed to take power after Mao Zedong's death. Why do you think the moderates succeeded in stopping them?

3 Southeast Asia Faced Major Challenges

As you read, look for answers to these questions:

◆ What is the geography of Southeast Asia like, and how has it affected the region's history?
◆ How do Filipinos view American involvement in their country?
◆ How did America become involved in the Vietnam War?
◆ What was the final outcome of the Vietnam War?

> **Key Terms:** domino theory (defined on p. 725), hawk (p. 726), dove (p. 726)

Over the past 30 years, the countries of Southeast Asia have made various degrees of progress. This area of the world has faced serious economic and political challenges. As you read the following section, you will learn about how some of these challenges were met.

Geography Was Important to Emerging Southeast Asia

Southeast Asia includes the island archipelagoes of Indonesia and the Philippines, the peninsula of Malaysia, the tiny island country of Singapore, and the peninsula of Indochina, which now includes the countries of Vietnam, Laos, and Kampuchea. On the mainland of Asia are Burma and Thailand. Because geography has kept most of the countries separated from one another, each country has developed its own traditions and ways of life.

A thousand different languages and dialects are spoken in Southeast Asia, and the people follow many different religions. Indonesia and Malaysia are mostly Muslim; Thailand, Burma, Vietnam, Kampuchea, and Laos are mostly Buddhist. The people of the Philippines are 95 percent Christian, of whom 80 percent are Catholic.

Southeast Asia is a strategically vital part of the world. It is a crossroads for the trade and commerce of many nations as well as a treasury of resources including tin, petroleum, bauxite, chromite, rubber, quinine (a medicine used to fight malaria), tea, palm oil, spices, and fine woods. (See the map on page 723.) Rice is Southeast Asia's most important agricultural commodity.

Because of their location and their resources, the people of Southeast Asia have been invaded often, and they are often suspicious of "outsiders."

Indonesia Achieved a Fragile Stability

Indonesia, a country of over 176 million people, became independent in 1945. Achmed Sukarno became its first president in 1949 and governed for nearly 28 years. Sukarno's government brought terror to Indonesia. He encouraged the forming of a large Communist party in Indonesia, which, in 1965, attempted to take over the government. The non-Communists fought back vigorously, killing more than 500,000 Communists or suspected Communists. Sukarno was forced to give up all powers of government, and the Communist party was banned.

In 1967, General Suharto, who had led the rebellion against the Communists, became president of Indonesia. He sought ties with the West, encouraged foreign investments, and promoted friendship with Malaysia and other nations of the area. Indonesia, however, continued to have problems. Oil profits dwindled in the 1980s due to falling oil prices, and Indonesia had trouble growing enough rice to feed its rapidly growing population. Other problems included widespread corruption in government and a growing gap between the rich and the poor. Despite these difficulties, Suharto was reelected for his fourth five-year term in 1983 and continued to lead the nation in 1988.

Unrest Continued in the Philippines

Since the end of World War II, the Philippines have been the scene of political and social unrest. Granted independence by the

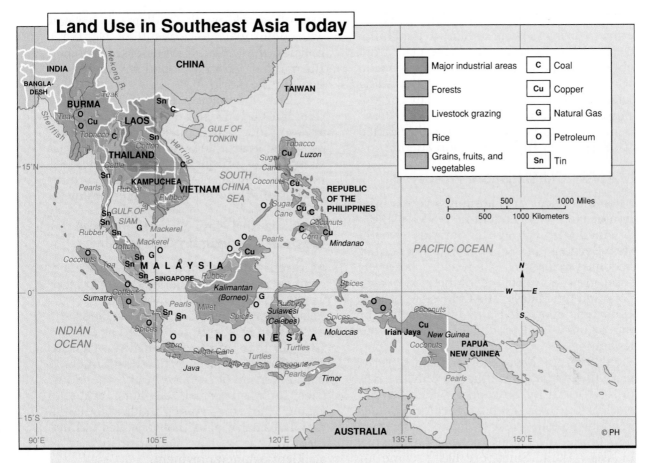

Land Use in Southeast Asia Today

Legend:
- Major industrial areas
- Forests
- Livestock grazing
- Rice
- Grains, fruits, and vegetables
- **C** Coal
- **Cu** Copper
- **G** Natural Gas
- **O** Petroleum
- **Sn** Tin

0 500 1000 Miles
0 500 1000 Kilometers

Focus on Geography

Interaction The map shows how land is used in Southeast Asia today. Locate the mainland of Southeast Asia. Instead of natural forest, much of the forest in mainland Southeast Asia is commercial forest. What kind of trees are cultivated?

United States in 1946, the Republic of the Philippines allied itself with the United States by permitting American military bases in the Philippine Islands. The American presence has not helped to ease political problems between parties competing for control of the country.

Ferdinand Marcos. In 1965, Ferdinand Marcos was elected president of the Philippines. In response to the political uprisings and terrorism in the country, Marcos declared martial law in 1972. He made half-hearted and unsuccessful attempts to limit price increases and to provide land to poor peasants. The United States supported Mar-

cos throughout most of his administration, and many people in the Philippines resented American involvement in their affairs.

In 1983, Benigno Aquino, a popular leader who opposed Marcos, was murdered, and many blamed Marcos for this crime. The result was violent and widespread opposition to his government.

Corazon Aquino. In a corrupt election in 1986, Marcos was declared the victor. However, Corazon Aquino, the wife of the slain opposition leader, challenged his right to office. President Reagan urged Marcos to yield, and Marcos fled to Hawaii. Corazon Aquino thus became president.

723

President Aquino has had enormous difficulty in trying to bring stability to the Philippines. She has sought to make land available to the poor, but the country is faced with rapid population growth, continuing widespread poverty, and persistent corruption in the government. Late in 1989, President Aquino's government was threatened with a serious, but failed, coup attempt.

Malaysia and Singapore Prospered

After the defeat of Communist rebels, Malaya became independent in 1957. In 1963, it joined with Singapore, Sarawak (Northwest Borneo), and Sabah (North Borneo) to become Malaysia. Differences, however, soon grew between the Chinese in Singapore and the Malays. The Chinese were well educated, controlled the business life of the country, and tended to dominate the federation.

In 1965, the Malays forced Singapore to leave the federation. Although only the size of New York City, Singapore, which has the world's fourth largest port, became an independent nation. Next to Japan, Singapore now boasts the highest per person income in Asia. While Singapore has become an economic "tiger," under its prime minister, Lee Kuan Yew, it also has developed an authoritarian form of government. The people do not enjoy many freedoms.

Malaysia has made excellent economic progress as well. The Chinese make up much of the wealthy class, but the Malays control the government. This situation has caused racial tension between Chinese and Malays in recent years.

Revolution Came to Burma

Burma's 38 million people live in a potentially rich country, and yet they are among the world's poorest. Until 1937, Britain governed Burma as part of India. Burma became an independent nation in 1948. U Nu, the hero of independence, became the first premier of his country. In 1962, General U Ne Win staged a successful political uprising, and since then, Burma has been dominated by the Socialist government that he established. Ne Win isolated Burma

from the world much as Albania is isolated within Europe. As a result of Ne Win's policies, the United Nations has designated Burma the "least developed developing nation" in the world.

Burma was once a leading exporter of rice, but by 1987, there were serious shortages of food. Since Burma has petroleum, precious gems, and rich teak forests, it should be a prosperous nation. In 1988, Burmese students began a revolution to try to change the government and economy.

Australia and New Zealand Became Western Outposts in Asia

As discussed in Chapter 21, Australia became a member of the British Commonwealth in 1901 and New Zealand in 1907. Australia and New Zealand developed the Australian, or secret, ballot, and as early as 1893 all men and women had the right to vote. The two countries have experimented with government ownership of some industries, such as railroad, telephone, and telegraph. They were among the first to have a national health plan that provides old age insurance as well as insurance in case of accident or unemployment.

Australia and New Zealand share with the United States a common interest in the Pacific. In 1986, however, New Zealand refused to allow American nuclear ships to enter its ports. As a result, the Australia-New Zealand-United States Defense Alliance (ANZUS), which had been in effect since 1951, was cancelled. Even so, the alliance between the United States and Australia remains intact.

War Came to Vietnam

In 1940, when France surrendered to the Nazis, the Japanese occupied Vietnam. At the end of the war, however, Vietnam was returned to France. Although President Franklin D. Roosevelt and other people felt Vietnam should become independent, this opinion was not accepted, and France once more gained control of Vietnam.

On September 2, 1945, Ho Chi Minh (hoh chee min), a Vietnamese revolutionary devoted to communism and Vietnamese nation-

724

alism, announced a declaration of Vietnamese independence from France that began with words borrowed from the American Declaration of Independence. His words clearly indicated that the return of the French was unwelcome and would be resisted.

Ho Chi Minh's defeat of the French. The war that followed between France and the Vietnamese Communists was a bitter one. After a decisive victory by the Communist forces at Dien Bien Phu (dyen byen foo) on May 6, 1954, France looked to the United States for aid. However, although President Eisenhower had supported the French with money and arms, he refused to send American troops to Vietnam.

After the French were driven out of Vietnam in 1954, a peace conference was held in Geneva, Switzerland. Delegates from France, Great Britain, the United States, the Soviet Union, Vietnam, Laos, Cambodia, and the People's Republic of China attended. Far from ending the war, the conference seemed to lay the foundation for renewed fighting.

Growth of United States involvement. Although there was no final agreement between the nations at the Geneva conference, one decision was made: to divide Vietnam at the 17th parallel. North Vietnam was left to the Communists under Ho Chi Minh. In the newly formed South Vietnam, Ngo Dinh Diem (noh din dyem) agreed to head the government.

The North Vietnamese, however, were not satisfied with the division of the country and tried to unite Vietnam under Communist control. Armed North Vietnamese sympathizers, known as the Viet Cong, hid throughout South Vietnam. They were prepared to use terrorist tactics to bring about Communist rule. In response to the threat of a Communist takeover in Southeast Asia, the United States organized the Southeast Asia Treaty Organization (SEATO) to protect the independence of South Vietnam. In 1954, President Eisenhower sent United States military advisers to South Vietnam. Eisenhower still would not send American soldiers to fight in Vietnam, however.

Many people in the United States believed in an idea known as the **domino theory.** This theory stated that just as pushing one domino causes a whole row to fall, one nation falling under communism would lead to the fall of other nearby nations. By late 1961, increased attacks by North Vietnam made it clear that the United States would have to offer more help if South Vietnam (and perhaps all of Southeast Asia) was to remain free of Communist control.

In August of 1964, President Johnson announced that North Vietnamese gunboats had attacked American warships in the

▼ **Illustrating History** *In the photograph below, American soldiers lead a South Vietnamese family away from a Vietnam War battle zone.*

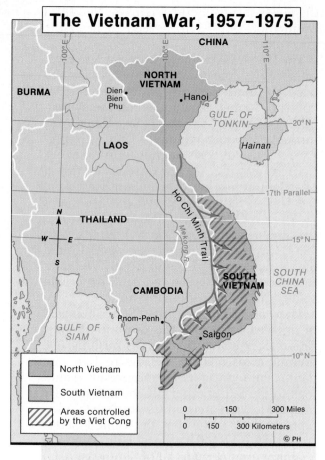

The Vietnam War, 1957–1975

North Vietnam

South Vietnam

Areas controlled by the Viet Cong

0   150   300 Miles

0   150   300 Kilometers

© PH

Focus on Geography

Movement Find the Ho Chi Minh Trail on the map. The Ho Chi Minh Trail was a supply route. Who was supplying whom?

fighting to celebrate Tet, the Vietnamese New Year, Communist forces launched what was called the *Tet offensive*. The Viet Cong and the North Vietnamese attacked 30 South Vietnamese cities, among them Saigon (SY gon), the capital of South Vietnam, and Hue (hway). The Communists held Hue for 25 days and killed many people before they were finally forced out.

While the Tet offensive was not really a great military success for the North Vietnamese, the event had a major impact on American public opinion. In the United States, an unpopular war became even less popular. Many Americans could see nothing to be gained by fighting in Vietnam, and many soldiers' lives had been lost already. People who urged a decisive defeat of North Vietnam were called **hawks,** while people who wanted the United States to withdraw from the war immediately were known as **doves.** President Johnson's popularity reached a new low, and in March 1968, he withdrew from the presidential race.

America's withdrawal. A limited bombing halt allowed peace talks to begin in Paris in January 1969. The United States, North Vietnam, South Vietnam, and the Viet Cong (also called the National Liberation Front) were represented in the talks. Richard Nixon, who had been elected president of the United States in 1968, began to reduce gradually the number of American troops in South Vietnam. Ho Chi Minh died in 1969, but the peace talks dragged on for years. Finally, a complex agreement was reached, and Nixon, now in his second term of office, appeared on television to announce that a cease-fire would go into effect on January 27, 1973 at 7:00 P.M.

North Vietnam's victory. Although American involvement in Vietnam came to an end, peace did not follow. In April 1975, the armies of South Vietnam, without consulting the United States, suddenly began a retreat. As the armies fled south, they left behind over 1 billion dollars worth of American military equipment. Many South Vietnamese soldiers deserted the army altogether and refused to protect defenseless

Gulf of Tonkin. Although the incident was never confirmed, Johnson asked Congress to expand his powers in dealing with the situation. On August 7, 1964, Congress passed the Gulf of Tonkin Resolution, and Johnson was able to commit troops and planes in increasing numbers to protect SEATO countries. The resolution also allowed him to justify bombing raids over North Vietnam. North Vietnam is shown on the map above. The Gulf of Tonkin lies off its coast.

A turning point in the war. The year 1968 was a turning point in the war. For the United States and South Vietnam, it was a turn for the worse. During a pause in the

726

women and children. Few military retreats in history have been so disorderly or so shameful.

Soon after the retreat, South Vietnamese President Thieu resigned, and the Communist grip on Saigon tightened. Foreign embassies closed their buildings, and it was clear that the final victory of North Vietnam over South Vietnam had occurred.

By the end of the Vietnam War, the United States had lost 58,000 soldiers, and the South Vietnamese over 200,000. Over 1 million civilians had been murdered, and there were 6.5 million homeless war refugees in South Vietnam. On July 2, 1978, the Socialist Republic of Vietnam, with its capital at Hanoi, was established.

Cambodia Became a Victim of War

In Cambodia, Prince Norodom Sihanouk (SEE uh nook) kept his country out of the war by allowing North Vietnam to set up bases in Cambodia. In March 1970, while Sihanouk was visiting Moscow, Lon Nol, an army general, seized control of the Cambodian government. Because Lon Nol supported the Americans and South Vietnam, Cambodia was quickly drawn into the war. The Khmer Rouge, Cambodian Communists, sprang into action and captured the capital of Cambodia. Lon Nol fled.

The Khmer Rouge took control of Cambodia in 1975. They renamed the country Kampuchea. Pol Pot, the new leader, began a policy of mass killing to rid the country of his non-Communist enemies. Pol Pot's regime killed over 2 million people during this effort, which has been called "the killing fields."

In 1979, Vietnamese troops, supported by many Communists in Kampuchea, combined forces to overthrow the Khmer Rouge government. Pol Pot and the Khmer Rouge have continued to fight the Vietnamese as guerrillas. In late 1989, Vietnamese troops withdrew from Kampuchea and negotiations began to install a stable government there. Many feared that the Khmer Rouge will try to take advantage of the Vietnamese withdrawal and renew their attacks.

▲ **Illustrating History** *These Cambodians, now living as refugees in Thailand, left their country to escape the Khmer Rouge.*

SECTION 3 REVIEW

Knowing Key Terms, People, and Places
1. Define: **a.** domino theory **b.** hawk **c.** dove
2. Identify: **a.** General Suharto **b.** Corazon Aquino **c.** Ho Chi Minh **d.** SEATO

Focus on Geography
3. Why was Kampuchea strategically located for the North Vietnamese?

Reviewing Main Ideas
4. What made the people of Southeast Asia suspicious of outsiders?
5. How did Corazon Aquino come to power in the Philippines?
6. How did the United States become involved in the Vietnam conflict?

Critical Thinking
Distinguishing Fact from Opinion
7. Explain why you agree or disagree with the statement, "America should never have gotten involved in the Vietnam War."

4 South Asia Made Slow but Steady Progress

As you read, look for answers to these questions:

◆ What challenges has India faced since gaining independence in 1947?
◆ What conflicts are going on in Sri Lanka?
◆ How was the nation of Bangladesh formed?
◆ Why did the Soviets invade Afghanistan?

Key Terms: pariah (defined on p. 728), sabotage (p. 729)

India's independence, which was discussed in Chapter 28, presented new challenges to the country. Independence set the stage for a division between Muslim Pakistan and Hindu India. West Pakistan, East Pakistan —which eventually became the separate state of Bangladesh—Sri Lanka, and Afghanistan will be the focus of the last section in this chapter.

Independence Brought Problems to India

When the Republic of India was established in 1947, Jawaharlal Nehru became India's first prime minister. Under his leadership, a democratic constitution was drafted and adopted, and free elections were held. Under the constitution, the **pariahs,** the lowest of India's social castes, could no longer be discriminated against. Women gained the right to vote and the right to hold property.

In foreign affairs, India tried to remain neutral. The country sought to maintain friendly relations with the People's Republic of China as well as with the Soviet Union and the United States. However, violence occurred when India was forced to defend her borders against both China and Pakistan during the 1960s.

Nehru's daughter, Indira Gandhi, became India's prime minister in 1966. (See the Biography feature on page 729.) After her death, Mrs. Gandhi's son, Rajiv, became prime minister.

For all its troubles, India has made good economic progress. The country has a great number of modern industries, and an economy that is largely self-sufficient. Famines no longer happen frequently. In spite of India's progress, however, problems remain. What Jawaharlal Nehru once said about India remains true today: "India must run very hard just to stand still."

Violence Erupted in Sri Lanka

One of Rajiv Gandhi's problems was how to bring peace to Sri Lanka, which was formerly known as Ceylon. This pear-shaped island is close to India and almost linked to it by a series of sandbars. Ceylon was seized by the British from the Dutch in 1796. It became a Commonwealth country in 1948 and the Republic of Sri Lanka in 1972.

The majority of the people of Sri Lanka are Buddhist Sinhalese (SIN huh LEEZ). However, there is an outspoken minority of Tamils who are descended from Indian Hindus. The extremists among the Tamils seek an independent state in the northwestern part of the island where they are numerous. Despite the presence of Indian troops, violence between Sinhalese and Tamils has led to the death of more than 8,500 people.

The Military Governed Pakistan

In 1948, Mohammed Ali Jinnah, the founding father of Pakistan, died. This left the new nation without a strong leader, and a series of weak governments followed. In 1956, a new constitution went into effect, and the nation adopted the name Islamic Republic of Pakistan. In a political crisis during which the constitution was annulled, General Mohammed Ayub Khan became president. Although Ayub Khan's regime was authoritarian, he allowed some communities to make their own decisions. However, by 1969, there were antigovernment riots and demonstrations, and General Mohammed Yahya Khan replaced Ayub Khan.

Indira Gandhi

"I had an advantage," Indian leader Indira Gandhi once said, "because of the education my father gave me and the opportunities of meeting some great people . . . but in politics one has to work doubly hard to show one is not merely a daughter but is also a person in her own right." Wielding power for nearly two decades, Indira Gandhi defined herself through a life of action.

Born in 1917, Gandhi (pictured on the right) was the only child of prominent politician Jawaharlal Nehru and his wife. Her parents were leaders in the movement seeking Indian independence from Britain. In 1946, when her father became independent India's first prime minister, Indira served by his side as an adviser. In 1966, she was elected prime minister.

Indira Gandhi (no relation to Mohandas Gandhi) was a tough, determined leader. She led the nation into the nuclear and space ages with the explosion of an underground nuclear device and the launching of India's first satellite. There was another side to Gandhi's toughness. When an Indian court found her guilty of illegal practices in the 1971 elections, she declared a state of emergency and arrested thousands of her critics. Gandhi's ca-

reer ended tragically in 1984 when she was assassinated by Sikh terrorists.

1. How was Indira Gandhi's early family life an advantage to her?
2. Why did critics accuse Gandhi of ruling like a dictator?

West Pakistan. In 1971, Zulfikar Ali Bhutto became the president of West Pakistan. Under Bhutto, Pakistan sought to rebuild its economy and improve poor health conditions. Although Bhutto was popular with the people, in July 1977, he was overthrown in a military coup and replaced by Mohammed Zia ul-Haq.

Mohammed Zia ul-Haq followed an anti-Soviet course, and under his leadership, Pakistan became an important outpost for Western influence in that part of the world. The United States provided Pakistan with 7 billion dollars in military aid. President Zia improved the Pakistani economy somewhat and kept the country stable. However, this stability was at the expense of political freedom. In 1986, Benazir Bhutto, the daughter of Ali Bhutto, returned to Pakistan from exile in Europe. She pledged to revive her father's party and to become active in the nation's political affairs.

Benazir Bhutto's opportunity came sooner than she expected. President Zia and the U.S. ambassador to Pakistan were killed in 1988 when the plane carrying them exploded. The possibility of **sabotage,** or intentional destruction, was not ruled out.

A free election was held, and on December 2, 1988, Benazir Bhutto was sworn in as prime minister of Pakistan. She was the first woman ever to be elected leader of a Muslim nation. After being sworn in, Bhutto said, "I think it's a great day for women, a great day for youth, a great day for Islam, and above all a great day for Pakistan."

729

▲ Illustrating History *Above, Soviet tanks arrive in Kabul, Afghanistan. They are greeted by some Afghan supporters.*

Bangladesh. In 1970, the East Pakistanis won enough votes in the national election to have the head of their political party become prime minister. West Pakistanis, led by Yahya Khan, refused to accept the results and sent soldiers to arrest the East Pakistani leaders. A massacre followed in which thousands of people were killed. East Pakistan, with help from India, went to war with West Pakistan in 1971. In 1972, East Pakistan became the independent nation of Bangladesh.

Bangladesh has accepted help from India and the Soviet Union. It has also attempted to control its economy by nationalizing industry. However, problems such as political instability, inadequate health care, chronic hunger, housing shortages, and annual flooding continue to plague Bangladesh.

The Soviet Union Invaded Afghanistan

In December 1979, between 60,000 and 100,000 Soviet troops invaded Afghanistan in order to put into place a pro-Soviet Marxist government. Since Afghanistan borders the Soviet Union, a pro-Soviet government could provide a strategic base for greater Soviet influence in South Asia. Under Communist leadership, there was

widespread torture and bloodshed. Whole villages were destroyed, and approximately 12,000 political prisoners were held without trial. About 2 million Afghan people became refugees in Pakistan and Iran. After several years of fighting, Soviet forces controlled Kabul, the capital, but the countryside was still held by Muslim guerillas.

To protest the invasion, United States President Jimmy Carter imposed an American boycott of the 1980 Summer Olympic Games in Moscow. He also stopped the sale of American grain to the Soviet Union.

The invasion of Afghanistan was a move that the Soviet Union would regret. The Soviets had not really understood the depth of Muslim opposition to communism. The war dragged on until 1988, when the Soviet Union agreed to begin a troop withdrawal.

South Asia today remains the scene of hardship and violence. However, in the next chapter you will learn about some of the steps that are being taken toward global peace and prosperity.

SECTION 4 REVIEW

Knowing Key Terms, People, and Places
1. Define: **a.** pariah **b.** sabotage
2. Identify: **a.** Indira Gandhi **b.** Mohammed Zia ul-Haq **c.** People's Republic of Bangladesh

Focus on Geography
3. Why was Afghanistan strategically located for Soviet takeover?

Reviewing Main Ideas
4. What did Indira Gandhi attempt to do as prime minister of India?
5. How did Bangladesh become an independent nation?
6. Why did the Soviets invade Afghanistan?

Critical Thinking
Formulating Questions
7. Imagine that you are trying to come up with some ideas to solve one of the problems facing Bangladesh. Make a list of questions that you would need to have answered before attacking the problem.

Developing Criteria for Making Judgments: Testing Conclusions

Criteria are standards that you use to judge or evaluate something. You use criteria to test the accuracy and the validity of conclusions. For example, data that are known to be valid could be used as criteria for testing a conclusion. If the data support the conclusion, then you have reason to believe that the conclusion is sound.

A series of untested conclusions, accompanied by a table of reliable data, is shown below. Use the following steps to test the validity of the conclusions.

1. **Study the conclusions to recognize the kind of data needed to verify them.** If supporting data is provided, decide if they are useful for testing the conclusions. Answer the following questions: (a) Upon what economic measurement are all the conclusions based? (b) Is there a relationship between the conclusions and the evidence provided?

2. **Decide on the criteria by which the conclusions could be tested most effectively.** Some conclusions are based upon trends and must be tested against data that cover a period of time. Other conclusions are more specific and may need exact data for verification. Answer the two following questions: (a) Does conclusion 5 below deal with a trend or with a specific point in time? (b) Would data covering a period of time be needed to support conclusion 2?

3. **Test the conclusions by comparing them with the criteria.** Decide if the data support or contradict the conclusions. Additional data may be needed to determine the validity of some conclusions. Answer the following questions: (a) Do the data support or contradict conclusion 4? (b) According to the data, is conclusion 3 valid or not? (c) Do you agree with conclusion 5? Explain.

---

1. The 10-year period between 1975 and 1984 saw significant economic growth in many parts of Asia.
2. The economic giant of Asia in 1984 was clearly Japan.
3. In terms of percentages, the rate of China's economic growth was actually greater than that of Japan between 1975 and 1984.
4. Of the two Koreas, North Korea's economy lagged far behind South Korea's, but North Korea will draw even by 1990.
5. Indonesia's economy was greater than that of South Korea in 1975, but the Indonesian economy probably will never again equal or exceed South Korea's economy.

Gross National Product (GNP) of Selected Asian Nations, 1975−1984 (in billions of constant [1983] U.S. dollars)			
Nation	1975	1980	1984
China*	167.5	219.0	310.5
Indonesia	46.7	67.1	82.0
Japan	827.8	1,062.0	1,249.0
North Korea*	15.6	18.8	22.2
South Korea	42.5	60.5	82.5

*Estimated

REVIEW

Section Summaries

Section 1 Japan and Korea Developed Rapidly
Japan was occupied by United States forces from the end of World War II until 1951. During these years, Japan ratified a democratic constitution and started on the road to becoming an industrial power. South Korea, also a modernizing and prosperous nation, finally achieved democratic elections by the late 1980s. Improved relations with North Korea remained a high priority for South Korea.

Section 2 China Reentered World Affairs Mao Zedong hoped to make important economic and political changes in the People's Republic of China. His Great Leap Forward, however, failed to produce more and better goods, and the Cultural Revolution turned into a reign of terror. During the 1970s, relations with the United States improved. After Mao's death in 1976, moderates came to power with the goal of modernizing the nation and creating a more flexible economy. Meanwhile, the non–Communist Republic of China on the island of Taiwan gave up the goal of taking control of mainland China. Eventually, the United Nations and the United States gave full recognition to the People's Republic. The Republic of China on Taiwan lost its status as a recognized nation yet remained prosperous.

Section 3 Southeast Asia Faced Major Challenges The diverse and resource-rich region of Southeast Asia remained an important crossroads for trade and defense. Indonesia overthrew its dictator during the 1960s, but poverty, hunger, and dwindling oil prices plagued the nation into the 1980s. Similarly, the Philippines overthrew Ferdinand Marcos, yet problems such as poverty and corruption continued. Malaysia and Singapore both prospered, however, although Singapore had an authoritarian government. Burma's dictators led that nation into poverty, despite its rich resources. In Vietnam, war raged for years. The Vietnamese defeated the French, yet they then fell into a civil war in which the United States was heavily involved. The United States supported non-Communist South Vietnam. The war became unpopular in the United States, however, and American forces left in 1973. By 1975, Communist North Vietnam controlled the entire nation. Soon, the Vietnamese overthrew neighboring Kampuchea's ruler and set up a new government there.

Section 4 South Asia Made Slow but Steady Progress After winning independence, India became a democracy. Jawaharlal Nehru was India's first prime minister, followed by his daughter, Indira Gandhi. Serious problems arose, including conflict with Pakistan, government corruption, and uprisings by the Sikhs. India's economy made progress, however. Sri Lanka was plagued by violence between Buddhists and Tamils. In Pakistan, weak governments were followed by an authoritarian regime. In 1970, impoverished East Pakistan won its independence and became Bangladesh. Bangladesh remained a poor country, however. In 1988, Pakistan's pro-Western prime minister died when his plane exploded. Pakistanis then elected Benazir Bhutto, the first woman to lead a Muslim nation. In nearby Afghanistan, Muslim rebels fought to topple a Soviet-supported government.

Key Facts

1. Use each vocabulary word in a sentence.
   a. stereotype   e. hawk
   b. commune   f. dove
   c. indoctrinate   g. pariah
   d. domino theory   h. sabotage
2. Identify and briefly explain the importance of the following names, places, or events.
   a. North Korea   f. North Vietnam
   b. South Korea   g. South Vietnam
   c. Mao Zedong   h. Kampuchea
   d. Ferdinand Marcos   i. Indira Gandhi
   e. Corazon Aquino   j. Benazir Bhutto

Main Ideas

1. How has a low military budget helped Japan become an economic power?
2. How did South Koreans win free elections?
3. What were the problems of China's Great Leap Forward and Cultural Revolution?
4. List Indonesia's major problems under the leadership of Suharto.
5. How did the North Vietnamese Communists unite all of Vietnam?
6. What democratic advances were made in India under Nehru?
7. How did East Pakistan win its independence?

Developing Skill in Reading History

Read the following quotation. Tell who the speaker was and briefly explain the situation that prompted the quotation and what the quotation means.

> "I think it's a great day for women, a great day for youth, a great day for Islam, and above all a great day for Pakistan." (page 729)

Using Social Studies Skills

Developing Criteria for Making Judgments: Testing Conclusions Evaluate the following opinion: "Prosperity usually comes soon after a nation overthrows its dictator." Support your evaluation with facts from the chapter.

Critical Thinking

1. **Making Comparisons** After Mao Zedong's death, there was a struggle for power between the Gang of Four and a group of moderates. In what ways were these two groups different?
2. **Perceiving Cause and Effect** What were the long-term causes that drove Ferdinand Marcos from power in the Philippines? What were the immediate causes?
3. **Formulating Questions** Imagine that you are the president of the United States during the early 1970s. You are trying to decide whether U.S. troops should remain in Vietnam or withdraw. Create a list of questions to help you make such a decision.

Focus on Writing

Interpreting Essay Exam Questions

When you read a question on an essay exam, look for words that offer clues about what kind of information is expected. The chart below shows some of these word clues. Study the chart. Then, read each essay question below and tell what kind of question it is.

1. Show how one geographical factor adds to the severe problems of Bangladesh.
2. Why did the Soviets invade Afghanistan? Why do you think the rebels continued to fight against government and Soviet forces?
3. Give the major differences between Indonesia's two rulers, Sukarno and Suharto.

Word Clues in Essay Exam Questions	
Kind of Question	**Words That Offer Clues**
Compare	Compare, similarities, resemblances, likenesses
Contrast	Contrast, differ, differences
Define	Define, explain
Describe	Describe
Diagram	Diagram, draw, chart
Discuss	Discuss, explain
Explain	Explain, why, what, how
Illustrate	Illustrate, show

Contemporary Global Issues

1 **Population Growth Has Stretched Resources**

2 **The Environment of Planet Earth Is Fragile**

3 **The World's Economy Has Become Global**

▲ **Illustrating History** *This photograph shows a withered corn field in Iowa during the 1988 drought. Millions of dollars worth of crops were destroyed by the extremely hot weather.*

The weather in the United States was big news during the summer of 1988. Newspaper headlines proclaimed it the hottest summer on record. People across the country suffered in 100° heat day after day. Particularly hard hit were the Great Plains, where a punishing drought accompanied the heat wave. By summer's end, millions of acres of wheat and corn had withered in the fields.

Some scientists blame the high temperatures on an environmental condition known as the greenhouse effect. They believe this warming trend is caused by gases from the earth rising into the atmosphere. There, like a roof over a greenhouse, the gases trap the sun's heat. Although the process is a natural one and has been going on for billions of years, modern air pollution has greatly increased the volume of gas rising into the air. More and more heat is being trapped this way.

The trend concerns experts who watch the world's environmental health. Whether or not the 1988 heat wave can be blamed on the greenhouse effect, most scientists agree that the earth is steadily warming up. Any change in surface temperatures on the earth, they say, is bound to cause dramatic changes in the world's weather. The problem is a global one. In this chapter, you will learn about many problems, environmental and otherwise, that tie the countries of the world together in a common search for solutions.

▲ **Illustrating History** *The planet Earth, shown above from space, needs special care if it is to continue supporting life.*

1 Population Growth Has Stretched Resources

As you read, look for answers to these questions:

◆ How is population growth affecting the world?
◆ What are the major causes of hunger and starvation?
◆ How have cities responded to growth?

Key Terms: population growth (defined on p. 736), population base (p. 736), genetic engineering (p. 737), squatter (p. 739), host country (p. 739)

History is an unending conversation between the past and present. We study the past because it sheds light on who we are and where we are going as a people.

The past has shown us that our survival as a species depends to a large degree on our ability to solve problems. One of the major problems the world faces today is its sheer number of people. How many of us are there? How many will there be? How can this beautiful but small planet provide for all of us comfortably?

The World's Population Has Grown Rapidly

By 1630, the world's population had grown to half a billion people. By 1830, there were 1 billion people in the world. It had taken only 200 years for the world population to double. One hundred years later, there were 2 billion people on the planet. The world's population had doubled again in half the time. Today, less than 100 years later, the global population is about 5 billion, an increase of two and a half times what it was in 1930. (See the graph on page 738.)

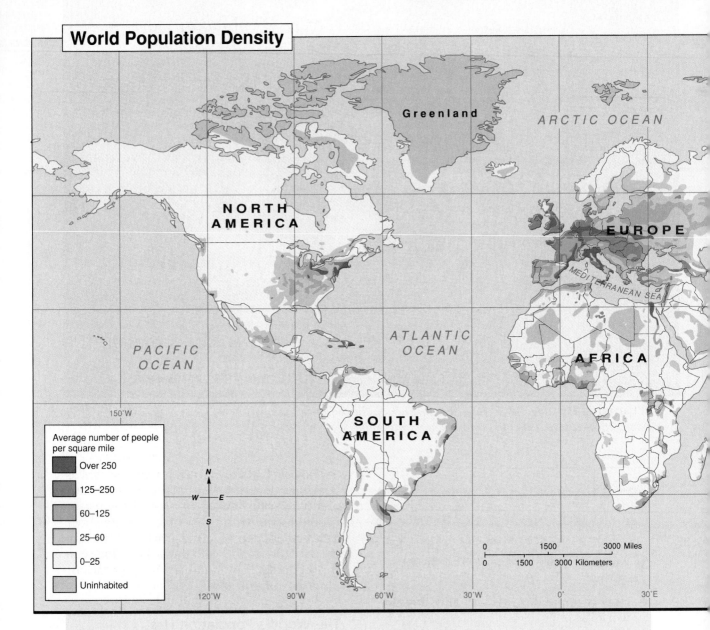

World Population Density

Greenland

ARCTIC OCEAN

NORTH AMERICA

EUROPE

MEDITERRANEAN SEA

PACIFIC OCEAN

ATLANTIC OCEAN

AFRICA

150°W

SOUTH AMERICA

Average number of people per square mile

Over 250

125–250

60–125

25–60

0–25

Uninhabited

N
W — E
S

0   1500   3000 Miles
0   1500   3000 Kilometers

120°W   90°W   60°W   30°W   0°   30°E

Focus on Geography

1. **Location** What two continents have the highest population density?
2. **Regions** As you know, the higher the latitude, the colder the climate. Look at the Northern Hemisphere and explain the link between climate and population.

Birth rates. The rate of **population growth,** or increase in the size of population, is declining. Nevertheless, the population is increasing rapidly because the **population base,** or the number of people who can have children, grows bigger each year.

(See the map above.) By the year 2000, the United Nations expects a world population of over 6 billion, and over 8 billion by 2025. Most of this increase will occur in the less developed areas, including Africa, Asia (except Japan), and Latin America.

was estimated at 62 years. Africa has the lowest life expectancy at 50 years. In Japan, life expectancy for girls born in 1984 has reached 80 years. One dramatic prospect for future progress lies in the field of **genetic engineering,** the science that adjusts the molecular structure of living organisms. Genetic engineering may create plants that are resistant to disease, vegetables that are larger in size, hogs that are meatier, and cows that can give more milk. Genetic engineering research also explores how hereditary, or family, diseases may be prevented or cured.

Agricultural research. Through experiments involving such foods as soybeans and amaranth—both extremely high in protein—scientists are exploring new sources of nutrition. Soybeans can be added to meat or even bread to enhance nutrition. Amaranth, once cultivated by the ancient Aztecs, has been called the "grain of the future."

Surprisingly, the harsh life endured by people in underdeveloped nations has also contributed to world population growth. Where farming is central to a nation's economy, parents want large families so that they will have as many laborers as possible on hand to help with the chores.

Some poor, overcrowded nations have tried to encourage birth control among their people as a means of checking explosive growth. A program launched in China has attempted to limit family size to a single child per couple—or, in rural areas of the country, to a maximum of two children.

Problems Have Accompanied Large Population Growth

As world growth accelerates, pressure increases on the world's resources to feed, house, and clothe the new members of society. Most of the world's population is born into raw poverty without any of the benefits of industrialization. But, some problems bridge the rich and the poor.

Health. One troubling health concern in the 1980s was Acquired Immune Deficiency Syndrome, or AIDS. This disease, which has

Medical breakthroughs. Enormous progress in medical research, especially in disease control and sanitation, has contributed greatly to population growth. In 1953, for example, Jonas Salk developed a vaccine to combat polio. Now measles, mumps, smallpox, yellow fever, and malaria are among the illnesses from which people are immunized or protected.

Improved medical care has increased longevity and reduced infant mortality. In a recent survey, worldwide life expectancy

737

attracted global attention, can be transmitted sexually, through blood transfusions, or by intravenous drug use. In 1988, AIDS was considered such a serious threat that the United States surgeon general, Dr. C. Everett Koop, mailed a warning about the disease to every household in the United States in a effort to educate the public.

The use of illicit drugs has become yet another global problem, and commonly used illegal substances, such as cocaine, heroin, and marijuana, have become widely available through a network of international criminals. Efforts, sometimes between countries, to catch and convict drug smugglers have not stopped the traffic. Because no community made up of addicted people can prosper, stamping out drug addiction should have a high priority worldwide. As the last decade of the twentieth century begins, a cure for AIDS and a solution to the illegal drug crisis are still awaited.

Overcrowding and poverty. You learned that urbanization is the name given to the movement of people from rural areas to cities or urban areas. According to United Nations statistics, there will be 93 cities worldwide with populations of over 5 million by the year 2000. The largest will include: Tokyo, Japan (30 million), Mexico City, Mexico (27.3 million), São Paulo, Brazil (25.4 million), and Seoul, South Korea (22 million).

Improved means of transportation and communication make rapid urbanization possible. People can now live far from their food supplies. When cities become too large too fast, however, particularly in developing countries, services such as schools, hospitals, mass transportation, and police and fire protection often deteriorate.

Mexico City is just one example of urban growth running out of control. In this city, modern buildings and boutiques for the

▼ **Graph Skill** *By how much did the world's population grow from 1950 to 1988? How much did the average life expectancy rise in that period?*

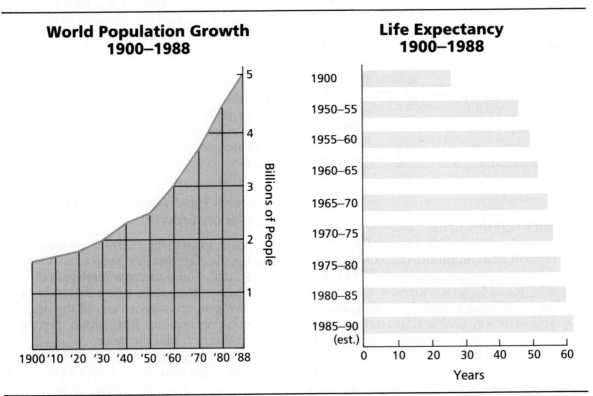

wealthy are ringed by clusters of people living in conditions of appalling poverty. All around the world, millions of **squatters,** as they often are called, live on the outskirts of urban centers in shacks or on rooftops. In Cairo, millions live in cemeteries among the tombstones. In India, the squatter population is estimated at 30 million.

Refugees. People who have lost their homes and countries, known as refugees, numbered about 12 million in the late 1980s. These people become homeless for many reasons, including unchecked population growth and political unrest. When Israel was created, Palestinians left for other Arab lands. The division of India created millions of homeless people. Sadly, the list is endless.

You read how Laos, Kampuchea, and Vietnam, in particular, were devastated by wars and Communist takeovers. These events led to an onrush of refugees who became known as boat people. In order to live in freedom, refugees left by boat for other countries and sometimes roamed the oceans for weeks until a country would allow them to enter. Death and starvation were common among these people. The resources of **host countries,** that is, the places that accept refugees for temporary or permanent resettlement, were stretched by the challenge of feeding and housing large numbers of refugees. As a result, some countries became more and more reluctant to accept these homeless people.

In May 1979, an agreement was reached between the United Nations High Commission for Refugees and the Social Republic of Vietnam to establish the Orderly Departure Program, or ODP. By 1985, the ODP had resettled large numbers of refugees in many countries, including the United States. However, thousands of refugees still waited for new homes in the late 1980s.

Hunger. The Sudan is a good example of how hunger in less developed areas becomes compounded by political turmoil. Hunger in the Sudan is the product of the five-year civil war between the Islamic dominated government in the north and the

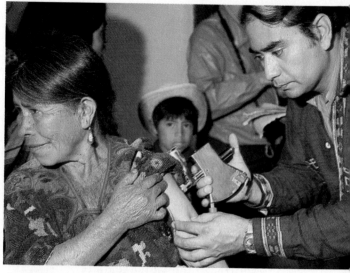

▲ **Illustrating History** *The spread of modern medical care has raised the world's average life expectancy in recent decades. The Guatemalan woman shown above is receiving a vaccination from her doctor.*

Christians in the south. Both sides used food as a weapon of war and blocked food from reaching their enemies. From time to time, fearing adverse public opinion, the government reluctantly allowed United Nations and private relief agencies to deliver food, but government troops blocked the efficient distribution of that food by withholding planes and trucks.

Drought, poor soil conditions caused by primitive methods of farming, and rapidly growing populations are among the causes of hunger in the less developed countries of Africa, Asia, and Latin America. Important as these causes of hunger are, however, the political and economic causes are, in many cases, even greater.

In poor countries, most of those who starve work on farms, but they generally do not own the land on which they work and do not have the knowledge or tools to make the land productive. Often government policies, designed to keep down the price of bread in the cities, mean that farmers must sell grains for less than it costs to grow them. These policies do not provide farmers with an incentive to be productive.

739

Overcoming World Hunger

Since the early 1970s, Frances Moore Lappé has been arguing that world hunger can be solved. Lappé, an analyst of developmental policies, believes that hunger results from political, not agricultural, problems. In the following excerpt, she explains why a shortage of food and agricultural land are not the basic causes of world hunger.

"Even in the worst years of famine in the early 70s there was plenty to go around—enough in grain alone to provide everyone in the world with 3000 to 4000 calories a day. . . .

We looked at the most crowded countries in the world to see if we could find a [relationship] between land density and hunger. We could not. Bangladesh, for example, has just half the people per cultivated acre that Taiwan has. Yet Taiwan has no starvation while Bangladesh is thought of as the world's worst basketcase. . . .

Finally, when the pattern of *what* is grown sank in, we simply could no longer subscribe to a 'scarcity' diagnosis [explanation] of hunger. In Central America and in the Caribbean, where as much as 70 percent of the children are undernourished, at least half of the agricultural land, and the best land at that, grows crops for export, not food for the local people.**"**

1. According to Lappé, what is the relationship between the amount of land a country has in cultivation and the amount of hunger?
2. Explain how a country could have increasing agricultural output and still have increasing hunger.

In many of the less developed countries, there is a wide gap between the rich and the poor, with the result that the rich own most of the land. Small landowners cannot borrow money readily to buy the farm machinery needed. The plots of land on which they work are often too small for machinery.

Making matters worse, many poor countries rely on a single crop. Brazil depends on coffee, Sri Lanka depends on tea, Thailand depends on rice. They must sell these products to obtain the money they need to buy other foods for their people. When the market collapses for these crops, the country cannot get the money to feed itself.

As in most developed countries, poorer nations spend too much money on wars and weapons to build strong economies. Civil wars in Ethiopia and the Sudan prevented gifts of food sent by sympathetic countries from reaching starving people. Only when public opinion was against them did warring forces allow the United Nations and other agencies to deliver some relief.

Implications for the United States. In 1986, Congress passed the Immigration Reform and Control Act, which offered amnesty to millions of refugees who have lived in the United States since before January 1, 1982. Many people praised the amnesty program of 1986 as a humanitarian gesture on the part of the United States government.

The feelings of support, however, were not unanimous. Many people in the United States resented the recognition of illegal aliens as full citizens at a time when millions of Americans could not find jobs. The move meant more competition and further hardship for such Americans. The debate over the amnesty was furious at times, but finally the bill was passed.

A Variety of Organizations Have Fought World Hunger

Henry Kissinger, the former American secretary of state, once declared the following goal concerning world hunger: "that . . . no child will go to bed hungry, that no family will fear for its next day's bread, and that no human being's future and capacities will be stunted by malnutrition." Although that goal has not been realized yet, many people and organizations now are committed to achieving it.

In 1954, the United States adopted Public Law 480, the Food for Peace Program. The law provided long-term credit at low rates of interest to enable poor countries to buy food from the United States.

In 1974, the World Food Conference proposed the creation of a system of international wheat reserves. During periods of worldwide food crises, these resources would be available to poor nations at prices they could afford. While the worldwide wheat reserve system did not develop, the United States did guarantee a reserve of 4 million metric tons that can be used in cases of severe hardship.

Many international organizations have been developed to help fight hunger. The United Nations has several such organizations, including the World Health Organization (WHO), the United Nations Children's Fund (UNICEF), the Food and Agriculture Organization (FAO), and the International Fund for Agricultural Development. The World Bank, or International Bank for Reconstruction and Development, makes loans to poor countries to help them solve many different problems, including hunger. The Peace Corps, a United States government organization, trains volunteers to help communities in developing nations.

Many private organizations also try to relieve world hunger. The International Red Cross (IRC), for example, sends food and other emergency aid to victims of natural disasters such as floods and hurricanes. OXFAM and CARE also collect food and money for food to send to famine-stricken areas. In the 1980s, popular rock musicians formed groups such as "USA for Africa" and gave benefit concerts or recorded songs such as "We Are the World" to raise money for the world's hungry.

Through further cooperative efforts, even more progress can be made to end world hunger. In the words of the poet W. H. Auden, "Hunger allows no choice. . . . We must love one another or die."

▲ **Illustrating History** *When famine struck Ethiopia in the mid-1980s, relief organizations sent food for the hungry.*

SECTION 1 REVIEW

Knowing Key Terms, People, and Places
1. Define: **a.** population growth **b.** population base **c.** genetic engineering **d.** squatter **e.** host country
2. Identify: **a.** refugees **b.** Orderly Departure Program **c.** Immigration Reform and Control Act

Focus on Geography
3. Identify the areas of fastest population growth.

Reviewing Main Ideas
4. How did the United States help the refugee problem?
5. Name some of the reasons it is difficult to provide food relief to victims of famine and war.

Critical Thinking
Perceiving Cause and Effect
6. How have advances in medical and other technology contributed to an increase in the world's population?

741

2 The Environment of Planet Earth Is Fragile

As you read, look for answers to these questions:

◆ What is the relation between the amount of wealth and the amount of waste a society creates?
◆ How did garbage disposal become a global problem?
◆ What happened at Chernobyl?

> **Key Terms:** nonbiodegradable product (defined on p. 742), acid rain (p. 742), greenhouse effect (p. 742), deforestation (p. 743)

If you had been riding on the American space shuttle *Discovery*, you would have enjoyed quite a splendid view from outer space. There below you would be planet Earth: a planet of rare beauty with its blue seas, sandy beaches, snowcapped mountains, vast forests, and rippling grasslands.

At closer range, the view might have proved less pleasant. Erosion by wind and water, pollution from factory smoke-stacks and car exhausts, and chemical contamination of lakes and rivers have all damaged the fragile environment. Our planet may be in danger for its life. Yet the very technology that made the journey of *Discovery* possible enables us to study the earth so that we may avert further damage.

Our Environment Is Besieged

When the residents of earth were living in caves, the environment was almost completely unchanged by their presence. But progress—the advance of civilization—has made a big difference in the condition of the world's land, water, and air.

Waste. Environmental pollution is created by people. The greater the number of people on earth, the more garbage they create. The more wealthy the society, the greater the waste it pours out. With 6 percent of the world's population, the United States produces more than 70 percent of the world's garbage and waste.

Industries in most countries have found ways to convert ordinary waste into energy, but the plastic bags, hamburger containers, and styrofoam cups, which are part of our culture today, are only a few examples of **nonbiodegradable products.** That is, they are materials that essentially last forever because they will not break down and become part of the earth, as does food waste, for example.

Even space is polluted. There are 48,000 manufactured objects that are one centimeter or larger in size orbiting the earth. So congested with junk has space become that future space vehicles may have to be armor-plated in case they crash into the debris.

Acid rain. Environmental problems are plentiful closer to home, too. **Acid rain** is caused by smoke from factory chimneys and from the exhausts of automobiles, which contain sulfur and nitrogen oxides. These poisons are carried into the atmosphere, where they become acidic and return to earth as acid rain.

Acid rain weakens all our natural resources and has already damaged historic monuments such as the Acropolis in Athens, Greece, and the Taj Mahal in India. Plants, animals, and drinking water slowly become poisonous. Fish and other foods that become contaminated represent a clear danger to public health. In 1986, the United States and Canada began a detailed study of how best to control acid rain on both sides of the border.

Greenhouse effect. The earth has undergone periods of warming and cooling in the past. In our time, a warming trend known as the **greenhouse effect** may be taking place. By 2050, if not earlier, planet Earth may be so much warmer than it is today that global patterns of climate will be disrupted and many fragile life forms will be threatened with extinction.

The greenhouse effect is caused mainly by burning fossil fuels such as oil, coal, and gasolines. Burning releases carbon dioxide into the atmosphere, where it gradually accumulates. Sunlight is admitted to the earth's atmosphere, but then becomes trapped there beneath a shield of airborne pollution. The heat is absorbed rather than reflected and brings a sharp warming effect in the earth's atmosphere.

Deforestation. Some things can be done to reduce the greenhouse effect, or at least to prepare for it. The United Nations Environment Program, UNEP, reports that if **deforestation,** that is, the cutting down of forests, could be stopped, then the greenhouse effect would be delayed. The wildlife that lives in the forests also would be protected. At present, deforestation occurs in Brazil, West Africa, and Indonesia at a rate of 50 acres every minute.

The natural desire of people to own and cultivate their own land has contributed to the loss of forests around the world. In the jungle of the Amazon, for example, the Brazilian government has encouraged rapid growth over the past 15 years. Brazil built a major highway into the densely forested regions at the heart of the country, then promoted settlement by using a slogan that said, "The Bold Ones March Westward." Many poor Brazilians, starved for land, took advantage of the offer.

Experts estimate that 20 percent of Brazil's rain forest already has been cut down and burned, and that it may be stripped entirely away by the end of the century. The consequences of this action are serious. Not only is the greenery that creates oxygen destroyed, but the tremendous bonfires that are used to remove the felled trees produce carbon dioxide. The carbon dioxide further clogs our atmosphere.

Animals. People aren't the only ones who suffer under these conditions. When wilderness is cleared to create level land for housing, roads, and industry, the environmental impact is severe. Many animals lose their homes and must flee the region or die.

Extinction awaits those plant and animal forms that are unable to stand the shock of sudden change. This fate already strikes thousands of species a year around the

▲ **Illustrating History** *This desolate area near the Amazon River in Brazil was once a lush rain forest.*

world. Black rhinos are nearly extinct in Africa, and Florida manatees are endangered in our country. At the same time, through careful handling, certain species have regained their foothold in the biological chain. Sea otters, gray whales, and whooping cranes are among the animals that have been nursed back to health from the edge of extinction.

The search for resources. There is a constant tension between the need for natural resources and the protection of the environment that holds them. Miners seeking gold and tin in the Amazon, for example, have helped destroy the Brazilian rain forest where these deposits lie hidden.

In our country, rich Alaskan oil fields pose a similar dilemma. The deposits of oil located in central Alaska are considered to rank among the most promising anywhere in North America. Unfortunately, the oil is buried beneath a fragile crust of ice and snow, in the middle of a wilderness. So the nation's need for fuel must be weighed against the likely damage from further drilling and exploration.

743

Rachel Carson

Rachel Louise Carson (shown above) was born on May 27, 1907, in Springdale, Pennsylvania. As a small child, she was fascinated by the outdoors. As an adult, Carson would spend most of her life working in the field she loved—marine biology—for the United States Fish and Wildlife Service.

Carson wrote several books during her career as a biologist. In her writings, Carson stressed the interdependence of all living things. She argued that even when a seemingly unimportant species of creatures became extinct, it was a sign that the entire ecological system was out of balance. Sooner or later, she warned, human beings would feel the effect of this imbalance.

It was Carson's 1962 book, *Silent Spring*, that had the greatest impact. *Silent Spring* awakened the American public to the serious dangers involved in the widespread use of pesticides (chemicals used to kill insects on crops). She argued in the book that such pesticides not only kill many birds, fish, and animals but also find their way into the human food supply. *Silent Spring* set off a controversy that resulted in increased research on the effects of pesticides and, finally, to restrictions on the use of these deadly chemicals in many parts of the world.

1. Why should humans be concerned when other species become extinct?
2. What were the results of Carson's *Silent Spring*?

Environmental Issues Have Raised Serious Questions

As with any public policy issue, the debate surrounding the proper course of action for the environment is hotly argued at times. Those most concerned with shaping the debate include individuals, communities of people drawn together by their specialized training, and activist groups.

Conservation groups. In the United States, as well as in many European countries, private citizens have organized to stop urban growth and rural development from ruining the environment. People are taking a much closer look when shopping malls and other commercial ventures threaten to destroy forests, wetlands, or public recreational areas.

Many environmental groups have sprung up to answer these concerns. Greenpeace is the largest private group in the United States and was formed to fight every type of environmental decay. It has acted aggressively, for example, to block illegal whaling expeditions on the high seas and to save whales from slaughter. Another such group, the Nature Conservancy, buys unspoiled land and then sets it aside as a nature preserve. Over the past few decades, working in all 50 states, this businesslike organization has acquired 3.5 million acres of wilderness for the public good.

The scientific community. Scientists, too, are concerned by the deterioration of the environment. Many have formed organizations designed to research and clarify technical issues for the general public and to recommend policy based on their findings. One such group is the Union of Concerned Scientists (UCS), founded in 1969 by physics professors at the Massachusetts Institute of Technology. Among other issues, the UCS is concerned with defining a more efficient energy policy for the United States and with reducing national reliance on the use of fossil fuels. Solar and wind power are possible alternative sources of energy that might be used in a mix with other types of fuels to lessen environmental damage.

Biologists also have taken an active role in monitoring plants and animals that are in danger of becoming extinct. Often, this concern has meant acquiring land. The endangered bald eagle, for example, has been returned to health slowly by scientists working to protect the bird's nesting places around the country. At many other sites, tracts of land have been set aside to protect delicate desert, lake, and woodland plants.

Individual efforts. In recent years, news bulletins have brought the environmental crisis home to every citizen of the world. In 1979, for example, a nuclear accident at a power plant at Three Mile Island in Pennsylvania almost led to disaster and made the public fearful of nuclear power. In 1984, in history's worst industrial accident, deadly gas escaped from a chemical plant and killed 2,500 people in Bhopal, India. In 1986, at Chernobyl, near the Soviet city of Kiev, an accident at a nuclear plant led to the fallout of radioactivity over many European cities. In 1989, huge oil spills occurred off the coasts of Alaska and Morocco.

Americans have responded to the threat of environmental damage in positive ways. In addition to concern expressed at the community level, private habits also have been altered by a growing awareness of the environment and its fragility. Many families have moved toward a better use of resources in their daily lives. Homes have been better insulated to conserve energy. Automobiles and appliances now are rated on the basis of their efficiency. At the supermarket, many shoppers avoid foods that contain high levels of chemical preservatives or elaborate packaging that will only be thrown away once the food is eaten.

More choices than ever before are available to consumers seeking to live in balance with the natural world. The desire to save our environment from destruction must begin in the individual heart and mind and spread outward from there. Viewed from space, the earth may be a planet of rare beauty. But, as we have seen, the life on the surface of the earth is a delicate mesh. The best chance for the survival of our planet lies in an environmental awareness that touches everyone.

SECTION 2 REVIEW

Knowing Key Terms, People, and Places
1. Define: **a.** nonbiodegradable product **b.** acid rain **c.** greenhouse effect **d.** deforestation
2. Identify: **a.** Greenpeace **b.** Nature Conservancy **c.** Union of Concerned Scientists **d.** Chernobyl

Focus on Geography
3. Why was the nuclear accident at Chernobyl of concern to the whole world?

Reviewing Main Ideas
4. Explain some possible ways to reduce the greenhouse effect.
5. How does the destruction of rain forests in Brazil hurt the environment?

Critical Thinking
Synthesizing Information
6. Why is global waste disposal such a difficult problem to solve?

3 The World's Economy Has Become Global

As you read, look for answers to these questions:

◆ How does the global economy affect our everyday lives?
◆ How do trade deficits affect business?
◆ What led to "Black Monday" of 1987?

> **Key Terms:** global economy (defined on p. 746), rate of exchange (p. 747), trade deficit (p. 747)

Some years ago, in its annual report to its shareholders, ITT, International Telephone and Telegraph Company, declared, "[ITT] is constantly at work around the clock—in 67 nations on six continents . . . and quite literally from the bottom of the sea to the moon. . . ." What this company wrote 20 years ago is true of an even greater number of businesses today.

A Global Product Market Has Appeared

While we may not as yet be trading with the moon, we are becoming part of a **global economy,** or the worldwide development, distribution, and sale of goods. In the 1980s, Americans bought jeans from Taiwan, sweaters from New Zealand, and shirts and gifts from the People's Republic of China, to cite just a few examples. On our highways, Japanese and Korean cars could be seen more often than American makes.

That Japanese auto makers have caught up with and, in some cases, surpassed American automobile manufacturers is a well-known story. Indeed, in the manufacture of automobiles, the dividing line between foreign and domestic has become so fuzzy that there are few American cars made entirely in the United States. Some American cars are made abroad, and in turn, about half of the production of the Hyundai from South Korea is done in the United States.

United States consumption.   With about 6 percent of the world's population, the United States consumes one-third of the world's minerals annually. It needs 35 percent of the non-Communist world's silver and more than 30 percent of all lead. The United States must import nearly all of its chromium, cobalt, aluminum, nickel, platinum, manganese, and tin. Most of the these vital raw materials are found in the less developed countries of the world. While America has substantial oil reserves, it relies upon Middle Eastern oil for much of its needs. The price American citizens pay for gasoline for their cars or fuel oil for their homes is determined both by consumption here and the level of profit desired by the producers. One-third of the profits of American corporations come from their exports or from foreign investments. One out of every eight factory workers makes something for export. One-sixth of everything that is grown or made in America is sold abroad.

The stock market crash.   Just as the global markets for cars and televisions are tightly linked, so too are the international markets for stocks and bonds. Each stock market in the world watches closely what occurs in the other major markets. In the fall of 1987, when the American market suddenly collapsed following an enormous rise in value, stock markets in London and Tokyo felt the blow. A pattern of furious selling in these foreign markets prompted a dip in the value of stock on an international scale. New York Exchange stocks fell about 30 percent in value on October 19, 1987, or "Black Monday." Foreign markets registered somewhat smaller losses.

A Global Money Market Has Developed

Nations do more than sell each other goods, however. They also sell their currencies back and forth.

Buying and selling currency.   The world's leading financial centers are in London, New York, and Hong Kong. These cities are linked electronically to form a huge money market. One purpose of such a market is to exchange the currency, or money, of one country into that of another in order to make trade easier. (Speculation in currencies also may be undertaken for the sake of profit.) For example, when an American company buys computer chips from Japan, it must convert its dollars into Japanese currency, or yen. Americans visiting England have to change American dollars to British pounds to pay for travel expenses there.

Dollars are exchanged for pounds or yen in accordance with a **rate of exchange,** or the amount of one currency that can buy a certain amount of another currency. When the United States runs a **trade deficit,** that is, when America buys more goods from foreign nations than it sells, then foreign countries have a great many dollars. Since these countries do not need more dollars, they will pay less in their currency for American dollars.

The American dollar declines when there is a trade deficit in the United States—a situation that can be both good and bad for the United States. On the positive side, it encourages foreign industries to buy from American manufacturers. When there is a trade deficit, an American tractor, for example, is cheaper abroad than it used to be. This enables the United States export industry to prosper and provide more jobs. On the negative side, a drop in the price of the dollar makes imported goods more costly for American buyers, and opens our nation to possible control and partial ownership by foreign investors.

International loans. The International Bank for Reconstruction and Development, known as the World Bank, makes loans to build up the economies of struggling nations. Money is lent for such things as building dams or generating electric power. Loans for education, roads, and hospitals also are made to poor countries. The World Bank must design international guidelines in the best interests of all people for the sake of global prosperity and peace and, at the same time, not interfere with the internal affairs of other countries.

▲ **Illustrating History** *The New York Stock Exchange, shown above, is electronically linked to other stock markets around the world.*

Various Organizations Help World Trade

The International Monetary Fund, IMF, was established to help world trade. It has 140 members, mostly from the non-Communist countries, but it also includes Romania, Yugoslavia, Kampuchea, Laos, and Vietnam. The IMF makes loans for short periods to countries that have little or no foreign exchange, and looks out for any signs of unfair or dishonest trading practices. The IMF has a form of currency of its own called *special drawing rights,* or SDRs, which enables countries to free themselves from over-reliance on gold, dollars, or any other international currency. SDRs may be viewed as a form of global money.

International trade is dominated by industrial giants, including the United States, the Soviet Union, and Japan. By 1992, the international trade market will also include the European Community, which was discussed in Chapter 29. In Eastern Europe, the Council for Mutual Economic Assistance, or COMECON, also seeks to become an important international trading partner.

747

Bill Haley Goes to Japan

It is a bright Sunday in May in Tokyo, Japan. The year is 1982. Soon, the first bunch of teenagers arrives, each member of the group dressed in identical 50s-style clothing. A boy sets down a huge tape recorder. The music of Bill Haley and the Comets, a popular American rock group in the 1950s, comes blaring out. The young people begin to dance. Another song comes on and then another. Before long, the street is jammed with over 1,000 twisting forms.

This was how Calvin Trillin, an American writer, described a Sunday afternoon in Tokyo in his book *Third Helpings*. The scene points out a visible blending of two cultures—Japanese and Western. While Japanese teenagers value the time-honored traditions of their parents and grandparents, they also love the look and sound of Western things—like rock 'n roll.

1. Besides music, what other links between Japanese and Western cultures might you expect to see in Japan?
2. What links to other cultures exist in your community today?

More People Seek Work Abroad

Just as huge corporations have crossed national boundaries, so have many people moved from one country to another in search of jobs. During the postwar years, the economically healthier European nations, such as Germany, France, and Switzerland, have had a shortage of unskilled workers. People have been needed to fill lower-paying jobs, such as seasonal harvesting, that their own citizens will not, or cannot, do.

People from the poorer countries, such as Greece, Turkey, and Yugoslavia, have gone to the developed countries in Europe as *"guest workers."* They are called guest workers because they are not expected to settle permanently in the country, and usually they are not allowed to bring their families with them. Guest workers improve the economies of their homelands by sending back money to their families.

Knowing Key Terms, People, and Places
1. Define: **a.** global economy **b.** rate of exchange **c.** trade deficit
2. Identify: **a.** IMF **b.** COMECON **c.** World Bank **d.** guest workers

Reviewing Main Ideas
3. What does a trade deficit mean for United States business?
4. Explain the functions of the IMF and the World Bank.
5. How do guest workers improve the economies of their homelands?

Critical Thinking
Making Comparisons
6. Explain why the fall of the American stock market in 1987 had consequences around the world.

Predicting Consequences

Though no one can be absolutely certain about what will happen in the future, social scientists attempt to predict the consequences of events and trends. Such projections help prepare for future events.

Practice your skill of predicting consequences by following the steps below.

1. **Have a clear and accurate understanding of the event or trend.** Your predictions can only be as valid as the information upon which you based them. Read Passage 1 and answer the following questions: (a) In what year will this United Nations prediction occur? (b) How many large urban areas will be found in developing nations at that time?
2. **Predict and evaluate all possible consequences.** Study the facts and then ask yourself, "What consequences can occur as a result of the event?" Evaluate each projection by asking, "How likely is it that any of these consequences will occur?" Answer the following questions: (a) Read Passage 2 and list three possible consequences. (b) Rank your projections from 1 to 3, with 1 being the most likely projection to occur.
3. **Use your knowledge of history when predicting consequences.** The pattern of events in the past can be helpful, particularly when strong parallels exist. Review Passage 1 and answer the following questions: (a) List three results of nineteenth-century urbanization. (b) Are similar events likely to occur with current urbanization? Explain.
4. **Predict consequences for different groups involved.** Read Passage 3 and answer the following questions: Predict at least one consequence for (a) the host nation, (b) the country of origin, and (c) the families of the guest workers.

Passage 1

In the nineteenth century, rapid growth took place in the cities of those nations undergoing industrialization. These urban areas did not immediately respond to this growth. Housing and sanitation facilities were inadequate, local transportation systems were poor, and social services—such as schools and private charities—were unable to meet the demands placed upon them.

Another period of rapid urban development is underway. The United Nations predicts that by 2025, the world will have 93 urban areas with populations of 5 million or more. All but 13 will be in developing nations.

Passage 2

Because of rapid technological change, weapons produced by the United States and the Soviet Union tend to become outdated quickly. However, while such conventional weapons lose their usefulness for the two superpowers, other nations of the world still want them. Today, the two superpowers are major arms sellers, though neither is willing, at this point, to sell nuclear weapons to other nations.

Passage 3

One occurrence of the modern world is the legal and illegal movement of millions of workers across national borders. Thus, you find Italians working in Germany and Mexicans working in the United States. The most common pattern is for migrants to remain in the host country for a short period of time and then return to their country of origin. These workers usually labor for lower wages than are earned by most citizens of the host nation.

REVIEW

Section Summaries

Section 1 Population Growth Has Stretched Resources The world's population has grown rapidly, from about half a billion people in 1630 to about 5 billion today. Much of this increase has occurred in the world's less developed areas. One reason for the rapid population growth has come from the great advances in medicine. Breakthroughs have decreased infant mortality, cured diseases, and extended life expectancy. Agricultural research has provided another spur to population growth, developing new ways to feed the world's people. Many problems accompany rapid population growth, however. These include overcrowding, poverty, homelessness, and famine.

Section 2 The Environment of Planet Earth Is Fragile The advance of civilization brings more and more assaults on our fragile environment. Modern society produces too much garbage, for example, and needs new methods of waste disposal. Acid rain, another problem of modern life, is a danger to public health. In addition, the burning of fossil fuels is creating a warming trend called the greenhouse effect, which can disrupt many life forms. Similarly, deforestation is decreasing one source of oxygen and robbing animals of their homes. Numerous groups have formed to protect the environment, and many individuals are now making personal choices that show concern for the environment.

Section 3 The World's Economy Has Become Global Today, American consumers buy products from all over the world. U.S. industries depend on imports for many important raw materials. There is even a global market for money. Financial centers exchange the currency of many nations to make international trade easier. A number of worldwide organizations have arisen to help world trade. Even the job market is now international, as "guest workers" from poorer nations come to economically healthier nations.

Key Facts

1. Use each vocabulary word in a sentence.
   - **a.** population growth
   - **b.** population base
   - **c.** genetic engineering
   - **d.** squatters
   - **e.** host countries
   - **f.** nonbiodegradable products
   - **g.** acid rain
   - **h.** greenhouse effect
   - **i.** deforestation
   - **j.** global economy
   - **k.** rate of exchange
   - **l.** trade deficit
2. Identify and briefly explain the importance of the following names, places, or events.
   - **a.** Jonas Salk
   - **b.** Mexico City
   - **c.** the Sudan
   - **d.** World Food Conference
   - **e.** the rain forest
   - **f.** the central Alaskan oil fields
   - **g.** Black Monday of 1987

Main Ideas

1. List some ways in which medical breakthroughs and advances in agriculture have contributed to rapid population growth.
2. List five organizations that presently fight world hunger.
3. List and briefly explain three major environmental problems.
4. List five important minerals that the United States must import.
5. Why do nations sell currency back and forth?
6. How does the International Monetary Fund help world trade?

Developing Skill in Reading History

Study the words or names in each set below. Then, based on what you have learned in this chapter, write a sentence for each set describing what its members have in common.
1. sea otters, gray whales, bald eagles
2. Greenpeace, Nature Conservancy, Union of Concerned Scientists
3. Three Mile Island, Bhopal, Chernobyl
4. Tokyo, Mexico City, São Paulo
5. OXFAM, CARE, USA for Africa

Using Social Studies Skills

1. **Understanding Economic Concepts** Review the discussion of a trade deficit on page 747. Then, draw a diagram or a cartoon that helps explain what a trade deficit is or what its effects may be.
2. **Reading a Diagram** The diagram below shows how the "greenhouse effect" works to trap heat from the sun and thus warm the earth. Study the diagram. Then, decide whether each statement below is true or false.
   a. Infrared rays are part of sunlight.
   b. Clouds and pollution can trap infrared rays.
   c. Sunlight does not reflect off the earth's surface.
   d. The greenhouse effect was just as strong in the days before factories and cars.

Critical Thinking

1. **Translating Information from One Medium to Another** Use the information on pages 735 and 736 to create a two-column chart, called "World Population Growth: 1630 to 2025." The left-hand column should be headed Year, and the right-hand Population (actual or projected). Use the years 1630, 1830, the current year, 2000, and 2025.
2. **Identifying Assumptions** Explain the following quote from the French magazine *L'Express:* "We know that, sooner or later, we will need global management of wastes that grow steadily in volume."
3. **Predicting Consequences** Experts predict that some cities will have populations ranging from 20 million to 30 million by the year 2000. List at least five ways that life might become different in such populous and overcrowded cities.

Focus on Writing

Writing a Descriptive Paragraph

Look through magazines to find one or more pictures of any endangered feature of nature, such as the Amazon rain forest, the central Alaskan wilderness, a bald eagle, or a gray whale. *(Readers Guide to Periodical Literature* may be helpful.) Then, write a paragraph describing the great beauty of your subject. Be sure that your topic sentence presents one dominant impression. Include as many specific details as possible, and use vivid language and sensory images.

The Greenhouse Effect

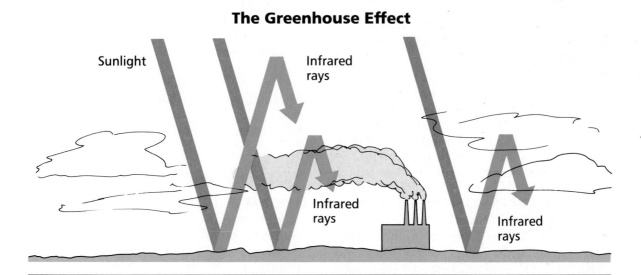

Sunlight

Infrared rays

Infrared rays

Infrared rays

Geography in History

Acid Rain—A Problem in Geography

In the 1960s, scientists in Sweden realized that many of the high-altitude lakes in their country were so acidic that their fish were dying in the bitter waters. The whole system of life in the lakes had been disturbed. In the 1970s, similar effects were noticed in North America. By studying the soils and wind and weather patterns, scientists soon had a good idea where the acid was coming from (see page 742).

Finding the Culprit

Coal, oil, and gas give off pollutants, or unwanted chemicals, when they are burned. Factory smokestacks spew tons of pollutants into the atmosphere every day. Exhaust from cars also pollutes the air. These pollutants combine with rain in clouds to turn ordinary water into a substance that is sometimes powerfully acidic. It is called acid rain.

Researchers also found that not all the places that lay in the path of acid rain were affected by it. The dying lakes tended to be those at high altitudes where pollutants were thickest. The soil around these lakes is thin and rocky. Instead of being absorbed by the soil, acids run quickly through it and into the lakes.

By the early 1980s, about one-fifth of the 100,000 lakes in Sweden were dead or dying. In 1986, the Environmental Protection Agency in the United States estimated that over 2,400 lakes in 14 eastern states also had harmful levels of acids. Whole forests were dying. Stone buildings were crumbling. Iron and steel bridges were being eaten away by the acid.

An International Problem

If the source of the problem lay in one country, a solution might have been simple. But, in Sweden, for example, about three-quarters of the pollutants were coming from other countries in Europe. Wind currents blow across the heaviest industrial regions of Europe directly into Sweden and Norway.

Pollutants were crossing borders in North America, too. In Canada and the United States, over 50 million tons of pollutants are released into the atmosphere every year, nearly as much as in all of Europe.

Weather and wind concentrate most of these pollutants in what is called a "core area" of acid rain from Illinois eastward and from Kentucky and Virginia northward into southern Quebec. In that region, industry is heavy, and there are high concentrations of car exhaust.

As in Sweden, mountain lakes are affected the most. The lakes in the Adirondack Mountains of New York, for example, have been severely damaged by acid rain probably caused by pollutants from the Ohio River valley.

Conflicting Priorities

The acid rain poses this problem: What is more important, the industry that generates acid-rain pollution or the lakes that are destroyed by it? Much of the pollution in the eastern United States is made by electric power plants. Changing those plants to reduce emissions could cost up to 5 billion dollars. For consumers, the cost of electricity would rise very dramatically. Utility companies argue that it would be cheaper to try to reverse the effects of acid rain. People in Sweden have been dumping lime into lakes as a way to reduce acidity. Scientists are experimenting with breeding fish to tolerate acidity. Environmentalists argue that these are short-term cures only and that choosing the quick fix frequently risks the health of the entire planet.

Experts estimate that if international action were taken, emissions could be reduced enough by the year 2000 to halt the harmful effects of acid rain. But will people pay the costs? And, if one country acts, will its polluting neighbor act as well?

Focus on Geography

1. **Place** What makes a place vulnerable to acid rain?

2. **Location** Define the boundaries and routes of the core area of acid rain in North America.

3. **Interaction** Besides killing wildlife in lakes, what effects does acid rain have?

Critical Thinking

Predicting Consequences

4. Do you think it would help solve the problem of acid rain if one country in Europe cut its use of automobiles by 50 percent? Why or why not?

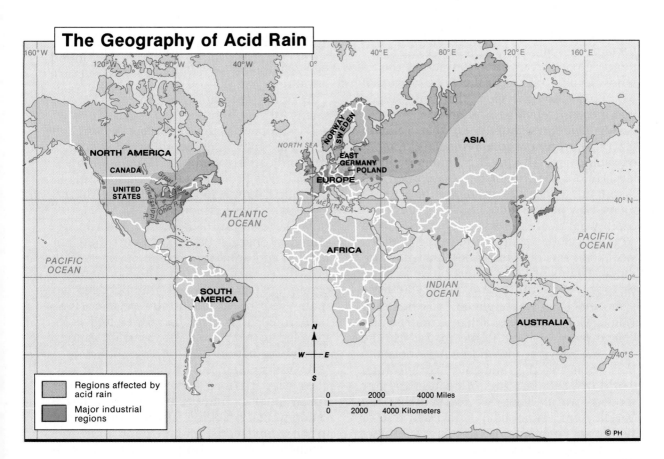

The Geography of Acid Rain

Regions affected by acid rain

Major industrial regions

As a conclusion, it would be nice to be able to write the words "THE END" and put the book down with a sense of having finished the story. Although this story has been brought up to the present, you know that the "end" of the human story is a long way off. There is a great deal of historical detective work still to be done.

Do you remember Colin Fletcher in the Prologue, who used bits of evidence to reconstruct the life of a drifter? Like Colin Fletcher, we used bits of evidence to reconstruct the lives of early people, and we watched as they crossed that invisible line that separated the prehistoric from the historic eras. Using bits of evidence, we reviewed the contributions of the Fertile Crescent to the growth of civilization. We saw how certain bits of evidence directed our attention across the island stepping stones of the Aegean so that we could study the glory that was Greece and the grandeur that was Rome.

> "Although this story has been brought up to the present . . . the 'end' of the human story is a long way off."

Our evidence showed us that religion played a prominent role in the development of civilization. The great religions of Judaism, Hinduism, Buddhism, Christianity, and Islam influenced, as they continue to do today, how people thought, whom they honored, what institutions they cherished, and what moral ideals they held. In the Western world, we saw how the Judeo-Christian tradition established the values of work, honesty, peace, tolerance, and family stability.

As detectives, we sought clues to the fall of Rome. The evidence enabled us to cross the bridge from ancient Rome to the Middle Ages. We saw that the Middle Ages not only had roots in the ancient Greco-Roman world but also laid the foundation for our modern world. Thus, we learned that the Middle Ages were not dark ages but a time of significant political, economic, scientific, and artistic advancement.

Brave mariners during the Age of Discovery pieced together the evidence and concluded that the world was not flat but round and that one could reach the East by sailing west. In this quest, fearless European navigators circumnavigated the globe, discovered North and South America, rounded the Cape of Africa, and finally reached the Eastern worlds of India and Asia.

The discovery of new worlds inspired people to explore their own creative talents, so that by the mid-fifteenth century, historians spoke about a "rebirth" or Renaissance. Actually, the evidence demonstrated that creativity had never really died, but that during the Renaissance, there was simply a new burst of creative energy in art and literature. The development of vernacular, or national, languages allowed more people to enjoy great works of literature.

At about the same time as the Renaissance, the role of religion in the lives of men and women became apparent when evidence mounted that incompetence and corruption had scarred the Roman Catholic church. The Protestant Reformation and the Catholic Counter-Reformation were the responses to these discoveries.

As the medieval system of feudalism declined, monarchs began to assert their authority and establish national states. The growth of nations strengthened national economies and reduced the burdens on many—but by no means all—people. However, intense rivalries for power and colonies led to nearly chronic warfare among developing nations.

As we studied the evidence, it became clear that in Asia, Africa, and North and South America, important centers of civilization were developing. The American Revolution established a republican form of government for the United States. That a government could exist without an absolute monarch was a lesson not lost on other nations of the world. The French followed the American example in a revolution that overthrew their monarchy and set the pace for other revolutions in Europe.

Perhaps the most important revolution of all was the change from hand to machine labor, from work at home to work in factories, from the importance of the farm to the importance of cities. These developments we called the Industrial Revolution. In Western Europe and America, political democracies generally prevailed. At the same time, market economies were established in which the demands of consumers determined what products manufacturers made and how much they charged for them.

Between two world wars, Communist, Fascist, and Nazi dictatorships were established. World War II was fought to end the Nazi and Fascist tyrannies and to halt Japanese aggression in Asia. Before the war was over, the United States had dropped an atomic bomb on Hiroshima, Japan. This event made it clear that the world had become a vastly different place.

As the twentieth century progressed, people sought to conquer new frontiers. Satellites were rocketed into orbit, human beings were landed on the moon, and space probes explored the reaches of our solar system. All of these events demonstrated the emerging technologies that bound the world together so tightly that, as the former American Secretary of State Henry Kissinger said, "a short circuit could fry us all."

As the 1990s begin, the signs for a more peaceful world are more hopeful than they have ever been. However, there is still plenty of room for historical detective work, as the following unanswered questions suggest:

· The earth's environment remains fragile and requires the cooperation of all nations if problems of global pollution are to be resolved. Will the nations of the world be able to work together on this issue?

· Does the historical evidence suggest that today's general global peace will be temporary or permanent?

· While a period of better East-West relationships may be at hand, what is the evidence that this new openness will be long-lasting?

· In 1992, a conference on human rights will be held in Moscow. Will the Soviet Union by then have made sufficient progress in human rights to deserve the privilege of hosting such a conference?

· Today it is clear that in every corner of the world, people yearn for democracy. Can they expect to achieve it? Once achieved, as in some parts of Latin America, will the new democracies survive?

· In a world where food is plentiful, no person should starve. Does the evidence suggest that civilized people have the will to solve this problem?

Such is the unfinished detective work of world history. What "bits of evidence" have we left for future historians?

Gerald Leinwand
West Hyannisport,
Massachusetts

755

UNIT 6: An Age of Revolution
(1600–1848)

On a hot and humid day in June, 1776, Richard Henry Lee, the delegate from Virginia to the Continental Congress, introduced the following resolution, ". . . that these united colonies are, and of right ought to be, free and independent states." A few days later, the congress voted to name a committee to write a declaration of independence. On July 4, the congress adopted a draft written by Thomas Jefferson. The document was signed by most of the delegates on July 8, and the American nation was born.

The new American nation was a lesson to the world. It showed that a revolution for freedom was possible and that there are times when a revolution is necessary. It showed that a government could be formed without a monarch. These lessons were not lost on the people and nations of the world.

▼ **Illustrating History**   *In the engraving below, the Declaration of Independence is read to an enthusiastic Philadelphia crowd in 1776.*

18 A Revolution in Government and Thought

As you read, look for answers to these questions:

◆ How did the power of the monarchy become limited in England?
◆ How was the American Revolution influenced by the ideas of the Age of Reason?

In both England and America, revolutionary leaders created new forms of government. Their struggles contributed significantly to the rights and freedoms we associate with democracy today.

England Changed the Monarchy

During the 1600s, the kings of England and the English Parliament engaged in a battle over political control. The kings claimed to rule by divine right and to have absolute power. The Parliament sought a greater voice in government for themselves and for the people they represented.

When King Charles I abolished Parliament by force, a civil war broke out. A group led by Oliver Cromwell defeated the king and his supporters. The victorious Cromwell set up a dictatorship, but when he died, Parliament reinstalled the monarchy to prevent a new civil war. Parliament once again became unhappy with the monarchy, and it invited William and Mary of the Netherlands to become the new king and queen. Their peaceful arrival is often referred to as the Glorious Revolution. It established a **limited monarchy** in England—a system that restricted the powers of the king—and was a giant step toward democracy.

The Age of Reason Encouraged Change

The Age of Reason, or the Enlightenment, was a movement that began in the late 1600s and lasted 100 years. During this period, scientists, writers, philosophers, and artists sought to free people from ignorance. Their ideas prepared the way for future changes in government and society. Scientists of the Enlightenment used the **scientific method**—drawing conclusions from observations—to gain new knowledge. Their findings caused people to question traditional ways of viewing the world. Writers also made new observations of human behavior, using new forms of literature such as the novel.

The American Revolution Brought Independence and Democracy

The American Revolution had its roots in the Glorious Revolution and the ideas of the Age of Reason. Most American colonists thought of themselves as English, having the same rights as those living in England. Revolutionary leaders in the colonies became angered by laws such as those that raised taxes and took away American land rights. They declared independence in 1776.

Americans expressed the political, social, and economic ideals of the Age of Reason in the Declaration of Independence, the Constitution, and the Bill of Rights. The Declaration of Independence restated the philosopher John Locke's idea that every person has the right to life, liberty, and pursuit of happiness. The Constitution applied Locke and Baron de Montesquieu's concept of checks and balances to keep political leaders from gaining too much power. The Bill of Rights guaranteed the rights of individuals, which Locke, Thomas Jefferson, and others had written about.

REVIEW

1. Define: limited monarchy, scientific method
2. Identify: Oliver Cromwell, Glorious Revolution, John Locke
3. What was the Age of Reason?
4. What were two causes of the American Revolution?

19 The French Revolution and Napoleon

As you read, look for answers to these questions:

◆ How did the French Revolution change the government of France?
◆ How did Napoleon change France and Europe?

France was ripe for revolution in 1789. Its undemocratic government had changed little since feudal times. The rich paid few taxes, the growing middle class—the **bourgeoisie** (BOOR zhwah ZEE)—had few rights, and the king maintained absolute power over the lives of his subjects.

Poor Economic Conditions Began the French Revolution

The French monarchy was bankrupt in 1789. The king, desperate for money, needed the help of the nobles, bourgeoisie, farmers, and workers. The bourgeoisie and the working class, seeing a chance to take control, declared themselves the National Assembly of France and invited the nobles and king to join them. At first, the nobles and king rejected the offer. But when angry mobs attacked the fortress prison of the *Bastille,* the nobles agreed to make some democratic reforms. The National Assembly then set up a constitutional monarchy and passed the Declaration of the Rights of Man, which declared that all citizens were equal before the law.

The Declaration of the Rights of Man, however, extended rights only to middle-class men. Peasants and workers were disappointed that the new government failed to provide them with any benefits. War provided an excuse to remove the king and to form a republic. In time, the king was put to death. The queen, Marie Antoinette, was put to death not long after, during the Reign of Terror. Robespierre led the Terror, during which people who opposed the violence of the revolution were beheaded. The Reign of Terror gradually ended, and a new government was set up.

The people of France wanted a leader who could solve the nation's problems and bring peace. Napoleon became the leader they were seeking.

Napoleon Changed the Goals of the French Revolution

Napoleon Bonaparte became dictator of France through a **coup d'état** (KOO day TAH)—a sudden overthrow of a government by a small group of people. By 1802, Napoleon had brought victory to France and peace to Europe. He brought about changes that helped solve the economic problems. He organized the Bank of France and centralized power through the Napoleonic code of law. The French people adored him. Napoleon asked the people to elect him emperor by **plebiscite** (PLEHB uh SYT), a vote on a political issue.

Armed now with even greater power, Napoleon conquered Austria, Prussia, and Spain, although he failed to defeat Britain. Napoleon then made a mistake; he tried to invade Russia. The long march to Moscow and the cold Russian winter wiped out his army. By the time he returned to France, European nations had united against him, and he was eventually defeated by English forces at the Battle of Waterloo. He was exiled to St. Helena, a British island in the South Atlantic, where he died.

REVIEW

1. Define: bourgeoisie, coup d'état, plebiscite
2. Identify: National Assembly, Reign of Terror, Napoleon
3. Why did the bourgeoisie and workers form the National Assembly?
4. What reforms did Napoleon bring to France?

20 The Congress of Vienna and Its Aftermath

As you read, look for answers to these questions:

◆ How did the Congress of Vienna change Europe after Napoleon?
◆ Why did revolutions continue to take place in Latin America and Europe?

After Napoleon, the leaders of the victorious European powers met at the Congress of Vienna. The delegates decided to bring back the monarchs that had lost their thrones to Napoleon.

New Political Patterns Emerged After Napoleon

Throughout the 1800s, two political philosophies—liberalism and conservatism—influenced events. The philosophy of **liberalism** supports the ideas of individual freedom, political change, and social reform. **Conservatism,** on the other hand, is a philosophy that favors the traditional political and social order and resists change.

▼ **Illustrating History** *The 1834 painting Allegory of Independence (below) draws a contrast between monarchy and freedom.*

The delegates to the Congress of Vienna in 1814 were conservatives. They paid little attention to the wishes of people and pledged to use their armies to put down revolution. The delegates created a plan that maintained peace in Europe for over 100 years, but they did so at the cost of many political freedoms.

Latin American Nations Gained Independence

For over 300 years, Spain and Portugal ruled Latin America. Both countries established a caste system that denied political or economic power to people born in the colonies. Furthermore, Spain bound Indians to the land, like the serfs in medieval Europe. This system of labor was called **encomienda.**

While Spain and Portugal were fighting for their own independence from the forces of Napoleon, Latin Americans fought to gain their independence. Great revolutionary leaders, such as Francisco Miranda (mee RAHN duh), Simon Bolivar (baw LEE vahr), and José de Sucré (day SOO kray), freed most of Latin America by 1825.

Revolutions Continued in Europe

For over 30 years, political stability was maintained in Europe by the conservative policies of the Congress of Vienna. But liberalism was not dead. In 1848, revolutions sprang up in many European countries. These revolutions led to a new generation of leaders and some democratic reforms.

REVIEW

1. Define: liberalism, conservatism, encomienda
2. Identify: Congress of Vienna, Simon Bolivar
3. How did the Congress of Vienna "turn back the clock" of European history?
4. What events in Spain and Portugal helped Latin America achieve independence?

Knowing Key Terms, People, and Places

Match each term with its definition.

1. limited monarchy
2. scientific method
3. bourgeoisie
4. coup d'état
5. plebiscite
6. liberalism
7. conservatism
8. encomienda
   a. drawing conclusions through observation
   b. a sudden overthrow of a government by a small group of people
   c. a vote by the people on a political issue
   d. a system that restricts the power of the king
   e. philosophy that favors the current social and political order
   f. the middle class
   g. supports ideas of individual freedom and political reform
   h. a system of labor that bound Indians to the land like serfs
9. Identify: Glorious Revolution, American Revolution, National Assembly, Reign of Terror, Napoleon, Francisco Miranda

Focus on Geography

10. How did the location of the American colonies contribute to their independence?
11. How did geography play a part in Napoleon's defeat in Russia?

Reviewing Main Ideas

12. What did the English Parliament do when Oliver Cromwell died?
13. What is another name for the Enlightenment?
14. What American documents have ideas based on ideas of the Enlightenment?
15. How did Napoleon gain control of France?
16. What were the purposes of the Congress of Vienna? How successful was the Congress in accomplishing its goals?
17. Describe the social structure in Latin America before independence.

Critical Thinking

18. **Drawing Conclusions** Why do you think the French Revolution led to a Reign of Terror?
19. **Recognizing Ideologies** What are two basic differences between the philosophies of liberalism and conservatism?

◀ **Illustrating History** *In this painting, a patriotic women's club meets during the French Revolution.*

UNIT 7: The Dominance of Europe

(1700–1914)

When railroads began to replace wagons and river traffic as the main form of transportation during the 1850s, railroad engineers found that iron rails wore out quickly. They knew that steel rails would last much longer, but it was too expensive to produce steel in the quantities needed.

Scientists and engineers throughout the world experimented with inexpensive ways to produce steel. Henry Bessemer, an Englishman, and William Kelly, an American, independently developed a cheap steel-making process. They found that blasting air over molten iron purified the iron and changed it into steel. Molten iron, from a blast furnace, was poured into a huge pear-shaped container called a converter. Air was then blown into the bottom of this container. The oxygen in the air combined with the impurities in the iron, causing it to separate into molten slag and steel. The molten steel then was cast into rails to be used throughout the world. Transportation then entered an age of rapid growth, development, and major change that has continued to the present day.

Illustrating History ▶
Railways like the Liverpool and Manchester Railway, at right, made transporting goods much faster.

21 Nationalism: New European Nations Are Born

As you read, look for answers to these questions:

◆ How did nationalism help to unify Italy and Germany?
◆ How did nationalism divide the Austrian and Ottoman Empires?

Nationalism refers to the desire of people with common interests, background, and history to become a nation. Sometimes nationalism unites countries, while at other times it shatters nations that have been joined together for many centuries.

Italy and Germany Unify

In the late 1850s, Camillo di Cavour, the prime minister of the Italian state of Sardinia, succeeded in unifying the northern Italian states. Shortly thereafter, Giuseppe Garibaldi conquered the kingdom of the Two Sicilies (southern Italy and the island of Sicily) and urged its people to become part of a unified Italian kingdom. Even after unification in 1861, many Italian-speaking areas were not united with the central government. Italians tried to make their government **annex,** or add, these regions to Italy.

At the Congress of Vienna, Germany was divided into 39 independent states. The first attempt to unify the country was an agreement for free trade among the German states, including Prussia. The second step toward union was orchestrated by Otto von Bismarck, the Prussian chief minister. The Second German Empire unified all the German states with the exception of Austria.

Austrian and Ottoman Empires Wanted Independence

Austria was made up of many **nationalities** —groups of people who share common history, customs, beliefs, and language but who do not necessarily have a country of their own. The Austrian Empire ruled over groups of Germans, Hungarians, Italians, Russians, Poles, Czechs, Croats, and Slovenes. Each of these groups wanted to govern themselves.

The Ottoman Empire was centered in Turkey and extended to the Middle East and eastern Europe. Russia tried to destroy the Ottoman Empire in the 1800s, but other European countries prevented Russia from breaking the empire up. For example, during the Crimean War, which lasted from 1853 to 1856, Great Britain saved the Ottoman Empire. Even though European countries tried to maintain the Ottoman Empire, some groups within the empire gained independence, setting up the countries of Romania, Montenegro, and Serbia.

Nationalism Spread Through the British Empire

Nationalism also played a part in gaining some independence for people living in the British Empire. The British North American Act united all the provinces of Canada and gave its people limited self-government, except in foreign affairs. Both Australia and New Zealand gained their independence in a similar way 40 years later. Canada, Australia, and New Zealand are dominions; that is, they are completely self-governing nations within the British Commonwealth. After a bitter civil war, the United States reaffirmed a system of government known as **federalism,** in which power is divided among national and state governments.

REVIEW

1. Define: annex, nationality, federalism
2. Identify: Camillo di Cavour, Otto von Bismarck, Ottoman Empire
3. How was Italy unified?
4. How did European nations help keep the Ottoman Empire intact?
5. How did Canada win self-government?

22 People, Money, and Machines

As you read, look for answers to these questions:

◆ What was the Industrial Revolution?
◆ What reform movements resulted from the Industrial Revolution?

Until the mid-1700s, manufacturing of products such as cloth was done in homes. This process was known as the **domestic system.** But this system could not keep pace with the demand for goods. A **factory system** developed in which goods were made on machines in large buildings.

The Industrial Revolution, which began in England, brought many changes. Transportation networks were built and cities grew. An educated middle class developed. The **corporation,** a form of business in which people have government permission to sell stock, became common. Many people began to invest in businesses.

Groups Tried to Correct Labor Problems

Most middle-class people believed in laissez faire economics—the point of view that the marketplace should regulate the economy. They thought the economy would prevent poverty from being very deep or long lasting, and that government interference would limit the ability of the marketplace to correct abuses.

The greatest evils of the Industrial Revolution developed in the factory system. Many children and women had to work fourteen to sixteen hours a day under life-threatening conditions. Wages for factory workers were low; slums developed, and crime increased in cities.

Some groups felt government intervention was necessary. Believers in utopian **socialism** hoped to establish a perfect society in which poverty would not exist. Followers of **communism** believed that the workers should control industrial production.

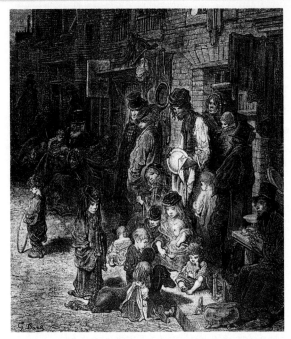

▲ **Illustrating History** *This painting of a London street scene depicts the wretched poverty of the masses in the 1800s.*

Their leader, Karl Marx, believed that a class struggle between workers and owners was inevitable and that the workers would win. Followers of **anarchism** sought the overthrow of all government.

Science, literature, music, and art made great advances. One major development in science was Charles Darwin's theory of **evolution,** which explained the process of change from simple forms of life to more complex ones. The forms that are best fitted to their environment survive.

REVIEW

1. Define: domestic system, factory system, corporation, socialism, communism, anarchism, evolution
2. Identify: Industrial Revolution, Karl Marx
3. How did the manufacture of goods change after about 1750?
4. How did the Industrial Revolution change society?

23 The Age of Democratic Reform

As you read, look for answers to these questions:

◆ How did democracy expand in England during the 1800s?
◆ How did Britain and France change their parliamentary systems?

Democracy expanded in England and France in the late 1800s. Some people say that democracy in England developed by evolution, while in France it developed by revolution. This is a convenient way to remember how democracy was achieved in those countries.

Democratic Reforms Occurred in Great Britain

Following the Glorious Revolution of 1688, more progress had to be made before England could be considered a democratic nation. As late as 1832, few men could vote. The House of Lords, in which membership was determined by birth, was far more powerful than the House of Commons, whose members were elected. The House of Lords could stop attempts at reform. People living in the new cities that sprung up during the Industrial Revolution often had no representation in Parliament.

Between 1832 and 1928, Britain became more democratic. Workers' groups and reformers forced Parliament to pass a number of reform measures that gave more men **suffrage**—the right to vote. Later, in 1925, Parliament extended suffrage to women. Legislation also gave the House of Commons more power than the House of Lords.

New Parliamentary Forms Developed in England and France

Great Britain's constitution is made up of a series of great documents rather than a single one. The prime minister of Great Britain gains power by being head of the party that has a majority in the House of Commons. The prime minister serves as long as he or she retains a majority. Elections must be held every five years, or sooner if the party in power calls for them. In England, the prime minister is both a law enforcer and a lawmaker because separation of powers does not exist.

In France, Napoleon III, the nephew of Napoleon Bonaparte, became emperor in 1852. He was overthrown in 1871 and the Third French Republic was set up. This parliamentary government ruled France between 1871 and 1940.

Living Conditions Improved

Among the working class of the city, life was hard. The city was crowded and many people shared apartments with little heat and little privacy. Working hours were long. However, life in the nineteenth century was filled with hope. Democratic reforms and industrial growth were gradually making everyday life more comfortable and enjoyable for most people.

Many improvements took place. The death rate declined as health care and sanitation improved. **Immunization,** or the process of building up resistance to disease, and **pasteurization,** or the method of killing bacteria in foods, especially milk, were both discovered at this time. People convicted of crime were treated more humanely. Education was valued and most children attended school.

REVIEW

1. Define: suffrage, immunization, pastuerization
2. Identify: House of Commons, Napoleon III
3. Which house in the British Parliament holds the most power today?
4. What form of government replaced Napoleon III in France?
5. How did living conditions improve in the nineteenth century?

24 Imperialism in Africa and Asia

As you read, look for answers to these questions:

◆ How did Europeans gain control of Africa?

◆ How did Europeans gain control of Asia?

Throughout history, strong nations have dominated weaker nations. This process is called **imperialism.** Europeans used their colonies as sources of cheap raw materials and places to sell products of the Industrial Revolution.

Europeans Carved Up Africa

Britain, France, Belgium, Italy, and Germany each scrambled for colonies in Africa. By World War I, nearly all of Africa was occupied by European powers. Britain possessed South Africa and the Suez Canal in Egypt. Belgium controlled the Congo. Germany and Italy were among the last to acquire colonies in Africa.

Imperialism brought some benefits to Africa, but it also brought many evils. The European powers drained the natural wealth of their colonies without compensating the native inhabitants. The worst evil of imperialism in Africa, however, was slavery and slave trading. African men, women, and children were snatched from their homes and sold as slaves in Europe and the New World. Following World War II, all the African colonies finally freed themselves from foreign rule.

The British Secured India

A trading company, the British East India Company, ruled India for Britain for more than 100 years. After the British army put down an Indian uprising called the Sepoy Mutiny in 1857, the British Parliament decided to rule India directly rather than through the trading company. The British sent many able and devoted soldiers and statesmen to India; however, the people of India were not content under British rule.

The British helped India in many ways. They built schools and hospitals, constructed a transportation system, and improved farming methods. But the British also hurt Indians by forcing them to live in poverty and denying them freedoms. During British rule, many famines occurred as Indians were directed away from farming.

Europeans Dominated China and Japan

The Chinese rulers resisted European imperialism for a long time. But Britain forced them to open trade by defeating China in wars known as the Opium Wars. Europeans then began to stake their claims over parts of China and to demand ports and special trading privileges.

The United States did not want to see China divided up by the Europeans. The U.S. introduced the *open door policy* in China, which sought to open China to trade with all nations.

The principle of **extraterritoriality** also caused hard feelings between the Chinese and the Europeans. This principle permitted Europeans to break Chinese laws and be tried by the courts of their home lands.

In Japan, Commodore Perry of the United States opened Japan to American and European trade by a threat of military force. Japan had been a country in which changes were discouraged, but it soon began to copy the West. The old system, in which a powerful feudal noble ruled and the emperor was only a figurehead, was overthrown. The emperor became the real ruler.

REVIEW

1. Define: imperialism, extraterritoriality
2. Identify: British East India Company, open door policy, Commodore Perry
3. Why were colonies useful for Europeans?
4. How did the British help and hurt India?

Knowing Key Terms, People, and Places

1. Define: federalism, domestic system, factory system, corporation, socialism, communism, anarchism, suffrage, imperialism, extraterritoriality
2. Identify: Ottoman Empire, British North American Act, Industrial Revolution, House of Lords

Match each person or event with its correct identification.

3. Camillo di Cavour
4. Otto von Bismarck
5. Karl Marx
6. Commodore Perry
   a. leader of Communist movement
   b. unified Italian states
   c. opened Japan to world trade
   d. unified German states

Focus on Geography

7. Why do you think that control of the Suez Canal was important for Britain's colonies in India and China?

Reviewing Main Ideas

8. How did nationalism affect the Ottoman Empire?
9. Use the map on page 499 to tell the date when most of Italy was unified.
10. What is the political relationship between Great Britain and Canada today?
11. What are three problems that arose as a result of the Industrial Revolution?
12. What are some reforms that made life better for the average person in nineteenth-century Britain?
13. Why did European countries want to acquire colonies?
14. What wars forced China to open up to foreign trade?

Critical Thinking

15. **Making Comparisons** Compare England's parliamentary form of government with the government of the United States.
16. **Drawing Conclusions** Was the Industrial Revolution really a revolution? Cite evidence to support your conclusion.

▼ **Illustrating History** *In 1871, American suffragist Victoria Woodhull read her argument for women's suffrage before members of Congress.*

UNIT 8: The World in Crisis

(1914–1960)

The little man in the diplomat's black frock coat and striped trousers stepped off the aircraft into a fine drizzle. He waved a single sheet of paper before the breathless crowd and grandly announced that it was a promise from the German leader for "peace in our time." Then he stepped into a waiting automobile and hurried back to Number 10 Downing Street—one of London's most famous addresses—with a satisfied smile on his face.

The man was Neville Chamberlain, prime minister of Great Britain, and he had just returned from a talk with Adolf Hitler. He had agreed with the German Führer's demands for more land—this time land that belonged to Czechoslovakia. It was September 1938, and Chamberlain believed that he had ensured world peace by once again bowing to Hitler's ambitions. World War II was less than one year away.

▼ **Illustrating History**   *Hitler used new weapons of war, such as the dive-bombers shown in the painting below, to invade and subdue Poland.*

25 World War I and Its Aftermath

As you read, look for answers to these questions:

◆ What were the causes of World War I?
◆ How did the world order change as a result of the war?

The nations of Europe were once again plunged into conflict in 1914, in a war that was truly global in scale. Much of Europe was devastated by this war, which brought an end to the old world order.

Many Factors Caused World War I

Europe on the eve of World War I was a hotbed of nationalism and **militarism**, which glorifies war and encourages arms-building. The continent was divided by secret military alliances, such as the Triple Alliance of Germany, Austria-Hungary, and Italy and the Triple Entente of France, Britain, and Russia. Struggles between the major European powers in northern Africa and in the Balkans further aggravated the tense situation.

The war was triggered by the murder of Archduke Francis Ferdinand by Serbian nationalists. The major powers quickly mobilized their huge forces, and the war began.

The Allies Defeat the Central Powers

The attacks by the Central Powers —Germany and Austria—against the British and French in the west and against Russia in the east were successful at first. But the Germans' western drive soon broke down in France. The Central Powers' eastern attack was more successful, and by 1917, Russia was forced out of the war. The czar was overthrown, and Russia came under Communist control.

Germany used unrestricted submarine warfare in the Atlantic to prevent supplies from reaching Britain. This action brought the United States into the war on the side of the Allies—Britain, France, and Italy. America's great military and industrial strength changed the balance of power in the Allies' favor. By late 1918, the Central Powers had been crushed, and Germany agreed to an **armistice**—a temporary agreement to end the fighting.

After the armistice, a meeting was called to write a treaty to establish peace. The Versailles Treaty, which was drawn up by the Big Four—Wilson of the United States, Clemenceau (KLEHM uhn SOH) of France, Orlando of Italy, and Lloyd George of Britain—redrew the map of Europe and forced Germany to accept blame for the war. A League of Nations was formed to insure world peace. Because the United States did not join the league, it was weak and could not enforce its decisions.

The Postwar Era Saw New Struggles

Like Germany, Britain and France were greatly changed by the war. France, where much of the war in the west had been fought, faced years of rebuilding. The British created a commonwealth and granted gradual self-government and independence to many of its former colonies. However, in some British lands, such as India, independence was slow, and violence broke out. Britain also faced new difficulties in Ireland and the Middle East.

In China, the last dynasty was overthrown, and a dictatorship headed by Chiang Kai-shek (chang ky SHEK) united the country. However, China was no match for the growing power of Japan. In 1931, Japan invaded China and gradually occupied most of China's major cities.

REVIEW

1. Define: militarism, armistice
2. Identify: Triple Entente, President Wilson
3. What effect did the war in eastern Europe have upon Russia?
4. In what ways did the British Empire change during the postwar years?

26 The Rise of Dictatorships

As you read, look for answers to these questions:

◆ How did Russia change after 1918?
◆ What was the impact of totalitarianism upon the European political scene?

World War I had a major impact on many nations. In Russia, Communists under Lenin fought forces seeking to restore the czar. By the early 1920s, Lenin and his backers were clearly victorious. They set up a "dictatorship of the **proletariat**"—a term that means the working class—and renamed the country the Union of Soviet Socialist Republics.

In the Soviet Union, the state became both owner and director of all economic activity. Farms were combined into huge collectives, in which land was held and worked in common and all members of the farming community shared equally in the group's output.

Lenin and his sucessor, Joseph Stalin, established an iron dictatorship in which the needs of the individual were viewed as sub-ordinate to those of the state. Those who resisted the Communist program were executed or sent to remote prison camps called **gulags.**

Fascism Emerged in Italy and Germany

In Italy, the Fascist Benito Mussolini (moos soh LEE nee) overthrew the monarchy in the 1920s. **Fascism** is based on a dictatorship in which there is one party, strict censorship, strong nationalism, and complete control of the people by the government. Mussolini, like Lenin, stressed state power over individual liberty.

The 1920s saw another Fascist—Adolf Hitler—rise to prominence in Germany. By 1933, Hitler and his National Socialists, known as Nazis, had gained control of the German government. Hitler succeeded in rebuilding German industries and reestablishing German military strength. He also preached racial superiority and attempted to destroy the Jews and other ethnic and opposition groups.

Smaller European Countries Faced Challenges

Democracy survived in parts of Europe, including the Netherlands, Belgium, Norway, Switzerland, and Denmark. Totalitarian governments took over many countries, however. In Hungary, a Fascist dictatorship was set up. In Poland, the Soviets and the Germans competed for power. Spain experienced a bloody civil war during the mid-1930s that ended with the victory of the Fascist dictator Francisco Franco. By the late 1930s, Europe was once again moving toward international conflict.

▼ **Illustrating History** *Below, Lenin is shown speaking to a crowd in 1917.*

REVIEW

1. Define: proletariat, gulag, fascism
2. Identify: Lenin, Nazis, Francisco Franco
3. What was Mussolini's platform?
4. What actions did Hitler take as leader of Germany?

27 World War II

As you read, look for answers to these questions:

◆ How did the doctrine of appeasement encourage Hitler's aggression?
◆ What was the impact of World War II on America's global position?

The rise of totalitarian dictatorships in Europe and of Japanese power in the Far East ultimately led to the outbreak of World War II in 1939. At the war's end in 1945, new hopes arose for world peace.

World Tensions Led to World War II

The Axis powers—Germany, Japan, and Italy—sought to expand in the 1930s. Japan's desire for land and resources led that nation to invade Manchuria in northern China. Germany occupied the Rhineland and annexed Austria in 1938. At the same time, Italy extended its power into Africa.

The western democracies criticized these acts of aggression but followed the policy of **appeasement,** or giving in to the demands of a strong power in hopes of avoiding trouble. In Munich in 1938, for example, the Allies, led by Britain and France, accepted Hitler's invasion of part of Czechoslovakia. The Allies' attempts to maintain peace ended in September 1939, however, with the German invasion of Poland. World War II began.

Axis Power Led to Early Allied Defeats

Hitler's armies were very successful at the beginning of the war. They used the tactic of **blitzkrieg**—a sudden, swift, and overwhelming attack by massed armor and infantry—to overrun much of western Europe. By 1941, France, Norway, Belgium, and Luxembourg had fallen, and only Britain held out against Germany.

The British Royal Air Force succeeded in turning back the worst air raids Hitler could send against England's cities. Then Hitler ordered an invasion of the Soviet Union in June 1941. He thus brought upon himself a war in which he was fighting enemies on two fronts.

In the Far East, Japan conquered much of China, Southeast Asia, and the East Indies. On December 7, 1941, the Japanese launched a surprise attack against a United States base at Pearl Harbor, Hawaii. This action brought America into the war.

The United States fought against Japan on the Pacific islands and in Asia, and it battled Germany in Europe and northern Africa. At the same time, the flow of United States supplies to Britain and the Soviet Union enabled those two nations to overcome the initial success of the Axis and fight back.

By 1944, the German army had been stopped and was fighting on the defensive. In June of that year, the United States, Britain, Canada, and other Allies invaded German-occupied France in a massive attack known as *D-Day*. The German army, squeezed between the western Allies in France and the Soviets in the east, was forced to retreat.

The Allies Gained a Total Victory

By the spring of 1945, Hitler's armies were driven back into Germany. Germany surrendered in May 1945. In August 1945, Japan gave up when atomic bombs were dropped on two cities, Hiroshima and Nagasaki.

When the war ended, the Allied nations united to create a new organization, the United Nations. They hoped that they could work as well together to preserve peace as they had to win World War II.

REVIEW

1. Define: appeasement, blitzkrieg
2. Identify: Axis powers, D-Day
3. What event ended the Allies' policy of appeasement?
4. What event brought the United States into the war?

28 The Aftermath of World War II

As you read, look for answers to these questions:

◆ What were the causes of the cold war?
◆ Why were the nations of Western Europe able to recover after World War II?

After World War II, the world was plunged into the **cold war.** The cold war is a condition of tension between the free countries, led by the United States, and the Communist countries, led by the Soviet Union.

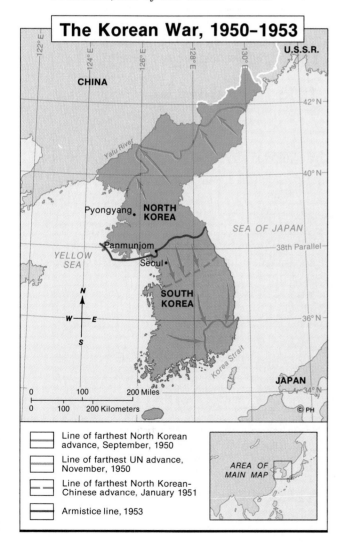

The Korean War, 1950–1953

CHINA

U.S.S.R.

Yalu River

Pyongyang • NORTH KOREA

SEA OF JAPAN

Panmunjom
YELLOW SEA
Seoul •
38th Parallel

SOUTH KOREA

Korea Strait

JAPAN

| 0 | 100 | 200 Miles |
| 0 | 100 | 200 Kilometers |

© PH

Line of farthest North Korean advance, September, 1950

Line of farthest UN advance, November, 1950

Line of farthest North Korean-Chinese advance, January 1951

Armistice line, 1953

AREA OF MAIN MAP

To help European nations recover from the war, the United States began a program of economic help known as the Marshall Plan. Destroyed by war, France, Germany, and Italy achieved economic and political progress.

The Cold War Divided the World

In 1950, troops from Communist North Korea invaded South Korea. (See the map on this page.) A United Nations army under United States leadership turned back the invasion, but not before Chinese soldiers had come to the aid of North Korea. By 1953, an uneasy truce was reached.

In Eastern Europe, several attempts to shake off Soviet control took place during the 1950s. Unrest erupted into violence and rebellion in Poland, East Germany, and Hungary.

New Nations Formed

In Asia, India achieved its independence from Britain in 1947. The fighting between Hindus and Muslims that followed led to the formation of two countries: India, a Hindu nation, and Pakistan, a Muslim nation.

Because of Hitler's persecution of Jews, the movement known as **zionism** became stronger among Jews. Zionists favored the establishment of a Jewish country in Palestine. Arabs who lived in Palestine opposed the idea of a Jewish state, but with the approval of the United Nations, the Jewish state of Israel was founded in 1948. Israel has fought several wars since then against neighboring Arab countries to preserve its existence.

REVIEW

1. Define: cold war, zionism
2. Identify: Marshall Plan
3. What did the U.S. do to help European nations recover from World War II?
4. What two nations were formed after the British left India?

771

Knowing Key Terms, People, and Places

1. Define: proletariat, gulag, fascism, appeasement, cold war, zionism
2. Identify: the Central Powers, Chiang Kai-shek, Joseph Stalin, Adolf Hitler, Pearl Harbor, D-Day

Focus on Geography

Use the map on this page to answer questions 3 and 4.

3. Which alliance, NATO or the Warsaw Pact, is aligned with the United States?
4. What part of Europe would probably see the first fighting in the event of a war between the two alliances?

Reviewing Main Ideas

5. How did Germany's use of unrestricted submarine warfare help to broaden the scope of World War I?

6. Name some changes that the Communists made after they took control of Russia.
7. Why did the Allies' policy of appeasement toward Adolf Hitler fail to prevent the outbreak of World War II?
8. Name one major conflict that resulted from the cold war.

Critical Thinking

9. **Making Comparisons** Compare the opposing sides in World War II. In what ways are they similar? In what ways do they differ?
10. **Recognizing Ideologies** Judging from the way the Soviets set up their government, do you think that they really believed that a "dictatorship of the proletariat" would help Russia's people?

Military Alliances in Postwar Europe, 1955

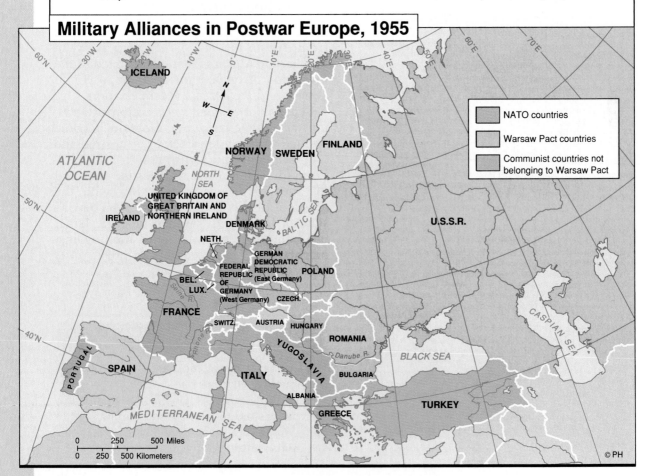

772

UNIT 9: The World Today

(1960–Present)

In February of 1972, a president of the United States shook hands with a leader of the People's Republic of China for the first time. President Richard Nixon stepped off Air Force One in Beijing for a historic eight-day visit. His presence in China signalled a new American desire to normalize relations with the government of the Asian giant. It also demonstrated the president's understanding that new international conditions demanded closer cooperation among the world's people and their leaders. At the same time, Nixon's visit reflected the wish of China—once the mortal enemy of the West—to open its doors to new ideas and to participate more fully in the evolving world community.

The world of the late twentieth century is truly "shrinking" as new efforts to achieve global peace and cooperation among nations emerge. Much remains to be done if these goals are to be fully met, but great strides already have been taken.

November 1989, for example, was notable for the opening of the Berlin Wall, communism's most visible symbol since 1961. With this dramatic event, a new era began. The countries of Eastern Europe, the Soviet Union, and the United States all have important decisions to make as 1990 begins a decade of remarkable change.

◀ **Illustrating History** *At a formal banquet, hosted by Chinese Premier Zhou Enlai (left), President and Mrs. Nixon celebrate the reopening of communications between the United States and China.*

773

29 Europe and the Soviet Union Today

As you read, look for answers to these questions:

◆ What factors account for Western Europe's growing economic strength?
◆ How have conditions in Eastern Europe changed since the cold war era?

The nations of Western Europe are global economic leaders with great political influence. Political changes in some Eastern European nations also have led to energetic growth and to potentially greater freedom.

Western Europe Experienced Great Progress

Great Britain has moved away from its postwar socialism in recent years. Since 1979, Prime Minister Margaret Thatcher's laissez-faire ideas have emphasized private enterprise. Britain continues to face major political problems, however, including unrest in Northern Ireland.

During the 1960s, President Charles de Gaulle of France worked to rebuild his nation's power and prestige. De Gaulle did much to restore French leadership in Europe, but in 1968, the French defeated a **referendum**—a vote of public support—for his policies. Today, the country is led by François Mitterrand, a moderate Socialist.

Throughout the 1970s, West German Chancellor Willy Brandt sought to build closer ties between his country and Communist East Germany. Brandt's *Ostpolitik*, or eastern policy, aimed for economic and political cooperation between East and West Germany. At the same time, the West German economy has thrived.

Terrorism and political instability have troubled Italy often since 1960. Economic problems have continued into the present, although the country has made progress. Spain and Portugal also have experienced unrest. In Greece and Turkey, political problems often have slowed progress.

Economic growth and development has characterized Western Europe since 1960. At the same time, the trend toward greater regional cooperation has grown. The establishment of the first European parliament in 1970 represented new efforts to achieve cooperation in Western Europe. The European Economic Community (EEC) also aims to achieve complete economic unity by 1992. If this goal is met, there will be no trade barriers among member nations.

Soviet Failures Led to New Reforms

The years since 1960 have led to a new reality in Soviet-dominated Eastern Europe. In 1964, Leonid Brezhnev (BREZH nev) rose to power in the Soviet Union and soon ended the limited freedoms of the Khrushchev (KROOS chev) era. Dissidents, such as Alexander Solzhenitsyn (SOHL zhuh NEET sihn), were jailed, and opposition to the regime was harshly suppressed.

In 1985, Mikhail Gorbachev (mee KAYL GOR buh CHEV) became the Soviet leader. Gorbachev faced massive economic and social problems. Recognizing the need for change, Gorbachev declared a new era of openness, called **glasnost,** and a program of economic reform known as **perestroika.** Gorbachev also worked with President Reagan to reduce the nuclear arms race.

With new Soviet openness, however, came demands from East-bloc nations for greater freedom. In Poland, the first non-communist government in over 40 years was set up in 1989. With the opening of the Berlin Wall, other Eastern European nations also called for more freedoms. At the start of the 1990s, the future of Soviet domination was in doubt.

REVIEW

1. Define: referendum, *glasnost, perestroika*
2. Identify: Margaret Thatcher, Willy Brandt
3. Why is the EEC's goal of economic unity significant?
4. Why is the future of *glasnost* in doubt?

30 The Western Hemisphere Today

As you read, look for answers to these questions:

◆ How has the United States expanded its global leadership since 1960?
◆ What major challenges have faced Latin America during the 1980s?

The election of President John F. Kennedy in 1960 seemed a symbol of the optimism and progress that characterized the nation. His assassination in 1963 ended that dream.

The civil rights struggle gained momentum under the leadership of Martin Luther King, Jr. Public protests led to passage of the Civil Rights Act of 1964. The law was aimed at ending **discrimination,** that is, showing preference for one person over another based on race or religion.

President Lyndon Johnson expanded America's role in the Vietnam conflict. Opposition to the war grew. Under President Nixon, relations with the Soviets and the Communist Chinese eased, and America gradually withdrew from Vietnam. During his second term, however, scandal forced Nixon to resign.

President Carter helped fashion the Camp David Agreement between Israel and Egypt. But Carter faced inflation, an energy crisis, and American hostages in Iran.

Ronald Reagan was elected president in 1980. These were times of major economic recovery and of renewed national confidence. To reduce the arms race, Reagan secured a major **arms limitation** treaty with the Soviets. Reagan also worked to improve United States relations with Canada.

During the postwar years, Canada grew in strength and in independence from British control. Today, Canada is one of the world's leading food producers and exporters. In 1988, Canada and the United States reached a free trade agreement.

Latin America Continued to Face Turmoil

The nations of Latin America share many problems, including widespread poverty, poor health care, political instability, and a gulf between rich and poor. In parts of Latin America, inequality and discontent have led to revolutions and to the establishment of Communist regimes, as in Cuba and Nicaragua. Other countries have suffered under military dictators who have jailed and executed dissidents, or people who oppose the government. In 1989, a United States invasion of Panama ousted military strongman Manuel Noriega.

▼ **Illustrating History** *In 1983, people showed names of loved ones who disappeared during Argentina's military rule.*

REVIEW

1. Define: discrimination, arms limitation
2. Identify: Martin Luther King, Jr., Civil Rights Act of 1964
3. How did President Reagan help to reduce the nuclear arms race?
4. What are some problems faced by countries in Latin America?

31 The Middle East and Africa

As you read, look for answers to these questions:

◆ What is the source of the Arab-Israeli dispute?
◆ How did colonialism affect the peoples of Sub-Saharan Africa after 1960?

Since 1960, the Middle East has witnessed an ongoing cycle of conflict and truce. The Arab-Israeli dispute lies at the root of modern Middle Eastern violence. Since 1948, Israel has gone to war four times to defend its existence against its surrounding Arab neighbors.

President Anwar Sadat of Egypt was the first major Arab leader to discuss peace with Israel in 1977. A year later, he signed the historic Camp David Peace Agreement in which Egypt recognized Israel's right to exist, and Israel gave occupied land back to Egypt. However, other Arab leaders rejected the accord. Sadat was assassinated in 1981.

▼ **Illustrating History** *Yasir Arafat heads the Palestine Liberation Organization.*

Other events in the Middle East destabilized the region. In Iran, the shah was overthrown by Muslim fundamentalists led by the Ayatollah Khomeini (koh MAY nee). This action was followed by war between Iran and Iraq. In Lebanon, civil war between Christian and Muslim groups has destroyed the country's economy and weakened its fragile political structure.

New Troubles Arose in Africa

New world tensions developed in northern Africa in the years after 1960. In Libya, the extremist leadership of Muammar el-Qaddafi (guht DAW fee) added to regional unrest. Qaddafi became an enemy of the United States because of his close ties with the Soviets and his program of terrorism, that is, random acts of violence intended to cause fear. Qaddafi's attacks on the neighboring country of Chad also added to the strain in the area.

The nations of sub-Saharan Africa also face major problems of poverty, illiteracy, and political unrest. **Tribalism,** or tribal conflicts, in such places as Uganda and Nigeria have resulted in oppression and civil war. Opposition to colonial and white minority rule in countries such as Angola and Zimbabwe have led to violent rebellions.

Today, the white minority government of South Africa faces a major crisis as it seeks to uphold its policy of **apartheid** (ah PART hite), which is complete segregation of whites and blacks. World leaders continue to pressure South Africa to change its racial policy, and violence in the country continues to grow.

REVIEW

1. Define: tribalism, apartheid
2. Identify: Anwar Sadat, Ayatollah Khomeini
3. Why is the United States opposed to Libya's Qaddafi?
4. What problem is presently causing unrest in South Africa?

32 Asia in Today's World

As you read, look for answers to these questions:

◆ What factors account for Japan's postwar economic success?
◆ Why did the United States seek diplomatic relations with Communist China?

Many Asian nations, including Japan, China, and South Korea, have made enormous progress since the 1960s. Today, the region is gaining economic and political strength in the world.

Asian Nations Became Economic Powers

During the immediate postwar years, Asia was a scene of economic and political ruin. During the 1960s, however, both Japan and South Korea began full-scale programs of economic recovery and growth. Japan, under a democratic constitution modeled upon that of the United States, recovered quickly from its wartime devastation.

Because of a very small military budget, industrial and commercial development in the country restored the power of the economically and politically powerful corporations. The nation turned its energies to international business and, by the decade of the 1980s, Japan had become the world's third-leading economic power.

South Korea, too, has become a world economic power and is a major trading partner of the United States and Western Europe. By 1988, in fact, South Korea enjoyed a trade surplus of 10 billion dollars and a generally high standard of living. But South Korea continues to experience political unrest because of increasing opposition to repressive government policies.

North Korea, under a rigid and oppressive Communist regime, continues to depend heavily upon other Communist nations for trade and support.

The People's Republic of China, under Mao Zedong (mow dzoo dong), joined the United Nations and resumed diplomatic relations with the United States in the early 1970s. He organized Chinese farms and factories into communities called **communes.** After Mao's death in 1976, some political liberalization took place. In 1989, however, the Chinese government crushed a popular, pro-democracy student uprising in Tiananmen Square in Beijing. Thousands of students were arrested and hundreds killed.

Other Asian Countries Faced Challenges

Much of Southeast Asia, including Vietnam, Laos, and Kampuchea (formerly Cambodia), has long been a scene of war and civil turmoil. Throughout the 1960s, the leaders of North Vietnam sought to impose communism on South Vietnam. The United States became involved in the long war aimed at keeping South Vietnam free. After the United States withdrew its forces in 1973, the North Vietnamese took control of South Vietnam.

In the Philippines, the overthrow of Ferdinand Marcos in 1986 led to the establishment of a new and more liberal government under President Corazon Aquino (ah KEE noh). Having survived a serious coup attempt late in 1989, the new government is working to restore stability to the island nation.

During the postwar years, India was divided along religious lines, and the nations of Pakistan and Bangladesh were created. India continues working to improve its economy.

REVIEW

1. Define: commune
2. Identify: Corazon Aquino
3. In what ways has Communist China sought to liberalize its economy?
4. What conflict led to United States involvement in the Vietnam War?

33 Contemporary Global Issues

As you read, look for answers to these questions:

◆ Why has the world's economy become global in nature?
◆ What are some of the major environmental issues facing the world today?

Increasing economic, environmental, and demographic problems confront today's world. As we move toward the next century, new solutions to these problems are being sought.

Overpopulation Has Become a Global Issue

By the late 1980s, a global population crisis had emerged as a major threat to world peace and order. Improved medical care and greater agricultural productivity were among the reasons for our world's rising population. But poor nutrition and hunger cause suffering or death to millions of people. The issue is especially critical in the less developed nations of the world, which, by about 2025, will account for more than 80 percent of the earth's population.

▼ **Illustrating History** *This Guatemalan woman is receiving a vaccination from her doctor.*

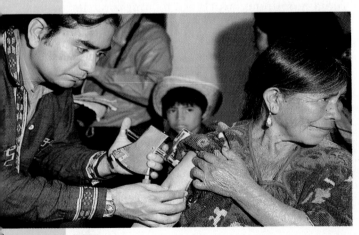

Rapid urbanization is another issue confronting our world. Urban growth has been speeded by improved transportation and communication systems and by the attraction of economic and cultural opportunities in cities. Some urban areas, such as Tokyo and Mexico City, have become megalopolises or sprawling urban networks with no real boundaries. Urban growth will continue to place new demands upon city services and support facilities.

A Global Economy Has Developed

The growth of international trade during the late years of the twentieth century led to the creation of a **global economy** in which huge corporations produce goods and services for markets throughout the world. These corporations buy raw materials and finished goods from many different countries, and because labor costs vary enormously, they often employ workers around the world. Today, it is no longer possible for a nation to expand its economy and to remain isolated at the same time.

Complex Issues Received Growing Attention

During the late 1980s, people became increasingly aware of the dangers of industrial wastes and other forms of pollution to our environment. New efforts to combat environmental damage were initiated, but much remains to be accomplished.

Another major issue confronting the world was the **greenhouse effect**—the warming trend that could disrupt global patterns of climate by the year 2050.

REVIEW

1. Define: global economy, greenhouse effect
2. Identify: megalopolis
3. How has improved medical care affected world population?
4. What factors have caused cities to grow rapidly?

UNIT NINE REVIEW

Knowing Key Terms, People, and Places
1. Define: referendum, *glasnost,* dissident
2. Identify: Martin Luther King, Jr., Ayatollah Khomeini, Muammar el-Qaddafi, Corazon Aquino

Focus on Geography
Use the map on this page to answer questions 3–5.
3. What Arab nations border the country of Israel?
4. Why do you think the Israelis are concerned about recent upheavals in the country of Lebanon?
5. Does Israel have major oil fields within its borders?

Reviewing Main Ideas
6. What was the purpose of the West German "eastern policy"?

7. Why did Mikhail Gorbachev of the Soviet Union declare a new policy of *glasnost* during the mid-1980s?
8. What factors have enabled Japan to recover from the effects of World War II and to build its economic might?
9. How many major wars has Israel fought to preserve its existence?
10. Name four key issues facing the world today.

Critical Thinking
11. **Determining Relevance** In what way is our global ability to produce food relevant to the issue of the growth of world population?
12. **Perceiving Cause and Effect** In what way did Israel's victory in the Six-Day War create new problems for Israel?

North Africa and the Middle East Today

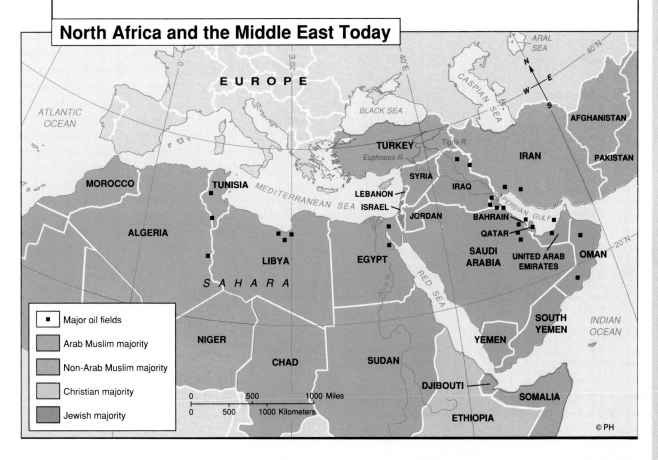

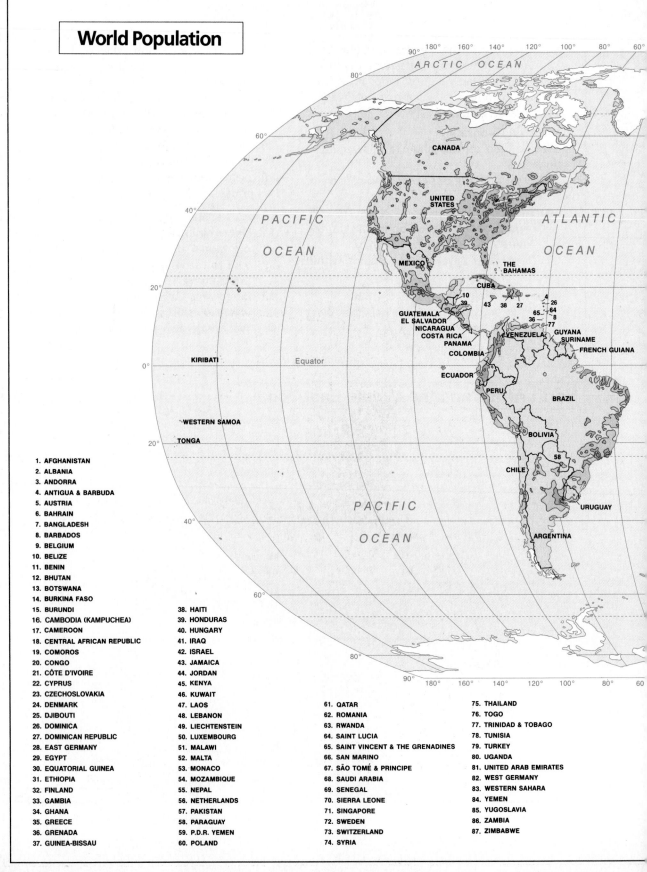

World Population

ARCTIC OCEAN

80°

CANADA

PACIFIC OCEAN

ATLANTIC OCEAN

UNITED STATES

MEXICO

THE BAHAMAS

CUBA

10
39
4
26
64
8
77

43 38 27
65
36

GUATEMALA
EL SALVADOR
NICARAGUA
COSTA RICA
PANAMA
COLOMBIA

VENEZUELA

GUYANA
SURINAME
FRENCH GUIANA

KIRIBATI

Equator

ECUADOR

PERU

BRAZIL

WESTERN SAMOA

TONGA

BOLIVIA

58

CHILE

URUGUAY

PACIFIC

OCEAN

ARGENTINA

1. AFGHANISTAN
2. ALBANIA
3. ANDORRA
4. ANTIGUA & BARBUDA
5. AUSTRIA
6. BAHRAIN
7. BANGLADESH
8. BARBADOS
9. BELGIUM
10. BELIZE
11. BENIN
12. BHUTAN
13. BOTSWANA
14. BURKINA FASO
15. BURUNDI
16. CAMBODIA (KAMPUCHEA)
17. CAMEROON
18. CENTRAL AFRICAN REPUBLIC
19. COMOROS
20. CONGO
21. CÔTE D'IVOIRE
22. CYPRUS
23. CZECHOSLOVAKIA
24. DENMARK
25. DJIBOUTI
26. DOMINICA
27. DOMINICAN REPUBLIC
28. EAST GERMANY
29. EGYPT
30. EQUATORIAL GUINEA
31. ETHIOPIA
32. FINLAND
33. GAMBIA
34. GHANA
35. GREECE
36. GRENADA
37. GUINEA-BISSAU

38. HAITI
39. HONDURAS
40. HUNGARY
41. IRAQ
42. ISRAEL
43. JAMAICA
44. JORDAN
45. KENYA
46. KUWAIT
47. LAOS
48. LEBANON
49. LIECHTENSTEIN
50. LUXEMBOURG
51. MALAWI
52. MALTA
53. MONACO
54. MOZAMBIQUE
55. NEPAL
56. NETHERLANDS
57. PAKISTAN
58. PARAGUAY
59. P.D.R. YEMEN
60. POLAND

61. QATAR
62. ROMANIA
63. RWANDA
64. SAINT LUCIA
65. SAINT VINCENT & THE GRENADINES
66. SAN MARINO
67. SÃO TOMÉ & PRINCIPE
68. SAUDI ARABIA
69. SENEGAL
70. SIERRA LEONE
71. SINGAPORE
72. SWEDEN
73. SWITZERLAND
74. SYRIA

75. THAILAND
76. TOGO
77. TRINIDAD & TOBAGO
78. TUNISIA
79. TURKEY
80. UGANDA
81. UNITED ARAB EMIRATES
82. WEST GERMANY
83. WESTERN SAHARA
84. YEMEN
85. YUGOSLAVIA
86. ZAMBIA
87. ZIMBABWE

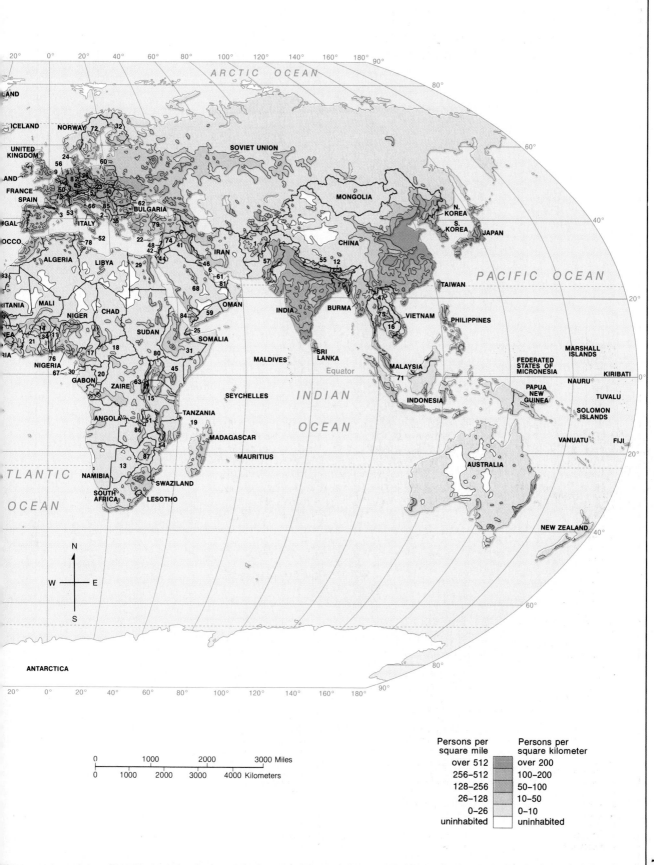

ARCTIC OCEAN

20° 0° 20° 40° 60° 80° 100° 120° 140° 160° 180° 90°

80°

LAND

ICELAND

NORWAY 72   32

60°

UNITED
KINGDOM   24   60

56
9

AND

82
FRANCE   50   62
SPAIN   66 85   BULGARIA   79
3 53   2   35
ITALY   74
52   22 48 41
78   42
29   44   IRAN
ALGERIA   LIBYA   46
6   61
83   81
68
ITANIA   MALI
OMAN   59
NIGER   CHAD   84
NEA 34 11
21   SUDAN   25
76   17   18   31 SOMALIA
NIGERIA   80
67 30 20   45
GABON   63
ZAIRE
15

ANGOLA   51 TANZANIA
86   19

54   MADAGASCAR
87
13   MAURITIUS
TLANTIC NAMIBIA

OCEAN   SOUTH   LESOTHO
AFRICA SWAZILAND

SOVIET UNION

MONGOLIA

N.
KOREA
S.
KOREA   JAPAN

CHINA

TAIWAN

55 12

BURMA
INDIA   47
75   VIETNAM
16   PHILIPPINES

SRI
MALDIVES LANKA
Equator
MALAYSIA
71
SEYCHELLES   INDONESIA

INDIAN

OCEAN

PACIFIC OCEAN

MARSHALL
ISLANDS

FEDERATED
STATES OF
MICRONESIA   KIRIBATI
NAURU
PAPUA   TUVALU
NEW
GUINEA   SOLOMON
ISLANDS

VANUATU   FIJI

AUSTRALIA

NEW ZEALAND

80°

60°

40°

20°

0°

20°

40°

60°

80°

N

W   E

S

ANTARCTICA

20° 0° 20° 40° 60° 80° 100° 120° 140° 160° 180° 90°

0	1000	2000	3000 Miles
0	1000	2000	3000 4000 Kilometers

Persons per   Persons per
square mile   square kilometer
over 512   over 200
256–512   100–200
128–256   50–100
26–128   10–50
0–26   0–10
uninhabited   uninhabited

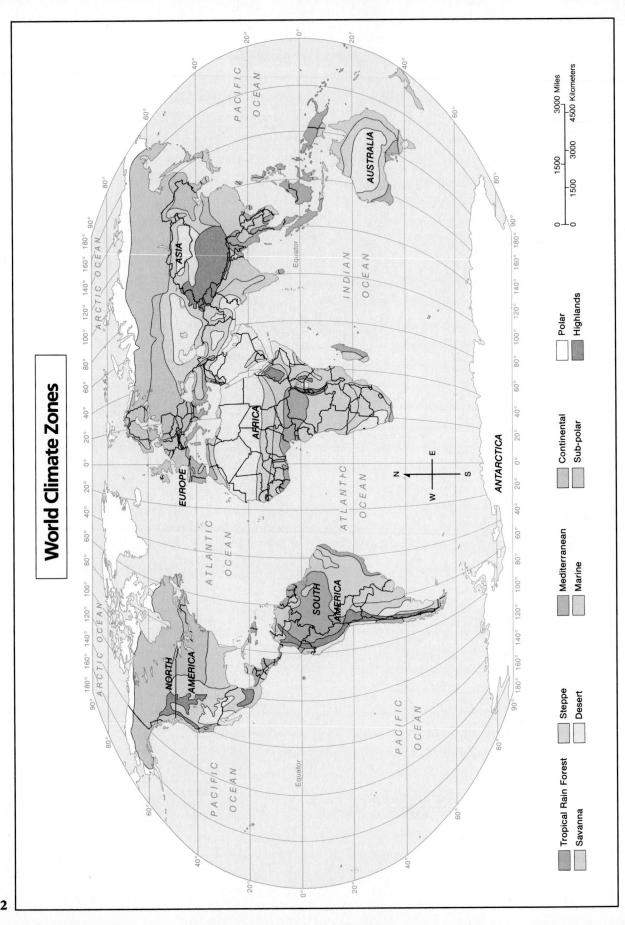

World Climate Zones

ARCTIC OCEAN

PACIFIC OCEAN

ATLANTIC OCEAN

INDIAN OCEAN

Equator

ASIA

EUROPE

AFRICA

AUSTRALIA

NORTH AMERICA

SOUTH AMERICA

ANTARCTICA

N
W — E
S

0   1500   3000
0   1500   3000 Miles
0   4500 Kilometers

Tropical Rain Forest

Savanna

Steppe

Desert

Mediterranean

Marine

Continental

Sub-polar

Polar

Highlands

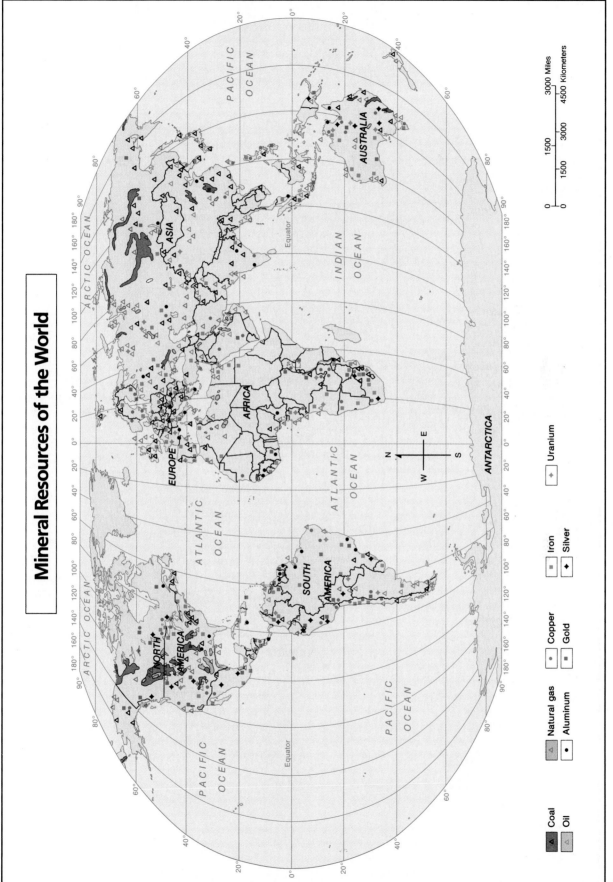

Mineral Resources of the World

PACIFIC OCEAN

ARCTIC OCEAN

ASIA

EUROPE

AFRICA

AUSTRALIA

INDIAN OCEAN

ATLANTIC OCEAN

ATLANTIC OCEAN

NORTH AMERICA

SOUTH AMERICA

PACIFIC OCEAN

PACIFIC OCEAN

ANTARCTICA

Equator

Equator

N
W   E
S

| | | 1500 | 3000 | | 3000 Miles |
| 0 | | 1500 | 3000 | 4500 Kilometers |

Coal

Oil

Natural gas

Aluminum

Copper

Gold

Iron

Silver

Uranium

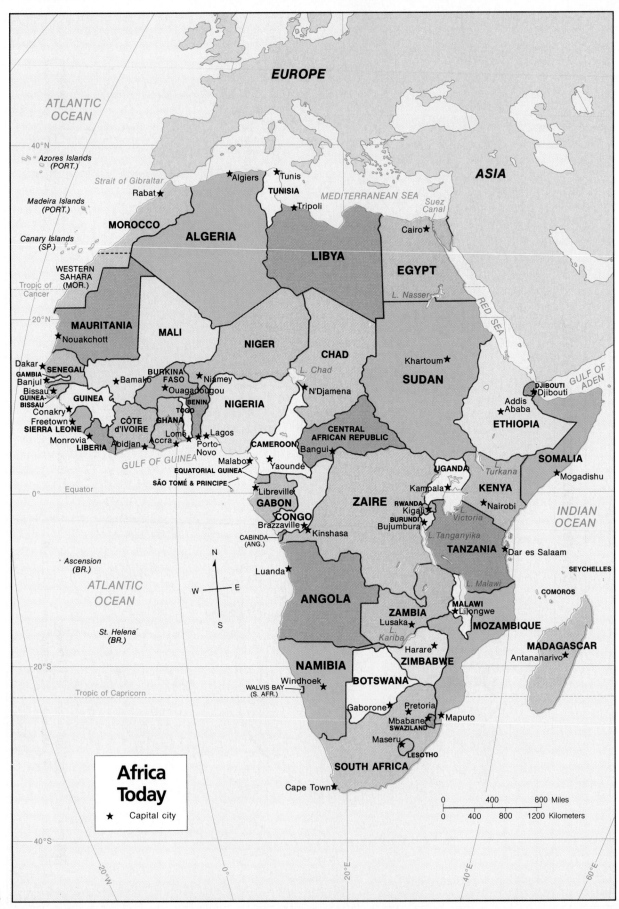

ATLANTIC
OCEAN

EUROPE

ASIA

40°N

Azores Islands
(PORT.)

Strait of Gibraltar

Algiers★ ★Tunis

TUNISIA

MEDITERRANEAN SEA

Suez
Canal

Madeira Islands
(PORT.)

Rabat★ ★Tripoli

Cairo★

MOROCCO

ALGERIA

LIBYA

EGYPT

Canary Islands
(SP.)

WESTERN
SAHARA
(MOR.)

Tropic of
Cancer

L. Nasser

RED SEA

20°N

MAURITANIA

Nouakchott★

MALI

NIGER

CHAD

Khartoum★

GULF OF
ADEN

Dakar★

SENEGAL

BURKINA
FASO

★Niamey

SUDAN

DJIBOUTI
Djibouti

GAMBIA
Banjul

Bamako★

N'Djamena★

Addis
Ababa

Bissau

Ouagadougou★

L. Chad

GUINEA-
BISSAU

GUINEA

NIGERIA

BENIN
TOGO

CENTRAL
AFRICAN REPUBLIC

ETHIOPIA

Conakry

CÔTE
d'IVOIRE

GHANA

SOMALIA

Freetown★

Lomé★ ★Lagos

SIERRA LEONE

Accra★ Porto-
Novo

CAMEROON

Bangui★

Mogadishu★

Monrovia

Abidjan★

LIBERIA

UGANDA

L.
Turkana

GULF OF GUINEA

Malabo★ ★Yaoundé

KENYA

EQUATORIAL GUINEA

Kampala★

Equator

SÃO TOMÉ & PRINCIPE

Libreville★

ZAIRE

Nairobi★

INDIAN
OCEAN

Ascension
(BR.)

GABON

CONGO

RWANDA
Kigali

L.
Victoria

Brazzaville★

BURUNDI
Bujumbura

CABINDA
(ANG.)

★Kinshasa

L. Tanganyika

TANZANIA

★Dar es Salaam

SEYCHELLES

ATLANTIC
OCEAN

Luanda★

L. Malawi

COMOROS

St. Helena
(BR.)

ANGOLA

ZAMBIA

MALAWI
★Lilongwe

MADAGASCAR

Lusaka★

MOZAMBIQUE

Antananarivo★

20°S

L.
Kariba

NAMIBIA

Harare★

Tropic of Capricorn

ZIMBABWE

Windhoek★

BOTSWANA

WALVIS BAY
(S. AFR.)

Gaborone★ Pretoria★

Maputo★

Mbabane

SWAZILAND

Maseru

LESOTHO

SOUTH AFRICA

N

W   E

S

**Africa
Today**

★ Capital city

Cape Town★

0   400   800 Miles

0   400   800   1200 Kilometers

40°S

20°W

0°

20°E

40°E

60°E

784

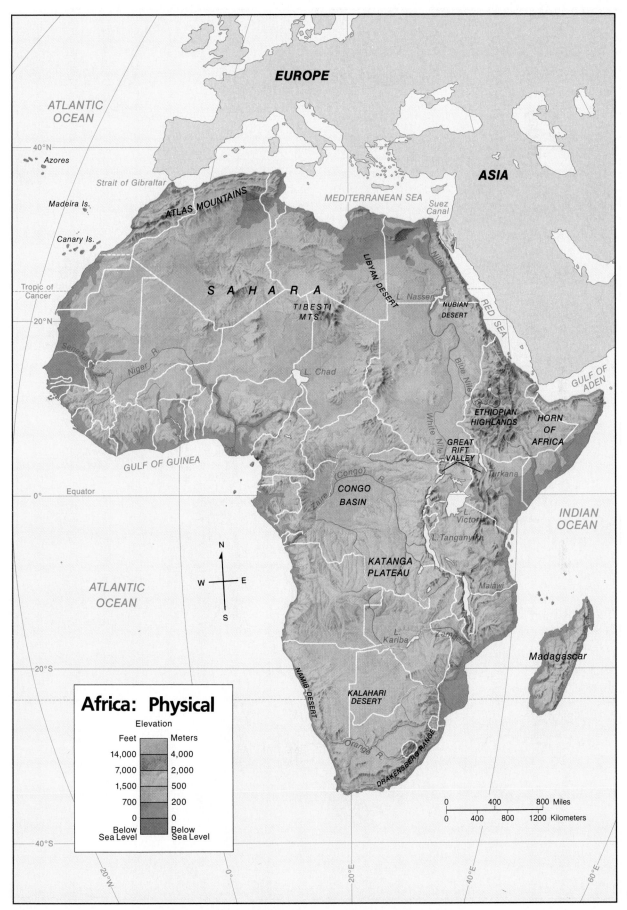

Africa: Physical

ATLANTIC OCEAN

EUROPE

ASIA

Azores

Strait of Gibraltar

Madeira Is.

ATLAS MOUNTAINS

MEDITERRANEAN SEA

Suez Canal

Canary Is.

SAHARA

Tropic of Cancer

LIBYAN DESERT

L. Nasser

NUBIAN DESERT

RED SEA

TIBESTI MTS.

Senegal R.

Niger R.

Niger R.

Blue Nile

GULF OF ADEN

L. Chad

White Nile

ETHIOPIAN HIGHLANDS

HORN OF AFRICA

GULF OF GUINEA

GREAT RIFT VALLEY

L. Turkana

Equator

(Congo) R.

Zaire R.

CONGO BASIN

L. Victoria

INDIAN OCEAN

L. Tanganyika

N

KATANGA PLATEAU

L. Malawi

W   E

ATLANTIC OCEAN

S

L. Kariba

Zambezi

Madagascar

NAMIB DESERT

KALAHARI DESERT

Orange R.

DRAKENSBERG RANGE

Elevation

Feet		Meters
14,000		4,000
7,000		2,000
1,500		500
700		200
0		0
Below Sea Level		Below Sea Level

0	400	800 Miles
0	400	800 1200 Kilometers

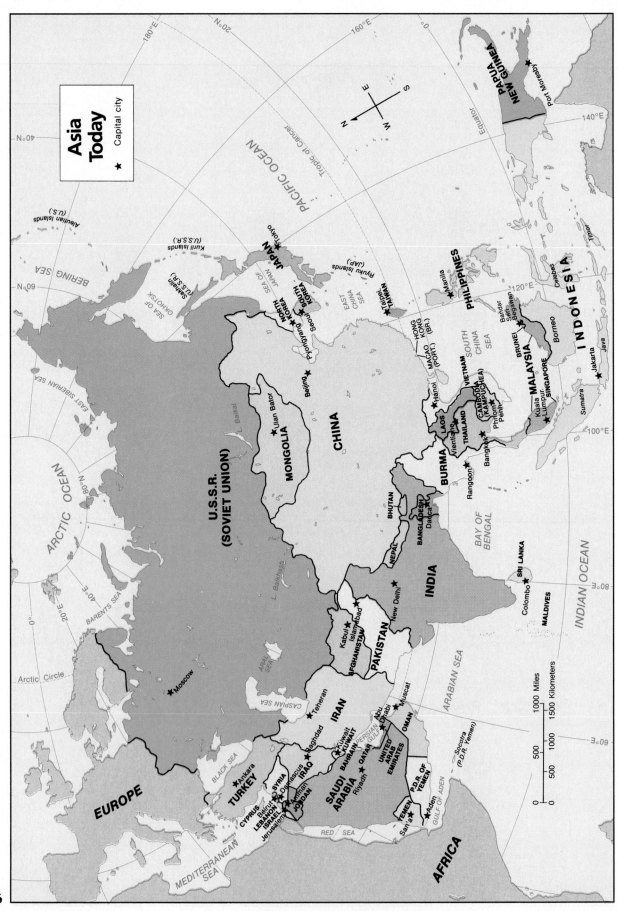

Asia Today

★ Capital city

786

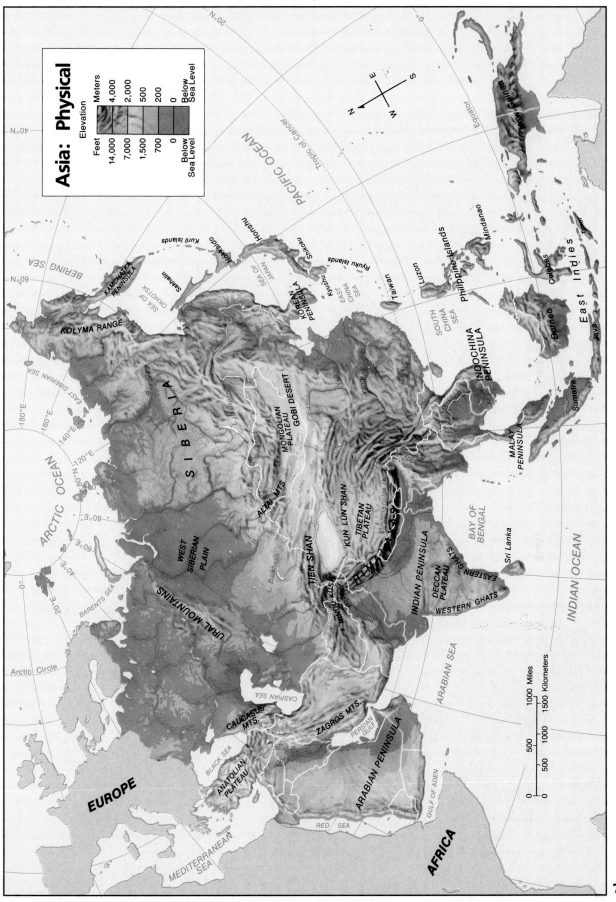

Asia: Physical

Elevation

Feet	Meters
14,000	4,000
7,000	2,000
1,500	500
700	200
0	0
Below Sea Level	Below Sea Level

ARCTIC OCEAN

PACIFIC OCEAN

Tropic of Cancer

Equator

BERING SEA

SEA OF OKHOTSK

SEA OF JAPAN

EAST SIBERIAN SEA

BARENTS SEA

KAMCHATKA PENINSULA

KOLYMA RANGE

Kuril Islands

Sakhalin

Hokkaido

Honshu

Shikoku

Kyushu

Ryuku Islands

KOREAN PENINSULA

EAST CHINA SEA

Taiwan

SOUTH CHINA SEA

Luzon

Mindanao

Philippine Islands

New Guinea

Celebes

Borneo

Java

Sumatra

East Indies

Timor

SIBERIA

WEST SIBERIAN PLAIN

URAL MOUNTAINS

ALTAI MTS.

MONGOLIAN PLATEAU

GOBI DESERT

L. Balkhash

L. Baikal

Yenisey

Ob

Lena

TIEN SHAN

KUN LUN SHAN

TIBETAN PLATEAU

HINDU KUSH

HIMALAYAS

Brahmaputra

Ganges

Indus

INDOCHINA PENINSULA

MALAY PENINSULA

INDIAN PENINSULA

DECCAN PLATEAU

WESTERN GHATS

EASTERN GHATS

BAY OF BENGAL

Sri Lanka

INDIAN OCEAN

ARABIAN SEA

CASPIAN SEA

CAUCASUS MTS.

ZAGROS MTS.

PERSIAN GULF

ARABIAN PENINSULA

GULF OF ADEN

RED SEA

BLACK SEA

ANATOLIAN PLATEAU

Tigris

Euphrates

MEDITERRANEAN SEA

EUROPE

AFRICA

Arctic Circle

Arctic Circle

1000 Miles

1500 Kilometers

0   500   1000

0   500   1000   1500

Europe Today

★ Capital city

● Other city

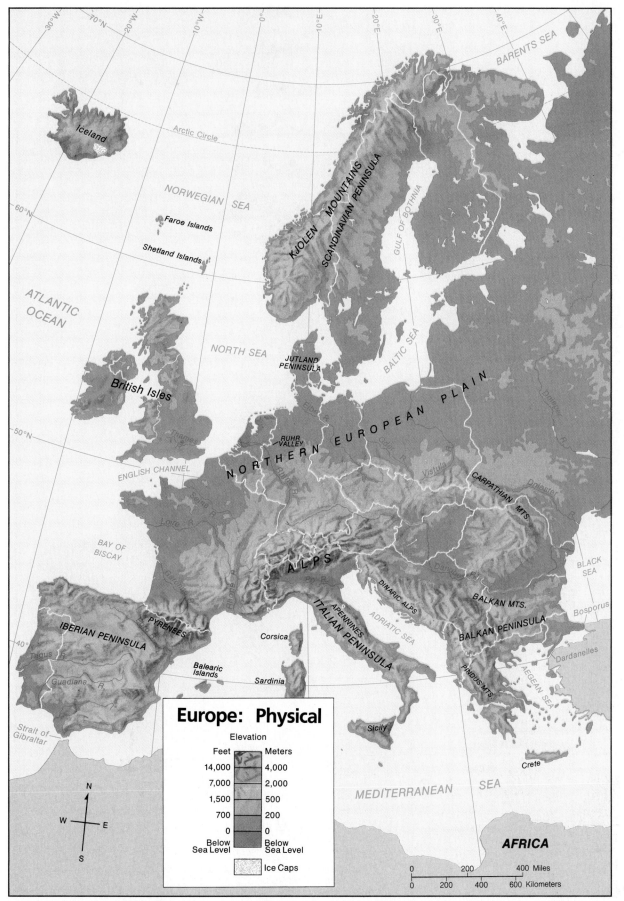

Europe: Physical

Elevation

Feet	Meters
14,000	4,000
7,000	2,000
1,500	500
700	200
0	0
Below Sea Level	Below Sea Level

Ice Caps

N
W — E
S

0   200   400 Miles
0   200   400   600 Kilometers

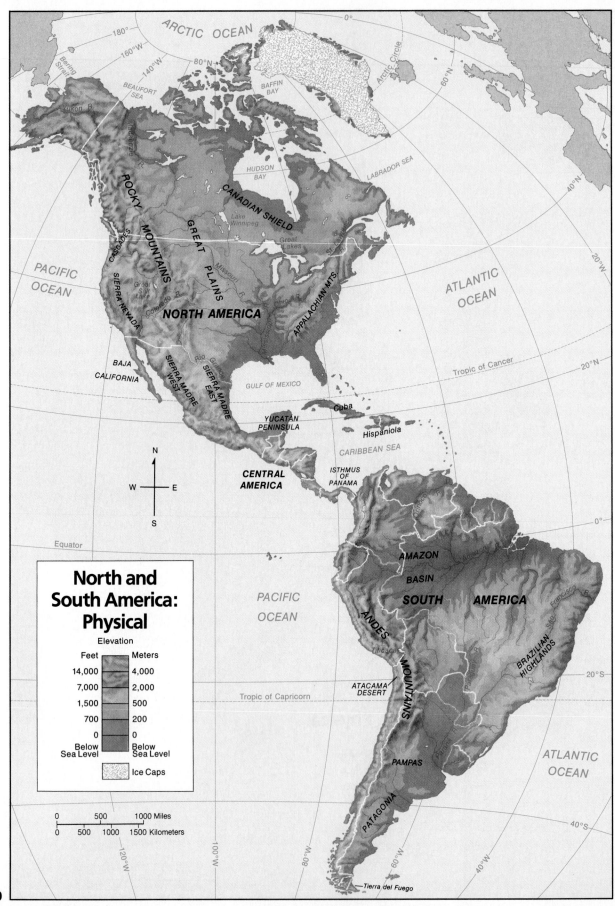

North and South America: Physical

Elevation

Feet		Meters
14,000		4,000
7,000		2,000
1,500		500
700		200
0		0
Below Sea Level		Below Sea Level

Ice Caps

0 500 1000 Miles

0 500 1000 1500 Kilometers

ARCTIC OCEAN

180°
160°W
140°W
80°N
0°
Arctic Circle
60°N

BEAUFORT SEA
BAFFIN BAY
Yukon R.

Mackenzie R.

HUDSON BAY
LABRADOR SEA
40°N

ROCKY MOUNTAINS
CANADIAN SHIELD
Lake Winnipeg
Great Lakes
St. Lawrence R.

GREAT PLAINS
CASCADES
SIERRA NEVADA
Great Salt Lake
Colorado R.
Missouri R.
Mississippi R.
Ohio R.
APPALACHIAN MTS.

NORTH AMERICA

PACIFIC OCEAN
ATLANTIC OCEAN
20°W

BAJA CALIFORNIA
SIERRA MADRE WEST
SIERRA MADRE EAST
Rio Grande

Tropic of Cancer
20°N

GULF OF MEXICO
Cuba
YUCATÁN PENINSULA
Hispaniola
CARIBBEAN SEA

N
W   E
S

CENTRAL AMERICA

ISTHMUS OF PANAMA

Equator
0°

Orinoco R.
AMAZON BASIN
SOUTH AMERICA
Amazon R.
São Francisco R.
BRAZILIAN HIGHLANDS

PACIFIC OCEAN

ANDES MOUNTAINS
Lake Titicaca
ATACAMA DESERT

Tropic of Capricorn
20°S

Paraná R.
Paraguay R.
PAMPAS
ATLANTIC OCEAN

PATAGONIA

120°W
100°W
80°W
60°W
40°W
40°S

Tierra del Fuego

790

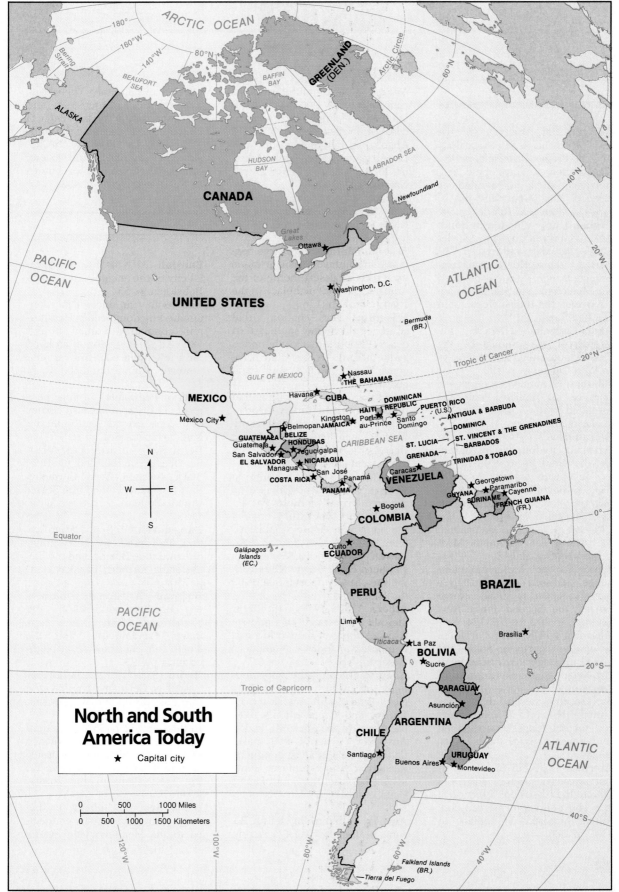

ARCTIC OCEAN

180°
160°W
140°W
80°N
Arctic Circle
60°N
40°N
20°W
0°

BEAUFORT
SEA

BAFFIN
BAY

GREENLAND
(DEN.)

Bering
Strait

ALASKA

PACIFIC
OCEAN

HUDSON
BAY

LABRADOR SEA

CANADA

Newfoundland

Great
Lakes

Ottawa ★

ATLANTIC
OCEAN

Washington, D.C. ★

UNITED STATES

Bermuda
(BR.)

Tropic of Cancer
20°N

GULF OF MEXICO

Nassau ★
THE BAHAMAS

MEXICO

Havana ★ CUBA

DOMINICAN
REPUBLIC

Mexico City ★

Kingston
JAMAICA

HAITI
Port-
au-Prince

PUERTO RICO
(U.S.)

ANTIGUA & BARBUDA

Santo
Domingo

DOMINICA

Belmopan

CARIBBEAN SEA

ST. LUCIA

ST. VINCENT & THE GRENADINES
BARBADOS

GUATEMALA BELIZE
Guatemala   HONDURAS
San Salvador Tegucigalpa
EL SALVADOR NICARAGUA
Managua

GRENADA

TRINIDAD & TOBAGO

San José

Caracas ★

COSTA RICA
PANAMA

Panamá

VENEZUELA

Georgetown
★ Paramaribo
★ Cayenne

Bogotá ★

GUYANA
SURINAME
FRENCH GUIANA
(FR.)

COLOMBIA

0°

Galápagos
Islands
(EC.)

Quito ★
ECUADOR

Equator

PERU

BRAZIL

PACIFIC
OCEAN

Lima ★

Brasília ★

L.
Titicaca

★ La Paz

BOLIVIA

★ Sucre

20°S

Tropic of Capricorn

PARAGUAY

North and South
America Today

★ Capital city

Asunción ★

ARGENTINA

CHILE

URUGUAY

Santiago ★

Buenos Aires ★

★ Montevideo

ATLANTIC
OCEAN

40°S

N
W   E
S

0   500   1000 Miles
0   500   1000   1500 Kilometers

120°W
100°W
80°W

Falkland Islands
(BR.)

Tierra del Fuego

60°W
40°W

791

A

Adriatic Sea, an arm of the Mediterranean Sea between Italy and the Balkan Peninsula. p. 96

Aegean Sea, an arm of the Mediterranean Sea; surrounded by Greece, Asia Minor, and the islands of Crete and Rhodes. p. 96

Afghanistan, a nation in South Asia; bordered by the Soviet Union, Pakistan, and Iran. p. 730

Africa, the world's second largest continent; located between the Mediterranean Sea, the Atlantic Ocean, the Indian Ocean, and the Red Sea. p. 34

Aix-la-Chapelle (51°N/6°E), the capital of the empire of the Franks; now called Aachen, a city in West Germany. p. 198

Albania, a nation in the western part of the Balkan Peninsula; bounded by the Adriatic Sea, Yugoslavia, and Greece. p. 618

Alexandria (31°N/30°E), the Egyptian city founded by Alexander the Great; became the center of Hellenistic culture; today, a modern Egyptian city. p. 114

Algeria, a nation in northern Africa; bounded by Morocco, the Western Sahara, Mauritania, Mali, Libya, Tunisia, and the Mediterranean Sea. p. 648

Alps, Europe's major mountain range; crossed by Carthage's army in order to invade Rome during the Second Punic War (219 B.C. to 202 B.C.). p. 124

Altamira (43°N/3°W), an area of caves in northern Spain; the site of an important discovery of Cro-Magnon cave paintings. p. 28

Amazon River, a river in northern South America; the largest river in the world by volume and the second longest; surrounded by the world's largest rain forest. p. 284

Amritsar (32°N/75°E), a city in northwestern India; the site where British troops fired on a peaceful political demonstration, killing hundreds of Indians in 1919. p. 586

Andes, a vast mountain range running about 4,000 miles (6,440 kilometers) along the western coast of South America. p. 284

Angola, a nation in southwestern Africa; bordered by the Atlantic Ocean, Zaire, Zambia, and Namibia. p. 710

Appian Way, an ancient 360-mile (500-kilometer) road from Rome to the Adriatic Sea; still in use. p. 133

Arabian Peninsula, a large peninsula in southwestern Asia; made up mostly of desert; home of the Arab people and birthplace of the Islamic faith. p. 176

Argentina, the nation that stretches down the southeastern coast of South America; bounded by the Atlantic Ocean, Chile, Uruguay, Brazil, Bolivia, and Paraguay. p. 485

Armenia, a Soviet republic that borders Iran and Turkey. p. 669

Asia, the world's largest continent; located between the Arctic Ocean, the Pacific Ocean, the Indian Ocean, and Europe. p. 34

Asia Minor, the peninsula in western Asia that now makes up the greater part of Turkey. p. 97

Assyria, a powerful ancient Mesopotamian empire that lasted from 1100 B.C. to 612 B.C. p. 56

Aswan (24°N/33°E), a city in southern Egypt on the Nile River; the site of two important dams on the Nile. p. 44

Athens (38°N/24°E), the most famous city-state in ancient Greece; home of the world's first democracy; today, a modern Greek city. p. 97

Atlantic Ocean, the enormous body of water that separates North and South America from Europe and Africa; extends from the Arctic to the Antarctic. p. 198

Australia, a nation that makes up the world's smallest continent; located in the Southern Hemisphere between the South Pacific Ocean and the Indian Ocean. p. 508

Austria, a nation in central Europe; bounded by West Germany, Czechoslovakia, Italy, Yugoslavia, Switzerland, Liechtenstein, and Hungary; until 1919, the center of an empire that included the lands of present-day Hungary, Czechoslovakia, Yugoslavia, and Poland; after 1867, the empire was known as Austria-Hungary. p. 402

B

Babylon (33°N/44°E), the capital city of the ancient kingdom of Babylonia. p. 55

Babylonia, an ancient Mesopotamian kingdom; leader Hammurabi conquered Sumer around 1800 B.C.; the kingdom flourished for a few hundred years; became powerful again around 600 B.C. p. 55

Balkan Peninsula, a huge peninsula in the southeastern corner of Europe; extends south into the Mediterranean Sea. p. 95

Baltic Sea, an arm of the Atlantic Ocean; surrounded by Denmark, Sweden, West Germany, East Germany, Poland, the Soviet Union, Finland, and Sweden. p. 198

Bangladesh, a South Asian nation; bordered by the Indian Ocean, India, Burma, and the Bay of Bengal; formerly East Pakistan. p. 730

Belgium, a nation in northwestern Europe; bounded by the Netherlands, France, West Germany, Luxembourg, and the North Sea; once part of the Netherlands. p. 323

Berlin (53°N/13°E), the former capital of Germany; now divided into East Berlin and West Berlin. p. 637

Bethlehem (32°N/35°E), a small village in the Palestinian province of Judea; the birthplace of Jesus, around 4 B.C.; today, a town on the West Bank of the Jordan River. p. 144

Black Sea, an inland sea between Europe and Asia; connected to the Mediterranean by the

Bosporus, the Sea of Marmara, and the Dardanelles. p. 176

Bosporus (41°N/33°E), the narrow strait that separates Europe and Asia Minor; connects the Black Sea and the Sea of Marmara. p. 176

Boston (42°N/71°W), the major city and capital of the U.S. state of Massachusetts; in colonial times, the site of the Boston tea party. p. 444

Brazil, a vast nation in eastern and central South America; a colony of Portugal until 1822. p. 483

Bulgaria, a nation on the eastern part of the Balkan Peninsula; bounded by Romania, Yugoslavia, Turkey, Greece, and the Black Sea. p. 577

Burma, a nation in Southeast Asia. p. 250

Byzantine Empire, also known as the Eastern Roman Empire; its changing boundaries at times included the lands of present-day Greece, Turkey, Bulgaria, Hungary, Yugoslavia, and Romania; the empire lasted from A.D. 395 to 1453. p. 175

Byzantium (41°N/29°E), an ancient city, founded in 667 B.C.; the city of Constantinople was built there by the Roman emperor Constantine in A.D. 330. p. 175

C

Cairo (30°N/31°E), an Egyptian city that became a prosperous and important part of the Muslim Empire; today, the capital of Egypt. p. 191

Cambodia, a nation in Southeast Asia; now known as Kampuchea. p. 250

Canada, a nation in the northern part of North America; bounded by the United States, the Pacific Ocean, Alaska, the Arctic Ocean, Baffin Bay, the Davis Strait, the Labrador Sea, and the Atlantic Ocean. p. 380

Cape of Good Hope, the land at the southern point of Africa. p. 552

Cape Trafalgar, the site off the southwest coast of Spain where Admiral Nelson's British navy defeated the combined fleets of France and Spain in 1805. p. 468

Caribbean Sea, an arm of the Atlantic Ocean; located between the West Indies and Central and South America. p. 284

Carthage, a great trading city founded by the Phoenicians on the northern coast of Africa; destroyed by the Romans in 146 B.C. after the Third Punic War. p. 124

Caspian Sea, an inland sea between the Soviet Union and Iran; makes up part of the geographical boundary between Europe and Asia. p. 198

Caucasus Mountains, a major mountain system in the Soviet Union that forms part of the geographical boundary between Europe and Asia. p. 198

Central America, a land bridge connecting North and South America; made up of seven nations: Guatemala, El Salvador, Belize, Honduras, Nicaragua, Costa Rica, and Panama. p. 283

Chaldea, an ancient Mesopotamian Empire that lasted only 74 years, from 612 B.C. to 538 B.C.; also known as the Neo-Babylonian Empire. p. 56

Chile, the nation that stretches down the southwest coast of South America; bounded by the Pacific Ocean, Argentina, Bolivia, and Peru. p. 485

China, an enormous land that covers much of East Asia; home of the early civilization in the Huang River Valley; united in 221 B.C.; a Communist republic since 1949. p. 80

Colombia, a nation in northwestern South America; bounded by Panama, the Caribbean Sea, the Pacific Ocean, Venezuela, Brazil, Ecuador, and Peru. p. 482

Congo River, Africa's second largest river; located in central and western Africa. p. 553

Constantinople (41°N/29°E), the capital of the Byzantine Empire and, later, of the Ottoman Empire; located on both sides of the Bosporus and, thus, the only city that lies on two continents; the Turkish city of Istanbul since 1930. p. 152

Corinth (38°N/23°E), an independent city-state of ancient Greece; today, a town in Greece, 4.4 miles (7 kilometers) from the original site. p. 98

Corsica (9°E/42°N), a Mediterranean island and region of France; birthplace of Napoleon. p. 124

Costa Rica, the second smallest nation in Central America; bounded by the Pacific Ocean, Nicaragua, the Caribbean Sea, and Panama. p. 687

Crécy, the site in France of a major battle of the Hundred Years' War, 1346. p. 319

Crete (36°N/25°E), an island located about 60 miles (96 kilometers) south of the mainland of Greece; home of Minoan civilization, which flourished between 2000 B.C. and 1300 B.C. p. 97

Crimea, a peninsula in the Soviet Union; won by Russia from the Turks in 1793; site of battles in the Crimean War, the Russian Revolution, World War I, and World War II. p. 402

Cuba, an island nation in the Caribbean Sea; located between Haiti, Jamaica, and Florida. p. 378

Cyprus (35°N/33°E), an island nation in the northeastern Mediterranean Sea. p. 643

Czechoslovakia, a landlocked nation of central Europe; bordered by East Germany, Poland, West Germany, Austria, Hungary, and the Soviet Union. p. 671

D

Danube River, a river in central and southeastern Europe; an important border of the Roman Empire. p. 198

Dardanelles, the narrow straits that connect the Black Sea with the Aegean and Mediterranean seas; located between Europe's Gallipoli Peninsula and Asia Minor. p. 176

Delhi (29°N/77°E), the capital of the powerful Delhi sultanate in India, which flourished during the 1200s and 1300s; today, the capital of India. p. 240

Denmark, a nation in northern Europe; the smallest and farthest south of the Scandanavian nations; made up of the peninsula of Jutland and a number of islands. p. 201

E

Ecuador, a nation in northwestern South America on the equator; surrounded by Colombia, Peru, and the Pacific Ocean. p. 482

Egypt, a land in northeastern Africa; the home of an ancient civilization that flourished during three periods—2780 B.C. to 2180 B.C., 2100 B.C. to 1788 B.C., and 1580 B.C. to 1090 B.C.; also the site of the modern nation of Egypt since 1936. p. 44

El Salvador, the smallest nation in Central America; bounded by Hondurus, Guatemala, and the Pacific Ocean. p. 686

Elba (43°N/11°W), the island between Italy and Corsica where Napoleon was sent after his defeat at Leipzig. p. 469

English Channel, an arm of the Atlantic Ocean that separates Britain from the continent of Europe. p. 313

Ethiopia, a nation in northeastern Africa; one of the world's oldest nations; known as Aksum in ancient times; also formerly known as Abyssinia. p. 294

Europe, the world's second smallest continent; forms an enormous peninsula from the Eurasian landmass; located between the Arctic Ocean, the Atlantic Ocean, the Mediterranean Sea, and Asia. p. 21

F

Fertile Crescent, a horseshoe, or crescent-shaped, area of good farmland that begins in the valleys of the Tigris and Euphrates rivers and runs along the coast of the Mediterranean Sea as far as Egypt; the "crossroads of the an-cient world" and site of ancient civilizations. p. 54

Florence (44°N/11°E), an ancient Italian city that became a center for world trade during the Middle Ages; later, an important center of the Renaissance; today, a city in Italy. p. 220

France, a western European nation; bounded by Belgium, Luxembourg, West Germany, Switzerland, Italy, Monaco, Spain, and Andorra. p. 197

G

Ganges River, one of India's two great rivers; flows eastward to the Bay of Bengal, forming wide and fertile valleys along the northern plains. p. 71

Gaza Strip (31°N/34°E), a small strip of land on the Mediterranean, northeast of the Sinai Peninsula; occupied by Israel since 1967. p. 650

Gdansk (54°N/19°E), a port city in Poland; formerly called Danzig; the scene of strikes by Polish workers in 1980. p. 670

Genoa (44°N/9°E), an Italian seaport on the Mediterranean that was a center of world trade during the Middle Ages; today, a city in Italy. p. 220

Germany, a European nation, united in 1871; at that time, bounded by the Baltic Sea, Denmark, the North Sea, the Netherlands, Belgium, France, Switzerland, Austria, and Russia; today, divided into East Germany and West Germany. p. 323

Ghana, a powerful trading kingdom in western Africa until the late 1000s; today, the name of a nation on the Gulf of Guinea. p. 292

Great Britain, a nation of western Europe made up of England, Scotland, and Wales; with Northern Ireland, makes up the United Kingdom of Great Britain and Northern Ireland. p. 437

Great Lakes, a chain of lakes in central North America on the U.S.-Canada border; the largest group of freshwater lakes in the world. p. 682

Greece, the land that occupies the southern end of the Balkan Peninsula; surrounded on three sides by seas—the Adriatic, Ionian, Mediterranean, and Aegean; the home of great ancient civilizations; today, a modern, independent nation since 1829. p. 95

Guadalcanal (9°S/160°E), an island in the southwestern Pacific Ocean; the largest of the Solomon Islands; captured by U.S. Marines from the Japanese during World War II. p. 623

Guam (13°N/144°E), an island in the western Pacific Ocean; the largest and farthest south of the Mariana Islands; captured by the Japanese a few days after the attack on Pearl Harbor. p. 623

Gulf of Tonkin, an inlet of the South China Sea; located east of Vietnam; the site of a conflict that began the commitment of American troops to the Vietnam War. p. 725

H

Hague (the) (52°N/4°E), a city in the Netherlands; the headquarters of the International Court of Justice. p. 590

Haiti, a nation in the Caribbean Sea; located on the western third of the island of Hispaniola. p. 378

Himalayas, one of the two great mountain ranges on India's northern border; includes Mount Everest, the world's highest peak. p. 71

Hindu Kush, one of the two great mountain ranges on India's northern border. p. 71

Hiroshima (34°N/132°E), a city in Japan; located on the southern part of Honshu Island; the U.S. dropped an atomic bomb on Hiroshima, August 6, 1945, in an attempt to end World War II. p. 275

Hong Kong (24°N/114°E), a British colony in East Asia; obtained in 1842 as a result of the First Opium War. p. 562

Huang River, one of China's three great rivers; one of the world's earliest civilizations developed in its valley. p. 80

Hungary, a nation in central Europe; bounded by Czechoslovakia, the Soviet Union, Romania, Yugoslavia, and Austria. p. 322

I

Iberian Peninsula, the area of southwestern Europe that includes Spain and Portugal. p. 189

India, the land that makes up most of the South Asian subcontinent, the home of one of the earliest civilizations; a modern, independent nation since 1947. p. 71

Indian Ocean, the world's third largest ocean; lies between Africa, Asia, and Australia. p. 555

Indonesia, a nation in Southeast Asia; makes up the world's largest island group with more than 13,600 islands and islets; once known as the Dutch East Indies. p. 250

Indus River, a river in northwestern India; India's earliest civilizations developed in the Indus Valley. p. 69

Ionian Sea, a part of the Mediterranean Sea, west of Greece and south of Italy. p. 96

Iran, a nation in southwestern Asia; bounded by the Soviet Union, the Caspian Sea, Afghanistan, Pakistan, the Gulf of Oman, the Persian Gulf, Iraq, and Turkey; known as Persia until 1935. p. 588

Iraq, a nation in southwestern Asia; bounded by Iran, Turkey, Syria, Jordan, Saudi Arabia, Kuwait, and the Persian Gulf. p. 588

Israel, a nation in the Middle East; bounded by the Mediterranean Sea, Lebanon, Syria, Jordan, and Egypt; established as a Jewish state in 1948. p. 648

Istanbul (41°N/29°E), the major city and seaport of modern Turkey; lies on both sides of the Bosporus, partly in Asia, partly in Europe; formerly known as Byzantium and later as Constantinople. p. 581

Isthmus of Panama (9°N/79°W), the narrow strip of land connecting North and South America; site of the Panama Canal. p. 378

Italy, a boot-shaped peninsula that reaches into the central Mediterranean Sea; the modern nation of Italy since 1861. p. 120

J

Jamestown, the first permanent English settlement in the New World; established in 1607 in the colony of Virginia. p. 381

Japan, an eastern Asian nation made up of four large islands: Hokkaido, Honshu, Shikoku, and Kyushu. p. 274

Jerusalem (32°N/35°E), an ancient city on a plain west of the Dead Sea and the Jordan River; traditionally, a holy city for Christians, Jews, and Muslims; conquered by Crusaders, 1099; recaptured by Muslims, 1187; today, the capital and largest city of Israel. p. 209

Johannesburg (26°S/28°E), the largest city in South Africa. p. 708

Jordan, a Middle East nation; located between Syria, Iraq, Saudi Arabia, and Israel. p. 53

Jordan River, a river in the Middle East that runs from the Lebanon-Syria border to the Dead Sea; its fertile West Bank lands are now ruled by Israel p. 649

K

Kampuchea, a nation of Southeast Asia, formerly known as Cambodia. p. 252

Kenya, a nation in eastern Africa, bounded by Tanzania, Uganda, Sudan, Ethiopia, Somalia, and the Indian Ocean; a British colony until 1961. p. 648

Khyber Pass (34°N/71°E), a mountain pass in the northeastern part of South Asia; a historical invasion route into India; today, on the border between Afghanistan and Pakistan. p. 71

Korea, an eastern Asian nation lying on a peninsula that extends 600 miles (966 kilometers) into the Yellow Sea off northern Asia; today, divided into North Korea and South Korea. p. 271

L

Laos, a nation in southeast Asia. p. 250

Lascaux, an area of caves in southern France; the site of a well-known discovery of Cro-Magnon cave art. p. 28

Latin America, the region that includes Mexico, Central America, and South America; the most common languages—Spanish and Portuguese—are based on Latin. p. 284

Lebanon, a nation in southwestern Asia on the Mediterranean coast; located between Syria and Israel. p. 53

Leningrad (60°N/30°E), a major city and seaport of the Soviet Union; was called St. Petersburg from 1703 to 1914 and Petrograd from 1914 to 1924. p. 401

Libya, an oil-producing North-African nation; located on Africa's Mediterranean coast between Tunisia, Algeria, and Egypt. p. 700

London (52°N/0°W), an ancient city on the Thames River in southeastern England; today, the capital of England and the United Kingdom; a major trade center and one of the world's most populous cities. p. 224

M

Malay Peninsula, a peninsula in Southeast Asia; forms part of modern Thailand and part of Malaysia; long an object of European imperialism since it lies on the shortest water route from Europe to the Far East. p. 566

Malaysia, a nation in Southeast Asia; made up of lands on the Asian mainland and on the island of Borneo. p. 250

Mali, a powerful western African trading kingdom from the eleventh century to the fifteenth

South Pole, the southern point at which the earth's axis meets the surface; covered by the landmass of Antarctica. p. 378

Southeast Asia, the region that includes the nations of Thailand, Burma, Vietnam, Laos, Kampuchea, Malaysia, Singapore, the Philippines, and Indonesia. p. 250

Soviet Union, a federation of 15 Socialist republics; stretches from the Baltic Sea to the Bering Strait and from the Arctic Ocean to Asia Minor; formed in 1922 by the leaders of the Russian Revolution; the official name is the Union of Soviet Socialist Republics. p. 601

Spain, a western European nation that occupies the Iberian Peninsula along with Portugal. p. 198

Sparta (37°N/22°E), a warlike Greek city-state and rival of Athens located at the southern end of the Greek peninsula; today, a town in Greece. p. 99

Sri Lanka, an island nation in the Indian Ocean; formerly Ceylon. p. 728

Stalingrad (49°N/44°E), a city in the Soviet Union where Soviet troops made a heroic stand to stop the Nazi advance during World War II; today, known as Volgograd. p. 623

Strait of Gibraltar (36°N/5°W), the passage between the Atlantic Ocean and the Mediterranean Sea; lies between Europe and Africa. p. 198

Sudetenland, an area of Czechoslovakia bordering on Germany; annexed by Germany in 1938; returned to Czechoslovakia after World War II. p. 617

Suez Canal (31°N/32°E), the canal in northeastern Egypt that connects the Mediterranean Sea with the Red Sea and the Indian Ocean. p. 555

Sumer, an ancient Mesopotamian kingdom that lasted from about 2500 B.C. to about 1800 B.C. p. 55

Sweden, a nation in northern Europe; located on the eastern side of the Scandanavian Peninsula. p. 201

Switzerland, a landlocked European nation; bounded by Liechtenstein, Austria, Italy, France, and West Germany. p. 322

Syria, a nation of the Middle East; bounded by the Mediterranean Sea, Israel, Jordan, Iraq, and Turkey. p. 46

T

Taiwan, an island nation made up of Taiwan Island and several other islands; where Nationalist forces fled after China's Communist revolution in 1949; then known as Formosa. p. 562

Tanzania, a nation in eastern Africa; located on the Indian Ocean coast between Kenya and Mozambique; formed in 1964 by the joining of Tanganyika and Zanzibar. p. 703

Teheran (36°N/52°E), the capital of Iran; located in northern Iran. p. 699

Tenochtitlán, the capital of the Aztec civilization in Mexico. p. 286

Texas, a state in the southwestern United States that was a part of Mexico until declaring its independence in 1836. p. 485

Thailand, a nation in Southeast Asia; formerly known as Siam. p. 250

Thebes, the capital city of ancient Egypt during the Middle Kingdom. p. 46

Thermopylae, the narrow Greek mountain pass where the Persians defeated the Spartans in 480 B.C. p. 103

Tiber River, a river that runs through central Italy; Rome was founded on the banks of the Tiber. p. 119

Tokyo (36°N/140°E), the capital and major city of Japan. p. 274

Toledo (40°N/4°W), a city on the Iberian Peninsula that was a center of the Muslim Empire and helped spread Muslim learning to the rest of western Europe; today, a city in Spain. p. 192

Tours (47°N/40°E), the site of an important battle where the Franks stopped the Muslim advance into western Europe in 732; today, a city in France. p. 189

Troy, an ancient city; according to legend destroyed by a Greek army around 1300 B.C. p. 94

Tunisia, a nation in northern Africa; bounded by Algeria, Libya, and the Mediterranean Sea. p. 648

Turkey, a nation that lies mostly on the Anatolian Peninsula and on a small, adjoining strip of land in Europe; made up the remains of the Ottoman Empire after World War I; won independence in 1922. p. 503

U

Uganda, a nation in eastern Africa; located between Rwanda, Tanzania, Kenya, Sudan, and Zaire. p. 703

United Arab Emirates, a federation of lands on the eastern central part of the Arabian Peninsula; an oil-producing region. p. 701

United States of America, a North American nation bounded by Canada, the Atlantic Ocean, the Gulf of Mexico, Mexico, and the Pacific Ocean; also includes Alaska and Hawaii. p. 446

Ural Mountains, a mountain range in the Soviet Union that forms part of the geographical boundary between Europe and Asia. p. 198

V

Vatican City (42°N/13°E), the tiny area of Rome ruled by the pope. p. 499

Venezuela, the northernmost nation of South America; a Spanish colony until 1823; part of Great Colombia until 1830. p. 482

Vietnam, a nation in Southeast Asia; divided into North and South Vietnam until 1975. p. 250

W

Washington, D.C. (39°N/77°W), the capital of the United States; located between Maryland and Virginia. p. 678

Waterloo (51°N/4°E), the site of the battle near Brussels, Belgium, where Napoleon met his final defeat by the combined forces of Europe in 1815. p. 469

West Indies, the region made up of Cuba, Jamaica, Haiti, and other islands of the Caribbean Sea. p. 372

Wittenberg (52°N/13°E), the German town where Martin Luther posted his *Ninety-Five Theses*; today, a town in East Germany. p. 356

Worms (50°N/8°E), the German town where the Diet, or assembly, of the Holy Roman Empire declared Martin Luther an outlaw in 1521; today, a town in West Germany. p. 357

Y

Yalta (45°N/34°E), a resort town in the Soviet Union on the Crimean Peninsula; the site of an important World War II meeting of Allied leaders in February of 1945. p. 626

Yugoslavia, a nation on the Balkan Peninsula; bounded by the Adriatic Sea, Romania, Bulgaria, Albania, Austria, Hungary, and Greece. p. 638

Z

Zaire, a central African nation with a strip of land extending to the Atlantic Ocean; formerly the Republic of the Congo. p. 704

Zambezi River, one of Africa's major rivers; located in the southeastern part of the continent. p. 290

Zimbabwe, a nation in southern Africa; bordered by Zambia, Mozambique, and Botswana; formerly Rhodesia. p. 706

A

abdicate, for a ruler to abandon the throne. p. 487

absentee landlord, owner of property who does not live on it or care about it except as a source of rent. p. 538

absolute location, exactly where something is located on the earth. p. 9

absolutism, complete or absolute control of a monarch over his or her people. p. 391

acid rain, rain that contains sulfur and nitrogen oxides gathered from factory smoke and automobile exhaust. p. 742

alchemy, early form of chemistry in which scientists tried to change inferior metals into gold. p. 225

alliance, agreement between nations to help each other when threatened. p. 576

anarchism, political belief that all governments and rule under law are unnecessary. p. 524

annexation, illegal, forceful takeover of adjoining territory by a nation. p. 617

anthropologist (AN thruh PAHL uh jihst), scientist who studies the customs, organization and relationships of a society. p. 24

anti-Semitism, hatred of Jews and the taking of action purposely prejudicial to them. p. 542

apartheid (ah PART hite), policy of strict racial separation in South Africa. p. 707

appeasement, policy of a nation giving in against its principles to a strong power in the hope of avoiding trouble. p. 617

Arabic numerals, number symbols from zero to nine developed in the third century B.C. and used by Indian mathematicians. p. 249

archaeologist (AHR kee AHL uh jihst), scientist who studies the remains of early peoples to learn about their cultures. p. 24

archipelago (ahr kih PELL uh goh), chain of islands. p. 252

aristocracy, rule by a privileged group, usually an upper-class minority. p. 99

armistice, a temporary agreement to stop fighting. p. 584

arms limitation, agreement between nations to limit the armaments produced, especially nuclear armaments. p. 680

artifact (AHR tuh FAKT), any object made by human such as tools, pottery or jewelry. p. 24

asiento (ah see EN toh), a Spanish trading privilege that allowed African slaves to be sold in the New World. p. 481

assimilation, a policy under which colonies were to be absorbed culturally and politically into the systems of the ruling nation. p. 554

atom, the smallest part of an element that can exist alone or in combination. p. 527

autocrat, ruler with total power. p. 322

axis, alliance between Germany, Italy, and Japan to promote the common purposes of these countries. p. 616

ayatollah, Muslim holy man, especially in the Middle East and Iran. p. 699

B

balance of power, plan to keep any one nation from becoming too strong. p. 392

Bantustan, so-called homelands for blacks in South Africa but actually large-scale reserves or isolated compounds for blacks. p. 707

barter, exchange of one product for another. p. 64

basilica, Christian church built according to a particular architectural plan. p. 340

blitzkrieg (BLITZ kreeg), from the German for "lightning war," the military method that uses sudden, swift, and overpowering attacks of air and ground forces. p. 619

borough, voting district from which representatives were elected to the House of Commons. p. 536

bourgeoisie (BOOR zhwah ZEE), members of the middle class in France. p. 454

boycott, refusal to buy goods produced by one group, especially another country. p. 586

buffer zone, neutral area that separates nations. p. 617

burgess (BUR jess), citizen of a borough or town in England, especially one who served in Parliament. p. 315

bushido, samurai code, or "the way of the warrior," that contained the precepts of loyalty, bravery, and discipline. p. 277

C

cahier (kah YAY), book containing lists of grievances and criticisms against the government drawn up by French Third Estate. p. 456

caliph (KAY lihf), Muslim leader with total power, except over religious teachings. p. 190

canton, one of the independent communities that joined to form Switzerland. p. 406

capitalism, economic system based on the private ownership of the means of producing goods and services. p. 231

caravel (KAHR uh VEHL), small, fast-sailing ship, such as Columbus's *Nina*. p. 373

caste system (kast), system that divided Indian society into four main groups according to occupation. p. 73

cataract, waterfall or series of rapids. p. 43

cavalry, soldiers on horseback. p. 105

censorship, system exercised by totalitarian governments to control public information and free speech. p. 670

chivalry (SHIV uhl ree), courtesy and highly developed court manners and procedures during Middle Ages. p. 207

circumnavigate, to sail completely around (the world). p. 376

citizen, a person who owes loyalty to a country and is entitled to that country's protection. p. 100

city-state, formerly polis, ruled by military nobles and later kings. p. 97

civil disobedience, tactics of nonviolent resistance to government action. p. 586

civil service, body of employees trained in government administration. p. 242

civilization, advanced society marked by use of a written language, government by law, and advances in science and the arts. p. 34

clan, community of people whose allegiance to each other is based on family ties. p. 274

cold war, condition between nations of hostility without armed conflict. p. 636

collaborate, to work in cooperation with another, particularly a defeated government working with its conqueror. p. 620

common law, system of laws developed in England, based on judges' decisions influenced by the customs of the people. p. 314

commune, community organized by a Communist government to control and direct the people and their industries. p. 718

communism, extreme form of socialism in which the state owns all land and means of production. p. 524

confederation, loose association of states, wherein the states are largely independent and the central government is limited. p. 500

conquistador (kon KEES tah dor), Spanish conqueror in the New World. p. 377

conservatism, political philosophy that resists changes in the traditional political and social order. p. 476

consul, Roman official and lawmaker chosen from patrician class. p. 121

corporate state, political system combining politics with the economy, especially in Mussolini's Italy. p. 604

corporation, a business organized by people who are permitted by law to sell shares of stock (ownership) in that business. p. 518

coup d' état (KOO day TAH), revolution in which a government is suddenly overthrown by a small group of people. p. 467

creole (KREE ohl), person of Spanish descent who was born in the colonies. p. 481

Crusades, holy wars organized by Christians to drive the Muslims from Palestine. p. 209

culture, the language, customs, and values followed by people in a society. p. 24

cuneiform (kyoo NEE uh FORM), early form of writing in Mesopotamia in which the characters were wedge-shaped. p. 55

czar (zar), title of princes of Moscow, from the word *caesar*, meaning emperor. p. 322

D

daimyo (DY myoh), a lord and landlord of feudal Japan. p. 276

dauphin (DAW fihn), title held by the eldest son of the king of France. p. 319

deforestation, the cutting down of forests at a rate greater than the planting and growth of new trees. p. 743

delta, area of soil washed down to the mouth of a river in the form of a triangle or Greek letter △ (delta). p. 43

demesne (dih MAYN), the best land in a medieval manor, belonging to the lord. p. 204

democracy, government in which the citizens rule, first developed in Athens. p. 101

despotism, term meaning government by a ruler with unlimited power. p. 137

dialect (DY uh LEKT), one of the various ways of pronouncing words in a language, such as Chinese. p. 269

dictator, ruler who reigns with absolute power and authority. p. 467

diplomatic revolution, shift of loyalties between countries, especially when a former enemy becomes an ally. p. 404

disciple, one who believes in and follows the teachings of another person. p. 144

discrimination, preferring one person over another often based on race, religion, or sex. p. 678

dissident, person who opposes the policies of his or her government. p. 666

dividend, a share of the profits of a corporation paid to its stockholders. p. 518

divine right, rule by the will of God, as claimed by some European monarchs. p. 391

domestic system, practice of entrepreneurs, or owners, of supplying raw materials to others to make at home a product for the owner. p. 514

domino theory, belief that countries near countries of Communist domination will fall to communism, as dominoes in a row will fall when the first one falls. p. 725

dove, one who opposes military action in resolution of an international problem, especially during the Vietnam War. p. 726

dynasty, family of rulers in which heirs to the throne are members of ruler's family. p. 45

E

embargo, restriction on international trade, often imposed in time of war. p. 622

encomienda (ehn koh mee EHN dah), system of labor used by Spain in the New World that bound Indians to the land as serfs. p. 481

entente (ahn TANT), understanding or agreement between nations. p. 576

entrepreneur (AHN truh pruh NOOR), individual who risks beginning a new business to make a profit. p. 384

epic, a long poem that describes the deeds of a hero. p. 111

epistle, letter included in the New Testament, especially of St. Paul. p. 147

estate, one of the three classes (clergy, nobles, and townspeople) of French society. p. 316

evangelist, preacher and writer of the gospels of the New Testament. p. 144

evolution, theory that states that the process of change from simple to complex forms of life takes place over a long period of time. p. 527

excommunicate (EKS kuh MYOO nuh kayt), to cut off from participation in the rituals and the blessings of the church and its priests. p. 208

expansionism, drive of a nation to increase its territory. p. 635

extraterritoriality, the right of a citizen accused of a crime in a foreign country to be tried under his or her country's law, not under the law of the foreign country. p. 562

F

factory system, practice of manufacturing goods by workers at a central place using power machines. p. 514

fallow, term used for land left untilled to restore its fertility. p. 204

fascism, political philosophy calling for the glorification of the state, a single-party system with a strong ruler, and aggressive nationalism. p. 603

federalism, system of government in which power is divided between the national (central) and state governments. p. 506

federation, form of government in which smaller states unite and give up some power to a central government. p. 106

feudal system, system in which the king grants land to nobles in return for military allegiance. p. 81

feudalism (FYOOD uh LIZ uhm), political organization of powerful lords, landowners, and tenants. p. 203

fossil, preserved remains of plants and animals. p. 24

freemen, artisans and merchants in feudal society who were not lords or serfs. p. 204

G

galley, Venetian ship propelled by oars and sails. p. 337

genetic engineering, science that adjusts the molecular structure of organisms. p. 737

genocide (JEN uh side), attempt to wipe out an entire religious or racial group. p. 607

geography, study of where things are on the earth, why they are there, and their relationships to people, things, or other places. p. 5

gladiator, armed fighter in the Roman circus. p. 126

glasnost (GLAHS NOHST), Russian word meaning openness, attributed to the political philosophy of Mikhail Gorbachev. p. 666

global economy, worldwide development, distribution, sale, and use of goods. p. 746

glyph (glif), picture writing used by early peoples of Mexico and Central America. p. 284

grand jury, in England under Henry II, those jurors who reported to the king's judges the names of those accused of crimes. p. 314

greenhouse effect, warming trend over parts of the earth caused by reflected sunlight trapped beneath a shield of pollution created by the burning of fossil fuels. p. 742

griots (GREE ohts), trained storytellers of Africa. p. 298

guild, organization of artisans that regulated business and trained workers. p. 181

gulag, forced-labor camp in Siberia or elsewhere in the Soviet Union. p. 602

H

hawk, one who urges military action in the resolution of an international problem, especially during the Vietnam War. p. 726

helot (HEHL uht), defeated enemy of Sparta who was treated as a slave. p. 99

heresy (HEHR ih see), belief that is contrary to those taught by a church. p. 208

hierarchy, organization of the officials of a government or religion, ranked according to their authority. p. 154

hieroglyphic (HI eroh GLIF ik), writing of ancient Egypt that used pictures to represent words and sounds. p. 41

historic period, period since the beginning of written records to the present day. p. 23

history, study of what human beings have done on earth. p. 2

home rule, the power of the people to make their own laws on domestic affairs. p. 539

host country, country that has accepted refugees for temporary or permanent resettlement. p. 739

human geography, study of the patterns and changes humans have made on the earth. p. 6

humanism, focus on the talents and strengths of the individual in the optimistic belief that humans can improve their society. p. 330

I

immunization, process of building up a resistance to a disease, especially through vaccination. p. 544

imperialism, the domination of the political, economic, and cultural life of one country or region by another country. p. 551

imperium, supreme authority in ancient Rome. p. 121

indoctrinate, instruct or provide strenuous teaching of a political philosophy, especially communism. p. 718

indulgence, a full or partial pardon for one's sins that was first granted by the medieval church. p. 352

interdependent, the condition in which continents and countries need each other for trade, protection, and natural resources. p. 36

infantry, footsoldiers. p. 105

isolationism, policy of government to stay out of international affairs. p. 616

J

jihad (jih HAHD), Muslim holy war. p. 187

joint-stock company, business in which a number of people invest their money by buying shares. p. 384

journeyman, rank in a guild of one who has learned the craft or trade. p. 220

K

kami (KAH mee), in Japanese history, nature spirits that may inhabit a mountain or waterfall or be represented in a jewel or mirror. p. 274

karma, force of a person's good or bad actions that will determine his place in the future life. p. 73

kismet (KIHZ met), fate, especially the Muslim belief in predetermination. p. 187

kowtow, deep bow of respect practiced by the ancient Chinese. p. 85

L

labor union, organization of workers whose representatives pursue the workers' interests and negotiate with owners of industry. p. 523

laissez faire (LES ay FAYR), French for "let people do as they choose," and meaning government should keep hands off business. p. 443

land reform, government division among the poor of land once owned by the wealthy. p. 685

landform, physical feature of the earth, such as a mountain, island, or valley. p. 6

latitude, the distance north or south as measured from the equator. p. 16

lend-lease, agreement of the United States to lend or lease military equipment to Great Britain and her allies during World War II. p. 622

liberalism, political philosophy that seeks individual freedom, political change, and social reform. p. 475

limited monarchy, monarchy in which the powers of the ruler are restricted, usually by a constitution or legislative body. p. 436

longitude, the distance east or west as measured from the prime meridian. p. 17

M

mandate system, system under which a nation is placed in charge of a colony until the colony can rule itself. p. 591

maniple (MAN uh puhl), subgroup of Roman legion of about 60 to 120 men. p. 123

marathon, long-distance race named after site of Greek victory and in honor of runner who brought news to Athens. p. 103

maritime, sea-going, a term applied to a country's tradition of building a navy. p. 371

martyr, person who dies for his or her faith. p. 149

mayor of the palace, adviser to a Frankish king. p. 198

mercantilism (MER kun til izm), the practice of colonists producing raw materials for the parent country and providing a market for that country's manufactured products. p. 385

mercenary, professional soldier usually hired by a country other than his or her own. p. 138

meridian, an imaginary line running north and south on the globe; vertical aspect of grid system. p. 16

mestizo (mee STEE zoh), child of Spanish and Indian parents. p. 481

metic (MEH teek), foreigner living in Greek city. p. 109

middle class, that class of people between the nobles and the peasants or serfs. p. 312

militarism, strong national feeling that glorifies war and encourages arms-building and readiness for battle. p. 576

mimicry (MIHM ik ree), entertainment of African origin in which the sounds of birds and animals are imitated. p. 300

minuteman, American citizen at time of the Revolution who volunteered to fight at a minute's notice. p. 446

missionary, person who works to teach and spread a particular religion. p. 147

mixed economy, combination of government controls and free trade, used especially to describe the economy of Hungary. p. 671

monarchy, rule of a single person who inherited the right and power to rule. p. 98

monastery, buildings that provide a home for a religious order, especially monks. p. 154

monotheism (MAHN uh thee ihzm), worship of a single God. p. 62

monsoon, heavy, seasonal rains in Asia. p. 251

movable type, separate pieces of wood or metal representing symbols, letters, and words that can be reused in printing. p. 273

mullah (MUL ah), prayer leader who is highly educated in Muslim teachings. p. 187

N

nationalism, desire of a people to form a nation to promote their common culture and interests. p. 309

nationality, group of people who share common history, customs, and language. p. 502

nationalization, taking over of industry by the government of a nation. p. 641

neutrality, policy of a nation to not participate in a war between other nations. p. 323

nirvana, ultimate goal of life in Hinduism and Buddhism. p. 76

nomad, person who moves in search of food and has no permanent home. p. 27

nome, province in ancient Egypt ruled by a warrior noble. p. 44

nonaggression pact, agreement between nations not to war against each other. p. 618

nonbiodegradable product, material that will last forever because it cannot break down and become part of the earth. p. 742

northwest passage, water route from Europe around or through North America to Asia, sought by European explorers. p. 380

novel, long story with a complex plot and human characters. p. 441

O

oasis, fertile area in a desert. p. 184

oracle, priest consulted by Greeks to foretell events through signs and omens. p. 108

orthodoxy, religion in which all members must accept its teachings and practices. p. 152

P

pain d'égalité (pan day GAHL ee TAY), "equality bread," bread made from whole wheat rather than white flour during the French Revolution. p. 464

pan-Arabism, movement to unite Muslim people in a common language and one religion and political system. p. 700

pantomime (PAHN tuh MYME), entertainment of African origin in which the actor shows the action of characters without using words. p. 300

papal bull, serious decree issued by a pope indicated by papal seal or "bulla." p. 357

papyrus (puh PY ruhs), reed plant used for making baskets, sandals, and paperlike writing material. p. 43

parable, short story that illustrates a moral or religious principle. p. 146

parallel, an imaginary line running east and west on a globe; horizontal aspect of grid system. p. 16

pariah, member of India's lowest social caste. p. 728

pasteurization, process of killing bacteria in foods through heat to make them safe for consumption. p. 544

paternalism, policy wherein the ruling country plays a parental role over the colony in all areas of its life. p. 554

patrician, upper class of Rome. p. 121

patron, an individual who sponsors arts and learning generally or the particular artistic endeavor of an individual. p. 336

perestroika (PEHR uh STROY kuh), Russian term meaning less government control, as explained by Mikhail Gorbachev. p. 668

petit (PEH tee) **jury**, in England under Henry II, the twelve jurors who discussed what they knew about a crime before a judge. p. 314

phalanx (FAY langks), group in Roman army comprised of 8000 soldiers. p. 123

pharaoh (FEHR oh), Egyptian ruler with absolute authority and glorified as a god. p. 45

philosophe (fee law ZAWF), French intellectual who thought, discussed, and wrote about the conduct of men and governments. p. 442

philosopher, serious thinker, so called from Greek words for "lover of wisdom," who sought knowledge through reasoning. p. 112

physical geography, study of the natural world. p. 6

plebeian (plih BEE uhn), common citizen of Rome. p. 121

plebiscite (PLEHB uh SYT), vote of people by direct ballot on a political issue. p. 467

polis, originally a fortress but later the town that developed within it together with the surrounding farms. p. 97

polytheism (PAHL ih thee ihzm), worship of many gods. p. 58

population base, number of people who are capable of having children. p. 736

population growth, increase in the size of a population. p. 736

prehistory, period before the appearance of written records. p. 23

primary source, document, record, or written account made by someone who took part in or witnessed an event. p. 2

princeps, title granted Octavian, meaning "first citizen." p. 135

printing press, machine used to make multiple copies of typeset information by pressing sheets of paper against a body of type. p. 344

privateers, English sea raiders who attacked Spanish treasure ships. p. 381

proletariat, the working class. p. 599

propaganda, a communications technique for shaping public opinion. p. 579

protectorate, a country with limited self-government under the control of a stronger country. p. 588

provisional government, temporary government established between legal or elected governments, especially in a time of crisis. p. 599

purdah (PUR dah), practice of wearing veils by Indian women. p. 246

Q

quipu (KEE poo), cord containing knots used by the Incas in place of a written language to keep records and send messages. p. 289

R

rajah (RAH jah), king of ancient India. p. 73

rajput, warrior class in ancient India. p. 79

rate of exchange, amount of one currency that can buy a certain amount of another currency. p. 747

realism, a movement in creative expression that emphasized portraying things as they are, with both ugly and beautiful aspects. p. 528

recant, to take back what has been said or written. p. 357

redcoat, British soldier in the American revolution, so called because of the color of his uniform. p. 446

reeve, foreman who supervised the work of serfs and served as their spokesperson. p. 206

referendum, vote by the people on a policy or measure. p. 660

relative location, location of a place relative to a known, familiar place. p. 9

religious toleration, the acceptance of the fact that different religions have different religious beliefs. p. 362

Renaissance (REHN uh sahns), from the Latin word for rebirth, a major cultural movement that began in Italy in the 1300s and spread throughout Europe. p. 329

reparations, payments for the costs of war demanded by the victorious nations from the defeated nations. p. 585

republic, form of government in which elected representatives of the people govern. p. 121

revenue, government income used to offset government expenses. p. 397

right of petition, freedom to make formal requests to the monarch. p. 437

Romance language, a language that developed in an area that had been part of the Roman Empire, such as French, Spanish, or Italian. p. 130

romanticism, a movement in creative expression that emphasized feeling and emotion and a love of nature, liberty, and beauty. p. 528

ronin (ROH nin), mercenary warriors of Japan who served no overlord. p. 276

S

sabotage, intentional destruction of property without concern for life by political foes of an individual, party, or government. p. 729

sacraments, solemn religious rites in which spiritual grace is bestowed. p. 352

salon, a gathering of talented and distinguished men and women who openly discuss their ideas. p. 443

samurai (SAH muh rye), vassal warriors in the feudal system of Japan. p. 276

sanction, restriction imposed on a country's trade by another country as a penalty for its political activities. p. 708

satellite country, a country controlled by the Soviet Union. p. 636

savanna, broad grassland with shrubs and trees in much of Africa. p. 290

scapegoat, a person, group, or thing wrongfully blamed for the mistakes or crimes of others. p. 607

schism (SIZ ehm), division with discord, particularly between factions of a church. p. 180

scholasticism (skuh LAS tih SIZ ahm), philosophy that held that faith could be achieved through logical reasoning. p. 228

scientific method, method requiring observation, writing down facts, and drawing conclusions about natural phenomena. p. 439

scurvy, disease caused by a lack of vitamin C. p. 371

secede, action of withdrawing, as a state from a confederation or union of states that form a nation. p. 506

secondary source, written account made some time after an event has taken place by a person who was not an eyewitness. p. 2

sepoy, Indian soldier in the British army. p. 558

serf, peasant who farmed and did other duties for the lord who owned the land. p. 203

shogun (SHOH GUHN), title of supreme military leader in Japan. p. 276

smelting, removal of metal from ore. p. 32

socialism, economic and political system in which society, rather than individuals, owns and operates businesses. p. 523

society, group of people who live together and share common goals, fortunes, and misfortunes. p. 24

Socratic method, teaching method that involves asking and answering questions. p. 113

sovereignty (SOV er uhn TEE), the power of a nation to establish policy, make decisions, and do as it wishes within its borders. p. 310

soviet, term used for a government council, especially in the Soviet Union. p. 599

specialization of labor, separation and assignment of jobs according to the skills of individuals. p. 30

squatter, economically poor individual or family who lives on property not personally owned or rented. p. 739

stadholder, ruler of sixteenth-century Holland. p. 407

stereotype, fixed, generalized ideas that ignore facts about individual situations. p. 715

stylus (STY luhs), sharp, hard-pointed instrument used for writing in damp clay. p. 61

subcontinent, very large landmass attached to a continent, such as India. p. 69

sub-Saharan, all that part of the continent of Africa south of the Sahara Desert. p. 290

suffrage, the right to vote. p. 501

suffragist, a person who worked for the right to vote, especially for women. p. 539

sultan, in India, ruler of a small state, especially Muslim. p. 241

sultanate, state governed by a sultan. p. 242

suttee (SU tee), expected death of a widow on the funeral pyre of her husband. p. 246.

T

tariff, tax on goods coming into a country. p. 399

theater of war, one of the four main areas in which World War II was fought. p. 623

theocracy (thee OCK rah see), form of government shaped by a religion. p. 359

theology, body of beliefs about God as professed by a particular religion. p. 153

theses (THEE seez), arguments carefully arranged to support a particular view, generally new and different. p. 356

tithe (tyth), tax imposed by a church, usually one-tenth of one's income. p. 208

totalitarian government, government in which one leader or party has total political control. p. 609

tournament, scheduled games of combat and horsemanship in medieval times. p. 207

trade deficit, financial imbalance resulting when the sales of a country's products are less than its purchase of foreign products. p. 747

tribalism, loyalty of members of a tribe that disrupts national unity. p. 704

tribune, Roman officials in the Assembly of Tribes, elected by plebeians. p. 122

tribute, money or goods exacted from weaker countries for protecting them. p. 265

troubadour, poet-musician who wandered from castle to castle singing songs of love and adventure. p. 226

trust territory, term given to former colony of defeated nation in World War II and held in trust by United Nations. p. 630

turtle ship, ship of the Korean navy protected by plates of iron armor. p. 272

tyrant, any harsh ruler. p. 99

U

underground, secret, generally illegal movement or organization determined to overthrow the existing government. p. 598

urbanization, growth of cities due to migration of people to them. p. 32

usury, in Middle Ages, practice of charging interest on money loaned to another. p. 208

V

vassal (VAS uhl), landowner who served a nobleman in return for his protection. p. 203

vernacular, everyday language of the people. p. 130

veto, power to stop an act of government officials. p. 121

veto power, power of each permanent member of the United Nations Security Council to prohibit any proposed action. p. 629

viceroy, ruler sent by Spain to govern a colony in the New World. p. 379

vote of confidence, vote taken within a parliamentary body to show that the majority support a particular leader. p. 683

Z

ziggurat (ZIHGG uh rat), Sumerian temple with shape of pyramid and outside staircases. p. 55

zionism, drive to establish a Jewish nation in Palestine. p. 648

GLOSSARY

Athens, 97, 98; first democracy of, 101–2; as leading city-state, 103

Attila the Hun, 137

Austerlitz, battle of, 468

Australia: and formation of commonwealth, 508; independence of, 641; settlement of, 508; western outpost in Asia, 724

Austria: absolutism in, 405; and Congress of Vienna, 478; Hapsburg family of, 324; Hitler invades, 617; nationalist groups in, 502–3; in Quadruple Alliance, 479; revolution in, 488; in Seven Years' War, 404; and War of Austrian Succession, 403

Austria-Hungary: annexations of, 577; declares war on Serbia, 578; establishment of, 502

Austro-Prussian War, 499, 501

Austro-Sardinia War, 498

Avignon popes, 354

Azerbaijan, 669

Aztecs, 286–88, 377–78

B

Babur, 242

Babylonia, 54, 55–56, 71; contributions of, 58–60; organized society of, 58–59

Babylonian Captivity, 354

Bach, Johann Sebastian, 441

Bacon, Francis, 439

Bacon, Roger, 225

Baghdad, 190, 191

Bakunin, Mikhail, 524

balance of power, 392, 398, 404

Balboa, Vasco Nuñez de, 377

Baltic states, 95–96; interest in, 577; and Soviet Union, 669

Balzac, Honoré de, 529

Bangladesh, 8, 730

banking: in Antwerp, 345; and Bank of France, 467; and Crusades, 211; feudal, 218; Florentine families in, 335; and Fugger family, 355; and great fairs, 216; Medici family and, 335; in medieval China, 267; Renaissance, 335

Bantus, 707

Bantustans, 707

barter, 218

Basil I, 176

Basil II, 176, 177

Basques, 662

Bastille, 457

Bay of Bengal, 71

Bay of Pigs incident, 685

Bedouins, 184

Beethoven, Ludwig von, 529

Begin, Menachem, Prime Minister, 694, 697

Behistun Rock, 58

Beijing (formerly Peking), 718 720, 777

Belgian Congo, 556

Belgium: and Africa, 556; Antwerp stock exchange of, 345; and Battle of Bulge, 624; and Battle of Waterloo, 469; becomes part of Netherlands, 478; invaded by Germany in WW I, 578; invaded by Hitler, 620; and Locarno Pacts, 592; and Peace of Westphalia, 407

Benedictines, 154, 155

Benin, artists of, 298–99

Ben-Gurion, David, 648

Bentham, Jeremy, 523

Beowulf, 226

Bering Strait, 283

Berlin: divided after WW II, 637; revolution in, 487

Berlin airlift, 637

Berlin Wall, 6, 643, 658, 773, 774

Bernadotte, Count Folke, 649–50

Bessemer, Henry, 515

Bhutto, Benazir, 729

Bhutto, Zulfikar Ali, 728–29

"Big Four," in Congress of Vienna, 477; in WW I, 585

Bill of Rights (England), 437

Bill of Rights (United States), 448

birth rates, 736

Bismarck: and Austria, 502; and Triple Alliance, 576; and unification of Germany, 501

Black Death, 232

Black Sea, 99, 176

Blackwell, Elizabeth, 546

blitzkrieg, 619

"Bloody Sunday," 596, 598

Body of Civil Law **(Byzantine),** 182

Boer War, 554

Boers, 381, 554

Boleyn, Anne, 360

Bolívar, Simón, 482, 484

Bolsheviks, 599

Bonaparte, Louis Napoleon. *See* Louis Napoleon

Bonaparte, Napoleon, 41; changes made by, 467–68; defeat of, by Russia, 469; exile to Elba, 469; exile to St. Helena, 469–70; profile of, 466–67; and war in Europe, 468–69

Borneo, 256

Bosporus, 176

Boston tea party, 445

Botha, Prime Minister Pieter William, 709

Boulanger, Georges, 542

Bourbons, 477

bourgeoisie, 454

Bourguiba, President Habib, 702

Boxer Rebellion, 550, 562–64, 586; China's punishment for, 563–64

Brahma, 74

Brahmans, 73, 244

Brandenburg, 403

Brandt, Willy, 661, 672

Brazil: becomes republic, 485; deforestation of, 743; peaceful revolution in, 483–84; returns to democracy, 688

Brest-Litovsk, Treaty of, 600

Brezhnev, Leonid, 666

British Commonwealth of Nations, 555

British East India Company, 381, 557–58

Bronze Age, 24, 31–33

Brunelleschi, Filippo, 333–34

bubonic plague, 232

Buddhism, 75–76, 266–67; growth of, in China, 262; in Japan, 275; in Korea, 272; in Southeast Asia, 253

Bulge, Battle of the, 624–25

Bunche, Dr. Ralph, 649–50

burgesses, 315

Burgundians, 198, 320

Burma, 252, 253–54, 588, 722; revolution in, 724

bushido, 277

business: in ancient Greece, 108; in ancient Rome, 129; in Babylonia, 59; changes brought by the Age of Discovery, 384; French, under Colbert, 399; and guilds, 220; in medieval China, 268; in Middle Ages, 208

Byron, George Gordon, Lord, 528

Byzantine Empire, 211; contributions of, 181–83; development of, 175–80; fall of, 182–83; military power, 178–79; religion in, 180; rules of, 176

C

Cabot, John, 380
Caesar, Julius, 124, 127–28
Caligula, 136
Calvin, John, 358–59, 434
Calvinism, 358–59, 364
Cambodia, 252, 305, 722, 727
Camp David Accords, 694
Canada: and alliance with United States, 682; dominion formed in, 508; and economic ties with United States, 684; French Nationalists in, 683; government of, 507–8, 682–83; impact of geography on, 682; as independent nation, 682–84; provinces and territories of, 682; Quebec Act of 1774, 507
Canossa, 212
Canterbury Tales, The (Chaucer), 333
Cape Colony, 554
Cape Horn, 284
Cape of Good Hope, 552–53
Capet, Hugh, 316
capitalism: described, 385; growth of, 364, 518; roots of, 231–32
Carter, President Jimmy, 694, 697, 719, 730; administration of, 678–79
Carthage, trade of, 124
Cartier, Jacques, 380
Cartwright, Edmund, 515
caste system, 73, 244, 558
Castile, 322
Castlereagh, Lord, 476
castles, 205–6
Castro, Fidel, 685, 710
cathedrals, medieval, 226–28
Catherine of Aragon, 360
Catherine the Great, 401–2; absolutism of, 408
Catholic church: England breaks with, 320; and National Assembly, 459–60; reforms from within, 360. *See also* Church, the
Cavaliers, 435
Cavour, Camilo di, 498–99
Celtic people, 36
censors, 121

censorship: in Brazil, 688; in Chile, 688; in czarist Russia, 598; under Louis Napoleon, 540; in Nazi Germany, 606; in Poland, 670; in Soviet Union, 667
Central America, conflicts in, 686–88
Central Powers, composition of, in WW I, 578
Ceylon. *See* Sri Lanka
Cezanne, Paul, 529
Chabray, Madelaine, 457
Chaldean Empire, 54, 56
Chamberlain, Prime Minister Neville, 614, 618
Champollion, Jean, 41
Chang (Yangtze) River, 80
Charlemagne, 180, 198, 202, 309, 316; reign of, 200–1
Charles I, King (England): beheading of, 435; rule of, 434–35; and war with Scotland, 434
Charles II, King (England), 436
Charles II, King (Spain), 398
Charles IV, King (France), 317
Charles V, Emperor (Holy Roman Empire), 357, 358, 360
Charles V, King (Spain), 378, 392
Charles VI, Emperor (Austria), 405
Charles VII, King (France), 319, 320
Charles X, King (France), 486
Charles XII, King (Sweden), 401
Charles the Bold, 201
Chartists, 537–38
checks and balances, 447–48
Chernenko, Konstantin, 666
Chernobyl (Soviet Union), 745
Chiang Kai-shek, 587, 646, 721
child labor, 521, 523
Children's Crusade, 211
Chile, 485, 688–89; stability in, 485
China: art and inventions of medieval, 269–70; and Boxer Rebellion, 562–64; under Chiang, 587; civil war in, 587; under Communist rule, 646; Cultural Revolution in, 718; cultural traditions of, 266–70; dynasties of, 81–82; early history of, 80–83; economy of medieval, 267–68; establishment of two Chinas, 646; European imperialism in, 561; family life in medieval, 266–67; feudalism in, 81; foreign powers mistreat,

562; geography of, 80–82; golden ages of, 261–70; influence of, on Japan, 275–76; in the 1980s, 720; pottery of, 267–68; reentry to world affairs, 718–21; as a republic, 586–87; unification of, 84; United States recognition of, 719; and war with Vietnam, 719. *See also* Republic of China.
chivalry, 207, 223, 226
Chopin, Frederic, 529
Chou dynasty. *See* Zhou dynasty
Chou En-lai. *See* Zhou Enlai
Christianity: appeal of, 151; beginnings of, 143–56; in Ethiopia, 294; under Hitler, 607; literature of, 152–53; as major force in western civilization, 152; missionaries of, in Japan, 276; as official religion of empire, 150–51; persecution of members of, 147; religious and political differences of, 179–80; and Renaissance art, 343; and Roman Empire, 148–51. *See also* Catholic Church, Reformation, Protestantism
"chunnel," 665
Church, the: canon law of, 231; on equality of men, 230–31; and government, 154–55; internal divisions of, 354–55; and medieval economy, 208; and medieval education, 224–25; and medieval government, 208–9; and moneylending, 218; principal beliefs of, 352; becomes Roman Catholic church, 179; as successor to Rome, 155; supremacy of, in Middle Ages, 352, 353. *See also* Catholic church, Christianity
Church of England, 360. *See also* Anglican church
Churchill, Prime Minister Winston, 620, 626, 635, 641
Cicero, 126, 130–31
cities: and civilization, 34; European, in Middle Ages, 197; growth of, 543; Renaissance, 335
citizens: of ancient Greece, 109; in ancient Rome, 130; in Sparta, 100
city-states, 97–98, 99; Italian, 331, 499
Civil Rights Act of 1964, 678
civil service: in ancient India, 242; Inca, 289; in medieval China, 268–69; during Tang dynasty, 263

D

ancient, 99; independence of, 503; lasting cultures of, 110–14; life in ancient, 107–9; natural resources of, 108; philosophies of ancient, 112–14; after WW II, 643; wars in ancient, 103–6

Greek Dark Age, 97, 99
"Greek fire," 179
Greek Orthodox church, 179
greenhouse effect, 734
Greenpeace, 744
Gregory VII, Pope, and Henry IV, 212
griots, 298
guilds: and business life, 220–21; in China, 267; in Constantinople, 181; student, 224–25
gulags, 602
Gulf of Tonkin Resolution, 725–26
gunpowder, 269, 318
Guptas, 78–79
Gustav I, King (Sweden), 324
Gustavus Adolphus, King (Sweden), 364
Gutenberg, Johann, 344

H

habeas corpus, 231, 432
Habeas Corpus Amendment Act, 432
Hadrian, Emperor, 133, 136, 182
Hague, The, 590
Haile Selassie, Emperor, 703
Hammarskjold, Dag, 629
Hammurabi, 55–56
Hammurabi's Code, 55, 59, 62
Han dynasty (China), 83, 85; fall of, 261–62
Handel, George Frederick, 441
Hannibal, 124
Hanseatic League, 219
Hapsburg family, 323, 324, 363, 392
Harappa, 71
Hargreaves, James, 514
Harold, King (England), 313
Harun al-Rashid, 190
Harvey, William, 441
Hassan, King (Morocco), 720
Hastings, Battle of, 313
Hastings, Warren, 558
Hatshepsut, 47, 48
Hausa tribe, 704
Hawkins, Sir John, 381, 395
health: improvements in nineteenth century, 543–44; and population growth, 737

Hebrews, 60, 61–63
Hegira, 186
Heian period, 276
Hellenes, 97
Hellenic civilization, 97
Hellenistic culture, 106, 114
helots, 99
Helvetii, 406
Henry I (England), 207
Henry II (England), 222, 313
Henry IV, King (France), 342, 397; and Pope Gregory VII, 212
Henry VI, King (England), 320
Henry VIII, King (England), 320, 360, 380, 392, 394
Henry of Navarre, 363
Henry the Navigator, Prince, 375
Herbart, Johann, 545
heresy, 208
Herodotus, 5, 42, 103
Hidalgo, Miguel, 482
Hideyoshi, 272, 276
hieroglyphics, 41, 45, 50
Himalaya Mountains, 68, 71
Hindenburg, General Paul von, 580, 606
Hindu Kush, 71
Hinduism: 73–75; and absorption of Buddhism, 79; in Indonesia, 256; in Southeast Asia, 253
Hindus: under Akbar, 243; conflict with Muslims, 645–46; persecuted by Muslims, 244
Hippocrates, 114
Hirohito, Emperor (Japan), 626
Hiroshima, 275, 626
historians, 2–4, 5
history, defined, 2, 735
Hitler, Adolf, 605–7, 609, 625; and Nazi party, 606; terrorizes Europeans, 620
Hittites, 48, 56
Ho Chi Minh, 724–25
Hobbes, Thomas, 311
Hohenzollerns, 404, 501
Hokkaido, 274
Holland, and absolutism of Philip II, 406–7
holocaust, 607
Holy Alliance, 479, 590
Holy Roman Empire: and Charlemagne, 200, 201; under Charles V, 392–93; creation of, 200; and Diet of Worms, 357; end of, 478; German states of, 324; and Hapsburgs, 405
Homer, 111–12
Hong Wu, 265
Horace, 130, 131

House of Burgesses (Virginia), 382–83
House of Commons, 315
House of Lancaster, 320
House of Lords, 315
House of York, 320
Hsia dynasty. *See* Zia dynasty
Hsuan Tsung. *See* Xuan Zong
Huang (Yellow) River, 69
Hudson, Henry, 380
Hugo, Victor, 529
Huguenots, 359, 363, 400
human geography, 6–7
humanism, 330
humanitarianism, 525
Hundred Years' War, 308, 317–20
Hungary: Communist rule of, 639–40, 671; economic prosperity in, 671; fascism in, 609; kingdom of, 501
Huns, 79, 137, 198
Huss, John, 354
Hussein, President Sadam (Iraq), 699
Hyksos, 46–47

I

Iberian Peninsula, 321–22
Ibn Saud, 588
Ibo tribe, 704
Ice Age, 28, 283
Ikhnaton (Amenhotep IV), 49, 56
Illiad **(Homer),** 94, 97, 111–12
imperialism, 617; in Africa, due to geography, 552–53; as factor leading to World War I, 576; reasons for, 551–52
Impressionists, 529
Inca empire, 288–89
India: ancient traditions of, 245–48; under British control, 557–60; caste system of, 244; contributions of, 249–51; families in, 245; geography of, 69–71; Golden Age of, 78–79; and independence, 586, 645–46, 728; invaded by Muslims, 241–42; kingdoms of ancient, 77; post-Vedic age of, 246; religion in, 73–76, 250; slavery in, 241; village life in, 247
India Act, 558
indirect rule, of colonies, 554
Indo-Aryans, 72–73
Indochina, 255, 588

INDEX

815

Koryo dynasty, 272
Krishna, 250
Kshatriyas, 73
Kuang Hsu, Emperor, 562–63
Kublai Khan, 253, 263–64, 276
Kush, 46
Kushan Empire, 78
Kushites, 292

L

La Marseillaise, 461
labor union, 523
Labour party (Britain), 641
laissez faire, 443; philosophy of, 520
landform, 6
Lao-tse. *See* Laozi
Laos, 252, 722
Laozi, 82
Las Casas, Bartolome de, 379, 481
Lascaux (France), 28
Last Supper, The (Da Vinci), 144, 153, 338, 339
Latin, 130
Latin America: challenges to, 685–89, 690; forced labor in, 481; formation of countries of, 484–85; geography of, 287; origin of term, 284; revolutions in, 482–84
Latins, 119
latitude, 15–17
law: in ancient Athens, 101; Church, 208; in English nation, 313–14; Roman, 122, 130. *See also* Bill of Rights; Constitution; Hammurabi's Code; International Court of Justice; Magna Carta; Napoleonic code
League of Nations, 585; condemns Japan, 587, 617; peace goals of, 590; purpose of, 590–91; successes and failures of, 592
leagues, town, 219
Leakey, Richard E., 26
Lebanon, 53
Lee Kuan Yew, 724
Leeuwenhoek, Anton van, 441
legions, 123
Leipzig, battle of, 469
lend-lease agreements, 622
Lenin, Vladimir Ilyich Ulyanov, 583, 599–600
Leo I, Pope, 138, 179
Leo III (Byzantine Emperor), 176, 180

Leo X, Pope, 355, 357
Leon, Ponce de, 377
Leopold II, King (Belgium), 556
Lespinasse, Julie de, 444
Letters on the English (Voltaire), 442
Leviathan (Hobbes), 312
Li Yuan (China), 260
liberalism, 475–76
Libya, terrorism in, 700–1
limited monarchy, 436–38, 459, 460, 486
Lin Ze Xu, 561
Lincoln, President Abraham, 506
literature: Africa, 298; ancient China, 84; ancient Greece, 110–11, 113–14; ancient India, 74–75, 249, 250–51; of Christianity, 143–45, 149; early Russia, 183; Egypt, 46; of Hebrews, 62; Islam, 186; medieval, 226; medieval China, 269; Muslim, 191; nineteenth century, 528–29; Renaissance, 330–31, 342; Rome, 130; vernacular, 331
Lithuania, 669
Liu Bang, 85
Liu Pang. *See* Liu Bang
Livingston, David, 553–54
Lloyd George, David, 585
Locke, John, 442, 446, 447
Lombards, 178, 198
Lombardy, 497, 498
London: blitz of, 619; fire of, 437
"long armistice," 616
Long March, 719
Long Parliament, 435
longitude, 15–17
Louis VII, King (France), 222
Louis XI, King (France), 320
Louis XIII, King (France), 397–98
Louis XIV, King (France): absolutism of, 390, 398–400; culture during reign of, 399; and divine right, 391; mistakes of, 400
Louis XV, King (France), 454
Louis XVI, King (France), 454, 455; and Estates-General, 456–57; execution of, 461
Louis XVIII, King (France), 469, 477, 486
Louis the German, 201
Louis Napoleon, Emperor (France), 487, 498, 501, 540–41; and Crimean War, 540
Louis Philippe, King (France), 486
Luddites, 536
Luxembourg, 620, 644

Lusitania, 582
Luther, Martin, 355, 356–58, 364, 446; and Charles V, 392; excommunication of, 357
Lutheranism, 358
Luthuli, Albert John, 708
Luxor, 41, 49
Lydians, 48, 61, 64

M

MacArthur, General Douglas, 625–26; and Korean "police action," 647; and President Truman, 647–48
Macedonia, conquests of, 104–6
Macedonian Wars, 124
Machiavelli, Niccolò, 336, 498
Machu Picchu, 282
Mackenzie, William, 507
Magellan, Ferdinand, 376
Maginot Line, 620
Magna Carta, 231, 314–15
Mahmud of Ghazni, 241
Malay Peninsula, 566
Malaya, 645
Malays, 253
Malaysia, 252, 256, 722, 724
Mali, 292
Malta, summit at, 680
Malthus, Thomas, 520
Manchu dynasty, 562
Manchuria, invaded by Japan, 587
Manchus, 265
Mandela, Nelson, 708
maniples, 123
manor, 204; life in, 206–7; replaced by towns, 218–20
Mansa Musa, 292–93
Mao Tse-tung. *See* Mao Zedong
Mao Zedong, 646, 718, 719
Maoris, 508
maps: information on, 17–18; kinds of, 14; uses for, 14–18
Marcos, President Ferdinand (Philippines), 723
Marcus Aurelius, Emperor, 136–37, 148–49
Margrethe I, Queen (Denmark), 324
Maria Theresa, Empress (Austria), 403, 405; letters of, 404
Marie Antoinette, Queen (France), 452, 454, 455, 462
Mark Antony, 129
marriage: in ancient Rome, 138; in medieval China, 266; in Middle Ages, 222

N

nationalism, 476, 528; in Austria-Hungary, 502; and breakup of Ottoman Empire, 503–5; defined, 497; and division of Austrian Empire, 502; as force in history, 309; in Germany, 617; influence of, beyond Europe, 506–8; Italy, 617; Japan, 617

Nationalist People's Party (Kuomintang), 586

nationalization, in Great Britain, 641

nations: characteristics of, 310–11; formation of, throughout Europe, 321–24; growth of, 308–26

NATO (North Atlantic Treaty Organization), 638

Nazi-Soviet pact of 1939, 618

Ne Win, U, 724

Neanderthal people, 26–28

Nebuchadnezzar, King, 56, 62

Nehru, Prime Minister Jawaharlal, 586, 645, 728

Neolithic Revolution, 29

Nero, Emperor, 136, 147, 148

Nerva, Emperor, 136

Netherlands, the, 11, 323–24; colonies of, 381; under Philip II, 393

neutrality: defined, 323; of Swiss, 406; and Treaty of Paris, 504

New Economic Policy (NEP), 600

New Kingdom (Egypt), 45, 47–48

New Model Army, 435

New Stone Age (Neolithic Age), 26; changes of, 29–30

New Testament, 143–45, 147; composition of, 152

New Zealand, 724; joins British Empire, 508

Newton, Sir Isaac, 439, 440–41

Nicaragua, 687; in Reagan administration, 680

Nicene Creed, 152

Nicholas II, Czar (Russia), 480, 503, 590, 596, 598

Niger River, 290, 553

Nigeria, 704

Nile River, 42–44, 290, 553

Ninety-Five Theses, 356

Nixon, President Richard M.: administration of, 678; and Vietnam War, 726; visit to China, 718–19

Nkrumah, Kwame, 648, 704–5

Nobel, Alfred, 590

Noriega, Manuel, 775

Norman conquest, 313

Normans, 202

North German Confederation, 501

North Korea *vs.* South Korea, 717

North Sea, 324

Northern Society, 480

northwest passage, 380–81

Nu, U, 724

Nubia, 46, 48

nuclear arms race, 627

Nuclear Test Ban Treaty, 680

Nuremberg trials, 636

Nyerere, President Julius K. (Tanzania), 703

O

ocean voyages, dangers of, 370–71

Octavian (Augustus), 118, 129, 135

***Odyssey* (Homer),** 97, 111–12

O'Higgins, Bernardo, 482–83

oil, importance of Arab, 588; of Middle East, 696, 746; in Nigeria, 704

oil spills, 745

Old Kingdom (Egypt), 44, 45–46

Old Regime, 453–55

Old Stone Age (Paleolithic Age), 26

Old Testament, 152

Olmecs, 284

Olympic Games, 107

Omar (caliph), 190

Open Door Policy, 562, 564

Opium Wars, 561–62

oracle, 108

Orange Free State, 555

Organization of American States (OAS), 690

Organization of Petroleum Exporting Countries (OPEC), 696

Orlando, Vittorio, 585

Orléans, battle of, 319

Ortega Sanvedra, Daniel, 687

Orthodox church, 179

Ostpolitik, 661, 672

Ostrogoths, 198

Oswald, Lee Harvey, 678

Othman (Caliph), 190

Ottoman Empire: nationalist groups in, 503

Ottoman Turks, 183

Ovid, 130, 131

Owen, Robert, 525

OXFAM, 741

P

Paine, Thomas, 446, 447

Pakistan, 68, 646, 728–29

Palestine, 46, 48, 61; divided by United Nations, 648

Palestine Liberation Organization (PLO), 698

Palestine National Council (PNC), 698, 699

Palestinians, displaced, 698

Panama Canal, 687; invasion of, 775

Panchatantra, 250

Pantheon, 133

Papal States, 198, 208, 497, 499

Papandreou, President Andreas (Greece), 662

Papineau, Louis Joseph, 507

papyrus, 43, 50

Paris, Treaty of, 445, 507

Parliament, 315; under Stuarts, 433–35; and Tudors, 396

Parthenon, 103, 110

Pasteur, Louis, 544

Pataliputra, 77

patriarchs, 180

patricians, 121–22, 125

Paul, St., achievements of, 146, 147

Pax Romana, 129

Peace Corps, 676, 678, 741

Peace of Augsberg, 358

Peace of Westphalia, 364, 406, 407

Pearl Harbor, 622

Pearson, Prime Minister Lester (Canada), 683

peasants: China, 81, 267; Egypt, 50; Greece, 108; Sparta, 99

Peasants Rebellion, 232

Pedro II, Emperor (Brazil), 485

Peking. *See* Beijing

Peloponnesian Wars, 104

Peloponnesus, 97

People's Republic of China, 646. *See also* China

Pepin the Short, 198

Pepys, Samuel, 437

perestroika, 668–69

Pericles, 103–4

Perón, Isabel, 688

Perón, Juan, 688

Perry, Commodore, 277, 565

Persians, 48, 56, 103, 178

Pétain, Henri Philippe, 581, 582, 620

Peter, St., 147

Peter the Great, Czar (Russia), 401; goals of, 602

bia (1819), 482; in Cuba, 685; in Ecuador (1822), 482; in France (1848), 486–87; in Hungary (1849), 488; in Mexico (1824), 485; in Russia, 480, 597–601

Reza Khan, 588

Reza Pahlavi, Mohammed, 699

Rhee, President Syngman, 647

Rhine River, 345

Rhineland, occupied by Germany, 617

Rhodes, Cecil, 554

Ricardo, David, 520

Richard II, King (England), 232

Richard III, King (England), 320

Richard the Lion-Hearted, King, 209, 222, 314

Richelieu, Cardinal, 364, 397–98

Rig-Veda, 74

right of petition, 437

Rio Grande, 284

Robespierre, Maximilien de, 462

Roh Tae Woo, 717

Roland, Madame, 463

Roman Catholic church, 130, 179. *See also* Church, the

Roman Empire, 106, 123–30; African province of, 292; and Christianity, 143–56; history of, 155; persecution of Christians by, 148–51

Roman Republic, 121–22

Romania, 672

Romanov family, 322, 599

romanticism, 528

Rome: capital of united Italy, 499; fall of, 138, 175; geography of, 120; government of ancient, 121; growth of, 119–20; heritage of ancient, 331; influence of, on western civilization, 130–33; invasions of, 137, 198; as monarchy, 129; practical gifts of, 132–33; values of, 131–32; as world power, 124

Rome-Berlin-Tokyo Axis, 616

Roosevelt, Eleanor, 644

Roosevelt, President Franklin D., 616, 625, 626, 724

Rosas, Juan de, 485

Rose, Lisa A., 651

Rosetta Stone, 41, 58

Roundheads, 435

Rousseau, Jean Jacques, 443, 446

Rubens, Peter Paul, 441

Rubicon River, 128

Runnymeade, 314

Rurik, 322

Russia: civil war in, 600; and entry in WW I, 598–99; and nationhood, 322; in Quadruple Alliance, 479; revolution in, 480, 597–601; in WW II, 580–81, 582–83. *See also* Soviet Union

Russian Orthodox church, 598, 600

Russo-Japanese War, 598

Russo-Turkish War, 505

S

Sabuco, Olivia, 342

Sadat, President Anwar (Egypt), 694, 697

Sahara, 290, 552

Saigon, 726

St. Bartholomew's Day Massacre, 363

St. Peter's Basilica, 340

St. Sophia, Church of, 182

Sakharov, Andrei, 667

Saladin, 209

Salamis, 103

Salk, Jonas, 737

samurai, 276, 277–78

San Martín, José de, 482

Sandinista National Liberation Front (Sandinistas), 687

Sanskrit, 75, 79

Santa Anna, Antonio Lopez, 485

Sarajevo, 578

Sardinia, 124, 497, 498

Sargon I, 55

Saudi Arabia, 588

savannas, 290

Saxons, 198, 202

Scandinavia, and nationhood, 324

scholarship, in medieval China, 268

Scholasticism, 288

science: in ancient India, 249; Arabic contributions to, 190; in Hellenistic culture, 114; and Industrial Revolution, 527; in Middle Ages, 225; in nineteenth century, 543–44

scientific method, 225, 439

scientists, work of, with historians, 23–25

Sea of Marmara, 176

Second Balkan War, 577–78

Second French Republic, 487

Second Hundred Years' War, 557–58

secondary source, 2–3, 279

Secretariat, of United Nations, 629

Security Council, of United Nations, 628

self-government, and WW I, 586

Seljuk Turks, 183, 190, 209

senate, of Sparta, 100

Seneca, 130, 131

Seoul, ancient Korea, 272

Sepoy Mutiny, 558

Serbia, and Balkan wars, 577

serfdom, disappearance of, 231

serfs: American Indians as, 481; in Austria, 405; daily life, 203, 204–5; defined, 203; emigration to towns of, 218, 220; and Magna Carta, 314; in Old Regime, 454; in Russia, 598, 602

Seven Years' War, 403–4, 445

Shakespeare, William, 333, 392, 395

Shang dynasty, 81

shelter: in ancient Greece, 109; of Cro-Magnon, 28; of Neanderthals, 28; in New Stone Age, 30

Shi-Huang, 84

Shiites, 699

Shinto, 274

shogunates, 276

Shotoku, Prince (Japan), 275

Sicily, 124

Siddhartha Gautama, 75

Sihanouk, Prince Norodom, 727

silk industry, 181, 267

Sinai, 43, 46

Singapore, 252, 566, 722, 724

Sinhalese, as Buddhists, 728

Sinn Fein, 539

Sino-Japanese War, 562

Six-Day War, 696

slave labor, German, 621

slavery and slaves: abolished in Brazil, 485; abolished in French colonies, 464; in ancient Africa, 294; in ancient Greece, 99, 108, 109; in Babylonia, 58, 59; Carthaginians as, 125; condemned at Congress of Vienna, 479; in Egypt, 48, 50; Hebrews as, 61, 62; in India, 73, 241, 245; introduced to America, 386; in Latin America, 481; and League of Nations, 591; as major issue in United States, 506; in Rome, 125, 132; in Sumer, 55

Slavs, 198; intense nationalism of, 577

Smith, Adam, 443, 520

Social Darwinism, 528

T

Illustrations and Maps

Matthew S. Pippin: 45, 127, 227, 255, 288, 395, 664.

Lonnie S. Knabel: 111, 205.

Sanderson Associates: 15, 16, 17, 35, 46, 47, 54, 58, 65, 80, 100, 105, 125, 150, 177, 190, 201, 210, 242, 265, 287, 295, 317, 321, 323, 331, 362, 374, 382, 387, 417, 425, 447, 467, 478, 483, 489, 499, 500, 504, 516, 564, 577, 583, 591, 624, 625, 639, 645, 649, 663, 689, 698, 701, 705, 717, 720, 723, 736.

Mapping Specialists Ltd: 20, 35, 42, 57, 70, 74, 77, 78, 91, 92, 96, 121, 161, 172, 199, 237, 238, 252, 262, 264, 271, 285, 291, 305, 306, 413, 430, 493, 494, 571, 572, 647, 655, 656, 726, 753.

R.R. Donnelley & Sons Company: 780–781, 782, 783, 784, 785, 786, 787, 788, 789, 790, 791.

Photos

Front Cover: Giraudon/Art Resource

Back Cover: Robert Frerck/Woodfin Camp and Associates, William Hubbell/Woodfin Camp and Associates, Robert Harding Picture Library, Laurie Platt Winfrey, Inc., NASA

Text: ii–iii, Art Resource **v,** *top,* The Ancient Art and Architecture Collection, *bottom,* Art Resource **vi,** *top,* Art Resource, *bottom,* The Ancient Art and Architecture Collection **vii,** *top,* Laurie Platt Winfrey, Inc., *center,* Art Resource, *bottom,* Art Resource **viii,** *top and center,* The Ancient Art and Architecture Collection, *bottom,* Lee Boltin **ix,** *top,* The Granger Collection, *center,* Susan Van Etten/National Portrait Gallery, *bottom,* Art Resource **x,** *top,* The Granger Collection, *center,* Historical Pictures Service, *bottom,* The Granger Collection **xi,** *both,* The Granger Collection **xii,** *top,* The Granger Collection, *center,* The Bettmann Archive, Bildarchiv Preussischer Kultur Besitz, *bottom,* The Granger Collection **xiii,** *top,* Elliott Erwitt/Magnum, *center,* Uniphoto, *bottom,* Anthony Suau/Black Star **xiv,** L. Gubb/Gamma-Liaison **xv,** John Carter Brown Library/Yale University **xvi,** *left,* Lee Boltin, *right,* Laurie Platt Winfrey, Inc. **xvii,** *left,* Art Resource, *right,* Paul Conklin **xviii,** *top left,* Nik Wheeler/Black Star, *top right,* The Ancient Art and Architecture Collection, *bottom,* The Granger Collection **xx,** The Bettmann Archive **1,** Susan Van Etten/Alfred A. Knopf **3,** Robert Harding Picture Library **4,** Bill Curtsinger/Photo Researchers **5,** Susan Van Etten/NASA **7,** *left,* Susan Van Etten, *right,* Robert Frerck **9,** Paul Conklin **10,** Muncel Chang **11,** Muncel Chang **12,** Robert Harding Picture Library **20–21,** Scala/Art Resource, *left,* Giraudon/Art Resource, *right,* Wan-go Wen **22,** Bill Curtsinger **23,** Bill Curtsinger **24,** Dan Budnik/Woodfin Camp and Associates **25,** The Ancient Art and Architecture Collection **27,** *insert,* Art Resource, D. Mazonowicz/Art Resource **29,** Laurie Platt Winfrey, Inc. **30,** The Ancient Art and Architecture Collection **33,** *both,* Scala/Art Resource **36,** *The New York Times* News Service **40,** Lee Boltin **41,** Robert Frerck/Woodfin Camp and Associates **44,** Michael Yamashita/Woodfin Camp and Associates **48,** The Ancient Art and Architecture Collection **49,** *left,* Scala/Art Resource, *right,* Art Resource **52,** *left,* Michael Holford, *right,* John G. Ross/Robert Harding Picture Library **53,** The Ancient Art and Architecture Collection **55,** *top,* Scala/Art Resource, *bottom,* The Ancient Art and Architecture Collection **60,** Art Resource **61,** Scala/Art Resource **63,** *both,* The Ancient Art and Architecture Collection **67,** Robert Harding Picture Library **68,** Borromeo/Art Resource **69,** The Ancient Art and Architecture Collection **71,** Lindsay Hebberd/Woodfin Camp and Associates **72,** Jehangir Gadzar/Woodfin Camp and Associates **75,** Giraudon/Art Resource **81,** Art Resource **82,** The Ancient Art and Architecture Collection **86,** Robert Harding Picture Library **89,** Wan-go Wen, Boris Malkin/Anthrophoto **94,** The Ancient Art and Architecture Collection **95,** William Hubbell/Woodfin Camp and Associates **98,** Boris Malkin Anthrophoto **101,** The Ancient Art and Architecture Collection **102,** The Ancient Art and Architecture Collection **106,** The Ancient Art and Architecture Collection **107,** The Ancient Art and Architecture Collection **108,** *top and bottom,* The Ancient Art and Architecture Collection **109,** The Ancient Art and Architecture Collection **110,** Paul Conklin **112,** The Ancient Art and Architecture Collection **113,** SEF/Art Resource **117,** The Granger Collection **118,** Scala/Art Resource **120,** The Ancient Art and Architecture Collection **122,** Scala/Art Resource **123,** Scala/Art Resource **124,** *both,* The Ancient Art and Architecture Collection **126,** The Ancient Art and Architecture Collection **128,** Giraudon/Art Resource **129,** *right,* Scala/Art Resource, *left,* Art Resource **131,** Giraudon/Art Resource **133,** The Ancient Art and Architecture Collection **134,** *left,* Scala/Art Resource, *top right,* Robert Harding Picture Library, *right,* Laurie Platt Winfrey, Inc. **135,** The Ancient Art and Architecture Collection **136,** Scala/Art Resource **137,** The Ancient Art and Architecture Collection **141,** Scala/Art Resource **142,** Art Resource **143,** Scala/Art Resource **144,** Robert Harding Picture Library **146,** The Ancient Art and Architecture Collection **147,** The Ancient Art and Architecture Collection **148,** Robert Harding Picture Library **153,** *right,* Robert Harding Picture Library, *left,* The Ancient Art and Architecture Collection **154,** The National Gallery of Art, Washington, D.C. **155,** Beiniche Library/Yale University **156,** *left,* Richard Pasley/Stock Boston, *right,* Michael Holford **159,** Scala/Art Resource **162,** Scala/Art Resource **165,** The Ancient Art and Architecture Collection **166,** Robert Frerck/Woodfin Camp and Associates **167,** *left,* The Ancient Art and Architecture Collection, *top right,* Art Resource, *bottom center,* Art Resource, *bottom right,* Art Resource **169,** Art Resource **171,** Dale Ahern/TexaStock **172,** Laurie Platt Winfrey, Inc. **173,** The Granger Collection **174,** The Metropolitan Museum of Art, Gift of J. J. Kluejman, 1962 **175,** Laurie Platt Winfrey,

Inc. **176,** *top,* Robert Harding Picture Library, *bottom,* The Ancient Art and Architecture Collection **178,** The Ancient Art and Architecture Collection **180,** Laurie Platt Winfrey, Inc. **181,** Laurie Platt Winfrey, Inc. **183,** Roland and Sabrina Michaud/Woodfin Camp and Associates **184,** Alon Reininger/Woodfin Camp and Associates **185,** Robert Harding Picture Library **187,** *top,* Robert Azzi/Woodfin Camp and Associates **188,** Art Resource **189,** Adam Woolfit/ Woodfin Camp and Associates **195,** Susan Van Etten/ Musée Guiment, Paris **196,** The Ancient Art and Architecture Collection **197,** Dallas and John Heaton Uniphoto **202,** The Ancient Art and Architecture Collection **203,** Laurie Platt Winfrey, Inc. **206,** Robert Harding Picture Library **209,** The Bettmann Archive **215,** Laurie Platt Winfrey, Inc. **216,** Laurie Platt Winfrey, Inc. **218,** The Ancient Art and Architecture Collection **219,** *top,* The Ancient Art and Architecture Collection, *bottom,* The Granger Collection **220,** The Ancient Art and Architecture Collection **222,** Laurie Platt Winfrey, Inc. **223,** Laurie Platt Winfrey, Inc. **224,** Laurie Platt Winfrey, Inc. **226,** Robert Harding Picture Library **229,** *both,* Robert Harding Picture Library **230,** Scala/Art Resource **235,** Robert Harding Picture Library **238–239,** The Ancient Art and Architecture Collection, *left,* The Ancient Art and Architecture Collection, *center,* Robert Harding Picture Library, *right,* Robert Harding Picture Library **241,** The Ancient Art and Architecture Collection **248,** Roland Michaud/Woodfin Camp and Associates **241,** Robert Harding Picture Library **243,** Art Resource **244,** Roland Michaud/Woodfin Camp and Associates **245,** Marc and Evelyn Bernheim/ Woodfin Camp and Associates **246,** Jagdish Agarwal/ Uniphoto **248,** Michael Yamashita/Woodfin Camp and Associates **250,** Borromeo/Art Resource **251,** Borromeo/ Art Resource **252,** Thomas Hoepker/Woodfin Camp and Associates **253,** Robert Harding Picture Library **259,** Robert Harding Picture Library **260,** Wan-go Wen **261,** Wan-go Wen **263,** Laurie Platt Winfrey, Inc. **266,** The Metropolitan Museum of Art, Anonymous gift, 1942 **268,** Wan-go Wen **270,** *left,* Laurie Platt Winfrey, Inc., *right,* Wan-go Wen **273,** Lee Boltin **275,** Sekai Bunka **277,** Laurie Platt Winfrey, Inc. **278,** The Granger Collection **281,** Robert Harding Picture Library **282,** Laurie Platt Winfrey, Inc. **283,** Ulrike Welsch **293,** *top,* The Granger Collection, *bottom,* Mitchell Funk/The Image Bank **294,** Paul Conklin **297,** *left,* The Ancient Art and Architecture Collection, *center,* Laurie Platt Winfrey, Inc., *right,* Michael Holford **298,** Art Resource **299,** Lee Boltin **300,** *left, center, right,* Michael Holford **306–307,** Ulrike Welsch, *left,* Art Resource, *center,* Bridgeman Art Library, *right,* The Ancient Art and Architecture Collection **308,** The Granger Collection **309,** The Granger Collection **310,** Ulrike Welsch **327,** The Ancient Art and Architecture Collection **328,** Art Resource **329,** Art Resource **330,** Scala/ Art Resource **332,** *both,* Scala/Art Resource **334,** *left,* Scala/Art Resource, *right,* Art Resource **337,** Scala/Art Resource **338,** Art Resource **339,** Wide World Photos **340,** *top,* Malyszko/Stock Boston, *bottom,* Scala/Art Resource **341,** The Bettmann Archive **343,** *left,* Scala/Art Resource, *top right,* Scala/Art Resource, *bottom right,* Walter Rawlings/Robert Harding Picture Library **344,** The Ancient Art and Architecture Collection **345,** Historical Pictures Service **346,** Art Resource **347,** Scala/Art Resource **349,** Scala/Art Resource **350,** Susan Van Etten/ The National Portrait Gallery **351,** Walter Rawlings/

Robert Harding Picture Library **352,** Loris Renault/Photo Researchers **353,** The Granger Collection **354,** Historical Pictures Service **356,** Giraudon/Art Resource **357,** The Bridgeman Art Library **359,** The Ancient Art and Architecture Collection, **367,** New York Public Library/Prints Division **369,** Robert Harding Picture Library **371,** The Bridgeman Art Library **373,** *both,* The Granger Collection **375,** Michael Holford **376,** The Granger Collection **378,** *left,* The Granger Collection, *right,* The Bettmann Archive **381,** The Granger Collection **385,** Historical Pictures Service **386,** Bettmann Archive **389,** Susan Van Etten/Bridgeman Art Library **390,** The Ancient Art and Architecture Collection **391,** Laurie Platt Winfrey, Inc. **393,** Laurie Platt Winfrey, Inc. **395,** The Bettmann Archive **396,** *left,* The Ancient Art and Architecture Collection, *right,* Susan Van Etten/National Portrait Gallery **397,** Laurie Platt Winfrey, Inc. **399,** The Bettmann Archive **401,** Michael Holford **402,** Michael Holford **403,** Historical Pictures Service **407,** Historical Pictures Service **411,** Scala/Art Resource **414,** *left and right,* The Ancient Art and Architecture Collection **418,** Roland and Sabrina Michaud/Woodfin Camp and Associates **421,** Laurie Platt Winfrey, Inc. **422,** Michael Schneps/The Image Bank **423,** Art Resource **427,** The Granger Collection **429,** The Ancient Art and Architecture Collection **430–431,** Mansell Collection, *left,* Laurie Platt Winfrey, Inc., *right,* The Granger Collection **432,** Historical Pictures Service **433,** The Granger Collection **435,** Historical Pictures Service **436,** Historical Pictures Service **438,** Susan Van Etten **439,** The Granger Collection **440,** Historical Pictures Service **443,** The Granger Collection **444,** The Granger Collection **448,** Historical Pictures Service **451,** Giraudon/Art Resource **452,** The Granger Collection **453,** The Granger Collection **454,** The Granger Collection **458,** The Granger Collection **460,** The Granger Collection **461,** The Granger Collection **462,** Laurie Platt Winfrey, Inc. **463,** The Granger Collection **464,** The Granger Collection **465,** *right,* Art Resource, *left,* Laurie Platt Winfrey, Inc. **467,** Giraudon/Art Resource **470,** The Granger Collection **473,** The Mansell Collection **474,** The Granger Collection **475,** The Granger Collection **477,** Robert Harding Picture Library **481,** Art Resource **484,** Laurie Platt Winfrey, Inc. **491,** Laurie Platt Winfrey, Inc. **494–495,** The Granger Collection, *right,* Peabody Museum, Salem/ Photo by Mark Sexton, *left,* The Granger Collection **497,** The Granger Collection **503,** Laurie Platt Winfrey, Inc. **505,** The Bettmann Archive **507,** National Archives of Canada **512,** Historical Pictures Service **513,** Historical Pictures Service **515,** The Granger Collection **519,** *left,* Susan Van Etten, *right,* Historical Pictures Service **522,** Susan Van Etten/National Portrait Gallery **523,** The Granger Collection **524,** The Granger Collection **525,** The Granger Collection **526,** *left,* The Granger Collection, *right,* Art Resource **528,** Susan Van Etten/National Portrait Gallery **530,** Connie Geocaris/Click-Chicago **533,** The Granger Collection **534,** Historical Pictures Service **535,** The Metropolitan Museum of Art, Purchase, Lyman G. Bloomingdale Gift, 1901 **537,** Laurie Platt Winfrey, Inc. **541,** Art Resource **542,** The Granger Collection **544,** The Bettmann Archive **545,** The Bettmann Archive **550,** Art Resource **551,** Library of Congress, Washington, D.C. **553,** The Granger Collection **557,** Laurie Platt Winfrey, Inc. **558,** Laurie Platt Winfrey, Inc. **560,** The Granger Collection **563,** The Granger Collection **569,** The Granger Collection **572–573**, The Granger Collection, *left*, U.S. Air Force Museum, *right*, Franklin Delano Roosevelt Library **574**, The Granger Collection **575**, Laurie Platt Winfrey, Inc. **579**, Historical Pictures Service **580**, Lee Boltin **582**, The Bettmann Archive **585**, The Granger Collection **587**, Sigma **589**, *left*, Vasily Kandinsky: *Violet-Orange, October 1935*, Collection, Solomon R. Guggenheim Museum, N.Y.: Photo: Myles Aronowitz, *right*, Susan Van Etten/Meštrović Studio, Zagreb **595**, Susan Van Etten **596**, The Bettmann Archive **597**, Sovfoto **598**, Sovfoto **600**, Sovfoto **601**, Wide World Photos **605**, Historical Pictures Service **606**, Yivo Institute **608**, Bettmann Newsphotos **610** Robert Capa/Magnum **611**, Daniel Bishop/*St. Louis Star Times* **613**, D. R. Fitzpatrick/*St. Louis Post Dispatch* **614**, Wide World **615**, Bildarchiv Preussischer Kultur Besitz **617**, Wide World **618**, The Bettmann Archive **619**, Wide World **621**, Bettmann News Service **622**, Sovfoto **629**, George Halton/Photo Researchers **633**, Alfred Eisenstadt/Life Magazine, c TIME, INC. **634**, Wide World **635**, Bob Henriques/Magnum **637**, Wide World **640**, Wide World **642**, Steele Perkins/Magnum **646**, Eastfoto/Sovfoto **650**, Paul Conklin **653**, Wide World **656–657**, Robert Frerck, *left*, Sygma, *center*, Wide World, *right*, Wide World **658**, Jacques Witt/Sipa Press **659**, Sichov/Sipa Press **661**, Wide World **667**, Wojtek Laski/Sipa Press **671**, Eric Bouvet/Gamma-Liaison **672**, Dennis Brack/Black Star **675**, *Chicago Sun-Times* **676**, Elliott Erwitt/Magnum **677**, Paul Conklin **679**, Fred Ward/Black Star **681**, *left*, Romare Bearden/Art Resource, *right*, Paul Conklin **683**, Valan Photos **684**, M. Ponomareff/Gamma-Liaison **686**, Juergen Schmitt/The Image Bank **690**, Wide World **693**, Susan Van Etten **694**, David Rubinger/*Time Magazine* **695**, David Rubinger/*Time Magazine* **697**, Eve Arnold/Magnum **700**, Gaillarde/Gamma-Liaison **702**, Gamma-Liaison **706**, Sovfoto **709**, Wide World **710**, Jordan/Gamma-Liaison **714**, Nik Wheeler/Black Star **715**, Eiji Miyazawa/Black Star **721**, Bob Davis/Woodfin Camp and Associates **725**, Vernon Merritt/Black Star **727**, Sygma **729**, Paul Conklin **730**, Andy Hernandez/Picture Group **734**, Paul Conklin **735**, NASA **739**, Dr. A. C. Twomey/Photo Researchers **741**, L. Gubb/Gamma-Liaison **743**, Kevin Horan/Picture Group **744**, Magnum **747**, P. J. Griffiths/Magnum **748**, Nik Wheeler/Black Star **756**, Historical Pictures Service **755**, NASA **757**, Laurie Platt Winfrey, Inc. **760**, The Granger Collection **761**, Historical Pictures Service **763**, The Granger Collection **766**, The Granger Collection **767**, Bildarchiv Preussischer Kultur Besitz **769**, Sovfoto **773**, Magnum **775**, Claude Urraca/Sygma **776**, Reglain/Gamma-Liaison **778**, Dr.A. C. Twomey/Photo Researchers

Text Acknowledgments:

32 Excerpted from *The Anthropology of Sport: An Introduction*, by Kendall Blanchard and Alyce Cheska. Granby, MA: Bergin & Garvey Publishers, Inc., 1985.

50 Excerpted from *The Tomb of Tutankhamen*, by Howard Carter. New York: E. P. Dutton & Co., Inc., 1972.

76 Excerpted from *The Buddhist Bible*, ed. by Dwight Goddard. New York: E. P. Dutton & Co., Inc., 1938.

104 Excerpted from *The Greek Historians*, vol. 1, ed. by Francis R. B. Godolphin. New York: Random House Publishers, 1942.

128 Excerpted from *Women in Greece and Rome*, by Mary R. Lefkowitz and Maureen B. Fant. Toronto: Samuel-Stevens, 1977.

149 Excerpted from *Tacitus on Britain and Germany*, trans. by H. Mattingly. New York: Penguin Books, 1954.

179 Excerpted from *Justinian and the Later Roman Empire*, by John W. Barker. Chicago, IL: University of Chicago Press, 1960.

211 Excerpted from "Le lettere di Margherita Datini a Francesco di Marco," in *Women in the Middle Ages*, by Frances and Joseph Gies. New York: Barnes and Noble Books, 1978.

225 Excerpted from *Life in the Middle Ages*, vol. 3, by G. G. Coulton. New York: Cambridge University Press, 1929.

247 Excerpted from *Sources of Indian Tradition: From the Beginning to 1800*, vol. 1, ed. by Ainslie T. Embree. New York: Columbia University Press, 1988.

267 Excerpted from *Chinese Civilization and Society*, ed. by Patricia Buckley Ebrey. New York: The Free Press, 1981.

299 Excerpted from *Wit and Wisdom from West Africa*, ed. by Richard F. Burton. Westport, CT: Greenwood Press, Inc., 1969.

311 Excerpted from *The Book of the City of Ladies*, by Christine de Pizan, et al. New York: Persea Books, Inc., 1982.

336 Excerpted from *The Prince*, by Niccolò Machiavelli. New York: The Bobbs-Merrill Company, Inc., 1976.

358 Excerpted from *Three Treatises*, by Martin Luther, trans. by W. A. Lambert. Philadelphia: The Muhlenberg Press, 1943.

371 Excerpted from *Age of Exploration*, by John R. Hale and the Editors of TIME-LIFE Books. New York: Time, Inc., 1966.

377 Excerpted from *The Voyage of Magellan: The Journal of Antoinio Pigafetta*, trans. by Paula Spurlin Paige. Englewood Cliffs, NJ: Prentice-Hall, Inc., 1969.

404 Excerpted from *Maria Theresa*, by Edward Crankshaw. New York: Atheneum Publishers, 1986.

437 Excerpted from *The Shorter Pepys*, ed. by Robert Latham (from *The Diary of Samuel Pepys*, ed. by Robert Latham and William Matthews). Berkeley, CA: University of California Press, 1985.

457 Excerpted from *The French Revolution*, by G. Pernoud and S. Flaissier, trans. by Richard Graves. New York: G. P. Putnam's Sons, 1961.

487 Excerpted from *Rhyme and Revolution in Germany*, by J. C. Legge. London: Constable and Company, Ltd., 1918.

498 Excerpted from *Life and Writings of Joseph Mazzini*, vol. 5. London: Smith, Elder, & Co., 1891.

521 Excerpted from *The Curse of the Factory System*, by John Fielden, 4th ed. London: Charles Knight, 1835.

538 Excerpted from "My Own Story," by Emmeline Pankhurst, in *Shoulder to Shoulder*, ed. by Midge Mackenzie. New York: Alfred A. Knopf, 1975.

552 Excerpted from *I Was Savage*, by Prince Modupe, trans. by Paul R. Reynolds. New York: Harcourt Brace Jovanovich, Inc., 1957.

581 Excerpted from *The German Student's War Letters*, ed. by Dr. Philipp Witkop, trans. by A. F. Wedd. New York: E. P. Dutton & Co., Inc., 1929.

609 Excerpted from a letter in *Hitler's Words*, by Adolf Hitler, ed. by Gordan Prange. Washington, D.C.: American Council on Public Affairs, 1944.

626 Excerpted from "The Effects of the Atomic Bombs on Health and Medical Services in Hiroshima and Nagasaki," in *The United States Strategic Bombing Survey*. Washington, D.C.: Department of the Air Force, 1947.

644 Excerpted from *On My Own*, by Eleanor Roosevelt. San Leandro, CA: The Curtis Publishing Company, 1958.

668 Excerpted from *Perestroika: New Thinking for Our Country and the World*, by Mikhail Gorbachev. New York: Harper & Row, 1987.

687 Excerpted from *Stanford Central American Action Network: Education and Revolution in Central America*.

708 Excerpted from *Classic Speeches: Words That Shook the World*, ed. by Richard Crosscup. New York: Philosophical Library, Inc., 1965.

719 Excerpted from a New China News Agency release, November 19, 1966.

740 Excerpted from "Food First," by Frances Moore Lappé and Joe Collins. *The New Internationalist*, August 1976, pp. 5–9.

TERMS & CONDITIONS

Allows only one book at £7.99 per qualifying transaction. This voucher is valid from 15th September 2009 to 15th October 2009 subject to publication date. It can only be redeemed in WHSmith High Street Stores, airports and railways. Excludes Outlet stores, Online, motorway service stations, hospitals and work places. Subject to availability. Cannot be used in conjunction with any other promotional voucher or offer. Only one voucher can be redeemed per transaction and it must be surrendered upon use. No cash alternative. Photocopies will not be accepted and the voucher is not transferable. WHSmith reserves the right to reject any voucher it deems, in its sole discretion, to have been forged, defaced or otherwise tampered with.

Customers must retain their receipt as proof of pre-order and receipt must be presented, together with this voucher, upon collection of The Lost Symbol . This voucher does not guarantee you a copy on day of release.

3390 6522

------------------------------✂------------------------------

TERMS & CONDITIONS

Only one half price book per qualifying transaction. This voucher is valid from 11th June 2009 to 10th September 2009. It can only be redeemed in WHSmith High Street Stores, airports and railways. Excludes Outlet stores, Online, motorway service stations, hospitals and work places. Subject to availability. Cannot be used in conjunction with any instore multi-buy or promotional voucher. Only one voucher can be redeemed per transaction and it must be surrendered upon use. No cash alternative. Photocopies will not be accepted and the voucher is not transferable. WHSmith reserves the right to reject any voucher it deems, in its sole discretion, to have been forged, defaced or otherwise tampered with.

3388 7548

------------------------------✂------------------------------

TERMS & CONDITIONS

Both items must be purchased in the same transaction. Cheapest item is free. This voucher is valid from 25th May 2009 to 14th September 2009. It can only be redeemed in WHSmith High Street Stores, airports and railways. Excludes Outlet stores, Online, motorway service stations, hospitals and work places. Subject to availability. Cannot be used in conjunction with any instore multi-buy or promotional voucher. Only one voucher can be redeemed per transaction and it must be surrendered upon use. No cash alternative. Photocopies will not be accepted and the voucher is not transferable. WHSmith reserves the right to reject any voucher it deems, in its sole discretion, to have been forged, defaced or otherwise tampered with.

< 3388 9009 >

--- ✂ --

--- ✂ --

Deadline

Simon Kernick

CORGI BOOKS

TRANSWORLD PUBLISHERS
61–63 Uxbridge Road, London W5 5SA
A Random House Group Company
www.rbooks.co.uk

DEADLINE
A CORGI BOOK: 9780552160902

First published in Great Britain
in 2008 by Bantam Press
a division of Transworld Publishers
Corgi edition published 2008
Corgi edition reissued 2009

Addresses for Random House Group Ltd companies outside
the UK can be found at: www.randomhouse.co.uk
The Random House Group Ltd Reg. No. 954009

The Random House Group Limited supports The Forest
Stewardship Council (FSC), the leading international forest
certification organisation. All our titles that are printed on
Greenpeace approved FSC certified paper carry the FSC logo.
Our paper procurement policy can be found at
www.rbooks.co.uk/environment

Typeset in Palatino by Falcon Oast Graphic Art Ltd.

Printed in the UK by CPI Cox & Wyman, Reading, RG1 8EX.

2 4 6 8 10 9 7 5 3 1

For Anna Bridges.
May your spirit never stop soaring.

Prologue

When his girlfriend greeted him at the door dressed only in a T-shirt and thong, then kissed him hard on the mouth without a word before pulling him into her ground-floor bedroom, she was so worked up she didn't even notice that he was wearing gloves. They'd talked on the phone five minutes earlier and in that conversation he'd explained in intimate detail what he planned to do with her when he got to her place. So it was with a hint of regret that, as her hands headed southwards, he kicked shut the bedroom door, slipped the knife from the concealed sheath beneath his cheap suit jacket, and drove it silently between her ribs and directly into her heart. In the short time he'd known her, the girl had proved to be adept and enthusiastic in bed, and it would have been a pleasant distraction to have had sex with her one last time. But that would have meant leaving behind incriminating evidence, and he was a professional who didn't let the desire for cheap gratification get in the way of business.

He clasped her close to him while she died. The single blow had been enough, as he knew it would be, having used this method of killing on several occasions in the past. The girl made barely a sound. There was the surprised, pained gasp as the blade went in, of course, which was accompanied by a single juddering spasm, not unlike an orgasm, as her muscles tensed for a final time and her fingernails dug into the material of his suit jacket, but it didn't last long and was quickly followed by the long, slow release of breath as she relaxed in his arms.

He counted to ten in his head, then, still holding on to her, reached into the inside pocket of his jacket with his knife hand and produced a handkerchief. The blade made a strange hissing sound as it was slowly withdrawn, and he used a well-practised combination of both hands to wipe it clean, before replacing it in its sheath. When this was done, he placed the body on the carpet next to the unmade bed and briefly admired his handiwork. Because she'd died so quickly, there was very little blood, and she looked remarkably peaceful lying there with her eyes closed. It was the quietest he'd seen her. In life, she'd been quite a talker.

Leaning down, he tried to push her under the

bed, but there wasn't enough of a gap between the bottom of the frame and the floor, so he squeezed her in as far as she would go, then covered the rest of the body with one end of the duvet cover. It was only a tidying-up gesture. Concealing the body would do nothing to mask the smell that would soon be coming from it, but he wasn't overly concerned about that. He doubted if she'd be discovered for a while. She lived alone in her tiny ground-floor flat, and had few friends in the city, which had always been one of her complaints about it. He knew she spoke to her mother back home once a week but that was always on a Sunday, so it would be another six days before the mother had a reason to worry about her daughter, and several days more, at least, before anyone did anything about it.

No one had ever seen him with her. Their few clandestine meetings had always been in this flat. As far as he knew, she hadn't told anyone about him either, although even if she had it would make no difference. He'd given her a false name and background, one of four different identities he periodically used in order always to keep one step ahead of the authorities. His DNA would be in this room, of course, but then so would the DNA of those few friends the girl had, and since they were mainly illegals, it would be difficult to trace them.

He saw the girl's pink Nokia mobile phone on the bedside table. He picked it up and put it in his pocket to be disposed of later, then took a last look round. Seeing nothing else that might incriminate him, he left the bedroom, shutting the door behind him, leaving the girl in her makeshift tomb.

As he stepped out of the front door and into the bright sunlight, he looked at his watch.

It was time.

Part One

One

The first thing Andrea Devern noticed when she stepped out of her Mercedes C-Class Cabriolet was that there were no lights on in the house. It was 8.45 p.m. on a breezy Tuesday night in mid-September, and she had only a minute of normality left in her life.

Clicking on the Mercedes' central locking, she walked the five yards to her front gate, glancing both ways along the quiet residential street because as a Londoner born and bred Andrea was never complacent about the potential for street crime, even in an area as upmarket as Hampstead. Criminals moved around these days. They no longer kept to their own patches. They gravitated towards the money, and on Andrea's tree-lined avenue of grand three-storey townhouses, barely spitting distance from the Heath, there was plenty of that.

15

But there was nothing out of place tonight, unless you counted the fact that her house was in darkness. Andrea tried to remember if Pat had told her that he had arrangements, or whether he'd taken Emma off somewhere. She'd had a stressful day dealing with the management team of one of the five health spas she and her business partner owned. They'd taken it over a year ago and it had underperformed ever since. Now they were going to have to make redundancies, something that Andrea never liked doing, and it was up to her to decide who was for the push. She'd been mulling over who was going to have to go all the way back from Bedfordshire, and still she couldn't decide. By rights, it should be the manager. He was paid well over the odds, and since he was the one who'd presided over the mess the spa was now in, it appealed to Andrea's sense of justice to give him the boot; but with no one to replace him, that was looking less and less viable. Better the devil you know, and all that.

Andrea decided to worry about it tomorrow. For now, she needed a long, slow glass of Sancerre and a relaxing cigarette. Not the healthiest of options, but a woman needs some pleasures in life, especially when she worked as hard as she did.

She pressed the card key against the pressure

pad on the security system and stepped through the gap as the gate slid open smoothly. As always when she entered her front garden and left the outside world behind her, she experienced a familiar sense of relief and pleasure. Sheltered by a high brick wall, the garden was a riot of colour, courtesy of the eight hundred quid a month she paid to the gardening company responsible for making it look like something from the front cover of a magazine.

She breathed in the thick, heady smell of jasmine and honeysuckle, relaxing already as she opened the front door and deactivated the alarm.

Then the phone rang.

It was her mobile. She reached into her limited-edition Fendi Spy Bag and fished it out. The ringtone was 'I Will Survive', Gloria Gaynor's classic anthem of feminine defiance. It was only later that she realized how much grim irony there was in this.

The screen said 'Anonymous Call', and though she never liked answering her phone to anyone she couldn't identify, she also knew that it was possible it was business, even at this hour, and Andrea never said no to business, particularly when the market was as tough as it was at the moment. As she stepped into her empty hallway she put the phone to her ear and said, 'Hello, Andrea Devern.'

'We have your daughter.'

The words were delivered in a high-pitched, artificial voice which sounded vaguely like a man impersonating a woman.

At first she thought she'd misheard, but in the slow, heavy silence that followed, the realization came upon her like an approaching wave.

'What? What do you mean?'

'We have your daughter,' repeated the caller, and now Andrea could tell that he was using something to disguise his voice. 'She's not there, is she? Look around. Can you see her?' His tone was vaguely mocking.

Andrea looked around. The hallway was bathed in gloom, the rooms leading off it silent. There was no one there. She felt a rising sense of helpless panic, and fought to keep herself calm.

'You can't see her, can you? That's because we have her, Andrea. And if you ever want to see her again, you'll do exactly as you're told.'

Andrea felt faint. Needing some kind of support, she leaned back against the front door, her movement clicking it shut. Keep calm, she told herself. For God's sake, keep calm. If they're phoning you, then it's got to be a good sign. Surely?

'What do you want?' she whispered, her whole body tensing as she waited for the answer.

'Half a million pounds in cash.'

'I haven't got that sort of money.'

'Yes, you have. And you're going to get hold of it for us as well. You've got exactly forty-eight hours.'

'Please, I'm going to need longer than that.'

'There's no compromise. You have to get us that money.'

Andrea began to shake. She couldn't believe this was happening. One minute she'd been thinking about winding down after her meeting, the next she was plunged into a crisis involving the most precious person in the world to her: Emma, her only daughter. She exhaled slowly. It was still possible this was some kind of hoax.

'How do I know you're not lying?' she asked.

'Do you want to hear your daughter scream?' replied the caller matter-of-factly.

Oh, Jesus, no.

'Please, for God's sake, don't do anything to her. Please.'

'Then do exactly as we say, and don't ask stupid questions.'

'She's fourteen years old, for Christ's sake! What sort of animal are you?'

'One who doesn't care,' he snapped. 'Do you understand that? I don't give a toss.' His tone became more businesslike. 'So listen closely. It's ten to nine now. At nine o'clock on Thursday, in forty-eight hours' time, you're going to receive a phone call on your landline. At that point you'll have the half a million ready in used notes, denominations of fifties and twenties. Do you understand that?'

Andrea cleared her throat. 'Yes,' she said.

'You'll be told where and when to deliver it. As soon as we've received it, you get her back.'

'I want you to let me speak to her now. Please.'

'You'll speak to her when we're ready.'

'No.'

'No? I'm afraid you're not in any position to argue with us. We have your child, remember?'

She took a deep breath. 'Please. Let me speak to her. I need to know she's OK.'

'You can speak to her next time we call. When you have the money.'

'How do I know she's even alive?' Andrea shouted, determined not to cry even though she felt the tears stinging her eyes.

'Because,' said the caller calmly, 'she's no use to us dead. Now go and get that money, Andrea. Then you can speak to her. And don't even think about going to the police. Because if you do, we'll know about it. We're watching you. The whole time. The first sign of the police and Emma dies. Slowly and painfully.' There was a pause. 'Nine o'clock Thursday night. Be ready.' The line went dead.

For several seconds Andrea remained frozen to the spot, the shock of what was happening still seeping through her system. Someone had taken her daughter. Her lively, pretty fourteen-year-old girl who did well at school and who'd never hurt anyone. A complete innocent. Her poor baby must be absolutely terrified. 'Please don't hurt her,' Andrea whispered aloud, her words sounding hollow in the empty hallway.

Andrea Devern was a tough woman, and her life hadn't been easy. A successful, financially independent entrepreneur, she'd had to fight hard to get to the position she was in now. She'd taken one hell of a lot of knocks on the way, knocks that would have finished a lot of other, more privileged people, and she'd always held firm. But nothing could have prepared her for this. Emma was Andrea's world, no question, and to think of her now, trapped and frightened with no understanding of what was going on, filled her with a helpless dread. And that was the worst part, the sheer helplessness. Her daughter was missing, and there was absolutely nothing she could do.

Except satisfy the demands of the anonymous caller and find him half a million pounds.

My only child . . . If anything happens to her . . .

She flicked shut the phone and walked into the kitchen, the heels of her court shoes clicking loudly on the mahogany floorboards. She grabbed a glass from one of the cupboards and filled it with water from the tap, then drained it in one go.

She had to keep calm, but it was hard when you were alone. And that was when her thoughts turned to Pat.

Pat Phelan. Andrea's husband of two years, and Emma's stepfather. Charming, good-looking and five years younger than her, she'd been infatuated with him when they met. A whirlwind romance had been followed by a marriage barely four months later. Her mother had described her as a 'fool' and Pat as a 'ne'er do well'. At the time Andrea had thought her mother was being short-sighted, and maybe even a little jealous, but in recent months she'd begun to get the first hints that maybe the old woman, spiteful as she'd always been, had a point. After all, it takes one to know one.

She needed Pat now, more than she ever had.

So where the hell was he?

She refilled her glass with water and swallowed another couple of large gulps, then walked over to the landline and punched in the number of his mobile. Pat didn't work. He was between jobs. It seemed he'd been between jobs pretty much ever since they'd met. His trade, if you could call it that, was bar work. He'd been working in a bar in

Holborn when she'd first seen him. A month later he'd had an argument with the owner, and the job was history. He tended to be something of a house husband now. He ferried Emma to and from school most days, and picked her up from friends' houses when Andrea was at work, but more and more in the evenings he liked to go out for a couple of drinks at the local pub, or to one of his old haunts down the road in Finchley, which was where he'd been brought up. Sometimes he didn't come home until well after she was in bed.

But the thing was, Pat didn't leave Emma alone in the house. He'd only ever go out when Andrea got back from work. It was a situation that suited her well, although occasionally she wished he'd show a bit of get up and go, and maybe secure some gainful employment.

The phone rang and rang, but Pat wasn't answering. It went to message and, keeping her voice even, Andrea left one, asking – no, telling – him to call her back as soon as possible.

She slammed the receiver back in its cradle, cursing the fact that he hadn't picked up, then stood by the sink, her eyes closed, taking slow, deep breaths, trying to make sense of the situation she found herself in. Emma had been kidnapped by a ruthless individual who, from the way he spoke, clearly had an accomplice, or accomplices.

She forced herself to look at things logically. The motive for abducting Emma was money. Which meant there was a good chance of getting her back. There had to be. Andrea knew she could raise half a million in the time given. It wouldn't be easy, but she had access to ready cash in a way that other people didn't. There were numbered accounts, and cash that had been squirrelled away, far from the prying eyes of the taxman, in a safety deposit box in Knightsbridge. Probably just enough to cover this amount. If she did what she was told and delivered the money to where they wanted it, she'd have her daughter back.

The thought filled her with relief, but it was an emotion that lasted barely seconds, because it relied on trusting Emma's kidnappers. What if they didn't release her? What if, God forbid, she was already dead? A spasm of sheer terror shot up her spine. If anything happened to Emma, she was finished. The thought of life without her was simply too much to bear.

Andrea reached into her handbag and pulled out a cigarette, lighting it with shaking hands. She took a long drag and tried Pat's number again, but there was still no answer. She left a second, curt message: 'Call me now. It's urgent.'

She leaned back against one of the kitchen's spotless worktops. This house had been Andrea's

dream home when she bough..............
for close to a million cash, whic..........
proceeds of the 40 per cent stake s...........
current business partner. It had cha...........
land, everything that had been missing...........
flat in which she'd grown up with her tv...........
and mother. It was her and Emma's sa.... and
private haven, where they could relax and spend
time together. Yet tonight it felt alien, like a place
she'd just stepped into for the very first time.
Normally at this time there'd be noise: music
playing in Emma's room; the tinny blare of the
TV; the sounds of life. Tonight her home was
dead, and she wondered whether it would ever
feel the same again.

She went into the lounge and over to the drinks
cabinet, avoiding turning on the lights. There
were photos in here, of her and Emma – Emma as
a toddler; her first day at school; at the beach. She
didn't want to see them. Not now. She averted her
eyes and poured herself a large brandy in the
gloom, taking a big hit of it. It didn't make her
feel any better, but at the moment nothing was
going to.

With the drink in one hand and a succession of
cigarettes in the other, she paced the darkening
house, upstairs and down, walking fast but
heading nowhere, eyes straight ahead so she
didn't have to see any reminder of Emma.

thinking, worrying, trying to keep a lid on the terror and frustration that infected every ounce of her being. She wondered where they'd snatched Emma, and how. There were no signs of a struggle anywhere in the house, and besides, the alarm had been on when she came in.

But they have her, Andrea, said a voice in her head. *That's the only thing that matters. They have her.*

Half an hour passed. In that time she stopped walking only once, to refill her brandy tumbler, and to look out of the French windows and into the darkness beyond, wondering if even now there was someone out there watching her, checking her reactions. She drew the curtains and resumed her pacing. She knew now she wouldn't be able to sleep until Emma was safe, and in her arms. In the meantime, all she could do was pace the prison of her house alone.

Where was Pat?

An hour passed. She called him again. Still no answer. This time she didn't bother leaving a message.

She was getting a bad feeling about this. It wasn't like him not to answer his mobile. He carried it with him everywhere. It finally occurred to her that he might be at the Eagle, a pub he often liked to drink in on his evenings out. She didn't know the number, so she looked it up in the Yellow Pages and gave them a call.

A young woman with a foreign accent answered. In the background Andrea could hear the buzz of conversation, and immediately felt a pang of jealousy. Sounding as casual as possible, she asked if Pat Phelan was in tonight.

'I'll ask,' the girl replied. 'Hold on, please.'

Andrea waited, the phone clutched tight to her ear.

Thirty seconds later the girl came back on the line. 'I'm afraid no one has seen him for a long time,' she said politely.

Andrea's jaw tightened. Tonight was Tuesday. Pat had told her he'd been at the Eagle the previous Friday night, and last Wednesday.

'Is that everything?' asked the girl.

'Yes,' said Andrea quickly. 'Thank you.'

She hung up and stared at the phone. So Pat had been lying about his whereabouts. But why?

An unpleasant thought began to form in her mind. Could he possibly be involved in this? It was difficult to believe. After all, they'd been together nearly two and a half years, and although, if she was honest, she didn't entirely trust him, particularly where other women were concerned, he'd always got on all right with Emma. They hadn't been the best of friends, and Emma had certainly not welcomed his arrival into their close family unit, but she'd come round in the end. If anything, their relations had been improving in recent months. It was too much of a step to imagine him hurting her like this.

And yet . . . Pat was one of the only people in the world who knew she had cash reserves she could call upon without attracting too much attention. Near enough half a million pounds of cash reserves, in fact. Nor was he whiter than white. He'd admitted to her that years earlier, as a young man, he'd had a few scrapes with the law, and had even served a few months for receiving stolen goods. Receiving stolen goods was a long, long way from abduction, but even so, in her weakened state the thought preyed on Andrea's mind that the man who, for all his faults, she still loved might have betrayed her dramatically.

'Please don't let it be you,' she whispered, staring at the phone. Because she knew if that was the case, she'd be totally on her own.

Another hour passed, and as the clock ticked towards midnight with still no word from him, her doubts grew stronger. It crossed her mind more than once to call the police, but the people she was dealing with were ruthless, and clearly well organized, and they'd already told her what would happen to Emma if she did. Andrea didn't have much faith in the forces of law and order anyway. She'd had too much experience of them for that.

No, she needed someone she could trust. Someone who'd know what to do.

There was one person who could help. She might not have spoken to him for more than a decade but she was sure he would respond in this, her hour of need. The problem was, if she brought him back, she might also be unleashing forces outside her control.

But what choice did she really have? She couldn't do this alone.

There was a grandfather clock in the hallway, bought from an Islington antique dealer at an exorbitant price several years earlier, which had always looked out of place. Something about its relentless ticking tended to soothe her, though, and when it chimed midnight she stubbed out her latest cigarette in the ashtray and made her decision.

She retrieved a small black address book from her handbag on the kitchen top and found the number she wanted in the back, with no name next to it. She turned on the overhead light to dial, stopping at the last second. Thinking. They might have bugged the landline, and if they heard her ... She couldn't risk it. Instead, she fed the digits into her mobile and stepped out into the back garden.

The night was silent as she walked to the pear trees at the end, thirty yards from the house, and stopped. She looked round, listening, remembering what the kidnapper had said: *We're watching you.* But they couldn't see her in the back of the garden, she was sure of it.

So, taking a deep breath, she pressed the call button on the mobile.

And took her situation to a whole new level.

Two

Jimmy Galante answered on the third ring. 'Hello,' he said quietly, his accent still firmly east London.

There was no background noise that Andrea could make out, which surprised her. Jimmy had always been something of a nightbird. Maybe he'd changed.

'It's me,' she said, keeping her voice low, knowing the risk she was taking.

'Who's me?' he asked.

'Andrea. Andrea Devern.'

He gave a raucous laugh down the phone. 'Jesus, now there's a ghost from the past. How you doing?'

'Bad. Very bad.'

'Shit, I'm sorry to hear that,' he said, but she could almost hear the smirk in his voice. Jimmy Galante was not the kind of man who wasted time or effort on sympathy. 'How did you get my number? You been keeping tabs on me, Andrea?'

She had, but she wasn't going to tell him that. At least not yet. 'Someone gave it to me.'

'Oh yeah? Who?'

'That doesn't matter. What matters is I need your help.'

'To do what?'

Andrea took a deep breath, looked round in the gloom. 'My daughter's been kidnapped. I need you to help me get her back.'

Jimmy's husky trademark chuckle rumbled down the line again. There was something inherently cruel in it. It made Andrea think of a child pulling the wings off a butterfly, or cutting a worm into quarters, and it still made her nervous, even now, years afterwards.

'Sure, Andrea, whatever you say. You don't speak to me for God knows how many years—'

'You haven't been here. You've been in Spain.'

'You could have called,' he snapped. 'In all that time, you could have fucking called. But you didn't bother, did you? Because you didn't want nothing then, but now you do, so it's' – and here he did a nasty, high-pitched imitation of Andrea – 'please, Jimmy, help me find my daughter, some nasty man's kidnapped her.' He chuckled again. 'It don't work like that, babe. I've got business interests over here now. What do I want to come back to a shithole like England for? Fuck that for a game of soldiers.'

Andrea sighed. She'd been expecting this, but it still hurt to hear his complete lack of interest, either in her or in Emma. But his reaction told her something else too. Jimmy Galante, for all his faults, wasn't involved in this. If he had been, he'd have asked more questions.

'I want you to help me, Jimmy,' said Andrea, knowing that the sudden firmness in her tone was born of desperation.

'Sorry, babe, forget it. You still ain't given me a good reason why I should.'

'Because,' she answered, 'Emma isn't just my daughter. She's yours too.'

There was a long silence at the other end, and then Jimmy started to say something, but Andrea cut him off, pressing her advantage. 'Emma's fourteen years old. Her birthday's April the second. Think of the timing, Jimmy.'

'I can't think that far back. It's been too long.'

'Try. Fifteen years ago, the summer of 1992. We were together, weren't we? That's when I got pregnant. Just before you left.'

'How the fuck do I know she's mine?' he barked. 'You was married, Andrea. Remember? You was the one shagging around behind your old man's back. Or has that conveniently slipped your mind now as well?'

'Billy was impotent,' she said, not wanting to speak ill of her dead husband, but knowing that she had no choice. 'And you were the only man I was sleeping with then. She's yours, Jimmy. Face it. Your child. And now some bastard's taken her.'

She could almost hear the cogs whirring as he thought things over down the other end of the phone. This time she left him to it.

'What's happened then?' he asked eventually, a tone of resignation in his voice.

For the first time since the phone call more than three hours earlier, Andrea experienced a tiny, barely perceptible twinge of optimism. It seemed like she might be getting Jimmy Galante onside, which meant there was a chance she was no longer facing this nightmare alone.

Constantly mentioning Emma by name, and keeping her voice as quiet as possible, she detailed the evening's events, trying not to leave anything out. When she was finished, Jimmy asked her if she could raise the money in the time she'd been given, and she told him that she reckoned she could. 'It's not going to be easy, but I can manage it,' she said.

'And your new old man . . . he's missing?'

'Yes,' she said slowly. 'He is.'

'You certainly know how to pick 'em, don't you, babe?'

'Don't, Jimmy.'

'Think he might be involved?'

'To be honest, I can't see it, but . . .' She paused a moment. 'But I can't say for sure.'

'All right. What's his name?'

'Pat Phelan.'

'Don't know the name.'

'He's from Finchley.'

'I know a couple of people up that end of town. I'll ask around. You haven't gone to the cops, then?'

'No. And I don't intend to either.'

'Good, no point involving those bastards. So, what do you need me to do?'

'I just need you here with me, OK? I'd feel better. After all, you are her dad.'

'I'd better be, Andrea,' he said ominously, his voice barely more than a whisper. 'Because if I'm not, and you've dragged me back under false pretences, then I really ain't going to be very happy at all. You understand what I mean?'

There was no doubt at all what he meant. There never was when Jimmy talked like that. 'Yeah, I understand,' she answered. 'But you are. I promise you that. You are.'

There was another pause.

'I'll be on the first available flight into Heathrow tomorrow,' he said at last. 'I'll call you.'

'Thanks.'

'Don't thank me,' he said blankly. 'I ain't doing it for you.' And he hung up.

Andrea exhaled loudly as she flicked the phone shut. Now there really was no going back. Part of her was afraid of what involving Jimmy was going to mean for Emma's safe release. Jimmy was a violent man. He was capable of inflicting serious injury, even killing someone, but perhaps, in the end, that was what she wanted. Revenge on the people who'd abducted her daughter and put her through such pain. And Jimmy was no fool. He wouldn't rush in guns blazing and put Emma and everyone else in danger. He possessed an animal cunning, an ability to sniff out danger, something that had served him well in the past and something, she knew, he wouldn't have lost, even during his years in Spain. You didn't lose cunning like that. It was instinctive. And she needed someone with it in her corner.

She went back inside and locked the door behind her, feeling a little better. At least she'd actually done something now, and the paralysis born of utter helplessness which had affected her all evening seemed to dissipate a little. She drank another glass of water, smoked a last cigarette, and thought about having another brandy, but decided against it. Andrea had a strong tolerance of alcohol, having consumed it regularly throughout her adult life, but she'd had more than enough tonight. She needed to keep her wits about her. It would have been all too easy simply to lose herself in the oblivion of the bottle, and behaviour like that wouldn't help Emma.

Emma. Her baby. A fourteen-year-old girl enduring her first night as the prisoner of those animals.

If she's still alive . . .

Andrea stopped the thought, took a deep breath and told herself not to weaken.

'Think positive. They won't hurt her. They want money.'

She repeated it to herself three times, praying to God that it was true. Then, with slow, listless movements, she got herself ready for bed knowing that, for better or for worse, Jimmy would be here tomorrow. Jimmy Galante. Armed robber, violent thug, and possibly her only hope.

As she lay under the silk sheets in the master bedroom, staring at the ceiling, with a gap beside her where Pat usually lay, it wasn't her husband she was thinking about. It was Emma.

And Jimmy.

Three

Jimmy Galante had always been a smooth bastard. Now forty, two years older than Andrea, he still looked damn good as he walked out of the arrivals gate at Heathrow's Terminal One, dressed in a tailored suit and open-neck shirt, and Andrea noticed more than one pair of female eyes glancing at him as he walked across the concourse with a casual confidence that bordered on arrogance. Tall, broad-shouldered and tanned, his thick wavy black hair was longer than she remembered, but still as lustrous as it had been all those years ago. Even under the current circumstances, even after all these years, Andrea still felt a twinge of excitement. She wondered what it was about her, why she always seemed to go for the smooth bastards. It was something her business partner, Isobel, had once asked her, with more than a hint of disapproval in her voice, and it was a question she hadn't attempted to answer. Some women just go for the wrong sort of men, Andrea told herself, and maybe she was one of them.

As Jimmy approached her, he smiled, and there was something so knowing and cocky about his expression that it made her realize immediately why their relationship had ended. Up close the lines on his face were more pronounced, and the scar that ran down in a jagged line from just below his earlobe to his chin seemed deeper than before. But the eyes, so dark they were almost black, still commanded attention.

'Hello, babe,' he said, looking her up and down. 'You look good.'

She knew he was just saying that. She felt awful, and she was pretty sure she looked awful as well. She'd hardly slept the previous night, tossing and turning in the silence, knowing that Emma was out there somewhere, desperate for her mother's help. Emma was a tough young thing – she took after her mother in that respect – but there was no way she could have been prepared for what she had to be going through now. Andrea had always protected her from the darker things the world had to offer. She wanted for nothing materially (although she wasn't spoiled); she was being well educated at a decent private school (girls only); and her mother had always been there for her, never failing to make time in her busy schedule for her daughter and providing her with the nurturing hand any child needs. They'd always been a team, the two of them, with Andrea the senior partner.

Today had been easier than the previous night because she'd been able to keep busy. Having called Isobel to tell her that she wasn't feeling too good and was going to take the day off, she'd then phoned the dentist's and found out that Emma had kept her 4.45 appointment. She didn't know how this helped her, but for some reason the knowledge that Emma had been alive and well the previous afternoon, only a few hours before the kidnapper had called her, made it feel more likely that she was alive now.

Andrea had then spent the remainder of the morning and much of the first half of the afternoon raising the half a million she needed. This had involved emptying the two private deposit boxes she rented in separate banks in Knightsbridge, which gave her the grand total of £439,000. It was money that had been built up over a number of years as a result of various cash deals, and she'd viewed it as her retirement fund, her nest egg should things ever go badly wrong. And now they had. She'd then called the three banks where she had personal accounts, and organized the transfer of cleared funds between accounts to secure the remaining £61,000, which had proved a lot less easy than she'd anticipated, since no one these days seemed to want to hand over large sums of cash. When this had been done, she was left with a total of £11,561 in liquid assets – a pretty poor return for fourteen years of hard graft.

There'd still been aspects of the business to attend to as well. She'd received a number of calls from the company accountants regarding the Bedfordshire Spa, and even a couple of semi-apologetic ones from Isobel on the same subject. She'd dealt with them as best she could but it was hard to concentrate on anything other than Emma. Andrea had built up her company, Feminine Touch Health and Beauty Spas, from absolutely nothing into a thriving business which generated turnover in excess of five million cash. Yet ultimately, when it came down to it, this huge achievement and all the hard work that had brought it about would count for absolutely nothing if her daughter didn't come home.

Which was why Jimmy was here. To make sure she did.

'Any news?' he asked as they stood there looking at each other.

'No, nothing yet.'

'You got the money?'

She thought she saw a glint in his dark eyes when he said this, and felt a twinge of unease. The expression on his face remained irritatingly casual, and his lips formed the vague, knowing half-smile of someone who always has the answers. It concerned her that he didn't seem to be too worried about his daughter.

'I'll have it by tomorrow night,' she told him. 'Come on, let's go. I want to beat the rush-hour traffic.'

They walked in silence through the arrivals hall and into short-term parking.

'My, my, you are doing well,' said Jimmy when he saw the Mercedes.

'I've worked hard for it,' she answered curtly.

'You didn't tell me what you did for a living.'

'I know,' she said, getting inside.

They didn't speak again until they were through the slip road and on to the M4, heading back into London. Even though it was still before five, the traffic both ways was heavy, and the atmosphere in the car was tense.

'Why didn't you tell me about my daughter, Andrea?'

Andrea sighed. 'Because I thought we'd be better off without you.'

'*You're* certainly better off. That's for sure.'

'You know something, Jimmy? You haven't even asked her name. Your own daughter.'

Now it was Jimmy's turn to sigh. 'You already told me, Andrea. Her name's Emma. And cut me a bit of slack here, please. Number one, I didn't even know I had a daughter until last night. I still ain't seen a photo of her so I don't even know what she looks like. And number two, and much more important, I'm here, aren't I? I didn't have to come.'

'OK, OK, point taken.'

Andrea wiped sweat from her brow. The car's interior was cold with the air con blasting out on full, but she felt hot and vaguely nauseous.

'Are you all right, love?' he asked, leaning over towards her.

She could smell his cologne. It was strong but pleasant.

'Yeah, I'm fine. I think I need to eat something. I haven't had anything since a sandwich yesterday night.'

'We'll get something for you. What about your old man? Mr Phelan. Any sign of him yet?'

She shook her head. 'Nothing.'

She remembered how strange it had seemed waking up this morning without him there. He never stayed away from home. She did occasionally, for business, but not Pat. He always made it back to their bed, even if sometimes it was in the early hours. She still prayed that he had nothing to do with this, but with each hour that passed without any word from him it became more and more difficult to believe otherwise. But she didn't want to say that to Jimmy. It was bad enough that he was probably thinking it, without her admitting that once again she'd ended up with the wrong kind of man.

'I found out a little bit about him,' said Jimmy. 'He's a bit of a crook, ain't he?'

Although his tone was remarkably free of any gloating, she couldn't let it go.

'That's rich, Jimmy.'

'I was never a small-time little peasant like him, peddling dope and knock-off electrical goods.'

'He's not like that any more.'

'He doesn't need to be any more, does he? He's got you.'

Andrea fell silent. Conceded the point.

'Listen,' he said, putting a hand on her shoulder, 'I'm not trying to score points. I'm just trying to work out whether he's involved or not.'

'And do you think he is?'

Jimmy shrugged. 'Hard to tell. He's still missing, ain't he? That doesn't look too good. But it's a big step from flogging hookey gear to kidnapping.'

'Oh God, Jimmy. I don't know what to think, I really don't.'

'It'll be all right, babe. Don't worry. I'm here now.'

But it wouldn't be all right, Andrea knew that. Whatever happened, the life she'd worked so hard to build up, and the life of her precious daughter, had changed irreversibly. Even in the best-case scenario, with Emma returned to her physically unharmed, she would be a different person, permanently scarred by the trauma of this situation. And Pat ... well, Pat wasn't coming back. There was no doubt about that. And the thing was, she thought they'd been pretty happy. She would miss him, too – unless, of course, he was involved. But her instincts told her he wasn't; that he wasn't capable of putting Emma through such an ordeal. Because the thing was, as Jimmy had pointed out, he really didn't need to. He had access to money, he drove a nice car, he didn't need to work for a living, he enjoyed two or three foreign holidays a year, and he had freedom, too. Andrea cut Pat a lot of slack, so why put it all at risk for a share in half a million pounds, and the possibility that he'd end up in jail for the next ten years? She didn't buy it.

But she still couldn't explain his absence.

Jimmy's hand massaged her shoulder, slowly and deliberately. The sensation filled her with conflicting feelings. She still loved Pat, or at least she thought she did, but Jimmy had always done something to her, and even now she felt the first stirrings of arousal, accompanied by sharp pangs of guilt that she could even think about sex when her daughter was in the position she was in. Yet she couldn't help feeling much more secure with Jimmy here with her. He was strong, stronger than Pat could ever be, and she needed that now. But he was also trouble, and there was no part for him in her life now. Once this was over, she'd say goodbye to him for ever.

Although something told her it wasn't necessarily going to be as easy as that.

Four

'Half a million quid. It looks beautiful.'

Jimmy Galante had always loved money. He just hadn't liked the part where you had to work for it, which was why he'd chosen armed robbery and major drug dealing as his means of making a living.

The ransom was in a large Adidas holdall that Andrea had dug out from the loft, which was now sitting open on the coffee table in her living room. Jimmy was sitting on one of the leather armchairs with a large wad of fifties secured by a rubber band in his hand. His dark eyes moved from the wad to the contents of the holdall, then back again. The expression on his face was pure, unadulterated excitement.

'It's not all there yet,' she told him. 'I'm still sixty short. I need to pick up the rest at the bank tomorrow.'

'Where did all this lot come from, then?'

'Never you mind.'

He grinned. 'Been hiding it from the taxman, have you?'

'It's none of your business, Jimmy. The lucky thing is I've got it. It means our daughter can come home.'

The grin disappeared, and he nodded soberly, returning the wad of fifties to the holdall.

Initially, Andrea had been reluctant to bring Jimmy back here. She knew the kidnappers had been watching her and was afraid they might have bugged the house, so on Jimmy's advice they'd driven to a shop in Kensington which sold surveillance products and Andrea had bought a bug finder for a hundred pounds.

When they'd got back it was already dark, and after checking there was no one watching from the street, she and Jimmy had hurried inside, and he'd gone to work with the bug finder. It had taken him only seconds to locate a tiny electronic trip switch attached to the bottom of the skirting on the front door which would have alerted the kidnappers remotely as soon as the front door was opened, and was clearly how they'd known to phone her as soon as she'd got home the previous night.

Inside the house, though, the bug finder hadn't picked up anything, but this didn't stop Andrea feeling that the place had been violated by the kidnappers. It was now twenty-four hours since she'd found out about Emma's disappearance.

She watched Jimmy carefully as she sat smoking what was probably her fortieth cigarette of the day and drinking her third glass of red wine, and wondered if she could trust him. She'd hoped that telling him that Emma was his daughter would stir his parental instinct, but now she wasn't so sure it even existed. In the four hours since she'd picked him up from the airport, he'd hardly asked about Emma at all, seeming far more concerned about filling his stomach. He'd insisted on ordering an Indian takeaway, at the same time bemoaning the quality of them in his little corner of the Costa del Sol. Andrea had hardly been able to touch hers, but Jimmy had fallen upon his food ravenously. He'd eaten enough for two men, and washed it all down with four cans of Stella.

When Andrea had shown him a picture of Emma she'd brought with her to the airport, she'd said quietly, and with a sense of awe in her voice, 'This is your daughter, Jimmy. This is Emma.' His reaction had been a vague half-smile and a murmured, 'She's pretty.' Nothing else. Just those two words. She's pretty. For Andrea, this hadn't been enough. She'd wanted more. In truth, Emma didn't look much like Jimmy, but then again she didn't look much like either of them. Andrea was a natural brunette, with features that were sharp and well defined – a very attractive woman, but one with a hard edge to her. Emma, meanwhile, was a natural blonde, with small, delicate features, a round snub nose, and lively blue eyes. She was pretty in a sweet, cherubic way, and looked young for her age. The photo Andrea had shown Jimmy was a head-and-shoulders shot taken on Hampstead Heath the previous summer. Emma was grinning at the camera, showing a neat row of white teeth courtesy of the brace she'd been wearing for the previous six months, and which had been taken out the week before that shot. It was a celebration smile, and to Andrea the most beautiful smile in the world. It killed her to look at it. But not Jimmy. All he could manage was, 'She's pretty.'

She wondered if he genuinely believed he was the father or whether he'd concluded she was bullshitting in order to get his help. It was difficult to tell. That was the thing with Jimmy. He rarely let on what he was thinking, preferring to play mind games and keep people guessing.

As she sat there watching him, she realized she'd never really known him. On the one hand he was a ruthless bastard capable of terrible violence. On the other, he was also capable of great shows of affection. She remembered how once, not long after she'd first started seeing him, she arrived at his flat for a prearranged visit only to find that he wasn't there. Even though it was the early days of mobile phones, both of them had one, and she called him. He didn't answer so she took a walk round his neighbourhood before trying his number again. This time he answered, and he sounded breathless. Apologizing for the delay but not going into any detail as to what had caused it, he told her that he'd be back at the flat in fifteen minutes, although it was actually nearer half an hour before he finally pulled up in his Jaguar XJ6.

As he stepped out, Andrea could tell that something wasn't right. He was looking worn out, and his hair, usually so immaculately styled, was unkempt. His shirt was partly untucked, and as he jogged across the road towards her she saw a handkerchief tied tightly round his left hand.

'What happened to you?' she asked with a smile, looking towards the hand.

'Nothing for you to worry about,' he answered with a smile of his own, kissing her on the lips before ushering her inside the building. 'Sorry I'm late.'

Andrea knew better than to ask too many questions. She was aware that Jimmy operated outside the law. That much was obvious. He didn't appear to have a proper job but always had plenty of money. He'd told her he owned a construction business but was suitably vague, and tended to keep very odd hours for someone running his own company, often staying in bed with her until mid-afternoon on a weekday. Andrea was no fool. She knew. And the truth was that at the time it didn't bother her unduly. In fact, she found the whole thing very exciting. Jimmy was handsome and mysterious, a fantastic lover, and possessed the kind of wild streak a young woman like her couldn't help but find attractive.

Once they were inside the flat, Jimmy showed that wild streak by pulling her close and kissing her hard, then lifting her in his arms and taking her through to the bedroom, where he flung her on the bed and tore off her clothes. They made intense, passionate love, several times in quick succession, and when they were lying, sated, in each other's arms, his free hand – the one with the handkerchief wrapped round it – gently stroking her belly, he said he had something for her.

'What?' she asked, intrigued, trying to ignore the tiny flecks of blood on his fingers, just visible beneath the fabric.

He clambered off the bed and walked over to where his jeans lay on the floor. She watched as he leaned down to pick them up, admiring his naked body, thinking about the orgasm she'd just had, thinking about how happy Jimmy made her, wondering how she was ever going to tell her husband.

When he returned to the bed he had a small black box in the palm of his good hand.

'For you, my lady,' he said with a mock bow.

She smiled. 'What is it?'

'Open it and find out.'

So she did. And let out a little gasp. It was a gold necklace, eighteen carat at least, with a gold-lined emerald heart roughly the size of a five-pence piece on the end.

'Oh, Jimmy,' she whispered. 'It's beautiful.'

'I bought it this morning,' he told her.

She reached up and kissed him tenderly on the lips, feeling for that moment like the happiest woman in the world.

'I love it. Thank you.'

They spent the rest of the afternoon and much of the evening in bed. The lovemaking was some of the best Andrea had ever experienced. She could remember what they'd done together even now. The following morning, wearing that beautiful necklace and thinking that she'd really landed on her feet, she cooked Jimmy breakfast in bed, then went out to get the papers.

Glancing through the *Sun* on the way back to the flat, a photo caught her eye. It was of an ordinary-looking middle-aged man with a beard and a side-parting, and the headline beside him read 'Hundred K Robbery: Security Guard Fights for Life'. Even before she read the article, Andrea knew instinctively that Jimmy was involved. What followed simply confirmed her suspicions. It seemed that a gang of four robbers armed with a variety of firearms had held up a security van as it made a cash pick-up from a branch of Barclays Bank in Wembley. The security guard carrying the case containing the money, whom the paper identified as forty-seven-year-old father of two Alan Jones – the man in the photograph – had tried to resist when one of the gang had grabbed the case. In the ensuing mêlée he was punched savagely in the face several times and knocked unconscious, having struck his head on the concrete as he fell. An eyewitness was quoted as saying that the robber had then kicked him several times, even though it was obvious he was no longer any threat. He was now in intensive care where his condition was described as 'poorly but stable'.

Andrea saw that the time of the robbery was 2.10 the previous afternoon, barely an hour before Jimmy had turned up back at the flat looking dishevelled and wearing a makeshift bandage on his left hand. Jimmy had told her that at one time he'd been an amateur middleweight boxer and had won eleven of his twelve bouts, six by knockout. Not exactly overwhelming proof of guilt, but it didn't need to be. Andrea just knew.

Stupidly, she didn't say anything. Instead, trying to be as casual as possible, she watched him out of the corner of her eye as he lay in bed, casually perusing the paper, a cigarette in his mouth, as calm as you like. He went straight to the robbery story – she counted the pages – and read it twice before running through the sports pages at the back. Then, with a predatory half-smile, he chucked the paper aside and patted the sheets.

'Why don't you come back to bed, love? We've got some unfinished business to attend to.'

And she had, too, something which when she thought about it now made her cringe with shame. They'd made love again twice, and all the time she couldn't stop thinking about the security guard lying in a hospital bed connected to a load of tubes while his family sat round him, waiting for news. But Jimmy . . . Jimmy had forgotten him already. The whole thing was simply business to him, nothing more and nothing less.

After they'd finished, he got a call on his mobile and went out of the room, talking quietly. He returned a few minutes later, saying he had to go out. He was still acting casually, but she could tell he was tense.

And that's when she came out with it.

'You didn't have anything to do with yesterday, did you, Jimmy? You know, that robbery where the guard got hurt?'

'Course I didn't,' he answered, but she could tell that she'd rattled him. It was something in his eyes.

She looked at his hand. The handkerchief was gone now, but the knuckles were dark with bruises. He glanced down at them as well, then back at her. This time his expression had changed. There was a darkness in it.

'Why'd you think that?'

She immediately regretted asking. What, after all, was the point? He was always going to deny it.

'I don't know. I . . .' She stopped, not sure how to finish the sentence.

'I told you, I work in the building trade.'

She nodded. 'Sure, Jimmy.'

He came over to the side of the bed.

'Don't I treat you right or something?'

'Course you do,' she answered, feeling a little uneasy, not liking the way he was looking at her.

He crouched down so they were level, the smile he was giving her devoid of any warmth, his dark eyes boring into her.

'You know, I like you a lot, Andrea. I think we could do real well together. That's why I bought you the necklace.' He paused, touching the emerald heart. 'But don't go asking silly questions, all right? About stuff that doesn't concern you.' The fingers of his good hand stroked her

56

cheek tenderly but she felt herself tensing under the touch. The truth was, she was scared. 'Because otherwise . . .' He wrapped a lock of her hair round his middle finger. 'Otherwise we're going to fall out. Understand?'

She nodded.

'And I don't want that to happen. Because I like you. I really do.'

She felt a sharp pang of pain as he yanked the lock of hair, and she cried out. Immediately he let go, his lips parted in a pleasant, loving smile that almost made her think she'd imagined what had just happened. He leaned forward and kissed her gently on the lips, before pulling back.

'I've really got to go, luv. I'll call you later. Let yourself out, OK?'

And that was that. Chucking on some clothes, he'd left her there alone, wondering what on earth she'd got herself into.

She should have finished it there and then, of course. Someone who could beat and kick an innocent man to within an inch of his life and then, an hour later, come back home as if nothing had happened and make love to his girlfriend clearly had no conscience. And already he was exerting his dominance over her. If he could pull her hair like that, it wouldn't be much of a jump to hitting her. She didn't need this. She had a husband, a man who looked after and cared for her. It wasn't as if she was one of those women who put up with abusive partners because they had no self-esteem. Andrea knew she was a good-looking woman. She'd always been able to attract men.

But she hadn't finished it. To her eternal regret. And now, years later, Jimmy Galante was back, staring at money that she, Andrea, had worked so hard to earn. And she still feared him, although in her current situation she feared not having him around even more.

He drank from the tumbler of whisky she'd poured for him and looked over with one of his mocking smiles.

'Half a million quid, eh, Andrea? Who'd have thought you'd ever have that kind of money.'

'I always did,' she answered firmly.

'You know,' he said, watching her over the rim of the glass, 'I've been following your progress over the years. I'm impressed by how far you've come, living in a nice, big, flash pad like this.' He gestured vaguely with an arm.

'Money isn't everything, Jimmy.'

'It is when you ain't got none.'

'I'm sure you manage. You don't look like you're starving.'

'You think there's money out in Spain? There's fuck all. I get by, that's all.'

He sounded bitter, which was Jimmy all over.

Andrea had no sympathy. No one had ever given her anything. She'd had to go out and graft for it and had proved that you could be successful if you were willing to put in the sweat and the tears. No one had ever given Jimmy anything, either. He'd grown up in a Hackney council flat, with damp on the walls and cockroaches in the grime-encrusted spaces behind the cheap, flimsy kitchen units. The difference was that he hadn't wanted to work, and had taken what wasn't his, and by any means necessary. His fly-by-night lifestyle might have been exciting to her once, but she was young then. Now it simply depressed her that she'd ever fallen for his charms.

Andrea changed the subject. 'If you've been following my progress all these years, you must have known I had a daughter.'

He nodded. 'Yeah, I did.'

'And it never occurred to you that Emma might have been yours?'

He shrugged. 'No, it didn't. I mean, let's face it, babe, you weren't exactly whiter than white where men were concerned, were you?'

It was a cheap shot, but she let it go.

'I mean, she doesn't exactly look like me, does she?' he continued.

'She doesn't exactly look like me either, Jimmy, but I can tell you with total and utter certainty that she's mine.' She paused. 'And yours.'

He nodded, conceding the point, then once again his eyes drifted down towards the holdall of money. 'I'm looking forward to meeting her,' he said, but his tone was vague and it was clear his attention was focused elsewhere.

'You'll love her,' said Andrea quietly, feeling a sudden and terrible longing for her daughter. Tears stung at her eyes. She'd held it together so well today, but now, more than thirty-six hours since she'd last seen and touched Emma, the grim reality of her situation once again took her in its grip.

And there was something else, too. Could she really trust Jimmy?

The phone rang. The landline. It startled her. She and Jimmy exchanged glances. She got to her feet, walked out into the hallway and picked up the receiver.

'Hello?'

'Mum?'

Relief and shock soared through her. It was Emma. Her Emma!

'Darling, oh God, is that you?'

'Yeah, it's me.'

'Are you OK, baby? Is everything OK?' Tears were streaming down her face, but she didn't care. She was just ecstatic to be hearing her daughter's voice.

'I'm fine,' answered Emma, her voice small. She

60

sounded afraid. 'They say I should be home tomorrow, if you've got the money.'

'I've got the money, baby, don't worry. We're going to have you home by tomorrow night, I swear it. God, it's so good to hear you're all right. They haven't hurt you, have they?'

'No, but it's . . .'

Emma broke off, and there was a minor commotion at the other end. It sounded like she was being moved away from the phone, and Andrea felt a wave of panic, as if she was losing her all over again. Emma cried out, but the cry was cut short. It sounded as if it was being muffled.

'Emma?' she shouted as the panic shot through her. 'Emma, darling, are you OK?'

For a few seconds there was silence. Then came the sound of a door being shut and a new voice came on the line.

'You've spoken to her, and you know she's alive, so we've kept our side of the bargain.' Once again the voice was disguised but the tone was more aggressive. Andrea thought it might be a different person from the one who'd called the previous night. 'Now it's your turn to keep yours. Have you got the money?'

'Most of it,' she answered breathlessly. 'I'll have the rest by tomorrow.'

'Good. Then you'll be hearing from us

tomorrow night to make the final arrangements.'

'Don't hurt her, please,' begged Andrea, hating herself for showing her desperation, but unable to stop. The line, however, was already dead.

Slowly, she put down the phone. Jimmy had followed her out into the hallway and was staring at her with a look of concern. He didn't say anything for a couple of seconds, then he stepped forward and took her in his arms. She sank into them, burying her head against his chest.

'It's going to be all right,' he said quietly, the deep, gruff intonation of his voice suddenly making her feel safe.

That was the thing with Jimmy. Even now, he could inspire so many different and conflicting emotions. She breathed in his scent. He must have splashed on some more cologne after he'd had a shower earlier. It smelled strong, but somehow comforting.

'I spoke to her,' said Andrea, pulling away and looking at Jimmy. 'She's alive, Jimmy. She's alive.'

'See, I told you it was going to be all right, babe,' he said, continuing to hold her. 'These guys are professionals. They're not going to do anything to hurt her. She's their prime asset.'

Andrea didn't like his choice of words, nor the fact that he still hadn't referred to Emma by name, but she was too excited by the fact that she'd spoken to her to pay too much attention to that.

Finally, she had confirmation that Emma was OK. She was scared, but it didn't sound like they'd hurt her, which meant she was going to get her back. This time tomorrow, she'd be safe and sound.

Jimmy's hand ran down her back and moved across her buttocks. At the same time, he pulled her closer, and she could feel the hardness growing between his legs. 'It's going to be OK, babe. I'm here now. I'm back.' His grip on her tightened as he rubbed his cock against the material of her gypsy skirt.

She thought of Pat. Her husband. How their love life, once so vigorous, had slackened in recent months until, in the past few weeks, it had evaporated to almost nothing. Pat wasn't coming back. She was sure of that. One man leaves her life, another returns.

Jimmy lifted her chin so she was looking up into his dark eyes, seeing the lust in them.

'You still look beautiful, babe,' he whispered.

But she didn't want Jimmy. Not like that. She'd already betrayed one husband with him. Whatever Pat's faults, whatever he might have done, she wasn't going to betray a second. She pulled away from his kiss, trying to move backwards, but his hand grabbed her chin roughly and turned it back so she was facing him.

'Come on, I know you feel the same way.'

He was smiling now. As cocky as ever, forcing her towards him. She could smell the booze on his breath. Anger overtook her – anger that the bastard could be so cold to both her and Emma's plight – and she slapped his hand away, wrenching herself free from his grasp with more force than she'd intended.

'You fucking bitch,' he snarled, clenching his fists; but she stood her ground, glaring back at him.

'I'm not the little girl you used to know, Jimmy. So don't you dare try it. Think of someone else for a change. Like Emma . . . your daughter.'

'Still a tease, ain't you, babe?' he said quietly, and then with a snort of derision he walked past her back into the living room.

Five

The next day, Thursday, was excruciating. It was the waiting.

Jimmy apologized for his behaviour in the morning, which was typical of him. Always changing tack. She accepted the apology but she didn't believe it was genuine. Jimmy Galante was not the sort of person to feel remorse about anything he'd done. If he was, he'd never sleep at night, and she knew from experience that he slept like a log.

Their conversation over coffee in the kitchen was strained, and she was pleased to get out of the house and leave him behind. He'd wanted to come with her as she drove to the bank to pick up the remainder of the money, but she told him it would be easier if he didn't. 'It'll just arouse suspicions,' she explained, knowing that this was just an excuse. She took the holdall containing the money with her as well.

'Don't you trust me or something?' he asked her at the door.

And the truth, of course, was that she didn't. But she didn't say this. Instead she looked him right in the eye and said, 'This money represents our daughter's freedom. It's not going out of my sight today.'

Jimmy nodded and left it at that.

The bank were reluctant to part with the money, even though it was hers, and she had to go into the back and endure a lecture from the manager about the perils of being in possession of large sums of cash and sign a load of paperwork before they let her out with what was rightfully hers.

For lunch she grabbed a sandwich and took a walk on Hampstead Heath, leaving the money locked in the boot of the car. Usually it was a place of tranquillity where she could relax and enjoy the illusion of being somewhere in the country. Today, however, she paced relentlessly, counting down the minutes and hours, worrying about someone stealing the car and therefore the money, and when she encountered passers-by she felt bitterness and jealousy at the way they went about their easy lives while she suffered alone in hers. Waiting, always waiting.

She was home by mid-afternoon, and carried the holdall with difficulty up to the front door. Half a million pounds, she was discovering, weighed one hell of a lot. Jimmy was out, for which she was thankful, and she took the opportunity to sit on a lounger in the back garden, look out at the trees and listen to the sounds of early autumn. This was her refuge, her place of peace, and today it gave her hope. There was still that numb fear that it could all go wrong, and that these people, whoever they were, were simply stringing her along, but Andrea was a pragmatist, and the more she thought about it the more she shared Jimmy's view that their primary motive was money. If she did what she was told, they would release Emma. And then maybe, just maybe, things could start to get back to normal. Just the two of them together again.

Jimmy returned at seven o'clock, telling her not to worry because he'd been careful leaving and coming back. She didn't bother asking him where he'd been, assuming he'd been visiting associates. Frankly, she didn't care. She just wanted tonight sorted, and then she wanted rid of him for ever. It remained to be seen whether she'd made a mistake by involving him at all, but it was too late to worry about that now. Tonight she had to focus on the task ahead.

And so, for the next two hours, the waiting continued. They didn't speak much. There was little to say, and it was difficult to plan anything given that neither of them knew what procedures the kidnappers intended to set for them. Andrea kept looking at her watch. Sometimes she counted the seconds ticking on the clock in the hallway, and all the time the tension cranked up inside her little by little.

The clock struck nine.

She looked across at Jimmy. Her mouth was dry. He looked back, and for the first time she saw that he too was worried. He was frowning, his eyebrows almost touching, the lines on his forehead heavily pronounced and suddenly making him look his age. The room was thick with silence.

A minute passed. Andrea counted the seconds on the clock. Neither of them spoke, but Jimmy looked at his watch several times and sighed. It was a cheap thing with a black plastic strap, not like the Cartier he'd worn when she'd first known him. Times had obviously been hard for Jimmy. Maybe even hard enough for him to consider getting involved in a kidnap ... No, she didn't want to go down that route. She had to trust somebody, and right now there was no one else.

The phone rang. The receiver was next to her on the coffee table. She picked up immediately.

'Yes?'

'Have you got a pen and paper?' asked the disguised voice – the one that had first called her, she thought.

'Yes.'

'Good. Do exactly what I say and you'll have your daughter back before the end of the night.'

'That's all I want,' she told him.

'Fuck us about, though, and she dies. Painfully. Do you understand?'

She tensed, thinking of Jimmy. Was it a big mistake bringing him in? She said that she understood.

'Here are your instructions. Get in your car – the Mercedes – and drive up to the junction of the M1 and the M25, then proceed eastbound on the M25 to junction twenty-five. Turn left on to the A10, then turn left again at the next roundabout on to the B198 signposted to Rosedale.' He waited while she wrote all this down. His breathing was audible on Andrea's end of the phone. 'There's a turning on the left about two hundred metres down. Follow the road for approximately three quarters of a mile until you see a sign on the right for Gabriel's Saw Mill. Drive down there two hundred metres.' He paused again. 'At that point the track forks. Take the right-hand fork and follow it approximately fifty metres. A burnt-out single-storey building with no front door will appear on your right. You can't miss it. Stop the car but leave the engine running. Take the bag containing the money inside, and drop it against the front wall so that it can't be seen from outside.

69

There's a turning circle another twenty metres down the track. Drive down to that, turn round and leave.'

'What about Emma?'

'When you get back on to the road, turn right and keep going about half a mile and you'll come to a phone box on the left. Go inside and wait for our call. As soon as we've confirmed that all the money's there, and you haven't tried anything stupid, we'll make contact and give you instructions on where to collect your daughter.'

'I need to speak to her.'

'Not now. Do as you're instructed and you'll be seeing her soon enough. One other thing: turn off your mobile and don't bring it with you.'

'OK,' she said reluctantly. She didn't like the idea of being without it.

'Now get moving. You've got exactly forty-five minutes to get to the drop-off point. And remember, we're watching.'

The line went dead and Andrea put the receiver down.

'What's the plan?' asked Jimmy, looking at her closely.

Briefly, she went through the instructions she'd been given. 'I don't think you should come,' she added when she'd finished. 'They said they were going to be watching me. If they see you, it could jeopardize things. I can't afford that.'

'She's my daughter too,' he answered. 'I'm coming with you.'

'What's the point, Jimmy? I'm delivering the money, that's all.'

'Because I don't trust them. That's the point. What if they're bullshitting about letting her go?'

'But you were the one who told me they just wanted cash. That they didn't want to hurt her.'

'Well, maybe that is all they want, but there's still no guarantee they'll release her. They might hold out for more cash. But if you drop me off a couple of hundred yards from where you're making the drop, I'll make my own way down there and keep an eye on the place. I'll see who goes in, see if I recognize them. I might be able to get their registration number.'

'What good'll that do?'

'There's still a couple of coppers I know. They'll be able to trace who the car belongs to.'

Andrea didn't like the sound of this at all.

'But it's risky, isn't it? What happens if they see you? Then they're not going to let Emma go, are they? They might kill her.'

Jimmy shook his head. 'They ain't going to kill her. She's worth more to them alive. And they ain't going to see me, either. I'll be quiet. And I'll be careful. I don't want anything to happen to Emma either, you know.'

Andrea sighed, trying to think. Not following

the kidnappers' instructions to the letter was a huge risk, but what if Jimmy was right? What if they weren't going to let Emma go? Surely it was better to have an insurance policy in the form of Jimmy watching the place – someone cunning enough to spot a double-cross, and hard enough, if necessary, to do something about it. But, did she even trust him? She wiped sweat from her brow, wrestling with the alternatives, knowing she had only seconds to make up her mind. Knowing that even one wrong move could end the life of her only child.

She took several deep breaths, telling herself to keep calm, for Emma's sake.

'What if they're out there now watching the house?' she asked. 'If they see us leaving together . . .'

He shook his head. 'They're not watching the house. If they were, they'd already know I was here. Anyway, there won't be enough of them to do that.'

'How do you know?' she demanded.

'This ain't a big firm, babe. No way. There'll only be a couple of them. Any more and there'd be too much chance of a leak. Also, they'd stand out sitting in a car in a nice, quiet street like this for hours on end. They won't want to risk that. But we'll play it safe. You go out the front, and I'll come out nice and quiet behind you, and I'll stay down in the seat. It'll be dark, no one'll see.'

His words were filled with a quiet confidence that was proving seductive.

'What happens afterwards? Where will I pick you up from? They told me not to bring my mobile phone.'

He reached into his pocket and retrieved a cheap Nokia handset. 'Take this,' he said. 'It's a spare one of mine.'

'I told you, they don't want me to take one.'

'No, babe, they don't want you to bring *your* mobile phone. There's a difference.'

'What do you mean?'

'They're just covering themselves. If you have gone to the police then one of the ways they can track your movements would be using your mobile. That's why they don't want you to have it. They probably know your number so they can phone to check whether it's switched off.' He handed her the Nokia. 'But they don't know the number of this one.'

'OK,' she said uncertainly as he gave her the handset.

'Put it on vibrate, OK? I've got another phone. You drop me off just before we get to the ransom drop. Then an hour after we part company, I'll text you. If it's safe for you, you call my number and we can arrange to meet.'

She nodded, coming to a decision. 'All right, let's go.'

Six

At 9.47 p.m. Andrea's Mercedes was moving at a steady thirty miles an hour along a quiet country B road with a cornfield stretching into the darkness on one side and a bank of beech and oak trees rising up on the other. A car passed them going the other way and moving far too fast, but there was no traffic behind. Andrea slowed as she spotted the dilapidated sign for Gabriel's Saw Mill nailed to a tree up ahead.

'This is it,' she whispered, indicating right.

Jimmy was hunched down in the front passenger seat, a position he'd adopted ever since they'd left the motorway.

'All right, babe,' he whispered. 'I'm out as soon as you make the turning, unless I hear any different.'

'I don't like this, Jimmy, I really don't like this.' The doubts were savaging her now. *If he makes a mistake . . .*

'It's just an insurance policy. Better safe than sorry.'

She steered the Mercedes into the turning, little more than a dirt track which was only just wide enough for the car. Ahead, the trees loomed, blotting out the light of the moon.

'Wish me luck, babe.'

'Good luck,' she answered without looking at him as she peered through the windscreen into the darkness.

A second later the door opened – a foot, maybe a foot and a half – and Jimmy slid through the gap. Then he shut the door silently behind him and Andrea drove on, risking a brief glance in the rear-view mirror as he disappeared into the woods.

Suddenly she was on her own.

Up ahead the trees seemed to rise up to greet her, and the only sounds were the tyres crunching on the track's loose gravel and her own low, tense breathing. This was it, the moment of truth. Close to all of Andrea's life savings were in the holdall in the footwell of the front passenger seat. She would have given everything, down to the clothes on her back, to have Emma returned to her safely, but if this failed and her tormentors didn't keep their side of the bargain she didn't know what else she could do, or where she could get any more money from.

The track forked as the kidnapper had said it would, and she followed it to the right as instructed. The road surface became pitted and potholed and she was forced to slow right down as she manoeuvred the Mercedes round the worst of the holes. Nothing moved in the darkness up ahead and on either side of her the wall of trees looked impenetrable.

And then it appeared to her right, a concrete outbuilding with blackened walls set back a few yards from the track, its roof all but gone, a black hole where the front door was.

She stopped the car and jerked on the handbrake, slipping the gearstick into neutral. For a few seconds she just sat there, listening to the silence, wondering if the man on the phone was watching her now, the man who'd abducted her daughter. Wondering too whether he'd hear Jimmy's approach and call the whole thing off.

Nothing moved. Andrea could hear her heart beating.

Finally, she bent down and pulled up the holdall, leaning back against the weight, and manoeuvred it awkwardly out of the car. As she stood up, she took one last look around before walking slowly up to the building, carrying the holdall two-handed, stopping at the gap where the front door had been.

It suddenly occurred to her that it might well be

easier for the kidnappers simply to lie in wait, take the money and kill her, then go back and do exactly the same to Emma. Job done. *Right now, Andrea, there could be someone just inside this door, a crowbar in his hand, ready to smash your skull in.*

'Just do as he said,' she muttered to herself: drop the money, leave, go to the phone box and wait for the call that would reunite her with her daughter.

She stepped inside. Pale shards of moonlight shone through the huge hole in the roof, revealing an empty room with cement flooring, and a few tins of paint in one corner. To her right, a wooden door hanging off one of its hinges led into a poky little room which had probably once been a storage cupboard. The air smelled musty and vaguely of turps. There was no one there, no crowbar-wielding maniac. Taking a deep breath, she put the holdall on the floor next to the wall, then quickly turned and walked back outside.

And stopped.

She thought she saw movement in the trees ahead of her, something rustling. She stood still, staring, but as she watched, the movement stopped. But she knew she hadn't imagined it, and, feeling a new and very strong urge to get out of this place, she hurried over to where the car sat idling and jumped inside, reversing back the way she'd come in rather than going any further into the woods and using the turning circle she'd been told to use.

It was only when she was back on the road that she sighed with relief. She may have just parted with half a million pounds of her hard-earned money, with still no sign of her daughter, but at least she was out of that place. She wondered if it had been Jimmy she'd heard. She hoped it wasn't. If he could draw attention to himself like that then it might not just be her who'd noticed his presence. It wasn't something she wanted to think about.

A few minutes later the phone box she was after – a modern glass BT one – came into view at the edge of a village which was little more than a tiny collection of houses. It was up on a verge just beyond a bus stop, and partly concealed by the branches of a large oak tree. She pulled up twenty yards short of it, parking her car as close to the verge as possible, and banged on the hazard lights.

Once she was inside the phone box, she stood and waited for the last act, praying that this was finally it. The end of the nightmare.

The time was 9.56 p.m.

Seven

The phone didn't ring. Ten minutes passed, then twenty, and still Andrea stood in the bright light of the booth, staring at the receiver as the occasional car hissed past in the darkness outside, willing the call to come through. Hoping, praying . . .

A memory came back to her of a time years ago when she'd lost Emma on a crowded beach in Spain. They'd been on holiday with a new boyfriend of Andrea's, an Aussie bar manager called Bryan she'd met a few months earlier. Andrea had been besotted with Bryan, who was tall, blond and a lot younger, and for a very short time she'd even thought he was going to be the one. She was all over him on the beach that day, and for just a few moments – no more than that, because Emma was always the most important thing in the world to her – just for those few moments, she hadn't paid attention to her four-year-old daughter, and when she'd pulled away from Bryan and looked around, Emma wasn't there any more.

God, the terror she'd felt. It had almost been worse than when she'd got the call from the kidnapper. She'd jumped up, called out her daughter's name, looked round desperately, but all she could see was a sea of half-naked strangers stretching in both directions as far as the eye could see, like something out of the worst kind of nightmare. She'd panicked, really panicked. All she could think was that Emma had been taken. *My baby's been snatched by paedophiles, predators who'll abuse her and kill her. I'll never see her again, and it will all be my fault. Because I put myself before her.* She'd run round, not sure which way to go, knowing that the wrong decision would take her even further from Emma, ignoring the blank, uncaring stares of the other beachgoers as she called out, her voice an anguished howl.

In the end it was Bryan who found her, walking along the shore several hundred yards away, all alone, crying her eyes out. She was only missing five minutes, but Andrea could still recall the intense, almost physical joy she'd felt when she saw Bryan coming back with Emma in his arms. She'd never experienced anything like it, either before or since.

Within weeks she'd finished with Bryan – not because he was at fault, but because she would forever associate him with her own selfishness – and she'd sworn then never to let anyone get in the way of her and Emma. She'd kept to her vow, too. Until now.

There was a vibration in her jeans pocket. It was the mobile Jimmy had given her. She looked at her watch. It was 10.18. Pulling it from her pocket, she saw that he'd sent a text.

She read the words on the screen, then read them again.

GET BACK TO DROP-OFF POINT NOW.

It was half an hour since she'd dropped him off. He'd specifically told her he wouldn't contact her for an hour. Something had made him change his mind. Could it be good news? But if so, why hadn't he just called? She thought about calling him back, but stopped herself. Far better simply to wait here, as she'd been instructed, until the kidnappers called. But why hadn't they done so already? They must have counted the money by now.

The minutes passed. Outside, another car drove past, slowed down, then accelerated again. She suddenly felt very exposed out here in the middle of the country late at night, illuminated for all to see by the phone booth's light.

God, what the hell was Jimmy doing? Had he

done something stupid, like confront the kidnappers? Had he beaten a confession out of one of them? If he had, she'd kill him. All she wanted was her daughter back. Christ, they could have the money. It was totally and utterly irrelevant to her now without Emma. Everything was.

The phone vibrated again. It was another message from Jimmy.

GET BACK TO DROP-OFF POINT NOW. URGENT!

Andrea leaned against the glass panel of the phone booth, staring down at the screen, her stomach churning, wondering what the hell she should do. Then she made a decision and called Jimmy's number.

It rang and rang. She counted each ring, and when the number hit twelve she hung up. What the hell was he playing at?

She replaced the mobile in her pocket and stared at the phone unit on the booth's wall. The gunmetal-grey stand was covered in carved teenage graffiti, and the receiver was scratched and old. It was also not ringing.

What are you going to do, babe? They're not calling, are they? You could be here for hours.

But if I go . . . If I go and they call . . . What then?

Andrea agonized. She clenched her fists, and gritted her teeth, squeezed her eyes shut. Tried, tried, tried to make the right decision. Cursed herself for bringing in Jimmy. Cursed Jimmy for complicating things, and then not being there when she needed to talk to him. And still the fucking phone wasn't ringing, and it was now 10.35.

Flinging open the door in one angry movement, Andrea hurried out of the phone booth, jumped back in the car and executed a rapid three-point turn in the road before driving back the way she'd come, going fast and trying her best not to think about the fact that even now the phone might be ringing away as the kidnapper called to give her instructions about where to find Emma.

She was back at the turning to Gabriel's Saw Mill in under two minutes. Once again the track was empty and silent as she drove down it, taking the right-hand fork, looking for but not seeing any sign of Jimmy. She could only assume that he'd meant the abandoned outbuilding when he'd said in the message to get back to the drop-off point, but when she stopped the car outside, it looked just as deserted as it had done before.

This time she killed the lights and the engine, and put the keys in her pocket as she got out. It was a risk – she might need to make a quick getaway – but if she moved away from an idling car, she fancied the idea of someone driving it off and leaving her out here alone even less.

'Jimmy?' she called out, trying to keep her

voice down as she slid her gaze along the silent tree line.

No answer.

She turned in the direction of the outbuilding, and swallowed. She didn't want to go back in there, but nor did she want to stay out here, with just the slow, quiet rustling of the leaves in the breeze for company.

'Jimmy?' she called again, a little louder this time, but with exactly the same effect.

She walked up to the hole in the outbuilding where the door had once been, and slowly poked her head inside. The holdall containing the money was gone. Aside from that, everything was just like it was before. The smell of turps, the inner door hanging off its hinges . . .

Except, now there was the sound of dripping.

At first she thought she was imagining it, that it was the wind playing tricks. But it wasn't. It was definitely there.

Drip, drip, drip . . .

Coming from the room off to the right.

'Jimmy,' she hissed, 'are you there?'

Nothing.

Fear ran its fingers up Andrea's spine. She wanted to run. But where?

Get back to the phone box. Now. They might be calling. You could miss them!

But where's that dripping coming from?

Suddenly every drop seemed loud inside her head, and as her fear built, so too did her curiosity. She took three paces inside the room, turned her head and looked into the gloom beyond the hanging door.

'Oh Jesus,' she gasped. 'Oh no.'

Her hand shot to her mouth, covering her scream as she took a step backwards, unable to take her eyes off Jimmy Galante's corpse. They'd impaled him on a rusty butcher's hook, which had been rigged up on an exposed wooden beam running below the ceiling join. He hung there unsteady and sprawling, like a stringless marionette, head slumped forward, feet just about touching the grimy stone floor, arms dangling uselessly at his side. The sky blue polo shirt he'd been wearing earlier was stained black in the semi-darkness, and the dripping she could hear was the blood splattering steadily on to the floor from the gaping wound in his neck where his throat had been sliced wide open.

But there was worse. All his fingers were missing, on both hands. They'd been crudely hacked off, leaving nothing more than uneven, bloodied stumps.

She couldn't believe what she was seeing. Jimmy had been such a powerful presence, and to see him butchered like this was almost too much to bear.

'Oh Jimmy,' she whispered. 'What have they done to you?'

His right arm twitched. She was sure of it. She stared hard into the darkness, asking herself if she'd imagined it.

But then it twitched again.

Oh God, he was still alive.

She rushed forward, half-slipping in the pool of blood that was forming on the floor, and leant down in front of him.

'Jimmy, it's me,' she said urgently, putting one arm round his shoulders and using her free hand to lift up his chin. 'We're going to get you . . .'

She never finished the sentence, the shock of Jimmy's sightless, dead eyes staring back at her stopping her dead in her tracks. He was gone. The man she'd been relying on was gone. She let go of him and staggered backwards, wondering how this nightmare could get any worse, unable to believe what she'd just witnessed because to believe it was to admit to herself that the animals she was dealing with were capable of the worst kind of atrocity.

And as she leaned against the opposite wall, unable to move, she barely noticed the mobile phone in her pocket as it started to vibrate.

Eight

Andrea ran outside into the darkness, desperate to put some distance between her and Jimmy as the mobile continued to vibrate. This wasn't a message. It was a call.

She pulled it from her pocket and said 'Hello?' breathlessly into the mouthpiece.

'Hello, Andrea.' It was the artificial voice of the kidnapper, his tone neutral.

'You've got the money. Now where's my daughter?'

'She's safe.'

'But where is she? I've given you the money, every penny of it. I've kept my side of the bargain—'

'But you haven't though, Andrea, have you? I told you to come alone, didn't I?' He paused, taking his time. 'And you didn't. You decided it would be better to bring someone along to spy on us. That was very stupid. I told you we were watching your every move.'

Andrea felt her heart lurch. 'Please, I'm so sorry. I just wasn't sure what to do. You've got your money. Please let my daughter go.'

'It's going to cost you.'

'For Christ's sake, I've got no more money. You've had everything.'

'There's always more.'

'Listen, please—'

'No, you listen, and you listen very carefully. You fucked up. You didn't follow the simple instructions you were given. So now it's going to cost you another half a million if you want to see your daughter alive again.'

'But I told you, I haven't got that sort of money.'

'You've got another forty-eight hours to find it. That's the deadline. Use the time wisely. And remember, do not tell anyone this time. No one at all. Or Emma dies.'

'Let me speak to my daughter. You've got to let me speak to her.'

'You'll speak to her again, but when we're ready. Not now.'

The line went dead while Andrea was still talking desperately into the mouthpiece, the knowledge that she had indeed totally screwed up ringing round her head. It was all Jimmy's fault. Even after all these years he still had the capacity to cause her pain. But this was pain like she'd never felt before.

Hold together, Andrea. You owe it to Emma. Hold together.

But God it was hard. It was so damn hard. Tears stung her eyes and she wiped them away angrily as she ran over to the car and jumped inside, switching on the engine. She lit a cigarette and took urgent drags, then drove down to the end of the track and turned round.

As she got back on the main road and drove back in the direction of London, she stared wide-eyed out of the windscreen, silently repeating the mantra over again: *Stay strong, stay strong, stay strong.* She knew she couldn't collapse under the pressure, because if she did she would never get up again, and right now she couldn't afford that, not while Emma remained in the clutches of those animals.

She thought about them now, the people she was up against. Jimmy Galante was no pushover. He was a hard man, a street fighter with the kind of low cunning that only the truest criminals possess, and yet he'd been discovered by the man or men he was supposed to be watching, and butchered like a dog. These people were ruthless. And worse, they knew exactly what they were doing. She couldn't fight them alone, she knew that. Yet involving others had already backfired. Which left what?

There was, of course, only one alternative. The police. At least they might know what to do. It was a huge risk, given how brutally efficient Emma's kidnappers were. If they found out that the police were involved, they might panic and kill her, but then they might well kill her anyway, especially if Andrea couldn't raise the new money fast enough. Once again she was being forced into a corner, knowing that the wrong move would have terrifying ramifications.

So intensely was she concentrating that she didn't notice that her car was veering into the centre of the road until she saw headlights rushing towards her and heard the sound of the other car's horn. She swung the wheel hard left and slammed on the brakes, going into a wild skid that whirled the car round a hundred and eighty degrees in a screech of tyres before she finally came to a halt, facing the wrong way down the empty road.

Except it wasn't empty. The car that had been coming towards her had now stopped about thirty yards ahead. As she watched, her hands gripping the steering wheel as if it was the edge of a cliff she was hanging from, it did a three-point turn and started driving back towards her, the lights on its roof flashing a bright blue against the night sky.

Andrea cursed. Of all the bad luck, she had to

run into probably the only police patrol car in a ten-mile radius.

Act natural. For Christ's sake, act natural.

She glanced briefly in the rear-view mirror and was shocked by the face that stared back at her. Her expression was tight and haunted, making her look a good five years older than she was, her hair a tangled mess.

Stay calm. Act natural.

The police car came to a halt five feet in front of her bumper, and its two occupants slowly clambered out of each side, donning their caps.

She wound down her window as the driver stopped beside it and leaned down. He was middle-aged, heavy-set but running to fat, with a thick moustache and a gruff expression that suggested whatever she said wasn't going to be enough to stop her getting booked for careless driving. But she had to try.

'I'm sorry, officer,' she announced before he had a chance to speak. 'I think I must just have lost concentration. I've had a very busy day at work.'

'I'm afraid that's not an excuse, madam,' he told her sternly. 'You really shouldn't be driving if you're tired.'

Typical copper, she thought. *Always acting holier than thou. I bet he's driven knackered plenty of times.* But she knew she couldn't say anything to antagonize him. Instead, she apologized for a second time.

'Where have you been this evening?' he asked, his expression unchanged.

Belatedly, she realized her hands were still gripping the steering wheel. She removed them, saw that they were shaking, put them in her lap.

'Work,' she answered.

'Where do you work?'

Her mind went blank. Completely. For a moment, she couldn't even remember where she was. 'Erm . . .' Her hesitation sounded ridiculous, she knew it. But she just couldn't think. 'Er . . .'

'Would you mind stepping out of the car, madam?' he asked, reaching in with a gloved hand and removing her keys from the ignition. 'I have to tell you that I've got reason to believe you've been drinking, so we're going to ask you to take a breath test. Do you understand?'

She nodded weakly. 'Sure.'

Stay calm, Andrea, stay calm. You haven't been drinking. One shot of brandy two hours ago, nowhere near enough to make you over the limit. The worst that can happen is they book you for dangerous driving. They'll issue you with a ticket, let you go, and you can go home and try to think of a way of finding another half a million pounds in cash by Saturday to save your fourteen-year-old daughter's life.

She stepped out of the car, unsteady on her feet as all the knocks of the past forty-eight hours rose up and battered her like winter waves on a sea wall. She was finally crumbling, and she knew it.

'Are you all right, madam?' It was the driver's colleague. He was a taller, younger guy, with the air of the college graduate about him, and he was holding a breathalyser under his arm.

'Yeah, thanks. I'm fine.' She tried to smile but didn't quite make it.

The young cop was staring at her chest. 'What's that?'

'What's what?'

She looked down, saw what he was staring at. There was a thick patch of blood on her jacket where she'd grabbed hold of Jimmy. Jesus, how could she have missed that? There were further flecks of it lower down, as well as a single thumb-sized spot on her T-shirt, which suddenly seemed to stick out a mile in the flashing lights.

The older cop stepped forward, staring too.

'Have you been hurt?' he asked.

She turned round quickly. 'No, I'm fine. Honestly.'

'This is blood,' he said. 'You'd better take your jacket off. You might have cut yourself.'

'I haven't.'

The two cops were watching her closely. The older one seemed to come to a decision.

'Take your jacket off, madam.'

She felt like asking why, but knew she was going to have to cooperate eventually, so she slipped it off and gave it to the older cop, who lifted it to his nose and sniffed it suspiciously.

'This is definitely blood,' he said.

Andrea stood there, her heart pounding. Now that they could see she wasn't hurt, one of them was going to ask the obvious question. It was the younger one who did.

'Care to explain how it got on your shirt and jacket, madam?'

Andrea took a deep breath. The decision about what her next move would be had finally been made for her.

'Yes,' she said, looking at them both in turn. 'I think I'd better.'

Part Two

Part Two

Nine

When SG3 Mike Bolt of SOCA, the Serious and Organized Crime Agency, was woken at just after 5.30 a.m. on a Friday morning in mid-September by a call from his boss telling him to get down to their offices fast, he had no idea that one of the hardest days of his life had just begun.

His team had just come off a job tracking a gang of professional money-launderers who were now safely banged up awaiting trial, and he'd booked the day off as holiday. He had big plans for the coming weekend, his first off in close to a month, which involved driving down to Cornwall to spend a few relaxing days with a twenty-eight-year-old artist from St Ives with raven hair and a dirty laugh. He'd been introduced to Jenny Byfleet a couple of months earlier when she'd been up in London, and he was very keen to get to know her better. Jenny was the kind of girl a man could really fall for, and Bolt felt that he deserved a bit of romance in his life, even the long-distance kind. Things had been a bit sparse in that department for some time now.

But the romantic weekend was going to have to wait because this was an emergency: an ongoing kidnap situation, according to the boss.

Most of the public don't know it, but kidnapping is a comparatively common crime. On average, there's one every day in London alone, but the vast majority of these are drugs-related, involving squabbles over money between criminal gangs, particularly those from ethnic minorities. This case was totally different, and far, far rarer. A fourteen-year-old middle-class white girl abducted for ransom was a frightening development, and a senior cop's worst nightmare. Although none of the top brass would ever admit it, Bolt knew that the police service had no real problem tolerating kidnappings involving a few thugs snatching and torturing a crack addict over an unpaid couple of hundred quid, because frankly the press, and therefore the public, weren't really that interested. But if the media got hold of something like this, they'd have a field day. It had all the elements of a great story, particularly now that the kidnapper or kidnappers had murdered a friend of the victim's mother during an attempted ransom drop the previous evening.

The stakes, then, were extremely high, and the pressure for a successful result was going to be enormous.

And Mike Bolt was the one who was about to be chucked headfirst into the eye of the storm.

The details he'd been given were still sketchy. The victim's mother had been stopped at just before eleven o'clock the previous night, having been spotted driving erratically by a police traffic vehicle containing two officers from Hertfordshire Constabulary. As she'd got out of her car, she was seen to have bloodstains on her clothing, and when questioned about this, the woman, who'd been in a distressed state, had told them about the kidnapping and the subsequent murder of her friend.

The woman had refused to return to the spot where her friend's body was, claiming that the kidnappers might still be there, but a second patrol car had eventually been dispatched, only to discover that the body had been set on fire and was already badly burned. There was no sign of anyone else in the vicinity and so, despite her protestations of innocence, the woman had been arrested on suspicion of murder and transferred to Welwyn Garden City police station where she'd given a lengthy statement explaining what had happened to her over the previous two days.

It was a difficult and highly unusual situation

for Hertfordshire police. On the one hand they had an obvious murder suspect in custody, but one who nevertheless remained insistent that her daughter had been kidnapped, and was acting like someone telling the truth. In the end they'd decided to escalate the inquiry, and because she'd been picked up outside London's city limits, the senior investigating officer on the case had approached SOCA rather than the Met's over-stretched Kidnap Unit, hence the call to Bolt.

It had just turned seven a.m. when he arrived at the office where his team was based. The Glasshouse, as it was known, was a 1960s ten-storey office block with windows that were tinted with the grime of age rather than lavishness of design, set on the corner of a lacklustre shopping street a few hundred metres south of the river in Vauxhall. It was a fine sunny morning, the fifth such day in a warm spell that had followed one of the wettest, most disappointing summers on record – which for England was really saying something – and if it hadn't been for the fact that he was missing out on seeing Jenny, Bolt would have been in a good mood. He liked cases he could get his teeth into, and they didn't come much more meaty than this. More and more these days, his work took him and his team into long-drawn-out inquiries where the slow and usually laborious process of evidence-gathering took weeks, sometimes months, to complete. The money-laundering job they'd just finished was a case in point, having started right back in early June; and he'd once been part of a people-smuggling investigation that had lasted the best part of a year. During a career that had spanned two decades, Bolt had learned the art of patience, but even so, the idea of taking charge of a case whose resolution could be measured in hours was one he was never going to pass up.

Bolt's team was based in an open-plan office on the fourth floor of the Glasshouse, and when he arrived about half of its dozen members were already there, drinking coffee and generally looking pretty groggy. They'd all been rousted from their beds earlier than they'd been expecting, and Bolt knew he wasn't the only one whose day off had been interrupted before it had even got going. The team had had a major drink-up two nights earlier in the West End to celebrate the arrests of the money-launderers, and it looked like one or two of his people had continued the cele-bration the previous night as well.

At least Mo Khan looked fairly ship-shape. Mo was one of Bolt's team leaders and the guy he trusted most. They'd been colleagues for close to five years now, first in the National Crime Squad, then at SOCA, and though, with his big round face and friendly, twinkling eyes, he bore more than a passing resemblance to a short, squat cuddly bear, the appearance was deceptive. Mo Khan was tough, efficient and unflappable under pressure, and these were three traits Bolt knew were going to come in very useful today. There was no sign yet of Tina Boyd, his other team leader, or his overall boss, SG2 Barry Freud, although Bolt knew he would be around somewhere since he was the one phoning everyone up at half past five.

He'd only just managed to say his hellos to the team members when Mo came over and collared him.

'Our mystery lady got here twenty minutes ago,' he said as Bolt poured himself a cup of strong black coffee from the percolator. 'Big Barry wants us to start the interview straight away. She's been up all night and he thinks that if we leave it much longer she's going to be too exhausted to talk.'

'Fair enough. Where is she?'

'Over in Interview Room B. Everything's set up and we're ready to go.'

'Blimey, you're quick off the mark this morning,' said Bolt, following him out the door and down the corridor. 'What time did you get in?'

'Half an hour ago. I was moving fast.'

Bolt grinned and gave him a playful punch on

the arm. 'You never move fast, Mr Khan. How did you get here? Levitate?'

'I'm a man of many talents, boss.'

'So, have you seen her yet? This Mrs Devern?'

He nodded. 'I spoke to her briefly. She looks absolutely shattered, but she's very keen to talk to us.'

'I'll bet she is.'

Bolt slowed down to take a sip from his coffee, burning his lip in the process.

'Have the Hertfordshire cops checked her story out?'

'Parts of it. She's definitely got a fourteen-year-old daughter, but they haven't searched her house yet to check that she's actually missing. They're leaving that to us, in case the place is bugged.'

'So this whole thing could still be a load of bull-shit?'

Mo shrugged. 'I talked to the cops who brought her in. They think that if this is all an act, then she's one hell of a good actress – but, yeah, it's possible.' He stopped outside Interview Room B. 'Guess there's only one way to find out, isn't there?'

Mo entered first, and as Bolt followed him in he experienced a lurch of shock that almost knocked him backwards. It had been a long, long time, but even looking as drawn and exhausted as she was now, with all the life sucked out of her features by whatever ordeal she'd endured these past few days, there was definitely no mistake. He knew the woman sitting in front of him.

And at one time he'd known her far too well.

Ten

Andrea Devern stood up as they came in. Mo introduced Bolt to her and they shook hands formally. Knowing that he couldn't let on that he recognized her, Bolt sat down opposite Andrea. Pleased that she made no sign of recognition either, he explained that they were only talking in such formal surroundings because their conversation could be monitored and recorded. 'This way, it'll allow us to go back over your statement more easily. But don't worry. It's not an interview under caution. We just want you to go through everything from the beginning, trying not to leave anything out, so we've got a full picture of what's happened.'

This wasn't entirely true. Given that the truth of her story had yet to be confirmed, making her repeat it would give them an opportunity to check for discrepancies later, should the need arise.

Andrea yawned, putting a hand over her mouth, and Bolt noticed that one of her manicured nails had been broken. 'I've already told everything to the detectives in Welwyn Garden City. I just want you to find my daughter.' Her tone was weary, almost irritable.

'It's important for us to hear it from you. Just in case there's anything you've forgotten. That way it'll help us to get your daughter back safely.' He gave her a reassuring smile.

'OK,' she said, meeting his eyes. 'I understand. Can I smoke in here?'

'Well, this is a non-smoking building, and Mo here has just given up a forty-a-day habit, but . . . What do you think, Mo?' Bolt smiled. 'Will you be able to concentrate?'

Mo didn't look too happy about it but he nodded his assent. He'd only quit the dreaded weed six weeks earlier and by his own admission was still wobbling at the precipice, but Bolt was one of those people who still believed in a common-sense approach to how the law was enforced, and it seemed churlish to deny Andrea a small pleasure at a time like this. Big Barry would probably have something to say about it, given that he usually had something to say about everything, but Bolt would worry about that later.

Andrea thanked him, removed a pack of Benson and Hedges from an expensive-looking handbag on the desk in front of her, drew out a cigarette and lit it. She took a long drag, clearly enjoying it, before blowing a thin column of blue smoke skywards. And then she started talking. As she spoke, Bolt listened carefully, taking notes, only occasionally interrupting her narrative to question her about points that needed clarification.

It's possible to tell a great deal from a person's body language about whether or not he or she is telling the truth. Liars tend to limit their physical movements, and those they do make are towards their own body rather than outwards. They touch their face, throat and mouth a lot, and will often turn their head or body away from their questioner when they talk, so that they're not facing him or her directly. Andrea exhibited none of these tendencies. Hers might have been a highly unusual story, but from Bolt's point of view she was telling the truth.

There were three reasons for this. First, she came across as genuine. Second, there was, in the end, no real point in her lying, since it would take very little time for him to verify the truth of many of her claims. And third, and perhaps most importantly, he knew her, or at least had known her once, and didn't think she was capable of a charade like this. Underneath a hard, occasionally defensive exterior, she'd always been a good-hearted person.

It was why he'd once been in love with her.

Having no children of his own, Bolt couldn't begin to appreciate the extent of the ordeal Andrea was going through, but it was clearly taking a terrible toll. She was still a very attractive woman, with thick, shoulder-length auburn hair and well-defined, striking features that would make most people look twice, but today her face was haggard and puffy from lack of sleep, with dark bags under the eyes and a greyish, unhealthy tinge to the pale skin. The eyes themselves, a very light and unusual hazel that he remembered being so pretty, now appeared haunted and torn, and more than once when she looked at him as she spoke he felt an urge to reach across the table and touch her. It was an urge he fought down. There was no room for personal involvement in something like this.

'I made one mistake,' she said when she'd finished, looking at both men in turn. 'I trusted them.'

'No, Andrea,' Bolt told her, 'you made two mistakes. You trusted them, and you didn't come to us first.'

'I thought I was doing the right thing.' She sighed, stubbing out her third cigarette in the coffee cup in front of her. 'I guess I was wrong.'

Mo looked up from his notes and spoke for the first time. 'Do you have a picture of Emma we can copy, Andrea?'

108

She nodded and produced a small colour photo from her purse, handing it to him. 'This was taken last year. I'd like it back, please. It's very precious to me.'

'I'm sure it is,' he answered, his tone sympathetic. He gave it only the briefest of glances, not wanting to make the moment any more painful than it had to be, before slipping it inside a small clear wallet.

'Do either of you two gentlemen have children?'

'I'm afraid I don't,' answered Bolt.

'I have,' said Mo. 'Four of them.'

Andrea looked at him with new interest, as if he was a kindred spirit in a way that Bolt could never be. 'You're very lucky,' she told him. 'I hope what happens to me never happens to you. You can't imagine what it's like.' And in that moment, her features, tight with tension and pain, almost cracked. Almost, but not quite.

'I promise you we'll all do everything in our power to help you and bring your daughter back,' Mo told her. 'But you're going to need to help us as much as you can. Now, there are some points that need clarifying, and some questions that need answering. Can I speak frankly?'

She nodded. 'Of course.'

'Your husband's missing, and he has been since Tuesday, the same day that Emma was kidnapped. Do you think he could be involved?'

She paused for several seconds. 'I've thought about that a lot but I just can't see it. He's always got on well with Emma, and he's not the sort to do something like this to her.'

'Has he acted at all differently around you and your daughter in the last few weeks?' asked Bolt.

'Not that I've noticed.'

'So, where do you think he might be?'

She threw up her hands. 'I honestly don't know. Maybe they've taken him as well.'

Mo made a show of consulting his notes. 'According to what you've told us, you never asked the kidnapper who phoned you whether he was also holding your husband, or what might have happened to him?'

'It's about priorities, isn't it? I've only had a few very short conversations with the man holding my daughter, and in all of them that's who I've been focusing on: Emma.' She sighed. 'Look, the thing is, I don't know whether Pat was involved or not, but I'm pretty damn certain he wasn't. He's not that sort of bloke. Besides, why would he bother? He's got a pretty good life. He doesn't have to do a lot. He drives a nice car, gets decent holidays. Goes out when he wants. If he asks me for money, I give it to him. I probably shouldn't do, because I'm hardly motivating him to get off his arse and get a proper job, but I do. So, why would he put all that at risk? For a share in half a million quid? I don't think so.'

It was, thought Bolt, a good point.

'Kidnapping a child for this kind of ransom is highly unusual,' he said, 'and it's clear that you weren't chosen at random. Is there anyone you can think of, in either your personal or your business life, who might have a motive for putting you through this?'

Andrea was silent again, then shook her head firmly. 'I can't think of anyone, no.'

But there was just the briefest flickering of hesitation in her eyes when she spoke, and Bolt, who was trained in such things, noticed it.

He looked at Mo. 'I think that's everything for the moment, isn't it?'

Mo nodded. 'I haven't got anything else.'

'So what happens now?' Andrea asked, her voice shaking.

'The kidnapper gave you forty-eight hours,' said Bolt, leaning forward in his seat. 'There's still nearly forty left until he makes contact again. During that time we're going to be gathering what clues we can as discreetly as possible in an attempt to ID him.'

'If they find out about you, though . . . I mean, these guys know what they're doing.'

Bolt fixed her with a calm stare. 'So do we, Andrea, so do we. In the meantime, you'll be supplied with a team of trained liaison officers. They'll look after your day-to-day needs and provide support until the situation's resolved. We'll also house you in secure and comfortable accommodation. Any calls to your home landline will be automatically re-directed to you there, so when the kidnapper makes contact you'll still be able to speak to him and we'll be able to monitor the conversation.'

'No. I want to go home.'

'That's not going to be possible,' said Mo. 'The logistics would be too difficult.'

'I don't care. I want to go home.' Her voice was panicky now. 'These people have been watching the house. They must have been to know that Jimmy was there. If they're watching it now and they see that I'm not at home, they'll suspect that I've gone to you. I can't risk it. They said they'd kill Emma if I went to the police, and I believe them.'

'It's very unlikely that your kidnapper or any of his accomplices are watching your house,' Bolt explained, knowing that Mo was right: letting her back home would be a real problem. 'They won't want to risk drawing attention to themselves, and there won't be many people involved in this either. Two, possibly three at most, so they won't be able to spare the manpower to keep watch on all your movements.'

112

'That's what Jimmy said,' Andrea countered, 'and look what happened to him. I'm sorry, but I want to go home. That's all there is to it.'

Bolt sighed, knowing from the decisive expression on her face that she wasn't going to budge on this. 'All right, we'll see what we can do.' He stood up, and Mo followed suit. 'Someone'll be along shortly to take you to a more comfortable room. But don't worry, I'll be giving you regular updates.'

He turned to go.

'Mike?'

Bolt flinched at her sudden familiarity, and Mo looked at him. He turned back, avoiding his colleague's gaze. Andrea's hazel eyes were full of anguish.

'Promise me you'll get her back. Please.'

Bolt felt his mouth go dry. This was hard, far harder than he was used to. He wanted to promise her but knew that there was absolutely no way he could. It would be a dereliction of duty. Emma's kidnappers had already killed once; it was entirely possible they could kill again. If he said one thing, and then another happened . . . well, it wouldn't look good.

'I can't provide a cast-iron guarantee on anything. I'm sorry.'

She turned to Mo. 'You've got children. You must have some idea of the pain I'm feeling.'

'I do,' he said softly. 'I really do.'

'Please . . .'

'We'll do absolutely everything in our power to get Emma back,' Bolt told her firmly. 'Absolutely everything.'

She gave a slight nod and reached for her cigarettes with shaking hands, ignoring a single tear that ran down her cheek.

For the moment, there was nothing more to say.

Eleven

When he first started out as a nineteen-year-old probationary constable, having failed to secure the A Level results needed to get into the universities and polytechnics he'd applied for, Mike Bolt's first posting was Holborn Nick in the heart of central London, directly between the West End and the City. Having grown up on a diet of 1970s cop shows from *Z Cars* to *Starsky and Hutch*, he'd always quite fancied the idea of joining the police, but in an abstract way, like someone wanting to be an astronaut or a jockey. Had he made university, his life would probably have taken a completely different turn.

He'd spent five and a half years at Holborn, the first three in uniform, before joining the station's CID. One of his first cases as a detective was the death of Sir Marcus Dallarda, a fifty-eight-year-old City financier who'd made a fortune in the late 1980s developing rundown inner-city brown-field sites and turning them into blocks of luxury flats. Sir Marcus was one of the few people to foresee the end of the property boom and had sold virtually all his property holdings before the great crash, and as interest rates soared, he'd lent his profits to the money markets where the returns were suddenly enormous. To some people Sir Marcus was the worst kind of capitalist, a man who created nothing and simply sat on a growing pot of money that had been gained through other people's sweat. But the media loved him. He was a good-looking, flamboyant figure with a ready stream of amusing one-liners, and he exuded the kind of unashamed joie-de-vivre that made him difficult to dislike. With two divorces, more than one love child, and a string of mistresses under his belt, he was tabloid heaven, and he possessed that strange upper-class ability of creating an affinity with the masses that someone middle-class could never dream of achieving.

So when he was found, after an anonymous tip-off, naked and dead in the penthouse suite of a renowned five-star hotel in the Strand, with several thin lines of white powder on the table beside him and a condom hanging rather forlornly from his flaccid penis, it was always going to be big news. Although a DCI was made the senior investigating officer in charge of the case, it was Bolt and his boss at the time, DS Simon Grindy, a world-weary forty-year-old for whom the term 'half-empty' could have been invented, who'd been given most of the legwork.

'Dirty old bastard,' Grindy had mused, with a gruff mixture of admiration and jealousy, as he and Bolt stood in the opulent bedroom looking down at Sir Marcus's rather spindly body. 'If you've got to go, I could think of worse ways.'

Bolt wasn't so sure. He always felt sorry for those whose deaths had to be investigated by the police. There was a certain indignity about being inspected by various people while you lay helpless, and in Sir Marcus's case in a somewhat humiliating pose. Like most people at the time, Bolt had enjoyed reading about Sir Marcus's rakish antics, and he remembered thinking at the time how powerful death was that it could crush even the most larger-than-life characters. It was something that had remained with him ever since.

It hadn't taken long to determine what had happened in this particular case, though. The post-mortem concluded that he'd died of a massive and sudden heart attack, at least partly brought on by the cocaine in his bloodstream. If he'd been indulging in intense physical activity before his death this could also have been a contributory factor.

Since Sir Marcus's friends and colleagues

insisted he would never normally touch drugs, it was concluded by the media that whoever had been with him that night, and had made the anonymous call, had also supplied him with the illegal contraband. There was an appeal for witnesses and it turned out that two young women had been seen leaving the hotel in a hurry shortly before the call to the police, which had been made from a nearby phone box. At the same time, a search of the room and Sir Marcus's possessions turned up a business card in the name of a 'Fifi' who provided 'relief for all your tensions'. On it was an east London telephone number.

A call to BT had provided a name and address for the number in Plaistow, and so it was on a grey drizzling afternoon, three days after Sir Marcus had shuffled off his mortal coil, that Bolt and Grindy knocked on the door. The address itself was a small 1950s grey-brick terrace on a lonely back street in the shadow of a monolithic tower block. 'This girl ain't going to be pretty,' was Grindy's less than deductive take on things. 'If she was making money there's no way she'd be cooped up in a shithole like this.'

But Simon Grindy had not been the best of detectives, the accuracy of his predictions never likely to be giving Mystic Meg cause for concern, and this one was no exception. The girl who answered the door was a very attractive willowy brunette in her early twenties, wearing a pleasant smile, a black negligee and not a great deal else. The smile disappeared the moment she saw the two men in suits and raincoats standing on her doorstep.

'Whatever it is, I'm not buying,' she'd said dismissively in a strong east London accent.

'I can see that, Fifi,' Grindy had replied with a leer. 'If I was a betting man, I'd say you were selling.'

She'd pulled a face. 'Not to you, mate. Everyone's got to have minimum standards.'

Bolt had almost laughed but managed to stop himself. He hadn't been working with Grindy long and had no wish to fall out with him. But he liked this girl. She had balls.

'We're police officers,' he'd told her, pulling out his warrant card, 'and we want to speak to a Miss Andrea Bailey. Are you her?'

She seemed to notice him for the first time then, and gave him a quick appraising look that would have made him blush if he'd been five years younger before reluctantly opening the door and leading them into a cramped living room. She motioned for them to take a seat on a threadbare sofa while she put on a dressing gown and asked them what they wanted.

Andrea Bailey was a cool customer. When Grindy told her harshly that they knew she was the woman who'd been with Sir Marcus Dallarda and demanded that she tell them who her companion was, she'd sat in the chair opposite and flatly denied it, and for the next ten minutes batted off their questions with a quiet confidence that Bolt couldn't help but admire. When asked how her business card had got into Sir Marcus's wallet, she'd replied that she had no idea. 'I've got hundreds of business cards. I give them out. That's what they're for. I can't keep track of where they end up.'

'And what exactly is your business, Miss Bailey?' Grindy had growled menacingly.

'Read the card. Massage, of course.'

And so it had gone on, with Grindy's attempts at intimidation failing dismally.

'We can get a warrant to search this place,' he'd said at last.

'I'm sure you can,' she'd answered with just the hint of a smirk. 'You're a policeman.'

'In fact we've got it here,' he'd added, producing it from his raincoat pocket with a flourish, as if this would throw her off-balance.

It didn't. She remained casually impassive, even giving Bolt a cheeky wink.

Bolt knew she was trying to embarrass him, and didn't rise to the bait.

'Have you got something in your eye, Miss Bailey?' he'd asked her coolly.

'Just a twinkle,' came her answer, and he'd always remembered that. Cool and witty. It made Bolt wonder what she was doing in such a dump when there was a whole world out there she could have conquered.

They'd searched the house from top to bottom, supposedly looking for the same kind of drugs that had killed Sir Marcus, and Bolt had had to go through her underwear drawer while she watched.

'I don't enjoy doing this, you know,' he'd told her as he rummaged through the various lacy little numbers.

'Course you don't,' she'd said with a chuckle. 'But ask yourself this: how many other blokes get into a pretty girl's knickers as part of their job?'

They'd bantered on and off throughout the search. Andrea was a terrible flirt but there was something hugely engaging about the way nothing seemed to faze her, and Bolt was pleased she hadn't taken offence to them turning her house upside down.

There hadn't been any drugs – there hadn't been anything illegal anywhere – and Grindy was in a horrendous mood when they left. 'Cheeky bitch,' he'd complained bitterly. 'You want to keep away from women like her, Mike. They're trouble. Take it from me. I know.'

Grindy had never struck Bolt as an expert on

women, but in this case his boss was right. Andrea, however, had definitely got under his skin, and he'd thought about her often afterwards.

It was three years before he saw her again. He was still living in Holborn but had joined the Flying Squad, and was walking down the Strand one afternoon when he heard a woman's voice call out, 'Mr Bolt, are you ignoring me?' He'd turned round to see a woman with jet black hair, a good suntan and big sunglasses coming out of a designer clothes shop. She was dressed in a white sleeveless top, figure-hugging jeans and high-heeled black court shoes, and was carrying several bags. There was something familiar about her, the voice especially.

She smiled. 'Plaistow, 1989. My knickers drawer.' Then she removed the sunglasses and it came back to him in an instant.

'Andrea Bailey?'

She shook her head, coming forward. 'No, Andrea Bailey's dead. Meet Andrea Devern.' She put out a manicured hand, and they shook. 'I'm a married woman now,' she added, just in case he hadn't noticed the wedding band and diamond-encrusted engagement ring.

'Congratulations. You've dyed your hair.'

She shrugged. 'I fancied a change.'

'It's good to see you again,' he told her, and it was. 'You look well.'

'Thanks. You don't look so bad yourself. Still a copper?'

He nodded. 'Yeah, but not at Holborn any more. I'm in the Flying Squad these days.'

She raised her eyebrows. '*The Sweeney*? Very glamorous. So' – she looked around – 'you fancy buying me a drink, or are you too busy?'

Bolt was single at the time. It was a Saturday afternoon and he'd just been wondering about doing a bit of shopping without any real plans.

'Sure,' he answered, 'why not?'

So they'd found a wine bar round the corner, got themselves a nice quiet table and proceeded to demolish a bottle of Chablis.

It was one of those occasions when everything just clicked. They'd only met that one time years earlier, and hardly under ideal circumstances, but even so they talked like old friends. Andrea told him about her upbringing in a council flat, the middle of three daughters brought up by a single mother; how she'd left school at a young age with no qualifications and got herself a job in a local corner shop which she really enjoyed, before a friend turned her on to drugs. 'I got in far too deep, far too fast. Problem was, with my wages, I couldn't pay for them, so my mate told me a great way of earning big money.' She rolled her eyes. 'I was young, and I suppose it seemed like a good idea at the time. I didn't want to work for some pimp, though, so I set up on my own, got business cards printed, and worked through recommendations. I didn't enjoy it, but . . .' She shrugged. 'It got me money. My idea was to kick the coke, raise a couple of grand and put myself through college. I wanted to do a business course.'

'But you never made it?'

'Oh, I made it all right,' she told him with a smile. 'I kicked the gear, but I took a quicker route to the real money and married it.'

'Always a good move,' he said.

'He's a nice guy,' she told him, her expression suddenly serious. 'He looks after me.'

But on that day at least, Andrea hadn't been in a hurry to get back to him, and with one bottle consumed she'd asked Bolt if he fancied sharing another. He knew it wasn't right to fool around with married women, but he was twenty-four, and the sad truth of the matter was that he was never going to say no.

And so the afternoon drifted lazily on, the conversation veering here and there, covering both their lives. Andrea now lived in Cobham with her husband, a businessman twenty-five years her senior who was, she claimed, one of the nicest guys she'd ever met. 'Present company excepted, of course.'

'Of course,' said Bolt with a smile.

Eventually they got round to how they'd

originally met, and with the case of Sir Marcus Dallarda now firmly set in the past, Andrea admitted that she'd been with him that night. 'I'd never met him before but a girl I knew in the business had and she said he was a decent bloke and a good payer, so I went along with her. I never normally did threesomes – I'm not that kind of girl, believe it or not.'

Bolt wasn't sure that he did believe it, but as a trained detective he preferred to listen rather than pass immediate judgement.

'Well,' she continued, 'to cut a long story short, there we were, doing the business, and he conked out. Just like that. Grabbed his chest and keeled over.' Her eyes widened as she recalled the events, and although she was clearly trying to stop herself, a small smile appeared. 'It was comical really, the way it happened. Like something off the TV. I know I shouldn't say that, but it just didn't seem real.

'Anyway, we didn't know what to do. My friend was panicking. She thought we might get the blame for it, especially as he was a bit of a celebrity as well. So I said, let's just get the hell out of here. And that's what we did. But obviously we didn't want him to get found by the cleaner the next day, so we phoned the police and told them. I didn't want to bullshit you when you came round to interview me, but I didn't actually think

I was doing anything wrong, you know.' She paused, fixing him with an expression of mild amusement, her eyes twinkling. 'So, what do you think of me now?'

Bolt may have been mildly drunk, but what he thought was that Andrea was a liar. A funny, engaging, attractive and intelligent one, with beautiful twinkling eyes, and loyal too, because she'd never given up her friend, even when he and Grindy had turned her house upside down, but a liar nonetheless, and one who wasn't much good at remembering the details of the past either. Otherwise she would have recalled that the police had originally been led to her by the fact that it was her business card in Sir Marcus's wallet, and not her friend's, meaning that Sir Marcus had almost certainly known her before that night. It seemed a strange lie to tell, given that she'd already admitted that she'd been a prostitute. Why not simply admit that she was the one who'd approached her friend about the threesome, not the other way round?

Not that Bolt said any of this, of course. Instead, he put down his glass and returned her gaze.

'I think,' he said quietly, 'that if I stay here much longer I'll do something I regret.'

'Here's to regrets,' she said, and lifted her glass.

Don't get involved, he told himself. *You will regret it.*

126

'You're a married woman, Andrea,' he said, but it sounded lame, even to his own ears.

She sat back in her seat with a wide smile on her face. She was a little drunk too, but her eyes remained sharp and focused. 'Ah, I forgot, I'm talking to a policeman.' She raised her hands in mock surrender. 'All right, you've convinced me. I shouldn't even think about making love to you.'

But it was clear that neither of them was thinking about anything else. Andrea was in London on a weekend shopping trip, and she was staying at a hotel in Bloomsbury on her own. So once they'd finished their second bottle of Chablis Bolt had walked her back. She'd invited him in. This time he hadn't even bothered to resist, and they'd gone to her room and made love before ordering room service, making love again, and finally sinking into the slumber of the drunk and the contented.

The next morning they'd made love a final time before Andrea told him she had to get back to Surrey. 'I'm really glad we met up,' she'd whispered, touching his cheek and leaning over to kiss him on the lips before getting off the bed and walking naked into the bathroom to shower.

Bolt remembered what an effect she'd had on him: a potent mixture of lust, satisfaction, jealousy and anger. The anger was the worst part, because he wasn't used to getting so worked up over a woman. He'd had a great time with her, a fantastic time, but he couldn't get over the feeling that he'd been used and was now being discarded, which hurt his young man's pride. Even in those days he'd known that the best way to woo a woman was to play it cool, to pretend you didn't care that much, but it hadn't worked and he'd still left his card on top of her handbag, hating himself for it, before walking out and shutting the door behind him.

And here he was fifteen years later, and still she was having an effect on him. The shock of seeing her again that morning was wearing off as the operation to find Emma cranked rapidly into gear and the team focused on the hunt for the kidnapper, but Andrea still possessed that 'something' Bolt had always found so irresistible, even in her current state. He wanted to help her. He told himself it was because she and her daughter were both crime victims, but he knew it was more than that. A part of him still wanted to impress her, to prove that he was the tough guy who could rescue a damsel in distress.

As he walked down the corridor to his boss's office for a strategy meeting, he knew that, just like last time, Andrea's presence in his life spelled trouble.

Twelve

'What do you mean she wants to go home?' SG2 Barry Freud, the SOCA equivalent of a DCS, sat behind the huge slab of glass he called a desk, looking incredulous. 'That's not how we do things. There are procedures to follow in cases like this.'

Bolt, who was sitting on the other side of the slab, told him she was insistent. 'She says that otherwise she's not going to cooperate.'

'What choice does she have? She's got to co-operate if she wants her daughter back. It'll be far too much hassle allowing her to go home. I can tell you that for free, old mate. Far too much hassle.'

Big Barry Freud called every man he knew 'old mate'. It was supposed to be a term of endearment, but it never came across like that. As bosses went, Bolt scored Barry as decent enough. A big bluff Yorkshireman with a bald, egg-shaped head and a pair of peculiarly small ears, he made a hearty effort to come across as one of the lads, but never quite managed to make it look natural. Like a lot of senior officers, both in SOCA and the police services beyond, he always had one eye on the next rung of the ladder and did what he thought would go down well with his own bosses. He also had an inflated idea of his own importance. Word, probably put about by Barry himself, had it that he was a distant relation to the great psychoanalyst with the same last name, which gave him a natural insight into the minds of the people he was paid to catch. But Bolt couldn't see it himself. If you were part of such a distinguished family tree, you really weren't going to name your first-born son Barry. However, he was a decent enough organizer and he usually left Bolt alone to do his job, for which he was thankful.

That wasn't going to be the case today, though. Today, it was all hands on deck, and Big Barry was looking excited. He was the kind who tended to look at a crisis as a potential career opportunity.

'Can't you persuade her to see sense? The logistics of getting her home'll be a nightmare.'

'I've tried. I think it's going to be easier just to live with it.'

'That's your opinion, is it?'

Bolt nodded.

'She's still under suspicion of murder.'

'And we'll still be able to keep an eye on her there. I know it's unusual, but if we play it right, it won't compromise the op.'

Barry sighed. 'Well, if she absolutely insists, I suppose we can do it. I'm going to trust your judgement on this one, old mate. But make sure she knows that it means using resources that could be used helping to locate her daughter.'

'I will.'

Barry lifted a huge mug of coffee to his lips and took a loud slurp.

'What do you think of her story?' he asked.

Bolt hadn't mentioned the fact he knew Andrea because to do so would almost certainly mean him being removed from the case, but he answered honestly. 'I think it's true. You don't make something like that up. We know her daughter kept her dental appointment on Tuesday afternoon at a quarter to five, but that's the last confirmed sighting.'

'Have they got CCTV at the dentist's?'

'They have. It covers the car park and the front entrance, but it works on a loop and gets wiped every forty-eight hours, so it's already gone.'

Barry looked annoyed. 'Stupid woman. She should have come to us earlier. We could have had the daughter back by now if we'd been involved

131

from the start. We need to know where she was snatched from, Mike. If it was in a public place, someone might have seen it.'

'I've got Mo and his people on that,' said Bolt, 'but this is the interesting thing. So far there's been not a single reported abduction anywhere in Greater London on Tuesday between four forty-five, when we know Emma was at the dentist's, and eight forty-five, when Andrea received the first phone call from the kidnappers. Also, when Andrea arrived home that night, she specifically said in both her statements that the alarm was on. If anyone had snatched Emma from the house, there's no way they would have stopped to reset the alarm.'

'So it looks like it could be an inside job? What about the old man, Phelan? What have we got on him?'

Bolt consulted his notebook, even though he already knew Patrick Phelan's form. 'He's got old convictions for drug dealing and receiving,' he answered, wondering why a livewire like Andrea was so often attracted to deadbeats. 'Nothing major, but he served a year behind bars in the late nineties for receiving a load of hi-fis that had been lifted in a hijack a few weeks earlier. That was his last conviction. He's been straight since then. For what it's worth, Andrea doesn't think he was involved.'

Barry grunted. 'She wouldn't, would she? It wouldn't say much for her judgement if her old man was capable of kidnapping his stepdaughter and holding her to ransom. The fact is, he's missing. Which means he's either dead, or he's one of the kidnappers. Fact.'

'Phelan's car's missing too,' said Bolt. 'I've got Mo's people checking the ANPR to see if we can track it that way.'

The automatic number plate recognition system was the latest technological tool available to the police in the twenty-first-century fight against crime. It used a huge network of CCTV cameras which automatically read car number plates to log the movement of vehicles along virtually every main road in Britain. These images – some thirty-five million a day – were then sent to a vast central database housed alongside the Police National Computer at Hendon HQ where they were stored for up to two years. Not only was it possible to trace the movements of Phelan's car on the day, but also where it had been in the days and weeks leading up to the kidnap, although Bolt knew it would take time and effort to gather this information.

'What are Tina Boyd's people doing?' Barry asked, taking another noisy slurp of his coffee.

'Background checks on everyone involved in this. Looking for motives. Andrea told us she had a lot of cash stored in deposit boxes, which made up most of the half million she paid out to the kidnapper. I think someone knew she had those deposits, and we need to find out who.'

Barry nodded. 'If it is personal, then it's someone who really hates her, isn't it? To kidnap her only child, take the half million, and then renege on the deal. You've got to be a truly nasty piece of work to do that.'

'Well, these people are certainly nasty, and they took out Jimmy Galante, so they know what they're doing.'

'You knew him?'

'I knew the name from my days in the Flying Squad. He had a reputation as a hard bastard. We had him down as a suspect in a couple of armed robberies but we never pinned anything on him, and he ended up running a bar in Spain, like Andrea said.'

'But why are they asking for more money? That's what I can't understand. They've got what they wanted. Why not just release the girl and have done with it?'

Bolt shrugged. 'Because they're greedy, I suppose. Maybe they figure that if it only took Andrea forty-eight hours to come up with half a million, then maybe they were selling themselves short. I don't suppose the fact that she brought someone along to the ransom drop made any difference. I think that was just an excuse for them.'

'So they were always going to keep squeezing . . .' Barry shook his head slowly. 'We're going to have to catch these bastards, Mike.'

'All I'd say, sir, is, don't expect miracles. We haven't got a lot of time until the next deadline.' He looked at his watch and saw that it had just turned ten a.m. 'It's only about thirty-six hours until she's meant to come up with the next tranche of money.'

'All right, point taken.' Barry put down his mug. 'So, what are we going to do about this one, old mate? Negotiate, or take them out?'

It was the big question. Bolt knew only too well that the problem with kidnap cases, what made them so different from other equally serious crimes, was the fact that the investigators had far less control over events. It was the kidnapper who set the tempo, and since the circumstances of kidnappings varied so much, the police procedures for dealing with them had to be far more flexible than they would be in, say, a murder case where a set of very specific rules applied.

There was an uncomfortable silence.

'I think the girl's still alive,' Bolt said at last. 'And I think they'll keep her alive while they need her as a bargaining chip. They've already said that

Andrea can speak to her again before the next ransom drop, and there's no reason at the moment to believe that they'll renege on that.'

'But?'

'But, as we both know, they're ruthless. They've killed once. They may well have killed Phelan too for all we know. So if we spook them by trying to negotiate when they next make contact, my guess is they'll disappear back into the woodwork and that'll be the last we see of them. And there's no guarantee they'll let Emma go either. Especially if they think there's the remotest chance she can identify them. To them, she's just a loose end. We go the negotiation path, I think there's a good chance they'll kill her.'

Barry didn't look convinced. 'But there are a lot of things that can go wrong if we try to trap them, and if we mess it up it could be disastrous for SOCA. We're in need of some high-profile successes at the moment, so the public can see where all their tax money's going. A high-profile failure's going to set us back years.'

'You asked my opinion, sir. I think negotiation's the wrong move. If we can put trackers with the ransom money and play things right, we should be able to get our kidnappers to lead us right to Emma. It's risky, and there's a chance it might not work, but there's also a chance she's dead already. If we want to catch these guys, and we can't ID them before they make contact, then this is the best way.'

Barry massaged his head with pudgy hands, and tipped his chair back. 'Well, I'm going to send it upstairs. See what the head honchos have to say. I'll let you know their decision as soon as I've got it.'

As Bolt got to his feet, sensing that the meeting was over, there was a knock on the door and Tina Boyd entered the room, carrying several sheaves of paper in one hand.

Tina was a relatively new member of the team, whom Bolt had brought on board after he'd met her during a case a few years earlier. At the time she'd just resigned from the force, and it had taken a lot of persuading to get her to join the team. An attractive woman just short of thirty, with dark hair cut into a jaunty bob and smooth, delicate features that shaved five years off her easily, she had that look that was unmistakably educated and middle-class, and she could have passed as a primary school teacher just as much as a cop. But the look belied the tough time she'd had down the years. Bolt knew that Tina had seen and done it all. Shot during a hostage-taking drama four years earlier, she'd also lost two colleagues, both murdered. One of them had been her lover, earning her the unwelcome nickname of the Black Widow in some quarters.

When she'd finally joined the team a year or so back, Bolt had harboured the odd romantic aspiration where Tina was concerned, but any attempt at warmth or even flattery had come up against a brick wall, and he'd quickly realized that he was on a hiding to nothing. Tina was polite and she was pleasant, but it seemed you didn't get close to her. Even when she socialized with the team, she was always one of the first to leave, making her excuses before heading home alone.

'I've got some interesting news,' she said, approaching the giant glass desk.

'Tell us more, Tina,' said Barry with something approaching a leer.

She looked at them both in turn. 'Andrea Devern might be a high-flying businesswoman but her company's not doing that well. Turnover in the last financial year was £4.81 million but the overall operating profit was only forty-eight thousand pounds, which for a company that size is piss poor. It's also a seventy per cent drop on the year before on a higher turnover, and they've got serious debt to service with the banks. Andrea owns sixty per cent of the company. Her main business partner, and fellow director, is a woman called Isobel Wheeler.' Tina consulted one of the sheets of A4. 'She's a forty-two-year-old lawyer, divorced with no children, who bought into the company ten years ago and now owns the

138

remaining forty per cent. Both women pay themselves generously. They draw salaries of one hundred and sixty grand each.'

'Nice work if you can get it,' grunted Barry.

'Very nice, but it's not going to last. With profits that feeble, the banks are going to be having serious words. And Andrea and her husband are big spenders. Their joint credit card bills mount up to a hundred and twenty K a year.'

'So, what's the interesting part, Tina?' asked Barry, cutting to the chase. 'They're big spenders. So are most other people in this country. It's why the economy keeps doing so well.'

Tina gave him a mildly dismissive look, but when she spoke her tone was even. 'Well, I Googled Andrea's name and her company, and it seems that there've been a couple of articles about her in trade publications, but nothing of any significance. She certainly hasn't got a public profile. She earns good money but nothing special, so the question is, why on earth target her?'

Bolt nodded. 'It's what I've been thinking. This isn't random. It's personal.'

'You need to talk to Andrea herself, old mate,' Barry told him, manoeuvring himself slowly to his feet, 'and find out who the hell knew she was sitting on that half million in cash.'

'I will, but I reckon we can count in Pat Phelan

straight away, and I reckon her business partner's a strong possibility too. Which means we need to turn up everything we can on the two of them.'

'We're on it already,' said Tina.

Bolt felt a rush of excitement. It was the knowledge that the clock was ticking; the realization that this case was going to be concluded in hours rather than months; and that he was in the centre of things.

It was a good feeling.

And one that wasn't going to last.

Thirteen

She had to be brave.

Emma Devern had said this to herself countless times since they'd brought her here. But as the hours dragged into days and still there remained no prospect of her being released back to her mum, it became harder and harder for her to manage it.

They were keeping her in a dank, carpetless cellar with one narrow window coated in grime, high up on one wall and well out of reach, which let in thin shafts of daylight. She had to wear a pair of handcuffs, and was chained to the wall by one ankle. The chain was long enough so she could move around, but she couldn't reach the steps at the end of the room or the far wall, and she knew in her heart that there was no way she was going to be able to escape.

She thought this was the third day she'd been

here, which meant it was Friday. It was difficult to know for sure because the days simply flowed into one another, but she was trying hard to keep track. At nights it was cold. She slept on a horrible little bed with filthy sheets and she was forced to wrap herself up in them to keep warm, even though they smelled awful.

On the first night she'd been too shocked about what had happened even to cry. She remembered very little about how it had all started. She was going back to the car after the dentist appointment. Her dentist was called Mr Vermont, after the American state. He always said what good teeth she had, and she did too, because she looked after them well and didn't stuff her face with sweets like a lot of her friends. It had just been a standard check-up. She liked Mr Vermont. He was good-looking with a nice tan, even though he was a bit old and his hair was beginning to go a bit thin on top. The check-up had gone well. For the third visit running nothing needed doing – which was just as well because she hated having her teeth messed about with – and she'd been in a good mood as she crossed the car park at the front of the building.

Pat had been in the driver's seat with the paper in front of him, checking the sports pages, like he always did, but as she opened the door and got inside, something immediately felt wrong. He didn't greet her like he usually did, with a big grin and an 'All right, baby, how'd everything go?' in his rough London accent. Instead, he turned and stared at her, and she saw that he looked really frightened. His eyes were wide and there was sweat running down his forehead.

Then she heard a noise behind her, a kind of shuffling, and before she could even take in what was happening she was grabbed round the neck and pulled back into the seat. The next second, a wet cloth that smelled of chemicals was pushed against her face, and suddenly she couldn't breathe any more and she was struggling and kicking, trying to attract attention, help, anything . . .

It was all over so quickly, even now it didn't feel quite real. Her last image was Pat turning away from her and starting the car's engine with a low rumble. Then everything went black, and she couldn't remember another thing until she'd woken up in this cold, featureless room with a terrible headache and feeling really sick.

She wondered what had happened to Pat. She'd always liked him. He was good fun. They liked to joke together, and he seemed to make her mum happy. At first she hadn't been sure about him. She was used to it being just her and her mum. That was the way it had always been, the way she'd always preferred it. She didn't know her real dad. She'd never met him and she didn't even know who he was. Whenever she asked her mum about him, she'd always said that it was just a man from a long time ago, that he'd gone away, and that it would be best just to forget about him. She wanted to find her dad, but she didn't push it with her mum, and anyway, Pat made quite a good dad. And her friends were jealous because he was nice-looking, and not too old either.

She hoped they hadn't done anything bad to him.

'They' were the two men who were keeping her prisoner. She was not allowed to see them, and had to put on a black hood like something an executioner in a medieval history book might wear whenever the cellar door opened. One of them wheezed when he walked, making a horrible sound like something out of a horror film. She might not have been able to see him, but she could always hear his approach. And she could smell him too. He absolutely stank, a really horrible combination of BO, old socks and toilets that was so bad she thought she might gag whenever he got too close to her. He was the one who usually came down twice a day to check up on her. He'd bring food – Marmite or jam sandwiches, and fruit – and change the bucket they made her use as a toilet.

When he'd come down on that first night,

telling her to put on the hood, she'd been absolutely terrified. But he'd told her not to worry, that no one would hurt her, and that she'd be going home soon, and even though he'd talked in a strange rasping voice as if he was trying to disguise it, and had stroked her arm with cold, gloved hands, his touch lingering that little bit too long, something told her that he meant what he said.

As time wore on she'd begun to lose hope of going home and being reunited with her mum and her friends, and everyone she cared about. But she had to be brave. She just had to be. It was just that she really didn't want to die. She was happy. She'd never done anything wrong, and she couldn't see why anyone would do this to her. It wasn't fair. And when she thought about what might happen to her, she got really scared. Although she trusted the smelly one, she definitely didn't trust the one he was working with.

He'd only been down once, on the second night. When he'd called out to her from the top of the stairs, telling her to put on the hood, his voice was harsh and cruel, with no kindness in it at all. She'd done what she was told to do and had then sat there waiting, but she hadn't heard his approach. He was that silent on his feet it was like he was a phantom. All that told her he was in the room was the faint smell of cigarettes, and a feeling that someone was watching her.

After a while she'd asked uncertainly whether there was anyone there.

'Yeah,' came the reply, like he was mocking her. 'I'm here.'

'What do you want?'

'You're going to talk to your mum. You're going to tell her that if she pays the money, then you'll be going home tomorrow.'

She felt a rush of excitement. 'And will I?'

'If she does what she's told, yeah,' he answered, but it didn't sound like he meant it. 'Now turn round on the bed so you're facing the wall.'

She did what she was told.

'Bet you're not used to being told what to do, are you? Little rich girl like you. Bet you usually tell the servants what to do, don't you?'

'I don't have servants,' she said quietly. 'I'm just normal.'

'You don't know what normal is, you little bitch.'

'Why are you doing this to me?' she asked, because she really didn't understand why he was being so cruel to her.

'You don't ask the questions,' he said, ripping the hood from her head in one movement. 'You obey orders. Keep staring at the wall, and remember what you've got to tell your mum. If she does what we say, you go home tomorrow.'

He'd pushed a phone roughly against her ear and a couple of seconds later her mum had come on the line. Emma felt a huge burst of emotion. She wanted to cry so much but she knew she had to hold it together for her mum's sake, so she'd said she was fine and that if the money was paid she'd be back tomorrow. She'd wanted to say more but the phone had been snatched away with a hissed 'Don't turn round', and then a few seconds later she'd heard the key turn in the lock of the cellar door.

After he'd gone, she'd sat there shaking for several minutes, part of her feeling hope now that she'd heard her mum's voice, but a much bigger part feeling fear. She'd never come across anyone truly evil before, and now that she had, it made her wonder whether she was ever going to get out of here alive. Because they hadn't let her go, like he'd said they would. She was still here, hoping that the smelly one would keep the cruel one from doing anything to her, which was why she'd been as nice as possible to him whenever he came down.

They were talking upstairs now, their voices muffled, and she wondered what time it was. They'd taken her watch, or at least she thought they had. When she'd woken up in this place for the first time, it was gone, as was her handbag, which had had her mobile phone in it. All she'd been left with were the clothes she was wearing when she'd been taken – a black T-shirt, denim skirt and her favourite wedge-heeled sandals – and she was still in them now.

The smelly one had already been in that morning to give her sandwiches – Marmite this time – and to change the bucket. That was a while back now. He'd seemed in a strange mood. Normally he was quite friendly, but today he'd been quiet, and it had worried her. She'd asked him if everything was all right, and when they were going to let her go like they'd said they would, and he'd come over, sat down and put his arm round her, telling her it was going to be fine and that she'd be home very soon. Even though she'd felt like throwing up with him so close to her, she'd told him once again that she just wanted to be back with her mum and her friends, because she thought that if she said it enough times he'd feel sorry for her and would help to make it happen. He'd told her not to worry, everything would be all right, like he always did, but this time it seemed as if he was making an effort to say it, and that maybe it wasn't true.

The voices were getting louder. They were arguing. She got up from the bed and walked as far as the chain would allow until she was almost at the bottom of the steps, then stopped and listened, straining hard to hear what they were saying.

The voices stopped before she could make out any words, and then suddenly the key turned in the lock and the door flew open, slamming hard against the wall.

Emma darted back, rushing for the bed, but not before she'd seen the man at the top of the stairs, partly silhouetted by the bright light behind him. She'd only got the barest of glimpses, just enough time to note that he was of normal height and build and had dark hair. For just half a second their eyes had met, but she knew straight away that she'd made a terrible mistake.

'Get your hood on. Now,' the cruel one called out from the top of the steps.

Shaking with fear, trying hard not to cry, Emma sat on the bed and pulled the hood over her head. She heard the door shutting, followed by a pause that lasted long enough that she began to hope he wasn't coming down at all, and then she heard the footfalls moving fast, louder than last time. She tensed as she heard him stop in front of her.

'Did you see me?' he hissed, venom in his voice.

'No,' she answered, shaking her head vigorously.

'Did you see me, bitch? Tell me the truth.'

'No, I promise.' She pushed herself back against the cold stone wall, her heart pounding.

He tore the hood off and she turned her head away from him, shutting her eyes, not wanting to see him, knowing only too well what seeing him would mean. He grabbed her roughly by the chin, squeezing the flesh, and pulled her towards him.

'Look me in the eye, bitch. Did you fucking see me?'

She opened her eyes and saw that he'd put on a black balaclava. His face was only inches away from hers.

'No, honestly, I didn't,' she said, finding it hard to get the words out. 'Please, you're hurting me.'

'This ain't hurt, bitch. You don't know the fucking meaning of the word. But you will if you're lying. I'll hurt you good. I'll hurt you until you're screaming with the pain. Do you understand?'

She nodded rapidly, feeling the tears well up, but determined not to cry in front of him. 'Yes, yes. I'm not lying, I promise.'

He released his grip on her chin. Behind the slits his eyes were dark and cold. 'Good.' He pushed the hood back over her head. 'Now, we're going to send your mummy a little message. So you can let her know how much fun you're having.'

His tone had changed again. He was mocking her, pleased that she seemed so terrified. He was enjoying this. It was difficult, almost impossible to believe, but he was actually enjoying this. Underneath the hood, away from his terrible gaze, the tears flowed freely down Emma's face.

And then she felt something touch the bare skin of her arm. Something cold and sharp.

Oh God, no. He's got a knife.

Fourteen

There were serious logistical issues to be addressed in order to get Andrea back home, and Bolt spent most of the remainder of Friday morning organizing them. He had to operate on the assumption that the kidnappers were watching the place, even though he thought it highly unlikely. It didn't take long to confirm that no properties with views on to Andrea's house had been rented out for more than eighteen months, so any observation point being used by the kidnappers would have to be on the street itself. With Big Barry's authorization, he managed to get a twelve-person surveillance team from another area of SOCA pulled off their current job, and they were sent to Andrea's neighbourhood. Having discreetly confirmed that there was no one suspicious hanging about, either on foot or in a car, they'd set up at various points and now had the street under continuous observation.

With the area secure, Bolt had given Andrea's card key, house keys and the burglar alarm code to one of his team, SG5 Matt Turner, who'd gone to check out the property. Although Jimmy Galante had searched the place for bugs, he'd bought a cheap device from a spy shop, so it was likely he'd only have been using a radio frequency detector, and not a very good one either, which would have been inadequate for the task at hand. Bolt knew that RF detectors were designed to pick up signals from active transmitters and radio telephone taps, but couldn't detect switched-off or remote control devices, nor could they find hard-wired microphones and telephone taps, or recorders. In other words, the place could have been bugged to the hilt and neither Jimmy nor Andrea would have known about it. Turner was armed with the latest cutting-edge counter-surveillance equipment, including a Time Domain Reflectometer used to detect breaks and splices in cables; a Harmonic Radar to find cables and mikes buried in walls, cavities and furniture; and a Multi-Meter to measure line voltages within the telephone line.

However, when he called Bolt just after midday, Turner hadn't found anything either. 'The place is clear, sir. I've given it a complete once-over, and there's nothing here.'

Bolt trusted Turner's judgement on this kind of thing.

'Any sign of a struggle in there, Matt? Something that might suggest Emma Devern was snatched at the house?'

'Nothing like that. The place is spotless. Also, I reckon it'd be too risky trying to abduct someone here. There's a security gate running round the property, with only one entrance from the front, and it's pedestrian access only. No room to get a car through it. So the kidnappers would have had to take her out on to the street, and I think that would have been too risky in broad daylight. That's my take on it, anyway.'

Bolt sighed. The kidnappers had managed to track Emma's movements on Tuesday, and find out about Jimmy Galante's involvement in the ransom drop, but for the moment, how they'd done so remained a mystery.

He thanked Turner and rang off, then went to tell Andrea that he would drive her home. She'd been kept in the only office in the building with a sofa all morning and, according to the female liaison officer assigned to her, had spent most of the time asleep on it. She was awake when he went in there, though, and seemed pleased by the news that she was going back to her house, even if it was without her daughter.

It felt strange for Bolt being so close to Andrea

again, and their conversation for much of the journey was stilted. He wanted to bring up the past, to talk about the old days, but Marie Cohen, the very short, very earnest liaison officer, was in the back seat of his car, which made any such conversation impossible. Eventually Andrea fell asleep again, leaning against the passenger side window. Occasionally Bolt glanced across at her, trying to look natural in front of Marie Cohen. Andrea was still a very attractive woman, but the lively spark in her eyes that had drawn him in all those years ago had long since gone.

Poor, rich Andrea. She'd never really had much luck with men, and Bolt wondered whether in Phelan she'd made the worst choice of all.

She woke up when they were stuck in traffic on Hampstead high street.

'How long have I been out for?' she asked, rubbing her eyes.

Bolt checked the clock on the dashboard: 12.49. 'A while. The traffic's been murder.' In his rear-view mirror, he saw that Marie had also gone to sleep in the back. Clearly his effect on women wasn't quite as electric as he would have liked.

Andrea yawned. 'Do you mind if I smoke?'

He smiled. 'Well, technically it's illegal as this is a work car, but I guess under the circumstances we can make an exception. I'd ask Marie, but she looks flat out.'

Andrea looked round, checked that she was, and opened her window halfway before lighting up.

'Thank God for that,' she whispered, looking at Bolt. 'She means well, but I wish she'd just leave me alone.'

'She's just trying to help.'

'Yeah, but sometimes you can try too hard.'

Bolt watched as she put the cigarette to her lips. Her hands were trembling and the drags she took were short and urgent. The tension was coming off her in waves.

'You know, Andrea,' he said, turning off the high street, 'we've checked out your house, and the area round it, and we can't work out how the kidnapper could have known Emma's movements so thoroughly.'

'So you still think it might be an inside job?'

'It's a strong possibility.'

Andrea sighed, taking another drag on the cigarette. 'I just can't see it being Pat, that's all. He's got faults – big ones, like the fact that he's a waster – and if I'd known about them when I first met him I'd never have married him, but he wouldn't have done something like this to Emma. He's not cold enough. And I've met some cold people in my time.'

Bolt thought of Jimmy Galante. She was right on that score.

They were almost there now, and Bolt used a

dual-band radio to call the surveillance team. He needed confirmation that the area round Andrea's house was still secure. When this had been given by the team leader, he slowed the car down and turned into Andrea's road.

It was a leafy avenue of grand semi-detached houses, lined with mature oak trees planted fifteen yards apart, with expensive-looking sports cars and 4×4s parked on both sides. Instinctively, Bolt checked for occupants, but they were all empty, although he spotted a white van with blacked-out windows and the name of a plumbing firm down the side, which he recognized as a SOCA surveillance vehicle. A pretty young woman with oversized sunglasses who was busy putting a toddler in the car seat of a brand-new Range Rover seemed to be the only person around.

Andrea's place, one half of an impressive-looking three-storey Edwardian redbrick building, was about halfway down on the right-hand side. It was fronted by a brick wall approximately head height, mounted with freshly painted black railings, which enclosed the entire property but wouldn't have put off a determined intruder. Bolt found a parking spot about thirty yards further down between a Mercedes and a BMW people carrier. In the back, Marie woke up with a start.

As Bolt got out of the car he saw a shadow move across one of the upstairs windows of the house opposite. It had been turned into an observation post by the surveillance team, giving them a perfect view of the portion of the street to the front of Andrea's house.

Bolt let Andrea lead the way, with Marie bringing up the rear. He thought about how much Andrea had moved on since the old days when he'd first known her. It was all down to her own efforts as well. He admired her for that, but then she'd never been short of spirit and drive. It was spirit she was going to need now.

'We've got something called a trace/intercept set up on your landline,' he told her as she pressed the buzzer on the security gate and waited for Turner to let them in. 'It means that if they make a call to your home, we'll be able to pinpoint the location of the caller very quickly.'

'I don't want you to do anything that risks hurting Emma, Mike.'

'We won't,' said Bolt, but it was a lie, and he knew it. Whatever they did, they risked hurting Emma.

Matt Turner buzzed them in, and as they stepped inside the gate Bolt was immediately struck by the strong scent of flowers. The garden was a riot of colour, well kept with neat flowerbeds bordering the house's exterior wall. It was also very well stocked, with thick walls of greenery rising all round the terraced lawn. His wife Mikaela would have loved this place. She'd always wanted to live in a big, rambling house with a couple of kids and a couple of dogs and plenty of space, somewhere that with his copper's salary and hers as a primary school teacher they were never going to be able to afford.

Turner met them both at the door, greeting Andrea with a formal 'Mrs Devern' and moving out of the way to let her pass.

The front door led into a rather grand tiled hallway with a flight of stairs disappearing up to the next floor. The decor was all very neutral, with off-white colours dominating, which in Bolt's opinion gave it a rather soulless feel – not that he was any kind of expert in interior design. Straight ahead of him, above a vase containing partially wilted orchids, was a large professional portrait photograph of Andrea and Emma. It was a good shot of both mother and daughter, who were smiling widely at the camera, their faces side by side and touching, and the twinkle was firmly in Andrea's eye. Emma was a pretty kid with dark blonde hair down to her shoulders and a cute button nose. She looked young in the picture, probably no more than ten.

Bolt looked away quickly, not wanting to draw

attention to the photo. Marie asked whether anyone would like a cup of tea.

Bolt smiled at her. 'I'll take coffee, thanks, if it's going.'

Turner said he'd have the same.

Andrea didn't appear to have heard her. She was staring at the picture.

'What do you think of her, Mike? Isn't she beautiful?'

'Yes,' he said, keen to keep Andrea's spirits up. 'She's beautiful. And we're going to bring her back.'

'You've got to.'

The hallway fell silent and Marie and Turner went into the kitchen, leaving Bolt and Andrea alone. She ran a hand through her hair, turning away from the photo.

'I don't know what to do, Mike. It's the waiting. It's killing me.'

'Why don't you lie down for a bit?' He felt uneasy standing so close to her. 'We'll let you know of any developments.'

She nodded, and started up the staircase.

Bolt watched her go, then went to get his coffee.

The kitchen was large and modern with a breakfast island in the middle, and gleaming pots and pans hanging from hooks all around. Again, he thought about how much Mikaela would have loved a place like this. She'd been a great cook, but had had to do all her cooking in a place about a quarter of this size.

Marie and Turner were at the far end of the room, talking while she poured boiling water into the cups. Turner was approaching thirty and still resolutely single, a situation he seemed increasingly desperate to remedy. He tended to get first dates – he was a proud member of at least a dozen internet agencies, so was always getting introductions – but second ones proved a lot more elusive, which Bolt thought was a pity. Prematurely balding with a long hangdog face designed for frowning, and an obsession with the technical, the guy was definitely the kind of acquired taste a lot of people never get round to acquiring, but Bolt liked him. Turner might have had a geeky exterior, but he also had a bone-dry sense of humour, he never moaned, and there was a certain vulnerability about him that Bolt found endearing. Lately, he'd been smiling a lot more, as if he'd been taking charm lessons.

When Bolt walked in, Marie was laughing at something Turner had said, and he almost felt as if he was interrupting something. They both stopped speaking and turned his way, and Marie looked a bit sheepish.

'Andrea's gone to lie down,' he told them with a smile to show he hadn't seen or heard anything untoward.

He took the coffee cup from Marie and added a couple of sugars to it. There was another photo of Emma attached to the cupboard above the kettle, this time just a snapshot. In it she was flanked by her mother on one side and a lean, good-looking guy with unkempt brown hair on the other. They looked like a typical family. It made Bolt feel slightly jealous, although he wasn't a hundred per cent sure why.

'Do you think the husband's involved, sir?' asked Turner, seeing Bolt looking at the photo.

'Part of me says definitely,' he answered quietly, aware that he had to be careful what he said in front of Marie, who wasn't officially part of this inquiry, 'because it would explain how the kidnappers knew Emma's movements. But the other part says that if he is, why on earth did he then disappear? Surely he'd have known it would only arouse suspicion. It'd be far better to let the kidnappers know when and where to make the snatch, then act completely innocent. Even if we suspected him, there'd be nothing we could do about it.'

'That's what I was thinking,' said Turner. 'It's all wrong somehow, isn't it?'

Bolt was about to tell him not to speculate too much out loud when he heard a rapid set of footfalls on the stairs, and Andrea came rushing into the room dressed in a full-length dressing gown, her mobile phone in her right hand.

'They've called.'

'When? Just now?'

'Yes. On the mobile.'

'What did they say?'

'He asked if I was getting the money together for tomorrow night. I said I was, and he told me to turn my computer on and check my emails.'

She took a deep breath, and Bolt could tell she was using all her strength to hold things together.

'They said they've sent me a warning.'

Fifteen

While Andrea fetched her laptop and turned it on, Matt Turner called in to HQ and asked them to run an urgent trace on the last number to call Andrea's mobile. 'They'll get back to us in five,' he said as he and Bolt followed Andrea through the hallway and into a large, spacious study at the back of the house.

Andrea set the laptop down on a desk at the far end of the room which faced out on to the back lawn, and sat down to wait while it booted up. Bolt and Turner stood behind her while Marie Cohen remained further back, in the doorway. The desk itself was expensive mahogany and scrupulously tidy. There were two framed photos on it: one of Emma as a toddler, dressed in a pink swimming costume and playing with a hosepipe, laughing at the camera; another more recent one of mother and daughter smiling.

'What do you think they mean by sending me a warning?' asked Andrea, turning round in her seat and looking up at Bolt.

'Let's just see,' he said calmly.

'That's easy for you to say, isn't it?' she snapped, turning back and double-clicking on her internet icon.

Bolt didn't answer. The problem was that he wasn't very good around victims of crime. He never had been. He much preferred the process of detective work, of breaking up criminal enterprises. Of identifying targets and hitting them. He might have suffered his own private tragedy but the fact remained that he wasn't trained for this, and being intimately acquainted with this particular victim wasn't helping either. He looked over at Marie Cohen, wondering if she was going to intervene with soothing words, but she remained silent, motioning him just to leave it.

Andrea's homepage appeared on the screen and she clicked on her emails. There were a dozen or so unread messages but it was the one at the top, sent from a numbered hotmail account, which was the one they wanted. The word WARNING was written in block capitals in the subject column, and there was an mpeg attachment.

Without speaking, Andrea opened it. The message said simply WATCH THE FILM.

'Oh God,' she whispered.

Bolt tensed. 'Maybe it's best if we watch it first, Andrea,' he told her, putting a reassuring hand on her shoulder. He didn't add 'just in case', but he knew he might as well have done.

She took another deep breath. 'No. She's my daughter. I've got to watch it.'

'It might not be a good idea, Andrea,' said Marie, moving into the study.

'I am going to watch it. End of story.' Her words were loud and decisive, cutting across the room.

She clicked on the mpeg file and waited the twenty seconds while it downloaded. The room was silent, with just the peaceful sound of birdsong coming from outside. With trembling fingers, Andrea pressed play.

Immediately the screen was filled with the top half of a person sitting against a wall in a darkened room lit by a bulb somewhere off camera. The quality of the recording was very good, and Bolt knew that he was looking at Emma even though she had a black hood over her head. The arms beneath the black T-shirt she was wearing were pale and skinny – kid's arms.

Andrea let out an audible gasp.

For two or three seconds Emma sat there, absolutely still, then very slowly she lifted a copy of *The Times* until it was in full view. The main headline was about the run on the Northern Rock bank. The camera panned forward until it was fixed on the date in the top right-hand corner. It was today's.

'See, Andrea, she's alive,' said Bolt, trying to sound positive. 'And it's in their interests to keep her that way.'

Andrea didn't reply, but her shoulders were shaking, and he realized she was crying silently as she stared at the screen.

The camera panned back so that Emma's upper body filled the screen again, and then the camera suddenly jerked as the cameraman reached forward with a gloved hand and roughly removed the hood, revealing the pretty teenage girl with the dark blonde hair and blue eyes whose photo was all over Andrea's house.

Her face was terrified and wet with tears as she stared uncertainly at the cameraman. He appeared to give her some sort of off-camera prompt because she started to speak slowly and carefully, her voice shaking with fear. 'Mum, they say that if you get the money, they'll let me go tomorrow night.' There was a pause again while she appeared to get a second prompt. 'But Mum . . . they said that if you don't pay, or you call the police . . . they said they'd hurt me really bad.' As she spoke these last words, the tears began streaming down her face again.

Then she gave a short, tight gasp. She was

staring at something they couldn't see, her eyes widening.

'Oh God, Emma,' whispered Andrea, her own voice cracking under the strain. 'My darling.'

And then they all saw it. The long, gleaming blade of a hunting knife, held in a black-gloved hand, moving slowly across the screen from right to left, mocking the viewers with its presence. It belonged to the cameraman. His camera shook very slightly as he moved it. The knife then changed direction as he leaned forward, pointing the tip of the blade at Emma's neck. His arm beyond the glove was covered by a black sweater. There was no flesh showing, nothing that might even hint at a possible ID.

A torturous wail came from Andrea. 'No, Jesus, no. Please. Don't hurt her.'

Bolt felt his mouth go parchment dry. This was total sadism, something that, thank God, was rare. In twenty years of law enforcement he'd only seen something similar once before when he'd been forced to watch an old amateur videotape showing the sexual abuse and torture of a three-year-old child by her father. That was a long time ago now, yet he could still remember every single moment of it. It was etched on his brain, like a hideous tattoo, for ever. This was similar, and in a way all the more painful in that the victim's mother was someone he'd once cared so much for.

'Let's turn it off, Andrea,' he said. 'We can watch it again in a minute.'

She shook her head angrily. 'No. I've got to see. I've got to.'

On the film, Emma pushed her body back into the wall, craning her head away from the blade, her pale blue eyes never leaving it.

Andrea's moaning grew louder. It stopped abruptly when the point touched Emma's neck. Ever so gently.

No one moved a millimetre. It was as if they'd been frozen to the spot, staring hypnotized at the screen. Waiting.

The blade traced a slow path up the contours of Emma's jawline and on to her cheek, brushing the pale skin but not breaking it, stopping at the fold of skin just below her left eye. Half a centimetre more and it would be caressing the eyeball.

Bolt steeled himself for what might be coming next. He prided himself on being a hard man, able to take some of the worst experiences the world had to offer, but this was tearing him up inside, and he wondered how many times this scene would be revisiting his dreams in the coming months.

The knife jerked suddenly to the side, moving like a flash. Disappeared from view.

Emma cried out. Andrea gasped. Bolt stopped breathing.

The camera panned inwards. Emma's face filled the screen. Terrified, but unmarked. Then it panned slowly outwards as Emma crumpled into a fetal position on the bed she'd been sitting on, dropping the newspaper to the floor. She was wearing handcuffs, and there was a chain attached to her ankle by a metal loop.

Something dark rose up from the bottom of the screen, blocking out everything else, and the camera took several seconds to focus on it. It was a piece of paper. Five words were written on it in bold capitals: NO POLICE OR SHE DIES. The camera stayed on it for a full three seconds. Then abruptly the film ended and the screen returned to Andrea's homepage.

For a long moment, no one spoke. Bolt was just about to open his mouth to tell Andrea to be strong, that this was just a method for the kidnappers to cow her into submission so that she'd get them the next tranche of the ransom money – even though he wasn't at all sure he still believed it – when in one ferocious movement Andrea swept the laptop off the table, sending it crashing to the floor, and jumped to her feet. She grabbed the photo of Emma as a toddler from the desk and hugged it to her chest. Pushing Turner out of her way, she swung round to face Bolt, her tear-stained face a twisting combination of torment and rage.

'They're going to kill her, aren't they? That's it. They're going to kill her.'

Bolt put a hand on her arm, trying to calm her. 'No, Andrea, they won't. They're far better off keeping her alive.'

'They told me not to involve the police, and now look at you all here.' She yanked herself free and swept an arm dismissively round the room. 'Standing around while my daughter's tortured by these bastards. Oh God. If they kill her . . . if they kill her, it's all going to be my fault!'

'You can't think like that, Andrea,' said Bolt, but she was no longer listening. She strode rapidly past them and out the door, leaving behind only grim silence.

Sixteen

Marie went after Andrea, and Bolt heard them both going up the stairs, Andrea shouting at Marie to leave her alone. He stood staring at the upended laptop, wondering how Andrea was ever going to recover from this. Finally he broke his reverie and turned away.

Turner was speaking into the phone. When he hung up a few seconds later, Bolt asked him if they'd got a trace.

'He called from a mobile on a back street in the N18 postcode. But he switched off straight away so we can't follow him.'

'So he knows what we can do with mobile phones.'

'Looks that way, doesn't it?'

'Any chance of getting anything from the email he sent?'

'We won't get much out of the email address

itself. Anyone can set up a hotmail account anonymously. But we should be able to locate the computer he sent it from. It might take some time.'

'Get the team on to it straight away. We've just got to hope this guy makes a mistake.'

'He hasn't made any so far.'

Bolt might have liked Turner, but his occasional habit of accentuating the negatives could grate at times. Especially times like this. 'Just do it,' he said, turning away and pulling out his own mobile. 'And get the local cops down the street where the call was made from, just in case he's still there.'

He unlocked the French windows in the living room and went out into the back garden, dialling his boss's number. When Big Barry answered, he explained to him what the kidnappers had done. 'These guys are good, sir. They know exactly which buttons to press. But there's something else too. The way they're tormenting her – this is personal. I'm sure of it. Someone really wants Andrea Devern to suffer.'

'Well, let's hope you're right, because that might help lead us to them. The woman can't have that many enemies. In the meantime, though, I've had authorization for us to set up a sting. Looks like the ladies and gents upstairs agreed with you about negotiation. It's pointless with people as ruthless as this.'

'It's definitely the right move. This way we'll be the ones in control.'

'We'll use bundles of counterfeit notes fitted with trackers.'

'These people are professionals, sir. They're going to spot something like that.'

'We'll be right on their tails. By the time they realize the notes are fake it'll be too late and they'll be in custody.'

Bolt wasn't convinced. 'But it also might be too late for Emma. If they pick up the money, then check the notes in the car, see that they're not real, they'll know we're involved. In that case, they might never lead us to her.'

'Come on, old mate, how am I going to get authorization to use half a million pounds of real money? And where am I going to get it from? The Christmas kitty? Think about it.'

'You said we're not going to lose them.'

'We're not.'

'So we can afford to use the real thing, surely?' Bolt thought of the photo of Emma as a toddler, playing with the hosepipe in her pink swimming costume. 'This is a young girl's life we're talking about.'

'Let's not get sentimental, Mike.'

'I'm not. But if we use fake money and it all goes wrong, it's not going to look good for any of us, is it? That we thought the money was more important than our kidnap victim.' He resisted adding 'heads will roll', but the point was a valid one. Bolt was appealing to Barry's innate arse-covering instincts, knowing that there lay his greatest chance of success.

And it seemed to be working. 'I'll talk to them upstairs, but I can't see them going for it.' Barry sighed. 'Look, this whole operation needs to be well planned, so I want you back here so we can discuss the details. As soon as poss. Keep Turner and the liaison there with Mrs Devern, just in case they make contact again.'

Bolt hung up, and looked at his watch. It was ten past one. His stomach was growling and he realized that he hadn't eaten a thing all day. He'd grab some lunch on the way back. He took a deep breath. One way or another, he was going to get these bastards. And get Emma back for Andrea as well. The hunt was on now, and on the ground at least, he was the one in charge. This was the part of the job he loved, when the battle lines were drawn and it was all about you and them. Pushing the images of the video aside, he felt a renewed sense of determination.

He became aware of a presence behind him. It was Turner, looking vaguely sheepish.

'Everything all right, Matt?'

'Mrs Devern wants a word with you upstairs. Alone. She doesn't want to talk to Marie.' There was a vague disapproval in his tone.

'OK, thanks.'

Bolt walked back into the house through the French windows. Marie was standing at the bottom of the stairs, looking concerned.

'She's in the first room on the left,' she said wearily.

Bolt smiled, feeling sorry for her. 'Thanks. I don't see there's much I'm going to be able to do either, but I'll give it a try.'

Andrea was in the master bedroom, sitting in a white leather armchair and staring out of the bay window, a cigarette in her hand. She turned as he came inside and shut the door behind him. Her face was set hard, the tears wiped away now.

'You've got to get her back, Mike.' She spoke the words firmly.

'And we're doing absolutely everything we can to bring that about. I know how hard it must be, but you've got to try to sit tight and be patient.'

'Did you never want children, Mike?'

She watched him closely, waiting for an answer, the cigarette burning, forgotten, in her hand. He sighed, wondering how he was going to extricate himself from this conversation.

'The opportunity never arose. Maybe one day.'

'Have you ever been married?'

'I was. Once.'

'What happened?'

'She died. In a car crash. Five years ago.'

Five years. It felt like such a long time, yet in truth it had gone fast. He could still picture Mikaela perfectly, could still hear her voice. But she was someone he didn't like to be reminded of by other people. He liked to keep his thoughts and memories of her to himself.

'I'm sorry,' she said, sounding like she meant it.

'It's OK.'

Silence. He sensed there was something she wanted to add, so he waited for it.

And it came.

'Listen, Mike, I don't know how to say this, but . . .'

She noticed the cigarette then, and flicked the ash into an ashtray on the windowsill before it spilled into her lap.

'What is it, Andrea?'

'I told you about Jimmy Galante, didn't I? About the reason I involved him.'

'Because you needed his help.'

'Yes, and because he was her father as well.'

'That's right.'

'The thing is, I was lying.'

Bolt tensed. 'What do you mean?'

'I mean I was lying when I told Jimmy he was the father. He wasn't.'

She looked him squarely in the eye. 'You are.'

Seventeen

One of Mike Bolt's problems in his younger days was an inability to say no. He should never have carried on the affair with Andrea Devern after that first night of passion in the Bloomsbury hotel. She was a married woman, with a wealthy husband who looked after her, and he was an impetuous twenty-four-year-old cop, so it was always going to end in tears. But Bolt had somehow convinced himself that this didn't really matter. He was just going to see how things went and not get too involved.

But he had got involved, and in the eight weeks the affair had lasted he'd found himself driven ever deeper into Andrea's web. In the beginning he'd been in control, but that control had evaporated rapidly as he'd become more and more obsessed with her. He was driven to distraction by the difficulties in getting hold of her, and in meeting up for their illicit liaisons. In those eight weeks they slept together on only six occasions, and then suddenly it was all over. Just like that. Not with a whimper either, but with a bang he'd never forget.

But could he really have fathered her child? The thought nagged at him ferociously as he drove back to HQ. But the dates fit. Andrea had convinced him of that back at the house. 'Our daughter's birthday's the second of April,' she'd said. 'We were seeing each other in June and July.'

Our daughter. His daughter. She could be wrong, of course. As he'd found out afterwards, she was also seeing Jimmy Galante at the time. And she was married too, although she'd always claimed that her husband, Billy Devern, was impotent, which was why he'd allowed her to take lovers. Whether that was true or not was still largely immaterial, because the dates fitted. Check them, Andrea had said, and he had, going back in his head to those giddy days, and the truth shouted at him so loudly he could barely hear anything else. It was possible Emma Devern wasn't his child, but there was a damn good chance that she was.

On the seat next to him were photographs of Emma and Pat Phelan which he was taking back to the incident room. Phelan's was face up, but Emma's was face down. He couldn't bear to look at her. Couldn't bear to think that she might be his flesh and blood, and the first he'd known about it was when he'd been put in charge of investigating her kidnapping.

He thought of Mikaela, the woman he'd met a couple of years after Andrea, who'd gone on to be his wife. Mikaela had always wanted children. A boy and a girl, she'd always said. Children, and the big, rambling house with a nice garden. It was Bolt who'd always held back. He'd feared the immense commitment required; with the long hours he worked, he didn't think he could provide the necessary support. But eventually, after seven years together, he'd reluctantly agreed to Mikaela's increasingly persistent requests that they should start trying for a baby.

She was two months pregnant when the car he was driving left the road and smashed into an oak tree, crunching it into a shape that made it unrecognizable. He'd spent six weeks in hospital and now carried three small scars on his face as a permanent reminder of that night. Mikaela's life support system was turned off three days later, without her ever regaining consciousness. Bolt had been too ill to leave his bed to say goodbye. He hadn't even been told of the decision, made by her parents, until almost two days later because it was thought the news would be so traumatic it would worsen his condition.

And all that time – all the time he'd ever been with Mikaela, and through those long hard years since – he might already have had a child. A child growing up whom he'd never seen, and knew absolutely nothing about.

His fingers tightened on the steering wheel and he clenched his jaw, feeling a sudden burst of furious resentment towards Andrea. If he was the father, why had she said nothing to him all these years? And if he wasn't, how could she manipulate him like this?

He pulled over to the side of the road before the fury got the better of him, and took some long, deep breaths, trying to calm himself down. But it was hard. Incredibly hard. That morning he'd been a reasonably happy man with a new girl-friend, coasting towards his fortieth birthday – now only a few months away – having got used to the idea that he was probably never going to have children. And now he'd been told not only that he might have one, but that her life was in terrible danger, and he was the one responsible for getting her back safely.

He sat there for a full minute, his heart thumping so loudly it felt like the only thing he could hear. Then he picked up the photo of Emma – blonde, smiling, fourteen years old, in her school uniform – and stared at it, searching for resemblances. Was she his? There were similarities, there were differences. He thought of the man – the men – holding her. The men who might not want to return her alive. The men they were now going to try to set up. For the first time, he truly imagined what could happen if their plan went wrong, and his stomach lurched violently. The girl who could be his only child would die.

He put down Emma's photo, but he kept it face up so that he could see the girl he had to rescue. It was time to take responsibility and think straight. Technically, the position hadn't changed; it was just that the stakes had now become infinitely higher.

He took a final deep breath, flicked on the indicator, and pulled out into the traffic.

Part Three

Part Three

Eighteen

It was half past two on Friday afternoon when SG4 Tina Boyd stopped outside the Lively Lounge Club and Casino, a turd-coloured slab of a building straight out of the 1960s school of bland architecture, which sat at the Colindale end of the Edgware Road, about three miles and a thousand years as the crow flies from the leafy Hampstead suburb where Pat Phelan now lived. Looking at it made her feel mildly pleased that gambling wasn't one of her vices. It wasn't that she wasn't interested. She just didn't dare place a bet, even on something like the Grand National, because she knew if she got a bit of beginner's luck and started winning, she'd probably never stop. Tina had an addictive personality. It was part of her genetic make-up. All through her early and mid-teens she'd resisted the peer pressure to start smoking, then at seventeen she'd tried her first cigarette at a party and she'd been putting away twenty a day ever since, with every attempt to stop ending in rapid failure.

She wondered if Phelan was the same. Because he definitely had a gambling problem, and the Lively Lounge Club and Casino was where he sank the lion's share of the money he spent on his betting. And he spent a lot. Tina's team had got hold of copies of the previous year's statements for the five credit cards and one debit card held in his name, and during that period his outgoings amounted to a grand total of £87,288.36 – and this from a man with no actual income that they could find, other than a £1,500-a-month standing order paid into his personal bank account from Andrea's own account, which was held at a separate bank. There'd been a number of further payments into his account over the course of the year, more than twenty-five grand's worth in all, but they were sporadic which meant they almost certainly represented winnings. Even with his wife's £160,000-a-year salary it was an unsustainable amount, and already Phelan's credit limit was maxed out on every one of the credit cards, while he was currently overdrawn at the bank by more than six thousand.

It wasn't that someone getting himself into this situation was all that uncommon. As Big Barry had pointed out earlier that morning, people got themselves into serious debt the whole time. What was interesting about Pat Phelan's finances from a SOCA point of view was that his spending had tailed off dramatically in the last two months, by more than 90 per cent, and in the same period there'd been no deposits of winnings in his bank account. Either he'd turned over a new leaf or, in Tina's opinion far more likely, he was funding his habit from a different source. Since the financial statements all pointed to the Lively Lounge as the venue of choice for his gambling, Tina had decided that it was as good a place as any to start digging into Phelan's background. She could have left it to one of the more junior members of the team but, like a lot of detectives, she liked to get out and about; and if she was entirely honest with herself, she wasn't much of a delegator, preferring to rely on her own ability to get things done.

The needs of the compulsive gambler tend to be of the twenty-four-hour variety, and the club was open. Tina went through the tinted double doors and into the darkened lobby. A blonde girl was at the reception desk talking to an older woman with hair extensions and far too much make-up. The girl smiled politely as Tina approached, wishing her a good afternoon in a Polish accent. Her colleague, meanwhile, said nothing but gave her a more suspicious look, clocking immediately that she was police, even though Tina wasn't wearing a uniform and always made a conscious effort never to give off that aura. Some people simply have a nose for spotting coppers, and they're usually the ones who have the most to fear from them.

Tina smiled at the girl. 'Good afternoon, my name's Tina Boyd from the Serious and Organized Crime Agency.' She held up her warrant card. 'I'd like to speak to the owner, please.'

'I'll deal with this, Barbara,' said the older woman in a deep voice that was midway between a bear and Demi Moore. 'The owners aren't here. They're not based in this country.' Her expression seemed to add, so what the hell are you going to do about that? 'Is there anything I can help with?'

'That depends. Are you the most senior person in the building at the moment?'

There was a moment's hesitation that told Tina the answer was no.

'Well, Mr McMahon's here, but—'

'And what's his position?'

'He's the manager, but I think he's—'

'Well, I'll see him then, thank you.'

'He's busy, Miss whatever-your-name-was,' the woman growled.

Tina wasn't deterred. 'That makes two of us. Can you take me to him, please?'

'I'll call up and see if he's available.'

She picked up a phone behind the desk,

scowling at Tina, who stared back at her impassively, amazed why some people always had to put up a token resistance to the police before they acquiesced, even though the end result was inevitable.

The woman hung up. 'OK, he can see you now.'

Tina followed her through the main gambling area, a big, windowless place with all the charm of an aircraft hangar. Only a handful of the gaming tables were in use, the clientele mainly quiet Chinese men wearing inscrutable expressions as they placed their bets. None of them looked up as Tina and her guide passed by in silence.

Mr McMahon's office was at the far end of the building, up a flight of stairs and along a short corridor. The woman knocked on his door and moved out of the way for Tina to go in, giving her a last glare of defiance as she did so.

'The Serious and Organized Crime Agency,' said the man standing behind the desk as Tina shut the door behind her. 'I've not had any dealings with them. Malcolm McMahon,' he said, putting out a hand. 'Pleased to meet you, Miss . . .'

'Boyd. Tina Boyd.'

They shook hands, and Tina took the seat on her side of the desk.

Malcolm McMahon was a big man who looked like he enjoyed a drink. He was good-looking in a brutish sort of way, with slicked-back grey hair fashioned into a widow's peak as sharp as an arrowhead, and a straight one-inch scar edging away from his top lip. He was dressed in a badly ironed shirt and unfashionable striped tie, while his casino clothes – black suit and dress shirt – were hanging up on one wall, next to a bank of eight small screens that showed the gaming area from various angles.

'I hear you SOCA people aren't even police any more,' he said with a smile. 'You're special agents or something. So, what do I call you?'

'Miss Boyd'll do fine.'

He nodded slowly, accepting this. 'Well, Miss Boyd, we run a tight ship here, and we don't tolerate anything illegal, so I don't know how we came to the attention of SOCA. Do you mind if I check your ID again? Just to make sure you are who you say you are. It's amazing how many charlatans there are these days.'

'Sure.'

Tina produced the warrant card from the back pocket of her jeans and handed it to him, noticing the nicotine stains on his thick, stubby fingers as he took it. He examined it carefully before thanking her and handing it back.

'It's about one of your customers.'

'I don't like talking about our customers, Miss Boyd. They value their privacy, and so do we.'

'This is a very serious case, Mr McMahon. If

you want me to get official and bring officers down here to interview all your staff, I can. But I'm also prepared to talk off the record, and I can guarantee that anything you tell me will be treated in the strictest confidence.'

'So, you want me to grass up one of my paying punters?' he asked evenly.

Now it was her turn to smile. 'No, I want you to help him. His name's Patrick Phelan, and I know he spends a lot of money in your establishment, and has done so for a long time.' McMahon didn't say anything, so she continued. 'Mr Phelan's gone missing, and we're extremely concerned about his welfare.'

'I don't see how I can help.'

'But you know him?'

McMahon sighed and sat back in his seat. 'Yeah, I know him. He's been coming here for a while. Nice bloke, friendly enough. Not the sort to piss people off.'

'When was the last time you saw him?'

He drummed his fingers on the desk. 'Last week some time. I can't remember for sure, but I definitely haven't seen him this week, and I don't think he's been in. I could check for you.'

'No, it's fine. Who does he usually come in with?'

'Various people. The occasional girl, sometimes with a couple of mates. Sometimes alone.' He shrugged. 'I didn't really know any of them.'

Tina reached into her jeans pocket and pulled out a pack of Silk Cut. 'Do you mind if I smoke?' She knew from the way McMahon wasn't settling that he was itching for a cigarette, and from the stale smell in the room it was obvious he usually puffed away in here.

He grinned, and leaned down behind the desk. When his hand re-emerged, it was holding a huge half-full ashtray.

'Didn't realize you were a smoker,' he said. 'Now that it's against the law to have a fag in your own office, I thought I'd best be careful when you came in.'

'That's one law I'm happy to break,' she said, offering him a cigarette.

He took it, and she lit for both of them. A rapport had been struck based on their shared identity as social outcasts, just as Tina had hoped. It was amazing what you could do with a rapport.

'According to his bank statements, Mr Phelan was a big spender, and it didn't look like he was very successful.'

'He wasn't. He'd have a few drinks and he'd start getting reckless. Sometimes it worked – you know, who dares wins and all that – but most of the time it didn't.'

Tina took a drag on her cigarette. 'The thing is, the statements also show that his spending plummeted in the last couple of months, but it sounds like he was still coming here.' She paused. 'Any idea where he might have been getting his money from?'

'We've got credit lines we can extend to valued customers. Pat's a valued customer.'

'But you weren't extending credit to him for two months solid, were you?'

He shook his head. 'No, we weren't. We stopped a few weeks back. He still owes us more than three grand. He asked the other week for more time to pay. He told me he had what he called an alternative means of income. I wasn't happy. I like Pat, but this is business.'

Tina kept her interest in check. 'Did he give you any idea what this alternative means of income was?'

'Nah. He just promised me it was kosher.'

'Was he borrowing money from any other sources, as far as you know?'

This time, McMahon's silence didn't sit naturally. He looked evasive.

'Remember, Mr McMahon, this talk's purely off the record. If you know anything, I can guarantee it won't get back to you.'

McMahon continued to sit there smoking. Tina didn't push things. She waited.

'Look,' he said at last, 'I like Pat. He's a nice bloke. I wouldn't want to think anything bad's happened to him. But if it has, I'd want whoever's involved to suffer. You know what I mean?'

'Sure.'

'This is definitely, definitely off the record, right?'

Tina nodded, realizing something significant was coming.

'Pat doesn't just owe us. He also owes someone you really don't want to be in hock to. Man by the name of Leon Daroyce.'

'I don't know him,' she said, making no attempt to write the name down. Producing a notebook might give this talk an official air and spook him, and she didn't want that. She'd remember the name easy enough.

'He's a loan shark, and a big player round these parts,' McMahon continued. 'I think a few of our punters have used his services, but you've got to be pretty desperate. The rates he charges are high and, like I said, he really ain't a nice bloke.'

'Have you got any idea how much Phelan owes him?'

He shook his head. 'Pat never told me about Daroyce. I just heard rumours. It was one of the reasons I cut the credit lines to him. I was worried we wouldn't get paid.'

Tina was going to have to find out as much as she could about Leon Daroyce and how much Phelan was in the can to him. If Daroyce was such a brutal operator – and with a man like McMahon, clearly no stranger to violence himself, saying it then she was inclined to believe he must be – it was also possible that Pat Phelan had gone to extraordinary lengths to get the money to pay him. Maybe even resorting to the kidnap of his stepdaughter.

'I think that's everything, Mr McMahon,' she said, standing up. 'Thanks for your time, and for being so candid with me.'

He stubbed out his cigarette. 'I'm trusting you, Miss Boyd. If word gets out that I pointed you in Leon Daroyce's direction, things ain't going to look good for me.'

'I keep my word.'

'Yeah,' he said, watching her carefully. 'You look like you do.' He lit another cigarette, blew out some smoke. 'A word of advice. Be careful. Leon Daroyce tends to take things personal.'

Tina opened the door, gave him a cool smile. 'Don't worry about me, Mr McMahon, I'm always careful.'

Nineteen

There was one reason above any other why Tina Boyd was always careful. She attracted trouble. It hadn't always been like that. She'd had a happy middle-class upbringing in the country, the product of two parents who appeared to love each other, and certainly loved her. She'd gone to private school, then to university, studied English and Psychology, did her time on the well-worn backpacking trail. And then, while all her friends took up their office jobs, she'd joined the police. It hadn't been on a whim – well, not entirely anyway. She'd never fancied office work, and she'd always had an inquisitive mind. She was interested in what made people tick. Maybe she should have been a psychiatrist, but somehow she thought she'd learn more about the human condition as a cop. And she had, too, although she wasn't at all sure that it had been a positive development.

For the first few years of her police career things had been remarkably trouble-free. She'd spent two years in uniform – and was one of the few officers in her station who was never assaulted once – before joining Islington CID as a detective constable. As a graduate, she was on the fast track. A senior position looked inevitable, and sooner rather than later.

But then things had started to go wrong. First, she was taken hostage by a suspect she'd been investigating and was hit in the crossfire when he was shot dead by armed CO19 officers. The wound she suffered was comparatively light, and she was back at work within six weeks, to much fanfare and an immediate promotion to detective sergeant. They'd even put her on the cover of one of the issues of *Police Review* shortly afterwards. It should have made her happy, but she knew she didn't deserve the praise. She'd made a mistake which had got her into the position of being shot in the first place, and it looked like she was being rewarded for that. If she was honest with herself – something that she was constantly – then this was the part of the whole incident that had scarred her the most. Tina was a perfectionist, and when it came down to it she'd been found wanting.

Barely six months later, trouble came calling again, except this time it was with a vengeance. A detective she'd been working with closely was murdered while on a case they were both involved in, followed only weeks later by the apparent suicide of her long-term lover, also a police officer, which turned out to be a murder indirectly related to the same case. Suddenly, from being the next big thing, she'd become tainted by association, the kind of cop everyone wants to avoid in case something should happen to them. Someone had even nicknamed her the Black Widow, and the name had stuck.

She never saw the people who'd killed the two men so close to her brought to justice. It was possible that not all of them had been. This knowledge had scarred her too, and she'd resigned from the force, hit the rails, and become very depressed. She might never have recovered – at one point, things had genuinely felt that bad – but then she'd met Mike Bolt, who was then working for the National Crime Squad, and he must have seen something in her because he persuaded her to join his team, and to move across with them when the NCS became SOCA.

She appreciated what he'd done for her, and she worked hard at her job to demonstrate this. Sometimes she thought Bolt was attracted to her, occasionally even that this was the reason he'd hired her in the first place, and consequently she tended to keep her distance from him in the work-place. He was a good-looking guy, there was no question about that. Tall, broad-shouldered, with blond hair only just beginning to fleck with grey, and piercing blue eyes that were so striking she'd thought at first (wrongly) that he wore contact lenses. She almost certainly would have gone for him at one time, but things were different for her now. She'd had her fingers burned far too badly, and the experience had made her more cautious. She'd become a loner, someone who kept herself to herself both inside and outside a work environment, and she knew that some of the team resented her for it, putting her manner down to a brusqueness that wasn't there.

She'd been a fun girl once. Had got drunk, got laid, travelled the world. Smoked dope so strong in northern Thailand she'd hallucinated. Swum, awestruck, with dolphins on the Great Barrier Reef. Had a real life. She didn't really have one any more, and there were times – more often than she'd like – when she was filled with an angry regret over the path she'd chosen, and its bitter consequences, wondering how things might have turned out if she'd taken the office job.

But today wasn't one of those times. She was actually feeling good as she walked along Colindale Avenue in the direction of the Underground, the autumn sun warming the back of her neck. She was on her way back to the Glasshouse and had already called ahead and told

Bolt about Pat Phelan's alleged debt problems, as well as asking him to check out anything they had on Leon Daroyce.

Bolt had seemed pleased with the lead – which he should have been, because it provided them with a motive for the kidnap – but he'd also sounded under strain, which wasn't like him. Mike Bolt was generally calm and level-headed, the type of guy who was able to withstand pressure. It was one of the reasons she enjoyed working with him. She felt she could trust his leadership.

'Hey lady, how you doin'?'

The words, delivered in a deep baritone with a faux American twang, snapped her straight out of her thoughts. She turned to see a silver Merc pull up beside her. The man addressing her through the open window was a well-built, smooth-headed black man in his thirties, wearing shades and an expensive-looking suit.

'I'm not buying, I'm not available, and I'm not interested. So piss off.' She looked away and kept walking, but the car kept pace with her.

Tina didn't take kindly to being accosted in the street by strangers. It happened now and again. This was London, after all. She tended to ignore them, and usually they went away, but it didn't look like this guy was going to. She was a hundred metres from the Tube station now, the irony of the fact that she was only spitting distance from Hendon Police College not lost on her. God knows why this guy was picking on her, but if he decided to jump out of the car and cut up rough, then he'd get a lot more than he bargained for.

She heard the guy chuckle. 'You got some spirit, lady. I like that. A friend of mine would like to speak to you. I hear you might want to speak to him too.'

She stopped, turned his way, saw a white guy with a tight T-shirt and big biceps beyond him in the driver's seat.

'Is that right?' she said. 'And who's your friend?'

'His name's Leon, but to you he's Mr Daroyce.'

Tina cursed to herself. How the hell had he found out about her this fast? Then she thought of that brassy bitch who'd taken her up to McMahon's office, and it came to her. She must have been listening at the door. And there she'd been, saying how careful she always was. *Not careful enough, darling*.

'Thanks for the offer, but I have a rule never to get into cars with strangers.'

'Does it still count if we know you, Tina Boyd?' The man gave her a predatory smile as he made a great show of emphasizing the pronunciation of those last two words.

The use of her name made Tina feel naked and exposed. 'No, it doesn't,' she answered, beginning to turn away.

'If you don't come now, we might have to come and find you, Tina Boyd.' His voice had hardened now, laced with threat.

She turned back. 'What does your friend want?'

'He just wants to talk.' He shrugged his powerful shoulders. 'That's it. Nothing more. I think he might have some information for you.'

He leaned behind him and opened the back door of the Mercedes for her.

Tina made a quick calculation. If they knew her name, they knew she was a SOCA agent. That meant it was unlikely they were going to risk hurting her. Especially when their car, and possibly even their faces, would already have been picked up somewhere on CCTV. And when it came down to it, there was no reason for them to hurt her anyway. She didn't owe Daroyce money, had in fact never met him, which meant the guy in front of her was almost certainly telling the truth.

Those were the pros. There was only one con, but it was a big one. What if she was wrong?

It was a big decision, but in the end – although she'd never admit it to herself – part of the reason Tina Boyd attracted trouble was that she was always prepared to put herself in situations where encountering it was inevitable. And this was one of them. Taking a long look round so that the people walking up and down the street might remember her face if it came to it, she got inside the Merc and shut the door.

'Let's go then,' she said, lighting a cigarette.

Twenty

They drove through back streets heading west in
the direction of Queensbury. Tina tried to make
conversation, knowing how important it was to
create a rapport with the black guy, who was
clearly the senior of the two. But now she was in
the car, both men were worryingly reticent. The
white guy said nothing at all, his friend either
answering her questions with an uninterested yes
and no or ignoring them altogether.

The journey didn't last long, ten minutes at
most, before they pulled into a dingy dead-end
road lined with brand-new low-rise council flats
on one side and a pair of grim-looking tower
blocks on the other. The car pulled into a parking
space in front of the first of the blocks, next to an
overflowing bright orange wheelie bin that
seemed to be attracting the flies. A gang of half a
dozen kids on mountain bikes were messing

about by a rusty climbing frame over to one side.

'Nice place,' said Tina, wrinkling her nose against the smell from the bin as she got out of the car.

'Mr Daroyce likes to stay close to his roots,' answered the black guy as they walked over to the front entrance.

Tina noticed the kids give him respectful looks as he passed, before passing more hostile eyes over her. *Jesus*, she thought. *What is it about me? I might as well be wearing a flashing blue light on my head.*

They went up to the tenth floor in a graffiti-strewn lift with black smoke stains running down two sides as if someone had tried to set it alight, travelling in silence with only the creaking of the cables for company. Tina was getting more and more nervous. She didn't much like going alone to isolated places with the kind of men your mother warned you about, particularly when she was unarmed and out of contact with her colleagues. She thought about trying to leave but had a strong feeling that they wouldn't let her.

As they emerged from the lift into a dingy corridor only partly illuminated by noisy over-head strip lighting, dark shadows flickering at the edges, she was reminded of something that had happened during her backpacking days. She'd been caught in a sudden storm while travelling by fishing boat between islands in southern Indonesia. Huge dark waves had reared up and crashed over the deck, sending the tiny boat spinning and lurching. The fishermen had looked terrified, their expressions terrifying Tina even more as she clung desperately to her seat, genuinely believing she was going to die. Then the friend she was travelling with leaned over and, with a grim smile on his face, had shouted above the noise, 'It's not much consolation now, but you're going to love telling this story one day!' And she had, too. They'd made it across, the storm had passed, and life had moved on. The moral being, things are never as bad as they seem.

She told herself she'd be out of there soon enough, life would move on, and she'd have a good laugh about it over a long gin and tonic, curled up on her sofa.

The flat they wanted was at the end of the corridor. She knew which one it was going to be straight away, because it looked like Fort Knox. The doorway was covered with an iron security grille, the door behind it reinforced with a series of home-cut steel plates. No fewer than five separate locks ran up one side, and attached to the doorframe was a tiny CCTV camera, its lens pointing out at head height through one of the gaps in the grille.

The black guy produced a set of keys and let

them in, a process that took the best part of a minute. The interior was cloyingly warm and smelled of dope as they made their way through a narrow hallway and into a dimly lit backroom which was furnished with just a table and two chairs facing each other on either side.

Sitting in one of the chairs, with his legs crossed and his back to them, was a short, well-built black man in a peach-coloured suit and fedora of the same colour. The fedora was set at a jaunty angle and had two small peacock feathers jutting from the rim, giving the man the overall appearance of a 1970s New York pimp. He didn't turn round as the black guy moved out of the way and Tina stepped inside, just motioned with a casual wave of a hand for her to take the vacant seat.

'I hear you been asking questions about Patrick Phelan,' said the man from beneath the fedora as she sat down opposite him. 'You a cop, yeah?'

His voice was softer than she'd been expecting, the accent local but with just a hint of something more exotic. As he lifted his head she could see that he was young, probably no more than late twenties, with a round boyish face and dark intelligent eyes. He was definitely not what she'd been expecting, and now that the two men who'd brought her here had disappeared into another room, she felt herself relax a little.

'Yes,' she answered, 'I'm a cop.' She wasn't

technically, she was an agent, but it was never worth explaining it like that since no one ever seemed to understand the difference. 'I work for the Serious and Organized Crime Agency. You must be Leon Daroyce.'

He touched a finger to his hat and half-smiled. 'That's me.'

'And yes, I have been asking questions about Patrick Phelan,' Tina continued. 'We're looking for him.'

Daroyce nodded slowly. 'So am I,' he said softly, hardly moving his lips as he spoke, so that his words came out almost as a hiss.

He leaned forward in his seat and crossed his hands on the table. They were small and surprisingly dainty considering his build, dwarfed by the gold sovereign rings on most of his fingers. He exhaled slowly through pursed lips and fixed her with a gaze that was almost hypnotic.

'Let me tell you something, Miss Boyd,' he hissed. 'I'm an entrepreneur, a small businessman. I lend money like a bank, except unlike a bank I don't ask hundreds of questions. I don't make my customers fill out a pile of forms. You know what someone once said? A banker's a man who lends you his umbrella when the sun's shining, then asks for it back as soon as it starts raining.'

'Mark Twain.'

He shrugged, uninterested. 'Well, I'm not like

that. I don't turn people away. All I ask is you pay me back the money you've borrowed, and the interest on it. That's it. I'm providing a service. And I provided a service to Pat Phelan. Except he seems to have welshed on the deal. He owes me thirty-five thousand pounds, Miss Boyd. And I need to get that money back.'

'I don't see how I can help.'

'Because you're looking for him. What is it that you people want to speak to him about?'

'We think he's involved in a fraud case,' she lied. If Daroyce and his friends were involved in the kidnapping then they'd know she wasn't telling the truth, but she was beginning to think that they couldn't be. Otherwise, why on earth would they have brought her here?

'That sounds like Phelan. The guy's a snake. Is he likely to get bail?'

'I don't know.'

'Listen, Miss Boyd, perhaps you and me can help each other. I need to get my money back from Pat Phelan, because if I let something like this go, then it's going to look very bad on me and my business. Do you understand what I'm saying?'

'I think so, yes.'

'Now, if you hear where he is, all you need to do is give me a call, let me and my people get there first, and I'll pay you ten grand in cash.' He reached inside his peach suit and produced a huge wad of used notes, putting it down on the table in front of her. 'Not bad for five minutes' work, is it?'

She looked at the money, wondered who'd suffered for him to get it, then back at Daroyce. 'I'll see what I can do.'

'No,' he said quietly, 'that's not good enough. I want you to say you'll do it.'

His tone was cold now.

Tina made another quick calculation. She had no intention of helping Daroyce, and she certainly couldn't take his money. However, it seemed prudent to say yes, just so she could get out of there.

'OK, I'll do it. If we locate him, of course. Have you got a number I can get you on?'

His half-smile returned. 'Sure.' He took a card from his pocket and handed it to her. It was blank except for a handwritten mobile number.

She put it in her pocket.

'I still don't understand why you need me, though. It looks like you've got eyes and ears all over the place. You certainly found out about me easily enough.'

'I've looked everywhere for Phelan, but he seems to have done a better job at disappearing than he ever did at gambling. He was supposed to give me a fifteen grand down payment last Sunday. He didn't turn up; neither did it. He asked for a few more days. I told him he had twenty-four hours. But he didn't come through again. So, I've been hunting for him. I know where he lives, but his car hasn't been there, and from what I hear, neither has he. But,' he added, regarding her almost playfully, 'I've got a little clue that you might be able to use.'

'What's that?' Tina sat forward, interested.

'The thing is, Miss Boyd, can I trust you?'

Tina met his gaze, held it firmly. 'Yes, you can trust me. If we find him, I'll let you know. What you do after that is your concern.'

Daroyce nodded, seeming to accept this. 'Phelan's got a girlfriend. Good-looking chick. A little bit old for my tastes, but she carries it well.'

'Are you sure it's not his wife?'

He shook his head. 'No, I know what his wife looks like. It's not her. She's been here, too. The girlfriend. She came with him to deliver a five grand down payment on the debt a couple of weeks ago. I don't know who she is, or where she lives, but they were definitely close, and I had the feeling that, you know, the five grand was her money.'

'Can you describe her?'

'I can do better than that. I can show you a picture.'

He leaned down behind the table and picked up an envelope which he handed her. There was a

211

single photograph inside, a still from the security camera outside Daroyce's door. It showed the faces of a man and a woman, both of whom looked nervous. The man's face was in the foreground, and Tina recognized him as Pat Phelan. The picture quality wasn't fantastic and the woman's face appeared slightly grainy, but even so there was no mistaking who it was, since Tina had seen her picture on the website of Feminine Touch Health and Beauty Spas only hours before.

It was Isobel Wheeler. Andrea Devern's business partner.

Twenty-one

'Do you know her?'

'No, but I should be able to find out.'

Tina was a good liar. She knew how to wear a poker face.

'Good.'

Leon Daroyce smiled properly now, and Tina had to fight to maintain her poker face as she saw his teeth for the first time. There was enough gold in there to stock a small jewellery shop, but it wasn't that which grabbed her attention. It was the fact that every single one of them was filed to a razor-sharp point. Daroyce's mouth was a lethal weapon, those jaws easily capable of murder.

Seeing her reaction, he chuckled – a strange, high-pitched little sound that made her skin crawl. 'You like them, baby? The girls always get a little frightened at first, but when they see what I can do with them, they always come back for more.' He waggled his tongue at her, running it along the points of his fangs.

Tina needed to get out of there. The room suddenly felt hot and claustrophobic. She picked up the envelope, slipped the photo back inside, and stood up.

'Let me get on with things, then.'

'Haven't you forgotten something?' He motioned towards the wad of money.

'I can't take it now. I haven't done anything yet.'

'But you're going to, though. Aren't you?'

'If we find him, yes.'

'You look thirsty,' he said, changing the subject. 'Do you want a drink?'

Tina took a sharp breath. 'Thanks, but I need to get going.'

'Sit down there for a couple of seconds. I want to show you something. Go on,' he said, waving towards the seat, 'it won't take long.'

Reluctantly, she did as requested.

'What is it?'

'Power,' he whispered.

'Sorry?'

He mouthed the word again, then turned towards the door. 'Woman, bring me water!' he called out, and a few seconds later a skinny mixed-race girl, no more than eighteen, with unkempt hair, hurried into the room. She was dressed in a dirty white T-shirt and a black thong, and Tina noticed that there were bruises on her bare legs. Avoiding their eyes, the girl put a small bottle of Evian on the table in front of Daroyce and quickly turned to go, but his hand whipped out like a flailing cord and grabbed her wrist in a tight, visibly painful grip. The girl looked scared, but didn't say anything.

'You know what power is, Miss Boyd?' asked Daroyce, tightening his grip on the girl's wrist, making her wince. 'Power is when you're respected; when you're feared; when people will do anything you tell them. Let me show you what I mean.' He looked up at the girl with gleaming eyes. 'You're mine, aren't you, woman?'

'Yes,' she whispered.

'You're hurting her, Mr Daroyce. Why don't you let go of her arm?'

He ignored her, pulling the girl towards him.

'Now, get on your knees.'

The girl knelt down.

'You don't have to do this,' said Tina firmly, horrified by what might be about to take place. 'I believe you.'

Daroyce backhanded the girl across the face. Hard. The slap rebounded around the room. Tina flinched as the girl's head snapped sideways under the blow before quickly righting itself. She didn't cry out or make a sound. Instead, she remained kneeling, staring straight ahead, her jaw quivering as it tightened against the pain. The fear had gone from her eyes now, replaced by the submissiveness of the defeated.

Tina stood up and addressed the girl. 'I'm a police officer,' she said, pulling out her warrant card and showing it to her. 'You can leave with me now. You don't have to stay here.' She didn't add that the girl could also press charges if she wanted to; they could talk about that later, when they were in a safer location.

The girl said nothing, continued to stare straight ahead.

'Come on,' said Tina, putting out a hand. 'You can come with me now.'

Daroyce chuckled. 'Tell her to fuck off, woman.'

This time the girl looked at Tina. There was a red mark covering the entire left side of her face, several small cuts on the cheek where Daroyce's rings had made contact.

'Fuck off,' she said, without feeling or passion.

'Please. I can take you home.'

But Tina knew it was no use. Even the girl's eyes were blank.

Daroyce's smile grew wider, the teeth showing, as he saw Tina's frustration. Then it disappeared altogether. 'Get out, woman!' he snapped, and immediately the girl got to her feet and hurried out of the door.

Tina shoved the warrant card back in her

pocket. 'I'm leaving, and I want to take her with me.'

'You don't get it, do you, Miss Boyd? She won't go with you. Not in a thousand years. Because she's mine.'

'Slavery was outlawed in this country two hundred years ago, Daroyce. Maybe you missed the bicentennial celebrations.'

'She can leave if she wants to, Boyd. But she won't. Because she owes me, and she's paying her debt.'

'I don't care about—'

'Enough!' His hand slammed down on the table, silencing her. 'The reason I showed you that is so you know I don't fuck about.'

'You're a bully.'

He wagged a finger at her. 'No, I'm no bully. Bullies only pick on the weak. I'm prepared to take on everyone. And I'm also a man of my word, so when people break theirs, I take great offence. And I make them suffer. That little whore fucked me about once, and now she's paying for her stupidity. Just like Pat Phelan will pay for it when I get hold of him.' He stood up, and even though at full height he was still shorter than Tina, he radiated the kind of cruel, low menace that would have intimidated men twice his height. 'Now you've made me a promise as well,' he said quietly, making a point of showing his teeth as he spoke. 'So, if you find the whereabouts of Phelan, I want to hear about it. Otherwise, Miss Boyd, my people will come for you too. Do you understand?'

Again, Tina held his gaze, but she was finding it hard to keep her nerve. She was scared, and he knew it.

'I understand,' she answered.

'Good. Would you like my men to drop you off where they picked you up?'

She shook her head. 'No, it's OK. I'll walk.'

He moved aside to let her pass, and she caught a subtle waft of expensive and very nice cologne that almost made her pause to take in more of it, until she thought about what he'd just done.

'Watch yourself out there,' he whispered. 'The streets round here can be very, very dangerous.'

She ignored him and kept walking, out into the narrow hallway. The big black guy in the shades materialized from a room ahead of her, unlocking the front door for her in silence. She couldn't see the girl anywhere, but if she was honest with herself, she wasn't looking too hard, so eager was she just to get out of there.

There were all kinds of things Tina could have taken from the conversation she'd just had: the large amount of cash Pat Phelan owed Daroyce; the way he'd recently asked Daroyce for just a few more days to pay the money; the fact that he was having an affair with his wife's business partner . . . But she couldn't seem to concentrate on any of them as she walked rapidly through the back streets, going in no particular direction, haunted by the face of an anonymous girl who got down on her knees and waited to be beaten by a thug – a man who'd just threatened to turn on Tina as well if she didn't do what she was told.

She felt the pressure building inside her head. She was a tough person. She'd had to be to put up with what life had thrown at her these past few years, but occasionally her strength wavered, and it was wavering now.

She needed a drink. Badly.

There was a pub up ahead, a spit-and-sawdust type of place with a chalkboard outside advertising football games on Sky, and a couple of potbellied builders standing by the door smoking. The door was open. It seemed to welcome her.

She knew she shouldn't do it. Knew what one drink meant. But it was hard. So damn hard. She felt a desperate need to put a glass to her lips, to soften the blows that had rained down on her this afternoon – no, shit, that had rained down on her over the last four years.

You never drink on duty, she told herself. *Never. You work hard, you do well. They might not all like you, but they respect you. If you weaken now, you're finished.*

A picture of her dead lover walked uninvited into her mind's eye. John Gallan. He'd been a good man, a nicer, better person than she could ever be. He'd loved her; he'd said so many times and she'd believed him. John wasn't the sort to lie. Part of her had loved him back, too. Thought that maybe it could come to something. And then he died.

And then he fucking died.

She walked inside the pub, ignoring the slimy look she got from the jaundiced old codger sitting at the bar, and ordered a double gin, no ice, ignoring the voice inside her head that screamed for her not to do it. The decision had been made.

She drank it down in one.

'Bad day?' asked the barman, a gangly teenager with a haystack's worth of red hair.

'Fucking fantastic,' she said, and ordered another.

She put a tenner on the bar and drank the gin slower this time, savouring the fiery taste as the alcohol slipped down her throat. The kick was instantaneous, and she felt the familiar lightheadedness come on, knowing that if she had another, that would be it. There'd be no going back. The work day would be written off. The leads she'd gained, leads that could help save a teenage girl from death, wouldn't emerge until she'd sobered up. Tina wasn't the sort who could work drunk.

She became clumsy and lethargic. Her colleagues would notice it straight away, and her guilty little secret, the one she'd carried for so long, would suddenly be out there for all to see. And she couldn't have that. Tina had her pride. She suffered, but she suffered alone. She didn't want pity, she didn't want help, and right now, she really didn't want to be off this case.

Fuck Leon Daroyce. He wasn't going to beat her. She finished the drink and banged the glass on the bar harder than she'd planned before picking up her change and heading back out into the sunlight.

It was time to get back to work.

Part Four

Part Four

Twenty-two

'I've got authorization for the money,' said Big Barry grimly, looking across his desk at Bolt. 'It wasn't easy. One or two of the top people favoured calling in the negotiators. It took some persuading that not letting on about our involvement was the best course of action. And as you can imagine, no one wanted the responsibility of signing off half a million pounds.'

Bolt nodded. It had just turned four o'clock and he was back in Big Barry's office. Despite the sunny day, the heating was on full blast and the room felt hot and airless. Bolt had an empty feeling in his stomach. He'd tried to eat on the way back to HQ, stopping off at a Pret a Manger to buy a sandwich and a bottle of juice, but two bites and the juice was all he'd managed. The tension running through him made it hard to sit still, let alone concentrate on what Barry was saying.

'If we lose this money,' Barry continued, 'both you and I are going to be in serious trouble. We really can't afford to screw this one up, old mate.'

Bolt nodded again, didn't say anything.

'We'll be providing the bag containing the ransom, and I'm going to have two separate tracking devices sewn into the material where there's absolutely no chance they'll be found. We'll also have two more trackers buried right in among the money, just in case they change bags. Obviously, though, these things aren't foolproof. They can lose their signal. We all know that. So we're going to need major surveillance back-up. I suggest two ground teams. One will follow Mrs Devern, the other will be sent to stake out the rendezvous as soon as the kidnappers confirm where it's going to be, so we have complete coverage of the area and the ransom itself. Then, as a final layer of surveillance, I want a helicopter on standby to take over the pursuit of the money so we make absolutely sure it doesn't disappear on us. Then it's simply a matter of following it to its destination, and that's the moment we bring in the negotiators and try to end things peacefully. The girl gets released, the perpetrators get nicked, and the money lands safely back in our hands.'

He paused, looking pleased with himself.

'What do you think?'

'I think,' said Bolt, trying desperately to be objective, 'that it's very risky.'

Barry looked mildly irritated. He didn't quite roll his eyes but the movement wasn't far off. 'Of course it's risky. This is a professional kidnapping we're dealing with, Mike. It's the type of op that's always risky. It was risky this morning, and you were arguing for it then.'

But this morning there hadn't been the possibility that 'the girl', as Barry had described her so dispassionately, was his daughter. On the way over, Bolt had thought about laying things on the line. Admitting everything. But he'd quickly dismissed this as a bad move. With such a huge personal involvement, Barry would have had no choice but to remove him from the case and there was no way he was going to allow that to happen.

'I've had time to think,' Bolt said. 'These people haven't put a foot wrong so far. If we don't get this exactly right, then they're likely to kill her.'

'Then we get it right,' said Barry firmly.

'You don't think we might be better off bringing in the negotiators? It's possible that if they realize we're on to them, they might cut their losses and let Emma go.'

'And it's also possible that they might not. You said that yourself.'

Bolt exhaled. 'I guess that's true.'

Barry frowned. 'Are you all right, old mate?'

Bolt nodded. 'Yeah, I'm fine.' But he was sweating, and his shirt felt clammy against his skin.

'We've made the decision now,' Barry continued. 'There's no point going back on it. SOCA needs a nice high-profile success. If we get this right – and, make no mistake about it, we will, because we're going to plan it properly – then it's going to look extremely good on the organization, and on us in particular. We don't often get much in the way of praise. Let's make sure we get some this time.'

'OK, but I don't like the idea of the helicopter. The kidnappers get so much as a sniff of it, they're going to panic.'

'We'll keep it well away from whatever rendezvous they choose, don't worry. And it'll only be used as a back-up.'

Bolt wasn't convinced, but he didn't argue. There was no point. Barry had made up his mind about how they were going to play it. In fact, he'd made up his mind before the meeting had even started, which made Bolt feel that his presence was largely irrelevant.

'How's Mrs Devern?' asked Barry.

'She's holding up.'

'Hertfordshire CID still aren't entirely happy with her story.'

Bolt wiped sweat from his forehead with the back of his hand. 'Why not?'

'Well, their officers did find her covered in blood having just left the scene of the violent murder of her former lover.' Barry allowed himself a thin smile. 'You have to admit it's more than a little suspicious.'

Bolt felt like slapping that smile off his boss's face. For the first time in his life he suddenly had an insight into what it must be like to be a victim of crime – the lonely frustration of dealing with officials who were never going to care enough to deal with your plight.

'I'm sure they don't like her story,' he said, trying to keep his voice as calm as possible, 'but her child's definitely been kidnapped. I saw her on the video the kidnappers sent just three hours ago. And the people holding her are definitely after a ransom. So, unless Mrs Devern somehow set this all up herself, and is deliberately putting her daughter through a huge trauma, then we've got to accept that her story's true.'

Barry waited for Bolt to finish. 'I agree with you,' he said eventually, 'but I do get the idea with Mrs Devern that all is not what it seems. I think we need to watch her.'

Bolt nodded. 'Fair point.'

His boss was right. Andrea was a frighteningly enigmatic woman. She was also a manipulator, as Jimmy Galante had found to his cost, and Bolt himself was finding now.

There was a knock on the door, and one of the newer team members, Kris Obanje, a tall, good-looking black man with a fondness for amateur dramatics, appeared.

'There's been a development,' he said with a typical flourish.

Bolt felt his heart race and he clenched his teeth. What the hell kind of development?

'We've just heard back from the phone provider who runs the network Emma Devern and Pat Phelan both use,' he continued, his voice a rich baritone that seemed to resound around the room. 'Phelan's phone was switched off at 4.47 p.m. on Tuesday afternoon in the car park of the dental practice. According to the receptionist, this would have been while Emma was in with the dentist. Emma's own mobile was turned off twelve minutes later at 4.59, a few hundred metres from the surgery, and on the same street. It would have been just after she'd left.'

'That solves the mystery of where they snatched her from, then,' said Barry. 'It must have been in the car park. Shows our kidnappers are willing to take risks.'

'It also shows how technology savvy they are,' said Bolt, 'getting rid of the mobiles straight away.'

'That's the media for you,' snorted Barry. 'They publicize all the ways we can track people. It's no wonder the criminals catch on. We're going to have to interview everyone who was at the surgery that afternoon, see if anyone saw anything.'

'We've also managed to trace the route the car took away from the surgery,' Obanje told them. He unfolded a sheet of A3 paper and laid it on the desk between the two men. It was a photocopied large-scale map of north London, with a curving line of red crosses drawn on it in marker pen running from Hampstead in the south to Barnet and the M25 in the north. 'Here's the surgery,' he said, pointing at the bottom-most cross. 'Here's where Emma's phone was turned off. And here's where they went afterwards.' He traced a finger along the line of crosses, stopping at one in the middle. 'We got a good CCTV shot of Phelan's car here at 5.14.' He unfolded a second piece of paper, this time showing an overhead black and white camera shot of a Range Rover. 'It looks like it might be Phelan driving, and it looks like it might be an adolescent in the seat next to him. We've sent the image over for enhancement. We should have the results back by tomorrow.'

'We're going to have to,' said Bolt, 'because after tomorrow they'll be irrelevant.'

He looked more carefully at the photo as Obanje moved his finger away. The figure in the passenger seat – the girl who might be Bolt's daughter – was a lot smaller than the man next to her, and she had her head turned to one side, making a positive ID impossible. But it was Emma. There was no doubt about that, and he felt a twinge of emotion as he stared at her image.

'If this is Phelan driving, and he's involved in the kidnap, why on earth did he bother taking her to the dentist's first?' demanded Barry.

'Look at this,' said Obanje, producing a third piece of paper. It was another overhead camera shot but this time it was a close-up taken of the rear of the Range Rover. 'This is from another camera on the same street, two minutes later at 5.16. You have to look closely.'

Bolt and Barry both leaned forward so their heads were almost touching. It wasn't difficult to see what Obanje was referring to. There was no mistaking the figure in the back seat, directly behind the driver.

'So there was someone else involved in the initial snatch,' said Barry. 'He gets in the car, presumably at the dental surgery, and either forces Phelan to drive, or it's possible that Phelan's involved, and this gentleman's just helping him.' He turned to Obanje. 'Have we got any better shots than this?'

Obanje shook his head. 'No, this is the best we've got at the moment. And after the car crosses the M25 on the A1 at 5.49, we lose it altogether.

Hendon haven't got a single sighting of it after that.'

'So, Phelan's Range Rover could have been abandoned round here somewhere,' said Bolt, prodding the map near to the final cross.

'Could have been, but it's also possible that if they turned off the A1 and took back roads, they could have driven miles without being picked up by cameras. I'll keep on to Hendon, see if we can come up with any more sightings, but I wouldn't hold out much hope.'

'We'll also have a word with the local police, see if they've got any reports of the car being abandoned on their manor,' Barry said. He turned to Obanje. 'Thanks, Kris. Keep up with the good work.'

'It's coming along,' he said. 'She's a sweet-looking kid. We all want to get her back.' He picked up the papers and left the room, the other two watching him go.

The tightness in Bolt's stomach had eased just a little. If the man in the back of the Range Rover had got in the car in the dentist's car park, then it was possible he might have been seen by a passer-by. It wasn't much, but it represented a chink of hope.

He stood up. He needed to get out of Barry's stifling office. 'I'll get a couple of the team to go down to the surgery,' he said, and went outside.

But he didn't go back to the incident room straight away. Instead, he walked down the empty corridor and into the toilet. He splashed water on his face and stared at himself in the mirror.

He wasn't a bad-looking guy. His hair was still more blond than grey, although turning faster than he'd have liked, and he had a long, lean face with well-defined features and the kind of strong jaw that would stand up in a fight. Even the scars – an S-shaped slash on his chin, two small ragged lumps on his left cheek – added to rather than detracted from his appearance, and their effect was softened by his eyes. 'Laughing eyes' Mikaela used to call them. They were a bright, lively blue, and shone with a friendly and disarming interest.

But today they were duller, more brooding, and Bolt could see that he looked haggard and stressed. All his adult life he'd had to cope with pressure. The pressure of being a young man in uniform policing the streets of modern-day London had given way to the pressure of chasing some of the capital's most dangerous armed robbers during the ten years he'd spent with the Flying Squad. He'd been involved in some extremely dangerous operations, but the difference was that in those days he'd been part of a team, sharing the tension with a group of men and women who knew exactly how he was feeling, their support always providing a measure of comfort. Today he was completely on his own as the investigation into the kidnapping of the girl who could be his daughter went on around him.

He'd been operating pretty much on autopilot all afternoon, constantly turning over the various scenarios in his head, thinking back to those long-ago days when he and Andrea had had their brief and passionate affair, trying to work out whether he really was the father of someone he'd never met, and whose first fourteen years he'd completely missed. Wondering now whether he was ever going to meet her, or whether he'd be the man staring down at her dead, broken body. Every time this last thought took hold, he felt himself wince and his heart pound faster.

He forced himself to concentrate on the task at hand. They desperately needed a break, a single mistake by the kidnappers that would provide them with a clue to their identity, and hopefully their whereabouts. But if no one had seen the kidnapper get into Pat Phelan's Range Rover in the surgery car park, it was looking less and less likely that they were going to get one.

For a long moment, Bolt stood there watching the water drip down his face, listening to the constant drumbeat of his heart, knowing that whatever happened today, his life would never be the same again. 'Pull yourself together,' he whispered. 'She needs you.' And he vowed then and there that if he got Emma out of this, he was going to introduce himself to her, and if he was her father – and Christ knows he might never know for sure – he was going to make her part of his life whether Andrea liked it or not.

But in the meantime, he had to force her out of his mind.

His mobile started to ring. He looked at his watch. Twenty past four. He pulled it from his pocket.

It was Tina calling.

Twenty-three

From the moment the cruel one had run the blade of the knife across her face, smiling behind the balaclava at her fear, Emma knew there was no way he was ever going to let her go.

Afterwards, when he'd turned off the camera, he'd stared at her for a long time with his dead fish eyes. 'I think you're lying, you little bitch. You saw my face, didn't you?' He leaned forward so his face was almost touching hers, and sniffed loudly. 'I can smell the bullshit on you,' he whispered.

She promised him again that she wasn't lying, even sworn on her mum's life. Because it was true, she hadn't really seen anything – only that he had dark hair. But he didn't believe her, and just kept staring until finally she shut her eyes because she couldn't bear to see him looking at her like that any more.

'If you are lying, you little bitch, then you're going to fucking die,' he said as he headed towards the steps.

She shouted again that she wasn't, honestly, that he had to believe her, but he didn't reply and a few seconds later he was gone, locking the basement door behind him.

For a long time afterwards she sat hunched up on the bed, her knees pressed against her chest, too shocked and terrified to move, wondering why he wanted to kill her when it must have been obvious that she was telling the truth. Why did he have to be so cruel? She'd never done anything bad to him. She'd never done anything bad to anyone. Her mum called her a carer, and she was. She looked after people. There was a girl at school, Natalie, who was getting picked on by some of the Year 12 girls, and Emma had stepped in, even squared up to one of them to get them to stop (and they had: they'd backed off, even though they were bigger), because she didn't like people being bullied.

But now none of this counted for anything.

When she realized that this was it, that the cruel one really might kill her, the fear was like nothing she'd ever experienced before, far worse than the previous days when she'd at least had some kind of hope that the nightmare might end with her being reunited with her mum. Now she was sure this wasn't going to be the case. As soon as she was no longer needed, that'd be it. The cruel one would get rid of her, and there'd be nothing she could do about it, because she was totally helpless down here.

She wondered how they were going to do it. With a gun, or a pillow over her head? Or maybe with that knife of his? She couldn't bear that. To be stabbed to death. It would be slow, horrible, and there'd be blood everywhere. She couldn't bear the idea of her mum having to identify her in some morgue somewhere when they finally discovered her body. If they ever did find it, of course. She might end up missing for ever, like one of those kids who disappear and are never heard from again. If they had to do it, she hoped they'd give her pills so she could just go to sleep, and that would be the end of everything. It would be awful, and she'd miss her mum and her friends, and even her teachers – well, a couple of them – but at least it would be painless.

But she didn't want to die. God, she didn't. And just thinking about it made her cry again.

And then, as she sat there all alone, something within her changed. She realized that she couldn't just lie there weeping. She had to do something, anything. There was a topic they'd covered in history when she was in Year 9. It was about British prisoners in Germany during the Second

World War and how they were always trying to escape. How often they weren't successful, and got punished for it, but how they kept on trying, and some – quite a few – even managed it.

It was hard, but once the thought of escape was in her head, she got this weird burst of hope. She stood up and tugged frantically at her handcuffs. In the days since they were first put on she'd lost weight, and with a lot of effort she was able to pull the cuff a half inch or so up over her left hand. It wasn't nearly enough to release her, but at least it was a start. Another half inch and she'd be in with a chance. She decided not to eat again. It would make her feel sick and weak, but it had to be worth a try.

Then she pulled at the chain attached to her ankle, trying to yank it free from the wall. It didn't budge the first few times, but then she gave it a huge tug, leaning back and putting all her weight into it as if she was doing a tug of war, and she was sure she heard something give. The metal plate attaching the chain to the wall was brand new and had obviously been put there just for her, but it felt very slightly loose in her hands, and because the wall itself was so old, she felt sure she could get it out somehow. It would still leave her handcuffed, and trailing a chain, but at least she'd be mobile.

She started scraping at the brickwork round the

plate with her fingernails, breaking most of them in the process. Some flakes came away, but the plate didn't get any looser. She needed a tool of some kind, so she scoured the floor all over, hunting in every nook and cranny, until she found an old rusty nail in the corner just beneath the bed frame. Slowly, carefully, she began cutting away at the brickwork with the nail, methodically chipping away at it. It was a slow, painful job, but every time more brick dust fell to the floor she knew she was getting that little bit closer.

She just had to keep praying she had enough time.

Twenty-four

'So, Pat Phelan might be in the frame after all?' said Mo Khan as he and Bolt drove to Andrea's house.

'Well, he's certainly got a motive. He owes a lot of money to a very dangerous man who's likely to use some pretty extreme violence to get it back. He also called that man two days before the kidnapping to ask him for a few more days to get the money he owed him. That's a pretty big co-incidence if he wasn't involved, isn't it?'

Mo nodded. 'And he's not exactly the most upstanding citizen. A layabout and petty criminal who's sleeping with his wife's business partner. The problem is, it doesn't lead us to Emma, and if Phelan is involved, and she knows he's involved, he's not going to want to let her go.'

'I don't know,' said Bolt slowly. 'I would hope that it would mean he's less likely to hurt her because of the personal relationship they have.'

'That's assuming he's got a conscience. Anyone who can kidnap their own stepdaughter and put her through a living hell that's going to scar her for life just to pay off a gambling debt is capable of most things in my book.'

Bolt's fingers tightened on the steering wheel. 'But what I still can't work out is that if he is involved, why did he disappear too? Why not set everything up, make sure he's got an alibi for the time Emma's snatched, and simply stay behind and act innocent, advise Andrea not to go to the police, and wait for his money? Why implicate yourself?'

Mo shrugged. 'Maybe he's stupid.'

Bolt shook his head. 'No, one thing we do know for sure is the people behind this aren't stupid.'

The reason they were going to Andrea's house was to talk to her about these latest developments. Bolt had spoken on the phone to Tina Boyd for more than fifteen minutes and had been impressed by her detective work in uncovering the leads, but also concerned that she'd been abducted from the street and threatened by Leon Daroyce. Bolt was unfamiliar with the name, but a quick check on the PNC had revealed Daroyce as an unpleasant thug with several convictions for violence. He'd also been charged with a number of offences over the years, including extortion and, more ominously, attempted murder, all of which had ended up being dropped as witnesses retracted their statements, refused to testify, or in one case simply disappeared. Clearly he was a dangerous man.

But Tina hadn't sounded unduly distressed. If anything, she'd sounded excited, which wasn't like her. The thing with Tina was that she tended to keep her emotions in check, and usually exhibited a businesslike calm that her colleagues occasionally found disconcerting. He'd offered her the rest of the day off, knowing that however brave a face she put on it she was still going to be shocked by what had happened, but knowing too that she'd refuse the offer, which of course she had. Tina Boyd wasn't the type who liked being treated with kid gloves, something that Bolt had always admired about her, and he'd told her to return to the Glasshouse and help out there.

Bolt was finding it increasingly hard to concentrate on anything but Emma's whereabouts and he knew he looked under stress. His fingers were glued to the steering wheel, and twice Mo had asked him whether everything was OK. He'd replied that he was fine, just tired, which wasn't an uncommon occurrence on his team. They regularly did sixty-, even seventy-hour weeks when they were on a job, but he'd felt bad not saying something to Mo about his plight. They were good friends who knew each other well. But Bolt was well aware that the moment he opened his mouth he'd put his colleague in an impossible situation. He'd done that once before, and had sworn then that he wouldn't risk their friendship a second time.

It had just turned twenty to six when they pulled up outside Andrea's house, having called through to the surveillance team to announce their arrival. Not surprisingly, the team leader reported that there'd been no suspicious activity in the street all day. The kidnappers, it seemed, were continuing to keep a low profile.

Bolt pressed the buzzer on the security gate, and they were let through without preamble. The garden looked even prettier in the dappled late-afternoon sunshine as he and Mo walked towards the front door. It opened and Andrea appeared, dressed in a white LA Fitness T-shirt and ill-fitting trackpants. She'd removed her make-up, and looked older. Her eyes were red, and there'd been recent tears.

'Any news?' she asked.

'I'm afraid not,' answered Bolt as she moved aside to let them in, 'but we've got a few questions we need to ask you.'

Matt Turner and Marie Cohen, the liaison officer, were in the hallway and Bolt nodded to them both as Andrea led them through to her living room. She took a seat on a long leather sofa while Bolt and Mo sat down in armchairs opposite her.

Marie leaned round the door and asked if anyone fancied a cup of tea. Bolt declined. Mo and Andrea both asked for coffee.

'What do you want to know?' she asked, lighting a cigarette with shaking hands and blowing out a line of pale blue smoke.

Bolt wasn't looking forward to this. It felt akin to kicking her when she was already down.

'We've heard from very reliable sources that Mr Phelan has a very large gambling debt. Did you know anything about that?'

She looked genuinely shocked. 'Are you sure? How big?'

'We believe it's tens of thousands of pounds.'

'Oh God, no. He's been staying out late quite a bit, but I had no idea he was gambling. What's he been betting on?'

'He's been losing it in a casino, but the point is, he owes a lot of money to some very nasty people.'

'Have you ever heard the name Leon Daroyce, Mrs Devern?' asked Mo, speaking for the first time.

She shook her head. 'Is he the person Pat owes the money to? Do you think he's the one who snatched Emma?'

'It's possible,' Bolt conceded. 'We don't know for certain. We think it might be that Mr Daroyce is currently looking for your husband to get the money he's owed.'

Andrea took another urgent drag on the cigarette. 'But surely he's the one with the motive. Are you not going to arrest him? Do something?'

'Mr Daroyce and his people are currently under surveillance, so if they are involved, we'll know about it very quickly.' Bolt paused. 'But our source tells us that your husband phoned Daroyce last Sunday night, saying he was going to get him his money in the next few days. That was only two days before the kidnapping.'

'So you're saying he is involved?' she asked, her voice cracking.

'We have to face up to the possibility that he is, yes.'

'He wouldn't do this, you know. He really cares for her.'

The room fell silent. Bolt leaned forward in his seat.

'What we keep coming back to, Andrea, is that if your husband wasn't a part of this conspiracy, how did the kidnappers know his and Emma's movements? We think the abduction happened in the car park of the dental surgery where Emma had her appointment.'

Andrea's eyes filled with tears. 'Don't use that

word, abduction. It makes it seem, I don't know, like some paedophile snatched her and she's not coming back.'

'I'm sorry. Snatched. But the point is, the kidnappers knew she was going to be there. And we need to know how.'

Marie came back into the room with the coffee for Mo and Andrea. Andrea waved hers away.

'Who's got access to this house, Mrs Devern?' asked Mo, taking his coffee and thanking Marie. 'And who knows the code to your burglar alarm, aside from you, Mr Phelan and your daughter?'

'No one except the cleaner, and she's been doing the house for years.'

As Mo took down the cleaner's details, Bolt's mobile rang. It was the surveillance team leader. Bolt excused himself and walked to the other side of the room out of earshot.

'We've got an IC1 female stopping at Mrs Devern's security gate. Black hair, early forties. She'll be ringing the bell any moment now.'

The buzzer sounded in the hallway, and Matt Turner poked his head round the living-room door.

'Are we expecting anyone?' Bolt asked him.

'Not that I'm aware of.'

'OK, ignore it, then. Let's hope they go away.'

A few seconds later the buzzer sounded again, longer this time.

'Oh shit,' said the surveillance team leader down the phone.

'What is it?'

'She's unlocking the gate, and now she's coming through.'

Bolt cursed. This was the problem with operating out of a private address. He hung up as the key turned in the lock and the front door opened.

'Andrea?' came a woman's voice, followed immediately by an accusatory 'Who are you?' as she saw Turner.

'It's all right, Isobel, I'm in here,' Andrea called out, getting to her feet quickly. 'It's my business partner,' she added by way of explanation.

Bolt and Mo exchanged glances as Isobel Wheeler, the other half of Feminine Touch Health and Beauty Spas, came into view. She was a striking woman in her mid-forties whose shoulder-length black hair and olive skin suggested eastern Mediterranean parentage. She was wearing a short black dress that finished halfway down her thigh, and which Bolt thought would have suited a slightly younger woman, and black high-heeled court shoes. She didn't do a lot for Bolt, but he could see why some men might go for her.

Isobel and Andrea greeted each other with a kiss on both cheeks.

'I came to see whether you were feeling any better,' Isobel said, breaking away and surveying the room with a cool confidence that was only a hair's breadth short of arrogance. 'What's going on? Who are all these people?'

Bolt opened his mouth to reply but Andrea beat him to it. 'Pat's gone missing,' she said worriedly. 'I haven't seen him for days.'

Isobel looked shocked. 'Is that why you haven't been in this week? You weren't ill, then?'

Andrea shook her head. 'No. I've been waiting for him to come home, and he hasn't. The police are looking for him.'

'What do you think's happened? Did you have an argument or something?' There was something accusatory in Isobel's tone.

'No, it wasn't like that. He just didn't come home one night. I don't know what's happened.'

Isobel turned to Bolt. 'Why aren't you out there looking for him?'

'I don't believe we've been introduced,' he said coolly. 'You are?'

'Isobel Wheeler,' she snapped. 'Why aren't you looking for him?'

Bolt didn't like this woman at all, but knew better than to react to her rudeness.

'We are looking for him,' he explained calmly, 'but unfortunately there's no law against a man

250

leaving his house, even for an extended period of time, and at the moment there's no suggestion of foul play.'

'Pat wouldn't just walk out,' she said firmly.

'You know him well, do you?'

'I know him well enough,' she said curtly before turning back to Andrea. 'And you can't think where he might be, Andi?'

Once again, Andrea shook her head. 'I've tried everywhere. I've got no idea where he is, or why he went.'

Bolt was impressed by the way she was holding up, but he also found the smooth and natural manner in which she lied unnerving.

Isobel stared at Andrea for a couple of seconds, then leaned forward and gave her a hug.

'Do you want me to stay here with you?' she asked.

'I'll be all right, I promise.'

'Keep me posted of progress, OK?'

'Of course I will.'

'And don't worry about anything at work; it's all being sorted.'

Andrea managed a weak smile. 'Thanks, Iz. I appreciate it.'

'Now, if you'll excuse us, Miss Wheeler,' said Bolt, 'there are details we need to take down from Mrs Devern.'

Isobel nodded brusquely. 'Call me,' she told

Andrea, then pushed past Turner and walked back out into the hallway.

Bolt followed her out and opened the front door for her.

'Have you any idea what's happened to him?' Isobel whispered as she stepped past him on to the steps. 'I mean, really? Because four police officers seems an awful lot to come round to take a missing person's details.'

Bolt shook his head. 'No, we haven't, I'm afraid.'

She gestured in the direction of the living room. 'Watch her,' she said, but before Bolt could ask her to elaborate she'd turned and walked away down the garden path.

Bolt watched her go, wondering what she meant. And wondering too why at no point had she asked where Emma was.

Twenty-five

'I thought you said only the cleaner had access to the house, Mrs Devern,' said Mo as Bolt re-entered the living room.

Andrea was back on the sofa, looking flustered. 'Sorry, I forgot that I'd given a key to Isobel. It was last year. I asked her to check the place while we were on holiday.'

'And there's definitely no one else we should know about?'

She shook her head firmly. 'Definitely not.'

Bolt thought of what Isobel had said on the doorstep.

'Do the two of you get on well?' he asked.

Andrea nodded. 'Well enough. She's my business partner. I've known her for years.' Then her expression changed. 'You're not saying she's got something to do with this as well, are you? First you accuse Pat—'

'No, no,' he said hastily, 'of course not. But we don't think this is a random act. If your husband wasn't involved, we still need to know how the people targeting you knew your movements, and one of the ways would be by bugging your house.'

'But you said you found no bugs.'

'There were none when we looked this morning, but if someone other than you had access, they could have removed any listening devices.'

'Jesus, this is ridiculous. Isobel's a lawyer, not something out of MI5. What would she gain by any of this?'

'We're just trying to cover every angle, that's all,' he said, knowing that if he told her about Isobel's affair with her husband it would probably prove the last straw.

Andrea reached over to the coffee table and picked up her cigarettes again, taking one out of the pack and lighting it.

'Mike,' she said, looking him squarely in the eye, 'is there something you're not telling me?'

The question caught him off guard, as did the fact that she'd called him by his first name again in Mo's presence. Bolt had to consciously resist looking at him.

'No,' he said, shaking his head. 'As I say, these are just routine enquiries.'

As he spoke, he caught sight of an old framed photo of Emma on top of an antique chest of drawers in the corner next to the French windows – a smiling child's face staring at him from an odd angle. For a second he couldn't drag his gaze away, and he felt a bead of sweat run down his temple.

Andrea stood up. 'Well, if you haven't got any other questions, I'd like to lie down for a while.'

He nodded. 'Of course. Matt and Marie will stay here with you.'

She left the room, and Bolt wiped the bead of sweat from his brow. It had been a long day, and he knew that tomorrow was going to be an even longer one. There wasn't much more they could do, so, having instructed Turner and Marie to keep a close eye on Andrea, and promising Turner that he'd be relieved later, he and Mo said their goodbyes and went outside.

Bolt felt a surge of relief to be away from the pictures of Emma. It was torture looking at them.

'I still get the feeling Mrs Devern's not telling us everything,' said Mo as they walked back to the car.

'Shit, Mo,' Bolt snapped, 'her daughter's missing. She's going to tell us everything she can to get her back, isn't she?'

He stopped by the car and took a deep breath, surprised by the anger in his tone. Mo looked taken aback.

Bolt sighed. 'Sorry, I shouldn't have said it like that. It's just, you know ... I don't think she's going to be holding anything back.'

They got into the car in silence. Bolt took another deep breath. The pressure was getting to him. The knowledge that he might lose the only child he'd ever had, and before he'd even met her, was affecting every step he took, and he was beginning to doubt his ability to handle it.

'What is it, boss? What's wrong with you?'

Bolt avoided Mo's concerned gaze. 'Nothing. I'm fine.' It was his stock response, and it sounded utterly hollow. He couldn't even bring himself to instil any meaning into it.

'No, you're not. This isn't like you. I've worked with you, how long now? Four years, five? You never let things get to you. Not like this. You care, but not so much it brings you right down. And you're down now. You haven't been right all day.'

There was a long pause. Bolt sat there with the key in his hand, inches from the ignition, unmoving.

'Come on, tell me,' said Mo eventually, his voice quiet. 'We've shared things in the past.'

'I know.'

'Important things. Things that no one else knows.'

'I know.'

'So, talk to me now.'

In that moment, Bolt knew that the dam had to give, whatever the consequences. He put the key in the ignition but made no move to start the car.

'I had an affair with Andrea Devern fifteen years ago.'

'I thought there was something between the two of you. Back at the house—'

'There's more.'

Mo didn't say anything for a moment, then it seemed to click.

'Oh shit, boss. You're not saying that . . . that Emma's something to do with you?'

'It looks that way.'

He told Mo what Andrea had told him earlier.

'How do you know Mrs Devern, Andrea, isn't bullshitting you?' Mo asked when Bolt had finished. 'Especially as that's exactly what she told Jimmy Galante as well.'

Bolt sighed. 'I don't know, Mo, but the dates fit. I checked them.'

'But she was seeing Galante at the same time, right?'

'That's right. And she was married too.'

'Well, she certainly got around,' Mo said, a hint of disapproval in his voice.

'I don't know what to do. It's ripping me to shreds.'

'Chances are she isn't yours, boss. That's the way you've got to look at it. No offence, but if she was married, seeing another man, and seeing you, it's likely there were others as well.'

'But if it's true . . .'

'If it's true . . .' Mo paused, thinking. Choosing his words carefully. 'Then we've got to make sure we bring her back.'

Bolt ran a hand across his face, the fingers finding the scars on his left cheek. He rubbed hard at the shallow divots in his flesh.

'You saw what those bastards did to Galante. They're not going to let her go, are they?'

'You've got to have faith, boss.'

'Faith in what, Mo? Faith in what?'

'If you haven't got faith in God, and I know that you haven't, then at least have faith in our abilities. We've got out of tight corners before.'

'It's a lot easier said than done, Mo. It really is.'

'I know.'

'Do you?'

'I've got four children, boss. Believe me, I know.'

They were silent again. Bolt felt the tension flowing through his veins, tightening every muscle in his body.

'You know,' said Mo eventually, staring out of the window, 'there's a village in India, somewhere along the Ganges, where they consider cobras sacred. It means they're not allowed to harm them, and because of that, the whole village is teeming with them. In schools; in people's kitchens; in kids' bedrooms; all over the place. But no one takes a blind bit of notice because they're convinced they're not going to get bitten. And, you know, even when one of the villagers is bitten, they think it's a mistake on the cobra's part, and that the poison won't have any long-lasting effect because they worship it. Now, cobra venom can kill if it's not treated. That's a medical fact. But do you know what? In that village there's not one recorded incident of anyone dying of a snake bite. Like I said, boss, you've got to have faith. It'll be OK.'

They looked at each other, and Bolt was impressed by the determination in the other man's expression. It made him feel a little better, glad that he had shared his feelings. He was also surprised by the fact that Mo hadn't suggested he say something to Barry Freud. Mo was his friend, but he was also a professional, and he would know that he was taking a risk by keeping his boss's relationship with both the kidnap victim and her mother silent.

'Not a word about this, OK?' Bolt told him. 'It won't affect how I run this op, I promise.'

Mo nodded. 'OK, boss, but only as long as it doesn't. If it looks like the pressure's getting too much . . .'

'It won't. I promise.'

'But if it does, I'm going to have to say something. You understand that, don't you?'

'Yeah, I understand that.'

Bolt started to turn the key in the ignition, but Mo's next words stopped him dead.

'You were in the Flying Squad when you were seeing Andrea, weren't you?'

Although there was nothing accusatory in the tone, the meaning was clear. The Flying Squad dealt with armed robberies. The woman Bolt had been having an affair with was also sleeping with an armed robber. The potential for corruption was obvious, and it wasn't as if the Flying Squad hadn't had its fair share of corruption problems in the past. Bolt wasn't offended, but it hurt him that his friend had felt the need to ask the question.

'As soon as I found out she was seeing Galante, I finished it,' he said firmly.

'Good. That's all I wanted to know.'

There was another awkward silence. Bolt had crossed the line with Mo once before, two years earlier, and the implicit trust that had always existed between them had come under a lot of strain. It felt like something similar was happening again.

'Come on,' he said, starting the engine, 'let's go.'

Twenty-six

Home for Mike Bolt was a spacious studio apartment on the third floor of a converted warehouse in Clerkenwell, one of the quietest places in central London, and not far from where he'd first been based as a uniformed cop. He'd been there for four years now, having moved in the year after his wife's death, and ordinarily he'd never have been able to afford a place one quarter of the size on his SOCA salary, but the rent he paid was minimal. The reason for this was that it belonged to a wealthy Ukrainian businessman, Ivan Stanevic, whom Bolt had helped out years before in his National Crime Squad days.

The case was remarkably similar to the one he was involved in now. Stanevic's twelve-year-old daughter Olga had been abducted from the street by business rivals of her father's, and Bolt had led the team tasked with getting her back. On that occasion it hadn't taken long to find out who they were dealing with and consequently where Olga was being held. It was Bolt who'd personally negotiated her release with the kidnappers, and she'd been freed unharmed, for which her father had been eternally grateful. It was the only other kidnap case he'd ever been involved with, and the grim irony wasn't lost on him as he stepped inside his apartment and shut the door behind him.

Usually he loved this place. It was hard not to love it since it had been refurbished with absolutely no expense spared. The floors were polished teak; the high, angular ceiling was criss-crossed with mighty timber beams carefully restored to their former glory; but the *pièce de résistance* was the way the old windows had been knocked out and replaced by a huge strip of floor-to-ceiling tinted glass that ran the entire length of one side of the apartment, facing east out on to the bright lights of London, with the high towers of the Barbican rising up behind the buildings opposite. Only the night before he'd sat in his armchair with a glass of 2005 Côtes du Rhône staring out across the city while an old Herbie Hancock CD played on the stereo, feeling quietly satisfied that the money-laundering case had been brought to a successful conclusion, and looking forward to a weekend away with Jenny Byfleet. The world then had seemed a good, decent place, and for the first time in a while he'd actually felt contented. And all the time the clock was counting down to when it would all go suddenly and horribly wrong. Just like it had that night five years ago when he and Mikaela waved goodbye to the friends they'd spent the evening with, got into his car and driven off to their doom.

It had just turned eight o'clock as Bolt kicked off his shoes and poured the remainder of the previous night's Côtes du Rhône into an oversized wine glass, taking a big slug and trying hard to relax. He'd phoned Jenny on the way home and, trying to sound as casual as possible, had apologized for the fact that he was going to have to postpone. She'd asked if he wanted to rearrange, and he'd said he'd get back to her, hearing her disappointment down the other end of the line as he'd hung up. That was probably it for the two of them, but he was past caring about that. All he could think about was the case, about how Andrea had come back into his life and, even after all these years, managed once again to turn everything upside down for him.

He sat down in his armchair, but almost immediately stood up again. It didn't feel right resting his legs. Not with his mind going like the clappers. Instead he paced the room, thinking about what Mo had said about Andrea not being entirely truthful, and holding something back. He remembered Isobel Wheeler's words: *Watch her*. And most of all he thought back to his own experience with Andrea, and of how one night fifteen years ago, a mere eight weeks into their relationship, she'd dropped such a bombshell that it had ended everything between them with a bang that echoed even now.

He recalled the night perfectly. It was in the days when mobile phones were still the size of house bricks, and long before Bolt had taken to carrying one as a matter of course. He'd arrived home after a few drinks with a couple of Flying Squad buddies to find that he had a message from Andrea on his answerphone, asking him to call her urgently if he received the message before 10.30, giving him a number he didn't recognize, and adding that under no circumstances was he to call the number after that time. If she didn't hear from him before then, she'd call back later when she got a chance. The message had been left at twenty to ten, just fifteen minutes earlier, and Andrea had sounded uncharacteristically scared. He'd called her back immediately, and she'd picked up on the first ring, obviously waiting for the call.

'Mike, thank God you've called. I don't know how to tell you this.'

'Whatever it is, you can talk to me about it, OK? I can help.'

She took a deep breath and spoke quietly. 'There's going to be an armed robbery. Tomorrow morning, between ten and ten thirty. A police van carrying a load of cocaine for incineration from Lewisham Nick to Orpington.'

The shock of her announcement left Bolt cold.

'How do you know about this, Andrea?' he asked.

'I just do,' she said unconvincingly.

'You're going to have to do better than that. I need details. Like where you got the information.'

There was a silence at the other end of the line.

'Andrea, I can't go to my bosses and get authorization to do anything about this until I know more.'

This wasn't entirely true. He could have done if he really wanted to, but the most important thing was to find out how the woman he, a Flying Squad officer, had been seeing for the past two months had details of exactly the kind of major crime he specialized in investigating.

'I've been seeing a guy,' she said. 'His name's Jimmy Galante.'

'While you've been seeing me?' he asked, knowing the answer already.

'Yes.' Pause. 'I'm sorry, Mike. I've been seeing him a while. Since before you.'

He resisted the urge to shout at her, even though he wanted to. Instead, he listened while she continued, telling him how she'd always known that Jimmy was a bit dodgy and operated on the wrong side of the law, but hadn't ever realized the extent of his misdemeanours. Until that evening, when she'd been at his place and overheard a conversation he'd had on the phone in which he'd discussed the robbery with a fellow conspirator. 'He was in the other room, and thought I couldn't hear him, but he's been jumpy all day so when the phone rang I listened at the wall and heard everything he said. When he came back in the bedroom, I was in bed, so he didn't suspect a thing. Then he said he had to go out, and he'd be back about half ten.'

To this day, Bolt remembered how gutted he felt when she told him about getting back into another man's bed, how he'd got that wrenching feeling in his stomach as if someone was tying it in knots. He hadn't seen Andrea for close to a week because she'd said she'd been so busy, and all the time she was fucking some lowlife robber.

'So, you're at his place now?' he said.

'Yeah. I'm meant to be staying tonight. Billy's away on business.'

Bolt sighed. 'And you're absolutely sure about this?'

'Positive. I'd bet my life on it.'

'So why are you telling me this now?'

'Isn't it obvious?'

'Not really, no. I'm surprised you're so keen to shop your . . . your boyfriend.'

'I'm scared of him, Mike. I've been wanting to finish it for a while, but he's not the sort to take no for an answer. He even threatened to hurt Billy if I left him.'

'Tell me something. When you met me, was it a coincidence, or did you plan it?'

'Course I didn't plan it. How could I have done that?'

Bolt was silent. He wanted to believe her, but even though he was a lot younger then, he wasn't entirely naive. Something didn't feel right with her story. But she was giving him a tip, and he felt duty bound to act.

'Do you know where they're meeting up to do this robbery?'

'No. I've given you all the details I know.'

'If we try to stop them, and they're armed, you know what might happen, don't you? Your boyfriend, the guys he's with . . . They might end up getting shot.'

Andrea said that she understood. 'He's the one going out there with a gun,' were her exact words.

And that had been that. The next day the Flying Squad had hastily set up an ambush, following the police van and its cargo of more than a hundred kilos of cocaine, which was being driven by their officers, on its journey from Lewisham police station to an incinerator in Orpington. Sure enough, the robbers made their move, boxing the van in on a busy dual carriageway and forcing it to a halt before appearing, balaclava-clad, weapons in hand. Such was their speed and brazenness that they caught the Flying Squad team off guard, but only for a couple of seconds.

The Flying Squad ambush ethos is surprise, aggression and overwhelming force. As their own cars roared on to the scene, forming a loose cordon around the van and the robbers' vehicles, and disgorged their screaming officers, the back of the security van flew open and more gun-wielding cops leapt out. The shouts of 'Armed police, drop your weapons!' filled the air and Bolt felt an adrenalin kick like he'd never felt before as he stood, legs apart, Colt revolver held two-handed in front of him.

Which was the moment it all went wrong.

There were four robbers with guns outside the car, two more – the drivers – inside. One of them opened fire and a Flying Squad guy called Hammond, who was thirty-one and just cel-ebrating the birth of his child, got hit in the shoulder. Passers-by dived for cover as another of the robbers raised his shotgun, but this time he never got the chance to pull the trigger. Bolt and the guy standing next to him both opened fire, hitting the robber a grand total of four times. Dean Hayes was twenty-five, only months older than Bolt, with a criminal record stretching back into his mid-teens. He died three hours later on the operating table. Only one of the bullets was fatal. It had pierced his heart. A later PCC investigation revealed that it was Bolt who'd fired it.

The cops from the back of the security van grabbed another of the robbers and slammed him to the tarmac with guns in his back, while the fourth robber got off a wild shot before taking a bullet in the shoulder that sent him sprawling. But the first robber, the one who'd shot Hammond, had managed to scramble into the back of one of the getaway cars, a powerful Sierra Cosworth, whose driver then reversed suddenly, knocking down one of the advancing cops and breaking his hipbone. It then smashed into the Flying Squad car that was blocking it in, pushing it into the central reservation and narrowly missing Bolt in the process, before accelerating through the narrow gap it had created.

Several of Bolt's team had been carrying pickaxe handles, and one of them managed to smash the driver's side window as the getaway car passed, showering the driver with glass, and another threw his into the windscreen; but, faced with no direct threat to their lives, they were unable to shoot at the occupants. Bolt remembered being cool-headed enough, even after shooting a person for the first time, to take aim at the Cosworth's tyres, but the car had taken off at such a speed that it was thirty metres away before he had a chance to fire, and with civilians everywhere he knew it would be too dangerous to pull the trigger again.

Police patrol cars from Lewisham station had descended rapidly on the scene and there was a high-speed chase which ended only minutes later when the Cosworth crashed into a parked van. The driver, a well-known face in the criminal fraternity, was captured, but the gunman was nowhere to be seen, having fled the vehicle on foot, still wearing his balaclava.

With the other five gang members accounted for, it soon became clear that none of them was the mysterious Jimmy Galante, a man who at that time had never shown up on the Flying Squad radar. An arrest warrant was hastily put together, and at four a.m. the following morning a Flying Squad team that included Bolt had raided his flat, finding him apparently asleep. Bolt had half expected to find Andrea there still, having not heard from her the previous day, but it turned out Galante was alone, and remarkably unfazed at being prematurely woken from his slumber by half a dozen men in black, all shouting and pointing guns at him.

Galante was a cocky bastard from the start. Even if he hadn't been sleeping with the woman Bolt had fallen in love with, he would have hated him anyway. It just made it worse that he was a criminal, and a good-looking one at that. But his cockiness was justified. Although he had several cuts to his head and bruised ribs, strongly suggesting that he'd been involved in the Cosworth's crash, he'd denied involvement in any robbery and produced a cast-iron alibi for his whereabouts at the time (a café in Islington where he'd apparently been seen by at least half a dozen witnesses, including the owner). Worse, there was no sign of the clothes he'd been wearing, or any firearms residue on his hands. Everyone knew that he could have removed this simply by washing them thoroughly, but there was nothing they could do about it, and because none of the surviving robbers fingered him, Galante wasn't even charged with, let alone convicted of, any offence.

Bolt burned with the intense frustration any police officer feels when a criminal he or she knows is guilty gets off through lack of evidence; the fact that he'd shot one of Bolt's colleagues made it almost unbearable. But bear it he had to, and shortly afterwards Galante disappeared off the scene, moving to Spain, away from the watchful eyes of a vengeful Flying Squad.

Bolt had never heard from Andrea again after that. He'd tried to make contact with her several times but she hadn't returned his calls, and he'd been forced to accept that their relationship was over. But for him, personally, it had been a coup. His information had led to a huge result for the Flying Squad, marred only by wounding and injury to two of their own, and the fact that he'd shot dead one of the gang only increased his kudos among his colleagues. There'd been no repercussions from the PCC – his shooting of Hayes was considered totally justified – and although he'd been asked on several occasions to name the source who'd told him about the robbery, he'd always claimed that it was an informant, and gave no further details. Because the op had been a success, no one had ever pushed him on it.

He continued to pace the room. Continued to think. Always about Andrea. How her information had foiled a major robbery and put a lot of very nasty people out of business, at least one permanently. How she seemed to have turned her life around so formidably in the years since. And how she could have made some serious enemies along the way.

He stopped pacing and put down his wine on

the marble kitchen top. He had an idea, and for the first time in the last few hours he felt a twinge of hope, coupled with something approaching excitement.

Pulling the mobile from his pocket, he dialled a number he hadn't called in far too long.

Twenty-seven

Emma dug away in the gloom with the rusty nail, trying to shut the constant fear out of her mind, forcing herself to concentrate totally on what she was doing. It had been dark for over an hour now but still she kept going, even though every part of her body seemed to ache with the effort. It was a slow, painful job, but she was getting somewhere. She'd created a gap of almost a quarter of an inch between the wall and the plate on the left-hand side, enough almost to get a finger underneath, and when she tugged at the chain it definitely felt looser. If she could just keep at it, eventually it was going to come free. She was sure of it. But God, it was hard.

She heard a noise upstairs – footsteps. She froze. If they saw what she was doing, they'd punish her. The cruel one might even decide that keeping her alive was now too risky, that it was time to get rid of her altogether.

She jumped up, lifted the bed, straining with the effort, and pushed it back against the wall, trying to be as quiet as possible but unable to stop it from scraping loudly on the stone floor.

Please don't let them hear it.

Gritting her teeth, she lay back on the bed, put the nail under her pillow, and reached for the hood.

The footsteps stopped. Was one of them outside the door?

She put on the hood and closed her eyes, hardly daring to breathe, terrified that this might be it. The last few seconds of her life. Had all her efforts of the last few hours been wasted?

But the door didn't open.

Five minutes passed. Then ten.

She lay there in the darkness, her heart going faster and faster, cold beads of sweat running down her forehead as she listened as hard as she could for any sound in the room, knowing that the cruel one always liked to creep up on her.

But she could hear nothing. Only silence. And eventually she plucked up the courage to remove the hood and look around. But the room was empty.

So, he wasn't coming for her tonight.

But she couldn't help thinking it was just a stay of execution.

Twenty-eight

In the old days, everyone in the Flying Squad had had a nickname. Bolt's, not altogether surprisingly, was Nuts, while Jack Doyle, the man he was going to meet, had been known as Dodger. Although he was five years older, Doyle had probably been Bolt's best mate in the squad. He was also the most accident-prone guy Bolt had ever known.

Doyle's long litany of injuries was legendary: three months in traction after falling off a ladder trying to retrieve a football from his roof; a rare and potentially deadly blood infection when he'd stepped on a fishbone on the first day of his honeymoon; and in the most bizarre instance of all, a month off sick with concussion after a pool tournament during which a wildly mishit cueball flew off the table, hit him in the temple and knocked him spark out. Somehow his injuries always coincided with times when the squad were in action, hence the nickname, and it irritated him hugely because he'd always been one of its hardest members, and as a highly successful former amateur boxer was not afraid of a fight. He simply considered himself unlucky.

Jack (Bolt had never called him Dodger) was one of the few of the old team still left at Finchley. He'd moved up the ranks and was now a DI. His experience, coupled with a near photographic memory, meant that if there was ever anyone who could provide Bolt with the information he needed, it was him. Although they'd kept in touch over the years, and still did the occasional fishing weekend away, it had been months since they'd last spoken. Even so, as soon as Bolt explained that he needed to meet up with him urgently, Doyle hadn't hesitated, and told him to name the time and place.

And so it was that barely an hour after arriving home Bolt walked in through the door of the King's Arms, a busy, old-fashioned drinkers' pub just off the King's Cross end of the Gray's Inn Road. He had to look around for a few seconds, pushing his way through the buzzing crowd of drinkers, before he saw Doyle sitting in a booth in the corner, two pints of lager set out on the table in front of him.

Doyle stood up as Bolt approached and they shook hands. As always, the other man's grip was vice-like. With his jutting, granite jaw and square-shaped head, topped with thick black hair, Jack Doyle bore a strong resemblance to a *Thunderbirds* puppet – not that it was advisable to tell him that. He wasn't a particularly big man – no more than five nine, and of slim build – but the look was deceptive. He was all sinewy muscle, and even now, in his mid-forties, there wasn't an ounce of fat on him.

'How are you, Mike?' he asked in a thick Glasgow accent that hadn't mellowed, even after more than a quarter of a century down south. He gestured at one of the pints. 'I got you one in.'

Bolt smiled as they sat down opposite each other.

'Thanks, Jack, I'm all right,' he said, determined not to show the turmoil he was going through. 'You?'

'Not bad,' said the other man wearily. 'Counting the days until retirement.'

They clinked glasses.

'What is it you've got left now? Five years?'

'Four. And I tell you, pal, I can't bloody wait. How's life at SOCA?'

Bolt took a gulp of his beer. It tasted good.

'Busy,' he answered. 'That's why I need your

help. You remember the Lewisham robbery, back in ninety-two? The police van carrying the coke for incineration?'

'How could I forget? It's the one where you made your spurs. Took out that toe rag Dean Hayes.'

Bolt nodded. 'That's the one.' He'd never been proud of the fact that he'd killed Hayes. He might have been, as Doyle put it, a toe rag, but that didn't make ending his life any easier, and Bolt felt mildly uncomfortable at it being mentioned now. 'Do you remember what happened to the people who got put away for it?'

'Is this to do with a case you're working on?'

He knew there was no point denying it. 'Yeah, it is.'

'It must be a pretty big case if you wanted to see me this urgently. Can you give me any details?'

'It's an ongoing op, so I can't say too much at the moment.'

'Not even to an old mate?'

'You know I'd tell you if I could, Jack.'

'Fair enough. And you think some of the guys we put away might be involved in it?'

'We don't know yet. But at the moment, I'd like to know their current status, and any intelligence you've got on any of them.'

'Well, you tagged one, and we put away four,

didn't we? Vernon Mackman – he was one of the drivers. One of the best there was, I always thought. He died of cancer five years back while he was still in the Scrubs. As for Barry Tadcaster, he's back inside. He was out six months, then teamed up with a couple of old-style blaggers and got done for conspiracy to rob when one of them turned grass. I don't think he's expected out until after I retire.'

'And the others? Marcus Richardson, and who was the other? Scott somebody?'

'Scott Ridgers. They've been in and out since they got released for the Lewisham job. You know what it's like with blokes like that, professional robbers – they never change. Ridgers carried on blagging; Richardson branched out into smuggling coke into the country. But as far as I know they're both on parole and keeping their noses clean. I haven't heard anything about either of them for a while now.'

'How long did they go down for?'

Doyle thought for a moment. 'Ridgers got fourteen years, I think, and served seven. Richardson got longer – seventeen, eighteen, something like that – because he fired a shot before he got hit himself, so he did time on an attempted murder charge as well, even though he always claimed the gun went off by accident. He served eight or nine.'

'You got an address for either of them?'

Doyle's face broke into a craggy smile. 'My memory's good, Mike, but it's not that bloody good. They'll be on the PNC, though. I'm sure they're both still on licence.'

'I'll check them out.'

'You haven't asked about the one who got away. Jimmy Galante.'

'Oh yeah, I remember him. He ended up in Spain, didn't he?'

Doyle nodded. 'He did, but I heard from one of my snouts that he was back in the country. Someone saw him the other day in a pub in Islington.'

Bolt feigned interest. 'Really? I must look into that.'

Doyle took a slug of his own beer and at least a quarter of it disappeared. For a small guy, he'd always had a prodigious capacity for the booze.

'Whatever you think our boys Richardson and Ridgers might be involved in, you've got to remember they weren't the brightest of sparks. Galante was always the brains of the outfit.'

Bolt tried to picture the two men, to remember anything about them, but they were a blank. It was all too long ago. He wondered whether he was wrong to think that there might be a connection. The Lewisham robbery was ancient history, and as far as he was aware no one, either inside or outside the Flying Squad, knew that it was Andrea who'd helped to foil it. And even if someone had found out, there was still no reason to wait until now, fifteen years later, to do something about it. When he thought about it like that, the whole thing didn't make much sense. But it was all he had, and the fact that Jimmy Galante had been involved in both cases meant that it was better to be here asking questions than sitting around at home.

They sat in silence for a few moments, finishing their drinks, oblivious to the noise around them.

'How well do you remember Richardson and Ridgers?' asked Bolt.

'Not very. There wasn't much to say about either of them. They were just two robbers prepared to get nasty to get what they wanted. I doubt many people'll have fond memories of them when they're gone.'

'Do you think either of them could be capable of the kidnap of a young girl? A fourteen-year-old?'

Doyle frowned. 'Is that what this is about?'

'Between you and me, yes.' Bolt knew he was treading on shaky ground here, talking about the investigation to someone outside it, but he also knew it was the only way he was going to get answers.

'A kidnap for ransom?'

'Yeah. But I can't tell you any more than that, and you've got to keep what I do tell you under wraps, OK?'

'You know me, Mike. I don't blab. What makes you think those two are anything to do with it?'

'Just a hunch.'

'Shit, pal, you sound just like Columbo.' Doyle fingered his empty glass. 'I wouldn't put it past either of them to be involved in something like that. They're criminals, and they're greedy bastards, so if there's money to be had, there's a good chance they'll be there.'

'Do you think they'd hurt her? The girl?'

'Christ, Mike, I don't know. The one thing about armed blaggers is they're pros. They don't add years on to their sentences unless they absolutely have to.'

Bolt felt relieved, even though he knew this was irrational. Jack Doyle was no criminal psychologist.

'You look shattered,' Doyle told him.

'I am. It's been a long day.'

'Maybe you should get home.'

But Bolt didn't want to go back yet. He picked up the empty glasses. 'No, let me get you a drink.'

'Cheers. I'll have a pint of Stella.'

When he returned with the drinks they made small talk for a while, but Bolt found it hard to concentrate on anything other than Emma, and he was conscious that he wasn't good company. It angered him that he couldn't relax with an old friend over a few beers at the end of a long, hard day, and the anger was aimed at Andrea, because it was her doing. If she'd just kept her mouth shut, he might have been able to do his job properly instead of flailing round from place to place, tearing himself apart.

He finished his second pint and got to his feet. 'I'd better go, Jack. Early start tomorrow.'

Doyle stood up as well and they shook hands.

'Good luck with the case, Mike.'

'Thanks. I hope we don't need it.'

'Don't worry, she'll be all right. Blokes like that, they just want the money. They won't risk going down an extra twenty years by killing her.'

Easy for you to say, thought Bolt as he said his goodbyes and walked outside into the cool night air. It was a two-minute taxi ride home or a fifteen-minute walk. He decided to walk, hoping it might calm him down a little, but he'd only got a few hundred yards when his mobile started ringing.

It was Mo. Bolt had left him back at the Glasshouse a few hours earlier. He'd said he was just finishing up and was about to go home, but maybe he'd decided to stay later. He flicked open the phone and put it to his ear.

'Mo?'

'There's been a development.'

His tone was grim, and Bolt felt his stomach constrict at the prospect of bad news.

'What is it?'

'I'm at a house in Tufnell Park. I think you'd better get over here.'

Twenty-nine

It had just turned twenty past ten when Bolt arrived at the address Mo had given him – a bedsit on a residential road of rundown white-brick Georgian townhouses on a hill a few hundred yards north of Tufnell Park Tube station. There were a dozen or so police vehicles as well as an ambulance double-parked on both sides of the street, blocking it off entirely, and small clusters of onlookers, some of them in dressing gowns, standing at the edges of the cordon talking quietly among themselves, clearly both appalled and fascinated by the crime that had taken place in their midst.

Bolt's taxi stopped a few yards short of the bright yellow lines of scene-of-crime tape.

'Christ, what's going on here?' asked the driver as he took the fare.

'Murder,' Bolt told him, and got out of the car.

He showed his ID to one of the uniforms ringing the cordon and was directed to a van where he put on the plastic coveralls all officers are obliged to wear when entering crime scenes. He was exhausted, the remnants of the two pints of Stella he'd had with Jack tasting sour and dry in his mouth.

Mo met him in front of number 42. He looked a little queasy. 'It's pretty bad in there, boss. You might want some of this.' He produced a tube of Vicks and Bolt dabbed some under his nostrils.

Bolt sighed. The last thing on earth he wanted to see right now was a body, and it wasn't essential to the inquiry that he did so since he could easily get the details of what happened from other people, but he wasn't the sort to shirk the unpleasant aspects of the job. 'Let's get it over with,' he said, following Mo through the open front door and into a dusty foyer with plastic sheeting over the bare stone floor. Long threads of cobweb hung from the corners of the ceiling and there was a stale, airless smell, mixed with something else. Something much more pungent.

'She's down here,' said Mo, walking past a threadbare-looking staircase and down a dark, very narrow hallway to an open door at the end, the smell of decay getting stronger with each step.

By the time they reached it, it was pretty much unbearable, and Bolt had to stop himself from gagging.

'Jesus,' he whispered.

'It looks like she's been dead for days,' said Mo, moving aside to allow him access.

The room was small and cramped, dominated by an unmade double bed which took up well over half the floor space. Flies were everywhere, their buzzing irritatingly loud as they vied for space with the four white-overalled SOCOs inside, who were testing the various surfaces for DNA, and taking samples from the body. Bolt could get no further than the doorway, which suited him fine.

A woman lay on her side in an approximate fetal position, her feet and ankles wedged under the bed. She was wearing a pink T-shirt with writing on it that Bolt couldn't make out, and a lacy black thong. Her body was bloated and discoloured where the first stages of decomposition were beginning to take effect, but the maggots that were eating her up on the inside had yet to burst out. From his basic knowledge of forensics, Bolt knew this meant that although death had definitely not been recent, it was also unlikely to be more than four days ago, particularly in comparatively warm weather such as they'd been having.

He stood still for several seconds, staring at her dead, ruined body. The abject humiliation of death depressed and horrified Bolt. It always brought home his own mortality, and the sure knowledge that one day he too would end up like this. Nothing more than rotting flesh, all thoughts and memories of a lifetime gone.

'Have we ID'd her yet?'

Mo nodded. 'That's why I called you. Her name's Marie Aniewicz. She's Mrs Devern's cleaner.'

'Jesus Christ,' he whispered, tensing. 'How old was she?'

'Twenty-five,' answered Mo. 'She'd worked at Mrs Devern's place for just under three years.'

He thought of Emma, only eleven years younger, and was unable to stop himself from picturing her here in the same position.

'It's no age, is it?'

'No, it's not.'

Bolt took a deep breath, temporarily forgetting the thick stench of rancid meat.

'What a waste.'

No one said anything for a while. The SOCOs continued to work methodically, as if this was just a routine task for them, which of course to a large extent it was.

'Do we know how she died yet?'

The SOCO nearest to Bolt, who was kneeling

289

down beside the body taking photographs, heard the question and looked up.

'Looks like a single stab wound to the heart,' he said, his voice muffled by his face mask. 'No other obvious injuries on her.'

He gently lifted her right arm with his free hand and touched a thin tear in her T-shirt at roughly the level of her third and fourth ribs. A small dark patch on the T-shirt, not much bigger than two fifty-pence pieces, marked the spot. The fact that there was so little blood, either on the body or anywhere else in the room, suggested to Bolt that she'd died quickly.

'How was she found?' he asked.

'Like this,' answered the SOCO, 'but with the duvet covering her.'

'It's an unusual position to be in for someone who's just been stabbed. I'd have thought she'd be more sprawled out.'

'It looks like she was stabbed, then placed in this position almost immediately. You can see from the lividity that this is where she's been lying most of the time since death.' He pointed to her underside which was darker than the rest of the body where the blood had slowly collected there.

Bolt nodded, and looked around the room. There were no signs of a struggle. The two lamps on either side of the bed were still upright, as were the handful of framed photos and the pot plant on the chest of drawers against one wall. Bolt didn't look at the photos. He didn't want to see what Marie Aniewicz had been like in life.

'Looks like a professional job,' he said when he and Mo were back outside on the pavement, breathing in the comparatively fresh air, glad to be out of the stifling tomb that was the young cleaner's bedroom.

'No one heard a thing, and there's no sign of forced entry, either to the house itself or her bedsit. And it's been difficult to get hold of witnesses. The other ground-floor bedsit's empty, and the rest of the people in the house are apparently illegals, so they've made themselves scarce. The local cops got an anonymous call reporting a nasty smell coming from her room about six o'clock this evening.'

'Does Barry know? And Tina?'

'I got hold of Barry, and he told me to get you down here. He's at some charity function tonight. He wants a full update in the meeting tomorrow morning. I couldn't get hold of Tina. She left before I found out about this, and now she's not answering her phone.'

Bolt exhaled air through his nostrils. 'This puts a whole new perspective on things, doesn't it?'

'Well, there's no way it's unconnected. We haven't got an exact time of death yet, but according to the doctor who examined the body she's been dead somewhere between three and five days. About the time of the kidnapping.'

'There's only one motive for killing the cleaner, then: they found out the alarm code from her and got access to Andrea's house. Which is how they would have placed the trip switch on the front door and found out what Emma was planning on Tuesday. So it's not an inside job.'

'And Phelan's probably not involved.'

'Almost certainly not. Killing the cleaner was a risk. You'd only do that if you had to.'

'So, either they've got Phelan as well as Emma . . .'

'Or he's dead.' Bolt thought of Andrea, wondered how much more bad news she could take. 'They've already killed two people that we know about. There's no reason why they won't have made it three.' Or four, whispered an uninvited voice at the back of Bolt's mind. The fact that the kidnappers could plan to murder a cleaner just to get access to a house meant that it was highly unlikely they'd lose too much sleep over the prospect of killing Emma.

Bolt wiped a hand across his brow. The night was unseasonably warm for September, and he was conscious that he was sweating again.

'These guys really mean business, Mo.'

Mo nodded slowly, his dark eyes full of

sympathy. 'I know. But as you've said, they took a risk killing the cleaner. Someone somewhere might have seen something. Sooner or later they're going to make a mistake. Remember that, boss. No one's luck lasts for ever.'

Thirty

It was close to midnight by the time Bolt walked through his apartment door for the second time that day. He and Mo had stayed at the crime scene for a further half an hour to talk to the senior investigating officer from Tufnell Park CID. They shared what information they could, but were deliberately vague about most of it because of the secrecy of their own op. Bolt had been apologetic about this but it hadn't prevented the senior investigating officer from getting seriously pissed off and threatening to talk to the head of SOCA to get further details if he had to.

After saying his goodbyes to Mo, he'd found a taxi on Junction Road to take him home. On the way back he'd tried Tina's number to bring her up to date with developments but again she wasn't answering, and he decided to leave speaking to her until the morning. He hoped she hadn't suffered any ill effects from her earlier ordeal, and it struck him that maybe he should have done more to check she was OK. At the Glasshouse earlier she'd been quieter than usual, and they'd hardly had a chance to speak. But Tina was a tough cookie. She'd be all right. And at the moment he had enough on his plate without worrying about her.

The first thing he did when he got back inside the apartment was gulp down a large glass of water in an effort to rehydrate himself and get the taste of stale beer off his breath. The remainder of his glass of red wine was on the kitchen top and he was tempted to finish it off, but quickly dismissed the idea. Instead, he threw off his clothes and jumped in the shower, trying hard to relax himself. He was still tense but less so than he had been, even given what he'd just seen. Perhaps he was simply getting more used to it.

It occurred to him as he towelled himself dry that this had possibly been the worst day of his life, and there'd certainly been a fair share of contenders for that accolade over the years. Mainly because it had been so totally and utterly unexpected, and he'd had so little time to react to the speed and ferocity of events as they'd buffeted him again and again.

He was also aware that tomorrow could turn out to be even worse.

Part Five

Part Five

Thirty-one

Bolt tossed and turned all night, his sleep a series of fitful dozes. In those rare times when he did go under, the dreams came, unwelcome and unnerving. In one of them he and Mikaela were living in Andrea's house with two young children of their own. But the children were nameless, faceless wraiths. He wasn't even sure if they were boys or girls, only that he loved them with an intensity he didn't realize he was capable of. Yet every time he went to hold one of them, they would float out of his grip, leaving him feeling progressively more angry and frustrated. He tried to talk about this to Mikaela but she didn't seem to understand. 'They're our children,' was all she said, and she was smiling as she spoke, because Mikaela had always wanted children. It was he who hadn't . . .

Some time later, in the grey time before dawn,

he'd found himself slipping into another dream, this one far clearer and more violent. He was back at the Lewisham robbery – the gunfight that in reality had lasted a matter of seconds, but which had remained etched on his mind for ever. Only this time the robbers were unarmed. They were standing in a line and trying to surrender, hands in the air, their balaclavas removed, all but one of their faces blurred. The one Bolt could see properly was Dean Hayes, a scraggy-faced youth with a hook nose that had been broken more than once, and dyed blond hair. His eyes were wide with fear and he was trying to say something. But in the dream, Bolt was filled with a ferocious rage. These were the bastards responsible for kidnapping his daughter – all of them. The rage made the gun quiver and twitch in his hands, but that didn't stop him from opening fire, the shock of the retorts echoing in his head. Dean Hayes bucked crazily as he was hit repeatedly, until finally he fell sprawling to the pavement. Then Bolt moved the gun in a slow, careful arc, pulling the trigger again and again, experiencing a burst of elation as one after another they went down, hardly hearing the shouts of his colleagues as they tried to get him to stop shooting.

The last thing he remembered was seeing Andrea standing beside him, dressed in the lacy black negligee she was wearing when he'd first met her all those years ago, the gun in her hand kicking as she too opened fire on the men in front of her, her expression a picture of controlled calm.

And then suddenly the dream ended with the shriek of the alarm, and it was back to a reality he'd rather not have had to face.

He was shattered by the time he got into the office that morning. There was a 7.30 meeting for everyone involved in the operation, except those who were on surveillance duty, either watching the area around Andrea's house or keeping tabs on the movements of Leon Daroyce and his close associates. It was led by Big Barry Freud, and was at least partly overshadowed by the discovery of Marie Aniewicz's body the previous evening. There were no further details on her death, although the initial results of her autopsy were expected by mid-afternoon. One thing, though, was clear: she'd been deliberately targeted, and her murder was linked to the kidnap inquiry. Barry seemed unduly hopeful that the results of the house-to-house enquiries in the area, and a search of the murder scene itself, might elicit clues as to the identity of the kidnappers, conveniently glossing over the fact that they had only a matter of hours left before any such clues became irrelevant. There'd been no breaks in the case anywhere else, and the Daroyce surveillance team had nothing to report to suggest that either he or his people were directly implicated, so, once again, everything hinged on the success of the sting operation they were setting up to catch the kidnappers during the ransom drop.

The bulk of the meeting was spent going over the details of the sting itself and everyone's part in it, and Bolt sensed the growing excitement among those present in the incident room as it became clear they were going to get a chance to bring some truly brutal individuals to justice.

Bolt shared none of this excitement. The tension was building in him again, rising to almost intolerable levels as he heard his colleagues discuss the proposed arrest of the kidnappers and the rescue of his daughter, noting grimly that there seemed to be more emphasis on the first objective than on the second, and that Emma was rarely mentioned by name. Once during the meeting he caught Tina's eye. She was looking tired, but she mouthed the words 'You OK?' at him. He managed a small smile and a nod in return, wondering if his stress was that obvious, and she turned away. He watched her for a second, feeling a sudden urge to unburden himself – somehow he knew she'd understand – but he dismissed it immediately, telling himself not to weaken. There were things he needed to do.

When the meeting was over, Bolt asked to see Barry alone.

'You look bloody awful, old mate,' said his boss when they were in his office.

Bolt was already on his fourth coffee of the day. He hadn't eaten anything more substantial than half a sandwich for more than twenty-four hours now, and the lack of food was making him nauseous.

'I feel it.'

'I'd say take a holiday, but we're far too busy for that.'

'I've got a possible lead,' Bolt told him.

Barry frowned. 'Why didn't you mention it in the meeting?'

'I didn't want to muddy the waters. Everyone's got enough to think about without me complicating matters.'

'If it's a lead, it's a lead. What is it?'

Bolt told him about the armed robbery fifteen years ago, how Galante was strongly suspected of being involved, and how Andrea's information had scuppered it, leaving the other robbers dead or behind bars.

Barry looked incredulous. 'So what you're telling me is that you knew Andrea Devern from the past? Why the hell haven't you said anything before now?'

'I only knew her vaguely. She was a friend of a snout.' He could see that Barry didn't entirely believe him. 'Anyway, two of the gang – Marcus

Richardson and Scott Ridgers – are out now, and I think we should view them as potential suspects.'

'Why? Were either of them aware that it was Mrs Devern who shopped them?'

Bolt shook his head. 'No, not that I know of. I was deliberately vague about who'd given me the information so that I could protect Mrs Devern. You know what it was like back then. You didn't have to give too many details.'

'So why do you think they'd be targeting her if they didn't know about her part in putting them away?'

It was a good question, and one Bolt had been thinking about a lot.

'They were probably aware that Jimmy Galante was seeing Andrea – Mrs Devern – at the time, so they may well have known her too. Then, when they come out of prison years later, looking for a way to make money and see how well she's doing, they think, well, why not hit on her?'

'Was any reward money paid to Mrs Devern for the information she gave?'

'No.'

'So they couldn't have found out that way.'

Bolt shook his head.

Barry leaned forward in his seat, adopting one of his thoughtful poses, which consisted of steepling his hands together as if in prayer, his index fingers touching his nostrils.

'It's not much, is it?' he said finally.

It wasn't. But for Bolt it was still something.

'These guys are villains, sir. Hardened criminals. Richardson fired at us when we tried to arrest him. He didn't hesitate. There aren't many people around like that. People willing to kill for financial gain like our kidnappers. They've got to be worth looking into.'

Barry sighed loudly. 'I haven't got the resources, Mike. We've got two surveillance teams out already, and everyone else is concentrating on the ransom drop.'

Bolt knew he wasn't going to win, but when he was back in his own office the first thing he did was access the PNC and check the details of Marcus Richardson and Scott Ridgers.

Richardson was the more brutal of the two, having amassed a total of twenty-three convictions in his forty-two years, including one for stabbing a teacher in the eye with a screwdriver when he was only fifteen years old. He'd been released from his sentence for armed robbery and attempted murder in the summer of 2001 and since then had been back inside twice: once for possession of cocaine with intent to supply, the other time for assault, after he'd beaten his girlfriend so badly she'd been in hospital for three days. He'd been out for just over two years now and it looked like he'd kept his nose clean, although someone with a criminal record as long as his was unlikely to have turned over a new leaf. He was currently living in his native Kilburn, and remained on parole, as he would do until his original eighteen-year sentence ran out some time in 2010.

Ridgers had a similar, if slightly less violent, record. Since he hadn't discharged the handgun he was carrying during the robbery, his sentence had been only fourteen years, which Bolt noted wryly didn't say much for how the courts treated the attempted murder of police officers. He'd been released in 1999 but had gone back in three years later, once again for armed robbery, after he'd held up a betting shop at gunpoint, firing several shots into the ceiling. He was caught minutes later by the occupants of an armed response vehicle that had been passing. It seemed that Ridgers wasn't the luckiest armed robber around, and he'd spent a further four years inside before being released back into an unsuspecting community late in 2006.

Bolt stared at their pictures and tried to remember the initial police interviews with them, but after fifteen years and several hundred other suspects his memory of them both was sketchy. Jack Doyle had said neither man was a budding Einstein, so it was unlikely they had organized something like this, but even so, he couldn't get the feeling out of his head that they were worth pursuing.

Throughout the morning the sense of anticipation in the incident room grew. Although most of those present were still involved in the mundane tasks of sifting through camera footage, everyone knew that later on they were going to be in action. That sense became heightened when it was reported that the ransom money, half a million pounds in cash, had arrived in the building and was under armed guard in the basement.

Bolt was on his sixth cup of coffee, feeling wired and knowing he was going to have to eat soon, when Andrea phoned, asking for him. He refused to take the call, making an excuse. For the moment, he had nothing to say to her. He still had doubts that she was telling the truth about his relationship with Emma. The more he thought about her actions, both in the present and in the distant past, the more manipulative he found her.

Yet, as she'd told him, the dates fitted. There was no way round that. Within minutes he was feeling guilty about not taking her call, so he phoned Matt Turner – who was back on babysitting duties, along with Marie Cohen the liaison officer – and asked him what she wanted.

'She just wants to speak to you, sir,' Turner told him when he came back on the line. 'She wouldn't say what it's about.'

'Tell her I'm very busy at the moment. I'll talk to her later. How's she bearing up?'

'Same as she was yesterday. Tired, emotional . . . like you'd expect.'

'OK. Keep an eye on her, can you?'

'Sure – but, boss?'

'Yes.'

'When exactly am I going to get relieved? I'd like to get where the action is. You know, there's not a lot happening here.'

Bolt sympathized with him. He'd have felt the same way too, but he didn't have the time or the inclination to start shuffling resources.

'Soon,' he said. 'I'll sort something.'

He hung up and stared out of the window at the street below. The sun was shining, a few puffy clouds trailed in an otherwise blue sky, and it looked like it was going to be another warm day, the sixth or seventh in a row after the wet summer. When Bolt craned his neck, as he was doing now, he could see one half of a small park, little more than a thin strip of land with a climbing frame and a couple of trees, set between two office buildings. There was a man sitting on one of the benches, a pushbike propped up beside him, and he was looking up at the sky. Bolt was too far away to see his expression, but he knew from the man's casual demeanour that it was one of satisfaction.

Bolt watched him enviously. He'd always been a level-headed man. You needed to be in his line of business, where part of the job involved stalking your target for weeks, sometimes months, at a time. He was finding this sudden change in him just too much to bear.

He turned away and stood up. He could stand it no more. He had to do something other than sit and wait to react to events that might well shatter his life for ever. He had to get out and start influencing them.

Grabbing his jacket, he walked out of the office, telling Kris Obanje, who was the nearest person to him, that he was off for an early lunch.

It was time to renew some old acquaintances.

Thirty-two

Marcus Richardson's bail address was the third floor of a five-storey block of 1960s flats, one of about a dozen identical buildings built in a loose square, which made up an isolated estate just off London's North Circular Road. Even on a sunny, warm day like this one it seemed a bleak place to live, and the streets were near enough deserted as Bolt parked on the opposite side of the road to Richardson's block.

Because all the flats were reached via an open-air walkway running along each floor, Bolt could see directly to his front door. As he stared up at it, he wondered what he was going to do now that he was here. The need for action had been so great that it had driven him out of the office, but he hadn't thought much beyond that. A recent mugshot of Richardson staring moodily at the camera was on the seat beside him. Balding and unshaven, with a double chin and narrow eyes as cold as flint, he looked like the kind of guy who didn't turn down many things for moral reasons, which was the reason Bolt had focused on him first.

He stared at the photo for several seconds, concentrating on the eyes, imagining the man behind them running a knife across Emma's neck, then turned it over and grabbed the ham and cheese baguette he'd bought at a corner shop on the way over, unwrapping it furiously. The idea of eating made him nauseous but he had to have something to keep him going; he couldn't make it through the day on adrenalin alone. He forced down a mouthful while he pondered his next move. Almost immediately he felt his hunger pangs returning, and he demolished the baguette in the space of a minute, washing the bread down with a half-litre bottle of mineral water.

A couple of kids, one carrying a football, walked past chatting, paying him no heed. He was used to waiting around. It was what a surveillance cop did. But this time things were different and it wasn't long before he was fidgeting. He looked at his watch. It was half past twelve. As one of the senior guys on this case, it wasn't going to be long before he was missed. If he was going to do anything, he had to do it now.

He decided on the simple option. Knock on the

door, identify himself, and if Richardson exhibited absolutely no signs of fear or panic he could probably be eliminated from their enquiries. Hardly scientific, but at the moment Bolt was operating on the hoof.

There was only one problem. When he got up there, there was no answer. He knocked a second time, hard and decisive, so that Richardson would know he meant business. But nothing happened. Either he wasn't there, or he wasn't opening up.

Bolt peered through the letterbox, ignoring the stale smell of socks and old food that came back his way. He was looking straight into a small lounge with a cheap sofa and matching chairs. It was empty. A door directly opposite was partly ajar. There didn't seem to be any activity beyond it.

He stood up and looked around. The walkway was empty, the only sound a crying baby beyond one of the doors further up. He knew the risk he was about to take, but it was all about priorities and right now keeping his job wasn't that high on the list. He didn't like breaking the laws he was paid to uphold, but he'd always been a pragmatic man, and like a lot of surveillance cops he was also a highly competent burglar. It took him less than a minute to open the door using the set of picks he always carried with him. Richardson hadn't even bothered to double lock it, which told

Bolt that even if he was involved in the kidnapping he was coming back to the flat regularly. He was also probably not intending to be out for that long, which meant Bolt was going to have to be quick.

He stepped inside, shut the door behind him and gave the room a quick scan, putting on a pair of evidence gloves as he did so. The furnishings were cheap and old; the only thing of any value was a brand-new LCD TV on a stand. There were a couple of lads' magazines and old copies of the *Sun* spread about, and a pile of DVDs stacked up in front of the TV, but it wasn't as messy as many of the bachelor pads Bolt had seen in his time. He noticed that one of the papers was this Thursday's, and by the look of it had been read from cover to cover.

Bolt knew that most armed robbers tended to be big spenders; it was the nature of their business. They lived life fast and hard because they knew their profession could be ended at any time. They snorted coke, they gambled, they bought women. Bolt had always understood why that sort of life held an appeal for certain people. When times were good, the life of an outlaw must have been a lot of fun, and he wondered how well someone like Richardson coped now, living in a poky little place like this. Not very, was his guess. Like all these guys, he'd want to take a shortcut to easy money, and kidnap could be an attractive option.

It was obvious that Richardson lived alone. There were no photos or pictures on the walls, nothing to give it the appearance of a home, and no self-respecting woman would put up with the stale smell, which got worse as he went through the lounge and into the kitchen. Washing up was piled high in the sink, which was half full of rusty-coloured water, and there were plastic fast food containers everywhere, some still with the remnants of earlier meals.

He gave the bathroom a cursory glance, then carried on through into a bedroom with an unmade double bed and a view straight out on to the next block of identical flats. There was no landline in the flat, and it was definitely empty. There was also no evidence that someone had been held there against their will, or even that anyone female had been there at all recently. Bolt felt a surge of disappointment. He'd been positive he was on to something with Richardson; now unwelcome realization began to break over him.

There was a small cabinet beside the bed with a lamp on it. He checked through the drawers, moving quickly, but found nothing other than underwear and socks. Sighing, he stood back up.

Which was when he heard the movement behind him and the menacing, aggression-laced growl, 'Who the fuck are you?'

Thirty-three

Bolt swung round fast, adrenalin surging through him as he came face to face with Marcus Richardson. The first thing that crossed his mind was that Richardson was a lot stockier than he remembered him. The second thing that crossed it was that the former armed robber wasn't going to be waiting for an answer to his question. Instead he came forward fast, his face set hard, and Bolt saw that he had a small wooden cosh in his hand.

'Thought you could fucking rob me, did ya?' he demanded, raising up the cosh for Bolt to see, his biceps rippling beneath his sweat-stained Lonsdale T-shirt, the eyes just as cold and unpitying as they were in the mugshot.

Bolt had to make a decision, fast. He was trapped, with his back to the wall. He could identify himself, say he just wanted to talk, but he knew it would make little difference. In fact, it might make things worse. Richardson had already worked himself up for violence and Bolt knew that if he got the shit kicked out of him now he'd be out of action for days, and with Emma needing him as much as she did he couldn't have that. Not because of the actions of a low-life bottom-feeder like Marcus Richardson.

He experienced a sudden and ferocious sense of injustice, and in that single moment something inside him just snapped. All the tension that had been building up over the past twenty-four hours – the constant frustration, the crushing feeling of impotence – finally found the kind of outlet it had been waiting for. But he knew better than to go in guns blazing.

'Listen, I'm sorry,' he stammered, raising his hands, palms outwards, in a non-confrontational pose.

Richardson grinned, still coming forward, raising his free hand to grab Bolt by the collar.

'You will be, mate.'

Without a sound, or even a change in his contrite expression, Bolt lunged at Richardson, moving so fast that he took the other man completely by surprise. He grabbed both wrists and yanked them apart to create a gap, and before Richardson had time to react Bolt slammed his forehead into the bridge of his opponent's nose.

It was a good hit, but Richardson was no pushover, and though he stumbled, he didn't lose his footing. With an angry, pained grunt, he pulled his weapon hand free of Bolt's grip. But Bolt still had the advantage, and he used it, butting him a second and third time in rapid succession, creating a deep cut just above Richardson's eye.

This time Richardson did fall backwards, landing on the bed, Bolt going down on top of him with as much force as he could muster. The blood was running into his eyes but Richardson still managed to drive the cosh into Bolt's ribs. Bolt grunted in pain but knew he had to keep up the momentum before the other man got his act together, so he rolled over on to Richardson's weapon arm, effectively limiting the cosh's swing to only a few inches. In such a close-quarters position his head remained his best weapon, and he smashed it down into Richardson's face again and again, feeling a blind, furious elation. He heard bones crack under his blows and felt blood slick against his forehead.

Richardson struggled under him. He finally managed to get his other hand free, and used it to grab Bolt by the collar of his shirt and push his face away, but on this day of all days Bolt wasn't stopping for anyone. Spotting an opportunity, and with his usual inhibitions temporarily absent, he rammed two fingers first into Richardson's left eye, then into his right, digging them in as far as he could, ignoring the high-pitched shrieks of pain coming from the other man.

Of all his tactics, this was by far the most effective. Temporarily blinded, Richardson howled and waved his arms about uselessly. Bolt jumped up from the bed, twisting the cosh out of his hand and throwing it against the far wall.

'Jesus, stop it! Take what you want!' wailed the ex-con, writhing about on the bed, pawing at a face that had become a mask of blood.

Bolt stared down at him, panting. His head hurt where he'd been using it as a battering ram, and the baguette was lurching around his stomach. But he was still in the zone, his anger not yet sated, the realization of what he was doing still way off in the distance.

'Have you been keeping your nose clean, Richardson?' he demanded.

'What?'

'You heard me. What have you been doing the last few days?'

'What the fuck are you talking about?'

Bolt lunged forward and pulled him up by his T-shirt, slapping him hard across the face.

'I said, what the fuck have you been doing the last few days?' He stuck his face so close to Richardson's he could smell his blood, confident he was beyond fighting back. 'Tell me where you've been. Now!'

Bolt threw him roughly to the floor. Richardson lay there, squinting up at him. He used his T-shirt to wipe the blood from his eyes, leaving behind a thick stain. His nose looked broken and he was bleeding from several cuts.

'Nowhere,' he answered. 'Just doing my job.'

'What's your job?'

'I'm a labourer. On a site near Wembley. Why do you want to know? And anyway, who the fuck are you?'

'I'm the person who's asking the questions,' Bolt answered, speaking loudly, knowing that the best way of getting answers was to continue the quickfire questions, taking advantage of his dominant position. 'So unless you want more of the same, you answer them.' He stamped a foot down hard on Richardson's chest as he tried to sit up, knocking him back down. 'Now, where have you just been?'

Richardson looked as if he might make a grab for Bolt's leg, then evidently thought better of it.

'Out,' he said. 'Getting lunch.' He motioned towards the kitchen. 'Check if you don't fucking believe me. It's KFC. Three pieces with fries and coleslaw.'

Bolt had stopped panting now. Above the general stench that pervaded the flat was the unmistakable odour of freshly fried chicken. Realizing he might have made a big mistake, he turned back to Richardson, who was a picture of righteous indignation. In no way whatsoever did he look guilty, and in Bolt's experience people who didn't look guilty generally weren't.

'Are you a copper or something?' demanded Richardson, more confident now as he sensed the doubt in Bolt. 'Because I'm going to fucking sue you if you are, you bastard.' He touched a hand to his face, wiped off more blood. 'Look what you've done to me. That's serious assault, that is.'

But Bolt wasn't going to let things go just yet.

'Scott Ridgers. When was the last time you saw him?'

'You are a fucking copper, aren't you?' Richardson said, sitting back up again.

Bolt took a step back and kicked him hard in the chest, knocking him backwards a second time. 'Answer the question!'

'I ain't seen him in years,' Richardson hissed through gritted teeth. 'I don't socialize with perverts.'

Bolt's jaw tightened. 'What do you mean?'

Richardson saw his reaction, and managed a small, mean grin. 'Oh, didn't you know, copper? Scottie Ridgers is a kiddy fiddler. He likes 'em nice and young. Why? He hasn't been after one of your kids, has he?'

Bolt drove the heel of his shoe into Richardson's face, stamping down hard, then kicked him savagely in the ribs, the force of the blow shunting him across the carpet. The anger roared through him. He spat out curses and kicked him again, even though a voice inside his head was screaming at him to stop, stop, stop! But he couldn't. When the red mist came down, as it did so rarely in his life, he had no control over it.

Richardson wailed in pain, but Bolt kept kicking, conscious enough of what he was doing to concentrate on the body and not the head, but still too lost in the rage and emotion of the past twenty-four hours to cease until his victim was curled up in a ball, silent, unmoving and beaten.

Then the full extent of what he was doing hit Bolt like an express train, and he stepped backwards, retreating into the wall, wondering what the hell he'd become. He had to get out of there.

Turning away quickly, he strode through the stinking flat, past the greasy box of KFC and out the front door. And all the time he was thinking, *What the hell is happening to me?* Acting on nothing more than a general hunch, he'd deliberately disobeyed orders, broken into a suspect's flat and beaten the living shit out of him. And now it looked like his victim was almost certainly innocent.

But he'd got some answers. Not the ones he

wanted maybe, but he'd been doing something to get Emma back, and it had felt good. He'd crossed the line before, and had sworn then he wouldn't cross it again. Yet he just had. And the terrifying thing was, part of him had enjoyed it.

Thirty-four

Upstairs they were arguing again. It was the second time she'd heard them today. Emma couldn't hear what they were saying – the voices were too muffled for that – but she knew it was about her, and was pretty sure what the subject would be: whether she lived or died. She wondered which of the two of them was in charge. She prayed it was the smelly one, but something told her he wouldn't be.

Neither man had been down to see her today. This was unusual. It had been light for hours now, and the bucket she was going to the toilet in needed changing. She was also hungry, and though she'd vowed not to eat anything until she could slip off her handcuffs, she thought she might have to relent on that one. She was using up plenty of energy, scraping away at the wall – a task that had become something of a full-time

323

activity. The chain was definitely getting looser, but it still wasn't budging, and she knew she was beginning to run out of time. The nail had worn down by about a third, and her fingers were stiff and aching. If she stopped eating altogether, she ran the risk of being too weak to escape if an opportunity did somehow arise, although she was still unsure exactly how she'd get out anyway, even if she got the chain free from the wall.

Take it one step at a time, she told herself.

Upstairs the voices stopped, and she broke off what she was doing too, replacing the nail under her pillow and pushing the bed back against the wall so that the metal plate wasn't showing.

For a few minutes she sat there in silence, the butterflies racing around her stomach as she wondered if they'd come to a decision about what to do with her. Maybe they had; maybe they'd agreed it was best simply to kill her. 'Calm down,' she whispered out loud. 'Calm down. Remember what Mum always says. It's the tough ones who rise to the top.'

But when the cellar door opened she had to stop herself from crying out as she pushed herself back against the wall, praying that this wasn't the end, reaching for the hood she had to wear and thrusting it over her head, not wanting to give them any more of an excuse for getting rid of her.

It was the smelly one. She could hear his heavier footfalls as he came down the steps, that wheezing of his. She felt a surge of relief, even enjoyed the familiar odour of his BO, which was stronger than usual today. She heard him stop at the bed, put some food down on the floor, and change the waste bucket.

'Hello,' she said uncertainly.

'All right, love?' he answered, in his gruff voice. 'Did you sleep all right?'

She nodded. 'OK, I guess.'

She could smell his breath as he crouched down in front of her.

'I just need you to do another little message for your mum. I want you to let her know what day it is, so she knows you're OK.'

'OK.'

'So, I'm going to lift your hood up, all right? Just a little bit so you can see the date on the paper.'

She nodded again, waiting patiently while he lifted up the hood and placed the newspaper in front of her face, obscuring her view of anything else. He held it there, giving her plenty of time to see it, and she stared straight ahead obediently, confirmed that it was indeed Saturday, and the hood was replaced. He then recorded a very short

325

message from her before switching off the tape player.

'Well done, love,' he said, trying to sound all cheery, but not quite making it. 'Not long now and you'll be home in front of the telly.'

'What are you arguing about up there?'

'Can you hear us?' He seemed surprised.

'I can't hear what you're saying, but I know you're arguing, because your voices are very loud. Is it about me?'

'Course not.'

She didn't believe him. 'He wants to kill me, doesn't he?'

'No, no, it's not like that,' he said quickly, but he sounded flustered, like one of her friends who'd been caught out telling a lie.

'Please don't let your friend kill me. Please. I never saw his face, I promise, whatever he says.'

'I won't, love, it's all right.'

'Because I know how cruel he is. When he came down here yesterday, he really scared me.'

Beneath the hood, she pretended to cry (she'd vowed not to cry for real any more), hoping this would make him feel sorry for her. And it seemed to work. He put an arm around her and pulled her into his shoulder. The smell of BO coming from his armpit made her want to gag but she forced herself to ignore it. She had to keep him on her side.

'I promise you, darling, no one's going to hurt you while I'm here. I wouldn't let anyone hurt defenceless kids.' His hand stroked her head. 'Tonight it's all going to be over and you'll be going home. I'm sorry my friend had to come down yesterday. I didn't want him to, but it was important your mum took things seriously, you know.'

'He put a knife to my face.'

His arm tensed, almost crushing her. She realized then how strong he was.

'Bastard,' he hissed angrily. 'Did he?'

'Yes.'

'Don't worry, he won't be coming down here again. And he won't touch you, I promise. No one hurts kids on my watch.'

His hand continued to stroke her hair, his gloved fingers slowly massaging her head. It was a horrible, creepy sensation, like spiders running across it, and she really wanted to move away, but she couldn't. He had her pinned.

'Who's in charge?' she whispered, trying to ignore what he was doing. 'You or him?'

'Neither,' he answered, but she heard him hesitate. And that told her everything.

It was the cruel one.

She desperately wanted to feel better, had hoped that his words might soothe her, but as he got up and left, telling her to enjoy her meal, the

327

waste bucket sloshing and slapping against the banister as he mounted the steps, she felt instead a growing sense that something dark and terrible was about to happen.

And it was going to happen soon.

Thirty-five

Scott Ridgers' place was no palace either. He lived in the basement flat of a dilapidated post-war townhouse situated on a back street near Finsbury Park, the paintwork so faded that the people who'd last given it a lick probably owned ration books. The stone steps that led down to Ridgers' front door were caked in an unpleasant combination of dried and fresh pigeon shit, and Bolt had to tread carefully to avoid taking away any unwanted souvenirs from his visit.

The curtains were pulled, and when Bolt knocked on the door, it quickly became clear that Ridgers wasn't in either, although unlike Richardson, he was far less blasé about personal security. The single window, not much bigger than a porthole, was barred, and there were no fewer than three locks on the front door, including two five-levers. They were all in use as well. Bolt wasn't put off.

He could get past almost any locks. The problem was he'd had his fingers burned once already today. Richardson had had no idea who he was, but if he made a fuss and reported what had happened to the local cops, there might be ramifications.

Bolt was in no mood for a further confrontation. His head still hurt from the last one, as did his ribs, where Richardson had dug his cosh into them. But he also knew that having driven over here, he needed to do something. It was ten to two now. He'd turned his mobile off but knew he couldn't keep it off for much longer, and when he did switch it back on he knew he was going to have to come up with a decent reason why he'd gone AWOL on arguably the most important day for his team since it had first been formed eighteen months earlier. It was now or never.

But as he took out the picks, he heard a noise above him.

'He's been gone for days,' said a female voice. 'Your lot probably frightened him off.'

Bolt looked up and saw a short, grey-haired woman in her late sixties dressed in a black trouser suit more suited to a Khmer Rouge guerrilla than a London senior citizen.

'What do you mean, your lot?' he asked with a puzzled smile, wondering how on earth she'd recognized him as a copper. He was dressed casually in jeans and trainers, and that, coupled with the flecks of blood on his shirt, made him sure he didn't look like one at all.

'Are you working for him?' she continued, her tone suspicious. 'The dad?'

'I don't know who you're talking about, I'm afraid.'

'Who are you, then?'

Bolt saw no point in denying his official role. 'I'm a police officer.'

Her expression didn't lighten. It seemed even the nation's senior citizens were against the police these days.

'Haven't you got anything better to do than harass a poor man who's just trying to get on with his life? Scott's a lovely lad. Who sent you? The dad? Can't he let it go?'

'I think you've got me wrong, madam. I'm here to let Scott know that a friend of his has been badly hurt in an accident.'

'Oh, I'm sorry, I didn't realize. Who's that, then? Scott doesn't have many friends.'

'It's someone from the past,' he answered with suitable vagueness, coming back up the steps so he no longer had to crane his neck to talk to her, stepping in pigeon shit on the way. 'You don't happen to know where he is, do you?'

She shook her head. 'I haven't seen him for a few days now. He's probably run off somewhere to escape her dad.'

'Whose dad?'

'Lisa's. That's Scott's girlfriend. I haven't seen her yet, but Scott thinks the world of her. He says she's beautiful.'

Bolt looked puzzled. 'So why's her dad after him?'

'Because he says she's too young,' she answered in a tone that suggested he was being entirely unreasonable. It was clear this lady had a lot of time for Scott.

'And how old is she?'

'It's hard to tell these days, but Scott says she's quite old enough to make her own decisions.'

'I know what you mean,' Bolt agreed. 'Can you remember the last time you saw Scott?'

She thought about it for a moment. 'It was at the beginning of the week, I think. Monday or Tuesday. To be honest, I've been a bit worried. It's not like him not to be around. I usually see him most days when I'm passing. He likes to sit out the front here on his deckchair, watching the world go by. Do you think he's all right?'

'It might be worth checking. Do you have keys to his flat?'

She shook her head. 'Sorry, no.'

The timing of Ridgers' absence was certainly interesting. However, it didn't bring Bolt any closer to finding him now.

'Do you know where Scott's girlfriend lives?' he asked.

She shrugged. 'Over in Paddington some-where.'

'That's a long way from here.'

'They met on the internet,' she said with a conspiratorial whisper, as if this was some kind of magic.

'That doesn't really help me much.'

'I know her last name, though. Scott told me because it's so pretty.' She pronounced it Boo-sha-ra, with something of a flourish, but then had the good sense to spell it for him. 'Lisa B-o-u-c-h-e-r-a. It's French, apparently,' she explained as Bolt memorized it.

He felt a glimmer of hope. London was a big city, but there weren't going to be many people of that name floating around Paddington. It wasn't much, but he was beginning to grow used to getting by on slim pickings. He thanked the old lady and walked back to his car, without looking back.

When he was inside, he switched on his mobile, dialled 118 118 and asked for the number of a Bouchera in the W2 postcode area. He could have got the information faster by phoning the Glasshouse, but he wanted to avoid speaking to anyone there for the moment.

There was one number listed under that name,

and he called it straight away. A man answered after three rings.

'Hello, is that Mr Bouchera?' asked Bolt.

'Who's asking?' came the gruff reply.

Bolt identified himself, and asked if he was the same man whose daughter Lisa was seeing a Mr Scott Ridgers.

'That bloody pervert. Yes, my daughter has been seeing him. I'm glad you lot are finally taking it seriously now. I want him arrested.'

'I'm sorry, sir, but we can't arrest him if your daughter's over the legal age of consent.'

'What do you mean, the legal age of consent? She's fifteen, for God's sake!'

Bolt's mouth went dry. 'What?'

'She's fifteen years old, mate,' he snapped, disgust in his voice. 'Only just turned as well. Why on earth do you think I called the police about it? They've been getting up to all sorts as well. She even filmed some of it on her mobile phone. He should be locked up.'

Bolt thought of Emma at the mercy of a murdering thug with a predilection for young girls.

'Didn't you know any of this? What the hell are you phoning for?'

'Listen to me,' Bolt snapped. 'Is your daughter still seeing him?'

'Course not. What do you take me for? I

grounded her as soon as I found out about it. And confiscated her mobile. But she's been sneaking out to see him. I got the police round here to talk to her but she wouldn't tell them anything. Denies everything. He even gave her this software that wiped all their conversations off her computer. I've been at my wits' end trying to sort it out. I've threatened her, locked her in her room, even found out where he lived and went round. But the bastard wasn't there.'

'Is Lisa at home now?'

'Yeah. She hasn't been out for the last few days, except for school. She's just moping about, not speaking. I'm hoping she's over him.'

'Have you still got her mobile phone?'

'I gave it back to her yesterday if she promised not to call him. So far, I don't think she has. She's a good girl, you know. That bastard corrupted her. If I could get my hands on him . . .'

'I know exactly how you feel,' Bolt told him, 'but in the meantime you can help us locate him, because we're very interested in talking to him about a number of matters.'

'What kind of matters?'

'The kind that'll put him away for a very long time.'

Bouchera grunted. 'Good.'

'But I need to know straight away if Lisa hears from him, or if you hear him speaking to her.

Understand? And if you can get the number he's speaking to her from, even better.' Bolt gave Bouchera his mobile number, then wrote down the daughter's number and the name of her service provider. 'It doesn't matter what time of day or night it is, call immediately. It's extremely urgent.'

'Course I will,' replied Bouchera. 'I want to see that bastard suffer.'

Bolt thanked him and ended the call. There was still no proof Ridgers was involved, but Bolt's gut instinct was telling him he was definitely on to something here.

Ordinarily, the excitement at getting a lead like this would have been surging through him, but instead he felt a growing sense of dread. Time was running out and Scott Ridgers could be anywhere. If he didn't find him, and the ransom op failed, then he was convinced now that Emma was as good as dead. But he wasn't going to give up. Not while there was still an ounce of fight in him.

Thirty-six

The phone rang as he pulled out into the road. It was a message from Mo, wondering where he was. There was obvious concern in his colleague's voice. The time of the message was 1.27 – just over half an hour ago.

But Bolt didn't call him back. Instead he called Tina. 'I need you to check on whether there are any mobile numbers registered to a Mr Scott Ridgers of Hanbury Gardens, N19,' he told her. It was a long shot that someone like Ridgers would have registered anything in his name, particularly a mobile phone. Criminals don't like giving the authorities a means of tracing them. And even if he'd done so, Bolt doubted whether he would have taken it with him on a job as important and risky as a kidnap. But it was still worth a try.

Tina asked who Scott Ridgers was.

'I'll explain later, I promise.'

'You sound excited. Where are you? People have been asking. I mean, it's a big day, and you've been gone a long time.'

There was a trace of criticism in her voice, something Bolt hadn't heard from Tina before, and he wondered if his team were beginning to lose respect for him. If so, it was something he was going to have to counter. Just not now.

'I've been following something up, and I'm on the way back. I won't be long.'

He hung up and called Mo, telling him a briefer version of the same story – that he'd been following up on a lead – deliberately keeping details scarce. He didn't want to tell his friend too much about Ridgers, still less ask him a favour, because Bolt had the distinct feeling he would refuse.

Mo told him to hold on while he went somewhere private.

'Why are you working on a lead that no one knows anything about?' he asked. 'On a day as important as this one.'

'It's just something that's come up, OK? From the past.'

'Do you want to share it?'

'I'll tell you about it later.'

There was a pause.

'I think this is getting too personal for you, boss,' he said eventually.

338

It was the first time Bolt could remember Mo questioning his abilities, and it galled him. He felt like telling his old friend to butt out.

'I'm not going to mess this up, Mo.'

'Don't, please. I respect you, boss. Don't make me lose that respect.'

There was a genuine pain in his voice that cut into Bolt, and neither man spoke for a few seconds, both unsure what to say. It was Bolt who finally broke the silence.

'This time, Mo, I'm going to have to ask you to be the one to have faith. I promise you I know what I'm doing.'

'OK. That's good enough for me. But don't try to do everything on your own. It won't work.'

Bolt said he wouldn't, and it was with an element of genuine relief that he ended the call.

There was a traffic snarl-up around Millbank and it wasn't until twenty to three that he finally reached the office, having already found out from Tina that there was no mobile anywhere in the UK registered in the name of a Scott Ridgers of Hanbury Gardens, N19. He hadn't even made the incident room before Barry collared him. He didn't look very happy at all.

'Where the hell have you been?' he demanded.

Bolt knew immediately that he was going to have to tell him, but as soon as he started talking, Barry's expression darkened.

'Let's get to my office,' he snapped, looking round to make sure that no one was witnessing his wrath.

'What's going on, Mike?' he asked, his voice laden with exasperation, when they were behind closed doors. 'I thought I told you not to go running off on a wild goose chase.'

'With all due respect, sir, I don't think it is a wild goose chase.'

Bolt explained about Scott Ridgers' absence over the past few days, though he didn't mention his taste for underage girls, since he wasn't sure what relevance this had.

'So, what the hell does that prove? Maybe he's gone on holiday.'

'He's been gone since Monday. You've got to admit, it's coincidental.'

Barry nodded furiously. 'Yes, it is coincidental, isn't it? But that's all it is. A coincidence. It doesn't help us one fucking iota.'

Bolt couldn't remember the last time his boss had sworn. It was a measure of his anger and the pressure he and they were all under.

'I thought it was better than just waiting around. I'm convinced I'm on to something.'

'Did Tina say there was a mobile registered in his name?'

Bolt admitted there wasn't.

'So you're not on to something, are you? Listen,

Mike, you're going to have to pull yourself together. I don't know what the hell's got into you over this, but whatever it is, it's got to stop. And what's happened to your face? You've got a bloody great bruise coming up.'

'I had an accident. Banged my head against the car door.'

Barry's gaze then dropped to the bloodstains on his shirt.

'Are you all right to go through with this tonight? Because if you're not ... if you're not well or something ...'

'I'm fine, I promise.'

But even as Bolt spoke, he wondered for the first time whether he really was capable of operating effectively. He thought of Marcus Richardson, his face smeared with blood as he lay curled up in a defenceless ball against his flailing kicks; of Emma, a girl he might never know, chained to a rusty iron bed, a black hood over her head, while an unseen man ran a knife across her neck. Then he forced out the thoughts and focused on his boss.

'I won't mess this up,' he said firmly.

Barry nodded once, accepting the answer. 'Good. I need you fine. In fact, I need you more than fine. You were the one who initiated this op, and it's got to work.' He looked at his watch. 'We've got a final briefing at three thirty for everyone taking part. After that, I want you and Mo to get down to Mrs Devern's place and brief her. It's essential she doesn't mess things up either. There's going to be a lot riding on her.'

'She knows that.'

'Make sure she knows it again.'

'What about the ransom money?'

'You're taking it with you, so don't suddenly go AWOL again.' He smiled to show he was joking, but Bolt wasn't entirely sure he was. 'The rest of the team are going to be following you,' he continued, 'so we'll be ready to move as soon as they call. You'll be in charge on the ground. I'll be overseeing things from here.'

'No problem.'

Bolt nodded decisively because he had a feeling this was the kind of encouraging gesture Barry wanted to see. His boss looked more stressed than Bolt had seen him for a while, and he knew that his own actions weren't exactly helping.

'If this goes well, it'll be a huge boost for SOCA, and for us,' said Barry, watching Bolt closely, looking, it seemed, for answers. 'But if things go wrong . . .' He let the words hang in the air for several seconds. 'If they go wrong, then you and me, we're going to be in a lot of shit, old mate.'

More than you'll ever know, thought Bolt. *More than you'll ever know.*

Thirty-seven

The briefing was short and to the point. It focused purely on how the operation to follow the money, apprehend the kidnapper and rescue Emma was going to work. It seemed like a good plan with an extremely high chance of success to most people. To Bolt it was full of holes.

Afterwards, when he and Mo were in the Jaguar driving to Andrea's place in a convoy of cars containing the rest of the team, the canvas holdall with the half a million pounds locked safely in the boot, Mo asked him about the lead he'd been working on all day. Bolt knew he had to tell his friend the truth now, so he told him about his visits to Richardson's and Ridgers' addresses, leaving out the part where he beat the shit out of Richardson.

'Why didn't you tell me any of this earlier?' Mo asked.

'I didn't want you thinking that I'd lost control – you know, after what I told you yesterday.'

'But you spoke to Tina. Do you trust her more than me?'

'No, I don't. Of course not. I just wasn't sure what you'd say if I asked you to look up Ridgers' number. Also, Tina's got good contacts at the phone companies.'

'And you really think I wouldn't have helped you?' Mo looked deflated.

'Look, I'm sorry.'

Bolt wished he wasn't having this conversation. He wished too that he hadn't opened his mouth the previous day and put himself in such a vulnerable position with one of his most trusted colleagues.

'How did you get that bruise on your head? And the blood on your shirt?'

'I had an accident. Banged my head on the car doorframe.'

'I'm a detective, boss, not a ten-year-old.'

Bolt sighed. 'I broke into Richardson's place. He attacked me. We had a fight. That's how I got it.'

'What the hell is happening to you?' demanded Mo.

'What's happening to me is that it could be my daughter who's imprisoned by the kind of scum who've already killed at least twice, and so won't hesitate a single minute to kill again. That's what's happening. OK?'

'But you can't go round breaking into people's houses and having fights with them. It's just not the way to get things done.'

'What is the way, then? Tell me!'

'To focus,' snapped Mo. 'To focus on making sure this operation's a success. Not on running round on a wild goose chase.'

'It's not a wild goose chase.'

'It is, boss. What proof have you got that either of them has any involvement whatsoever? Absolutely none.' Mo shook his head angrily. 'If it wasn't so bloody late in the day, I'd be talking to Barry about it right now.'

They continued the rest of the journey in brooding silence. They'd never argued before, not like this. They'd had the occasional niggling disagreement and cross words, but it had never got anywhere near the position they were in now. Mo was openly questioning his ability to do the job, and, though Bolt desperately didn't want to admit it, he had some justification too. Another line had been crossed, one from which it was going to be a hard journey back, and he knew exactly whose fault it was.

Thirty-eight

It was after five when he and Mo left the convoy and turned into Andrea's street, having been given the all-clear by the surveillance team watching the house. It was the third time in a little over twenty-four hours that he'd been here, and each time Bolt arrived he felt worse than the time before. He couldn't help wondering how he was going to be feeling the next time he came – if there was a next time.

Heaving the bag containing the money out of the boot, he walked to the gate in silence, Mo following behind. Marie the liaison officer buzzed them through. She was wearing a more concerned expression than usual as she opened the door to him.

'Still no word from the kidnappers,' she told him.

'How's Andrea?'

'She's bearing up, but her nerves are shot with all this waiting. I think all of ours are.'

It was the first sign from Marie that she was getting personally involved in the case. Bolt wasn't surprised. Liaison officers might be highly trained but they were still human, and, he noted wryly, someone like Andrea had always been good at tugging on other people's heartstrings.

'They'll be in contact soon enough,' he said, nodding to Matt Turner who'd poked his head round the door of the study. 'Is she upstairs?' he asked Marie.

'She's in the lounge,' she answered quietly. 'She's been there most of the afternoon. She said she wanted to be left alone.'

Andrea was on the same sofa she'd been on yesterday afternoon. Apart from the change of clothes – she was smarter today, in a white blouse and black knee-length skirt – she might as well not have moved. Her haunted, almost hypnotized expression remained the same, and she only gave him the barest of glances as he and Mo entered the room.

Bolt felt a sudden, almost overwhelming urge to take her in his arms, but he fought it back down. He put the holdall on the floor between them and took a seat opposite her. Mo remained standing near the door.

'They haven't called, Mike.'

'I know. But they will. They want the money, Andrea. That's their sole motivation for this.'

She stared into space. 'I can't lose her. I . . . I just don't know what I'd do.'

Bolt leaned forward in the seat, willing her to look at him. 'You've got to be strong, Andrea. Do you understand?'

'OK,' she said quietly in a voice that didn't fill Bolt with confidence. For the first time he wondered if she'd be able to do what they needed her to do.

'For Emma's sake.'

She nodded, a little more decisively this time, and looked down at the holdall.

'Is that the money?'

'Yes. There's a tracking device attached to the lining on the inside. It's so small it'll be almost impossible to find. There are also two further devices, also very tiny, attached to the notes inside.'

'But surely the kidnappers'll find them?'

'Eventually they will, yes, if they know what they're looking for.'

'Which they do, Mike. You know they do.'

'But we're not going to let them run with this money for long. We'll be following you the whole way as you deliver it. There'll be surveillance teams travelling in front of you and behind. There'll also be helicopter back-up. There's no way you're going to be in any danger.'

'I'm not worried about me, Mike, I'm worried about Emma. We're putting her life in danger here, and I can't stop thinking about it.'

'Look, we'll keep back so we're not noticeable, and you'll be wearing a mike so we can monitor any conversation you have, and a tracking device so we don't lose you either. Mo, can you put them on for Andrea?'

Mo nodded curtly, and attached the devices to Andrea's blouse while Bolt continued.

'When you've delivered the money and withdrawn from the scene, we'll track the money to its destination. The kidnappers may put the money in a different bag but they won't have a chance to check half a million pounds in cash for trackers. We'll then follow them and the money to that destination and arrest them there.'

'But what if Emma isn't there? What if they're hiding her somewhere else?'

It was the big question, one that Bolt really didn't want to think about, because it represented the biggest flaw in their plan.

'The chances are she will be, Andrea. If all the kidnappers are involved in the drop – and given that there are only two of them, three at the most, they probably will be – then they won't want to leave her alone for long, I promise you.'

'It's all chances and likelys though, isn't it, Mike?' she said as Mo moved aside. 'That's the problem. There are no guarantees. They've already killed Jimmy. What if they kill Emma too?'

Bolt could have added that they'd also killed her cleaner, but he didn't. Back at the Glasshouse it had been decided not to tell Andrea about this latest development until after the ransom drop, because of how it might affect her mental state.

'There are no guarantees, Andrea. Not in something like this. But you've got to trust us. We know what we're doing.' He decided to change the subject. 'Have you ever heard of anyone by the name of Scott Ridgers?'

She lit a cigarette with shaking hands, and blew out a thin plume of smoke. 'No. Should I have? Who is he?'

Bolt told her about the possible connection. When he'd finished, she looked shocked.

'You're not saying this has got anything to do with what happened all those years ago, are you?'

'It's possible. We can't find him at the moment.'

'Was it common knowledge that I told you about the robbery, then?' She glanced at Mo as she spoke. 'I swore you to secrecy.'

'And I kept it secret, I promise. It's just a possibility that he's involved.'

'I only ever met a couple of Jimmy's friends, and I don't remember a Scott Ridgers,' she mused.

'Fair enough,' he said, not entirely able to mask the disappointment in his voice. He wasn't totally surprised. Ridgers was a vague lead at best, and now he was beginning to get vaguer.

It was a long shot, but he pulled out of a pocket an A4-sized copy of Scott Ridgers' latest mugshot and unfolded it.

'This is a photo of him.'

The moment she took it, her eyes widened.

'I know him,' she said simply.

Thirty-nine

'He's done work in the garden here before,' said Andrea, still staring at the photo. 'For the firm I use. I've seen him here a couple of times.'

Bolt looked at Mo. His colleague's face was impassive.

'What's the name of the firm?'

'Brandon Landscapes. I've got a business card with all their details round here somewhere.'

She got up and rummaged round in the top drawer of the pine cabinet next to the sofa until she found what she was looking for.

'And when did you see the man in the photo here?'

'He's only been here recently,' she said, handing Bolt the card. 'In the last few weeks. I hadn't seen him before that.'

'Did he act suspiciously at all?' asked Mo, speaking for the first time.

Andrea shook her head, sitting back down. 'No. Just did his job.'

'Did he ever come inside the house?'

'No. I never let any of the gardeners inside the house. There was never any need. And also, quite a few of the people who work for Mike Brandon have criminal records.'

Bolt raised his eyebrows. 'Really?'

'The idea's to help them get back on their feet. I've always thought it was a good idea but, you know, I'm not entirely stupid. I'm not going to give them the run of the place. Not with their backgrounds.' She picked up the photo again. 'God, do you really think he might be involved?'

Bolt suddenly wished he wasn't, after what Bouchera and Richardson had both said about him, but he nodded. 'Yes, I do. And it shows we're on the right track.' He glanced at Mo as he said this.

Bolt looked at the card Andrea had given him and saw that Brandon was a local Hampstead firm.

'Well, we're going to need to get on to them straight away and see if they've got any other contact details for Mr Ridgers.'

He stood up and excused himself and Mo.

As soon as they were out in the hall, Bolt let out a deep breath. He turned to his colleague, hoping for some form of acknowledgement that he'd been right to follow up the lead.

'I still don't agree with how you went about it,' he said grudgingly.

'This is my daughter we're talking about,' Bolt hissed, leaning close to Mo. 'I had no choice. And now we're getting somewhere, aren't we? Because this is way too coincidental. Ridgers is involved. No question.'

'OK, but we still don't know where he is and we haven't got a lot of time to find him.'

Bolt nodded. 'But I was right to do what I did.'

He turned away before Mo could say anything else and dialled the number for Brandon Landscapes. The call went straight to message and he left one, asking Mike Brandon to get back to him urgently. Then he called Big Barry and gave him the news.

Barry seemed to forget his earlier irritation with Bolt, and praised him for his good work. 'We don't want to put out an alert in case any local copper tries to nick him before he's picked up the money. But it's good to be able to put a name to one of them, Mike. Well done.'

Matt Turner emerged from the study as Bolt came off the phone.

'Any chance of getting relieved here, boss?' he asked. 'I'm going stir crazy.'

'Don't worry,' Bolt told him wearily, 'this is all going to be over soon.'

He wasn't sure what else to say so he left Turner

and Mo there and went and stood out in the garden. He had a strong need to get away from everyone. It was a beautiful early autumn afternoon, with only a few wispy strands of cloud and aircraft trails crossing an otherwise perfect azure sky, but he was unable to enjoy the solitude. Like Andrea, he couldn't stand the waiting. It gave him far too much time to think, and the fact that his hunch had paid off was proving to be a double-edged sword. As Barry had said, it was good to be able to ID one of the kidnappers, but the fact remained that he'd also been accused of being a paedophile, and he was quite possibly holding Bolt's daughter. That thought made relaxation of any kind impossible.

He paced the garden for quite a while, then went back inside. He could hear Mo, Turner and Marie talking quietly in the study but couldn't make out what they were saying. Not wanting to interrupt them, he knocked on the living-room door and was unsurprised to see Andrea still in her seat, smoking.

'You know what?' she said through the smoke, without looking at him. 'The contents of that bag . . .' She motioned with a flick of her head towards the holdall on the floor. 'It's just a load of fucking paper, isn't it? I've spent my whole life trying to earn as much as I can of those little bits of paper, and all for what? A nice big house.

A big car. A daughter I might never see again . . .'

'You can't think like that, Andrea. You've got to be positive.'

She managed a weak smile. 'We'll get through it. Won't we?'

'If we're strong, we'll get through it. And tonight we both need to be very strong, and very focused.'

She stubbed the cigarette out in the ashtray and stood up, taking a step towards him. 'Will you hold me?' she asked him. 'Just for a moment?'

She looked so vulnerable that Bolt knew there was no way he could resist, and he went to take her in his arms.

And then stopped, startled by a sound that inspired hope and fear in equal measure.

The ringing of the phone.

Forty

Emma's voice came over the line on loudspeaker. Like the previous day, it was a recording. Unlike the previous day, Bolt's relationship with her had changed, and he experienced a wrenching in his stomach as she spoke, her words nervous and halting.

'Hi Mum, it's me. I'm OK. It's Saturday. I've seen the paper.' A short pause. 'They say that they'll let me go tonight if you give them the money. But you can't involve the police. Please. Otherwise . . .' Another pause, longer this time.

They were in the study. All five of them. Turner, Marie, Mo, Bolt and Andrea. Turner clicked frantically on his laptop, trying to secure a trace. The others stood silent, waiting. Bolt couldn't look at Andrea, even though he knew she was looking at him. The receiver was shaking in her hand. He caught Mo's eyes and saw sympathy there. He didn't acknowledge it. Instead, he stared at a fixed point high on the ceiling, his jaw set hard.

There was a click at the other end of the phone, and then the familiar disguised voice came on the line.

'Do you have the money yet, Mrs Devern?'

'Yes.' Delivered firmly.

'Good. And have you spoken to the police?'

'No.' Delivered just as firmly.

'We have someone with your daughter. He has instructions to kill her at ten p.m. exactly if he hasn't heard from us, so I would advise you strongly to do the right thing this time.'

Bolt flinched at his words, and for a moment Andrea appeared unsteady on her feet; then she began to speak confidently into the phone.

'I told you, I haven't,' she said. 'I just want to get this thing over with.'

'Good. You have sat-nav in your car, don't you?'

'Yes.'

'Munroe Drive in N7 is a six-minute drive away from you in normal traffic. You've got four minutes to get there or the deal's off. Drive to the end and await my call.'

'But—'

The line went dead. Andrea let the receiver drop to the floor.

'Jesus, where are my keys? I've only got four minutes.'

'Don't panic, Andrea,' Bolt told her sharply. 'He's bluffing. Remember, he wants the money. Just stay calm and get to Munroe Drive as soon as you can.' He looked at Turner. 'Trace?'

'Mobile, north London. That's all I've got. If he's following the same MO as yesterday, he'll have switched the phone off by now.'

But Bolt was no longer listening. Pressing his mobile to his ear, he put a call in to Barry in the control room. 'It's on,' was all he said. Then, as he followed Andrea out of the room, he called the surveillance team leader outside.

'It's clear,' came the reply.

'We're on the move,' Bolt told him.

'Good luck.'

I'm going to need more than that, Bolt thought as he hung up. But for the first time in over twenty-four hours he felt better. He was taking charge of a well-rehearsed operation. The stakes were higher than he'd ever known, but at least it was now up to him.

'The mobile he called on was a different one from yesterday,' said Turner, coming out of the study, 'and it is already switched off. Somewhere in N17, not far from yesterday's.'

'Good work, Matt.'

'I want to come with you.'

Bolt looked at him.

'Please, boss. I don't want to stay here.'

There was no time to argue.

'All right, you can come with me and Mo.'

Bolt grabbed the holdall containing the money, and once Andrea had retrieved her keys from the kitchen, they left the house together. The money was heavy and he struggled to keep up with her as she ran down the street to her car. He pulled open the door and dropped it into the passenger seat as Andrea switched on the engine and hurriedly fed Munroe Drive N7 into her sat-nav. She looked terrified, but focused. He wished her luck but she didn't even glance his way. Instead she leaned over, shut his door and pulled away from the kerb.

One minute had passed.

'I'll drive,' Bolt announced, jumping in the Jag with Mo and Turner.

He shoved in his earpiece, switched on the loop mike he was wearing round his neck, and then they were away, doing a rapid three-point turn in the middle of the street. A middle-aged couple walking arm in arm stopped and watched them curiously. *Lucky sods*, Bolt thought. *Not a care in the world*.

There were five surveillance cars and two motorbikes involved in the convoy. As with all surveillance ops, they would switch position constantly so that no one vehicle stood out, just in case the kidnappers had decided to tail Andrea themselves. All communication would now be done by radio, using call signs, so that every person involved could hear what was being said and be able to act accordingly.

Bolt got into position behind a Toyota Auris with Tina Boyd and Kris Obanje inside.

'I think our targets are getting paranoid,' said Mo. 'Munroe Drive's a dead end.'

'Shit. They're obviously checking for tails. We're going to have to be very, very careful here.'

He turned right out of Andrea's road, pulled over while another of the surveillance cars overtook him, then accelerated, his fingers drumming on the wheel as the tension coursed through him. He looked at his watch.

Two minutes.

They turned again, this time on to the Finchley Road, heading north in the direction of the North Circular. Traffic was steady rather than heavy and one of the surveillance bikes roared past them, disappearing into the distance and tucking in behind Andrea's Mercedes, which was fifty yards ahead and weaving in and out of the lanes, moving fast. The surveillance vehicles would be travelling both behind and in front of her, so she could be kept under the eyeball at all times, but her speed and the erratic nature of her driving were making it difficult for them.

Bolt leaned against the window looking

skywards, hoping that Barry was being true to his word and keeping the helicopter back and out of sight. Even in a sprawling city like London, where helicopters are a common sight, it would stick out a mile to the kidnappers. But today the sky was clear.

Three minutes.

Up ahead, the lights went amber. Andrea accelerated through them, just as they went red, the surveillance bike going through just behind her. The two cars in front of Bolt stopped, giving him no choice but to do the same. He cursed, and his finger-tapping on the seat intensified as he counted the seconds in his head as Andrea's car disappeared from sight.

One, two, three . . . thirteen, fourteen, fifteen . . . twenty-two, twenty-three . . .

'Come on, come on,' he hissed.

As the lights turned green again, there was a crackle of static in Bolt's earpiece and a voice came on the line amid a lot of background noise.

'Bike two to all cars, target has just turned into Clearland Road, leading to Munroe Drive. Am taking the next road along, Boothby Avenue. Have lost eyeball.'

Tina's voice broke in. 'Car two to bike two, we're thirty seconds behind. Will turn into Clearland and take the eyeball.'

Four minutes.

Bolt accelerated, cutting inside to overtake the two cars in front before pulling back into the outside lane. He was making up ground fast but they were still way behind.

And then from inside their car they heard the sound of Andrea's mobile ringing, the mike on her blouse picking it up. They heard her say 'hello' and then the kidnapper's voice came on the line, faint but audible.

'Where are you?' he demanded, the voice warped by the suppressor.

'I'm just turning into Munroe Drive now.'

'Drive to the end. Stop outside number twenty on the left. There's a green Renault Scenic parked directly outside. In the driver's-side wheel arch, on top of the tyre, is a package. Pick it up and leave this phone in its place, making sure you switch it off. Then get back in your car and open the package. There'll be two items inside, one of which is another mobile phone. Turn it on, and you'll be called on it with further instructions. In the meantime, drive up to the North Circular and turn right, heading east.'

The line went dead.

'Christ, these guys aren't taking any chances, are they?' said Turner in the back.

Bolt shook his head angrily. 'The bastards know something. They must do.'

'How?' asked Mo. 'We've kept everything under wraps.'

'God knows. But they know. I'm sure of it.'

Tina's voice came over the airwaves, interrupting them. 'Car two to all cars. Target has stopped near bottom of Munroe Drive. She's picked up the package, and she's getting back in. She's turning round and coming back up Munroe Drive. Now turning left and heading back towards Finchley Road.'

'We'll take the eyeball,' said Bolt as he pulled over just before the entrance to Clearland Road, waiting for Andrea's Mercedes to emerge.

Seconds later, she pulled out of the junction, heading north, her driving even more erratic than it had been earlier.

'Car one to all cars,' announced Bolt, 'we're following the target north on Finchley Road, three cars back. She's driving fast. I can't get a good view, but it looks like she's on the phone. Her mike's not picking anything up so she can't be speaking.'

'Shit,' cursed Mo. 'What the hell's she doing?'

'Oh no,' said Bolt.

Barry's voice came over the radio, urgent. 'What's going on?'

'Target is opening the window and throwing something out.'

'That's her mike,' yelled Barry. 'And the tracker she's wearing.'

'She's just chucked something else out,' said Mo.

'I know!' Barry yelled. He sounded almost apoplectic now. 'It's the bloody trackers in the bag lining. How's she finding these things, and what on earth does she think she's doing?'

It was Bolt who answered the question. 'That package she just picked up. It doesn't just contain a phone, there's a bug finder in there as well. The bastards know we're on to them. That's what's happening.'

He couldn't believe it. The kidnappers had been tipped off. But by whom?

Forty-one

Andrea hit the North Circular at exactly 6.26 p.m. and proceeded east, driving fast. No longer able to hear what she was saying, the surveillance cars simply had to do their best to keep up, throwing all hopes of remaining inconspicuous out of the window. Not that that was such a priority now that it was obvious the kidnappers were assuming the police were involved.

In the control room, Big Barry Freud sounded as if he was fighting a losing battle to stay calm. As he sat grim-faced at the wheel of his car, conscious for the first time of the helicopter overhead, Bolt knew how he was feeling. This was no longer a surveillance job, it was a chase, and once again he cursed Andrea. He knew the kidnappers were telling her to get rid of anything which made it possible to trace the money, and knew too that they'd be lacing their instructions with murderous threats to ensure her obedience. Alone in the car with only her thoughts and fears for company, it would have been incredibly difficult for her to say no, but the fact remained, cold and hard, that her actions could also be costing her any chance of seeing Emma alive again. These guys were frighteningly ahead of the game. They were doing everything to make sure they got this money while at the same time minimizing their risk of getting caught. It would be a simple matter to put a knife through Emma's heart when they'd finished with her, just like they'd done to Andrea's cleaner. Bolt cursed himself, too, for going through with this charade. They should have gone the negotiation route from the start, laid their cards on the table, used trained people to get her back, instead of trying to come up with a sexy, headline-grabbing success story that was in danger of falling apart only minutes after it had started.

For twenty-four minutes Andrea drove along the North Circular. Traffic was busy but moving both ways, and though she continued to weave between lanes, there was never any danger that they were going to lose her. At 6.50, she turned on to the A10 going south, taking advantage of the lighter traffic to speed up.

'I can't understand why she's not trying to get rid of the trackers in the ransom money,' said Mo as they accelerated after her. 'They've obviously told her to remove anything that could trace them, and she seems to be cooperating.'

'Maybe she hasn't had a chance to look for them while she's driving,' answered Bolt.

'Or maybe she's only pretending to cooperate,' suggested Turner.

Bolt shook his head. 'No, she's definitely doing what they're telling her.' He took a deep breath. 'They're planning something,' he added quietly. 'God knows what. But they're planning something.'

Ten minutes later, Andrea turned again, this time into Lordship Lane, heading east into Tottenham. Then a strange thing happened. She slowed right down, managing barely fifteen miles per hour in the nearside lane. By this time Bolt and Mo were only twenty yards behind her.

'Car one to control,' said Bolt as he stared straight ahead.

Barry came back in the earpiece. 'Control receiving. What is it, car one?'

'Target driving very slowly. Now down to approximately fifteen miles an hour. Still looks to be on the phone. What do you want us to do? Over.'

'Stay behind her, car one. Just stay behind her. Important thing is not to lose her. Over.'

'Don't worry, there's no chance of that. We're

more likely to crash into the back of her. Over.'

They were coming up to the junction with Tottenham High Road. Andrea slowed down still further and the lights went red.

Bolt stared out of the windscreen. To his right were Tina and Kris Obanje in the Toyota, while one of the motorbike outriders was flanking them. He couldn't see the helicopter any more but knew it wouldn't be far away. There was no way Andrea was going to get out of their sight, so he couldn't see how the kidnappers would be able to pull off getting hold of the money without being spotted. Yet these guys were pros. So far they hadn't made a single slip-up. They had something up their sleeves. He was sure of it.

The lights seemed to stay red for a long time. Bolt desperately wanted to get out of the car, walk up to Andrea's Mercedes and ask her what the hell she thought she was doing, but he knew it would do no good. If they aborted the ransom drop now, their hopes of getting Emma back alive would diminish still further. They simply had to follow her.

He tried to second-guess the kidnappers. Clearly they suspected something was up. They'd originally tried to get Andrea to outrun the police, but had now changed tack, getting her to slow right down. Why? They were waiting for something. But what?

And then it hit him. 'Shit.'

Mo turned to him. 'What?'

'Are Tottenham playing today?'

The lights ahead went green, and the cars started pulling away.

'I'm not sure. I haven't had the time to check. You don't think—'

'Christ, they are,' said Turner, leaning forward between the front seats. 'Five fifteen kick-off.'

Bolt smacked the steering wheel. 'So they'll be finishing up about now. I bet the final whistle's just gone. It makes perfect sense.'

Before he had a chance to say another word, Barry's voice came over the airwaves, his tone frantic, his words immediately confirming Bolt's suspicions.

'Control to all cars, we have a situation. Football fans beginning to exit White Hart Lane on to Tottenham High Road in large numbers due north of target. This could be possible location for ransom exchange.'

Bolt felt a shot of adrenalin go through him. Possible location? It was damn near inevitable.

'Give me current target location.'

'Car one to control, she's turning left into Tottenham High Road, and she's accelerating fast.'

'Keep her in sight!' Barry howled. 'All cars, keep her and the money in sight! Over.'

But Andrea wasn't stopping for anyone. She weaved between the two lanes, driving like crazy, even though the traffic was slowing in front of her as, up ahead, a wave of close to forty thousand white-shirted football fans poured on to the street.

Bolt cursed loudly as they tried to keep pace, squeezing between two cars in a manoeuvre that smacked both wing mirrors out of position, and accelerating through the gap. Andrea's initial burst of pace had put thirty yards between them. No more than a hundred and sixty yards in front of them mounted police were in the road, stopping the traffic as the road became a sea of white. Already fans were crowding the pavements, coming towards them on both sides of the road, their raucous shouts filling the air.

Andrea suddenly pulled up on the kerb and stopped. A second later she was out of the car, the phone no longer to her ear. She ran round to the passenger door, pulled out the holdall, heaved it over her shoulder and started walking as fast as she could manage under its weight.

Bolt's earpiece was suddenly filled with every surveillance car and bike trying to talk.

'Car three to all cars, she's on the move. What do you want us to do? Over.'

'Bike one to control, I'm ten yards behind her vehicle. I have the eyeball. Do you want me to intercept? Over.'

'Control to bike one, does she have the bag? Over.'

'Yes, she has it. Over.'

'Shit. The money trackers say the damn thing's still in the car. The stupid bitch has removed them too. Control to all vehicles, follow on foot. Now. Do not lose her. Or the bag. Go! Go! Go!'

Bolt, Mo and Turner were out of the car like a shot, leaving it in the middle of the road as they ran to where Andrea was already being swallowed up by the advancing crowd. Bike one was ahead of them, pulling off his helmet as he ran, but Bolt was faster, overtaking him and dodging through the fans, his gaze fixed firmly on the back of Andrea's head.

Only fifteen yards and closing.

The explosion came out of nowhere, followed by a flash of very bright light somewhere in the crowd up ahead. Bolt shut his eyes and covered his head instinctively, but the moment he opened them again there was a second blast, coming from roughly the same direction. Panicked shouts broke out and there was a sudden surge of people barging and shoving into him as they attempted to get away from the explosion's source. He was knocked backwards and had to fight to keep his balance as he struggled through them, looking round frantically for Andrea but unable to see her among the mass of humanity blocking his view.

And then he was choking and his eyes began to water. It felt like someone had squirted ammonia in his face before dumping a load more down his throat. Tear gas. The bastards had let off tear gas grenades. The panic suddenly grew vastly worse as people began to experience its noxious effects, most of them doubtless fearing that this was some kind of terrorist attack. Bolt was battered like a ship in a storm as he tried to hold his ground amid the choking stampede, eyes squinting against the pain, his shirt pulled up to cover the lower half of his face.

Then a large empty space opened up in front of him. A handful of members of the public were on the ground, one with a cut on his head. Right in the middle, barely ten yards away, was Andrea. She was kneeling on the pavement, hands clutching her face. There was no sign of the holdall. Sirens were starting up now, and mounted police were galloping towards the scene, but they were still too far away to be of any immediate help.

Eyes still streaming, Bolt tried to focus on the backs of the fleeing people, his eyes scanning wildly in all directions. He saw Mo and Turner only a few yards away, standing close together. Mo's face was in his hands, while Turner had a handkerchief to his and was also looking around desperately.

And then he caught a glimpse of the holdall, slung over the shoulder of a guy in a black baseball cap. He was rounding the corner into an adjacent street, moving fast as he was carried along by the fleeing crowd, already disappearing from sight.

Still choking, Bolt leaned into the mike and spoke rapidly. 'Suspect fleeing with bag into . . .' He looked for a street sign, couldn't see one. 'Into one of the streets off the high road, heading due west.'

'Control to all units,' shouted Barry through the earpiece. 'Do not lose that bag! We are trying to get CCTV up and running.'

'There he is,' spluttered Bolt, still swallowing acrid-tasting gas as he pointed.

Turner had already spotted him and was pushing through the crowds of supporters in his direction, followed by Kris Obanje and Tina Boyd. It was Turner who was moving the fastest, as if being cooped up in Andrea's place had given him a huge new reservoir of energy, as well as a point to prove. He wasn't the biggest or strongest of guys but he ploughed through the mob, shoving people aside as he ate up the distance between himself and the holdall.

'Mo,' yelled Bolt, 'stay with Andrea!'

Before his colleague could reply, Bolt was past him and joining the chase, his eyes beginning to sting less as the fresher air hit them.

374

It was fifteen seconds since the first explosion, and already the gas was dissipating, and its effects wearing off on those who'd been affected. Now most of the crowd were coming to a halt as their more voyeuristic tendencies took over, creating a dense wall which acted as a perfect cover for the fleeing suspect. 'Police! Out the way!' Bolt screamed as loudly as he could as he charged into them, no longer seeing the point in trying to keep a low profile. Being football fans, they weren't in a desperate hurry to be cooperative, but Bolt was a big man, and one who knew that if he lost the guy with the holdall then he'd almost certainly lose the daughter he'd never known, so today he wasn't stopping for anyone. If he'd had a gun, he would have waved it, even fired off a couple of shots in the air and risked the sack.

Still yelling, he pushed right through them, ignoring the outraged cries and the insults, catching up with Tina and Obanje and passing them. Turner was ten yards further ahead, at a point in the street where the crowd was beginning to thin. Ten more yards separated him from the man with the holdall. Turner was running, the suspect walking quickly. In a few seconds he'd be on him, and that would be it because Bolt and the rest of them were only seconds behind.

And then there was a blurred movement in the corner of Bolt's eye. It was so quick that it took him a second to register the man in black cap and sunglasses and brand-new Tottenham shirt as he ran headlong into Turner from the side. Bolt caught a glint of metal as the man's hand shot out once, making contact, and then he was dancing past him and running for the other side of the road, in the opposite direction to the man with the holdall. Turner stopped running and seemed to stumble, his hand reaching to where the man had hit him, and then he fell to one knee, while fans milled about him, wearing vaguely curious expressions.

Bolt stopped when he reached him, putting a hand on his shoulder. 'Matt, you all right?'

Through the earpiece, Barry demanded to know what was going on. It was only then that Bolt saw the growing bloodstain on his colleague's shirt.

'Shit!'

Turner looked up, his eyes wide and fearful, his expression almost childlike. 'I think I've been stabbed, boss,' was all he said, and then he put a hand out to steady himself and lay down on his side, almost as if he was about to go to sleep.

'Officer down!' yelled Bolt into the mike. 'Stabbed by second suspect. We need urgent medical help immediately.'

'What the hell happened?' yelled Barry in his ear, his tone close to full-blown panic as the full enormity of what was happening began to hit home. 'Control to all units, secure the scene. Secure the money. Armed back-up is arriving shortly.'

Bolt knew that the important thing was to stay calm and take the lead. In the ten seconds since Turner had got hit, the man with the bag had disappeared. They had to get him. Obanje and Tina had arrived now and Bolt yelled at Obanje to keep up the chase and Tina to stay with her injured colleague.

'What about the one who stabbed him?' she demanded.

'He's mine,' hissed Bolt, jumping to his feet.

The knifeman had run off down Tottenham High Road and he, too, had disappeared from view, but Bolt wasn't going to give up that easily. He didn't give a toss about the money, that was irrelevant, but this bastard, whoever he was, had seriously injured one of his men, as well as put Bolt himself through over a day's worth of personal hell. He hadn't got a good enough look at him to see whether or not it was Ridgers, but he didn't think it was. Guessing that he would keep the black cap on to avoid being ID'd by CCTV cameras, and knowing he wouldn't have got far, Bolt took off after him, ignoring the frantic chatter in the earpiece.

He almost hit a police horse and took no notice

of the shouted command of its rider as he ran down the middle of the road between the lines of stationary cars, his eyes scanning the pavements and the legions of white-shirted fans. There was no black cap anywhere to be seen. Not on either side of the road. It was like looking for a needle in a haystack. Except for one thing. The herd mentality remained in full flow, which meant that almost everybody had turned in the direction of the mêlée behind, and some were actually moving towards it, their movement hesitant. One man, though, stood out, simply because he was walking purposefully away from the scene, his pace far too quick. He was keeping to the inside of the pavement, trying to remain out of view as he weaved between other fans. Bolt had hardly got a look at him earlier, but he was the right height and build, and he was thirty, maybe forty yards ahead.

It was him, Bolt was sure of it. He wiped his eyes, spat on the ground to get the taste of gas out of his mouth and kept running, going flat out in his desperation to get hold of him.

Thirty-five, thirty, twenty-five, twenty yards. His footfalls sounded artificially loud on the tarmac. Two uniformed cops in full riot gear stood in the road surveying the crowd uneasily, their batons drawn. One of them heard Bolt's rapid approach and, as if he was looking for someone to lash out at, lifted his baton menacingly and shouted at him to stop. Bolt didn't even slow down. He just pulled out his warrant card and yelled 'Police!' as loud as he could, and miraculously the cop simply got out of the way.

Unfortunately, the suspect also turned round. The expression on his face was one of pure shock, even behind the black shades, and in that single moment Bolt knew he was looking at the right man.

The suspect took off down the street, knocking over a middle-aged woman in his haste and stumbling before regaining his balance. Her husband shouted something and threw out a hand to grab him but he was nowhere near quick enough. This guy was speedy, and he had one hell of a lot of incentive to get away from his pursuers.

Bolt was less fit than he should have been. These days he only got to the gym once a week at best, and he was beginning to put on a few pounds round the middle. Today, though, he was powered by pure rage, and he kept pace with his target. He screamed at him to stop, loud enough so the whole street could hear it. People turned his way, then towards the fleeing suspect, who reacted by pulling out his knife and waving it wildly in front of him. It was an effective move. The crowds parted, no one wanting to tackle a knifeman.

Bolt sneaked a quick look over his shoulder.

Two of the team, Dan Blakeley and Cliff Yakonos, were running along behind him, but were still a good twenty-five yards back, while the helicopter continued to hover impotently overhead. And Bolt was unarmed. If he caught up with the suspect, he'd be taking a huge risk. He thought about this information, accepted the risk, and kept running, ignoring the pain in his lungs and beginning to gain on his target half-yard by half-yard.

'Suspect two running south on Tottenham High Road,' he shouted into the mike. 'He's armed and dangerous. Request immediate back-up.'

'This is control. Back-up on way. ETA one minute.'

Without warning, a large man in his thirties, with a kid of about ten who must have been his son, jumped at the suspect as he ran past, trying to grab him in a bear hug. It was a brave move. Brave, public-spirited and totally rash. He got a grip, knocked the suspect against the window of a charity shop, but wasn't quick enough to neutralize the knife. The suspect reacted ruthlessly and instinctively, driving it directly into the man's upper body with a single bloody lunge, his face contorted with rage and desperation. The man went down like a falling tree, probably dead before he hit the ground. His kid cried out, 'Dad!' It was a terrified, shocked howl, a sound that would live with Bolt for a long time. It was a savage reminder that death can be so quick. One second you're a living, breathing, smiling human being out with your boy to see your team play football on a glorious evening, the next you're gone. For ever.

'Suspect two has stabbed member of public; urgent medical assistance required,' Bolt yelled into his mike, but it wasn't urgent. The guy was dead. Like Andrea's cleaner and Jimmy Galante. Maybe even Emma. Laid low by a killer without the slightest regard for human life.

A fury filled Bolt. It was stronger than any he'd felt in a long, long time, maybe ever, dwarfing the emotion that had soared through him as he kicked and beat Marcus Richardson, and it seemed to give him a blind, terrible energy.

The man's intervention might have cost him his life but it also cost the suspect five or six yards. He took off again as soon as he could, waving his bloody knife as he ran past the son he'd just deprived of a father, but he now had only a handful of yards on Bolt. A junction was coming up ahead, and when he reached it he turned hard right, his body almost jack-knifing in his bid to keep momentum. Bolt kept coming, not even thinking about hesitating as he too took the corner, even though he knew the suspect could use the blind spot as an ambush point. He was moving beyond logical risk assessment and into the realms of pure revenge. He was going to beat the information he needed out of this bastard, would kill him if he had to, but there was no way he was losing him. No way at all. It was an incredibly liberating thought.

When he rounded the bend, the suspect had gained a few yards and was racing across to the other side of the road through the blocked traffic. There were fewer people milling about on the pavements here, and no sign of any police either. But also less cover for his quarry, and Bolt knew that as long as he kept pace, feeding the suspect's position into the mike, then he wasn't going to get away.

After thirty more yards, the suspect looked round and saw Bolt still right behind him. He turned back and kept running, but Bolt was conscious of the knife in his hand. It was a stiletto, the blade probably eight inches long, still slick with the blood of two men. All Bolt had to fight with was the standard-issue police pepper spray. That and the pure rage that was driving him on. Neither of which was any guarantee of success. He knew that if he'd had a gun on him he'd have used it without a second's hesitation to bring the bastard down. He'd have put a bullet in his leg, and beaten the whereabouts of his daughter out of him while he lay helpless. Because the fact remained – indeed, it was branded right on the front of his brain in flaming white-hot letters – that if he lost this man, Emma was as good as dead.

The suspect turned a hard left. Bolt did the same, shouting the street name into the mike, but he wasn't looking where he was going properly and he slipped and lost his balance, jarring his knee as he hit the deck hard, and rolling on to his side. He ignored the pain, jumped up and kept running, cursing the fact that his clumsiness had lost him five yards and counting.

The street led up to the entrance to a high-rise council estate. It was a dead end for cars. Bolt cursed. He knew that if the suspect got inside the warren of alleys that these characterless sixties estates always featured it would mean he'd almost certainly slip through the net. Jesus, where the hell was the back-up? Even the helicopter was no longer overhead; doubtless it had been sent to chase the money. It disgusted him that the recovery of the half a million pounds was more important to his bosses, and their bosses, than capturing a brutal knife-wielding killer and possibly saving the life of a fourteen-year-old girl, but then in his heart he'd always known it would be. The whole British justice system was built on the protection of property above the protection of lives, which was why armed robbers were always put away for two, three, sometimes even five times as long as child molesters.

Bastards. In those taut, desperate seconds, Bolt was a man entirely on his own, out on a limb and having to do everything himself, knowing that failure was unthinkable.

The armed response vehicle seemed to materialize from nowhere. In fact it had come out of a side road up ahead, just in front of the entrance to the estate. It stopped dead, blocking the way, and the three officers were out in an instant, their MP5s pointed straight at the suspect, who was twenty yards from them.

'Armed police! Drop your weapon!'

Bolt reached into his pocket for the pepper spray, knowing that the suspect was going to turn and run back his way, away from the guns, meaning it would be up to him to make an arrest.

But the suspect didn't. He kept on going. Charging right at them, yelling something that sounded remarkably like a battle cry.

'Don't shoot him!' shouted Bolt. 'Take him alive! For Christ's sake, we need him!'

'Armed police! Drop your weapon now!'

'Don't shoot!'

The suspect was only ten yards away from them. Still running, he pulled back his arm and threw the knife. It hit one of the ARV officers in the arm above the elbow, slicing right through the bicep. The cop dropped his gun and grabbed uselessly at the knife's handle, which was jammed halfway into his arm, stumbling as he did so. For the suspect, it was a suicidal move. Bolt knew it, and knew too what it meant. He saw a dead girl; a funeral; a lifetime of wondering how he could have done things differently.

The bullets sounded like firecrackers in the empty street, their noise reverberating hollowly off the high walls of the surrounding buildings. Two two-round bursts. The suspect flew backwards, arms flailing as he spun round before crashing to the ground, his sunglasses flying off and clattering across the tarmac.

'Police!' screamed Bolt to identify himself, holding up his warrant card as he ran over to where the suspect lay. He knelt down, felt for a pulse, knew it was pointless. There was something there, but it was fading fast, and even as his fingers squeezed the wrist and he shouted at him not to die, his voice full of desperation, it disappeared altogether. He was gone. His eyes were closed, his mouth ever so slightly open, a single drop of blood forming in one corner. It wasn't Scott Ridgers, either. This guy was young – late twenties, maybe thirty – an ordinary, unblemished face, olive skin and thick black hair suggesting a background from somewhere in southern Europe. Bolt had never seen him before, knew nothing about him, would probably never know anything about him, other than the fact that his death might have ramifications for him that lasted for the rest of his days.

And as he knelt there, staring down at the dead man, unable to understand why the ARV cops couldn't have used a non-lethal option like a taser or a baton round to bring him down, his worst fears were confirmed as Barry's frantic voice came over the earpiece.

'Control to all units. What do you mean you've lost suspect one? Find him! I want the whole fucking area locked down! We have to get hold of that money! Over.'

They'd failed. And God alone knew what happened now.

Forty-two

'Why the hell did you remove all the tracking devices, Mrs Devern?' demanded Mo Khan, barely able to contain his anger. 'You must have known it was going to help them get away.'

Andrea, ashen-faced, shocked like all of them, glared at him. 'Because they knew about them, that's why!' she yelled, her voice close to breaking. 'They knew you were there. How the hell did that happen?'

The question hung in the air.

Twenty minutes had passed since the fatal shooting of suspect two. Two police helicopters continued to hover overhead, moving in lazy circles, hunting for a quarry who had long since disappeared, leaving a trail of chaos in his wake. The worst of the crowds were gone too, although there were still large groups of pedestrians hanging around to see the aftermath of the action, and because they were spilling out into the road they were causing serious traffic congestion. The operation to clear the area to allow police forensic teams and ambulances in was being further complicated by an apparently unrelated outbreak of fighting between rival fans further up on White Hart Lane. The competing blare of sirens filled the air as Mo, Bolt and Tina stood beside one of a line of police vehicles clustered round the corner from the street where the body of suspect two still lay where it had fallen. Andrea was in the back of one of the cars, sitting with her legs out, holding a plastic bottle of water.

The mood among everyone at the scene was one of complete shock. The operation had been a complete failure. Half a million pounds of taxpayers' money had walked away from right under their noses; worse than that, a member of the public had been killed, one of the team's own number seriously wounded, and the one suspect they had managed to apprehend had decided to go out in a blaze of glory rather than be taken alive. It couldn't really have gone any more wrong. The only positive was that, unlike the stabbed fan, Turner was still alive, although the seriousness of his condition wasn't yet known. He'd been airlifted to the Homerton Hospital in Hackney whose expertise in dealing with knife injuries, honed through years of practice, was legendary, so he was in the best possible hands. Even so, as they all knew, that might not be enough.

Bolt felt as if he'd done ten rounds boxing a man twice his size and speed whose speciality was headshots. He couldn't seem to think straight, was finding it hard to come to terms with the fact that he and his people were being out-thought and outfought by the men who'd taken Emma. He knew he couldn't give up, but standing there among the wreckage of the op, he was getting perilously close.

'What happened, Andrea?' he asked. 'We lost communication with you after you stopped to pick up the package.'

'I got a call on the phone that was in it. It was Emma screaming.'

Bolt swallowed. Told himself to keep calm.

'Just this one terrified scream. Then it cut out and he came on the line. He said that this time Emma was screaming out of fear, but the next time it would be out of pain, unless I did exactly what I was told. Those were his exact words. He told me to use that thing to start removing all the bugs and trackers' – she pointed at the bug-finding device that was now in an evidence bag in Mo's hands – 'and I tried to tell him I didn't know what he was talking about, but he told me he knew I'd gone to the police, and if I tried to deny

389

it then he'd . . . he'd make Emma scream again.' She stared at them each in turn. 'I had no choice. Don't you see that? I had no choice. I want my daughter back.'

'Well, you went about it the wrong way,' said Tina, her tone exasperated.

'What do you know? Have you got children?'

'No, but—'

'But nothing. You have no idea what you're talking about.'

Tina opened her mouth to reply but Bolt stepped in. This was getting them nowhere.

'OK, Andrea, so you followed their instructions. You removed the tracking devices and threw them out of the car. But not the two that were attached to the money.'

'No, they told me to leave them in the car when I got out.'

It was a logical move from the kidnappers' point of view, lulling the team into a false sense of security by letting them think they'd still be able to follow the ransom. It also showed that at least one of those involved had fairly expert knowledge of tracking devices.

'What was the last instruction you received?'

'To get out of the car and start walking up the road. I was told I'd be met by someone. I started walking and the next thing I knew there were these loud bangs, everyone was running, there was that gas . . . I remember shutting my eyes, getting knocked about by all these people running, and then someone punched me in the side of the head and grabbed the bag.' She touched the left side of her face where she'd been struck. The area was red and beginning to swell.

'And did you get a look at your attacker at all, Mrs Devern?' asked Mo.

'No, I didn't see anything. It all happened so fast.'

She took a gulp from the water and hunted round for her cigarettes, but couldn't find them.

'Has anyone got a smoke?'

Tina reached into her jeans, pulled out a battered pack of Silk Cut and a cheap lighter, and lit two cigarettes, one for Andrea and one for her. Andrea gave her a curt nod of acknowledgement.

'So, the person on the phone made you remove all these devices,' said Tina, a hint of scepticism in her voice, 'which you did . . .'

'That's right.'

'And did he at any point tell you when you were going to see your daughter again?'

All three of them looked at Andrea.

'He said I'd be seeing her very soon. As soon as he'd verified that the money was all there.'

'When did he say that?'

'During the car journey. Twice. He said it twice.'

'How did he say he was going to make contact to tell you where to find her?'

'He didn't.'

'It seems like you were very trusting,' said Tina. 'You made it impossible for us to track either the suspects or the money, yet you were offered very little in return.'

'All right, Tina,' said Bolt, concerned about the aggressiveness of her questioning, 'there's no point going over all this now.'

Andrea shot Tina a look that was both angry and incredulous.

'What is it? Don't you believe me or something?'

'No,' Tina replied, 'it's just that I can't understand why you did it.'

'Look, don't blame me because someone leaked the fact that I'd brought the police in. This is your fault not mine.' She took an urgent drag on her cigarette and stood up. 'I'm going home.'

'I'm afraid that's not possible for the moment, Andrea,' Bolt informed her.

'Back off, Mike. They've still got my daughter. They could call. So, if you're not arresting me, I'm going, and I'm going to need a lift if you're holding on to my car.'

She pushed past them and started walking in the direction of Tottenham High Road.

'Wait here,' Bolt told the other two and hurried

after her. 'Listen, Andrea,' he said when he was alongside her, 'you've got to let me know the second you hear from the kidnappers, OK?'

'What, so you can fuck it up again?' she snapped, without breaking pace. 'No way. I'll take my own chances from now on.'

Bolt grabbed her by the shoulder and swung her round so that she was facing him.

'That's not fair, Andrea, and you know it. I did everything I could.'

'Let go of my arm. You're hurting me.'

Bolt was conscious of several uniformed cops watching him. He ignored them. 'Please,' he said, 'tell me when they call.'

'Mike, what the hell's going on?'

Bolt looked round into the eyes of Stephen Evans, the former head of the NCS, now the assistant head of SOCA, who was flanked by several other equally grim-faced men in suits. Bolt let go of Andrea's arm and she walked away rapidly, passing Evans and his colleagues before they had a chance to say anything. Evans whispered something to the men with him and they went after Andrea while he approached Bolt.

Bolt knew Evans from the past. A short, compactly built man in his late forties with a neatly clipped moustache and a military bearing courtesy of an earlier career in the army, he'd helped him once before when he'd found himself

393

in trouble, and had a well-deserved reputation for looking after the interests of the men and women in his charge. But this time it was different, and Bolt knew it.

'Hello, sir,' he said with a sigh. 'Long time no see.'

Evans stopped in front of him. 'Yes, it is. And I'm sorry we've got to meet again under these kinds of circumstances.'

Bolt nodded grimly. 'I know.'

'I'm afraid I'm taking over the running of this op from SG2 Freud. Because of the way it's gone, he's been suspended pending an investigation. The same goes for you, Mike. As the team leader of the central team on this, I can't afford to keep you on.'

Bolt took a step back as he absorbed the hit.

'Don't do this, sir. I've got a good lead. There's a guy called Scott Ridgers with a long criminal record who's been doing gardening work for Andrea – Mrs Devern – until very recently. He was part of a gang of robbers she informed on fifteen years back. I think he might be our suspect one.'

'I know all that, Mike,' said Evans coldly. 'We've already got surveillance in place outside his flat in Finsbury Park.'

'But he's not there, is he? And the guy's a paedophile—'

'We're dealing with it.'

'Listen, sir, please—'

'No,' Evans said with a brutal finality. 'You're off the case, Mike, suspended until further notice. The IPCC will be getting in touch with you for a witness statement, so don't go disappearing on holiday. I'm sorry, but that's the way it's going to have to be.'

Bolt knew there was no point arguing. The decision had been made. He watched as Evans walked past him and over to Mo and Tina. He caught their eyes but said nothing. Instead, he simply turned away. He was no longer wanted or needed here.

Forty-three

Emma scratched away at the brickwork with the nail. It was so worn down now that it stuck out barely half an inch from between her thumb and forefinger, the end blunt and splayed. Progress was desperately slow. She was on her hands and knees, the bed pushed out from the wall to give her room, but her back still ached from where she'd been bent over for what felt like hours, and her fingers were almost numb with the pain and stiffness. But she refused to stop because she knew that her life might depend on success. Even more so now, after what had happened earlier.

A couple of hours or so after she'd recorded the message to her mum, telling her it was Saturday and that she was coming home soon, there'd come the familiar sound of the cellar door being unlocked, and she'd wondered if it was the smelly one coming down to collect the plate she'd used for breakfast. She'd had to push the bed as hurriedly and as quietly as possible back against the wall, and slip on her hood.

But his footsteps hadn't come. There'd simply been a cold, dead silence, and she'd known without a shadow of a doubt that it was the cruel one who'd come to visit, the one whose footsteps she could never hear.

An icy sensation had crept slowly up her spine as she sensed his presence in the room with her. Watching. Could he have spotted what she'd been doing to the wall? Had he heard her move the bed? Was this the end? Right now?

'Die, bitch!'

The voice was mocking and close.

She'd felt a sudden rush of air, and his hand had grabbed her shoulder in a tight, vicious grip. She'd screamed, instinctively – a terrified wail – and he'd laughed.

And that had been it. He released his grip, and she thought she heard something click, like a tape recorder. His parting words were delivered in a quiet sing-song voice, just before the cellar door shut again: 'Back later, bitch, back later.'

Ever since then she'd been working frantically, stopping every so often to yank at the chain, ignoring the frustration when still it seemed no looser. The sheer terror she was feeling kept her going, but it was also tiring her out. She wanted to sleep desperately, to lie down and shut her eyes. Forget this awful nightmare. But she refused to stop, knew that if she did she'd probably never start up again.

And then finally she got her break. For the first time, the brickwork really started crumbling. Full of hope, she scratched away even harder, and a load more brick dust poured down so that two of the screws holding the plate in place were almost completely revealed. She grabbed the chain and pulled furiously. Something gave, and one of the screws came out completely. She kept at it, but she simply didn't have the strength to tear it free.

But she was nearly there. A quick rest, and she'd carry on.

She lay back on the bed, her eyes shutting almost immediately. She was so tired, so weak. She felt herself dozing, drifting away . . . tried to come back, but never quite made it . . .

Forty-four

Bolt was sitting in heavy traffic on Tottenham High Road, only a few hundred metres away from where it had all gone so badly wrong. Darkness had fallen, and the sound of the sirens was becoming more sporadic. The helicopters still flew overhead, but their constant circling felt pointless and redundant. Not for the first time in his life he was left on the outside, no longer wanted on an investigation he'd helped to get started.

He didn't want to go home, not with Emma still out there somewhere. The two mobile phone calls the kidnappers had made to Andrea's landline had come from round these streets, and he doubted that the guy with the money had gone far. Much easier to disappear into a nearby house, away from the helicopters, the pursuing cops and the prying eyes of the CCTV. It would take some nerve to organize the ransom drop so near to where they were holding Emma, but nerve had never been in short supply with these people. He was sure that suspect number one was Scott Ridgers, and if necessary he'd drive round and round hoping that at some point Ridgers emerged from his hideout. It was the longest of long shots but it had to be better than doing nothing.

The traffic was moving at a snail's pace, and the worn-out buildings around him – cheap take-aways, charity shops, a few boarded-up wrecks – felt foreboding and claustrophobic. It was on nights like this that he hated London with its noise, its litter and its gridlock, and he felt an almost physical yearning for space. He remembered back to the day he'd bumped into Andrea on the Strand, and how it had been the start of their affair. What if he hadn't been there? What if he'd been doing something different, and their paths had never crossed that second time? How much happier a man would he be now.

Which was when that old nagging thought struck him. What if their meeting hadn't been spontaneous? What if it had all been a set-up? Perhaps Andrea's lover, Jimmy Galante, had wanted inside information on the Flying Squad and had encouraged her to take up with Bolt in order to get it. He thought back, trying to remember if she'd ever pumped him for information, but nothing came to mind. But then, of course, she might not have been doing it on behalf of Galante. She might have taken up with Bolt of her own accord, using him to bring Galante down, either because she was genuinely desperate to leave him and could think of no other way of doing it, or . . . or what?

God knows. He sighed, wiping sweat from his brow and turning the air con higher.

The sound of his mobile ringing jolted him from his thoughts. He looked at the screen but didn't recognize the number. He flicked it on to hands-free and took the call.

'Mr Bolt?'

Bolt recognized the slightly officious tones of Lisa Bouchera's father and tensed a little.

'Mr Bouchera, how can I help you?'

'He's called my daughter.'

Bolt felt a sudden flash of excitement. 'When?'

'Just now. I was outside in the garden but when I came back inside she was crying. She told him she didn't want to see him any more and he started calling her all these filthy names.'

'I'm very sorry to hear that,' Bolt told him. 'We can make sure he doesn't call her again. Have you got access to your daughter's phone?'

'I can get it. Hold on.'

A few seconds later he was back on the line. Bolt asked him to go into the Calls Received screen.

'OK, let's have a look.' There was a pause. 'All right, I'm in.'

His hands shaking, Bolt pulled out his notebook and pen.

'Read me out the top number.'

The moment of truth.

Bouchera reeled off a mobile number and Bolt wrote it down. By using a mobile to make the call to his girlfriend, Scott Ridgers had effectively given out his location, and, Bolt hoped, Emma's location as well. The excitement he was feeling was so powerful it actually made him nauseous for a few seconds.

'And he was the last person who called her?'

'Yes. It was just now.'

Bolt looked at his watch. Five to eight. Just under an hour since the money had disappeared.

'Thank you, sir,' he said, 'you've been a great help.'

'And you. Let me know when you've got the bastard in custody.'

'Course I will,' Bolt said, ending the call.

He took a deep breath, brutally aware that he was suspended and that unless he played things right this lead counted for nothing. He had to do something, and fast. Mo or Tina – who did he call? Who did he trust?

Mo was the colleague he'd always trusted the most, but things had changed between them these past twenty-four hours, possibly irreversibly. Tina, meanwhile, was the person on the team with the best access to the phone companies, and he remembered the look she'd given him in the meeting that morning. Was it empathy? Some kind of understanding? He was stepping over a line by contacting her, he knew that. Asking her to put her own job in jeopardy as a favour to him. And she was such an enigmatic person, so difficult to read, that he had no idea whether she'd help him or not.

There was only one way to find out. He dialled her number, willing her to answer, concentrating so much on this latest development that he didn't even notice that the traffic ahead of him was moving until he heard the horns blaring. As he touched the accelerator and moved forward, her voice came on the line. Clear and businesslike as always.

'Tina Boyd.'

'Tina, it's Mike.'

He heard her sharp intake of breath.

'I didn't expect to hear from you. There's no more news. Matt's in surgery at the moment.'

His thoughts returned to Turner. Poor sod. If only he'd stayed behind at Andrea's house.

'Listen, sir, we're snowed under here. I'm going to have to go.'

'I need a favour.'

'But you're suspended.'

'I know that, but this is urgent, and it's to do with the case. I've got a mobile number for Scott Ridgers – that suspect I was talking to you about earlier who turned out to be one of Andrea's gardeners. He's just used it, literally minutes ago, to make a call. If we can get a trace on that number, it'll lead us straight to him.'

'How did you find this out?'

Bolt explained as briefly as he could.

'I can speak to Steve Evans, but I'm not sure he'll be able, or willing, to authorize it.'

'No, don't speak to him. I can tell you now, he won't authorize it. Just do it. Please.'

'I can't, sir. You're suspended. It could cost me my job.' She sighed. 'I'm sorry.'

'She's my daughter, Tina.'

'What?'

'Emma Devern. She's my daughter. Check with Mo if you don't believe me. It's why I've been so highly strung since this all began.'

'God, I . . . I don't know what to say.'

'Don't say anything. Just help me, please. If we don't act fast, Emma could die.'

'I can't believe you're putting me in this position, Mike.'

'Do you think I want to? Look, there's no way on God's earth I would ask you to do this unless I absolutely had to.' He could hear the desperation in his voice, hated it.

Tina was silent for two, maybe three seconds.

'OK, let me have the number.'

He reeled it off for her.

'I'll do what I can, but it might take some time.'

'This is my daughter. There is no time.'

'If you're lying to me,' she said evenly, 'I'll kill you.'

Forty-five

Emma awoke with a start, sitting bolt upright. It was dark in the room, and her mouth felt bone dry. She wondered how long she'd been out. Without a watch it was difficult to tell, but it was a while. Half an hour, something like that. She rubbed her eyes, swung her legs off the bed and remembered that she'd been very close to getting the chain free from the wall.

And then she heard a loud bang. It was the sound of the front door shutting.

They were back.

She grabbed the chain with both hands, closed her eyes and pulled as hard as she could. There was a crack – something giving – and more dust showered on to the stone floor. She could hear footfalls on the floor above, but no voices.

Clenching her teeth, ignoring the nauseous feeling flowing through her, she kept pulling, leaning back so her whole body was behind it, knowing this could well be her last chance.

Another crack.

Movement near the cellar door – a shuffling of feet.

They're coming.

She was out of time.

And then suddenly she was falling back off the bed, landing painfully on the floor with the chain uncoiling on top of her.

She'd done it. The metal plate had come free.

Forty-six

Bolt was driving aimlessly down yet another grimy terraced back street when the call came. The clock on his dashboard said 8.07. Only nine minutes since he'd got off the phone to Tina.

So much of a person's life seemed to him to boil down to those single, long, terrifying moments of anticipation when you're given the hugely important news you've been waiting for: the results of medical tests; exam results; a jury's verdict; the location of the man who's holding your daughter.

'Tina,' he said, his voice hoarse, 'what have you got?'

'The phone's still on. The location's been triangulated to an area around a farm called Woodlands in Crews Hill.'

'Where the hell's that?'

'Just north of Enfield, south of the M25.'

She gave him the address and he fed it into the car's sat-nav system. The distance was just over six miles from where he was now. He swung the car round in a rapid three-point turn so that he was heading back towards the main road.

'Thanks, Tina.'

'What are you going to do?'

'I'm going to go and check it out. If it looks like it's a lead, I'll call in straight away.'

'This could put me in huge amounts of trouble, Mike. They're going to know the info's come from me, and you know as well as I do that it's totally illegal to get an unauthorized triangulation.'

'If it comes to nothing, there's no way it'll ever get back to you. You've got my word on that. And if it does lead somewhere, I'll come up with a reason why I found out about Ridgers' location without mentioning your name. I really appreciate this, Tina.'

'I talked to Mo. Christ, I can't believe she could be your daughter.'

There was a silence then, because Bolt didn't really know what to say. Tina ended it by wishing him good luck.

'Call us as soon as you've checked it out,' she added.

'Sure.'

He cut the connection, and accelerated on to the main road, ignoring the blast of the horn from the driver he'd just cut up. All that mattered to him was getting to Scott Ridgers.

Six miles and counting.

Forty-seven

Emma put the bed back in its original position so that it covered the hole in the wall and the brick-dust on the floor, and waited in silence with the hood in her hands. Her elbow ached where she'd smacked it on the floor, and she felt sick and thirsty.

The movement upstairs had stopped a few minutes ago, and now she couldn't hear anything. She wondered what to do. The problem was, she might be mobile, but the fact remained that she was still handcuffed and locked in here, and the chain was still attached to her ankle, which was definitely going to slow her down if she did make a run for it. And the silence scared her, because silence was what she associated with the cruel one.

Back later, bitch.

Maybe he was sharpening his knife right now?

But she couldn't just sit there waiting for him to come and kill her. Otherwise all her efforts would be in vain. No, she had to do something. A plan formed in her mind. She'd hide at the top of the steps behind the door, and when he came inside she'd push him down them before he had a chance to spot her. Then she'd make a break for it. It was pretty lame as plans went, but it was the best she could think up at the moment.

She lifted up the ankle chain and started to get up from the bed. And then stopped as the key turned in the lock and the door opened.

She was too late.

Hurriedly, she got back on the bed and let the chain slip to the floor. Her hands were shaking and she felt fear running up her spine. Was this it? The last seconds of her life, in a dingy, cold basement miles from home?

Silence.

She made no move to put on the hood as she stared towards the staircase.

The light came on, and she squinted against its brightness.

'Emma,' came a voice from the top of the steps, 'it's me.'

She felt a surge of excitement. It was the smelly one. She was going to be OK.

'Hi,' she said quietly. 'I'm here.'

'Put your hood on, honey. OK? It's almost time to go home.'

She did as she was told, hardly able to believe her luck.

'Am I honestly going home?'

'That's right,' he answered in that wheezy voice of his. 'It's over. Your mum paid the money so you don't have to stay here any more.'

She heard him come close. Smelled him, too, the BO so strong now it made her gag beneath the hood. He put something down on the floor by the bed and she thought she heard water sloshing.

'Am I going to go now?'

'Very soon. We'll just get you ready. Then there'll be a little journey, and that'll be it. Back home to your mum. First I'm going to give you a little wash, though. So you're all nice and clean.'

She felt a wet sponge on her left arm. It made her feel cold and itchy. He ran it slowly up and down before starting on the other one.

'Bet that feels good, doesn't it?'

'You don't need to do this. I can wait until I'm home.'

'I want to do it.'

He moved her arms to one side and lifted up her T-shirt, rubbing the sponge on her tummy in small circles. Water dripped down towards the top of her skirt, and she heard him swallow. It was

413

a really horrible sound, like something a frog would make.

'What are you doing?' she whispered.

'Just washing you, darling,' he replied, lifting her T-shirt higher. Swallowing a second time.

That was when she realized with a sickening feeling that the nightmare hadn't ended after all.

Forty-eight

The driveway that led down to Woodlands Farm was situated on a quiet wooded road half a mile south of the M25, a simple wooden sign attached to a beech tree announcing its presence. There were no other houses in the immediate vicinity, making Bolt think that it would be an ideal place to hold someone without arousing suspicion.

The tension coursed through him. Scott Ridgers had motive; he'd worked at Andrea's place and then disappeared at the same time that Emma had gone missing. And as a fully fledged city boy, why else would he be out here in the back of beyond?

Not wishing to announce his presence, Bolt drove thirty yards further along the road before pulling up on the verge and manoeuvring his car as far into the trees as it would go. He killed the lights and got out. Through the darkness created by the thick concentration of trees, he thought he could just make out lights, but it was difficult to tell. According to the sat-nav, Woodlands Farm was set back at least a hundred yards from the road.

Knowing how short time was, he moved swiftly, making for the driveway. His plan was to approach from the front as quietly as possible and recce the place. If there was no sign of Ridgers, he'd break in. He'd taken the law into his own hands enough times today to worry about doing it again, and it was possible that his actions had already cost him his job.

The advantage, however, was that he now had nothing to lose.

Forty-nine

Emma knew what was coming. The dirty, stinking pervert wanted to have sex with her. Was *going* to have sex with her if she didn't do something about it.

A gloved hand touched her knee, and she gagged beneath the hood.

She had an idea. It was her only chance.

'Can you undo the handcuffs?' she asked, trying to make her voice sound as if she might be interested in what he was about to do to her. 'Then maybe we can . . .' She let the words trail off.

'You're not teasing me, are you?' he said, seriously. 'I don't like girls who tease me. I've had too much of that recently.'

'No, course not. I've done it before, you know.'

He chuckled. 'Ooh, you are a naughty girl, aren't you? I think maybe we can make things a bit more comfortable for you.'

He stopped sponging her and she heard him fiddling around for the key. She tensed as he found it and unlocked the cuffs, slipping them off. She heard him stand up, then the sound of a zipper being pulled.

Now! Now! Now! a voice in her head screamed.

She pulled off the hood and jumped up from the bed in one movement, kneeing him in the groin as hard as she could. He gasped in pain and staggered backwards, clutching himself with both hands.

For the first time, she got a look at him. He was dressed in jeans and a dirty white T-shirt, and his face was covered by a balaclava. Tattoos adorned his arms.

Picking up the chain, she ran past him, dodging beneath a flailing arm as he tried to grab her.

'You little cow!' he bellowed, lurching after her, still holding on to his balls.

She took the steps two at a time, the chain still in her hand. Her limbs felt stiff and painful from the sudden burst of exercise, but adrenalin drove her on because she knew that if he caught her, this time he'd kill her for sure. He hadn't locked the door from the inside, and she yanked it open and ran out, slamming it behind her.

She was in a hallway. A door ahead led through to a living room, one to the right looked like it led outside. She turned hard right, ran across the hall

418

and grabbed the handle. It turned, but the door didn't open. Panic flooded through her.

Behind her, the cellar door flew open and banged hard against the wall as he came stumbling out after her.

There was a second handle. Tucking the chain beneath her arm, she turned the two of them simultaneously, and this time the door opened.

A gloved hand snatched at her collar, but she kept going, hearing it rip as he lost his grip, and then she was out into the night, breathing in fresh air for the first time in days. There was a gate and fence ahead, beyond them trees. The gate was shut. She knew he'd catch her if she ran towards it, so she darted left, running along the front of the house, past an outbuilding, making for a field with long grass up ahead.

She could hear his footsteps on the gravel behind her, and the sound of his heavy breathing. He was only feet away now. Pure fear drove her on, the sure knowledge of what he'd do if he caught her making her legs pump far faster than she'd ever thought they were capable of. She'd never been much of a runner, and at school she'd hated athletics, even though her Games teacher, Miss Floyd, always said that she had the perfect build for it, being slim and small-chested. And now, finally, when it really mattered, she was proving Miss Floyd right.

His breathing got fainter as she began to open up some distance between them. She was running into the long grass now, and she felt a surge of elation which lasted no more than a second. As she pumped her arms to speed herself up, the movement tightened the chain and caused her to trip up and lose her footing. She fell forwards, the uneven, stony ground charging up to meet her, and her hands hit it palms first.

Desperately she scrambled to her feet, but it was too late. With a roar of triumph, he came down hard on her back, knocking the wind out of her in an agonizing rush.

'Oh God!'

'He can't help you now, you little tease!'

He laughed as he sat astride her and twisted her round roughly so that she was facing him, his knees digging into her upper arms. She stared into his balaclava-clad face, saw dark eyes glinting excitedly through the slits, and felt terror surge through her as his gloved hands fiddled impatiently with the zipper on his jeans, pulling them open.

He grabbed her wrist and thrust her hand towards his groin, pulling her upright as he did so. 'Feel me,' he hissed, and she cried out as the hand made contact. But he'd moved as well and his knee was no longer pinning her free arm. Taking her chance, with the free hand she scrabbled around in the grass until she found a sharp piece of flint half the size of her palm. It wasn't much of a weapon, but it was all she had. Operating entirely on instinct now, she drove it into the side of his head and dragged the sharp edge down the side of his balaclava.

He yelped in pain and smacked her hand away, letting go of the other one at the same time, but Emma pressed her advantage, ramming the flint into the top of his thigh, only centimetres from his balls. Cursing, he jumped off her, keen to get out of the way before she did any more damage, and she saw her opportunity. Scrambling to her feet, she took off again, the chain trailing loosely behind her as she made for the tree line, not daring to look back.

She hit the trees at a sprint, branches crunching underfoot as she was swallowed up by the darkness, tearing through brambles, ignoring the pain as they scratched and clawed her, just wanting to keep running, to get as far away from him as possible. Faster and faster, almost blind now in her desire to keep going.

She fell headfirst, landing on a bed of leaves. She could still hear him but it sounded as if he was some distance away. He hadn't seen or heard her fall, she was sure of that. Part of her wanted to jump back up and keep going, but a bigger part told her that it was best to stay put, hidden.

Slowly, very slowly, trying to control her breathing, she inched forward on her stomach, pushing herself under a thick holly bush until she'd got her whole body underneath it, the jagged leaves scraping against her head and back.

She could feel his heavy footfalls getting closer. Step by slow step. She'd never been so scared in her whole life and it took all her willpower just to stop herself from crying out. She squeezed her eyes shut and bit her lip.

'You've cut me, you little cow,' he hissed, his voice carrying through the darkness. 'And after all I've done for you as well. I kept you alive, and you do this.'

Another footstep. Almost next to her now. She forced her eyes open, and had to stifle a scream. He was right by the holly bush, his black Caterpillar boot only feet away from her face, a hulking black shadow blocking out the moonlight as he sniffed the air like some kind of predator.

She stayed utterly still, frozen to the spot, not even daring to breathe. Waiting. Hoping. Praying that he wouldn't discover her.

Please. I just want to go home. See my mum. End this nightmare.

He seemed to stand there for ever, and she felt her lungs tightening, crying out for air.

Move. Move, please. I can't hold it in much longer.

And then suddenly he did, the footfalls starting

again as he skirted the holly bush and began to move away.

She shut her eyes and thanked God, exhaling as silently as she could and slowly taking in much-needed air. Kept listening, telling herself that she only had to lie there another few minutes and everything would be all right. He'd give up his search, and she'd make a run for the nearest road. Get help. Go home.

She never heard the movement behind her, just caught a reek of stale sweat. And then the chain that was attached to her ankle was suddenly round her neck, choking her, and a triumphant voice was whispering in her ear, 'Found you.'

Fifty

Bolt walked slowly down the track as it ran in a curve through the woodland and then straightened as the tree line ended and an old two-storey cottage in need of a lick of paint appeared in front of him, nestled between two ramshackle outbuildings. There were lights on downstairs and the double-gates that led to the front of the house were wide open. A dark-coloured Range Rover was parked in the driveway.

He moved off the driveway and on to the long grass lining it so that his movements didn't trigger any lights, and approached the gates quietly using the darkness as cover.

But as he reached them he heard the sound of footsteps on gravel coming from somewhere up ahead. His view of whoever it was was blocked by the Range Rover as he crouched down behind the fence so that he couldn't be seen.

Then he heard it. A strangled sob, definitely female. He felt a ferocious jolt of emotion that almost knocked him off his feet as he realized that it was almost certainly coming from Emma.

This was confirmed in the next few seconds when she came into view, barely a silhouette in the gloom and smaller than he'd imagined, staring straight ahead. But it was definitely Emma, just as Bolt knew that the man dragging her by the length of chain round her neck was Scott Ridgers. He might have been wearing a bala-clava, but that didn't matter. It was him.

Bastard.

Ridgers had a small-bladed knife in his free hand which he kept close to Emma's side to ensure she didn't struggle. Even in the darkness, Bolt could see the terrified expression on her face, and he felt the rage build within him. But there were at least twenty yards between them, which would give Ridgers far too much time to react if Bolt charged him. He was going to have to be patient, look for an opportunity.

Then Ridgers said something to Emma that chilled Bolt's blood: 'We're going to have some fun now, baby.'

Emma managed a strangled sob, and Bolt had to shut his eyes and hold on to the fence for support.

When he opened them again, they'd reached

the front door. He watched as Ridgers pushed it open and shoved Emma inside, following her in without looking round.

And chuckling. The bastard was actually chuckling.

He also made the biggest mistake of his life. He didn't shut the door behind him.

Bolt took a deep breath. Moving as quietly and swiftly as he could, he followed them into the house.

Fifty-one

The chain round her neck was choking Emma so badly she could hardly breathe as he dragged her through the hallway. The cellar door was still open and he pushed her towards it.

Oh God, she couldn't go back in there again, not having come so close to freedom. And she knew that if she went back in, this time she definitely wouldn't be coming back out. Not alive, anyway.

She went limp in his arms, and he cursed.

'Come on, move it,' he snapped, angry now, pressing the blade of a penknife he'd produced earlier against her ribs.

She stayed limp, and started to make horrible choking sounds, as if she was dying.

'If you're fooling me about . . .'

He let her drop to her knees and loosened the chain a little.

'Water,' she gasped.

'All right,' he said, hauling her to her feet and manhandling her through the hallway in the direction of the kitchen. 'You can have some water. Then we'll have some—'

He suddenly stopped as they reached the kitchen door and he switched on the light. She felt him go tense.

'Where is it? Where the fuck is it?'

He shoved her roughly inside, letting go of the chain and sending her sprawling to the floor.

'The bag!' he yelled, his voice filling the room. 'The bag with the fucking money! It was on here!' He pointed a gloved hand at the empty kitchen table. 'Where the hell is it?' He paced about inside the room, rubbing a hand over his face beneath the balaclava, his eyes wide and angry. 'I can't believe this. Someone's taken it. Someone's taken my money.' He stopped and slammed his hand down on the table, hitting it so hard the legs wobbled. 'My fucking money!' he roared at the ceiling.

Emma cowered, terrified, pushing herself into the corner of the room, away from his rage and frustration.

'I'm going to find whoever's done this,' he muttered. 'I'm going to find him now. And when I get hold of him . . .' He shoved the penknife he was holding back into the pocket of his jeans, then yanked open one of the drawers, took out a huge kitchen knife and ran a finger along the blade. 'When I get hold of him, I'm going to fillet the bastard.'

He turned and pointed the knife at Emma. The blade shone in the glare of the overhead lights. 'Stay there, all right? Don't you dare move an inch if you ever want to see your mum again. OK?'

She nodded, trying not to sob. 'OK.'

He swung round and stormed out of the door, knife in hand.

And immediately cried out in surprise.

The next second he was flying back through the door with another man hanging on to him and shouting something that filled her with sudden and delirious relief: 'Armed police! Drop your weapon!'

Fifty-two

But that was the problem. Bolt wasn't armed when he charged Scott Ridgers. He wasn't even carrying standard-issue pepper spray, which had been taken off him earlier. He had nothing but surprise. He grabbed Ridgers' wrists and twisted them away from his body, paying particular attention to the hand holding the kitchen knife, and trying to butt him as he'd done Marcus Richardson earlier that day. But the blow he caught Ridgers with as they both crashed into the kitchen barely glanced the other man, who had the good sense to move his head, and as they hit the kitchen table, disaster struck. Bolt lost his footing and slipped, sliding along the tiled floor on one knee, desperately trying to keep hold of his foe, even though his head was now only level with the other man's groin.

Ridgers was fast, and he took advantage of

Bolt's plight to tug his wrists free and slam a knee into his face. A piercing, hot pain shot through Bolt's nose and he wobbled in his kneeling position, unable to react as Ridgers then lifted a leg and delivered an accurate kung-fu kick to the side of his head. This time he fell backwards, landing against something white and hard. His head throbbed savagely where Ridgers' boot had connected and he could feel the blood pouring out of his nostrils and on to his lips. He tried to focus through the pain, saw the huge knife in Ridgers' hand, and knew that he was helpless.

Jesus. After all this, he'd failed.

Then he saw Emma crouching in the corner of the room, her eyes wide with shock.

'Run, Emma!' he shouted. 'Run!'

Ridgers took a step forward, pointing the knife down at Bolt, ignoring Emma now. 'Where's my money?' he roared. 'Where's my fucking money?'

Bolt rolled on to his side, thinking fast, assessing his options . . . knowing full well that he didn't have any. Emma leapt to her feet, but instead of running for the door, she ran at Ridgers and sank her teeth into his knife arm, just above the elbow. He cried out but didn't relinquish his grip on the knife. Instead, he grabbed her by the hair and yanked her off in one movement, the force of his attack sending her crashing into one of the worktops.

Adrenalin born of pure rage shot through Bolt, briefly substituting the pain and dizziness. He started to get up.

But it was too late. Ridgers was bearing down on him, and there was murder in his eyes as he brought back his knife arm to deliver a blow that Bolt knew would not only end his life, but would mean the end of Emma's too.

And then there was a loud crack, followed a second later by the sound of breaking glass, and suddenly Scott Ridgers pitched forward as his legs went from under him. His head smacked hard against the fridge and he collapsed to the floor, landing on his side on Bolt's legs. A thin stream of blood poured from the smoking hole where his right eye had been.

Emma screamed as he convulsed in his death throes.

'Stay down!' Bolt yelled at her, kicking Ridgers' body off him.

Four more shots exploded through the night air in rapid succession, showering the table and floor with shards of glass. Emma screamed again, and Bolt crawled over to her, moving as fast as he could and ignoring the glass beneath him. Grabbing her in his arms, he pulled her under him so that she was shielded from the gunfire. She was shaking with fear and sobbing, and he held her tight, thinking how small and vulnerable she was.

Even in those dramatic moments he felt a kind of love he'd never experienced before.

'Just stay still,' he whispered. 'I'm here now. You're going to be all right.'

For ten seconds they lay there together in a tight, tangled embrace. There were no more shots. Silence had returned, and Ridgers had stopped moving. But the fact remained that someone had just murdered him, and that person was close by.

'Stay where you are,' Bolt told Emma as he got to his feet.

'Where are you going?'

'Just stay there, help's coming.'

Keeping low, he killed the kitchen light and crept over to the back door. A yard, with outbuildings to the left and right, ran about twenty yards to the beginning of the tree line. It looked empty, but, as Bolt turned the key in the lock and slowly opened the door, he knew he was being foolish. It was one thing risking your neck to save your daughter, it was quite another to chase a gunman while he was unarmed.

But whoever had fired the shot that killed Scott Ridgers was also involved in this, and Bolt was in no mood to let him get away. And if he was carrying half a million in cash, his escape was going to be a slow one.

Bolt slid through the gap in the door on his hands and knees, then made a dash for the nearest outbuilding, where he stopped and peered round at the trees. He could hear nothing. The night was silent with only the lightest of breezes. The gunman was gone.

He was being an idiot. He could never do this alone, and he couldn't leave Emma alone with a corpse either. He wiped the blood from his face, pulled his mobile from his pocket and put in a call to Tina as he jogged back the way he'd come.

'I've got Emma,' he told her once he'd briefly explained what had just happened. 'She's OK, but the guy who shot Ridgers is gone. You're going to have to get people over here quick. We need to get a security cordon in place and seal off the whole area.'

Ignoring the fact that she was being ordered around by someone who was suspended, Tina said she was on it and hung up.

Bolt stepped back inside the kitchen door. Emma was sitting on the floor, staring into space. She turned his way as he entered, and for several seconds they simply looked at each other in silence.

Emma looked utterly exhausted. Her clothes were torn and sweat-stained, and her blonde hair was matted and dishevelled, parts of it stuck to the thin layer of grime that covered her face. But none of that mattered. She was beautiful. And she was safe. He felt a wave of emotion sweep over him and he had to grit his teeth so that he didn't cry.

'Who are you?' she asked uncertainly.

Who am I? Your father, I think. A man you've never met before who's linked to you inextricably and for ever. Someone who's sweated blood these past hours trying to find you, who wants to get to know you, take you places, be a part of your life, and explain why he hasn't been there for so long. Who needs you so badly you can't imagine it.

'I'm the police,' he said.

'Will you take me home?'

He took a deep breath, fought back the tears. 'Of course I will.'

Fifty-three

But he didn't take her home. In fact, he hardly had
a chance to talk to her.

Within minutes, the first of a long line of police
and ambulance vehicles were on the scene, and
she was taken away from him. After checking that
she didn't need emergency medical treatment, the
paramedics whisked her off to the nearby Chase
Farm Hospital where she was to be reunited with
her mother before being debriefed, and for Bolt,
that was largely that. He was left alone on the
periphery, watching as the local police sealed off
the murder scene.

Within half an hour, the area around the farmhouse was teeming with activity, and floodlights
had been set up to illuminate proceedings. Bolt
was introduced briefly to a DI called Baker,
who was running the CID nightshift at Enfield
Nick, and who had the initial responsibility for

investigating Scott Ridgers' death. He looked more like an accountant than a copper and when he spoke it was in a flat estuary accent, but he had sharp, intelligent eyes that didn't look like they missed a lot, and Bolt had a feeling that when he went down to the station later to give his statement he was going to get a serious grilling about how he, a suspended SOCA agent, had ended up at the scene, particularly as the ransom money was missing. But he was ready for it. After everything else that had happened today, he was pretty much prepared for whatever was going to be thrown at him.

He was leaning against the farmhouse's front fence, drinking coffee from a plastic container, when a car pulled up just behind the line of police vans on the driveway, and Steve Evans got out, followed by Tina and Mo. Their expressions were grim and businesslike, but as they got closer Tina nodded at him from behind Evans's shoulder and gave him the barest hint of a smile. Mo just nodded.

Evans, meanwhile, was just plain pissed off. 'I thought I told you you were suspended, Mike,' he said, stopping in front of him.

'You did, sir. I got a lead on Scott Ridgers. I thought I'd check it out. As a concerned private citizen.'

Evans didn't look mollified. 'And you tracked

him down here, only for him to be shot dead by an unknown assailant while you were struggling with him. That's the story I'm getting from DI Baker.'

'Yes, sir. Someone shot Ridgers from outside the kitchen window while I was fighting with him inside. I'm assuming it's the same person who disappeared with the money from the ransom drop. I phoned Tina as soon as I could so that she could alert the local police, and I've been here ever since.'

Evans looked sceptical. 'It always seems to be you who gets in these situations, doesn't it? How did you end up here?'

Avoiding Tina's eyes, he told Evans the story he'd already rehearsed in his head.

'Ridgers told his girlfriend where he was staying in case she needed him. When her father told her that he was wanted for a very serious crime, she gave him this address. The father phoned me because we'd already spoken earlier today. Obviously I was suspended, and I didn't think my word would count for much, so I decided to come up here myself, just to check things out. As soon as I arrived, I saw Ridgers dragging Emma into the house, and decided I was going to have to intervene immediately.' He shrugged. 'The rest you know.'

Evans stared at him for several seconds. He had

a hard, intimidating gaze that carried the heavy weight of authority. Bolt, who was used to such looks and wasn't affected by them, held it firmly.

'Well, you're still suspended, Mike, and I don't want to see you around again until you're back on duty. Understood?'

The rebuke was painful, especially as he'd done so much to break a case that was about to go very high-profile, but not entirely unexpected. Evans was right. He still shouldn't have been there.

'Sure, I understand.'

'Good. Now, I need to go and see DI Baker. If you'll excuse me.'

Evans moved past Bolt, leaving him alone with Mo and Tina. Mo asked how Emma was. His tone was stiff and formal, and Bolt had noticed that he hadn't called him 'boss' for some time now.

'She's good,' he answered. 'As well as can be expected, anyway. But it's going to take her a while to recover.'

'But she will recover. Kids always do. They're resilient like that.' Mo looked towards the house. 'I'd better go inside.'

'OK.'

Mo managed a weak smile that confirmed to Bolt that their relationship had taken a serious beating.

'I hope you're back on duty soon,' he said.

'I will be.'

439

'Good luck.'

Mo turned and walked towards the gate. Tina made no move to follow him.

'You not going with him?'

She nodded. 'In a minute.'

Bolt smiled at her. He couldn't help but think she looked pretty in the moonlight.

'Thanks for what you did, Tina. It saved Emma's life.'

'Thanks for covering for me.'

'I couldn't really do anything else, could I? Not after you put your job on the line.' He sighed. 'How's Turner?'

'Still critical, but he's off the operating table now. It looks better than it did.'

'Thank God for that. Any other developments in the case?'

It was her turn to smile now. 'You're the one who seems to be creating the developments, Mike.'

'I didn't have anything to do with Ridgers' death, you know.'

'I never thought you would have done.'

He wondered why he'd felt the need to tell her that. Had he really moved so far from his position as law enforcer that he had to justify himself to his colleagues in case they suspected he might be a killer?

'It wouldn't surprise me if Mo thinks I did, though,' he said, rubbing his eyes.

'Mo likes to do things the right way. He's pissed off with you, but he still thinks you're a good cop.'

Tina was wrong. Mo didn't always have to do things the right way. Bolt remembered that at one time Mo had done things for him way above and beyond the call of duty, but that maybe now he'd grown weary of bailing his boss out.

'You look whacked, Mike.'

'I am. It's been a long day. But, you know, I don't like the idea of going home knowing there's still someone out there who's a kidnapper and a killer, and who's now at least half a million pounds richer.'

'The police here have found Phelan's car in one of the outbuildings. But no sign of Phelan.'

Bolt was surprised. He'd almost forgotten about Andrea's husband.

'I don't think it was Phelan who killed Ridgers,' he said slowly. 'I just can't see that he's the one behind this. I mean, the guy's a fly-by-night, a minor criminal, and an inveterate gambler. He's hardly a criminal mastermind.'

'But if his car's here, then why isn't he?' asked Tina. 'If he wasn't involved, I would have thought they'd've disposed of the car and the body together, because there'd be no point doing it separately.'

'I suppose so, but if he is part of this, then why did they bother killing Andrea's cleaner?'

Tina shrugged. 'Good point. God knows.'

They fell silent, and Bolt yawned.

'You'd better go in, Tina. Steve Evans won't be pleased if you're talking to me. You'll keep me posted of how things go though, yeah?'

She nodded. 'Of course I will.'

As she walked past him, she patted his arm reassuringly and he realized it was the first time in their two years working together that she'd ever touched him.

'You did a good job tonight, Mike,' she said. 'You'll be back on duty soon.'

He watched her go, thinking of all the things he'd done today, so many of which could still cost him his career. He'd been in law enforcement for twenty years. It was the only job he'd known, and despite the constraints it imposed and the huge tedium of much of the work, he loved it. If they sacked him, he had no idea what he'd do. But the fact remained, there was no way he'd have changed any of his actions because in the end, illegal or not, they had got him the one thing he wanted most: his daughter back.

He thought about Pat Phelan in the photograph with Emma and Andrea at Andrea's house, all close up together, the happy nuclear family. If he was involved, it would be a betrayal of epic proportions. Fear can make a man do some strange things, and owing big sums of money to a violent thug like Leon Daroyce was going to make someone like Pat Phelan very frightened. But even so, Bolt still didn't buy the fact that he was the man who'd escaped with the money.

The problem now, with the other conspirators dead, was finding out who was.

Part Six

Part Six

Fifty-four

Whatever doubts Bolt had about Pat Phelan's involvement in the kidnap of his stepdaughter, the fact remained that they were largely irrelevant. He was off the case and, for the moment at least, off the team.

It had been a long night. He'd been at Enfield Nick until the early hours, giving his statement to two of the local CID and taking their questions. He'd stuck to the story he'd told Steve Evans about why he'd been on the scene in the first place, but made sure he told the truth about everything else, and it soon became clear that they were treating him as a witness rather than a suspect in the murder of Scott Ridgers. Formalities complete, he'd eventually made it home a little after three a.m. and collapsed, exhausted, into his bed straight away, able to relax for the first time in close to forty-eight hours.

He slept late. It was gone eleven when he finally rose from his bed, cleaned himself up, and put on a fresh pot of coffee. There was a message on his mobile from Mo telling him that Matt Turner was still on the critical list but that the operation had been a success and the doctors were confident he was going to pull through. He also added that Emma had been debriefed and had confirmed Bolt's version of events, then finished by wishing his boss luck and hoping he'd be back on duty soon. He sounded a little contrite, and Bolt guessed that this was his apology for the way he'd been the previous day.

It was good news about Turner. He'd go down the hospital to visit him as soon as he was well enough to be seen.

As he poured the coffee and made himself a couple of slices of toast, his thoughts turned to Emma. It was a strange feeling knowing that he had a daughter who for fourteen years had grown up only a few miles away. But he felt happy about it, and hopeful too. He wanted to become a part of her life now, although he knew that this would have to wait a while, at least until she'd recovered from the worst of her ordeal.

But at the very least he needed to know how she was getting on, and when he'd finished his toast he called Andrea's landline. Marie the liaison officer answered. She sounded tired, but brightened a little when she recognized Bolt's voice.

'It's great news that we've got Emma back,' she said. 'Andrea's ecstatic, as you can imagine.'

'Is Andrea there?' he asked.

'Yes, they're both here. Do you want to speak to her?'

'Please. Just tell her it's a quick courtesy call. I'm sure she's busy.'

'I'll go and find her. Hold on.'

Marie clearly didn't know about his suspension. In fact, it didn't seem that she'd been told much, which under the circumstances was probably no bad thing.

A few seconds later he heard the receiver being picked up. But it wasn't Andrea. It was Marie again.

'She says she's very busy at the moment, Mr Bolt. Can she call you back later?'

He tried to keep the disappointment out of his voice. 'No problem. I'll wait to hear from her. But Emma's fine, yeah?'

'She's asleep at the moment, but yes, she's bearing up well, although the doctors say she's quite dehydrated.'

He wanted to ask something else, to keep the conversation going in the hope that Andrea would change her mind and take the call, but he wasn't sure what, so reluctantly he said his good-byes and hung up.

He turned on the TV and found Sky News. The main report was on the failed ransom drop. The man shot dead by police had not been named, but the young father he'd fatally stabbed had been identified as thirty-five-year-old Anthony Randolph of Waltham Abbey, Essex. A photo of him on his wedding day flashed up on the screen, followed by a photo of Matt Turner looking particularly deadpan, as the reporter described him as fighting for his life in intensive care. A camera panned round a largely empty Tottenham High Road, lined with strips of scene-of-crime tape, as the report continued, but it was clear that information was scarce, and there was no mention of the kidnapping, or of the separate but linked death of Scott Ridgers.

Bolt felt resentful that he was no longer involved in an investigation he'd done so much to break. He wondered whether Phelan had shown up yet, and briefly contemplated phoning Tina, but decided against it. She'd done more than enough for him already, and he didn't want to lose her respect by pushing her further.

Instead, he finished his coffee and got dressed, knowing that he had to do something, anything, to ease his frustration.

Which was when he had an idea. Outside, the

sun was shining and it looked like it was going to be another beautiful day. He grabbed his shoes and looked at his watch. Five minutes to midday.

It was time to catch up with some old friends.

Fifty-five

When Tina Boyd pressed the buzzer on Andrea's security gate at just after 2.30 p.m. she'd already done a seven-hour day and was finally on her way home, albeit in a slightly indirect way. She'd already spent more than two hours there that morning with Mo talking to Emma, listening to her harrowing account of the past few days while her mother sat beside her, holding her hand. Tina had been impressed by how brave and lucid Emma was in the interview, answering all their questions quietly and carefully, and although she'd looked tired, and thinner than she did in the photos that lined the house, her overall demeanour suggested that the damage she'd suffered wasn't irreversible. It was too early to say for sure, and Tina was no psychologist, but she'd come away feeling positive, and also proud of her boss, who according to Emma's testimony had saved her life and almost lost his own in the process. Emma had asked where Bolt was, saying she'd like to thank him properly, and Tina had told her that she was sure they'd get to meet soon, looking at Andrea as she did so.

Andrea had looked away.

Andrea's voice came on the line now, far brighter and chirpier now that she'd got her daughter back, but it immediately lost its lustre when Tina introduced herself.

'Oh, back again?' she said wearily. 'I'm afraid Emma's asleep at the moment, and I don't want her disturbed.'

'That's OK. It's you I've come to see. Can I come in?'

Andrea buzzed her through. She'd changed since Tina had left earlier and was now wearing a long T-shirt and a pair of khaki hotpants that showed off shapely legs and freshly painted, bright red toenails. The haggard, terrified woman of the last couple of days had now almost completely disappeared. It was quite a transformation.

'I've sent the liaison officer away,' she said as Tina stepped into the hallway. 'It's just me and Emma now. Like it's always been. Any word on Pat yet?'

'Nothing at the moment, I'm afraid.'

'God knows what's happened to him. I still

don't think he's involved, but if he is . . .' Her face darkened momentarily but then returned to normal as she pushed thoughts of her husband aside. 'Do you have more questions for me, then? Is that why you're here?'

'Shall we go through to the living room?'

'OK.'

Andrea stretched out the word, trying to gauge from Tina's expression what this might be about. Tina didn't give anything away, so Andrea led her through, taking her usual position on the sofa. Tina shut the door but remained standing.

'I wanted to ask you some questions about Emma's father. Her real one.'

Andrea sighed loudly. 'God, do we have to? I mean, is it important? I could do with a rest myself, you know.'

'We need to discuss it now.'

'Don't take that sort of tone with me.'

'You said in your statement on Friday that Emma's father was James Galante.'

'That's right.'

Tina pulled a folded sheet of paper from the back pocket of her jeans, holding it out in front of her.

'Do you know what it says on here?'

Andrea didn't say anything, but she was looking less sure of herself.

'It says that Emma was adopted.'

Andrea swallowed.

'By you and your then husband, Mr William Devern, in September 1994. When she was seventeen months old. I got a copy of the birth certificate from Somerset House this morning.'

'Christ. Keep your voice down. Emma doesn't know.'

'OK. But it makes me wonder, Mrs Devern, how many other things have you been lying about?'

Andrea reached for her cigarettes, which Tina now recognized as a sure sign that she was feeling stressed.

'It was only that I wanted Jimmy to help me and I thought if I convinced him he was Emma's dad then he'd never be able to say no.' She got up and opened the French windows, lighting up and blowing smoke out into the garden, her arms folded in a defensive gesture. 'You'd have done the same in my position, except you don't know that, because you've never had kids. She may not be my flesh and blood, but she's still my daughter. I brought her up. No one else, because Billy was dead within a year. Just me.' She blew out more smoke and glared defiantly at Tina.

'When are you intending to tell Mike Bolt that he's not Emma's father?'

The question made Andrea flinch.

'So, he told you about that, did he?'

'Only when he absolutely had to.'

'I'll tell him soon enough. When I've got my head back together.'

'You almost destroyed him, Mrs Devern. He's suspended from his job because of you, and it's possible he'll lose it over this. The least you can do is put him out of his misery.'

'I told you, I'll tell him soon.'

'No. Either you call him now, or I do. And I really think it would be best if it came from you, don't you?'

'Listen, Miss Boyd, you've got no idea what I've been through in the last week. What I've done, I've done to protect my daughter and help to get her away from those animals and back with me where she belongs, and I'm not going to make any apologies for that.'

'He still needs to know,' Tina insisted. 'Today.'

Andrea unfolded her arms, softening her stance.

'Can you tell him? Please? Say I'm very, very sorry and that I will call him, I promise. It's just . . .' She paused, and Tina could see that her eyes were filling with tears. 'Not today.'

'OK. I'll call him outside.'

As she walked through the French windows, Andrea stopped her with a hand on the arm.

'I do care for him, you know,' she said quietly, a tear running down one cheek. 'A lot more than you think.'

Tina nodded. She didn't believe a word of it.

She walked up to the end of the garden, well out of earshot, and dialled Mike's number, knowing that he was going to take this hard.

When he answered, he sounded in a good mood and there was a buzz of conversation in the background.

'Tina, how's it going?'

'Not bad. Where are you?'

'In a pub in Finchley. Relaxing with some old Flying Squad buddies. I figure, I'm suspended, I may as well enjoy myself. What can I do for you?'

The moment of truth. And straight away she knew she couldn't do it. Not when he was enjoying himself. It would just have to wait.

'I thought you might want a quick update on things, but if you're out with your friends—'

'No, I'd like to hear what you've got.'

She gave him a summary of where the investigation was, but there really wasn't a lot to say as things were running down now. There was still no sign of Pat Phelan. They'd put surveillance on Isobel Wheeler's house in case he turned up there, but that was pretty much it.

'And have you seen Emma?'

Tina stiffened. 'Yes, she's well. Back at home now.'

'And Andrea?'

'She's fine too.'

'Thanks, Tina. I really appreciate you keeping me in touch with things.'

'I'd want to be, if I was in your position. Anyway, you'd better get back to your friends.'

She rang off, cursing herself for being such a coward. Now she'd have to call him again later.

She sat down on the garden's loveseat and lit a cigarette, in no hurry to go back inside. As she basked in the mid-afternoon sunshine, she realized with surprise that she was going to miss Mike Bolt now that he was suspended. Things had changed between them these past few days. She'd seen a vulnerable side to him for the first time, and she was flattered that he'd turned to her when he needed help, seeing something beyond the hard shell she surrounded herself with. She hadn't had romance in a long time. It was over three years since John had died. Since then there'd been a couple of one-night stands and a brief holiday fling in Thailand. But now she felt the first hint of attraction, and it unnerved her.

She stubbed out the cigarette in the grass and stood up slowly. It was time to go home.

But as she reached the French windows, she stopped. Andrea was back on her sofa, but there were two men in suits in the room with her whom Tina recognized as detectives from the farm the previous night. They were obviously trying to keep their expressions as calm and inscrutable as possible as they turned towards her, but there was no escaping the excitement in them.

'We've got a new lead on Scott Ridgers' killer,' said the younger of the two, a fresh-faced youth with thinning hair and a spray of freckles. 'A big one.'

Fifty-six

The Coach and Horses was the pub where Finchley Flying Squad members past and present liked to drink. There were always a few old faces in on a Sunday lunchtime, mainly the local guys, but today was the first time in a long while that Bolt had made it.

The lunchtime crowd was thinning out now as Bolt came off the phone to Tina and returned to the table where he'd been drinking for the last two hours with today's Flying Squad contingent: Ron 'Scissors' Austin, silver-haired, still serving, nearing retirement; Marvin 'Mad Dog' Bennett, a huge black guy now working on the Met's Operation Trident; Big Tim Pritchard, once the squad's Romeo, but now a few stones above his ideal weight courtesy of his desk job at Scotland Yard; and the ever injury-prone Jack 'Dodger' Doyle.

'Who was that, your girlfriend?' grinned Scissors Austin as Bolt sat back down with his drink.

'No such luck. Colleague.'

'You want to get yourself out more, pal,' advised Jack Doyle before resuming his story, which involved a long-ago one-night stand he'd had with a female DCI from Hendon.

Bolt wasn't really listening to the story. His mind was elsewhere. He wanted to talk to Emma and had thought that Tina's call might have been her or Andrea getting in touch. The fact that it wasn't disappointed him. It had been good to catch up and trade war stories from the good old days, but now, as the conversation moved on to sexual conquests, he decided it was probably time to go.

Doyle finished his story of fumbled, drunken lovemaking (which had resulted, somewhat inevitably, in him falling over and twisting his ankle so badly he'd been off work for three days) with a flourish and plenty of illustrative hand movements, amid much laughter. When he went off to the toilet, Big Tim, not to be outdone, started on a story of his own, involving a relationship with a pretty uniformed PC from Finchley Nick.

'Tracey Bonham was her name. Anyone remember her?'

'Yeah, I do,' said Scissors. 'Pretty little thing.

Red hair. Don't tell me she had a fling with an ugly sod like you.'

Big Tim's seat creaked precariously as he leaned back on it. 'Watch it, old man. That girl was in love with me, I tell you. I liked her as well. We almost got engaged at one point.'

'I never knew that,' said Scissors sceptically. 'Are you sure you didn't dream it?'

'I don't remember her at all,' said Mad Dog, shaking his head.

Bolt swallowed the last of his pint. To be honest, he didn't either.

'Well, I didn't bloody dream it, all right? We did nearly get engaged, and I reckon we would have done as well, but then she ends up running off with some scuzzy little bastard who turns out to be one of Dodger Doyle's snouts.'

Scissors looked mortified. 'Christ, she dumped you for a snout?'

'All right, all right. Don't rub it in. He was one of these real charmers, you know. The sort gullible women go for.'

'What, like you, you mean?' chuckled Mad Dog.

'No, not like me. I'm sophisticated and good-hearted, as well as being beautiful. He was just a long-haired toe rag with a nice line in patter. But he had things with a couple of the girls at Finchley Nick. Then he got done for receiving a load of hijacked hi-fis, after he started trying to flood the market with them. He even sold one to Tracey.'

'Serious?'

'Yeah. She ended up leaving the force over it eventually. Christ, what was his name now?' Big Tim looked up and saw Doyle returning from the toilet. 'What was his name, Jack? That snout of yours a few years back. The one who got done for all them hi-fis. Pat somebody or other, wasn't it?'

'I've got it,' said Scissors, banging his empty pint glass on the table. 'It was Pat Phelan. Right long-haired nancy. He was one of yours, wasn't he, Jack?'

'Christ, I can't remember that far back,' said Doyle, re-taking his seat.

But as he spoke the words he glanced across at Bolt and their eyes met. Bolt felt his fingers tighten around his empty glass. Doyle looked away quickly and picked up his pint, trying too hard to appear natural.

Bolt stared at him, feeling adrenalin course through his body. There was a news blackout. Pat Phelan had not been mentioned at all in the media. Yet Jack Doyle clearly knew of his relevance to Bolt, which was why he'd instinctively glanced his way.

Their eyes met again, and it was suddenly as if everyone else in the room had melted away, leaving just the two of them there, at opposite ends of an empty, silent table.

Instincts. They shape so much of human behaviour. And in those single, dark moments, every instinct in Bolt's body told him that he was staring at the man who'd telephoned Andrea at home and in her car, and who one way or another had masterminded the whole thing.

Fifty-seven

Jack Doyle drained his pint and stood up. 'Well, boys, I've got to go. Things to do, people to see, you know the score.'

He shook hands with the boys.

'I've got to go as well,' said Bolt, getting to his feet.

'Don't fancy one more for the road, gents?' asked Big Tim, looking disappointed at the prospect of losing half his potential audience.

'No, sorry, I've had a long few days,' said Bolt, doing his own rounds and having to hurry as he followed Jack out of the pub.

'I'd give you a lift, Mike,' said Doyle, fumbling for his car keys, 'but I'm going in the wrong direction. See you soon, eh?'

He nodded briefly, a smile so tight on his face that it looked like it had been fixed there with botox, and made no attempt to shake hands as he started walking up towards the car park at the back of the pub.

Bolt kept pace alongside him.

'She was my daughter, Jack.'

Doyle looked at him with a puzzled expression. 'Who was?'

'Emma Devern. The girl whose kidnapping you organized.'

'What the hell are you talking about?'

'You know exactly what I'm talking about. Why did you target Andrea? Did Phelan get you in on it?'

'Whoa, Mike. I think the stress of this kidnap case you've been on's got to you. Why don't you go home and get some rest? Because I promise you, you're talking shit.'

He carried on walking, and once again Bolt kept pace, even though he was experiencing the first signs of doubt.

And then it struck him.

'You were off sick for the Lewisham job, weren't you? The one where I shot Dean Hayes.'

'I'm not talking about this, Mike. Now fuck off.'

Doyle clicked off the central locking as they reached his car, a silver Ford Mondeo, parked up against a fence round the back of the pub and out of sight of the front door.

'You were off sick, so you never knew about the ambush until afterwards. That's right, isn't it?

Shit, Jack. I never had you down for corrupt, but you were involved, weren't you? You were in on it.'

Doyle's features hardened as he opened the driver's door. 'You're pissing in the wind, Mike. And you can keep pissing as long as you like, because none of it's going to hit me.'

'There'll be evidence, Jack. You know it. I know it. So, where's the half million? Under your bed? Safe for a rainy day? We'll find it.'

Doyle shook his head. 'Well, *you* won't, will you? You're suspended.'

And with that he got inside the car.

Bolt felt rage bubble up inside him. He looked around. The car park was empty. He had to act. Now.

'You think I'm going to let you drive away after what you've done to my daughter?'

He strode round to the driver's door and yanked it open.

'No, I don't,' said Doyle as Bolt went to grab him. 'That's why I've got this.' There was a snub-nosed revolver with a scotch-taped handle in his left hand, and it was pointing up at Bolt. 'Now, step back from the car, nice and easy.'

'You won't shoot me here.'

'I wouldn't place a bet on that if I were you.'

The cold expression in Doyle's eyes told Bolt that it was best to comply, and he took a step backwards, realizing as he did so that he'd made a serious miscalculation. What the hell was he going to do now?

Doyle got out of the car, keeping the gun down by his side and glancing briefly over Bolt's shoulder to check that the car park was still clear. Then he threw his car keys on the driver's seat.

'OK, Mike, you're driving. Get in or I'll put a bullet in you right now.'

'Don't do this, Jack. It's over, can't you see that?'

'Get in.'

Bolt took a deep breath and complied, while Jack got in the back. He pointed the gun through the gap in the seats.

'All right, let's get moving.'

'Where are we going?'

'Just start driving and turn right out of here.'

Bolt started the car and pulled out, heading slowly through the car park, hoping that one of the Flying Squad boys would come out of the front door and ask for a lift.

'Go on, get moving,' Doyle snapped, shoving the gun in Bolt's ribs.

There was a big gap in the traffic and, knowing he had no choice, he pulled out on to the Finchley Road and started driving north, trying hard to figure out his options. He was certain Doyle wouldn't pull the trigger while he was driving, and pretty sure he wouldn't even if he stopped and jumped out – not in such a public place with pedestrians and other traffic about – but pretty sure wasn't good enough. Jack Doyle was both a killer and a desperate man. It was a bad combination.

It struck Bolt that Doyle was almost certainly trying to work out his own options, and he decided that his best policy was to distract him. He needed to keep Doyle talking.

'Why the hell did you have to do this, Jack?' he asked, his voice laced with disappointment.

'It's not like you think, and I didn't know she was your daughter. I just wanted my money back.'

'What do you mean?'

'That Lewisham job was going to be my retirement fund. Instead, the whole thing went tits up and almost cost me everything. If I hadn't got Galante out of the country he'd have definitely grassed me up. For years I never knew who'd fucked things up for us. You never named your source, remember?'

'Yeah, I remember.'

'Very chivalrous of you. Except the problem was one day you did tell me.'

Bolt frowned. 'When?'

'Remember that fishing trip you and me went on to Ireland a couple of years back, the last time you got yourself suspended? Well, it was then. We got pissed one night in that pub near Kilrush, the one with the big log fire. I asked you about the job then. I wasn't even that bothered about it. I just wanted to know.'

'And I told you?' Bolt vaguely remembered saying something now, but it had been an extremely drunken night.

'Yeah, you told me it was that bitch Andrea Devern. I didn't even know she was Galante's squeeze at the time.' Doyle cleared his throat. 'Anyway, I looked into things and saw she'd done very, very nicely for herself. Unlike me with a divorce, kids I don't see, and a whore of an ex-wife who's nicked all my money and half my pension.'

Bolt didn't bother telling him that this was hardly a reason for committing kidnap and murder. Instead, he kept quiet, letting Doyle talk. All the time pondering his options.

'And then I heard she'd married that piece of dirt Pat Phelan. You know, I met up with him a few months ago? I was going to sound him out about getting involved, but the flash bastard couldn't stop telling me how much money he had now that he was married to a rich girl, really rubbing it in. He laughed at me. You know that, Mike? The bastard laughed at me. Well, he ain't laughing now.'

'Where is he?'

'Not far away. I'm surprised you lot haven't found him yet.'

He pulled a crumpled pack of cigarettes from the sports jacket he was wearing, drew one out and lit it.

'You know what gets me? The whole thing was planned brilliantly. I really put effort into it. I let Ridgers and his prison buddy, a toe rag called Karl Roven, do all the hard work, and the idea was they'd turn up back at the farm last night and I'd take them both out. Bang bang, just like that. Then with Pat Phelan disappeared off the face of the earth, he'd end up getting the blame for organizing it all.'

'What about Emma? What were you going to do with her?'

'She was always going to get released. I'm not that cruel. I don't mind getting rid of scum like Ridgers and his mate, but I don't hurt kids.'

Somehow Bolt doubted it. If Doyle was cruel enough to lock Emma in a cellar and subject her to such a terrifying ordeal, he was definitely cruel enough to dispose of her afterwards.

'What about the cleaner? Was she scum as well?'

'That was a pity,' Doyle answered, sounding genuinely regretful. 'I got Ridgers' prison buddy, Roven, to get to know her. It was the only way we could get the alarm codes to plant the bugs. I tried

471

getting past the alarm a couple of times myself, but it was too sophisticated. And once Roven had the information, he had to get rid of her.'

'But we never found any bugs in the house.'

'We used the simplest ones of all: a couple of mobile phones planted in the house and set up to hands-free kits. All we had to do was put them on silent and auto answer, then dial the numbers, and we could hear everything. The reason you never found them was because they'd both run out of batteries by Friday, so they wouldn't have shown up on all the new-fangled stuff you use these days. I didn't think we'd need them beyond then.'

Bolt knew it was possible to turn standard mobile phones into covert listening devices with only a few standard modifications. They should have thought of that. Not that it would have made any difference in the end.

'You know, I can't believe a friend of mine – someone I've known for, God, how long is it? sixteen, seventeen years? – could do what you've done and sit here trying to justify it.'

Doyle sat up in his seat and glared at Bolt, blowing smoke into the front of the car.

'I saved your life last night, Mikey boy. Remember that. If I hadn't put a bullet in Ridgers, he'd have cut you to pieces, and you know it.' He dragged hard on the cigarette. 'I saved your life, even though you turning up there nearly ruined everything for me. Just like you turning up now has.'

'Forgive me if I don't apologize for wanting to rescue my daughter from the animals you hired.'

'You know I'd never have done it if I'd known she was anything to do with you. Like I say, all I wanted was my money.'

Bolt stared at him in the wing mirror.

'You keep saying that, "my money". Andrea ran a business she'd built up from scratch. What did she owe you?'

'How do you think she started that business? There was other money that Jimmy Galante had stashed away that went missing after he left the country. Money that she had. Don't ever make the mistake of thinking that bitch is whiter than white.'

Doyle opened the window and chucked his cigarette butt out.

'Go straight across at the lights, and don't try anything. There's a turning up here somewhere.'

'Where are we going?'

'Just for a little drive.'

Bolt knew what was coming. He slowed down as the lights went red, and the Mondeo came to a halt.

'So, you're going to kill me then?'

Doyle looked pained. 'Course not, Mike. We go back way too far for that.'

'Sure we do.'

The lights went green and Bolt pulled away. He knew that Doyle couldn't afford to leave him alive, even if he was an old friend. When you were responsible for as many killings as he'd been this past week, you became hardened to it, and Jack Doyle had always been a hard man, unafraid to make tough decisions.

The mobile in Bolt's pocket rang.

'Aren't you going to answer that?'

Bolt pulled it out, but Doyle extended his free hand. 'Give me that,' he said, taking it off him. He examined the screen as it continued to ring. 'Who's Tina Boyd?'

Bolt tensed. What could she want now?

'She's a friend.'

Doyle smiled knowingly. 'Friend, or girlfriend?'

'Friend.'

The mobile stopped ringing and went to voice-mail, before ringing again for a few seconds to announce a message. Doyle put it to his ear, still keeping the gun firmly on Bolt.

But as he listened to Tina's message, something happened. As Bolt watched in the rear-view mirror, Doyle's face, blotchy and lined after years of too much boozing, began to drain of colour, and his breathing rate increased.

'Shit!' he hissed, throwing the phone to the floor. It clattered under one of the seats. 'Shit,

shit, shit! How the hell do they know about me?'

Somehow they were on to him. Bolt wondered whether this was a good or a bad thing. He had a grim feeling it might be the latter.

'It's over, Jack,' he said, trying hard to stay calm, looking for a chance to get out of range of that gun. 'You can give yourself up. None of what you've said in here's admissible in court. You'll get done for kidnapping, but you'll miss the murder charge.'

Behind him, Doyle fidgeted in his seat.

'It ain't going to happen, pal,' he said after a short pause. 'They know. Somehow they know I pulled the trigger on Ridgers. What am I going to do?'

'Give up.'

'Fuck you. No way. Got to think, pal. That's what I've got to do.'

He exhaled deeply, still training the gun on Bolt, his expression distracted as he desperately weighed up his options.

Bolt noticed he wasn't wearing a seatbelt.

Without warning, he slammed his foot down on the accelerator and swung the wheel hard left, cutting up the car in the next lane.

'What the hell are you doing? Stop, or I'll shoot!'

Bolt's whole body stiffened, expecting a bullet any second, but he kept driving, aiming straight at a line of concrete bollards on the edge of the pavement.

'Stop, you bastard, stop!'

There was a tremendous bang as Bolt hit the nearest bollard head-on, his foot still flat on the floor, and the sound of shattering glass and crunching metal. At exactly the same time, a shot rang out in the car, louder than the initial crash and deafening Bolt as he was flung forward in his seat like a stringless puppet. Out of the corner of his eye he saw Doyle smash into the front passenger seat, then fly backwards, his legs flailing wildly, before disappearing altogether.

Then the airbag shot out, driving the wind out of Bolt as it smothered him in its rubbery grip. For a few seconds he was crushed against his seat, unable to move, not even sure whether or not the bullet had hit him. Then, realizing that it hadn't, he managed to yank open the door handle and struggle free, desperate to get out.

He staggered round the front of the Mondeo, conscious that he was outside a parade of shops, some of which were open. Shocked onlookers were gathering fast, the majority of them looking at something round the back of the car.

'He's got a gun!' someone called out, and the small crowd moved backwards quickly.

Doyle was lying on the pavement about ten feet from the back of the car, propped up precariously on one elbow, the revolver hanging loosely from his hand. He must have been flung out of the back window, but somehow had managed to retain his grip on the gun, which was typical of him. He'd always been single-minded. Blood stained his shirt and sports jacket, and a huge gash had opened up one cheek like a second, bleeding mouth. He was in a bad way, but when he saw Bolt, something flashed in his eyes and he tried hard to lift the gun.

For a long moment they simply watched each other, oblivious to everyone around them, each man trying hard to come to terms with this terrible turn of events that had destroyed things between them for ever. Then Bolt began walking towards him, steady, confident strides that ate up the distance fast.

Doyle's eyes narrowed, but he was having difficulty focusing and the gun was shaking in his hand. Several people in the crowd gasped but no one made a move to intervene. It was as if they were watching the last dramatic scene in a TV cop drama.

Blood leaked out of the corner of Doyle's mouth, running down his chin. Bolt saw his finger tighten on the trigger, the end of the barrel pointed towards his belly, and he felt a lurch of adrenalin that almost lifted him off his feet. In that second, he leapt forward, stamped on the wrist of

Doyle's shaking gun hand and drove it into the pavement. Doyle grunted and fell down on his back, losing his grip on the revolver.

Bolt snatched it up and pointed it, two-handed, down at Doyle's chest, holding it steady, his face as hard as stone.

'Don't do it!' someone in the crowd cried out, shrill and fearful.

But he was never going to. There was no point. Emma was safe, Jack Doyle was finished, and finally his rage was fading, to be replaced by a leaden sense of regret that an old friendship he'd once thought so strong could have ended up like this. Tattered, bleeding, and ultimately hollow.

Doyle's eyes closed and his head rolled to one side, more blood trailing out of his mouth and dripping on to the concrete.

Bolt took a step back, then another, until he reached the car. He propped himself up against it and noticed the crowd watching – twenty, thirty strong now – for the first time.

'Someone dial nine-nine-nine,' he said with as much strength as he could muster.

Then tiredness seemed to overwhelm him and, still clutching the revolver, he slid down the car and landed in a sitting position on the tarmac.

It was over.

Fifty-eight

Tina Boyd stood in the shadows thrown by the low-rise council flats and looked through the darkness at the brand-new four-door Lexus GS parked behind the chainlink fence on the other side of the road. It had just turned twenty past ten and she'd been standing there for more than an hour already. She wondered if she was wasting her time. Probably. But Tina wasn't the sort to give up that easily. She'd give it another half an hour before calling it a day.

She stifled a yawn. It had been a manic weekend but at least events had come to a comparatively clean conclusion, which, as most police officers would tell you, is very rarely the case. Pat Phelan had at last turned up, although the manner in which he did so left something to be desired. A thorough search by Enfield SOCO of one of the farm's outbuildings revealed his dismembered remains inside a barrel of sulphuric acid, where they were dissolving steadily; they would probably have been little more than sludge had they been left for another week. His teeth had been forcibly removed, and identification had only been possible because a large 'Ban the Bomb' tattoo on what was left of his upper arm was still just about visible, and was recognized by Andrea Devern.

The other main development that day had been the uncovering of the third person involved in the kidnap, DI Jack Doyle of the Flying Squad. A woman who lived a hundred yards from the farm had heard the gunshots the previous evening and had gone outside to investigate. She'd seen an unfamiliar car parked down the lane from her house, and because of the circumstances she'd written down the registration number. A few minutes later she'd seen a man return to the car and drive away. Because there were a number of farms in the area, and the sound of shotguns being fired wasn't that unusual, the woman hadn't called the police. But when they'd turned up at her door earlier that day as part of their general enquiries, she'd told them about what had happened. The car was quickly traced to DI Doyle, and when the witness was shown his photo she was able to say that it bore a very strong resemblance to the person she'd seen. Not enough for a conviction perhaps, but ample justification for an arrest warrant to be issued, and from that moment on his fate had been sealed. However, before he could be arrested, he'd been involved in a car crash, and was now seriously ill in hospital. A gun recovered from the scene with his finger-prints on it had subsequently been confirmed as the weapon used to murder Scott Ridgers at the farm.

The reason why it was only a comparatively clean conclusion rather than an absolutely perfect result was that Matt Turner was still very ill and Mike Bolt, who more than anyone deserved credit for the op's overall success, was suspended until further notice. It didn't seem fair. And this was the main reason Tina was hanging around in the dark in a bad part of town, waiting. Because sometimes doing the job and upholding the law didn't neces-sarily provide the justice it was meant to. Sometimes you had to dispense that justice your-self, as an individual. Like Mike had done yesterday.

There was movement across the road. A group of men emerged from the entrance to the mono-lithic tower block, three of them in all, moving purposefully, their voices low. They stopped at the Lexus and got inside, pulling out seconds later.

Tina retreated further into the shadows and

took out her mobile as they drove past her. It was an unregistered pay-as-you go she'd bought on Tottenham Court Road earlier that day, and as the Lexus came to the end of the road and turned left, she dialled 999, asking for police.

'Hello, can I help you?'

'I've just seen three men get into a car armed with guns.'

'Are you sure about this, madam?'

'Absolutely,' she said breathlessly. 'They walked right past me.'

She gave her location, the make and model of the car, and the direction it was travelling in, waiting patiently while the operator took all the information down.

'And can I have your name, madam?'

'I don't want to get involved, I'm too scared.'

And with that, she ended the call, switched off the phone, and walked back to her car.

When she'd phoned the number Leon Daroyce had given her an hour earlier she'd disguised her voice and said he could find Pat Phelan at a flat in Colindale, where he was holed up with a lover, hoping he'd take the bait. And now it looked like he had done. She had no idea whether Daroyce and his two associates would be armed or not, but it didn't really matter since when the police stopped the car they'd find the five grams of cocaine she'd planted in the glove compartment.

It had taken all the burglary skills she'd learned at SOCA to bypass the Lexus's sophisticated alarm system, as well as one hell of a lot of nerve, but it would be worth it. Armed with the coke, the police would be able to execute a search warrant on Daroyce's premises, a place she was absolutely sure would be full of illegal contraband.

It might not be enough to put him away for years, or even months, but at least she'd done something to disrupt his business and pay him back for the ordeal he'd put her through two days earlier, and a search of the flat would probably mean freedom for the girl he'd abused as well, which had to be a good thing. He would probably work out who'd been behind it, and might even want to extract some kind of revenge when he was back on the street, but she doubted he'd risk killing a SOCA agent. Whatever he might like to claim, Daroyce was a bully, and bullies tended to be cowards when it came down to it.

She knew what her former lover, John Gallan, would have thought of her actions. He'd have disapproved, not only because what she'd done was potentially so dangerous, but also because he'd always believed in the absolute sanctity of the law he'd been paid to uphold. But as Tina and countless many others had found to their cost down the years, the law didn't always punish the bad, just like it didn't always protect the good.

Sometimes you just had to bend the rules, even if that did mean planting evidence.

Somewhere deep inside, the realization of what she'd done and the huge risk she'd taken worried her. But nowhere near enough to regret it, and there was even something of a spring in her step as she walked down the quiet, litter-strewn street and heard the first of the sirens converging on Leon Daroyce.

Epilogue: Two Days Later

It was a cool, drizzly day, very different to the Indian summer of the past ten days or so, and Mike Bolt and Andrea Devern were standing on Hampstead Heath, looking up in the direction of Kenwood House.

Andrea looked good. She was dressed in a three-quarter-length raincoat, her long auburn hair flowing over the collar. Her eyes were bright and alive in a way Bolt hadn't seen since their affair all those years ago.

'I really didn't want to do it,' she was saying to him now. 'It's no consolation, I know, but I was under huge amounts of pressure. Will you forgive me?'

Bolt looked at her. Andrea Devern had put him through hell, there was no doubt about it, but she'd also had one of the best reasons going for doing so. The safety of her daughter. Not his, unfortunately, he knew that now, but he could still sympathize. Today was the first time the two of them had seen each other since the chaotic aftermath of the ransom drop, but what should perhaps have been an awkward meeting felt anything but.

But then, Bolt thought ruefully, *Andrea has always had a way of making me feel good.*

He smiled. 'Sure, I forgive you. Maybe I'd have done the same in your position.'

'No, you wouldn't. You're not like that. You're a good man, Mike. You've got too much integrity.'

He shrugged. 'Maybe. But we all do desperate things sometimes. I'd like to see Emma at some point, too. I know she's not mine, but it would be nice to see how she's getting on.'

'I'll get her to call you when she's feeling better. She's been sleeping most of the past few days.'

'But she's OK?'

'Yeah, she's doing well. She's a fighter, just like me. She's upset about Pat. She liked him.'

'How do you feel about it?'

'I've shed my tears. He wasn't such a bad bloke, and I'm glad he didn't betray either me or Emma. That's a comfort.'

'Good.'

'And what about your colleague, Turner? The one who was at my place. How's he getting on?'

'He's out of intensive care and they say he should make a full recovery, but he's going to be in hospital for a while yet.'

'I hope he's all right. He seemed a nice guy.'

Neither of them mentioned Jack Doyle. He was still in a bad way in hospital but Bolt had little doubt he'd survive. Jack wasn't the kind to give up. He'd always been too bloody-minded for that, although he had little to look forward to when and if he did finally make it.

'And how about you, Mike?' asked Andrea. 'How are you managing? What's going to happen about your suspension?'

'I don't know yet. I'm still waiting to hear what action they're planning to take against me.'

'They shouldn't take any. You were a bloody hero. If it wasn't for you . . .'

There was no need for her to finish the sentence. They both knew what she meant.

He wasn't sure that he had been a hero, though. More likely he'd been a fool, and it was foolishness that still might cost him his job. But he didn't regret his actions, had even stopped worrying about the whole thing these past couple of days. What would happen would happen anyway, so it was easier just to think about something else.

They were silent for a moment, each watching the other. Conscious that there was still something there. Finally, Bolt spoke again.

'The reason I wanted to meet you today was because I had a question.'

Andrea looked wary. 'OK . . .'

'That day we met in the West End all those years ago, when we went back to your hotel. That wasn't, you know . . .'

'What?'

He suddenly felt embarrassed to bring it up.

'It was genuine coincidence, right? You didn't know I was going to be there?'

'You asked me that before. A long time ago.'

'And now I'm asking it again.'

Andrea smiled a little sadly. 'Have I been that bad to you that you could believe it wasn't?'

'I just wanted to hear it from your own lips again. Now that this is all over.'

'It was genuine coincidence, Mike. I promise.'

She'd lied to him before, but he chose to believe her this time. Perhaps it was easier that way.

'So, what now?' she asked, and there was an element of invitation in her hazel eyes.

He'd thought a lot about this these past couple of days, and hadn't known the answer until he'd arrived here today and seen Andrea as she should have been – happy, attractive and spirited.

'Well?'

'We do the same thing we did fifteen years ago, Andrea.' He looked her in the eyes and smiled. 'We part company.'

Her expression didn't change. 'Are you sure? I thought maybe there was still something there between us. Something that might be worth exploring.'

He leaned forward and kissed her on the cheek, lingering just a second over her scent, wanting to hold her but not knowing where it would end if he did, before moving away.

'Good luck, Andrea,' he said.

The invitation remained in her eyes for another second, then faded as she accepted the inevitable.

'And to you, Mike, and to you.'

He turned and left her there, striding away purposefully, wishing perhaps that things could have been different – that Emma was his daughter, that Andrea genuinely loved him, that they could end up as the kind of happy family he and Mikaela had never had the chance to create. But knowing too that he'd made the right decision. It was time to make a clean break with the past, start looking towards the future.

And where better to start than with a twenty-eight-year-old artist from St Ives with raven hair and a dirty laugh.

As he walked out on to Spaniards Road, he took out his mobile and called Jenny Byfleet, hoping that she was in a forgiving mood.

THE END

THE BUSINESS OF DYING

**Featuring DS Dennis Milne:
full-time cop, part-time assassin.**

It's a cold November night and
DS Dennis Milne is waiting to kill
three unarmed men.

Cynical and jaded, Milne earns
money on the side by doing
what he does best: punishing
the bad guys.

But he's been set up. This time,
instead of shooting drug dealers,
he kills two customs officers
and an accountant.

The hunter has become the hunted.
With his colleagues and his enemies closing
in on him, Milne must use all his skills just to stay alive.

The explosive first novel by the bestselling author of *Deadline*.

'Caught me with its gut-wrenching reality. A compelling début'
Gerald Seymour

'A remarkable début...Pace, twists and a savage sense of place
make this a guilty pleasure' *Guardian*

THE EXPLOSIVE FIRST NOVEL
BY THE BESTSELLING AUTHOR OF
RELENTLESS

SIMON KERNICK
THE BUSINESS
OF DYING

THE MURDER EXCHANGE

FIVE GRAND FOR A COUPLE OF HOURS WORK?

It seems easy money, but the deal ex-mercenary **Max Iversson** is chasing has gone disastrously wrong. Two of his friends are dead. And now he wants to find out who's behind their killings.

Detective Sergeant **John Gallan** is also looking for answers. He's investigating the fatal poisoning of a nightclub doorman. But leads are scarce and, when they do appear, so do bodies.

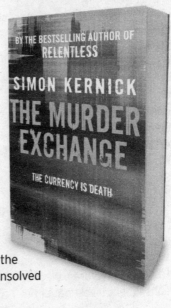

As Iversson struggles to stay alive, Gallan keeps on digging, unearthing in the process a shocking crime that's been unsolved for a long, long time.

What neither man knows is that they are heading towards a devastating confrontation that will see one of them staring down the wrong end of a gun.

'I love this book! It's hard, fast and tight and blasts through the London underworld like a speed boat on the Thames' Lee Child

'The next time I see Simon Kernick's name on a book I will pick it up. Brilliant!' Richard Madeley

THE CRIME TRADE

'Simon Kernick writes with his foot pressed on the pedal. Hang on tight' Harlan Coben

When Operation Surgical Strike goes horribly wrong, suspicion quickly falls on one of the officers involved: **Stegs Jenner**. No ordinary undercover cop, Stegs is a man who's always lived life on the edge.

Now he decides to go it alone.

DI John Gallan and his partner **DS Tina Boyd** are part of the subsequent investigation.

What they cannot know is that their enquiries will take both of them into the heart of one of London's most notorious criminal gangs – and one of them into the rifle sights of the enemy.

'Great plots, great characters, great action' Lee Child

BY THE BESTSELLING AUTHOR OF
RELENTLESS

SIMON KERNICK
THE CRIME
TRADE

THEY PLAY, YOU PAY

A GOOD DAY TO DIE

It's cold, it's December – and ex-cop Dennis Milne is intent on revenge.

BY THE BESTSELLING AUTHOR OF
RELENTLESS

SIMON KERNICK

A GOOD DAY TO DIE

YOU CAN RUN ...
BUT YOU CAN'T HIDE

His best friend has been brutally executed, and Milne wants to know who did it – and why.

But London is a dangerous place, especially for a man on his own.

And although his former colleagues don't know Milne's back in town, it soon becomes clear there are people who do. And that they'll stop at nothing to get him out of the way.

From the beaches of the Philippines to the mean streets of London, a hunt for justice becomes a terrifying battle for survival.

RELENTLESS

Tom Meron finds himself on the run, pursued by enemies he never knew he had...

3 o'clock. It's a normal Saturday afternoon. You're with the kids in the garden when the phone rings.

It's your best friend from school, the best man at your wedding. Someone you haven't seen for a few years.

It should be a friendly call making arrangements to see each other again, catching up on old times.

But it's not. This call is different.
Your friend is speaking quickly, panting with fear,
his breaths coming in tortured, ragged gasps.
It is clear that someone is inflicting terrible pain on him.

He cries out and then utters six words that will change your life forever...the first two lines of your address.

What do you do? Do you run or do you hide?

**'The pace is breakneck, the plot twists like a hooked eel...
The sort of book that forces you to read so fast you stumble
over the words'** *Evening Standard*

**'Simon Kernick writes with his foot pressed hard on the pedal.
Hang on tight!' Harlan Coben**

SEVERED

ONE NIGHT STAND.
ONE DEAD GIRL.
ONE BAD DAY.

You wake up in a strange
room on a bed covered
in blood. And you have
no idea how you got there.

Beside you is a dead girl.
Your girlfriend.

The phone rings, and a voice
tells you to press play on the
room's DVD machine.

The film shows you killing your girlfriend.
Then you're told to go to an address in East London
where you're to deliver a briefcase and await further instructions.

There's no way out. If you're to survive the next 24 hours,
you must find out who killed your girlfriend, and why.

Before they come for you too...

'Great plots, great characters, great action' Lee Child

'For those who like their thrillers breathless, as well as bloody,
this will be just the ticket' *The Times*

BY THE BESTSELLING AUTHOR OF
RELENTLESS

SIMON KERNICK
SEVERED

ONE NIGHT STAND
ONE DEAD GIRL
ONE BAD DAY

TARGET

DID SOMEONE TRY TO KILL ME OR AM I GOING MAD?

When writer Rob Fallon gets drunk one night and ends up joining his friend's girlfriend, Jenny, back at her apartment in London's West End, he's feeling guilty before anything's even happened.

But guilt quickly turns to shock when two men break into the apartment, and abduct Jenny.

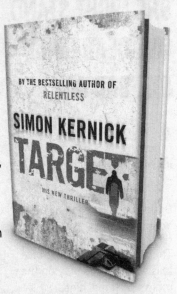

Somehow Rob manages to escape, but when he reports the abduction to the police no one believes him. Rob knows what he witnessed and he can't let things lie – not with Jenny's life in danger.

But when he starts asking questions, he finds himself the target of ruthless killers who'll stop at nothing to get him out of the way...

READ SIMON KERNICK'S NEW NOVEL
OUT NOW!